NEW
ENGLAND

27th Edition

**Where to Stay and Eat
for All Budgets**

**Must-See Sights
and Local Secrets**

Ratings You Can Trust

Fodor's Travel Publications   New York, Toronto, London, Sydney, Auckland
www.fodors.com

FODOR'S NEW ENGLAND

Editor: Kristin Moehlmann

Editorial Production: David Downing and Aviva Muse-Orlinoff

Editorial Contributors: Michelle Bodak Acri, Stephen and Neva Allen, Diane Bair, Michael Blanding, Catherine Bowen Brophy, Gail M. Burns, Lelah Cole, Andrew Collins, Matthew Cordell, Alexandra Hall, Sherry Hanson, Satu Hummasti, Sandy MacDonald, Phyllis Meras, Lori A. Nolin, Corey O'Hara, Carole Owens, Eileen Pierce, Andrew Rimas, James W. Rohlf, Mary Ruoff, Laura V. Scheel, Peggy Shinn, Erica Silverstein, David Simons, Emily J. Stebbins, Pamela Wright

Maps: David Lindroth, *cartographer;* Rebecca Baer and Bob Blake, *map editors*

Design: Fabrizio La Rocca, *creative director;* Guido Caroti, *art director;* Moon Sun Kim, *cover designer;* Melanie Marin, *senior picture editor*

Production/Manufacturing: Angela L. McLean

Cover Photo (Vermont): Mike Brinson/The Image Bank/Getty Images

Twenty-Seventh Edition

ISBN-10: 1–4000–1679–7

ISBN-13: 978–1–4000–1679–2

ISSN: 0192–3412

SPECIAL SALES

This book is available for special discounts for bulk purchases for sales promotions or premiums. Special editions, including personalized covers, excerpts of existing books, and corporate imprints, can be created in large quantities for special needs. For more information, write to Special Markets/Premium Sales, 1745 Broadway, MD 6-2, New York, New York 10019, or e-mail specialmarkets@randomhouse.com.

AN IMPORTANT TIP & AN INVITATION

Although all prices, opening times, and other details in this book are based on information supplied to us at press time, changes occur all the time in the travel world, and Fodor's cannot accept responsibility for facts that become outdated or for inadvertent errors or omissions. So **always confirm information when it matters,** especially if you're making a detour to visit a specific place. Your experiences—positive and negative—matter to us. If we have missed or misstated something, **please write to us.** We follow up on all suggestions. Contact the New England editor at editors@fodors.com or c/o Fodor's, 1745 Broadway, New York, NY 10019.

PRINTED IN THE UNITED STATES OF AMERICA

10 9 8 7 6 5 4 3 2 1

Be a Fodor's Correspondent

Your opinion matters. It matters to us. It matters to your fellow Fodor's travelers, too. And we'd like to hear it. In fact, we *need* to hear it.

When you share your experiences and opinions, you become an active member of the Fodor's community. That means we'll not only use your feedback to make our books better, but we'll publish your names and comments whenever possible. Throughout our guides, look for "Word of Mouth," excerpts of your unvarnished feedback.

Here's how you can help improve Fodor's for all of us.

Tell us when we're right. We rely on local writers to give you an insider's perspective. But our writers and staff editors—who are the best in the business—depend on you. Your positive feedback is a vote to renew our recommendations for the next edition.

Tell us when we're wrong. We're proud that we update most of our guides every year. But we're not perfect. Things change. Hotels cut services. Museums change hours. Charming cafés lose charm. If our writer didn't quite capture the essence of a place, tell us how you'd do it differently. If any of our descriptions are inaccurate or inadequate, we'll incorporate your changes in the next edition and correct factual errors at fodors.com *immediately.*

Tell us what to include. You probably have had fantastic travel experiences that aren't yet in Fodor's. Why not share them with a community of like-minded travelers? Maybe you chanced upon a beach or bistro or B&B that you don't want to keep to yourself. Tell us why we should include it. And share your discoveries and experiences with everyone directly at fodors.com. Your input may lead us to add a new listing or highlight a place we cover with a "Highly Recommended" star or with our highest rating, "Fodor's Choice."

Give us your opinion instantly at our feedback center at www.fodors.com/feedback. You may also e-mail editors@fodors.com with the subject line "New England Editor." Or send your nominations, comments, and complaints by mail to New England Editor, Fodor's, 1745 Broadway, New York, NY 10019.

You and travelers like you are the heart of the Fodor's community. Make our community richer by sharing your experiences. Be a Fodor's correspondent.

Happy traveling!

Tim Jarrell, Publisher

03059 5449

CONTENTS

MAPS

CLOSEUPS

New England

CANADA QUÉBEC

Rangeley
Mooselookmeguntic Lake
Newport
Colebrook
Enosburg Falls
St. Albans Orleans Barton Island Pond North Stratford Errol
Wilton
Lake Champlain
Morrisville Hardwick Lyndonville Groveton Rumford Newry
Lancaster Berlin
Burlington Stowe St. Johnsbury Bethel
Montpelier Littleton Gorham S. Paris
Vergennes Twin Mtn. Mechanic Falls
Barre Woodsville Bartlett Bridgton
Middlebury Lincoln North Conway Fryeburg
Brandon Randolph Conway Sebago Lake
Tamworth
VERMONT Sebago Lake Westbrook
Connecticut River Ossipee Portland
Rutland Woodstock Lebanon Meredith Lake Winnipesaukee Biddeford
Poultney Bristol Laconia Stratford
Wallingford Ludlow Claremont
Springfield NEW HAMPSHIRE Rochester 95
Manchester Concord Dover
Arlington Grafton Portsmouth
Keene Manchester
Bennington Milford Amesbury
Wilmington Brattleboro Nashua Haverhill Newburyport
Lawrence
Williamstown Athol Lowell Gloucester
Greenfield Fitchburg Danvers Beverly
Pittsfield Gardner Concord Lexington Salem
Northampton Leominster Cambridge
Stockbridge Amherst Marlborough Boston
MASSACHUSETTS Worcester
Sandisfield Chicopee Braintree 3
90 90 Brockton
Springfield 146 495
Winsted Putnam Bridgewater Plymouth
Windsor Locks 84 Providence Taunton
Torrington Manchester Willimantic 24 Sandwich
New Britain Warwick Fall River Cape
Bristol Hartford CONNECTICUT 395 95 Bristol 195 Hyannis
7 Waterbury Meriden RHODE New Bedford
84 Middletown ISLAND Newport Falmouth
Wallingford 91 Norwich Oak Bluffs
Danbury Wakefield Martha's Vineyard
New London Westerly
New Haven 1 Block Island Sound
15 Bridgeport Long Island Sound Block Island
Norwalk 95
Long Island (N.Y.)

NEW YORK

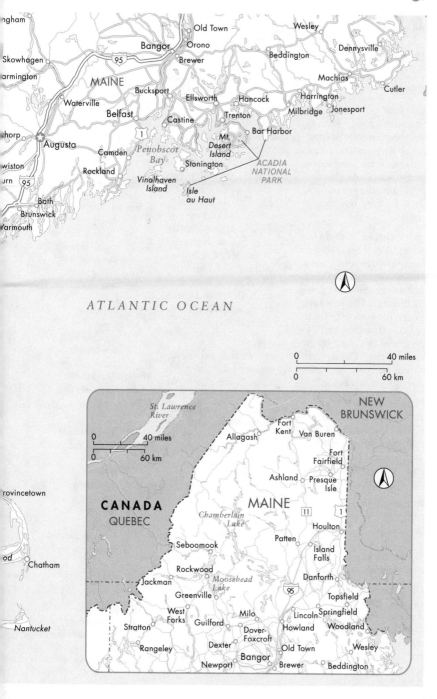

ABOUT THIS BOOK

Our Ratings

Sometimes you find terrific travel experiences and sometimes they just find you. But usually the burden is on you to select the right combination of experiences. That's where our ratings come in.

As travelers we've all discovered places whose worthiness is obvious. And sometimes a place is so wonderful that superlatives don't do it justice: you just have to see for yourself. These sights, properties, and experiences get our highest rating, **Fodor's Choice**, indicated by orange stars throughout this book.

Black stars highlight sights and properties we deem **Highly Recommended**, places that our writers, editors, and readers praise again and again for consistency and excellence.

By default, there's another category: any place we include in this book is by definition worth your time, unless we say otherwise. And we will.

Disagree with any of our choices? Care to nominate a place or suggest that we rate one more highly? Visit our feedback center at www.fodors.com/feedback.

Budget Well

Hotel and restaurant price categories from ¢ to $$$$ are defined in the opening pages of each chapter. For attractions, we always give standard adult admission fees; reductions are usually available for children, students, and senior citizens. Want to pay with plastic? **AE, D, DC, MC, V** following restaurant and hotel listings indicate if American Express, Discover, Diner's Club, MasterCard, and Visa are accepted.

Restaurants

Unless we state otherwise, restaurants are open for lunch and dinner daily. We mention dress only when there's a specific requirement and reservations only when they're essential or not accepted—it's always best to book ahead.

Hotels

Hotels have private bath, phone, TV, and air-conditioning and operate on the European Plan (a.k.a. EP, meaning without meals), unless we specify that they use the Continental Plan (CP, with a continental breakfast), Breakfast Plan (BP, with a full breakfast), or Modified American Plan (MAP, with breakfast and dinner) or are all-inclusive (including all meals and most activities). We always list facilities but not whether you'll be charged an extra fee to use them, so when pricing accommodations, find out what's included.

Many Listings
- ★ Fodor's Choice
- ★ Highly recommended
- ⊠ Physical address
- ✛ Directions
- 🗐 Mailing address
- ☎ Telephone
- 🖷 Fax
- ⊕ On the Web
- ✉ E-mail
- 🎫 Admission fee
- ☉ Open/closed times
- ▶ Start of walk/itinerary
- Ⓜ Metro stations
- ▭ Credit cards

Hotels & Restaurants
- 🏨 Hotel
- ᴝ Number of rooms
- ⚲ Facilities
- ⑂⚬⑂ Meal plans
- ✕ Restaurant
- ⚓ Reservations
- 🏛 Dress code
- ⟍ Smoking
- ⑧ BYOB
- ✕🏨 Hotel with restaurant that warrants a visit

Outdoors
- ⚐ Golf
- ⚐ Camping

Other
- ☝ Family-friendly
- 🛈 Contact information
- ⇨ See also
- ⊠ Branch address
- ☞ Take note

MAINE	Maine is by far the largest state in New England. At its extremes it measures 300 mi by 200 mi; all other New England states could fit within its perimeter. Maine's southernmost coastal towns are too overdeveloped to give you the rugged, "Down East" experience, but the Kennebunks will: classic townscapes, rocky shorelines punctuated by sandy beaches, quaint downtown districts. Purists hold that the Maine coast begins at Penobscot Bay, where the vistas over the water are wider and bluer, the shore a jumble of granite boulders. East of the bay is Acadia National Park, Maine's principal tourist attraction; Bar Harbor is one of the park's gateway towns. North of the bay is Bangor, on the Penobscot River. The vast North Woods region is a destination for outdoors enthusiasts.
NEW HAMPSHIRE	Portsmouth, the star of New Hampshire's 18-mi coastline, has great shopping, restaurants, music, and theater as well as one of the best historic districts in the nation. Exeter is New Hampshire's enclave of Revolutionary War history. The Lakes Region, rich in historic landmarks, also has good restaurants, several golf courses, hiking trails, and antiques shops. People come to the White Mountains to hike and climb, to photograph the dramatic vistas and the vibrant foliage, and to ski. Western and central New Hampshire have managed to keep the waterslides and the outlet malls at bay. The lures here include Lake Sunapee, the charming college town of Hanover, and Mt. Monadnock, the second-most-climbed mountain in the world.
VERMONT	Southern Vermont has farms, freshly starched New England towns, quiet back roads, bustling ski resorts, and strip-mall sprawl. Central Vermont's trademarks include famed marble quarries, just north of Rutland, and large dairy herds and pastures that create the quilted patchwork of the Champlain Valley. The heart of the area is the Green Mountains, and the surrounding wilderness of the Green Mountain National Forest. Both the state's largest city (Burlington) and the nation's smallest state capital (Montpelier) are in northern Vermont, as are some of the most rural and remote areas of New England. Much of the state's logging, dairy farming, and skiing takes place here. With Montréal only an hour from the border, the Canadian influence is strong, and Canadian accents and currency common.

WHAT'S
WHERE

MASSACHUSETTS	Much of what makes Massachusetts famous is in the eastern part of the state: academically endowed Boston, the historic South Shore town of Plymouth, chic Martha's Vineyard, scenic Cape Cod, and cozy Nantucket; witch-obsessed Salem and the port town of Gloucester are on the North Shore, which extends past grimy docklands to the picturesque Cape Ann region. But the western reaches of the state hold attractions as well: the Pioneer Valley is a string of historic settlements, and the Berkshires, in the western end of the state, live up to the storybook image of rural New England.
RHODE ISLAND	Wedged between Connecticut and Massachusetts, Rhode Island is the smallest of the 50 states. Providence, the state capital, is in the northeast portion of the state. To the southeast is Newport, the state's other well-known city and one of the great sailing capitals of the world. The area known as South County contains coastal towns along U.S. 1, rolling farmland, sparsely populated beaches, and wilderness; it's just a short ferry ride from the South County town of Galilee to scenic Block Island. The Blackstone Valley, in the northern portion of the state, was the cradle of the Industrial Revolution in the United States. The region, which includes the towns of Pawtucket, Woonsocket, and Slatersville, is beginning to blossom as a tourist destination.
CONNECTICUT	Southwestern Connecticut, the richest part of the richest state, is home to commuters, celebrities, and others who seek privacy, rusticity, and proximity to New York City. Far less touristy than other parts of the state, the Connecticut River valley is a stretch of small villages and uncrowded state parks punctuated by a few small cities and one large one: Hartford. The Litchfield Hills have grand old inns, rolling farmlands, and plenty of forests and rivers, making the area a popular retreat for New Yorkers. The Quiet Corner, a string of sparsely populated towns in the northeast known chiefly for their antiquing potential, is also becoming a weekend escape from New York City. New Haven has experienced a dramatic renaissance in recent years and is home to Yale and several fine museums. Along the southeastern coast lie quiet shoreline villages, and, a bit inland, both Foxwoods and Mohegan Sun casinos draw droves of gamblers.

GREAT ITINERARIES

ESSENTIAL NEW ENGLAND

14 to 19 days

In a nation where distances can often be daunting, New England packs its highlights into a remarkably compact area. Understanding Yankeedom might take a lifetime—but it's possible to get a good appreciation for the six-state region in a 2- to 2½-week drive.

Hartford

1 day. The Mark Twain House resembles a Mississippi steamboat beached in a Victorian neighborhood. Downtown, visit Connecticut's ornate State Capitol and the Wadsworth Atheneum, which houses fine Impressionist and Hudson River School paintings. ⇨ Hartford & the Connecticut River Valley *in* Chapter 6.

Lower Connecticut River Valley & Block Island Sound

1 or 2 days. Here centuries-old towns such as Essex and Chester coexist with a well-preserved natural environment. In Rhode Island, sandy beaches dot the coast in Watch Hill, Charlestown, and Narragansett. ⇨ Hartford & the Connecticut River Valley *in* Chapter 6, South County *in* Chapter 5.

Newport

1 day. Despite its Colonial downtown and seaside parks, to most people Newport means mansions—the most opulent, cost-be-damned enclave of private homes ever built in the United States. Turn-of-the-20th-century "cottages" such as the Breakers and Marble House are beyond duplication today. ⇨ Newport County *in* Chapter 5.

Providence

1 day. Rhode Island's capital holds treasures in places such as Benefit Street, with its Federal-era homes, and the Museum of Art at the Rhode Island School of Design. Savor a knockout Italian meal on Federal Hill and visit Waterplace Park. ⇨ Providence *in* Chapter 5.

Cape Cod

2 or 3 days. Meander along Massachusetts' arm-shape peninsula and explore Cape Cod National Seashore. Provincetown, at the Cape's tip, is Bohemian, gay, and touristy, a Portuguese fishing village on a Colonial foundation. In season, you can whale-watch here. ⇨ Cape Cod *in* Chapter 4.

Plymouth

1 day. "America's hometown" is where 102 weary settlers landed in 1620. You can climb aboard the replica *Mayflower II,* then spend time at Plimoth Plantation, staffed by costumed "Pilgrims." ⇨ Around Boston *in* Chapter 4.

Boston

2 or 3 days. In Boston, famous buildings such as Faneuil Hall are not merely civic landmarks but national icons. From the Boston Common, the Freedom Trail extends to encompass foundation stones of American liberty such as Old North Church. Walk the gaslit streets of Beacon Hill, too. On your second day, explore the Museum of Fine Arts and the grand boulevards and shops of Back Bay. Another day, visit the Cambridge campus of Harvard University and its museums. ⇨ Boston *in* Chapter 4.

GREAT
ITINERARIES

Salem & Newburyport

1 or 2 days. In Salem, many sites, including the Peabody Essex Museum, recall the dark days of the 1690s witch hysteria, and the fortunes amassed in the China trade. Newburyport's Colonial and Federal-style homes testify to Yankee enterprise on the seas. ⇨ The North Shore *in* Chapter 4.

Manchester & Concord

1 day. Manchester, New Hampshire's largest city, holds the Amoskeag Mills, a reminder of New England's industrial past. Smaller Concord is the state capital. Near the State House is the fine Museum of New Hampshire History, housing one of the locally built stagecoaches that carried Concord's name throughout the West. ⇨ The Monadnocks & Merrimack Valley *in* Chapter 2.

Green Mountains & Montpelier

1 or 2 days. Route 100 travels through the heart of the Green Mountains, whose rounded peaks assert a modest grandeur. Vermont's vest-pocket capital, Montpelier, has the gold-dome Vermont State House and the quirky Vermont Museum. ⇨ Central Vermont & Northern Vermont *in* Chapter 3.

White Mountains

1 day. U.S. 302 threads through New Hampshire's White Mountains, passing beneath brooding Mt. Washington and through Crawford Notch. In Bretton Woods, the Mt. Washington Cog Railway still chugs to the summit, and the Mount Washington Hotel recalls the glory days of White Mountain resorts. ⇨ The White Mountains *in* Chapter 2.

Portland

1 day. Maine's maritime capital shows off its restored waterfront at the Old Port. Nearby, two lighthouses on Cape Elizabeth, Two Lights and Portland Head, stand vigil. ⇨ Portland to Waldoboro *in* Chapter 1.

GREAT ITINERARIES

FALL FOLIAGE

7 to 12 days

In fall, New England's dense forests explode into reds, oranges, yellows, and purples. Like autumn itself, this itinerary works its way south from northern Vermont into Connecticut. Nature's schedule varies from year to year; as a rule, this trip is best begun around the third week of September. Book accommodations well in advance.

Northwestern Vermont

1 or 2 days. In Burlington, the elms will be turning color on the University of Vermont campus. A ferry ride across Lake Champlain affords great views of Vermont's Green Mountains and New York's Adirondacks. After visiting the resort town of Stowe, continue beneath the cliffs of Smugglers' Notch. The north country's palette unfolds in Newport, where the blue waters of Lake Memphremagog reflect the foliage. ⇨ Northern Vermont *in* Chapter 3.

Northeast Kingdom

1 day. After a side trip along Lake Willoughby, explore St. Johnsbury, where the St. Johnsbury Athenaeum and Fairbanks Museum reveal Victorian tastes in art and natural-history collecting. In Peacham, stock up for a picnic at the Peacham Store. ⇨ Northern Vermont *in* Chapter 3.

White Mountains & Lakes Region

1 or 2 days. In New Hampshire, Interstate 93 narrows as it winds through craggy Franconia Notch. The sinuous Kancamagus Highway passes through the mountains to Conway. In Center Harbor, in the Lakes

Region, you can ride the M/S *Mount Washington* for views of the Lake Winnipesaukee shoreline, or ascend to Moultonborough's Castle in the Clouds for a falcon's-eye look at the colors. ⇨ The White Mountains & Lakes Region *in* Chapter 2.

Mt. Monadnock

1 or 2 days. In Concord, stop at the Museum of New Hampshire History and the State House. Several trails climb Mt. Monadnock, near Jaffrey Center, and colorful vistas extend as far as Boston. ⇨ The Monadnocks & Merrimack Valley *in* Chapter 2.

The Mohawk Trail

1 day. In Shelburne Falls, Massachusetts, the Bridge of Flowers displays the last of autumn's blossoms. Follow the Mohawk Trail as it ascends into the Berkshire Hills—and stop to take in the view at the hairpin turn just east of North Adams. In Williamstown, the Sterling and Francine Clark Art Institute houses a collection of impressionist works. ⇨ The Pioneer Valley & the Berkshires *in* Chapter 4.

The Berkshires

1 or 2 days. The scenery around Lenox, Stockbridge, and Great Barrington has long attracted the talented and the wealthy. You can visit the homes of novelist Edith Wharton (the Mount, in Lenox), sculptor Daniel Chester French (Chesterwood, in Stockbridge), and diplomat Joseph Choate (Naumkeag, in Stockbridge). ⇨ The Berkshires *in* Chapter 4.

GREAT ITINERARIES

The Litchfield Hills

1 or 2 days. This area of Connecticut combines the feel of up-country New England with exclusive urban polish. The wooded shores of Lake Waramaug are home to country inns and wineries in New Preston and other pretty towns. Litchfield has a village green that could be the template for anyone's idealized New England town center. ⇨ The Litchfield Hills *in* Chapter 6.

GREAT ITINERARIES

THE SEACOAST

8 to 14 days

Every New England state except Vermont borders on saltwater. For history buffs, vivid links to the days when the sea was the region's lifeblood abound; for water-sports enthusiasts, the sea guarantees fun on beaches from the sandy shores of Long Island Sound to the bracing waters of Down East Maine. A journey along the coast also brings the promise of fresh seafood, incomparable sunrises, and a quality of light that has entranced artists from Winslow Homer to Edward Hopper.

Southeastern Connecticut & Newport

1 to 3 days. Begin in New London, home of the U.S. Coast Guard Academy, and stop at Groton to tour the *Nautilus* at the Submarine Force Museum. In Mystic, the days of wooden ships and whaling adventures live on at Mystic Seaport. In Rhode Island, savor the Victorian resort of Watch Hill and the Block Island Sound beaches. See the extravagant summer mansions in Newport. ⇨ New Haven & the Southeastern Coast *in* Chapter 6; South County, Block Island & Newport County *in* Chapter 5.

Massachusetts' South Shore & Cape Cod

2 to 4 days. New Bedford was once a major whaling center; exhibits at the New Bedford Whaling Museum capture this vanished world. Cape Cod can be nearly all things to all visitors, with quiet Colonial villages and lively resorts, gentle bay-side wavelets, and crashing surf. In Plymouth, visit the *Mayflower II* and Plimoth Plantation, the re-created Pilgrim village. ⇨ Boston & Cape Cod *in* Chapter 4.

Boston & the North Shore

2 days. To savor Boston's centuries-old ties to the sea, take a half-day stroll by Faneuil Hall and Quincy Market or a boat tour of the harbor. In Salem, America's early shipping fortunes are chronicled in the Peabody Essex Museum and the Salem Maritime National Historic Site. Spend a day exploring more of the North Shore, including the old fishing port of Gloucester and Rockport, one possible place to buy that seascape painted in oils. Newburyport, with its Federal-style shipowners' homes, is home to the Parker River National Wildlife Refuge, beloved by birders and beach walkers. ⇨ Boston & the North Shore *in* Chapter 4.

New Hampshire & Southern Maine

1 or 2 days. New Hampshire fronts the Atlantic for a scant 18 mi, but its coastal landmarks range from honky-tonk Hampton Beach to quiet Odiorne Point State Park in Rye and pretty Portsmouth, where the cream of pre-Revolutionary society built Georgian- and Federal-style mansions—visit a few at Strawbery Banke Museum and elsewhere. Between here and Portland, Maine's largest city and the site of a waterfront revival, you will find ocean-side resorts such as Kennebunkport. Near Portland is Cape Elizabeth, with its Portland Head and Two Lights lighthouses. ⇨ The Coast *in* Chapter 2; York County Coast & Portland to Waldoboro *in* Chapter 1.

Down East

2 or 3 days. Beyond Portland ranges the ragged, island-strewn coast that Mainers call Down East. On your first day, travel

GREAT
ITINERARIES

to Camden or Castine. Some highlights are the retail outlets of Freeport, home of L. L. Bean; Brunswick, with the museums of Bowdoin College; and Bath, with the Maine Maritime Museum. Perhaps you'll think about cruising on one of the schooners that sail out of Rockland. In Camden and Castine, exquisite inns occupy homes built from inland Maine's gold, timber. On your second day, visit the spectacular rocky coast of Acadia National Park, near the resort town of Bar Harbor. If you have another day, drive the desolately beautiful stretch of Maine's granite coast to the New Brunswick border, where President Franklin Roosevelt's "beloved island," Campobello, and Roosevelt Campobello International Park lie across an international bridge. ⇨ Portland to Waldoboro, Penobscot Bay, Mount Desert Island & Way Down East *in* Chapter 1.

WHEN TO GO

°F HARTFORD, CT °C

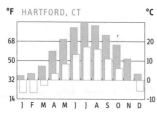

°F BOSTON, MA °C

All six New England states are largely year-round destinations. But you might want to **stay away from rural areas, especially in the northern states, during mud season in April and black-fly season from mid-May to mid-June.** Many smaller museums and attractions are open only from Memorial Day to mid-October, at other times by appointment only.

Memorial Day is the start of the migration to the beaches and the mountains, and summer begins in earnest on July 4. Those who are driving to Cape Cod in July or August should know that Friday and Sunday are the days weekenders clog the overburdened U.S. 6; a better time to visit the beach areas and the islands may be after Labor Day. The same applies to the Maine coast and its feeder roads, Interstate 95 and U.S. 1.

Fall is the most colorful season in New England, a time when many inns and hotels are booked months in advance by foliage-viewing visitors. New England's dense hardwood forests explode in color as the diminishing hours of autumn daylight signal trees to stop producing chlorophyll. As green is stripped away from the leaves of maples, oaks, birches, beeches, and other deciduous species, a rainbow of reds, oranges, yellows, purples, and other vivid hues is revealed. The first scarlet and gold colors emerge in mid-September in northern areas; "peak" color occurs at different times from year to year. Generally, it's best to **visit the northern reaches in late September and early October** and move southward as October progresses.

All leaves are off the trees by Halloween, and hotel rates fall as the leaves do, dropping significantly until ski season begins. November and early December are hunting season in much of New England; those who venture into the woods should wear bright orange clothing.

Winter is the time for downhill and cross-country skiing. New England's major ski resorts are well equipped with snowmaking equipment if nature falls short. Along the coast, bed-and-breakfasts that remain open will often rent rooms at far lower prices than in summer.

WHEN TO GO

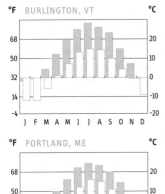

In spring, despite mud season, maple sugaring goes on in Maine, New Hampshire, and Vermont, and the fragrant scent of lilacs is never far away.

Climate

In winter, coastal New England is cold and damp; inland temperatures may be lower, but generally drier conditions make them easier to bear. Snowfall is heaviest in the interior mountains and can range up to several hundred inches per year in northern Maine, New Hampshire, and Vermont. Spring is often windy and rainy; in many years winter appears to segue almost immediately into summer. Coastal areas can be quite humid in summer, making even moderate temperatures uncomfortable. One of the delights of inland northern New England, particularly at higher elevations, is the prevalence of cool summer nights. Autumn temperatures can be quite mild in more southerly areas well into October, although northern portions of the region can be quite cold by Columbus Day. In some years, a period of unseasonably mild weather occurs in late October and early November.

⛏ Forecasts **Weather Channel** ⊕ www.weather.com.

The following are average daily maximum and minimum temperatures in Hartford, CT; Boston, MA; Burlington, VT; and Portland, ME.

ON THE CALENDAR

New England's top seasonal events are listed below. Reserve rooms far in advance for many of these events, especially those that fill up in the busy summer and fall high seasons, or in winter in ski areas.

WINTER	
Dec.	The reenactment of the Boston Tea Party takes place in Boston Harbor (MA). In Nantucket (MA), the first weekend of the month sees an early Christmas celebration with elaborate decorations, costumed carolers, theatrical performances, art exhibits, and a tour of historic homes. In Newport (RI), several Bellevue Avenue mansions open for the holidays, and there are candlelight tours of Colonial homes. At Mystic Seaport (CT), costumed guides escort visitors on lantern-lighted tours. Old Saybrook (CT) has a Christmas Torchlight Parade and Muster of Ancient Fife and Drum Corps, which ends with caroling. The little town of Bethlehem (CT) is the site of a large Christmas festival each December. Several hundred spectacularly decorated trees and wreaths grace the Wadsworth Atheneum in Hartford (CT) during its annual Festival of Trees. Historic Strawbery Banke (NH) has a Christmas Stroll, with carolers, through nine historic homes. Christmas Prelude in Kennebunkport (ME) celebrates winter with concerts, caroling, and special events. The final day of the year is observed with festivals, entertainment, and food in many locations during First Night Celebrations. Some of the major cities hosting First Nights are Portland (ME); Burlington, Montpelier, and St. Johnsbury (VT); Providence (RI); Boston, New Bedford, and Northampton (MA); and Danbury, Hartford, and Mystic (CT).
Jan.	The Maine WinterFest in Freeport (ME) gives professional and amateur ice carvers from around the world a chance to show off. Stowe's (VT) festive Winter Carnival heats up late in the month. Brookfield (VT) holds its Ice Harvest, one of New England's largest.
Feb.	The Camden Snow Bowl in Camden (ME) is the site of the U.S. National Toboggan Championships. On tap at the Brattleboro Winter Carnival (VT), held the last week of the month, are jazz concerts and an ice-fishing derby; Burlington has a similarly well-attended Winter Festival in February. The Mad River Valley Winter Carnival, in Warren (VT), is a week of winter festivities, including dogsled races, ski races, and fireworks. The 10-day Mt. Washington Valley Winter Carnival in Jackson, North Conway, and other towns along Route 16 in the White Mountains (NH), includes ski races and ice sculptures.
Mar.	This is the season for maple-sugaring festivals and events: throughout the month and into April, New England sugarhouses demon-

ON THE CALENDAR

	strate procedures from maple-tree tapping to sap boiling. On Maine Maple Sunday, Maine sugarhouses open for tours and tastings. Stratton Mountain (VT) hosts the U.S. Open Snowboarding Championships. Boston's (MA) St. Patrick's Day Parade is one of the nation's largest. Five acres of landscaped gardens bloom at Boston's (MA) New England Spring Flower Show. At Lyman Plant House on the Smith College Campus in Northampton (MA), more than 2,500 flowering bulbs and spring flowers are on display at the Spring Bulb Show.
SPRING Apr.	During Sugarloaf Reggae Weekend (ME), Caribbean reggae bands play outdoors and inside. At Sunday River's (ME) annual Bust 'n' Burn Mogul Competition, professional and amateur bump skiers test their mettle. Early blooms are the draw of Nantucket's (MA) Daffodil Festival, which celebrates spring with a flower show and a procession of antique cars along roadsides bursting with daffodils. You can gorge on sea grub at Boothbay Harbor's (ME) Fishermen's Festival, held at the end of April. Dedicated runners draw huge crowds to the Boston Marathon (MA), run each year on Patriot's Day (the Monday nearest April 19). Colonial minutemen battle the British at the annual Battle of Lexington and Concord Reenactment (MA). At the Maple Festival, held each April in St. Albans (VT), you can try Sugar on Snow, a taffylike treat.
May	The Shelburne Museum in Shelburne (VT) is awash in purple glory in mid-May, when the Lilac Festival blossoms. Lilac Sunday, at Boston's Arnold Arboretum (MA), celebrates the blooming of more than 250 varieties. If you want to see a moose, visit Greenville (ME) during MooseMainia, which runs from mid-May to mid-June. Events include moose safaris and mountain bike and canoe races. Lobsterfest kicks off Mystic Seaport's (CT) summer of festivities with live entertainment and good food. Holyoke's (MA) Shad Derby is said to be the largest freshwater fishing derby in North America.
June	In Vermont, you can listen to jazz at Burlington's Discover Jazz Festival. The Lake Champlain International Father's Day Derby (VT) entices anglers to try their fishing skills. Jacob's Pillow Dance Festival at Becket (MA) in the Berkshires hosts performers of various dance traditions in June through August. The Boothbay Harbor Windjammer Days starts the high season for Maine's boating set. The Blessing of the Fleet in Provincetown (MA) culminates a weekend of festivities celebrating the town's Portuguese heritage. Mystic Seaport in Mystic (CT) hosts its annual Small Craft Weekend. The Sea Music Festival, in Mystic (CT), is a celebration of New England's quintessential folk music. In Essex (CT), the Hot Steamed Jazz Festival

mingles the music of traditional jazz with the sounds of vintage lo-comotion at the Essex SteamTrain Station. A Taste of Hartford lets you eat your way through Connecticut's capital city while enjoying outdoor music, dance, comedy, and magic. Burlington's (VT) Green Mountain Chew Chew offers a variety of entertainment including outdoor music and comedy. New Haven (CT) hosts the two-week International Festival of Arts and Ideas, showcasing music, dance, theater, film, visual arts, and literature. During the Strawberry Festival in Wiscasset (ME), you can get your fill of strawberry goodies. At the Great Chowder Cookoff in Newport (RI), restaurants compete for the distinction of having the best chowder in New England.

SUMMER		During Bath's (ME) Heritage Days, Independence Day is celebrated with concerts, family entertainment, an art show, a parade, and fireworks.
	July	

Exeter (NH) holds the American Independence Festival at the American Independence Museum with battle reenactments and period crafts and antiques. The Mashpee Powwow (MA) brings Native Americans from North and South America to Cape Cod for three days of dance contests, drumming, a fireball game, and a clambake. The Marlboro Music Festival presents classical music at Marlboro College (VT) from mid-July to mid-August. Newport's (RI) Music Festival brings together celebrated musicians for two weeks of concerts in Newport mansions. The Tanglewood Music Festival, which begins in late June and perseveres through August, fills the air around Lenox (MA) with performances by the Boston Symphony Orchestra and major entertainers. Glorious outdoor concert sites and sumptuous picnics are sidelines to fine music at the Vermont Mozart Festival, held throughout central and northern Vermont in July and August. The two-day Stoweflake Hot Air Balloon Festival in Stowe (VT) is one of the state's most popular events. Admire the furnishings of homes during the annual Open House Tour in Litchfield (CT). Folks flock to the Mashantucket Pequot's Fireworks on the Thames River in New London (CT) to view one of the country's largest fireworks events. In Mystic (CT), vintage powerboats and sailboats are on view at the Antique and Classic Boat Rendezvous. The Yarmouth Clam Festival (ME) is more than a seafood celebration—expect continuous entertainment and a crafts show throughout the three-day event.

	Aug.	The Newport Folk Festival (RI) is one of the region's most popular musical events. Another top music event is the Newport Jazz Festival. Stowe (VT) hosts a popular Antique Car Show. The Bar Harbor Jazz Festival

ON THE CALENDAR

(ME) hosts classical, jazz, and popular music concerts. The Southern Vermont Art and Craft Festival in Manchester (VT) features popular arts, crafts, and antiques. The Outdoor Art Festival in Mystic (CT) presents the works of fine local artists. Sellers and collectors throng to the Maine Antiques Festival in Union. Waterfront activities, arts and crafts, entertainment, and succulent Maine lobster feature prominently at Rockland's (ME) Maine Lobster Festival. Everything's coming up blueberries at the Wild Blueberry Festival in Machias (ME). In Rangeley Lake (ME), the blueberry is king at the annual Blueberry Festival. Rhode Islanders honor their favorite shellfish at the International Quahog Festival in Wickford. A Bluefish Festival takes place in Clinton (CT). Brunswick's Maine Festival is a four-day celebration of Maine arts. The Annual Maine Highland Games, in Brunswick, feature traditional Scottish athletic events and music entertainment. The Martha's Vineyard Agricultural Fair (MA) includes animal shows, a carnival, and evening entertainment. In New Bedford (MA), the Feast of the Blessed Sacrament is the country's largest Portuguese feast.

FALL Sept.	New England's Labor Day fairs include the Vermont State Fair in Rutland, with agricultural exhibits and entertainment. The International Seaplane Fly-In Weekend sets Moosehead Lake (ME) buzzing. The Champlain Valley Fair, in Burlington (VT), has all the features of a large county fair. The Rhythm and Roots Festival of Cajun food, music, and dancing is held in Charlestown (RI). Many of the country's finest fiddlers compete at the Traditional Old-Time Fiddler's Contest in Barre (VT). In Stratton (VT), artists and performers gather for the Vermont Arts & Fine Craft Festival. Providence (RI) shows off its diversity during its Rhode Island Heritage Festival. The Common Ground Country Fair in Unity (ME) is an organic farmer's delight. The Deerfield Fair (NH) is one of New England's oldest agricultural fairs. The six small Vermont towns of Walden, Cabot, Plainfield, Peacham, Barnet, and Groton host the weeklong Northeast Kingdom Fall Foliage Festival. Crafts, entertainment, and fried scallops are served up at the Bourne Scallop Fest in Buzzards Bay Park in Bourne (MA). For the Martha's Vineyard Striped Bass and Bluefish Derby (MA), from mid-September to mid-October, locals cast their lines in search of a prizewinning whopper. The Maine Salmon Festival, in Eastport (ME), the first Sunday after Labor Day, hosts entertainers and crafts artists. At the annual Hampton Beach Seafood Festival (NH), you can sample seafood specialties, dance to live bands, and watch fireworks.
Oct.	The Fryeburg Fair (ME) presents agricultural exhibits, harness racing, and a pig scramble. The Nantucket Arts Festival in Massachu-

		setts is a 10-day celebration including performances, lectures, gallery exhibitions, walking tours, and other community events. Connecticut's Quiet Corner holds a Walking Weekend, with 50 guided scenic walks through the towns, along rivers, and in the woods of this rural area. The Vermont International Film Festival presents films dealing with environmental, human rights, and political issues for a week in Burlington (VT). Hildene Farm, Food and Folk Art Fair in Manchester (VT) has farm activities, entertainment, and lots of events for kids.
	Nov.	The Annual Wild Game Supper, in Bradford (VT), draws thousands to taste large and small game animals and birds. New Haven's (CT) Annual Celebration of American Crafts exhibits and sells works of more than 400 juried craftspeople.

IF YOU LIKE

Beaches

Long, wide beaches edge the New England coast from southern Maine to southern Connecticut; the most popular are on Cape Cod, Martha's Vineyard, Nantucket, and the shore areas north and south of Boston; on Maine's York County coast; Block Island Sound in Rhode Island; and the coastal region of New Hampshire. Many are maintained by state and local governments and have lifeguards on duty; they may have picnic facilities, restrooms, changing facilities, and concession stands. Depending on the locale, you may need a parking sticker to use the lot. The waters are at their warmest in August, though they're cold even at the height of summer along much of the Maine coast. Inland, small lake beaches abound, most notably in New Hampshire and Vermont.

Bicycling

Cape Cod, in Massachusetts, has miles of bike trails, some paralleling the national seashore, most on level terrain. On either side of the Cape Cod Canal is an easy 7-mi straight trail with views of the canal traffic. Other favorite areas for bicycling are the Massachusetts Berkshires, the New Hampshire Lakes Region, and Vermont's Green Mountains and Champlain Valley. Nantucket, Martha's Vineyard, and Block Island can be thoroughly explored by bicycle. Biking in Maine is especially scenic in and around Kennebunkport, Camden, Deer Isle, and the Schoodic Peninsula. The carriage paths in Acadia National Park are ideal. Many ski resorts allow mountain bikes in summer.

Boating

Along many of New England's larger lakes, sailboats, rowboats, canoes, and outboards can be rented at local marinas. Sailboats are available for rent at a number of seacoast locations; you may, however, be required to demonstrate competence. Lessons are also frequently available. In Rhode Island, Block Island Sound, Narragansett Bay, and Newport are revered by sailors worldwide. Maine's Penobscot Bay draws boaters, including windjammers. Lakes in New Hampshire and Vermont are splendid for all kinds of boating. In Massachusetts, the Connecticut River in the Pioneer Valley and the Housatonic River in the Berkshires are popular for canoeing. Maine's Allagash Wilderness Waterway is one of the region's premier places to canoe.

Dining

Seafood is king throughout New England. Clam favorites include chowder, made with milk or cream, unlike the tomato-based Manhattan version, and big, meaty quahogs; fried clams; and steamers. Some lobster classics include plain boiled lobster—a staple at "in the rough" picnic-bench-and-paper-plate spots along the Maine coast—and lobster rolls, a lobster meat and mayo (or just melted butter) preparation served in a hot dog bun. The leading fin fish is scrod—young cod or haddock—best sampled baked or broiled.

Inland specialties run to the plain and familiar dishes of old-fashioned Sunday-dinner America—pot roast, roast turkey, baked ham, hefty stacks of pancakes (with local maple syrup, of course), and apple pie. One regional favorite is Indian pudding, a long-boiled cornmeal-and-molasses concoction that's delicious with vanilla ice cream. As for ethnic menus, New England has welcomed Chinese, Thai, Middle Eastern, and all the other international cuisines popular in America. The region's deeper ethnic traditions, though, take in the hearty Portuguese pork and fish dishes and spicy sausages of southern Massachusetts and Rhode Island; the festival of Italian flavors that is Boston's North End and Providence's Federal Hill; and the pork pie (*tortière*) and pea soup of northern New England's French-Canadians.

Fishing

Anglers will find sport aplenty throughout the region—surf casting along the shore; deep-sea fishing in the Atlantic on party and charter boats; fishing for trout in streams; and angling for bass, landlocked salmon, and other fish in freshwater lakes. Maine's Moosehead and Rangeley lakes regions are draws for serious anglers, as are Vermont's Lakes Champlain and Memphremagog and the Connecticut Lakes of far northern New Hampshire. Coastal towns in southeastern Connecticut and Rhode Island (notably Narragansett) are home to scores of deep-sea charter boats. Sporting-goods stores and bait-and-tackle shops are reliable resources for licenses—necessary in freshwater—and leads to the nearest hot spots.

Golf

Golf caught on early in New England. The region has an ample supply of public and semiprivate courses, many of which are attached to distinctive resorts or even ski areas. One dilemma facing golfers is keeping their eyes on the ball instead of the scenery: in Manchester, Vermont, the Gleneagles Course at the Equinox Hotel is ringed by mountain splendor, as are the links at the Balsams Wilderness grand resort in Dixville Notch, New Hampshire, and the nearby course at the splendid old Mount Washington Hotel in Bretton Woods. During prime season, make sure you reserve ahead for tee times, particularly near urban areas and at resorts.

IF YOU LIKE

Hiking

Probably the most famous trails are the 255-mi Long Trail, which runs north–south through the center of Vermont, and the Maine-to-Georgia Appalachian Trail, which runs through New England on both private and public land. The Appalachian Mountain Club (AMC) maintains a system of staffed huts in New Hampshire's Presidential Range, with bunk space and meals available by reservation. You'll find good hiking in many state parks throughout the region.

National & State Parks & Forests

National parks and forests provide myriad facilities, including campgrounds, picnic grounds, hiking trails, nature walks, boating, and ranger programs. Contact the state tourism offices or specific national park or forest headquarters for more information on any of these.

Connecticut. Although Connecticut has no national parks or forests, stretched along 60 mi of its coastline from Norwalk to Westbrook are the eight units of the Stewart B. McKinney National Wildlife Refuge, popular with birders. A 52-mi swath of the Appalachian Trail, which is part of the national park system, cuts through Litchfield County, in the northwestern part of the state. The Litchfield Hills have a strong concentration of protected green spaces, of which the best include Kent Falls State Park, Mt. Tom, Dennis Hill, Haystack Mountain, Housatonic Meadows, and Burr Pond. Elsewhere in the state, Dinosaur State Park, north of Middletown in Rocky Hill, has dinosaur tracks dating from the Jurassic period. Gillette Castle State Park, an outrageous hilltop castle on 117 acres, has excellent hiking and picnicking.

Maine. Acadia National Park, which preserves fine stretches of shoreline and high mountains, covers much of Mount Desert Island and more than half of Isle au Haut on the mainland. Baxter State Park comprises more than 200,000 acres of wilderness surrounding Katahdin, Maine's highest mountain. Hiking and moose-watching are major activities. The Allagash Wilderness Waterway is a 92-mi corridor of lakes and rivers surrounded by vast commercial forest property. A number of state parks line Maine's fabled rockbound coast; at Camden Hills State Park, an auto road winds to the top of Mt. Battie for spectacular views of Penobscot Bay.

Massachusetts. Terrain of all kinds unfolds in Massachusetts state parks and forests, ranging from the heights of Mt. Tom State Reservation overlooking the Pioneer Valley near Holyoke to the many public lands in the Berkshire Hills, most spectacular of which is the Mt. Greylock State Reservation surrounding the state's highest peak. Cape Cod National Seashore, a 30-mi stretch of the Cape between Chatham and Provincetown, has excellent swimming, biking, bird-watching, and nature walks. Parker River National Wildlife Refuge, near Newburyport, is a jewel of the nation's refuge system, comprising a barrier island rich in birdlife and dune vegetation.

New Hampshire. New Hampshire state parklands vary widely, even within a region. Major recreation parks are at Franconia Notch, Crawford Notch, and Mt. Sunapee. Rhododendron State Park near Fitzwilliam in the Monadnock region has a singular collection of wild rhododendrons; Mt. Washington Park (White Mountains) is on top of 6,288-foot Mt. Washington, the highest point in the Northeast. Along New

Hampshire's short coastline, Hampton Beach and Odiorne Point state parks provide fine ocean swimming. The White Mountain National Forest covers 770,000 acres of northern New Hampshire, including Mt. Washington and the other peaks of the Presidential Range; several federally designated wilderness areas lie within its boundaries. Near the city of Portsmouth, Great Bay Estuarine Research Reserve has fine birding and canoeing opportunities on a shallow backwater of the Piscataqua River.

Rhode Island. Rhode Island makes up for its small size with 19 preserves, state parks, beaches, and forest areas, including a string of beautifully maintained public beaches along Block Island Sound and Narragansett Bay. Fifteen state parks in Rhode Island permit camping. Its federally protected areas consist of an impressive string of national wildlife refuges along the shores of Rhode Island Sound. These include Ninigret and Sachuest national wildlife refuges.

Vermont. Vermont has one of the Northeast's best developed systems of state parks, many of which are along the shores of lakes ideal for swimming, fishing, and boating. Most have campsites and boat rentals. Several of the most attractive are among the islands of northern Lake Champlain. The 350,000-acre Green Mountain National Forest consists of separate northern and southern portions in the center of the state. Hikers treasure the more than 500 mi of trails; canoeists work its white waters; and campers and anglers find plenty to keep them happy. Among the most popular spots are the Falls of Lana and Silver Lake near Middlebury. The Marsh-Billings-Rockefeller National Historical Park, in Woodstock, is dedicated to the legacy of conservation and land stewardship associated with the trio of local luminaries for which it is named. On the shores of Lake Champlain in the state's northwestern corner, the Missisquoi National Wildlife Refuge provides superb wildfowl habitat.

IF YOU LIKE

Shopping

Antiques, crafts, maple syrup and sugar, and fresh produce lure shoppers to New England's flea markets, bazaars, yard sales, country stores, and farmers' markets.

Antiques. Best bets for antiquing in Connecticut include U.S. 7 (in Wilton and Ridgefield, and also in western Litchfield County), New Preston, Putnam and Woodstock, Woodbury and Litchfield, and the area of West Cornwall just east of the covered bridge. Antiques stores are plentiful in Newport but are a specialty of Rhode Island's South County: the best places to browse are Wickford, Charlestown, and Watch Hill. In Massachusetts, the North Shore around Essex has a large concentration of antiques stores, but plenty of shops thrive in Salem and Cape Ann and along Boston's Charles Street at the base of Beacon Hill. Also try the Berkshires around Great Barrington, South Egremont, and Sheffield. One of America's biggest open-air antiques markets is held at Brimfield, Massachusetts, on several dates in summer and fall. Particularly in the Monadnock region of New Hampshire, dealers abound in barns and home stores strung along back roads—along Route 119, from Fitzwilliam to Hinsdale; Route 101, from Marlborough to Wilton; and in the towns of Hopkinton, Hollis, and Amherst. In southern New Hampshire, shops flourish along the stretch of U.S. 4 between Durham and Concord. In Vermont, antiques shops and barns are scattered just about everywhere but are especially concentrated along the southern portions of U.S. 7 and along Route 30, particularly in and around Newfane. In Maine, antiques shops are clustered in Wiscasset and Searsport and along U.S. 1 between Kittery and Scarborough.

Crafts. Try Washington Street in South Norwalk, Connecticut; in Massachusetts, Provincetown on Cape Cod and the Berkshires have some good shops. In Vermont, galleries in Burlington, Middlebury, and Windsor sell work by some of the best of the state's craftspeople, although artisans have set up shop throughout the state. The League of New Hampshire Craftsmen operates nine excellent shops, including locations in Concord, Exeter, and North Conway. On Maine's Deer Isle, Haystack Mountain School of Crafts attracts internationally renowned craftspeople to its summer institute. The Schoodic Peninsula is home to many skilled artisans. Passamaquoddy baskets can be found in Eastport.

Produce. Opportunities abound for obtaining fresh farm produce from the source; some farms allow you to pick your own strawberries, raspberries, blueberries, and apples. October in Maine is prime time for pumpkins and potatoes. Maple-syrup producers demonstrate the process to visitors, most notably in Vermont. Maple syrup is available in different grades; although Grade AA, "fancy," is the lightest in color and the most refined, many Vermonters prefer grade B, which has a deeper flavor and is often used in cooking. Grade A, medium amber in color, has a light caramel flavor and is often used with pancakes and hot cereals.

Skiing

New England resorts reflect New England values: independence, resourcefulness, and thriftiness. No two are alike. Although skiing may have changed the face of some resorts, it hasn't affected the charm of the New England village: the church on the town green, the barns and homesteads brimming with antiques for sale, the country inns.

Blending Old and New. New England areas have attitude and history on their side. Some of the first lifts in North America were located here: a shovel handle tow at Black Mountain, New Hampshire; single chairlifts at Stowe and Mad River Glen, Vermont. Many of these have given way to high-speed chairlifts, trams, and gondolas.

Sugar Hill, in Franconia, New Hampshire, was the site of America's first ski school. Today most areas have instructional programs for adults and children, including clinics for women, tree skiers, bump bashers, and extreme skiers. First-timers should ask about Learn-to-Ski-or-Ride programs that package lessons with equipment and a lift ticket. Discovery Centers at Mt. Snow and Killington, Vermont; Sunday River, Maine; and Attitash Bear Peak, New Hampshire, are excellent programs for families and beginners.

Perhaps nowhere is the blend of old and new more apparent than on the hill. Old-fashioned trails ebb and flow with the mountain's contours, weaving through woods, over knolls, and providing glimpses of the surrounding countryside. Newer trails were built to accommodate snowmaking and grooming equipment; they're usually wide and often follow the fall line. Often, at the same mountain, you can cruise down a steep, wide, perfectly groomed slope; experience the thrills of linking tight turns on a narrow, bump-choked trail; or ramble along a trail that takes the least direct route from summit to base.

Advanced skiers have even more options: tree skiers can snake their way through glades at most resorts, with Stowe Mountain and Jay Peak, Vermont, and Sugarloaf/USA and Sunday River, Maine, providing some of the best tree skiing in the country. For the true expert, Tuckerman Ravine in New Hampshire is the Holy Grail. This hike to–only terrain on Mt. Washington, New England's tallest peak, is a rite of passage.

New England's weather can be unpredictable: rain on the coast is often snow in the mountains, and sleet at lower elevations may be feathery powder at higher ones. For the most part, modern snowmaking and grooming produce reliable conditions from early December into April. Nevertheless, New England snow is not Western-style snow. What New Englanders consider hard-packed powder, Westerners often consider ice. Although powder days are a rare treat here, grooming means top-to-bottom cruising runs are the rule. It can get cold, but if you dress in layers and wear a neck warmer and face mask, you'll be prepared. As a general rule, the farther north the ski area, the longer the season and the more natural snow you can expect.

Riding, Gliding, Shoeing. Snowboarding has changed American resorts as riders have come to share the lifts, slopes, and trails with skiers. Most resorts have embraced snowboarding. Half pipes and terrain parks are popular not only with riders but also with skiers. New snow toys, such as the giant Zorb ball, ski bikes, and snow blades,

IF YOU LIKE

as well as tubing parks, provide alternative activities.

Off-the-hill activities abound. Cross-country centers such as Jackson, Bretton Woods, and the Balsams Wilderness, New Hampshire; Bethel, Maine; and Stowe, Vermont, have gained international recognition for their climate, terrain, and size. Bretton Woods and the Balsams are self-contained downhill and cross-country resorts anchored by historic grand resort hotels. In Jackson, you can ski from inn to inn, and Stowe has the Trapp Family Lodge. At many cross-country centers you can also snowshoe, a wonderful, easy-to-do sport.

Saving Big by Thinking Small. Although day tickets at the bigger resorts approach $60, those at smaller areas can be as low as $20. Some independently owned areas are bona fide bargains for skiers who don't require the glitz of the high-profile resorts. Family pricing, multiday tickets, frequent-skier programs, junior and senior rates, Web-site deals, and lift-and-lodging packages can all lower the price significantly. Midweek prices are often less expensive, and many areas offer incentives then, such as two-for-one days.

Most ski areas have a variety of accommodations—lodges, condominiums, hotels, motels, inns, bed-and-breakfasts—close to the action. For stays of three days or more, a package rate may be a good deal. Packages vary in composition, price, and availability; their components may include a room, meals, lift tickets, ski lessons, rental equipment, transfers to the mountain, parties, races, use of a sports center, tips, and taxes. In general, if you're willing to commute a few extra miles, off-site lodging offers good value.

Getting Practical. Rental equipment is available at all ski areas, at ski shops around resorts, and even in cities far from ski areas. Shop personnel will advise you on equipment and how to use it.

Ski areas have devised standards for rating and marking trails and slopes that offer fairly accurate guides. Trails are rated Easier (green circle), More Difficult (blue square), Most Difficult (black diamond), and Expert (double diamond). Keep in mind that trail difficulty is measured relative to that of other trails at the same ski area. A black-diamond trail at one area may rate only a blue square at a neighboring area. Unless you're able to handle any type of terrain, your best bet is to start on green-circle trails and work your way up in difficulty until you find the terrain where you're most comfortable.

If you're traveling with children, ask about programs geared to their age. Areas renowned for their family emphasis include Smugglers' Notch, Vermont, and Waterville Valley, New Hampshire. Both have plenty of activities, both on the snow and off, for all ages. Child-care centers can be found at virtually all ski areas and often accept children from ages six weeks to six years. Parents must usually supply formula and diapers for infants; reservations are advised at most, essential at some. Most programs also have instructional opportunities for children at least three years of age and older.

SMART TRAVEL TIPS

Finding out about your destination before you leave home means you won't squander time organizing everyday minutiae once you've arrived. You'll be more streetwise when you hit the ground as well, better prepared to explore the aspects of New England that drew you here in the first place. The organizations in this section can provide information to supplement this guide; contact them for up-to-the-minute details, and consult the A to Z sections that end each chapter for facts on the various topics as they relate to the different regions. Happy landings!

AIR TRAVEL

Most travelers visiting New England head for a major gateway, such as Boston, Providence, Hartford-Springfield, Manchester, or even New York City or Albany, and then rent a car to explore the region. The New England states form a fairly compact region, with few important destinations more than six hours apart by car. It's costly and generally impractical to fly within New England, the exceptions being the island resort destinations of Martha's Vineyard, Nantucket, and Block Island, which have regular service from Boston and a few other regional airports.

Boston's Logan Airport is one of the nation's most important domestic and international airports, with direct flights coming from all over North America and Europe as well as other continents. New England's other major airports receive few international flights (mostly from Canada) but do offer a wide range of direct domestic flights to East Coast and Midwest destinations, and to a lesser extent to the western United States.

BOOKING

When you book, look for nonstop flights and remember that "direct" flights stop at least once en route. Try to avoid connecting flights, which require a change of plane. Two airlines may operate a connecting flight jointly, so ask whether your airline operates every segment of the trip; you may find that the carrier you prefer flies you only part of the way. To find more booking tips and to check prices and make online flight reservations, log on to www.fodors.com.

CARRIERS

Numerous airlines, large and small, fly to and from Boston; additionally, the discount carrier Southwest Airlines flies to Albany, Hartford/Springfield (Bradley International Airport), Providence, and Manchester, New Hampshire. Smaller or discount airlines serving Boston include AirTran, Cape Air, JetBlue, and Midwest. Cape Air also provides service from Cape Cod and the islands to Providence and New Bedford. You can fly to Burlington from New York City on JetBlue, and you can fly to Providence from Fort Myers and Fort Lauderdale on Spirit Airlines. ATA serves Hartford from Dallas, and serves Manchester and Providence from Dallas, San Francisco, and Honolulu.

✈ Domestic Carriers **American** ☎ 800/433-7300 ⊕ www.americanairlines.com. **Continental** ☎ 800/525-0280 ⊕ www.continental.com. **Delta** ☎ 800/221-1212 ⊕ www.delta.com. **Northwest/KLM** ☎ 800/225-2525 ⊕ www.nwa.com. **United** ☎ 800/241-6522 ⊕ www.united.com. **US Airways** ☎ 800/428-4322 ⊕ www.usairways.com.

✈ International Carriers **Aer Lingus** ☎ 800/474-7424 ⊕ www.aerlingus.ie. **Air Canada** ☎ 888/247-2262 ⊕ www.aircanada.ca. **Air France** ☎ 800/237-2747 ⊕ www.airfrance.com. **Alitalia Airlines** ☎ 800/223-5730 ⊕ www.alitalia.com. **British Airways** ☎ 800/247-9297, 0870/85-098-50 in the U.K. ⊕ www.ba.com. **Lufthansa** ☎ 800/645-3880 ⊕ www.lufthansa.com. **Virgin Atlantic Airways** ☎ 800/862-8621, 01293/450-150 in the U.K. ⊕ www.virgin-atlantic.com.

✈ Smaller Airlines **AirTran Airways** ☎ 800/247-8726 ⊕ www.airtran.com. **ATA Airlines** ☎ 800/225-2995 ⊕ www.ata.com. **Cape Air** ☎ 800/352-0714 ⊕ www.flycapeair.com. **JetBlue** ☎ 800/538-2583 ⊕ www.jetblue.com. **Midwest** ☎ 800/452-2022 ⊕ www.midwestairlines.com. **Southwest Airlines** ☎ 800/435-9792 ⊕ www.southwest.com. **Spirit Airlines** ☎ 800/772-7117 ⊕ www.spiritair.com.

CHECK-IN & BOARDING

Always **find out your carrier's check-in policy.** Plan to arrive at the airport about 2 hours before your scheduled departure time for domestic flights and 2½ to 3 hours before international flights. You may need to arrive earlier if you're flying from one of the busier airports or during peak air-traffic times. Keep in mind you can probably arrive a bit later (60 to 90 minutes ahead of departure) for domestic flights from Albany, Hartford, Providence, and Manchester, which are smaller and more manageable than Logan and the New York City facilities. To avoid delays at airport-security checkpoints, try not to wear any metal. Jewelry, belt and other buckles, steel-toe shoes, barrettes, and underwire bras are among the items that can set off detectors.

Assuming that not everyone who has bought a ticket will show up for the flight, airlines routinely overbook planes. When everyone does check in, airlines ask for volunteers to give up their seats. In return, these volunteers usually receive a flight voucher worth several hundred dollars applicable toward the purchase of another ticket and are rebooked on the next flight out. If there are not enough volunteers, the airline must choose who will be denied boarding. The first to get bumped are passengers who checked in late and those flying on discounted tickets, so get to the gate and check in as early as possible, especially during peak periods.

Always **bring a government-issued photo ID** to the airport; even when it's not required, a passport is best.

CUTTING COSTS

The least expensive airfares to New England are priced for round-trip travel. Airlines generally allow you to change your return date for a fee; most low-fare tickets, however, are nonrefundable. It's smart to call a number of airlines and check the Internet; when you are quoted a good price, book it on the spot—the same fare may not be available the next day, or even the next hour. Always check different routings and look into using alternate airports. Also, price off-peak flights, which may be significantly less expensive than others. Travel agents, especially low-fare specialists (⇨ Discounts & Deals), are helpful.

Airlines often post discounted "cyberfares" on their Web sites. The best bargains are on unsold seats on upcoming flights. If your plans are flexible, you can often save 60% to 70% by booking on-line. Discount travel Web sites such as Travelocity and Priceline.com also offer reduced fares.

Consolidators are another good source. They buy tickets for scheduled flights at reduced rates from the airlines, then sell them at prices that beat the best fare available directly from the airlines. (Many also offer reduced car-rental and hotel rates.) Sometimes you can even get your money back if you need to return the ticket. Carefully read the fine print detailing penalties for changes and cancellations, purchase the ticket with a credit card, and confirm your consolidator reservation with the airline.

When you fly as a courier, you trade your checked-luggage space for a ticket deeply subsidized by a courier service. There are restrictions on when you can book and how long you can stay. Some courier companies list with membership organizations, such as the Air Courier Association and the International Association of Air Travel Couriers; these require you to become a member before you can book a flight.

⚑ Consolidators AirlineConsolidator.com ☎ 888/468-5385 ⊕ www.airlineconsolidator.com; for international tickets. **Best Fares** ☎ 800/880-1234 or 800/576-8255 ⊕ www.bestfares.com; $59.90 annual membership. **CheapTickets** ☎ 888/922-8849 or 615/874-4304 ⊕ www.cheaptickets.com. **Expedia** ☎ 800/397-3342 or 404/728-8787 ⊕ www.expedia.com. **Hotwire** ☎ 866/468-9473 or 920/330-9418 ⊕ www.hotwire.com. **Onetravel.com** ⊕ www.onetravel.com. **Orbitz** ☎ 888/656-4546 ⊕ www.orbitz.com. **Priceline.com** ⊕ www.priceline.com. **Travelocity** ☎ 888/872-8356, 877/282-2925 in Canada, 0870/876-3876 in the U.K. ⊕ www.travelocity.com.

⚑ Courier Resources Air Courier Association/Cheaptrips.com ☎ 800/280-5973 or 800/282-1202 ⊕ www.aircourier.org or www.cheaptrips.com; $39 annual membership, plus $15 processing fee. **International Association of Air Travel Couriers** ☎ 515/292-2458 ⊕ www.courier.org; $45 annual membership.

ENJOYING THE FLIGHT

State your seat preference when purchasing your ticket, and then repeat it when you confirm and when you check in. For more legroom, you can request one of the few emergency-aisle seats at check-in, if you're capable of moving obstacles comparable in weight to an airplane exit door (usually between 35 pounds and 60 pounds)—a Federal Aviation Administration requirement of passengers in these seats. Seats behind a bulkhead also offer more legroom, but they don't have under-seat storage. Don't sit in the row in front of the emergency aisle or in front of a bulkhead, where seats may not recline.

Airlines have cut back on in-flight meal service. Ask whether a snack or meal is served on the flight. If you have dietary concerns, request special meals when booking. These can be vegetarian, low-cholesterol, or kosher, for example. It's a good idea to pack some healthful snacks and a small (plastic) bottle of water in your carry-on bag. On long flights, try to maintain a normal routine, to help fight jet lag. At night, get some sleep. By day, eat light meals, drink water (not alcohol), and **move around the cabin** to stretch your legs. For additional jet-lag tips consult *Fodor's FYI: Travel Fit & Healthy* (available at bookstores everywhere).

All flights within the United States are strictly nonsmoking, as are international flights on American-based carriers. Smoking regulations vary among non-U.S.-based carriers, so call if this is important to you. It is uncommon for U.S. airports to allow smoking, although a few permit it in specially designated areas.

FLYING TIMES

Some sample flying times to Boston are: from Chicago (2½ hours), London (6½ hours), and Los Angeles (6 hours). Times from U.S. destinations are similar, if slightly shorter, to Albany and Hartford, assuming you can find direct flights.

HOW TO COMPLAIN

If your baggage goes astray or your flight goes awry, complain right away. Most carriers require that you **file a claim immediately.** The Aviation Consumer Protection Division of the Department of Transportation publishes *Fly-Rights*, which discusses airlines and consumer issues and is available online. You can also find articles and information on mytravelrights.com, the Web site of the nonprofit Consumer Travel Rights Center.

▶ Airline Complaints Aviation Consumer Protection Division ✉ U.S. Department of Transportation, Office of Aviation Enforcement and Proceedings, C-75, 400 7th St. SW, Room 4107, Washington, DC 20590 ☎ 202/366-2220 ⊕ airconsumer.ost.dot.gov. **Federal Aviation Administration Consumer Hotline** ✉ For inquiries: FAA, 800 Independence Ave. SW, Washington, DC 20591 ☎ 866/835-5322 ⊕ www.faa.gov.

RECONFIRMING

Check the status of your flight before you leave for the airport. You can do this on your carrier's Web site, by linking to a flight-status checker (many Web booking services offer these), or by calling your carrier or travel agent.

AIRPORTS

The main gateway to New England is Boston's Logan International Airport (BOS), the region's largest. Bradley International Airport (BDL), in Windsor Locks, Connecticut, 12 mi north of Hartford, is convenient to western Massachusetts and all of Connecticut. T. F. Green Airport (PVD), just outside Providence, Rhode Island, is another major airport. Additional New England airports served by major carriers include Manchester International Airport (MHT) in New Hampshire (a rapidly growing, lower-cost alternative to Boston); Portland International Jetport (PWM) in Maine; and Burlington International Airport (BTV) in Vermont. Other airports are in Bangor, Maine, and Hyannis, Massachusetts (Barnstable Municipal).

▶ Airport Information Bangor International Airport ☎ 207/992-4600 ⊕ www.flybangor.com. **Barnstable Municipal Airport** ☎ 508/775-2020 ⊕ www.town.barnstable.ma.us/departments/airport. **Bradley International Airport** ☎ 860/292-2000 ⊕ www.bradleyairport.com. **Burlington International Airport** ☎ 802/863-1889 ⊕ www.burlingtonintlairport.com. **Logan International Airport** ☎ 800/235-6426 ⊕ www.massport.com/logan. **Manchester International Airport** ☎ 603/624-6539 ⊕ www.flymanchester.com. **Portland International Jetport** ☎ 207/774-7301 ⊕ www.

portlandjetport.org. **T. F. Green Airport** ☎ 401/737-8222 or 888/268-7222 ⊕ www.pvdairport.com.

BIKE TRAVEL

Cyclists favor New England because overnight destinations are seldom far apart. Inns and B&Bs are plentiful, and some operators provide guided inn-to-inn tours. In general, northern (except for far northern Maine) and western New England have the best cycling opportunities, with plenty of lightly traveled secondary roads and pleasant small towns to explore en route. Make sure you're in shape if you plan to tackle the hills of Vermont and New Hampshire, and **consider a mountain bike** if you're going to be on dirt roads. Both mountain and touring bikes are available for rent in resort areas and in most larger towns and cities for as little as $20 a day.

BIKES IN FLIGHT

Most airlines accommodate bikes as luggage, provided they are dismantled and boxed; check with individual airlines about packing requirements. Some airlines sell bike boxes, which are often free at bike shops, for about $20 (bike bags can be considerably more expensive). International travelers often can substitute a bike for a piece of checked luggage at no charge; otherwise, the cost is about $100. Most U.S. and Canadian airlines charge $50–$80 each way.

BOAT & FERRY TRAVEL

Principal ferry routes in New England connect New Bedford on the mainland and Cape Cod with Martha's Vineyard and Nantucket, Boston with Provincetown, southern Rhode Island with Block Island, and Connecticut with New York's Long Island and Block Island. Other routes provide access to many islands off the Maine coast. In addition, ferries cross Lake Champlain between Vermont and upstate New York. International service between Portland and Bar Harbor, Maine, and Yarmouth, Nova Scotia, is also available. With the exception of the Lake Champlain ferries, which are first-come, first-served, car reservations are always advisable. *See* the individual state A to Z sections for specific information on ferry companies, fares, and schedules.

BUSINESS HOURS

Hours in New England differ little from those in other parts of the United States. Within the region, shops and other businesses tend to keep slightly later hours in larger cities and along the coast, which is generally more populated than interior New England.

MUSEUMS & SIGHTS

Most major museums and attractions are open daily or six days a week (with Monday being the most likely day of closing). Hours are often shorter on Saturday and especially Sunday, and some prominent museums stay open late one or two nights a week, usually Tuesday, Thursday, or Friday. New England also has quite a few smaller museums—historical societies, small art galleries, highly specialized collections—that open only a few days a week, and sometimes only by appointment in winter or slow periods.

SHOPS

Banks are usually open weekdays from 9 to 3 and some Saturday mornings. The post office is open from 8 to 5 weekdays and often on Saturday morning. Shops in urban and suburban areas, particularly in indoor and strip malls, typically open at 9 or 10 daily and stay open until anywhere from 6 PM to 10 PM on weekdays and Saturday, and until 5 or 6 on Sunday. Hours vary greatly, so call ahead when in doubt.

On major highways and in densely populated areas you'll usually find at least one or two supermarkets, drugstores, and gas stations open 24 hours, and in a few big cities and also some college towns you'll find a smattering of all-night fast-food restaurants, diners, and coffeehouses.

BUS TRAVEL

Regional bus service is relatively plentiful throughout New England. It can be a handy and somewhat affordable means of getting around, as buses travel many routes that trains do not; however, this style of travel prevents the sort of spontaneity and freedom to explore that you're afforded if traveling by car. Also, it's often

a good idea to compare travel times and costs between bus and train routes to and within New England; in some cases, it's faster to take the train. Still, if it's a simple matter of getting from one city to another and you've got a bit of time on your hands, consider this option. Remember that buses sometimes make frequent stops, which may delay you but may also provide you the chance to see parts of the region you might not otherwise see.

Reservations are not required on buses serving the region, but they're a good idea for just about any bus trip.

CUTTING COSTS

Greyhound offers the **North America Discovery Pass,** which allows unlimited travel in the United States within any 7-, 10-, 15-, 21-, 30-, 45-, or 60-day period ($229–$609, depending on length of the pass). You can also buy similar passes covering both the United States and Canada or limited to the West Coast or the East Coast of North America, and international travelers can purchase international versions of these same passes. Greyhound also has senior-citizen, military, children's, and student discounts applicable to individual fares and to the Discovery Pass.

FARES & SCHEDULES

Sample one-way bus fares (standard fare followed by the seven-day advance purchase fare, if any, in parentheses), with travel times (note that times vary greatly depending on the number of stops) to Boston from: New York City, 4–5 hours, $35 ($31 with 7-day advance purchase); Philadelphia, 7–8 hours, $55 ($43); Montréal, 7–8 hours, $63 ($43); Washington, DC, 9–11 hours, $66 ($43); Toronto, 13–15 hours, $82; and Cleveland, 15–16 hours, $81 ($55).

Sample one-way fares and travel times to other prominent New England destinations from other cities: New York City to Burlington, 8–10 hours, $67; New York City to Barnstable (Cape Cod), 6–7 hours, $51; Montréal to Pittsfield (MA), 7 hours, $63; Montréal to Portsmouth (NH), 13–14 hours, $76 ($53 with 7-day advance purchase); Philadelphia to Portland

(ME), 10–12 hours, $86 ($53 with 7-day advance purchase); Washington, DC, to Concord (NH), 12–14 hours, $89 ($55 with 7-day advance purchase); and Toronto to Burlington, 10–11 hours, $81.

Bus Information Bonanza Bus Lines ☎ 800/556-3815 ⊕ www.bonanzabus.com. **Greyhound Lines Inc.** ☎ 800/231-2222 ⊕ www.greyhound.com. **Peter Pan Bus Lines** ☎ 800/343-9999 or 413/781-3320 ⊕ www.peterpanbus.com. **Vermont Transit Lines** ☎ 800/552-8737 ⊕ www.vermonttransit.com.

CAMERAS & PHOTOGRAPHY

Seascapes and fall foliage are the most commonly photographed subjects in New England. Both can make for memorable images, provided you remember that saltwater and autumn leaves photograph better when something else is included in the picture. Look for a lighthouse or fog-shrouded sailboat in your ocean shots and a covered bridge or church steeple tucked among the birches and maples. The *Kodak Guide to Shooting Great Travel Pictures* (available at bookstores everywhere) is loaded with tips.

Photo Help Kodak Information Center ☎ 800/242-2424 ⊕ www.kodak.com.

EQUIPMENT PRECAUTIONS

Don't pack film or equipment in luggage that you intend to check. The X-ray machines used to view checked luggage are extremely powerful and therefore are likely to ruin your film. Try to ask for hand inspection of film, which becomes clouded after repeated exposure to airport X-ray machines, and keep videotapes and computer disks away from metal detectors. Always keep film, tape, and computer disks out of the sun. Carry an extra supply of batteries, and be prepared to turn on your camera, camcorder, or laptop to prove to airport security personnel that the device is real.

Be careful on sailboat cruises—saltwater can corrode metal camera parts. **Keep your camera in its case when not in use,** and wipe the lens and case with a soft cloth if it's sprayed with saltwater. Remember to **stock up on film at home or in big cities.**

Prices are a lot higher in airports, resort areas, and small towns, and the film options are often limited.

CAR RENTAL

Because a car is the most practical way to get around New England, it's wise to rent one if you're not bringing your own. The major airports serving the region all have on-site car-rental agencies. If you're traveling to the area by bus or train, you might consider renting a car once you arrive. A few train or bus stations have one or two major car-rental agencies on site.

Major Agencies Alamo ☎ 800/327-9633 ⊕ www.alamo.com. **Avis** ☎ 800/331-1212, 800/879-2847 or 800/272-5871 in Canada, 0870/606-0100 in the U.K., 02/9353-9000 in Australia, 09/526-2847 in New Zealand ⊕ www.avis.com. **Budget** ☎ 800/527-0700, 0870/156-5656 in the U.K. ⊕ www.budget.com. **Dollar** ☎ 800/800-4000, 0800/085-4578 in the U.K. ⊕ www.dollar.com. **Hertz** ☎ 800/654-3131, 800/263-0600 in Canada, 0870/844-8844 in the U.K., 02/9669-2444 in Australia, 09/256-8690 in New Zealand ⊕ www.hertz.com. **National Car Rental** ☎ 800/227-7368, 0870/600-6666 in the U.K. ⊕ www.nationalcar.com.

CUTTING COSTS

Rates at the area's major airports begin at around $35 a day and $150 a week for an economy car with air-conditioning, automatic transmission, and unlimited mileage. These rates do not include state tax on car rentals, which varies depending on the airport but generally runs 12% to 15%.

For a good deal, book through a travel agent who will shop around. Also, price local car-rental companies—whose prices may be lower still, although their service and maintenance may not be as good as those of major rental agencies—and research rates on the Internet. Consolidators that specialize in air travel can offer good rates on cars as well (⇨ Air Travel). Remember to ask about required deposits, cancellation penalties, and drop-off charges if you're planning to pick up the car in one city and leave it in another. If you're traveling during a holiday period, also make sure that a confirmed reservation guarantees you a car.

INSURANCE

When driving a rented car you are generally responsible for any damage to or loss of the vehicle. You also may be liable for any property damage or personal injury that you may cause while driving. Before you rent, see what coverage you already have under the terms of your personal auto-insurance policy and credit cards.

For about $9 to $25 a day, rental companies sell protection, known as a collision- or loss-damage waiver (CDW or LDW), that eliminates your liability for damage to the car; it's always optional and should never be automatically added to your bill. In Massachusetts the car-rental agency's insurance is primary; therefore, the company must pay for damage to third parties up to a preset legal limit, beyond which your own liability insurance kicks in. However, **make sure you have enough coverage to pay for the car.** If you do not have auto insurance or an umbrella policy that covers damage to third parties, purchasing liability insurance and a CDW or LDW is highly recommended.

REQUIREMENTS & RESTRICTIONS

Most agencies won't rent to you if you're under the age of 21. When picking up a rental car, non-U.S. residents need a voucher for any prepaid reservations that were made in their home country, a passport, a driver's license, and a travel policy that covers each driver.

SURCHARGES

Before you pick up a car in one city and leave it in another, ask about drop-off charges or one-way service fees, which can be substantial. Also inquire about early-return policies; some rental agencies charge extra if you return the car before the time specified in your contract, whereas others give you a refund for the days not used. To avoid a hefty refueling fee, fill the tank just before you turn in the car, but be aware that gas stations near the rental outlet may overcharge. It's almost never a deal to buy the tank of gas that's in the car when you rent it; the understanding is that you'll return it empty, but some fuel usually remains. Surcharges may apply if you're under 25 or if you take the car outside the area approved by the rental agency. You'll pay extra for child seats (about $8 a day), which are compulsory for children under 5, and usually for additional drivers (up to $25 a day, depending on location).

CAR TRAVEL

New England is best explored by car. Areas in the interior are largely without heavy traffic and congestion, and parking is consistently easy to find, even in cities like Hartford and Springfield. Coastal New England is considerably more congested, and parking can be hard to find or expensive in Boston, Providence, and the many smaller resort towns along the coast. Still, a car is typically the best way to get around even on the coast, though you may want to park it at your hotel in Boston or on Cape Cod and use it as little as possible, exploring on foot, on a bike, or by local transit and cabs once you arrive. In the interior, especially western Massachusetts, Vermont, New Hampshire, and Maine, public transportation options are more limited and a car is almost necessary. Morning and evening rush-hour traffic isn't usually much of a problem, except in larger cities and along the coast.

RULES OF THE ROAD

On city streets the speed limit is 30 mph unless otherwise posted; on rural roads, the speed limit ranges from 40 to 50 mph unless otherwise posted. Interstate speeds range from 50 to 65 mph, depending on how densely populated the area. Throughout the region, you're permitted to make a right turn on red except where posted. Be alert for one-way streets in some of the more congested communities, such as Boston and Providence.

State law requires that front-seat passengers wear seat belts at all times. Children under 16 must wear seat belts in both the front and back seats. Always **strap children under age 5 into approved child-safety seats.**

CHILDREN IN NEW ENGLAND

New England is an enjoyable part of the country for family road trips, and it's also relatively affordable, excepting some of the fancier resort towns and also Boston.

Throughout New England, however, you'll have no problem finding comparatively inexpensive child-friendly hotels and family-style restaurants—as well as some top children's museums, beaches, parks, planetariums, and lighthouses. Just keep in mind that a number of fine, antiques-filled B&Bs and inns punctuate the landscape, and these places are not always suitable for kids—many flat-out refuse to accommodate children. Also, some of the quieter and more rural areas—although exuding history—lack child-oriented attractions.

Favorite destinations for family vacations in New England include Boston, Cape Cod, the White Mountains, Mystic and southeastern Connecticut, and coastal Maine, but in general, the entire region has plenty to offer families. *Fodor's Around Boston with Kids* (available in bookstores everywhere) can help you plan your days together.

Be sure to plan ahead and **involve your youngsters** as you outline your trip. When packing, include things to keep them busy en route. On sightseeing days try to schedule activities of special interest to your children. If you are renting a car, don't forget to arrange for a car seat when you reserve. For general advice about traveling with children, consult *Fodor's FYI: Travel with Your Baby* (available in bookstores everywhere).

FLYING

If your children are two or older, ask about children's airfares. As a general rule, infants under two not occupying a seat fly at greatly reduced fares or even for free. But if you want to guarantee a seat for an infant, you have to pay full fare. Consider flying during off-peak days and times; most airlines will grant an infant a seat without a ticket if there are available seats.

Experts agree that it's a good idea to use safety seats aloft for children weighing less than 40 pounds. Airlines set their own policies: if you use a safety seat, U.S. carriers usually require that the child be ticketed, even if he or she is young enough to ride free, because the seats must be strapped into regular seats. And even if you pay the full adult fare for the seat, it may be worth it, especially on longer trips. Do **check your airline's policy about using safety seats during takeoff and landing.** Safety seats are not allowed everywhere in the plane, so get your seat assignments as early as possible.

When reserving, request children's meals or a freestanding bassinet (not available at all airlines) if you need them. But note that bulkhead seats, where you must sit to use the bassinet, may lack an overhead bin or storage space on the floor.

LODGING

Chain hotels and motels welcome children, and New England has many family-oriented resorts with lively children's programs. You'll also find farms that accept guests and can be lots of fun for children. Rental houses and apartments abound, particularly around ski areas; off-season, these can be economical as well as comfortable touring bases. Some country inns, especially those with a quiet, romantic atmosphere and those furnished with antiques, are less enthusiastic about little ones, so **be up front about your traveling companions** when you reserve. Many larger resorts and hotels will provide a babysitter at an additional cost. Others will provide a list of sitters in the area.

Most hotels in New England allow children under a certain age to stay in their parents' room at no extra charge, but others charge for them as extra adults; be sure to find out the cutoff age for children's discounts.

Most lodgings that welcome infants and small children will provide a crib or cot, but **be sure to give advance notice** so that one will be available for you. Many family resorts make special accommodations for small children during meals. Be sure to ask in advance.

SIGHTS & ATTRACTIONS

Throughout this book, places that are especially appealing to children are indicated by a rubber-duckie icon (🦆) in the margin.

TRANSPORTATION

Each New England state has specific requirements regarding age and weight requirements for children in car seats. If you're renting a car, **be sure to ask about the state(s) you're planning to drive in.** If you will need a car seat, make sure the agency you select provides them and **reserve well in advance.**

CONSUMER PROTECTION

Whether you're shopping for gifts or purchasing travel services, **pay with a major credit card** whenever possible, so you can cancel payment or get reimbursed if there's a problem (and you can provide documentation). If you're doing business with a particular company for the first time, contact your local Better Business Bureau and the attorney general's offices in your state and the company's home state as well. Have any complaints been filed? Finally, if you're buying a package or tour, always consider travel insurance that includes default coverage (⇨ Insurance).

🚩 BBBs **Council of Better Business Bureaus** ✉ 4200 Wilson Blvd., Suite 800, Arlington, VA 22203 ☎ 703/276–0100 🖷 703/525–8277 ⊕ www. bbb.org.

CUSTOMS & DUTIES

IN AUSTRALIA

Australian residents who are 18 or older may bring home A$400 worth of souvenirs and gifts (including jewelry), 250 cigarettes or 250 grams of cigars or other tobacco products, and 1,125 ml of alcohol (including wine, beer, and spirits). Residents under 18 may bring back A$200 worth of goods. Members of the same family traveling together may pool their allowances. Prohibited items include meat products. Seeds, plants, and fruits need to be declared upon arrival.

🚩 **Australian Customs Service** ⌀ Regional Director, Box 8, Sydney, NSW 2001 ☎ 02/9213–2000 or 1300/363–263, 02/9364–7222 or 1800/020–504 quarantine-inquiry line 🖷 02/9213–4043 ⊕ www. customs.gov.au.

IN CANADA

Canadian residents who have been out of Canada for at least seven days may bring in C$750 worth of goods duty-free. If you've been away fewer than seven days but more than 48 hours, the duty-free allowance drops to C$200. If your trip lasts 24 to 48 hours, the allowance is C$50.

You may not pool allowances with family members. Goods claimed under the C$750 exemption may follow you by mail; those claimed under the lesser exemptions must accompany you. Alcohol and tobacco products may be included in the seven-day and 48-hour exemptions but not in the 24-hour exemption. If you meet the age requirements of the province or territory through which you reenter Canada, you may bring in, duty-free, 1.5 liters of wine or 1.14 liters of liquor or 24 12-ounce cans or bottles of beer or ale. Also, if you meet the local age requirement for tobacco products, you may bring in, duty-free, 200 cigarettes and 50 cigars. Check ahead of time with the Canada Customs and Revenue Agency or the Department of Agriculture for policies regarding meat products, seeds, plants, and fruits.

You may send an unlimited number of gifts (only one gift per recipient, however) worth up to C$60 each duty-free to Canada. Label the package UNSOLICITED GIFT—VALUE UNDER $60. Alcohol and tobacco are excluded.

🚩 **Canada Customs and Revenue Agency** ✉ 2265 St. Laurent Blvd., Ottawa, Ontario K1G 4K3 ☎ 800/ 461–9999 in Canada, 204/983–3500, 506/636–5064 ⊕ www.ccra.gc.ca.

IN NEW ZEALAND

All homeward-bound residents may bring back NZ$700 worth of souvenirs and gifts; passengers may not pool their allowances, and children can claim only the concession on goods intended for their own use. For those 17 or older, the duty-free allowance also includes 4.5 liters of wine or beer; one 1,125-ml bottle of spirits; and either 200 cigarettes, 250 grams of tobacco, 50 cigars, or a combination of the three up to 250 grams. Meat products, seeds, plants, and fruits must be declared upon arrival to the Agricultural Services Department.

🚩 **New Zealand Customs** ✉ Head office: the Customhouse, 17–21 Whitmore St., Box 2218, Wellington ☎ 0800/428–786 or 09/300–5399 ⊕ www.customs. govt.nz.

IN THE U.K.

From countries outside the European Union, including the United States, you may bring home, duty-free, 200 cigarettes, 50 cigars, 100 cigarillos, or 250 grams of tobacco; 1 liter of spirits or 2 liters of fortified or sparkling wine or liqueurs; 2 liters of still table wine; 60 ml of perfume; 250 ml of toilet water; plus £145 worth of other goods, including gifts and souvenirs. Prohibited items include meat and dairy products, seeds, plants, and fruits.

HM Customs and Excise ✉ Portcullis House, 21 Cowbridge Rd. E, Cardiff CF11 9SS ☎ 0845/010–9000 or 0208/929–0152 advice service, 0208/929–6731 or 0208/910–3602 complaints ⊕ www.hmce.gov.uk.

DISABILITIES & ACCESSIBILITY

Although rural and historic in many places, New England has come a long way in making life easier for people with disabilities. The majority of businesses in the area are up to ADA standards (except some historic inns and restaurants), and you'll find plenty of people who are more than happy to help you get around.

Local Resources Cape Cod Chamber of Commerce ☎ 888/332–2732 or 508/862–0700 ⊕ www.capecodchamber.org produces two publications with accessibility ratings: "Visitor's Guide" and "Accommodations Directory." The **Cape Cod National Seashore** ☎ 508/349–3785 ⊕ www.nps.gov/caco publishes "Cape Cod National Seashore Accessibility." **Connecticut Office of Tourism** (⇨ Visitor Information) prints accessibility codes in the *Connecticut Vacation Guide.* The **Massachusetts Bay Transportation Authority** ☎ 617/222–3200, 800/222–32300, 617/222–5146 TTY ⊕ www.mbta.com distributes a brochure, "MBTA: Access." The **New Hampshire Office of Travel and Tourism Development**'s (⇨ Visitor Information) *New Hampshire Guide Book* includes accessibility ratings for lodgings and restaurants. The **Vermont Department of Tourism and Marketing** (⇨ Visitor Information) includes accessibility codes for attractions in the *Vermont Traveler's Guidebook.*

LODGING

Most hotels in New England comply with the Americans with Disabilities Act. However, the definition of accessibility may differ from hotel to hotel. Some properties may be accessible by ADA standards for people with mobility problems but not for people with hearing or vision impairments, for example.

When discussing accessibility with an operator or reservations agent, ask hard questions. If you have mobility problems, are there any stairs, inside *or* out? Are there grab bars next to the toilet *and* in the shower/tub? How wide is the doorway to the room? To the bathroom? For the most extensive facilities meeting the latest legal specifications, opt for newer accommodations. If you reserve through a toll-free number, consider also calling the hotel's local number to confirm the information from the central reservations office. Get confirmation in writing when you can.

If you have a hearing impairment, check whether the hotel has devices to alert you visually to the ring of the telephone, a knock at the door, and a fire/emergency alarm. Some hotels provide these devices without charge. Discuss your needs with hotel personnel if this equipment isn't available, so that a staff member can personally alert you in the event of an emergency.

If you're bringing a guide dog, get authorization ahead of time and write down the name of the person with whom you spoke.

SIGHTS & ATTRACTIONS

In Boston, many sidewalks are brick or cobblestone and may be uneven or sloping; many have curbs cut at one end and not the other. To make matters worse, Boston drivers are notorious for running yellow lights and ignoring pedestrians. Back Bay has flat, well-paved streets; older Beacon Hill is steep and difficult; Quincy Market's cobblestone and brick malls are crisscrossed with smooth, tarred paths. The downtown financial district and Chinatown are accessible, while areas such as the South End and the Italian North End may prove more problematic for people who use wheelchairs.

In Cape Cod, a number of towns such as Wellfleet, Hyannis, and Chatham have wide streets with curb cuts, and the Cape Cod National Seashore has several accessible trails. The narrow streets of Provincetown, the Cape's most popular destination, are difficult for anyone to navigate. Travelers using wheelchairs would be well advised to visit "P-town" in the off-season, when pedestrian and vehicular traffic is less chaotic.

In many other coastal towns throughout the region, travelers with mobility impairments will have to cope with crowds as well as with narrow, uneven steps and sporadic curb cuts. L. L. Bean's outlet in Freeport is fully accessible, and Acadia National Park has some 50 accessible miles of carriage roads that are closed to motor vehicles. In New Hampshire, many of Franconia Notch's natural attractions are accessible.

TRANSPORTATION

Many major rental agencies provide special cars for people with disabilities on request. Most ask that you provide your own handicapped sticker or plate, which will be honored throughout the region. Be sure to reserve well in advance.

◨ Complaints Aviation Consumer Protection Division (⇨ Air Travel) for airline-related problems. **Departmental Office of Civil Rights** ⊠ For general inquiries, U.S. Department of Transportation, S-30, 400 7th St. SW, Room 10215, Washington, DC 20590 ☎ 202/366-4648 🖷 202/366-9371 ⊕ www.dot.gov/ost/docr/index.htm. **Disability Rights Section** ⊠ NYAV, U.S. Department of Justice, Civil Rights Division, 950 Pennsylvania Ave. NW, Washington, DC 20530 ☎ 800/514-0301, 800/514-0383 TTY, 202/514-0301 ADA information line, 202/514-0383 TTY ⊕ www.ada.gov. **U.S. Department of Transportation Hotline** ☎ 800/778-4838 or 800/455-9880 TTY for disability-related air-travel problems.

TRAVEL AGENCIES

In the United States, the Americans with Disabilities Act requires that travel firms serve the needs of all travelers. Some agencies specialize in working with people with disabilities.

◨ Travelers with Mobility Problems B. Roberts Travel ⊠ 1876 East Ave., Rochester, NY 14610 ☎ 800/444-6540 or 585/256-1680 ⊕ www.brobertstravel.com, begun by a former physical-rehabilitation counselor. **Accessible Vans of America** ⊠ 9 Spielman Rd., Fairfield, NJ 07004 ☎ 877/282-8267, 888/282-8267, 973/808-9709 reservations 🖷 973/808-9713 ⊕ www.accessiblevans.com, for wheelchair-accessible van rentals. **CareVacations** ⊠ 5110-50 Ave., No. 5, Leduc, Alberta T9E 6V4, Canada ☎ 877/478-7827 or 780/986-6404 🖷 780/

986-8332 ⊕ www.carevacations.com, for group tours and cruise vacations. **Flying Wheels Travel** ⊠ 143 W. Bridge St., Box 382, Owatonna, MN 55060 ☎ 507/451-5005 🖷 507/451-1685 ⊕ www.flyingwheelstravel.com.

◨ Travelers with Developmental Disabilities Sprout ⊠ 893 Amsterdam Ave., New York, NY 10025 ☎ 888/222-9575 or 212/222-9575 🖷 212/222-9768 ⊕ www.gosprout.org.

DISCOUNTS & DEALS

Be a smart shopper and compare all your options before making decisions. A plane ticket bought with a promotional coupon from travel clubs, coupon books, and direct-mail offers or purchased on the Internet may not be cheaper than the least expensive fare from a discount ticket agency. And always keep in mind that what you get is just as important as what you save.

DISCOUNT RESERVATIONS

Discount reservations services use their buying power to get a better price on hotels, airline tickets (⇨ Air Travel), even car rentals. Look for those with Web sites and toll-free numbers. When booking a room, always **call the hotel's local toll-free number** (if one is available) rather than the central reservations number—you'll often get a better price. Always ask about special packages or corporate rates.

◨ Hotel Rooms Accommodations Express ☎ 800/444-7666 or 800/277-1064 ⊕ www.accommodationsexpress.com. **Central Reservation Service** (CRS) ☎ 800/555-7555 or 800/548-3311 ⊕ www.crshotels.com. **Hotels.com** ☎ 800/246-8357 ⊕ www.hotels.com. **Quikbook** ☎ 800/789-9887 ⊕ www.quikbook.com. **Turbotrip.com** ☎ 800/473-7829 ⊕ w3.turbotrip.com.

PACKAGE DEALS

Don't confuse packages and guided tours. When you buy a package, you travel on your own, just as though you had planned the trip yourself. Fly/drive packages, which combine airfare and car rental, are often a good deal. In cities, ask the local visitor's bureau about hotel and local transportation packages that include tickets to major museum exhibits or other special events.

EATING & DRINKING

Although there are certain ingredients and preparations that are common to the region as a whole, New England's cuisine varies greatly from place to place. Especially in such urban areas as Boston, Providence, New Haven, and Portland, and in upscale resort areas such as Newport, Litchfield County, the Berkshires, Martha's Vineyard, Nantucket, and coastal Maine, you can expect to find stellar restaurants, many of them with culinary luminaries at the helm and a reputation for creative, and occasionally daring, menus. Elsewhere, restaurant food tends more toward the simple, traditional, and conservative. Cities, collegiate communities, and other sophisticated New England areas also have a great variety of ethnic restaurants, especially excellent Italian, French, Japanese, Indian, and Thai eateries. There are also quite a few diners, which typically present patrons with page after page of inexpensive, short-order cooking and often stay open until the wee hours; for a road-tripper, these down-home, locals' favorites make great alternatives to fast-food chains. The proximity to the ocean accounts for a number of restaurants serving very fresh seafood, and the numerous boutique dairy, meat, and vegetable suppliers that have sprung up throughout New England in the past couple of decades account for other choice ingredients. In fact, menus in the more upscale and tourism-driven communities often note which Vermont dairy or Berkshires produce farm a particular goat cheese or heirloom tomato came from.

The restaurants we list are the cream of the crop in each price category. Properties indicated by an ✕⊡ are lodging establishments whose restaurant warrants a special trip.

MEALTIMES

In general, the widest variety of mealtime options in New England is in larger cities and at resort areas.

For an early breakfast, pick places that cater to a working clientele. City, town, and roadside establishments specializing in breakfast for busy people often open their doors at 5 or 6 AM. At country inns and B&Bs, breakfast is seldom served before 8; if you need to get an earlier start, ask ahead of time if your host or hostess can accommodate you. Lunch in New England generally runs from around 11 to 2:30; dinner is usually served from 6 to 9 (many restaurants have early-bird specials beginning at 5). Only in the larger cities will you find full dinners being offered much later than 9, although you can usually find a bar or bistro serving a limited menu late into the evening in all but the smallest towns. Many restaurants in New England are closed Monday, and sometimes Sunday or Tuesday, although this is never true in resort areas in high season. However, resort-town eateries often shut down completely in the off-season.

Credit cards are accepted for meals throughout New England in all but the most modest establishments. Unless otherwise noted, the restaurants listed in this guide are open daily for lunch and dinner.

RESERVATIONS & DRESS

Reservations are always a good idea; we mention them only when they're essential or not accepted. Book as far ahead as you can, and reconfirm as soon as you arrive. (Large parties should always call ahead to check the reservations policy.) We mention dress only when men are required to wear a jacket or a jacket and tie.

WINE, BEER & SPIRITS

New England is no stranger to microbrews. The granddaddy of New England's independent beer makers is Boston's Samuel Adams, producing brews available throughout the region since 1985. Following the Sam Adams lead in offering hearty English-style ales and special seasonal brews are breweries such as Vermont's Long Trail, Maine's Shipyard, and New Hampshire's Old Man Ale.

New England is beginning to earn some respect as a wine-producing region. Varieties capable of withstanding the region's harsh winters have been the basis of promising enterprises such as Rhode Island's Sakonnet Vineyards, Chicama Vineyards on Martha's Vineyard, and Connecticut's Hopkins Vineyard. Even

Vermont is getting into the act with the Snow Farm Vineyard in the Lake Champlain Islands and Boyden Valley Winery in Cambridge.

Although a patchwork of state and local regulations affect the hours and locations of places that sell alcoholic beverages, New England licensing laws are fairly liberal. State-owned or -franchised stores sell hard liquor in New Hampshire, Maine, and Vermont; many travelers have found that New Hampshire offers the region's lowest prices. Look for state-run liquor "supermarkets" on interstate highways in the southern part of New Hampshire; these also have good wine selections.

ECOTOURISM

Many state parks in New England request that when you leave the grounds, you carry your trash out with you. Connecticut, Massachusetts, Maine, and Vermont recycle cans and bottles and charge 5¢–15¢ per unit at time of purchase, refundable when the can or bottle is returned to a store or recycling center.

Throughout the region, particularly on beaches and in areas with high cliffs, markers forbid trespassing. These are generally nesting areas for endangered species, such as peregrine falcons in Smugglers' Notch, Vermont, and terns on beaches in Connecticut and Massachusetts.

GAY & LESBIAN TRAVEL

As one of the country's most socially and politically progressive regions, New England is almost invariably accepting of gay and lesbian travelers. Some exceptions might be found in some areas less frequented by visitors, but in general, people in the tourism business here are hospitable to travelers regardless of sexual orientation.

The hubs of gay New England are Boston, Northampton, and Provincetown, Massachusetts, with Providence, Rhode Island and Ogunquit, Maine also being quite popular. Most sizable college and university towns in New England have gay communities. Alternative publications in all of these areas carry listings of gay bars, nightclubs, and special events. For details about the gay and lesbian scene in Boston,

central Vermont, Hartford, New Haven, Northampton, Ogunquit, Portland, Providence, and southern Vermont, consult *Fodor's Gay Guide to the USA* (available in bookstores everywhere).

7 Gay- & Lesbian-Friendly Travel Agencies **Kennedy Travel** ⊠ 130 W. 42nd St., Suite 401, New York, NY 10036 ☎ 800/237–7433 or 212/840–8659 🖷 212/730–2269 ⊕ www.kennedytravel.com. **Now, Voyager** ⊠ 4406 18th St., San Francisco, CA 94114 ☎ 800/255–6951 or 415/626–1169 🖷 415/626–8626 ⊕ www.nowvoyager.com. **Skylink Travel and Tour/ Flying Dutchmen Travel** ⊠ 1455 N. Dutton Ave., Suite A, Santa Rosa, CA 95401 ☎ 800/225–5759 or 707/546–9888 🖷 707/636–0951 ⊕ www.flyingdutchmentravel.com, serving lesbian travelers.

HEALTH

LYME DISEASE

Lyme disease, so named for its having been first reported in the town of Lyme, Connecticut, is a potentially debilitating disease carried by deer ticks, which thrive in dry, brush-covered areas, particularly on the coast. Always **use insect repellent**; outbreaks of Lyme disease all over the East Coast make it imperative that you protect yourself from ticks from early spring through summer. To prevent bites, **wear light-color clothing and tuck pant legs into socks.** Look for black ticks about the size of a pinhead around hairlines and the warmest parts of the body. If you have been bitten, **consult a physician, especially if you see the telltale bull's-eye bite pattern.** Influenza-like symptoms often accompany a Lyme infection. Early treatment is imperative.

PESTS & OTHER HAZARDS

New England's two greatest insect pests are black flies and mosquitoes. The former are a phenomenon of late spring and early summer and are generally a problem only in the densely wooded areas of the far north. Mosquitoes, however, can be a nuisance just about everywhere in summer—they're at their worst following snowy winters and wet springs. The best protection against both pests is repellent containing DEET; if you're camping in the woods during black fly season, you'll also want to **use fine mesh screening in eating and**

sleeping areas, and even wear mesh head-gear. A particular pest of coastal areas, especially salt marshes, is the greenhead fly. Their bite is nasty, and they are best repelled by a liberal application of Avon Skin So Soft.

SHELLFISHING

Coastal waters attract seafood lovers who enjoy harvesting their own clams, mussels, and even lobsters; permits are required, and casual harvesting of lobsters is strictly forbidden. Amateur clammers should be aware that New England shellfish beds are periodically visited by red tides, during which microorganisms can render shellfish poisonous. To keep abreast of the situation, inquire when you apply for a license (usually at town halls or police stations) and pay attention to red tide postings as you travel.

HOLIDAYS

Expect banks and post offices to be closed on all national holidays. Exceptions are restaurants and hotels, which, depending on location, may be even busier at holiday times. Christmas in Boston or in ski country, for instance, will require early advance dining and lodging reservations. Public transportation schedules will also be affected on major holidays; in general, schedules will be similar to those of a normal Sunday.

Major national holidays are New Year's Day (January 1); Martin Luther King Day (third Monday in January); Presidents' Day (third Monday in February); Memorial Day (last Monday in May); Independence Day (July 4); Labor Day (first Monday in September); Columbus Day (second Monday in October); Thanksgiving Day (fourth Thursday in November); Christmas Eve and Christmas Day (December 24 and 25); and New Year's Eve (December 31).

Patriots' Day (the Monday closest to April 19) is a state holiday in Massachusetts.

INSURANCE

The most useful travel-insurance plan is a comprehensive policy that includes coverage for trip cancellation and interruption,

default, trip delay, and medical expenses (with a waiver for preexisting conditions).

Without insurance you'll lose all or most of your money if you cancel your trip, regardless of the reason. Default insurance covers you if your tour operator, airline, or cruise line goes out of business—the chances of which have been increasing. Trip-delay covers expenses that arise because of bad weather or mechanical delays. Study the fine print when comparing policies.

U.K. residents can buy a travel-insurance policy valid for most vacations taken during the year in which it's purchased (but check preexisting-condition coverage).

Always **buy travel policies directly from the insurance company**; if you buy them from a cruise line, airline, or tour operator that goes out of business you probably won't be covered for the agency or operator's default, a major risk. Before making any purchase, review your existing health and home-owner's policies to find what they cover away from home.

⁊ Travel Insurers In the United States: **Access America** ✉ 2805 N. Parham Rd., Richmond, VA 23294 ☎ 800/729–6021 🖷 800/346–9265 ⊕ www.accessamerica.com. **Travel Guard International** ✉ 1145 Clark St., Stevens Point, WI 54481 ☎ 800/826–4919 or 715/345–1041 ⊕ www.travelguard.com.

FOR INTERNATIONAL TRAVELERS

For information on customs restrictions, *see* Customs & Duties.

CAR RENTAL

When picking up a rental car, non-U.S. residents need a reservation voucher for any prepaid reservations that were made in the traveler's home country, a passport, a driver's license, and a travel policy that covers each driver.

CAR TRAVEL

Gas stations are easy to find along major highways and in most communities throughout the region. The average price of a gallon of regular unleaded gas is $2.38 throughout the area. However, prices vary from station to station within any city. Most stay open late (24 hours along large highways and in some larger towns), except in rural areas, where Sunday hours are limited and where you may drive long stretches without a refueling opportunity. Highways are well paved. Interstate highways—limited-access, multilane highways whose numbers are prefixed by "I–"—are the fastest routes. Interstates with three-digit numbers encircle urban areas, which may have other limited-access expressways, freeways, and parkways as well. Tolls may be levied on limited-access highways. So-called U.S. highways and state highways are not necessarily limited-access but may have several lanes.

Along larger highways, roadside stops with restrooms, fast-food restaurants, and sundries stores are well spaced. State police and tow trucks patrol major highways and lend assistance. If your car breaks down on an interstate, pull onto the shoulder and wait for help, or have your passengers wait while you walk to an emergency phone (available in most states). If you carry a cell phone, dial *55, noting your location on the small green roadside mileage markers.

Driving in the United States is on the right. Do obey speed limits posted along roads and highways. Watch for lower limits in small towns and on back roads. On weekdays between 6 and 10 AM and again between 4 and 7 PM expect heavy traffic. To encourage carpooling, some freeways have special lanes for so-called high-occupancy vehicles (HOV)—cars carrying more than one passenger.

Bookstores, gas stations, convenience stores, and rest stops sell maps (about $3) and multiregion road atlases (about $10).

For more information, *see* Car Travel.

CONSULATES & EMBASSIES

🄵 Australia **Consulate** ⊠ 150 E. 42nd St., 34th fl., New York, NY 10017 ☏ 212/351-6500.
🄵 Canada **Consulate** ⊠ 3 Copley Pl., Suite 400, Boston, MA 02116 ☏ 617/262-3760.
🄵 New Zealand **Consulate** ⊠ 222 E. 41st St., Suite 2510, New York, NY 10017 ☏ 212/832-4038.
🄵 United Kingdom **Consulate** ⊠ 1 Memorial Dr., Boston, MA 02142 ☏ 617/245-4500.

CURRENCY

The dollar is the basic unit of U.S. currency. It has 100 cents. Coins are the copper penny (1¢); the silvery nickel (5¢), dime (10¢), quarter (25¢), and half dollar (50¢); and the occasionally encountered golden $1 coin, replacing a now-rare silver dollar. Bills are denominated $1, $5, $10, $20, $50, and $100, all mostly green and identical in size; designs and background tints vary. In addition, you may come across a $2 bill, but the chances are slim.

ELECTRICITY

The U.S. standard is AC, 110 volts/60 cycles. Plugs have two flat pins set parallel to each other.

EMERGENCIES

For police, fire, or ambulance, **dial 911** (0 in rural areas).

INSURANCE

Britons and Australians need extra medical coverage when traveling overseas.
🄵 Insurance Information In Australia: **Insurance Council of Australia** ⊠ Insurance Enquiries and Complaints, Level 12, Box 561, Collins St. W, Melbourne, VIC 8007 ☏ 1300/780-808 or 03/9629-4109 🖷 03/9621-2060 ⊕ www.iecltd.com.au. In Canada: **RBC Insurance** ⊠ 6880 Financial Dr., Mississauga, Ontario L5N 7Y5 ☏ 800/668-4342 or 905/816-2400 🖷 905/813-4704 ⊕ www.rbcinsurance.com. In New Zealand: **Insurance Council of New Zealand** ⊠ 111-115 Customhouse Quay, Level 7, Box 474, Wellington ☏ 04/472-5230 🖷 04/473-3011 ⊕ www.icnz.org.nz. In the United Kingdom: **Association of British Insurers** ⊠ 51 Gresham St., London EC2V 7HQ ☏ 020/7600-3333 🖷 020/7696-8999 ⊕ www.abi.org.uk.

MAIL & SHIPPING

You can buy stamps and aerograms and send letters and parcels in post offices. Stamp-dispensing machines can occasionally be found in airports, bus and train stations, office buildings, drugstores, and the like. You can also deposit mail in the stout, dark blue, steel bins at strategic locations everywhere and in the mail chutes of large buildings; pickup schedules are posted. You can deposit packages at public collection boxes as long as the parcels are affixed with proper postage and weigh less than one pound. Packages weighing one or more pounds must be taken to a post office or handed to a postal carrier.

To send mail to an address within the United States, you need a 39¢ stamp for first-class letters weighing up to 1 ounce (24¢ for each additional ounce) and 24¢ for postcards. You pay 84¢ for 1-ounce airmail letters and 75¢ for airmail postcards to most other countries; to Canada and Mexico, it costs 63¢ for a 1-ounce letter and 55¢ for a postcard. An aerogram—a single sheet of lightweight blue paper that folds into its own envelope, stamped for overseas airmail—costs 75¢.

To receive mail on the road, have it sent c/o General Delivery at your destination's main post office (use the correct five-digit ZIP code). You must pick up mail in person within 30 days and show a driver's license or passport.

PASSPORTS & VISAS

When traveling internationally, carry your passport even if you don't need one (it's always the best form of ID) and **make two photocopies of the data page** (one for someone at home and another for you, to be carried separately from your passport). If you lose your passport, promptly call the nearest embassy or consulate and the local police.

Visitor visas aren't necessary for Canadian or European Union citizens, or for citizens of Australia who are staying fewer than 90 days.

🇦🇺 Australian Citizens **Passports Australia** ☎ 131-232 ⊕ www.passports.gov.au. **United States Consulate General** ☒ MLC Centre, 19-29 Martin Pl., Level 59, Sydney, NSW 2000 ☎ 02/9373-9200, 1902/941-641 fee-based visa-inquiry line ⊕ usembassy-australia.state.gov/sydney.

🇨🇦 Canadian Citizens **Passport Office** ☒ To mail in applications: 200 Promenade du Portage, Hull, Québec J8X 4B7 ☎ 800/567-6868, 866/255-7655 TTY, 819/994-3500 ⊕ www.ppt.gc.ca.

🇳🇿 New Zealand Citizens **New Zealand Passports Office** ☒ For applications and information, Boulcott House, 47 Boulcott St., Level 3, Wellington ☎ 0800/225-050 or 04/474-8100 ⊕ www.passports.govt.nz. **Embassy of the United States** ☒ 29 Fitzherbert Terr., Thorndon, Wellington ☎ 04/462-6000 ⊕ usembassy.org.nz. **U.S. Consulate General** ☒ Citibank Bldg., 3rd fl, 23 Customs St. E, Auckland ☎ 09/303-2724 ⊕ usembassy.org.nz.

🇬🇧 U.K. Citizens **U.K. Passport Service** ☎ 0870/521-0410 ⊕ www.passport.gov.uk. **American Consulate General** ☒ Danesfort House, 223 Stranmillis Rd., Belfast BT9 5GR, Northern Ireland ☎ 028/9032-8239 🖷 028/9024-8482 ⊕ www.usembassy.org.uk. **American Embassy** ☒ For visa and immigration information or to submit a visa application via mail (enclose an SASE), Consular Information Unit, 24 Grosvenor Sq., London W1 1AE ☎ 09055/444-546 for visa information (per-min charges), 0207/499-9000 main switchboard ⊕ www.usembassy.org.uk.

TELEPHONES

All U.S. telephone numbers consist of a three-digit area code and a seven-digit local number. Within many local calling areas, you dial only the seven-digit number. Within some area codes, you must dial "1" first for calls outside the local area. To call between area-code regions, dial "1" then all 10 digits; the same goes for calls to numbers prefixed by "800," "888," "866," and "877"—all toll free. For calls to numbers preceded by "900" you must pay—usually dearly.

For international calls, dial "011" followed by the country code and the local number. For assistance, dial "0" and ask for an overseas operator. The country code is 61 for Australia, 64 for New Zealand, 44 for the United Kingdom. Calling Canada is the same as calling within the United States. Most local phone books list country codes and U.S. area codes. The country code for the United States is 1.

For operator assistance, dial "0." To obtain someone's phone number, call directory assistance at 555–1212 or occasionally 411 (free at many public phones). To have the person you're calling foot the bill, phone collect: dial "0" instead of "1" before the 10-digit number.

At pay phones, instructions often are posted. Usually you insert coins in a slot (usually 25¢–50¢ for local calls) and wait for a steady tone before dialing. When you call long-distance, the operator tells you how much to insert; prepaid phone cards, widely available in various denominations, are easier. Call the number on the back, punch in the card's personal identification number when prompted, then dial your number.

LODGING

New England is generally a bit more expensive than the rest of the country when it comes to accommodations, and some cities and coastal areas—Boston, the Cape, the islands—rank among the most expensive anywhere. Many areas are seasonal. Coastal sections tend to have the highest rates in summer, mountains regions can be pricey during the ski season, and virtually all of New England can be expensive during the peak fall foliage times. Keep in mind it can be tough to find weekend hotel rooms in summer and fall, so it's wise to book several weeks ahead. Also, rooms can often be hard to get on weekends in towns with a large college presence.

Assume that hotels operate on the European Plan (EP, with no meals) unless we specify that they use either the Continental Plan (CP, with a continental breakfast), Breakfast Plan (BP, with a full breakfast), or the Modified American Plan (MAP, with breakfast and dinner) or are all-inclusive (including all meals and most activities).

APARTMENT & VILLA (OR HOUSE) RENTALS

If you want a home base that's roomy enough for a family and comes with cooking facilities, consider a furnished rental. These can save you money, especially if you're traveling with a group. Home-exchange directories sometimes list rentals as well as exchanges.

In New England, you are most likely to find a house, apartment, or condo rental in areas in which ownership of second homes is common, such as beach resorts and ski country. A good strategy is to **inquire about rentals in what would be the off-season** for those resort areas—for instance, it's fairly easy to rent ski chalets in summer. Home-exchange directories sometimes list rentals as well as exchanges. Another good bet is to **contact real estate agents in the area in which you are interested.**

🛈 International Agents **Hideaways International** ✉ 767 Islington St., Portsmouth, NH 03801 ☎ 800/843–4433 or 603/430–4433 🖷 603/430–4444 ⊕ www.hideaways.com, annual membership $145.
🛈 Local Agents **Meadow Marsh Real Estate** ☎ Box 355, Eastham, MA 02642 ☎ 508/255–1500 ⊕ www.meadowmarsh.com, for Cape Cod rentals.
🛈 Listings Service **Cyberrentals.com** ✉ 3801 S. Capital of Texas Hwy., Austin, TX 78704 ☎ 512/684–1098 ⊕ www.cyberrentals.com.

BED & BREAKFASTS

Historic bed-and-breakfasts and inns proliferate throughout New England. In many rural or less-touristy areas, B&Bs offer an affordable alternative to chain properties, but in tourism-dependent communities (i. e., most of the major towns in this region), you can expect to pay about the same or more for a historic inn as for a full-service hotel. Many of the state's finest restaurants are also found in country inns. Although many B&Bs and smaller establishments continue to offer a low-key, homey experience without TVs or numerous amenities, in recent years, especially in upscale resort areas, many such properties have begun to cater to business and luxury leisure travelers with high-speed Internet, voice mail, whirlpool tubs, and VCRs. Quite a few inns and B&Bs serve substantial full breakfasts—the kind that may keep your appetite in check for the better part of the day.

CAMPING

The state offices of tourism (⇨ Visitor Information) supply information about privately operated campgrounds and campgrounds in parks run by state agencies and the federal government.

HOME EXCHANGES

If you would like to exchange your home for someone else's, join a home-exchange organization, which will send you its updated listings of available exchanges for a year and will include your own listing in at least one of them. It's up to you to make specific arrangements.

🛈 Exchange Clubs **HomeLink International** ✉ 2937 NW 9th Terr., Fort Lauderdale, FL 33311 ☎ 800/638–3841 or 954/566–2687 🖷 954/566–2783 ⊕ www.homelink.org; $80 yearly for a listing and online access; $45 additional to receive directories. **Intervac U.S.** ✉ 30 Corte San Fernando, Tiburon, CA 94920 ☎ 800/756-4663 🖷 415/435-7440 🌐 www.intervacus.com; $140 yearly for a listing, on-line access, and a catalog; $95 without catalog.

HOSTELS

No matter what your age, you can save on lodging costs by staying at hostels. In some 4,000 locations in more than 60 countries, Hostelling International (HI), the umbrella group for a number of na-tional youth-hostel associations, offers single-sex, dorm-style beds and, at many hostels, rooms for couples and families. New England communities with hostels include Boston, Burlington (VT), Conway (NH), Dudley (MA), Eastham (MA), Hartford, Littleton (MA), Martha's Vine-yard, Middlebury (VT), Nantucket, Truro (MA), West Bethel (ME), White River Junction (VT), and Woodford (VT). Membership in any HI national hostel as-sociation, open to travelers of all ages, al-lows you to stay in HI-affiliated hostels at member rates; one-year membership is $28 for adults in the U.S. (C$35 in Canada, £15.50 in the United Kingdom, A$52 in Australia, and NZ$40 in New Zealand); the bed rate in New England hostels ranges from $15 to $30 approxi-mately. Members have priority if the hos-tel is full; they're also eligible for discounts around the world, even on rail and bus travel in some countries.

🖪 Organizations **Hostelling International–USA** ✉ 8401 Colesville Rd., Suite 600, Silver Spring, MD 20910 ☎ 301/495-1240 🖷 301/495-6697 🌐 www.hiusa.org. **Hostelling International– Canada** ✉ 205 Catherine St., Suite 500, Ottawa, Ontario K2P 1C3 ☎ 800/663-5777 or 613/237-7884 🖷 613/237-7868 🌐 www.hihostels.ca. **YHA Aus-tralia** ✉ 422 Kent St., Sydney, NSW 2001 ☎ 02/ 9261-1111 🖷 02/9261-1969 🌐 www.yha.com.au. **YHA England and Wales** ✉ Trevelyan House, Dimple Rd., Matlock, Derbyshire DE4 3YH, U.K. ☎ 0870/870-8868 or 01629/592-700 🖷 0870/ 770-6127 or 01629/592-627 🌐 www.yha.org.uk. **YHA New Zealand** ✉ Moorhouse City, 166 Moor-house Ave., Level 1, Box 436, Christchurch ☎ 0800/278-299 or 03/379-9970 🖷 03/365-4476 🌐 www.yha.org.nz.

HOTELS

All hotels listed have private bath unless otherwise noted.

Hotel and motel chains are amply repre-sented in New England. Some of the large chains, such as Hilton, Holiday Inn, Hyatt, Marriott, and Ramada, operate all-suites, budget, business-oriented, or luxury resorts, often variations on the parent cor-poration's name (Courtyard by Marriott, for example). Though some chain hotels and motels may have a standardized look to them, this "cookie-cutter" approach also means that you can rely on the same level of comfort and efficiency at all prop-erties in a chain, and at a chain's premier properties—its so-called flagship hotels— the decor and services may be outstanding.

New England is liberally supplied with small, independent motels, which run the gamut from the tired to the tidy. Don't overlook these mom-and-pop operations; they frequently offer cheerful, convenient accommodations at lower rates than the chains.

Reservations are always a good idea, and they are particularly recommended in sum-mer and winter resort areas; in college towns in September and at graduation time in spring; and at areas renowned for autumn foliage.

Most hotels and motels will hold your reservation until 6 PM; **call ahead if you plan to arrive late.** All will hold a late reservation for you if you guarantee your reservation with a credit-card number.

When you call to make a reservation, **ask all the necessary questions up front.** If you are arriving with a car, ask if there is a parking lot or covered garage and whether there is an extra fee for parking. If you like to eat your meals in, ask if the hotel has a restaurant or whether it has room service (most do, but not necessarily 24 hours a day—and be forewarned that it can be ex-pensive). Most hotels and motels have in-room TVs, often with cable movies, but verify this if you like to watch TV. If you want an in-room crib for your child, there will probably be an additional charge.

🖪 Toll-Free Numbers **Best Western** ☎ 800/780-7234 🌐 www.bestwestern.com. **Choice** ☎ 877/424-

6423 @ www.choicehotels.com. **Clarion** 877/
424-6423 @ www.choicehotels.com. **Comfort Inn**
877/424-6423 @ www.choicehotels.com. **Days
Inn** 800/329-7466 @ www.daysinn.com. **Dou-
bletree Hotels** 800/222-8733 @ www.
doubletree.com. **Embassy Suites** 800/362-2779
@ www.embassysuites.com. **Fairfield Inn** 800/
228-2800 @ www.marriott.com/fairfieldinn. **Hilton**
800/445-8667 @ www.hilton.com. **Holiday Inn**
800/465-4329 @ www.ichotelsgroup.com.
Howard Johnson 800/446-4656 @ www.hojo.
com. **Hyatt Hotels & Resorts** 800/233-1234
@ www.hyatt.com. **La Quinta** 866/725-1661
@ www.lq.com. **Marriott** 888/236-2427
@ www.marriott.com. **Quality Inn** 877/424-6423
@ www.choicehotels.com. **Radisson** 888/201-
1718 @ www.radisson.com. **Ramada** 800/228-
2828 @ www.ramada.com. **Sheraton** 800/325-
3535 @ www.starwood.com/sheraton. **Sleep Inn**
877/424-6423 @ www.choicehotels.com. **Westin
Hotels & Resorts** 800/228-3000 @ www.
starwood.com/westin.

MEDIA

NEWSPAPERS & MAGAZINES
The *New York Times* and the national
USA Today are available in all but the
most remote regions of New England. The
Boston Globe, a respected morning daily,
is also available throughout the region.
Most communities with 25,000 or more
inhabitants generally have their own daily
newspapers, many of which carry comprehensive listings of local events at least once
a week. Larger cities and college towns
often have at least one alternative publica-
tion that provides extensive coverage on
the local cultural and social scene. Among
regional magazines, the most noteworthy
are *Yankee, Connecticut, Vermont Life,
Down East* (Maine), and *Boston.*

RADIO & TELEVISION
As in the rest of the United States, talk
shows are usually found on AM radio stations, while FM stations are devoted primarily to music. National Public Radio
(NPR), which has FM affiliates in each
New England state, provides a combination of both, including *Morning Edition*
and *All Things Considered,* the most comprehensive radio news programs in the
United States.

Although New England's half dozen or so
major metropolitan areas all have their
own local television stations and public
television affiliates, cable and satellite TV
bring dozens of channels to most hotels
and motels. Cable News Network (CNN)
offers the most comprehensive national
and international news coverage. Boston's
public television affiliate, WGBH, is a flagship station of the U.S. Public Broadcast-
ing Service network.

MONEY MATTERS
It costs a bit more to travel in most of
New England than it does in the rest of the
country, with the most costly areas being
Boston and the coastal resort areas. There
are also a fair number of somewhat posh
inns and restaurants in the Berkshires,
northwestern Connecticut, and parts of
Vermont and New Hampshire.

Prices throughout this guide are given for
adults. Substantially reduced fees are almost always available for children, students, and senior citizens. For information
on taxes, *see* Taxes.

ATMS
Cash machines are abundant throughout
New England and are found not only in
banks but in many grocery stores, Laun-
dromats, delis, and hotels. But beware,
many bank ATMs charge users a fee of up
to $2, and the commercial ATMs in retail
establishments can charge even more.

CREDIT CARDS
Using a credit card on the road allows
you to delay payment and gives you certain rights as a consumer (⇨ Consumer
Protection).

Throughout this guide, the following ab-
breviations are used: **AE,** American Express; **D,** Discover; **DC,** Diners Club; **MC,**
MasterCard; and **V,** Visa.

Reporting Lost Cards **American Express**
800/992-3404. **Diners Club** 800/234-6377.
Discover 800/347-2683. **MasterCard** 800/
622-7747. **Visa** 800/847-2911.

NATIONAL PARKS
Look into discount passes to save money
on park entrance fees. For $50, the Na-
tional Parks Pass admits you (and any pas-

sengers in your private vehicle) to all national parks, monuments, and recreation areas, as well as other sites run by the National Park Service, for a year. (In parks that charge per person, the pass admits you, your spouse and children, and your parents, when you arrive together.) Camping and parking are extra. The $15 Golden Eagle Pass, a hologram you affix to your National Parks Pass, functions as an upgrade, granting entry to all sites run by the NPS, the U.S. Fish and Wildlife Service, the U.S. Forest Service, and the Bureau of Land Management. The upgrade, which expires with the parks pass, is sold by most national-park, Fish-and-Wildlife, and BLM fee stations. A major percentage of the proceeds from pass sales funds National Parks projects.

Both the Golden Age Passport ($10), for U.S. citizens or permanent residents who are 62 and older, and the Golden Access Passport (free), for persons with disabilities, entitle holders (and any passengers in their private vehicles) to lifetime free entry to all national parks, plus 50% off fees for the use of many park facilities and services. (The discount doesn't always apply to companions.) To obtain them, you must show proof of age and of U.S. citizenship or permanent residency—such as a U.S. passport, driver's license, or birth certificate—and, if requesting Golden Access, proof of disability. The Golden Age and Golden Access passes are available only at NPS-run sites that charge an entrance fee. The National Parks Pass is also available by mail and via the Internet.
🔳 **National Park Foundation** ✉ 11 Dupont Circle NW, Suite 600, Washington, DC 20036 ☎ 202/238-4200 ⊕ www.nationalparks.org. **National Park Service** ✉ National Park Service/Department of Interior, 1849 C St. NW, Washington, DC 20240 ☎ 202/208-6843 ⊕ www.nps.gov. **National Parks Conservation Association** ✉ 1300 19th St. NW, Suite 300, Washington, DC 20036 ☎ 800/628-7275 ⊕ www.npca.org.
🔳 Passes by Mail & Online **National Park Foundation** ⊕ www.nationalparks.org. **National Parks Pass** National Park Foundation ⊄ Box 34108, Washington, DC 20043 ☎ 888/467-2757 ⊕ www.nationalparks.org; include a check or money order payable to the National Park Service, plus $3.95 for

shipping and handling (allow 10 to 13 business days from date of receipt for pass delivery), or call for passes.

PACKING

The principal rule on weather in New England is that there are no rules. A cold, foggy morning in spring can and often does become a bright, 60° afternoon. A summer breeze can suddenly turn chilly, and rain often appears with little warning. Thus, the best advice on how to dress is to **layer your clothing** so that you can peel off or add garments as needed for comfort. Showers are frequent, so **pack a raincoat and umbrella.** Even in summer you should bring long pants, a sweater or two, and a waterproof windbreaker, for evenings are often chilly and sea spray can make things cool.

Casual sportswear—walking shoes and jeans or khakis—will take you almost everywhere, but swimsuits and bare feet will not: shirts and shoes are required attire at even the most casual venues. Dress in restaurants is generally casual, except at some of the distinguished restaurants of Boston, Newport, and Maine coast towns such as Kennebunkport; a few inns in the Berkshires; and in Litchfield and Fairfield counties in Connecticut. Upscale resorts will, at the very least, require men to wear collared shirts at dinner, and jeans are often frowned upon.

In summer, **bring a hat and sunscreen.** Remember also to **pack insect repellent;** to prevent Lyme disease you'll need to guard against ticks from early spring through summer (⇨ Health).

In your carry-on luggage, pack an extra pair of eyeglasses or contact lenses and enough of any medication you take to last a few days longer than the entire trip. You may also ask your doctor to write a spare prescription (using the drug's generic name if you're coming from outside the U.S., as brand names can vary from country to country). **Never pack prescription drugs, valuables, or undeveloped film** in luggage you intend to check. And don't forget to carry with you the addresses of offices that handle refunds of lost traveler's checks.

Check *Fodor's How to Pack* (available at online retailers and bookstores everywhere) for more tips.

To avoid customs and security delays, carry medications in their original packaging. Note that such recently prohibited items as nail clippers, nail files, corkscrews, and safety razors are once again permitted in carry-on baggage. Plastic or round-bladed butter knives may also be packed in carry-on bags, but not any other kind of knife, box cutter, or razor blade. Similarly, plastic or metal scissors with blunt tips may be carried in hand luggage, but not metal scissors with pointed tips or blades longer than four inches. These rules pertain to flights originating in the U.S.; flights originating in Canada, including Canadian flights into the U.S., may be governed by different rules. For details of the prohibited list, contact the U.S. Transportation Security Administration Contact Center (if you go to the Web site, click on Travelers & Consumers/Air Travel) or the Canadian Air Transport Security Authority.

7 **U.S. Transportation Security Administration Contact Center** ☎ 866/289-9673 ⊕ www.tsa.gov. **Canadian Air Transport Security Authority** ☎ 888/294-2202 ⊕ www.catsa.gc.ca/english/travel voyage/list.htm.

CHECKING LUGGAGE

You're allowed to carry aboard one bag and one personal article, such as a purse or a laptop computer. Your carry-on bag must fit under the seat in front of you or be placed in the overhead bin. Get to the gate early, so you can board as soon as possible, before the overhead bins fill up.

Baggage allowances vary by carrier, destination, and ticket class. On international flights, you're usually allowed to check two bags weighing up to 70 pounds (32 kilograms) each, although a few airlines allow checked bags of up to 88 pounds (40 kilograms) in first class. Some international carriers don't allow more than 66 pounds (30 kilograms) per bag in business class and 44 pounds (20 kilograms) in economy. On domestic flights, the limit is usually 50 to 70 pounds (23 to 32 kilograms) per bag. In general, carry-on bags shouldn't exceed 40 pounds (18 kilograms). Most airlines

won't accept bags that weigh more than 100 pounds (45 kilograms) on domestic or international flights. Expect to pay a fee for baggage that exceeds weight limits. Check baggage restrictions with your carrier before you pack.

Airline liability for baggage is limited to $2,500 per person on flights within the United States. On international flights it amounts to $9.07 per pound or $20 per kilogram for checked baggage (roughly $640 per 70-pound bag), with a maximum of $634.90 per piece, and $400 per passenger for unchecked baggage. You can buy additional coverage at check-in for about $10 per $1,000 of coverage, but it often excludes a rather extensive list of items, shown on your airline ticket.

Before departure, itemize your bags' contents and their worth, and label the bags with your name, address, and phone number. (If you use your home address, cover it so potential thieves can't see it readily.) Include a label inside each bag and **pack a copy of your itinerary.** At check-in, make sure each bag is correctly tagged with the destination airport's three-letter code. Because some checked bags will be opened for hand inspection, the U.S. Transportation Security Administration recommends that you leave luggage unlocked or use a TSA-approved lock. TSA screeners place an inspection notice inside searched bags, which are resealed with a special lock.

If your bag has been searched and contents are missing or damaged, file a claim with the TSA Claims Management Office as soon as possible. If your bags arrive damaged or fail to arrive at all, file a written report with the airline before leaving the airport.

7 Complaints **U.S. Transportation Security Administration Contact Center** ☎ 866/289-9673 ⊕ www.tsaclaims.org.

SAFETY

Rural New England is one of the country's safest regions, so much so that residents often leave their doors unlocked. In the cities, particularly in Boston, observe the usual precautions; it's worth noting, however, that crime rates have been dropping in metropolitan areas. You should avoid out-of-the-way or poorly lighted areas at night; clutch handbags close to your body and don't let them out of your sight; and be on your guard in subways, not only during the deserted wee hours but in crowded rush hours, when pickpockets are at work. Keep your valuables in hotel safes. Try to use ATMs in busy, well-lighted places such as bank lobbies.

If your vehicle breaks down in a rural area, **pull as far off the road as possible,** tie a handkerchief to your radio antenna (or use flares at night—check if your rental agency can provide them), and stay in your car with the doors locked until help arrives. Don't pick up hitchhikers. If you're planning to leave a car overnight to make use of off-road trails or camping facilities, **make arrangements for a supervised parking area** if at all possible. Cars left at trailhead parking lots are subject to theft and vandalism.

The universal telephone number for crime and other emergencies throughout New England is 911.

SENIOR-CITIZEN TRAVEL

To qualify for age-related discounts, mention your senior-citizen status up front when booking hotel reservations (not when checking out) and before you're seated in restaurants (not when paying the bill). Be sure to have identification on hand. When renting a car, ask about promotional car-rental discounts, which can be cheaper than senior-citizen rates.

Members of AARP, an organization for people 50 years of age and older, are often eligible for discounts at attractions, lodgings, and restaurants. Elderhostel is a nonprofit organization that operates educational travel trips for people 55 and up to destinations worldwide.

🎫 Educational Programs **Elderhostel** ✉ 11 Ave. de Lafayette, Boston, MA 02111-1746 ☎ 877/426-8056, 877/426-2167 TTY, 978/323-4141 international callers 🖶 877/426-2166 ⊕ www.elderhostel.org.

SHOPPING

SMART SOUVENIRS

Distinctive New England souvenirs include Nantucket lightship baskets; authentic handbag versions are available at several Nantucket shops and will cost several hundred dollars (watch out for imported knockoffs). Less-expensive options are Blue Hill pottery, sturdy, brightly colored tableware made in Blue Hill, Maine, and available at several shops in the area; Bennington Pottery, attractive, utilitarian items made in the Vermont town (Bennington Potters North in Burlington sells inexpensive seconds); moccasins of moose and deer hide made by Maine Native Americans and sold throughout the state; and whimsical animal prints by Woody Jackson (cows) and Stephen Huneck (dogs), available at several Vermont galleries.

WATCH OUT

When you're looking for pure maple syrup, a sugarhouse can be the most or the least expensive place to shop, depending on how tourist-oriented it is. Small grocery stores are often a good source of less-expensive syrup. **Look for the word "pure" and the state designation;** much artificially flavored sugarcane syrup is sold as "maple."

With any crafts item, always **be aware that some vendors substitute mass-produced imports** for the real thing; if the price seems too good to be true, it probably is.

As the United States is signatory to treaties involving trade and products made from endangered animal species, you won't need to worry about purchasing souvenirs that you won't be able to bring into your home country. Visitors to New Hampshire should be aware that one item for sale in this state—fireworks, found at many roadside stands—is strictly forbidden as airline baggage and cannot be imported into most countries.

STUDENTS IN NEW ENGLAND

Most major attractions throughout New England offer discount admissions to students. This is particularly true in and around Boston, which has America's highest concentration of colleges and universities.

🎫 IDs & Services **STA Travel** ✉ 10 Downing St., New York, NY 10014 ☎ 800/771-4040 24-hr service center, 212/627-3111 ⊕ www.sta.com. **Travel Cuts** ✉ 187 College St., Toronto, Ontario M5T 1P7, Canada

☎ 800/592-2887 in the U.S., 866/246-9762 or 416/979-2406 in Canada ⊕ www.travelcuts.com.

TAXES

See Restaurant *and* Hotel charts at the beginning of each chapter for information about taxes on restaurant meals and accommodations.

SALES TAX

Sales taxes in New England are as follows: Connecticut 6%; Maine 5%; Massachusetts 5%; Rhode Island 7%; Vermont 6%. No sales tax is charged in New Hampshire. Some states and municipalities levy an additional tax (from 1% to 10%) on lodging or restaurant meals. Alcoholic beverages are sometimes taxed at a higher rate than that applied to meals.

TIME

New England operates on Eastern Standard Time. When it is noon in New England it is 9 AM in Los Angeles, 11 AM in Chicago, 5 PM in London, and 3 AM the following day in Sydney.

TIPPING

The customary tipping rate for taxi drivers is 15%–20%, with a minimum of $2; bellhops are usually given $2 per bag in luxury hotels, $1 per bag elsewhere. Hotel maids should be tipped $2 per day of your stay. A doorman who hails or helps you into a cab can be tipped $1–$2. You should also tip your hotel concierge for services rendered; the size of the tip depends on the difficulty of your request, as well as the quality of the concierge's work. For an ordinary dinner reservation or tour arrangements, $3–$5 should do; if the concierge scores seats at a popular restaurant or show or performs unusual services (getting your laptop repaired, finding a good pet-sitter, etc.), $10 or more is appropriate.

Waiters should be tipped 15%–20%, though at higher-end restaurants, a solid 20% is more the norm. Many restaurants add a gratuity to the bill for parties of six or more. Ask what the percentage is if the menu or bill doesn't state it. Tip $1 per drink you order at the bar, though if at an upscale establishment, those $15 martinis might warrant a $2 tip.

TOURS & PACKAGES

Because everything is prearranged on a prepackaged tour or independent vacation, you spend less time planning—and often get it all at a good price.

BOOKING WITH AN AGENT

Travel agents are excellent resources. But it's a good idea to collect brochures from several agencies, as some agents' suggestions may be influenced by relationships with tour and package firms that reward them for volume sales. If you have a special interest, find an agent with expertise in that area. The American Society of Travel Agents (ASTA) has a database of specialists worldwide; you can log on to the group's Web site to find one near you.

Make sure your travel agent knows the accommodations and other services of the place being recommended. Ask about the hotel's location, room size, beds, and whether it has a pool, room service, or programs for children, if you care about these. Has your agent been there in person or sent others whom you can contact?

Do some homework on your own, too: local tourism boards can provide information about lesser-known and small-niche operators, some of which may sell only direct.

BUYER BEWARE

Each year consumers are stranded or lose their money when tour operators—even large ones with excellent reputations—go out of business. So check out the operator. Ask several travel agents about its reputation, and try to **book with a company that has a consumer-protection program.** (Look for this information in the company's brochure.) In the United States, members of the United States Tour Operators Association are required to set aside funds ($1 million) to help eligible customers cover payments and travel arrangements in the event that the company defaults. It's also a good idea to choose a company that participates in the American Society of Travel Agents' Tour Operator Program; ASTA will act as mediator in any disputes between you and your tour operator.

Remember that the more your package or tour includes, the better you can predict the ultimate cost of your vacation. Make sure you know exactly what is covered, and beware of hidden costs. Are taxes, tips, and transfers included? Entertainment and excursions? These can add up.

🖪 Tour-Operator Recommendations **American Society of Travel Agents** (⇨ Travel Agencies). **National Tour Association** (NTA) ⊠ 546 E. Main St., Lexington, KY 40508 ☎ 800/682-8886 or 859/226-4444 🖷 859/226-4404 ⊕ www.ntaonline.com. **United States Tour Operators Association** (USTOA) ⊠ 275 Madison Ave., Suite 2014, New York, NY 10016 ☎ 212/599-6599 🖷 212/599-6744 ⊕ www.ustoa.com.

TRAIN TRAVEL

State-run and national train service are options in New England: the Massachusetts Bay Transportation Authority (MBTA) connects Boston with outlying areas on the north and south shores of the state; Amtrak offers frequent daily service along its Northeast Corridor route from Washington and New York to Boston. Amtrak's high-speed *Acela* trains link Boston and Washington, with a stop at Penn Station in New York. The *Downeaster* connects Boston with Portland, Maine, with stops in coastal New Hampshire.

Other Amtrak services include the *Vermonter* between Washington, D.C., and St. Albans, Vermont; the *Ethan Allen Express* between New York and Rutland, Vermont; and the *Lake Shore Limited* between Boston and Chicago, with stops at Worcester and Springfield, Massachusetts. These trains run on a daily basis. To avoid last-minute confusion, allow 15 to 30 minutes to make train connections.

Private rail lines have scenic train trips throughout New England, particularly during fall foliage season. Several use vintage steam equipment; the most notable is the Cog Railway to Mt. Washington in New Hampshire.

CUTTING COSTS

Amtrak offers a **North America rail pass** that gives you unlimited travel within the United States and Canada within any 30-day period ($799 peak, $543 off-peak),

and several kinds of **USA Rail passes** (for non-U.S. residents only) offering unlimited travel for 15 to 30 days. Amtrak also has senior-citizen, children's, disability, and student discounts, as well as occasional deals that allow a second or third accompanying passenger to travel for half price or even free. The **Amtrak Vacations** program customizes entire vacations, including hotels, car rentals, and tours.

FARES & SCHEDULES

Sample one-way fares and travel times (note that times vary greatly depending on the number of stops) on major routes to Boston from: New York City, 3½–4½ hours, $54–$117; Philadelphia, 5–6 hours, $68–$174; and Cleveland, 14–16 hours, $63–$101.

Sample one-way fares and travel times on other routes to New England: Philadelphia to Portland, 8–10 hours, $91–$135; Pittsburgh to New Haven, 8–13 hours, $77–$104; Washington, DC, to Providence, 6–7 hours, $73–$187.

🖪 Train Information **Amtrak** ☎ 800/872-7245 ⊕ www.amtrak.com. **Massachusetts Bay Transportation Authority** (MBTA) ☎ 617/222-3200, 800/392-6100, 617/222-5146 TTY ⊕ www.mbta.com.

TRANSPORTATION AROUND NEW ENGLAND

If you plan to travel around a sizable portion of New England, a car or car rental is a *must*. Frequent rail connections between major cities exist only within Amtrak's Northeast Corridor (most notably New Haven, Providence, Boston, Springfield, and Portland), and regional travel by air is expensive and limited. Buses connect major cities and towns, but schedules are often inconvenient. Since one of New England's primary attractions is its picturesque countryside and innumerable small villages, only the automobile traveler (or bicyclist) can really appreciate all the region has to offer. If, however, you plan to concentrate your trip in and around Boston, where streets and roads are tangled and hectic, you're better off relying on public transportation.

TRAVEL AGENCIES

A good travel agent puts your needs first. Look for an agency that has been in business at least five years, emphasizes customer service, and has someone on staff who specializes in your destination. In addition, **make sure the agency belongs to a professional trade organization.** The American Society of Travel Agents (ASTA) has more than 10,000 members in some 140 countries, enforces a strict code of ethics, and will step in to help mediate any agent-client disputes involving ASTA members. ASTA also maintains a directory of agents on its Web site; ASTA's TravelSense.org, a trip planning and travel advice site, can also help to locate a travel agent who caters to your needs. (If a travel agency is also acting as your tour operator, *see* Buyer Beware *in* Tours & Packages.)

 Local Agent Referrals **American Society of Travel Agents (ASTA)** ⊠ 1101 King St., Suite 200, Alexandria, VA 22314 ☎ 703/739-2782 ⊟ 703/684-8319 ⊕ www.astanet.com. **Association of British Travel Agents** ⊠ 68-71 Newman St., London W1T 3AH ☎ 0901/201-5050 ⊕ www.abta.com. **Association of Canadian Travel Agencies** ⊠ 350 Sparks St., Suite 510, Ottawa, Ontario K1R 7S8 ☎ 613/237-3657 ⊟ 613/237-7052 ⊕ www.acta.ca. **Australian Federation of Travel Agents** ⊠ 309 Pitt St., Level 3, Sydney, NSW 2000 ☎ 02/9264-3299 or 1300/363-416 ⊟ 02/9264-1085 ⊕ www.afta.com.au. **Travel Agents' Association of New Zealand** ⊠ Tourism and Travel House, 79 Boulcott St., Level 5, Box 1888, Wellington 6001 ☎ 04/499-0104 ⊟ 04/499-0786 ⊕ www.taanz.org.nz.

VISITOR INFORMATION

Each New England state provides a helpful free information kit, including a guidebook, map, and listings of attractions and events. All include listings and/or advertisements for lodging and dining establishments. Each state also has an official Web site with material on sights and lodgings; most of these sites have a calendar of events and other special features.

 Tourist Information **Connecticut Office of Tourism** ⊠ 505 Hudson St., Hartford, CT 06106 ☎ 800/282-6863 ⊕ www.ctbound.org. **Maine Office of Tourism** ⊠ 59 State House Station, Augusta, ME 04333 ☎ 888/624-6345 or 207/287-5711 ⊕ www.visitmaine.com. **Massachusetts Office of Travel and Tourism** ⊠ 10 Park Plaza, Suite 4510, Boston, MA 02116 ☎ 800/227-6277 or 617/973-8500 ⊕ www.massvacation.com. **New Hampshire Office**

of Travel and Tourism Development ⊠ Box 1856, Concord, NH 03302 ☎ 800/386-4664 or 603/271-2665 ⊕ www.visitnh.gov. **Rhode Island Department of Economic Development, Tourism Division** ⊠ 1 W. Exchange St., Providence, RI 02903 ☎ 800/556-2484 or 401/222-2601 ⊕ www.visitrhodeisland.com. **Vermont Department of Tourism and Marketing** ⊠ 6 Baldwin St., Drawer 33, Montpelier, VT 05633 ☎ 800/837-6668 brochures, 802/828-3237 ⊟ 802/828-3676 ⊕ www.vermontvacation.com.

 In the U.K. **Discover New England** ⊠ Cellet Public Relations, 16 Dover St., London W1S 4LR, U.K. ☎ 015/6479-4999 ⊕ www.discovernewengland.org.

WEB SITES

Do check out the World Wide Web when planning your trip. You'll find everything from weather forecasts to virtual tours of famous cities. Be sure to visit Fodors.com (⊕ www.fodors.com), a complete travel-planning site. You can research prices and book plane tickets, hotel rooms, rental cars, vacation packages, and more. In addition, you can post your pressing questions in the Travel Talk section. Other planning tools include a currency converter and weather reports, and there are loads of links to travel resources.

Check out the official home page of each New England state for information on state government, as well as for links to state agencies with information on doing business, working, studying, living, and traveling in these areas. Gorp.com is a terrific general resource for just about every kind of recreational activity; just click on the state link under "Destinations," and you'll be flooded with links to myriad topics, from wildlife refuges to ski trips to backpacking advice. Citysearch.com and Digitalcity.com both offer a wide range of reviews and links to dining, culture, and services in major cities and destinations throughout New England. The site www.visitnewengland.com provides tourism information on the entire region.

CONNECTICUT

Produced in conjunction with several of the state's leading news sources, **www.ctnow.com** has dining reviews, information on culture and attractions, and other helpful data. The **Connecticut Impressionist Art**

Trail (⊕ www.arttrail.org) lists museums containing the work of Connecticut's impressionist artists, the landscapes that inspired them, and other related sites. The **Connecticut Wine Trail** (⊕ www.ctwine. com) links all of the state's many wineries.

MAINE

MaineToday.com (⊕ www.travel. mainetoday.com) provides travel information. Maine's **Nordic Ski Council** (⊕ www. mnsc.com) provides cross-country info. The **Ski Maine** (⊕ www.skimaine.com) Web site has information about alpine snow sports.

MASSACHUSETTS

The home of the *Boston Globe* online, **www.boston.com,** has news and feature articles, ample travel information, and links to towns throughout Massachusetts. The *Boston Phoenix* (⊕ www.bostonphoenix. com), an arts and entertainment weekly, has nightlife, movie, restaurant, and fine- and performing-arts listings. At its site, the **Cape Cod Information Center** (⊕ www. allcapecod.com) carries events information

and has town directories with weather, sightseeing, lodging, and dining entries.

NEW HAMPSHIRE

Look to **www.nh.com** for features and anecdotes on New Hampshire, as well as advice on accommodations, dining, recreation, and other aspects of New Hampshire. For information on downhill and cross-country skiing, check out **Ski New Hampshire** (⊕ www.skinh.com).

RHODE ISLAND

The site of *The Providence Journal* (⊕ www.projo.com) contains loads of great information on what to see and do throughout the state.

VERMONT

The **Vermont Ski Areas Association** (⊕ www.skivermont.com) covers the downhill scene. Online **foliage reports** (⊕ www.foliage-vermont.com) will keep you up to date; the site also posts information on driving tours, accommodations, and attractions.

Maine

WORD OF MOUTH

"Getting up into Maine, the beach towns of York, Ogunquit, and Kennebunkport are wonderful. There are lighthouses, wide sandy beaches, and scenic rocky coastlines."

—zootsi

"Lobster. Views. Our favorite area of Maine is mid-coast, which is north of Portland. The only view that can beat the one overlooking Camden harbor from Mt. Battie (take auto road) is the one from the top of Cadillac in Acadia National Park."

—dfrostnh

"Acadia National Park is one of Maine's jewels. You can drive around the Loop Road—about 20 mi or so—and stop at the various overlooks."

—massteacher

By Stephen
and Neva
Allen, Lelah
Cole, Sherry
Hanson, Mary
Ruoff, Laura V.
Scheel

AS YOU DRIVE ACROSS THE BORDER INTO MAINE, a sign plainly announces the state's philosophy: THE WAY LIFE SHOULD BE. Romantics luxuriate in the feeling of a down comforter on a yellow pine bed or in the sensation of the wind and salt spray on their faces while cruising in a historic windjammer. Families love the unspoiled beaches and safe inlets dotting the shoreline and the clear inland lakes. Hikers are revived by the exalting and exhausting climb to the top of Katahdin. Adventure seekers raft the Kennebec and Penobscot rivers or kayak along the coast, and skiers head for the snow-covered slopes of western and northern Maine.

There is an expansiveness to Maine, a sense of distance between places that hardly exists elsewhere in New England and, along with the sheer size and spread of the place, a variety of terrain. People speak of "coastal" Maine and "inland" Maine as though the state could be summed up under the twin emblems of lobsters and pine trees. Yet the topography and character in this state are a good deal more complicated.

Even the coast is several places in one. Rapidly gentrifying Portland may be Maine's largest metropolitan area, but its attitude is decidedly more big town than small city. South of Portland, Ogunquit, Kennebunkport, Old Orchard Beach, and other resort towns predominate along a reasonably smooth shoreline. North of Portland and Casco Bay, secondary roads turn south off U.S. 1 onto so many oddly chiseled peninsulas that it's possible to drive for days without retracing your route. Slow down to explore the museums, galleries, and shops in the larger towns and the antiques and curio shops and harborside lobster shacks in the smaller fishing villages on the peninsulas. Freeport is an entity unto itself, a place where numerous name-brand outlets and specialty stores have sprung up around the retail outpost of famous outfitter L. L. Bean. And no description of the coast would be complete without mention of popular Acadia National Park, with its majestic mountains that are often shrouded in mist.

Inland Maine likewise defies easy characterization. For one thing, a lot of it is virtually uninhabited. This is the land Henry David Thoreau wrote about in his evocative mid-19th-century portrait, *The Maine Woods*; much of it hasn't changed since the writer passed through. Ownership of vast portions of northern Maine by forest-products corporations has kept out subdivision and development, but this, too, is changing; many of the roads here are private, open to travel only by permit.

If you come to Maine seeking an untouched fishing village with locals gathered around a potbellied stove in the general store, you'll likely come away disappointed; that innocent age has passed in all but the most remote spots. Tourism has supplanted fishing, logging, and potato farming as Maine's number-one industry, and most areas are well equipped to receive the annual onslaught of visitors. But whether you are stepping outside a cabin for a walk in the woods or watching a boat rock at its anchor, you can sense the infinity of the natural world. Wilderness is always nearby, growing to the edges of the most urbanized spots.

GREAT ITINERARIES

You can spend days exploring just the coast of Maine, as these itineraries indicate, so plan ahead and decide whether you want to ski and dogsled in the western mountains, raft or canoe in the North Woods, or simply meander up the coast, stopping at museums and historic sites, shopping for local arts and crafts, and exploring coastal villages and lobster shacks. Trying to see everything in one visit is complicated by the lack of east–west roads in the state and heavy traffic on popular routes, such as U.S. 1 and U.S. 302. Build extra time into your schedule and relax. You'll get there eventually, and in the meantime, enjoy the view.

IF YOU HAVE 2 DAYS

A two-day exploration of the southern coast provides a good introduction to different aspects of the Maine coast. Begin in **Ogunquit** ❸ with a morning walk along the Marginal Way. Then head north to the **Kennebunks** ❺, allowing at least two hours to wander through the shops and historic homes around Dock Square. Relax on the beach for an hour or so before heading to 🚘 **Portland** ❼–⓬. If you thrive on arts and entertainment, spend the night here. Otherwise, continue north to 🚘 **Freeport** ⓯, where you can shop all night at L. L. Bean. On Day 2, head north, stopping in **Bath** ⓱ to tour the Maine Maritime Museum, and finish up with a lobster dinner on **Pemaquid Peninsula** ❷⓪.

IF YOU HAVE 4 DAYS

A four-day tour of mid-coast Maine up to Acadia National Park is one of New England's classic trips. From New Harbor on **Pemaquid**

Peninsula ❷⓪, take the boat to 🚘 **Monhegan Island** ㉔ for a day of walking the trails and exploring the artists' studios and galleries. The next day, continue northeast to **Rockland** ㉕ and 🚘 **Camden** ㉖. On Day 4, visit the Farnsworth Museum in Rockland, hike or drive to the top of Mt. Battie in Camden, and meander around Camden's boat-filled harbor. Or bypass mid-coast Maine in favor of 🚘 **Mount Desert Island** ㊱–㊹ and Acadia National Park. To avoid sluggish traffic on U.S. 1, from Freeport, stay on Interstate 95 to Augusta and the Maine Turnpike; then take Route 3 to Belfast and pick up U.S. 1 north there.

IF YOU HAVE 8 DAYS

An eight-day trip allows time to see a good portion of the coast. Spend two days wandering through gentrified towns and weather-beaten fishing villages from 🚘 **Kittery** ❶ to 🚘 **Portland** ❼–⓬. On your third day explore Portland and environs, including a boat ride to **Eagle Island** ⓮ or one of the other Casco Bay islands and a visit to Portland Head Light and Two Lights in Cape Elizabeth. Continue working your way up the coast, letting your interests dictate your stops: outlet stores in **Freeport** ⓯, the Maine Maritime Museum in 🚘 **Bath** ⓱, antiques shops in **Wiscasset** ⓲, fishing villages and a much-photographed lighthouse on **Pemaquid Peninsula** ㉑. Allow at least one day in the **Rockland** ㉕ and 🚘 **Camden** ㉖ region before taking the leisurely route to **Bar Harbor** ㊶ via the **Blue Hill** ㉚ peninsula and 🚘 **Deer Isle Village** ㉛. Finish up with two days on 🚘 **Mount Desert Island** ㊱–㊹.

Exploring Maine

Maine is a large state that offers many different experiences. The York County Coast, in the southern portion of the state, is easily accessible and has long sand beaches, historic homes, and good restaurants. The coastal geography changes in Portland, the economic and cultural center of southern Maine. North of the city, long fingers of land jut into the sea, sheltering fishing villages. Penobscot Bay is famed for its rockbound coast, sailing, and numerous islands. Mount Desert Island lures crowds of people to Acadia National Park, which is filled with stunning natural beauty. Way Down East, beyond Acadia, the tempo changes; fast-food joints and trinket shops all but disappear, replaced by family-style restaurants and artisans' shops. Inland, the western lakes and mountains provide an entirely different experience. Summer camps, ski areas, and small villages populate this region. People head to Maine's North Woods to escape the crowds and to enjoy the great outdoors by hiking, rafting, camping, or canoeing.

Numbers in the text and in the margin correspond to numbers on the maps: Southern Maine Coast, Portland, Penobscot Bay, Mount Desert Island, Way Down East, Western Maine, and the North Woods.

About the Restaurants

Lobster and Maine are synonymous. As a general rule, the closer you are to a working harbor, the fresher your lobster will be. Aficionados eschew ordering lobster in restaurants, preferring to eat them "in the rough" at classic lobster pounds, where you select your dinner out of a pool and enjoy it at a waterside picnic table. Shrimp, scallops, clams, mussels, and crabs are also caught in the cold waters off Maine. Restaurants in Portland and in resort towns prepare shellfish in creative combinations with lobster, haddock, salmon, and swordfish. Blueberries are grown commercially in Maine, and local cooks use them generously in pancakes, muffins, jams, pies, and cobblers. In 1999, Maine passed a law prohibiting smoking in restaurants.

WHAT IT COSTS				
$$$$	**$$$**	**$$**	**$**	**¢**
AT DINNER over $28	$21–$28	$13–$20	$8–$12	under $8

Prices are per person, for a main course at dinner.

About the Hotels

The beach communities in the south beckon with their weathered look. Stately digs can be found in the classic inns along the York County Coast. Bed-and-breakfasts and Victorian inns furnished with lace, chintz, and mahogany have joined the family-oriented motels of Ogunquit, Boothbay Harbor, Bar Harbor, and the Camden-Rockport region. Although accommodations tend to be less luxurious away from the coast, Bethel, Carrabassett Valley, and Rangeley have sophisticated hotels and inns. Greenville has the largest selection of restaurants and accommodations in the North Woods region. Lakeside sporting camps, which range from the primitive to the upscale, are popular around Rangeley and the North Woods. Many have cozy cabins heated with woodstoves and serve three

PLEASURES & PASTIMES

BOATING

Maine's long coastline is justifiably famous: be sure to get on the water, whether on an excursion headed for Monhegan Island for the day or on a windjammer for a relaxing vacation. Windjammer trips last from just a few hours to a full week. Longer trips include hearty, home-style meals and a traditional lobster bake often held on a remote island. Windjammers may sail past long, craggy fingers of land that jut into a sea dotted with more than 2,000 islands. Sail among these islands and you'll see hidden coves, lighthouses, boat-filled harbors, and quiet fishing villages. Some windjammers, traditional two- or three-masted tall ships, are historic vessels that have been modified to carry passengers, whereas others have more modern amenities. Most windjammers depart from Rockland, Rockport, or Camden, all ports on Penobscot Bay. Boating trips, including whale-watching, run from mid- to late May through September or mid-October.

HIKING

From seaside rambles to backwoods hikes, Maine has a walk for everyone. This state's beaches are mostly hard-packed and good for walking. Many coastal communities, such as York, Ogunquit, and Bar Harbor, have shoreside paths for people who want to keep sand out of their shoes yet enjoy the sound of the crashing surf and the cliff-top views of inlets and coves. Those who like to walk in the woods will not be disappointed: 90% of the state is forested land. Acadia National Park has more than 150 mi of hiking trails, and within Baxter State Park are the northern end of the Appalachian Trail and Mt. Katahdin.

SKIING

Weather patterns that create snow cover for Maine ski areas may come from the Atlantic or from Canada, and Maine may have snow when other New England states do not—and vice versa. Sunday River and Sugarloaf are the state's largest ski areas. Both are full-service destination resorts with a choice of lodging, dining, and shopping as well as more than enough terrain to keep skiers and riders content for days. It's worth the effort to get to Sugarloaf, which provides the only above-tree-line skiing in New England.

Saddleback, in Rangeley, and Squaw Mountain, in Greenville, have big-mountain skiing at little-mountain prices.

WHITE-WATER RAFTING

From early May through September, Maine has consistent white-water rafting on three dam-controlled, Class III–V rivers: the Kennebec, the Penobscot, and the Dead. Both the Kennebec and the Dead are good day trips, with the Kennebec being the most popular—like a white-water roller coaster: big thrills but few chills. The Penobscot, which flows near Baxter State Park in the shadow of Mt. Katahdin, provides a remote trip with challenging white water and beautiful views of the mountain. It's not uncommon to see moose or deer while on the river. Most outfitters have facilities in this area, and most offer both day and overnight trips.

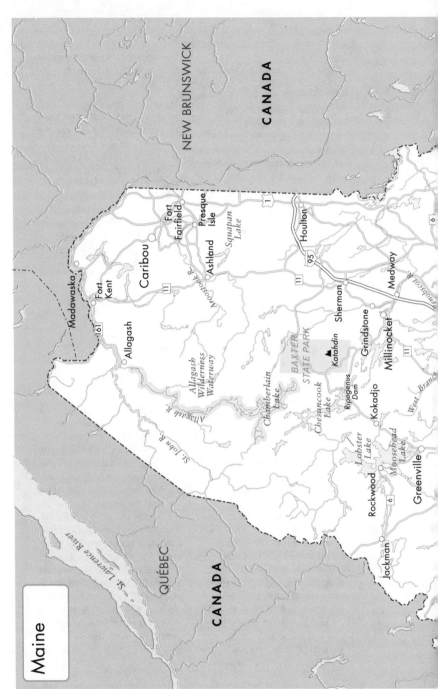

6

Maine

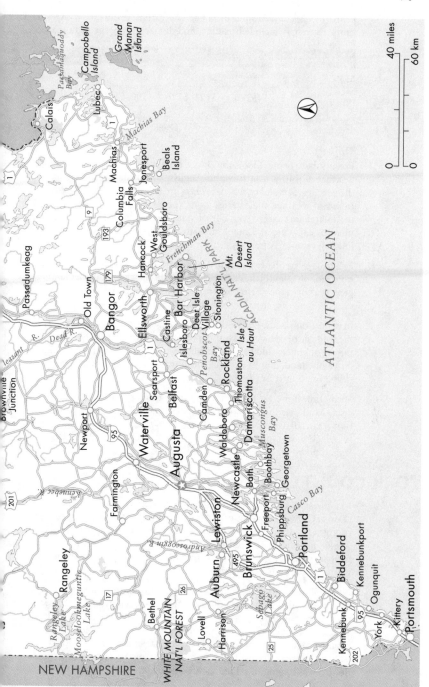

hearty meals a day. At some of Maine's larger hotels and inns with restaurants, rates may include breakfast and dinner during the peak seasons.

	WHAT IT COSTS				
	$$$$	$$$	$$	$	¢
FOR 2 PEOPLE	over $220	$171–$220	$121–$170	$80–$120	under $80

Prices are for a standard double room during peak season and not including tax or gratuities. Some inns add a 15% service charge.

Timing

From July to September is the choice time for a vacation in Maine. The weather is warmest in July and August, so throngs of people head to the beaches. September, when the days are still sunny, is far less crowded. In warm weather, the arteries along the coast and lakeside communities inland are clogged with out-of-state license plates, campgrounds are filled to capacity, and hotel rates are high. Midweek is less busy, and lodging rates are often lower then than on weekends.

Fall foliage can be brilliant in Maine and is made even more so by its reflection in inland lakes or streams or off the ocean. Late September is peak season in the north country, whereas in southern Maine the prime viewing dates are usually the first few weeks of October.

In winter, only a few places along the coast stay open for those who enjoy the solitude of the winter landscape. If the sidewalks could be rolled up, they probably would be. Maine's largest ski areas usually open in mid-November and, thanks to excellent snowmaking facilities, provide good skiing often into April.

Springtime is mud season here, as in most other rural areas of New England. Mud season is followed by spring flowers and the start of wildflowers in roadside meadows. Mid-May to mid-June is the main season for black flies, especially inland. It's best to schedule a trip after mid-June if possible, though this is prime canoeing time.

YORK COUNTY COAST

Maine's southern coast is extremely popular in summer—an all-too-brief period. Crowds converge on these otherwise quiet towns and gobble up rooms and dinner reservations at prime restaurants. You'll have to work a little harder to find vestiges of the "real" Maine. Still, even day-trippers who come for a few fleeting hours will appreciate the magical warmth of the sand along this coast.

North of Kittery, the coast has long stretches of hard-packed white-sand beach, crowded by nearly unbroken ranks of oceanfront cottages, motels, and restaurants. The summer colonies of York Beach and Wells Beach suffer from ticky-tacky overdevelopment, but quiet wildlife refuges promise an easy escape. York's historic district is on the National Register of Historic Places. Ogunquit is more upscale and offers much to do, from shopping to taking a cliff-side walk.

More than any other region south of Portland, the Kennebunks—and especially Kennebunkport—provide the complete Maine-coast experience: classic townscapes where white clapboard houses rise from manicured lawns and gardens; rocky shorelines punctuated by sandy beaches; quaint downtown districts packed with gift shops and ice-cream stands; harbors where lobster boats bob alongside yachts; rickety lobster pounds and well-appointed dining rooms.

Kittery

❶ *55 mi north of Boston; 5 mi north of Portsmouth, New Hampshire.*

Known as the "Gateway to Maine," Kittery lacks a large beach of its own. It has become a major shopping destination, thanks to its complex of factory outlets. Travel east on Route 103 for a peek at the hidden Kittery most people miss: the lands around Kittery Point. Here you'll find hiking and biking trails and, best of all, great views of the water.

Built in 1690 to protect the mouth of the Piscataqua River, **Fort McClary** (⊠ Rte. 103, Kittery Point ☎ 207/439–2845) is notable for its hexagonal blockhouse, which sits on a scenic harbor. **Fort Foster** (⊠ Pocahontas Rd., Kittery Point ☎ 207/439–3800), constructed in 1872, is an ideal place for picnics and explorations into the rocky crevices along the beach.

Where to Stay & Eat

$–$$ ✕ **Warren's Lobster House.** A local institution, this waterfront restaurant specializes in seafood and has a huge salad bar. The pine-sided dining room leaves the impression that little has changed since the restaurant opened in 1940. In season, you can dine outdoors overlooking the water. ⊠ *U.S. 1 and Water St.* ☎ *207/439–1630* ▭ *AE, MC, V.*

$$–$$$ ⊞ **Portsmouth Harbor Inn & Spa.** Renovations have added a bit more decadent luxury to this inn, but the antique beauty of the place remains the same. The brick Victorian was built in 1889 on the old Kittery town green. It overlooks the Piscataqua River and Portsmouth Harbor. An easy walk over the bridge takes you to nearby Portsmouth, New Hampshire. ⊠ *6 Water St., 03904* ☎ *207/439–4040* 📠 *207/438–9286* ⊕ *www.innatportsmouth.com* ⇥ *5 rooms ⚹ Cable TV, in-room data ports, spa; no kids under 16, no smoking* ▭ *MC, V* ⦿ *BP.*

Shopping

Kittery has more than 120 outlet stores. Along a several-mile stretch of U.S. 1 you can find just about anything, from hardware to underwear. Among the stores are Crate & Barrel, Eddie Bauer, Jones New York, Esprit, Waterford/Wedgwood, Lenox, Ralph Lauren, Tommy Hilfiger, DKNY, and J. Crew.

The Yorks

❷ *4 mi north of Kittery.*

The Yorks—York Village, York Harbor, York Beach, and Cape Neddick—are typical of small-town coastal communities in New England. Many of their nooks and crannies can be explored in a few hours. The beaches are the big attraction here.

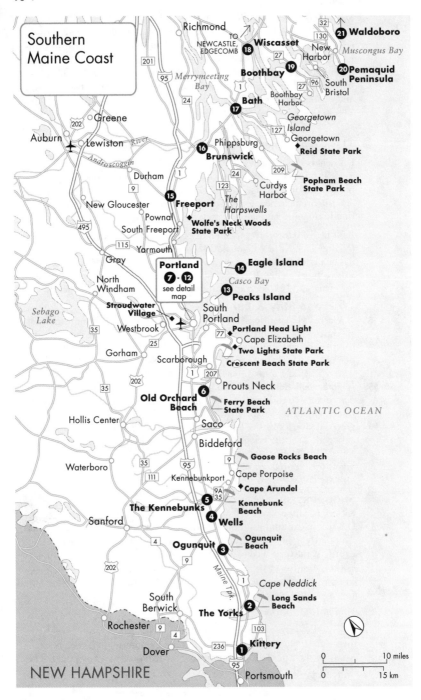

Southern Maine Coast

Richmond
TO NEWCASTLE, EDGECOMB
18 **Wiscasset**
32
130
21 **Waldoboro**
New Harbor
Muscongus Bay
27
Boothbay **19**
20 **Pemaquid Peninsula**
Merrymeeting Bay
201
95
27 **96** South Bristol
Boothbay Harbor
1
24
17 **Bath**
Georgetown Island
127 Georgetown
◆ **Reid State Park**
202 Greene
Auburn
Lewiston
Androscoggin River
Phippsburg
16 **Brunswick**
209
Popham Beach State Park
Durham
1
9
24
123
Curdys Harbor
15 **Freeport**
New Gloucester
The Harpswells
495
Pownal
South Freeport
◆ **Wolfe's Neck Woods State Park**
115 Yarmouth
Gray
Portland
7 - **12**
see detail map
14 **Eagle Island**
Casco Bay
North Windham
Sebago Lake
Stroudwater Village
South Portland
13 **Peaks Island**
35
Westbrook
◆ **Portland Head Light**
77 Cape Elizabeth
25
Gorham
Scarborough
◆ **Two Lights State Park**
1
207
◆ **Crescent Beach State Park**
202
35
6 Prouts Neck
Old Orchard Beach
Ferry Beach State Park
ATLANTIC OCEAN
Hollis Center
Saco
Biddeford
Waterboro
35
95
9 **Goose Rocks Beach**
111
Kennebunkport
Cape Porpoise
9A **35**
◆ **Cape Arundel**
5
The Kennebunks
Kennebunk Beach
Sanford
4
4 **Wells**
202
9
3
Ogunquit
Ogunquit Beach
South Berwick
Cape Neddick
1
Maine Tpke.
2
Long Sands Beach
The Yorks
Rochester
9
4
103
Dover
236
1 **Kittery**
95
NEW HAMPSHIRE
Portsmouth

0   10 miles
0   15 km

Most of the 18th- and 19th-century buildings within the **York Village Historic District** are clustered along York Street and Lindsay Road in York Village. You can buy tickets to see the seven owned by the Old York Historical Society at the **Jefferds Tavern** (✉ U.S. 1A at Lindsay Rd.), a restored late-18th-century inn. The **Old York Gaol** (1720) was once the King's Prison for the Province of Maine; inside are dungeons, cells, and the jailer's quarters. Theatrical jailbreak tours are staged Friday and Saturday nights. The 1731 **Elizabeth Perkins House** reflects the Victorian style of its last occupants, the prominent Perkins family. ☎ *207/363–4974* ⊕ *www.oldyork. org* ✉ *All buildings $10* ☺ *Early June–mid-Oct., Mon.–Sat. 10–5.*

The waterfront **Sayward-Wheeler House** was built in 1718. In the 1760s, Jonathan Sayward, a local merchant who had prospered in the West Indies trade, remodeled and furnished the house. By 1860 his descendants had opened it to the public. Guided tours of the house reveal both the simple decor of the 18th century and the more opulent and elaborate furnishings of the 19th century. ✉ *9 Barrell La. Extension, York Harbor* ☎ *207/384–2454* ⊕ *www.historicnewengland.org* ✉ *$5* ☺ *June–Oct., first Sat. of month 11–5.*

If you drive down Nubble Road from U.S. 1A and go to the end of Cape Neddick, you can park and gaze out at the 1879 **Nubble Light,** which sits on a tiny island just offshore. The keeper's house has gingerbread woodwork and a red roof.

Where to Stay & Eat

★ **$$–$$$$**   ✕ **Clay Hill Farm.** If you can bear to forgo the lobster crepe—a scallion crepe wrapped around fresh Maine lobster, caramelized onions, and spinach served over toasted almond rice pilaf and drizzled with Newburg sauce—find out what the intriguing nightly chef's special might be. An extensive wine list complements the menu. The setting, on 30 acres of pastoral farmland, is perfect. ✉ *220 Clay Hill Rd., Cape Neddick* ☎ *207/361–2272* ⌂ *Reservations essential* ▭ *AE, D, MC, V.*

¢   ✕ **Flo's Steamed Hot Dogs.** Who would guess that a hot dog could make it into both *Saveur* and *Gourmet* magazines? But there is something grand about this shabby, red-shingled shack that has been dealing dogs since 1959. The line is out the door most days but the operation is so efficient that the wait is not long at all. ✉ *1359 U.S. 1, Cape Neddick* ☎ *No phone* ▭ *No credit cards* ☺ *Closed Wed.*

★ **$$–$$$$**   ✕▣ **York Harbor Inn.** A mid-17th-century fishing cabin with dark timbers and a fieldstone fireplace forms the heart of this inn. The rooms are furnished with antiques and country pieces; many have decks overlooking the water, and some have whirlpool tubs or fireplaces. The nicest rooms are in two adjacent buildings, Harbor Cliffs and Harbor Hill. Still more rooms are in the Yorkshire Building and the "newest" addition, the 1730 Harbor Crest Inn, a ½-mi away. The dining room ($$–$$$$) has great ocean views. For dinner, start with Maine crab cakes and then try the lobster-stuffed chicken breast. ✉ *Rte. 1A* 🕮 *Box 573, York Harbor 03911* ☎ *207/363–5119* 🖷 *207/363–7151* ⊕ *www.yorkharborinn. com* ⇆ *53 rooms, 3 suites* ⌂ *Restaurant, cable TV, in-room data ports, pub, meeting rooms; no smoking* ▭ *AE, DC, MC, V* ⥮ *CP.*

$$–$$$$ ▣ **Chapman Cottage.** Set proudly atop a grassy lawn is this impeccably
Fodor'sChoice   restored inn, named for the woman who had it built as her summer cot-
★   tage in 1899. The luxuriant bedspreads, antiques, and beautiful rugs only
hint at the indulgence found here. Innkeepers Donna and Paul Archibald
spoil their guests with sumptuous breakfasts, afternoon hors d'oeuvres,
port, sherry, and homemade chocolate truffles. Most rooms have fire-
places and whirlpool tubs. A restaurant with full bar is the latest addi-
tion. ⊠ *370 York St., York Harbor 03911* ☎ *207/363–2059 or 877/
363–2059* ⊕ *www.chapmancottagebandb.com* ⤳ *3 rooms, 3 suites*
⚭ *Restaurant, Wi-Fi; no room phones, no room TVs, no kids under 12,
no smoking* ⊟ *AE, D, MC, V* ⎮◎⎮ *BP.*

Sports & the Outdoors

BEACHES   U.S. 1A runs right behind **Long Sands Beach,** a 1½-mi stretch of sand in
York Beach that has roadside parking and a bathhouse. **Short Sands Beach**
in York Beach has a bathhouse and is convenient to restaurants and shops.

Ogunquit

❸ *10 mi north of the Yorks, 39 mi southwest of Portland.*

Probably more than any other south-coast community, Ogunquit blends
coastal ambience with style and good eating. A resort since the 1880s,
the village gained fame as an artists' colony. Ogunquit has a gay pop-
ulation that swells in summer; many inns and small clubs cater to a pri-
marily gay and lesbian clientele. Families love the protected beach area
and friendly environment. Shore Road, which takes you into downtown,
passes the 100-foot Bald Head Cliff, with views up and down the coast.
On a stormy day the surf can be quite wild here.

Perkins Cove, a neck of land connected to the mainland by Oarweed Road
and a pedestrian drawbridge, has a jumble of sea-beaten fish houses.
These have largely been transformed by the tide of tourism into shops
and restaurants. When you've had your fill of browsing and jostling the
★   crowds, stroll out along the **Marginal Way,** a mile-long footpath that hugs
the shore of a rocky promontory known as Israel's Head. Benches along
the route let you appreciate the open sea vistas.

The small but worthwhile **Ogunquit Museum of American Art,** dedicated
to 20th-century American art, overlooks the ocean and is set amid a 3-
acre sculpture garden. Inside are works by Henry Strater, Marsden
Hartley, Winslow Homer, Edward Hopper, Gaston Lachaise, Mar-
guerite Zorach, and Louise Nevelson. The huge windows of the sculp-
ture court command a superb view of cliffs and ocean. ⊠ *543 Shore
Rd.* ☎ *207/646–4909* ⊕ *www.ogunquitmuseum.org* ⊠ *$5* ☉ *July–Oct.,
Mon.–Sat. 10:30–5, Sun. 2–5.*

Where to Stay & Eat

★ **$$–$$$$**   ✕ **98 Provence.** A country French interior provides a fitting backdrop
for chef Pierre Gignac's French fare. Begin with the duck foie gras or
country-style rabbit pâté, and follow it up with a cassoulet or medal-
lion of veal tenderloin with a wild mushroom cream sauce. ⊠ *262
Shore Rd.* ☎ *207/646–9898* ⚭ *Reservations essential* ⊟ *AE, MC, V.*

$$–$$$ ✕**Arrows.** Elegant simplicity is the hallmark of this restaurant in an 18th-century farmhouse. Grilled salmon and radicchio with marinated fennel and baked polenta, and Chinese-style duck glazed with molasses are typical entrées on the daily-changing menu. The Maine crabmeat mousse and lobster risotto appetizers, and desserts such as strawberry shortcake with Chantilly cream, are also beautifully executed. ⊠ *Berwick Rd.* ☎ *207/361–1100* ⌕ *Reservations essential* ▭ *MC, V* ⊗ *Closed Mon. and mid-Dec.–mid-Apr. No lunch.*

$$–$$$ ✕**Gypsy Sweethearts.** The multiethnic fare at this popular bistro ranges from shrimp margarita to chili-crusted rack of lamb to Jamaican jerk-rubbed chicken. In the dining area, cobalt-blue glassware accents the white-draped tables. ⊠ *10 Shore Rd.* ☎ *207/646–7021* ▭ *MC, V* ⊗ *Closed Mon. and Jan.–Apr. No lunch.*

$$$ ▥ **Black Boar Inn.** The original part of this inn dates to 1674, an era that
Fodor'sChoice   is reflected in the beauty of the wide-pine floors and the fireplaces in
★   every room. A sense of absolute luxury pervades here. The interior is immaculate and exquisite, with bead board walls, richly colored rugs and comforters, and many antiques. Wine and hors d'oeuvres are served in the afternoon and can be enjoyed on the front terrace, overlooking the massive gardens and the world of Main Street beyond. ⊠ *277 Main St., 03907* ☎ *207/646–2112* ⊕ *www.blackboarinn.com* ▱ *6 rooms, 2 cottages* ⌕ *Cable TV; no TV in some rooms* ▭ *MC, V* ▯⊖▯ *BP.*

$ ▥ **Yardarm Village Inn.** With stenciling winding up stairs and along many of its walls, colorful quilts, and tin ceilings, this inn has been lovingly cared for since its construction in the late 19th century. Set near the now defunct trolley bed of the same era, the peaceful home is a very short walk from the activity of Perkins Cove. Standard rooms are large and suites have separate sitting rooms. Those eager to get on the water can cruise with the innkeepers on their 26-foot single sail. ⊠ *406 Shore Rd., 03907* ☎ *207/646–7006* ⊕ *www.yardarmvillageinn.com* ▱ *5 rooms, 3 suites* ⌕ *Refrigerators, cable TV; no room phones* ▭ *No credit cards* ⊗ *Closed Nov.–Apr.*

Nightlife & the Arts

The **Ogunquit Playhouse** (⊠ U.S. 1 ☎ 207/646–5511 ⊕ www. ogunquitplayhouse.org), one of America's oldest summer theaters, mounts plays and musicals with well-known actors of both stage and screen from late June to Labor Day.

Sports & the Outdoors

Ogunquit Beach, a 3-mi-wide stretch of sand at the mouth of the Ogunquit River, has snack bars, a boardwalk, restrooms, and, at the Beach Street entrance, changing areas. Families gravitate to the ends; gay visitors camp at the beach's middle.

Wells

❹ *5 mi north of Ogunquit, 34 mi southwest of Portland.*

Don't breeze past Wells—this little community has some of the best beaches on the coast. There are also nature preserves where you can explore salt marshes and tidal pools and see birds and waterfowl.

In the **Wells Reserve at Laudholm Farm,** extensive trails lace the 1,600 acres of meadows, orchards, fields, and salt marshes. Laudholm Farm, an 18th-century saltwater farm, houses a visitor center filled with historical exhibits. A separate ecology center has learning exhibits geared mainly for kids. ⊠ *342 Laudholm Farm Rd.* ☎ *207/646–1555* ⊕ *www.wellsreserve. org* ⚑ *Parking fee $2* ⊙ *Grounds daily dawn–dusk; visitor center late May–mid-Oct., weekdays 8–4, Sat. 10–4, Sun. noon–4; mid-Oct–late May, weekdays 10–4.*

At the **Rachel Carson National Wildlife Refuge** (⊠ Rte. 9 ☎ 207/646–9226), a 1-mi-long nature trail loops through a salt marsh. The trail borders the Little River and a white-pine forest where migrating birds and waterfowl of many varieties are regularly spotted.

Where to Stay & Eat

¢–$$$ ✕ **Billy's Chowder House.** Locals head to this simple restaurant in a salt marsh for the generous lobster rolls, haddock sandwiches, and chowders. Big windows in the bright dining rooms overlook the marsh. ⊠ *216 Mile Rd.* ☎ *207/646–7558* ▤ *AE, D, MC, V* ⊙ *Closed mid-Dec.–mid-Jan.*

$–$$ ✕▨ **Grey Gull Inn.** This Victorian inn, built in 1893, has views of the open sea and rocks on which seals like to sun themselves. Most of the unpretentious, simply furnished rooms have ocean views. Overnight guests have access to nearby pool, golf, and tennis privileges. The restaurant ($$–$$$$) serves excellent seafood dishes such as soft-shell crabs amandine, and regional fare such as Yankee pot roast, and chicken breast rolled in walnuts. ⊠ *475 Webhannet Dr., at Moody Point 04090* ☎ *207/646–7501* ⊟ *207/646–0938* ⊕ *www.thegreygullinn.com* ⚑ *5 rooms, 4 with bath* ⚐ *Restaurant, cable TV; no smoking* ▤ *AE, D, MC, V* ¶⊙¶ *CP.*

$–$$ ▨ **Beach Farm Inn.** Innkeepers Nancy and Craig painstakingly renovated and decorated this 19th-century farmhouse. Craig, also a woodworker, made a good portion of the furniture as well. With a multitude of antiques, four-poster beds, artful rugs, and ample sitting areas, the home is a place of real peace among the general busyness of Wells. The beach is about a ½-mi walk down the country road. ⊠ *97 Eldredge Rd., 04090* ☎ *207/646–8493* ⊟ *207/646–5738* ⊕ *www.beachfarminn.com* ⚑ *8 rooms, 3 with bath; 2 cottages* ⚐ *Pool; no a/c in some rooms, no room phones, no room TVs, no kids under 12* ▤ *AE, MC, V* ¶⊙¶ *BP.*

Sports & the Outdoors

Kayaking is popular along the coast, and **World Within Sea Kayaking** (☎ 207/646–0455) conducts guided tours with lessons. Departure points depend on time and tide.

The Kennebunks

❺ *5 mi north of Wells, 29 mi southwest of Portland.*

The Kennebunks encompass Kennebunk, Kennebunk Beach, Goose Rocks Beach, Kennebunkport, Cape Porpoise, and Arundel. This cluster of seaside and inland villages provides a little bit of everything, from salt marshes to sand beaches, jumbled fishing shacks to architectural gems.

All About Lobsters

JUDGING FROM THE CURRENT PRICE of a lobster dinner, it's hard to believe that lobsters were once so plentiful that servants in rich households would have contracts stating they could be served lobster "no more than two times a week."

The going price for lobsters in the 1840s was 3¢ per lobster—not per pound, but per lobster. Today, of course, lobster fishing has become one of Maine's primary industries. You can find old-style, wood-slatted lobster traps in front of nearly every seafood restaurant in the state.

The coast of Maine, which is relatively new geologically speaking, is ideal for the breeding of lobsters. The floor of the ocean here is rocky, not sandy or silty like most ocean floors. This gives the baby lobsters places to hide from predators until they are big enough to fend for themselves.

To make sure the lobsters are not fished out, the state now has strict rules governing the catch. If a lobster is undersize, the fisherman has to throw it back. If it is oversize (and therefore a stud), he has to throw it back. If it's a female carrying eggs, he has to throw it back—but not before "v-notching" a flipper. Because it takes about two years for the notched tail to be shed, a v-notch is a sign to the next lobsterman that the female is of reproductive age. Obviously, v-notched females must also be thrown back. Thanks to these conservation laws—and the overfishing of cod, the baby lobsters' natural predator—the harvest is getting bigger all the time.

Because of the size restrictions, most of the lobsters you'll find in restaurants weigh 1¼ to 1½ pounds. However, lobsters can grow much larger and live to a ripe old age. The largest lobster ever caught off the coast of Maine weighed in at nearly 45 pounds and was more than 50 years old!

For an authentic, Maine-style lobster dinner, you must go to a lobster pound. Generally, these places are rustic and simple—they look more like fish-packing plants than restaurants. Hundreds of freshly caught lobsters of varying sizes are kept in pens, waiting for customers. Service is simple in the extreme. You usually sit at a wooden picnic table, and eat off a thick paper plate. A typical dinner consists of lobster—boiled or steamed—with a cup of clam chowder, and an ear of corn. Most lobster pounds offer beer and wine but usually no hard mixed drinks. The two biggest and best lobster pounds are the Lobster Pound Restaurant, in Lincolnville; and the Lobster Pound, a little north of Belfast. Both are on U.S. 1.

—Stephen Allen

Handsome white clapboard homes with shutters give Kennebunk, a ship-building center in the first half of the 19th century, a quintessential New England look. If you enjoy shopping, plan to spend the better part of a day exploring the boutiques and galleries in Dock Square.

The cornerstone of the **Brick Store Museum,** a block-long preservation of early-19th-century commercial buildings, is **William Lord's Store.** Built as a dry-goods store in 1825 in the Federal style, the building has an open-work balustrade across the roofline, granite lintels over the windows, and paired chimneys. The museum leads architectural walking tours of Kennebunk's historic Summer Street on Tuesday, Wednesday, and Friday mornings (but call to verify) from mid-June through September. ⊠ *117 Main St., Kennebunk* ☎ *207/985–4802* ⊕ *www. brickstoremuseum.org* ☞ *Donations accepted, walking tours $5* ⊗ *Tues.–Fri. 10–4:30, Sat. 10–1.*

The drive from Kennebunk to Kennebunkport will take you by the **Wedding Cake House** (⊠ 104 Summer St. [Rte. 35], Kennebunk). The legend behind this confection in fancy wood fretwork is that its builder, a sea captain, was forced to set sail in the middle of his wedding; the house was his bride's consolation for the lack of a wedding cake.

The **Nott House,** also known as White Columns, is an imposing Greek-revival mansion with Doric columns. The 1853 house is furnished with the belongings of four generations of the Perkins-Nott family and is open for guided tours. The Kennebunkport Historical Society, which maintains the house, also offers guided walking tours of Kennebunkport. ⊠ *8 Maine St., Kennebunkport* ☎ *207/967–2751* ⊕ *www. kporthistory.org* ☞ *House tours $5, walking tours $5; combination ticket $7* ⊗ *Mid-June–Labor Day, Tues., Wed., and Fri. 1–4; Thurs. 10–4, Sat. 10–1; Labor Day–mid-Oct., Wed.–Fri. 1–4; Thurs. 10–4, Sat. 10–1. Walking tours July–Labor Day, Thurs. and Sat. at 11, Labor Day–mid-Oct., Sat. at 11.*

★ ⓒ The **Seashore Trolley Museum** displays streetcars built from 1872 to 1972 and includes trolleys from major metropolitan areas and world capitals—Boston to Budapest, New York to Nagasaki, and San Francisco to Sydney—all beautifully restored. Best of all, you can take a trolley ride for nearly 4 mi over the tracks of the former Atlantic Shoreline trolley line, with a stop along the way at the museum restoration shop, where trolleys are transformed from junk into gems. ⊠ *195 Log Cabin Rd., Kennebunkport* ☎ *207/967–2800* ⊕ *www.trolleymuseum.org* ☞ *$7.50* ⊗ *Early May–mid-Oct., daily 10–5.*

Where to Stay & Eat

★ **$$$$** ✕ **White Barn Inn.** Formally attired waiters, meticulous service, and exquisite food have earned this restaurant accolades as one of the best in New England. Regional New England fare is served in a rustic but elegant dining room. The three-course, prix-fixe menu might include steamed Maine lobster nestled on fresh fettuccine with carrots, ginger, and snow peas. ⊠ *37 Beach Ave., Kennebunkport* ☎ *207/967–2321* ☞ *Reservations essential* ⓜ *Jacket required* ⊟ *AE, MC, V* ⊗ *Closed 3 wks in Jan. No lunch.*

$$–$$$$ ✕ **Mabel's Lobster Claw.** Mabel's has long been serving lobsters, homemade pies, and lots of seafood for lunch and dinner in this tiny dwelling out on Ocean Avenue. With its paneled walls, wooden booths, autographed photos of various TV stars, and paper place mats that illustrate how to eat a Maine lobster, this place is a simple little classic. ⊠ *124 Ocean Ave., Kennebunkport* ☎ *207/967–2562* ⊟ *AE, D, MC, V* ⊗ *Closed Nov.–Mar.*

$$–$$$$ ✕ **Pier 77.** The emphasis is on seafood at this pretty harbor-front restaurant where the view takes center stage. You can begin with the smoked chowder, then move on to grilled diver-harvested scallops, or try the ginger-garlic rack of lamb. Accompany it all with a selection from the excellent wine list. ⊠ *77 Pier Rd., Cape Porpoise* ☎ *207/967–8500* ⊟ *AE, MC, V* ⊘ *Closed Jan. and Feb.*

¢–$$ ✕ **Cape Pier Chowder House.** From this oceanfront eatery, you can watch the surf crash in the distance near the Goat Island lighthouse and see lobster boats returning with their day's catch. Seating is on the deck or inside. The fare includes lobster, clams, and fried foods. ⊠ *79 Pier Rd., Cape Porpoise* ☎ *207/967–0123* ⊟ *AE, D, MC, V* ⊘ *Closed early Nov.–Mar.*

$$$$ ✕🏨 **Cape Arundel Inn.** This shingle-style inn commands a magnificent ocean view that takes in the Bush estate at Walker's Point. The spacious rooms are furnished with country-style furniture and antiques, and most have sitting areas with ocean views. You can relax on the front porch or in front of the living room fireplace. In the candlelit dining room ($$$–$$$$), open to the public for dinner, every table has a view of the surf. The menu changes seasonally. ⊠ *208 Ocean Ave., Kennebunkport 04046* ☎ *207/967–2125* 🖷 *207/967–1199* ⊕ *www.capearundelinn. com* ➡ *19 rooms, 1 suite* ⚒ *Restaurant, in-room data ports, bicycles; no a/c, no room phones, no TV in some rooms, no smoking* ⊟ *AE, D, MC, V* ⊘ *Closed Jan. and Feb.* ⊺⊙⊦ *CP.*

$$$$ 🏨 **Beach House.** Gooch's Beach is out the front door of this elegant late-19th-century inn. Rooms are individually decorated, with most colored in shades of beige and accented with country antiques that are comfortable rather than fussy. Featherbeds and down comforters and pillows add a luxurious touch. Watch the sunrise from the wraparound porch, or sleep in, lulled by the sounds of the water. ⊠ *211 Beach Ave., Kennebunk 04046* ☎ *207/967–3850* 🖷 *207/967–4719* ⊕ *www.beachhseinn. com* ➡ *34 rooms* ⚒ *Some in-room hot tubs, cable TV, in-room VCRs, beach, boating, bicycles; no smoking* ⊟ *AE, MC, V* ⊺⊙⊦ *CP.*

$$$$ 🏨 **Captain Lord Mansion.** Of all the mansions in Kennebunkport that have
Fodor'sChoice been converted to inns, the 1812 Captain Lord Mansion is the most stately
★ and sumptuously appointed. Distinctive architecture, including a suspended elliptical staircase, gas fireplaces in all rooms, and near-museum-quality accoutrements, make for a formal but not stuffy setting. Six rooms have whirlpool tubs. The extravagant suite has two fireplaces, a double whirlpool, and a king-size canopy bed. ⊠ *6 Pleasant St.* ⬠ *Box 800, Kennebunkport 04046* ☎ *207/967–3141 or 800/522–3141* 🖷 *207/ 967–3172* ⊕ *www.captainlord.com* ➡ *15 rooms, 1 suite* ⚒ *In-room data ports, Wi-Fi, bicycles, meeting rooms; no room TVs, no kids under 12, no smoking* ⊟ *AE, D, DC, MC, V* ⊺⊙⊦ *BP.*

★ **$$$$** 🏨 **White Barn Inn.** For a romantic overnight stay, you need look no further than the exclusive White Barn Inn, known for its attentive, pampering service. No detail has been overlooked in the meticulously appointed rooms, from plush bedding and reading lamps to robes and slippers. Rooms are in the main inn and adjacent buildings. Some have fireplaces, hot tubs, and luxurious baths with steam showers. ⊠ *37 Beach Ave.* ⬠ *Box 560C, Kennebunkport 04046* ☎ *207/967–2321* 🖷 *207/*

967–1100 ⊕ *www.whitebarninn.com* ☛ *16 rooms, 9 suites* ⅋ *Restaurant, cable TV, in-room VCRs, in-room data ports, pool, spa, bicycles, piano bar, dry cleaning, concierge, meeting room; no kids under 12, no smoking* ⊟ *AE, MC, V* ◯|❄ *BP.*

$–$$ ⊞ **Franciscan Guest House.** Those in search of a quiet, contemplative retreat may want to choose one of the unadorned rooms in this former dormitory on the grounds of a riverside monastery. The landscaped grounds with Frederick Law Olmsted gardens have trails and shrines. The monks live in a Tudor mansion on the property, where Mass is said daily. ⊠ *28 Beach Ave., Kennebunkport 04043* ☎ *207/967–4865* ⊟ *207/967–0423* ⊕ *www.franciscanguesthouse.com* ☛ *57 rooms* ⅋ *Cable TV, saltwater pool; no room phones* ⊟ *MC, V* ⊗ *Closed Nov.–May* ◯|❄ *BP.*

Sports & the Outdoors

BEACHES   **Kennebunk Beach** has three parts: Gooch's Beach, Mother's Beach, and Kennebunk Beach. Beach Road, with its cottages and old Victorian boardinghouses, runs right behind them. Gooch's and Kennebunk attract teenagers; Mother's Beach, which has a small playground and tidal puddles for splashing, is popular with families.

BOATING   *First Chance* (⊠ 4-A Western Ave., Kennebunk ☎ 207/967–5507 or 800/967–2628) leads whale-watching cruises and guarantees sightings in season. Daily scenic lobster cruises are also offered aboard *Kylie's Chance.*

Shopping

The **Gallery on Chase Hill** (⊠ 10 Chase Hill Rd., Kennebunk ☎ 207/967–0049) presents original artwork by Maine and New England artists. **Marlow's Artisans Gallery** (⊠ 64 Main St., Kennebunk ☎ 207/985–2931) carries a large and eclectic collection of crafts. **Mast Cove Galleries** (⊠ Mast Cove La. and Maine St. [Rte. 9], Kennebunkport ☎ 207/967–3453) sells graphics, paintings, and sculpture by 105 artists. **Tom's of Maine Outlet Store** (⊠ 106 Lafayette Center, Kennebunk ☎ 207/985–6331 ⊕ www.tomsofmaine.com) sells all-natural personal-care products.

Old Orchard Beach

❻ *15 mi north of Kennebunkport, 18 mi south of Portland.*

During the 1940s and '50s, in the heyday of the Big Band era, the pier at Old Orchard Beach had a dance hall where stars of the time performed. Fire claimed the end of the pier (there are plans to rebuild it), but booths with carnival games and concession stands still line both sides. Despite summertime crowds, this smaller version of Coney Island can be captivating. Fireworks light the sky Thursday at 9:30 from late June through Labor Day.

♺ **Palace Playland,** open from Memorial Day to Labor Day, has rides, booths, and a roller coaster that drops almost 50 feet. ⊠ 1 Old Orchard St. ☎ 207/934–2001 ☒ Free ⊗ Mid-June–Labor Day, daily 10–4:30.

Where to Stay & Eat

$$–$$$$ ✕ **Joseph's by the Sea.** Large windows frame the ocean opening up beyond the dunes at this fine restaurant, which offers outdoor dining in season. Appetizers may include goat cheese terrine and lobster potato pancake. Try the grilled Tuscan swordfish or seared sea scallops for your main course. ⊠ *55 W. Grand Ave.* ☎ *207/934–5044* ▭ *AE, MC, V.*

$–$$$$ ▦ **Old Orchard Beach Inn.** Dating from 1730, this is Old Orchard Beach's oldest inn. Saved from impending demolition in the late 1990s, the entire place was completely renovated with great care and attention to historic detail. The spacious guest rooms are furnished with antiques, area rugs cover the pine floors, quilts brighten the beds, and lace curtains frame the windows. Many rooms have views over the town and of the shimmering Atlantic beyond. ⊠ *6 Portland Ave., 04064* ☎ *207/934–5834 or 877/700–6624* 🖷 *207/934–0782* ⊕ *www.oldorchardbeachinn. com* ⮌ *17 rooms, 1 suite* ⚭ *Cable TV, in-room data ports; no smoking* ▭ *AE, D, MC, V* ⏻ *CP.*

Sports & the Outdoors
Not far from Old Orchard Beach is the Maine Audubon–run **Scarborough Marsh Nature Center** (⊠ Rte. 9, Scarborough ☎ 207/883–5100 ☉ Memorial Day–mid-Oct.). You can rent a canoe and explore this natural haven on your own, or sign up for a guided trip. The salt marsh is Maine's largest and is an excellent place for bird-watching.

York County Coast A to Z

To research prices, get advice from other travelers, and book travel arrangements, visit www.fodors.com.

BUS TRAVEL
The Shuttlebus-Zoom is a localized bus service connecting the communities of Biddeford, Saco, Old Orchard Beach, Scarborough, South Portland, and Portland. The larger Vermont Transit Lines has service throughout northern New England and within Maine.
🚍 **Shuttlebus-Zoom** ☎ 207/282-5408 ⊕ www.shuttlebus-zoom.com. **Vermont Transit Lines** ☎ 800/552-8737 ⊕ www.vermonttransit.com.

CAR TRAVEL
U.S. 1 from Kittery is the shopper's route north; other roads hug the coastline. Interstate 95 is usually a faster route for travelers headed to towns north of Ogunquit.

Route 9 goes from Kennebunkport to Cape Porpoise and Goose Rocks. Parking is tight in Kennebunkport in peak season. Possibilities include the municipal lot next to the Congregational Church ($2 an hour from May through October) and 30 North Street (free year-round).

EMERGENCIES
🚑 Hospitals & Emergency Services **Maine State Police** ⊠ Gray ☎ 207/624-7000. **Southern Maine Medical Center** ⊠ 1 Medical Center Dr., Biddeford ☎ 207/283-7000, 207/283-7100 emergency room. **York Hospital** ⊠ 15 Hospital Dr., York ☎ 207/351-2157 or 800/283-7234.

LODGING
For home rentals in the Kennebunks, try Port Properties. For rentals on the Southern Coast, try Seaside Vacation Rentals. Garnsey Brothers rents

condominiums and housekeeping cottages in Wells, Moody Beach, and Drakes Island.

⚑ **Garnsey Bros** ✉ 510 Webhannet Dr., Wells 04090 ☎ 207/646-8301 ⊕ www.garnsey. com. **Port Properties** ⬀ Box 799, Kennebunkport 04046 ☎ 207/967-4400 or 800/443-7678 ⊕ www.portproperties.com. **Seaside Vacation Rentals** ⬀ Box 2000, York 03909 ☎ 207/646-7671, 207/363-1825, or 866/681-8081 ⊕ www.seasiderentals.com.

TOURS

Intown Trolley conducts 45-minute sightseeing tours of the Kennebunks. The York Trolley Company has tours that start at $7.

⚑ **Tour Operators Intown Trolley** ✉ Dock Square, Ocean Ave., Kennebunkport ☎ 207/967-3686 ⊕ www.intowntrolley.com. **York Trolley Company** ☎ 207/748-3030 ⊕ www. yorktrolley.com.

TRANSPORTATION AROUND YORK COUNTY COAST

Forget about your car, as trolleys serve several areas. A trolley circulates among the Yorks from late June to Labor Day. A trolley fleet serves Ogunquit in July and August. Trolleys circulate in Wells on weekends from Memorial Day to Columbus Day and daily from late June to Labor Day. Trolleys circulate through Kennebunkport to Kennebunk Beach from Memorial Day to Columbus Day. A trolley also circulates through Old Orchard Beach.

VISITOR INFORMATION

⚑ **Kennebunk-Kennebunkport Chamber of Commerce** ⬀ Box 740, Kennebunk 04043 ☎ 207/967-0857 ⊕ www.visitthekennebunks.com. **Maine Tourism Association Visitor Information Center** ✉ U.S. 1 and I-95, Kittery 03904 ☎ 207/439-1319 ⊕ www. mainetourism.com. **Ogunquit Chamber of Commerce** ✉ 36 Rte. 1 ⬀ Box 2289, Ogunquit 03907 ☎ 207/646-2939 ⊕ www.ogunquit.org. **Old Orchard Beach Chamber of Commerce** ✉ 1st St. ⬀ Box 600, Old Orchard Beach 04064 ☎ 207/934-2500 or 800/365-9386 ⊕ www.oldorchardbeachmaine.com. **Wells Chamber of Commerce** ⬀ Box 356, Wells 04090 ☎ 207/646-2451 ⊕ www.wellschamber.org. The **Greater York Region Chamber of Commerce** ✉ 1 Stonewall La., York 03903 ☎ 207/363-4422 or 800/639-2442 ⊕ www.gatewaytomaine.org.

PORTLAND TO WALDOBORO

Portland, the state's largest city, holds some pleasant surprises, including the atmospheric streets filled with shops and restaurants that surround the Old Port. North of Portland, Freeport was made famous by its L. L. Bean store, whose success led to the opening of scores of other outlets. The Boothbays—including Boothbay, Boothbay Harbor, East Boothbay, Linekin Neck, and Southport Island—attract hordes of vacationing families and flotillas of pleasure craft. Near Pemaquid Beach you can view the objects unearthed at the Colonial Pemaquid Restoration, including the remains of an old customs house, a tavern, a jail, a forge, and homes.

Portland

105 mi northeast of Boston; 320 mi northeast of New York City; 215 mi southwest of St. Stephen, New Brunswick.

When its residents refused to surrender arms, the British burned this bustling port town in 1775. Much of Portland was again destroyed in the Great Fire of 1866, when a boy celebrating Independence Day threw a firecracker into a pile of wood shavings. Urban decay was the most recent threat, but a successful campaign to restore the downtown area has changed all that. Portland's beautifully restored Old Port balances modern commercial enterprise and salty waterfront character in an area bustling with restaurants, shops, and galleries. Tours of the harbor and excursions to islands in Casco Bay depart from the piers of Commercial Street.

Congress Street, where L. L. Bean operates a factory store, runs the length of the peninsular city from alongside the Western Promenade in the southwest to the Eastern Promenade on Munjoy Hill in the northeast, passing through the small downtown area.

❼ On Munjoy Hill, **Portland Observatory** was built in 1807 by retired sea captain Lemuel Moody. It used lights both as an aid to sea navigation and as a warning of the approach of enemy forces. It is the last remaining signal tower in the country and is held in place by 122 tons of ballast. After visiting the small museum, climb to the observation deck and take in views of the city. ⊠ *138 Congress St.* ☎ *207/774–5561* ⊕ *www.portlandlandmarks.org* ⊠ *$5* ☉ *Memorial Day–Columbus Day, daily 10–5.*

★ ❽ The Italianate-style Morse-Libby Mansion, known as **Victoria Mansion,** is widely regarded as the most sumptuously ornamented dwelling of its period remaining in the country. Architect Henry Austin designed the house for hotelier Ruggles Morse and his wife, Olive. Inside the elegant brownstone exterior of this National Historic Landmark are colorful frescoed walls and ceilings, ornate marble mantelpieces, gilded gas chandeliers, a magnificent 6-foot-by-25-foot stained-glass ceiling window, and a freestanding mahogany staircase; guided tours cover all the details. ⊠ *109 Danforth St.* ☎ *207/772–4841* ⊕ *www. victoriamansion.org* ⊠ *$10* ☉ *May–Oct., Mon.–Sat. 10–4, Sun. 1–5; Dec., Tues.–Sun. 11–5.*

☾ ❾ Touching is okay at Portland's relatively small but fun **Children's Museum of Maine,** where kids can pretend they are lobster fishermen, shopkeepers, or computer experts. The majority of the museum's exhibits, many of which have a Maine theme, are best for children 10 and younger. The newest addition, L. L. Bear's Discovery Woods, takes imagination to the great outdoors, with explorations below the sea, up a tree, and within a flowing stream. ⊠ *142 Free St.* ☎ *207/828–1234* ⊕ *www. childrensmuseumofme.org* ⊠ *$6* ☉ *Memorial Day–Labor Day, Mon.–Sat. 10–5, Sun. noon–5; early Sept.–Memorial Day, Tues.–Sat. 10–5, Sun. noon–5.*

★ ❿ The American collection of the **Portland Museum of Art,** Maine's largest public art institution, is strong in seascapes and landscapes by Winslow Homer, John Marin, Andrew Wyeth, Edward Hopper, and Marsden Hartley. Homer's *Pulling the Dory* and *Weatherbeaten,* two quintessential Maine coast images, are here, along with 17 others. The collection of

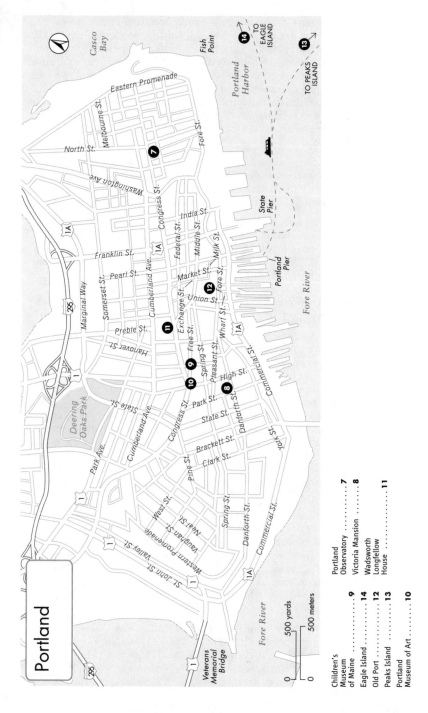

Portland

0 500 yards

0 500 meters

European impressionist and postimpressionist art includes works by Monet, Picasso, and Renoir. Harry N. Cobb, an associate of I. M. Pei, designed the strikingly modern Charles Shipman Payson building. The nearby and entirely renovated McLellan House contains additional galleries housing the museum's 19th-century collection. ⊠ *7 Congress Sq.* ☎ *207/775–6148, 207/773–2787 recorded information* ⊕ *www.portlandmuseum.org* ⊡ *$8; free Fri. 5–9* ☉ *Memorial Day–Columbus Day, Mon.–Thurs. and weekends 10–5, Fri. 10–9; Columbus Day–Memorial Day, Tues.–Thurs. and weekends 10–5, Fri. 10–9.*

⓫ The **Wadsworth Longfellow House,** the boyhood home of the poet and the first brick house in Portland, is particularly interesting because most of the furnishings are original to the house. The late-Colonial-style structure, built in 1785, has a small portico over its entrance and four chimneys surmounting the roof. ⊠ *489 Congress St.* ☎ *207/774–1822* ⊕ *www.mainehistory.org* ⊡ *$7* ☉ *May–Oct., Mon.–Sat. 10–5, Sun. noon–5; last tour at 4. Nov. and Dec., call for hrs.*

★ **⓬** The **Old Port** bridges the gap between the city's 19th-century commercial activities and those of today. The brick buildings and warehouses of the Old Port were built following the Great Fire of 1866 and were intended to last for ages. When the city's economy slumped in the mid-20th century, however, the Old Port declined and seemed slated for demolition. Then artists and craftspeople began opening shops in the late 1960s, and restaurants, boutiques, and bookstores followed. Allow a couple of hours to wander at leisure on Market, Exchange, Middle, and Fore streets. Park your car at the city garage on Fore Street, between Exchange and Union streets.

OFF THE BEATEN PATH

PORTLAND HEAD LIGHT – Familiar to many from photographs and Edward Hopper's painting, this white-stone lighthouse was commissioned by George Washington in 1791. Besides a harbor view, its park has walking paths and picnic facilities. The keeper's house is now the Museum at Portland Head Light. ⊠ *1000 Shore Rd., Cape Elizabeth* ☎ *207/799–2661* ⊡ *$2* ☉ *June–Oct., daily 10–4; mid-Apr.–May and Nov.–mid-Dec., weekends 10–4.*

TWO LIGHTS STATE PARK – sits on just over 40 acres of Maine's quintessential rocky shoreline. Named for the two lighthouses atop the hill (one is now privately owned, the other is still in use), the park has great views of Portland Harbor. ⊠ *7 Tower Dr., Cape Elizabeth* ☎ *207/799–5871* ⊡ *$3* ☉ *Daily 9–½ hour before sunset.*

Where to Stay & Eat

$$$$ ✕ **Hugo's.** Chef-owner Rob Evans has turned Hugo's, always a popular eatery, into one of the city's best restaurants. The subdued yet elegant dining room is a perfect background for Evans's masterful, creative cuisine. The four-course fixed-price menu, which may include pistachio-crusted lobster or panfried scallops, changes weekly. For a splurge, ask for the 8- to 12-course Chef's Menu ($120, reservations essential): Evans will send out multiple courses of his choosing. There is also a fixed-price vegetarian menu and a moderately priced, à la carte bar menu. ⊠ *88*

Middle St. ☎ *207/774–8538* ▭ *AE, MC, V* ⊘ *Closed Sun. and Mon. No lunch.*

★ **$$–$$$$** ✕ **Fore Street.** Two of Maine's best chefs, Sam Hayward and Dana Street, opened this restaurant in a renovated, cavernous warehouse on the edge of the Old Port. Every table in the two-level main dining room has a view of the enormous brick oven and hearth and the open kitchen, where creative entrées such as roasted Maine lobster, apple-wood-grilled Atlantic swordfish loin, and wood oven–braised cassoulet are prepared. ⊠ *288 Fore St.* ☎ *207/775–2717* ▭ *AE, MC, V* ⊘ *No lunch.*

★ **$$–$$$** ✕ **Cinque Terre.** The passionate and traditional art of Italian dining is celebrated at this Old Port spot, encouraging a long, relaxing eating experience that covers up to five courses and even more northern Italian flavors. Half portions are available, allowing you to savor more of the many choices. Start with an appetizer such as the pan-roasted clams, mussels, and hot salami on grilled focaccia; move on to salad, pasta, and a main entrée, which could be anything from seafood to veal, quail to venison. ⊠ *36 Wharf St.* ☎ *207/347–6154* ▭ *AE, MC, V* ⊘ *No lunch.*

$$–$$$ ✕ **Street and Co.** Fish and seafood are the specialties here, and you won't

Fodor'sChoice find any better or fresher. You enter through the kitchen, with all its won-

★ derful aromas, and dine, amid dried herbs and shelves of staples, at one of a dozen copper-topped tables (so your waiter can place a skillet of steaming seafood directly in front of you). Some good choices are lobster diavolo for two, scallops in Pernod and cream, and sole Française. ⊠ *33 Wharf St.* ☎ *207/775–0887* ▭ *AE, MC, V* ⊘ *No lunch.*

$$–$$$ ✕ **Walter's Cafe.** Brick walls and wood floors in this popular two-story restaurant capture the 19th-century spirit of the Old Port. Begin with lobster bisque or deep-fried lemongrass shrimp sticks; then move on to a shrimp and andouille bake. This casual, busy place in the heart of the Old Port's shopping area manages a good balance of local seafood and meats with Asian and more eclectic flavors. ⊠ *15 Exchange St.* ☎ *207/ 871–9258* ▭ *AE, MC, V* ⊘ *No lunch Sun.*

$–$$ ✕ **Pepperclub.** A hot spot for vegetarians and a young, casual crowd, this funky little restaurant features its nightly offerings on handwritten, colorful chalkboards propped up about the place. If the portobello pie doesn't tickle your fancy, choose from selections of beef, seafood, pasta, and chicken. Especially tasty is the Middle Eastern–influenced ground lamb with rice and warmly spiced yogurt-based sauce. ⊠ *78 Middle St.* ☎ *207/772–0531* ▭ *AE, D, MC, V* ⊘ *No lunch.*

¢–$$ ✕ **Portland Public Market.** Nibble your way through this handsome, airy market where 20 locally owned businesses sell fresh foods, organic produce, and imported specialty items, including fresh baked goods, soups, smoked seafood, rotisserie chicken, aged cheeses, and free-range meats. The market is open Monday through Saturday from 9 AM to 7 PM, Sunday from 10 AM to 5 PM; some vendors open at 7 AM. ⊠ *25 Preble St.* ☎ *207/228–2000.*

$$$$ ▥ **Portland Harbor Hotel.** One of Portland's newest giant hotels, the Harbor Hotel makes luxury its primary focus. Business travelers favor it for meetings on a more intimate scale, whereas vacationing guests appreciate the high quality of service and amenities. The location, in the middle of the Old Port, puts you right in the midst of the action.

✉ *468 Fore St., 04101* ☎ *207/775–9090 or 888/798–9090* 🖷 *207/ 775–9990* ⊕ *www.portlandharborhotel.com* ➳ *85 rooms, 12 suites* ⚘ *Restaurant, cable TV, in-room data ports, Wi-Fi, gym, dry cleaning, business services, meeting rooms, no-smoking rooms, parking* ▤ *AE, D, DC, MC, V.*

★ **$$$–$$$$** 🏨 **The Danforth.** This beautiful 1821 brick home has white columns, a cupola, and a prominent place in the Spring Street historic district. Rooms have fireplaces and are plush with simple Colonial furnishings and couches. Just three blocks from the Old Port, the inn overlooks the working waterfront and is also an easy stroll to the downtown area. ✉ *163 Danforth St., 04102* ☎ *207/879–8755 or 800/991–6557* 🖷 *207/879– 8754* ⊕ *www.danforthmaine.com* ➳ *10 rooms* ⚘ *Cable TV, in-room data ports, some pets allowed (fee)* ▤ *AE, MC, V* ⑩ *BP.*

$$$–$$$$ 🏨 **Pomegranate Inn.** The classic architecture of this handsome inn in the
Fodor'sChoice architecturally rich Western Promenade area gives no hint of the sur-
★ prises within. Vivid hand-painted walls, floors, and woodwork combine with contemporary artwork, and the result is both stimulating and comforting. Rooms are individually decorated, and five have fireplaces. Room 8, in the carriage house, has a private garden terrace. ✉ *49 Neal St., 04102* ☎ *207/772–1006 or 800/356–0408* 🖷 *207/773–4426* ⊕ *www.pomegranateinn.com* ➳ *7 rooms, 1 suite* ⚘ *In-room data ports; no kids under 16, no smoking* ▤ *AE, D, DC, MC, V* ⑩ *BP.*

$$$–$$$$ 🏨 **Portland Regency Hotel.** One of the few major hotels in the center of the Old Port, the brick Regency building was Portland's armory in the late 19th century. Most rooms have four-poster beds, tall standing mirrors, floral curtains, and love seats. You can walk to shops, restaurants, and museums from the hotel. ✉ *20 Milk St., 04101* ☎ *207/774– 4200 or 800/727–3436* 🖷 *207/775–2150* ⊕ *www.theregency.com* ➳ *87 rooms, 8 suites* ⚘ *Restaurant, minibars, cable TV, in-room data ports, Wi-Fi, health club, hot tub, massage, sauna, steam room, dry cleaning, business services, meeting rooms, no-smoking rooms* ▤ *AE, D, DC, MC, V.*

$$–$$$$ 🏨 **Inn on Carleton.** After a day of exploring Portland's museums and shops, you'll find a quiet retreat at this elegant brick town house on the city's Western Promenade. Built in 1869, it is furnished throughout with period antiques as well as artwork by contemporary Maine artists. A restored trompe l'oeil painting by Charles Schumacher greets you at the entryway. ✉ *46 Carleton St., 04102* ☎ *207/775–1910 or 800/639–1779* 🖷 *207/761–0956* ⊕ *www.innoncarleton.com* ➳ *6 rooms* ⚘ *No room phones, no room TVs, no kids under 9, no smoking* ▤ *D, MC, V* ⑩ *BP.*

Nightlife & the Arts

NIGHTLIFE **Asylum** (✉ 121 Center St. ☎ 207/772–8274) oozes with live entertainment and dancing on two levels and a sports bar; it books local and regional rock, pop, and hip-hop groups. For live blues every night of the week, try the **Big Easy Blues Club** (✉ 55 Market St. ☎ 207/871–8817). **Brian Boru** (✉ 57 Center St. ☎ 207/780–1506) is an Irish pub with occasional entertainment, ranging from Celtic to reggae, and an outside deck. **Gritty's** (✉ 396 Fore St. ☎ 207/772–2739) brews fine ales and serves British pub fare and seafood dishes.

THE ARTS **Portland City Hall's Merrill Auditorium** (✉ 20 Myrtle St. ☎ 207/874–8200) hosts numerous theatrical and musical events including performances by the Portland Symphony Orchestra, Portland Concert Association, and Portland Opera Repertory Theater. On most Tuesdays from mid-June to September, recitals are given on the huge 1912 Kotzschmar Memorial Organ. The **Center for Cultural Exchange** (✉ 1 Longfellow Sq. ☎ 207/761–0591) presents music, dance, and theater performances.

Sports & the Outdoors

BEACHES **Crescent Beach State Park** (✉ Rte. 77, Cape Elizabeth ☎ 207/799–5871), about 8 mi south of Portland, has a sand beach, picnic tables, a seasonal snack bar, and a bathhouse. Popular with families with young children, it charges a nominal fee for admittance in season. From Columbus Day to Memorial Day, the park is closed to vehicles but not to pedestrians.

BICYCLING **Portland Trails** (✉ 305 Commercial St. ☎ 207/775–2411 ⊕ www.trails. org), a group devoted to blazing (literally) new trails for cyclists, can tell you about designated, paved routes that wind along the water, through parks, and beyond.

BOAT TRIPS For tours of the harbor, Casco Bay, and the scenic nearby islands, try **Bay View Cruises** (✉ Fisherman's Wharf ☎ 207/761–0496). For an extra treat, request the Lobster Bake on the Bay—a full meal of chowder, bread, mussels, lobster, and dessert. **Lucky Catch Cruises** (✉ 170 Commercial St. ☎ 207/761–0941 ⊕ www.luckycatch.com) sets out to sea in a real lobster boat so passengers can get the genuine experience, which includes hauling traps and the chance to purchase the catch. **Portland Schooner Co.** (✉ Maine State Pier ☎ 207/766–2500 ⊕ www. portlandschooner.com) offers daily sails aboard a 72-foot 1924 vintage schooner, the *Bagheera*, or the 88-foot 1912 vintage *Wendameen*.

Shopping

For a city this size, you'll find a plethora of locally owned stores and art and crafts galleries, particularly those in or near the Old Port; trendy Exchange Street is great for browsing.

ART & ANTIQUES **F. O. Bailey Antiquarians** (✉ 35 Depot Rd. ☎ 207/781–8001), a large retail showroom, carries antique and reproduction furniture and jewelry, paintings, rugs, and china. **Greenhut Galleries** (✉ 146 Middle St. ☎ 207/772–2693) shows contemporary art and sculpture by New England artists. The **Bayview Gallery** (✉ 58 Market St., Brunswick ☎ 207/729–5500 or 800/244–3007) has original art and prints by prominent New England painters.

BOOKS **Carlson and Turner** (✉ 241 Congress St. ☎ 207/773–4200) is an antiquarian-book dealer with an estimated 70,000 titles. **Longfellow Books** (✉ 1 Monument Way ☎ 207/772–4045) is known for its good service and thoughtful literary selection.

CLOTHING Family-owned **Casco Bay Wool Works** (✉ 10 Moulton St. ☎ 207/879–9665) sells beautiful, handcrafted wool capes, shawls, blankets, and scarves. Retro, rockabilly, and suave, **Stitchez Clothing** (✉ 574 Congress St. ☎ 207/780–8340) is a great find for hip male fashions.

Casco Bay Islands

The islands of Casco Bay are also known as the Calendar Islands because an early explorer mistakenly thought there was one for each day of the year (in reality there are only 140). These islands range from ledges visible only at low tide to populous Peaks Island, which is a suburb of Portland. Some islands are uninhabited, others support year-round communities as well as stores and restaurants. Fort Gorges commands Hog Island Ledge, and Eagle Island is the site of Arctic explorer Admiral Peary's home. The brightly painted ferries of Casco Bay Lines are the islands' lifeline. There is frequent service to the most-populated ones, including Peaks, Long, Little Diamond, and Great Diamond. A ride on the bay is a great way to experience the Maine coast.

⓭ Peaks Island, nearest to Portland, is the most developed of the Calendar Islands, but you can still commune with the wind and the sea, explore an old fort, and ramble along the alternately rocky and sandy shore. The trip to the island by boat is particularly enjoyable at or near sunset. Order a lobster sandwich or cold beer on the outdoor deck of **Jones' Landing** restaurant, steps from the dock. A circle trip without stops takes about 90 minutes. On the far side of the island you can stop on the rugged shoreline and have lunch. A small museum with Civil War artifacts, open in summer, is maintained in the **Fifth Maine Regiment** building. When the Civil War broke out in 1861, Maine was asked to raise only a single regiment to fight, but the state raised 10 and sent the Fifth Maine Regiment into the war's first battle, at Bull Run.

⓮ Eagle Island, owned by the state and open to the public for day trips in summer, was the home of Admiral Robert E. Peary, the American explorer of the North Pole. Peary built a stone-and-wood house on the 17-acre island as a summer retreat in 1904 but made it his permanent residence. Filled with Peary's stuffed Arctic birds, the quartz he brought home and set into the fieldstone fireplace, and other objects, the house remains as it was when Peary lived in it. A boat ride here offers a classic Maine experience as you pass by forested islands, and the island has a rocky beach and some trails to explore. The *Kristy K.* and *Fish Hawk* depart from Long Wharf in Portland (you can also visit the island from Freeport) and make four-hour narrated tours; tours of Portland Head Light and seal-watching cruises are also conducted. ⊠ *Long Wharf* ☎ *207/774–6498* ⌨ *$12–$24, depending on tour* ☉ *Departures late May–Labor Day, daily beginning 10 AM.*

Freeport

⓯ *17 mi northeast of Portland, 10 mi southwest of Brunswick.*

Most people come to Freeport simply to shop—L. L. Bean is the store that put this town on the map, and plenty of outlets and some specialty stores have moved in. But Freeport, on U.S. 1, has charming backstreets lined with historic buildings and old clapboard houses, and the pretty little harbor on the Harraseeket River is a relaxing place to linger. The **Freeport Historical Society** mounts exhibits pertaining to the town's history. You can also pick up a walking map of the village here. ⊠ *45*

Main St. ☎ *207/865–3170* ⊕ *www.freeporthistoricalsociety.org* ⊙ *Tues., Thurs., and Fri. 10–2:30; Wed. 10–7.*

Bradbury Mountain State Park has moderate trails to the top of Bradbury Mountain. There are lovely views of the sea from the peak. A picnic area and shelter, a ball field, a playground, and 41 campsites are among the facilities. ☒ *Rte. 9 (I–95, 5 mi from Freeport-Durham exit), Pownal* ☎ *207/688–4712* ☒ *$3 Memorial Day–Labor Day, $2 off-season.*

🖑 At the **Desert of Maine,** a 40-acre natural desert, you can tour the sand dunes in a safari coach, walk nature trails, hunt for gemstones, and watch sand artists at work. Poor agricultural practices in the late 18th century combined with massive land clearing and overgrazing uncovered this desert, which was actually formed by a glacier during the last Ice Age. ☒ *I–295, Exit 20* ☎ *207/865–6962* ⊕ *www.desertofmaine.com* ☒ *$7.75* ⊙ *Early May–mid-Oct., daily 9–5.*

Wolfe's Neck Woods State Park has 5 mi of good hiking trails along Casco Bay, the Harraseeket River, and a fringe salt marsh. Naturalists lead walks on a regular basis in summer and on weekends and holidays in spring and fall; it's an excellent place to view nesting ospreys. ☒ *Wolfe's Neck Rd. (follow Bow St. opposite L. L. Bean off U.S. 1)* ☎ *207/865–4465* ☒ *$3 high season (Memorial Day–Labor Day); $1.50 off-season* ⊙ *Daily Apr.–Oct.*

Where to Stay & Eat

$$$–$$$$ ✕🏠 **Harraseeket Inn.** Despite modern appointments such as elevators and whirlpool baths in some rooms, this 1850 Greek-revival home provides a pleasantly old-fashioned, country-inn experience just a few minutes' walk from L. L. Bean. Guest rooms have print fabrics and reproductions of Federal quarter-canopy beds. The formal Maine Dining Room ($$–$$$$) specializes in contemporary American regional cuisine such as green apple and sarsaparilla short ribs and pan-roasted halibut with potato chowder. The casual Broad Arrow Tavern ($–$$$) serves heartier fare. ☒ *162 Main St., 04032* ☎ *207/865–9377 or 800/342–6423* 🖶 *207/865–1684* ⊕ *www.harraseeketinn.com* ☜ *82 rooms, 2 suites* ♦ *2 restaurants, some microwaves, some refrigerators, cable TV, in-room data ports, indoor pool, croquet, meeting room, some pets allowed (fee), no-smoking rooms* ⊟ *AE, D, DC, MC, V* ⦿ *BP.*

$$ 🏠 **James Place Inn.** Set on a quiet side street yet within easy walking distance of shopping paradise, this peaceful inn is tastefully decorated with brightly painted walls, colorful floral bedspreads, hooked rugs, and four-poster beds. Maine-inspired artwork and fresh flowers add to the simple elegance of the place, which serves a full hot breakfast in a light-dappled sunroom. Some marbled bathrooms even provide two-person Jacuzzis. For winter visits, choose the room with a working fireplace. One room has a kitchenette. ☒ *11 Holbrook St., 04032* ☎ *207/865–4486 or 800/964–9086* ⊕ *www.jamesplaceinn.com* ☜ *7 rooms* ♦ *Cable TV* ⊟ *AE, D, MC, V* ⦿ *BP.*

¢ 🏠 **Maine Idyll Motor Court.** The Marsteller family has operated this simple 1932 cottage colony for four generations. The tidy white cabins are shaded by towering pines and popular with families. Wood floors and paneling enrich the rustic interior of each cabin. ☒ *1411 U.S. 1, 04032*

☎ 207/865–4201 ✆ 20 1- *to 3-bedroom cottages* ⚵ *Some microwaves, refrigerators, cable TV, 2 playgrounds, some pets allowed, no-smoking rooms; no a/c in some rooms* ▤ *No credit cards* ⊘ *Closed mid-Nov.–mid-Apr.* CP.

Sports & the Outdoors

Atlantic Seal Cruises (⊠ South Freeport ☎ 207/865–6112, 877/285–7325 seasonal) operates day trips to Eagle Island and Seguin Island lighthouse, as well as evening seal and osprey watches.

L. L. Bean's year-round **Outdoor Discovery Schools** (⊠ Freeport ☎ 888/552–3261 ⊕ www.llbean.com/ods) include half- and one-day classes, as well as longer trips that teach canoeing, shooting, photography, kayaking, fly-fishing, cross-country skiing, and other sports. It's best to sign up several months in advance.

Shopping

The *Freeport Visitors Guide* (☎ 207/865–1212, 800/865–1994 for a copy) lists the more than 100 shops and factory outlet stores that can be found on Main Street, Bow Street, and elsewhere, including such big-name designers as Coach, Brooks Brothers, Polo Ralph Lauren, and Cole-Haan. Don't overlook the specialty stores and crafts galleries.

Cuddledown of Maine (⊠ 475 U.S. 1 ☎ 207/865–1713) has a selection of down comforters, pillows, and luxurious bedding. Head upstairs for discounted merchandise. The giant **L. L. Bean Flagship Store** (⊠ 95 Main St. ☎ 800/341–4341), open 24 hours a day, 365 days a year, attracts 3½ million shoppers annually to the heart of Freeport's shopping district. Founded in 1912 as a mail-order merchandiser of products for hunters, guides, and anglers, the company still makes and sells the original hunting boots, along with cotton, wool, and silk sweaters; camping and ski equipment; comforters; and hundreds of other items for the home, car, boat, or campsite. The **L. L. Bean Hunting & Fishing Store** (⊠ 8 Nathan Nye St. ☎ 800/341–4341), next door, keeps similarly long hours. The **L. L. Bean Factory Store** (⊠ Depot St. ☎ 800/341–4341), open from 9 to 9 daily except Christmas Day, has seconds and discontinued merchandise at discount prices.

Kids get their chance to shop at the educational toy store **Play and Learn** (⊠ 200 Lower Maine St. ☎ 207/865–6434).

Brunswick

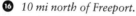 *10 mi north of Freeport.*

Lovely brick and clapboard homes and other structures are the highlights of the town's Federal Street Historic District, which includes Federal Street and Park Row and the stately campus of Bowdoin College. Bowdoin's imposing neo-Gothic Hubbard Hall, on the campus quadrangle, is home to the **Peary–MacMillan Arctic Museum**, where you'll find navigational instruments and other artifacts from the first successful expedition to the North Pole, in 1909. The journey was headed by two of Bowdoin's most famous alumni, Admiral Robert E. Peary and shipmaster Donald B. MacMillan. ⊠ *Junction Bath Rd. and Upper Maine St.* ☎ *207/725–3416* 🖼 *Free* ☉ *Tues.–Sat. 10–5, Sun. 2–5.*

The **Bowdoin College Museum of Art,** in a splendid Renaissance-revival–style building designed by Charles F. McKim in 1894, displays small but good collections encompassing Assyrian and classical art and works by Dutch, Italian, French, and Flemish old masters; superb Colonial and Federal paintings, notably Gilbert Stuart portraits of Madison and Jefferson; the Winslow Homer Collection of watercolors, engravings, etchings, and memorabilia donated by the artist's family; and works by Mary Cassatt, Andrew Wyeth, and Robert Rauschenberg. Closed for renovation in mid-2005, the museum should be open again by spring 2007. ⊠ *Junction Bath Rd. and Upper Maine St.* ☎ *207/725–3275* 🖼 *Free* ☉ *Tues.–Sat. 10–5, Sun. 2–5.*

The **General Joshua L. Chamberlain Museum** displays memorabilia and documents the life of Maine's most celebrated Civil War hero. The general, who played an instrumental role in the Union Army's victory at Gettysburg, was elected governor of Maine in 1867. From 1871 to 1883 he served as president of Bowdoin College. ⊠ *226 Maine St.* ☎ *207/ 729–6606* 🖼 *$5* ☉ *Late May–mid-Oct., Tues.–Sat. 10–4.*

**OFF THE
BEATEN
PATH**

THE HARPSWELLS – A side trip from Bath or Brunswick onto Route 123 or Route 24 takes you to the peninsulas and islands known collectively as the Harpswells. Small coves along Harpswell Neck shelter the boats of lobstermen, and summer cottages are tucked away amid the birch and spruce trees. Along Route 123, signs with blue herons mark the studios and galleries of the Harpswell Craft Guild.

Where to Stay & Eat

$$–$$$
Fodor's Choice
★

✕ **Cook's Lobster House.** You cross the world's only cribstone bridge (designed so that water flows freely through gaps between the granite blocks) on your way to this famous seafood restaurant on Bailey Island. Try the lobster casserole, one of the signature dishes. Come for lunch or dinner and watch men checking the lobster pots that dot the surface of the water. ⊠ *68 Garrison Cove Rd., Bailey Island* ☎ *207/833–2818* ⊕ *www.cookslobster.com* ⌦ *Reservations not accepted* ☰ *D, MC, V.*

¢–$
✕ **Fat Boy Drive-In.** Turn on your lights to catch the attention of the servers at this old-fashioned drive-in restaurant. The eatery is renowned for its BLTs made with Canadian bacon. Order one with onion rings and a frappé (try the blueberry). Baskets of fried clams and shrimp are the menu's most popular items. ⊠ *111 Bath Rd.* ☎ *207/729–9431* ☰ *No credit cards* ☉ *Closed mid-Oct.–mid-Mar.*

$$$–$$$$
✕🖼 **Captain Daniel Stone Inn.** This Federal-style inn, built by Captain Daniel Stone in 1819, looks down on the Androscoggin River. In the main house, a grand stairway winds down to the sun-filled lobby. No two rooms are identical, but most have comfortable furnishings such as four-poster beds. Excellent service distinguishes the Narcissa Stone Restaurant ($$–$$$). Look for entrées such as mariner's stew, which combines lobster, scallops, and shrimp in a seafood broth. ⊠ *10 Water St., 04011* ☎ *877/573–5151 or 207/725–9898* 🖨 *207/725–9898* ⊕ *www.captaindanielstoneinn.com* ⇄ *34 rooms, 4 suites* ⌂ *Restaurant, cable TV, no-smoking rooms* ☰ *AE, D, DC, MC, V* ⏐◎⏐ *CP.*

$–$$$ ☐ **Brunswick Bed & Breakfast.** Near the shops and restaurants of downtown Brunswick, this gracefully restored Greek-revival house couldn't have a more central location. Crackling fires in the main room and breakfast room keep out the chill in winter. Eight units grace the main house, with six more in the carriage house (including two that are wheelchair accessible). Look for thoughtful touches such as terry robes in the baths. ⊠ *650 Park Row, 04011* ☎ *207/729–4914 or 800/299–4914* ⊕ *www.brunswickbnb.com* ⮑ *15 rooms, 2 suites* ⚲ *In-room data ports; no TV in some rooms, no smoking* ▭ *AE, MC, V* ⊘ *Closed Jan.* �ⓞⓘ *BP.*

Nightlife & the Arts

A six-week concert series at Bowdoin College, the **Bowdoin International Music Festival** (⊠ Bowdoin College ☎ 207/373–1400 ⊕ www.bowdoinfestival.org) runs from late June to early August. The series features performances by students, faculty, and guest artists.

Sports & the Outdoors

★ **H2Outfitters** (⊠ Rte. 24, Orr's Island ☎ 207/833–5257 or 800/205–2925 ⊕ www.H2outfitters.com) provides top-notch sea-kayaking instruction for people of all skill levels. The company also rents all the gear you'll need to strike out on your own and leads day and overnight excursions.

Shopping

Ash Cove Pottery (⊠ 75 Ash Cove Rd., Harpswell ☎ 207/833–6004 ⊕ www.mainepotters.com) is worth a trip to see how pottery is fired. This cooperative gallery is open all year. **Georgetown Pottery** (⊠ 755 Five Islands Rd., Georgetown ☎ 207/371–2801 ⊕ www.georgetownpottery.com) fires all its pieces on the premises.

Bath

⓱ *11 mi northeast of Brunswick, 38 mi northeast of Portland.*

Bath has been a shipbuilding center since 1607. These days the Bath Iron Works turns out guided-missile frigates for the U.S. Navy and merchant container ships. On Front and Centre streets in the heart of Bath's historic district, amid 19th-century Victorian homes, antiques shops and intriguing specialty shops invite browsing.

★ In a cluster of buildings that once made up the Percy & Small Shipyard, the **Maine Maritime Museum** examines the world of shipbuilding. A number of impressive ships, including the 142-foot Grand Banks fishing schooner *Sherman Zwicker,* are on display in the port. Exhibits use ship models, paintings, photographs, and historical artifacts to tell the history of the region. From Memorial Day to Columbus Day weekend, hour-long tours of the shipyard show you how these massive wooden ships were built. In summer, boat tours sail the scenic Kennebec River. ⊠ *243 Washington St.* ☎ *207/443–1316* ⊕ *www.mainemaritimemuseum.org* 🎟 *$9.75* ⊙ *Daily 9:30–5.*

On Georgetown Island, **Reid State Park** (⊠ Rte. 127 ☎ 207/371–2303) has 1½ mi of sand split among three beaches. From the top of Griffith Head, a rocky headland overlooking the park, you can spot the lighthouses on Seguin Island, the Cuckolds, and Hendricks Head.

OFF THE
BEATEN
PATH

POPHAM – Follow Route 209 south from Bath to Popham, the site of the short-lived Popham Colony, the first attempt to establish an English colony in New England—it endured from summer 1607 to fall 1608, enough time to build a ship, the *Virginia,* to take some of the colonists back to England. Benedict Arnold set off from Popham in 1775 on his ill-fated march against the British in Québec. Granite-walled **Fort Popham** (⊠ Rte. 209, Phippsburg ☎ 207/389–1335) was built in 1861, for use during the Civil War. It was employed subsequently in the Spanish-American War and World War I. **Popham State Park,** at the end of Route 209, has a sandy beach. At low tide you can walk to a nearby island and explore tide pools.

Where to Stay & Eat

★ $$–$$$$ ✕**Robinhood Free Meetinghouse.** Michael Gagne, one of Maine's best chefs, prepares his classic yet creative cuisine in this 1855 Greek-revival–style meetinghouse. The dining room evokes the past with its cream-color walls, pine floorboards, and cherry Shaker-style chairs. Crisp linens add an elegant touch. You might begin with the artichoke strudel, then move on to the veal saltimbocca or the confit of duck. Finish up with Obsession in Three Chocolates, his signature decadent dessert. ⊠ *210 Robinhood Rd., Georgetown* ☎ *207/371–2188* ⊕ *www.robinhood-meetinghouse. com* ⊟ *AE, D, MC, V* ☉ *No lunch.*

$–$$ ✕**Beale Street Barbecue.** Ribs are the thing in this barbecue joint. Jalapeño popovers and chili served with corn bread are popular appetizers. For hearty eaters, there are platters piled high with pulled pork, pulled chicken, or shredded beef. ⊠ *215 Water St.* ☎ *207/442–9514* ⊟ *MC, V.*

★ $$–$$$ ⊞**Inn at Bath.** Filled with antiques, this handsome 1820 Greek-revival–style lodging sits in the middle of Brunswick's historic district. Many of the downtown sights, shops, and restaurants, including the local library with its distinctive shaded gazebo, are within easy walking distance. The romantic guest rooms are tastefully decorated with works by local artists. Four have wood-burning fireplaces and two have two-person whirlpool tubs. ⊠ *969 Washington St., 04530* ☎ *207/443–4294 or 800/423–0964* ⊟ *207/443–4295* ⊕ *www.innatbath.com* ⊃ *8 rooms* ⚇ *Cable TV, in-room VCRs, in-room data ports, Wi-Fi, meeting rooms, some pets allowed* ⊟ *AE, D, MC, V* ⧖ *BP.*

$–$$$ ⊞ **1774 Inn.** Listed on the National Register of Historic Places, this Georgian-style mansion dating from before the Revolutionary War has handsome interior detailing and magnificent antiques. The former McCobb-Hill-Minott House, on a bend in the Kennebec River, it has spacious corner guest rooms, including two with fireplaces and two with shared baths. One room has a deck overlooking the river. A four-bedroom cottage facing the river has its own kitchen, two baths, and four bedrooms. ⊠ *44 Parker Head Rd., Phippsburg 04562* ☎ *207/389–1774* ⊟ *207/389–9076* ⊕ *www.1774inn.com* ⊃ *7 rooms, 1 cottage* ⚇ *Dining room; no room TVs, no kids under 12* ⊟ *MC, V* ⧖ *BP.*

$–$$ ⊞ **Pryor House Bed & Breakfast.** An elegant double staircase in the foyer welcomes visitors to this 1820s Federal-style home gazing down on the Kennebec River. It's in the historic district of Bath, so shops and restaurants are nearby. The Tall Chimney Room has a railroad theme, with a working model train that runs around the chimney. There's also a hot tub big enough for two. Nautical themes are reflected in the Washington Room, with its wide pine floorboards and windows overlooking the river. ✉ *360 Front St., 04530* ☎ *207/443–1146* ⊕ *www. pryorhouse.com* ➬*3 rooms* ⚭ *Dining room; no kids under 12* ☴ *AE, D, DC, MC, V* ¶◯∣ *BP.*

Nightlife & the Arts

The **Chocolate Church Arts Center** (✉ 804 Washington St. ☎ 207/442–8455) hosts folk, jazz, Celtic, blues, and classical concerts, as well as theatrical performances for adults and children. The gallery space exhibits works in various media by local artists. Classes in watercolors and pastels are available.

Shopping

You'll spot an authentic teepee as you approach **Native Arts** (✉ 813 U.S. Rte. 1, Woolwich ☎ 207/442–8399), which carries fine crafts made by 50 different Native peoples, from carvings made in Alaska to beadwork produced in South America. Stop in and see the drums and birch-bark canoes on display.

Wiscasset

18 *10 mi north of Bath, 46 mi northeast of Portland.*

Settled in 1663 on the banks of the Sheepscot River, Wiscasset fittingly bills itself as Maine's Prettiest Village. Stroll through town and you'll pass by elegant sea captains' homes (many now antiques shops or galleries), old cemeteries, churches, and public buildings.

★ The 1852 **Musical Wonder House,** formerly a sea captain's home, is now a museum with a collection of thousands of antique music boxes from around the world. Come and see player pianos and other musical rarities; for an extra fee you can arrange for a tour of the main floor or the entire house. ✉ *18 High St.* ☎ *207/882–7163 or 800/336–3725* ⊕ *www. musicalwonderhouse.com* ✉ *$2* ⊙ *Memorial Day–mid-Oct., daily 10–5.*

The **Nickels-Sortwell House** is an outstanding example of Federal architecture. Built by Captain William Nickels, a shipowner and trader, the house recalls the prosperity of those times. Tours begin every hour on the hour between 11 and 4. ✉ *121 Main St., Rte. 1* ☎ *207/882–6218* ✉ *$5* ⊙ *June–mid-Oct., Fri.–Sun. 11–5.*

The 1807 **Castle Tucker** is known for its extravagant architecture, Victorian appointments, and freestanding elliptical staircase. Standing on top of a hill overlooking the Sheepscot River, the structure was built by Judge Silas Lee when Wiscasset was the busiest port east of Boston. ✉ *2 Lee St.* ☎ *207/822–7169* ✉ *$5* ⊙ *June–mid-Oct., Fri.–Sun. 11–5; tours on the hr 11–4.*

Where to Stay & Eat

$–$$$ ✕ **Le Garage.** The best tables at this former service station are on the glassed-in porch overlooking the Sheepscot River and Wiscasset Harbor. Entrées include homemade chicken pie, sea scallops au gratin, and stuffed fillet of sole. The broiled lamb-and-vegetable kebabs are especially tasty. Portions are large, but you can always ask for a half order. Sample something from the wine list while you gaze across the river. ⊠ *Water St.* ☎ *207/882–5409* ⊟ *D, MC, V* ⊘ *Closed Jan.*

¢ ✕ **Red's Eats.** You've probably driven right past this little red shack on the Wiscasset side of the bridge if you've visited this area. Red's is famous for its hot dogs and onion rings, as well as its lobster and crab rolls. Watch out for the seagulls; they like lobster rolls, too. ⊠ *41 Water St.* ☎ *207/882–6128* ⊟ *No credit cards* ⊘ *Closed mid-Oct.–mid-Apr.*

$ ⊡ **Marston House.** Two rooms in a carriage house provide a quiet retreat from the hustle and bustle of Main Street, yet they are just a stone's throw from the galleries and shops. Both have private entrances and fireplaces and are simply furnished with Shaker- and Colonial-style pieces. The rooms can be joined to make a suite perfect for families. The inn, which has been serving guests since 1987, has retained its 19th-century character. ⊠ *101 Main St.* ⊅ *Box 517, 04578* ☎ *207/882–6010 or 800/852–4137* ⊕ *www.marstonhouse.com* ⊟ *207/882–6965* ↩ *2 rooms* ⌕ *Fans; no a/c, no room TVs* ⊟ *AE, MC, V* ⊘ *Closed Nov.–Apr.* ⊠⊡ *CP.*

Shopping

The Wiscasset area rivals Searsport as a destination for antiquing. Shops line Wiscasset's main and side streets and extend over the bridge into Edgecomb. The **Butterstamp Workshop** (⊠ 55 Middle St. ☎ 207/882–7825) carries handcrafted folk-art pieces made from antique molds. Not to be missed is **Edgecomb Potters** (⊠ 727 Boothbay Rd., Edgecomb ☎ 207/882–9493 ⊕ www.edgecombpotters.com), which specializes in pricey exquisitely glazed porcelain. Open year-round, the shop has one of the best selections in the area. With beautifully glazed kitchen tiles, **Sheepscot River Pottery** (⊠ 34 Rte. 1, Edgecomb ☎ 207/882–9410 ⊕ www.sheepscot.com) also displays other fine pottery.

Boothbay

⑲ *10 mi southeast of Wiscasset, 60 mi northeast of Portland, 50 mi southwest of Camden.*

When Portlanders want a break from city life, many go north to the Boothbay region, which comprises Boothbay proper, East Boothbay, and Boothbay Harbor. This part of the shoreline is a craggy stretch of inlets where pleasure craft anchor alongside trawlers and lobster boats. Commercial Street, Wharf Street, the By-Way, and Townsend Avenue are filled with shops, galleries, and ice cream parlors. You can browse for hours in the trinket and T-shirt shops, crafts galleries, clothing stores, and boutiques that line the streets around the harbor. Excursion boats leave from the piers off Commercial Street. From the harbor, you can catch a boat to Monhegan Island.

♻ At the **Boothbay Railway Village,** about 1 mi north of Boothbay, you can ride 1½ mi on a coal-fired, narrow-gauge steam train that takes you through a model of a century-old New England village. Here you'll find more than 50 antique automobiles. ⊠ *Rte. 27* ☎ *207/633–4727* ⊕ *www.railwayvillage.org* ⊠ *$8* ⊘ *Memorial Day–Columbus Day, daily 9:30–5.*

You Gotta Lotta Moxie, Kid!

IT'S DIFFICULT TO GET VERY FAR IN MAINE without running into Moxie—the nation's oldest soft drink. You'll recognize it by its bright orange label. It comes in bottles and cans and is sold in just about every supermarket and convenience store in Maine.

Moxie was invented by Dr. Augustin Thompson of Union, Maine, who introduced the stuff in 1884. Moxie's big claim to fame is that it's the only brand name in the dictionary that is associated with a human quality: "energy, pep, courage, determination." If you drink it, you'll know why.

Dr. Thompson touted his gentian-root-based drink as a medicine guaranteed to cure just about any illness, including "softening of the brain." He eventually had to drop those claims when the Pure Food & Drug Act was enacted. Despite this and many other setbacks, Moxie has continued to prosper and be consumed by Mainers and visitors all over the state.

And how does it taste? It tastes *awful*.

—Stephen Allen

The **Department of Marine Resources Aquarium** has a shark you can pet, tide pools where you can see marine creatures up close, and tanks with rare blue lobsters. Bring a picnic lunch and enjoy the views of Boothbay Harbor. ⊠ *194 McKown Point Rd., Boothbay Harbor* ☎ *207/633–9559* ⊕ *www.maine.gov/dmr* 🗃 *$5* ⊙ *Memorial Day–late Sept., daily 10–5.*

Where to Stay & Eat

$$–$$$$ ✕ **Lobstermen's Co-op.** Crustacean lovers will find something to satisfy their craving at this dockside working lobster pound. Needless to say, you won't find fresher lobster anywhere. Eat in the dining room or outside where you can watch the lobstermen at work. For landlubbers, there are also hamburgers and sandwiches on the menu. ⊠ *99 Atlantic Ave., Boothbay Harbor* ☎ *207/633–4900* ▤ *D, MC, V* ⊙ *Closed mid-Oct.–mid-May.*

$–$$ ✕ **Lobster Dock.** Dine inside or outside at this waterfront restaurant, built on the site of the Reed Shipyard, which operated here from the late 1800s to the early 1900s. Specialties of the house include the area's only hot lobster roll. Start off with the seafood chowder, then move on to the yellowfin tuna, rack of lamb, or slow-roasted prime rib. No meal is complete without a slice of the homemade pie. ⊠ *49 Atlantic Ave., Boothbay Harbor* ☎ *207/633–7120* ⊕ *www.thelobsterdock.com* ▤ *MC, V* ⊙ *Closed Oct.–May.*

$$–$$$$ 🏨 **Spruce Point Inn.** Escape the hubbub of Boothbay Harbor at this sprawling resort spread over 15 beautifully landscaped acres. There are plenty of activities here, from a game of tennis to a dip in one of the pools. Guest rooms in the main inn are comfortable, and most have fireplaces, whirlpool baths, and a view of the ocean. A full-service spa offers massages and other treatments. The formal dining room serves dishes such as fillet of sole stuffed with crabmeat, shallots, and Asiago and chèvre cheese. ⊠ *88 Grandview Ave.* ☏ *Box 237, Boothbay Harbor 04538* ☎ *207/633–4152 or 800/553–0289* ⊟ *207/633–7138* ⊕ *www.sprucepointinn.com* ⌲ *48 rooms, 32 suites, 5 cottages* ♿ *2 restaurants, microwaves, cable TV, 2 tennis courts, 2 pools (1 saltwater), massage, spa, dock, lounge, meeting rooms; no a/c in some rooms* ⊟ *AE, D, DC, MC, V* ⊘ *Closed late Oct.–mid-May.*

$$–$$$ ⊞ **Welch House Inn.** This 1889 shipbuilder's house sits high on a hill near

Fodor'sChoice Boothbay Harbor. Antiques, artworks, and bric-a-brac from the owner's

★ travels around the world adorn the rooms. From the shared third-floor deck, you can take in the 180-degree views of the water. Breakfast on the lower deck usually includes one of the chef's specialties, which might mean caramel-apple and pecan-crusted French toast. ⊠ *56 McKown St., Boothbay Harbor 04538* ☎ *207/633–3431 or 800/279–7313* ⊕ *www.welchhouseinn.com* ⌲ *14 rooms* ♿ *Cable TV, in-room VCRs, some pets allowed* ⊟ *MC, V* ⫶○⫶ *BP.*

$–$$$ ⊞ **Admiral's Quarters Inn Bed & Breakfast.** Open all year, this renovated 1830 sea captain's house is ideally situated for exploring Boothbay Harbor. Many shops, galleries, and restaurants are within easy walking distance. Fresh baked goods greet you upon your return. All rooms have fireplaces, and some have private decks overlooking the water. On rainy days you can relax by the cozy woodstove in the sunroom. ⊠ *71 Commercial St., Boothbay Harbor 04538* ☎ *207/633–2474 or 800/644–1878* ⊟ *207/633–5904* ⊕ *www.admiralsquartersinn.com* ⌲ *2 rooms, 5 suites* ♿ *Cable TV; no kids under 12* ⊟ *AE, D, MC, V* ⫶○⫶ *BP.*

$–$$$ ⊞ **Hodgdon Island Inn.** Every room in this restored 1810 sea captain's house has a view of a quiet cove, and two open out onto a shared sundeck. Sunsets from here, or from the porch where you're served afternoon tea or lemonade, are spectacular. The location puts you within walking distance of a lobster pound and a botanical garden. ⊠ *374 Barters Island Rd., 04537* ☎ *207/633–7474* ⊕ *www.hodgdonislandinn.com* ⌲ *9 rooms* ♿ *Fans, pool; no room phones* ⊟ *MC, V* ⫶○⫶ *BP.*

Sports & the Outdoors

BOAT TRIPS On Pier 8, **Balmy Day Cruises** (⊠ 62 Commercial St., Boothbay Harbor ☎ 207/633–2284 or 800/298–2284 ⊕ www.balmydaycruises.com) offers day trips to Monhegan Island and tours of the harbor. A guided tour of the Burnt Island Lighthouse is available. Setting sail from Pier 6, **Boothbay Whale Watch** (⊠ Pier Six, Boothbay Harbor ☎ 207/633–3500 or 800/942–5363 ⊕ www.boothbaywhalewatch.com) conducts whale-watching tours and sunset cruises. On Pier 1 you'll find **Cap'n Fish's Boat Trips** (⊠ Pier 1, Boothbay Harbor ☎ 207/633–3244 or 800/636–3244 ⊕ www.capnfishmotel.com), which runs regional sightseeing cruises, including puffin-watching adventures. You can also join lobster-hauling and whale-watching rides.

KAYAKING **Tidal Transit Ocean Kayak Co.** (⊠ 18 Granary Way, Boothbay Harbor ☎ 207/633–7140 ⊕ www.kayakboothbay.com) has equipment to rent and offers guided tours of the coastline.

Shopping

Wind chimes and streamers greet you at the door of **Enchantments** (⌧ 10 Boothbay House Hill Rd., Boothbay Harbor ☎ 207/633–4992), a spiritual retreat filled with magical gifts. You'll find extraordinary cards, carvings, mobiles, and jewelry. **Mung Bean** (⌧ 37 Townsend Ave., Boothbay Harbor ☎ 207/633–5512) is open until 9:30 PM in summer so it's perfect for after-dinner browsing. You'll find pottery and wood carvings, jewelry and collectibles, and fruit preserves. No trip to Boothbay Harbor is complete without a stop at **Orne's Candy Shop** (⌧ 11 Commercial St., Boothbay Harbor ☎207/633–2695 ⊕www.ornescandystore.com), a must for anyone with a sweet tooth.

Pemaquid Peninsula

❷⓪ *8 mi southeast of Wiscasset.*

A detour off U.S. 1 via Routes 130 and 32 leads to the Pemaquid Peninsula and a satisfying microcosm of coastal Maine. Art galleries, country stores, antiques and crafts shops, and lobster shacks dot the country roads that meander to the tip of the point, where you'll find a much-photographed lighthouse perched on an unforgiving rock ledge. Exploring here reaps many rewards, including views of salt ponds, the ocean, and boat-clogged harbors. The twin towns of Damariscotta and Newcastle anchor the region, but small fishing villages such as Pemaquid, New Harbor, and Round Pond give the peninsula its purely Maine flavor.

At the **Colonial Pemaquid Restoration,** set on a small peninsula jutting into the Pemaquid River, English mariners established a fishing and trading settlement in the early 17th century. The excavations at Fort William Henry, begun in the mid-1960s, have turned up thousands of artifacts from the settlement, including the remains of an old customs house, a tavern, a jail, a forge, and several homes. Some older items are from earlier Native American settlements. The state operates a museum that displays many of these artifacts. ⌧ *Rte. 130, New Harbor* ☎ *207/677–2423* ▱ *$2* ☉ *Memorial Day–Labor Day, daily 10–7.*

★ Route 130 terminates at the **Pemaquid Point Light,** which looks as though it sprouted from the ragged, tilted chunk of granite that it commands. The former lighthouse keeper's cottage is now the Fishermen's Museum, which displays historic photographs, scale models, and artifacts that explore commercial fishing in Maine. Also here is the Pemaquid Art Gallery, which mounts exhibitions in July and August. Restrooms, picnic tables, and barbecue grills are all available. ⌧ *Museum: Rte. 130 (Bristol Rd.)* ☎ *207/677–2494* ▱ *$2* ☉ *Memorial Day–Columbus Day, daily 9–5.*

Where to Stay & Eat

★ **$$–$$$** ✕ **Round Pond Lobstermen's Co-op.** Lobster doesn't get any fresher or any cheaper than what's served at this no-frills dockside takeout. The best deal in town is the nightly dinner special: a 1-pound lobster, steamers, corn-on-the-cob, and a bag of chips. Regulars often bring their own beer, wine, bread, and salads. ⌧ *Town Landing Rd., Round Pond* ☎ *207/529–5725* ▭ *MC, V.*

$$–$$$$ ✕▦ **Bradley Inn.** When you think of a country inn, you probably picture something like this. Within walking distance of Pemaquid Point Light, this former rooming house was built as a private residence for sea captain John Bradley. The lovingly restored building now has guest rooms that are comfortable and uncluttered; some have fireplaces, and those on the third floor have ocean views. The Bradley Inn has one of the region's best dining rooms ($$$–$$$$). The menu changes nightly, but always emphasizes fresh local foods. You can eat in the dining room or outside on the deck. ⊠ *3063 Bristol Rd., New Harbor 04554* ☏ *207/677–2105 or 800/942–5560* 🖷 *207/677–3367* ⊕ *www.bradleyinn.com* ⇗ *12 rooms, 4 suites* ⚠ *Restaurant, fans, bicycles, boccie, croquet, lounge, piano bar, babysitting, meeting rooms; no a/c, no TV in some rooms* ⊟ *AE, MC, V* ⏀ *BP.*

$$–$$$$ ✕▦ **Newcastle Inn.** A riverside location and an excellent dining room make this country inn a classic. All the guest rooms are filled with antiques and decorated with sumptuous fabrics; some rooms have fireplaces and whirlpool baths. On pleasant mornings, breakfast is served on the back deck overlooking the river. The dining room ($$$$), which is open to the public by reservation, serves five-course meals. ⊠ *60 River Rd., Newcastle 04553* ☏ *207/563–5685 or 800/832–8669* 🖷 *207/563–6877* ⊕ *www.newcastleinn.com* ⇗ *15 rooms, 3 suites* ⚠ *Restaurant, some hot tubs, pub; no room phones, no TV in some rooms, no kids under 12* ⊟ *AE, D, MC, V* ⏀ *BP.*

$$–$$$ ▦ **Inn at Round Pond.** Once a stagecoach stop, this 1830s mansard-roof Colonial sits on the eastern shore of Pemaquid Peninsula. At this restful retreat you won't be bothered by ringing telephones or blaring televisions. The trio of tastefully appointed suites—the Foster Suite, the Prentice Suite, and the Monhegan Suite—have separate sitting rooms decorated with original works by local artists. All have harbor views. A full country breakfast is served each morning. ⊠ *1442 Rte. 32, Round Pond 04564* ☏ *207/529–2004* ⊕ *www.theinnatroundpond. com* ⇗ *3 suites* ⚠ *No room phones, no room TVs, no kids under 8* ⊟ *AE, D, MC, V* ⏀ *BP.*

$–$$ ▦ **Hotel Pemaquid.** Step back in time at this beautifully restored 1888 inn located less than 500 feet from the lighthouse at Pemaquid Point. The main building is Victorian in style; cottages and bungalow units have a more contemporary feel. The carriage-house suite is ideal for honeymooners or others seeking a romantic retreat. Relax on the big wraparound porch or enjoy a fire in the stone fireplace. ⊠ *3098 Bristol Rd., New Harbor 04554* ☏ *207/677–2312* ⊕ *www.hotelpemaquid. com* ⇗ *28 rooms, 6 suites, 2 cottages, 1 apartment* ⚠ *No-smoking rooms; no a/c, no room phones* ⊟ *No credit cards* ⊘ *Closed mid-Oct.–mid-May.*

Sports & the Outdoors

You can take a cruise to Monhegan with **Hardy Boat Cruises** (⊠ Shaw's Wharf, New Harbor ☏ 207/677–2026 ⊕ www.hardyboat.com). On the sightseeing cruises you can spot seals and puffins. At **Salt Water Charters** (⊠ Round Pond Harbor ☏ 207/677–6229 ⊕ www.saltwatercharters.com), the fishing vessel *Paige Elizabeth* takes passengers on sightseeing cruises.

Shopping

Of the villages on and near the Pemaquid Peninsula, downtown Damariscotta has boutiques, a bookshop, clothing stores, and galleries. New Harbor and Round Pond have crafts and antiques shops as well as artisans' studios. Antiques shops dot the region's main thoroughfares.

If plants are your passion, **Bramble's** (⊠ 132 Main St., Damariscotta ☎ 207/563–2800) carries gardening tools, topiaries, and pots. The **Granite Hall Store** (⊠ 9 Backshore Rd., Round Pond ☎ 207/529–5864) has everything from penny candy to antiques. Order ice cream cones through a window on the side. The work of more than 50 Maine artisans is displayed in the 15 rooms of the **Pemaquid Craft Co-op** (⊠ 2545 Bristol Rd., New Harbor ☎ 207/677–2077). The barnlike **Stable Gallery** (⊠ 26 Water St., Damariscotta ☎ 207/563–1991) stocks paintings and prints by more than 100 artists.

Waldoboro

㉑ *10 mi northeast of Damariscotta.*

Veer off U.S. 1 onto Main Street or down Route 220 or Route 32, and you'll discover a seafaring town with a proud shipbuilding past, its Main Street lined with houses and businesses representing numerous architectural styles, including Cape Cod, Queen Anne, Stick, Greek-revival, and Italianate. Several buildings make up the **Waldoborough Historical Society Museum,** including the one-room Boggs Schoolhouse, built in 1857; the Town Pound, built in 1819; and a barn filled with artifacts such as hooked rugs, antique toys, tools, clothing, and housewares. ⊠ *Main St. and Rte. 220* ☎ *No phone* 🖾 *Free* ☉ *July–Labor Day, daily 1–4:30.*

🖰 **Fawcett's Toy Museum** delights adults and children with collectible toys, from Betty Boop and Popeye to Charlie Brown and Mickey Mouse. There's also original comic art. ⊠ *3506 U.S. 1* ☎ *207/832–7398* 🖾 *$3* ☉ *Memorial Day–Columbus Day, Thurs.–Mon. 10–4; Columbus Day–Christmas Eve, weekends noon–3:30.*

One of the oldest churches in Maine, the **Old German Church** was built in 1772. It originally sat on the eastern side of the Medomak River, then was moved across the ice to its present site in 1794. Inside you'll find box pews and a 9-foot-tall chalice pulpit. ⊠ *Rte. 32* ☎ *No phone* ☉ *July and Aug., daily 1–3.*

Where to Stay & Eat

¢–$ ✕ **Moody's Diner.** Settle into one of the well-worn wooden booths or snag a counter stool at this old-style diner known for its home cooking. Breakfast is served all day at this local landmark where coffee is still only 70¢. Don't miss the legendary walnut pie. ⊠ *1885 U.S. 1* ☎ *207/ 832–7785* 🖃 *D, MC, V.*

$ 🏠 **Roaring Lion Bed & Breakfast.** Tin ceilings, hand-carved woodwork, and other Victorian-era architectural details highlight this friendly B&B. Built in 1905, this house has two fireplaces and a large screened porch where guests tend to congregate. One of the country-style guest rooms has a fireplace. The location is convenient to local sights. ✉ *995 Main St., 04572* ☎ *207/832–4038* 🖶 *207/832–7892* ⊕ *www.roaringlion. com* ⇨ *4 rooms, 1 with bath* ♻ *No a/c, no room phones, no room TVs* 🖃 *No credit cards* ⦿| *BP.*

Shopping
The **S. Fernald's 5 & 10** (✉ 17 Friendship St. ☎ 207/832–4624) is the oldest continually operated five-and-ten in the country. It has an old-fashioned soda fountain that serves sandwiches, soups, and ice cream. There's even a penny-candy counter that's popular with the kids.

Portland to Waldoboro A to Z

To research prices, get advice from other travelers, and book travel arrangements, visit www.fodors.com.

BOAT & FERRY TRAVEL
Casco Bay Lines provides ferry service from Portland to the islands of Casco Bay.

🚹 Boat & Ferry Information **Casco Bay Lines** ☎ 207/774-7871 ⊕ www.cascobaylines. com.

CAR TRAVEL
Congress Street leads from Interstate 295 into the heart of Portland; the Gateway Garage on High Street, off Congress, is a convenient place to leave your car downtown. North of Portland, U.S. 1 takes you to Freeport's Main Street, which continues on to Brunswick and Bath. East of Wiscasset you can take Route 27 south to the Boothbays, where Route 96 is a good choice for further exploration. To visit the Pemaquid region, take Route 129 off U.S. 1 in Damariscotta; then pick up Route 130 and follow it down to Pemaquid Point. Return to Waldoboro and U.S. 1 on Route 32 from New Harbor.

In Portland, metered on-street parking is available at 25¢ per half hour, with a two-hour maximum. Parking lots and garages can be found near the Portland Public Market, downtown, in the Old Port, and on the waterfront; most charge $1 per hour or $8–$12 per day. If you're shopping or dining, remember to ask local vendors if they participate in the Park & Shop program, which provides an hour of free parking for each participating vendor visited.

EMERGENCIES
🚹 Hospitals **Maine Medical Center** ✉ 22 Bramhall St., Portland ☎ 207/662-0111. **Mid-Coast Hospital** ✉ 123 Medical Center Dr., Brunswick ☎ 207/729-0181. **Miles Memorial Hospital** ✉ 35 Miles St., Damariscotta ☎ 207/563-1234. **St. Andrews Hospital** ✉ 6 St. Andrews La., Boothbay Harbor ☎ 207/633-2121.

LODGING
Your Island Connection manages vacation home rentals near Brunswick.
🚹 Lodging **Your Island Connection** ☎ 207/833-7779 or 207/833-7705 ⊕ www. mainerentals.com.

TOURS

BUS TOURS   In Portland, the informative trolley tours of Mainely Tours cover the city's historical and architectural highlights from Memorial Day through October. Other tours combine a city tour with a bay cruise or a trip to four lighthouses.

🛈 Tour Operator **Mainely Tours** ⊠ 3 Moulton St. ☎ 207/774-0808 ⊕ www.mainelytours.com.

WALKING TOURS   Greater Portland Landmarks conducts 1½-hour walking tours of the city from July through September; tours cost $8. Sagadahoc Preservation leads walking tours of historic homes and buildings in Bath on Tuesday and Thursday afternoons from mid-June to early September. Many old ship captains' and shipbuilders' homes are on this tour. Tours cost $10.

🛈 Tour Operators **Greater Portland Landmarks** ⊠ 165 State St., Portland ☎ 207/774-5561 ⊕ www.portlandlandmarks.org. **Sagadahoc Preservation** ⊠ 165 State St., Bath ☎ 207/443-2174.

VISITOR INFORMATION

🛈 **Boothbay Harbor Region Chamber of Commerce** ⌻ Box 356, 04538 ☎ 207/633-2353 ⊕ www.boothbayharbor.com.

Damariscotta Region Chamber of Commerce ⌻ Box 13, Damariscotta 04543 ☎ 207/563-8340 ⊕ www.damariscottaregion.com.

Freeport Merchants Association ⊠ 23 Depot St., Freeport 04032 ☎ 207/865-1212 or 800/865-1994 ⊕ www.freeportusa.com.

Convention and Visitors Bureau of Greater Portland ⊠ 245 Commercial St., Portland 04101 ☎ 207/772-5800 ⊕ www.visitportland.com.

Portland Regional Chamber ⊠ 60 Pearl St., Portland 04101 ☎ 207/772-2811 ⊕ www.portlandregion.com.

Southern Midcoast Maine Chamber ⊠ 59 Pleasant St., Brunswick 04011 ☎ 207/725-8797 ⊕ www.midcoastmaine.com.

Maine Tourism Association Visitor Information Center ⊠ 1100 U.S. 1 (I-295, Exit 17), Yarmouth 04096 ☎ 207/846-0833 ⊕ www.mainetourism.com.

PENOBSCOT BAY

Purists hold that the Maine coast begins at Penobscot Bay, Maine's largest bay, where the vistas over the water are wide and blue, the shore a jumble of broken granite boulders, cobblestones, and gravel punctuated by small sand beaches, and the water numbingly cold. Port Clyde, in the southwest, and Stonington, in the southeast, 35 mi apart across the bay waters but separated by a drive of almost 100 mi on scenic but slow two-lane highways, are its outer limits.

Thomaston, on the western edge of the region, has a fine collection of sea captains' homes. Rockland, the largest town on the bay, is a growing arts center, home of the Maine Lobster Festival and the port of departure for trips to Vinalhaven, North Haven, and Matinicus islands. The Camden Hills, looming green over Camden's fashionable waterfront, turn bluer and fainter as you head toward Castine, the small town across the bay. In between Camden and Castine are Belfast and the antiques and flea market of Searsport. Deer Isle is connected to the mainland by a slender, high-arching bridge, but Isle au Haut can be reached only by passenger ferry from the fishing town of Stonington on Deer Isle. More than half of the steep, wooded Isle au Haut is wilderness, the most remote section of Acadia National Park.

Thomaston

㉒ *10 mi northeast of Waldoboro, 72 mi northeast of Portland.*

This is a delightful town, full of beautiful sea captains' homes and dotted with antiques and specialty shops. A National Historic District encompasses parts of High, Main, and Knox streets.

Built in 1930, **Montpelier** is a replica of the late-18th-century mansion of Major General Henry Knox, a commander in the Revolutionary War and secretary of war in George Washington's cabinet. Antiques, including many Knox family possessions, fill the interior. Architectural appointments include an oval room and a double staircase. Call ahead to reserve a place on the half-hourly tours. ⊠ *U.S. 1 and Rte. 131* ☎ *207/354–8062* ⊕ *www.generalknoxmuseum.org* ✎ *$6* ☉ *Memorial Day–Columbus Day, Tues.–Sat. 10–3.*

Where to Stay & Eat

$$–$$$ ✕ **Thomaston Café & Bakery.** A changing selection of works by local artists adorns the walls of this small café. Entrées, prepared with locally grown ingredients, include seared fresh tuna on soba noodles, lobster ravioli with lobster sauce, and filet mignon with béarnaise sauce. ⊠ *154 Main St.* ☎ *207/354–8589* ▭ *MC, V* ☉ *No dinner Sun.–Thurs.*

$ ▣ **Chestnut Tree Bed & Breakfast.** Maine's fleet of windjammers are anchored close to this restored 1850s Colonial-style house. Each of the comfortably furnished guest rooms has a private bath. Coffee and tea are served each afternoon in the lounge, where you can play board games or a hand of cards. ⊠ *12 Wadsworth St., 04861* ☎ *207/354–0089 or 866/745–3723* ⊕ *www.chestnuttreebandb.com* ⇲ *4 rooms* ♨ *Cable TV* ▭ *MC, V* ☉ *Closed mid.-Oct.–mid-May* ⵙ *BP.*

Shopping

The **Maine State Prison Showroom Outlet** (⊠ Main St. ☎ 207/354–9237) carries furniture and other wooden items fashioned by prisoners. Browse the comprehensive selection of books and original art at the **Personal Book Shop** (⊠ 144 Main St. ☎ 207/354–8058).

Tenants Harbor

㉓ *13 mi south of Thomaston.*

Tenants Harbor is a quintessential coastal town—its harbor is dominated by lobster boats, its shores are rocky and slippery, and its downtown streets are lined with clapboard houses, a church, and a general store. It's a favorite with artists, and galleries and studios welcome browsers. The fictional Dunnet Landing of Sarah Orne Jewett's classic *The Country of the Pointed Firs* (1896) is based on towns in this region.

The 1895 keeper's house at the **Marshall Point Lighthouse** has been turned into a museum containing memorabilia from the town of St. George (a few miles north of Tenants Harbor). The lighthouse is about 1 mi from the Port Clyde boat landing. ⊠ *Marshall Point Rd., Port Clyde* ☎ *207/ 372–6450* ☞ *Free* ⊙ *June–Sept., weekdays 1–5, Sat. 10–5; May and Oct., weekends 1–5.*

Where to Stay & Eat

$–$$$$ ✕⊡ **East Wind Inn & Meeting House.** Built as a sail loft in 1830, this comfortably old-fashioned inn has a wraparound porch with a dreamy view of the island-studded harbor. Some of the guest rooms in the Meeting House, a converted sea captain's house, are warmed by fireplaces. A grand piano graces the great room. The inn's restaurant ($$–$$$) emphasizes local seafood and a take-out restaurant on the wharf serves lighter fare. ⊠ *21 Mechanic St., 04860* ☎ *207/372–6366 or 800/241–8439* 🖶 *207/ 372–6320* ⊕ *www.eastwindinn.com* ☞ *18 rooms, 12 with bath; 3 suites; 4 apartments* ⚭ *2 restaurants, some microwaves, cable TV, meeting rooms, some pets allowed; no a/c* ▭ *AE, D, MC, V* ⊙ *Closed Dec.–Apr.* ◯ *BP.*

Shopping

The **Port Clyde Arts & Crafts Society Gallery** (⊠ Rte. 131, Tenants Harbor ☎ 207/372–0673) showcases members' works in a colorful garden.

Monhegan Island

★ ㉔ *10 mi south of Port Clyde.*

Remote Monhegan Island, with its high cliffs fronting the sea, was known to Basque, Portuguese, and Breton fishermen well before Columbus discovered America. About a century ago, Monhegan was discovered again by some of America's finest painters, including Rockwell Kent, Robert Henri, A. J. Hammond, and Edward Hopper, who sailed out to paint its open meadows, savage cliffs, wild ocean views, and fishermen's shacks. Tourists followed, and today three excursion boats dock here. The village bustles with activity in summer, when many artists open their studios. You can escape the crowds on the island's 17 mi of hiking trails, which lead to the lighthouse and to the cliffs.

The **Monhegan Museum,** housed in an 1824 lighthouse and the adjacent assistant keeper's house, has wonderful views of nearby Manana Island. Inside, informative displays depict island life and local flora and fauna. ⊠ *White Head Rd.* ☎ *207/596–7003* ⊕ *www.monheganmuseum.org* ☞ *Donations accepted* ⊙ *July–mid-Sept., daily 11:30–3:30.*

Where to Stay

$$–$$$$ ⊡ **Island Inn.** This three-story inn, which dates from 1807, has a commanding presence on Monhegan Island's harbor. The waterfront rooms are the nicest, with views of the sunset over stark Manana Island. Avoid the meadow-view rooms, which have the distinct disadvantage of being over kitchen vents. The property includes a small café and a dining room that serves breakfast, lunch, and dinner. ⊠ *1 Ocean Ave., 04852* ☎ *207/ 596–0371* 🖶 *207/594–5517* ⊕ *www.islandinnmonhegan.com* ☞ *30 rooms, 15 with bath; 4 suites* ⚭ *Restaurant, café; no a/c, no room*

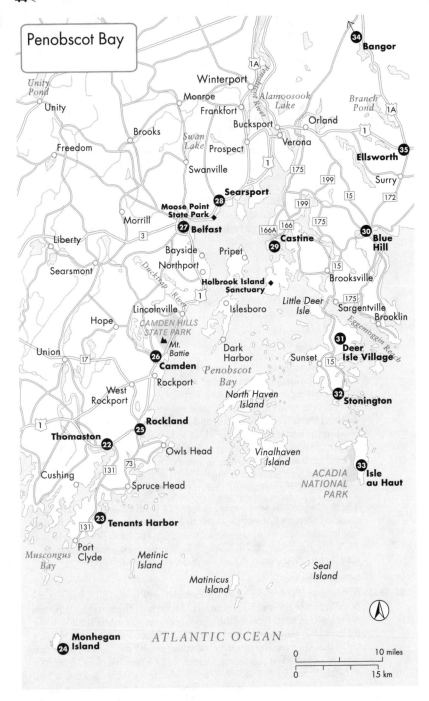

Penobscot Bay

phones, no room TVs ⊟ *MC, V* ⊘ *Closed Columbus Day–Memorial Day* ⦿ *BP.*

Sports & the Outdoors

The **Balmy Days** (☎ 207/633–2284 or 800/298–2284) sails from Boothbay Harbor to Monhegan on daily trips in summer. **Hardy Boat Cruises** (☎ 207/677–2026 or 800/278–3346) leave daily from Shaw's Wharf in New Harbor. The **Monhegan Boat Line** (☎ 207/372–8848 ⊕ www. monheganboat.com) operates the *Laura B.* and the *Elizabeth Ann,* carrying mail, freight, and passengers daily year-round between Port Clyde and Monhegan Island. In summer, nature cruises are offered.

Rockland

㉕   *4 mi northeast of Thomaston, 14 mi northeast of Tenants Harbor.*

Though it was once a place to pass through on the way to tonier ports like Camden, Rockland now attracts attention on its own, thanks to the renowned Farnsworth Art Museum, the increasingly popular summer Lobster Festival, and the North Atlantic Blues Festival. Rockland's Main Street Historic District, with its Italianate, Mansard, Greek-revival, and Colonial-revival buildings, is on the National Register of Historic Places. Specialty shops and galleries line the main street, and restaurants and inns continue to open.

Rockland Harbor is the berth of more windjammer ships than any other port in the United States. The best place in Rockland to view these beautiful vessels is the mile-long granite breakwater that bisects the outer portion of Rockland Harbor. To get there, go north on U.S. 1, turn right on Waldo Avenue, and turn right again on Samoset Road. The breakwater is at the end of this short road.

Fodor'sChoice   The **Farnsworth Art Museum and Wyeth Center** is one of the most impor-
★   tant small museums in the country. Its permanent collection, entitled Maine in America, consists of some 9,000 paintings, drawings, sculpture, photographs, and decorative objects—not all on view at all times—by artists from Maine or of Maine-related subjects. The museum is especially strong in American landscape painting from the 19th century on, and also includes an extensive collection of works by Louise Nevelson (a native of Rockland) and works by Edward Hopper (his paintings of old Rockland are a highlight). Works by living Maine artists are in the **Jamien Morehouse Wing.** The **Wyeth Center** is devoted to Maine-related works of the famous Wyeth family: N. C. Wyeth, an accomplished illustrator whose works were featured in many turn-of-the-20th-century books; his son Andrew, one of America's best-known painters; and Andrew's son James, also an accomplished painter, who lives nearby on an island. The **Farnsworth Homestead,** a handsome circa-1852 Greek-revival dwelling that is part of the museum, retains its original lavish Victorian furnishings. The museum also operates the **Olson House** (⊠ Hathorn Point Rd., Cushing), which is depicted in Andrew Wyeth's famous painting *Christina's World.* ⊠ *16 Museum St.* ☎ *207/596–6457* ⊕ *www. farnsworthmuseum.org* ⧑ *Museum, Olson House, and Farnsworth*

Homestead $10 ☉ Memorial Day–Columbus Day, daily 10–5; Colum-bus Day–Memorial Day, Tues.–Sun. 10–5.

★ ☾ The **Maine Lighthouse Museum** contains the largest collection of light-house memorabilia and Coast Guard lighthouse artifacts in the world, including an extensive collection of Fresnel lenses. You can hear the moaning of a foghorn and the clanging of a buoy bell, and see the whirling of a light behind a Fresnel lens. The museum also houses a large collection of model ships and lifesaving gear. Lighthouse souvenirs are available in the store. *⊠ 1 Park Dr. ☎ 207/594–3301 ⊕ www.mainelighthousemuseum.com ⊠ $5 ☉ Memorial Day–Columbus Day, Mon.–Sat. 9–5, Sun. 10–4; Columbus Day–Memorial Day, week-days 9–5, Sat. 10–4.*

At Owls Head Light State Park, the beautifully maintained **Owls Head Light** (⊠ Rte. 73, Owls Head ☎ 207/941–4014) has shown the way since 1825. Located on West Penobscot Bay, the local landmark indicates the entrance to Rockland Harbor. The grounds are open to the public, but not the lighthouse or keeper's house.

⌐ OFF THE
BEATEN
PATH

VINALHAVEN – You can take the ferry from Rockland to this island for a pleasant day of bicycling or walking. A number of parks are within walking distance of the ferry dock, including Armbrust Hill, the site of an abandoned quarry, and Lane's Island Preserve, a 40-acre site of moors, tidal pools, and beaches. You can learn about the island's quar-rying history at the Historical Society Museum on High Street and even take a dip in the cool, clear waters of two quarries. For ferry informa-tion, call **Maine State Ferry Service** (☎ 207/596–2202).

Where to Stay & Eat

★ $$$–$$$$ ✕ **Amalfi.** A well-chosen and affordable wine list and excellent service have made this storefront bistro a hit with locals and visitors alike. Chef-owner David Cooke serves delicious Mediterranean cuisine, influenced by the culinary traditions of France, Spain, Italy, Greece, and Morocco. The menu changes seasonally but may include the house paella with chorizo, or duck risotto. Ask about the oysters and the Chocolate Soup. *⊠ 421 Main St. ☎ 207/596–0012 ⊕ www.amalfi-tonight.com ⊟ AE, MC, V ☉ Closed Mon. No lunch.*

$$$–$$$$
Fodor$Choice
★

✕ **Primo.** This restaurant has won so many awards it would be impos-sible to list them all here. The cuisine combines fresh Maine ingredients with Mediterranean influences. The menu, which changes weekly, may include wood-roasted black sea bass, local crab-stuffed turbot, or diver-harvested-scallop and basil ravioli. The eatery grows much of its own food in an extensive organic garden. *⊠ 2 S. Main St. (Rte. 73) ☎ 207/596–0770 ⊟ AE, D, DC, MC, V ☉ Closed Jan.–Apr.*

$$ ✕ **Café Miranda.** At this cozy little bistro with a brick oven and open kitchen, the huge menu changes daily to include fresh seasonal ingredi-ents. Chef-owner Kerry Alterio has come up with creative ideas to re-flect the cuisines of Italy, Thailand, Mexico, Armenia, and other countries. You could make a full meal just from the 20 or so imaginative appetiz-ers. The many entrées may include crispy panfried soft-shell crabs with red bean ragout and yellow jasmine rice. *⊠ 15 Oak St. ☎ 207/594–2034 ⊕ www.cafemiranda.com ⊟ MC, V ☉ No lunch.*

$$$$ ✗▥ **Samoset Resort.** This 230-acre oceanside resort on the Rockland-
Fodor'sChoice Rockport town line offers luxurious rooms, all with a private balcony
★ or patio. The 18-hole championship golf course is ranked among the
best in New England. The formal restaurant, Marcel's ($$–$$$), fea-
tures French and American cuisine, as well as specials from the sea. The
menu includes chicken and scallops Chambord, rack of lamb for two,
chateaubriand for two, Steak Diane, and blueberry duck breast. For a
less-formal affair, try the Breakwater Cafe, which offers basic New
England fare. ⊠ *220 Warrenton St., Rockport 04856* ☎ *207/594–
2511 or 800/341–1650* 🖷 *207/594–0722* ⊕ *www.samoset.com* ⇌ *156
rooms, 22 suites △ 3 restaurants, some minibars, cable TV with movies
and video games, in-room data ports, Wi-Fi, 18-hole golf course, putting green, 4 tennis courts, pro shop, 2 pools (1 indoor), health club,
hot tub, massage, sauna, dock, racquetball, lounge, babysitting, children's
programs (ages 3–12), playground, dry cleaning, laundry service,
concierge, business services, meeting rooms, airport shuttle; no smoking* ▭ *AE, D, MC, V.*

$$–$$$$ ▥ **Berry Manor Inn.** Built in 1898, this inn is located in a historic resi-
dential neighborhood. Originally, it was the residence of Charles H. Berry,
a prominent Rockland merchant. The large guest rooms all have fire-
places and are elegantly furnished with antiques and reproduction
pieces. A guest pantry is stocked with sweets. The inn is within walk-
ing distance of downtown and the harbor. ⊠ *81 Talbot Ave., 04841*
☎ *207/596–7696 or 800/774–5692* 🖷 *207/596–9958* ⊕ *www.
berrymanorinn.com* ⇌ *12 rooms △ Some in-room hot tubs, in-room
data ports, Wi-Fi, library, Internet room, meeting room; no smoking*
▭ *AE, MC, V* ⧖❘ *BP.*

$$–$$$ ▥ **Limerock Inn.** This inn is literally in the center of town (Limerock is
the street that bisects Rockland into two halves), so you can easily walk
to the Farnsworth or any of the other downtown attractions. The house
is built in the Queen Anne–Victorian style, and among the meticulously
decorated rooms is one called Island Cottage, which features a whirlpool
tub and doors that open onto a private deck overlooking a garden. The
Grand Manan room has a fireplace, a whirlpool tub, and a four-poster
king-size bed. ⊠ *96 Limerock St., 04841* ☎ *207/594–2257 or 800/546–
3762* ⊕ *www.limerockinn.com* ⇌ *8 rooms △ In-room data ports; no
room phones, no room TVs, no smoking* ▭ *AE, D, MC, V* ⧖❘ *BP.*

Sports & the Outdoors

BOAT TRIPS A windjammer excursion can be the highlight of your trip. Contact the
Maine Windjammer Association (☎ 800/807–9463 ⊕ www.sailmainecoast.
com), which represents operators based in Rockland, Rockport, and Cam-
den, for general information about windjammers or for information about
specific ships and cruises offered by the MWA fleet. Prices are about $395
to $875 for a three- to six-day cruise, all meals included.

Shopping

The **Caldbeck Gallery** (⊠ 12 Elm St. ☎ 207/594–5935 ⊕ www.caldbeck.
com) displays contemporary Maine works by artists such as William Thon,
Lois Dodd, Alan Bray, and Dennis Pinette. **Élan Fine Arts** (⊠ 8 Elm St.
☎ 207/596–9933 ⊕ www.elanfinearts.com) displays works by con-

temporary American artists. **The Gallery** (✉ 357 Main St. ☎ 207/596–0084) specializes in marine paintings. **Harbor Square Gallery** (✉ 374 Main St. ☎ 207/594–8700) has roomfuls of Maine-related arts and crafts.

Camden

❷❻ *8 mi north of Rockland, 19 mi south of Belfast.*

"Where the mountains meet the sea," Camden's longtime publicity slogan, is an apt description, as you will discover when you look up from the harbor. The town is famous not only for geography but for its large fleet of windjammers—relics and replicas from the age of sailing. At just about any hour during the warm months you're likely to see at least one windjammer tied up in the harbor. The excursions, whether for an afternoon or a week, are best from June through September. Eggemoggin Reach is a famous cruising ground for yachts, as are the coves and inlets around Deer Isle and the Penobscot Bay waters between Camden and Castine. Busy downtown Camden has some of the best shopping in the region. The district's compact size makes it perfect for exploring on foot: shops, restaurants, and galleries line Main Street (U.S. 1) and Bayview, as well as side streets and alleys around the harbor.

★ Although their height may not be much more than 1,000 feet, the hills in **Camden Hills State Park** are lovely landmarks for miles along the low, rolling reaches of the Maine coast. The 5,500-acre park contains 25 mi of hiking trails, including the easy Nature Trail up Mt. Battie. Hike or drive to the top for a magnificent view over Camden and island-studded Penobscot Bay. ✉ *U.S. 1* ☎ *207/236–3109 for park camping information.*

☺ **Merryspring Nature Park** is a 66-acre retreat with herb, rose, rhododendron, hosta, and children's gardens as well as 4 mi of walking trails. ✉ *Conway Rd. off U.S. 1* ☎ *207/236–2239* ⊕ *www.merryspring.org* ▭ *Free* ☉ *Daily dawn–dusk.*

Where to Stay & Eat

$$$–$$$$ ✕ **Atlantica Restaurant.** In a historic clapboard building, this restaurant is right on the water's edge. The lower deck is cantilevered over the water offering a romantic setting with great views. The inside has a combination of white walls and contemporary paintings. Fresh seafood with French and Asian accents is the specialty here. Favorites include pan-roasted split lobster tails with lemon butter, lobster stuffed with scallops, and the seldom-found skate with brown butter. ✉ *Bay View Landing* ☎ *207/236–6011 or 888/507–8514* ⊕ *www.atlanticarestaurant.com* ▭ *AE, MC, V.*

$$–$$$$ ✕ **Lobster Pound Restaurant.** If you're looking for the real Maine, you've
FodorsChoice come to the right place. This summertime favorite is right on the beach,
★ off U.S. 1—you can't miss it. The place is so huge—seating for 260 inside and 40 outside—that you won't have to wait long for a table. The traditional meal is a Shore Dinner, which includes fish, clam, or lobster chowder; steamed mussels or clams; a fresh boiled lobster; and corn on the cob. ✉ *U.S. 1, Lincolnville Beach* ☎ *207/789–5550* ▭ *AE, D, MC, V* ☉ *Closed mid-Oct.–early May.*

$–$$ ✕ **Cappy's Chowder House.** Cappy's has been around for so long it's become something of an institution. As you would expect from the name, the "chowdah" is the thing to order here—it's been written up in the *New York Times* and in *Bon Appetit* magazine—but there are plenty of other seafood specials to choose from. ⊠ *1 Main St.* ☎ *207/236–2254* ⊕ *www.cappyschowder.com* ⇗ *Reservations not accepted* ⊟ *MC, V.*

$$–$$$ ✕⌂ **Whitehall Inn.** One of Camden's best-known inns, the Whitehall is an 1834 white clapboard sea captain's home. The Millay Room, off the lobby, preserves memorabilia of the poet Edna St. Vincent Millay, who grew up in the area and who read her poetry here. The sparsely furnished rooms have dark-wood bedsteads, white bedspreads, and claw-foot tubs. The dining room, which serves creative American cuisine as well as many seafood specialties, is open to the public for dinner. ⊠ *52 High St., 04843* ☎ *207/236–3391 or 800/789–6565* ⊟ *207/236–4427* ⊕ *www.whitehall-inn.com* ⇗ *50 rooms, 45 with bath* ⚴ *Restaurant, tennis court, shuffleboard; no a/c, no phones in some rooms, no room TVs* ⊟ *AE, MC, V* ⊘ *Closed mid-Oct.–mid-May* ❢⃝ *BP.*

$$–$$$ ✕⌂ **Youngtown Inn & Restaurant.** Inside this white Federal-style farmhouse you'll find a French-inspired country retreat. The country location, which is closer to Lincolnville than Lincolnville Beach, guarantees quiet, and the inn is a short walk from the Fernald Neck Preserve on Lake Megunticook. Simple, airy rooms open to decks with views of the rolling countryside. Four have fireplaces. The restaurant ($$–$$$) serves entrées such as rack of lamb and breast of pheasant with foie-gras mousse. ⊠ *Rte. 52 at Youngtown Rd., Lincolnville 04849* ☎ *207/ 763–4290 or 800/291–8438* ⊟ *207/763–4078* ⊕ *www.youngtowninn. com* ⇗ *5 rooms, 1 suite* ⚴ *Restaurant, cable TV; no smoking* ⊟ *AE, MC, V* ❢⃝ *BP.*

FodorśChoice
★

★ **$$–$$$$** ⌂ **Camden Maine Stay.** This 1802 clapboard inn is listed on the National Register of Historic Places. The grounds are classic and inviting, from the flowers lining the granite walk in summer to the snow-laden bushes in winter. The fresh and colorful rooms contain Eastlake and other period furniture; six have fireplaces. ⊠ *22 High St., 04843* ☎ *207/236– 9636* ⊟ *207/236–0621* ⊕ *www.camdenmainestay.com* ⇗ *4 rooms, 4 suites* ⚴ *Cable TV; no room phones, no smoking* ⊟ *AE, MC, V* ❢⃝ *BP.*

★ **$$–$$$$** ⌂ **Hartstone Inn.** This downtown 1835 Mansard-roofed Victorian home has been turned into an elegant and sophisticated retreat and a fine culinary destination. No detail has been overlooked, from soft robes, down comforters, and chocolate truffles in the guest rooms to china, crystal, and silver in the dining room. The specialty is a five-course prix fixe menu. The inn also hosts seasonal food festivals and off-season cooking classes. ⊠ *41 Elm St., 04843* ☎ *207/236–4259 or 800/788–4823* ⊟ *207/236– 9575* ⊕ *www.hartstoneinn.com* ⇗ *6 rooms, 6 suites* ⚴ *Restaurant, cable TV, in-room data ports; no smoking* ⊟ *MC, V.*

$$–$$$$ ⌂ **Victorian by the Sea.** With a quiet waterside location, the Victorian Inn feels as if it's a world away from all the hustle and bustle of town. Most rooms and the wraparound porch have magnificent views over island-studded Penobscot Bay. Romantic touches include canopied brass beds, braided rugs, white wicker furniture, and floral wallpapers. Six guest rooms have fireplaces. ⊠ *33 Sea View Dr., Lincolnville* ▱ *Box 1385, Camden 04843* ☎ *207/236–3785 or 800/382–9817* ⊟ *207/236–*

0017 ⊕ *www.victorianbythesea.com* ⤳ *5 rooms, 2 suites* ♻ *No a/c in some rooms, no room TVs, no smoking* ⊟ *AE, MC, V* ⦿ *BP.*

$$–$$$ ⌂ **Belmont Inn.** This attractive inn, with its wraparound porch, is in a quiet, off-the-main-street location, yet is only a five-minute walk from the harbor. The rooms are large, bright, and airy and are decorated in either a Federal, French, or country style; a few have gas-fired fireplaces. ⊠ *6 Belmont Ave., 04843* ☎ *207/236–8053 or 800/238–8053* ⊕ *www. thebelmontinn.com* ⤳ *6 rooms* ♻ *Wi-Fi; no room TVs, no smoking* ⊟ *AE, D, MC, V* ⦿ *BP.*

Nightlife & the Arts

Gilbert's Publick House (⊠ 12 Bay View Landing ☎ 207/236–4320), the favorite drinking place of the windjammer crowd and other boat people, offers live music, dancing, pub food, and some local brews. The **Whale's Tooth Pub** (⊠ U.S. 1, Lincolnville Beach ☎ 207/789–5200) hosts live folk music on weekends.

Sports & the Outdoors

BOATING The *Betselma* (⊠ Camden Public Landing ☎ 207/236–4446) offers one- and two-hour powerboat trips. For the voyage of a lifetime, consider a
★ ♻ **windjammer trip.** Windjammers leaving from Camden Harbor, most of the schooner type, include: *Lazy Jack* (☎ 207/230–0602); *Olad* (☎ 207/ 236–2323 ⊕ www.maineschooners.com); *Shantih II* (☎ 207/236–8605 or 800/599–8605 ⊕ www.woodenboatco.com); and *Windjammer Surprise* (☎ 207/236–4687 ⊕ www.camdenmainesailing.com). Prices range from $395 to $875 for a three- to six-day cruise, all meals included— and often that means a lobster bake on a deserted beach somewhere.

SKI AREAS There are 10 mi of cross-country skiing trails at **Camden Hills State Park**
★ (⊠ U.S. 1 ☎ 207/236–0849).

★ ♻ The Maine coast isn't known for skiing, but the **Camden Snow Bowl** (⊠ 20 Barnstown Rd. ☎ 207/236–3438, 207/236–4418 snow phone ⊕ www. camdensnowbowl.com) has a 950-foot-vertical mountain with 11 trails accessed by one double chair and two T-bars. The complex also includes a small lodge with a cafeteria, a ski school, and ski and toboggan rentals. Activities include skiing, night skiing, snowboarding, tubing, to-bogganing, and ice-skating—plus magnificent views over Penobscot Bay. The North American Tobogganing Championships, a tongue-in-cheek event open to anyone, is held annually in early February.

Shopping

Bayview Gallery (⊠ 33 Bay View St. ☎ 207/236–4534 ⊕ www. bayviewgallery.com) specializes in original art, almost all with a Maine theme. **Maine Gathering** (⊠ 21 Main St. ☎ 207/236–9004) is a premier showplace for Maine crafts and Native American arts and crafts. **ABCD Books** (⊠ 23 Bay View St. ☎ 207/236–3903 or 888/236–3903) has a discriminating selection of quality antiquarian and rare books. **Owl & Turtle Bookshop** (⊠ 32 Washington St. ☎ 207/236–4769 ⊕ www. owlandturtle.com), in business for 35 years, sells books, CDs, cassettes, and cards. The two-story shop has rooms devoted to marine and children's books. **Windsor Chairmakers** (⊠ U.S. 1, Lincolnville ☎ 207/789–5188 or 800/789–5188) sells custom-made handcrafted beds, chests, china cabinets, dining tables, highboys, Shaker furniture, and chairs. You can even go to the back of the shop and watch the furniture being made.

Belfast

㉗ *19 mi north of Camden, 46 mi east of Augusta.*

A number of Maine coastal towns, such as Wiscasset and Damariscotta, like to think of themselves as the prettiest little town in Maine, but Belfast has equal claim to this title. It has a full variety of charms: a beautiful waterfront; an old and interesting main street climbing up from the harbor; a delightful array of B&Bs, restaurants, and shops; and a friendly population. The downtown even has old-fashioned street lamps, which set the streets aglow at night. The only thing Belfast does not have is traffic jams.

Where to Stay & Eat

$–$$$ ✕ **Darby's Restaurant & Pub.** Tin ceilings and a friendly bar create a comfortable atmosphere for the creative casual fare served here. The eclectic menu lists hearty soups and sandwiches as well as dishes with an international flavor. A couple of examples are Darby's monsoon curry, pad Thai, and seafood à la Grecque. ⊠ *155 High St.* ☎ *207/338–2339* ⊟ *AE, D, MC, V.*

$–$$$ ✕ **Young's Lobster Pound.** The place looks more like a corrugated-steel
Fodor'sChoice fish cannery than a restaurant, but this is pure Maine. Young's sits right
★ on the edge of the water, across the river from the Belfast Harbor (cross Veterans Bridge to get here). When you first walk in, you'll see tanks and tanks and tanks of live lobsters of varying sizes. The traditional meal here is the Shore Dinner: fish or clam chowder; steamed clams or mussels; a 1½-pound boiled lobster; corn on the cob; and rolls and butter. ⊠ *2 Fairview St. (go north over U.S. 1 Veterans Bridge, turn right on Mitchell Ave.)* ☎ *207/338–1160* ⊟ *MC, V* ✷ *Closed Nov.–Easter.*

★ **$–$$$** ▦ **White House.** This 1840 landmark by Maine architect Calvin Ryder is considered one of the most sophisticated examples of Greek-revival architecture in New England. An eight-sided cupola tops the house; inside are ornate plaster ceiling medallions, Italian marble fireplaces, an elliptical flying staircase, and intricate moldings. Crystal chandeliers, oriental rugs, antiques, and reproduction pieces elegantly decorate the spacious rooms. ⊠ *1 Church St., 04915* ☎ *207/338–1901 or 888/290–1901* ▦ *207/338–5161* ⊕ *www.mainebb.com* ➥ *4 rooms, 2 suites* ⚟ *Some cable TV, some in-room VCRs; no smoking* ⊟ *D, MC, V* ¶◯ *BP.*

★ **$–$$** ▦ **Jeweled Turret Inn.** Turrets, columns, gables, and magnificent woodwork embellish this inn, built in 1898 as the home of a local attorney. The inn is named for the jewel-like stained-glass windows in the stairway turret. The gem theme continues in the den, where the ornate fireplace is said to include rocks from every state in the Union. Elegant Victorian pieces furnish the rooms: the Opal Room has a French armoire and a four-poster bed. ⊠ *40 Pearl St., 04915* ☎ *207/338–2304 or 800/ 696–2304* ⊕ *www.jeweledturret.com* ➥ *7 rooms* ⚟ *No a/c in some rooms, no room phones, no room TVs, no smoking* ⊟ *AE, MC, V* ¶◯ *BP.*

Sports & the Outdoors

BOATING **Belfast Bay Cruises** (✉ Thompson's Wharf ☎ 207/322–5530 ⊕ www. belfastbaycruises.com) offers bay cruises, sometimes with sightings of seals and porpoises. The cruises stop at historic Castine for lunch. A lobstering cruise, on which you'll learn how the crustaceans are caught, is also available.

KAYAKING **Water Walker Sea Kayak** (✉ 152 Lincolnville Ave. ☎ 207/338–6424 ⊕ www.touringkayaks.com) provides guided sea kayak trips among the islands of Penobscot Bay.

Shopping

The **Fertile Mind Book Shop** (✉ 105 Main St. ☎ 207/338–2498) has all kinds of reading matter, much of it about Maine. The **Green Store** (✉ 71 Main St. ☎ 207/338–4045) sells nothing but environmentally friendly products from lightbulbs to clothing.

The **Shamrock, Thistle & Rose** (✉ 48 Main St. ☎ 207/338–1864 ⊕ www. shamrockthistlerose.com) sells clothing, jewelry, art, and music from Ireland, Scotland, and England.

Searsport

❷❽ *11 mi northeast of Belfast, 57 mi east of Augusta.*

Searsport, Maine's second-largest deepwater port (after Portland), has a rich shipbuilding and seafaring history. In the 1880s, 10% of all captains under deepwater sail hailed from here. Many of the former sea captains' homes are now bed-and-breakfasts. They make an ideal base for exploring the multitude of antiques shops and flea markets lining U.S. 1 that have earned Searsport the title of Maine's Antiques Capital.

★ The **Penobscot Marine Museum** is dedicated to the history of Penobscot Bay and the maritime history of Maine. The museum's exhibits, artifacts, souvenirs, and paintings are displayed in a unique setting: seven historic buildings, including two sea captains' houses, in an original seaside village. The various exhibits provide fascinating documentation of the region's seafaring way of life. The outstanding collection of marine art includes the largest gathering in the country of works by Thomas and James Buttersworth. Also of note are photos of local sea captains; a collection of China-trade merchandise; artifacts of life at sea (including lots of scrimshaw); navigational instruments; antique logging, granite cutting, fishing, and ice-cutting tools; treasures collected by seafarers from around the globe; and models of famous ships. ✉ *5 Church St. (U.S. 1)* ☎ *207/548–2529* ⊕ *www.penobscotmarinemuseum.org* 🎫 *$8* ☉ *Memorial Day–mid-Oct., Mon.–Sat. 10–5, Sun. noon–5.*

Where to Stay & Eat

★ **$$$** ✕ **Rhumb Line.** This upscale restaurant in an 18th-century sea captain's home delivers fine dining, with formally attired waitstaff and excellent food. Specials include pan-seared peppered swordfish with Vidalia onion piccalilli, horseradish-crusted salmon with rémoulade sauce, and grilled rack of lamb with blackberry mint vinegar. ✉ *200 E. Main St.* ☎ *207/ 548–2600* ⊕ *www.therhumblinerestaurant.com* ▱ *MC, V* ☉ *No lunch.*

1

$–$$$ ⊞ **Inn Britannia.** Each of the rooms here is named after a place in England—such as the Cotswolds, Warwick, and Dover—and they are all decorated in an elegant modern British style. Some of the rooms have fireplaces, and some have four-poster beds. In addition to the beautiful gardens, the inn has the only Backyard Wildlife Habitat on Maine's Mid-Coast that has been certified by the National Wildlife Foundation. ⊠ *132 W. Main St. (U.S. 1), 04974* ☎ *207/548–2007 or 866/466–2748* ⊕ *www.innbritannia.com* ⇆ *8 rooms* ⚬ *Cable TV, some pets allowed; no a/c, no room phones, no TV in some rooms, no smoking* ☐ *D, MC, V* ⊺⊙⊺ *BP.*

★ $ ⊞ **Carriage House Inn.** This stately Victorian mansion is listed on the National Register of Historic Places. A rambling yellow clapboard house, it was built in 1874 by one of Searsport's many clipper ship captains, John McGilvery. Later, it became the home of the impressionist painter Waldo Pierce. Pierce was close friends with Ernest Hemingway, whom he knew from the ambulance corps, and the two met here often. One can only imagine what their conversations in the lavish library must have been like. ⊠ *120 E. Main St., 04974* ☎ *207/548–2167 or 800/578–2167* ⊕ *www.carriagehouseinmaine.com* ⇆ *3 rooms* ⚬ *Library; no a/c, no room phones, no room TVs, no smoking* ☐ *D, MC, V* ⊺⊙⊺ *BP.*

Shopping

In the very heart of town, **Captain Tinkham's Emporium** (⊠ 34 E. Main St. ☎ 207/548–6465) offers antiques, collectibles, old books, magazines, records, paintings, and prints. **Pumpkin Patch Antiques** (⊠ 15 W. Main St. ☎ 207/548–6047) displays such items as quilts, nautical memorabilia, and painted and wood furniture from about 20 dealers. The biggest collection of antiques is in the **Searsport Antique Mall** (⊠ 149 E. Main St. ☎ 207/548–2640), which has more than 70 dealers.

Castine

㉙ *30 mi southeast of Searsport.*

Federal- and Greek-revival–style architecture, spectacular views of Penobscot Bay, and a peaceful setting make Castine an ideal spot to spend a day or two. Well worth exploring are its lively harbor front, two small museums, and the ruins of a British fort. For a nice stroll, park your car at the landing and walk up Main Street toward the white Trinitarian Federated Church, which has a tapering spire. Among the white clapboard buildings that ring the town common are the Ives House (once the summer home of the poet Robert Lowell), the Abbott School, and the Unitarian Church, capped by a whimsical belfry. The Maine Maritime Academy is also here, and its training ship often can be seen in port. Historical markers are posted throughout town, making it ideal for a self-guided walking tour. You can also pick up a map detailing the historic sites at most local businesses.

The **Wilson Museum** is made up of four historic structures. The main building houses anthropologist-geologist John Howard Wilson's collection of prehistoric artifacts from around the world, including rocks, minerals, and intriguing objects. The **John Perkins House** is a restored Colonial-era house originally built on what is now Court Street, in 1763, and enlarged in 1774 and 1783. Inside you'll find Perkins family heirlooms and 18th- and early-19th-century furnishings. The kitchen and four front rooms appear as they did in 1783. The **Blacksmith Shop** holds demonstrations showing all the tricks of this old-time trade. Inside the **Hearse House** you can see the summer and winter hearses that serviced Castine more than a century ago. ⊠ *107 Perkins St.* ☎ *207/326–9247* ⊕ *www.wilsonmuseum.org* ▭ *Museum, Blacksmith Shop, and Hearse House free; John Perkins House $5* ⊙ *Museum late May–late Sept., Tues.–Sun. 2–5; John Perkins House, Blacksmith Shop, Hearse House July and Aug., Sun. and Wed. 2–5.*

Where to Stay & Eat

¢–$$$ ✕ **Dennett's Wharf.** Built as a sail-rigging loft in the early 1800s, this waterfront restaurant is a longtime favorite. A good place for fresh seafood, it also serves burgers, sandwiches, and other light fare. Several microbrews are on tap, including the tasty Dennett's Wharf Rat Ale. Eat in the dining room or outside on the deck. ⊠ *15 Sea St.* ☎ *207/326–9045* ▭ *AE, D, MC, V* ⊙ *Closed Columbus Day–May.*

$–$$$$ ✕▥ **Castine Inn.** This historic inn, built in 1898, is a delightful place to
Fodor'sChoice stay. Most of the guest rooms are rather simple, but they are bright and
★ airy, and have views of the ocean. A seascape mural covers the walls of the dining room ($$$$; reservations essential), where chef Tom Gutow serves an excellent prix-fixe menu. You might try an appetizer of Penobscot Bay crab cakes with mustard vinaigrette and herb mayonnaise, followed by the pork with spinach, chard, and fingerling potatoes. The staff is happy to suggest the correct wine pairings for each course. ⊠ *33 Main St., 04421* ☎ *207/326–4365* ▤ *207/326–4570* ⊕ *www.castineinn.com* ⥱ *15 rooms, 4 suites* △ *Restaurant, sauna, pub; no a/c, no room phones, no room TVs, no kids under 8, no smoking* ▭ *MC, V* ⊙ *Closed Nov.–late Apr.* ⎮⊙⎮ *BP.*

$–$$$ ✕▥ **Pentagoet Inn.** With period lithographs in the common rooms, clawfoot tubs in the bathrooms, and a cozy pub, the owners of this inn strive to create a romantic air. Guest rooms are in the main inn, a Queen Anne–style building with a three-story turret and numerous gables, or a nearby 18th-century sea captain's home. The most memorable is Room 3, which has a balcony covered with flowers and views of town. The restaurant ($$–$$$), with tables in the dining room or on a porch, specializes in fresh fish, but not only. You might try the Stonington crab-cake appetizer, followed by the seared duck on a Belgian endive salad. ⊠ *26 Main St., 04421* ☎ *207/326–8616 or 800/845–1701* ▤ *207/326–9382* ⊕ *www. pentagoet.com* ⥱ *16 rooms* △ *Restaurant, pub; no a/c, no room phones, no room TVs, no smoking* ▭ *MC, V* ⊙ *Closed late Oct.–May* ⎮⊙⎮ *BP.*

Sports & the Outdoors

Castine Kayak Adventures (⊠ Dennett's Wharf ☎ 207/326–9045 or 207/266–2841) customizes kayaking tours and will teach beginners the basics of kayaking.

Shopping

Compass Rose Bookstore & Café (⊠ 3 Main St. ☎ 207/326–9366) carries books, music, and games. The coffee shop has cookies and a self-serve lunch. **Four Flags** (⊠ 19 Water St. ☎ 207/326–8526) has nautical charts, prints of old maps, and other souvenirs. **Leila Day Antiques** (⊠ 53 Main St. ☎ 207/326–8786) specializes in interesting antiques, colorful quilts, and nautical accessories.

Blue Hill

 19 mi east of Castine.

Snuggled between 943-foot Blue Hill Mountain and Blue Hill Bay, Blue Hill has a dramatic perch over a harbor popular with sailors and sea-kayakers. Originally known for its granite quarries, copper mining, and shipbuilding, today the town flourishes with pottery and artisans. You'll find a plethora of galleries, small shops and studios, as well as bookstores and antiques shops.

Jonathan Fisher was the first permanent minister of Blue Hill. The **Parson Fisher House,** which he built from 1814 to 1820, provides a fascinating look at his many accomplishments and talents, which included writing and illustrating books, painting, farming, and building furniture. Also on view is a wooden clock he crafted while a student at Harvard; the face holds messages about time written in English, Greek, Latin, Hebrew, and French. ⊠ *Rte. 15/176, west of the intersection with Rte. 172* ☎ *207/374–2459* ⊕ *www.jonathanfisherhouse.org* 🖾 *$5* ☉ *July–mid-Sept., Tues.–Fri. 1–4, Sat. 11–2.*

Where to Stay & Eat

$$–$$$ ✕ **Arborvine.** Crackling fireplaces, period antiques, exposed beams, and
Fodor's Choice hardwood floors covered with Oriental rugs create an elegant and com-
★ forting atmosphere in each of the four candlelit dining rooms in this renovated Cape Cod–style house a quarter mile west of Blue Hill center. You might begin with a salad of mixed greens, sliced beets, and sliced pears with blue cheese crumbled on top. For your entrée, choose from dishes like medallions of beef and goat cheese with fingerling potatoes, or pork tenderloin with sweet cherries in a port-wine reduction. ⊠ *Main St., Tenney Hill* ☎ *207/374–2119* ☰ *MC, V* ☉ *Jan.–late May closed Mon.–Thurs., late May–mid-Oct. closed Mon., mid-Oct–Dec. closed Mon.–Wed. No lunch.*

$ ✕🖼 **Brooklin Inn.** A comfortable yet elegant atmosphere distinguishes this B&B in the neighboring town of Brooklin. There are plenty of homey touches like hardwood floors and an upstairs deck. The sunny rooms have attractive bureaus and beds piled with cozy quilts. The restaurant ($$–$$$$) offers meals made from scratch and specializes in fresh fish and locally raised beef, poultry, and lamb. You'll also find soups, salads, and desserts worth saving room for. ⊠ *Rte. 175, Brooklin 04616* ☎ *207/359–2777* ⊕ *www.brooklininn.com* 🛏 *5 rooms, 3 with bath* ⚘ *Restaurant; no a/c, no room phones, no room TVs* ☰ *AE, D, DC, MC, V.*

$$–$$$$ 🖼 **Blue Hill Inn.** This rambling inn dating from 1830 is a comfortable place to relax after exploring nearby shops and galleries. Original pumpkin pine and painted floors set the tone for the mix of Empire and early Victorian pieces that fill the two parlors and guest rooms, several of which have working fireplaces. One of the nicest rooms is Number 8, which has exposures on three sides and views of the flower gardens and apple trees. The spacious Cape House Suite (available after the rest of the inn has closed for the season) has a bed as well as two pullout sofas, a full kitchen, and a private deck. ⊠ *40 Union St., 04614* ☎ *207/374–2844 or 800/826–7415* ⊞ *207/374–2829* ⊕ *www.bluehillinn.com* ⇔ *11 rooms, 1 suite* ♿ *Bar; no room phones, no room TVs, no kids, no smoking* ⊟ *AE, MC, V* ⊗ *Closed Nov.–mid-May* ⏍ *BP.*

Sports & the Outdoors

You can rent sea kayaks, canoes, and bicycles at the **Activity Shop** (⊠ 61 Ellsworth Rd. ☎207/374–3600). Pick them up at the shop, or have them delivered. **Rocky Coast Outfitters** (⊠ Grindleville Rd. ☎ 207/374–8866) has sea kayaks, canoes, and bicycles, which are rented by the week. Delivery is available.

Shopping

Blue Hill Bay Gallery (⊠ 11 Tenney Hill ☎ 207/374–5773 ⊕ www. bluehillbaygallery.com) sells oil and watercolor paintings of the local ★ landscape. **Handworks Gallery** (⊠ 48 Main St. ☎ 207/374–5613) carries unusual crafts made by local artists such as bookshelves and clothes trees fashioned from bark-peeled tree branches, wooden boxes, jewelry, ★ dishes, and other items. **Jud Hartmann Gallery** (⊠ Main and Pleasant Sts. ☎ 207/359–2544 ⊕ www.judhartmanngallery.com) displays bronze sculptures of Iroquois and Abenaki Native Americans. **L. Balombini** (⊠ 54 Main St. ☎ 207/374–5142 ⊕ www.lbalombini.com) uses wire, buttons, and other materials to create whimsical sculptures of people, fish, and other creatures.

North Country Textiles (⊠ 36 Main St. ☎ 207/374–2715 ⊕ www. northcountrytextiles.com) specializes in fine woven shawls, throws, baby blankets, place mats, and pillows in subtle patterns and color schemes. **Rackliffe Pottery** (⊠ 132 Ellsworth Rd. ☎ 207/374–2297) sells colorful pottery made with lead-free glazes. **Rowantrees Pottery** (⊠ 84 Union St. ☎ 207/374–5535) has an extensive selection of dinnerware, tea sets, vases, and decorative items.

EN
ROUTE

Scenic Route 15 south from Blue Hill passes through Brooksville and takes you over the graceful suspension bridge that crosses Eggemoggin Reach to Deer Isle. The turnout and picnic area at **Caterpillar Hill,** 1 mi south of the junction of Routes 15 and 175, commands a fabulous view of Penobscot Bay, hundreds of dark-green islands, and the Camden Hills across the bay.

Deer Isle Village

③ *16 mi south of Blue Hill.*

In Deer Isle Village, thick woods give way to tidal coves. Stacks of lobster traps populate the backyards of shingled houses, and dirt roads lead to summer cottages. The region is prized by craftspeople and artists, and studios and galleries are plentiful.

The **Haystack Mountain School of Crafts** offers two- and three-week-long courses for people of all skill levels in such crafts as blacksmithing, basketry, printmaking, and weaving. Artisans from around the world present evening lectures throughout summer. You can attend the lectures or take a campus tour at 1 PM on Wednesday; otherwise, the facility is closed to visitors. ⊠ *89 Haystack School Dr., Deer Isle* ☎ *207/348–2306* ⊕ *www.haystack-mtn.org* ⊠ *$5* ⊙ *June–Sept.*

Where to Stay & Eat

$$$–$$$$ ✕⊞ **Goose Cove Lodge.** A country lane leads to this spectacular oceanfront property, where cottages and suites are scattered through the woods and along a sandy beach. Most of the guest rooms have fireplaces to keep out the chill. At low tide you can walk across a sandbar to the beautiful Barred Island Preserve. Reservations are essential at the superb restaurant ($$–$$$). The expertly prepared contemporary American fare includes at least one vegetarian entrée. ⊠ *300 Goose Cove Rd.* ⟲ *Box 40, Sunset 04683* ☎ *207/348–2508 or 800/728–1963* 🖷 *207/348–2624* ⊕ *www.goosecovelodge.com* ⥱ *2 rooms, 7 suites, 13 cottages* ⚭ *2 restaurants, beach, boating, hiking; no a/c, no room phones, no room TVs, no smoking* ⊟ *AE, D, MC, V* ⊙ *All but 3 units closed mid-Oct.–mid-May* ⦿| *BP.*

★ **$$–$$$$**   ✕⊞ **Pilgrim's Inn.** A four-story gambrel-roof house, this inn dates from about 1793. Wing chairs and Oriental rugs fill the library; a downstairs taproom has a huge brick fireplace and pine furniture. Individually furnished guest rooms overlook a millpond. Three cottages—the Rugusa Rose, Ginny's One, and Ginny's Two—are perfect for families. The dining room (¢–$$$) is rustic yet elegant with exposed beams, hardwood floors, and French oil lamps. Try traditional boiled Maine lobster, or go for something entirely different like sautéed venison with shiitake mushrooms. Be sure to save room for desserts like the mocha mousse. ⊠ *20 Main St., 04627* ☎ *207/348–6615 or 888/778–7505* 🖷 *207/346–6615* ⊕ *www.pilgrimsinn.com* ⥱ *12 rooms, 3 cottages* ⚭ *Restaurant, bicycles, some pets allowed; no a/c, no room phones, no room TVs, no smoking* ⊟ *AE, D, MC, V* ⊙ *Closed mid-Oct.–mid-May* ⦿| *BP.*

Sports & the Outdoors

One- and two-person canoes and kayaks are available at **Finest Kind Canoe & Kayak Rentals** (⊠ Center District Rd. near Rtes. 15 and 15A, Deer Isle ☎ 207/348–7714 ⊕ www.finestkindenterprises.com).

Shopping

Purchase a handmade quilt from **Dockside Quilt Gallery** (⊠ 33 Church St. ☎207/348–2849 or 207/348–7712 ⊕www.docksidequiltgallery.com). If you don't see anything you like, you can always commission a custom-designed quilt. **Harbor Farm** (⊠ 29 Little Deer Isle Rd. ☎ 207/348–7737) carries wonderful products for the home, such as pottery, linens, and folk art. **Nervous Nellie's Jams and Jellies** (⊠ 598 Sunshine Rd. ☎ 207/348–6182) sells jams and jellies and operates a café. **Turtle Gallery** (⊠ 61 N. Deer Isle Rd. ☎ 207/348–9977) exhibits contemporary painting and sculpture.

Stonington

🟢 *7 mi south of Deer Isle.*

Stonington's isolation at the tip of the Deer Isle Peninsula has helped it retain its fishing-village flavor, but this is changing, as boutiques and galleries open in summer now line its main thoroughfare. Still, Stonington remains a working port town—the principal activity is at the waterfront, where fishing boats arrive with the day's catch. At night the town can be rowdy. The high, sloped island that rises beyond the archipelago known as Merchants Row is Isle au Haut, which contains a remote section of Acadia National Park; it's accessible by mail boat from Stonington.

The tiny **Deer Isle Granite Museum** documents Stonington's quarrying tradition. The museum's centerpiece is an 8-by-15-foot working model of quarrying operations on Crotch Island and the town of Stonington at the turn of the last century. ⊠ *Main St.* ☎ *207/367–6331* 🖼 *Free* ☉ *Memorial Day–Labor Day, Mon.–Sat. 10–5, Sun. 1–5.*

Where to Stay & Eat

¢–$$ ✕ **Fisherman's Friend.** For an extensive list of seafood specials, stop by this family-style restaurant. Look for crabmeat and clam rolls, fried clam and shrimp baskets, and other seafood platters. Pies and other desserts are made on the premises. The decor isn't fancy—this is a paper-place-mat kind of place. ⊠ *40 School St.* ☎ *207/367–2442* ▭ *D, MC, V* ☉ *Closed late Oct.–Apr.*

★ ¢–$$ ✕ **Lily's.** Homemade baked goods, delicious sandwiches, and fresh salads are on the menu at this eatery. Try the Italian turkey sandwich, which has slices of oven-roasted turkey and Jack cheese on homemade sourdough bread. The dining room's glass-top tables let you gaze at the shells and various treasures inside. A produce stand behind the restaurant sells some of the same organic foods used by the chefs here. ⊠ *Rte. 15 and Airport Rd.* ☎ *207/367–5936* ▭ *MC, V.*

$–$$$ 🛏 **Inn on the Harbor.** From the front, this inn made up of four century-old Victorian buildings is as plain and unadorned as the town in which it is located. But in the rear is an expansive deck over the harbor—a pleasant spot for morning coffee or afternoon cocktails. Rooms on the harborside have lovely views, and some have fireplaces and private decks. Those facing the street side can be noisy at night. ⊠ *45 Main St.* ☍ *Box 69, 04681* ☎ *207/367–2420 or 800/942–2420* 🖷 *207/367–5165* ⊕ *www.innontheharbor.com* ↵ *12 rooms, 2 suites* ♦ *Coffee shop, cable TV, in-room data ports; no a/c, no kids under 12, no smoking* ▭ *AE, D, MC, V* ⦿ *CP.*

Sports & the Outdoors

Old Quarry Ocean Adventures (⊠ 130 Settlement Rd. ☎ 207/367–8977 ⊕ www.oldquarry.com) rents bicycles, canoes, and kayaks and offers guided tours of the bay. Captain Bill Baker's three-hour boat tours take you past Stonington Harbor on the way to the outer islands.

Shopping

Art and antiques are for sale at the **Clown** (⊠ 6 Thurlow's Hill ☎ 207/367–6348), as well as specialty foods and a good wine selection. Facing the harbor, **Dockside Books & Gifts** (⊠ 62 W. Main St. ☎ 207/367–2652) stocks an eclectic selection of books. **Isalos** (⊠ 26 Main St. ☎ 207/367–2700 ⊕ www.isalosfineart.com), named for the Greek word for "waterline," sells paintings and photography by area artists.

Isle au Haut

③③ *14 mi south of Stonington.*

The steeply ridged back of Isle au Haut juts up from the sea south of Stonington. Accessible only by passenger mail boat (☎ 207/367–5193), the island is worth visiting for the ride itself, a half-hour cruise amid the tiny islands of Merchants Row, where you might see terns, guillemots, and harbor seals.

★ Half of Isle au Haut is part of beautiful **Acadia National Park.** More than 18 mi of trails wind through quiet spruce woods, along beaches and seaside cliffs, and over the spine of the central mountain ridge. The park's small campground, with five lean-tos, is open from mid-May to mid-October and fills up quickly. Reservations are essential. You can access Acadia National Park by turning right when you arrive at the dock; the ranger station is a short walk or bike ride away. Public restrooms are here, as is the trailhead for the Duck Harbor Trail. ⊠ *Isle au Haut* ☎ *207/ 288–3338* ⊕ *www.nps.gov/acad.*

Where to Stay

$$$$ ◫ **Keeper's House.** Hidden by thick woods, this converted lighthouse keeper's home is an ideal spot to unwind. The ecofriendly inn has a reverse-osmosis system that purifies the drinking water, and solar-power and wind-power generators. There's no electricity in the guest rooms, however, so in the evening you can dine by candlelight and read by kerosene lantern. The spacious rooms are filled with painted wood furniture and decorated with local crafts. Package rates apply here: stays are for a minimum three nights and include meals; a cottage with a kitchen is rented by the week. ⊠ *Lighthouse Point* ✉ *Box 26, 04645* ☎ *207/ 460–0257* ⊕ *www.keepershouse.com* ⇆ *2 rooms, 1 with bath; 1 cottage* ⚴ *Dining room, bicycles, hiking; no a/c, no room phones, no room TVs* ▭ *No credit cards* ☉ *Closed mid-Oct.–mid-May* ▮❍▮ *FAP.*

Penobscot Bay A to Z

To research prices, get advice from other travelers, and book travel arrangements, visit www.fodors.com.

CAR TRAVEL

U.S. 1 follows the west coast of Penobscot Bay, linking Rockland, Rockport, Camden, Belfast, and Searsport. On the east side of the bay, Route 175 (south from U.S. 1) takes you to Route 166A (for Castine) and Route 15 (for Blue Hill, Deer Isle, and Stonington). A car is essential for exploring the bay area.

EMERGENCIES

▣ Hospitals **Blue Hill Memorial Hospital** ⊠ 57 Water St., Blue Hill ☎ 207/374–2836 ⊕ www.bhmh.org. **Island Medical Center** ⊠ 354 Airport Rd., Stonington ☎ 207/367– 2311. **Penobscot Bay Medical Center** ⊠ 6 Glencove Dr., U.S. 1, Rockport ☎ 207/596– 8000. **Waldo County General Hospital** ⊠ 118 Northport Ave., Belfast ☎ 207/338–2500 or 800/649–2536.

VISITOR INFORMATION

Belfast Area Chamber of Commerce ⌂ Box 58, Belfast 04915 ☎ 207/338-5900 ⊕ www.belfastmaine.org. **Blue Hill Peninsula Chamber of Commerce** ⊠ 28 Water St., Blue Hill 04614 ☎ 207/374-3242 ⊕ www.bluehillpeninsula.org. **Camden-Rockport-Lincolnville Chamber of Commerce** ⌂ 2 Public Landing, Box 919, Camden 04843 ☎ 207/236-4404 or 800/223-5459 ⊕ www.camdenme.org. **Castine Town Office** ⊠ Emerson Hall, Court St., Castine 04421 ☎ 207/326-4502. **Deer Isle-Stonington Chamber of Commerce** ⊠ Rte. 15, Deer Isle 04627 ☎ 207/348-6124 ⊕ www.deerisle.com. **Rockland-Thomaston Area Chamber of Commerce** ⌂ Box 508, Rockland 04841 ☎ 800/562-2529 ⊕ www.therealmaine.com.

BANGOR TO MOUNT DESERT ISLAND

Just over an hour from the coast, Bangor anchors northern and eastern Maine. Its plethora of cultural and shopping spots and its convenient access, via Bangor International Airport, make it an ideal starting point for visits to Maine's North Woods and Acadia National Park. Acadia is the informal name for the area east of Penobscot Bay that includes Mount Desert Island (pronounced "dessert") as well as Blue Hill Bay and Frenchman Bay. Mount Desert, 13 mi across, is Maine's largest island, and it encompasses most of Acadia National Park, an astonishingly beautiful preserve with rocky cliffs, crashing surf, and serene mountains and ponds. Maine's number-one tourist attraction, it draws more than 4 million visitors a year. The 40,000 acres of woods and mountains, lake and shore, footpaths, carriage roads, and hiking trails that make up the park extend to other islands and some of the mainland. Outside the park, on Mount Desert's eastern shore, is Bar Harbor, a busy tourist town. Less commercial and congested are the smaller island towns, such as Southwest Harbor and Northeast Harbor, and the outlying islands.

Bangor

❸❹ *133 mi northeast of Portland, 46 mi north of Bar Harbor.*

The second-largest city in Maine, Bangor is about 20 mi from the coast and is the unofficial capital of northern Maine. Back in the 19th century its most important product and export was lumber from the state's vast North Woods. Bangor's location right on the Penobscot River helped to make it the largest lumber port in the world. Today, a 31-foot-tall statue of the legendary lumberman Paul Bunyan stands in front of the Bangor Auditorium.

The **Cole Land Transportation Museum** chronicles the history of transportation in Maine through historical photographs and more than 200 vehicles. ⊠ *405 Perry Rd.* ☎ *207/990–3600* ⊕ *www.colemuseum.org* ⌑ *$6* ☉ *May–mid-Nov., daily 9–5.*

The **Maine Discovery Museum** is the largest children's museum in the state. It has three floors of interactive and hands-on exhibits. Kids can explore Maine's ecosystem in Nature Trails, travel to foreign countries in Passport to the World, and walk through Maine's literary classics in Book-town. ⌂ *74 Main St.* ☎ *207/262–7200* ⊕ *www.mainediscoverymuseum. org* ⌦ *$6* ⊙ *Tues.–Sat. 9:30–5, Sun. noon–5.*

Where to Stay & Eat

$$–$$$ ✕ **Thistle's.** Paintings by local artists adorn the walls in this bright storefront restaurant. The diverse menu includes entrées such as Argentinian steak with chimichurri sauce, pickled ginger salmon piccata, and roast duckling. Musicians often perform during dinner. ⌂ *175 Exchange St.* ☎ *207/945–5480* ▤ *AE, D, MC, V* ⊙ *Closed Sun.*

$–$$$ ✕▥ **Lucerne Inn.** One of the most famous and respected inns in New Eng-
Fodor'sChoice   land, the Lucerne is nestled in the mountains, overlooking Phillips Lake.
★   It was established in 1814, and every room is furnished with antiques. The restaurant ($$–$$$$), nearly as famous as the inn itself, draws people for its lavish Sunday brunch buffet. The traditional dinner for guests is the boiled Maine lobster. ⌂ *2517 Main Rd. (Rte. 1A) 15 mins east of Bangor* ⌖ *R.R. 3, Box 540, Dedham 04429* ☎ *207/843–5123 or 800/325–5123* ⎙ *207/843–6138* ⊕ *www.lucerneinn.com* ⋑ *31 rooms, 4 suites* ⌂ *Restaurant, cable TV, pool, hot tubs, lounge, meeting rooms, no-smoking rooms* ▤ *AE, D, MC, V* ⎊ *CP.*

The Arts

The **Bangor Symphony Orchestra** (⌂ 51A Main St. ☎ 207/942–5555 or 800/639–3221) performs at the Maine Center for the Arts from September through mid-May. The **Penobscot Theatre Company** (⌂ 131 Main St. ☎ 207/942–3333 ⊕ www.ptc.maineguide.com) stages live classic and contemporary plays from October to May.

Ellsworth

㉟   *140 mi northeast of Portland, 28 mi south of Bangor.*

Ellsworth, the shire town of Hancock County, fills with traffic during summer months. Route 1 passes through an inviting downtown lined with shops and a strip of shopping plazas and factory outlets, including L. L. Bean, between downtown and where Route 3 splits to Mount Desert.

At the 130-acre **Stanwood Homestead Museum & Bird Sanctuary** you can look for birds along the trails and visit the 1850 Stanwood House Museum, a Cape Cod–style house. Cordelia Stanwood, born in 1856, was one of Maine's earliest ornithologists. ⌂ *Rte. 3* ☎ *207/667–8460* ⌦ *Free* ⊙ *Trails daily sunrise–sunset; museum mid-May–mid-Oct., daily 10–4.*

Between 1824 and 1828, Colonel John Black built **Woodlawn,** an elegant Georgian mansion. Inside are an especially fine elliptical flying staircase and period artifacts from the three generations of the family that lived here. Outside, you can wander through several different gardens. The formal garden, enclosed by a lilac hedge, features flowers that were popular in the 19th century, including iris, daylilies, and phlox. ⌂ *Surrey Rd.* ☎ *207/667–8671* ⊕ *www.woodlawnmuseum.org* ⌦ *$7.50, free access to gardens and grounds* ⊙ *May and Oct., Tues.–Sun. 1–4; June–Sept., Tues.–Sat. 10–5, Sun. 1–4.*

Fiddling with Fiddleheads

AS YOU HEAD TOWARD MOUNT DESERT ISLAND, it's common to see vendors on the side of the roadways selling produce from the back of a pickup truck. In spring, you're likely to see signs offering CLEAN FIDDLEHEADS. Unknown to many Americans, the fiddlehead fern is one of nature's true delicacies. Fiddleheads are the tightly coiled tips of newly emerging fronds, and are about the size of two or three quarters stacked on top of each other.

Fiddleheads come from different varieties of ferns. The best fiddleheads come from ostrich ferns, which, unlike most ferns, have hairless casings. You can also eat the fiddleheads from cinnamon ferns but they have a fuzzier casing. You shouldn't fiddle with some ferns, however. The bracken fern is similar to the ostrich fern, but it's hairy and can give you quite a stomachache. It can be difficult to identify ferns, but if you are determined to forage, you can identify the type of fern by examining the dead stalks from the previous year. Often these stalks will hold firmly to the plant even after a winter of heavy snow and ice.

Even the best fiddleheads require a good cleaning, and should be thoroughly cooked. If you pick some fiddleheads, be sure to boil them for 10 to 15 minutes. The best method is to boil them for about 7 minutes in one pot, then discard the water and boil them in fresh water until they are tender. Fiddleheads have a distinct flavor that aficionados say is somewhere between asparagus and spinach. Many area restaurants offer them as a side dish, toss them with pasta, or add them to other dishes. Be sure to give them a try if you are visiting in springtime.

Acadia National Park

4 mi northwest of Bar Harbor (to Hulls Cove).

There is no one Acadia. The park holds some of the most spectacular and varied scenery on the eastern seaboard: a rugged coastline of surf-pounded granite and an interior graced by sculpted mountains, quiet ponds, and lush deciduous forests. Cadillac Mountain, the highest point of land on the eastern coast, dominates the park. Although it's rugged, Acadia National Park also has graceful stone bridges, horse-drawn carriages, and the elegant Jordan Pond House. The 27-mi Park Loop Road provides an excellent introduction, yet to truly appreciate the park you must get off the main road and experience it by walking, biking, or taking a carriage ride on the carriage trails, or perhaps sea kayaking. If you get off the beaten path, you'll find places in the park that you can have practically to yourself, despite the millions of visitors who descend in summer.

The popular Hulls Cove approach to Acadia National Park, northwest of Bar Harbor on Route 3, takes you to the start of the **Park Loop Road.** Even though it is often clogged with traffic in summer, the road provides the best introduction to the park. You can drive it in an hour, but allow at least half a day or more to explore the many sites along the route. At the visitor center at the start of the loop, you can watch a free 15-minute orientation film and pick up a schedule of ranger-led nature walks and hikes, children's programs, photography programs, and evening talks. You can also pick up the *Acadia Beaver Log* (the park's free newspaper), books, maps of hiking trails and carriage roads, and cassettes for drive-it-yourself tours. Traveling south on the Park Loop Road, you'll reach a small ticket booth where you pay an entrance fee of about $20 per vehicle, good for seven consecutive days. ✉ *Park Loop Rd., Hulls Cove* ☎ *207/288–3338* 🌐 *www.nps.gov/acad* ⏲ *Visitor center July and Aug., daily 8–6; mid-Apr.–June, Sept., and Oct., daily 8–4:30.*

㊲ **Sand Beach** is a small stretch of pink sand backed by the mountains of Acadia and the odd lump of rock known as the Beehive. The Ocean Trail, which runs from Sand Beach to the Otter Point parking area, is an easily accessible walk with some of the most awesome scenery in Maine: huge slabs of pink granite heaped at the ocean's edge.

㊳ The**Thunder Hole** is a popular stop along Park Loop Road, especially on stormy or windy days. The ocean "thunders" into this natural seaside cave, spraying water all the way up to the viewing area. Although the closest view of this attraction is reached by a stairway, a wheelchair-accessible path provides fairly good views. A parking area and gift shop are located across the road.

㊴ The water source for the village of Seal Harbor, **Jordan Pond** is best seen from the observation deck next to the Jordan Pond House restaurant. Rising above the water are the Bubbles, two mountains of similar size and shape. Maps and other items are available at the information booth beside the restaurant.

★ ㊵ **Cadillac Mountain,** at 1,532 feet, is the highest point on the eastern seaboard. From the smooth, bald summit you have an awesome 360-degree view of the ocean, islands, jagged coastline, and woods and lakes of Acadia and its surroundings. You can drive or hike to the summit.

Abbe Museum at Sieur de Monts Spring. The original Abbe Museum (there's a newer, larger museum in Bar Harbor) has exhibits on the history of the Abbe people who once inhabited this area. The museum is on the National Register of Historic Places. ✉ *Sieur de Monts Spring exit from Rte. 3 or Park Loop Rd.* ☎ *207/288–3519* 🌐 *www.abbemuseum.org* 🎟 *$2* ⏲ *Memorial Day–mid-Oct., daily 9–4.*

Where to Eat

$$–$$$ ✕ **Jordan Pond House.** Oversize popovers with strawberry jam or homemade ice cream are a century-old tradition at this restaurant overlooking Jordan Pond. Dine outside on the tea lawn or the brick patio, or inside an enclosed porch or dining room. The lunch menu emphasizes sandwiches and salads, whereas the dinner menu includes seafood as well as beef and chicken. With two satellite parking lots, the restaurant makes an ideal base for hiking or biking along the nearby carriage roads. You can also use the adjacent boat launch for canoeing or kayaking on Jordan Pond. ✉ *Park Loop Rd.* ☎ *207/276–3316* 💳 *AE, D, MC, V* ⏲ *Closed late Oct.–mid-May.*

Sports & the Outdoors

BIKING　The 45 mi of carriage roads that wind through the woods and fields of Acadia National Park, built from 1915–1933 by John D. Rockefeller Jr., are ideal for biking and jogging when the ground is dry and for cross-country skiing in winter.

HIKING　Acadia National Park maintains approximately 120 mi of hiking trails, from easy strolls along flatlands to rigorous climbs that involve ladders and hand holds on rock faces. Among the more rewarding hikes are the Precipice Trail to Champlain Mountain, the Great Head Loop, the Gorham Mountain Trail, and the path around Eagle Lake. The Hulls Cove Visitor Center has trail guides and maps and will help you match a trail with your interests and abilities. The park's 45 mi of carriage roads are also used by hikers.

Bar Harbor

🕗 *160 mi northeast of Portland, 22 mi southeast of Ellsworth on Rte. 3.*

An upper-class resort town in the 19th century, Bar Harbor now serves as a gateway to Acadia National Park. Most of its grand mansions were destroyed in a fire that devastated the island in 1947, but many surviving estates have been converted into businesses. Shops, restaurants, and hotels are clustered along Main, Mount Desert, and Cottage streets. Take a stroll down West Street, a National Historic District, where you can see some of the grand cottages that survived the fire.

The only museum devoted solely to Maine's Native American heritage, the **Abbe Museum** houses a collection of artifacts that spans 10,000 years. The museum has both permanent and changing exhibitions. ⊠*26 Mount Desert St.* ☎*207/288–3519* ⊕*www.abbemuseum.org* ⊠*$6* ☉ *June–Sept., daily 9–5; Oct.–May, by appointment.*

The **Bar Harbor Historical Society Museum** displays photographs of Bar Harbor from the days when it catered to the very rich. Other exhibits document the great fire that devastated the town in 1947. ⊠ *33 Ledgelawn Ave.* ☎ *207/288–3807 or 207/288–0000* ⊠ *Free* ☉ *June–Oct., Mon.–Sat. 1–4.*

☺ **Bar Harbor Whale Museum.** Bone up on the history of whaling, the anatomy of whales, and how biologists are working to gain more information about these massive creatures at this interesting museum. All proceeds from the gift shop benefit Allied Whale, a nonprofit organization that conducts marine mammal research. ⊠ *52 West St.* ☎ *207/288–0288* ⊕ *www.barharborwhalemuseum.org* ⊠ *Free* ☉ *June, Sept., and Oct., daily 10–8; July and Aug., daily 9–9.*

☺ At the College of the Atlantic, the **George B. Dorr Museum of Natural History** has wildlife exhibits, a hands-on discovery room, interpretive programs, and summer field studies for children. ⊠ *105 Eden St.* ☎ *207/288–5395 or 207/288–5015* ⊕ *www.coa.edu/nhm* ⊠ *$4* ☉ *Mid-June–Labor Day, Mon.–Sat. 10–5; Labor Day–mid-Nov. and mid-Jan.–mid-June, Fri. and Sun., 1–4, Sat. 10–4.*

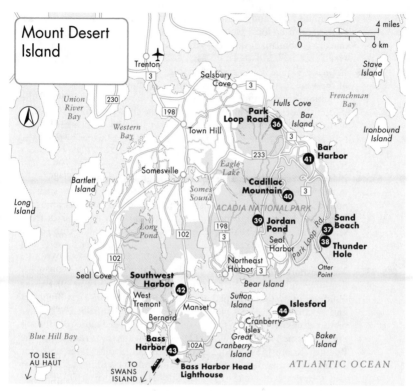

Mount Desert Island

0   4 miles
0   6 km

Trenton
Salsbury Cove
Union River Bay
230
198
Western Bay
Town Hill
3
Hulls Cove
Park Loop Road 36
Bar Island
Stave Island
Frenchman Bay
Ironbound Island
233
Bar Harbor 41
Eagle Lake
Somesville
Bartlett Island
Some Sound
Cadillac Mountain 40
3
ACADIA NATIONAL PARK
Long Island
Long Pond
102
198
3
39 **Jordan Pond**
37 **Sand Beach**
38 **Thunder Hole**
Seal Harbor
Park Loop Rd.
Otter Point
102
Northeast Harbor 3
Seal Cove
Southwest Harbor 42
West Tremont
Manset
Bernard
Sutton Island
Bear Island
44 **Islesford**
Cranberry Isles
Baker Island
Blue Hill Bay
TO ISLE AU HAUT
Bass Harbor 43
102A
Great Cranberry Island
ATLANTIC OCEAN
TO SWANS ISLAND
Bass Harbor Head Lighthouse

Where to Stay & Eat

$$–$$$
Fodor'sChoice
★

✕ **Burning Tree.** Local art adorns the walls in the two dining rooms and on the porch at this restaurant in Otter Creek. The ever-changing menu emphasizes freshly caught seafood. Entrées include pan-sautéed monkfish, Cajun-style lobster, and crab au gratin. Delicious dishes such as chicken pot roast hold their own on the menu. There are always two or three vegetarian choices. ⊠ *Rte. 3, Otter Creek* ☎ *207/288–9331* ▤ *D, MC, V* ⊘ *Closed Tues. and mid-Oct.–June.*

$$–$$$
✕ **Havana.** Soft jazz playing in the background sets the tone at this storefront restaurant on the edge of downtown Bar Harbor. The pumpkin-color walls and wood floors lend an air of sophistication. The Latin-influenced menu, which emphasizes local ingredients and changes weekly, may include crab-and-roasted-corn cakes or grilled swordfish marinated in ginger and lime and finished with a scallion vinaigrette. ⊠ *318 Main St.* ☎ *207/288–2822* ⊕ *www.havanamaine.com* ▵ *Reservations essential* ▤ *AE, MC, V* ⊘ *Closed Sun.–Tues. Nov.–mid-May.*

$$–$$$
✕ **Mache.** Painted with muted earth tones and decorated with flickering candles, this low-key restaurant allows the food to take center stage. The menu changes weekly, but always begins with freshly baked bread. Choose from appetizers such as seared scallops and fiddlehead ferns tossed with penne and Alfredo sauce. Entrées include a seared salmon fillet with

ginger and basil, and panfried tofu with apricots. There's also a cheese course featuring local blue cheese and chèvre. Be sure to save room for one of the homemade desserts—the lemon tart is excellent. ⊠ *135 Cottage St.* ☎ *207/288–0447* ⊟ *AE, MC, V* ⊗ *Closed Mon.*

$–$$$ ✕ **George's.** Fine linens grace the tables, and original art fills the walls of the four small dining rooms in this charming old house. It may be difficult to choose among the entrées, but you won't go wrong with the lobster strudel with chanterelle ragout or the charcoal-grilled swordfish with salsa served over couscous. Whatever you pick, remember to save room for dessert. The restaurant always has 10 to 12 wines by the glass. ⊠ *7 Stephen's La.* ☎ *207/288–4505* ⊟ *AE, D, DC, MC, V* ⊗ *Closed Nov.–mid-June.*

$–$$$ ✕ **McKay's Public House.** Low lighting and glowing candles set the right mood for relaxed but elegant dining. The pub menu includes such familiar favorites as fish-and-chips, lamb burgers, corned beef and cabbage, and bangers and mash. The restaurant also emphasizes fresh seafood, offering crab cakes, seafood risotto, seared scallops, and other dishes. Key lime pie, crème brûlée, cheesecake, and other desserts will tempt your palate. ⊠ *231 Main St.* ☎ *207/288–2002* ⊟ *AE, MC, V.*

$$$–$$$$ ✕🖾 **Bar Harbor Inn.** Established in the late 1800s, originally as a men's drinking club, this waterfront inn has rooms spread out over three buildings on well-landscaped grounds. Most rooms have gas fireplaces and balconies with great views. Rooms in the Oceanfront Lodge have private decks overlooking the ocean. Should you need more room, there are also some two-level suites. The elegant waterfront restaurant, the Reading Room ($$–$$$$), serves mostly continental fare. Look for Maine specialties such as lobster pie and Indian pudding. ⊠ *Newport Dr., 04609* ☎ *207/288–3351 or 800/248–3351* 🖷 *207/288–8454* ⊕ *www.barharborinn.com* ⇝ *138 rooms, 15 suites* ⚭ *2 restaurants, in-room safes, refrigerators, cable TV, in-room VCRs, pool, gym, business services, meeting room; no smoking* ⚮ *Reservations essential* ⊟ *AE, D, DC, MC, V* ⊗ *Closed late Nov.–late Mar.* ⦿❘ *CP.*

★ $$$$ 🖾 **Balance Rock Inn.** This grand summer cottage built in 1903 commands a prime waterfront location. An expansive lawn and gardens full of annuals lead down to the ocean. Even if your room doesn't have an ocean view, you can enjoy it from a wicker chair on the porch. Rooms are spacious and meticulously furnished with reproduction pieces—four-poster and canopy beds in guest rooms, crystal chandeliers and a grand piano in common areas. All rooms have whirlpool tubs, and some have fireplaces. ⊠ *21 Albert Meadow, 04609* ☎ *207/288–2610 or 800/753–0494* 🖷 *207/288–5534* ⊕ *www.barharborvacations.com* ⇝ *14 rooms, 3 suites* ⚭ *Cable TV, in-room VCRs, in-room data ports, pool, gym, bar, concierge* ⊟ *AE, D, MC, V* ⊗ *Closed late Oct.–early May* ⦿❘ *BP.*

$$–$$$$ 🖾 **Ullikana.** Inside the stucco-and-timber walls of this traditional Tudor
Fodor'sChoice cottage, antiques are juxtaposed with contemporary country pieces; vi-
★ brant color with French country wallpapers; and abstract art with folk creations. The combination not only works—it shines. Rooms are large; many have fireplaces, and some have decks. Breakfast is an elaborate multicourse affair. The refurbished Yellow House across the drive has six additional rooms. ⊠ *16 The Field, 04609* ☎ *207/288–9552* 🖷 *207/ 288–3682* ⊕ *www.ullikana.com* ⇝ *16 rooms* ⚭ *No a/c in some rooms,*

no room phones, no room TVs, no smoking ⊟ *MC, V* ⊘ *Closed Nov.–May* ⫯◯⫰ *BP.*

$–$$ ⊞ **Cromwell Harbor Motel.** Less than a mile from downtown Bar Harbor, this clean and pleasant motel is set amid pretty gardens. From here you can walk to a quiet section of Acadia National Park. ⊠ *359 Main St., 04069* ☎ *207/288–3201 or 800/544–3201* ⊕ *www.cromwellharbor. com* ⇖ *26 rooms* ♿ *Some microwaves, some refrigerators, cable TV, pool, no-smoking rooms* ⊟ *AE, D, MC, V.*

$–$$ ⊞ **Seacroft Inn.** It's an easy walk to Bar Harbor or the shore path from this rambling, multigabled inn. The property has seven efficiency units, including one two-bedroom unit that is a good choice for families. A breakfast basket is delivered to your room each morning. ⊠ *18 Albert Meadow, 04609* ☎ *207/288–4669 or 800/824–9694* ⊕ *www.seacroftinn. com* ⇖ *6 rooms, 1 two-bedroom unit* ♿ *Microwaves, refrigerators, cable TV* ⊟ *MC, V* ⊘ *Closed mid.-Nov.–Apr.* ⫯◯⫰ *CP.*

Nightlife & the Arts

The **Arcady Music Festival** (☎ 207/669–4225 ⊕ www.arcady.org) schedules classical concerts at locations around Mount Desert Island throughout the year. The **Bar Harbor Music Festival** (⊠ 59 Cottage St. ☎ 207/288–5744, 212/222–1026 off-season ⊕ www.barharbormusicfestival. org) hosts jazz, classical, and pop concerts by young professionals from July to early August.

If you want to shoot some pool or throw some darts, try the **Carmen Verandah** (⊠ 119 Main St. ☎ 207/288–2766 ⊕ www.carmenverandah. com). The upstairs bar also has live music and dancing. **Geddy's Pub** (⊠ 19 Main St. ☎ 207/288–5077) hosts local musicians early in the evening and DJs spinning later at night.

Sports & the Outdoors

BIKING **Acadia Bike Rentals** (⊠ 48 Cottage St. ☎ 207/288–9605 or 800/526–8615) rents mountain bikes good for negotiating the trails in Acadia National Park. The **Bar Harbor Bicycle Shop** (⊠ 141 Cottage St. ☎ 207/288–3886 or 800/824–2453) rents bikes by the half or full day.

BOATING **Acadia Outfitters** (⊠ 106 Cottage St. ☎ 207/288–8118) rents canoes and sea kayaks. **Coastal Kayaking Tours** (⊠ 48 Cottage St. ☎ 207/288–9605 or 800/526–8615) conducts tours of the rocky coastline led by registered guides.

The four-masted schooner *Margaret Todd* (⊠ Bar Harbor Inn Pier ☎ 207/288–2373 ⊕ www.downeastwindjammer.com) operates 1½- to 2-hour tours three times a day from mid-May to mid-October. The schooner *Rachel B. Jackson* (⊠ Harborside Hotel & Marina, 56 West St. ☎ 207/288–2216 or 888/405–7245) offers three daytime cruises and one sunset cruise.

WHALE-WATCHING **Acadian Whale Adventures** (⊠ 55 West St. ☎ 207/288–9800 ⊕ www.barharborwhales.com) has three different whale-watching cruises: just whales, whales and lighthouses, or whales and puffins. **Bar Harbor Whale Watch Co.** (⊠ 1 West St. ☎ 207/288–2386 ⊕ www.whalesrus.com) operates the catamaran *Friendship V,* for whale-watching, and the *Katherine,* for lobster-fishing and seal-watching.

Shopping

The **Alone Moose** (⊠ 78 West St. ☎ 207/288–4229) has bronze wildlife sculptures and other interesting artwork in clay, pottery, and wood. The **Birdsnest Gallery** (⊠ 12 Mount Desert St. ☎ 207/288–4054) sells paintings and sculpture. The **Eclipse Gallery** (⊠ 12 Mount Desert St. ☎ 207/288–9048) carries handblown glass, ceramics, lighting, and wood furniture.

Fodor'sChoice ★ **Island Artisans** (⊠ 99 Main St. ☎ 207/288–4214) sells basketry, pottery, fiber work, and jewelry created by Maine-based artisans. **Native Arts Gallery** (⊠ 99 Main St. ☎ 207/288–4474 ⊕ www.nativeartsgallery. com) sells Native American silver and gold jewelry.

Ben and Bill's Chocolate Emporium (⊠ 66 Main St. ☎ 207/288–3281) is a chocolate lover's nirvana. The shop also has more than 20 flavors of ice cream. **Song of the Sea** (⊠ 47 West St. ☎ 207/288–5653 ⊕ www. songsea.com) specializes in folk music, especially Celtic, and sells hand-crafted musical instruments such as bagpipes and harps.

Southwest Harbor

❷ *5 mi south of Somesville via Rte. 102 South.*

On what is known as the "quiet side" of Mount Desert Island, Southwest Harbor has fewer attractions than other towns. It can still be quite busy in summer, however. This working port is home to well-known boat-building companies, a major source of employment in the area. To reach the harbor from Route 102, make a left onto Clark Point Road.

The **Mount Desert Oceanarium** has exhibits on the fishing and sea life of the Gulf of Maine, a live-seal program, and hands-on exhibits such as a touch tank. ⊠ *Clark Point Rd.* ☎ *207/244–7330* ⊕ *www. theoceanarium.com* ⊠ *$8* ⊙ *Mid-May–late Oct., Mon.–Sat. 9–5.*

The **Wendell Gilley Museum** showcases bird carvings by Gilley and has carving demonstrations and workshops. Carvings are to scale, and include the ruffed grouse, upland sandpiper, American goldfinch, Atlantic puffin, and loon. ⊠4 *Herrick Rd.* ☎207/244–7555 ⊕*www.wendellgilleymuseum. org* ⊠ *$5* ⊙ *July and Aug., Tues.–Sun. 10–5; June, Sept., and Oct., Tues.–Sun. 10–4; May, Nov., and Dec., Fri.–Sun. 10–4.*

Where to Stay & Eat

$$–$$$ ✕ **Beal's Lobster Pier.** You can watch lobstermen hauling in their catch at this working lobster pound. Lobster, clams, and other seafood make up most of the menu. Eat your meal outside on the picnic tables or, if you want to organize your own lobster bake, order the critters to go. ⊠ *182 Clark Point Rd.* ☎ *207/244–7178* ⊕ *www.bealslobster.com* ▤ *AE, MC, V* ⊙ *Closed Columbus Day–mid-May.*

★ $$–$$$ ✕ **Fiddler's Green.** Perhaps the most difficult part of dining at this harborside restaurant is selecting just one entrée. It's hard to choose between dishes such as pan-seared yellowfin tuna with wasabi-and-tamari sauce or scallops with asparagus, spinach, tomato, pancetta, and grilled polenta. Everything here is fresh, including the locally grown organic produce. The desserts—such as vanilla-bean crème brûlée and Grand Marnier Bundt cake—make for hard decisions. Choose a bottle from a wine list that regularly includes 130 selections, and has as many as 180 at the height of summer. ⊠ *411 Main St.* ☎ *207/244–9416* ▤ *AE, MC, V* ☉ *Closed Columbus Day–Memorial Day; Memorial Day–June and Sept.–Columbus Day, Mon.–Wed.; July and Aug., Mon.*

$$$ ▥ **Claremont Hotel.** Built in 1884, the Claremont calls up memories of the long, leisurely vacations of days gone by. The inn commands a view of Somes Sound. Croquet is taken seriously here—a tournament is held on the lawn during the first week in August. Rooms are simply—some would say sparsely—decorated; cottages are more rustic. Breakfast and dinner are served in the waterfront dining room, where the menu changes weekly. It's popular, so make sure to call ahead. ⊠ *Clark Point Rd.* ⌂ *Box 137, 04679* ☎ *207/244–5036 or 800/244–5036* ⎙ *207/244–3512* ⊕ *www.theclaremonthotel.com* ⇆ *30 rooms, 2 suites, 14 cottages* ⌂ *Restaurant, tennis court, dock, bicycles, croquet; no a/c, no room TVs, no smoking* ▤ *No credit cards* ☉ *Hotel closed mid-Oct.–mid-June; cottages closed mid-Oct.–mid-May* ⋈ *BP, MAP.*

¢–$$ ▥ **Moorings Inn & Cottages.** Nothing is fancy here except the jaw-dropping view of Somes Sound. The main house, which dates back to the late 18th century, is decorated with period antiques and has more charming rooms, but those in a newer wing have sliding-glass doors leading to private decks. ⊠ *135 Shore Rd., Manset* ⌂ *Box 744, Southwest Harbor 04679* ☎ *207/244–5523 or 800/596–5523* ⊕ *www.mooringsinn. com* ⇆ *13 rooms, 5 cottages, 1 apartment* ⌂ *Some kitchenettes, some microwaves, some refrigerators, boating, bicycles; no a/c, no room phones, no room TVs* ▤ *No credit cards* ☉ *Closed mid-Oct.–mid-May* ⋈ *CP.*

Sports & the Outdoors

Acadia Adventures Sea Kayak Tours (⊠ 19 Clark Point Rd. ☎ 207/244–0680) runs morning and afternoon tours in two-person sea kayaks. Tours are tailored for different skill levels. **Manset Yacht Service** (⊠ Shore Rd., Manset ☎ 207/244–4040) charters powerboats and sailboats.

Southwest Cycle (⊠ 370 Main St. ☎ 207/244–5856) rents bicycles by the day or week.

Bass Harbor

❹❸ *4 mi south of Southwest Harbor via Rte. 102 or Rte. 102A.*

Bass Harbor is a tiny lobstering village with a relaxed atmosphere and a few accommodations and restaurants. If you're looking to get away from the crowds, consider using this hardworking community as your base.

★ **Bass Harbor Head Light.** Originally built in 1858, this lighthouse is one of the most photographed in Maine. The light, now automated, marks the entrance to Blue Hill Bay. Two trails around the facility provide excellent views. ⊠ *Rte. 102, Bass Harbor* ▱ *Free* ☉ *Daily 9–sunset.*

Where to Stay & Eat

¢–$$ ✕ **Thurston's Lobster Pound.** Located on the peninsula across from Bass Harbor, Thurston's Lobster Pound is easy to spot because of its bright yellow awning. You can buy fresh lobsters to go or sit at outdoor tables. Order everything from a grilled cheese sandwich to a boiled lobster served with clams or mussels. ⊠ *Steamboat Wharf and Bernard Rds., Bernard* ☎ *207/244–7600* ۝ *Closed Columbus Day–Memorial Day.*

$–$$ ▣ **Bass Harbor Inn.** If you're looking for someplace away from the crowds, consider this lodging near the harbor. Built in 1870, the inn is relaxed, and many of the bright and airy rooms lead out to sunny decks. ⊠ *Shore Rd., 04653* ☎ *207/244–5157* ⊕ *www.acadiavacations.com* ⇨ *6 rooms, 1 studio* ⚓ *No a/c, no room phones, no room TVs* ▤ *AE, MC, V* ۩ *CP.*

Cranberry Isles

1–5 mi south of Mount Desert Island via boat.

Off the southeast shore of Mount Desert Island lie the five Cranberry Isles—Great Cranberry, Islesford (also frequently called Little Cranberry), Baker Island, Sutton Island, and Bear Island. Ferry trips to **Islesford,** the island that has the closest thing to a village, are a great way to escape the crowds on Mount Desert Island. You'll find a cluster of houses, a church, a market, and a fishermen's co-op, near the ferry dock.

Sailing from from Northeast Harbor, the **Beal & Bunker Mail Boat Ferry Service** (☎ 207/244–3575) serves Islesford, as well as Great Cranberry and Sutton Island. The **Cranberry Cove Boating Company** (☎ 207/244–5882 ⊕ www.barharborferry.com) runs from Southwest Harbor to Islesford, Great Cranberry, and Sutton Island.

Bangor to Mount Desert Island A to Z

To research prices, get advice from other travelers, and book travel arrangements, visit www.fodors.com.

BOAT & FERRY TRAVEL

Bar Harbor Ferry provides passenger service between Bar Harbor and Winter Harbor, on the Schoodic Peninsula, from mid-May to early October. ▟ Boat & Ferry Information **Bar Harbor Ferry** ☎ 207/288-2984 ⊕ www. barharborferry.com.

BUS TRAVEL

The free Island Explorer shuttle service operates several routes around Mount Desert Island from mid-June to September, with limited service continuing through mid-October. Buses are equipped with racks for stowing bicycles and service the major campgrounds, Acadia National Park, and the Bar Harbor–Hancock County Airport. Concord Trailways operates shuttle service from Bangor International Airport to Bar Harbor, with stops along the way in Bangor and Ellsworth. Vermont Transit Lines runs between Bangor and Bar Harbor; if the bus isn't delayed by traffic, it takes about an hour. Downeast Transportation operates buses from

Ellsworth to various locations on Mount Desert Island. Greyhound services Bangor. West's Coastal Connection is a public bus operated by the Maine Department of Transportation. You can take it from the Bangor International Airport to Ellsworth, where you can transfer to another bus to the island.

🚌 **Concord Trailways** ☎ 207/945-4000 or 800/639-3317 ⊕ www.concordtrailways.com. **Downeast Transportation** ☎ 207/667-5796. **Greyhound Lines Inc.** ☎ 800/231-2222 ⊕ www.greyhound.com. **Island Explorer** ☎ 207/667-5796 ⊕ www.exploreacadia. com. **Vermont Transit Lines** ☎ 800/552-8737 ⊕ www.vermonttransit.com. **West's Coastal Connection** ☎ 800/596-2823 ⊕ westbusservice.com.

CAR TRAVEL

From the gateway towns of Ellsworth and Trenton, Route 3 leads to Mount Desert Island. When you reach the island, Route 3 continues to Bar Harbor. Route 102 heads toward Somesville and Southwest Harbor. In summer months, traffic can slow considerably, especially in the afternoon. If Northeast Harbor is your first destination when arriving on the island, take Route 102 to Somesville, then turn onto Route 198.

In Acadia National Park, the 27-mi Park Loop Road is accessible from Hulls Cove (visitor center entrance), Otter Creek (Sieur de Monts Spring entrance), and Seal Harbor (Jordan Pond House entrance). You can also access Park Loop Road from Bar Harbor (Cadillac Mountain entrance).

EMERGENCIES

🚑 **Hospitals Eastern Maine Medical Center** ✉ 489 State St., Bangor ☎ 207/973-8000. **Maine Coast Memorial Hospital** ✉ 50 Union St., Ellsworth ☎ 207/664-5311 ⊕ www. mainehospital.org. **Mount Desert Island Hospital** ✉ 10 Wayman La., Bar Harbor ☎ 207/288-5081. **Northeast Harbor Clinic** ✉ Kimball Rd., Northeast Harbor ☎ 207/ 276-3331, part of Mount Desert Island Hospital and open only in July and August. **Southwest Harbor Medical Center** ✉ 45 Herrick Rd., Southwest Harbor ☎ 207/244-5513.

LODGING

Several companies can help you find vacation rental accommodations, from in-town cottages to secluded estates.

🏠 **Davis Agency** ✉ 363 Main St., Southwest Harbor 04679 ☎ 207/244-3891 ⊕ www. davisagencyrealty.com. **Janet Moore Real Estate** ✉ 12B Main St., Northeast Harbor 04662 ☎ 207/276-5080 ⊕ www.moore-realestate.com. **Knowles Company** ✉ 1 Summit Rd., Northeast Harbor 04662 ☎ 207/276-3322 ⊕ www.knowlesco.com. **Maine Island Properties** ✎ Box 1025, Mount Desert 04660 ☎ 207/244-4348 ⊕ www. maineislandproperties.com. **Mount Desert Properties** ✎ Box 536, Bar Harbor 04609 ☎ 207/288-4523 ⊕ www.barharborvacationhome.com.

SPORTS & THE OUTDOORS

FISHING Maine residents 16 and older and non-Maine residents 12 and older must have a license to fish in fresh waters. Fishing licenses may be purchased at town halls and at some stores. Fishing licenses are not required for ocean fishing.

🎣 **Bar Harbor Municipal Office** ✉ 93 Cottage St., Bar Harbor ☎ 207/288-4098. **Mount Desert Municipal Office** ✉ Sea St., Northeast Harbor ☎ 207/276-5531. **Southwest Harbor Town Office** ✉ 26 Village Green Way, Southwest Harbor ☎ 207/244-5404.

TOURS

Acadia National Park Tours operates a 2½-hour bus tour of Acadia National Park, narrated by a naturalist, from May through October. Down East Nature Tours leads small-group tours highlighting the island's flora and fauna.

Acadia Air, at Hancock County Airport between Ellsworth and Bar Harbor, rents aircraft and flies seven aerial sightseeing routes from spring to fall. A Step Back in Time uses Victorian-costumed guides to lead walking tours that highlight the 1890s in Bar Harbor. Tours leave from 48 Cottage Street.

🔊 **A Step Back in Time** ☎ 207/288-9605. **Acadia Air** ☎ 207/667-5534. **Acadia National Park Tours** ☎ 207/288-0300 ⊕ www.acadiatours.com. **Down East Nature Tours** ☎ 207/288-8128.

VISITOR INFORMATION

🔊**Acadia Information Center** ⊠ 1201 Bar Harbor Rd., Trenton 04605 ☎ 207/667-8550 ⊕ www.acadiainfo.com. **Acadia National Park** �🖉 Box 177, Bar Harbor 04609 ☎ 207/288-3338 ⊕ www.nps.gov/acad. **Bangor Convention & Visitors Bureau** ⊠ 1 Cumberland Pl., Suite 300, Bangor 04401 ☎ 207/947-5205 or 800/916-6673 ⊕ www.bangorcvb.org. **Bangor Region Chamber of Commerce** ⊠ 519 Main St., Bangor 04401 ☎ 207/947-0307 ⊕ www.bangorregion.com. **Bar Harbor Chamber of Commerce** ⊠ 93 Cottage St. �🖉 Box 158, Bar Harbor 04609 ☎ 207/288-3393, 207/288-5103, or 800/288-5103 ⊕ www.barharborinfo.com. **Ellsworth Area Chamber of Commerce** ⊠ 161 High St., Ellsworth ☎ 207/667-5584 ⊕ www.ellsworthchamber.org. **Mount Desert Island Information Center** ⊠ Rte. 3, Thompson Island ☎ 207/288-3411. **Southwest Harbor/Tremont Chamber of Commerce** ⊠ Main St. �🖉 Box 1143, Southwest Harbor 04679 ☎ 207/244-9264 or 800/423-9264 ⊕ www.acadiachamber.com.

WAY DOWN EAST

East of Ellsworth on U.S. 1 is a different Maine, a place pretty much off the beaten path that seduces with a rugged, simple beauty. Red-hued blueberry barrens dot the landscape, and scraggly jack pines hug the highly accessible shoreline. The quiet pleasures include hiking, birding, and going on whale-watching and puffin cruises. Many artists live in the region; you can often purchase works directly from them.

Hancock

45 *9 mi east of Ellsworth.*

A small triangular green with a Civil War monument marks the center of Hancock. Not far away are the summer cottages at Hancock Point, where stunning views await, especially at sunset, across Frenchman Bay. You can pick up items for an impromptu picnic in Hancock or across the bridge in Sullivan, where there are more mountain-framed views.

Where to Eat & Stay

★ $-$$ ✕ **Tidal Falls Lobster Restaurant.** This lobster stand overlooks one of New England's best known reversing falls, a phenomenon created when the current "reverses" from the bay to the harbor and white water roils from an hour before to an hour after low tide. The menu eschews fried foods,

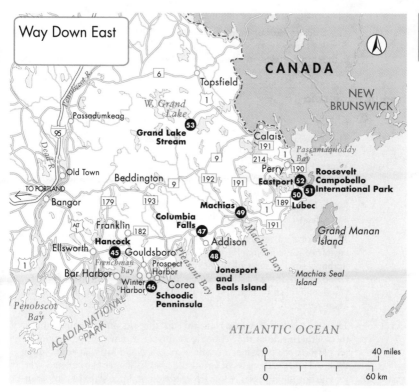

Way Down East

CANADA

NEW BRUNSWICK

opting instead for dishes such as steamed mussels. Look for sides such as garlic bread and mesclun salad. You can eat outdoors or inside a screened room. ⊠ *Tidal Falls Rd.* ☎ *207/422–6457* ⊟ *MC, V* ⊙ *Closed mid-Sept.–mid-June. No lunch weekdays.*

$$$–$$$$ ✕📷 **Le Domaine Inn.** In the French country-style dining room ($$$$; closed Mon., no lunch) the owner serves classic dishes such as *coquilles St. Jacques* (scallops) and *ris de veau pané à l'Anglaise* (veal sweetbreads with capers). The French cuisine is accompanied by the more than 5,000 bottles in the wine cellar. Le Domaine is known primarily for its food, but the French-influenced guest rooms are also inviting. They open onto private decks overlooking the perennial gardens, a pond, and trails that meander through the property's 100 acres. ⊠ *1513 U.S. 1, 04640* ☎ *207/422–3395 or 800/554–8498* 📠 *207/422–3916* ⊕ *www.ledomaine. com* 🛏 *3 rooms, 2 suites* ⚭ *Restaurant, fans, hiking, some pets allowed (fee); no room TVs* ⊟ *AE, MC, V* ⊙ *Closed late Oct.–May* ⦿ *CP.*

Sports & the Outdoors

You can paddle on open water in Frenchman Bay or follow the shores of Taunton Bay on kayak excursions with **Hancock Point Kayak Tours** (⊠ 58 Point Rd. ☎ 207/422–6854).

Shopping

The **Sullivan Harbor Farm Smokehouse** (⊠ U.S. 1 ☎ 800/422–4014
⊕ www.sullivanharborfarm.com) cold-smokes salmon and other seafood
in the traditional Scottish manner. Load up for a picnic—insulated bags
are available.

Schoodic Peninsula

46 *23 mi southeast of Hancock, 32 mi east of Ellsworth.*

The landscape of Schoodic Peninsula makes it easy to understand why
the overflow from Bar Harbor's wealthy summer population settled in
Winter Harbor. The craggy coastline, the towering evergreens, and views
over Frenchman Bay are breathtaking year-round. A drive through the
community of Grindstone Neck shows what Bar Harbor might have been
like before most of it was destroyed in the Great Fire of 1947. Artists
and artisans have opened galleries in and around Winter Harbor.

The Schoodic Peninsula also has several smaller coastal villages. The
largest of these is **Birch Harbor.** Near Birch Harbor you'll find **Prospect
Harbor,** a small fishing village nearly untouched by tourism. There's also
Corea, where there's little to do besides watch the fishermen at work,
wander along stone beaches, or gaze out to sea—and that's what makes
it so special.

Fodor'sChoice
★
The only section of **Acadia National Park** that sits on the mainland is at
the southern side of the Schoodic Peninsula. A few miles east of Winter Harbor, the park has a scenic 6-mi one-way loop that edges along
the coast and yields views of Grindstone Neck, Winter Harbor, and Winter Harbor Lighthouse. At the tip of the point, huge slabs of pink granite lie jumbled along the shore, thrashed unmercifully by the crashing
surf, and jack pines cling to life amid the rocks. The Fraser Point Day-
Use Area at the beginning of the loop is an ideal place for a picnic. Work
off your lunch with a hike up Schoodic Head for the panoramic views
up and down the coast. One of the Island Explorer bus routes takes passengers from Prospect Harbor, Birch Harbor, and Winter Harbor and
drops them off anywhere in the park. ⊠ *Rte. 186* ☎ *207/288–3338*
⊕ *www.nps.gov/acad* ⌨ *$20 per car* ⊙ *Daily.*

Where to Stay & Eat

$$–$$$$ ✕ **West Bay Lobsters in the Rough.** Lobsters and steamers, accompanied
by corn on the cob, coleslaw, or baked beans, are among the dishes served
at this lobster pound. Eat in the greenhouse, at the outdoor tables, or
have meals packed up to take on a picnic. Remember, your bill will be
proportional to the size of the lobster you pick. ⊠ *W. Bay Rd., Prospect
Harbor* ☎ *207/963–7021* ☰ *AE, D, DC, MC, V* ⊙ *Closed Nov.–May.
No lunch.*

$$–$$$ ✕ **Fisherman's Inn.** The house specialty, lobster pie, is one of the many
seafood dishes on the menu at this casual eatery founded in 1947. Beef,
chicken, and vegetarian dishes are also available. An appetizer of cheese
spread and salmon pâté comes from a local smokehouse run by the cou-
ple that owns the restaurant. ⊠ *7 Newman St., Winter Harbor* ☎ *207/
963–5585* ☰ *AE, D, MC, V* ⊙ *Closed mid-Oct.–late May.*

★ **$$–$$$** ✕**Mama's Boy Bistro.** With a lovely mahogany-and-ash bar, this bistro may be Way Down East's fanciest dining spot. The building, with soaring gables and a stone hearth, is typical of this part of the state. There is balcony seating overlooking an open kitchen, where you can watch the chefs prepare entrées such as grilled sablefish and beef tenderloin with a Gruyère cheese and red onion tart. ⊠ *10 Newman St., Winter Harbor* ☎ *207/963–2365* ▭ *AE, D, MC, V* ⊘ *Closed Mon. in season and mid-Oct.–mid May. No lunch except Sun. brunch.*

$$–$$$
Fodor'sChoice
★
▨ **Oceanside Meadows Inn.** This place is a must for nature lovers. Trail maps guide you through a 200-acre preserve dotted with woods, streams, salt marshes, and ponds. Inspired by the moose, eagles, and other wildlife that thrive here, the innkeepers created the Oceanside Meadows Innstitute for the Arts & Sciences, which holds lectures, musical performances, art exhibits, and other events in the restored barn. Furnished with antiques, country pieces, and family treasures and scented with flowers from the gardens, the inn has sunny, inviting living rooms with fireplaces and a separate guest kitchen. ⊠ *202 Corea Rd., Rte. 195, Prospect Harbor 04669* ☎ *207/963–5557* ⊟ *207/963–5928* ⊕ *www. oceaninn.com* ⇌ *12 rooms, 3 suites* ⬧ *Beach, croquet, hiking, horseshoes, concert hall, meeting rooms, some pets allowed (fee); no a/c, no room TVs, no smoking* ▭ *AE, D, DC, MC, V* ⊘ *Closed Nov.–Apr.* ⏉*BP.*

$–$$$
▨ **Black Duck Inn.** The comfortable common areas and guest rooms at this B&B are tastefully furnished with antiques, including the owner's toy collection. The walls are decorated with works by artists who have stayed here. A beachstone fireplace is the focal point of the cozy den. The first-floor guest room has a separate entrance and a private deck. If you're traveling with a small group, the two-bedroom suite is a great value. Two tiny cottages are perched on the harbor. ⊠ *36 Crowley Island Rd., Corea 04624* ☎ *207/963–2689* ⊟ *207/963–7495* ⊕ *www. blackduck.com* ⇌ *2 rooms, 1 suite, 2 cottages* ⬧ *No a/c, no room phones, no room TVs, no kids under 7, no smoking* ▭ *D, MC, V* ⊘ *Closed Nov.–Apr.* ⏉ *BP.*

Sports & the Outdoors

MooseLook Guide Service (⊠ 150 Corea Rd., Prospect Harbor ☎ 207/963–7223 ⊕ www.mooselookguideservice.com) rents canoes, kayaks, and bikes and leads canoeing and kayaking trips.

Departing from Bunker's Wharf, **Robertson Sea Tours Adventures** (⊠ 260 E. Schoodic Dr., Birch Harbor ☎ 207/546–3883 ⊕ www. robertsonseatours.com) takes up to six passengers out on a lobster boat.

Shopping

The wines sold at **Bartlett Maine Estate Winery** (⊠ U.S. 1, Gouldsboro ☎ 207/546–2408 ⊕ bartlettwinery.com) are produced from locally grown apples, pears, blueberries, and other fruit. Smoked salmon and mussels, and cheese and salmon pâté are among speciality foods sold at **Grindstone Neck of Maine** (⊠ Rte. 186, Winter Harbor ☎ 207/963–7347 or 866/831–8734 ⊕ www.grindstoneneckofmaine.com), which gives tours of its smokehouse. Glass wildlife sculptures, flowers, goblets, and beads are for sale at **Gypsy Moose Glass Co.** (⊠ 20 Williamsbrook Rd., Gouldsboro ☎ 207/963–2674 ⊕ www.oceaninn.com/gypsymoose).

Hand-cast bronze doorbells are among the items sold at **U.S. Bells** (✉ Rte. 186, Prospect Harbor ☎ 207/963–7184 ⊕ www.usbells.com). You are often able to tour the foundry.

Columbia Falls

47 *41 mi east of Ellsworth, 78 mi west of Calais.*

Founded in the late 18th century, Columbia Falls is a pretty village along the Pleasant River. As its name suggests, a waterfall tumbles into the river in the center of town. Columbia Falls was once a shipbuilding center and still has a number of stately homes dating from that prosperous time. U.S. 1 used to pass through the center of town, but now it passes to the west.

★ Judge Thomas Ruggles, a wealthy lumber dealer, store owner, postmaster, and Justice of the Court of Sessions, built **Ruggles House** in 1818. The house's distinctive Federal architecture, flying staircase, Palladian window, and intricate woodwork were crafted over a period of three years by Massachusetts wood-carver Alvah Peterson using a penknife. ✉ *146 Main St.* ☎ *207/483–4637* ⊕ *www.ruggleshouse.org* 🏷 *$5* ⊙ *June–mid-Oct., Mon.–Sat. 9:30–4:30, Sun. 11–4:30.*

Where to Stay

¢–$$ 🏨 **Pleasant Bay Bed & Breakfast.** This Cape Cod–style inn takes advantage of its riverfront location. Stroll the nature paths on the 110-acre property, which winds around a peninsula and out to Pleasant Bay—you can even take one of the inn's llamas along for company. A screened porch and deck overlooks the Pleasant River. The county-style rooms, all with water views, are decorated with antiques. A two-room suite has a private deck. A full breakfast is served before 8 AM, and a continental breakfast is available for late risers. ✉ *386 W. Side Rd.* ⌂ *Box 222, Addison 04606* ☎ *207/483–4490* 🖷 *207/483–4653* ⊕ *www.pleasantbay. com* ➪ *3 rooms, 2 with shared bath; 1 suite* ⚒ *Some refrigerators; no a/c, no room phones, no TV in some rooms, no smoking* ▭ *MC, V* ⦿*BP.*

Shopping

Yes, the deep-blue geodesic dome housing **Wild Blueberry Land** (✉ U.S. 1, at Rte. 187 ☎ 207/483–2583) is supposed to resemble a giant blueberry. In addition to foods filled with blueberries, the shop has displays about the local cash crop.

Jonesport & Beals Island

48 *12 mi south of Columbia Falls, 20 mi southwest of Machias.*

The birding is superb around Jonesport and Beals Island, a pair of fishing communities joined by a bridge over the harbor. A handful of stately homes are tucked away on Jonesport's Sawyer Square, where Sawyer Memorial Congregational Church's exquisite stained-glass windows are illuminated at night. But the towns are less geared toward travelers than those on the Schoodic Peninsula.

At the tip of Beals Island, **Great Wass Island Preserve** (✉ Beals Island ☎ 207/729–5181) is a 1,540-acre preserve where you'll find stunted pines and raised peat bogs. Trails lead through the woods and emerge onto the undeveloped coast, where you may spot gray seals as you make your way among the rocks and boulders. Admission is free.

Where to Stay & Eat

¢–$$ ✕**Tall Barney's.** Salty accents add plenty of flavor at this down-home restaurant. Reserved for fishermen, the "liar's table" near the entrance is about as legendary as the restaurant's namesake, a brawny fisherman who left truly tall tales in his wake. Lobstermen arrive when the place opens at 4 AM, and tourists show up somewhat later. The menu includes five types of seafood stew, "tall" and "small" burgers, and oversize desserts such as "no bakes" (a candylike chocolate cookie—a local favorite). ⊠ *52 Main St.* ☎ *207/497–2403* ▭ *MC, V.*

★ $ 🏠 **Harbor House on Sawyer Cove.** The two spacious rooms on the third floor of this harborfront building have big windows overlooking the water. Both have separate sitting areas and are tastefully furnished with Victorian flourishes such as cabbage-rose wallpaper and handwoven rugs. Breakfast is served on the enclosed porch. You can relax on the lawn, which is flanked by beach roses. ⊠ *27 Sawyer Sq.* ✑ *Box 468, Jonesport 04649* ☎ *207/497–5417* ⊕ *www.harborhs.com* ✑ *2 rooms* ⟁ *Cable TV; no a/c, no room phones, no kids under 12* ▭ *D, MC, V* ⯐ *BP.*

Sports & the Outdoors

In business since 1940, **Norton of Jonesport** (☎ 207/497–5933 ⊕ www.machiassealisland.com) takes passengers on day trips out into the Atlantic beyond Machias Bay to Machias Seal Island, where thousands of puffins nest. Arctic terns, razorbill auks, common murres, and many other seabirds also nest on the rocky island. Trips cost $100 per person.

Shopping

Years ago, many Down East fishermen hunted sea ducks to help feed their families, and the area's decoy-carving tradition lives on at **Nelson Decoys** (⊠ 13 Cranberry La. ☎ 207/497–3488), whose owners carve and paint wood eiders, puffins, and other waterfowl.

Machias

🌑 *20 mi northeast of Jonesport.*

Machias lays claim to being the site of the first naval battle of the Revolutionary War. Despite being outnumbered and outarmed, a small group of Machias men under the leadership of Jeremiah O'Brien captured the armed British schooner *Margaretta*. That battle, fought on June 12, 1775, is now known as the "Lexington of the Sea." The town's other claim to fame is its wild blueberries. On the third weekend in August, the annual Machias Wild Blueberry Festival is a community celebration complete with parade, crafts fair, concerts, and plenty of blueberry dishes.

★ The **Burnham Tavern Museum,** housed in a building dating from 1770, details the colorful history of Job Burnham and other early residents of the area. It was in this tavern that the men of Machias laid the plans that culminated in the capture of the *Margaretta* in 1775. Period furnishings show what life was like in Colonial times. ⊠ *Rte. 192* ☎ *207/ 255–4432* ⊕ *www.burnhamtavern.com* ⊡ *$5* ☉ *Mid-June–early Sept., weekdays 9–5; early-Sept.–mid-June, by appointment.*

Built in 1810, the **Nathan Gates House** houses the Machiasport Historical Society. The museum contains an extensive collection of old photographs, period furniture, housewares and tools, and other memorabilia. There's also a genealogical library. The Marine Room highlights the area's seafaring and shipbuilding past. A model school room and post office occupy the adjacent Cooper House, a utilitarian building constructed in 1850. ⊠ *Rte. 92, Machiasport* ☎ *207/255–8461* ⊡ *Free* ☉ *Late June–early Sept., Tues.–Sat. 12:30–4:30.*

Where to Stay & Eat

$$–$$$$ ✕ **Artist's Café.** In an old house across from the University of Maine, this restaurant has garnered a strong local following. The white-walled dining rooms provide a simple backdrop for eye-catching works by local artists and the palate-pleasing work of the chefs. The menu changes weekly, but a beloved appetizer called Horses Standing Still—hand-rolled Thai dumplings filled with chicken and shrimp and served with a dipping sauce—is almost always available. ⊠ *3 Hill St.* ☎ *207/255–8900* ▤ *MC, V* ☉ *Closed mid-Oct.–mid-Apr. No lunch Sat. Sept.–June.*

$–$$ ✕▦ **Riverside Inn & Restaurant.** A bright yellow exterior invites a stop at this delightful inn perched on the banks of the Machias River. Inside you'll find hammered tin ceilings and lots of hand-carved wood. The spacious guest rooms have antique furnishings and colorful quilts. The two-bedroom suite has a private balcony and a full kitchen. The restaurant ($$–$$$; closed Jan.–mid-Feb., mid-Feb.–May, Mon.–Wed., June–Dec., Mon.; reservations essential) has maintained its excellent reputation. The chef brings a special flair to traditional dishes such as London broil, as well as local dishes such as hake cakes and sautéed shrimp and scallops. ⊠ *U.S. 1* ⌂ *Box 373, East Machias 04630* ☎ *207/255–4134 or 888/ 255–4344* ⊕ *www.riversideinn-maine.com* ⌑ *2 rooms, 2 suites* � *Restaurant, cable TV; no a/c, no room phones, no smoking* ▤ *MC, V* ⦿ *BP.*

Sports & the Outdoors

Sunrise Canoe & Kayak (⊠ Hoytt Rd., Machias ☎ 207/255–3375 or 877/ 980–2300 ⊕ www.sunrisecanoeandkayak.com) offers sea-kayaking day trips to petroglyphs carved on slate ledges in Machias Bay.

Lubec

⑤⓪ *28 mi east of Machias.*

Lubec is the first town in the United States to see the sunrise. The village is perched at the end of a narrow strip of land, so you often can see water in three directions. Abandoned smokehouses once used to process sardines are clustered on the piers along Water Street, awaiting restoration. Lubec is a good base for day trips to New Brunswick's Campobello Island, which is reached by a bridge—the only one to the island— from downtown Lubec.

★ The easternmost point of land in the United States, **Quoddy Head State Park,** is marked by candy-striped West Quoddy Head Light. In 1806, President Thomas Jefferson signed an order authorizing construction of a lighthouse on this site. You can't climb the tower, but its interior is visible in a video shown at the museum in the former light-keeper's house; it also has displays on Lubec's maritime past and the region's marine life. ☒ *S. Lubec Rd. off Rte. 189* ☎ *No phone* ☜ *$2* ☉ *May 15–Oct. 15.*

★ ⑤ **Roosevelt Campobello International Park** is crisscrossed with interesting hiking trails. Eagle Hill Bog has a wooden walkway and signs identifying rare plants. Neatly manicured Campobello Island has always had a special appeal for the wealthy and famous. It was here that President Franklin Roosevelt and his family spent summers. The 34-room Roosevelt Cottage was presented to Eleanor and Franklin as a wedding gift, and the wicker-filled structure looks essentially as it did when the family was in residence. ☒ *Rte. 774, Campobello Island, Welshpool, New Brunswick, Canada* ☎ *506/752–2922* ☜ *Free* ☉ *House Memorial Day–Columbus Day, daily 10–6; grounds daily.*

Also on Campobello Island is **East Quoddy Head Lighthouse.** This distinctive lighthouse is marked with a large red cross and accessible only at low tide. ☒ *End of Rte. 774, Wilson's Beach.*

Where to Stay & Eat

¢–$$ ✕ **Uncle Kippy's.** There isn't much of a view from the picture windows, but locals don't mind—they come here for the satisfying seafood. There's one large dining room with a bar beside the main entrance. The menu includes seafood dinners and combo platters. ☒ *Rte. 189* ☎ *207/733–2400* ☰ *MC, V* ☉ *Closed Mon.*

$ ✕🏠 **Home Port Inn.** In a Colonial-style house perched high atop a hill, this grand lodging dating from 1880 has generously sized guest rooms, some with water views. All are furnished with family antiques, including several stately beds. Warm up by the fireplace in the large cherry-red living room's two sitting areas. The elegant restaurant ($$), one of the best in town, opens onto a deck overlooking Cobscook Bay. Lobster is served in a casserole with drawn butter, sherry, and bread crumbs, or in a salad with artichoke hearts and a creamy tarragon dressing. ☒ *45 Main St., 04652* ☎ *207/733–2077 or 800/457–2077* ⊕ *www. homeportinn.com* ☞ *7 rooms* ☍ *Restaurant; no a/c, no room phones, no room TVs, no smoking* ☰ *AE, D, MC, V* ☉ *Closed mid-Oct.–Apr.* ¶◯ *CP.*

Shopping

Pick up a six-pack—of smoked salmon kabobs—at **Bold Coast Smokehouse** (☒ 224 County Rd. ☎ 207/733–8912 or 888/733–0807 ⊕ www. boldcoastsmokehouse.com). Other offerings include trout pâté and gravlax from Scandinavia.

Eastport

⑤ *39 mi north of Lubec, 102 mi east of Ellsworth.*

Known for its architecture, Eastport was one of the nation's busiest seaports in the early 1800s. In the late 19th century, 14 sardine canneries operated here. The industry's decline in the 20th century left the city economically depressed, but it has now set its sights on salmon farming.

Anchoring downtown Eastport is the **National Historic Waterfront District,** which extends from the customs house down Water Street to Bank Square and the Peavey Library. Spanning such architectural styles as Federal, Victorian, Queen Anne, and Greek-revival, the district was largely built in the 19th century. The tides at Eastport, among the highest in the world, fluctuate as much as 28 feet. That explains the ladders and steep gangways necessary to access boats.

Shakford Head State Park has wonderful views over Passamaquoddy Bay to Campobello and Grand Manan islands. From here you can see the pens used by Eastport's salmon-farming industry. ⊠ *Deep Cove Rd.* ☎ *207/941–4014* ⊕ *www.state.me.us/doc/parks* ⊠ *Free* ☉ *Daily.*

Where to Stay

¢–$ ⊡ **Todd House.** This pre–Revolutionary War home has changed little over the years. Latched plank doors, wood floors, hearth, and a two-sided "good morning" staircase are all original. Antiques and artifacts add to the feeling you've stepped back in time. Two parlors downstairs have been converted into guest rooms with a shared bath. ⊠ *1 Capen Ave., 04631* ☎ *207/853–2328* ⮡ *6 rooms, 2 with bath* ⚇ *Some kitchenettes, cable TV; no a/c, no room phones, no smoking* ⊟ *No credit cards* ⦁○⦁ *CP.*

Sports & the Outdoors

Operated by a family that's plied local waters for five generations, **Eastport Windjammers/Harris Whale Watching & Fishing** (⊠ 104 Water St. ☎ 207/853–2500 or 207/853–4303 ⊕ www.eastportwindjammers.com) offers whale-watching and sunset cruises on the 50-passenger *Sylvina W. Beal.* Deep-sea fishing trips are available on the 35-passenger *Quoddy Dam.* The newly launched *Halie & Matthew* takes up to 30 passengers on overnight cruises.

Shopping

Joe's Basket Shop (⊠ Rte. 190, Pleasant Point ☎ 207/853–2840) has fancy and coarse baskets and other items made by members of the Passamaquoddy tribe. **Quoddy Wigwam** (⊠ U.S. 1, Perry ☎ 207/853–4812) sells handcrafted moccasins and other Native American crafts.

Grand Lake Stream

⑤ *50 mi northwest of Eastport, 108 mi east of Bangor.*

This tiny community, on Grand Lake Stream between West Grand Lake and Big Lake, was once one of the largest tannery centers in the world. Today it's renowned for fishing, especially for landlocked salmon and smallmouth bass. It's also known for the Grand Laker, a square-ended cedar canoe built specifically for use on the often windy lakes in this region. Along the Canadian border, outdoors lovers will find lakes and rivers for swimming, boating, and fishing; trails for hiking; and plenty of places to spot wildlife.

The tiny **Grand Lake Stream Historical Society & Museum** is jam-packed with artifacts from the town's early days. Here you can learn more about the Grand Laker canoes, the town's tannery years, and its fishing heritage. ✉ *10 Brown La.* ☎ *207/796–5562* 🖵 *Free* ⊗ *Mid-May–mid-Sept., Sun. 2–4.*

Where to Stay

$$ 🏠 **Weatherby's.** Nicknamed "the fishermen's resort," Weatherby's is ideal for anglers who want to be in the center of the action. The cottages, each with a fireplace, surround the main lodge. Breakfast and dinner are served in the dining room, and boxed lunches are provided for guests exploring the area. ✉ *112 Millford Rd.* ⌂ *Box 69, 04637* ☎ *207/796–5558* ⊕ *www.weatherbys.com* ➷ *15 cottages* ⚬ *Some pets allowed (fee); no a/c, no room phones, no room TVs* ☰ *D, MC, V* ⊗ *Closed Nov.–Apr.* ❍*FAP.*

$ 🏠 **Leen's Lodge.** Rustic cabins varying in size from one to four bedrooms are nestled on 23 wooded acres on West Grand Lake. All have woodstoves or fireplaces and big windows to take in the views. A country-style breakfast and a hearty, home-style dinner are served in a central lodge, where you'll also find a television, card tables, books, and games. Boat rentals are available. ✉ *368 Bonney Brook Rd.* ⌂ *Box 40, 04637* ☎ *207/796–2929 or 800/995–3367* ⊕ *www.leenslodge.com* ➷ *10 cabins* ⚬ *Some kitchenettes, beach, boating, hiking, recreation room, some pets allowed; no a/c, no room phones, no room TVs* ☰ *AE, MC, V* ⊗ *Closed Nov.–Apr.* ❍ *MAP.*

Sports & the Outdoors

The **Grand Lake Stream Guides Association** (✉ Grand Lake Stream, 04637 ☎ No phone ⊕ www.grandlakestreamguides.com) maintains more than 25 launch sites at area lakes.

Shopping

Shamel Boat & Canoe Works (✉ 42 Tough End Rd. ☎ 207/796–8199) specializes in Grand Laker canoes. Watch the owner make these traditional cedar canoes by hand.

Way Down East A to Z

To research prices, get advice from other travelers, and book travel arrangements, visit www.fodors.com.

BOAT & FERRY TRAVEL

East Coast Ferries provides ferry service between Eastport and Deer Island and Deer Island and Campobello from late June to mid-September. Ferries run on Atlantic time, which is one hour earlier than Eastern time. Bar Harbor Ferry provides passenger service between Bar Harbor and Winter Harbor from mid-May to early October.

🚩 Boat & Ferry Information **Bar Harbor Ferry** ☎ 207/288-2984 ⊕ www.barharborferry. com. **East Coast Ferries** ☎ 506/747-2159 ⊕ www.eastcoastferries.nb.ca.

BUS TRAVEL

West's Coastal Connection provides bus service between Calais and Bangor via Ellsworth, stopping at towns en route on U.S. 1.

🚍 **West's Coastal Connection** ☎ 207/546-2823 or 800/596-2823 ⊕ www. westbusservice.com.

CAR TRAVEL

U.S. 1 is the primary coastal route, with smaller roads leading to towns along the coast. Route 182 between Franklin and Cherryfield, a pleasant inland route, is a Maine Scenic Byway. The Schoodic National Scenic Byway follows U.S. 1 through Sullivan, then turns south on Route 186 on its way to the Schoodic Peninsula. Route 1A shaves several miles off a coastal trip north of Milbridge but bypasses historic Cherryfield. The most direct route to Lubec is Route 189, but Route 191 between East Machias and West Lubec is a scenic coastal drive through Cutler. Coastal U.S. 1 winds its way to Calais, but the quickest route from Bangor is Route 9, known as the "Airline." Route 191 is a scenic route from the Calais area back Down East. From Machias take Route 192 to Route 9.

EMERGENCIES

🚑 Hospitals **Calais Regional Hospital** ⊠ 22 Hospital La., Calais ☎ 207/454-7521. **Down East Community Hospital** ⊠ Court St., Machias ☎ 207/255-3356.

LODGING

Cabins and campgrounds are common Way Down East. Black Duck Properties specializes in rental properties on the Schoodic Peninsula. Hearts of Maine has waterfront listings from Steuben to Eastport, with the largest concentration in the Machias and Jonesport areas. The Maine Campground Association provides information on private campgrounds.

🏠 **Black Duck Properties** ⌖ Box 39, Corea 04624 ☎ 207/963-2689 ⊕ www.blackduck. com. **Hearts of Maine** ⊠ 5 Ocean Whisper Dr., Addison 04606 ☎ 207/483-4396 ⊕ www.heartsofmaine.com. **Maine Campground Association** ☎ 207/782-5874 ⊕ www.campmaine.com.

VISITOR INFORMATION

🏛 **Campobello Island Tourism Association** ⊠ 1977 Rte. 774, Wilson's Beach, New Brunswick E5E1J7 Canada ☎ 506/752-2419. **Eastport Area Chamber of Commerce** ⌖ Box 254, Eastport 04631 ☎ 207/853-4644 ⊕ www.eastport.net. **Grand Lake Stream Chamber of Commerce** ⌖ Box 124, Grand Lake Stream 04637 ⊕ www.grandlakestream.com. **Machias Bay Area Chamber of Commerce** ⊠ 12 E. Main St. ⌖ Box 606, Machias 04654 ☎ 207/255-4402 ⊕ www.machiaschamber.org. **Schoodic Peninsula Chamber of Commerce** ⌖ Box 381, Winter Harbor 04693 ☎ 207/963-7658 ⊕ www.acadia-schoodic. org. **Sunrise County Economic Council** ⌖ Box 679, Machias 04654 ☎ 207/255-0983 ⊕ www.sunrisecounty.org.

WESTERN LAKES & MOUNTAINS

Less than 20 mi northwest of Portland and the coast, the sparsely populated lake and mountain areas of western Maine stretch north along the New Hampshire border to Québec. In winter this is ski country; in summer the woods and waters draw vacationers.

The Sebago–Long Lake region bustles with activity in summer. Harrison and the Waterfords are quieter, Lovell is a dreamy escape, and Kezar

Lake, tucked away in a fold of the White Mountains, has long been a hideaway of the wealthy. Bethel, in the Androscoggin River valley, is a classic New England town, its town common lined with historic homes. The more rural Rangeley Lake area brings long stretches of pine, beech, spruce, and sky—and stylish inns and B&Bs with access to golf, boating, fishing, and hiking. Snow sports, especially snowmobiling, are popular winter pastimes. Carrabassett Valley, just north of Kingfield, is home to Sugarloaf/USA, a major ski resort with a challenging golf course.

Sebago Lake

 17 mi northwest of Portland.

Sebago Lake, which provides all the drinking water for Greater Portland, is Maine's best-known lake after Moosehead (⇨ *see* The North Woods). Many camps and year-round homes surround Sebago, which is popular with water-sports enthusiasts.

At the north end of the lake, the **Songo Lock** (☎ 207/693–6231), which permits the passage of watercraft from Sebago Lake to Long Lake, is the lone surviving lock of the Cumberland and Oxford Canal. Built of wood and masonry, the original lock dates from 1830 and was expanded in 1911; today it sees heavy traffic in summer.

The 1,300-acre **Sebago Lake State Park** on the north shore of the lake provides swimming, picnicking, camping (250 sites), boating, and fishing (salmon and togue). ☒ *11 Park Access Rd., Casco* ☎ *207/693–6613 May–mid-Oct., 207/693–6231 mid-Oct.–Apr.* ⊕ *www.maine.gov/doc/ parks/index.html* ☜ *$4.50* ☼ *Daily 9–8.*

OFF THE BEATEN PATH **SABBATHDAY LAKE SHAKER MUSEUM –** Established in the late 18th century, this is the last active Shaker community in the United States, with fewer than 10 members. Open to view are the 1794 meetinghouse and the ministry shop with rooms of Shaker furniture, folk art, tools, farm implements, and crafts from the 18th to the early 20th century. There is also a small gift shop; alongside the road out front, there are usually vegetables for sale; visitors can pick their own apples in autumn. ☒ *707 Shaker Rd. (Rte. 26, 20 mi north of Portland, 12 mi east of Naples, 8 mi west of Lewiston), New Gloucester* ☎ *207/926–4597* ⊕ *www. shaker.lib.me.us* ☜ *Tour $6.50* ☼ *Memorial Day–Columbus Day, Mon.–Sat. 10–4:30; open early Dec. for Christmas Fair.*

Naples

 32 mi northwest of Portland.

Naples occupies an enviable location between Long and Sebago lakes. On clear days, the view down Long Lake takes in the Presidential Range of the White Mountains, highlighted by often-snowcapped Mt. Washington. The Causeway, which divides Long Lake from Brandy Pond, pulses with activity. Cruise and rental boats sail and motor on the lakes, open-air cafés overflow, and throngs of families parade along the sidewalk edging Long Lake. The town swells with seasonal residents and visitors in summer and all but shuts tight for winter.

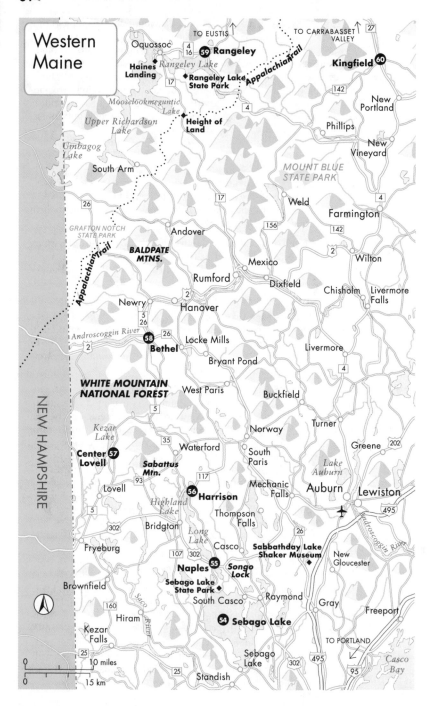

Western Maine

TO EUSTIS ↑

TO CARRABASSET VALLEY ↑ 27

Oquossoc 4 16 **59 Rangeley**

Rangeley Lake

Kingfield 60

Haines Landing

17

♦ Rangeley Lake State Park

Appalachian Trail

142

New Portland

Mooselookmeguntic Lake

Upper Richardson Lake

♦ Height of Land

4

Phillips

New Vineyard

Umbagog Lake

South Arm

MOUNT BLUE STATE PARK

26

Andover

17

156

142

Weld

Farmington

4

GRAFTON NOTCH STATE PARK

BALDPATE MTNS.

Appalachian Trail

Rumford

Mexico

Dixfield

2

Wilton

Chisholm Livermore Falls

Newry

5 26

Hanover

2

58

26

Bethel

Locke Mills

Livermore

Androscoggin River

2

Bryant Pond

4

WHITE MOUNTAIN NATIONAL FOREST

West Paris

Buckfield

5

Turner

Kezar Lake

35

Waterford

Norway

Greene 202

Center 57 Lovell

Sabattus Mtn.

South Paris

Lake Auburn

N
E
W

H
A
M
P
S
H
I
R
E

Lovell

93

117

56 Harrison

Mechanic Falls

Auburn **Lewiston**

Highland Lake

Bridgton

Thompson Falls

26

495

Long Lake

Casco

Androscoggin River

302

Fryeburg

107

302

Naples 55 *Songo Lock*

Sabbathday Lake Shaker Museum ♦

New Gloucester

Brownfield

Sebago Lake State Park ♦

South Casco

Raymond

Gray

Freeport

160

Hiram

Saco River

54 Sebago Lake

TO PORTLAND ↓

Kezar Falls

25

Sebago Lake

302

495

95

Casco Bay

0 —— 10 miles

0 —— 15 km

25

Standish

1

⏱ **Songo River Queen II,** a 92-foot stern-wheeler, takes passengers on hour-long cruises on Long Lake and longer voyages down the Songo River and through Songo Lock. ⊠ *U.S. 302, Naples Causeway* ☎ *207/693–6861* ⊕ *www.songoriverqueen.net* ⊠ *Long Lake cruise $8, Songo River ride $10* ⊘ *July–Labor Day, 5 cruises daily.*

Where to Stay

$$$$ ⌂ **Migis Lodge.** The lodge's pine-paneled cottages, scattered among 100 shorefront acres, have fieldstone fireplaces and are handsomely furnished with braided rugs and handmade quilts. A warm, woodsy feeling pervades the main inn. The deck has views (marvelous at sunset) of Sebago Lake. All kinds of outdoor and indoor activities are included in the room rate, and canoes, kayaks, and sailboats are available. Three fancy meals are served daily in the main dining room. ⊠ *Migis Lodge Rd. off U.S. 302* ⌂ *Box 40, South Casco 04077* ☎ *207/655–4524* ⊠ *207/655–2054* ⊕ *www.migis.com* ⇨ *35 cottages, 6 rooms* ⚹ *Dining room, refrigerators, cable TV, 2 tennis courts, gym, massage, spa, beach, boating, waterskiing, fishing, recreation room, playground, meeting rooms; no a/c in some rooms* ⊟ *No credit cards* ⏇ *FAP.*

$$–$$$$ ⌂ **Augustus Bove House.** Built as the Hotel Naples in the 1820s, this rambling brick B&B sits across from the Naples Causeway and has views down Long Lake. Rooms are furnished with antiques. ⊠ *11 Sebago Rd., 04055* ☎ *207/693–6365 or 888/806–6249* ⊕ *www.naplesmaine.com* ⇨ *5 rooms, 3 suites* ⚹ *Some microwaves, some refrigerators, cable TV, in-room VCRs, Wi-Fi; no smoking* ⊟ *AE, D, MC, V* ⏇ *BP.*

Harrison

⑯ *10 mi north of Naples, 25 mi south of Bethel.*

Harrison anchors the northern end of Long Lake but is less commercial than Naples. The combination of woods, lakes, and views makes it a good choice for leaf-peepers. The nearby towns of North Waterford, South Waterford, and tiny Waterford, a National Historic District, are ideal for outdoors lovers who prefer to get away from the crowds.

Where to Stay

★ $–$$$$ ⌂ **Bear Mountain Inn.** This rambling farmhouse inn has been meticulously decorated in a woodsy theme. The luxurious Great Grizzly Suite has a fireplace, whirlpool bath for two, and mesmerizing views; the cozy Sugar Bear Cottage is a romantic retreat. Breakfast is served in the dining room, which has a fieldstone fireplace and lake views. ⊠ *Rte. 35, South Waterford 04084* ☎ *207/583–4404* ⊠ *207/583–2437* ⊕ *www. bearmtninn.com* ⇨ *8 rooms, 2 suites, 2 cabins* ⚹ *Cable TV, some in-room VCRs, Wi-Fi, beach, boating, fishing, badminton, croquet, horseshoes, volleyball, cross-country skiing, ice-skating, snowmobiling; no kids under 8, no smoking* ⊟ *MC, V* ⏇ *BP.*

$ ⌂ **Harrison House.** When it was built in 1867, this house at the head of Long Lake was one of the most costly and elegant residences in town. Today it charms with featherbeds, quilts, and a porch swing. Most rooms have lake views; all have private baths, but four of the baths are adjacent to or across the hall from the rooms. ⊠ *16 Waterford Rd., 04040*

☎ *207/583–6564* ⊕ *www.harrisonhousebedandbreakfast.com* ➥ *5 rooms* ⚴ *No a/c, no room phones, no room TVs, no smoking* ⊟ *AE, MC, V* ⦾ *BP.*

Center Lovell

⑤⑦ *17 mi northwest of Harrison, 28 mi south of Bethel.*

At Center Lovell you can glimpse the secluded Kezar Lake to the west, the retreat of wealthy and very private people. Sabattus Mountain, which rises behind Center Lovell, has a public hiking trail and stupendous views of the Presidential Range from the summit.

Where to Stay & Eat

¢–$$$$ ✕⬚ **Center Lovell Inn.** The eclectic furnishings blend mid-19th and mid-20th centuries in a pleasing, homey style. The best tables for dining ($$–$$$$) are on the wraparound porch, which has sunset views over Kezar Lake and the White Mountains. Entrées may include pan-seared Muscovy duck, fillet of bison, or fresh swordfish. Rooms are upstairs and in the adjacent Harmon House. ⊠ *Rte. 5* ⚓ *Box 261, 04016* ☎ *207/925–1575 or 800/777–2698* ⊕ *www.centerlovellinn.com* ➥ *9 rooms, 6 with bath; 1 suite* ⚴ *Restaurant; no a/c, no room phones, no room TVs, no smoking* ⊟ *D, MC, V* ⊘ *Closed Nov.–late Dec. and Apr.–mid-May.*

$$$$ ⬚ **Quisisana.** This delightful cottage resort on Kezar Lake makes music a main focus. The staff—students and graduates of the country's finer music schools—perform everything from Broadway tunes to concert-piano pieces throughout your stay. Most of the white clapboard cottages have screened porches, pine-paneled living areas, fireplaces, and simple wicker and country furnishings. For most of the resort's season, a one-week stay beginning Saturday is required. ⊠ *Pleasant Point Rd., 04016* ☎ *207/925–3500* 🖷 *207/925–1004 in season* ⊕ *www.quisisanaresort. com* ➥ *11 rooms in 2 lodges, 32 cottages* ⚴ *Restaurant, 3 tennis courts, boating, waterskiing, Ping-Pong, recreation room; no a/c, no room phones, no room TVs, no smoking* ⊟ *No credit cards* ⊘ *Closed Sept.–mid-June* ⦾ *FAP.*

Sports & the Outdoors

BOATING & **Kezar Lake Marina** (⊠ W. Lovell Rd. at the Narrows, Lovell ☎ 207/925– FISHING 3000 ⊕ www.kezarlake.com) rents boats.

Bethel

⑤⑧ *28 mi north of Lovell, 66 mi north of Portland.*

Bethel is pure New England, a town with white clapboard houses and white-steeple churches and a mountain vista at the end of every street. In winter, this is ski country: Sunday River ski area in Newry is only a few miles north.

A stroll in Bethel should begin at the Bethel Historical Society's **Regional History Center.** The center's campus comprises two buildings, the 1821 O'Neil Robinson House and the 1813 Dr. Moses Mason House; both are listed on the National Register of Historic Places. The Robinson

House has exhibits pertaining to the region's history; the Moses Mason House has nine period rooms and a front hall and stairway wall decorated with murals by Rufus Porter. Pick up materials here for a walking tour of Bethel Hill Village. ⊠ *10–14 Broad St.* ☎ *207/824–2908 or 800/824–2910* ⊕ *www.bethelhistorical.org* ⤳ *$3* ⊙ *O'Neil Robinson House Tues.–Fri. 10–noon and 1–4; July, Aug. and Dec., also weekends 1–4. Dr. Moses Mason House July–Labor Day, Tues.–Sun. 1–4; also by appointment.*

Where to Stay & Eat

$–$$$$ ✕⊡ **L'Auberge.** Built as a barn in the late 1850s, L'Auberge has evolved into a casual inn with a French country accent and one of the area's best restaurants. The inn is on 5 acres just off the Bethel Common. The menu ($$–$$$) changes seasonally but might include hors d'oeuvres such as pâté de campagne or escargots and entrées such as sea bass Provençale or caramelized duck breast. ⊠ *15 L'Auberge La., 04217* ☎ *207/824– 2774 or 800/760–2774* ⊕ *www.laubergecountryinn.com* ⤳ *6 rooms, 1 apartment* ⚘ *Restaurant, babysitting, some pets allowed, Wi-Fi; no a/c, no room phones, no room TVs* ⊟ *AE, D, DC, MC, V* ⍥ *BP.*

$–$$ ✕⊡ **Victoria Inn.** It's hard to miss this turreted inn, with its beige-, mauve-, and teal-painted exterior and attached carriage house topped with a cupola. Inside, Victorian details include ceiling rosettes, stained-glass windows, elaborate fireplace mantels, and gleaming oak trim. Guest rooms vary in size; most are furnished with reproductions of antiques. The restaurant is open to the public for dinner ($$–$$$; closed Monday); choose from entrées such as lobster ravioli and filet mignon. ⊠ *32 Main St.* ⟟ *Box 249, 04217* ☎ *207/824–8060 or 888/774– 1235* ᐱ *207/824–3926* ⊕ *www.thevictoria-inn.com* ⤳ *15 rooms* ⚘ *Restaurant, cable TV, in-room data ports; no smoking* ⊟ *AE, MC, V* ⍥ *BP.*

Sports & the Outdoors

CANOEING **Bethel Outdoor Adventures** (⊠ 121 Mayville Rd. ☎ 207/824–4224) rents canoes, kayaks, bikes, and snowmobiles.

CROSS-COUNTRY SKIING **Bethel Inn Touring Center** (⊠ Village Common ☎ 207/824–6276) has 25 mi of cross-country trails and provides ski and snowshoe rentals and lessons. **Carter's Cross-Country Ski Center** (⊠ 786 Intervale Rd. ☎ 207/ 539–4848) has 31 mi of trails for all levels of skiers; lessons and snowshoe, ski, and sled rentals are provided.

DOGSLEDDING **Mahoosuc Guide Service** (⊠ 1513 Bear River Rd., Newry ☎ 207/824– 2073 ⊕ www.mahoosuc.com) leads day and multiday dogsledding expeditions on the Maine–New Hampshire border, as well as canoeing trips.

HIKING **Telemark Inn & Llama Treks** (⊠ King's Hwy., Mason Township ☎ 207/ 836–2703 ⊕ www.telemarkinn.com) operates one- to six-day llama-supported hiking trips in the White Mountain National Forest.

HORSEBACK RIDING **Sparrowhawk Mountain Ranch** (⊠ 120 Fleming Rd. ☎ 207/836–2528 ⊕ www.maineranch.com) leads one-hour to daylong trail rides and also has an indoor arena.

NATIONAL
FORESTS & PARKS At **Grafton Notch State Park** (⊠ Rte. 26, 14 mi north of Bethel ☏ 207/
824–2912) you can take an easy nature walk to Mother Walker Falls
or Moose Cave and see the spectacular Screw Auger Falls, or you can
hike to the summit of Old Speck Mountain, the state's third-highest peak.
If you have the stamina and the equipment, you can pick up the Appalachian Trail here, hike over Saddleback Mountain, and continue on
to Katahdin. The **Maine Appalachian Trail Club** (⌀ Box 283, Augusta
04330 ⊕ www.matc.org) publishes a map and trail guide.

White Mountain National Forest straddles New Hampshire and Maine.
Although the highest peaks are on the New Hampshire side, the Maine
section has magnificent rugged terrain, camping and picnic areas, and
hiking from hour-long nature loops to a 5½-hour scramble up Speck-
led Mountain. ⊠ *Evans Notch Visitor Center, 18 Mayville Rd., 04217*
☏ *207/824–2134* ⊠ *Parking pass (good 1–7 days) $5* ☺ *Center
Memorial Day–Columbus Day, Tues.–Sat. 8–4:30, rest of year, weekdays 8–4:30.*

SKI AREAS **Sunday River.** What was once a sleepy little ski area with minimal facilities has evolved into a sprawling resort that attracts skiers from as far
away as Europe. Spread throughout the valley are three base areas, two
condominium hotels, trailside condominiums, town houses, and a ski
dorm. Sunday River is home to the Maine Handicapped Skiing program,
which provides lessons and services for skiers with disabilities. There's
plenty else to do in all seasons, including cross-country skiing, ice-skating, tubing, hiking, and mountain biking. ⊠ *Sunday River Rd. off U.S.
2, Newry* ⌀ *Box 450, Bethel 04217* ☏ *207/824–3000, 207/824–5200
snow conditions, 800/543–2754 reservations* ⊕ *www.sundayriver.com.*

SNOWMOBILING **Sun Valley Sports** (⊠ 129 Sunday River Rd. ☏ 207/824–7533 or 877/
851–7533 ⊕ www.sunvalleysports.com) rents snowmobiles and gives
tours. It also operates fly-fishing trips, canoe and kayak rentals, and moose
and wildlife safaris.

**EN
ROUTE** The routes north from Bethel to the Rangeley district are all scenic, particularly in autumn when the maples are aflame with color. In the town
of Newry, make a short detour to the **Artist's Bridge** (turn off Route 26
onto Sunday River Road and drive about 3 mi), the most painted and
photographed of Maine's eight covered bridges. Route 26 continues north
to the gorges and waterfalls of **Grafton Notch State Park.** Past the park,
Route 26 continues to Errol, New Hampshire, where Route 16 will return you east around the north shore of Mooselookmeguntic Lake,
through Oquossoc, and into Rangeley.

A more direct route (if marginally less scenic) from Bethel to Rangeley
still allows a stop in Newry. Follow U.S. 2 north and east from Bethel
to the twin towns of Rumford and Mexico, where Route 17 continues
north to Oquossoc, about an hour's drive. The high point of this route
is **Height of Land,** with its unforgettable views of mountains ranges and
the island-studded blue mass of Mooselookmeguntic Lake. At **Haines
Landing** on Mooselookmeguntic Lake, you can stand at 1,400 feet above
sea level and face the same magnificent scenery you admired at 2,400
feet from Height of Land on Route 17.

Rangeley

1

59 *67 mi north of Bethel.*

Rangeley, north of Rangeley Lake on Route 4 and 16, has long lured anglers and winter-sports enthusiasts to its more than 40 lakes and ponds and 450 square mi of woodlands. Equally popular in summer or winter, Rangeley has a rough, wilderness feel to it. Lodgings are in the woods, around the lake, and along the golf course.

The **Wilhelm Reich Museum** interprets the life and work of controversial physician-scientist Wilhelm Reich (1897–1957), who believed that a force called orgone energy was the source of neurosis. The Orgone Energy Observatory exhibits biographical materials, inventions, and the equipment used in his experiments. Also on view are Reich's library, personal memorabilia, and artwork. Trails lace the 175-acre grounds, and the observatory deck has magnificent views of the countryside. ⊠ *Dodge Pond Rd.* ☎ *207/864–3443* ⊕ *www.wilhelmreichmuseum.org* 💷 *$6* ⊙ *July and Aug., Wed.–Sun. 1–5; Sept., Sun. 1–5.*

Where to Stay & Eat

$$–$$$ ✕ **Gingerbread House.** A big fieldstone fireplace, well-spaced tables, and an antique marble soda fountain, all with views of the woods beyond, make for comfortable surroundings at this gingerbread-trim house, which is open for breakfast, lunch, and dinner. Soups, salads, and sandwiches at lunch give way to entrées such as shrimp scampi, roasted cranberry-maple chicken, and Maine crab cakes. ⊠ *Rtes. 17 and 4, Oquossoc* ☎ *207/864–3602* ⊟ *AE, D, MC, V* ⊙ *Closed Nov. and Apr.; Dec.–Mar., Mon. and Tues.*

$–$$$ ✕🔲 **Country Club Inn.** Built in the 1920s on the Mingo Springs Golf Course, this retreat has a secluded hilltop location and sweeping lake and mountain views. Fieldstone fireplaces anchor both ends of the inn's living room. Rooms downstairs in the main building and in the 1950s motel-style wing are cheerfully if minimally decorated. Inside the glassed-in dining room ($$)—open to nonguests by reservation only—you can dine on such entrées as veal Gruyère and roast duck Montmorency. ⊠ *56 Country Club Rd., 04970* ☎ *207/864–3831* ⊕ *www.countryclubinnrangeley. com* 💷 *19 rooms* ♿ *Restaurant, cable TV, 18-hole golf course, pool, bar, no-smoking rooms; no a/c* ⊟ *AE, MC, V* ⊙ *Closed Nov. and Apr.* ⅠⓄⅠ *BP, MAP.*

$–$$ ✕🔲 **Rangeley Inn and Motor Lodge.** From Main Street you see only the three-story blue inn building (circa 1907), but behind it is a motel wing with views of Haley Pond, a lawn, and a garden. Some of the inn's sizable rooms have iron-and-brass beds and subdued wallpaper, some have claw-foot tubs, and others have whirlpool tubs. The dining room ($$$–$$$$) has continental-style choices, including chicken in creamy champagne sauce and filet mignon; the tavern serves casual fare such as soups, sandwiches, steaks, and ribs. ⊠ *2443 Main St.* ⌂ *Box 160, 04970* ☎ *207/864–3341 or 800/666–3687* 🖷 *207/864–3634* ⊕ *www. rangeleyinn.com* 💷 *36 inn rooms, 15 motel rooms* ♿ *Restaurant, some microwaves, some refrigerators, cable TV, bar, meeting rooms, some pets allowed (fee); no a/c in some rooms* ⊟ *AE, D, MC, V.*

$$ ⊞ **Grant's Kennebago Camps.** People have been roughing it in comfort at this traditional sporting camp on Kennebago Lake for more than 100 years, lured by the mountain views, excellent fly-fishing, and hearty home-cooked meals. The wilderness setting is nothing less than spectacular. The cabins, whose screened porches overlook the lake, have wood-stoves and are finished in knotty pine. Meals are served in the cheerful waterfront dining room. ⊠ *Off Rte. 16* ⬧ *Box 786, 04970* ☎ *207/864–3608 or 800/633–4815* ⊕ *www.grantscamps.com* ⬦ *18 cabins* ⬧ *Dining room, lake, windsurfing, boating, fishing, mountain bikes, hiking, playground, some pets allowed (fee); no a/c, no room phones, no room TVs* ⊟ *D, MC, V* ⊗ *Closed Oct.–mid-May* ⏧ *FAP.*

Sports & the Outdoors

BOATING & **FISHING** Rangeley and Mooselookmeguntic lakes are good for canoeing, sailing, and motorboating. Several outfits rent equipment and provide guide service if needed. Fishing for brook trout and salmon is at its best in May, June, and September; the Rangeley area is especially popular with fly-fishers.

SKI AREAS **Saddleback Ski & Summer Lake Preserve.** A down-home atmosphere prevails at Saddleback, where the quiet and the absence of crowds, even on holiday weekends, draw return visitors—many of them families. The Appalachian Trail crosses Saddleback's summit ridge. There are 57 trails accessed by five lifts; most are intermediate to novice level. Cross-country skiing is big here as well; there are 25 mi of groomed trails surrounding the mountain and base area. On-site is also a day-care center, ski school, rental and retail shop, and trailside condominium lodging. Hiking is the big sport in warm weather. ⊠ *Saddleback Rd. off Rte. 4* ⬧ *Box 490, 04970* ☎ *207/864–5671, 207/864–3380 snow conditions, 207/864–5364 reservations* ⊕ *www.saddlebackmaine.com.*

STATE PARK On the south shore of Rangeley Lake, **Rangeley Lake State Park** (⊠ Off Rte. 17 ☎ 207/864–3858) has superb lakeside scenery, swimming, picnic tables, a boat ramp, showers, and 50 campsites.

Kingfield

⑥ *33 mi east of Rangeley, 15 mi west of Phillips.*

In the shadows of Mt. Abram and Sugarloaf Mountain, Kingfield has everything a "real" New England town should have: a general store, historic inns, and a white clapboard church. Sugarloaf/USA has golf and tennis in summer.

The **Stanley Museum** houses a collection of original Stanley Steamer cars built by the Stanley twins, Kingfield's most famous natives. ⊠ *40 School St.* ☎ *207/265–2729* ⬧ *$4* ⊗ *May–Oct., Tues.–Sun. 1–4; Nov.–Apr., Tues.–Fri. 1–4.*

Sports & the Outdoors

SKI AREAS **Sugarloaf/USA.** Abundant natural snow, a huge mountain, and the only above-tree-line skiing in the East have made Sugarloaf one of Maine's best-known ski areas. Two slope-side hotels and hundreds of slope-side condominiums provide ski-in, ski-out access, and the base village has restaurants and shops. The Outdoor Center has over 60 mi of cross-country ski trails as well as snowshoeing, snow tubing, and ice-skating activities; there's also plenty for the kids, from day care to special events. Once you are here, a car is unnecessary—a shuttle connects all mountain operations. Summer is much quieter than winter, but you can bike, hike, golf at the superb 18-hole, Robert Trent Jones Jr.–designed golf course, and fish. ✉ *5092 Access Rd., Carrabassett Valley 04947* ☎ *207/ 237–2000, 207/237–6808 snow conditions, 800/843–5623 reservations* ⊕ *www.sugarloaf.com.*

Western Lakes & Mountains A to Z

To research prices, get advice from other travelers, and book travel arrangements, visit www.fodors.com.

AIR TRAVEL

Lake Region Air provides access to remote areas, scenic flights, and charter-fishing trips.

🛈 Airlines & Contacts **Lake Region Air** ✉ Rangeley ☎ 207/864–5307.

CAR TRAVEL

A car is essential to tour the western lakes and mountains. To travel from town to town in the order described in this section, drive U.S. 302 to Naples, then Route 35 to Harrison and the Waterfords. Take the Sweden Road, an ideal pick for autumn due to its vistas of the White Mountains, across to Lovell and pick up Route 5 to Bethel. From there, take Route 26 to U.S. 2 to Route 17 to Oquossoc, then head east on Route 16 through Rangeley to Kingfield.

EMERGENCIES

🛈 Hospitals **Bethel Family Health Center** ✉ 32 Railroad St., Bethel ☎ 207/824–2193 or 800/287–2292. **Bridgton Hospital** ✉ 10 Hospital Dr., Bridgton ☎ 207/647–6000. **Mt. Abraham Regional Health Center** ✉ 25 Depot St., Kingfield ☎ 207/265–4555. **Rangeley Regional Health Center** ✉ 42 Dallas Hill Rd., Rangeley ☎ 207/864–3303.

LODGING

Krainin Real Estate specializes in lakefront rentals in the Sebago area. Morton & Furbish has extensive rental listings in the Rangeley Lakes region. For reservations at Sugarloaf/USA, contact Sugarloaf Area Reservations Service. Bethel's Chamber of Commerce has a reservations service.

🛈 **Bethel's Chamber of Commerce Reservation Service** ☎ 207/824–3585 or 800/442–5826 ⊕ www.bethelmaine.com. **Krainin Real Estate** ✉ Rte. 302, Naples ☎ 207/693–5000 or 800/682–0963 ⊕ www.krainin.com. **Morton & Furbish** ✉ Rangeley ☎ 207/ 864–5777 or 888/218–4882 ⊕ www.rangeleyrentals.com. **Sugarloaf Area Reservations Service** ☎ 207/235–2100 or 800/843–2732.

SPORTS & THE OUTDOORS

SKIING   Sunday River and Sugarloaf/USA are the state's largest alpine areas. Family-friendly Mt. Abram also has night skiing. Saddleback delivers a back-to-basics ski experience. You can cross-country ski at Nordic centers with groomed trails or go on a backcountry excursion. For information on cross-country ski centers, shops, and lodging packages, contact the Maine Nordic Ski Council. For information on alpine skiing, contact Ski Maine.

🎿 **Maine Nordic Ski Council** ⬠ Box 645, Bethel 04217 ☎ 207/824–3694 ⊕ www.mnsc. com. **Ski Maine** ⬠ Box 7566, Portland 04112 ☎ 207/622–6983 or 207/761–3774, 888/624–6345 snow conditions ⊕ www.skimaine.com.

VISITOR INFORMATION

🎿 **Bethel Area Chamber of Commerce** ✉ 8 Station Pl. ⬠ Box 1247, Bethel 04217 ☎ 207/824–2282 ⊕ www.bethelmaine.com. **Greater Bridgton–Lakes Region Chamber of Commerce** ✉ U.S. 302 ⬠ Box 236, Bridgton 04009 ☎ 207/647–3472 ⊕ www.mainelakeschamber.com. **Greater Windham Chamber of Commerce** ✉ U.S. 302 ⬠ Box 1015, Windham 04062 ☎ 207/892–8265 ⊕ www.windhamchamber.sebagolake.org. **Maine Tourism Association Welcome Center** ✉ U.S. 2 ⬠ Box 1084, Bethel 04217 ☎ 207/824–4582. **Rangeley Lakes Region Chamber of Commerce** ✉ Main St. ⬠ Box 317, Rangeley 04970 ☎ 207/864–5571 or 800/685–2537 ⊕ www.rangeleymaine.com. **Sugarloaf Area Chamber of Commerce** ⬠ R.R. 1, Box 2151, Kingfield 04947 ☎ 207/235–2100.

THE NORTH WOODS

Maine's North Woods, the vast area in the north-central section of the state, is best experienced by canoe or raft, on a hiking trip, or on a fishing trip. Some great theaters for these activities are Moosehead Lake, Baxter State Park, and the Allagash Wilderness Waterway—as well as the summer resort town of Greenville. Maine's largest lake, Moosehead supplies more in the way of rustic camps, guides, and outfitters than any other northern locale. Its 420 mi of shorefront, three-quarters of which is owned by paper manufacturers, is virtually uninhabited.

Greenville

61 *160 mi northeast of Portland, 71 mi northwest of Bangor.*

Greenville, the largest town on Moosehead Lake, is an outdoors lover's paradise. Boating, fishing, and hiking are popular in summer; snowmobiling and skiing in winter. The town has the greatest selection of shops, restaurants, and inns in the region, though many of these are closed mid-October–mid-June.

The **Moosehead Historical Society** leads guided tours of the Eveleth-Crafts-Sheridan House, a late-19th-century Victorian mansion filled with period antiques. Special exhibits and displays change annually. A small lumberman's museum and a fine exhibit of Native American artifacts dating from 9,000 BC to the 1700s are in the Carriage House. ✉ *444 Pritham Ave.* ☎ *207/695–2909* ⊕ *www.mooseheadhistory.org* 🎫 *$4* ⊙ *Mid-June–Sept., Wed.–Fri. 1–4.*

The Moosehead Marine Museum runs three-, five-, and eight-hour trips

★ on Moosehead Lake aboard the **Katahdin,** a 115-foot 1914 steamship (now diesel). Also called *The Kate,* the ship carried passengers to Kineo until 1942 and then was used in the logging industry until 1975. The trips range in price from $30 to $45. ✉ *12 Lily Bay Rd.* ☞ *(boarding*

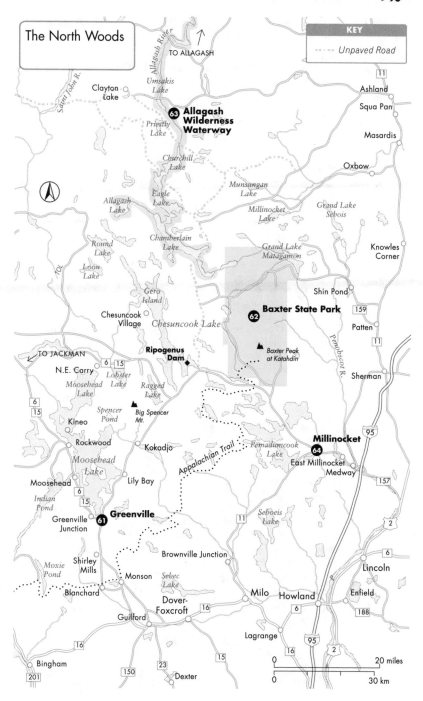

The North Woods

KEY
----- *Unpaved Road*

Saint John R.

Clayton Lake

Umsakis Lake

Ashland

11

Squa Pan

Masardis

53 **Allagash Wilderness Waterway**

Priestly Lake

Oxbow

Churchill Lake

Munsungan Lake

Grand Lake Seboeis

Knowles Corner

Eagle Lake

Allagash Lake

Millinocket Lake

Chamberlain Lake

Grand Lake Matagamon

Shin Pond

159

Round Lake

Gero Island

62 **Baxter State Park**

Patten

Loon Lake

Chesuncook Village

Chesuncook Lake

11

TOL

TO JACKMAN

6 15

N.E. Carry

Ripogenus Dam

Baxter Peak at Katahdin

Penobscot R.

Sherman

95

Moosehead Lake

Lobster Lake

Ragged Lake

6 15

Spencer Pond

Big Spencer Mt.

Kineo

Kokadjo

Pemadumcook Lake

Millinocket

64

Rockwood

East Millinocket

Medway

Moosehead Lake

Appalachian Trail

157

Moosehead

Lily Bay

6 15

Indian Pond

Seboeis Lake

Greenville Junction

61 **Greenville**

11

2

Brownville Junction

Lincoln

Moxie Pond

Shirley Mills

Monson

Sebec Lake

Enfield

Blanchard

Dover-Foxcroft

Milo

Howland

188

Guilford

16

16

95

201

Bingham

150

23

Dexter

Lagrange

16

2

0   20 miles

0   30 km

on shoreline by museum) ☎ *207/695–2716* ⊕ *www.katahdincruises. com* ☉ *Memorial Day–Columbus Day.*

MT. KINEO – Once a thriving summer resort, the original Mount Kineo Hotel (built in 1830 and torn down in the 1940s) was accessed primarily by steamship. Today Kineo makes a pleasant day trip. You can take the Kineo Shuttle, which departs from the State Dock in **Rockwood,** or rent a motorboat in Rockwood and make the journey across the lake in about 15 minutes. You can hike to Kineo's summit for awesome views down the lake. A map is available at the Moosehead Area Chamber of Commerce.

Where to Stay & Eat

★ **$$$$** ✕⌂ **Blair Hill Inn.** Beautiful gardens and a hilltop location with marvelous views over the lake distinguish this 1891 estate. Guest rooms are spacious, and four have fireplaces. A restaurant, open to the public by reservation, serves a five-course dinner ($$$$) from late May to mid-October on Friday and Saturday nights. Arrive early to enjoy cocktails on the wraparound porch. The inn hosts a music series from June through September and cooking school weekends in the off-season. ⊠ *351 Lily Bay Rd.* ⌖ *Box 1288, 04441* ☎ *207/695–0224* 🖷 *207/695–4324* ⊕ *www. blairhill.com* ↯ *6 rooms, 2 suites* ⌂ *Restaurant, cable TV, gym, outdoor hot tub; no a/c, no room phones, no kids under 10, no smoking* ⊟ *D, MC, V* ⍾⊙⍾ *BP.*

$$$ ⌂ **Little Lyford Pond Camps.** When you want to get away from everything—electricity, plumbing, phones—this remote and rustic wilderness retreat with llamas and sheep, dogs, and chickens casts a magical spell. Gulf Hagas is a half-day hike, moose are abundant, and the fly-fishing is excellent. Cabins have woodstoves, gas lanterns, and small libraries. The home-cooked fare is vegetarian oriented with some fish and poultry. Winter access is by cross-country ski. ⌖ *Box 340, 04441* ☎ *603/466–2727* ⊕ *www.outdoors.org/lodging* ↯ *9 cottages* ⌂ *Ponds, sauna, boating, fishing, hiking, cross-country skiing, some pets allowed (fee); no a/c, no room phones, no room TVs, no smoking* ⊟ *No credit cards* ☉ *Closed Apr. and Nov.–early Dec.* ⍾⊙⍾ *FAP.*

Sports & the Outdoors

Beaver Cove Marina (☎ 207/695–3526) rents boats and snowmobiles. **Big Lake Marina** (☎ 207/695–4487) is a full-service marina with boat rentals. **Moose Country Safaris and Dogsled Trips** (☎ 207/876–4907) leads moose safaris, dogsled trips, and canoe and kayak trips. **Northwoods Outfitters** (☎ 207/695–3288) outfits a variety of sports and offers tours, moose safaris, dogsledding, and trail advice.

FISHING   Togue, landlocked salmon, and brook and lake trout lure thousands of anglers to the region from ice-out in mid-May until September; the hardiest return in winter to ice fish. Call for current **information** (☎ 207/ 695–3756).

RAFTING   The Kennebec and Dead rivers and the west branch of the Penobscot River provide thrilling white-water rafting (guides are strongly recommended). These rivers are dam-controlled, so trips run rain or shine daily from May to October (day and multiday trips are conducted). Many rafting outfitters operate resort facilities in their base towns. **Raft Maine** (☎ 800/723–8633 ⊕ www.raftmaine.com) has lodging and rafting packages and information about outfitters.

SKI AREA   **Big Squaw Mountain Resort.** At this remote but pretty resort overlooking Moosehead Lake, the emphasis is on affordable family skiing—prices are downright cheap compared with those at other in-state areas. The 33 trails are mainly intermediate to novice. There's on-site lodging and food, as well as child care. ⊠ *Rte. 6/15* ⌂ *Box D, 04441* ☎ *207/695–1000* ⊕ *www.bigsquawmountain.com.*

STATE PARK   **Lily Bay State Park** (⊠ Lily Bay Rd. ☎ 207/695–2700), 8 mi northeast of Greenville, has a good swimming beach, two boat-launching ramps, and two campgrounds with 91 sites.

Baxter State Park

★ ⑥ *24 mi northwest of Millinocket.*

Baxter, a gift from Governor Percival Baxter, is the jewel in the crown of northern Maine, a 204,733-acre wilderness area that surrounds Katahdin, Maine's highest mountain (5,267 feet at Baxter Peak) and the terminus of the Appalachian Trail. Day-use parking areas fill quickly in season; it's best to arrive early, before 8 AM. The park is intersected by more than 180 mi of trails. No pets, domestic animals, oversize vehicles, cell phones, radios, all-terrain vehicles, motorboats, or motorcycles are allowed in the park, and there are no pay phones, gas stations, stores, or running water or electricity. The one visitor center is at Togue Pond, for which Millinocket is the nearest gateway. ⊠ *64 Balsam Dr., Millinocket 04462* ☎ *207/723–5140* ⊕ *www.baxterstateparkauthority. com* ⊠ *$12 per vehicle, free to Maine residents.*

OFF THE
BEATEN
PATH
LUMBERMEN'S MUSEUM – This museum comprises 10 buildings filled with exhibits depicting the history of logging in Maine, including models, dioramas, and equipment. ⊠ *61 Pond Rd. (Rte. 159), 22 mi east of Baxter State Park, Patten* ☎ *207/528–2650* ⊕ *www.lumbermensmuseum. org.* ⊠ *$7* ⊙ *July and Aug., Tues.–Sun. 10–4; Memorial Day–June and Sept.–Columbus Day, Fri.–Sun. 10–4.*

Where to Stay

$ ⛺ **Baxter State Park Authority.** Camping spaces at the 10 campgrounds here can be reserved only by mail or in person. Reservations can be made beginning the first working day in January—some sites are fully booked for midsummer weekends soon after that. The state also maintains primitive backcountry sites. ⊠ *64 Balsam Dr., Millinocket 04462* ☎ *207/723–5140* ⊕ *www.baxterstateparkauthority.com.*

Sports & the Outdoors

Katahdin, in Baxter State Park, draws thousands of hikers every year for the daylong climb to the summit and the stunning views of woods, mountains, and lakes from the hair-raising Knife Edge Trail along its ridge. The crowds can be formidable on clear summer days, so if you crave solitude, tackle one of the 45 other mountains in the park, 17 of which exceed an elevation of 3,000 feet and all of which are accessible from a 150-mi network of trails. South Turner can be climbed in a morning (if you're fit)—it has a great view of Katahdin across the valley. On the way you'll pass Sandy Stream Pond, where moose are often seen at dusk. The Owl, the Brothers, and Doubletop Mountain are good day hikes.

Allagash Wilderness Waterway

63 *22 mi north of Ripogenus Dam.*

The Allagash is a spectacular 92-mi corridor of lakes and rivers that cuts across 170,000 acres of wilderness, beginning at the northwest corner of Baxter State Park and running north to the town of Allagash, 10 mi from the Canadian border. From mid-May to October, this is prime canoeing (and camping) country, but it should not be undertaken lightly. On the lakes, strong winds can halt your progress for days; on the river, conditions vary greatly with the depth and volume of water, and although the Allagash rapids are ranked Class I and Class II (very easy and easy), the river is not a piece of cake. The complete 92-mi course requires 7 to 10 days. The best bet for a novice is to go with a guide; a good outfitter will help plan your route and provide your craft and transportation. For information, contact the **Allagash Wilderness Waterway** (✉ 106 Hogan Rd., Bangor 04401 ☎ 207/941–4014 ⊕ www.maine.gov/doc/parks/index.html).

Millinocket

64 *19 mi southeast of Baxter State Park, 70 mi north of Bangor, 90 mi northwest of Greenville.*

Millinocket, a paper-mill town with a population of 7,000, is a gateway to Baxter State Park and Maine's North Woods. Although it has a smattering of motels and restaurants, Millinocket is the place to stock up on supplies, fill your gas tank, or grab a hot meal or shower before heading into the wilderness. Numerous rafting and canoeing outfitters and guides are based here.

OFF THE
BEATEN
PATH

GULF HAGAS – From the site of the old Katahdin Iron Works, a hiking trail leads over fairly rugged terrain to Gulf Hagas, with natural chasms, cliffs, a 3½-mi gorge, waterfalls, pools, exotic flora, and rock formations.

Where to Stay

$$ 🏨 **Libby Camps.** Matt Libby, along with his wife, Ellen, represent the fifth generation of Libbys to run this sporting camp on Millinocket Lake, the headwaters of the Allagash and Aroostook rivers. Skylights brighten the well-kept cabins, where handmade quilts cover the beds and woodstoves keep the chill at bay (there's no electricity). The main lodge is open and airy with a magnificent central stone fireplace. Rates include all meals as well as use of sea kayaks, canoes, and sail and motor boats. ✉ Box 810, Ashland 04732 ☎ 207/435–8274 ⊕ www.libbycamps.com ➵ 8 cabins, 12 rustic outpost cabins ⚏ Beach, boating, fishing, hiking; no a/c, no room phones, no room TVs ☰ MC, V ⊗ Closed late Nov.–Apr. ⊙| FAP.

Sports & the Outdoors

Katahdin Outfitters (⊠ Baxter State Park Rd. ☎ 207/723–5700 or 800/862–2663 ⊕ www.katahdinoutfitters.com) outfits canoeing and kayaking expeditions. **New England Outdoor Center** (☎ 207/723–5438 or 800/766–7238 ⊕ www.neoc.com) rents snowmobiles and offers guided trips.

The North Woods A to Z

To research prices, get advice from other travelers, and book travel arrangements, visit www.fodors.com.

AIR TRAVEL

Charter flights, usually by seaplane, from Bangor, Greenville, or Millinocket to smaller towns and remote lake and forest areas can be arranged with a number of flying services, which will transport you and your gear and help you find a guide.

🚹 Airlines & Contacts **Currier's Flying Service** ⊠ Greenville Junction ☎ 207/695–2778. **Folsom's Air Service** ⊠ Greenville ☎ 207/695–2821. **Katahdin Air Service** ⊠ Millinocket ☎ 207/723–8378. **Scotty's Flying Service** ⊠ Shin Pond ☎ 207/528–2626.

CAR TRAVEL

A car is essential to negotiate this vast region but may not be useful to someone spending a vacation entirely at a wilderness camp. Public roads are scarce in the north country, but lumber companies maintain private roads that are often open to the public (sometimes by permit only). When driving on a logging road, always give lumber-company trucks the right of way. Be aware that loggers often take the middle of the road and will neither move over nor slow down for you.

Interstate 95 provides the quickest access to the North Woods. U.S. 201 is the major route to Jackman and to Québec. Route 15 connects Jackman to Greenville and Bangor. The Golden Road is a private, paper company–operated road that links Greenville to Millinocket. Be sure to have a full tank of gas before heading onto the many private roads in the region.

EMERGENCIES

🚹 Hospitals **Charles A. Dean Memorial Hospital** ⊠ Pritham Ave., Greenville ☎ 207/695–5200. **Mayo Regional Hospital** ⊠ 897 W. Main St., Dover-Foxcroft ☎ 207/564–8401. **Millinocket Regional Hospital** ⊠ 200 Somerset St., Millinocket ☎ 207/723–5161.

LODGING

CAMPING   Reservations for state park campsites (excluding Baxter State Park) can be made through the Bureau of Parks and Lands, which can also tell you if you need a camping permit and where to obtain one. Maine Sporting Camp Association publishes a list of its members, with details on the facilities available at each camp.

The Maine Campground Owners Association publishes a helpful annual directory of its members. Maine Tourism Association publishes a listing of private campsites and cottage rentals. North Maine Woods maintains 500 primitive campsites on commercial forest land.

7 **Bureau of Parks and Lands** ⊠ State House Station 22, Augusta 04333 ☎ 207/287–3821, 800/332–1501 in Maine ⊕ www.maine.gov/doc/parks/index.html. **Maine Campground Owners Association** ⊠ 10 Falcon Rd., Lewiston 04240 ☎ 207/782–5874 ⊕ www.campmaine.com. **Maine Sporting Camp Association** ⌂ Box 119, Millinocket 04462 ⊕ www.mainesportingcamps.com. **Maine Tourism Association** ⊠ 327 Water St., Hallowell 04347 ☎ 207/623–0363 or 800/767–8709 ⊕ www.mainetourism.com. **North Maine Woods** ⊠ 92 Main St. ⌂ Box 425, Ashland 04732 ☎ 207/435–6213 ⊕ www.northmainewoods.org.

SPORTS & THE OUTDOORS

BIKING Mountain biking is popular in the Greenville area, but bikes are not allowed on logging roads. Expect to pay $20–$25 for a rental bicycle.

7 **Northwoods Outfitters** ⊠ 5 Lily Bay Rd., Greenville ☎ 207/695–3288 ⊕ www.maineoutfitter.com.

CANOEING Most canoe-rental operations will arrange transportation, help plan your route, and provide a guide. Transport to wilderness lakes can be arranged through the flying services listed under Air Travel.

The Bureau of Parks and Lands (⇨ Lodging) provides information on independent Allagash canoeing and camping. Allagash Canoe Trips operates guided trips on the Allagash Waterway, plus the Moose, Penobscot, and St. John rivers. North Woods Ways is a Maine Master guide service on the state's rivers and lakes.

7 **Allagash Canoe Trips** ⌂ 8 Bigelow, Carrabassett Valley 04947 ☎ 207/237–3077 ⊕ www.allagashcanoetrips.com. **North Woods Ways** ⌂ R.R. 2, Box 159A, Guilford 04443 ☎ 207/997–3723 ⊕ www.northwoodsways.com.

FISHING For information about fishing and licenses, contact the Maine Department of Inland Fisheries and Wildlife. Guides are available through most wilderness camps, sporting goods stores, and canoe outfitters. For assistance in finding a guide, contact Maine Professional Guides Association or North Maine Woods (⇨ Camping).

7 **Maine Department of Inland Fisheries and Wildlife** ⊠ 284 State St., Augusta 04333 ☎ 207/287–8000 ⊕ www.mefishwildlife.com. **Maine Professional Guides Association** ⌂ Box 847, Augusta 04332 ☎ No phone ⊕ www.maineguides.org.

HORSEBACK Northern Main Riding Adventures, owned by registered Maine guides
RIDING Judy Cross-Strehlke and Bob Strehlke, conducts one-day, two-day, and weeklong pack trips (10 people maximum) through parts of Piscataquis County.

7 **Northern Maine Riding Adventures** ⊠ 186 Garland Line Rd., Dover-Foxcroft 04426 ☎ 207/564–3451 ⊕ www.mainetrailrides.com.

RAFTING Raft Maine is an association of white-water outfitters licensed to lead trips down the Kennebec and Dead rivers and the west branch of the Penobscot River. Rafting season begins May 1 and continues through mid-October.

7 **Raft Maine** ☎ 800/723–8633 ⊕ www.raftmaine.com.

VISITOR INFORMATION

7 **Baxter State Park Authority** ⊠ 64 Balsam Dr., Millinocket 04462 ☎ 207/723–5140 ⊕ www.baxterstateparkauthority.com. **Katahdin Area Chamber of Commerce** ⊠ 1029 Central St., Millinocket 04462 ☎ 207/723–4443 ⊕ www.katahdinmaine.com. **Moose-**

head Lake Region Chamber of Commerce ⊙ Box 581 Greenville ☎ 207/695–2702 or 888/876–2778 ⊕ www.mooseheadlake.org.

MAINE A TO Z

To research prices, get advice from other travelers, and book travel arrangements, visit www.fodors.com.

AIR TRAVEL

Regional flying services, operating from regional and municipal airports, provide access to remote lakes and wilderness areas as well as to Penobscot Bay islands.

AIRPORTS

The two primary airports serving the Maine coast area are Portland International and Bangor International. Logan International in Boston is the closest major international airport; Boston is about 65 mi (three hours' driving time) from the southern end of the Maine coast. Manchester Airport, in New Hampshire, is only 45 mi from the beginning of the Maine coast and is becoming an increasingly popular airport because of the number of discount airlines, such as Southwest, that fly there.

🚺 Airport Information **Bangor International (BGR)** ⊠ 287 Godfrey Blvd., Bangor ☎ 207/992–4600 ⊕ www.flybangor.com. **Logan International (BOS)** ⊠ 600 Tower Rd., East Boston, MA ☎ 800/235–6426 ⊕ www.massport.com/logan. **Manchester** ⊠ 1 Airport Rd., Manchester, NH ☎ 603/624–6539 ⊕ www.flymanchester.com. **Portland International (PWM)** ⊠ 1001 Westbrook St., Portland ☎ 207/774–7301 ⊕ www. portlandjetport.org.

BIKE TRAVEL

For information on bicycling in Maine and a list of companies operating tours, contact the Bicycle Coalition of Maine. The Maine Department of Transportation Web site has information on bike tours.

🚺 Bike Information **Bicycle Coalition of Maine** ⊙ Box 5275, Augusta 04332 ☎ 207/ 623–4511 ⊕ www.bikemaine.org. **Maine Department of Transportation Bike and Pedestrian Section** ⊕ www.exploremaine.org/bike/bike_tours.html.

BUS TRAVEL

Concord Trailways operates a luxury bus service (including snacks, drinks, and an "in-flight" movie) that travels the length of the coast from Orono (not far from Bangor) to Logan International Airport in Boston, stopping in every major town along the way. Greyhound and Vermont Transit Lines also operate bus services from the bus terminal in Bangor.

🚺 **Concord Trailways** ☎ 207/945–4000 or 800/639–3317 ⊕ www.concordtrailways.com. **Greyhound** ☎ 207/945–3000. **Vermont Transit Lines** ☎ 800/552–8737 ⊕ www. vermonttransit.com.

CAR TRAVEL

Interstate 95 is the fastest route to and through the state from coastal New Hampshire and points south; it turns inland at Brunswick and goes on to Bangor and the Canadian border. U.S. 1, more leisurely and scenic, is the principal coastal highway from New Hampshire to Canada.

The speed limit on major highways is 65 mph. The speed limit on secondary roads is 35 to 50 mph. Maine has zero tolerance for driving under the influence of alcohol—the legal limit is .08—and penalties are severe.

LODGING

APARTMENT & HOUSE RENTALS Seasonal apartments and houses for rent are common along the coast of Maine, but they are also popular and expensive. You can find out about them by picking up one of the local weekly newspapers or by contacting a real estate agent. The following are some of the best property rental agencies along the coast.

🖪 **Local Agents** All of Maine coast: **A1 Vacations** ⊕ www.A1vacations.com. **Cottage Connection of Maine** ☎ 800/823-9501 ⊕ www.cottageconnection.com. **Find Vacation Rentals** ⊕ www.findvacationrentals.com. **Great Rentals** ⊕ www.greatrentals.com. **Vacation Rentals by Owner** ⊕ www.vrbo.com.

Camden area: **Camden Real Estate** ☎ 207/236-6171. **Camden Vacation Rentals** ⊕ www.camdenac.com.

Mid-Coast area: **Jaret and Cohn** ⊕ www.jaretcohn.com.

Mount Desert Island: **Hinckley Real Estate** ☎ 207/244-7011.

BED & BREAKFASTS The B&Bs of Maine offer some of the region's most distinctive lodging. Many are in historic homes, have beautiful views of the ocean, and provide full American-style breakfasts, often with homemade pastries. For more information contact the Maine State Tourism office. For reservations log on to Bed & Breakfast Inns Online.

🖪 **Bed & Breakfast Inns Online** ⊕ www.bbonline.com/me. **Maine Tourism Association** ✉ 327 Water St., Hallowell 04347 ☎ 207/623-0363 or 800/767-8709.

MEDIA

The *Portland Press Herald* is published Monday–Saturday; the *Maine Sunday Telegram* is published on Sunday. The *York County Coast Star* is published weekly. The *Portland Phoenix,* published each Thursday, is an essential free weekly for those interested in Portland's many entertainment and arts offerings. The *Casco Bay Weekly,* free and available on Thursday, publishes local happenings and events as well as features of regional interest. Each major town along Penobscot Bay has its own traditional weekly newspaper (Courier Publications in Rockland owns many of them), but the major daily along the coast is the *Bangor Daily News.* Weekly Bar Harbor regional papers include the *Bar Harbor Times, Ellsworth American, Ellsworth Weekly,* and the *Islander.*

Portland Magazine and the bimonthly *Port City Life* cover Portland, whereas the *Maine Times* extends throughout the state.

SPORTS & THE OUTDOORS

BIRDING The Maine Audubon Society provides information on birding in Maine and hosts field trips for novice to expert birders.

🖪 **Maine Audubon Society** ✉ 20 Gilsland Farm Rd., Falmouth 04105 ☎ 207/781-6180 ⊕ www.maineaudubon.org.

FISHING For information about fishing and licenses, contact the Maine Department of Inland Fisheries and Wildlife. The Maine Professional Guides

Association maintains and mails out listings of its members and their specialties.

🛈 **Maine Department of Inland Fisheries and Wildlife** ✉ 284 State St., Augusta 04333 ☎ 207/287-8000 ⊕ www.mefishwildlife.com. **Maine Professional Guides Association** ☎ Box 847, Augusta 04332 ☎ No phone ⊕ www.maineguides.org.

KAYAKING The Maine Professional Guides Association represents kayaking guides.

🛈 **Maine Professional Guides Association** ☎ Box 847, Augusta 04332 ☎ No phone ⊕ www.maineguides.org.

RAFTING Raft Maine provides information on white-water rafting on the Kennebec, Penobscot, and Dead rivers.

🛈 **Raft Maine** ☎ Box 3, Bethel 04217 ☎ 800/723-8633 ⊕ www.raftmaine.com.

SKIING For information on alpine skiing, contact Ski Maine. For information on cross-country ski centers, shops, and lodging packages, contact the Maine Nordic Ski Council.

🛈 **Maine Nordic Ski Council** ☎ Box 645, Bethel 04217 ☎ 207/824-3694 or 800/754-9263 ⊕ www.mnsc.com. **Ski Maine** ☎ Box 7566, Portland 04112 ☎ 207/622-6983, 207/761-3774, 888/624-6345 snow conditions ⊕ www.skimaine.com.

SNOWMOBILING The Maine Snowmobile Association distributes an excellent statewide trail map of about 8,000 mi of trails.

🛈 **Maine Snowmobile Association** ☎ Box 77, Augusta 04332 ☎ 207/622-6983 ⊕ www.mesnow.com.

TRAIN TRAVEL

Amtrak's *Downeaster* connects Portland with Boston. The train makes four runs to and from Boston each day and makes seven stops along the way, with stops in Wells and Saco and a seasonal stop in Old Orchard Beach.

🛈 Train Information **Amtrak** ☎ 800/872-7245 ⊕ www.amtrak.com.

VISITOR INFORMATION

Contact the Maine Tourism Association for additional information about the state.

🛈 **Maine Tourism Association** ✉ 327 Water St., Hallowell 04347 ☎ 207/623-0363 or 800/767-8709.

New Hampshire

WORD OF MOUTH

"One of the most fantastic views of Lake Winnipesaukee can be had from the rocky flat top of Mt. Major. The summit is wide, flat, and offers panoramic views of the entire Lakes Region. This climb is especially stunning during the fall foliage season."

—clarkgriswold

"Definitely see the White Mountain area of N.H. b-e-a-u-t-i-f-u-l."

—aprilkrueg

"Littleton is a classic New England small town. There is a row of shops along main street, the classic church and steeple, and an angry little mountain river rushing along through town."

—Person_X

By Andrew
Collins

CRUSTY, AUTONOMOUS NEW HAMPSHIRE is often defined more by what it is not than by what it is. It lacks Vermont's folksy charm, and its coast isn't nearly as grand as that of Maine. Its politics tend toward conservative (with a distinctly libertarian slant), unlike the decidedly more liberal Massachusetts. It was the first colony to declare independence from Great Britain, the first to adopt a state constitution, and the first to require that constitution to be referred to the people for approval.

From the start, New Hampshire residents took their hard-won freedoms seriously. Twenty years after the Revolutionary War's Battle of Bennington, New Hampshire native General John Stark, who led the troops to that crucial victory, wrote a letter to be read at the reunion he was too ill to attend. In it, he reminded his men, "Live free or die; death is not the worst of evils." The first half of that sentiment is now the Granite State's motto. Nothing symbolizes those freedoms more than voting, not only for government officials but also on issues during an annual town meeting. And residents truly relish their role as host of the nation's earliest presidential primary.

New Hampshire's independent spirit, mountain peaks, clear air, and sparkling lakes have attracted trailblazers and artists for centuries. The first hiker to reach the top of Mt. Washington was Darby Field, in 1642. The first summer home appeared on one of the state's many lakes in 1763. Ralph Waldo Emerson, Henry David Thoreau, Nathaniel Hawthorne, and Louisa May Alcott all visited and wrote about the state, sparking a strong literary tradition that continues today. Filmmaker Ken Burns, writer J. D. Salinger, and poet Donald Hall all make their homes here.

Portsmouth has several theater groups, both cutting-edge and mainstream, and Tamworth's Barnstormers is the oldest professional summer stock theater in the country. Shops throughout the state often display the work of local artisans. On back roads and in small towns, you can find makers of fine furniture, glassblowers, potters, weavers, and woodworkers.

The state's diverse terrain makes it popular with everyone from avid adventurers to young families looking for easy access to nature. You can hike, climb, ski, snowboard, snowshoe, and fish as well as explore on snowmobiles, sailboats, and mountain bikes. Natives have no objection to others enjoying the state's beauty as long as they leave some money behind. New Hampshire has long resisted both sales and income taxes, so tourism brings in much-needed revenue.

With a few of its cities consistently rated among the most livable in the nation, New Hampshire has seen considerable growth over the past decade or two. Longtime residents worry that the state will soon take on two personalities: one of rapidly growing cities to the southeast and the other of quiet villages to the west and north. Although the influx of newcomers has brought change, the independent nature of the people and the state's natural beauty remain constant.

Exploring New Hampshire

The main attractions of southern New Hampshire's coast are historical Portsmouth and bustling Hampton Beach; several somewhat quieter communities such as Durham and Exeter are a bit farther inland. The east-central Lakes Region has good hiking trails, antiques shops, and, of course, water sports. To hike, ski, and photograph vibrant foliage, head to the north's White Mountains. The southwest is hemmed in to the east by the central Merrimack Valley, which has a string of fast-growing communities along Interstate 93 and U.S. 3.

Numbers in the text and in the margin correspond to numbers on the maps: New Hampshire Coast, New Hampshire Lakes, The White Mountains, Dartmouth–Lake Sunapee, and Monadnock Region and Central New Hampshire.

About the Restaurants

New Hampshire prides itself on seafood—not just lobster but also salmon pie, steamed mussels, fried clams, and seared tuna. Across the state you'll find country taverns with upscale continental and American menus, many of them embracing regional ingredients and cutting-edge preparations. Alongside a growing number of contemporary eateries are such state traditions as greasy-spoon diners, pizzerias, and pubs that serve hearty comfort fare.

	WHAT IT COSTS				
	$$$$	**$$$**	**$$**	**$**	**¢**
AT DINNER	over $28	$21–$28	$13–$20	$8–$12	under $8

Prices are per person, for a main course at dinner.

About the Hotels

In the mid-19th century, wealthy Bostonians retreated to imposing New Hampshire country homes in summer months. Many of these houses have been converted into inns. The smallest have only a couple of rooms and are typically done in period style. The largest contain 30 or more rooms and have in-room fireplaces and even hot tubs. Amenities increase each year at some of these inns, which, along with bed-and-breakfasts, dominate New Hampshire's lodging scene. You'll also find a great many well-kept, often family-owned motor lodges—particularly in the White Mountains and Lakes regions. A few of the grand old resorts still stand, with their world-class cooking staffs and tradition of top-notch service. In the Merrimack River valley, as well as along major highways, chain hotels and motels prevail.

	WHAT IT COSTS				
	$$$$	**$$$**	**$$**	**$**	**¢**
FOR 2 PEOPLE	over $220	$171–$220	$121–$170	$80–$120	under $80

Prices are for a standard double room during peak season and not including tax or gratuities. Some inns add a 15% service charge.

Timing

In summer, people flock to seaside beaches, mountain trails, and lake boat ramps. In the cities, festivals showcase music, theater, and crafts.

GREAT ITINERARIES

Some people come to New Hampshire to hike or ski the mountains, fish and sail the lakes, or cycle along the back roads. Others prefer to drive through scenic towns, visiting museums and shops. Although New Hampshire is a small state, roads curve around lakes and mountains, making distances longer than they appear. You can get a taste of the coast, lake, and mountain areas in three to five days; eight days gives you time to make a comprehensive loop.

IF YOU HAVE 3 DAYS

Drive along Route 1A to see the coast or take a boat tour of the Isles of Shoals before exploring 🔲 **Portsmouth** 1. The next day visit 🔲 **Wolfeboro** 7, on the eastern edge of Lake Winnipesaukee, good for an overnight stop. The following morning drive across the scenic **Kancamagus Highway** 28 (Route 112) from Conway to **Lincoln** 18 to see the granite ledges and sparkling streams of the White Mountains.

IF YOU HAVE 5 DAYS

After visiting 🔲 **Portsmouth** 1 and 🔲 **Wolfeboro** 7, explore Squam and Ossipee lakes and the charming towns near them: **Holderness** 14, **Center Sandwich** 15, and **Tamworth** 16. Spend your third night in the White Mountains town of 🔲 **Jackson** 24. After crossing the **Kancamagus Highway** 28 (Route 112) to **Lincoln** 18, tour the western part of the White Mountain National Forest via Route 112 to Route 118. Take Route 25A and then Route 10 south through the upper Connecticut River valley to 🔲 **Hanover** 31,

home of Dartmouth College, for an overnight. Follow Interstate 89 back by way of **Newbury** 30 and the Lake Sunapee region.

IF YOU HAVE 8 DAYS

Spend your first two nights in 🔲 **Portsmouth** 1, allowing a chance to visit Strawbery Banke Museum and soak up the city's history as well as explore the short, scenic shoreline. Then follow the five-day itinerary above as far as 🔲 **Hanover** 31. From here, visit the Shaker Community at **Enfield,** then take either Route 12A along the Connecticut River or Route 10 south to 🔲 **Keene** 40. Route 119 leads east to Rhododendron State Park in 🔲 **Fitzwilliam.**

2

Fall brings leaf-peepers, especially to the White Mountains and along the Kancamagus Highway (Route 112). Skiers take to the slopes in winter, when Christmas lights and carnivals brighten the long, dark nights. Spring's unpredictable weather—along with April's mud and late May's black flies—tends to deter visitors. Still, the season has its joys, not the least of which is the appearance of the state flower, the purple lilac, from mid-May to early June.

THE COAST

New Hampshire's 18-mi stretch of coastline packs in a wealth of scenery and diversions. The honky-tonk of Hampton Beach gets plenty of attention, good and bad, but first-timers are often surprised by the significant chunk of shoreline that remains pristine—especially through the town of Rye. This tour begins in the regional hub, Portsmouth; cuts down the coast to the beaches; branches inland to the quintessential prep-school town of Exeter; and then runs back up north through Dover, Durham (home of the University of New Hampshire), and Rochester. From here it's a short drive to the Lakes Region.

Portsmouth

★ ❶ *47 mi southeast of Concord; 50 mi southwest of Portland, Maine; 56 mi north of Boston.*

Settled in 1623 as Strawbery Banke, Portsmouth became a prosperous port before the Revolutionary War, and like similarly wealthy Newport, Rhode Island, it harbored many Tory sympathizers throughout the campaign. Filled with grand residential architecture spanning the 18th through early 20th century, this city of 23,000 has numerous house-museums, including the collection of buildings that make up the Strawbery Banke Museum. With hip eateries, quirky shops, swank cocktail bars, respected theaters, and jumping live-music venues, this sheltered harbor city is a hot destination. Downtown, especially around elegant Market Square, buzzes with conviviality.

The **Portsmouth Harbour Trail** passes more than 70 18th- and 19th-century structures downtown, through the South End, and along State and Congress streets. You can purchase a tour map ($2.50) at the information kiosk in Market Square, at the chamber of commerce, and at several house-museums. Guided walks are conducted late spring to early fall ☎ *603/436–3988 for guided tour* ⊕ *www.seacoastnh.com/harbourtrail* ✉ *$8 for guided tour* ☉ *Early July–mid-Oct., Thurs.–Mon.*

The **Portsmouth Black Heritage Trail** (☎ 603/431–2768 ⊕ www.seacoastnh.com/blackhistory) is a self-guided walk that visits sites important to African-American history in Portsmouth. Included are the **New Hampshire Gazette Printing Office,** where skilled slave Primus Fowle operated the paper's printing press for some 50 years beginning in 1756, and the city's 1866 **Election Hall,** outside of which the city's black citizens held annual celebrations of the Emancipation Proclamation.

PLEASURES & PASTIMES

BEACHES & LAKES

New Hampshire makes the most of its 18-mi coastline with several good beaches, among them Hampton Beach and Wallis Sands in Rye. For warmer, fresh waters, head to pristine Lake Winnipesaukee, Lake Sunapee, Squam Lake, and Newfound Lake.

BIKING

A safe, scenic route along New Hampshire's seacoast is the bike path along Route 1A, for which you can park at Odiorne Point and follow the road 14 mi south to Seabrook. (Some bikers begin at Prescott Park in Portsmouth and take Route 1B into New Castle, but beware of the traffic.) Another pretty route is from Newington Town Hall to the Great Bay Estuary. White Mountains routes are detailed in "The White Mountain Ride Guide," sold at area sports and bookshops. There's also a bike path in Franconia Notch State Park at the Lafayette Campground and a mountain-biking center, Great Glen Trails, at the base of Mt. Washington. Many ski areas have lift-serviced mountain biking in summer.

PARKS & FORESTS

The awesome White Mountain National Forest covers 770,000 acres in northern New Hampshire, and Mt. Washington Park crowns the Northeast's highest peak. You can camp, picnic, hike, fish, swim, bike, and ski at numerous other park and recreation areas, including Franconia Notch, Crawford Notch, and Mt. Sunapee. Rhododendron State Park, in Fitzwilliam in the Monadnock region, has a singular collection of wild rhododendrons.

SKIING & SNOW SPORTS

Scandinavian settlers who came to New Hampshire's high, handsome, rugged peaks in the late 1800s brought their skis with them. Skiing got its modern start here in the 1920s with the cutting of trails on Cannon Mountain. You can now ski or snowboard at nearly 20 areas, from the old, established slopes (Cannon, Cranmore, Wildcat) to more contemporary ones (Attitash, Loon, Waterville Valley). Packages assembled by the ski areas allow you to sample different resorts.

SHOPPING

The absence of sales tax makes New Hampshire a hugely popular shopping destination. Outside the outlet meccas of North Conway and Tilton, this pastime revolves around antiques and local crafts, though in the southern Lakes Region and Hampton Beach, tacky souvenirs are the norm.

Summertime fairs, such as the one operated by the League of New Hampshire Craftsmen at Mt. Sunapee State Park, are a good way to see the best arts and crafts. Look for pottery, jewelry, and wooden boxes. Antiques shops appear in clusters along U.S. 4, between Route 125 and Concord; along Route 119, from Fitzwilliam to Hinsdale; along Route 101, from Marlborough to Wilton; and in the towns of North Conway, North Hampton, Hopkinton, Hollis, and Amherst. In the Lakes Region, most shops are along the eastern side of Winnipesaukee, near Wolfeboro. Many stores are in barns and homes along back roads; quite a few are open by chance or by appointment.

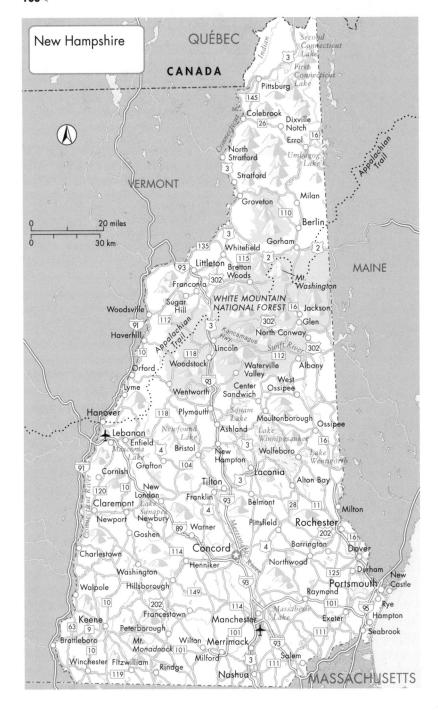

New Hampshire

The **Seacoast Trolley** (✉ Market Sq. ☎ 603/431–6975 ⊕ www.locallink.com/seacoasttrolley) conducts a narrated tour of Portsmouth, Rye, and New Castle, with views of the New Hampshire coastline and area beaches. The 17-mi trip operates from mid-June through Labor Day, departing from Market Square or from 14 locations en route. It costs $5 per person. Portsmouth is also served by the **Downtown Loop Coastal Trolley** (☎ 603/743–5777), which runs late June to early September and gives a narrated tour through downtown and around the waterfront. The whole loop takes about 90 minutes, but you can hop on and off at numerous stops; the fare is 50¢, or $2 for a three-day pass.

One of the questions visitors to Portsmouth ask most frequently is whether they can tour the familiar red tugboats plying the waters of Piscataqua River and Portsmouth Harbor. Unfortunately, the answer is no, but you can get a firsthand look at Portsmouth's working waterfront aboard the **Tug Alley Too** (✉ 2 Ceres St. ☎ 603/430–9556 ⊕ www.tugboatalley.com), a six-passenger replica. The 90-minute tours pass lighthouses, the Portsmouth Naval Shipyard, and Wentworth Marina. Tours are conducted daily from July through September, Monday through Saturday.

The **Isles of Shoals Steamship Company** (✉ Barker Wharf, 315 Market St. ☎ 603/431–5500 or 800/441–4620 ⊕ www.islesofshoals.com) runs a 3-hour Isles of Shoals, lighthouses, and Portsmouth Harbor cruise out of Portsmouth aboard the *Thomas Laighton,* a replica of a Victorian steamship, from April through December (twice daily in summer). Lunch and light snacks are available on board or you can bring your own. There are also fall foliage cruises, narrated sunset cruises visiting five local lighthouses, and special holiday cruises.

Granite State Whale Watch (✉ Rye Harbor State Marina, Rte. 1A, Rye ☎ 603/964–5545 or 800/964–5545 ⊕ www.whales-rye.com) conducts naturalist-led whale-watching tours aboard the 150-passenger M/V *Granite State* out of Rye Harbor State Marina from May to early October, and narrated Isles of Shoals cruises in July and August. From May to October, **Portsmouth Harbor Cruises** (✉ Ceres Street Dock ☎ 603/436–8084 or 800/776–0915 ⊕ www.portsmouthharbor.com) operates tours of Portsmouth Harbor, foliage trips on the Cocheco River, and sunset cruises aboard the M/V *Heritage.*

The yellow, hip-roof **John Paul Jones House** was a boardinghouse when the Revolutionary War hero lived here while supervising shipbuilding for the Continental Navy. The 1758 structure, now the headquarters of the Portsmouth Historical Society, contains furniture, costumes, glass, guns, portraits, and documents from the late 18th century. ✉ *43 Middle St.* ☎ *603/436–8420* ⊕ *www.seacoastnh.com/touring/jpjhouse.html* 📧 *$5* ☉ *June–Oct., daily 10–5.*

The period interior of the **Moffatt-Ladd House,** built in 1763, tells the story of Portsmouth's merchant class through portraits, letters, and fine furnishings. The Colonial-revival garden includes a horse chestnut tree planted by General William Whipple when he returned home after signing the Declaration of Independence in 1776. ✉ *154 Market St.* ☎ *603/436–*

New Hampshire Coast

TO ROCHESTER

6 Dover

MAINE

9

202 108 16

4 202

TO CONCORD

5

Durham 4

125

108

4

16

Newmarket

Great Bay

Portsmouth

New Castle

1

Greenland

♦ **Odiorne Point State Park**

TO MANCHESTER

85 33 1

Rye 2

Wallis Sands State Beach

Stratham

95

Jenness State Beach

Exeter

4

88

Rye Beach

Isles of Shoals

Exeter R.

Winnicut

North Hampton

101

Hampton

1A

108

Hampton Falls

3 Hampton Beach

ATLANTIC OCEAN

111

108

107

Hampton Beach State Park

Country Pond

Seabrook

95 1

MASSACHUSETTS

0 — 10 miles

0 — 15 km

MAINE 95

8221 ⊠ $6, garden and house tour $1 ⊙ Mid-June–mid-Oct., Mon.–Sat. 11–5, Sun. 1–5.

NEED A BREAK? Drop by **Annabelle's Natural Ice Cream** (⊠ 49 Ceres St. ☎ 603/436-3400) for a dish of Ghirardelli chocolate chip or Almond Joy ice cream. **Breaking New Grounds** (⊠ 14 Market Sq. ☎ 603/436-9555) serves coffee, pastries, and gelato.

The first English settlers named the area around today's Portsmouth for the wild strawberries abundant along the shores of the Piscataqua River. ★ The name survives in the **Strawbery Banke Museum**, a 10-acre neighborhood continuously occupied over 300 years and now doing duty as an outdoor history museum, one of the largest in New England. The compound has 46 buildings dating from 1695 to 1820—some restored and furnished to a particular period, some used for exhibits, and some viewed from the outside only—as well as restored or recreated period gardens. Half the interior of the Drisco House, built in 1795, depicts its use as a dry-goods store in Colonial times, whereas the living room and kitchen are decorated as they were in the 1950s, showing how buildings were adapted over time. The Shapiro House has been restored to reflect the life of the Russian Jewish immigrant family who lived in the home in the early 1900s. Perhaps the most opulent house, done in decadent Victorian style, is the 1860 Goodwin Mansion, former home of Governor Ichabod Goodwin. ⊠ *Marcy St.* ☎ *603/433–1100* ⊕ *www. strawberybanke.org* ⌚ *$15* ☉ *May–Oct., daily 10–5; Feb.–Apr., Nov., and Dec., Wed.–Sat. 10–2.*

The murals lining the hall staircase of the 1716 **Warner House** might be the oldest-known murals still in their original place in the United States. The house itself is a noted example of Georgian architecture, with 18-inch-thick brick walls. The west-wall lightning rod is believed to have been installed in 1762 under the supervision of Benjamin Franklin. ⊠ *150 Daniel St.* ☎ *603/436–5909* ⊕ *www.warnerhouse.org* ⌚ *$5* ☉ *June–Oct., Mon.–Sat. 11–4, Sun. noon–4.*

Picnicking is popular in **Prescott Park,** on the waterfront between Strawbery Banke Museum and the Piscataqua River. A large formal garden with fountains is perfect for whiling away an afternoon. The park also contains Point of Graves, Portsmouth's oldest burial ground, and two 17th-century warehouses.

☺ Nineteen hands-on exhibits at the **Children's Museum of Portsmouth** explore lobstering, sound and music, computers, space travel, and other subjects. Some programs require reservations. ⊠ *280 Marcy St.* ☎ *603/ 436–3853* ⊕ *www.childrens-museum.org* ⌚ *$6* ☉ *Tues.–Sat. 10–5, Sun. 1–5; also Mon. 10–5 in summer and during school vacations.*

The **Wentworth-Coolidge Mansion Historic Site,** a National Historic Landmark that's now part of Little Harbor State Park, was originally the residence of Benning Wentworth, New Hampshire's first royal governor (1753–70). Notable among its period furnishings is the carved pine mantelpiece in the council chamber. Wentworth's imported lilac trees bloom each May. The visitor center stages lectures and exhibits and contains a gallery with changing exhibits. ⊠ *375 Little Harbor Rd., near South Street Cemetery* ☎ *603/436–6607* ⌚ *$3* ☉ *Grounds daily; mansion mid-May–Aug., Wed.–Sat. 10–3, Sun. 1–5; Sept.–mid-May, by appointment.*

Docked at the **Port of Portsmouth Maritime Museum** in Albacore Park is the USS *Albacore,* built here in 1953. You can board this prototype submarine, which was a floating laboratory assigned to test an innovative hull design, dive brakes, and sonar systems for the Navy. The nearby Memorial Garden and its reflecting pool are dedicated to those who have lost their lives in submarine service. ⊠ *600 Market St.* ☎ *603/436–3680* ⌚ *$5* ☉ *Daily 9:30–5.*

The **Redhook Ale Brewery,** visible from the Spaulding Turnpike, conducts tours that end with a beer tasting. If you don't have time to tour, you can stop in the Cataqua Public House to sample the fresh ales and have a bite to eat (open daily for lunch and dinner). ⊠ *Pease International Tradeport, 35 Corporate Dr.* ☎ *603/430–8600* ⊕ *www.redhook.com* ⌚ *$1* ☉ *Tours weekdays at 2, weekends at 2 and 4; additional tours at noon, 1, and 3 summer weekends.*

Though it consists of a single square mile of land, the small island of **New Castle,** 3 mi southeast from downtown via Route 1B, was once known as Great Island. The narrow roads lined with prerevolutionary houses and upscale condos make the island, which is accessible from the mainland by car, perfect for a stroll.

Wentworth-by-the-Sea, the last of the state's great seaside resorts, is impossible to miss as you approach New Castle on Route 1B. It was the site of the signing of the Russo-Japanese Treaty in 1905, a fact that attracts many Japanese tourists. The long-vacant property reopened as a luxury resort in 2003.

Also on New Castle Island, **Ft. Constitution** was built in 1631 and then rebuilt in 1666 as Ft. William and Mary, a British stronghold overlooking Portsmouth Harbor. The fort earned fame in 1774, when patriots raided it in one of revolutionary America's first overtly defiant acts against King George III. The rebels later used the captured munitions against the British at the Battle of Bunker Hill. Panels throughout the fort explain its history. ⊠ *Rte. 1B at the Coast Guard Station* ☎ *603/436–1552* ☜ *Free* ☉ *Mid-June–Labor Day, daily 9–5; Labor Day–mid-June, weekends 9–5.*

OFF THE
BEATEN
PATH

ISLES OF SHOALS – Many of these nine small, rocky islands (eight at high tide) retain the earthy names—Hog and Smuttynose, to cite but two—given them by transient 17th-century fishermen. A history of piracy, murder, and ghosts surrounds the archipelago, long populated by an independent lot who, according to one writer, hadn't the sense to winter on the mainland. Not all the islands lie within the state's border: after an ownership dispute, five went to Maine and four to New Hampshire.

Celia Thaxter, a native islander, romanticized these islands with her poetry in *Among the Isles of Shoals* (1873) and celebrated her garden in *An Island Garden* (1894; now reissued with the original color illustrations by Childe Hassam). In the late 19th century, **Appledore Island** became an offshore retreat for Thaxter's coterie of writers, musicians, and artists. The island is now used by the Marine Laboratory of Cornell University. **Star Island** contains a nondenominational conference center and is open to those on guided tours.

Where to Eat

$$$–$$$$ ✕ **The Library.** Most of this 1785 mansion, a former luxury hotel, has been converted to condominiums, but the restaurant retains hand-carved mahogany paneling, a marble-top bar, and bookcases on every wall. Although the kitchen churns out such light dishes as pan-roasted salmon with olive oil, garlic, lemon, tomatoes, and basmati rice, the mainstays are thick-cut steaks and chops. The check arrives between the pages of a vintage best-seller. Order an ale in the English-style pub. Sunday brunch is a big to-do. ⊠ *401 State St.* ☎ *603/431–5202* ⊟ *AE, D, DC, MC, V.*

$$–$$$ ✕ **Blue Mermaid Island Grill.** The chefs at Blue Mermaid prepare Caribbean-influenced fare on a wood-burning grill. Specialties include plantain-encrusted grouper topped with grilled mango vinaigrette and served with black-eyed pea sweet-potato hash; and wood-grilled flat-iron steak with a cilantro-hoisin glaze, cucumber-citrus relish, and noodles. In summer you can eat on a deck that overlooks the historical Hill neighborhood.

Entertainers perform (outdoors in summer) on Friday and Saturday. ⊠ *409 The Hill* ☎ *603/427–2583* ▭ *AE, D, DC, MC, V.*

$$–$$$ ✕ **Forty-Three Degrees North.** Sage-green and mustard-yellow walls, dark woods, and large framed artworks give this popular, upscale restaurant a European look. Most of the menu changes daily, but standbys include grilled elk medallions with ginger-blueberry chutney, and pumpkin seed–crusted halibut with roasted butternut squash spaetzle and green-chili horseradish aioli. ⊠ *75 Pleasant St.* ☎ *603/430–0225* ▭ *AE, MC, V* ✆ *Closed Sun.*

$$–$$$ ✕ **Jumpin' Jay's.** A wildly popular spot downtown, this offbeat, dim-lighted eatery presents a changing menu of world-beat seafood, and nary a red-meat platter is served. Try the steamed Prince Edward Island mussels with a spicy lemongrass and saffron sauce, Jonah crab–and–vegetable lasagna, or the Chilean sea bass with a ginger-orange marinade. Singles often gather at the central bar for dinner and schmoozing. ⊠ *150 Congress St.* ☎ *603/766–3474* ▭ *MC, V* ✆ *No lunch.*

★ $$–$$$ ✕ **Pesce Blue.** Sleek, modern, and hip, this restaurant specializes in fresh seafood blended with simple Italian flavors. You pass a wall of flickering votives before entering the main dining room, which has an industrial feel: cinder-block walls, black industrial grid ceiling, wood and chrome accents, and mosaic blue tiles. Chef Mark Segal, who trained under Lydia Shire at Biba, serves some of the freshest, finest seafood dishes in town. The menu changes daily but may include grilled Greek sardines, fried anchovies, grilled jumbo prawns with sweet garlic custard, and a selection of local catches. There's patio dining in summer. ⊠ *103 Congress St.* ☎ *603/430–7766* ⊕ *www.pesceblue.com* ▭ *AE, D, MC, V* ✆ *No lunch weekends.*

$–$$$ ✕ **Muddy River Smokehouse.** Red-check tablecloths and murals of trees and meadows evoke an outdoor summer barbecue joint—even when the weather turns cold. Roll up your sleeves and dig into corn bread and molasses baked beans as well as blackened catfish or a burger. Devotees swear by the Pig City platter of grilled ribs, smoked sweet sausage, and pulled pork. There's live music many nights. ⊠ *21 Congress St.* ☎ *603/430–9582* ▭ *AE, MC, V.*

$–$$ ✕ **Chiangmai Thai.** Portsmouth's first authentic Thai restaurant remains one of its favorites among locals and visitors. The dining room is small, but the menu lists an extensive array of creative Thai dishes. Duck is a specialty (try it roasted, then lightly fried in egg batter; topped with ginger, scallions, and a spicy red-chili sauce; and served over crispy noodles and roasted pine nuts). Or you can create your own dish with an assortment of sauces and curries. ⊠ *128 Penhallow St.* ☎ *603/433–1289* ▭ *AE, D, MC, V* ✆ *Closed Mon.*

★ $–$$ ✕ **Poco's.** Sure, Poco's boisterous downstairs bar and spacious outside deck have earned it a reputation as a collegiate hangout, but the upstairs dining room turns out exceptional Southwest and pan-Latin cuisine—and at great prices. Avocado-wrapped fried oysters with chipotle tartar sauce, and lobster quesadilla with Brie, caramelized onions, and roasted corn–tomato salsa are among the better choices. Most tables have great views of the Piscataqua River. ⊠ *37 Bow St.* ☎ *603/431–5967* ▭ *AE, D, MC, V.*

$ ✕ **Radici.** Keeping it simple could be the motto of this small downtown restaurant, which serves old-world cuisine. The dining room is a lesson in minimalism—blond woods, putty-color walls hung with framed color photos of Italy, and soft, white lights. Menu classics include choice of pasta and freshly made sauces, *cioppino* (seafood stew) with roasted fennel, and chicken and sausage cacciatore. There's also a wide selection of such creative vegetarian dishes as wild mushroom cannelloni stuffed with roasted garlic, ricotta, and Asiago in a creamy sauce. ⊠ *142–144 Congress St.* ☎ *603/373–6464* ⊟ *AE, MC, V* ⊘ *No lunch.*

¢–$ ✕ **Friendly Toast.** The biggest and best breakfast in town is served at this funky, diner-style restaurant in downtown. Almond Joy cakes (buttermilk pancakes, chocolate chips, coconut, and almonds), orange French toast, and hefty omelets (lots of combinations) are favorites. The homemade breads and muffins are a hit, too. A late-night crowd gathers in the wee hours after the bars close, since the restaurant is open 24 hours on weekends. ⊠ *121 Congress St.* ☎ *603/430–2154* ⊟ *AE, D, MC, V.*

Where to Stay

★ $$–$$$$ ✕▥ **Wentworth by-the-Sea.** New Hampshire's only seaside resort hotel, this luxury property, which dates to 1874, was once a summer resort for East Coast socialites, wealthy patrons, and former presidents. The resort and spa, on New Castle island, a few minutes' drive from downtown Portsmouth, was boarded up for years; it reopened in spring 2003 after literally being rebuilt. All of the bright airy rooms have ocean and harbor views—the huge sunny suites occupy a new building right on the water, facing the marina. There are two first-rate restaurants: the Dining Room ($$$–$$$$) occupies the main hotel and is somewhat formal, serving rich contemporary American fare; the breezier and more casual Latitudes ($–$$$) overlooks the marina and waterfront and serves an artful raw bar platter for two as well as beer-battered–haddock sandwiches and wood-grilled filet mignon. ⊠ *588 Wentworth Rd., New Castle 03854* ☎ *603/422–7322 or 866/240–6313* ⊟ *603/422–7329* ⊕ *www.wentworth.com* ⊷ *127 rooms, 34 suites* ♻ *2 restaurants, room service, in-room hot tubs, cable TV, 18-hole golf course, 4 tennis courts, pro shop, 2 pools (1 indoor), health club, spa, bar, lobby lounge, dry cleaning, laundry service, concierge, meeting rooms* ⊟ *AE, D, DC, MC, V.*

★ $$$–$$$$ ▥ **Governor's House.** Small, plush, and quiet, this four-room inn, 1 mi from the historic downtown area, is the perfect place for discerning couples. It was once the home of Charles Dale, formerly the governor of New Hampshire. Frette linens, down comforters, in-room Bose CD stereos, high-speed wireless, a guest computer, in-room massages, and a private tennis court are some of the extras at this 1917 Georgian Colonial house turned bed-and-breakfast. ⊠ *32 Miller Ave., 03801* ☎ *603/427–5140 or 866/427–5140* ⊕ *www.governors-house.com* ⊷ *4 rooms* ♻ *Cable TV, in-room VCRs, tennis court, hot tub, massage, bicycles, library, business services; no kids under 15* ⊟ *D, MC, V* ⓞ *CP.*

$$$–$$$$ ▥ **Sheraton Harborside Portsmouth Hotel.** This five-story redbrick luxury hotel is within easy walking distance of shops and attractions. Many rooms have large windows overlooking Portsmouth Harbor and the Piscataqua River. The elegant suites have full kitchens and living rooms

2

as well as fireplaces and large balconies. The Harbor's Edge Restaurant serves a popular Sunday brunch. The hotel also rents out several luxury town homes across the street, geared more toward longer stays. ⊠ *250 Market St., 03801* ☎ *603/431–2300 or 800/325–3535* 🖷 *603/431–7805* ⊕ *www.sheratonportsmouth.com* ⇨ *179 rooms, 24 suites* △ *2 restaurants, room service, some kitchens, cable TV, indoor pool, health club, sauna, bar, nightclub, business services, meeting rooms* ⊟ *AE, D, DC, MC, V.*

\$\$\$–\$\$\$\$ 🏨 **Sise Inn.** Close to Market Square, this 1880s Queen Anne–style town house is decorated in Victorian style, with designer fabrics, antiques, and reproductions. Some rooms have fireplaces, and about half are in a 1980s carriage house that blends well with the older section. ⊠ *40 Court St., 03801* ☎ *603/433–1200 or 877/747–3466* ⊕ *www.siseinn.com* ⇨ *34 rooms, 8 suites* △ *Some in-room hot tubs, cable TV, in-room VCRs, laundry service, meeting rooms* ⊟ *AE, D, DC, MC, V* ⚟ *CP.*

\$\$–\$\$\$\$ 🏨 **Wren's Nest Village Inn.** With standard rooms, suites, efficiencies, and cottages, the Wren's Nest draws lots of families and groups of friends; many regulars rent for weeks at a time. Guest quarters are clean, well maintained, and decorated with nautical artwork and modern if rather ordinary furniture, and the 4 acres of lawns and gardens are attractive. A few units have unusual themes—the Harley-Davidson and Papa Hemingway suites, for example. It's a 10-minute drive south of downtown Portsmouth and convenient to Rye and the beaches. There is a charming restaurant and pub, Chestnut's. ⊠ *3548 Lafayette Rd. (U.S. 1), 03801* ☎ *603/436–2481* ⊕ *www.wrensnestinn.com* ⇨ *25 rooms, 8 suites, 3 cottages* △ *Restaurant, some in-room hot tubs, some kitchens, refrigerators, some in-room VCRs, volleyball, pub* ⊟ *AE, D, MC, V.*

\$\$–\$\$\$ 🏨 **Martin Hill Inn.** Within walking distance of the historic district and the waterfront, this inn consists of one building from 1815 and another from 1850 surrounded by extensive gardens. The quiet rooms are furnished with antiques and decorated in formal Colonial or country-Victorian styles. The Greenhouse Suite has a solarium. ⊠ *404 Islington St., 03801* ☎ *603/436–2287* ⊕ *www.martinhillinn.com* ⇨ *4 rooms, 3 suites* △ *Wi-Fi, no-smoking rooms; no room phones, no room TVs, no kids under 14* ⊟ *MC, V* ⚟ *BP.*

\$–\$\$ 🏨 **Inn at Christian Shore.** Perennial gardens surround this handsome, yellow clapboard Federal house, which is equidistant to downtown and the Maritime Museum. Original beam ceilings and rough-hewn hardwood floors reveal the building's rich history, and an eclectic mix of pre-Columbian, African, and European art makes a distinctive statement. The breakfast is memorable—the frittata-like Spanish tortillas are a specialty. ⊠ *335 Maplewood Ave., 03801* ☎ *603/431–6770* ⊕ *www.innatchristianshore.com* ⇨ *5 rooms* △ *No room phones, no room TVs, no kids, no smoking* ⊟ *MC, V* ⚟ *BP.*

Nightlife & the Arts

NIGHTLIFE The **Portsmouth Gas Light Co.** (⊠ 64 Market St. ☎ 603/430–9122), a brick-oven pizzeria and restaurant, hosts local rock bands in its lounge, courtyard, and slick upstairs space. People come from as far away as Boston and Portland to hang out at the **Press Room** (⊠ 77 Daniel St.

☎ 603/431–5186), which showcases folk, jazz, blues, and bluegrass performers.

Beloved for its acoustics, the 1878 **Music Hall** (✉ 28 Chestnut St. ☎ 603/436–2400, 603/436–9900 film line ⊕ www.themusichall.org) brings the best touring events to the seacoast—from classical and pop concerts to dance and theater. The hall also hosts art-house film series. From September through June the **Players' Ring** (✉ 105 Marcy St. ☎ 603/436–8123 ⊕ www.playersring.org) stages more than 15 original and well-known plays and performances by local theater groups.

The **Pontine Movement Theatre** (✉ 959 Islington St. ☎ 603/436–6660 ⊕ www.pontine.org) presents dance performances in a renovated warehouse. The company also tours throughout northern New England. The **Prescott Park Arts Festival** (✉ 105 Marcy St. ☎ 603/436–2848 ⊕ www.prescottpark.org) presents theater, dance, and musical events outdoors from June through August. The **Seacoast Repertory Theatre** (✉ 125 Bow St. ☎ 603/433–4472 or 800/639–7650 ⊕ www.seacoastrep.org) has a year-round schedule of musicals, classic dramas, and works by up-and-coming playwrights, as well as a youth theater.

Sports & the Outdoors

Just inland from Portsmouth, the **Great Bay Estuarine Research Reserve** is one of southeastern New Hampshire's most precious assets. Amid its 4,471 acres of tidal waters, mudflats, and about 48 mi of inland shoreline, you can spot blue herons, ospreys, and snowy egrets, particularly during spring and fall migrations. Winter eagles also live here. The best public access is via the **Sandy Point Discovery Center** (✉ 89 Depot Rd., off Rte. 33, Stratham ☎ 603/778–0015 ⊕ www.greatbay.org ☉ May–Sept., Wed.–Sun. 10–4; Oct., weekends 10–4). The facility has year-round interpretive programs, indoor and outdoor exhibits, a library and bookshop, and a 1,700-foot boardwalk as well as other trails through mudflats and upland forest. The center, about 15 mi southeast of Durham and 6 mi west of Exit 3 from Interstate 95 in Portsmouth, also distributes maps and information. ✉ *Information: New Hampshire Fish & Game Dept., 225 Main St., Durham 03824* ☎ *603/868–1095* ➴ *Free* ☉ *Daily dawn–dusk.*

New Hampshire's largest water park, **Water Country** (✉ Rte. 1 ☎ 603/427–1112 ➴ $29 ☉ Mid-June–Labor Day, daily 10–6 [until 7:30 in July and early Aug.]), 3 mi south of downtown Portsmouth, has a river tube ride, a large wave pool, white-water rapids, and 12 large waterslides.

The **Urban Forestry Center** (✉ 45 Elwyn Rd. ☎ 603/431–6774) has gardens and marked trails appropriate for short hikes on its 180 acres. Explore the waters, sites, and sea life of the Piscataqua River Basin and the New Hampshire coastline on a guided kayak tour with **Portsmouth Kayak Adventure** (✉ 185 Wentworth Rd. ☎ 603/559–1000). Beginners are welcome (instruction is included). Tours are run daily from June through mid-October, at 10 and 2. Sunset tours take off at 6. If you'd rather pedal than drive, stop by **Portsmouth Rent & Ride** (✉ 37 Hanover St. ☎ 603/433–6777) for equipment, maps, and suggested bike routes to Portsmouth sites, area beaches, and attractions. Guided two-hour tours of the seacoast area are also offered.

Shopping

Market Square, in the center of town, has gift and clothing boutiques, book and card shops, and exquisite crafts stores. **Byrne & Carlson** (✉ 121 State St. ☎ 888/559–9778) produces handmade chocolates in the finest European tradition. **N. W. Barrett** (✉ 53 Market St. ☎ 603/431–4262) specializes in leather, jewelry, pottery, and other arts and crafts. It also sells furniture, including affordable steam-bent oak pieces and one-of-a-kind lamps and rocking chairs. **Three Graces Gallery** (✉ 105 Market St. ☎ 603/436–1988) has prints and paintings of the Maine and New Hampshire coasts and also specializes in custom framing.

Rye

❷ *8 mi south of Portsmouth.*

In 1623 the first Europeans established a settlement at Odiorne Point in what is now the largely undeveloped and picturesque town of Rye, making it the birthplace of New Hampshire. Today the area's main draws are a lovely state park, oceanfront beaches, and the views from Route 1A.

★ ☾ **Odiorne Point State Park** encompasses more than 330 acres of protected land, on the site where David Thompson established the first permanent European site in what is now New Hampshire. Stroll several nature trails with interpretive panels describing the park's military history or simply enjoy the vistas of the nearby Isles of Shoals. The rocky shore's tidal pools shelter crabs, periwinkles, and sea anemones. Throughout the year, the **Seacoast Science Center** conducts guided walks and interpretive programs and has exhibits on the area's natural history. Displays trace the social history of Odiorne Point back to the Ice Age, and the tidal-pool touch tank and 1,000-gallon Gulf of Maine deepwater aquarium are popular with kids. Day camp is offered for grades K–8 throughout summer and during school vacations. Popular music concerts are held here on Thursday evenings in summer. ✉ *570 Ocean Blvd. (Rte. 1A), north of Wallis Sands, Rye State Beach* ☎ *603/436–8043 science center, 603/436–1552 park* ⊕ *www.seacentr.org* 🎟 *Science center $3, guided walks and some interpretive programs $4, park Memorial Day–Columbus Day and weekends $3* ☉ *Science center daily 10–5, park daily 8 AM–dusk.*

Where to Stay & Eat

★ $$–$$$$ ✕ **The Carriage House.** Walk across scenic Ocean Boulevard from Jenness Beach to this elegant cottage eatery that serves innovative dishes with a continental flair. Standouts include crab cakes served with a spicy jalepeño sauce, a penne alla vodka teeming with fresh seafood, creative madras curries, and a delectable steak au poivre. You can also order from a small plates menu for a lighter meal. Savor a hot fudge ice cream croissant or an indulgent tiramisu for dessert while enjoying the ocean views. ✉ *2263 Ocean Blvd.* ☎ *603/964–8251* 🖃 *AE, MC, V* ☉ *No lunch.*

$$–$$$ ✕ **Saunders at Rye Harbor.** Folks have been lazing about on the waterfront deck at sunset or over lunch since this place opened in the 1920s. Freshly caught lobster, broiled scallops with a butter-and-crumb topping, feta-crusted salmon with a citrus-tarragon sauce, and baked-stuffed shrimp are among the specialties. ⊠ *175 Harbor Rd.* ☎ *603/964–6466* ▭ *AE, D, MC, V.*

$$–$$$ 🏠 **Rock Ledge Manor.** Built out on a point, this mid-19th-century gambrel-roof house with a wraparound porch once anchored a resort colony. Rooms have water views, brass-and-iron beds, and marble-top dressers; the family suite has a balcony. Owners Stan and Stella Smith serve breakfast in the sunny dining room overlooking the Atlantic. Although rooms have no phones, the whole property has wireless high-speed Internet. ⊠ *1413 Ocean Blvd., 03870* ☎ *603/431–1413* ⊕ *www. rockledgemanor.com* ⬳ *2 rooms, 1 suite* ♢ *Dining room, Wi-Fi; no room phones, no room TVs, no kids under 11, no smoking* ▭ *No credit cards* ⧆ *BP.*

Sports & the Outdoors

Good for swimming and sunning, **Jenness State Beach** (⊠ Route 1A ☎ 603/436–1552) is a favorite with locals. The facilities include a bathhouse, lifeguards, and metered parking ($1.50 per hour). **Wallis Sands State Beach** (⊠ Route 1A ☎ 603/436–9404) is a swimmers' beach with bright white sands and a bathhouse. There's plenty of parking; the rate is $10. If you've got active kids with you, consider spending the day at **Rye Airfield** (⊠ U.S. 1 ☎ 603/964–2800), an extreme-sports park with an indoor in-line-skate and skateboard arena and two BMX tracks.

For a full- or half-day deep-sea angling charter, try **Atlantic Fishing and Whale Watch Fleet** (⊠ Rye Harbor ☎ 603/964–5220 or 800/942–5364).

Hampton Beach

🌙 ❸ *8 mi south of Rye.*

Hampton Beach, from Route 27 to where Route 1A crosses the causeway, is an authentic seaside amusement center—the domain of fried-dough stands, loud music, arcade games, palm readers, parasailing, and bronzed bodies. An estimated 150,000 people visit the town and its free public beach on the Fourth of July, and it draws plenty of people until late September, when things close up. The 3-mi boardwalk, where kids can play games and see how saltwater taffy is made, looks like a leftover from the 1940s; in fact, the whole community remains remarkably free of modern franchises. Free outdoor concerts are held on many a summer evening, and once a week there's a fireworks display. Talent shows and karaoke performances take place in the Seashell Stage, right on the beach. Each August, locals hold a children's festival, and they celebrate the end of the season with a huge seafood feast on the weekend after Labor Day.

Away from the beach crowds, you'll find **Fuller Gardens,** a late-1920s estate garden (the mansion was razed in 1961) designed in the Colonial-revival style by landscape architect Arthur Shurtleff, with a 1938 addition by the Olmsted brothers. With 2,000 rosebushes, a hosta garden, an annual display garden, a Japanese garden, and a tropical conservatory, it blooms all summer long. ⊠ *10 Willow Ave., North Hampton* ☎ *603/ 964–5414* ⊕ *www.fullergardens.org* 🖻 *$6* ☉ *Mid-May–mid-Oct., daily 10–5:30.*

Where to Stay & Eat

$$–$$$$ ✕ **Ron's Landing at Rocky Bend.** Amid the motels lining Ocean Boulevard is this casually elegant restaurant. Pan-seared ahi over mixed greens with a Thai peanut dressing makes a tempting starter. For an entrée, try the oven-roasted salmon with a hoisin (soybeans, garlic, and chili peppers) glaze, a Fra Angelico cream sauce, slivered almonds, and sliced apple or the baked haddock stuffed with scallops and lobster and served with lemon-dill butter. From many tables you can enjoy a sweeping Atlantic view. ⊠ *379 Ocean Blvd.* ☎ *603/929–2122* 🖃 *AE, D, DC, MC, V* ☉ *No lunch except Sun. brunch.*

$–$$$$ ✕🖭 **Ashworth by the Sea.** This family-owned hotel was built across the street from Hampton Beach in 1912, though furnishings vary from period to contemporary. Most rooms have decks, but request a beachside room for an ocean view; otherwise you'll look out onto the pool or street. The Ashworth Dining Room ($$–$$$) serves steaks, poultry, and seafood. Of the seven lobster variations, the lobster meat wrapped in haddock with a crawfish-sherry sauce stands out. ⊠ *295 Ocean Blvd., 03842* ☎ *603/926–6762 or 800/345–6736* 🖷 *603/926–2002* ⊕ *www. ashworthhotel.com* ⇗ *105 rooms* ♿ *3 restaurants, cable TV, indoor pool* 🖃 *AE, D, DC, MC, V.*

$$–$$$ 🖭 **D. W.'s Oceanside Inn.** The square front and simple awnings of this inn look much the same as those on all the other buildings lining Ocean Boulevard. Individually decorated rooms have carefully selected antiques and collectibles. You can curl up with a book by the fireplace in the living room or watch the waves from the second-floor veranda. Should Hampton Beach's crush of people and noise begin to overwhelm, you'll appreciate the soundproofing. A separate three-bedroom cottage sleeps up to six guests and has a kitchen. ⊠ *365 Ocean Blvd., 03842* 🖷🖷 *603/ 926–3542* ⊕ *www.oceansideinn.com* ⇗ *9 rooms, 1 cottage* ♿ *In-room safes; no room TVs, no kids, no smoking* 🖃 *AE, D, MC, V* ☉ *Closed mid-Oct.–mid-May* 🍽 *BP.*

Nightlife

Despite its name, the **Hampton Beach Casino Ballroom** (⊠ 169 Ocean Blvd. ☎ 603/929–4100) isn't a gambling establishment but rather a late-19th-century, 2,000-seat performance venue that has hosted everyone from Janis Joplin to Jerry Seinfeld, George Carlin, and B. B. King. Performances are scheduled weekly from April through October.

Sports & the Outdoors

BEACHES **Hampton Beach State Park** (⊠ Rte. 1A ☎ 603/926–3784) is a quiet stretch of sand on the southwestern edge of town at the mouth of the Hampton River. It has picnic tables, a store (seasonal), parking ($8 on summer weekends, $5 weekdays in summer), and a bathhouse.

FISHING & WHALE-WATCHING Several companies conduct whale-watching excursions as well as half-day, full-day, and nighttime cruises. Most leave from the Hampton State Pier on Route 1A. **Al Gauron Deep Sea Fishing** (☎ 603/926–2469) maintains a fleet of three boats for whale-watching cruises and fishing charters. **Eastman Fishing Fleet** (✉ Seabrook ☎ 603/474–3461) offers whale-watching and fishing cruises, with evening and morning charters. **Smith & Gilmore Deep Sea Fishing** (☎ 603/926–3503 or 877/272–4005) conducts deep-sea fishing expeditions and whale-watching trips.

⌐ EN
  ROUTE

At the 400-acre **Applecrest Farm Orchards** you can pick your own apples and berries or buy fresh fruit pies and cookies. Fall brings cider pressing, hay rides, pumpkins, and music on weekends. In winter a cross-country ski trail traverses the orchard. Author John Irving worked here as a teenager, his experiences inspiring the book *The Cider House Rules.* ✉ *133 Rte. 88, Hampton Falls* ☎ *603/926–3721* ⊕ *www.applecrest. com* ☺ *Daily 9–5.*

Exeter

❹ *9 mi northwest of Hampton, 52 mi north of Boston, 47 mi southeast of Concord.*

In the center of Exeter, contemporary shops mix well with the buildings of the esteemed Phillips Exeter Academy, which opened in 1783, and other equally historical structures. During the Revolutionary War, Exeter was the state capital, and it was here amid intense patriotic fervor that the first state constitution and the first Declaration of Independence from Great Britain were put to paper. These days Exeter shares more in appearance and personality with Boston's blue-blooded satellite communities than the rest of New Hampshire—indeed, plenty of locals commute to Beantown. There are a handful of cheerful cafés and coffeehouses in the center of town, making it a nice spot for a snack break.

The **American Independence Museum,** adjacent to Phillips Exeter Academy in the Ladd-Gilman House, celebrates the birth of our nation. The story unfolds during the course of a guided tour focusing on the Gilman family, who lived in the house during the Revolutionary era. Along the way, you'll see drafts of the U.S. Constitution and the first Purple Heart. Other items include letters and documents written by George Washington and the household furnishings of John Taylor Gilman, one of New Hampshire's early governors. The museum also hosts the American Independence Festival, formerly the Revolutionary War Festival, in July. ✉ *1 Governor's La.* ☎ *603/772–2622* ⊕ *www.independencemuseum. org* 🎟 *$5* ☺ *May–Oct., Wed.–Sat. 10–4 (last tour at 3).*

Where to Stay & Eat

$$–$$$ ✕ **Tavern at River's Edge.** A convivial downtown gathering spot on the Exeter River, this tavern pulls in parents of prep-school kids, University of New Hampshire (UNH) students, and suburban yuppies. It may be informal, but the kitchen turns out surprisingly sophisticated chow. You might start with sautéed ragout of portobello and shiitake mushrooms, sun-dried tomatoes, roasted shallots, garlic, and Asiago cheese. Move on to New Zealand rack of lamb with rosemary-port demi-glace and minted risotto. In the bar, lighter fare is served daily 3–10. ✉ *163 Water St.* ☎ *603/772–7393* 🖃 *AE, D, DC, MC, V* ☺ *No lunch.*

2

¢ ✕ **Loaf and Ladle.** Chowders, soups, and stews as well as huge sandwiches on homemade bread are served cafeteria-style at this understated eatery overlooking the river. Check the blackboard for the ever-changing rotation of specials, breads, and desserts, and don't miss the fresh salad bar. Although dinner is available, the restaurant closes at 8 PM. ⊠ *9 Water St.* ☎ *603/778–8955* ♿ *Reservations not accepted* ☰ *AE, D, DC, MC, V.*

$$–$$$$ ✕▥ **Inn and Conference Center of Exeter.** This brick Georgian-style inn on the Phillips Exeter Academy campus has been the choice of visiting parents since it opened in the 1930s. It's furnished with antique and reproduction pieces and possesses plenty of modern amenities. Among the Terrace Restaurant's ($$–$$$) specialties are chili-glazed monkfish with teardrop-tomato salsa, citrus-herb jasmine rice, and coconut-ginger coulis. On Sunday, the line forms early for brunch. ⊠ *90 Front St., 03833* ☎ *603/772–5901 or 800/782–8444* ☒ *603/778–8757* ⊕ *www. someplacesdifferent.com/exeter.htm* ⬦ *43 rooms, 3 suites* ♿ *Restaurant, some in-room hot tubs, cable TV, meeting rooms* ☰ *AE, D, DC, MC, V.*

$$–$$$ ▥ **Inn by the Bandstand.** Common rooms in this 1809 Federal mansion, within a stone's throw of shops and restaurants, are decorated in period style. Seven guest rooms have working fireplaces; some have marble baths, CD players, and curtained four-poster beds. After a day of sightseeing, you can relax with a glass of complimentary sherry. ⊠ *4 Front St., 03833* ☎ *603/772–6352 or 877/239–3837* ☒ *603/778–0212* ⊕ *www.innbythebandstand.com* ⬦ *7 rooms, 2 suites* ♿ *Some in-room hot tubs, cable TV, bicycles, business services; no smoking* ☰ *AE, D, MC, V* ⎪⊙⎪ *CP.*

¢ ⛺ **Exeter Elms Family Campground.** This 50-acre campground along the Exeter River has 200 sites (some riverfront), a swimming pool, canoe and kayak rentals, basketball, a playground, a video arcade, and a recreation program. ⊠ *188 Court St., 03833* ☎ *603/778–7631* ⊕ *www.exeterelms.com* ✉ *$24–$36* ♿ *Pool, playground, laundry facilities, flush toilets, full hookups, partial hookups, dump station, drinking water, showers, fire pits, picnic tables, electricity, public telephone, general store* ☰ *MC, V* ⊙ *Closed Oct.–mid-May.*

Shopping
A Picture's Worth a Thousand Words (⊠ 65 Water St. ☎ 603/778–1991) stocks antique and contemporary prints, old maps, town histories, and rare books. Prestigious **Exeter Fine Crafts** (⊠ 61 Water St. ☎ 603/778–8282) shows an impressive selection of juried pottery, paintings, jewelry, textiles, glassware, and other fine creations by some of northern New England's top artists. The **Travel and Nature Bookshop** (⊠ 45 Water St. ☎ 603/772–5573) has a wide selection of travel books including guides to New Hampshire hiking spots and other specialized titles. **Water Street Books** (⊠ 125 Water St. ☎ 603/778–9731) carries new fiction and nonfiction with an emphasis on New Hampshire authors.

Sports & the Outdoors
The New Hampshire Division of Parks and Recreation maintains the **Rockingham Recreation Trail,** which wends 27 mi from Newfields, just north of Exeter, to Manchester and is open to hikers, bikers, snowmobilers, and cross-country skiers.

Durham

❺ *12 mi north of Exeter, 11 mi northwest of Portsmouth.*

Settled in 1635 and the home of General John Sullivan, a Revolutionary War hero and three-time New Hampshire governor, Durham was where Sullivan and his band of rebel patriots stored the gunpowder they captured from Ft. William and Mary in New Castle. Easy access to Great Bay via the Oyster River made Durham a maritime hub in the 19th century. Among the lures today are the water, farms that welcome visitors, and the University of New Hampshire (UNH), which occupies much of the town's center.

The **Art Gallery** at UNH occasionally exhibits items from a permanent collection of about 1,100 pieces but generally uses its space to host traveling exhibits. Noted items in the collection include 19th-century Japanese wood-block prints and American landscape paintings. ⊠ *Paul Creative Arts Center, 30 College Rd.* ☎ *603/862-3712* ⊕ *www.arts. unh.edu* ☜ *Free* ☉ *Sept.–May, Mon.–Wed. 10–4, Thurs. 10–8, weekends 1–5.*

Emery Farm, which has been in the same family for 11 generations, sells fruits and vegetables in summer (including pick-your-own raspberries, strawberries, and blueberries), pumpkins in fall, and Christmas trees in December. The farm shop carries breads, pies, and local crafts. Children can pet the resident goats and sheep and attend the storytelling events that are often held on Tuesday mornings in July and August. ⊠ *U.S. 4, 1½ mi east of Rte. 108* ☎ *603/742-8495* ☉ *Late Apr.–Dec., daily 9–6.*

Several dozen American bison roam the farm run by the **Little Bay Buffalo Company.** Visitors cannot roam the range here, but the animals are visible from an observation area and the parking lot. The store on the property sells bison-related gifts and top-quality bison meat. ⊠ *50 Langley Rd.* ☎ *603/868-3300* ☉ *Store Tues.–Sun. 10–5.*

Where to Stay & Eat

$$–$$$$ ✕🏠 **Three Chimneys Inn.** This stately yellow structure has graced a hill overlooking the Oyster River since 1649. Rooms in the house and the 1795 barn are named after plants from the gardens and filled with Georgian- and Federal-style antiques and reproductions, canopy or four-poster beds with Edwardian drapes, and Oriental rugs; half have fireplaces. Specialties in the Maples dining room ($$–$$$) include tamarind-glazed warm duck salad, and calamari stuffed with sweet Italian sausage with tomato sauce, fried eggplant, and sweet-and-sour caponata vegetables. The comfy Ffrost Sawyer Tavern ($–$$) serves simpler fare as does the outdoor conservatory, which is open spring through fall. ⊠ *17 Newmarket Rd., 03824* ☎ *603/868-7800 or 888/399-9777* 🖶 *603/868-2964* ⊕ *www.threechimneysinn.com* ⇄ *23 rooms* ⚖ *3 restaurants, some in-room hot tubs, cable TV, business services, meeting room; no smoking* ⊟ *AE, D, MC, V* ⦿ *BP.*

$$ ✕🏠 **New England Conference Center and Hotel.** In a wooded area on the UNH campus, this contemporary hotel is large enough to be a full-service conference center but quiet enough to seem like a retreat. Acorns

Restaurant ($$–$$$), with tall windows overlooking the forest, special-izes in American regional cuisine and is a favorite place for Sunday brunch. A signature dish is roasted lobster tail over rosemary-garlic pappardelle in a lemon-herb beurre blanc. ✉ *15 Strafford Ave., 03824* ☎ *800/909–6931* 🖷 *603/862–4897* ⊕ *www.newenglandcenter.com* ➟ *115 rooms* ⚘ *Restaurant, cable TV, health club, bar, business services, meeting rooms* ▭ *AE, D, DC, MC, V.*

Nightlife & the Arts

The **Celebrity Series** (☎ 603/862–2290 ⊕ www.unh.edu/celebrity) at UNH brings music, theater, and dance to several venues.

The **UNH Department of Theater and Dance** (✉ Paul Creative Arts Cen-ter, 30 College Rd. ☎ 603/862–2919) produces a variety of shows. UNH's **Whittemore Center Arena** (✉ 128 Main St. ☎ 603/862–4000 ⊕ www. whittemorecenter.com) hosts everything from Boston Pops concerts to home shows, plus college sports.

Students and local yupsters head to the **Stone Church** (✉ 5 Granite St., Newmarket ☎ 603/659–6321)—in an authentic 1835 former Methodist church—to listen to live rock, jazz, blues, and folk. The restaurant on the premises serves dinner Wednesday through Sunday.

Sports & the Outdoors

An excellent 1-mi trail reaches the summit of **Blue Job Mountain,** where a fire tower provides a good view. The trailhead is on Crown Point Road, off Route 202A, 13 mi northwest of Dover. You can hike several trails or picnic at 130-acre **Wagon Hill Farm** (✉ U.S. 4 across from Emery Farm ☎ No phone), overlooking the Oyster River. The old farm wagon on the top of a hill is one of the most-photographed sights in New Eng-land. Park next to the farmhouse and follow walking trails to the wagon and through the woods to the picnic area by the water. Sledding and cross-country skiing are winter activities.

Dover

⑥ *6 mi northeast of Durham.*

Dover Point was settled in 1623 by fishermen who worked Great Bay. By the end of the century, the town center had moved inland to its pres-ent location. The falls on the Cocheco River made Dover a prolific tex-tile-mill town. Many of the brick mill buildings have been converted to restaurants and shops.

The **Woodman Institute** is a campus of museums consisting of four build-ings: the 1675 William Damm Garrison House, the 1813 J. P. Hale House (home to abolitionist Senator John P. Hale from 1840 to 1873), the 1818 Woodman House, and the 1827 Keefe House, added to the museum hold-ings in 2004. Exhibits focus on early-American cooking utensils, cloth-ing, furniture, New Hampshire's involvement in the Civil War, and natural history. ✉ *182–190 Central Ave.* ☎ *603/742–1038* ⊕ *www. seacoastnh.com/woodman* 🖃 *Free* ⏱ *Apr.–Nov., Wed.–Sun. 12:30–4:30; Dec. and Jan., weekends 12:30–4:30.*

NEW HAMPSHIRE FARM MUSEUM – Roughly 20 mi north of Dover in Milton, a sleepy Colonial village that stretches along the Salmon Falls river, this facility houses more than 60,000 artifacts, retelling New Hampshire farm life from 1700 to the early 1900s. Take a guided tour through the Jones Farmhouse and then explore the Grand Barn—filled with vehicles and implements—the gardens, and the nature trails at your leisure. Special events demonstrating farm-related crafts take place throughout the season. ✉ *1305 White Mountain Hwy.* ☎ *603/652–7840* ⊕ *www. farmmuseum.org* ✍ *$6* ☯ *June–Oct., Wed.–Sun. 10–4.*

Where to Stay & Eat

¢–$$$ ✕ **Newick's Seafood Restaurant.** Newick's, which also has locations in Merrimack and in Portland, Maine, might serve the best lobster roll on the New England coast, but regulars cherish the scallop pies and onion rings, too. This oversize shack serves seafood in heaping portions. Picture windows allow terrific views over Great Bay. ✉ *431 Dover Point Rd.* ☎ *603/742–3205* ▤ *AE, D, MC, V.*

$–$$ ✕▣ **Governor's Inn.** Just north of downtown Rochester, this pair of neighboring, early-20th-century Georgian-style mansions are the former homes of state governors (and brothers) Huntley and Roland Spaulding. Guests now make their way about the homes' stately marble fireplaces, elliptical staircases, garden patios, and lavishly furnished bedrooms. The restaurant ($$–$$$; closed Monday) presents an often-changing menu of regional American dishes such as baked seafood pie with lobster cream sauce, and filet mignon with a crab cake and shiitake demi-glace. Lighter fare is served in the Café in the Carriage House, which has a delightful garden. ✉ *78 Wakefield St., Rochester 03867* ☎ *603/332–0107* ▤ *603/ 335–1985* ⊕ *www.governorsinn.com* ⇨ *16 rooms, 4 suites* ♨ *Restaurant, café, some kitchenettes, cable TV, bar, no-smoking rooms* ▤ *D, MC, V.*

Shopping

Just the Thing! (✉ 451 Central Ave. ☎ 603/742–9040) carries an engaging mix of vintage collectibles and contemporary handicrafts. You can watch artisans work at **Salmon Falls Stoneware** (✉ Oak Street Engine House ☎ 603/749–1467 or 800/621–2030), which is known for its salt-glaze stoneware made using a method favored by early-American potters. **Tuttle's Red Barn** (✉ 151 Dover Point Rd. ☎ 603/742–4313) carries jams, pickles, and other farm products.

LAKES REGION

Lake Winnipesaukee, a Native American name for "smile of the great spirit," is the largest of the dozens of lakes scattered across the eastern half of central New Hampshire. With about 240 mi of shoreline full of inlets and coves, it's the largest in the state. Some claim Winnipesaukee has an island for each day of the year, but the total actually falls well short: 274.

In contrast to Winnipesaukee, which bustles all summer long, is the more secluded Squam Lake. Its tranquillity is what no doubt attracted the producers of *On Golden Pond*; several scenes of the Oscar-winning film were shot here. Nearby Lake Wentworth is named for the state's first royal governor, who, in building his country manor here, established North America's first summer resort.

Well-preserved Colonial and 19th-century villages are among the region's many landmarks, and you'll find hiking trails, good antiques shops, and myriad water-oriented activities. This tour begins at Laconia, just off Interstate 93, and more or less circles Lake Winnipesaukee clockwise, with several side trips.

Wolfeboro

➐ *40 mi northeast of Concord, 49 mi northwest of Portsmouth.*

Quietly upscale and decidedly preppy Wolfeboro has been a resort since Royal Governor John Wentworth built his summer home on the shores of Lake Wentworth in 1768. The town center, bursting with tony boutiques, fringes Lake Winnipesaukee and sees about a tenfold population increase each summer. The century-old, white clapboard buildings of the Brewster Academy prep school bracket the town's southern end. Wolfeboro marches to a steady, relaxed beat, comfortable for all ages.

Uniforms, vehicles, and other artifacts at the **Wright Museum** illustrate the contributions of those on the home front to America's World War II effort. ⊠ *77 Center St.* ☎ *603/569–1212* ⊕ *www.wrightmuseum.org* 🖾 *$6* ⊙ *May–Oct., Mon.–Sat. 10–4, Sun. noon–4; Apr. and Nov., Sat. 10–4, Sun. noon–4.*

Two miles northeast of downtown, the **New Hampshire Boat Museum** celebrates the Lakes Region's boating legacy with displays of vintage Chris-Crafts, Jersey Speed Skiffs, 3-point hydroplanes, and other fine watercraft, along with model boats, antique engines, racing photography and trophies, and old-time signs from marinas. ⊠ *397 Center St.* ☎ *603/569–4554* ⊕ *www.nhbm.org* 🖾 *$5* ⊙ *Memorial Day–Columbus Day, Mon.–Sat. 10–4, Sun. noon–4.*

NEED A BREAK?

Brewster Academy students and summer folk converge upon groovy little **Lydia's** (⊠ 33 N. Main St. ☎ 603/569–3991) for espressos, hearty sandwiches, homemade soups, bagels, and desserts. Picking up pastries, cookies, freshly baked breads, and other sweets in the **Yum Yum Shop** (⊠ 16 N. Main St. ☎ 603/569–1919) has been a tradition in these parts since 1948—the buttercrunch cookies are highly addictive.

The artisans at the **Hampshire Pewter Company** (⊠ 43 Mill St. ☎ 603/569–4944 or 800/639–7704) use 16th-century techniques to make pewter tableware and accessories. Free tours are conducted at 9:30, 11, 1:30, and 3 most days, Memorial Day–Columbus Day, and by appointment at other times. The gift shop is open year-round.

Where to Stay & Eat

$$ ✕ **East of Suez.** Set in a countrified lodge on the south side of town, this warm and friendly restaurant serves creative Pan-Asian cuisine, with an emphasis on Philippine fare, such as *lumpia* (pork-and-shrimp spring

New Hampshire Lakes

WHITE MOUNTAIN NATIONAL FOREST

WHITE LAKE STATE PARK

Silver Lake 153

Tamworth **16**

SQUAM MOUNTAINS **13**

Plymouth

113

West Ossipee 25

Ossipee Lake

25

15 Center Sandwich

Squam Lake

OSSIPEE MOUNTAINS

Center Ossipee

Holderness **14**

Ashland

93

East Hebron

Bridgewater

Lake Waukewan

3 25

Lake Kanasatka

Center Harbor

171

Tuftonboro

PINE RIVER STATE FOREST 153

Province Lake

MAINE

Newfound Lake

104

New Hampton

11 Meredith

Ossipee

109

16

Pine River Pond

12 Bristol

Winnisquam Lake

Lake Winnipesaukee

109

Lake Wentworth

109

9 Gilford

11

7 Wolfeboro

Wakefield

3A 132

Laconia **10**

Gunstock Recreation Area

11A

28

Sanbornton

3

Tilton

Silver Lake

107

Manning Lake

Alton Bay **8**

Merrymeeting Lake

Milton Mills

Franklin

140

Belmont

Crystal Lake

140

Alton

Sunrise Lake

Milton

125

Northfield

4 127

93

106

107

Gilmanton Iron Works

11

Farmington

16

Canterbury
◆Shaker Village

Canterbury Center

TO CONCORD

132

Pittsfield

Center Barnstead

Rochester

28

0   10 miles

0   15 km

---

rolls with a sweet-and-sour fruit sauce) and Philippine *pancit canton* (pan-fried egg noodles with sautéed shrimp and pork and Asian vegetables with a sweet oyster sauce). You can also sample Thai red curries, Japanese tempura, and Korean-style flank steak. ⊠ *775 S. Main St.* ☎ *603/569–1648* ▭ *AE, MC, V* ☉ *Closed Oct.–mid-May.*

¢–$$ ✕ **Wolfetrap Grill and Raw Bar.** The seafood at this festive shanty on Lake Winnipesaukee comes right from the adjacent fish market. You'll find all your favorites here, including a renowned clam boil for one that includes steamers, corn on the cob, onions, baked potatoes, sweet potatoes, sausage, and a hot dog. The raw bar has oysters and clams on the half shell. ⊠ *19 Bay St.* ☎ *603/569–1503* ▭ *MC, V* ☉ *Closed Oct.–mid-May.*

$–$$$$ ✕▥ **Wolfeboro Inn.** Built in the early 1800s, this white clapboard house has later additions with lake views. Rooms have polished cherry and pine furnishings, armoires, stenciled borders, and country quilts but could stand a little updating, especially the bathrooms and toiletries. Pub fare and more than 70 brands of beer are available at Wolfe's Tavern ($–$$), where fireplaces take the chill off cool evenings. The 1812 Steakhouse ($–$$$) serves a popular slow-roasted prime rib. ⊠ *90 N. Main St.* ⬠ *Box 1270, 03894* ☎ *603/569–3016 or 800/451–2389* 🖷 *603/569–5375* ⊕ *www.wolfeboroinn.com* ⬠ *41 rooms, 3 suites, 1 apartment* ⬠ *2 restau-*

rants, some refrigerators, cable TV, beach, boating, bar, meeting room ▭ *AE, D, MC, V* ¹⊙¹ *CP.*

★ **$–$$$** ▦ **Topsides B & B.** Wolfeboro got a real boost with the opening of this stylish retreat, each of whose refined rooms subtly conveys the allure of a particular region, from coastal France to Martha's Vineyard to Virginia fox-hunting country. Lavish, custom bedding, Persian rugs, marble dressers, and fresh flowers lend an eclectic sophistication to this pale-gray clapboard inn that's steps from downtown shops and restaurants. High-speed wireless, homemade bath amenities, and highly personalized attention complete the experience. ✉ *209 S. Main St., 03894* ☎ *603/569–3834* ⊕ *www.topsidesbb.com* ⟿ *5 rooms* ⚬ *Cable TV, Wi-Fi; no kids under 12, no smoking* ▭ *D, MC, V* ¹⊙¹ *CP.*

Sports & the Outdoors

BEACHES **Wentworth State Beach** (✉ Rte. 109 ☎ 603/569–3699) has good swimming, fishing, picnicking areas, ball fields, and a bathhouse; admission is $3.

BOATING **Wet Wolfe Boat Rentals** (✉ 17 Bay St. ☎ 603/569–1503) rents motorboats and personal watercraft.

Winnipesaukee Kayak Company (✉ 17 Bay St. ☎ 603/569–9926 ✉ 290 U.S. 3, Meredith ☎ 603/279–8147) gives kayak lessons and leads group excursions on the lake.

GOLF The Donald Ross–designed **Kingswood Golf Club** (✉ Rte. 28 ☎ 603/569–3569) has an 18-hole, par-72 course; greens fees are $55.

HIKING A short (¼-mi) hike to the 100-foot post-and-beam **Abenaki Tower,** followed by a more rigorous climb to the top, rewards you with a vast view of Lake Winnipesaukee and the Ossipee mountain range. The trailhead is a few miles north of town on Route 109.

WATER SPORTS Scuba divers can explore a 130-foot-long cruise ship that sank in 30 feet of water off Glendale in 1895. **Dive Winnipesaukee Corp** (✉ 4 N. Main St. ☎ 603/569–8080) runs charters out to wrecks and offers rentals, repairs, scuba sales, and lessons in waterskiing.

Shopping

American Home Gallery (✉ 49 Center St., Wolfeboro Falls ☎ 603/569–8989) mixes an amazing array of antiques and housewares in with its architectural elements. You'll find an excellent regional-history section and plenty of children's titles at Wolfeboro's fine general-interest bookstore, the **Country Bookseller** (✉ 23A N. Main St. ☎ 603/569–6030). **Made on Earth** (✉ 33 Main St. ☎ 603/569–9100) carries new age gifts, clothing, books, and crafts.

Alton Bay

❽ *10 mi southwest of Wolfeboro.*

Lake Winnipesaukee's southern shore is alive with visitors from the moment the first flower blooms until the last maple sheds its leaves. Two mountain ridges hold 7 mi of the lake in Alton Bay, which is the name of both the inlet and the town at its tip. Cruise boats dock here, and small planes land here year-round, on both the water and the ice. There's a dance pavilion, along with miniature golf, a public beach, and a Victorian-style bandstand.

Mt. Major, 5 mi north of Alton Bay on Route 11, has a 2½-mi trail with views of Lake Winnipesaukee. At the top is a four-sided stone shelter built in 1925.

Where to Eat

★ **$$$$** ✕ **Crystal Quail.** This 12-table restaurant, inside an 18th-century farmhouse, is worth the drive for the sumptuous meals prepared by longtime proprietors Harold and Cynthia Huckaby, who use free-range meats and mostly organic produce and herbs in their cooking. The prix-fixe contemporary menu changes daily but might include saffron-garlic soup, a house pâté, quenelle-stuffed sole, or goose confit with apples and onions. ✉ *202 Pitman Rd., 12 mi south of Alton Bay, Center Barnstead* ☎ *603/269–4151* ⊕ *www.crystalquail.com* ⚐ *Reservations essential* ▭ *No credit cards* ☞ *BYOB* ⊘ *Closed Mon. and Tues. No lunch.*

Gilford

❾ *15 mi northwest of Alton Bay.*

One of the larger public beaches on Lake Winnipesaukee is in Gilford. When the town was incorporated in 1812, the inhabitants asked the oldest resident to name it. A veteran of the Battle of the Guilford Courthouse, in North Carolina, he borrowed that town's name—though apparently he didn't know how to spell it. Quiet and peaceful, Gilford remains decidedly uncommercial.

🄲 Nearby **Weirs Beach** is Lake Winnipesaukee's center for arcade activity. Anyone who loves souvenir shops, fireworks, waterslides, and hordes of children will feel right at home. Several cruise boats depart from the town dock. The period cars of the **Winnipesaukee Scenic Railroad** carry you along the lakeshore on one- or two-hour rides; boarding is at Weirs Beach or Meredith. Special trips that include dinner are also available, as well as foliage trains. ✉ *U.S. 3, Weirs Beach* ☎ *603/279–5253 or 603/745–2135* ⊕ *www.hoborr.com* ▭ *$9–$71* ⊘ *July–mid-Sept., daily; Memorial Day–late June and mid-Sept.–mid-Oct., weekends only. Call for hrs and for special Santa trains in Dec.*

🄲 The mother ship of Lake Winnipesaukee's several giddy family-oriented amusement parks, **Funspot** claims to be the second-largest arcade in the country, but it's much more than just a video-game room. Here you can work your way through a miniature golf course, a golf driving range, an indoor golf simulator, 20 lanes of bowling, cash bingo, and more than 500 video games. Some outdoor attractions are closed in winter months. ✉ *Rte. 3, Weirs Beach* ☎ *603/366–4377* ⊕ *www.funspotnh.com* ▭ *Entrance free; charge for each activity* ⊘ *Mid-June–early Sept., daily 9* AM*–midnight; early Sept.–mid-June, Sun.–Thurs. 10–10, Fri. and Sat. 10* AM*–11* PM*.*

2

☺ The lake's ultimate water park, **Surf Coaster** has seven waterslides, a wave pool, and the Barefoot Action Lagoon, a large area for young children. Teams of six can also duke it out in a massive inflatable maze for a game of water tag. ☒ *1085 White Oaks Rd., Weirs Beach* ☎ *603/366–5600* ⊕ *www.surfcoasterusa.com* ☒ *$25* ☉ *Late June–early Sept., daily 10–6.*

The 230-foot **M/S Mount Washington** (☎ 603/366–5531 or 888/843–6686 ⊕ www.cruisenh.com ☒ $20 adults, $5 children) makes 2½-hour scenic cruises of Lake Winnipesaukee from Weirs Beach, mid-May–late October, with stops in Wolfeboro, Alton Bay, Center Harbor, and Meredith (you can board at any of these stops). Evening cruises include live music and a buffet dinner. The same company operates the M/V *Sophie C.*, which has been the area's floating post office for more than a century. The boat departs from Weirs Beach with mail and passengers Monday–Saturday, mid-June–Labor Day; call for stops. Additionally, the M/V *Doris E.* runs between Meredith and Weirs Beach throughout summer.

Where to Stay

$$–$$$ ☒ **B. Mae's Resort Inn.** All the rooms in this contemporary resort and conference center are large, if nondescript, and have a deck or patio; some are suites with kitchens. Close to the Gunstock ski area and within walking distance of Lake Winnipesaukee, B. Mae's is popular with skiers in winter and boaters in summer. ☒ *Rtes. 11 and 11B, 03249* ☎ *603/293–7526 or 800/458–3877* ☏ *603/293–4340* ⊕ *www. bmaesresort.com* ⬍ *59 rooms, 24 suites* ♨ *In-room safes, some kitchens, cable TV, some in-room VCRs, in-room data ports, 2 pools (1 indoor), gym, hot tub, bar, recreation room* ⊟ *AE, D, DC, MC, V.*

$–$$$ ☒ **Gunstock Inn & Fitness Center.** The original building of this Colonial-style inn, just up the road from the Gunstock ski area, was constructed in the 1930s by Civilian Conservation Corps workers who cut the area's first ski trails. The inn has individually decorated rooms, some of them large enough to accommodate families. Many rooms have views of the mountains and Lake Winnipesaukee. The snug tavern serves everything from seafood to burgers. In the fitness center, you can take water aerobics and body-toning classes free of charge. ☒ *580 Cherry Valley Rd., 03246* ☎ *603/293–2021 or 800/654–0180* ☏ *603/293–2050* ⊕ *www. gunstockinn.com* ⬍ *23 rooms, 2 suites* ♨ *Restaurant, some refrigerators, cable TV, indoor pool, health club, sauna, steam room* ⊟ *D, MC, V* ⑩ *BP.*

¢ ☒ **Gunstock Campground.** The campground at the Gunstock ski and recreation area has a pool and 300 tent and trailer sites as well as several cabins. ☒ *Rte. 11A* ☐ *Box 1307, Laconia 03247* ☎ *603/293–4341 or 800/486–7862* ⊕ *www.gunstock.com* ☒ *$25–$70* ⬍ *300 sites, 2 cabins* ♨ *Snack bar, playground, flush toilets, full hookups, dump station, drinking water, showers, fire grates, picnic tables, electricity, public telephone, general store* ⊟ *AE, D, MC, V.*

Nightlife & the Arts

The outdoor stage (with 2,500 covered seats) at **Meadowbrook** (☒ 72 Meadowbrook La., off Rte. 11B ☎ 603/293–4700 ⊕ www. meadowbrook.net) hosts top music acts. The **New Hampshire Music Festival** (☎ 603/279–3300 ⊕ www.nhmf.org) presents award-winning orchestras from early July to mid-August; concerts are held either at the Festival House on Symphony Lane in Center Harbor or at the Silver Cultural Arts Center on Main Street in Plymouth.

Sports & the Outdoors

Ellacoya State Beach (✉ Rte. 11 ☎ 603/293–7821) covers just 600 feet along the southwestern shore of Lake Winnipesaukee. In season, there's a bathhouse, picnic tables, and a fee ($3 from mid-May to Labor Day) for parking.

Thurston's Marina (✉ U.S. 3 at the bridge, Weirs Beach ☎ 603/366–4811) rents pontoon boats, powerboats, and personal watercraft.

GOLF **Pheasant Ridge Golf Club** (✉ 140 Country Club Rd. ☎ 603/524–7808) has an 18-hole layout with great mountain views. Greens fees range from $31 to $40.

SKI AREA **Gunstock USA.** High above Lake Winnipesaukee, this all-purpose area dates from the 1930s. It once had the country's longest rope tow lift—an advantage that helped local downhill skier and Olympic silver medalist Penny Pitou perfect her craft. Thrill Hill, a snow-tubing park, has 10 runs, multipassenger tubes, and lift service. Clever trail cutting along with grooming and surface sculpting three times daily has made this otherwise pedestrian mountain good for intermediates. That's how most of the 44 trails are rated, with a few more challenging runs as well as designated sections for slow skiers and learners. It's the state's largest night-skiing facility. Gunstock has 30 mi of trails for cross-country skiing and snowshoeing. In summer you'll find a swimming pool, a playground, hiking trails, mountain-bike rentals and trails, a skateboarding-blading park, guided horseback rides, pedal boats, and a campground. ✉ *Rte. 11A ⌂ Box 1307, Laconia 03247 ☎ 603/293–4341 or 800/486–7862 ⊕ www.gunstock.com.*

Shopping

Pepi Herrmann Crystal (✉ 3 Waterford Pl. ☎ 603/528–1020) sells handcut crystal chandeliers and stemware. You can take a tour and watch the artists at work.

Laconia

❿ *4 mi west of Gilford, 27 mi north of Concord.*

The arrival in Laconia—then called Meredith Bridge—of the railroad in 1848 turned the once-sleepy hamlet into the Lakes Region's chief manufacturing hub. It acts today as the area's supply depot, a perfect role given its accessibility to both Winnisquam and Winnipesaukee lakes as well as Interstate 93. Come here when you need to find a chain superstore or fast-food restaurant.

Belknap Mill (✉ Mill Plaza, 25 Beacon St. ☎ 603/524–8813 ⊕ www.belknapmill.org), the oldest unaltered, brick-built textile mill in the United States (1823), contains a knitting museum devoted to the textile industry and a year-round cultural center that sponsors concerts, workshops, exhibits, and a lecture series.

Where to Stay

$–$$ ⚏ **Ferry Point House.** Built in the 1800s as a summer retreat for the Pillsbury family of baking fame, this red Victorian farmhouse has superb views of Lake Winnisquam. White wicker furniture and hanging baskets of flowers grace the 60-foot veranda, and the gazebo by the water's edge is a pleasant place to lounge and listen for loons. A pedal boat and a rowboat await those eager to get in the water. The pretty rooms have Oriental rugs and Victorian furniture. ⊠ *100 Lower Bay Rd., Sanbornton 03269* ☎ *603/524–0087* ⊕ *www.new-hampshire-inn.com* ➳ *6 rooms* ⚲ *Beach, boating, fishing, no-smoking rooms; no room phones, no room TVs* ⊟ *No credit cards* ☉ *Closed Nov.–Mar.* ❄ *BP.*

Sports & the Outdoors

Bartlett Beach (⊠ Winnisquam Ave.) has a playground and picnic area. **Opechee Park** (⊠ N. Main St.) has dressing rooms, a baseball field, tennis courts, and picnic areas.

Shopping

The **Belknap Mall** (⊠ U.S. 3 ☎ 603/524–5651) has boutiques, crafts shops, and a New Hampshire State Liquor Store. The more than 50 stores at the **Tanger Outlet Center** (⊠ 120 Laconia Rd., I–93 Exit 20, Tilton ☎ 603/ 286–7880) include Brooks Brothers, Eddie Bauer, Coach, Geoffrey Beene, and Mikasa.

<table>
<tr><td>

OFF THE
BEATEN
PATH

</td><td>

CANTERBURY SHAKER VILLAGE – Shaker furniture and inventions are well regarded, and this National Historic Landmark helps illuminate the world of the people who created them. Established as a religious community in 1792, the village flourished in the 1800s and practiced equality of the sexes and races, common ownership, celibacy, and pacifism. The last member of the community passed away in 1992. Shakers invented such household items as the clothespin and the flat broom and were known for the simplicity and integrity of their designs. Engaging 90-minute tours pass through some of the 694-acre property's more than 25 restored buildings, many of them still with original Shaker furnishings, and crafts demonstrations take place daily. The Shaker Table restaurant ($$–$$$$) serves lunch daily and candlelight dinners Thursday–Sunday (reservations essential); the food blends contemporary and traditional Shaker recipes to delicious effect. A large shop sells fine Shaker reproductions. ⊠ *288 Shaker Rd., 15 mi south of Laconia via Rte. 106, Canterbury* ☎ *603/783–9511 or 866/783–9511* ⊕ *www. shakers.org* ⊠ *$15, good for 2 consecutive days* ☉ *Mid-May–Oct., daily 10–5; Apr., Nov., and Dec., weekends 10–4.*

</td></tr>
</table>

Meredith

⑪ *11 mi north of Laconia.*

Meredith, a onetime workaday mill town on U.S. 3 at Lake Winnipesaukee's western end, has watched its fortunes change for the better over the past decade or so. The opening of the Inns at Mills Falls has attracted hundreds of visitors, and crafts shops and art galleries have sprung up. You can pick up area information at a kiosk across from the town docks.

At **Annalee's Doll Museum,** you can view a collection of the famous felt dolls that Annalee Davis Thorndike began making after her graduation from high school in 1933. The poppets caught on with collectors, and the company grew into an empire. ☒ *Annalee Place off Rte. 104* ☎ *603/ 279–3333 or 800/433–6557* ⊕ *www.annalee.com* ☒ *Free* ☺ *Memorial Day–mid-Oct.; call for hrs.*

Where to Stay & Eat

$–$$ ✕ **Mame's.** This 1820s tavern, once the home of the village doctor, now contains a warren of convivial dining rooms with exposed-brick walls, wooden beams, and wide-plank floors. Expect mostly American standbys of the fish, steak, veal, and chicken variety, including very good seafood Diane (shrimp, scallops, and salmon sautéed in butter and white wine); the mud pie is highly recommended. ☒ *8 Plymouth St.* ☎ *603/279–4631* ▭ *AE, D, MC, V.*

$$–$$$$ ✕▥ **Inns and Spa at Mill Falls.** Overlooking Lake Winnipesaukee and in-
Fodor'sChoice corporating sections of the 19th-century Meredith Linen Mills, this
★ complex has all the amenities of a full resort as well as warmth and personality. The central-most Inn at Mills Falls, which adjoins an 18-shop market, has a pool and 54 spacious rooms. The lakefront Inn at Bay Point has 24 rooms—most with balconies, some with fireplaces. The 23 rooms at the lake-view Chase House at Mill Falls all have fireplaces; some have balconies. Many of the rooms at the posh Church Landing, a dramatic lakefront building, have double whirlpool tubs, gas fireplaces, and expansive decks with terrific water views. At the snazzy Cascade Spa, you can get a sea-salt glow or a Tribal Essence massage. Restaurants include the upscale Lakehouse ($$–$$$), which serves stellar contemporary dishes, and Lago ($$–$$$), which serves trendy Italian fare. ☒ *312 Daniel Webster Hwy U.S. 3 at Rte. 25, 03253* ☎ *603/279–7006 or 800/622–6455* ⊕ *www.millsfalls.com* ⇱ *146 rooms, 14 suites* ♿ *5 restaurants, some in-room hot tubs, cable TV, indoor pool, sauna, beach, dock, boating, ice-skating, bar, shops, meeting rooms* ▭ *AE, D, DC, MC, V.*

¢ ⛺ **Clearwater Campground.** This wooded tent and RV campground on Lake Pemigewasset has 153 shady sites, several well-outfitted cabins with fireplaces, a large sandy beach, a recreation building, a playground, basketball and volleyball courts, and boat rentals and slips. ☒ *26 Campground Rd., off Rte. 104, 03253* ☎ *603/279–7761* ⊕ *www. clearwatercampground.com* ⇱ *156 sites, 5 cabins* ♿ *Snack bar, playground, laundry facilities, flush toilets, full hookups, dump station, drinking water, showers, fire grates, picnic tables, electricity, public telephone, general store* ☺ *Closed mid-Oct.–mid-May.*

The Arts

The **Lakes Region Summer Theatre** (☒ Interlakes Auditorium, Rte. 25 ☎ 603/279–9933 ⊕ www.lakesregionsummertheatre.com) presents Broadway musicals during its 10-week season of summer stock.

Sports & the Outdoors

Red Hill, a hiking trail on Bean Road off Route 25, northeast of Center Harbor and about 7 mi northeast of Meredith, really does turn red in autumn. The reward at the end of the route is a view of Squam Lake and the mountains.

BOATING Meredith is also near the quaint village of Center Harbor, another boating hub that's in the middle of three bays at the northern end of Lake Winnipesaukee. **Meredith Marina and Boating Center** (⊠ 2 Bayshore Dr. ☎ 603/279–7921) rents powerboats. **Wild Meadow Canoes & Kayaks** (⊠ Rte. 25 between Center Harbor and Moultonboro ☎ 603/253–7536 or 800/427–7536) has canoes and kayaks for rent.

GOLF **Waukewan Golf Club** (⊠ 166 Waukewan Rd. ☎ 603/279–6661) is an 18-hole, par-71 course. Greens fees are $35–$40.

Shopping

About 170 dealers operate out of the three-floor **Burlwood Antique Center** (⊠ U.S. 3 ☎ 603/279–6387), open May–October. **Keepsake Quilting & Country Pleasures** (⊠ Senter's Marketplace, Rte. 25B, Center Harbor, 5 mi northeast of Meredith ☎ 603/253–4026 or 800/965–9456), reputedly America's largest quilt shop, contains 5,000 bolts of fabric, hundreds of quilting books, and countless supplies as well as handmade quilts.

The **Meredith League of New Hampshire Craftsmen** (⊠ 279 U.S. 3, ½ mi north of Rte. 104 ☎ 603/279–7920) sells works by area artisans. **Mill Falls Marketplace** (⊠ U.S. 3 at Rte. 25 ☎ 603/279–7006), part of the Inns at Mills Falls, contains shops with clothing, gifts, and books. The **Old Print Barn** (⊠ 343 Winona Rd., New Hampton ☎ 603/279–6479) carries rare prints—Currier & Ives, antique botanicals, and more—from around the world.

Bristol

⑫ *15 mi west of Meredith, 20 mi northwest of Laconia.*

The small workaday town of Bristol serves as a base for exploring one of the Lakes Region's greatest treasures: 4,000-acre Newfound Lake, one of the state's deepest bodies of water and also one of the purest. You reach the spring-fed lake by driving 2 mi north along Route 3A, along which are several beaches. Bristol is also close to several popular hiking areas, including 3,121-foot Mt. Cardigan, in nearby Alexandria, and Bit and Little Sugarloaf peaks, the trailhead for which is reached along West Shore Road, near the entrance to Wellington State Beach. The Newfound River runs through town and is great for fishing salmon, rainbow trout, and largemouth bass.

The best public access is on the lake's western shore, at 204-acre **Wellington State Park** (⊠ W. Shore Rd., off Rte. 3A ☎ 603/744–2197). Here you can swim, picnic, hike along the ½-mi shoreline, or use the boat launch. Admission is $3.

Where to Stay

$–$$ 🏠 **Henry Whipple House.** In downtown Bristol, 2 mi south of Newfound Lake, this magnificent turreted Queen Anne house with such original details as bronze fireplaces, chandeliers, and stained-glass windows has six antiques-filled rooms, two of them with wood-burning fireplaces. An adjacent carriage house contains a pair of suites, able to accommodate five or eight guests respectively. Breakfast is generous and delicious, using organic produce and free-range meats. ⊠ *75 Summer St., 03222* ☎ *603/744–6157* ⊕ *www.thewhipplehouse.com* ⟿ *6 rooms, 2 suites* ⚬ *Some kitchens, cable TV; no smoking* ═ *D, MC, V* ¶⃝ *BP.*

Shopping

More than 170 artisans show their offbeat crafts and decorative arts, including stunning hand-forged ironwork and fine jewelry, at **Earthly Treasures** (⊠ 150 Lake St. ☎ 603/744–5331 or 800/480–0380).

Plymouth

⓭ *16 mi north of Bristol, 18 mi south of Woodstock.*

Home to Plymouth State College, whose small but attractive campus clings to a steep hill looming over a bustling downtown, Plymouth acts as a bridge between the Lakes Region and the White Mountains. There's a very good ski resort, some engaging shops downtown, and one of the most impressive new hotels in northern New Hampshire, the Common Man Inn.

Where to Stay & Eat

$–$$$ ✕▦ **Common Man Inn.** Opened in 2003 by the same team behind the acclaimed Common Man restaurant group, which has popular eateries throughout central and northern New Hampshire, this contemporary hotel with country lodge–inspired furnishings sits within walking distance of downtown shopping and the college. Rooms are elegantly appointed and come in many different configurations; some have whirlpool tubs and fireplaces, and a few have cozy sleeping lofts. Foster's Steakhouse ($$–$$$) serves creative renditions of steaks and chops and also hosts one of the most popular Sunday brunches around. At the spa, you can indulge yourself with a massage, facial, or body treatment. ⊠ *231 Main St., 03264* ☎ *603/536–2200 or 866/843–2626* ⊕ *www.thecmaninn. com* ⟿ *3 suites, 3 lofts* ⚬ *Restaurant, some in-room hot tubs, cable TV, in-room broadband, Wi-Fi, spa, bar, meeting rooms, some pets allowed,* ═ *MC, V* ¶⃝ *BP.*

Sports & the Outdoors

SKI AREA   **Tenney Mountain.** At the southern edge of the White Mountains, this low-key and friendly facility provides mostly intermediate skiing, with about 46 trails, and a vertical drop of around 1,450 feet. The longest run floats down the mountain for nearly 2 mi. ⊠ *151 Tenney Mountain Rd. 03264* ☎ *603/536–4125* ⊕ *www.tenneymtn.com.*

Holderness

⓮ *8 mi southeast of Plymouth, 8 mi northwest of Meredith.*

Routes 25B and 25 lead to the small prim town of Holderness, between Squam and Little Squam lakes. *On Golden Pond,* starring Katharine Hepburn and Henry Fonda, was filmed on Squam, whose quiet beauty attracts nature lovers.

★ ☼ Trails at the 200-acre **Squam Lakes Natural Science Center** include a ¼-mi path that passes black bears, bobcats, otters, and other native wildlife in trailside enclosures. Educational events such as the "Up Close to Animals" series in July and August also allow you to study a species in an intimate setting. The Gordon Children's Activity Center has interactive exhibits. A ride on a 28-foot pontoon boat is the best way to tour the lake and observe the loons. The center runs all kinds of boat trips through **Golden Pond Tours,** including sunset excursions, dinner-and-cruise packages in conjunction with Walter's Basin restaurant, and full-moon jaunts. ⊠ *Rte. 113* ☎ *603/968–7194* ⊕ *www.nhnature.org* ▤ *$12, boat tour $16, combination boat tour $24* ☉ *May–Oct., daily 9:30–4:30 (last entry at 3:30).*

Where to Stay & Eat

$–$$$ ✕ **Walter's Basin.** A former bowling alley in the heart of Holderness makes an unlikely but charming setting for meals overlooking gentle Little Squam Lake—local boaters dock right beneath the dining room. Among the specialties on this seafood-intensive menu are crostini topped with lobster and fontina cheese, and almond-crusted rainbow trout with hazelnut beurre blanc. Burgers and sandwiches are served in the adjoining tavern. ⊠ *15 Main St. (U.S. 3)* ☎ *603/968–4412* ▤ *AE, D, MC, V.*

$$$$ ✕▥ **Manor on Golden Pond.** This stately, baronial stucco-and-shingle inn
Fodor'sChoice sits on a slight rise overlooking Squam Lake, on 15 acres of towering
★ pines and hardwood trees. You can sit on the lawn in one of the Adirondack chairs, gazing out at the lake in one direction or toward the distant White Mountains in the other. Rooms in this house carry out a British country theme, most with wood-burning fireplaces and more than half with double whirlpool tubs. Canopy beds, vintage blanket chests, and tartan fabrics fill the sumptuous bedchambers. In the first-rate restaurant ($$$–$$$$), three-, four-, or five-course prix fixe dinners may include roasted breast and confit of Maine duck on a bed of creamy polenta served with glazed root vegetables and a port wine sauce. Stroll down to the sandy private beach for a dip in the lake, or paddle a canoe for a bit, keeping an eye out for ever-elusive loons or even the occasional bald eagle. ⊠ *U.S. 3 and Shepard Hill Rd., 03245* ☎ *603/968–3348 or 800/545–2141* ▤ *603/968–2116* ⊕ *www.manorongoldenpond.com* ▱ *20 rooms, 3 cottages, 1 carriage house* ♿ *Restaurant, some in-room hot tubs, cable TV, in-room VCRs, 2 tennis courts, pool, beach, boating, fishing, badminton, croquet, pub, library; no kids under 12, no smoking* ▤ *AE, MC, V* ⊙| *BP.*

$$–$$$$ ▥ **Glynn House Inn.** Jim and Gay Dunlop run this swank, three-story, 1890s Queen Anne–style Victorian with a turret and wraparound porch and, next door, a handsome 1920s carriage house. Many rooms have fireplaces; the bi-level Honeymoon Suite has a whirlpool tub and fireplace downstairs and a four-poster bed and skylights above. Breakfast usually includes freshly baked strudel. Squam Lake is minutes away. ⊠ *59 Highland St., Ashland 03217* ☎ *603/968–3775 or 800/ 637–9599* ▤ *603/968–9415* ⊕ *www.glynnhouse.com* ▱ *5 rooms, 8 suites* ♿ *Some in-room hot tubs, cable TV, in-room VCRs; no smoking* ▤ *MC, V* ⊙| *BP.*

$$–$$$ ⊡ **Inn on Golden Pond.** This informal country home, built in 1879 and set on 50 wooded acres, is just up the road from Squam Lake. Rooms have hardwood floors, braided rugs, easy chairs, and calico-print bedspreads and curtains. The homemade jam at breakfast is made from rhubarbs grown on the property. ⊠ *U.S. 3* ☏ *Box 680, 03245* ☎ *603/968–7269* 🖷 *603/968–9226* ⊕ *www.innongoldenpond.com* ⮑ *6 rooms, 2 suites* ⚷ *Hiking; no room phones, no room TVs, no kids under 12, no smoking* ⊟ *AE, D, MC, V* ⧑ *BP.*

$$ ⊡ **Squam Lake Inn.** Graceful, simple Victorian furnishings fill the eight stylish rooms and suites at this peaceful farmhouse inn just a short stroll from Squam Lake. In each you'll find Crabtree & Evelyn bath amenities, hair dryers, alarm clocks, and downy bathrobes. The inn is well away from the bustle of Winnipesaukee's amusements but within an easy drive of area eateries and shops. A full country breakfast and Saturday-afternoon hors d'oeuvres are served by candlelight. ⊠ *Shepard Hill Rd., 03245* ☎ *603/968–4417 or 800/839–6205* 🖷 *603/968–3661* ⊕ *www.squamlakeinn.com* ⮑ *6 rooms, 2 suites* ⚷ *No room phones, no room TVs, no kids under 10, no smoking* ⊟ *AE, D, MC, V* ⧑ *BP.*

¢–$$ △ **Yogi Bear's Jellystone Park.** This family-oriented camping resort has wooded, open, or riverfront sites; basic and deluxe cabins; and trailers. There's also a pool, a water playground, a hot tub, a miniature golf course, a basketball court, canoe and kayak rentals, and daily supervised activities. ⊠ *Rte. 132, Ashland* ☏ *R.R. 1, Box 396, 03217* ☎ *603/968–9000* ⊕ *www.jellystonenh.com* ⊠ *$51–$132* ⮑ *275 sites, 43 cabins, 7 trailers* ⚷ *Snack bar, pool, playground, laundry facilities, flush toilets, full hookups, dump station, drinking water, showers, fire grates, picnic tables, electricity, public telephone, general store.*

Sports & the Outdoors
White Mountain Country Club (⊠ N. Ashland Rd., Ashland ☎ 603/536–2227) has an 18-hole, par-71 golf course. Greens fees are $32–$40.

Center Sandwich

★ ⓯ *12 mi northeast of Holderness.*

With Squam Lake to the west and the Sandwich Mountains to the north, Center Sandwich claims one of the prettiest settings of any Lakes Region community. So appealing are the town and its views that John Greenleaf Whittier used the Bearcamp River as the inspiration for his poem "Sunset on the Bearcamp." The town attracts artisans—crafts shops abound among its clutch of charming 18th- and 19th-century buildings.

The **Historical Society Museum** traces Center Sandwich's history through the faces of its inhabitants. Works by mid-19th-century portraitist and town son Albert Gallatin Hoit hang alongside a local photographer's exhibit portraying the town's mothers and daughters. The museum houses a replica country store and local furniture and other items. ⊠ *4 Maple St.* ☎ *603/284–6269* ⊕ *www.sandwichhistorical.org* ⊠ *$3* ☽ *Late June–early Oct., Thurs.–Sat. 10–4.*

The **Old Country Store and Museum** (⊠ Moultonborough Corner, 5 mi south of Center Sandwich ☎ 603/476–5750) has been selling maple products, cheeses aged on site, penny candy, and other items since 1781. Much of the equipment still used in the store is antique, and the museum (free) displays old farming and forging tools.

Castle in the Clouds is an odd, elaborate stone mansion built without nails; it has 16 rooms, 8 bathrooms, and doors made of lead. Construction began in 1911 and continued for three years. Owner Thomas Gustave Plant spent $7 million, the bulk of his fortune, on this project and died penniless in 1946. A tour includes the mansion and the Castle Springs spring-water facility on this 5,200-acre property; there's also hiking and pony and horseback rides. ⊠ *Rte. 171* ☎ *603/476–2352 or 800/729–2468* ⊕ *www. castleintheclouds.org* 🖾 *$10* ☉ *Mid-May–mid-Oct., daily 10–4:30.*

The **Loon Center** at the **Frederick and Paula Anna Markus Wildlife Sanctuary** is the headquarters of the Loon Preservation Committee, an Audubon Society project. The loon, recognizable for its eerie calls and striking black-and-white coloring, resides on many New Hampshire lakes but is threatened by boat traffic, poor water quality, and habitat loss. Besides the changing exhibits about the birds, two trails wind through the 200-acre property: vantage points on the Loon Nest Trail overlook the spot resident loons sometimes occupy in late spring and summer. ⊠ *Lee's Mills Rd.* ☎ *603/476–5666* ⊕ *www.loon.org* 🖾 *Free* ☉ *July–Columbus Day, daily 9–5; Columbus Day–June, Mon.–Sat. 9–5.*

Where to Eat

$$–$$$ ╳ **Coe House Restaurant.** Occupying a handsomely restored 18th-century mansion, this grand restaurant turns out expertly prepared contemporary American and continental fare. Start with the glazed cherrywood-smoked duck breast with toasted pecans and a cognac blackberry sauce before moving on to grilled maple-porterhouse pork chops with garlic-mashed potatoes and a black pepper–cider sauce. ⊠ *Rte. 25B, Center Harbor Village* ☎ *603/253–8617* ▭ *AE, MC, V* ☉ *Closed Mon.–Wed. Nov.–Apr. No lunch.*

$$–$$$ ╳ **Corner House Inn.** This restaurant, in a converted barn adorned with local arts and crafts, serves classic American fare. Before you get to the white-chocolate cheesecake with key-lime filling, try the chef's lobster-and-mushroom bisque or tasty garlic-and-horseradish-crusted rack of lamb. There's storytelling Thursday evening. ⊠ *Rtes. 109 and 113* ☎ *603/284–6219* ▭ *AE, MC, V* ☉ *Closed Nov.–May. No lunch.*

$$–$$$ ╳ **The Woodshed.** Farm implements and antiques hang on the walls of this enchanting, romantic 1860 barn. The fare is mostly traditional New England—sea scallops baked in butter and lamb chops with mint sauce—but with some occasional surprises, such as Cajun-blackened pork tenderloin. Either way, the exceptionally fresh ingredients are sure to please. ⊠ *128 Lee Rd. Moultonborough* ☎ *603/476–2311* ▭ *AE, D, DC, MC, V* ☉ *Closed Mon. No lunch.*

Tamworth

🔟 *13 mi east of Center Sandwich, 20 mi southwest of North Conway.*

President Grover Cleveland summered in what remains a village of almost unreal quaintness—it's equally photogenic in verdant summer, during the fall foliage season, or under a blanket of winter snow. Cleveland's son, Francis, returned to stay and founded the acclaimed Barnstormers Theatre in 1931. Tamworth has a clutch of villages within its borders. At one of them—Chocorua—the view through the birches of Chocorua Lake has been so often photographed that you may experience déjà vu.

For 99 years, Dr. Edwin Remick and his father provided medical services to the Tamworth area and operated a family farm. At the **Remick Country Doctor Museum and Farm,** exhibits focus on the life of a country doctor and on the activities of the still-working farm. There is always something hands-on going on, but try to visit when ice harvesting, stone-wall building, or the like is scheduled. ⊠ *58 Cleveland Hill Rd.* ☎ *603/323–7591 or 800/686–6117* ⊕ *www.remickmuseum.org* ⊠ *Free* ⊙ *Nov.–June, weekdays 10–4; July–Oct., Mon.–Sat. 10–4.*

Where to Stay & Eat

¢–$$$ ✕ **Jake's Seafood.** Oars and nautical trappings adorn the wood-paneled walls at this stop between West and Center Ossipee, about 8 mi southeast of Tamworth. The kitchen serves some of eastern New Hampshire's freshest and tastiest seafood, notably lobster pie, fried clams, and seafood casserole; other choices include steak, ribs, and chicken dishes. ⊠ *2055 Rte. 16* ☎ *603/539–2805* ▤ *D, MC, V* ⊙ *Closed Mon.–Wed.*

★ ¢–$$ ✕ **Yankee Smokehouse.** This down-home barbecue joint's logo depicting two happy pigs foreshadows the gleeful enthusiasm with which patrons dive into the hefty sandwiches of sliced pork and smoked chicken and immense platters of baby back ribs and smoked sliced beef. Ample sides of slaw, beans, fries, and garlic toast complement the hearty fare. Born-and-bred Southerners have been known to come away impressed. ⊠ *Rtes. 16 and 25, about 5 mi southeast of Tamworth* ☎ *603/539–7427* ▤ *MC, V.*

★ $$–$$$$ ✕▦ **Tamworth Inn.** This 1833 Victorian inn is a great base both for exploring the lakes and skiing in the White Mountains. Common rooms range from a beamed-ceiling pub to a dining room where tables are laid with white linen and crystal. Guest rooms have brass or antique beds, down comforters, CD players, and Caswell-Massey toiletries. The dining room ($$–$$$; closed Sunday and Monday in summer and Sunday–Wednesday in winter) serves seasonal cuisine with specialties such as grilled top sirloin with mushroom-leek ragout and whipped Red Bliss potatoes. It also serves an extensive full breakfast and afternoon tea. ⊠ *Main St., 03886* ☎ *603/323–7721 or 800/642–7352* 🖷 *603/323–2026* ⊕ *www.tamworth.com* ⇆ *10 rooms, 6 suites* ⚐ *Restaurant, some in-room hot tubs, pool, pub, some pets allowed (fee); no room phones, no room TVs, no smoking* ▤ *AE, MC, V* ⏅ *BP, MAP.*

$–$$$ ▦ **Lazy Dog Inn.** What began as a stagecoach stop has been operating as an inn almost continuously since 1845. Ideally located between the Lakes Region and the White Mountains, it draws many hikers and skiers. Guest rooms are welcoming with floral wallpapers, quilts, ceiling fans, and other personal touches. Common areas include a guest kitchen and a screened porch that might make hiking nearby Mt. Chocorua seem like too much work. ⊠ *Rte. 16* ✑ *Box 395, Chocorua*

03817 ☎ *603/323–8350 or 888/323–8350* ᵬ *603/323–3319* ⊕ *www. lazydoginn.com* ↝ *7 rooms, 4 with bath; 1 suite* ♿ *Gym, some pets allowed; no room phones, no room TVs* ⊟ *D, MC, V* ⅣⓄⅠ *BP.*

Nightlife & the Arts

The **Arts Council of Tamworth** (☎ 603/323–8104 ⊕ www.artstamworth. org) produces concerts—soloists, string quartets, revues, children's programs—from September through June and an arts show in late July. **Barn-stormers Summer Theatre** (⊠ Main St. ☎ 603/323–8500 ⊕ www. barnstormerstheatre.com) has performances in July and August. The box office opens in June.

Sports & the Outdoors

The 72-acre stand of native pitch pine at **White Lake State Park** (⊠ Rte. 16, Iamworth ☎ 603/323–7350) is a National Natural Landmark. The park has hiking trails, a sandy beach, trout fishing, canoe rentals, two camping areas, a picnic area, and swimming.

Shopping

The many theme rooms—a Christmas room, a bride's room, a children's room, among them—at the **Chocorua Dam Ice Cream & Gift Shop** (⊠ Rte. 16, Chocorua ☎ 603/323–8745) contain handcrafted items. When you've finished shopping, try the ice cream, coffee, or tea and scones. Local artisans create much of the jewelry, turned wooden bowls, pewter goblets, and glassware sold at **Tramway Artisans** (⊠ Rtes. 16 and 25, West Ossipee ☎ 603/539–5700).

THE WHITE MOUNTAINS

Sailors approaching East Coast harbors frequently mistake the pale peaks of the White Mountains—the highest range in the northeastern United States—for clouds. It was 1642 when explorer Darby Field could no longer contain his curiosity about one mountain in particular. He set off from his Exeter homestead and became the first man to climb what would eventually be called Mt. Washington. The 6,288-foot peak must have presented Field with formidable obstacles—its summit claims the highest wind velocity ever recorded and can see snow every month of the year.

Since Field's climb, curiosity about the mountains has not abated. Today an auto road and a cog railway lead to the top of Mt. Washington, and people come here by the tens of thousands to hike and climb, to photograph the vistas, and to ski. The peak is part of the Presidential Range, whose other peaks are also named after early presidents, and part of the White Mountain National Forest, whose roughly 770,000 acres extend from northern New Hampshire into southwestern Maine. Among the forest's scenic notches (deep mountain passes) are Pinkham, Kinsman, Franconia, and Crawford.

This tour begins in Waterville Valley, off Interstate 93, and continues to North Woodstock. It then follows portions of the White Mountains Trail, a 100-mi loop designated as a National Scenic & Cultural Byway.

Waterville Valley

⑰ *60 mi north of Concord.*

The first visitors began arriving in Waterville Valley in 1835. A 10-mi-long cul-de-sac cut by one of New England's several Mad rivers and circled by mountains, the valley was first a summer resort and then more of a ski area. Although it's now a year-round getaway, it still has a small-town charm. There are inns, condos, restaurants, shops, conference facilities, a grocery store, and a post office.

Where to Stay & Eat

¢–$$$ ✕ **Latitudes.** Southwest-inspired Latitudes caters to skiers, with fajitas, tacos, enchiladas, other Tex-Mex staples, and American fare. The food is well priced and filling. If you're solely into Tex, the lineup includes ribs, steak, seafood, and chicken. ⊠ *Town Sq.* ☎ *603/236–4646* ⊟ *AE, DC, MC, V.*

$$$$ 🏨 **Golden Eagle Lodge.** Waterville's premier condominium property—with its steep roof punctuated by dozens of gabled dormers—recalls the grand hotels of an earlier era. Rooms, however, are contemporary with upscale light-wood furniture and well-equipped kitchens; many have views of the surrounding peaks. The full-service complex has a two-story lobby and a capable front-desk staff. Guests have access to the White Mountain Athletic Club. ⊠ *6 Snow's Brook Rd.* ⓓ *Box 495, 03215* ☎ *603/236–4600 or 888/703–2453* 🖶 *603/236–4947* ⊕ *www. goldeneaglelodge.com* ⤳ *139 condominiums* ⚖ *Kitchenettes, cable TV, indoor pool, sauna, recreation room, laundry facilities* ⊟ *AE, D, DC, MC, V.*

$$$–$$$$ 🏨 **Black Bear Lodge.** This family-oriented property has one-bedroom suites that sleep up to six and have full kitchens. Each unit is individually owned and decorated. Children's movies are shown at night in season, and there's bus service to the slopes. Guests can use the White Mountain Athletic Club. ⊠ *3 Village Rd.* ⓓ *Box 357, 03215* ☎ *603/236–4501 or 800/ 349–2327* 🖶 *603/236–4114* ⊕ *www.black-bear-lodge.com* ⤳ *107 suites* ⚖ *Kitchens, cable TV, indoor-outdoor pool, gym, hot tub, sauna, steam room, recreation room; no a/c in some rooms* ⊟ *AE, D, MC, V.*

$–$$$$ 🏨 **Snowy Owl Inn.** You're treated to afternoon wine and cheese in the atrium lobby, which has a three-story fieldstone fireplace and many prints and watercolors of snowy owls. The fourth-floor bunk-bed lofts are ideal for families; first-floor rooms are suitable for couples seeking a quiet getaway. Four restaurants are within walking distance. Guests have access to the White Mountain Athletic Club. ⊠ *4 Village Rd.* ⓓ *Box 407, 03215* ☎ *603/236–8383 or 800/766–9969* 🖶 *603/236–4890* ⊕ *www. snowyowlinn.com* ⤳ *85 rooms* ⚖ *Some in-room hot tubs, some kitchens, cable TV, some in-room VCRs, 2 pools (1 indoor), gym, meeting rooms* ⊟ *AE, D, DC, MC, V* ⧖ *BP.*

Sports & the Outdoors

The **White Mountain Athletic Club** (⊠ Rte. 49 ☎ 603/236–8303) has tennis, racquetball, and squash as well as a 25-meter indoor pool, a jogging track, exercise equipment, whirlpools, saunas, steam rooms, and a games room. The club is free to guests of many area lodgings.

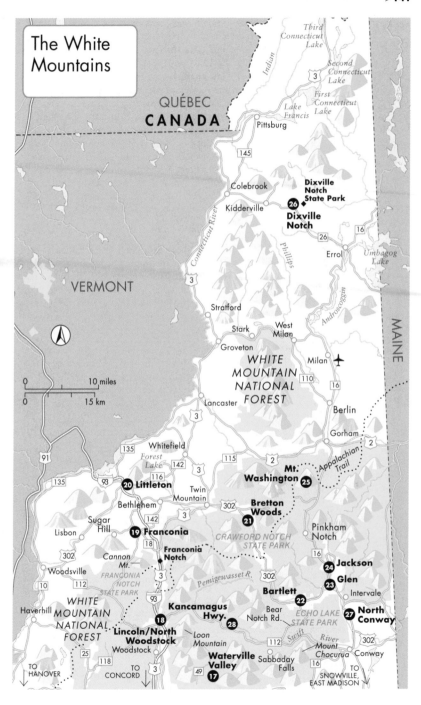

SKI AREA **Waterville Valley.** Former U.S. ski-team star Tom Corcoran designed this family-oriented resort. The lodgings and various amenities are about 1 mi from the slopes, but a shuttle renders a car unnecessary. This ski area has hosted more World Cup races than any other in the East, so most advanced skiers will be challenged. Most of the 52 trails are in-termediate: straight down the fall line, wide, and agreeably long. A 7-acre tree-skiing area adds variety. Snowmaking coverage of 100% ensures good skiing even when nature doesn't cooperate. The Water-ville Valley cross-country network, with the ski center in the town square, has 65 mi of trails. About two-thirds of them are groomed; the rest are backcountry. ⊠ *1 Ski Area Rd.* ✇ *Box 540, 03215* ☎ *603/236–8311, 603/236–4144 snow conditions, 800/468–2553 lodging* ⊕ *www.waterville.com.*

Lincoln/North Woodstock

⑱ *14 mi northwest of Waterville Valley, 63 mi north of Concord.*

Lincoln and North Woodstock, at the western end of the Kancamagus Highway (Route 112) or at Exit 32 off Interstate 93, combine to make one of the state's liveliest resort areas. They appeal more to the social set and families than to couples seeking a romantic retreat. Festivals, such as the New Hampshire Scottish Highland Games in mid-September, keep Lincoln swarming with people year-round; North Woodstock maintains more of a village feel.

Ⓒ A ride on the **Hobo Railroad** yields scenic views of the Pemigewasset River and the White Mountain National Forest. The narrated excursions take 80 minutes. ⊠ *Kancamagus Hwy. (Rte. 112), Lincoln* ☎ *603/745–2135* ⊕ *www.hoborr.com* ⊠ *$10* ⊗ *Late June–early Sept., daily; May–late June and early Sept.–Oct., weekends; call for schedule.*

Ⓒ At the **Whale's Tale Waterpark,** you can float on an inner tube along a gentle river, careen down one of five water slides, take a trip in a mul-tipassenger tube, or body-surf in the large wave pool. Whale Harbor and Orca Park Play Island contain water activities for small children and toddlers. ⊠ *U.S. 3, I–93 Exit 33, North Lincoln* ☎ *603/745–8810* ⊕ *www.whalestalewaterpark.net* ⊠ *$25* ⊗ *Mid-June–Labor Day, daily 10–6.*

Ⓒ It's undeniably hokey, but **Clarke's Trading Post** is a sure kids' favorite, consisting of a bear show, half-hour train rides over a 1904 covered bridge, a museum of Americana set inside an 1880s firehouse, a restored gas station filled with antique cars, and a replica of the Old Man of the Moun-tain that you can climb on. Tour guides tell tall tales and vendors sell popcorn, ice cream, pizza, and other snacks. There's also a mammoth gift shop, penny-candy store, and several other places to buy silly keep-sakes. ⊠ *U.S. 3, I–93 Exit 33, North Lincoln* ☎ *603/745–8913* ⊕ *www.clarkstradingpost.com* ⊠ *$12* ⊗ *Mid-May–mid June and early Sept.–mid-Oct., daily 9–5; mid-June–Aug., daily 9–6.*

Where to Stay & Eat

$–$$$ ✕☷ **Woodstock Inn.** Run by the Rice family since 1982, this social but laid-back inn occupies four buildings. Rooms range from simple to romantic (with canopy beds and free champagne), and many accommodate groups. The restaurants include the elegant Clement Room Grill ($$–$$$), an informal, plant-filled dining room that serves a mix of creative continental and American fare—bouillabaisse, jerk pork tenderloin, and ostrich quesadillas are favorites. The breakfasts here are bountiful and delicious—try the waffles slathered in peanut butter, marshmallow fluff, and walnuts. There's also Woodstock Station ($), where the menu lists everything from meat loaf to fajitas. The Woodstock Inn Brewery ($) serves the same dishes as the Woodstock Station as well as six year-round brews and four seasonal ones. ⊠ *U.S. 3* ⌂ *Box 118, North Woodstock 03262* ☎ *603/745–3951 or 800/321–3985* ⎘ *603/745–3701* ⊕ *www.woodstockinnnh.com* ⌁ *19 rooms, 5 suites, 2 with shared bath, 2 with hall bath* ↻ *2 restaurants, some inroom hot tubs, refrigerators, cable TV, outdoor hot tub, bar* ▭ *AE, D, MC, V* ⎮⊘⎮ *BP.*

$–$$$ ⊡ **Mountain Club on Loon.** This first-rate resort has an assortment of accommodations: suites that sleep as many as eight, studios with Murphy beds, and many units with kitchens. Many can be combined to form larger units. All rooms are within walking distance of the lifts, and condominiums are on or near the slopes. Entertainers perform in the lounge on most winter weekends. ⊠ *Kancamagus Hwy. (Rte. 112), Lincoln 03251* ☎ *603/745–2244 or 800/229–7829* ⎘ *603/745–2317* ⊕ *www. mtnclub.com* ⌁ *234 units* ↻ *Restaurant, some kitchens, cable TV, 2 tennis courts, 2 pools (1 indoor), fitness classes, health club, massage, sauna, spa, steam room, racquetball, squash, bar, lounge, video game room, meeting rooms* ▭ *AE, D, MC, V.*

¢–$$$ ⊡ **Indian Head Resort.** Views across the 180 acres of this motel near the Loon and Cannon Mountain ski areas are of Indian Head Rock Profile and the Franconia Mountains. Cross-country ski trails and a mountainbike trail from the resort connect to the Franconia Notch trail system. The Profile Room restaurant serves standard American fare. ⊠ *U.S. 3* ⌂ *R.R. 1, Box 99, North Lincoln 03251* ☎ *603/745–8000 or 800/343–8000* ⎘ *603/745–8414* ⊕ *www.indianheadresort.com* ⌁ *100 rooms, 40 cottages* ↻ *Restaurant, refrigerators, tennis court, 2 pools (1 indoor), lake, outdoor hot tub, sauna, fishing, bicycles, cross-country skiing, iceskating, bar, recreation room* ▭ *AE, D, DC, MC, V.*

Nightlife & the Arts

Skiers head to the **Black Diamond Lounge** (⊠ Kancamagus Hwy. [Rte. 112] ☎ 603/745–2244 ⊕ www.mtnclub.com) in the Mountain Club at the Loon Mountain resort. The **Olde Timbermill** (⊠ Mill at Loon Mountain, Kancamagus Hwy. [Rte. 112] ☎ 603/745–3603) has live dance music on weekends. The **North Country Center for the Arts** (⊠ Papermill Theatre, Kancamagus Hwy. [Rte. 112], Lincoln ☎ 603/745–6032, 603/745–2141 box office ⊕ www.papermilltheatre.org) presents theater for children and adults and art exhibitions in July and August. The draws at the **Thunderbird Lounge** (⊠ Indian Head Resort, 664 U.S. 3, North Lincoln ☎ 603/745–8000) are nightly entertainment year-round and a large dance floor.

The Old Man of the Mountain

NATHANIEL HAWTHORNE WROTE about it, New Hampshire resident Daniel Webster bragged about it, and P. T. Barnum tried to buy it. The New Hampshire Department of Motor Vehicles had its image etched onto every state license plate, and the U.S. Treasury imprinted it on the New Hampshire quarter in 2000. But ultimately, the fate of the Old Man of the Mountain rested with Mother Nature, not with the human beings who so admired it. And it was Mother Nature who dismantled the vaunted rock formation, just as surely as it had created it eons ago.

Those persons fortunate enough to have driven along Interstate 93 through Franconia Notch during the days preceding the early morning hours of May 3, 2003, were the last ever to lay eyes on this naturally formed granite profile, actually a series of five granite ledges, that so defined New Hampshire. It truly did look like the profile of an old, craggy man gazing out over Franconia Notch, some 1,200 feet above Spirit Lake, toward the Presidential Range.

In all likelihood, the bitter-cold winter of 2002–2003, along with especially harsh winds and heavy rains the weekend preceding its fall, contributed to the demise of the Old Man. But, of course, the rocky promontory, which measured 40 feet

from "chin" to "forehead," had withstood many brutal winters before this one—geologists believe the formation dated back at least 200 *million* years. Native Americans passed along legends of the peculiar likeness to Europeans in the early 1600s, and surveyors working in the region first claimed to have "discovered" the Old Man of the Mountain in 1805.

For a short time after the Old Man collapsed, some lively debates ensued regarding how to handle the loss of one of the White Mountains' favorite tourist attractions—one Connecticut businessman even proposed rebuilding the Old Man out of a patented polymer material. Most of the Old Man's fans, however, argued that any effort to reconstruct the formation would be an affront to its memory. And so it was decided simply to leave the remains of the formation as Mother Nature intended them.

Posted turnouts along Interstate 93's north- and southbound lanes still mark the parking areas where you can look up toward the Old Man's former perch. And at the Web page (⊕ www.franconianotchstatepark.com), you can admire an electronic "scrapbook" filled with remembrances from hundreds of saddened admirers.

—Andrew Collins

Sports & the Outdoors

ℭ At **Lost River Gorge in Kinsman Notch** (✉ Kancamagus Hwy. [Rte. 112], 6 mi west of North Woodstock ☎ 603/745–8720 or 800/346–3687 ⊕ www.findlostriver.com) you can hike along the sheer granite river gorge and view such geological wonders as the Guillotine Rock and the Lemon Squeezer or pan for gemstones. A cafeteria, garden, and gift shop round out the amenities. It's open daily from mid-May to mid-October; admission is $10. **Pemi Valley Excursions** (✉ Main St., I-93 Exit 32, Lincoln ☎ 603/745–2744 ⊕ www.i93.com/pvsr) offers a variety of recreational and scenic tours throughout the year. It's one of the best snowmobile outfitters in the region, offering one- to two-hour guided tours and half- and full-day snowmobile rentals. Spring through summer, you can ride horseback along wooded trails and along the Pemigewasset River, enjoy horse-drawn-carriage rides, and embark on moose-watching bus tours into the northernmost White Mountains.

SKI AREA **Loon Mountain.** Wide, straight, and consistent intermediate trails prevail at Loon, a modern resort on the Kancamagus Highway (Route 112) and the Pemigewasset River. Beginner trails and slopes are set apart. The most advanced among the 45 runs are grouped on the North Peak section farther from the main mountain. Snowboarders have a half-pipe and their own park; an alpine garden with bumps and jumps provides thrills for skiers. The vertical is 2,100 feet. In the base lodge and around the mountain are many food-service and lounge facilities. There's day and nighttime lift-served snow tubing on the lower slopes. The touring center at Loon Mountain has 22 mi of cross-country trails. ⊠ *Kancamagus Hwy. (Rte. 112)* ⬧ *Rte. 1, Box 41, Lincoln 03251* ☎ *603/745–8111, 603/745–8100 snow conditions, 800/227–4191 lodging* ⊕ *www.loonmtn.com.*

Shopping

The **Curious Cow** (⊠ Main St., North Woodstock ☎ 603/745–9230) is a multidealer shop selling country crafts. **Sunburst Fashions** (⊠ 108 Main St., North Woodstock ☎ 603/745–8745) stocks handcrafted gemstone jewelry and imported gifts.

Franconia

 16 mi northwest of Lincoln/North Woodstock.

Travelers have long passed through the White Mountains via Franconia Notch, and in the late 18th century a town evolved just to the north. It and the region's jagged rock formations and heavy coat of evergreens have stirred the imaginations of Washington Irving, Henry Wadsworth Longfellow, and Nathaniel Hawthorne, who penned a short story about the Old Man of the Mountain. The town remains enchanting, if sleepy, touched though it is by Interstate 93 (a.k.a. the Franconia Notch Parkway) and modern ski resorts.

At **Frost Place,** his home from 1915 to 1920, Robert Frost wrote one of his most-remembered poems, "Stopping by Woods on a Snowy Evening." Two rooms host occasional readings and contain memorabilia and signed editions of his books. Outside, you can follow short trails marked with lines from his poetry. ⊠ *Ridge Rd. off Rte. 116* ☎ *603/823–5510* ⊕ *www.frostplace.org* ⬧ *$4* ⊙ *Late May–June, weekends 1–5; July–early Oct., Wed.–Mon. 1–5.*

New Hampshire's famous **Old Man of the Mountain,** a naturally formed profile in the rock high above Franconia Notch, crumbled unexpectedly on May 3, 2003, from the strains of natural erosion. The iconic image had defined New Hampshire, and the Old Man's "death" stunned and saddened residents. You can still stop at the posted turnouts from Interstate 93 north- or southbound or along the shore of Profile Lake for the best views of the mountain face. There's also a small, free Old Man of the Mountain Museum administered by Franconia Notch State Park at the southbound viewing area (by the Cannon Mountain tram parking area); it's open daily 9–5.

The **Flume** is an 800-foot-long chasm with narrow walls that give the gorge's running water an eerie echo. The route through it has been built up with a series of boardwalks and stairways. The visitor center has exhibits on the region's history. ⊠ *Franconia Notch Pkwy. Exit 34A* ☎ *603/745–8391* ⊕ *www.nhstateparks.com/franconia.html* ▨ *$8* ☉ *Early May–late Oct., daily 9–5.*

Where to Stay & Eat

¢–$ ✕ **Polly's Pancake Parlor.** Originally a carriage shed built in 1830, this local institution was converted to a tearoom during the Depression, when the Dexters began serving all-you-can-eat pancakes, waffles, and French toast for 50¢. The prices have gone up some, but the descendants of the Dexters continue to serve pancakes and waffles made from grains ground on the property, their own country sausage, and pure maple syrup. The oatmeal-buttermilk pancakes with coconut, blueberries, or walnuts are other favorites. ⊠ *Rte. 117* ☎ *603/823–5575* ▤ *AE, D, MC, V* ☉ *Closed mid-Oct.–mid-May. No dinner.*

$$–$$$$ ✕▦ **Sugar Hill Inn.** The lawn's old carriage and the wraparound porch's wicker chairs put you in a nostalgic mood before you even enter this converted 1789 farmhouse. Antiques-filled guest quarters are in the main house or one of three cottages. Many rooms and suites have hand-stenciled walls and views of the Franconia Mountains; some have fireplaces. Bette Davis visited friends in this house—the room with the best vistas is named after her. The restaurant ($$$$; reservations essential) serves such haute American fare as peppercorn-crusted sirloin steak with grilled mushrooms and truffle oil; the homemade desserts are always delicious. ⊠ *Rte. 117* ▢ *Box 954, 03585* ☎ *603/823–5621 or 800/ 548–4748* ⊕ *www.sugarhillinn.com* ▭ *13 rooms, 5 suites* ⌂ *Restaurant, some in-room hot tubs, cross-country skiing, sleigh rides, pub; no room phones, no room TVs, no smoking* ▤ *AE, MC, V* ⊺◯ *BP, MAP.*

★ $$–$$$$ ✕▦ **Sunset Hill House.** Since opening in 1882, this inn has been famous as one of the best places in New England to watch the sun go down. It's along a 1,700-foot ridge with views not just west toward the sun but also east out toward the Presidential Range. Many of the meticulously kept rooms have antiques dating from the inn's early years; gas fireplaces and decks grace the upper units. The restaurant ($$$–$$$$) is highly acclaimed; try the cod Provençal or duck Bombay with almonds, smoked bacon, and mango-brandy sauce. A tavern ($–$$) serves lighter fare. ⊠ *Sunset Hill Rd., 03586* ☎ *603/823–5522 or 800/786–4455* ⊕*www.sunsethillhouse.com* ▭ *28 rooms* ⌂ *2 restaurants, some in-room hot tubs, pool, mountain bikes, hiking, cross-country skiing, ice-skating, bar; no room TVs* ▤ *AE, D, MC, V* ⊺◯ *BP, MAP.*

$$–$$$ ✕▦ **Franconia Inn.** At this 107-acre, family-friendly resort, you can play tennis, swim in the pool, and hike. The cross-country ski barn doubles as a horseback-riding center in the warmer months. The white, three-story inn has unfussy country furnishings—you'll find canopy beds and

country quilts in the rooms, most of which have period-style wallpapering or wood-paneling; many have working fireplaces. A sunny, plant-filled restaurant ($$–$$$) serves contemporary continental fare, such as hazelnut-crusted pork tenderloin with a raspberry demi-glace, and grilled yellowfin tuna with wasabi and purple, sticky Thai rice. ✉ *1300 Easton Rd., 03580* ☎ *603/823–5542 or 800/473–5299* ⊕ *www.franconiainn.com* ↪ *34 rooms, 3 suites, 2 2-bedroom cottages* ⚇ *Restaurant, some in-room hot tubs, some kitchenettes, cable TV, 4 tennis courts, pool, hot tub, mountain bikes, badminton, croquet, hiking, horseback riding, cross-country skiing, ice-skating, sleigh rides, bar* ⊟ *AE, MC, V* ⊗ *Closed mid-Apr.–mid-May.*

$–$$$ ⊡ **Hilltop Inn.** Staying here is just like dropping by Grandma's. Rooms in the 1895 farmhouse have a quirky mix of antiques as well as handmade quilts and piles of pillows. Watch one of the hundreds of videos in the TV room or take in the sunset from one of the rockers on the porch. Roughly 20 acres of backcountry terrain are perfect for cross-country skiing. The large country breakfast includes homemade jams, pancakes made with homegrown berries, soufflés, and smoked meats. ✉ *9 Norton La., Sugar Hill 03586* ☎ *603/823–5695 or 800/770–5695* 🖷 *603/823–5518* ⊕ *www.hilltopinn.com* ↪ *3 rooms, 3 suites* ⚇ *Cross-country skiing, bar, library, some pets allowed, no-smoking rooms; no room phones, no room TVs, no kids under 4* ⊟ *MC, V* ⊙ *BP.*

¢ ⚠ **Lafayette Campground.** This campground has hiking and biking trails, 97 tent sites on the Pemigewasset River, and easy access to the Appalachian Trail. There are no hookups, but RVs are permitted in any sites where they can fit. ✉ *Franconia Notch State Park, U.S. 3 and I–93 03580* ☎ *603/823–9513, 877/647–2757 reservations* ⊕ *www.nhstateparks.org* 🛏 *$19* ⚇ *Flush toilets, drinking water, showers, public telephone, general store* ⊟ *MC, V* ⊗ *Closed mid-Oct.–mid-May.*

Sports & the Outdoors

SKI AREAS **Cannon Mountain.** The staff at this state-run facility in Franconia Notch State Park is attentive to skier services, family programs, snowmaking, and grooming. All this makes Cannon—one of the nation's first ski areas—a very sound value. Cannon's 42 trails present challenges—among them narrow, steep pitches off the peak of a 2,146 foot of vertical rise—rarely found in New Hampshire, particularly after a fresh fall of snow. There are also two glade-skiing trails—Turnpike and Banshee—and a lift-service tubing park. Nordic skiing is on an 8-mi multiuse recreational path. In summer, for $10 round-trip, the Cannon Mountain Aerial Tramway can transport you up 2,022 feet. It's an eight-minute ride to the top, where marked trails lead to an observation platform. The tram runs daily from mid-May through late October.

The **New England Ski Museum** (☎ 603/823–7177 ⊕ www.skimuseum.org) sits at the base of the tramway and traces the history of the sport with displays of early gear as well as photos, books, and videos. Admission is free, and the museum is open daily 10–5 from late December through March and from late May through mid-October. ✉ *Franconia Notch State Park, I–93 Exit 34B, 03580* ☎ *603/823–8800, 603/823–7771 snow conditions, 800/237–9007 lodging* ⊕ *www.cannonmt.com* ⊙ *Late May–mid-Oct. and late Dec.–Mar., daily 10–5.*

Franconia Village Cross-Country Ski Center. The cross-country ski center at the Franconia Inn has 39 mi of groomed trails and 24 mi of back-country trails. One popular route leads to Bridal Veil Falls, a great spot for a picnic lunch. There are horse-drawn sleigh rides and ice-skating on a lighted rink. ✉ *1300 Easton Rd., 03580* ☎ *603/823–5542 or 800/473–5299* 🌐 *www.franconiainn.com.*

Littleton

⓴ *9 mi northeast of Sugar Hill, 7 mi north of Franconia, 86 mi north of Concord.*

One of northern New Hampshire's largest towns is on a granite shelf along the Ammonoosuc River, whose swift current and drop of 235 feet enabled the community to flourish as a mill center in its early days. Later, the railroad came through, and Littleton grew into the region's commerce hub. In the minds of many, it's more a place to stock up on supplies than a bona fide destination, but few communities have worked harder at revitalization. Today, intriguing shops and eateries line the main street, whose tidy 19th- and early-20th-century buildings suggest a set in a Jimmy Stewart movie.

Just off Main Street of bustling Littleton, stop by the restored 1798 **Littleton Grist Mill,** on the Ammonoosuc River. It contains a shop selling New England–made pottery, kitchenware, home accessories, and stone-ground flour products. You'll also find original mill equipment on display. There's a café on the second floor. ✉ *18 Mill St.* ☎ *603/444–7478 or 888/284–7478* 🌐 *www.littletongristmill.com* 🕒 *May–Dec., daily; Jan.–Apr., Wed.–Sat.*

NEED A BREAK?

Beside the Littleton Grist Mill, Miller's Café & Bakery (✉ 16 Mill St. ☎ 603/444–2146 🌐 www.millerscafeandbakery.com) serves coffees, microbrews and wines, baked goods, sandwiches, and salads. In warm weather dine on a deck overlooking the Ammonoosuc River.

OFF THE BEATEN PATH

WHITEFIELD – Like Dixville Notch and Bretton Woods, Whitefield, 11 mi northeast of Littleton, became a prominent summer resort in the late 19th century, when wealthy industrialists flocked to the small village in a rolling valley between two precipitous promontories to golf, ski, play polo, and hobnob with each other. The sprawling, yellow clapboard Mountain View hotel, which was established in 1865 and had grown to grand hotel status by the early 20th century, only to succumb to changing tourist habits and close by the 1980s, has been fully refurbished and is now open again as one of New England's grandest resort hotels. It's worth driving through the courtly Colonial center of town—Whitefield was settled in the early 1800s—and up Route 116 just beyond to see this magnificent structure atop a bluff overlooking the Presidentials.

Where to Stay & Eat

★ $$–$$$ ✕ **Tim-bir Alley.** This elegant restaurant is in the Adair Country Inn. The menu, which changes weekly, uses regional American ingredients in creative ways. Main dishes might include rosemary and garlic lamb chops with spinach, feta, and pine nuts, or sunflower-encrusted salmon with a smoked-tomato puree. Save room for such desserts as white chocolate–coconut tart. The hours here change seasonally (and they're sometimes sporadic within a given season); it's best to call ahead. ⊠ *80 Guider La.* ☎ *603/444–6142* ▭ *No credit cards* ⊘ *Closed Mon. and Tues. and Nov. and Apr. No lunch.*

★ $$$$ ╳▥ **Mountain View Grand Resort and Spa.** Built in 1865 and for decades one of New England's grandest of the grande dames, the Mountain View started to lose its cachet following World War II and actually sat shut from 1986 until developer Kevin Craffey bought the place and spent $20 million reviving it. This yellow, Colonial-revival structure reopened to great fanfare in summer 2002 and has already become a favorite of celebs and dignitaries. Nearly all the rooms afford vast vistas of the mountains or golf course, and all are outfitted with plush Colonial-style mahogany furniture and floral-print bedspreads. The main restaurant ($$$–$$$$), Juliet's, serves creative regional New England cuisine. The state-of-the-art Tower Spa provides myriad treatments, and a wide range of activities are offered, from horseback rides to golf to cross-country skiing. ⊠ *120 Mountain View Rd., Whitefield 03598* ☎ *603/837–2100 or 800/438–3017* 🖷 *603/837–8884* ⊕ *www.mountainviewgrand.com* ⌁ *145 rooms* ⚱ *2 restaurants, some in-room hot tubs, cable TV, 18-hole golf course, tennis court, pool, health club, hot tub, spa, badminton, hiking, horseback riding, horseshoes, volleyball, cross-country skiing, ice-skating, sleigh rides, lounge, children's programs, meeting rooms* ▭ *AE, D, MC, V.*

★ $$–$$$$ ╳▥ **Beal House Inn.** Pencil-post beds, marble nightstands, and fluffy upholstered chairs set a low-key, refined tone at this white 1833 Federal-style house. You can rent the two-bedroom suite—-with a claw-foot tub, TV/VCR, kitchenette, and fireplace—by the night or the week. The cozy restaurant ($$–$$$$; closed Monday and Tuesday, no lunch) has an eclectic menu. From the wood-grilled duck breast appetizer, you might move on to snapper sautéed with mango, bananas, grapes, and dark rum; or Black Angus tenderloin au poivre (in a Gorgonzola, chipotle-butter, and mushroom brandy sauce). Chef-owners José Luis and Catherine Pawelek prepare everything from scratch, including a lavish three-course breakfast. You can also relax in the Martini Bar, which has an astonishing 250-plus different kinds of martini. ⊠ *2 W. Main St., 03561* ☎ *603/ 444–2661 or 888/616–2325* 🖷 *603/444–6224* ⊕ *www.bealhouseinn. com* ⌁ *3 rooms, 5 suites* ⚱ *Restaurant, some in-room hot tubs, some kitchenettes, some refrigerators, cable TV, some in-room VCRs, bar, no-smoking rooms* ▭ *AE, MC, V* � *BP.*

★ $$$$ ▥ **Adair Country Inn.** In 1927 attorney Frank Hogan built this three-story Georgian-revival home as a wedding present for his daughter, Dorothy Adair. Today it's a luxurious country inn, with walking paths that wind through gardens on 200 acres. Rooms, which have garden or mountain views, are furnished with period antiques and reproductions; many have fireplaces. One suite has a large two-person hot tub, a fireplace, a balcony, and a king-size sleigh bed. Thoughtful touches include turndown service with Lindt chocolates, hair dryers and magnifying mirrors, and in-room CD players. A generous afternoon tea is served in the elegant living room. ✉ *80 Guider La., 03574* ☎ *603/444–2600 or 888/444–2600* ⊕ *www.adairinn.com* ➿ *9 rooms, 1 cottage* ⚫ *Restaurant, some in-room hot tubs, tennis court, billiards; no room phones, no room TVs, no kids under 12, no smoking* ⊟ *AE, D, MC, V* ⍩ *BP.*

¢–$$

Fodor's Choice

★

⊞ **Thayers Inn.** This stately 1843 Greek-revival hotel isn't luxurious, but it did undergo a complete room-by-room renovation throughout 2004, vastly improving the quality of furniture, linens, and decoration—the hotel also has high-speed wireless Internet. The well-kept rooms retain a quaintly old-fashioned look, with creaky floorboards, exposed pipes, vintage steam radiators, high ceilings, and comfy wing chairs. Passersby are welcome to have a look at a small third-floor room set up as it would have appeared in the 1840s or to visit the sixth-floor cupola, with its 360-degree views. There's no elevator—good to know if you planned to book an upper-floor room. Several restaurants and shops are within walking distance. It's one of the best values in New England. ✉ *111 Main St., 03561* ☎ *603/444–6469 or 800/634–8179* ⊕ *www.thayersinn.com* ➿ *22 rooms, 13 suites* ⚫ *Some refrigerators, cable TV, some in-room VCRs, no-smoking rooms, Wi-Fi* ⊟ *AE, D, MC, V* ⍩ *CP.*

Sports & the Outdoors

The Society for the Protection of New Hampshire Forests owns two properties open to visitors in Bethlehem, 5 mi southeast of Littleton. **Bretzfelder Park** (✉ Prospect St. ☎ 603/444–6228), a 77-acre nature and wildlife park, has a picnic shelter, hiking, and cross-country ski trails. The **Rocks Christmas Tree Farm** (✉ 4 Christmas La., Bethlehem ☎ 603/444–6228) is a working Christmas-tree farm with walking trails, historical buildings, and educational programs.

Shopping

In a restored mill on the Ammonoosuc River, **ADMAC Salvage at the Tannery Marketplace** (✉ 111 Saranac St. ☎ 603/444–1200) contains an amazing array of architectural relics, antiques, collectibles, and estate leftovers.

Potato Barn Antiques Center (✉ U.S. 3, 6 mi north of Lancaster, Northumberland ☎ 603/636–2611) has several dealers under one roof—specialties include vintage farm tools, clothing, and costume jewelry. The **Village Book Store** (✉ 81 Main St. ☎ 603/444–5263) has comprehensive selections of both nonfiction and fiction titles.

Bretton Woods

㉑ *14 mi southeast of Bethlehem, 28 mi northeast of Lincoln/Woodstock.*

In the early 1900s private railcars brought the elite from New York and Philadelphia to the Mount Washington Hotel, the jewel of Bretton Woods. The hotel was the site, in 1944, of a famous United Nations conference that created the International Monetary Fund and the International Bank for Reconstruction and Development and whose decisions governed international monetary and financial policy until the early 1970s. The area is also known for its cog railway and eponymous ski resort.

2

In 1858 Sylvester Marsh petitioned the state legislature for permission to build a steam railway up Mt. Washington. A politico retorted that he'd have better luck building a railroad to the moon. Just 11 years later, the **Mt. Washington Cog Railway** chugged its way along a 3-mi track up the west side of the mountain to the summit, and it is today one of the state's most beloved attractions—a thrill in either direction. Allow three hours round-trip; call for schedule information. ⊠ *U.S. 302, 6 mi northeast of Bretton Woods* ☎ *603/278–5404 or 800/922–8825* ⊕ *www.thecog.com* ☞ *$49* ☯ *Early May–late May, weekends; late May–Nov., daily.*

★ ☉

EN ROUTE

Scenic U.S. 302 winds through the steep, wooded mountains on either side of spectacular Crawford Notch, southeast of Bretton Woods, and passes through **Crawford Notch State Park** (⊠ U.S. 302, Harts Location ☎ 603/374–2272), where you can picnic and take a short hike to Arethusa Falls or the Silver and Flume cascades. The visitor center has a gift shop and a cafeteria; there's also a campground. ☎ *603/271–3628 reservations.*

Where to Stay & Eat

★ $–$$$$ ✕▦ **Mount Washington Resort at Bretton Woods.** Of Bretton Woods's three hotels, the most famous is the leviathan 1902 Mount Washington Hotel, a grand resort with a 900-foot-long veranda and full views of the Presidentials. With stately public rooms and large, Victorian-style guest quarters, the hotel retains an early-20th-century formality. A jacket and tie are required in the dining room ($$$–$$$$), which serves such seasonal dishes as lemon lobster ravioli with shrimp and scallops or roast pork with onions and mushrooms. The mid-price rooms at the 1896 Bretton Arms Country Inn are less formal. On arrival, make reservations for its contemporary dining room ($$$–$$$$). Rooms at the more modern Lodge at Bretton Woods have balconies or patios; Darby's Pizzeria ($–$$) serves pizza and other casual food. For long stays, look into the 55 town homes. ⊠ *U.S. 302, 03575* ☎ *603/278–1000 or 800/258–0330* 🖷 *603/278–8838* ⊕ *www.mtwashington.com* ⇗ *339 units* ♿ *8 restaurants, some in-room hot tubs, some kitchens, cable TV, driving range, 27-hole golf course, 12 tennis courts, 2 pools (1 indoor), health club, hot tub, massage, sauna, fishing, bicycles, hiking, horseback riding, cross-country skiing, downhill skiing, sleigh rides, 5 bars, recreation room, babysitting, children's programs (ages 5–12), meeting rooms* ➭ *AE, D, MC, V* ⑩ *MAP.*

¢ ⌂ **Dry River Campground.** This rustic campground in Crawford Notch State Park has 31 primitive tent sites and is a popular base for hiking the White Mountain National Forest. ⊠ *U.S. 302, Harts Location* ⌂ *Box 177, Twin Mountain 03595* ☎ *603/271–3628* ⊕ *www.nhstateparks.org* ☞ *$13* ♿ *Snack bar, flush toilets, drinking water, showers, public telephone, general store* ☯ *Closed mid-Dec.–mid-May.*

Sports & the Outdoors

SKI AREA **Bretton Woods Mountain Resort.** This expansive, well-run ski area has a tri-level base lodge, convenient parking and drop-off areas, and an uncrowded setting. The views of Mt. Washington alone are worth the visit; the scenery is especially beautiful from the Top o' Quad restaurant and from the former Cog Railway car atop West Mountain. Although its trails will appeal mostly to novice and intermediate skiers, steeper pitches near the top of the 1,500-foot vertical and glade skiing will satisfy experts. Skiers and snowboarders can try a terrain park with jumps and a half pipe. The Accelerator half pipe is for snowboarders only, and you can even do night skiing and snowboarding on weekends and holidays. The large, full-service cross-country ski center has 62 mi of groomed and double-track trails, many of them lift-serviced. ⊠ *U.S. 302, 03575* ☎ *603/278–3320, 603/278–3333 weather conditions, 800/232–2972 information, 800/258–0330 lodging* ⊕ *www.brettonwoods.com.*

Bartlett

㉒ *18 mi southeast of Bretton Woods.*

With Bear Mountain to its south, Mt. Parker to its north, Mt. Cardigan to its west, and the Saco River to its east, Bartlett, incorporated in 1790, has an unforgettable setting. Lovely Bear Notch Road (closed in winter) has the only midpoint access to the Kancamagus Highway (Route 112).

Where to Stay

$$$$ 🏨 **Grand Summit Hotel & Conference Center.** The gables and curves of this resort mimic the slopes of nearby Attitash Bear Peak. Attractive contemporary-style rooms have kitchenettes, VCRs, and stereos. The main dining room serves passable American fare; dishes at Crawford's Pub and Grill are lighter. ⊠ *U.S. 302* ☽ *Box 429, 03812* ☎ *603/374–1900 or 888/554–1900* 🖷 *603/374–3040* ⊕ *www.attitash.com* ⤴ *143 rooms* ♿ *2 restaurants, room service, some kitchens, cable TV, in-room VCRs, in-room data ports, pool, health club, 2 hot tubs, massage, steam room, downhill skiing, bar, recreation room, laundry facilities* ▤ *AE, D, MC, V.*

$–$$$$ 🏨 **Attitash Mountain Village.** The style at this condo-motel complex is alpine contemporary, and the staff is young and enthusiastic. Units, some with fireplaces, accommodate from 2 to 14 people. The restaurant, with a varied and family-friendly menu, has unobstructed mountain views. ⊠ *U.S. 302, 03812* ☎ *603/374–6501 or 800/862–1600* 🖷 *603/374–6509* ⊕ *www.attitashmtvillage.com* ⤴ *350 units* ♿ *Restaurant, some in-room hot tubs, some kitchens, cable TV, 2 tennis courts, 2 pools (1 indoor), gym, sauna, fishing, mountain bikes, hiking, cross-country skiing, downhill skiing, ice-skating, pub, recreation room, playground, laundry service, meeting rooms* ▤ *AE, D, MC, V.*

Sports & the Outdoors

SKI AREA **Attitash Ski Area.** Attitash has a computerized lift-ticket system that allows downhill skiers to pay as they run. Skiers can share the ticket, which is good for two years. Enhanced with massive snowmaking (98%), the trails number 70 on two peaks—Attitash and Attitash Bear Peak—both with full-service base lodges. The bulk of the skiing and boarding is geared to intermediates and experts, with some steep pitches and glades. At 500 feet, the Ground Zero half pipe is New England's longest. The Attitash Adventure Center has a rental shop, lessons desk, and children's programs. ⊠ *U.S. 302* ☽ *Box 308, 03812* ☎ *603/374–2368, 877/677–7609 snow conditions, 800/223–7669 lodging* ⊕ *www.attitash.com.*

Glen

❷❸ *6 mi northeast of Bartlett; 89 mi northeast of Concord; 71 mi northwest of Portland, Maine.*

Glen is hardly more than a crossroads between North Conway and Jackson, but its central location has made it the home of a few noteworthy attractions and dining and lodging options.

That cluster of fluorescent buildings on Route 16 is **Story Land,** a theme park with life-size storybook and nursery-rhyme characters. The 20 rides and five shows include a flume ride, a Victorian-theme river-raft ride, a farm tractor–inspired kiddie ride, swan boats, a pumpkin coach, and a farm-family variety show (presented in a new theater, which opened in 2004). In early spring, when only parts of the park are open, admission is reduced to $16. ☒ *Rte. 16* ☎ *603/383–4186* ⊕ *www.storylandnh. com* 🖃 *$21* ⊙ *Mid-June–Labor Day, daily 9–6; Memorial Day–mid-June and Labor Day–Columbus Day, weekends 10–5.*

Heritage New Hampshire uses theatrical sets, sound effects, and animation to render the state's history. A simulated voyage on the *Reliance* "sails" you from an English village of the mid-1600s to the New World, where you can then saunter along Portsmouth's streets in the late 1700s. Exhibits continue through to the present day. ☒ *Rte. 16* ☎ *603/383–4186* ⊕ *www.heritagenh.com* 🖃 *$11* ⊙ *Memorial Day–mid-June, weekends 9–5; mid-June–mid-Oct., daily 9–5.*

Where to Stay & Eat

$–$$$ ✕ **Red Parka Pub.** Practically an institution, the Red Parka Pub has been in downtown Glen for more than two decades. The menu has everything a family could want, from an all-you-can-eat salad bar to scallop pie. The barbecued ribs are favorites, and you'll find hand-carved steaks of every type, from aged New York sirloin to prime rib. ☒ *U.S. 302* ☎ *603/383–4344* 🍴 *Reservations not accepted* ▭ *AE, D, MC, V.*

$–$$ ✕ **Margarita Grill.** Après-ski and hiking types congregate here—in the dining room in cold weather and on the covered patio when it's warm—for homemade salsas, wood-fired steaks, ribs, burgers, and a smattering of Tex-Mex and Cajun specialties. Unwind at the tequila bar after a day on the mountains. ☒ *U.S. 302* ☎ *603/383–6556* ▭ *D, MC, V* ⊙ *No lunch weekdays.*

$–$$$ ✕🖫 **Bernerhof Inn.** With its hardwood floors, hooked rugs, and mix of antique and reproduction furniture, this hotel seems right at home in an alpine setting. The fanciest six rooms have brass beds and spa-size tubs; one suite has a Finnish sauna. The menu in the dining room ($$–$$$$) includes traditional Swiss specialties such as fondue and Wiener schnitzel as well as contemporary dishes—Asian duck breast or venison filet, for instance. The Black Bear pub ($–$$) pours microbrews and serves sandwiches and burgers, as well as shepherds' pie and other dishes. The CyBear Lounge ($) serves afternoon appetizers you can snack on while checking your e-mail. ☒ *U.S. 302* 🖃 *Box 240, 03838* ☎ *603/383–9132 or 800/548–8007* 📠 *603/383–0809* ⊕ *www. bernerhofinn.com* 🛏 *7 rooms, 2 suites* 🍴 *2 restaurant, snack bar, some in-room hot tubs, cable TV, Wi-Fi; no smoking* ▭ *AE, D, MC, V* ⭗ *BP.*

Jackson

★ ㉔ *5 mi north of Glen.*

Just off Route 16 via a red covered bridge, Jackson has retained its storybook New England character. Art and antiques shopping, tennis, golf, fishing, and hiking to waterfalls are among the draws. When the snow falls, Jackson becomes the state's cross-country skiing capital. Four downhill ski areas are nearby.

Where to Stay & Eat

$$–$$$$ ✕ **Thompson House Eatery.** One of the most innovative restaurants in generally staid northern New Hampshire, this romantic eatery inside a rambling red farmhouse serves such world-beat fare as applewood-smoked skewered shrimp over baby greens with fresh melon and balsamic vinegar. The entrée of grilled lamb chops with cucumber-tomato relish over Israeli couscous, Greek olives, and pancetta wins raves all around. ⊠ *Rte. 16A* ☎ *603/383–9341* ▤ *AE, D, MC, V.*

$–$$ ✕ **Red Fox Bar & Grille.** Some say this restaurant overlooking the Wentworth Golf Club gets its name from a wily fox with a penchant for stealing golf balls off the fairway. The wide-ranging menu has barbecued ribs, wood-fired pizzas, and blue-cheese-and-bacon burgers as well as more substantial dishes such as seared sea scallops with Grand Marnier sauce. The Sunday jazz breakfast buffet draws raves. ⊠ *Rte. 16* ☎ *603/383–4949* ▤ *AE, D, MC, V* ⊘ *No lunch weekdays.*

★ **$$$$** ✕🏠 **Inn at Thorn Hill.** Just steps from the cross-country trails and Jackson Village, this estimable Stanford White–designed Victorian inn completely burned to the ground in 2002 but was lavishly rebuilt and expanded in spring 2004. Although the main inn no longer feels quite so old-fashioned, it retains the original style and amazing attention to detail. All of the rooms in the new buildings abound with cushy amenities: two-person Jacuzzis, fireplaces, and TVs with DVDs. The top units have steam showers, wet bars, and refrigerators. Cottages and rooms in the carriage house harken back to an earlier period, but some do have whirlpool tubs and all are decorated beautifully. The restaurant ($$–$$$$; reservations essential) serves fine contemporary fare: braised pheasant with asparagus and dried cherries is a good bet. A full spa has been added to the new inn, providing a full range of beauty treatments and massages. Afternoon tea and a substantial full breakfast are included. ⊠ *Thorn Hill Rd.* ⬦ *Box A, 03846* ☎ *603/383–4242 or 800/289–8990* ⊞ *603/383–8062* ⊕ *www.innatthornhill.com* ⇗ *15 rooms, 7 suites, 3 cottages* ♿ *Restaurant, some in-room hot tubs, some refrigerators, cable TV, some in-room VCRs, pool, hot tub, spa, croquet, cross-country skiing, pub; no TV in some rooms, no smoking* ▤ *AE, D, MC, V* ❍❘ *BP.*

$$–$$$$ ✕🏠 **Wentworth.** This pale-yellow 1869 Victorian charms with individually decorated rooms—many with fireplaces—accented with antiques. Suites either have whirlpool tubs or private outdoor hot tubs. The Wentworth also rents out two- and three-bedroom condos, geared toward longer stays. The acclaimed restaurant ($$$) serves a five-course candlelight dinner with a menu that changes seasonally. Good choices are Australian rack of lamb with a carrot-ginger cream sauce, and grilled farm-raised salmon with potato and scallion pancakes and a baby spinach–and–bacon salad. The New England fish cakes with corn, sweet onions, and a celeriac rémoulade make a tempting starter. The 18-hole course at the Wentworth Golf Club is next door to the inn. ⊠ *1 Carter Notch Rd., 03846* ☎ *603/383–9700 or 800/637–0013* 🖷 *603/383–4265* ⊕ *www.thewentworth.com* ⤳ *44 rooms, 7 suites* ⌂ *Restaurant, some in-room hot tubs, cable TV, tennis court, pool, billiards, cross-country skiing, ice-skating, sleigh rides, bar* ▱ *AE, D, DC, MC, V* ⫿⃝⫿ *MAP.*

$–$$$$ ✕⌷ **Christmas Farm Inn.** Despite its wintery name, this 1778 inn is an all-season retreat. Rooms in the main building and the saltbox next door have Laura Ashley and Ralph Lauren prints. Other rooms are set in a delightful old barn, in a sugarhouse, and in a few cottages set about the wooded grounds. Suites have beamed ceilings and fireplaces. Standbys in the restaurant ($$–$$$$) are pan-seared sea scallops on shrimp risotto with coconut-mango cream sauce and crispy eggplant napoleon layered with portobello mushrooms, basil pesto, roasted red peppers, ricotta, and fresh mozzarella. The inn's gardens are spectacular. ⊠ *Rte. 16B* 🖉 *Box CC, 03846* ☎ *603/383–4313 or 800/443–5837* 🖷 *603/ 383–6495* ⊕ *www.christmasfarminn.com* ⤳ *22 rooms, 15 suites, 5 2-bedroom cottages* ⌂ *Restaurant, some in-room hot tubs, pool, health club, hot tub, massage, sauna, spa, volleyball, cross-country skiing, pub, recreation room, no-smoking rooms; no TV in some rooms* ▱ *AE, MC, V* ⫿⃝⫿ *MAP.*

$$ ✕⌷ **Wildcat Inn & Tavern.** After a day of skiing, you can collapse on a comfy sofa by the fire at this 19th-century inn. The fragrance of home baking wafts into the suite-style guest rooms, which are full of knick-knacks and furniture of various periods. The tavern, where bands often perform, attracts skiers. The restaurant ($–$$$) is a favorite with locals and serves very good, reasonably priced American fare, such as smoked salmon and avocado salad, Grand Marnier duck, lobster over fettuccine, and pulled-pork sandwiches; simpler food is served in the tavern. In summer, dining is available in the garden. ⊠ *Rte. 16A, 03846* ☎ *603/383–4245 or 800/228–4245* 🖷 *603/383–6456* ⊕ *www. wildcattavern.com* ⤳ *6 rooms, 4 with bath; 7 suites; 1 cottage* ⌂ *2 restaurants, some kitchenettes, cable TV, in-room VCRs, taproom* ▱ *AE, MC, V* ⫿⃝⫿ *BP.*

$$–$$$$ ⌷ **Eagle Mountain House.** With downhill slopes nearby and cross-country trails beginning at this mammoth 1879 country estate, skiing is the order of the day. Public areas are rustic but elegant and include a 280-foot-long wraparound porch, and the large guest rooms are furnished with late-Victorian pieces. Up to two kids under 17 stay free in the same room with parents (some rooms have pullout sofas and queen-size beds). ⊠ *179 Carter Notch Rd., 03846* ☎ *603/383–9111 or 800/966–5779* 🖷 *603/383–0854* ⊕ *www.eaglemt.com* ⤳ *63 rooms, 29 suites* ⌂ *2 restaurants, some refrigerators, driving range, 9-hole golf course, tennis court, pool, health club, hot tub, sauna, cross-country skiing, video game room, playground, meeting rooms; no room TVs* ▱ *AE, D, DC, MC, V.*

$$–$$$$ ⌷ **Inn at Ellis River.** Most of the Victorian-style rooms in this unabashedly romantic inn on the Ellis River have fireplaces; some have balconies. In winter, a snow bridge across the river connects you with the Ellis River Trail and Jackson's cross-country trail system. Dinner is served with 48 hours advance reservation. ⊠ *Rte. 16* ⬧ *Box 656, 03846* ☎ *603/383–9339 or 800/233–8309* 🖨 *603/383–4142* ⊕ *www.innatellisriver.com* 🛏 *17 rooms, 3 suites, 1 cottage* ⚘ *Dining room, some in-room hot tubs, cable TV, in-room DVD/VCR players, pool, hot tub, sauna, billiards, cross-country skiing, pub, no-smoking rooms; no kids under 12* ▭ *AE, D, MC, V* ⍾ *BP.*

$$–$$$$ 🏨 **Nordic Village Resort.** The light woods and white walls of these modern condos set in a series of three-story buildings are as Scandinavian as the snowy views. Larger units have fireplaces and full kitchens and sleep up to eight. The property is part of Luxury Mountain Getaways, which operates several upscale condos and hotels on 165 acres a mile south of Jackson covered bridge. ⊠ *Rte. 16, 03846* ☎ *603/383–9101 or 800/472–5207* 🖨 *603/383–9823* ⊕ *www.lmgnh.com* 🛏 *140 condominiums* ⚘ *Some in-room hot tubs, some kitchens, cable TV, tennis court, 3 pools (1 indoor), hot tubs (indoor and outdoor), steam room, boating, badminton, basketball, hiking, horseshoes, volleyball, cross-country skiing, ice-skating, sleigh rides, playground* ▭ *D, MC, V.*

$–$$$$ 🏨 **Inn at Jackson.** The builders of this 1902 Victorian, which overlooks the village, followed a design by Stanford White. Although the foyer's staircase is grand, everything else—from the braided rugs on the hardwood floors to the smattering of antiques—is unpretentious and a great value. The airy guest rooms have oversize windows; eight have fireplaces. The exceptional full breakfast may include anything from egg soufflé casserole to blueberry pancakes. ⊠ *Thorn Hill Rd.* ⬧ *Box 822, 03846* ☎ *603/383–4321 or 800/289–8600* 🖨 *603/383–4085* ⊕ *www. innatjackson.com* 🛏 *14 rooms* ⚘ *Cable TV, hot tub, cross-country skiing* ▭ *AE, D, MC, V* ⍾ *BP.*

$–$$ 🏨 **Briarcliff Motel.** This bright and clean motel is a short drive from outlet shopping and ½ mi south of North Conway Village along Route 16. Rooms have mini-refrigerators, coffeemakers, and utilitarian but perfectly pleasant furnishings. ⊠ *Rte. 16 (U.S. 302)* ⬧ *Box 504, 03860* ☎ *603/356–5584 or 800/338–4291* ⊕ *www.briarcliffmotel.com* 🛏 *31 rooms* ⚘ *Refrigerators, cable TV, pool, no-smoking rooms* ▭ *AE, D, MC, V* ⍾ *BP.*

Sports & the Outdoors

Nestlenook Farm (⊠ Dinsmore Rd. ☎ 603/383–9443) maintains an outdoor ice-skating rink with rentals, music, and a bonfire. Going snowshoeing or taking a sleigh ride are other winter options; in summer you can fly-fish or ride in a horse-drawn carriage.

SKI AREAS **Black Mountain.** Friendly, informal Black Mountain has a warming southern exposure. The Family Passport, which allows two adults and two juniors to ski at discounted rates, is a good value. Midweek rates here are usually the lowest in Mt. Washington Valley. The 40 trails and glades on the 1,100-vertical-foot mountain are evenly divided among beginner, intermediate, and expert. ⊠ *Rte. 16B, 03846* ☎ *603/383–4490, 800/475–4669 snow conditions, 800/698–4490 lodging* ⊕ *www. blackmt.com.*

Jackson Ski Touring Foundation. One of the nation's top four cross-country skiing areas has 97 mi of trails. About 60 mi are track groomed, and 53 mi are skate groomed. There are roughly 39 mi of marked backcountry trails. You can arrange lessons and rentals at the lodge, in the center of Jackson Village. ⊠ *153 Main St., Jackson 03846* ☎ *603/383–9355* ⊕ *www.jacksonxc.org.*

Mt. Washington

★ ㉕ *20 mi northwest of Jackson.*

In summer you can drive to the top of Mt. Washington, the highest peak (6,288 feet) in the northeastern United States and the site of a weather station that recorded the world's highest winds, 231 mi per hour, in 1934. The Mt. Washington Auto Road, opened in 1861, begins at the Glen House, a gift shop and rest stop 15 mi north of Glen on Route 16, and winds its way up the east side of the mountain, ending at the top an 8-mi and approximately half-hour drive later. At the summit is the Sherman Adams Summit Building, built in 1979 and containing a visitor center and a museum focusing on the mountain's geology and extreme weather conditions; you can stand in the glassed-in viewing area to hear the wind roar. The Mt. Washington Observatory is at the building's western end. There are rules limiting what cars may use the road. For instance, cars with automatic transmission must be able to shift down into first gear. It is also possible to reach the top along several rough hiking trails; those who hoof it can make the return trip via shuttle, tickets for which are sold at the Stage Office, at the summit at the end of the cog railway trestle. Remember that the temperature atop Mt. Washington will be much colder than down below—the average year-round is below freezing and the average wind velocity is 35 mph. ⊠ *Rte. 16, Pinkham Notch* ☎ *603/466–3988* ⊕ *www.mountwashingtonautoroad.com* ▨ *Car and driver $20, each additional adult passenger $7* ☽ *Open May–late Oct., daily (mid-June–early Sept. 7:30–6; otherwise 8–4, 8–5, or 8–5:30).*

In winter, when the road is closed to private vehicles, you can opt to reach the top of Mt. Washington via a guided tour in one of the **Snow-Coaches** that leave from Great Glen Trails Outdoor Center, just south of Gorham, on a first-come, first-served basis. Great Glen's 8-passenger vans are refitted with snowmobile-like treads and can travel to just above the tree line. You have the option of cross-country skiing, tubing, or snowshoeing down. ⊠ *Rte. 16, Pinkham Notch* ☎ *603/466–2333* ⊕ *www.greatglentrails.com* ▨ *$40 (includes all-day trail pass)* ☽ *Dec.–Mar., daily.*

Although not a town per se, scenic **Pinkham Notch** covers Mt. Washington's eastern side and includes several ravines, including Tuckerman Ravine, famous for spring skiing. The Appalachian Mountain Club maintains a large visitor center here on Route 16 that provides information to hikers and travelers and has guided hikes, outdoor skills workshops, a cafeteria, lodging, regional topography displays, and an outdoors shop.

Where to Stay

¢ ▣ **Joe Dodge Lodge at Pinkham Notch.** The Appalachian Mountain Club operates this rustic lodge at the base of Mt. Washington. Accommodations range from single-sex bunk rooms (rented by the bunk) for as many as five people, to private rooms—all have gleaming wood, cheerful quilts, and reading lights. The restaurant serves buffet breakfasts and lunches and family-style dinners. Packages include breakfast and dinner, plus skiing at Great Glen Trails and/or the Wildcat ski area. ⊠ *Rte. 16* ⌂ *Box 298, Gorham 03581* ☎ *603/466–2727* ☒ *603/466–3871* ⊕ *www.outdoors.org* ⤷ *102 beds without bath* ⚲ *Restaurant, no-smoking rooms; no a/c, no room phones, no room TVs* ⊟ *AE, MC, V* ⊺◉⊺ *MAP.*

Sports & the Outdoors

HIKING The **Appalachian Mountain Club Pinkham Notch Visitor Center** (⊠ Rte. 16 ⌂ Box 298, Gorham 03581 ☎ 603/466–2721, 603/466–2727 reservations ⊕ www.outdoors.org) has lectures, workshops, slide shows, and outdoor skills instruction year-round. Accommodations include the adjacent Joe Dodge Lodge, the Highland Center at Crawford Notch with 100-plus beds and a 16-bed bunk house next to it, as well as the club's eight high-mountain huts spaced one day's hike from each other in the White Mountain National Forest portion of the Appalachian Trail. The huts provide meals and dorm-style lodging from June to late September or early October; the rest of the year they are self-service.

SKI AREAS **Great Glen Trails Outdoor Center.** Amenities at this fabulous new lodge at the base of Mt. Washington include a huge ski-gear and sports shop, food court, climbing wall, observation deck, and fieldstone fireplace. In winter it's renowned for its dramatic 24-mi cross-country trail system. Some trails have snowmaking, and there's access to more than 1,100 acres of backcountry. It's even possible to ski or snowshoe the lower half of the Mt. Washington Auto Road. Trees shelter most of the trails, so Mt. Washington's infamous weather isn't a concern. In summer it's the base from which hikers, mountain bikers, and trail runners can explore Mt. Washington. The center also has programs in canoeing, kayaking, and fly-fishing. ⊠ *Rte. 16, Pinkham Notch* ☎ *603/466–2333* ⊕ *www.greatglentrails.com.*

Wildcat. Glade skiers favor Wildcat, with 28 acres of official tree skiing. The 47 runs include some stunning double-black-diamond trails. Skiers who can hold a wedge should check out the 2½-mi-long Polecat. Experts can zip down the Lynx. Views of Mt. Washington and Tuckerman Ravine are superb. The trails are classic New England—narrow and winding. Wildcat's expert runs deserve their designations and then some. Intermediates have mid-mountain–to–base trails, and beginners will find gentle terrain and a broad teaching slope. Snowboarders have several terrain parks and the run of the mountain. In summer you can ride to the top on the four-passenger gondola ($10) and hike the many well-kept trails. ⊠ *Rte. 16, Pinkham Notch, Jackson 03846* ☎ *603/466–3326, 888/754–9453 snow conditions, 800/255–6439 lodging* ⊕ *www. skiwildcat.com.*

Dixville Notch

 63 mi north of Mt. Washington, 66 mi northeast of Littleton, 149 mi north of Concord.

Just 12 mi from the Canadian border, this tiny community is known for two things. One is The Balsams, one of New Hampshire's oldest and most celebrated resorts. The other is the fact that Dixville Notch and another New Hampshire community, Hart's Location, are the first election districts in the nation to vote in presidential primaries and general elections. When the 30 or so Dixville Notch voters file into the little Balsams meeting room on the eve of election day and cast their ballots at the stroke of midnight, they invariably make national news.

One of the favorite pastimes in this area is spotting moose, those large, ungainly, yet elusive members of the deer family. Although you may catch sight of one or more yourself, **Northern Forest Moose Tours** (☎ 603/466–3103 or 800/992–7480) conducts bus tours of the region that have a 97% success rate for spotting moose.

OFF THE BEATEN PATH

PITTSBURG – Well north of the White Mountains, in the Great North Woods, Pittsburg contains the four Connecticut Lakes and the springs that form the Connecticut River. The state's northern tip—a chunk of about 250 square mi—lies within the town's borders, the result of a dispute between the United States and Canada that began in 1832 and was resolved in 1842, when the international boundary was fixed.

Remote though it is, this frontier town teems with hunters, boaters, fishermen, hikers, and photographers from early summer through winter. Especially in the colder months, moose sightings are common. The town has more than a dozen lodges and several informal eateries. It's about a 90-minute drive from Littleton and 40-minute drive from Dixville Notch; add another 30 minutes to reach Fourth Connecticut Lake, nearly at the Canadian border. On your way, you pass the village of Stewartson, exactly midway between the Equator and the North Pole.

Where to Stay & Eat

★ **$–$$$$** ╳▢ **The Balsams.** Nestled in the pine groves of the North Woods, this lavish grande dame has been rolling out the red carpet since 1866. The Balsams encompasses some 15,000 wooded acres—an area roughly the size of the New York City borough of Manhattan. Even when the resort is filled to capacity (figure about 400 guests and another 400 employees), it's still a remarkably solitary place. It draws families, golf enthusiasts, skiers, and others for a varied slate of activities—from dancing to cooking demonstrations. Rooms here are spacious, with large cedar-lined closets and ample dressers. Floral-print wallpaper, modern bathrooms, full-length mirrors, and reproduction antiques impart a dignified old-world grace. Most rooms have views overlooking the lake, gardens, and mountains; still, always inquire about the view when booking, as a handful afford less-promising vistas (the parking area, for example). In the dining room ($$$$; jacket and tie), you might sample a chilled strawberry soup spiked with Grand Marnier, followed by broiled swordfish with white beans and lemon coulis. Rates include breakfast and dinner and unlimited use of the facilities. ⊠ *Rte. 26, 03576* ☎ *603/255–3400, 800/255–0600, 800/255–0800 in NH* 🖶 *603/255–4221* ⊕ *www.thebalsams.com* 🛏 *184 rooms, 20 suites* ♨ *3 restaurants, room service, some in-room hot tubs, driving range, 18-hole golf course, 6 tennis courts, pool, gym, massage, boating, fishing, mountain bikes, hiking, cross-country skiing, downhill skiing, ice-skating, bar, library, recreation room, shops, children's programs (ages 1–12), dry cleaning, laundry service, business services; no TV in some rooms* 🖃 *AE, D, MC, V* 🍴 *FAP, MAP.*

$–$$ 🏠 **The Glen.** This rustic lodge with stick furniture, fieldstone, and cedar sits amid 180 pristine acres on First Connecticut Lake and is surrounded by log cabins, seven of which are right on the water. The cabins have efficiency kitchens and mini-refrigerators—not that you'll need either, because rates include hearty meals, served family-style, in the lodge restaurant. ⊠ *118 Glen Rd., 1 mi off U.S. 3, Pittsburg 03592* ☎ *603/538–6500 or 800/445–4536* ⊕ *www.theglen.org* 🛏 *6 rooms, 9 cabins* ♨ *Restaurant, kitchenettes, lake; no room phones, no room TVs* 🖃 *No credit cards* ⊙ *Closed mid-Oct.–mid-May* 🍴 *FAP.*

Sports & the Outdoors

Dixville Notch State Park (⊠ Rte. 26 ☎ 603/538–6707), in the northernmost notch of the White Mountains, has picnic areas, a waterfall, two mountain brooks, and hiking trails.

SKI AREA **Balsams.** Skiing was originally provided as an amenity for hotel guests at the Balsams, but the area has become popular with day-trippers as well. Slopes with such names as Sanguinary, Umbagog, and Magalloway may sound tough, but they're only moderately difficult, leaning toward intermediate. There are 16 trails and four glades for every skill level from the top of the 1,000-foot vertical. The Balsams has 59 mi of cross-country skiing, tracked and groomed for skating. Natural-history markers annotate some trails; you can also try telemark and backcountry skiing, and there are 21 mi of snowshoeing trails. ⊠ *Rte. 26, 03576* ☎ *603/255–3400, 603/255–3951 snow conditions, 800/255–0600, 800/255–0800 in New Hampshire* 🖶 *603/255–4221* ⊕ *www.thebalsams.com.*

North Conway

㉗ *76 mi south of Dixville Notch, 7 mi south of Glen, 41 mi east of Lincoln/North Woodstock.*

Before the arrival of the outlet stores, the town drew visitors for its inspiring scenery, ski resorts, and access to White Mountain National Forest. Today, however, shopping is as big a sport as skiing, and businesses line Route 16 for several miles.

🅒 The **Conway Scenic Railroad** operates trips aboard vintage trains from historic North Conway Station. The Notch Train, through Crawford Notch to Crawford Depot (a 5-hour round trip) or Fabyan Station (5½ hours), offers wonderful scenic views from the domed observation coach. The Valley Train provides views of Mt. Washington countryside on a 55-minute round trip to Conway or a 1¾-hour trip to

2

Bartlett—lunch and dinner are served on some departures. The 1874 station displays lanterns, old tickets and timetables, and other railroad artifacts. Reserve early during foliage season for the dining excursions. ⊠ *Rte. 16 (U.S. 302), 38 Norcross Circle* ☎ *603/356–5251 or 800/ 232–5251* ⊕ *www.conwayscenic.com* 🖾 *$12–$60* ☉ *Mid-Apr.–late Dec; call for times.*

At **Echo Lake State Park,** you needn't be a rock climber to catch views from the 700-foot White Horse and Cathedral ledges. From the top you'll see the entire valley, in which Echo Lake shines like a diamond. An unmarked trailhead another 7/10 mi on West Side Road leads to Diana's Baths, a series of waterfalls. ⊠ *Off U.S 302* 🖾 *$3* ☉ *Late May–mid-June, weekends dawn–dusk; mid-June–early Sept., daily dawn–dusk.*

🖑 The **Hartmann Model Railroad Museum** houses 14 operating layouts (from G to Z scales), about 2,000 engines, and more than 5,000 cars and coaches. A café, a crafts store, a hobby shop, and an outdoor ride-on train are on-site. ⊠ *Rte. 16 (U.S. 302) and Town Hall Rd., Intervale* ☎ *603/356– 9922* ⊕ *www.hartmannrr.com* 🖾 *$6* ☉ *Daily 10–5.*

Weather Discovery Center. The hands-on exhibits at this meteorological educational facility teach how weather is monitored and how it affects us. The center is a collaboration between the National and Atmospheric Administration Forecast Systems lab and the Mt. Washington Observatory at the summit of Mt. Washington. ⊠ *Rte. 16 (U.S. 302), 1/5 mi south of rail tracks* ☎ *603/356–2137* ⊕ *www.mountwashington.org* 🖾 *$5* ☉ *May–Oct., daily 10–5, Nov.–Apr., Sat.–Mon. 10–5 (also open daily during school vacation from mid-Feb. to early Mar.).*

Where to Stay & Eat

$–$$ ✕ **Delaney's Hole in the Wall.** This casual restaurant has eclectic memorabilia such as autographed baseballs and an early photo of skiing at Tuckerman Ravine hanging over the fireplace. Entrées range from fish-and-chips to fajitas to mussels and scallops sautéed with spiced sausage and Louisiana seasonings. There's live music most nights. ⊠ *Rte. 16, 1/4 mi north of North Conway Village* ☎ *603/356–7776* 🖃 *AE, D, MC, V.*

¢–$$ ✕ **Muddy Moose.** Especially popular with younger singles and families, the Muddy Moose is inviting and rustic thanks to its fieldstone walls, exposed wood, and understated lighting. Dig into a Greek salad, grilled chicken Caesar wrap, char-grilled pork chops with a maple-cider glaze, or muddy moose pie. ⊠ *Rte. 16 just south of North Conway* ☎ *603/ 356–7696* 🖃 *AE, D, MC, V.*

$$$–$$$$ ✕🖭 **White Mountain Hotel and Resort.** Rooms in this hotel at the base of Whitehorse Ledge have mountain views. Proximity to the White Mountain National Forest and Echo Lake State Park makes you feel farther away from the outlet malls than you actually are. Dinner at Ledges Dining Room ($$–$$$) might include a seafood medley in Alfredo sauce over fettuccine with a lobster tail, and sautéed chicken breast with a caramel glaze, apples, maple-smoked cheddar, and Yukon mashed potatoes. ⊠ *West Side Rd.* ☖ *Box 1828, 03860* ☎ *800/533–6301* ☎☎ *603/356–7100* ⊕ *www.whitemountainhotel.com* ⤶ *80 rooms, 13 suites* ⚘ *Restaurant, cable TV, 9-hole golf course, tennis court, pool,*

health club, hot tub, sauna, hiking, cross-country skiing, taproom, meeting rooms ⊟ *AE, D, MC, V* ⦿ *BP, MAP.*

$$–$$$$ ✕⊡ **Darby Field Inn.** After a day of activity in the White Mountains, warm up by this inn's fieldstone fireplace or by the bar's woodstove. Most rooms in this unpretentious 1826 farmhouse have mountain views; several have fireplaces. The restaurant ($$–$$$) prepares such haute regional American fare as roast duckling in a Chambord sauce and rack of lamb with a Dijon-burgundy sauce. The dark-chocolate pâté with white-chocolate sauce is a knockout dessert. ⊠ *185 Chase Hill, Albany 03818* ☎ *603/ 447–2181 or 800/426–4147* ⊟ *603/447–5726* ⊕ *www.darbyfield.com* ↪ *13 rooms, 4 suites* ᐃ *Restaurant, some in-room hot tubs, cable TV, some in-room VCRs, pool, hot tub, massage, mountain bikes, croquet, hiking, cross-country skiing, sleigh rides, bar; no smoking* ⊟ *AE, MC, V* ⊘ *Closed Apr.* ⦿ *BP, MAP.*

★ **$$–$$$$**   ✕⊡ **Snowvillage Inn.** Journalist Frank Simonds built the gambrel-roofed main house in 1916. To complement the tome-jammed bookshelves, guest rooms are named for famous authors; many have fireplaces. The nicest of the rooms, with 12 windows that look out over the Presidential Range, is a tribute to Robert Frost. Two additional buildings—the carriage house and the chimney house—also have libraries. The menu in the candlelit dining room ($$–$$$$; reservations essential) might include roasted rack of lamb with minted onion marmalade, pistachio-encrusted salmon, or a medley of young duckling prepared three ways. The inn is also home to the White Mountain Cooking School, and overnight packages with cooking classes are available. You can hike easily up to beautiful Foss Mountain, directly from the inn. ⊠ *Stewart Rd., 6 mi southeast of Conway* ⬒ *Box 68, Snowville 03832* ☎ *603/447–2818 or 800/ 447–4345* ⊟ *603/447–5268* ⊕ *www.snowvillageinn.com* ↪ *18 rooms* ᐃ *Restaurant, hiking, cross-country skiing; no room TVs, no kids under 6, no smoking* ⊟ *AE, D, MC, V* ⦿ *BP, MAP.*

$$–$$$ ⊡ **Buttonwood Inn.** A tranquil 17-acre oasis in this busy resort area, the Buttonwood is on Mt. Surprise, 2 mi northeast of North Conway Village. Rooms in the 1820s farmhouse are furnished in Shaker style. Wide pine floors, quilts, and period stenciling add warmth. Two rooms have gas fireplaces. Innkeepers Peter and Claudia Needham supply many thoughtful extras, such as backpacks and picnic baskets. ⊠ *Mt. Surprise Rd.* ⬒ *Box 1817, 03860* ☎ *603/356–2625 or 800/258–2625* ⊟ *603/356–3140* ⊕ *www.buttonwoodinn.com* ↪ *8 rooms, 2 suites* ᐃ *Some in-room hot tubs, pool, hiking, cross-country skiing; no a/c, no room TVs, no kids under 12, no smoking* ⊟ *AE, D, MC, V* ⦿ *BP.*

$–$$$ ⊡ **Inn at Crystal Lake.** Just 5 mi south of Conway in the quaint village of Eaton Center, this gracious Greek-revival inn dates to 1884 and contains 11 finely appointed rooms with dramatic themes, each filled with a mix of curious and whimsical art and collectibles from the innkeepers' travels. The gardens surrounding the inn are spectacular. Breakfast is a tasty and filling country spread, including delicious baked goods; you can also enjoy afternoon snacks in the on-site Palmer Pub, which serves light dinner fare throughout the evening. ⊠ *Rte. 15, Eaton Center* ⬒ *Box 12, 03832* ☎ *603/447–2120 or 800/343–7336* ⊕ *www. innatcrystallake.com* ↪ *11 rooms* ᐃ *Cable TV, in-room VCRs, lake, pub; no smoking* ⊟ *MC, V* ⦿ *BP.*

$–$$ ⬚ **Cranmore Inn.** This gambrel-roofed country inn opened in 1863, and many of its furnishings date from the mid-1800s. The stables have been remodeled to contain condo-style rooms with kitchens. A mere ⅓ mi from the base of Mt. Cranmore, the inn is within walking distance of North Conway Village. Guests have privileges at a nearby health club. ⬚ *80 Kearsarge St.* ⬚ *Box 1349, 03860* ☎ *603/356–5502* ⬚ *www. cranmoreinn.com* ⬚ *18 rooms* ⬚ *Restaurant, some kitchens, pool; no a/c, no room TVs* ⬚ *AE, MC, V* ⬚ *BP.*

Nightlife & the Arts

Horsefeather's (⬚ Main St. ☎ 603/356–6862), a restaurant and bar, often has rock, blues, and folk music, especially on weekends. **Mt. Washington Valley Theater Company** (⬚ Eastern Slope Inn Playhouse, Main St. ☎ 603/356–5776 ⬚ www.musical-theatre.org) stages four productions from mid-June to late August.

Sports & the Outdoors

CANOEING & KAYAKING   River outfitter **Saco Bound Canoe & Kayak** (⬚ Rte. 16 [U.S. 302], Conway ☎ 603/447–2177 ⬚ www.sacobound.com) leads gentle canoeing expeditions, guided kayak trips, and white-water rafting on seven rivers and provides lessons, equipment, and transportation.

FISHING   **North Country Angler** (⬚ 2888 White Mountain Hwy. ☎ 603/356–6000 ⬚ www.northcountryangler.com) schedules intensive guided fly-fishing weekends throughout the region. It's one of the best tackle shops in the state.

SKI AREAS   **Cranmore Mountain Resort.** This downhill ski area has been a favorite of families since it began operating in 1938. Five glades have opened more skiable terrain. The 39 trails are well laid out and fun to ski. Most runs are naturally formed intermediates that weave in and out of glades. Beginners have several slopes and routes from the summit; experts must be content with a few short, steep pitches. In addition to the trails, snowboarders have a terrain park and a half pipe. Night skiing is offered Thursday–Saturday and holidays. ⬚ *1 Skimobile Rd.* ⬚ *Box 1640, North Conway 03860* ☎ *603/356–5543, 603/356–8516 snow conditions, 800/786–6754 lodging* ⬚ *www.cranmore.com.*

King Pine Ski Area at Purity Spring Resort. Some 9 mi south of Conway, this family-run ski area has been going strong since the late 19th century. Some ski-and-stay packages include free skiing for midweek resort guests. Among the facilities and activities are an indoor pool and fitness complex, and ice-skating. King Pine's 16 gentle trails are ideal for beginner and intermediate skiers; experts won't be challenged except for a brief pitch on the Pitch Pine trail. There's tubing on weekend afternoons and night skiing and tubing on Friday and Saturday. There are 9 mi of cross-country skiing. An indoor fitness center is open year-round. In summer this lively place is a big hit for waterskiing, kayaking, loon-watching, tennis, hiking, and other activities; lodging packages are available. ⬚ *Rte. 153, East Madison 03849* ☎ *603/367–8896 or 800/ 373–3754* ⬚ *www.purityspring.com.*

Forty miles of groomed cross-country trails weave through North Conway and the countryside along the **Mt. Washington Valley Ski Touring As-**

sociation Network (⊠ Rte. 16, Intervale ☎ 603/356–9920 or 800/282–5220 ⊕ www.crosscountryskinh.com).

Shopping

ANTIQUES **Richard Plusch Antiques** (⊠ Rte. 16 [U.S. 302] ☎ 603/356–3333) deals in period furniture and accessories, including glass, sterling silver, Oriental porcelains, rugs, and paintings.

CRAFTS **Handcrafters Barn** (⊠ Main St. ☎ 603/356–8996) stocks the work of 350 area artists and artisans. The **League of New Hampshire Craftsmen** (⊠ 2526 Main St. ☎ 603/356–2441) carries the creations of the state's best artisans. **Zeb's General Store** (⊠ 2675 Main St. ☎ 603/356–9294 or 800/676–9294) looks just like an old-fashioned country store; it sells food items, crafts, and other products made in New England.

FACTORY More than 150 factory outlets—including L. L. Bean, Timberland,
OUTLETS Pfaltzgraff, London Fog, Polo, Nike, Anne Klein, and Woolrich—line Route 16.

SPORTSWEAR A top pick for skiwear is **Joe Jones** (⊠ 2709 Main St. ☎ 603/356–9411).

Kancamagus Highway

★ *36 mi between Conway and Lincoln/North Woodstock.*

Interstate 93 is the fastest way to the White Mountains, but it's hardly the most appealing. The section of Route 112 known as the Kancamagus Highway passes through some of the state's most unspoiled mountain scenery—it was one of the first roads in the nation to be designated a National Scenic Byway. This stretch, punctuated by overlooks and picnic areas, erupts into fiery color each fall, when photo-snapping drivers can really slow things down. There are campgrounds off the highway. In bad weather, check with the White Mountains Visitors Bureau for road conditions.

Sports & the Outdoors
A couple of short hiking trails off the Kancamagus Highway (Route 112) yield great rewards for relatively little effort. The **Lincoln Woods Trail** starts from the large parking lot of the Lincoln Woods Visitor Center, 4 mi east of Lincoln. You can purchase the recreation pass ($5 per vehicle, good for seven consecutive days) needed to park in any of the White Mountain National Forest lots or overlooks here; stopping briefly to take photos or to use the restrooms at the visitor center is permitted without a pass. The trail crosses a suspension bridge over the Pemigewasset River and follows an old railroad bed for 3 mi along the river. The parking and picnic area for **Sabbaday Falls,** about 15 mi west of Conway, is the trailhead for an easy ½-mi route to a multilevel cascade that plunges through two potholes and a flume.

DARTMOUTH–LAKE SUNAPEE

In the west-central part of the state, the towns around prestigious Dartmouth College and rippling Lake Sunapee vary from sleepy, old-fashioned outposts that haven't changed much in decades to bustling, sophisticated towns rife with cafés, art galleries, and boutiques. Among the latter, Hanover and New London are the area's main hubs, both of them becoming increasingly popular as vacation destinations and with telecommuters seeking a quieter, more economical home base. Although distinct from the Lakes Region, greater Lake Sunapee looks like a miniature Lake Winnipesaukee, albeit with far less commercial development. For a great drive, follow the Lake Sunapee Scenic & Cultural Byway, which runs for about 25 mi from Georges Mills (a bit northwest of New London) down into Warner, tracing much of the Lake Sunapee shoreline. When you've tired of climbing and swimming and visiting the past, look for small studios of area artists. This part of the state, along with the even quieter Monadnocks area to the south, has long been an informal artists' colony where people come to write, paint, and weave in solitude.

New London

🔞 *16 mi northwest of Warner, 25 mi west of Tilton.*

New London, the home of Colby-Sawyer College (1837), is a good base for exploring the Lake Sunapee region. A campus of stately Colonial-style buildings fronts the vibrant commercial district, where you'll find several cafés and boutiques. At the 10,000-year-old **Cricenti's Bog,** off Business Route 11, a short trail shows off the shaggy mosses and fragile ecosystem of this ancient pond.

★ ☺ About 15 mi southeast of New London, **Mt. Kearsarge Indian Museum, Education and Cultural Center** gives guided tours, which leave on the hour, of an extensive collection of Native American artistry, including moose-hair embroidery, quilt work, and basketry. Signs on the Medicine Woods trail identify plants and explain how Native Americans use them as foods, medicines, and dyes. ⊠ *Kearsarge Mountain Rd., Warner* ☎ *603/456–2600* ⊕ *www.indianmuseum.org* ⊠ *$8.50* ☺ *May–Oct., Mon.–Sat. 10–5, Sun. noon–5; Nov. and Dec., Sat. 10–5, Sun. noon–5.*

Near the Mt. Kearsarge Indian Museum, a 3½-mi scenic auto road at **Rollins State Park** (⊠ Off Rte. 103, Main St., Warner ☎ 603/456–3808) snakes up the southern slope of Mt. Kearsarge, where you can then hike the ½-mi trail to the summit. The road is closed mid-November through mid-June; park admission is $3.

Where to Stay & Eat

$$–$$$ ✕ **Jack's Coffee.** Nominally a coffeehouse, Jack's is actually much more, presenting a nice range of bountiful salads (try the lemon Caesar), designer sandwiches, and eclectic dinner entrées, such as duck cooked two ways: slow-roasted leg quarter or pan-seared breast with French lentils, grilled leeks, and duck demi-glace. The restaurant occupies a stately Greek-revival house in the heart of downtown, and a tree-shaded patio out front overlooks the pedestrian action. ⊠ *207 Main St.* ☎ *603/526–8003* ⊟ *D, MC, V* ☺ *No dinner Mon. and Tues.*

$–$$ ✕ **Four Corners Grille and Flying Goose Brew Pub.** South of downtown, this inviting restaurant and adjoining pub is known for massive burgers, pit-barbecued meats, calamari in basil pesto, great ales, and excep-

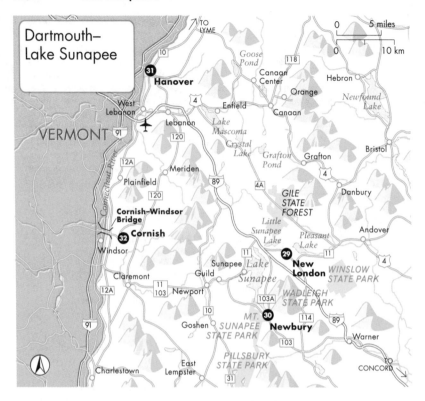

Dartmouth–
Lake Sunapee

tional views of Mt. Kearsarge. More substantial victuals include jam-
balaya with shrimp, scallops, mussels, and sausage, and char-grilled
teriyaki steaks. There's live folk and light rock music many nights.
⊠ *Rtes. 11 and 114* 🕾 *603/526–6899* ☰ *AE, D, MC, V.*

$ ✕ **Peter Christian's Tavern.** Exposed beams, wooden tables, a smattering
of antiques, and half shutters on the windows make Peter Christian's a
cool summer oasis and a warm winter haven. The fare tends toward the
traditional and the hearty, from beef stew to mustard-chicken cordon
bleu to an exceptional vegetarian-based onion soup. ⊠ *195 Main St.*
🕾 *603/526–4042* ☰ *D, MC, V.*

★ **$$–$$$** ✕▥ **Inn at Pleasant Lake.** This 1790s inn lies just across Pleasant Lake
from majestic Mt. Kearsarge. Its spacious rooms have country antiques
and modern bathrooms. The restaurant ($$$$; reservations essential)
presents a nightly changing prix-fixe menu that draws raves for such
entrées as roast tenderloin of Angus beef with a Calvados demi-glace
and watercress pesto and such desserts as white-chocolate mousse with
a trio of sauces. Afternoon tea and full breakfast are included. ⊠ *853
Pleasant St.* ⌂ *Box 1030, 03257* 🕾 *603/526–6271 or 800/626–4907*
🖷 *603/526–4111* ⊕*www.innatpleasantlake.com* ⇌ *10 rooms* ⌂ *Restaurant, some in-room hot tubs, gym, beach, boating, meeting rooms; no
room phones, no room TVs, no smoking* ☰ *MC, V* ⬭⫯ *BP.*

$–$$$ ✕🏠 **New London Inn.** The two porches of this rambling 1792 inn over-look Main Street. Rooms are relatively simple and cozy, with Victorian furnishings. Some have views of the Colby-Sawyer campus. The restaurant's ($$–$$$$) menu of innovative American cuisine has such starters as butternut squash with a sun-dried cranberry pesto and such entrées as grilled cilantro shrimp with a saffron risotto. ✉ *353 Main St.* 🕭 *Box 8, 03257* 🕾 *603/526–2791 or 800/526–2791* 🖷 *603/526–2749* ⊕ *www. newlondoninn.net* ⬱ *25 rooms* ♿ *Restaurant, cable TV; no TV in some rooms, no smoking* ▭ *AE, D, MC, V* ¶○¶ *CP.*

$–$$$ 🏠 **Follansbee Inn.** Built in 1840, this quintessential country inn on the shore of Kezar Lake is a perfect fit in the 19th-century village of North Sutton, about 4 mi south of New London. The common rooms and bed-rooms are loaded with collectibles—a traveling trunk here, a wooden school desk there. Each of the 18 rooms is filled with soft country quilts, and several of them overlook the water. In winter, you can ice-fish, borrow the inn's snowshoes, or ski across the lake; in summer you can swim or boat from the inn's pier. A 3-mi walking trail circles the lake. ✉ *Rte. 114, North Sutton 03260* 🕾 *603/927–4221 or 800/626–4221* ⊕ *www.follansbeeinn.com* ⬱ *18 rooms* ♿ *Some in-room hot tubs, lake, windsurfing, boating, fishing, bicycles, hiking, cross-country ski-ing, ice-skating; no room phones, no room TVs, no kids under 10, no smoking* ▭ *MC, V* ¶○¶ *BP.*

The Arts

The **New London Barn Playhouse** (✉ 84 Main St. 🕾 603/526–6710 or 800/633–2276) presents Broadway-style and children's plays every sum-mer in New Hampshire's oldest continuously operating theater.

Shopping

Artisan's Workshop (✉ Peter Christian's Tavern, 196 Main St. 🕾 603/ 526–4227) carries jewelry, glass, and other local handicrafts. Near New London in the tiny village of Elkins, **Mesa Home Factory Store** (✉ Elkins Bus. Loop 🕾 603/526–4497) carries striking hand-painted dinnerware, handblown glassware, wrought-iron decorative arts, and other house-wares at bargain prices.

Newbury

㉚ *8 mi southwest of New London.*

Newbury is on the edge of Mt. Sunapee State Park. The mountain, which rises to an elevation of nearly 3,000 feet, and the sparkling lake are the region's outdoor recreation centers. The popular League of New Hamp-shire Craftsmen's Fair, the nation's oldest crafts fair, is held at the base of Mt. Sunapee each August.

John M. Hay, who served as private secretary to Abraham Lincoln and secretary of state for Presidents McKinley and Roosevelt, built the **Fells** on Lake Sunapee as a summer home in 1890. House tours focus on his life in Newbury and Washington. Hay's son was responsible for the ex-tensive gardens, a mix of formal and informal styles that include a 75-foot perennial border and a hillside planted with heather. More than

800 acres of the former estate are open for hiking and picnicking. ⊠ *Rte. 103A* ☎ *603/763–4789* ⊕ *www.thefells.org* ⊠ *$6* ☉ *Labor Day–Columbus Day 10–5; grounds daily dawn–dusk.*

About midway between New London and Newbury on the west side of the lake, **Sunapee Harbor** is an old-fashioned, all-American summer resort community that feels a bit like a miniature version of Wolfeboro, with a large marina, a handful of restaurants and shops on the water, a tidy village green with a gazebo, and a small museum run by the historical society set in a Victorian stable. A plaque outside Wild Goose Country Store details some of Lake Sunapee's attributes—that it's one of the highest lakes in New Hampshire, at 1,091 feet above sea level, and that it's also one of the least polluted. An interpretive path runs along a short span of the Sugar River, the only outflow from Lake Sunapee, which winds for 18 mi to the Connecticut River.

Narrated cruises aboard the **M/V Mt. Sunapee II** (⊠ Main St., Sunapee ☎ 603/763–4030 ⊕ www.sunapeecruises.com) provide a closer look at Lake Sunapee's history and mountain scenery; they run from late May through mid-October, daily in summer and on weekends in spring and fall; the cost is $16. Dinner cruises are held on the **M/V Kearsarge** (☎603/938–6465 ⊕www.mvkearsarge.com); cruises leave from the dock at Sunapee Harbor, June through mid-October, Tuesday–Sunday evenings; the cost is $28.95, which includes a buffet dinner.

Where to Stay & Eat

$$–$$$　✕ **Anchorage at Sunapee Harbor.** Fans of this long gray restaurant with a sprawling deck overlooking Sunapee Harbor's marina come as much for the great views as for the dependable—and occasionally creative—American chow. It's as likely a place for a burger or fried seafood platter as for homemade lobster spring rolls. There's also live entertainment some nights—in fact, this is where the founders of the rock band Aerosmith first met back in the early 1970s. ⊠ *71 Main St., Sunapee Harbor* ☎ *603/763–3334* ▤ *D, MC, V* ☉ *Closed mid-Oct.–late Apr. and Mon.*

$$　✕ **Bellissima.** The hand-tossed brick-oven pizzas as well as the good views of the southern tip of Lake Sunapee make this lively Newbury restaurant a popular spot. Other options include rotisserie-grilled steaks and chicken, panini sandwiches, and hearty pasta fare, such as seafood pomodoro. Among the pizzas, you won't go wrong with the Romano Carni, topped with pepperoni, Italian sausage, grilled chicken, meatballs, bacon, mozzarella, and marinara sauce. More than 20 flavors of ice cream are offered, too. ⊠ *Newbury Harbor Plaza, Rte. 103 at Rte. 103A* ☎ *603/763–3290* ▤ *D, MC, V.*

$–$$$　✕▨ **Inn at Sunapee** A handsome, steep-roofed yellow farmhouse on a hill overlooking the ski slopes of Mt. Sunapee and the region's many other distant hills, this rambling 1870s inn lies just a short drive up the hill from Sunapee Harbor. Although fairly traditional looking from the outside, the inn contains a number of Asian decorative arts picked up during innkeepers Ted and Susan Harriman's years living in the Far East. Floral wallpaper, wicker chairs, and eclectic antiques also fill the rooms. The restaurant ($$) serves commendable continental fare, such as shrimp in lemon-thyme sauce. ⊠ *125 Burkehaven Hill Rd., Sunapee 03782*

☎ *603/763–4444 or 800/327–2466* 🖷 *603/763–9456* ⊕ *www. innatsunapee.com* ➾ *16 rooms* ⚄ *Restaurant; no room phones, no room TVs, no smoking* ⊟ *AE, D, MC, V* ¹⊙¹ *BP.*

★ **$$$–$$$$** 🖭 **Sunapee Harbor Cottages.** A luxurious take on the classic cottage compounds that dot the Sunapee and Lakes regions, this particular little collection of contemporary shingle bungalows tumbles down a gentle hillside just steps from Sunapee Harbor's marina and restaurants. Each light and airy unit sleeps from five to eight people, making this a good deal for larger groups and a bit of a splurge for couples—all have kitchens, gas fireplaces, porches, and a well-chosen mix of antiques and newer furnishings. Nice touches include grocery-delivery service, in-room massage, and even catered meals prepared by the nearby Millstone Restaurant. ⊠ *4 Lake Ave., Sunapee Harbor 03782* ☎ *603/763–5052 or 866/763–5052* ⊕ *www.sunapeeharborcottages.com* ➾ *6 cottages* ⚄ *Kitchens, cable TV, in-room VCRs, massage* ⊟ *MC, V.*

¢ 🏕 **Crow's Nest Campground.** Many of the sites at this campground sit directly on the Sugar River; some cabins have private baths. The facilities include a recreation hall, a pool, a children's wading pool, miniature golf, and a warm-up room with a fireplace. River swimming and fishing are summer pastimes; you can skate or sled in winter, and area snowmobile trails connect to the campground. ⊠ *529 S. Main St., Newport 03773* ☎ *603/863–6170* ⊕ *www.crowsnestcampground.com* 🖃 *$22–$65* ➾ *120 sites, 3 cabins* ⚄ *Pool, playground, laundry facilities, flush toilets, full hookups, dump station, drinking water, showers, fire grates, picnic tables, electricity, public telephone, general store, swimming (pond)* ⊟ *AE, D, MC, V* ☉ *Closed mid-Oct.–Nov. and Apr.–mid-May.*

Sports & the Outdoors

BEACHES **Sunapee State Beach** has picnic areas, a beach, and a bathhouse. You can rent canoes here, too. ⊠ *Rte. 103* ☎ *603/763–5561* 🖃 *$3* ☉ *Daily dawn–dusk.*

FISHING **Lake Sunapee** has brook and lake trout, salmon, smallmouth bass, and pickerel.

SKI AREA **Mount Sunapee.** Although the resort is state-owned, it's managed by Vermont's Okemo Mountain resort, known for being family friendly. The agreement has allowed the influx of capital necessary for operating extensive lifts, snowmaking (97% coverage), and trail grooming. This mountain is 1,510 vertical feet and has 60 trails, mostly intermediate. Experts can take to a dozen slopes, including three nice double-black diamonds. Boarders have a 420-foot-long half pipe and a terrain park with music. In summer, the Sunapee Express Quad zooms you to the summit. From here, it's just under a mile hike to Lake Solitude. Mountain bikers can use the lift to many trails, and an in-line skate park has beginner and advanced sections (plus equipment rentals). ⊠ *Rte. 103* 🖃 *Box 2021, 03772* ☎ *603/763–2356, 603/763–4020 snow conditions, 877/687–8627 lodging* ⊕ *www.mtsunapee.com.*

Shopping

Overlooking Lake Sunapee's southern tip, **Outspokin' Bicycle and Sport** (⊠ Rtes. 103 and 103A, at the harbor ☎ 603/763–9500) has a tremendous selection of biking, hiking, skateboarding, snow- and waterskiing,

Maple Sugaring

IT'S THE QUINTESSENTIAL CONDIMENT of New England breakfasts, the core ingredient of cutely shaped candies, and one of New Hampshire's legendary exports: maple syrup. In fact, the Granite State produces about 90,000 gallons of this sweet elixir every year. And throughout the state, particularly in the Monadnock and Sunapee regions, a number of private sugarhouses open their doors to the public—you can visit to watch maple-sugaring demonstrations, or just to buy fresh syrup. A few sugarhouses even hold parties and festivals.

The season generally runs from about mid-February through mid-April, depending on weather conditions. Sap runs best when daytime temperatures rise above freezing. Once collected in buckets from the trees, sap is taken to the sugarhouses, where it's boiled down and ultimately reduced to pure maple syrup. You need to boil down about 40 gallons of raw sap to get just a gallon of refined syrup. It's a time-consuming and rather painstaking process, which in part accounts for the relative high cost of pure maple syrup versus the treacly imitation variety sold in many grocery stores.

Make a note on your calendar to attend the state's foremost sugaring event, New Hampshire Maple Weekend, held in mid- to late March, when some 50 sugarhouses open their doors to guests, host pancake breakfasts, and show off their often impressive sugaring operations. For a list of syrup producers throughout the state, contact **New Hampshire Maple Producers** (⊠ 79 Fisherville Rd., Concord, 03303 ☎ 603/225-3757 ⊕ www.nhmapleproducers.com). The organization also produces a cookbook containing some 200 maple recipes; you can order this book from the Web site for $14, which includes shipping and handling.

−Andrew Collins

and snowboarding clothing and equipment. Right on the harbor in Sunapee village, on the marina, **Wild Goose Country Store** (⊠ 77 Main St. ☎ 603/763–5516) carries quirky gifts, teddy bears, penny candy, pottery, and other engaging odds and ends.

Hanover

 12 mi northwest of Enfield, 62 mi northwest of Concord.

Eleazer Wheelock founded Hanover's Dartmouth College in 1769 to educate the Abenaki "and other youth." When he arrived, the town consisted of about 20 families. The college and the town grew symbiotically, with Dartmouth becoming the northernmost Ivy League school. Today Hanover is still synonymous with Dartmouth, but the attractive town is also a respected medical and cultural center for the upper Connecticut River valley.

Robert Frost spent part of a brooding freshman semester at Ivy League **Dartmouth College** before giving up college altogether. The buildings that cluster around the green include the **Baker Memorial Library,** which houses such literary treasures as 17th-century editions of Shakespeare's works. The library is also well known for the 3,000-square-foot murals by Mexican artist José Clemente Orozco that depict the story of civilization on the American continents. If the towering arcade at the entrance to the **Hopkins Center** (☎ 603/646–2422) appears familiar, it's probably because it resembles the project that architect Wallace K. Harrison completed just after designing it: New York City's Metropolitan Opera House at Lincoln Center. The complex includes a 900-seat theater for film showings and concerts, a 400-seat theater for plays, and a black-box theater for new plays. The Dartmouth Symphony Orchestra performs here, as does the Big Apple Circus. In addition to African, Peruvian, Oceanic, Asian, European, and American art, the **Hood Museum of Art** (⊠ Wheelock St. ☎ 603/646–2808 ⊕ www.dartmouth.edu/hood 🎟 Free ⊗ Tues. and Thurs.–Sat. 10–5, Wed. 10–9, Sun. noon–5) owns the Picasso painting *Guitar on a Table,* silver by Paul Revere, and a set of Assyrian reliefs from the 9th century BC. The range of contemporary works, including pieces by John Sloan, William Glackens, Mark Rothko, Fernand Léger, and Joan Miró, is particularly notable. Rivaling the collection is the museum's architecture: a series of austere, copper-roofed, redbrick buildings arranged around a courtyard. Free guided tours are available on request

NEED A BREAK? Take a respite from museum-hopping with a cup of espresso, a ham-and-cheese scone, or a freshly baked brownie at the **Dirt Cowboy** (⊠ 7 S. Main St. ☎ 603/643–1323), a café across from the green and beside a used-book store. A local branch of a small Boston chain, **The Wrap** (⊠ 35 S. Main St. ☎ 603/643–0202), occupies a slick basement space with comfy sofas and has a small patio to the side. Drop by for healthful burritos, wraps, soups (try the carrot-ginger), and smoothies and energy drinks.

In 1782, two Shaker brothers from Mount Lebanon, New York, arrived on Lake Mascoma's northeastern side, about 12 mi southeast of Hanover. Eventually, they formed Enfield, the 9th of 18 Shaker communities in this country, and moved it to the lake's southern shore, where they erected more than 200 buildings. The **Enfield Shaker Museum** preserves the legacy of the Shakers, who numbered 330 members at the village's peak. By 1923, interest in the society had dwindled, and the last 10 members joined the Canterbury community, south of Laconia. A self-guided walking tour takes you through 13 of the remaining buildings, among them the Great Stone Dwelling (which served until recently as a hotel, the Shaker Inn) and an 1849 stone mill. Demonstrations of Shaker crafts techniques and numerous special events take place year-round. ⊠ *24 Caleb Dyer La., Enfield* ☎*603/632–4346* ⊕*www.shakermuseum.org* 🎟*$7* ⊗ *Late May–late Oct., Mon.–Sat. 10–5, Sun. noon–5; late Oct.–late May, Sat. 10–4, Sun. noon–4.*

OFF THE BEATEN PATH **UPPER VALLEY –** From Hanover, you can make a 60-mi drive up Route 10 all the way to Littleton for a highly scenic tour of the upper Connecticut River valley. You'll have views of the river and Vermont's Green Mountains from many points. The road passes through groves of evergreens, over leafy ridges, and through delightful hamlets. Grab gourmet picnic provisions at **Pat & Tony's General Store** (☎ 603/650–2015) on Lyme's village common, and stop at the bluff-top village green in historical Haverhill (28 mi north of Hanover) for a picnic amid the panorama of classic Georgian- and Federal-style mansions and faraway farmsteads. You can follow this scenic route all the way to the White Mountains region, or loop back south from Haverhill—along Route 25 to Route 118 to U.S. 4 west—to Enfield, a drive of about 45 mi (and 75 minutes).

Where to Stay & Eat

$$–$$$ ✕ **Canoe Club.** A snazzy newcomer to Hanover's burgeoning restaurant scene, this festive spot decked with canoes, paddles, and other boating paraphernalia presents live jazz and folk music many nights. The mood may be casual, but the kitchen presents rather fancy and imaginative food, including a memorable starter of shrimp, prosciutto, and almonds wrapped in bok choy with sweet-and-sour sauce. Among the main courses, roasted lamb sirloin with white beans, asparagus, and roasted garlic ragout stands out. There's also a lighter, late-night menu. ⊠ *27 S. Main St.* ☎ *603/643–9660* ⊟ *AE, D, DC, MC, V.*

$–$$ ✕ **Lui Lui.** The creatively topped thin-crust pizzas and huge pasta portions are only part of the draw at this chatter-filled eatery. It also has a dramatic setting inside a former power station on the Mascoma River. Pizza picks include the Tuscan (mozzarella on the bottom, tomato, and roasted garlic) and the grilled chicken with barbecue sauce. Pasta fans should dive into a bowl of linguine with prosciutto, spinach, and mushrooms. The owners also run Molly's Restaurant and Jesse's Tavern, which are both nearby. ⊠ *Adjacent to Powerhouse Mall, off Rte. 12A, West Lebanon* ☎ *603/298–7070* ⊟ *AE, MC, V.*

$–$$ ✕ **Murphy's.** Students, visiting alums, and locals regularly descend upon this wildly popular pub, whose walls are lined with shelves of old books. The varied menu of consistently tasty chow lists both familiar and innovative fare: blackened-chicken wraps, char-grilled Black Angus steaks, Szechuan yellowfin tuna with red curry sauce and ginger cakes, lobster ravioli, and fajitas. Check out the extensive beer list. ⊠ *11 S. Main St.* ☎ *603/643–4075* ⊟ *AE, D, DC, MC, V.*

¢ ✕ **Lou's.** A Hanover tradition for decades, this diner-cum-café-cum-bakery serves possibly the best breakfast in the valley—a plate of *migas* (eggs, cheddar, salsa, and guacamole mixed with tortilla chips) can fill you up for the better part of the day; blueberry-cranberry buttermilk pancakes also satisfy. Or grab a seat at the old-fashioned soda fountain and order an ice-cream sundae. ⊠ *30 S. Main St.* ☎ *603/643–3321* ⊟ *AE, MC, V* ⊘ *No dinner.*

★ $$$$ ✕▥ **Hanover Inn.** Owned by Dartmouth College, this sprawling, Georgian-style brick structure rises four white-trimmed stories. The original building was converted to a tavern in 1780, and this expertly run inn, now greatly enlarged, has been operating ever since. Rooms have Colonial reproductions, Audubon prints, large sitting areas, and marble-accented bathrooms. The formal Daniel Webster Room ($$–$$$$; no dinner Monday) serves regional American dishes such as sautéed sweetbreads with a beurre-blanc sauce, and trout over caramelized fennel, endive, and celeriac puree. The swank Zins Wine Bistro ($–$$) prepares lighter but still highly innovative fare. In warm weather, you can enjoy casual fare alfresco at the Terrace ($–$$). Guests have access to a local sports club. ⊠ *The Green, Main and Wheelock Sts.* ☎ *Box 151, 03755* ☎ *603/643–4300 or 800/443–7024* 🖷 *603/646–3744* ⊕ *www. hanoverinn.com* ⤷ *92 rooms, 22 suites* ♨ *2 restaurants, room service, cable TV, bar, business services, meeting rooms, some pets allowed (fee), no-smoking rooms* ☰ *AE, D, DC, MC, V.*

$$–$$$$ ⊞ **Trumbull House.** The sunny guest rooms of this white Colonial-style house—on 16 acres in Hanover's outskirts—have king- or queen-size beds, window seats, writing desks, feather pillows, and other comfortable touches, as well as wireless high-speed Internet. There is also a romantic guesthouse, complete with a private deck, whirlpool tub, refrigerator, and wet bar. Breakfast, with a choice of entrées, is served in the formal dining room or in front of the living room fireplace. Rates include use of a nearby health club. ⊠ *40 Etna Rd., 03755* ☎ *603/643–2370 or 800/651–5141* 🖷 *603/643–2430* ⊕ *www.trumbullhouse.com* ⤷ *4 rooms, 1 suite, 1 cottage* ♨ *Dining room, some in-room hot tubs, cable TV, in-room VCRs, pond, basketball, hiking, business services, meeting room; no smoking* ☰ *AE, D, DC, MC, V* ⧖ *BP.*

$–$$$$ ⊞ **Dowds Country Inn.** This 1780 Georgian-style house on 6 pastoral acres faces the village green and the vintage country store in the frozen-in-time river village of Lyme, about 10 mi north of Hanover. Rooms have a crisp, unfussy look, with Colonial antiques, quilted bedspreads, stenciled walls, and wide-plank floors. It's a relaxed and reasonably priced alternative to the accommodations in bustling Hanover. Breakfast is exceptional here, with delicious homemade pastries and pancakes or waffles with local syrup. ⊠ *On the Common, Lyme 03768* ☎ *603/795–4712 or 800/482–4712* 🖷 *603/795–4220* ⊕ *www.dowdscountryinn.com* ⤷ *19 rooms, 3 suites* ♨ *Pond, meeting room; no room TVs* ☰ *D, DC, MC, V* ⧖ *BP.*

Sports & the Outdoors

Ledyard Canoe Club of Dartmouth (☎ 603/643–6709) provides canoe and kayak rentals and classes on the swift-flowing Connecticut River, which isn't suitable for beginners and is safest after mid-June.

Shopping

Shops, mostly of the independent variety but with a few upscale chains sprinkled in, line Hanover's main street. The commercial district blends almost imperceptibly with the Dartmouth campus. West Lebanon, south of Hanover on the Vermont border, has many more shops. Goldsmith Paul Gross of **Designer Gold** (⊠ 3 Lebanon St. ☎ 603/643–3864) designs settings for gemstones—all one-of-a-kind or limited-edition. The **Powerhouse Mall** (⊠ Rte. 12A, 1 mi north of I–89 Exit 20, West Lebanon ☎ 603/298–5236), a former power station, comprises three buildings of specialty stores, boutiques, and restaurants.

EN ROUTE   From Hanover follow Route 10 south through West Lebanon to Route 12A. Then bear right directly onto scenic **River Road.** It hugs the shore of the Connecticut River, affording outstanding views of Vermont's countryside (try to ignore the occasional glimpse of busy Interstate 91).

The bucolic road also passes several old mansions, including Plainfield's stately Home Hill Inn. The narrow lane is slow going in places, all the better to take in the views. After about 7 mi, River Road puts you back onto the more prosaic Route 12A in Cornish.

Cornish

 22 mi south of Hanover.

Today Cornish is best known for its four covered bridges and for being the home of reclusive author J. D. Salinger, but at the turn of the 20th century the village was known primarily as the home of the country's then most popular novelist, Winston Churchill (no relation to the British prime minister). His novel *Richard Carvell* sold more than a million copies. Churchill was such a celebrity that he hosted Teddy Roosevelt during the president's 1902 visit. At that time Cornish was an enclave of artistic talent. Painter Maxfield Parrish lived and worked here, and sculptor Augustus Saint-Gaudens set up his studio and created the heroic bronzes for which he is known.

★ Just south of Plainfield, where River Road rejoins Route 12A, a small lane leads to the **Saint-Gaudens National Historic Site.** Here you can tour sculptor Augustus Saint-Gaudens's house, studio, gallery, and 150 acres of grounds and gardens. Scattered throughout are full-size casts of his works. The property has two hiking trails, the longer of which is the Blow-Me-Down Trail. Concerts are held every Sunday afternoon in July and August. ⊠ *Off Rte. 12A* ☎ *603/675–2175* ⊕ *www.sgnhs.org* ☞ *$5* ☉ *Buildings June–Oct., daily 9–4:30; grounds daily dawn–dusk.*

1½ mi south of the Saint-Gaudens National Historic Site you'll reach the 460-foot **Cornish-Windsor Bridge,** which connects New Hampshire to Vermont across the Connecticut River. It dates from 1866 and is the longest covered bridge in the United States.

Where to Stay & Eat

$$$$ ✕⌂ **Home Hill Inn.** Set back from the Connecticut River on 25 acres of
Fodor'sChoice meadow and woods, this tranquil 1818 mansion is best suited to adults.
★ The owners have given the inn a French influence with 19th-century antiques and collectibles. Rooms in the main house have canopy or four-poster beds; four have fireplaces. The carriage house contains six spacious rooms done with stunning country pine furniture; some have fireplaces. The dramatic dining room ($$–$$$$; closed Monday and Tuesday, no lunch) serves perhaps the best French and Mediterranean cuisine in the state, with specialties that include roasted Scottish partridge stuffed with savoy cabbage and served with wild huckleberry sauce, and pan-roasted sea bass with a ragout of confit tomatoes. Chef-owner Victoria du Roure runs the on-site L'École Culinaire; cooking classes are held one weekend each month in winter and spring and include two nights' accommodation and several meals. ⊠ *River Rd., Plainfield 03781* ☎ *603/675–6165* ⊕ *www.homehillinn.com* ☞ *9 rooms, 2 suites, 1 seasonal cottage* ♿ *Restaurant, putting green, tennis court, pool, massage, cross-country skiing, meeting rooms, no-smoking rooms; no room phones, no room TVs, no kids under 14* ═ *AE, D, DC, MC, V* ⦿ *CP.*

The Arts
The restored 19th-century **Claremont Opera House** (✉ Tremont Sq., Claremont ☎ 603/542–4433 ⊕ www.claremontoperahouse.com) hosts plays and musicals throughout summer.

Sports & the Outdoors
North Star Canoe Rentals (✉ Rte. 12A, Balloch's Crossing ☎ 603/542–6929) rents canoes for half- or full-day trips on the Connecticut River.

THE MONADNOCKS & MERRIMACK VALLEY

Southwestern and south-central New Hampshire mix village charm with city hustle across two distinct regions. The Merrimack River valley has the state's largest and fastest-growing cities: Nashua, Manchester, and Concord. To the west, in the state's sleepy southwestern corner, is the Monadnock region, one of New Hampshire's least-developed and most naturally stunning parts. Here you'll find plenty of hiking trails as well as peaceful hilltop hamlets that appear barely changed in the past two centuries. Mt. Monadnock, southern New Hampshire's largest peak, stands guard over the Monadnock region, which has more than 200 lakes and ponds. Rainbow trout, smallmouth and largemouth bass, and some northern pike swim in Chesterfield's Spofford Lake. Goose Pond in West Canaan, just north of Keene, holds smallmouth bass and white perch.

Two artsy communities in the area, Keene and Peterborough, have grown a bit in recent years and have even witnessed the opening of some urbane restaurants and inns.

Nashua

 98 mi south of Lincoln/North Woodstock, 48 mi northwest of Boston, 36 mi south of Concord, 50 mi southeast of Keene.

Once a prosperous manufacturing town that drew thousands of immigrant workers in the late 1800s and early 1900s, Nashua declined following World War II, as many factories shut down or moved to where labor was cheaper. Since the 1970s, however, the metro area has jumped in population, developing into a charming, old-fashioned community. Its low-key downtown has classic redbrick buildings along the Nashua River, a tributary of the Merrimack River. Though not visited by tourists as much as other communities in the region, Nashua (population 90,000) has some good restaurants and an engaging museum.

The city's impressive industrial history is retold at the **Florence Hyde Speare Memorial Museum,** which houses the Nashua Historical Society. In this two-story museum you'll find artifacts, early furnishings, photos, a vintage printing press, and a research library. Adjacent to the museum is the Federal-style **Abbot-Spalding House,** furnished with 18th- and 19th-century antiques, art, and household items. The house can be visited only on a guided tour that takes place one Saturday a month from April through November. ✉ *5 Abbot St.* ☎ *603/883–0015* ⊕ *www.nashuahistoricalsociety.org* ⌨ *Free ⊙ Mar.–Thanksgiving, Tues.–Thurs. 10–4 (also one Sat. a month by appointment).*

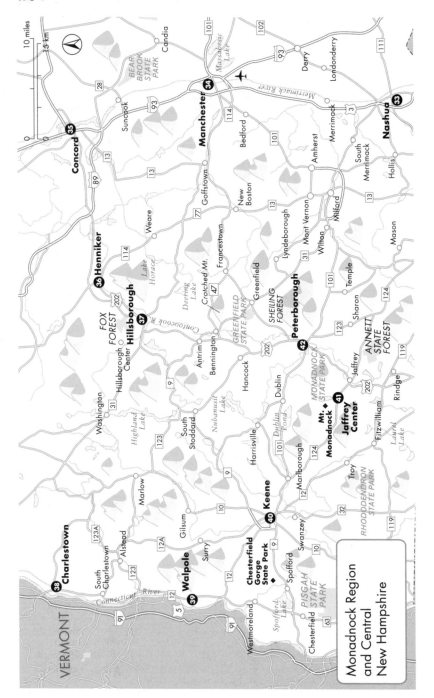

Monadnock Region
and Central
New Hampshire

Where to Eat

$$–$$$$ ✕ **Michael Timothy's Urban Bistro.** Part hip bistro, part jazzy wine bar (with
Fodor'sChoice live music many nights), Michael Timothy's is so popular that even food-
★ ies from Massachusetts drive here. The regularly changing menu might
include stuffed pheasant with foie gras risotto and cranberry-clove jus,
or wood-grilled venison loin with port reduction, herb spaetzle, creamed
morel mushrooms, and stewed lentils. Wood-fired pizzas are also a spe-
cialty—try the one topped with sirloin tips, caramelized onions, mush-
rooms, salami, sautéed spinach, and three cheeses. Sunday brunch is a
big hit here. ⊠ *212 Main St.* ☎ *603/595–9334* ▤ *AE, D, MC, V* ☉ *No
lunch Sat.*

$$–$$$ ✕ **Villa Banca.** On the ground floor of a dramatic, turreted office build-
ing, this airy spot with high ceilings and tall windows specializes in both
traditional and contemporary Italian cooking. Get a little taste of every-
thing by ordering a starter sampler platter consisting of seafood risotto
cakes, lobster-stuffed artichokes, chicken sausage, fried spinach-and-ar-
tichoke ravioli, chicken in phyllo dough, and fried calamari. Then move
on to the delicious pastas and grills, including gnocchi with wood-
grilled turkey and prosciutto, and chicken-and-sausage lasagna. Note
the exotic-martini menu—a big draw at happy hour. ⊠ *194 Main St.*
☎ *603/598–0500* ▤ *AE, D, DC, MC, V* ☉ *No lunch weekends.*

$ ✕ **Martha's Exchange.** A casual spot with copper brewing vats, original
marble floors, and booth seating, Martha's appeals both to the after-work
set and office workers on lunch breaks. Burgers and sandwiches, maple-
stout-barbecued chicken and ribs, Mexican fare, seafood and steak grills,
and salads—all in large portions—are your options here. There's also a
sweets shop attached, and you can buy half-gallon jugs of house-brewed
beers to go. ⊠ *185 Main St.* ☎ *603/883–8781* ▤ *AE, DC, MC, V.*

Manchester

34 *18 mi north of Nashua, 53 mi north of Boston.*

Manchester, with just over 108,000 residents, is New Hampshire's
largest city. The town grew up around the Amoskeag Falls on the Mer-
rimack River, which fueled small textile mills through the 1700s. By 1828,
Boston investors had bought the rights to the Merrimack's water power
and built, on its eastern bank, the Amoskeag Mills, which became a tes-
tament to New England's manufacturing capabilities. In 1906 the mills
employed 17,000 people and churned out more than 4 million yards of
cloth per week. This vast enterprise served as Manchester's entire eco-
nomic base; when it closed in 1936, the town was devastated.

Today Manchester is mainly a banking and business center. As part of
an economic recovery plan, the old mill buildings have been converted
into warehouses, classrooms, restaurants, museums, and office space. The
city has the state's major airport, as well as the Verizon Wireless Arena,
which hosts minor-league hockey matches, concerts, and conventions.

The **Amoskeag Mills** houses both restaurants and museums. The **SEE Sci-
ence Center** is a hands-on science lab and children's museum with more
than 70 exhibits. The **Millyard Museum** contains state-of-the-art exhibits
depicting the region's history, from when Native Americans lived along-

side and fished the Merrimack River to the heyday of Amoskeag Mills. The interactive Discovery Gallery is geared toward kids; there's also a lecture–concert hall and a large museum shop. ⊠ *Mill No. 3, 200 Bedford St. (entrance at 255 Commercial St.)* ☎ *603/625–2821, 603/669–0400 Science Center, 603/625–2821 Millyard Museum* ⊕ *www.seesciencecenter.org, www.manchesterhistoric.org/mill.htm* ☞ *Science Center $5, Millyard Museum $6* ☉ *Science Center weekdays 10–3, weekends noon–5; Millyard Museum Tues.–Sat. 10–4.*

At the neoclassical redbrick (1931) headquarters of the **Manchester Historic Association** you'll find a few exhibits on the city's history and information on the Amoskeag Mills. ⊠ *200 Bedford St.* ☎ *603/622–7531* ⊕ *www.manchesterhistoric.org* ☞ *Free* ☉ *Tues.–Sat. 10–4.*

★ The **Currier Museum of Art,** in a 1929 Italianate building, has a permanent collection of European and American paintings, sculpture, and decorative arts from the 13th to the 20th century, including works by Monet, Picasso, Hopper, Wyeth, and O'Keeffe. Also part of the museum is the Frank Lloyd Wright–designed Zimmerman House, built in 1950. Wright called this sparse, utterly functional living space "Usonian." It's New England's only Wright-designed residence open to the public. ⊠ *201 Myrtle Way* ☎ *603/669–6144, 603/626–4158 Zimmerman House tours* ⊕ *www.currier.org* ☞ *$7, free Sat. 10–1; Zimmerman House $11 (reservations essential)* ☉ *Sun., Mon., Wed., and Fri. 11–5; Thurs. 11–8; Sat. 10–5; call for Zimmerman House tour hrs.*

☺ From May to mid-June, salmon, shad, and river herring "climb" the fish ladder at **Amoskeag Fishways** near the Amoskeag Dam. The visitor center has an underwater viewing window, year-round interactive exhibits and programs about the Merrimack River, and a hydroelectric-station viewing area. ⊠ *6 Fletcher St.* ☎ *603/626–3474* ⊕ *www.amoskeagfishways.org* ☉ *Mon.–Sat. 9–5.*

Where to Stay & Eat

$$–$$$$ ✕ **Baldwin's on Elm.** Chef Nathan Baldwin has earned raves for his creative renderings of regional American fare, creating a mix of small and large plates, ideal if you want to nosh on a few different dishes at one seating. Among small plates, the Asian duck consommé with Napa cabbage–and–duck dumplings earns kudos, as does seared foie gras with huckleberry jam and a balsamic reduction. As an entrée, try grilled bluefish with haricots verts, salsify, lemon oil, and a smoked paprika reduction. Desserts here are incredible—finish off with warm chocolate-spiced soufflé cake with honey-chantilly cream. ⊠ *1105 Elm St.* ☎ *603/622–5975* ⊟ *AE, D, DC, MC, V* ☉ *No lunch.*

FodorsChoice ★

$$–$$$$ ✕ **Richard's Bistro.** Whether you want to celebrate a special occasion or just crave first-rate regional American cuisine, head to this romantic downtown bistro. The kitchen uses traditional New England ingredients in worldly preparations: try the char-broiled filet mignon with Gorgonzola, baked-stuffed potato, and strawberries or the broiled haddock topped with shrimp and scallops on an herb-risotto cake with a honey-peach sauce. ⊠ *36 Lowell St.* ☎ *603/644–1180* ⊟ *AE, D, MC, V* ☉ *No lunch Sun.*

★ **$$–$$$** ✕ **Cotton.** Mod lighting and furnishings and an arbored patio set a swanky tone at this restaurant inside one of the old Amoskeag Mills buildings. The kitchen churns out updated comfort food. Start with pan-seared crab cakes or the lemongrass-chicken salad. Stellar entrée picks include possibly the best steaks in the state, including a huge 20-ounce porterhouse, as well as superb grilled pork "mignon" with sweet-potato hash and a spicy honey-chipotle aioli. The same owners run the excellent and similarly hip seafood restaurant, Starfish Grill, at 33 South Commercial Street. ✉ *75 Arms Park Dr.* ☎ *603/622–5488* ▭ *AE, D, DC, MC, V* ☾ *No lunch weekends.*

$–$$ ✕ **Fratello's.** Despite a seemingly endless supply of seating, the wait for a table at this restaurant can be long on weekends. The huge bi-level space inside a redbrick building at the north end of Amoskeag Mills has high timber ceilings and exposed ducts. The kitchen prepares Italian food from a lengthy menu. Try any of several mix-and-match pastas and sauces, one of the wood-fired pizzas, or one of the many seafood dishes, such as lobster fra diavolo. ✉ *155 Dow St.* ☎ *603/624–2022* ▭ *AE, D, MC, V* ☾ *No lunch Sat.*

¢–$ ✕ **Red Arrow Diner.** A mix of hipsters and oldsters, including comedian
Fodor'sChoice and Manchester native Adam Sandler, favor this neon-streaked, 24-hour
★ greasy spoon, which has been going strong since 1922. Filling fare—platters of kielbasa, French toast, liver and onions, chicken Parmesan with spaghetti, and the diner's famous panfries—keeps patrons happy. ✉ *61 Lowell St.* ☎ *603/626–1118* ▭ *D, MC, V.*

★ **$$$$** ✕▣ **Bedford Village Inn.** The hayloft and milking rooms of this 1810 Federal farmstead, just a few miles southwest of Manchester, now contain lavish suites with king-size four-poster beds, plus such modern perks as two phones and high-speed wireless. The restaurant ($$–$$$$)—a warren of elegant dining rooms with fireplaces and wide-pine floors—presents contemporary fare that might include a starter of baked stuffed black mission figs with Gorgonzola, prosciutto, walnuts, and arugula, followed by pan-roasted sea bass with braised fennel and carrots, saffron-whipped potatoes, and rock-shrimp vinaigrette. There's also a casual tavern ($–$$$), where you might sample an herb-grilled steak Cobb salad or tortellini filled with whipped mascarpone cheese and pumpkin. ✉ *2 Olde Bedford Way, Bedford 03110* ☎ *603/472–2001 or 800/852–1166* 🖷 *603/472–2379* ⊕ *www.bedfordvillageinn.com* ⇥ *14 suites, 2 apartments* ⚴ *Restaurant, in-room hot tubs, cable TV, bar, meeting room; no kids under 12, no smoking* ▭ *AE, D, DC, MC, V.*

$$–$$$ ▣ **Radisson Manchester.** Of Manchester's many chain properties, the 12-story Radisson has the most central location—just steps from the Amoskeag Mills and the great dining along Elm Street. Rooms are simple and clean, perfect for business travelers, with high-speed wireless in many units. ✉ *700 Elm St., 03101* ☎ *603/625–1000 or 800/333–3333* 🖷 *603/625–4595* ⊕ *www.radisson.com/manchesternh* ⇥ *244 rooms, 6 suites* ⚴ *2 restaurants, cable TV, in-room data ports, indoor pool, gym, hot tub, sauna, bar, business services, meeting rooms, parking (fee)* ▭ *AE, D, DC, MC, V.*

Nightlife & the Arts

Revelers come from all over to drink and mingle at the **Yard** (✉ 1211 S. Mammoth Rd. ☎ 603/623–3545), which is also a steak house and seafood restaurant.

The **Palace Theatre** presents musicals and plays throughout the year. It also hosts the state's philharmonic and symphony orchestras and the Opera League of New Hampshire. ✉ *80 Hanover St.* ☎ *603/668–5588 theater, 603/647–6476 philharmonic, 603/669–3559 symphony, 603/647–6564 opera* ⊕ *www.palacetheatre.org.*

Concord

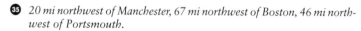 *20 mi northwest of Manchester, 67 mi northwest of Boston, 46 mi northwest of Portsmouth.*

New Hampshire's capital (population 42,000) is a quiet town that tends to the state's business but little else—the sidewalks roll up promptly at 6. The **Concord on Foot** walking trail winds through the historic district. Maps are available from the **Chamber of Commerce** (✉ 40 Commercial St. ☎ 603/224–2508 ⊕ www.concordnhchamber.com) or stores along the trail.

The **Pierce Manse** is the Greek-revival home in which Franklin Pierce lived before moving to Washington to become the 14th U.S. president. ✉ *14 Horseshoe Pond La.* ☎ *603/225–4555* ▱ *$5* ☉ *Mid-June–early Oct., Tues.–Sat. 11–3.*

At the neoclassical, gilt-domed **State House,** the legislature still meets in its original chambers. The building, which dates from 1819, is the oldest in the United States in continuous use as a state capitol. ✉ *107 N. Main St.* ☎ *603/271–2154* ⊕ *www.ci.concord.nh.us/tourdest/statehs* ▱ *Free* ☉ *Weekdays 8–4:30; guided tours by reservation.*

Among the artifacts at the **Museum of New Hampshire History** is an original Concord Coach. During the 19th century, when more than 3,000 such conveyances were built in Concord, this was about as technologically perfect a vehicle as you could find—many say it's the coach that won the West. Other exhibits provide an overview of state history, from the Abenaki to the settlers of Portsmouth up to current residents. ✉ *6 Eagle Sq.* ☎ *603/228–6688* ⊕ *www.nhhistory.org/museum.html* ▱ *$5.50* ☉ *Tues.–Sat. 9:30–5, Sun. noon–5 (also Mon. 9:30–5 in summer and Dec.).*

The **Christa McAuliffe Planetarium** presents shows on the solar system, constellations, and space exploration that incorporate computer graphics, sound, and special effects in a 40-foot dome theater. Children love seeing the tornado tubes, magnetic marbles, and other hands-on exhibits. Outside, explore the scale-model planet walk and the human sundial. The planetarium was named for the Concord teacher—and first civilian in space—who was killed in the Space Shuttle *Challenger* explosion in 1986. ✉ *New Hampshire Technical Institute campus, 2 Institute Dr.* ☎ *603/271–7831* ⊕ *www.starhop.com* ▱ *Exhibit area free, shows $8* ☉ *Tues.–Thurs. 9–5, Fri. 9–7, weekends 10–5; call for show times and reservations.*

Where to Stay & Eat

$–$$ ✕ **Barley House.** A lively, old-fashioned tavern practically across from the capitol building and usually buzzing with a mix of politicos, business folks, and tourists, the Barley House serves dependable American chow: chorizo-sausage pizzas, burgers smothered with peppercorn-whisky sauce and blue cheese, chicken potpies, Cuban sandwiches, beer-braised bratwurst, jambalaya, and Mediterranean chicken salad—it's an impressively comprehensive menu. The convivial bar turns out dozens of interesting beers, on tap and by the bottle, and there's also a decent wine list. ✉ *132 N. Main St.* ☎ *603/228–6363* ▭ *AE, D, DC, MC, V* ⊙ *Closed Sun.*

$–$$ ✕ **Siam Orchid.** This dark, attractive Thai restaurant with a colorful rickshaw gracing its dining room serves spicy and reasonably authentic Thai food. Try the fiery broiled swordfish with shrimp curry sauce or the pine-nut chicken in an aromatic ginger sauce. There's a second location in Manchester. ✉ *158 N. Main St.* ☎ *603/228–3633* ▭ *AE, D, DC, MC, V* ⊙ *No lunch weekends.*

★ ¢–$$ ✕ **Foodee's Pizzas.** A local chain with additional parlors in Keene, Dover, Tilton, Milford, and Wolfeboro, Foodee's serves creative pizzas with especially delicious crusts (sourdough, six-grain, deep-dish). The capital branch is in the heart of downtown and serves such pies as the Polish (with kielbasa, sauerkraut, and three cheeses) and the El Greco (with sweet onions, sliced tomatoes, olive oil, and feta). You can also order pastas, salads, and calzones. The all-you-can-eat buffet, Tuesday through Friday for lunch and dinner, is a great bargain. ✉ *2 S. Main St.* ☎ *603/225–3834* ▭ *MC, V.*

$$–$$$ ✕🏨 **Centennial Inn.** Built in 1892 for widows of Civil War veterans, this imposing brick-and-stone building is set back from busy Pleasant Street. Much of the original woodwork has been preserved. Each room is decorated with antiques and reproduction pieces, and all have ceiling fans. The kitchen at the somewhat stodgy Franklin Pierce Dining Room ($$–$$$$; closed Sunday) turns out genuinely appealing continental fare, such as beef tenderloin with béarnaise sauce, chive flan, and garlic-mashed potatoes. ✉ *96 Pleasant St., 03301* ☎ *603/225–7102 or 800/360–4839* 📠 *603/225–5031* 🌐 *www.someplacesdifferent.com/centennialinn.htm* ⇆ *27 rooms, 5 suites* ♁ *Restaurant, some in-room hot tubs, cable TV, in-room VCRs, bar, meeting rooms, no-smoking rooms* ▭ *AE, D, DC, MC, V.*

Nightlife & the Arts

The **Capitol Center for the Arts** (✉ 44 S. Main St. ☎ 603/225–1111 🌐 www.ccanh.com) has been restored to reflect its Roaring '20s origins. It hosts touring Broadway shows, dance companies, and musical acts. The lounge at **Hermanos Cocina Mexicana** (✉ 11 Hills Ave. ☎ 603/224–5669) stages live jazz Sunday through Thursday nights.

Sports & the Outdoors

Hannah's Paddles (✉ 15 Hannah Dustin Dr. ☎ 603/753–6695) rents canoes for use on the Merrimack River, which runs through Concord.

Shopping

Capitol Craftsman Jewelers (✉ 16 N. Main St. ☎ 603/224–6166) sells fine jewelry and handicrafts. The **Den of Antiquity** (✉ 74 N. Main St.

☎ 603/225–4505) carries handcrafted country gifts and accessories. The **League of New Hampshire Craftsmen** (✉ 36 N. Main St. ☎ 603/228–8171) exhibits crafts in many media. **Mark Knipe Goldsmiths** (✉ 2 Capitol Plaza, Main St. ☎ 603/224–2920) sets antique stones in rings, earrings, and pendants.

Henniker

36 *16 mi southwest of Concord.*

Governor Wentworth, New Hampshire's first Royal Governor, named this town in honor of his friend John Henniker, a London merchant and member of the British Parliament (residents delight in their town's status as "the only Henniker in the world"). Once a mill town producing bicycle rims and other light-industrial items, Henniker reinvented itself after the factories were damaged, first by spring floods in 1936 and then by the hurricane and flood of 1938. New England College was established in the following decade. One of the area's covered bridges is on its campus.

Where to Stay & Eat

★ **$$-$$$$** ✕⊡ **Colby Hill Inn.** There's no shortage of relaxing activities at this farmhouse: you can curl up with a book by the parlor fireplace, stroll through the gardens and meadows, or play badminton out back. Rooms in the main house contain antiques, Colonial reproductions, and lace curtains. In carriage-house rooms, plain country furnishings, stenciled walls, and exposed beams are the norm. Many rooms have fireplaces, and some have combo TV/VCR/CD players. The frequently changing menu ($$$-$$$$; no lunch) is excellent—fine choices include macadamia-crusted seared sea scallops, and plank-roasted loin of venison with a spiced-rhubarb barbecue sauce and barley-risotto sauce. ✉ *3 The Oaks ☐ Box 779, 03242* ☎ *603/428–3281 or 800/531–0330* ☐ *603/428–9218* ⊕ *www.colbyhillinn.com* ◁ *14 rooms, 2 suites* ♨ *Restaurant, some in-room hot tubs, cable TV, some in-room VCRs, pool, badminton, recreation room; no TV in some rooms, no smoking* ⊟ *AE, D, DC, MC, V* ⌖⊙⌗ *BP.*

Nightlife

There's often live folk music at **Daniel's** (✉ 30 Main St. ☎ 603/428–7621), which occupies a rambling wood-frame building with great views of the Contoocook River. It's a good restaurant, too, serving casual American food.

Shopping

The **Fiber Studio** (✉ 9 Foster Hill Rd. ☎ 603/428–7830) sells beads, handspun natural-fiber yarns, spinning equipment, and looms.

SKI AREA **Pats Peak.** A quick trip up Interstate 93 from the Massachusetts border, Pats Peak is geared to families. Base facilities are rustic, and friendly personal attention is the rule. Despite Pats Peak's short 710-vertical-foot rise, the 21 trails and slopes have something for everyone, and the resort has some of the best snowmaking capacity in the state. New skiers and snowboarders can take advantage of a wide slope and several short trails; intermediates have wider trails from the top; and experts have a couple of real thrillers. Night skiing and snowboarding take place in January and February. ⊠ *Flanders Rd., Rte. 114, 03242* ☎ *603/428–3245, 888/728–7732 snow conditions* ⊕ *www.patspeak.com.*

Hillsborough

🟤 *8 mi southwest of Henniker.*

Hillsborough comprises four villages, the most prominent of which lies along the Contoocook River and grew up around a thriving woolen and hosiery industry in the mid-1800s. This section, which is really considered Hillsborough proper, is what you'll see as you roll through town on Route 9 (U.S. 202).

Turn north from downtown up School Street, and continue 3 mi past Fox State Forest to reach one of the state's best-preserved historic districts, Hillsborough Center, where 18th-century houses surround a green. Continue north 6 mi through the similarly quaint village of East Washington, and another 6 mi to reach the Colonial town center of Washington. One of the highest villages in New Hampshire, this picturesque arrangement of white clapboard buildings made the cover of *National Geographic* several years back. You can loop back to Hillsborough proper via Route 31 south.

The nation's 14th president, Franklin Pierce, was born in Hillsborough and lived here until he married. He is, alas, one of the least-appreciated presidents ever to serve. The **Franklin Pierce Homestead,** operated by the Hillsborough Historical Society, welcomes visitors for guided tours. The house is much as it was during Pierce's life. ⊠ *Rte. 31 just north of Rte. 9* ☎ *603/478–3165* ⊕ *www.franklinpierce.ws/homestead* ☒ *$3* ☉ *June and Sept., Sat. 10–4, Sun. 1–4; July and Aug., Mon.–Sat. 10–4, Sun. 1–4.*

NEED A BREAK?

Families have been coming to **Diamond Acres Dairy Bar** (⊠ Rte. 9, ¼ mi west of Rte. 31 ☎ 603/478–3121), a short-order shanty attached to a gas station, for years to devour superfresh clam platters, lobster rolls, and frozen sweets.

Sports & the Outdoors

Fox State Forest (⊠ Center Rd. ☎ 603/464–3453) has 25 mi of hiking trails and an observation tower.

Shopping

At **Gibson Pewter** (⊠ 18 E. Washington Rd. ☎ 603/464–3410), Raymond Gibson and his son Jonathan create and sell museum-quality pewter pieces. Next door to the Franklin Pierce Homestead, **Richard Withington Antiques** (⊠ Rtes. 31 and 9 ☎ 603/464–3232) hosts some of the best antiques auctions in New England and stocks an impressive selection of fine pieces for general sale.

Charlestown

🟤 *40 mi northwest of Hillsborough, 20 mi south of Cornish.*

Charlestown has the state's largest historic district. About 60 homes, handsome examples of Federal, Greek-revival, and Gothic-revival architecture, are clustered about the town center; 10 of them were built before 1800. Several merchants on the main street distribute brochures that describe an interesting walking tour of the district.

In 1747, the **Fort at No. 4** was an outpost on the periphery of Colonial civilization. That year fewer than 50 militiamen at the fort withstood an attack by 400 French soldiers, ensuring that northern New England remained under British rule. Today, costumed interpreters at this living-history museum cook dinner over an open hearth and demonstrate weaving, gardening, and candle making. Each year the museum holds reenactments of militia musters and battles of the French and Indian War. ⊠ *Rte. 11, ½ mi north of Charlestown* ☎ *603/826–5700 or 888/367–8284* ⊕ *www.fortat4.com* ☜ *$8* ☉ *Early June–Oct., Wed.–Sun. 10–4:30.*

On a bright, breezy day you might want to detour to the **Morningside Flight Park** (⊠ Off Rte. 12/11 ☎ 603/542–4416 ⊕ www.flymorningside. com), not necessarily to take hang-gliding lessons, although you could. You can watch the bright colors of the gliders as they take off from the school's 450-foot peak.

Where to Stay

$–$$ ⬚ **Dutch Treat.** Formerly the MapleHedge, this was renamed in 2004 after an extensive renovation. The innkeepers live in the oldest section of this home, which dates from about 1755. Guest rooms, in the 1820 Federal-style part, are furnished with carefully chosen antiques. The Delfts Blue Room contains several pieces of the famed Dutch Delftware pottery, and in the Tulip Suite hangs a colorful history of the Netherlands' tulip-trade history. A bountiful breakfast is served in the formal dining room. ⊠ *355 Main St.* ⬚ *Box 1000, 03603* ☎ *603/826–5565 or 877/344–0944* ⊕ *www.thedutchtreat.com* ➾ *4 rooms, 1 suite* ⬚ *Hot tub, no-smoking rooms; no room TVs, no kids under 12* ⊟ *MC, V* ⦿ *BP.*

Walpole

39 *13 mi south of Charlestown.*

Walpole possesses one of the state's most perfect town greens. This one, bordered by Elm and Washington streets, is surrounded by homes built about 1790, when the townsfolk constructed a canal around the Great Falls of the Connecticut River and brought commerce and wealth to the area. The town now has 3,200 inhabitants, more than a dozen of whom are millionaires.

OFF THE BEATEN PATH

SUGARHOUSES – Maple-sugar season occurs about the first week in March when days become warmer but nights are still frigid. A drive along maple-lined back roads reveals thousands of taps and buckets catching the labored flow of unrefined sap. Plumes of smoke rise from nearby sugarhouses, where sugaring off, the process of boiling down this precious liquid, takes place. Many sugarhouses are open to the public; after a tour and demonstration, you can sample the syrup. **Bascom Maple Farm** (⊠ 56 Sugarhouse Rd., Alstead ☎ 603/835–6361) serves maple pecan pie and maple milk shakes. **Stuart & John's Sugar House & Pancake Restaurant** (⊠ Rtes. 12 and 63, Westmoreland ☎ 603/399–4486) conducts a tour and serves a pancake breakfast.

Where to Eat

$$–$$$$ ✕ **Restaurant at Burdick Chocolate.** Famous candy maker Larry Burdick,
Fodor'sChoice who sells his artful hand-filled and hand-cut chocolates to top restau-
★ rants around the Northeast, also operates this outstanding—and rea-
sonably priced—eatery adjacent to the candy shop. The
Mediterranean-inspired menu utilizes fresh, often local ingredients and
changes daily. Of course, dessert is a big treat here, featuring Burdick's
tempting chocolates and pastries. For dinner, you might start with a se-
lection of artisanal cheeses or the confit of duck with grilled plums and
a red wine reduction, followed by striped bass with eggplant, tomatoes,
and capers, or roasted chicken with garlic-mashed potato cake and
fresh tarragon. ✉ *47 Main St.* ☎ *603/756–2882* ▭ *AE, D, MC, V* ✆ *No
dinner Sun. and Mon.*

Shopping

Boggy Meadow Farm (✉ 13 Boggy Meadow La. ☎ 603/756–3300 or 877/
541–3953) sells the farm's Fanny Mason Farmstead Swiss cheese in its
store. A window overlooks the cheese-making area.

Keene

40 *17 mi southeast of Walpole; 20 mi northeast of Brattleboro, Vermont;
56 mi southwest of Manchester.*

Keene is the largest city in the state's southwest corner. Its rapidly gen-
trifying main street, with several engaging boutiques and cafés, is Amer-
ica's widest (8 rods, or 132 feet). Each year, on the Saturday before
Halloween, locals use the street to hold a Pumpkin Festival, where they
seek to retain their place in the record books for the most carved, lighted
jack-o'-lanterns—more than 25,000 some years.

Keene State College, hub of the local arts community, is on the tree-lined
main street. The **Thorne-Sagendorph Art Gallery** (☎ 603/358–2720
⊕ www.keene.edu/tsag) houses George Ridci's *Landscape* and pres-
ents traveling exhibitions. The **Putnam Theater** (☎ 603/358–2160)
shows foreign and art films.

**OFF THE
BEATEN
PATH**

CHESTERFIELD'S ROUTE 63 – If you're in the mood for a country drive or
bike ride, head west from Keene along Route 9 to Route 63 (about 11
mi), and turn left toward the hilltop town of Chesterfield. This is an es-
pecially rewarding journey at sunset, as from many points along the road
you can see west out over the Connecticut River valley and into Ver-
mont. The village center consists of little more than a handful of digni-
fied granite buildings and a small general store. You can loop back to
Keene via Route 119 east in Hinsdale and then Route 10 north—the
entire journey is about 40 mi.

Where to Stay & Eat

$$–$$$ ✕ **Luca's.** A snazzy storefront bistro overlooking Keene's graceful town
Fodor'sChoice square, Luca's dazzles with knowledgeable and helpful staff and some
★ of the most deftly prepared cooking in this part of the state. Pastas and
grills reveal Italian, French, Greek, Spanish, and North African influ-
ences—consider salmon tagine in a sun-dried-tomato-and-whole-grain

mustard cream sauce, or shrimp and scallops El Greco with plum tomatoes, feta, and baby spinach over linguine. Dine in the intimate art-filled dining room or at one of the sidewalk tables. ✉ *10 Central Sq.* ☎ *603/ 358–3335* ▭ *AE, MC, V* ✍ *No lunch weekends.*

$–$$$ ✕ **176 Main.** This grand mansard-roof house near the campus of Keene State College in the heart of downtown has a menu that runs the gamut from bourbon-glazed steak tips to maple-crusted salmon; sandwiches and burgers are also served throughout the day. The bar stocks an extensive selection of draft beers. Weekend brunch is a big event. ✉ *176 Main St.* ☎ *603/357–3100* ▭ *AE, D, MC, V.*

$$$$ ✕▦ **E. F. Lane Hotel.** Lending a rare touch of urbanity to the sleepy Monadnocks, this upscale redbrick hotel is inside a retrofitted department store on Keene's gentrified Main Street. It's within earshot of local church bells and is a 10-minute walk from Colony Marketplace. Rooms are furnished individually with reproduction Victorian antiques but have plenty of modern gadgets, such as high-speed Internet and individual climate control. The sky-lighted Salmon Chase Bistro ($$–$$$) serves excellent contemporary American fare and presents a terrific wine list. ✉ *30 Main St., 03431* ☎ *603/357–7070 or 888/300–5056* 🖷 *603/357–7075* ⊕ *www.someplacesdifferent.com/eflane.htm* ⇲ *33 rooms, 7 suites* ⅆ *Restaurant, some in-room hot tubs, cable TV, in-room data ports, bar, meeting rooms* ▭ *AE, D, MC, V* ⅋ *CP.*

★ $$–$$$ ✕▦ **Chesterfield Inn.** Surrounded by gardens, the Chesterfield sits above Route 9, the main road between Keene and Brattleboro, Vermont. Fine antiques and Colonial-style fabrics adorn the spacious guest quarters; 10 have fireplaces, and several have private decks or terraces that face the stunning perennial gardens and verdant Vermont hills. In the restaurant ($$–$$$$) rosemary- and walnut-crusted rack of lamb and grilled blue corn and smoked-cheddar polenta with black bean ratatouille are among the highlights. ✉ *Rte. 9* ⅆ *Box 155, Chesterfield 03443* ☎ *603/ 256–3211 or 800/365–5515* 🖷 *603/256–6131* ⊕ *www.chesterfieldinn. com* ⇲ *13 rooms, 2 suites* ⅆ *Restaurant, some in-room hot tubs, cable TV, some pets allowed* ▭ *AE, D, MC, V* ⅋ *BP.*

$$$ ▦ **Inn at East Hill Farm.** If you have kids, you'll be happy at this 1830 farmhouse resort, where children are not only allowed but seem to be expected. They can milk the cows; feed the animals; and try arts and crafts, storytelling, and hiking. The innkeepers arrange weekly sleigh (or hay) and pony rides. Twice weekly in July and August, trips are scheduled to a nearby lake for boating, waterskiing, and fishing. Rates include most activities and three meals in a camplike dining hall. The inn is 10 mi southeast of Keene. ✉ *460 Monadnock St., Troy 03465* ☎ *603/ 242–6495 or 800/242–6495* 🖷 *603/242–7709* ⊕ *www.east-hill-farm. com* ⇲ *65 rooms* ⅆ *Restaurant, cable TV, tennis court, 3 pools (1 indoor), wading pool, massage, sauna, hiking, horseback riding, sleigh rides, recreation room, babysitting, Internet room, some pets allowed (fee); no room phones, no TV in some rooms, no smoking* ▭ *D, MC, V* ⅋ *FAP.*

$ ▦ **Carriage Barn.** Antiques and wide pine floors give this inn across from Keene State College charm. An expansive buffet is served each morning in the breakfast room, but many guests savor a second cup of coffee in the summerhouse. ✉ *358 Main St., 03431* ☎ *603/357–3812*

⊕ *www.carriagebarn.com* ⟿ *4 rooms* ᗱ *No room phones, no room TVs, no smoking* ⊟ *AE, D, MC, V* ⫶⊙⫶ *CP.*

¢ ⚏ **Swanzey Lake Camping Area.** This 108-site campground on crystal-clear Swanzey Lake has a sandy beach, a dock, a ball field, a recreation area, and boat rentals. ⊠ *88 E. Shore Rd., West Swanzey 03469* ☎ *603/ 352–9880* ⊕ *www.swanzeylake.com* ⊴ *$20–$26* ⟿ *95 sites, 3 cabins* ᗱ *Full hookups, general store, swimming (pond)* ⊟ *AE, D, MC, V* ⊗ *Closed Nov.–Apr.*

Nightlife & the Arts

The **Colonial Theatre** (⊠ 95 Main St. ☎ 603/357–1233) opened in 1924 as a vaudeville stage. It now hosts folk and jazz concerts and has the town's largest movie screen. **Elm City Brewing Co.** (⊠ 222 West St. ☎ 603/355–3335), at the Colony Mill, serves light food and draws a mix of college students and young professionals. At Keene State College, the **Redfern Arts Center at Brickyard Pond** (⊠ 229 Main St. ☎ 603/ 358–2168) has year-round music, theater, and dance performances.

Shopping

Colony Mill Marketplace (⊠ 222 West St. ☎ 603/357–1240), an old mill building, holds 30-plus stores and boutiques such as the Toadstool Bookshop, which carries many children's and regional travel and history books, and Ye Goodie Shoppe, whose specialty is handmade confections. Also popular is Antiques at Colony Mill, which sells the wares of more than 200 dealers. There's a food court, too.

Country Artisans (⊠ 53 Main St. ☎ 603/352–6980) showcases the stoneware, textiles, prints, and glassware of regional artists.

Hannah Grimes Marketplace (⊠ 42 Main St. ☎ 603/352–686) overflows with mostly New Hampshire–made pottery, toys, kitchenware, soaps, greeting cards, and specialty foods.

The extraordinary collection of used books at the **Homestead Bookshop** (⊠ Rtes. 101 and 124, Marlborough ☎ 603/876–4213) includes biographies, cookbooks, and town histories.

Just touring the six furniture- and collectibles-filled rooms is part of the fun at **Stone House Antiques** (⊠ Rte. 9, Chesterfield ☎ 603/363–4866), a stately, restored stagecoach tavern.

Jaffrey Center

④① *16 mi southeast of Keene.*

Novelist Willa Cather came to Jaffrey Center in 1919 and stayed in the Shattuck Inn, which now stands empty on Old Meeting House Road. Not far from here, she pitched the tent in which she wrote several chapters of *My Ántonia*. She returned nearly every summer thereafter until her death and was buried in the Old Burying Ground. **Amos Fortune Forum**, near the Old Burying Ground, brings nationally known speakers to the 1773 meetinghouse on summer evenings.

The oft-quoted statistic about Mt. Monadnock in **Monadnock State Park** is that it's America's most-climbed mountain—second in the world to

Japan's Mt. Fuji. Whether this is true or not, locals agree that it's never lonely at the top. Some days more than 400 people crowd its bald peak. Monadnock rises to 3,165 feet, and on a clear day the hazy Boston skyline is visible from its summit. The park maintains picnic grounds and a small campground (RVs welcome, but no hookups) with 28 sites. Five trailheads branch into more than two dozen trails of varying difficulty that wend their way to the top. Allow between three and four hours for any round-trip hike. A visitor center has free trail maps as well as exhibits documenting the mountain's history. In winter, you can cross-country ski along roughly 12 mi of groomed trails on the lower elevations of the mountain. ⊠ *Off Rte. 124, 2½ mi north of Jaffrey Center, 03452* ☎ *603/532–8862* ⊠ *$3* ☉ *Daily dawn–dusk* ☞ *No pets.*

Cathedral of the Pines is an outdoor memorial to American soldiers and civilians who have sacrificed their lives in service to their country. There's an inspiring view of Mt. Monadnock and Mt. Kearsarge from the Altar of the Nation, which is composed of rock from every U.S. state and territory. All faiths are welcome to hold services here; organ music for meditation is played at midday from Tuesday through Thursday in July and August. The Memorial Bell Tower, with a carillon of bells from around the world, is built of native stone. Norman Rockwell designed the bronze tablets over the four arches. Flower gardens, an indoor chapel, and a museum of military memorabilia share the hilltop. It's 8 mi southeast of Jaffrey Center. ⊠ *10 Hale Hill Rd., off Rte. 119, Rindge* ☎ *603/899–3300 or 866/229–4520* ⊕ *www.cathedralpines.com* ⊠ *Donation suggested* ☉ *May–Oct., daily 9–5.*

More than 16 acres of wild rhododendrons bloom in mid-July at Fitzwilliam's **Rhododendron State Park,** which has the largest concentration of *Rhododendron maximum* north of the Allegheny Mountains. Bring a picnic lunch and sit in a nearby pine grove, or follow the marked footpaths through the flowers. On your way here, be sure to pass through Fitzwilliam's well-preserved historic district of Colonial and Federal-style houses, which have appeared on thousands of postcards. ⊠ *Rte. 119 W, off Rte. 12, 10 mi southwest of Jaffrey Center, Fitzwilliam* ☎ *603/239–8153* ⊠ *$3 weekends and holidays, free at other times* ☉ *Daily 8–sunset.*

Where to Stay & Eat

¢–$$ ✕ **Lilly's on the Pond.** An appealing choice either for lunch or dinner, this rustic-timbered dining room overlooks a small mill pond in Rindge, about 8 mi south of Jaffrey Center. The extensive menu of mostly American fare includes chicken sautéed with lime and tequila, shrimp scampi, and burgers. ⊠ *U.S. 202, Rindge* ☎ *603/899–3322* ⊟ *D, MC, V* ☉ *Closed Mon.*

$–$$ ✕⚏ **Inn at Jaffrey Center.** Rooms here are painted in lively lavenders, yellows, or peaches. Although full of period furnishings, they have a hip sensibility as well as high-thread-count bedding, fluffy towels, and fine toiletries. The restaurant ($$–$$$; no lunch Saturday) serves a mix of American, Asian, and Italian dishes; good bets include lobster-and-crab strudel and braised lamb shanks with rosemary and garlic. Sunday brunch is impressive, featuring enticing eggs Atlantis (English muffins topped with smoked salmon, sliced tomato, capers, poached eggs, and hollandaise sauce). ⊠ *379 Main St.* ⬦ *Box 484, 03452* ☏ *603/532–7800 or 877/510–7019* 🖷 *603/532–7900* ⊕ *www.theinnatjaffreycenter. com* ↝ *9 rooms, 2 suites* ♿ *Restaurant, cable TV, bar, no-smoking rooms; no TV in some rooms* ☰ *MC, V* ⑩ *CP.*

$–$$$$ 🏨 **Woodbound Inn.** A favorite with families and outdoors enthusiasts, this 1819 farmhouse became an inn in 1892. It occupies 200 acres on the shores of Contoocook Lake. Accommodations are functional but clean and cheerful; they range from quirky rooms in the main inn to modern hotel-style rooms in the Edgewood building to cabins by the water. ⊠ *247 Woodbound Rd., Rindge 03461* ☏ *603/532–8341 or 800/688–7770* ⊕ *www.woodboundinn.com* ↝ *44 rooms, 39 with bath; 11 cottages* ♿ *Restaurant, some refrigerators, cable TV, 9-hole golf course, tennis court, lake, fishing, croquet, hiking, horseshoes, shuffleboard, volleyball, cross-country skiing, ice-skating, tobogganing, bar, recreation room; no TV in some rooms* ☰ *AE, MC, V* ⑩ *BP, MAP.*

$–$$ 🏨 **Benjamin Prescott Inn.** Thanks to the working dairy farm surrounding this 1853 Colonial house—with its stenciling and wide pine floors—you feel as though you're miles out in the country rather than just minutes from Jaffrey Center. A full breakfast of Welsh miner's cakes and baked French toast with fruit and maple syrup prepares you for a day of antiquing or hiking. ⊠ *Rte. 124, 03452* ☏ *603/532–6637 or 888/950–6637* 🖷 *603/532–6637* ⊕ *www.benjaminprescottinn.com* ↝ *10 rooms, 3 suites* ♿ *No room phones, no room TVs, no kids under 10, no smoking* ☰ *AE, MC, V* ⑩ *BP.*

Shopping

You'll find about 35 dealers at **Bloomin' Antiques** (⊠ Rte. 12, 3 mi south of Rte. 119, Fitzwilliam ☏ 603/585–6688). The wares of some 40 dealers are for sale at **Fitzwilliam Antiques Centre** (⊠ Rtes. 12 and 119, Fitzwilliam ☏ 603/585–9092).

Peterborough

42 *9 mi northeast of Jaffrey Center, 30 mi northwest of Nashua.*

The nation's first free public library opened in Peterborough in 1833. The town, which was the first in the region to be incorporated (1760), is still a commercial and cultural hub.

🦆 A new addition to Peterborough, the **Mariposa Museum** opened in 2003 inside a grand redbrick Baptist church with the aim of celebrating international folklore and folk art. Galleries exhibit textiles, costumes, art, dolls, puppets, crafts, and instruments from around the world. Additionally, the museum hosts a number of workshops and presentations on dance and arts and crafts. Other features include a children's reading nook and a library. ⊠ *26 Main St.* ☏ *603/924–4555* ⊕ *www. mariposamuseum.org* 🖾 *$5* ☉ *July and Aug., daily noon–4; Sept.–May, weekdays 3–5; live music performances year-round, Sun. at 3.*

The **MacDowell Colony** was founded by the composer Edward MacDowell in 1907 as an artists' retreat. Willa Cather wrote part of *Death Comes for the Archbishop* here. Thornton Wilder was in residence when he wrote *Our Town* (Peterborough's resemblance to the play's Grover's Corners is no coincidence). Only a small portion of the still-active colony is open to visitors. ⊠ *100 High St.* ☎ *603/924–3886* ⊕ *www.macdowellcolony.org.*

In **Miller State Park**, 3 mi east of town, an auto road takes you almost 2,300 feet up Pack Monadnock Mountain. The road is closed mid-November through mid-April. ⊠ *Rte. 101* ☎ *603/924–3672* 🎫 *$3.*

Where to Stay & Eat

★ $$–$$$ ✕ **Acqua Bistro.** People like to congregate at the long bar of this smart bistro. You might join them before dining on a thin-crust pizza or an entrée of wild Arctic char with roasted vegetable-dill couscous and basil-walnut pesto. Save room for the bittersweet chocolate soufflé. ⊠ *9 School St.* ☎ *603/924–9905* ▤ *MC, V* ⊘ *Closed Mon. No lunch.*

$$–$$$$ ✕▥ **Hancock Inn.** This Federal-style 1789 inn, the oldest in the state, is the pride of the idyllic town it anchors. Common areas possess the warmth of a tavern, with fireplaces, big wing chairs, couches, dark-wood paneling, and Rufus Porter murals. Rooms, done in Colonial style, have antique four-poster beds. Updated Yankee fare is served by candlelight in the dining room ($–$$$); a specialty is maple roast duckling with sun-dried-cranberry pilaf and an apple-cider reduction, but also consider filet mignon with horseradish-Gorgonzola butter, portobello mushrooms, and garlic-mashed potatoes. ⊠ *33 Main St.* ⌂ *Box 96, Hancock 03449* ☎ *603/525–3318 or 800/525–1789* 📠 *603/525–9301* ⊕ *www. hancockinn.com* 🛏 *15 rooms* ⚘ *Restaurant, cable TV, bar; no smoking* ▤ *AE, D, DC, MC, V* ⦿∣ *BP.*

$–$$ ✕▥ **Inn at Crotched Mountain.** Three of the nine fireplaces in this 1822 inn are in Colonial-style guest rooms. The property, with stunning views of the Monadnocks, was once a stop on the Underground Railroad. In the restaurant ($$), where Singapore native Rose Perry is at the helm, you can sample both American and Asian-inspired fare, such as cranberry-port pot roast and Indonesian charbroiled swordfish with a sauce of ginger, green pepper, onion, and lemon. Weekend rates include breakfast and dinner. ⊠ *534 Mountain Rd., 12 mi northeast of Peterborough, Francestown 03043* ☎ *603/588–6840* 📠 *603/588–6623* 🛏 *13 rooms* ⚘ *Restaurant, 2 tennis courts, pool, cross-country skiing, bar, some pets allowed (fee)* ▤ *No credit cards* ⊘ *Closed Apr. and Nov.* ⦿∣ *BP, MAP.*

$ ✕▥ **Birchwood Inn.** Thoreau slept here, probably on his way to climb Monadnock or to visit Jaffrey or Peterborough. Country furniture and handmade quilts outfit the bedrooms, just as they did in 1775, when the house was new. Allow time to linger in the dining room ($$–$$$; reservations essential; BYOB; closed Sunday and Monday, no lunch). An 1820s Rufus Porter mural covers the dining room wall. She-crab soup, shrimp Parmesan, and pumpkin-applesauce tea bread are among the choices. ⊠ *Rte. 45* ⌂ *Box 23, Temple 03084* ☎ *603/878–3285* 📠 *603/ 878–2159* 🛏 *6 rooms, 4 with bath* ⚘ *Restaurant; no room phones, no room TVs, no kids under 10, no smoking* ▤ *MC, V* ⦿∣ *BP.*

$ ▥ **Apple Gate Bed and Breakfast.** With 90 acres of orchards across the street, this B&B is appropriately named. The four rooms (and the resident yellow labrador) are named for types of apples. Some guest quarters are small, but Laura Ashley prints and stenciling make them cheery.

The house dates from 1832, and the original beams and fireplace still grace the dining room. A music and reading room has a piano and a TV with a VCR tucked in the corner. From June through October, there's a two-night minimum on weekends. ⊠ *199 Upland Farm Rd., 03458* 🏠 *603/924–6543* 🛏 *4 rooms* ♿ *No room phones, no room TVs, no kids under 12, no smoking* ▭ *MC, V* ⑩ *BP.*

★ $ 🏠 **Jack Daniels Motor Inn.** With so many dowdy motels in southwestern New Hampshire, it's a pleasure to find one as bright and clean as the Jack Daniels, just ½ mi north of downtown Peterborough. The rooms are large and furnished with attractive cherrywood reproduction antiques and have high-speed wireless Internet; free local calls; complimentary coffee, tea, and juice; and well-tended bathrooms. ⊠ *U.S. 202, 03458* 🕾 *603/924–7548* 🖨 *603/924–7700* ⊕ *www.jackdanielsmotorinn.com* 🛏 *17 rooms* ♿ *Cable TV, Wi-Fi, no-smoking rooms* ▭ *AE, D, DC, MC, V.*

The Arts

From early July to late August, **Monadnock Music** (⊠ 2A Concord St. 🕾 603/924–7610 or 800/868–9613 ⊕ www.monadnockmusic.org) produces a series of solo recitals, chamber music concerts, and orchestra and opera performances by renowned musicians. Events take place throughout the area on Wednesday through Saturday evenings at 8 and on Sunday at 4; many are free. In winter, the **Peterborough Folk Music Society** (🕾 603/827–2905 ⊕ www.acousticmusic.com/pfms) presents folk music concerts. The **Peterborough Players** (⊠ Stearns Farm off Middle Hancock Rd. 🕾 603/924–7585 ⊕ www.peterboroughplayers.org) have performed since 1933. Productions are staged in a converted barn.

Sports & the Outdoors

GOLF   At the Donald Ross–designed **Crotched Mountain Golf Club** (⊠ Off Rte. 47 near Bennington town line, Francestown 🕾 603/588–2923), you'll find a hilly, rolling 18-hole layout with nice view of the Monadnocks. Greens fee are $30–$38.

SKI AREA   **Crotched Mountain.** New Hampshire's southernmost skiing and snowboarding facility opened in 2004 with 17 trails, half of them intermediate, and the rest divided pretty evenly between beginner and expert. There's an 875-foot vertical drop. The slopes have ample snowmaking capacity, ensuring good skiing all winter long. Other facilities include a 40,000-square-foot lodge with a couple of restaurants, a ski school, and a snow camp for youngsters. ⊠ *615 Francestown Rd. (Rte. 47), Bennington 03247* 🕾 *603/588–3668* ⊕ *www.crotchedmountain.com.*

Shopping

The corporate headquarters and retail outlet of **Eastern Mountain Sports** (⊠ 1 Vose Farm Rd. 🕾 603/924–7231) sells everything from tents to skis to hiking boots, gives hiking and camping classes, and conducts kayaking and canoeing demonstrations. **Harrisville Designs** (⊠ Mill Alley, Harrisville 🕾 603/827–3333) sells hand-spun and hand-dyed yarn as well as looms. The shop also conducts classes in knitting and weaving. **Sharon Arts Fine Crafts Store** (⊠ Depot Sq. 🕾 603/924–2787) has a gallery that exhibits locally made pottery, fabric, and woodwork and other crafts.

NEW HAMPSHIRE A TO Z

To research prices, get advice from other travelers, and book travel arrangements, visit www.fodors.com

AIRPORTS

Manchester Airport, the state's largest airport, has rapidly become a cost-effective, hassle-free alternative to Boston's Logan International Airport. It has nonstop service to more than 20 cities thanks to scheduled flights by Air Canada, American Eagle, Continental, Delta, Independence Air, Northwest, Southwest, United, and US Airways. Lebanon Municipal Airport, near Dartmouth College, is served by US Airways Express from New York.

🚩 Airport Information **Lebanon Municipal Airport** ⊠ 5 Airpark Rd., West Lebanon ☎ 603/298-8878. **Manchester Airport** ⊠ 1 Airport Rd., Manchester ☎ 603/624-6539 ⊕ www.flymanchester.com.

BIKE TRAVEL

Bike the Whites and New England Hiking Holidays organize bike tours.
🚩 Bike Information **Bike the Whites** ☎ 877/854-6535 ⊕ www.bikethewhites.com. **New England Hiking Holidays** ☎ 603/356-9696 or 800/869-0949 ⊕ www.nehikingholidays.com.

BUS TRAVEL

C&J Trailways serves the seacoast area of New Hampshire, with stops in Portsmouth and Dover. Concord Trailways links Boston's South Station and Logan International Airport with points all along Interstate 93 as far north as Littleton and, around Lake Winnipesaukee and the eastern White Mountains, along Route 16. Dartmouth Coach connects Boston's South Station and Logan International Airport with Hanover, Lebanon, and New London. Vermont Transit has service from Boston to Vermont that stops in southern and western New Hampshire.
🚩 Bus Information **C&J Trailways** ☎ 603/430-1100 or 800/258-7111 ⊕ www.cjtrailways.com. **Concord Trailways** ☎ 603/228-3300 or 800/639-3317 ⊕ www.concordtrailways.com. **Dartmouth Coach** ☎ 603/448-2800 or 800/637-0123 ⊕ www.concordtrailways.com. **Vermont Transit** ☎ 800/552-8737 ⊕ www.vermonttransit.com.

CAR TRAVEL

Interstate 93, running north from Massachusetts to Québec and passing through Manchester and Concord, is the principal south–north route through central New Hampshire. To the west, Interstate 91 traces the Vermont–New Hampshire border. To the east, Interstate 95, which is a toll road, passes through southern New Hampshire's coastal area on its way from Massachusetts to Maine. Interstate 89 travels from Concord to Montpelier and Burlington, Vermont.

Speed limits on interstate and limited-access highways are generally 65 mph, except in heavily settled areas, where 55 mph is the norm. On state and U.S. routes, speed limits vary considerably. On any given stretch, the limit may be anywhere from 25 mph to 55 mph, so watch the signs carefully. Right turns are permitted on red lights unless indicated.

Official state maps are available free from the New Hampshire Office of Travel and Tourism Development. They cite useful telephone numbers and information about bike, snowmobile, and scenic routes.

LODGING
Country Inns in the White Mountains handles reservations for a wide variety of B&Bs and inns throughout the region. For long-term rentals try Preferred Vacation Rental, Inc. and Strictly Rentals, Inc.

APARTMENT & VILLA RENTALS — 🗗 Local Agents **Country Inns in the White Mountains** ☎ 603/356-9460 ⊕ www.countryinnsinthewhitemountains.com. **Preferred Vacation Rentals, Inc.** ☎ 603/253-7811 ⊕ www.preferredrentals.com. **Strictly Rentals, Inc.** ☎ 603/253-9800 ⊕ www.strictlyrentals.biz.

CAMPING — The New Hampshire Campground Owners Association publishes a guide to private, state, and national-forest campgrounds. White Mountain National Forest campground reservations has 20 campgrounds with more than 900 campsites spread across the region; only some take reservations. All sites have a 14-day limit.

🗗 **New Hampshire Campground Owners Association** ✍ Box 320, Twin Mountain 03595 ☎ 603/846-5511 or 800/822-6764 ⊕ www.ucampnh.com. **White Mountain National Forest** ✉ U.S. Forest Service, 719 N. Main St., Laconia 03246 ☎ 603/528-8721 or 877/444-6777 ⊕ www.fs.fed.us/r9/forests/white_mountain.

SPORTS & THE OUTDOORS
BIRD-WATCHING — Audubon Society of New Hampshire schedules monthly field trips throughout the state and a fall bird-watching tour to Star Isle and other parts of the Isles of Shoals.

🗗 **Audubon Society of New Hampshire** ✉ 3 Silk Farm Rd., Concord 03301 ☎ 603/224-9909 ⊕ www.nhaudubon.org.

FISHING — Many companies along the coast offer rentals and charters for deep-sea fishing and cruises. Inland, for trout and salmon fishing, try the Connecticut Lakes, though any clear White Mountain stream (there are 650 mi of them in the national forest alone) will do. Many streams are stocked. Conway Lake—the largest of the area's 45 lakes and ponds—is noted for smallmouth bass and, early and late in the season, good salmon fishing. For information about fishing and licenses, call the New Hampshire Fish and Game Department.

🗗 **New Hampshire Fish and Game Department** ☎ 603/271-3211 ⊕ www.wildlife.state.nh.us.

HIKING — Among the 86 major peaks in the White Mountains, hiking possibilities are endless. Innkeepers can usually point you toward the better nearby trails; some inns schedule guided day trips for guests. The White Mountain National Forest office has information on hiking as well as on the parking passes ($5) that are required in the national forest. New England Hiking Holidays conducts hikes in the White Mountains with lodging in country inns for two to eight nights. Hikes, each with two guides, allow for different levels of ability and cover between 5 and 10 mi per day.

🎿 **New England Hiking Holidays** ☎ 603/356-9696 or 800/869-0949 ⊕ www. nehikingholidays.com. **White Mountain National Forest** ✉ U.S. Forest Service, 719 Main St., Laconia 03246 ☎ 603/528-8721 ⊕ www.fs.fed.us/r9/forests/white_mountain.

FOLIAGE HOTLINE A fall-foliage hotline is regularly updated with information on leaf-peeping conditions.

🎿 **Foliage hotline** ☎ 800/258-3608.

SKIING Ski New Hampshire has information on downhill and cross-country snow sports in the state.

🎿 **Ski New Hampshire** ✏ Box 10, North Woodstock 03262 ☎ 603/745-9396 or 800/887-5464 ⊕ www.skinh.com.

TRAIN TRAVEL

Amtrak's Downeaster service from Boston to Portland, Maine, stops along the seacoast in Exeter, Durham, and Dover, New Hampshire.

🎿 **Amtrak** ☎ 800/872-7245 ⊕ www.amtrak.com.

VISITOR INFORMATION

🎿 Tourist Information **Concord Chamber of Commerce** ✉ 40 Commercial St., Concord 03301 ☎ 603/224-2508 ⊕ www.concordnhchamber.com. **Exeter Area Chamber of Commerce** ✉ 120 Water St., Exeter 03833 ☎ 603/772-2411 ⊕ www.exeterarea.org. **Greater Portsmouth Chamber of Commerce** ✉ 500 Market St., Portsmouth 03802 ☎ 603/436-3988 ⊕ www.portcity.org. **Hanover Area Chamber of Commerce** ✉ 216 Main St., Hanover 03755 ☎ 603/643-3115 ⊕ www.hanoverchamber.org. **Keene Chamber of Commerce** ✉ 48 Central Sq., Keene 03431 ☎ 603/352-1303 ⊕ www.keenechamber. com. **Lakes Region Association** ✉ Rte. 104 off I-93 Exit 23 ✏ Box 430, New Hampton 03256 ☎ 603/744-8664 or 800/605-2537 ⊕ www.lakesregion.org. **Lake Sunapee Region Chamber of Commerce** ✏ Box 532, Sunapee 03782 ☎ 603/526-6575 or 877/526-6575 ⊕ www.sunapeevacations.com. **Manchester Area Convention & Visitors Bureau** ✉ 889 Elm St., Manchester 03101 ☎ 603/666-6600 ⊕ www.manchestercvb. com. **Monadnock Travel Council** ✏ Box 358, Keene 03431 ☎ 800/432-7864 ⊕ www. monadnocktravel.com.

New Hampshire Office of Travel and Tourism Development ✉ 172 Pembroke Rd. ✏ Box 1856, Concord 03302 ☎ 603/271-2665, 800/386-4664 free vacation guide ⊕ www.visitnh. gov. **New Hampshire Parks Department** ☎ 603/271-3556 ⊕ www.nhparks.state.nh. us. **New Hampshire State Council on the Arts** ✉ 40 N. Main St., Concord 03301 ☎ 603/271-2789 or 800/735-2964 ⊕ www.state.nh.us/nharts. **North Country Chamber of Commerce** ✏ Box 1, Colebrook 03576 ☎ 603/237-8939 or 800/698-8939 ⊕ www. northcountrychamber.org. **Seacoast New Hampshire Web site** ⊕ www.seacoastnh. com. **White Mountains Visitors Bureau** ✉ Kancamagus Hwy. (Rte. 112) at I-93 ✏ Box 10, North Woodstock 03262 ☎ 603/745-8720 or 800/346-3687 ⊕ www.whitemtn.org.

Vermont

WORD OF MOUTH

"Stowe is so cozy, and you don't need to be a ski enthusiast to take advantage of its rustic charm."
—cebubelle

"My favorite things to do in Vermont are bike rides, hikes, and just driving around the back roads. There are some very beautiful vistas, farms, old homes, and small villages tucked away on back roads."
—zootsi

"Things to do: Go to the Cabot Creamery in Cabot. Ride the gondola on Mt. Mansfield. Go see the floating bridge in Brookfield. Visit Burlington and have a picnic lunch on the waterfront. I could go on and on . . ."

—bm

By Peggy
Shinn

VERMONT IS AN ENTIRE STATE OF HIDDEN TREASURES. Highways are not marred with billboards, and on some roads, cows still stop traffic twice a day, en route to and from the pasture. In spring, sap boils in sugarhouses, some built generations ago. Yet up the road, a chef trained at the New England Culinary Institute in Montpelier might use the maple syrup to glaze a pork tenderloin.

Once a culinary backwater of pot roast and New England boiled dinners, Vermont now attracts chefs from some of the best restaurants in the world. You're just as likely to find pan-seared yellowfin tuna with wasabi on the menu as you are a roast turkey dinner with all the fixin's. Many of the state's restaurants belong to the Vermont Fresh Network, a partnership that encourages chefs to create menus from local produce. A participating chef might have picked the mesclun greens on your salad plate that morning, or the butternut squash in your soup might have been harvested by the restaurant's neighboring farmer. Not only is the food delicious, but the chefs are keeping Vermont's farmers in business.

And it's the landscape that, for the most part, attracts people to Vermont. The rolling hills belie the rugged terrain underneath the green canopy of forest growth. During the heyday of the wool industry in the mid-1800s, sheep farming denuded 85% of the landscape. Only when farming moved to the more profitable plains states with the opening up of the West after the Civil War did the landscape begin reclaiming itself.

Tourism is one of the state's main economic engines. In winter, Vermont's ski resorts are the prime attraction. In summer, clear lakes and streams provide ample opportunities for swimming, boating, and fishing; the hills attract hikers and mountain bikers. The more than 14,000 mi of roads, many of them only intermittently traveled by cars, are great for road biking. In fall, the leaves have their last hurrah, painting the mountainsides a stunning array of yellow, gold, red, and orange. The only time things really slow down is during "mud" season—otherwise known as late fall and spring. Even innkeepers have been known to tell guests to come another time.

Although Vermont may, in many ways, seem locked in time, technological sophistication appears where you least expect it. Like wireless Internet access in a 19th-century farmhouse-turned-inn and cell phone coverage from the state's highest peaks. But these 21st-century perks can infiltrate without many visual cues, and Vermont will likely stay this way. Like an old farmhouse under renovation, the historic exterior is what a passerby sees. The modern amenities are hidden inside.

Exploring Vermont

Vermont can be divided into three regions. The southern part of the state, flanked by Bennington on the west and Brattleboro on the east, played an important role in Vermont's Revolutionary War–era drive to independence (yes, there was once a Republic of Vermont) and its eventual statehood. The central part is characterized by rugged mountains and the gently rolling dairy lands near Lake Champlain. In northern Ver-

GREAT ITINERARIES

There are many ways to take advantage of Vermont's beauty–skiing or hiking its mountains, biking or driving its back roads, fishing or sailing its waters, shopping for local products, visiting its museums and sights, or simply finding the perfect inn and never leaving the front porch. Distances are relatively short, yet the mountains and many back roads will slow a traveler's pace. You can see a representative north–south section of Vermont in a few days; if you have up to a week you can hit the highlights around the state. But remember, many inns have two-night minimum stays on weekends and holidays. So plan accordingly.

IF YOU HAVE 3 DAYS

Spend a few hours in historic **Bennington** in the southern part of Vermont; then travel north to see Hildene and stay in **Manchester**. On your second day take Route 100 through Weston and travel north through the Green Mountains to Route 125, where you turn west to explore **Middlebury**. On Day 3, enter the Champlain Valley, which has views of the Adirondack Mountains to the west. Stop at Shelburne Farms and carry on to **Burlington**; catch the sunset from the waterfront and take a walk on Church Street.

IF YOU HAVE 5 TO 7 DAYS

Visit **Bennington** and **Manchester** on Day 1. Spend your second day walking around the small towns of **Chester** and **Grafton**. On Day 3 head north to explore **Woodstock** and **Quechee**, stopping at either the Billings Farm and Museum and Marsh-Billings-Rockefeller National Historical Park or the Vermont Institute of Natural Science. Head leisurely on your fourth day toward **Middlebury**, along one of Vermont's most inspiring mountain drives, Route 125 west of Route 100. Between Hancock and Middlebury, you'll pass nature trails and traverse a moderately steep mountain pass. Spend day five in **Burlington**. On Day 6 head east to **Stowe** and Mt. Mansfield for a full day. Begin your last day with a few hours in **Montpelier** on your way to Peacham, **St. Johnsbury**, **Lake Willoughby**, and the serenity and back roads of the Northeast Kingdom. Especially noteworthy are U.S. 5, Route 5A, and Route 14.

mont are the state's capital, Montpelier, and its largest city, Burlington, but also its most rural area, the Northeast Kingdom.

Numbers in the text correspond to numbers in the margin and on the Southern Vermont, Central Vermont, and Northern Vermont maps.

About the Restaurants

Home to the New England Culinary Institute, Vermont tends to keep the chefs who train here. The result: cuisine in Vermont is often exceptional. Seasonal menus use local fresh herbs and vegetables, along with native game. Look for imaginative approaches to native New England foods such as maple syrup (Vermont is the largest U.S. producer), dairy products (especially cheese), native fruits and berries, "new Vermont" products such as salsa and salad dressings, and venison, quail, pheasant, and other game.

Your chances of finding a table for dinner vary with the season: lengthy waits are common at peak times (a reservation is always advisable); the slow months are April and November. Some of the best dining is found at country inns.

	WHAT IT COSTS				
	$$$$	$$$	$$	$	¢
AT DINNER	over $28	$21–$28	$13–$20	$8–$12	under $8

Prices are per person, for a main course at dinner.

About the Hotels

Vermont's largest hotels are in Burlington. Elsewhere you'll find inns, bed-and-breakfasts, and small motels. The many lovely and sometimes quite luxurious inns and B&Bs provide what many people consider the quintessential Vermont lodging experience. Rates are highest during foliage season, from late September to mid-October, and lowest in late spring and November, when many properties close. Some offer package rates. Of note, almost all Vermont inns and B&Bs are no-smoking.

	WHAT IT COSTS				
	$$$$	$$$	$$	$	¢
FOR 2 PEOPLE	over $220	$171–$220	$121–$170	$80–$120	under $80

Prices are for a standard double room during peak season and not including tax or gratuities. Some inns add a 15% service charge.

Timing

The number of visitors and the rates for lodging reach their peaks along with the color of the leaves during foliage season, from late September to mid-October. But if you have never seen a kaleidoscope of autumn colors, it is worth braving the slow-moving traffic and paying the extra money. In summer the state is lush and green. Winter, of course, is high season at Vermont's ski resorts. Rates are lowest in late spring and November, although many properties close during these times.

PLEASURES & PASTIMES

BIKING

Vermont, especially the often deserted roads of the Northeast Kingdom, is great bicycle-touring country. Many companies lead weekend tours and weeklong trips throughout the state. If you'd like to go it on your own, most chambers of commerce have brochures highlighting good cycling routes in their area, including *Vermont Life* magazine's "Bicycle Vermont" map and guide, and many bookstores sell *25 Bicycle Tours in Vermont* by John Freidin.

FISHING

Central Vermont is the heart of the state's warm-water lake and pond fishing area. Harriman and Somerset reservoirs have both warm- and cold-water species; Harriman has a greater variety. Rainbow trout pulled out of Lake Dunmore have set state records; Lakes Bomoseen and St. Catherine are good for rainbows and largemouth bass. In the east, Lakes Fairlee and Morey hold bass, perch, and chain pickerel, while the lower part of the Connecticut River contains smallmouth bass, walleye, and perch; shad are returning via the fish ladders at Vernon and Bellows Falls.

In northern Vermont, rainbow and brown trout inhabit the Missisquoi, Lamoille, Winooski, and Willoughby rivers. Lakes Seymour, Willoughby, and Memphremagog and Great Averill Pond in the Northeast Kingdom are good for salmon and lake trout. The Dog River near Montpelier has one of the best wild populations of brown trout in the state, and landlocked Atlantic salmon are returning to the Clyde River following removal of a controversial dam.

Lake Champlain, stocked annually with salmon and lake trout, has become the state's ice-fishing capital; walleye, bass, pike, and channel catfish are also taken. Ice fishing is also popular on Lake Memphremagog.

SKIING

The Green Mountains run through the middle of Vermont like a bumpy spine, visible from almost every point in the state; generous accumulations of snow make the mountains an ideal site for skiing. Increased snowmaking capacity and improved, high-tech computerized equipment at many areas virtually assure a good day on the slopes. Vermont has 18 alpine ski resorts with nearly 1,000 trails and some 5,000 acres of skiable terrain. Combined, the resorts operate nearly 200 lifts and have the capacity to carry some 215,000 skiers per hour. Though grooming is sophisticated at all Vermont areas, conditions usually run to a typically Eastern hard pack, with powder a rare luxury and ice a bugbear after a January thaw. The best advice for skiing in Vermont is to keep your skis well tuned.

Route 100 is also known as Skier's Highway, passing by 13 of the state's ski areas. Vermont's major resorts are Stowe, Jay Peak, Sugarbush, Killington, Okemo, Mt. Snow, and Stratton. Midsize, less-hectic areas to consider include Ascutney, Bromley, Smugglers' Notch, Pico, Mad River Glen, Burke Mountain, and Bolton Valley Holiday Resort.

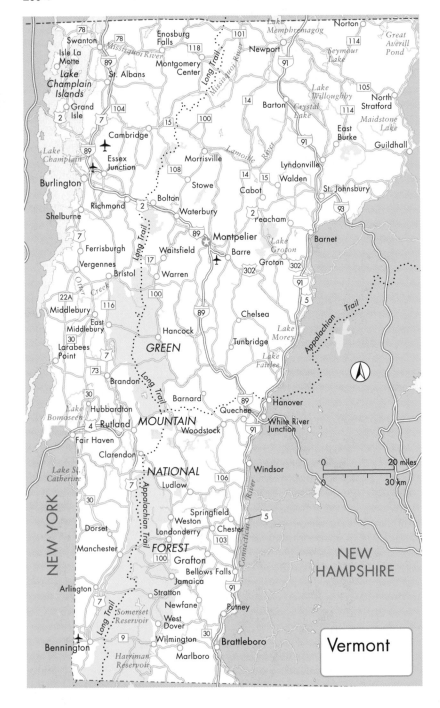

Vermont

SOUTHERN VERMONT

Cross into the Green Mountain State from Massachusetts on Interstate 91, and you might feel as if you've entered a new country. There isn't a town in sight, nor are there any billboards, which the state banned in the 1960s. The last one came down in 1975. What you see are forested hills punctuated by rolling pastures. When you reach Brattleboro, no fast-food joints or strip malls line the exits to signal your arrival at southeastern Vermont's gateway city. En route to downtown, you pass by Victorian-era homes on tree-lined streets. From Brattleboro, you can cross over the spine of the Green Mountains toward Bennington and Manchester. This area is the southern terminus of the Green Mountain National Forest, dotted with lakes, threaded with trails and old forest roads, and home to big ski resorts.

The towns are listed in counterclockwise order, beginning in the east in Brattleboro, then traveling west along Route 9 toward Bennington, then north to Manchester and Weston and south along scenic Routes 100 and 30 back to Townshend and Newfane.

Brattleboro

❶ *60 mi south of White River Junction.*

Since the 1960s, Brattleboro has drawn political activists and earnest counterculturists. Today, the city of 12,000 is still politically and culturally active, leading some people to call it Vermont's hippest town. Downtown is the hub of the art scene, led by the **Brattleboro Museum and Art Center.** Housed in historic Union Station, the museum presents changing exhibits created by locally, nationally, and internationally renowned artists. ✉ *10 Vernon St.* ☎ *802/257–0124* ⊕ *www.brattleboromuseum.org* 🖾 *$4* ☾ *Wed.–Mon. 11–5; open free 5:30–8:30 1st Fri. of month.*

The **Vermont Center for Photography** (✉ 49 Flat St. ☎ 802/251–6051) exhibits works from Vermont, New Hampshire, and Massachusetts photographers.

OFF THE BEATEN PATH

PUTNEY – Nine miles upriver, this small town, with a population of only 2,600, is the antithesis of bustling Brattleboro and is a haven for writers, artists, and craftspeople. Watch wool being spun into yarn at the **Green Mountain Spinnery** (✉ 7 Brickyard La., at Exit 4 off I–91 ☎ 802/387–4528 or 800/321–9665). The factory shop sells yarn, knitting accessories, and patterns. Tours are conducted at 1:30 on the 1st and 3rd Tuesday of the month. **Harlow's Sugar House** (✉ 563 Bellows Falls Rd., Putney ☎ 802/387–5852), 2 mi north of Putney, has a working cider mill and sugarhouse, as well as seasonal apple and berry picking. You can buy cider, maple syrup, and other items in the gift shop.

Where to Stay & Eat

$$$ ✕ **Max's.** Pasta and seafood are the theme at this trendy restaurant with an open kitchen. Pasta creations include artichoke-mascarpone ravioli or Tuscan-style cauliflower with linguine. Complementing this *nuovo* Ital-

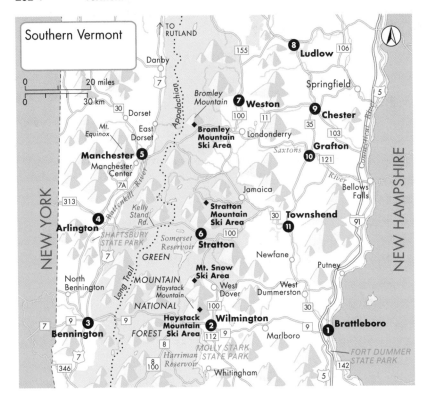

ian menu are eclectic entrées such as mahimahi in parchment, and laven-der-tea smoked salmon. Sunday brunch is both traditional and adventurous, with everything from eggs to curry rice kedgeree. ⊠ *1052 Western Ave., 2½ mi west of Brattleboro, West Brattleboro* ☎ *802/254–7747* 🖃 *MC, V* ⊗ *Closed Mon. and Tues. No lunch, except Sun. brunch.*

$$$ ✕ **Peter Havens.** In a town better known for tofu than toniness, this chic little bistro knows just what to do with a filet mignon: serve it with Roquefort walnut butter. Look for the house-cured gravlax made with lemon vodka and for fresh seasonal seafood, which even includes a spring fling with soft-shell crabs. The wine list is superb. ⊠ *32 Elliot St.* ☎ *802/ 257–3333* 🖃 *AE, MC, V* ⊗ *Closed Sun. and Mon. No lunch.*

¢–$$$ ✕ **Top of the Hill Grill.** Hickory-smoked ribs, beef brisket, apple-smoked
Fodor'sChoice turkey, and pulled pork are a few of the favorites at this barbecue just
★ outside town. Larger parties can opt for "family-style" dinners. Homemade pecan pie is the dessert of choice. You can sit indoors in the informal dining room with big windows, but the best seats are outdoors at picnic tables overlooking the West River. ⊠ *632 Putney Rd.* ☎ *802/ 258–9178* 🖃 *No credit cards* ⊗ *Closed Nov.–mid-Apr.*

¢–$ ✕ **Brattleboro Food Co-op.** Pick up a premade sandwich or order a plate of curry chicken at the deli counter, then eat it in a small sitting area in this busy market. The focus is on the natural and organic, with everything from tofu sandwiches to beef satay. The delicatessen is connected to a natural-food market. ☒ *2 Main St.* ☎ *802/257–0236* ☐ *MC, V.*

$$–$$$$ 🏨 **Forty Putney Road.** Lindsay and Lowell Hanson provide elegant yet comfortable accommodations in this French-style mansion. Rooms are furnished with antiques; the suite has a gas fireplace. A separate cottage with a full kitchen sleeps four. In warm weather, breakfast is served on the patio of the formally landscaped grounds, which lead to the shores of the West River. ☒ *192 Putney Rd., 05301* ☎ *802/254–6268 or 800/ 941–2413* 🖷 *802/258–2673* ⊕ *www.fortyputneyroad.com* ⮡ *3 rooms, 1 suite, 1 cottage* ⚒ *In-room VCRs, Wi-Fi, some pets allowed* ☐ *AE, MC, V* ⭗ *BP.*

$$–$$$ 🏨 **Hickory Ridge House.** On the National Register of Historic Places, this 1808 Federal-style mansion with a Palladian window has large comfortable guest rooms filled with antiques and country furnishings. Four rooms have Rumford fireplaces and en suite private baths. A two-bedroom cottage has a huge fireplace and full kitchen. The inn overlooks a large field, great for walking and cross-country skiing. ☒ *53 Hickory Ridge Rd., 11 mi north of Brattleboro, Putney 05346* ☎ *802/387–5709 or 800/ 380–9218* 🖷 *802/387–4328* ⊕ *www.hickoryridgehouse.com* ⮡ *6 rooms, 1 cottage* ⚒ *In-room VCRs, hiking, cross-country skiing; no kids under 10* ☐ *MC, V* ⭗ *BP.*

$ 🏨 **Latchis Hotel.** This restored 1938 three-story downtown art-deco landmark, with terrazzo floors and chrome fixtures, has simply furnished but comfortable rooms overlooking Main Street. You can catch a movie under the zodiac ceiling of the adjoining Latchis Theater. ☒ *50 Main St., 05301* ☎ *802/254–6300 or 800/796–6301* 🖷 *802/254–6304* ⊕ *www.latchis.com* ⮡ *30 rooms, 3 suites* ⚒ *Refrigerators, cable TV, Wi-Fi, pub* ☐ *AE, MC, V* ⭗ *CP.*

Nightlife & the Arts
Mole's Eye Cafe (☒ 4 High St. ☎ 802/257–0771) hosts an open-mike night every Thursday and live bands Friday and Saturday.

Sports & the Outdoors
BIKING **Brattleboro Bicycle Shop** (☒ 165 Main St. ☎ 802/254–8644 or 800/272– 8245) rents and repairs hybrid bikes. **Burrows Specialized Sports** (☒ 105 Main St. ☎ 802/254–9430) rents skis and snowshoes.

CANOEING **Vermont Canoe Touring Center** (☒ U.S. 5 ☎ 802/257–5008) conducts guided and self-guided tours, rents canoes and kayaks, and provides a shuttle service.

SKATING **Nelson Withington Skating Rink** (☒ Memorial Park, 4 Guilford St. ☎ 802/ 257–2311) rents skates.

STATE PARK The hiking trails at **Fort Dummer State Park** (☒ S. Main St., 2 mi south of Brattleboro ☎ 802/254–2610) afford views of the Connecticut River valley.

Shopping
Gallery in the Woods (☒ 143 Main St. ☎ 802/257–4777) sells art, jewelry, and glassware from around the world.

Vermont Artisan Designs (⊠ 106 Main St. ☎ 802/257–7044) displays ceramics, glass, wood, clothing, jewelry, and furniture.

EN
ROUTE
Tiny Marlboro, 10 mi west of Brattleboro, draws musicians from around the world each summer to the Marlboro College campus for the **Marlboro Music Festival** (⊠ Marlboro Music Center, Marlboro College ☎ 802/254–2394, 215/569–4690 Sept.–June). Founded by Rudolf Serkin, who was joined for many years by Pablo Casals, the festival presents weekend chamber music concerts from mid-July to mid-August. The **Southern Vermont Natural History Museum** houses one of New England's largest collections of mounted birds, including three extinct birds, and a complete collection of mammals native to the Northeast. The museum also has live hawk and owl exhibits. ⊠ *Rte. 9* ☎ *802/464–0048* 🖅 *$3* ⊙ *Memorial Day–late Oct., daily 10–5; late Oct.–Memorial Day, most weekends 10–4, call ahead.*

Wilmington

❷ *18 mi west of Brattleboro.*

The village of Wilmington, with its classic Main Street lined with 18th- and 19th-century buildings, anchors the Mt. Snow Valley. But most of the valley's lodging and dining establishments line Route 100 north to West Dover and Mt. Snow, where skiers flock on winter weekends. The area abounds with cultural activity year-round, from concerts to art exhibits.

The **Art of Humor Gallery** (⊠ 30 Not A-Rd. ☎ 802/464–5523) features the cartoons of Skip Morrow, who wrote *I Hate Cats*. **North River Winery,** in a converted farmhouse and barn, produces fruit wines such as Green Mountain Apple and Vermont Pear. ⊠ *Rte. 112, 6 mi south of Wilmington, Jacksonville* ☎ *802/368–7557* 🖅 *Free* ⊙ *Daily 10–5.*

Where to Stay & Eat

$$–$$$ ✕ **The Hermitage.** At this secluded 19th-century inn, executive chef David Vanderpoel has created an eclectic menu with, for example, cornish game hen with jalapeño cornbread stuffing and tequila shallot sauce or stuffed, bacon-wrapped roast-pork tenderloin with pomegranate reduction. The two dining rooms—the smaller front room and the expansive banquet hall—are adorned with such rustic antiques as birch-limb lamps. Tapas are served on Monday evenings. ⊠ *21 Handle Rd., 6 mi north of Wilmington, West Dover* ☎ *802/464–3511* ▬ *AE, MC, V* ⊙ *Closed Tues.*

$$$$ ✕▦ **Inn at Saw Mill Farm.** Full of character and charm, this inn in a converted barn has common rooms elegantly decorated with English chintzes, antiques, and Oriental rugs. Each of the guest rooms—in the main inn or in cottages scattered on the property's 22 acres—is individually decorated, and many have sitting areas and fireplaces. The restaurant's ($$$$) seasonal menu might include potato-crusted black sea bass with wild mushrooms and orzo or a grilled veal chop with wild mushroom risotto. The wine selection, with more than 30,000 bottles, is superb. ⊠ *Rte. 100 and Crosstown Rd., 6 mi north of Wilmington, West Dover 05356* ☎ *802/464–8131 or 800/493–1133* 🖷 *802/464–1130* ⊕ *www.*

FodorsChoice
★

theinnatsawmillfarm.com 🛏 *21 rooms* ⚴ *Restaurant, tennis court, pool, fishing; no room phones, no room TVs, no kids under 8* ▤ *AE, D, MC, V* ☉ *Closed Easter–late May* ¡◯¡ *MAP.*

$$–$$$$ ✕🖾 **Deerhill Inn.** This hillside country inn has wonderful views of the Mount Snow Valley. The living room has a large stone fireplace, and works by local artists hang on the walls of the common areas. Guest rooms are cozy and decorated with English floral linens; balcony rooms are more spacious. The restaurant's ($$$$; closed Wednesday) upscale comfort food might include a veal medallion with wild mushrooms in a lemon cream sauce or a black-pepper sirloin steak. A jazz pianist entertains diners most Saturday nights. ✉ *Valley View Rd., 6 mi north of Wilmington* ⌖ *Box 136, West Dover 05356* ☎ *802/464–3100 or 800/ 993–3379* 🖷 *802/464–5474* ⊕ *www.deerhill.com* 🛏 *14 rooms, 2 suites* ⚴ *Restaurant, some in-room DVDs, pool; no a/c, no kids under 12* ▤ *AE, MC, V* ¡◯¡ *BP, MAP.*

$–$$ ✕🖾 **Doveberry Inn and Restaurant.** After a day's skiing, this country lodge just a few minutes from the slopes provides a welcome haven. You can warm up by the fireplace in the living room with a glass of wine from the bar. Guest rooms are cheerful and bright, and four have fireplaces. The small restaurant ($$$–$$$$; closed Tuesday) serves northern Italian specialties such as wood-grilled veal chop with wild mushrooms and pan-seared salmon with herbed risotto. ✉ *Rte. 100, West Dover 05356* ☎ *802/464–5652 or 800/722–3204* 🖷 *802/464–6229* ⊕ *www. doveberryinn.com* 🛏 *11 rooms* ⚴ *Restaurant, some in-room VCRs, bar; no a/c in some rooms, no kids under 8* ▤ *AE, MC, V* ¡◯¡ *BP, MAP.*

$$–$$$$ 🖾 **White House of Wilmington.** The grand staircase in this Federal-style mansion leads to rooms with antique bathrooms and brass wall sconces; some rooms have fireplaces and lofts. Also here are a cross-country ski touring and snowshoeing center, a tubing hill, and 12 km (7 mi) of groomed trails. The restaurant has a prix-fixe Sunday brunch served from 11 to 2 for $12.95. ✉ *178 Rte. 9 E, 05363* ☎ *802/464–2135 or 800/ 541–2135* 🖷 *802/464–5222* ⊕ *www.whitehouseinn.com* 🛏 *25 rooms* ⚴ *Restaurant, some in-room hot tubs, 2 pools (1 indoors), sauna, steam room, cross-country skiing, pub; no a/c in some rooms, no TV in some rooms, no kids under 8* ▤ *AE, D, MC, V* ¡◯¡ *BP.*

Nightlife & the Arts

Deacon's Den Tavern (✉ Rte. 100 ☎ 802/464–9361) hosts bands on weekends from Thanksgiving through Easter.

A year-round roster of music, theater, film, and fine art is presented at the **Memorial Hall Center for the Arts** (✉ 14 W. Main St. ☎ 802/464–8411). In addition to steak and Mexican specialties, the standard fare on weekends at **Poncho's Wreck** (✉ S. Main St. ☎ 802/464–9320) is acoustic jazz or mellow rock. **Sitzmark** (✉ 55 East Dover Rd. ☎ 802/464–3384) hosts rock bands on weekends.

Sports & the Outdoors

PETTING FARM **Adams Farm** (✉ 15 Higley Hill Rd., off Rte. 100 ☎ 802/464–3762) is ⚘ a working farm where children and adults can collect fresh eggs from the chicken coop, feed a rabbit, milk a goat, ride a tractor or a pony, and jump in the hay. The indoor livestock barn is open Wednesday–Sunday from November to April; an outdoor version is open daily the rest of the year. The farm store sells more than 200 handmade quilts and sweaters. In winter, the farm gives sleigh rides.

SNOWMOBILE **High Country Tours** (✉ Rte. 100, West Dover ☎ 802/464–2108) runs one-
TOURS hour, two-hour, and ½-day snowmobile tours from two locations: one near the Mount Snow base area, the other west of Wilmington in Searsburg.

STATE PARK **Molly Stark State Park** (✉ Rte. 9 east of Wilmington ☎ 802/464–5460) has a hiking trail that leads to a vista from a fire tower on Mt. Olga.

WATER SPORTS Eight-mile-long **Lake Whitingham (Harriman Reservoir)** has good fishing. Boat-launch areas are at Wards Cove, Whitingham, Mountain Mills, and the Ox Bow. **Green Mountain Flagship Company** (✉ Rte. 9, 2 mi west of Wilmington ☎ 802/464–2975 ⊕ www.greenmountainflagship.com) runs a 65-passenger cruise boat on Lake Whitingham and rents canoes, kayaks, and sailboats from May to late October. The cruise takes you by New England's largest nudist beach.

High Country Waverunner and Water Sport Rentals (✉ Rte. 9, 2 mi west of Wilmington ☎ 802/464–2108) does what its name implies.

Shopping

Downtown Wilmington is lined with unique shops and galleries. **Quaigh Design Centre** (✉ W. Main St. [Rte. 9] ☎ 802/464–2780) sells artwork from Britain and New England—including works by Vermont wood-cut artists Sabra Field and Mary Azarian—and Scottish woolens and tartans. **Young and Constantin Gallery** (✉ 10 S. Main St. ☎ 802/464–2515) sells handblown glassware, ceramics, and art from local and nationally known artisans.

Ski Areas

MOUNT SNOW One of the state's premier family resorts has a full roster of year-round
RESORT activities. The almost 800-acre facility encompasses the **Grand Summit Hotel and Crown Club** (☎ 800/451–4211), a 201-room slope-side condo, hotel, and conference center; a golf course; 45 mi of mountain-biking trails; and an extensive network of hiking trails. One lift ticket lets you ski at Mount Snow and at nearby Haystack. A free shuttle con-nects the two ski areas.

Downhill. More than half of the 132 trails down its 1,700-foot verti-cal summit are intermediate, wide, and sunny. Most of the beginner slopes are toward the bottom, and the majority of expert terrain is on the North Face. The trails are served by 23 lifts, including 3 high-speed quads, 1 regular quad, 10 triple chairs, 4 double chairs, and 3 Magic Carpets (sim-ilar to a moving sidewalk). Snowmaking covers 85% of the terrain. The ski school's Perfect Turn instruction program is designed to help skiers of all ages and abilities.

Summer activities. Mount Snow has an 18-hole golf course, lift-served mountain biking and hiking trails, and a health club and spa.

✉ *400 Mountain Rd., Mount Snow 05356* ☎ *802/464–3333, 802/464–2151 snow conditions, 800/245–7669 lodging* ⊕ *www.mountsnow.com.*

Slopes Less Traveled

SINCE AMERICA'S FIRST SKI TOW opened in a farmer's pasture near Woodstock in January 1934, skiers have flocked to Vermont in winter. The Green Mountains are dotted with 18 ski resorts, from Mt. Snow in the south to Jay Peak near the Canadian border. They range in size from Killington, in central Vermont, with its 200 trails and 31 lifts, to the Bear Creek Mountain Club, also in central Vermont, with only 15 trails and one chairlift. On weekends and holidays, the bigger resorts—Mt. Snow, Stratton, and Okemo in southern Vermont; Killington, Sugarbush, and Mad River Glen in the central part of the state; and Stowe, Smuggler's Notch, and Jay Peak in the north—attract most of the skiers and snowboarders. To escape the crowds, try these smaller, less well-known ski resorts.

Southern Vermont:

Near Stratton, **Bromley** (✉ Rte. 11, Peru ☎ 802/824–5522 or 800/865–4786 ⊕ www.bromley.com) is a favorite with families. The 43 trails are evenly divided between beginner, intermediate, and expert. The resort runs a child care center, for kids ages 6 weeks to 4 years, and hosts children's programs, for ages 3–12. An added bonus: the trails face south, making for glorious spring skiing and warm winter days.

Central Vermont:

Once only a faint blip on skiers' radar, **Ascutney** (✉ Rte. 44, Brownsville ☎ 802/484–7711 or 800/243–0011 ⊕ www.ascutney.com) has remade itself into a bona-fide destination. The 56 trails on an 1,800 foot vertical drop are served by six lifts, including a high-speed quad chairlift accessing

double-diamond terrain near the summit. Day care is available for children ages 6 weeks to 6 years, with learn-to-ski programs for toddlers and up. On Saturday from 5–8 PM, children ages 4–12 can join Cheddar's Happy Hour and movie night. When weekend hordes hit Killington, the locals head to **Pico** (✉ Rte. 4, Killington ☎ 802/422–6200 or 866/667–7426 ⊕ www.picomountain. com). One of Killington's "seven peaks," Pico is physically separated from its parent resort. The 50 trails range from elevator-shaft steeps to challenging intermediate trails near the summit, with easier terrain near the bottom of the mountain's 2,000 foot vertical. The learning slope is separated from the upper mountain, so hotshots won't bomb through it. The lower express quad can get crowded, but the upper one rarely has a line.

Northern Vermont:

About an hour's drive from Montpelier is **Burke Mountain** (✉ Mountain Rd., East Burke ☎ 802/626–3322 ⊕ www.skiburke.com). Racers stick to the Training Slope, served by its own poma lift. The other 44 trails and glades are a quiet playground. Near Burlington, **Bolton Valley Resort** (✉ 4302 Bolton Valley Access Rd., Bolton ☎ 802/434–3444 or 877/926–5866 ⊕ www. boltonvalley.com) is a family favorite. In addition to 61 downhill ski trails (over half rated for intermediates), Bolton has night skiing Wednesday–Saturday, 100 km (62 mi) of cross-country and snowshoe trails, and a sports center.

3

CROSS-COUNTRY
SKIING
Two cross-country ski centers near Mount Snow provide more than 110 km (68 mi) of varied terrain. **Timber Creek** (⊠ Rte. 100 north of Mount Snow ☎ 802/464–0999) is appealingly small with 14 km (9 mi) of groomed loops. The groomed trails at the **White House of Wilmington** (⊠ Rtes. 9 and 100 ☎ 802/464–2135) cover 50 km (30 mi). Both areas have Nordic equipment and snowshoes for rent.

Bennington

❸ *21 mi west of Wilmington.*

Once a thriving commercial town, Bennington is well endowed with stately Colonial and Victorian mansions. The economy is less robust now, and not all these homes are well maintained. But downtown, where U.S. 7 and U.S. 9 intersect, has retained much of the industrial character it developed in the 19th century, when paper mills, gristmills, and potteries formed the city's economic base. West of downtown is **Old Bennington,** a National Register Historic District. Here, at the Catamount Tavern, Ethan Allen organized the Green Mountain Boys, who helped capture Ft. Ticonderoga in 1775. Two years later, American general John Stark urged his militia to attack the British-paid Hessian troops across the New York border: "There are the redcoats; they will be ours or tonight Molly Stark sleeps a widow!" In the graveyard of the **Old First Church,** at Church Street and Monument Circle, the tombstone of the poet Robert Frost proclaims, "I had a lover's quarrel with the world."

Ⅽ The **Bennington Battle Monument,** a 306-foot stone obelisk with an elevator to the top, commemorates General Stark's victory over the British, who attempted to capture Bennington's stockpile of supplies. The battle, which took place near Walloomsac Heights in New York State on August 16, 1777, helped bring about the surrender two months later of the British commander "Gentleman Johnny" Burgoyne. ⊠ *15 Monument Cir., Old Bennington* ☎ *802/447–0550* ☜ *$2* ☉ *Mid-Apr.–Oct., daily 9–5.*

The **Bennington Museum's** rich collections include military artifacts, early tools, dolls, and toys, and the Bennington Flag, one of the oldest Stars and Stripes in existence. One room is devoted to early Bennington pottery, and two rooms cover the history of American glass and contain fine Tiffany specimens. The museum displays the largest public collection of the work of Grandma Moses (1860–1961), the popular self-taught folk artist who lived and painted in the area. ⊠ *75 Main St. (Rte. 9)* ☎ *802/447–1571* ⊕ *www.benningtonmuseum.com* ☜ *$8* ☉ *Thurs.–Tues. 10–5.*

North of Bennington, the architecturally significant **Park-McCullough House** is a 35-room classic French Empire–style mansion, built in 1865 and furnished with period pieces. Several restored flower gardens grace the landscaped grounds, and a stable houses a collection of antique carriages. Call for details on the summer concert series and other special events. ⊠ *Corner of Park and West Sts., North Bennington* ☎ *802/442–5441* ⊕ *www.parkmccullough.org* ☜ *$8* ☉ *Mid-May–mid-Oct., daily 10–4; last tour at 3.*

Contemporary stone sculpture and white-frame neo-Colonial dorms surrounded by acres of cornfields punctuate the green meadows of **Bennington College**'s placid campus. The small liberal arts college is known for its progressive program in the arts. ⊠ *Rte. 67A off U.S. 7 (look for stone entrance gate)* ☎ *802/442–5401.*

Where to Stay & Eat

$–$$$$ ✕ **Pangaea.** Don't let the dusty old storefront fool you. Named after the Permian-era continent of Pangaea, when all the continents were one, this restaurant borrows cuisine from around the world. Owner-chef William Scully's ever-changing menu includes such delicacies as braised wild boar with porcini and beurre monté poached lobster. The lounge next door, complete with billiard table, serves eclectic pub fare such as pot roast chimichangas and Cobb salad with Danish blue cheese. ⊠ *1 and 3 Prospect St., 3 mi north of Bennington, North Bennington* ☎ *802/ 442–7171* ⊟ *AE, MC, V* ⊗ *Closed Mon. No lunch.*

¢–$ ✕ **Blue Benn Diner.** Breakfast is served all day in this authentic diner, where the eats include turkey hash and breakfast burritos, with scrambled eggs, sausage, and chilies, plus pancakes of all imaginable varieties. The menu lists many vegetarian selections. Lines may be long, especially on weekends. ⊠ *314 North St.* ☎ *802/442–5140* ⊕ *Reservations not accepted* ⊟ *No credit cards* ⊗ *No dinner Sat.–Tues.*

$–$$ ⌂ **South Shire Inn.** Canopy beds in lushly carpeted rooms, ornate plaster moldings, a mahogany fireplace, and leaded glass doors in the library re-create the grandeur of the Victorian past; fireplaces in some rooms add warmth. The South Shire is in a quiet residential neighborhood within walking distance of downtown. The carriage house has two airy, high-ceilinged rooms with fireplaces and modern baths; the two upstairs rooms have skylights. ⊠ *124 Elm St., 05201* ☎ *802/447–3839* 🖷 *802/442– 3547* ⊕ *www.southshire.com* 🖙 *9 rooms* ⚸ *Some in-room hot tubs; no TV in some rooms, no kids under 12* ⊟ *AE, MC, V* ⎊ *BP.*

Nightlife & the Arts

The **Bennington Center for the Arts** (⊠ Rte. 9 at Gypsy La. ☎ 802/442– 7158) hosts cultural events, including exhibitions by local and national artists. The **Oldcastle Theatre Co.** (☎ 802/447–0564) at the Bennington Center for the Arts, whose season runs from May through October, hosts fine regional theater.

Sports & the Outdoors

HIKING Four miles east of Bennington, the **Long Trail** crosses Route 9 and runs south to the top of Harmon Hill. Allot two or three hours for this hike.

STATE PARKS **Lake Shaftsbury State Park** (⊠Rte. 7A, 10½ mi north of Bennington ☎802/ 375–9978) has a swimming beach, nature trails, boat and canoe rentals, and a snack bar. **Woodford State Park** (⊠ Rte. 9, 10 mi east of Bennington ☎ 802/447–7169) has an activities center on Adams Reservoir, playground, boat and canoe rentals, and nature trails.

Shopping

The **Apple Barn and Country Bake Shop** (⊠ U.S. 7 S ☎ 802/447–7780) sells home-baked goodies, fresh cider, Vermont cheeses, and maple syrup, and has a cornfield maze. The shop is open from September to mid-October. The showroom at the **Bennington Potters Yard** (⊠ 324 County St. ☎ 802/447–7531 or 800/205–8033) stocks first-quality pottery and seconds from the famed Bennington Potters. Take a free tour on weekdays from 10 to 3 when the potters are working, or follow a self-guided tour around the yard. **Hemmings Motor News** (⊠ 222 Main St. ☎ 802/442–3101), publisher of the car-collector magazine, operates a full-service Sunoco filling station and store, selling scale models of classic cars, books, vintage license plates, and other motoring paraphernalia.

Arlington

❹ *15 mi north of Bennington.*

Smaller than Bennington and more down to earth than upper-crust Manchester to the north, Arlington exudes a certain Rockwellian folksiness. And it should. Illustrator Norman Rockwell lived here from 1939 to 1953, and many of the models for his portraits of small-town life were his neighbors. Although no original paintings are displayed at the **Norman Rockwell Exhibition,** the rooms are crammed with reproductions of the illustrator's works, arranged in every way conceivable: chronologically, by subject matter, and juxtaposed with photos of the models, several of whom work here. ⊠ *Main St. (Rte. 7A)* ☎ *802/375–6423* 🖾 *$3* ☉ *May–Oct., daily 9–5; Nov., Dec., and Feb.–Apr., daily 10–4.*

Where to Stay & Eat

$$$$ ✕▣ **West Mountain Inn.** Spectacular views, labyrinthine gardens, and pet
Fodor'sChoice llamas are hallmarks of this inn, built in the 1840s on 150 mountain-
★ side acres as an elegant summer retreat. The children's room, brightly painted with life-size Disney characters, is stocked with games and stuffed animals. Six-course prix-fixe dinners ($$$$) highlighting updated Continental cuisine are served in a low-beam country dining room. Request a table by the window. ⊠ *West Mountain Inn Rd., 05250* ☎ *802/ 375–6516* 🖹 *802/375–6553* ⊕ *www.westmountaininn.com* 🗗 *16 rooms, 6 suites* ⊘ *Restaurant, some microwaves, hiking, cross-country skiing, bar, recreation room, meeting room; no room phones, no room TVs* ▤ *AE, D, MC, V* ⌶◎⌶ *MAP.*

★ **$$–$$$$** ✕▣ **Arlington Inn.** Greek-revival columns at this 1848 home lend it an imposing presence, but the atmosphere is hardly forbidding. Victorian-style wallpaper, Louis XIV furniture, maple-paneled ceilings, and original moldings and wainscoting are highlights. Many of the rooms in the carriage house and old parsonage have fireplaces. The restaurant serves regional American dishes ($$$–$$$$). Landscaping includes a garden, gazebo, pond, and waterfall. ⊠ *Rte. 7A, 05250* ☎ *802/375–6532 or 800/443–9442* 🖹 *802/375–6534* ⊕ *www.arlingtoninn.com* 🗗 *13 rooms, 5 suites* ⊘ *Restaurant, cable TV, pond, meeting rooms* ▤ *AE, D, MC, V* ⌶◎⌶ *BP, MAP.*

$$–$$$$ ▣ **Hill Farm Inn.** Once a country farmhouse, this family-friendly inn on 50 acres near the Battenkill River has comfortable rooms furnished with sturdy antiques and even a spinning wheel in the upstairs hallway. The barn houses friendly goats and sheep, and chickens freely roam the property. The main inn, from 1830, has a large wraparound porch with sweeping views of Mt. Equinox. Other rooms are in the separate 1790 guesthouse; the charming one- and two-bedroom cabins are open from spring through fall. Along the Battenkill are 2½ mi of walking trails. ⊠ *458 Hill Farm Rd., off Rte. 7A, 05250* ☎ *802/375–2269 or 800/882–2545* ☒ *802/375–9918* ⊕ *www.hillfarminn.com* ⊅ *6 rooms, 5 suites, 4 cabins* ⚬ *Some kitchenettes, some refrigerators, some in-room VCRs, playground; no a/c in some rooms* ▭ *AE, D, MC, V* ⦿ *BP.*

Sports & the Outdoors

Battenkill Canoe, Ltd./Vermont Canoe Trips (⊠ Rte. 7A ☎ 802/362–2800 or 800/421–5268) rents canoes and runs inn-to-inn tours and day trips on the Battenkill.

Manchester

★ ❺ *9 mi northeast of Arlington.*

Manchester has been a popular summer retreat since the mid-19th century when city dwellers traveled north to take in the cool clean air at the foot of 3,816-foot Mt. Equinox. Manchester's tree-shaded marble sidewalks and stately old homes reflect the luxurious resort lifestyle of more than a century ago. But a mile away, Manchester Center's upscale factory outlets attract shoppers in droves, giving the place the feel of a crowded mall—with cars. If you're coming here from Arlington, take scenic Route 7A.

The **American Museum of Fly Fishing** houses the largest collection of angling art and angling-related objects in the world. Displays include more than 1,500 rods, 800 reels, 30,000 flies, and the tackle of famous people such as Winslow Homer, Bing Crosby, and Jimmy Carter. ⊠ *4070 Main St. (Rte. 7A)* ☎ *802/362–3300* ⊕ *www.amff.com* ⊡ *$5* ⊙ *Daily 10–4.*

★ **Hildene,** the summer home of Abraham Lincoln's son Robert Todd Lincoln, is a beautifully preserved 412-acre estate. The 24-room mansion, with its Georgian-revival symmetry, is unusual in that its rooms are not roped off. When the 1,000-pipe aeolian organ is played, the music reverberates as though from the mansion's very bones. Tours include a short film on the owner's life and a walk through the elaborate formal gardens. When snow conditions permit, you can cross-country ski on the property, which has views of nearby mountains. ⊠ *Rte. 7A* ☎ *802/ 362–1788* ⊕ *www.hildene.org* ⊡ *Tour $10, grounds pass $5* ⊙ *Mid-June–Oct., daily 9:30–4:30. Tours on the ½ hr (first tour at 9:30, last tour at 3). Nov.–May, Thurs.–Mon., 11–3.*

The **Southern Vermont Arts Center** showcases rotating exhibits and its permanent collection of more than 700 pieces of 19th- and 20th-century American art in a 12,500-square-foot museum. The arts center's original building, a graceful Georgian mansion set on 407 acres, is the frequent site of concerts, performances, and film screenings. In summer and fall, a pleasant restaurant with magnificent views serves lunch. ⊠ *West Rd.* ☎ *802/362–1405* ⊕ *www.svac.org* ⊡ *$6* ⊙ *Tues.–Sat. 10–5, Sun. noon–5.*

Where to Stay & Eat

$$$$ ✕ **Chantecleer.** Intimate dining rooms have been created in a former dairy barn with a large fieldstone fireplace. The menu reflects the chef's Swiss background: appetizers include *Bündnerfleisch* (air-dried Swiss beef) and frogs' legs in garlic butter. Rack of lamb, whole Dover sole filleted table-side, and veal chops highlight the entrées. ✉ *Rte. 7A, 3½ mi north of Manchester, East Dorset* ☎ *802/362–1616* ⌂ *Reservations essential* ☰ *AE, DC, MC, V* ⊗ *Closed Tues. in summer; Mon. and Tues. in winter; late Oct.–Thanksgiving; and mid-Apr.–mid-May. No lunch.*

★ $$$–$$$$ ✕ **Inn at West View Farm.** The country-style interior of this inn's restaurant belies its excellent cuisine. Chef Raymond Chen's continental menu has Asian influences, as in the coriander-crusted venison and sautéed skate. ✉ *2928 Rte. 30, 7 mi north of Manchester Center, Dorset* ☎ *802/867–5715 or 800/769–4903* ☰ *MC, V* ⊗ *Closed Tues. and Wed.*

$$$–$$$$ ✕ **Mistral's.** This classic French restaurant is tucked in a grotto off Route 11/30 on the climb to Bromley Mountain. The two dining rooms are perched over the Bromley Brook, and at night, lights magically illuminate a small waterfall. Ask for a window table. Specialties include chateaubriand béarnaise and rack of lamb with rosemary for two. Chef Dana Markey's crispy sweetbreads Dijonnaise are a favorite. ✉ *10 Toll Gate Rd.* ☎ *802/362–1779* ☰ *AE, DC, MC, V* ⊗ *Closed Wed. No lunch.*

$$–$$$$ ✕ **Bistro Henry.** This landmark building on the outskirts of town attracts a devoted clientele for its authentic Mediterranean fare. The menu lists fresh fish, seasonal game, and eclectic dishes such as rare tuna with wasabi and soy. The wine list is extensive. Order before 6:30 PM and enjoy a three-course prix-fixe dinner for $24.75. ✉ *1942 Rte. 11/30, 3 mi east of Manchester Center* ☎ *802/362–4982* ☰ *AE, D, DC, MC, V* ⊗ *Closed Mon. May–Oct.; closed Sun. and Mon. Nov.–Apr. No lunch.*

$–$$$ ✕ **Perfect Wife.** Owner-chef Amy Chamberlain, the self-proclaimed aspiring flawless spouse, creates such freestyle cuisine as turkey schnitzel and grilled venison with a caramelized shallot and dried cranberry demi-glace. The casual upstairs tavern serves burgers and potpies, along with Vermont microbrews on tap. Reservations are recommended for the dining room. ✉ *2594 Depot St. (Rte. 11/30), 2½ mi east of Manchester Center* ☎ *802/362–2817* ☰ *AE, D, MC, V* ⊗ *Closed Sun. No lunch.*

$$$$ ✕⌂ **The Equinox.** Commanding center stage in Manchester Village, this expansive white-columned hotel is truly grand. The high-ceilinged common areas and sunny, spacious rooms are furnished with antique reproductions. With Windsor chairs and Tartan wallpaper, the Marsh Tavern feels like a traditional Colonial pub. Next door, the exclusive Orvis Inn defines elegance: nine suites have marble baths, kitchens, and luxurious room appointments. Both the Colonnade dining room and its Sunday brunch, served noon–2:30, are spectacular. The Avanyu Spa offers a full menu of treatments. ✉ *3567 Main St. (Rte. 7A), 05254* ☎ *802/362–4700 or 888/367–7625* 📠 *802/362–4861* ⊕ *equinox.rockresorts.com* ⇝ *154 rooms, 29 suites* ⌂ *3 restaurants, cable TV, 18-hole golf course, 3 tennis courts, spa, cross-country skiing, ice-skating, snowmobiling, bar, meeting rooms* ☰ *AE, D, DC, MC, V.*

$$$–$$$$ 🏠 **1811 House.** Step into this restored 18th-century inn, and you're car-
Fodor'sChoice ried back 200 years. The sitting rooms and pub are paneled with rich,
★ dark wood and decorated with hand-stenciled walls, Oriental rugs, and
fine paintings. Behind the bar are 92 varieties of single-malt scotch, avail-
able to guests on the honor system. Outside, 7 acres of lawn and Eng-
lish gardens drop gently down to a golf course. Rooms contain period
antiques and original artwork; six have fireplaces and eight have four-
poster beds. ✉ *Rte. 7A* 📬 *Box 39, 05254* ☎ *802/362–1811 or 800/
432–1811* 📠 *802/362–2443* ⊕ *www.1811house.com* 🛏 *11 rooms, 2
suites* 🍴 *Pub, video game room; no TV in some rooms, no kids under
16* ☰ *AE, MC, V* 🍴 *BP.*

$$$–$$$$ 🏠 **Wilburton Inn.** Overlooking the Battenkill Valley, this turn-of-the-20th-
century Tudor mansion has 11 lovingly furnished bedrooms and suites,
and richly paneled common rooms decorated with part of the owners'
vast art collection. Five guest buildings are spread over the grounds, dot-
ted with sculpture. Twelve rooms have private decks with mountain views,
and 10 have fireplaces. The dining room is an elegant affair, with a menu
to match the surroundings. Entrées might include poached Maine lob-
ster with gnocchi or a roasted antelope chop with bordelaise sauce. One
note: weddings take place here most summer weekends. ✉ *River Rd.,
05254* ☎ *802/362–2500 or 800/648–4944* 📠 *802/362–1107* ⊕ *www.
wilburton.com* 🛏 *30 rooms, 4 suites* 🍴 *Restaurant, some microwaves,
cable TV, 3 tennis courts, pool* ☰ *AE, MC, V* 🍴 *BP.*

$–$$ 🏠 **Aspen Motel.** A rare find in this area, the immaculate, family-owned
Aspen is set well back from the highway and moderately priced. The
spacious, tastefully decorated rooms have Colonial-style furnishings. The
Birches cottage has two bedrooms and a fully equipped kitchen. ✉ *5699
Main St., 05255* ☎ *802/362–2450* 📠 *802/362–1348* ⊕ *www.
thisisvermont.com/aspen* 🛏 *24 rooms, 1 cottage* 🍴 *Some refrigerators, cable TV, some in-room DVDs, pool* ☰ *AE, D, MC, V.*

Nightlife & the Arts

The two pre–Revolutionary War barns of the **Dorset Playhouse** (✉ Off
town green, Dorset ☎ 802/867–5777) host a community group in winter and a resident professional troupe in summer. The **Marsh Tavern**
(☎ 802/362–4700) at the Equinox (⇨ Where to Stay & Eat) hosts folk
music and jazz from Thursday to Sunday in summer and on weekends
in winter. The **Perfect Wife** (✉ 2594 Depot St. [Rte. 11/30] ☎ 802/362–
2817) hosts live music in its tavern on Friday.

B. B. King, Lynyrd Skynyrd, and the Vermont Symphony Orchestra
have all played at **Riley Rink at Hunter Park** (✉ 410 Hunter Park Rd. ☎ 802/
362–0150 ⊕ www.hunterpark.com) during its summer concert series.

Near Bromley Mountain, **Johnny Seesaw's** (✉ 3574 Rte. 11 ☎ 802/824–
5533) is a classic rustic ski lodge, with live music on weekends and an
excellent "comfort food" menu. Closed April through Memorial Day.

Sports & the Outdoors

BIKING **Battenkill Sports** (✉ 1240 Depot St. [U.S. 7, Exit 4] ☎ 802/362–2734
or 800/340–2734) rents and repairs bikes and provides maps and route
suggestions.

FISHING **Battenkill Anglers** (✉ 6204 Main St., Manchester ☎ 802/379–1444) teaches the art and science of fly-fishing in both private and group lessons. The **Orvis Co.** (✉ Rte. 7A, Manchester Center ☎ 800/235–9763) hosts a nationally known fly-fishing school on the Battenkill, the state's most famous trout stream, with 2- and 2½-day courses offered weekly between June and October.

HIKING One of the most popular segments of Vermont's **Long Trail** starts from a parking lot on Route 11/30 and goes to the top of Bromley Mountain. The 6-mi round-trip trek takes about four hours. The **Mountain Goat** (✉ 4886 Main St. ☎ 802/362–5159) sells hiking and backpacking equipment and rents snowshoes and cross-country and telemark skis.

STATE PARK **Emerald Lake State Park** (✉ U.S. 7, North Dorset ☎ 802/362–1655), 9 mi north of Manchester, has a small beach, marked nature trail, an on-site naturalist, boat and canoe rentals, and a snack bar.

Shopping

ART & ANTIQUES Vermont-based artists display their oils, watercolors, and sculptures at **Gallery North Star** (✉ 3962 Main St. ☎ 802/362–4541). **Long Ago and Far Away** (✉ 4963 Main St. ☎ 802/362–3435) specializes in fine indigenous artwork, including Canadian Inuit stone sculpture. The large **Tilting at Windmills Gallery** (✉ 24 Highland Ave. ☎ 802/362–3022) displays and sells the paintings and sculpture of nationally known artists.

In Manchester Village, **Frog Hollow at Equinox** (✉ 3566 Main St. [Rte. 7A] ☎ 802/362–3321) sells such contemporary works as jewelry, glassware, and home furnishings from Vermont artisans.

BOOKS **Northshire Bookstore** (✉4869 Main St. ☎802/362–2200 or 800/437–3700) is a huge independently owned bookseller with a large children's section. Connected to the bookstore is the Spiral Press Café, where you can sit for a grilled pesto chicken on focaccia bread sandwich or a latte and scone.

CLOTHING Following L. L. Bean's model, the two-story **Orvis Flagship Store** (✉4200 Rte. 7A ☎ 802/362–3750), full of Orvis's latest clothing and accessories, feels like a large lodge and has an on-site trout pond.

MALLS & **Manchester Designer Outlets** (✉ U.S. 7 and Rte. 11/30 ☎ 802/362–3736
MARKETPLACES or 800/955–7467) line the streets in town and have such big-city names as Escada, Versace, Coach, Ralph Lauren, and Coldwater Creek.

Stratton

❻ *18 mi southeast of Manchester.*

Stratton is home to the exclusive Stratton Mountain Resort and has a self-contained town center with shops, restaurants, and lodgings clustered at the base of the slopes. When the snow melts, golf, tennis, and a host of other summer activities are big attractions, but the village remains quiet.

Where to Stay & Eat

$$–$$$$ ✕▦ **Three Mountain Inn.** A 1780s tavern, this inn in downtown Jamaica,
Fodor'sChoice 10 mi northeast of Stratton, feels authentically Colonial, from the wide
★ paneling to the low ceilings. Rooms are appointed with a blend of Colonial and modern furnishings, including featherbeds. Most rooms have

fireplaces and mountain views, and three have private decks. Dinner at the inn is a high point. The dining room ($$$$; closed Monday and Tuesday) serves a $55 five-course prix-fixe menu on Saturday that might include such entrées as infused roasted lobster or leek, potato, and hazelnut cakes. ☒ *Rte. 30, Jamaica 05343* ☎ *802/874–4140 or 800/532–9399* ⊕ *www.threemountaininn.com* ↻ *13 rooms, 1 suite, 1 cottage* ☐ *Restaurant, some in-room VCRs; no TV in some rooms* ⊟ *MC, V* ⧫○⧫ *BP.*

$$–$$$$ ☐ **Long Trail House.** This large complex is the newest property at Stratton Mountain. Within walking distance of the lifts, the lodge has well-equipped, nicely furnished studio to two-bedroom units. Ski packages that include lift tickets bring down room rates. ☒ *Middle Ridge Rd., 05155* ☎ *802/297–2200 or 800/787–2886* ⊕ *www.stratton.com* ↻ *100 units* ☐ *Kitchens, cable TV, in-room VCRs, pool, 3 outdoor hot tubs, sauna* ⊟ *AE, DC, MC, V.*

$$–$$$ ☐ **Red Fox Inn.** Tom and Cindy Logan's "white house," in an open meadow just 4 mi from Stratton and 8 mi from Bromley, provides pleasant and comfortable accommodations. Each room has a private bath, and the suite has a fireplace and hot tub. Dinner is served nightly in the restaurant next door; a full roster of entertainment in the Tavern includes Irish and folk music, as well as rock and roll. A special 50%-off room rate is offered Sunday–Thursday. ☒ *Winhall Hollow Rd., Bondville 05340* ☎ *802/297–2488* 🖶 *802/297–2156* ⊕ *www.redfoxinn.com* ↻ *8 rooms, 1 suite* ☐ *Restaurant, bar; no a/c, no room TVs* ⊟ *AE, MC, V.*

Nightlife & the Arts

Popular **Mulligan's** (☒ Mountain Rd. ☎ 802/297–9293) hosts bands or DJs in the late afternoon and on weekends in winter. Year-round, the **Red Fox Inn** (☒ Winhall Hollow Rd., Bondville ☎ 802/297–2488) hosts Irish music Wednesday night; an open mike Thursday night; and rock and roll at other times.

Ski Areas

STRATTON MOUNTAIN Sophisticated, exclusive Stratton is a popular destination for affluent families and young professionals from the New York–southern Connecticut corridor. An entire village, with a covered parking structure for 700 cars, is at the base of the mountain. Adjacent to the base lodge are a condo-hotel, restaurants, and about 25 shops lining a pedestrian mall. Stratton is 4 mi up its own access road off Route 30 in Bondville, about 30 minutes from Manchester's popular shopping zone.

Downhill. Stratton prides itself on its immaculate grooming, making it excellent for cruising. The lower part of the mountain is beginner to low-intermediate, served by several chairlifts. The upper mountain is served by several high-speed quads and a 12-passenger gondola. Down the face are the expert trails, and on either side are intermediate cruising runs with a smattering of wide beginner slopes. The third sector, the Sun Bowl, is off to one side with 2 high-speed, six-passenger lifts and 2 expert trails, a full base lodge, and plenty of intermediate terrain. Snowmaking covers 85% of the terrain. Every March, Stratton hosts the U.S. Open Snowboarding championships; its snowboard park has a 380-foot half pipe. A Ski Learning Park provides its own

Park Packages for novice skiers. In all, Stratton has 11 lifts that service 90 trails and 90 acres of glades.

Cross-country. The resort has more than 30 km (18 mi) of cross-country skiing and two Nordic centers: Sun Bowl and Country Club.

Summer and year-round activities. Stratton has 15 outdoor tennis courts, 27 holes of golf, horseback riding, hiking accessed by a gondola to the summit, and instructional programs in tennis and golf. The sports center, open year-round, contains two indoor tennis courts, three racquetball courts, a 25-meter indoor swimming pool, a hot tub, a steam room, a fitness facility with Nautilus equipment, and a restaurant. Stratton also hosts summer entertainment and family activities, including a climbing wall.

⌖ *R.R. 1, Box 145, Stratton Mountain 05155* ☎ *802/297–2200, 802/297–4211 snow conditions, 800/787–2886 lodging* ⊕ *www.stratton.com.*

Weston

➐ *17 mi north of Stratton.*

Best known for the Vermont Country Store, Weston was one of the first Vermont towns to discover its own intrinsic loveliness—and marketability. With its summer theater, pretty town green with a Victorian bandstand, and an assortment of shops, the little village really lives up to its vaunted image.

Where to Stay & Eat

$$$–$$$$ ✕▥ **Inn at Weston.** Highlighting the country elegance of this 1848 inn, a short walk from the Vermont Country Store and Weston Playhouse, is innkeeper Bob Aldrich's collection of 500 orchid species—rare and beautiful specimens surround the dining table in the gazebo and others enrich the indoors. Rooms in the inn, carriage house, and Coleman House (across the street) are comfortably appointed, and some have fireplaces. The restaurant ($$$–$$$$; closed Monday) serves contemporary regional cuisine amid candlelight. Vermont cheddar cheese and Granny Smith–apple omelets are popular choices for breakfast. ⊠ *Rte. 100* ⌖ *Box 66, 05161* ☎ *802/824–6789* 🖷 *802/824–3073* ⊕ *www.innweston.com* ⇆ *13 rooms* ⌂ *Restaurant, some in-room hot tubs, pub; no TV in some rooms, no kids under 12* ▭ *AE, DC, MC, V* ⫶⊙⫶ *BP.*

$ ▥ **Colonial House Inn & Motel.** You'll find warmth and charm at this family-friendly complex just 2 mi south of the village. Relax on comfortable furniture in the large living room or enjoy the sun in the solarium. Homey, country furnishings adorn both of the two inn rooms and the motel units. The complimentary breakfast includes fresh goodies from the family-owned bakery; a family-style dinner is served Thursday–Saturday nights. ⊠ *287 Rte. 100, 05161* ☎ *802/824–6286 or 800/639–5033* 🖷 *802/824–3934* ⊕ *www.cohoinn.com* ⇆ *9 motel units, 6 inn rooms without bath* ⌂ *Restaurant; no a/c, no TV in some rooms* ▭ *D, MC, V* ⫶⊙⫶ *BP, MAP.*

Nightlife & the Arts

The members of the **Weston Playhouse** (⊠ Village Green off Rte. 100 ☎ 802/824–5288 ⊕ www.westonplayhouse.org), the oldest professional theater in Vermont, produce Broadway plays, musicals, and other works. Their season runs from late June to early September. Also in summer, the **Kinhaven Music School** (⊠ 354 Lawrence Hill Rd. ☎ 802/824–4332) stages free student concerts on Friday at 4 and Sunday at 2:30. Faculty concerts are Saturday at 8 PM.

Shopping

The **Todd Gallery** (⊠ 614 Main St. ☎ 802/824–5606 ⊕ www.toddgallery.com) exhibits paintings, prints, and sculptures by Vermont artists and craftspeople. The gallery is open Thursday–Monday 10–5.

The **Vermont Country Store** (⊠ Rte. 100 ☎ 802/824–3184 ⊕ www.vermontcountrystore.com) sets aside one room of its old-fashioned emporium for Vermont Common Crackers and bins of fudge and other candy. The retail store and its mail-order catalog carry nearly forgotten items such as Lilac Vegetol aftershave and horehound drops, and practical items such as sturdy outdoor clothing and even typewriters. Nostalgia-evoking implements dangle from the store's walls and ceiling. (There's another store on Route 103 in Rockingham.)

Ludlow

8 *9 mi northeast of Weston.*

Ludlow was once a nondescript factory town that just happened to have a small ski area—Okemo. Today, that ski area is one of Vermont's largest and most popular resorts, and downtown Ludlow is a collection of restored buildings with shops and restaurants.

Where to Stay & Eat

$$–$$$ ✕ **Bear Creek Mountain Club.** A private ski club, the elegant clubhouse with mahogany doors and marble counters opens to the public at night for dinner (and for lunch from mid-December through March). A cathedral ceiling in the upstairs dining room gives an open, airy feel. The menu features such creations as cannelloni stuffed with butternut squash and grilled gingered pork tenderloin. Ski it off the next day with a $75 guest pass. A more economical tavern menu of burgers and salads is available downstairs. ⊠ *Rte. 100, 9 mi north of Ludlow, Plymouth* ☎ *802/672–4242* ▤ *MC, V* ⊗ *No dinner Sun.–Tues. mid-Dec.–Mar., Sun.–Wed. Apr.–mid-Dec. No lunch Mon. and Tues. Apr.–mid-Dec.*

$–$$$ ✕ **Cappuccino's.** Decorated somewhat like a Laura Ashley showroom, this downtown restaurant serves mostly Italian fare. Pasta dishes include Pasta Pink, which is loaded with crabmeat and shrimp in a sherry cream tomato sauce, and Pasta Balsamic, with chicken and tomatoes. ⊠ *41 Depot St.* ☎ *802/228–7566* ▤ *MC, V* ⊗ *No lunch.*

$–$$ ✕ **Harry's.** This casual roadside restaurant, about 5 mi northwest of Ludlow, is an oasis of eclectic food. The menu ranges from such traditional contemporary entrées as pork tenderloin to Mexican dishes. The large and tasty burrito, made with fresh cilantro and black beans, is one of the best bargains around. Chef-owner Trip Pearce also owns Little Harry's in Rutland. ⊠ *Rte. 103, Mount Holly* ☎ *802/259–2996* ▤ *AE, MC, V* ⊗ *Closed Mon. and Tues. No lunch.*

$$-$$$$ ⌂ **Andrie Rose Inn.** One block from Main Street, this 1829 inn has several sitting rooms and small dining rooms decorated in a country floral motif. Accommodations range from lavishly appointed rooms with whirlpool tubs in the main lodge to full-floor condo suites sleeping 12 in a Victorian townhouse of 1883. Luxury suites in the 1840 Solitude building have whirlpool tubs, fireplaces, and steam showers for two. Breakfast in a candlelit dining room is included in standard rooms; a breakfast basket is delivered to the luxury suites. A four-course dinner with a seasonal menu is served Friday and Saturday. ✉ *13 Pleasant St., 05149* ☎ *802/228–4846 or 800/223–4846* 🖷 *802/228–7910* ⊕ *www. andrieroseinn.com* ⇄ *9 rooms, 10 suites* ⌂ *Restaurant, some microwaves, some refrigerators, some cable TV, bicycles, bar; no a/c in some rooms, no phones in some rooms* ⊟ *AE, V* ⍀ *BP.*

$$-$$$$ ⌂ **Jackson Gore Inn.** This slope-side lodge is the centerpiece of Okemo's newest base village. The inn has regular hotel rooms, as well as studio to three-bedroom units, each with fireplace and full kitchen. At one end of the inn are three restaurants, including the excellent Coleman Brook Tavern, where ski-boot-wearing diners sit at linen-draped tables. Ask about ski-and-stay packages. ✉ *Okemo Ridge Rd. off Rte. 103, 05149* ☎ *802/228–1400 or 800/786–5366* 🖷 *802/228–1410* ⊕ *www.okemo. com* ⇄ *178 units* ⌂ *3 restaurants, kitchens, in-room VCRs, pool, gym, hot tub, sauna, bar* ⊟ *AE, MC, V.*

Sports & the Outdoors

Cavendish Trail Horse Rides (✉ 20 Mile Stream Rd., Proctorsville ☎ 802/226–7821) operates horse-drawn sleigh rides in snowy weather, wagon rides at other times, and guided trail rides from mid-May to mid-October.

Ski Areas

OKEMO
MOUNTAIN
RESORT
Family-owned Okemo has evolved into a major year-round resort, now with two base areas. Known for its wide, well-groomed trails, it's a favorite among intermediates. The Jackson Gore expansion, a new base village north of Ludlow off Route 103, opened in November 2003, has an inn, restaurants, a child-care center, and shops. The resort offers numerous ski and snowboarding packages.

Downhill. At 2,200 feet, Okemo has the highest vertical drop of any resort in southern Vermont. The beginner trails extend above both base areas, with more challenging terrain higher on the mountains. Intermediate trails are the theme here, but experts will find steep trails and glades at Jackson Gore and on the South Face. Of the 113 trails, 42% have an intermediate rating, 33% are rated novice, and 25% are rated for experts. They are served by an efficient system of 18 lifts, including 9 quads, 3 triple chairlifts, and 6 surface lifts; 95% are covered by snowmaking. Okemo has four terrain parks for skiers and snowboarders, including one for beginners; two 400-foot-long Superpipes, and a mini half pipe.

Cross-country skiing/snowshoeing. The **Okemo Valley Nordic Center** (✉ Fox La. ☎ 802/228–1396) has 26 km (16 mi) of groomed cross-country trails and 10 km (6 mi) of dedicated snowshoe trails, and rents equipment.

Summer activities. The Okemo Valley Golf Club has an 18-hole, par-70, 6,400-yard, Heathland-style course. Seven target greens, four putting greens, a golf academy, an indoor putting green, swing stations, and a simulator provide plenty of ways to improve your game year-round. In 2004 the resort added the 9-hole **Tater Hill Golf Course** (✉ 6802 Popple Dungeon Rd., Windham ☎ 802/875–2517) to its holdings.

✉ *77 Okemo Ridge Rd.* ☎ *802/228–4041, 802/228–5222 snow conditions, 800/786–5366 lodging* ⊕ *www.okemo.com.*

Chester

⑨ *13 mi southeast of Ludlow.*

At the junction of Routes 11 and 103, Chester is the town that time forgot. Gingerbread Victorians line the town green, the local pharmacy on Main Street has been in continuous operation since the 1860s, and the hardware store across from the train station is a living time machine. It opened in 1858.

From the Chester Depot, dating from 1852, you can board the **Green Mountain Flyer** for a two-hour round-trip journey to Bellows Falls. The cars date from railroading's golden age, and the route passes covered bridges and through the Brockway Mills gorge. Fall foliage trips are spectacular. ✉ *Rte. 103* ☎ *802/463–3069 or 800/707–3530* ⊕ *www.railsvt.com* ✉ *$14* ☉ *Late June–mid-Sept., Tues.–Sun.; mid-Sept.–late-Oct., daily. Call for schedule.*

Where to Stay & Eat

$-$$ ✕ **Raspberries and Thyme.** Breakfast specials, homemade soups, a large selection of salads, homemade desserts, and a menu listing more than 40 sandwiches make this one of the area's most popular spots for casual dining. ✉ *On the green* ☎ *802/875–4486* ▬ *AE, D, MC, V* ☉ *No dinner Tues.*

$-$$$ ⌂ **Chester House Inn.** All of the rooms in this handsomely restored 1780 historic inn on the green have private baths. Five have gas fireplaces, and three have hot tubs or steam showers. Breakfast is served in the elegant Keeping Room, which has a fireplace. ✉ *266 Main St., 05143* ☎ *802/875–2205 or 888/875–2205* ⊕ *www.chesterhouseinn.com* ⇆ *7 rooms* △ *Some in-room hot tubs, bar; no room TVs* ▬ *DC, MC, V* ⍓*BP.*

Shopping

More than 125 dealers sell antiques and country crafts at **Stone House Antique and Craft Center** (✉ Rte. 103 S ☎ 802/875–4477).

Grafton

★ ⑩ *8 mi south of Chester.*

Out-of-the-way Grafton is as much a historical museum as a town. During its heyday, citizens grazed some 10,000 sheep and spun their wool into sturdy yarn for locally woven fabric. When the market for wool declined, so did Grafton. Then in 1963, the Windham Foundation—Vermont's second-largest private foundation—commenced the town's rehabilitation. Not only was the Old Tavern preserved, but many other commercial and residential structures in the village center were as well. The **Historical Society** documents the town's renewal. ⊠ *Main St. (Rte. 121)* ☎ *802/843–1010* ⌚ *$3* ⊙ *Memorial Day–Columbus Day, weekends and holidays 10–noon and 2–4.*

Where to Stay & Eat

$$$–$$$$ ✕⊞ **Old Tavern at Grafton.** Two-story white-column porches wrap around the main building of this commanding 1801 inn. In the main building are 11 guest rooms; the rest are dispersed among six other close-by buildings. Two dining rooms ($$$–$$$$), one with formal Georgian furniture, the other with rustic paneling and low beams, serve inspired continental fare. The inn runs the nearby Grafton Ponds Cross-Country Ski Center. ⊠ *Rte. 121, 05146* ☎ *802/843–2231 or 800/843–1801* 🖶 *802/843–2245* ⊕ *www.old-tavern.com* ➷ *46 rooms, 8 suites* ♿ *2 restaurants, Wi-Fi, tennis court, pond, mountain bikes, paddle tennis, cross-country skiing, ice-skating, bar, meeting rooms; no a/c in some rooms, no room TVs* ☱ *AE, MC, V* ⊙ *Closed Apr.* ⍾ *BP.*

Shopping

Gallery North Star (⊠ 151 Townshend Rd. ☎ 802/843–2465) exhibits the oils, watercolors, lithographs, and sculptures of Vermont-based artists. Sample the best of Vermont cheddar at the **Grafton Village Cheese Company** (⊠ 533 Townshend Rd. ☎ 802/843–2221).

Townshend

⓫ *9 mi south of Grafton.*

One of a string of pretty villages along the banks of the West River, Townshend embodies the Vermont ideal of a lovely town green presided over by a gracefully proportioned church spire. The spire belongs to the 1790 Congregational Meeting House, one of the state's oldest houses of worship. Just north on Route 30 is the Scott Bridge (closed to traffic), the state's longest single-span covered bridge.

OFF THE BEATEN PATH **NEWFANE –** With a village green surrounded by pristine white buildings, Newfane, 6 mi southeast of Townshend, is sometimes described as the quintessential New England small town. The 1839 First Congregational Church and the Windham County Court House, with 17 green-shuttered windows and a rounded cupola, are often open. The building with the four-pointed spire is Union Hall, built in 1832.

Where to Stay & Eat

¢–$ ✕ **Townshend Dam Diner.** Folks come from miles around to enjoy traditional fare such as Mom's meat loaf, chili, and roast beef croquettes, as well as Townshend-raised bison burgers, and creative daily specials. Breakfast, served all day every day, includes such tasty treats as raspberry chocolate-chip walnut pancakes and homemade French toast. ⊠ *Rte. 30* ☎ *802/874–4107* ☱ *No credit cards* ⊙ *Closed Tues.*

$$$$ ✕⊞ **Windham Hill Inn.** Period antiques, Oriental carpets, and locally
Fodor'sChoice made furniture are hallmarks of this 1825 brick farmhouse and white
★ barn annex at the end of a country road. Most rooms have fireplaces; all have magnificent views of the West River valley. A prix-fixe, four-course candlelight dinner ($$$–$$$$; à la carte menu also available) is served

in the Frog Pond Dining Room. The chef will prepare a picnic lunch upon request. ✉ *311 Lawrence Dr., West Townshend 05359* ☎ *802/874–4080 or 800/944–4080* 🖷 *802/874–4702* ⊕ *www.windhamhill.com* ⌁ *21 rooms* ⌂ *Restaurant, tennis court, pool, hiking, cross-country skiing, ice-skating; no room TVs, no kids under 12* ▭ *AE, D, MC, V* ⦿ *BP.*

$$–$$$$ ✕⌨ **Four Columns Inn.** Rooms and suites in this white-columned, 1834 Greek-revival mansion were designed for luxurious romantic getaways. Some of the suites have cathedral ceilings; all have gas fireplaces and double whirlpool baths, and one has a rain shower. The elegant restaurant ($$$–$$$$; closed Tuesday) serves new American cuisine. ✉ *On the green, 6 mi southeast of Townshend, Newfane* ⬠ *Box 278, 05345* ☎ *802/365–7713 or 800/787–6633* 🖷 *802/365–0022* ⊕ *www.fourcolumnsinn.com* ⌁ *6 rooms, 9 suites* ⌂ *Restaurant, pool, hiking, bar, Internet room, some pets allowed (fee); no TV in some rooms* ▭ *AE, DC, MC, V* ⦿ *BP.*

¢–$ ⌨ **Boardman House.** This handsome Greek-revival home on the town green combines modern comfort with the relaxed charm of a 19th-century farmhouse. The uncluttered guest rooms are furnished with Shaker-style furniture, colorful duvets, and paintings. Both the breakfast room and front hall have trompe l'oeil floors. ✉ *On the green, 05353* ☎ *802/365–4086* ⌁ *5 rooms, 1 suite* ⌂ *Sauna; no TV in some rooms* ▭ *No credit cards* ⦿ *BP.*

Sports & the Outdoors

You can rent canoes, kayaks, tubes, cross-country skis, and snowshoes at **Townshend Outdoors** (✉ Rte. 30 ☎ 802/365–7309).

At **Townshend State Park,** you'll find a sandy beach on the West River and a trail that parallels the river for 2½ mi, topping out on Bald Mountain Dam. Up the dam, the trail follows switchbacks literally carved into the stone apron. ✉ *Rte. 30 N* ☎ *802/365–7500.*

Shopping

The **Big Black Bear Shop** (✉ Rte. 30 ☎ 888/758–2327) at Mary Meyer Stuffed Toys Factory, the state's oldest stuffed toy company, offers discounts of up to 70% on stuffed animals of all sizes. The **Newfane Country Store** (✉ Rte. 30, Newfane ☎ 802/365–7916) carries many quilts (which can also be custom ordered), homemade fudge, and other Vermont foods, gifts, and crafts.

Southern Vermont A to Z

To research prices, get advice from other travelers, and book travel arrangements, visit www.fodors.com.

BUS TRAVEL

Vermont Transit links Bennington, Manchester, and Brattleboro.
🚌 Bus Information **Vermont Transit** ☎ 800/552-8737 ⊕ www.vermonttransit.com.

CAR TRAVEL

In the south the principal east–west highway is twisty Route 9, the Molly Stark Trail, from Brattleboro to Bennington. The most important north–south roads are U.S. 7; the more scenic Route 7A; Route 100, which runs through the state's center; Interstate 91; and U.S. 5, which runs along the state's eastern border. Route 30 from Brattleboro to Manchester is a scenic drive.

EMERGENCIES

🏥 Hospitals **Brattleboro Memorial Hospital** ⊠ 17 Belmont Ave., Brattleboro ☎ 802/257-0341. **Southwestern Vermont Medical Center** ⊠ 100 Hospital Dr., Bennington ☎ 802/442-6361.

VISITOR INFORMATION

🏥 **Bennington Area Chamber of Commerce** ⊠ Veterans Memorial Dr., Bennington 05201 ☎ 802/447-3311 or 800/229-0252 ⊕ www.bennington.com. **Brattleboro Area Chamber of Commerce** ⊠ 180 Main St., Brattleboro 05301 ☎ 802/254-4565 or 877/254-4565 ⊕ www.brattleborochamber.org. **Chamber of Commerce, Manchester and the Mountains** ⊠ 5046 Main St., Manchester 05255 ☎ 802/362-2100 or 800/362-4144 ⊕ www.manchestervermont.net. **Mt. Snow Valley Chamber of Commerce** ⊠ W. Main St. ☐ Box 3, Wilmington 05363 ☎ 802/464-8092 or 877/887-6884 ⊕ www.visitvermont.com.

CENTRAL VERMONT

Central Vermont's economy once centered on marble quarrying and mills. But today, as in much of the rest of the state, tourism drives the economic engine. The center of the dynamo is Killington, the East's largest downhill resort. However, central Vermont has more to discover than high-speed chairlifts and slope-side condos. The old mills of Quechee and Middlebury are now home to restaurants and shops, giving wonderful views of the waterfalls that once powered the mill turbines. Woodstock has upscale shops and America's newest national historic park. Away from these settlements, the protected (except for occasional logging) lands of the Green Mountain National Forest are laced with hiking trails.

Our coverage of towns begins with Norwich, on U.S. 5 near Interstate 91 at the state's eastern edge; winds westward toward U.S. 7; then continues north to Middlebury before heading over the spine of the Green Mountains to Waitsfield.

Norwich

🔟 *6 mi north of White River Junction.*

On the shores of the Connecticut River, Norwich has beautifully kept 18th- and 19th-century homes surrounding a handsome green. Numerous hands-on exhibits in the **Montshire Museum of Science** explore nature and technology. Kids can make giant bubbles, watch fish and turtles swim in giant aquariums, explore wind, and wander a maze of outdoor trails by the river. An ideal destination for a rainy day, this is one of the finest museums in New England. ⊠ *1 Montshire Rd.* ☎ *802/649-2200* ⊕ *www.montshire.org* 🎫 *$7.50* ⊙ *Daily 10-5.*

FodorsChoice
★

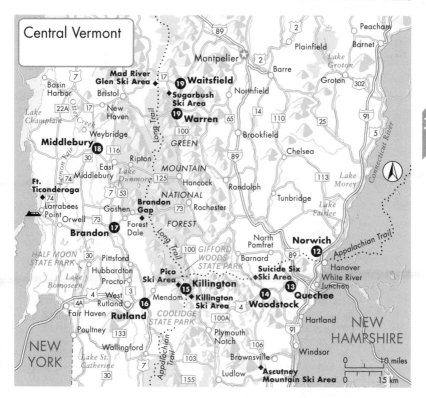

Central Vermont

Shopping

The shelves at **King Arthur Flour Baker's Store** (⊠ 135 Rte. 5 S ☎ 802/649–3881 or 800/827–6836) are stocked with all the ingredients and tools in the company's Baker's Catalogue, including flours, mixes, and local jams and syrups. The bakery has a viewing area where you can watch products being made.

Quechee

⓭ *11 mi southwest of Norwich, 6 mi west of White River Junction.*

A historic mill town, Quechee sits just upriver from its namesake gorge, an impressive 165-foot deep canyon cut by the Ottauquechee River. Most people view the gorge from U.S. 4. To escape the crowds, hike along the gorge or scramble down one of several trails to the river.

The main attraction in the village is **Simon Pearce,** a glassblowing factory that an Irish glassmaker by the same name set up in 1981 in a restored woolen mill by a waterfall. Water power still drives the factory's furnace. Visitors may take a free self-guided tour of the factory floor and see the glassblowers at work. The store in the mill sells contemporary glass and ceramic tableware and home furnishings, such as glass lamps and clocks. Seconds and discontinued items are reduced 25%.

✉ *The Mill, 1760 Main St.* ☎ *802/295–2711* ⊕ *www.simonpearce.com* ⊗ *Store daily 9–9; factory Tues.–Sat. 9–9, Sun. and Mon. 9–5.*

☾ The **Vermont Institute of Natural Science (VINS) Nature Center,** next to Quechee Gorge, has 17 raptor exhibits, including bald eagles, peregrine falcons, and a variety of owls. All the caged birds have been found injured and unable to survive in the wild. Predators of the Sky, a 30-minute-long live bird program, starts daily at 11, 1, and 3:30. ✉ *Rte. 4* ☎ *802/ 359–5000* ⊕ *www.vinsweb.org* ✍ *$8* ⊗ *May–Oct., daily 9–5:30; Nov.–Apr., daily 10–4.*

Where to Stay & Eat

$$–$$$$

Fodor'sChoice

★

✕ **Simon Pearce.** Candlelight, sparkling glassware from the studio downstairs, exposed brick, and large windows overlooking the roaring Ottauquechee River create an ideal setting for contemporary American cuisine. Sesame-seared tuna with noodle cakes and wasabi as well as roast duck with mango chutney sauce are house specialties; the wine cellar holds several hundred vintages. The lunch menu might include a roasted duck quesadilla or Mediterranean lamb burger. ✉ *The Mill, 1760 Main St.* ☎ *802/295–1470* ▭ *AE, D, DC, MC, V* ⌣ *Reservations not accepted.*

$$–$$$$

✕▣ **Quechee Inn at Marshland Farm.** Each room in this handsomely restored 1793 country home is decorated with Queen Anne–style furnishings and period antiques. From the old barn, the inn runs bike and canoe rentals, a fly-fishing school, and kayak and canoe trips. Guests also have privileges at the Quechee Club, a private golf, tennis, and ski club. The dining room's ($$–$$$) creative entrées include shellfish bouillabaisse and rack of lamb with green peppercorn pesto. ✉ *Main St., 05059* ☎ *802/ 295–3133 or 800/235–3133* 🖷 *802/295–6587* ⊕ *www.quecheeinn. com* ⬎ *22 rooms, 2 suites* ♿ *Restaurant, cable TV, golf privileges, fishing, bicycles, cross-country skiing, meeting room* ▭ *AE, D, DC, MC, V* ▮○▮ *BP.*

Sports & the Outdoors

FISHING

The **Vermont Fly Fishing School/Wilderness Trails** (✉ 1119 Main St. ☎ 802/ 295–7620) leads workshops, rents fishing gear and mountain bikes, and arranges canoe and kayak trips. In winter, the company conducts cross-country and snowshoe treks.

POLO

Quechee Polo Club (✉ Dewey's Mill Rd. ½ mi north of U.S. 4 ☎ 802/ 295–7152) draws hundreds of spectators on summer Saturdays to its matches near the Quechee Gorge. Admission is $8 per carload.

Shopping

The 40 dealers at the **Hartland Antiques Center** (✉ U.S. 4 ☎ 802/457– 4745) stock furniture, paper items, china, glass, and collectibles. **Ottauquechee Valley Winery** (✉ 5967 Woodstock Rd. [U.S. 4] ☎ 802/295– 9463), in a historic 1870s barn complex, has a tasting room and sells fruit wines, such as apple and blueberry.

More than 350 dealers sell their wares at the **Quechee Gorge Village** (✉U.S. 4 ☎ 802/295–1550 or 800/438–5565), an antiques and crafts mall in an immense reconstructed barn that also houses a country store and a classic diner. A merry-go-round and a small-scale working railroad op-

Spa Vacations

VERMONT'S DESTINATION SPAS have come a long way since the days its *au natural* mineral springs attracted affluent 19th-century city dwellers looking to escape the heat, but the overall principle remains the same. The state remains a natural place to restore mind and body. Since 2003, three world-class new or renovated destination spas have opened, and several other inns are associated with day spas.

The **Equinox Resort's Avanyu Spa** (✉ Rte. 7A, Manchester ☎ 802/362-4700 ⊕ equinox.rockresorts.com), with mahogany doors, high-ceilings with Vermont wood beams, bead-board wainscoting, and a leaf motif throughout, feels like a friend's country estate. At one end is a NCAA-length indoor pool and outdoor hot tub, at the other end are the treatment rooms. The signature 80-minute Spirit of Vermont combines Reiki, reflexology, and massage. In the co-ed relaxation room, spa-goers can nestle into overstuffed chairs next to a two-sided fireplace made of Vermont gneiss. The locker rooms, with native verde marble accents and pottery-bowl wash basins, have showers, steamrooms, and saunas.

Stowe has two destination spas. The largest spa in New England, **Spa at Stoweflake** (✉ 1746 Mountain Rd. [Rte. 108], Stowe ☎ 802/760-1083 or 800/253-2232 ⊕ www.stoweflake.com) features a massaging hydrotherapeutic waterfall, a Hungarian mineral pool, 30 treatment rooms, a hair and nail salon, and 120 services, such as the Bingham Falls Renewal, named after a local waterfall. This treatment begins with a seasonal body scrub (e.g., immune

builder in winter) that's rinsed in a Vichy shower, followed by an aromatherapy oil massage. The spacious men's and women's sanctuaries and locker rooms have saunas, steamrooms, and jacuzzis.

Opened in early 2005, the **Spa at Topnotch** (✉ 4000 Mountain Rd. [Rte. 108], Stowe ☎ 802/253-8585 ⊕ www.topnotchresort.com) provides an aura of calm, with its birch wood doors and accents, hardwood floors, natural light, chrome fixtures, and cool colors. Signature services include a Vermont wildflower or woodspice treatment, which includes a warm herb wrap, exfoliation, and massage. Locker areas are spacious, with saunas, steamrooms, and jacuzzis. The spa also has a full-service salon.

Next door to the swank Pitcher Inn, the **Alta Day Spa** (✉ 247 Main St., Warren ☎ 802/496-2582 ⊕ www.altadayspa.com) is an Aveda concept spa offering massage, masques, wraps, and facials in four light, airy treatment rooms in a renovated 19th-century house. A two-night spa package through the inn might include daily manicures and hydrating pedicures, facials, and massages, plus lodging and breakfast.

At Killington, the **Woods Resort and Spa** (✉ 53 Woods La., Killington ☎ 802/422-3139 ⊕ www.woodsresortandspa.com) is a European spa within an upscale condo complex. At the resort's clubhouse, the spa has a 75-foot indoor pool, a sauna, steamroom, and weight room. Spa services include massages, hot stone therapies, facials, salt scrubs, maple-sugar polishes, and mud treatments.

3

erate when weather permits. The **Vermont Toy and Train Museum** is the latest addition.

Scotland by the Yard (✉ U.S. 4 ☎ 802/295–5351 or 800/295–5351) sells all things Scottish, from kilts to Harris tweed jackets and tartan ties.

Woodstock

★ ⑭ *4 mi west of Quechee.*

Woodstock is a Currier & Ives print come to life. Well-maintained Federal-style houses surround the tree-lined village green, which is not far from a covered bridge. The town owes much of its pristine appearance to the Rockefeller family's interest in historic preservation and land conservation, and to town native George Perkins Marsh, a congressman, diplomat, and conservationist who wrote the pioneering book *Man and Nature* in 1864 about man's use and abuse of the land. Only busy U.S. 4 detracts from the town's quaintness.

The **Billings Farm and Museum,** on the grounds of George Perkins Marsh's boyhood home, was founded by Frederick Billings in 1871 as a model dairy farm and is one of the oldest dairy farms in the country. Concerned about the loss of New England's forests to overgrazing, Billings planted thousands of trees and put into practice Marsh's conservationist farming ideas. Exhibits in the reconstructed Queen Anne farmhouse, school, general store, workshop, and former Marsh homestead demonstrate the lives and skills of early Vermont settlers. ✉ *Rte. 12, ½ mi north of Woodstock* ☎ *802/457–2355* ⊕ *www.billingsfarm.org* 💲 *$9.50* ☉ *May–late Oct., daily 10–5; call for winter holiday and weekend schedules.*

The 500-acre **Marsh-Billings-Rockefeller National Historical Park** is Vermont's only national park and the nation's first to focus on natural resource conservation and stewardship. The park encompasses the forest lands planned by Frederick Billings according to Marsh's principles, as well as Frederick Billings's mansion, gardens, and carriage roads. The entire property was the gift of Laurance S. Rockefeller, who lived here with his late wife, Mary, Billings's granddaughter. The residential complex is accessible by guided tour only, but you can explore the extensive network of carriage roads and trails on your own. ✉ *Rte. 12* ☎ *802/457–3368* 💲 *Tour $6* ☉ *May–Oct., mansion and garden tours 10–5; grounds daily dawn–dusk.*

OFF THE BEATEN PATH

PLYMOUTH NOTCH HISTORIC DISTRICT – U.S. president Calvin Coolidge was born and buried in Plymouth Notch, a town that shares his character: low-key and quiet. The perfectly preserved 19th-century buildings look more like a large farm than a town. In addition to the homestead—where "Silent Cal" was sworn in as president at 2:47 AM on August 3, 1923, after the sudden death of President Harding—there is a visitor center, a general store once run by Coolidge's father (a room above it was once used as the summer White House), a cheese factory, two large barns displaying agricultural equipment, and a one-room schoolhouse. Coolidge's grave is in the cemetery across Route 100A. ✉ *Rte. 100A, 6 mi south of U.S. 4, 1 mi east of Rte. 100* ☎ *802/672–*

house rotates up to reveal the TV). Six rooms have gas fireplaces, four have whirlpool baths. In the intimate slate-floored dining ($$–$$$$; closed Monday and Tuesday), choose either a four-course fixe dinner or order à la carte. ☒ 37 Butler Rd., 05751 ☎ 802/ 4293 or 800/435–8566 🖷 802/422–3406 ⊕ www.birchridge.com 0 rooms ♿ Restaurant, Wi-Fi, lounge; no a/c in some rooms, no under 12 ⊟ AE, D, MC, V ⊗ Closed May ¶◯ BP, MAP.

oods Resort & Spa. These clustered upscale two- and three-bed-town houses stand in wooded lots along a winding road lead-the spa. Most units have master baths with saunas and two-person pool tubs. Vaulted ceilings in the living rooms give an open, airy The resort has a private shuttle to the ski area. ☒ 53 Woods La., 1 ☎ 802/422–3139 or 800/642–1147 ⊕ www.woodsresortandspa. 107 units ♿ Kitchens, cable TV, in-room VCRs, tennis courts, or pool, gym, hot tub, spa, some pets allowed (fee); no a/c ⊟ AE, V.

htlife & the Arts

weekends, listen to live music and sip draft Guinness at the **Inn at Trail** (☒ U.S. 4 ☎ 802/775–7181). The **Nightspot Outback** (☒ Killing-Rd. ☎ 802/422–9885) serves all-you-can-eat pizza on Monday s in winter, and $2 Long Trail pints on Sunday. It's open year-round. ng ski season, the **Pickle Barrel Night Club** (☒ Killington Rd. ☎ 802/ 3035) has a band every happy hour on Friday and Saturday. After crowd moves downstairs for dancing, sometimes to big-name bands. tysomethings prefer to dance at the **Wobbly Barn** (☒ Killington Rd. 02/422–3392), open only during ski season.

rts & the Outdoors

Wheels Bike Shop (☒ Killington Rd. ☎ 802/422–3234) sells and rents les and has information on local mountain and bicycle routes.

Pond in **Gifford Woods State Park** (☒ Rte. 100, ½ mi north of U.S. 802/775–5354) is a terrific fishing spot.

s namesake resort, **Killington Golf Course** (☒ 4763 Killington Rd., 1 ☎ 802/422–6700) has a challenging 18-hole course. Greens fees 52 midweek and $57 weekends; carts run for $17.

Areas

gamountain," "Beast of the East," and plain "huge" are apt de-tions of Killington. The American Skiing Company operates Killing-nd its neighbor, Pico, and over the past several years has improved and snowmaking capabilities. Thanks to its extensive snowmaking m, the resort typically opens in October and the lifts often run into . Killington's après-ski activities are plentiful and have been rated in the East by the national ski magazines. With a single call to Killing-s hotline or a visit to its Web site, skiers can plan an entire vaca-choose accommodations, book air or railroad transportation, and nge for rental equipment and ski lessons. Killington ticket holders also ski at Pico: a shuttle connects the two areas.

nhill. It would probably take several weeks to test all 200 trails on even mountains of the Killington complex, even though all except

3773 ⊕ www.historicvermont.org/coolidge ⊗ Late-May–mid-Oct., daily 9:30–5.

Where to Stay & Eat

★ **$$–$$$$** ✕ **Prince & the Pauper.** Modern French and American fare with a Vermont accent is the focus of this candlelit Colonial restaurant. The grilled duck breast might have an Asian five-spice sauce; lamb and pork sausage in puff pastry comes with a honey-mustard sauce. A three-course prix-fixe menu is available for $43; a less-expensive bistro menu is available in the lounge. ☒ 24 Elm St. ☎ 802/457–1818 ⊟ AE, D, MC, V ⊗ No lunch.

★ **$$–$$$** ✕ **Barnard Inn.** The dining room in this 1796 brick farmhouse breathes 18th century, but the food is decidedly 21st century. Former San Francisco restaurant chef-owners Will Dodson and Ruth Schimmelpfennig create inventive four-course prix-fixe menus with delicacies such as beef carpaccio and pan-seared escolar in lemon-and-caper herb butter. In the back is a local favorite, Max's Tavern, which serves upscale pub fare such as beef with Gorgonzola mashed potatoes and panfried trout with almond beurre noisette. Reservations are required in the dining room. ☒ 5518 Rte. 12, 8 mi north of Woodstock, Barnard ☎ 802/234–9961 ⊟ AE, MC, V ⊗ Closed Sun. and Mon. No lunch.

$–$$$ ✕ **EastEnder Restaurant.** The moderately priced food has made this restaurant a popular addition to Woodstock dining. A seasonal menu includes such entrées as chicken schnitzel with snap peas in a lemon-and-caper butter sauce and seafood stew. A full bar serves Vermont microbrews on tap. ☒ 442 Woodstock Rd., in Gallery Pl. ☎ 802/457–9800 ⊟ AE, MC, V ⊗ Closed Mon. No lunch.

$–$$$ ✕ **Keeper's Café.** Creative, moderately priced fare draws customers from all over the region to this café. Chef Eli Morse's menus include such light fare as pancetta salad and fresh corn soup as well as such elaborate entrées as herb garlic roast chicken with a sherry caper sauce. Blackboard specials change daily. Housed inside a former general store, the small dining room feels relaxed, with locals table-hopping to chat with friends. ☒ Rte. 106, 12 mi south of Woodstock, Reading ☎ 802/484–9090 ⊟ AE, MC, V ⊗ Closed Sun. and Mon. No lunch.

$$$–$$$$ ✕🛏 **Jackson House Inn.** European antiques, Oriental rugs, and French-cut crystal fill the formal parlor and cozy library at this inn. One wing houses suites with gas fireplaces, down duvets, and thermal massage tubs; the other wing has the restaurant ($$$$) with a freestanding, stone fireplace. Noted for its creativity and for attracting rising young chefs from around the country (Food & Wine voted previous chef Graham Elliott Bowles one of the top 10 best new chefs in America in 2004), the kitchen is now run by Jason Merrill, a Vermont native and adherent of Slow Food International, who is dedicated to celebrating the state's regional cuisine. You can choose from a prix-fixe, four-course menu or a 10-course chef's tasting menu. ☒ 114-3 Senior La., 05091 ☎ 802/457–2065 or 800/448–1890 🖷 802/457–9290 ⊕ www.jacksonhouse. com 9 rooms, 6 suites ♿ Restaurant, gym, sauna, Internet room, meeting room; no room TVs, no kids under 18 ⊟ AE, MC, V ¶◯ BP.

FodorsChoice ★

$$-$$$$ ╳▦ **Kedron Valley Inn.** Two 19th-century buildings and a 1968 log lodge make up this inn on 15 acres. Many of the rooms have a fireplace or a Franklin stove, and some have private decks or terraces. The motel units in the log lodge are decorated with country antiques and reproductions. In the restaurant ($$-$$$$), the chef creates French masterpieces such as fillet of Norwegian salmon stuffed with herb seafood mousse in puff pastry. ⊠ *Rte. 106, 05071* ☎ *802/457-1473 or 800/836-1193* 🖷 *802/457-4469* ⊕ *www.kedronvalleyinn.com* ⇆ *21 rooms, 6 suites* ♿ *Restaurant, pond, beach, bar, meeting room, some pets allowed (fee); no a/c in some rooms* ═ *AE, MC, V* ☯ *Closed Apr.* ¶⊙¶ *BP.*

$$-$$$$ ╳▦ **Woodstock Inn and Resort.** Resort entrepreneur and Woodstock resident Laurance Rockefeller made this elegant country inn a flagship property of his Rockresorts chain. Rooms are spacious, serene, and set well back from Woodstock's noisy main street. Dinner ($$$-$$$$), served by candlelight, highlights classic American and nouvelle New England. Lighter fare is served in the more casual café and tavern. ⊠ *14 The Green, U.S. 4, 05091* ☎ *802/457-1100 or 800/448-7900* 🖷 *802/457-6699* ⊕ *www.woodstockinn.com* ⇆ *142 rooms, 7 suites* ♿ *3 restaurants, cable TV, 18-hole golf course, 12 tennis courts, 2 pools (1 indoors), health club, sauna, croquet, racquetball, squash, cross-country skiing, downhill skiing, meeting room* ═ *AE, MC, V* ¶⊙¶ *MAP.*

$$$-$$$$ ▦ **Maple Leaf Inn.** Victorian appointments blend with modern amenities at this three-story inn on 16 wooded acres. The light and airy rooms have king-size beds; four have whirlpool tubs and two have soaking tubs. All rooms have wood-burning fireplaces and sitting areas. The inn includes a pillow library, where you can "check out" pillows of varying firmness. ⊠ *Rte. 12, 8 mi north of Woodstock, Barnard 05031* ☎ *802/234-5342 or 800/516-2753* ⊕ *www.mapleleafinn.com* ⇆ *7 rooms* ♿ *Cable TV, in-room VCRs; no kids under 16* ═ *AE, MC, V* ¶⊙¶ *BP.*

$$-$$$$ ▦ **Shire Riverview.** Some rooms in this immaculate motel have decks overlooking the Ottauquechee River. All are well appointed with four-poster beds and wing chairs; two rooms have hot tubs; and the suite has a full kitchen. Complimentary coffee is served each morning. ⊠ *46 Pleasant St., 05091* ☎ *802/457-2211* 🖷 *802/457-5836* ⊕ *www.shiremotel.com* ⇆ *42 rooms, 1 suite* ♿ *Refrigerators, cable TV* ═ *AE, D, MC, V.*

Sports & the Outdoors

BIKING **Biscuit Hill Bike and Outdoor Shop** (⊠ 490 Woodstock Rd. ☎ 802/457-3377) rents, sells, and services bikes and also distributes a free touring map of local rides.

CROSS-COUNTRY **SKIING** The **Woodstock Ski Touring Center** (☎ 802/457-6674), headquartered at the **Woodstock Country Club** (⊠ 14 The Green ☎ 802/457-1100), has 60 km (37 mi) of trails. Equipment and lessons are available.

GOLF Robert Trent Jones Sr. designed the 18-hole, par-70 course at **Woodstock Country Club** (⊠ 14 The Green ☎ 802/457-1100), which is run by the Woodstock Inn. Greens fees are $67 weekdays, $85 weekends; cart rentals are $18.

HORSEBACK **RIDING** **Kedron Valley Stables** (⊠ Rte. 106, South Woodstock ☎ 802/457-1480 or 800/225-6301) conducts one-hour guided trail rides and horse-drawn sleigh and wagon rides.

Shopping

In downtown Woodstock, ☎ 802/457-3206) invites c▮ filled with whimsical anima▮ **Butcher** (⊠ Elm St. ☎ 802/▮ mestibles. **Who Is Sylvia?** (⊠ ▮ firehouse, sells vintage cloth▮

The **Woodstock Farmer's Ma▮** round buffet of local produ▮ pastries. The maple-walnut ▮ day, when the market is clo▮

South on Route 106, the **S▮** South Woodstock ☎ 802/4▮ made gifts.

East of town, the **Taftsville** ▮ 457-1135 or 800/854-001▮ moderately priced wines, a▮

Near Taftsville, **Sugarbush Fa▮** 457-1757 or 800/281-175▮ You can sample and purcha▮ The farm also makes excelle▮ can be messy, so call ahead ▮

Killington

15 *15 mi east of Rutland.*

With only a gas station, po▮ tersection of Routes 4 and 1▮ ski resort is nearby. The villa▮ tunate strip development alo▮ 360-degree views atop Killi▮ dola, make it worth the driv▮

Where to Stay & Eat

★ **$$$$** ╳ **Hemingway's.** With a nati▮ as dining gets. Among the ho▮ and a seasonal kaleidoscope ▮ dulas. Native baby pheasant ▮ with truffles and caramelized ▮ pear on the menu. Diners ca▮ menu or the wine-tasting m▮ vaulted dining room, the in▮ ⊠ *4988 U.S. 4* ☎ *802/422-▮* *DC, MC, V* ☯ *Closed Mon.* ▮ *May. No lunch.*

$$$-$$$$ ╳▦ **Birch Ridge Inn.** A slate-c▮ Killington's newest inns, a fo▮ frames. Rooms range in style ▮ all have a sitting area with a ▮

Pico interconnect. About 70% of the 1,182 acres of skiing terrain can be covered with machine-made snow. Transporting skiers to the peaks of this complex are 32 lifts, including 2 gondolas, 12 quads (including 6 high-speed express quads), 6 triples, and a Magic Carpet. The K-1 Express Gondola goes to the area's highest elevation, 4,241-foot Killington Peak. The Skyeship Gondola starts on U.S. 4, far below Killington's main base lodge, and savvy skiers park here to avoid the more crowded access road. After picking up more passengers at a mid-station, the Skyeship tops out on Skye Peak. Although Killington has a vertical drop of 3,050 feet, only gentle trails—Juggernaut and Great Eastern—go from top to bottom. The skiing includes everything from Outer Limits, one of the East's steepest and most challenging mogul trails, to 11-km (6½-mi) Great Eastern. In the Fusion Zones, underbrush and low branches have been cleared away to provide tree skiing. Killington's Superpipe is one of the best rated in the East.

Summer activities. The Killington-Pico complex has a host of activities, including an alpine slide, a golf course, two waterslides, a skateboard park, and a swimming pool. The resort rents mountain bikes and advises hikers. The K-1 Express Gondola takes you up the mountain, Vermont's second-highest summit.

✉ *4763 Killington Rd., 05751* ☎ *802/422–6200, 802/422–3261 snow conditions, 800/621–6867 lodging* ⊕ *www.killington.com.*

CROSS-COUNTRY SKIING **Mountain Meadows** (✉ Thundering Brook Rd. ☎ 802/775–7077 or 800/221–0598) has 57 km (34½ mi) of groomed trails and a 1½-km (1-mi) loop with snowmaking coverage. **Mountain Top Inn and Resort** (✉ 195 Mountaintop Rd., Chittenden ☎ 802/483–6089 or 800/445–2100) has 80 km (50 mi) of hilly trails groomed for classic skiing, 60 km (37 mi) of which are also groomed for skate skiing.

Rutland

 15 mi southwest of Killington, 32 mi south of Middlebury, 31 mi west of Woodstock, 47 mi west of White River Junction.

On and around U.S. 7 in Rutland are strips of shopping centers and a seemingly endless row of traffic lights. Two blocks west, however, stand the mansions of the marble magnates. Preservation work has uncovered white and verd marble façades; the stonework harkens back to the days when marble ruled what was once Vermont's second-largest city. The highlight of downtown is the **Paramount Theater** (✉ 30 Center St. ☎ 802/775–0570), a 700-seat, turn-of-the-20th-century gilded playhouse.

The former mansion of the Paramount's founder, the **Chaffee Center for the Visual Arts** (✉ 16 S. Main St. ☎ 802/775–0356), exhibits the work of more than 200 Vermont artists. It's closed Tuesday.

North of Rutland, the **Vermont Marble Exhibit** highlights one of the main industries in this region, and illustrates marble's many industrial and artistic applications. The hall of presidents has a carved bust of each U.S. president, and in the marble chapel is a replica of Leonardo da Vinci's *Last Supper.* Elsewhere you can watch a sculptor-in-residence shape the stone into finished works of art, compare marbles from around the world, and also check out the Vermont Marble Company's original "stone library." Factory seconds and foreign and domestic marble items are for sale. A short walk away is the original marble quarry in Proctor. Marble from here became part of the U.S. Supreme Court building and the New York Public Library. ⊠ *52 Main St., 4 mi north of Rutland, off Rte. 3, Proctor* ☎ *802/459–2300 or 800/427–1396* ⊕ *www.vermont-marble.com* ✏ *$7* ☉ *Mid-May–Oct., daily 9–5:30.*

A 32-room mansion built in 1875, the **Wilson Castle** comes complete with 84 stained-glass windows (one inset with 32 Australian opals), hand-painted Italian frescos, and 13 fireplaces. It's magnificently furnished with European and Asian objets d'art. ⊠ *W. Proctor Rd., Proctor* ☎ *802/773–3284* ⊕ *www.wilsoncastle.com* ✏ *$8.50* ☉ *Late May–mid-Oct., daily 9–5:30.*

Where to Stay & Eat

¢–$$ ✕ **Little Harry's.** Locals have packed this restaurant ever since chef-owners Trip (Harry) Pearce and Jack Mangan brought Vermont cheddar-cheese ravioli and lamb lo mein to downtown Rutland in 1997. The 17 tabletops are decorated with laminated photos of the regulars. For big appetites on small budgets, the Pad Thai and burrito are huge meals for under $8. ⊠ *121 West St.* ☎ *802/747–4848* ▭ *MC, V* ☉ *No lunch.*

★ $$$$ ✕▣ **Red Clover Inn.** Nestled in a meadow beneath Pico Peak, this romantic 1840s hideaway is just 5 mi from Rutland. Among the antiques-filled rooms in the inn and carriage house, four have gas fireplaces, and three have whirlpool tubs for two. Many rooms have mountain views. A superb candlelit dinner ($$–$$$$) is served in four intimate dining rooms Thursday through Sunday year-round, daily in foliage season. ⊠ *7 Woodward Rd., Mendon 05701* ☎ *802/775–2290 or 800/752–0571* ▤ *802/773–0594* ⊕ *www.redcloverinn.com* ↳ *14 rooms* △ *Dining room, Wi-Fi, hiking, meeting rooms, some pets allowed (fee); no TV in some rooms, no kids under 12* ▭ *AE, D, MC, V* ⑩ *BP.*

$$–$$$ ▣ **Inn at Rutland.** This stately Victorian mansion on Main Street is a welcome respite from Rutland's chain motels. Large plate-glass windows illuminate the entryway, library, and sitting room, all lined with metallic embossed plaster wainscoting. A large table with chairs for 10 dominates the dining room, which has hand-tooled leather wainscoting. Upstairs, the rooms are individually decorated with antiques; two rooms have private porches and whirlpool tubs. ⊠ *70 N. Main St., 05701* ☎ *802/773–0575 or 800/808–0575* ▤ *802/775–3506* ⊕ *www.innatrutland.com* ↳ *8 rooms* △ *Dining room, cable TV, library* ▭ *AE, D, MC, V.*

Nightlife & the Arts

Crossroads Arts Council (⊠ 39 E. Center St. ☎ 802/775–5413) presents films, music, opera, dance, jazz, and theater year-round at venues throughout the region.

Sports & the Outdoors

BOATING   Rent pontoon boats, speedboats, waterskiing boats, Wave Runners, and water toys at **Lake Bomoseen Marina** (⊠ 145 Creek Rd., off Rte. 4A, 1½ mi west of Castleton ☎ 802/265–4611).

HIKING **Deer's Leap** is a short hike to a great view overlooking Sherburne Gap and Pico Peak. The 3-mi round-trip hike starts at the Inn at Long Trail on Route 4 west of Rutland. **Mountain Travelers** (✉ 147 Rte. 4 E ☎ 802/775–0814) sells hiking maps and guidebooks, and gives advice on local hikes.

Shopping

Tuttle Antiquarian Books (✉ 28 S. Main St. ☎ 802/773–8229) stocks more than 35,000 rare and out-of-print books, genealogies, local histories, and miniature books; you will also find a large collection of books on Asia.

Brandon

⓱ *15 mi northwest of Rutland.*

Thanks to an active artists' guild, Brandon is making a name for itself. In 2003 the Brandon Artists Guild, led by American folk artist Warren Kimble, auctioned 40 life-size fiberglass pigs painted by local artists. The "Really Really Pig Show" raised money for the guild (as well as other organizations) and brought fame to this once overlooked community. In 2004 the theme was birdhouses ("Brandon is for the birds"), and in 2005 the theme was rocking chairs—"Brandon Rocks." The painted works are distributed throughout town, and maps show the location of each. Galleries like the **Brandon Artists Guild** (✉ 7 Center St. ☎ 802/247–4956) and Warren Kimble's **Kimble House** (✉ 4 Conant Sq. ☎ 802/247–3026) are right on the town's main street and invite browsing.

Maple syrup is Vermont's signature product, and south of Brandon, the **New England Maple Museum and Gift Shop** explains the history and process of turning maple sap into syrup with murals, exhibits, and a slide show. ✉ *U.S. 7, 9 mi south of Brandon, Pittsford* ☎ *802/483–9414* 🎟 *Museum $2.50* ⊙ *Late May–Oct., daily 8:30–5:30; Nov., Dec., and mid-Mar.–late May, daily 10–4.*

Where to Stay & Eat

$$–$$$ ✕ **Café Provence.** One story above the main street, this large, high-ceilinged café with hints of Provence (flowered seat cushions and dried-flower window valences) specializes in eclectic farm-fresh dishes. Goat-cheese cake with mesclun greens, braised veal cheeks and caramelized endive, and a portobello pizza from the restaurant's hearth oven are just a few of the choices. Breakfast offerings include buttery pastries, eggs benedict, and breakfast pizza. Umbrellas shade outdoor seating. ✉ *11 Center St.* ☎ *802/247–9997* ▭ *MC, V.*

$$$–$$$$ ✕▥ **Blueberry Hill Inn.** In the Green Mountain National Forest and 5½ mi off a mountain pass on a dirt road, the inn has lush gardens and a pond with a wood-fired hot tub on its bank. Many rooms have views of the mountains; all are furnished with antiques and quilts. The restaurant prepares a four-course prix-fixe ($$$$) menu nightly, with dishes such as venison fillet with cherry sauce. The cross-country ski center has 70 km (43 mi) of trails. ✉ *1307 Goshen–Ripton Rd., Goshen 05733* ☎ *802/247–6735 or 800/448–0707* 🖶 *802/247–3983* ⊕ *www.*

blueberryhillinn.com ⤴ *12 rooms* ⌂ *Restaurant, Wi-Fi, pond, sauna, fishing, mountain bikes, hiking, volleyball, cross-country skiing, some pets allowed; no a/c, no room phones, no room TVs* ⊟ *AE, MC, V* ⦿ *MAP.*

$$$–$$$$ ✕⊞ **Lilac Inn.** This Greek-revival mansion's spacious common areas are filled with lovely antiques. The rooms, all furnished with claw-foot tubs and handheld European showerheads, are charming, and the grand suite has a pewter canopy bed, whirlpool bath for two, and fireplace. Overlooking the gardens, the elegant dining room ($$–$$$) serves unique creations such as fig-mango pork short ribs. The inn is a popular spot for weddings on summer weekends. ⌧ *53 Park St. (Rte. 73), 05733* ☎ *802/247–5463 or 800/221–0720* 🖷 *802/247–5499* ⦿ *www. lilacinn.com* ⤴ *9 rooms* ⌂ *Restaurant, cable TV, meeting rooms, some pets allowed (fee); no a/c, no kids under 12* ⊟ *AE, MC, V* ⦿ *BP.*

$$–$$$ ⊞ **Brandon Inn.** Built in 1786, this large hotel exudes an aura of elegance from centuries past. The foyer has marble flooring, and this decorative theme continues throughout the three-story inn. The Victorian-furnished common rooms and multipillared dining room, used only for special groups, are expansive (and underutilized). In the main lobby, the state's oldest elevator (circa 1901) leads to two upper floors with comfortable and spacious guest rooms. ⌧ *20 Park St., 05733* ☎ *800/639–8685* 🖷 *802/247–5768* ⦿ *www.historicbrandoninn.com* ⤴ *39 rooms* ⌂ *Restaurant, pool; no room TVs* ⊟ *AE, D, MC, V* ⦿ *BP.*

Sports & the Outdoors

The **Moosalamoo Association** (☎ 800/448–0707) manages, protects, and provides stewardship for more than 20,000 acres of the Green Mountain National Forest, just northeast of Brandon. More than 60 mi of trails take hikers, mountain bikers, and cross-country skiers through some of Vermont's most gorgeous mountain terrain. Attractions include Branbury State Park, on the shores of Lake Dunmore; secluded Silver Lake; and sections of both the Long Trail and Catamount Trail (the latter is a Massachusetts-to-Québec ski trail). Both the Blueberry Hill Inn and **Churchill House Inn** (☎ 802/247–3078) have direct public access to trails.

GOLF   **Neshobe Golf Club** (⌧ Rte. 73 east of Brandon ☎ 802/247–3611) has 18 holes of par-72 golf on a bent-grass course totaling nearly 6,500 yards. The Green Mountain views are terrific. Several local inns offer golf packages.

HIKING   For great views from a vertigo-inducing cliff, hike up the Long Trail to **Mt. Horrid.** The steep, hour-long hike starts at the top of Brandon Gap (about 8 mi east of Brandon on Route 73). A large turnout on Route 53 marks a moderate trail to the **Falls of Lana.** West of Brandon, four trails—two short ones of less than 1 mi each and two longer ones—lead to the old abandoned Revolutionary War fortifications at **Mt. Independence.** To reach them, take the first left turn off Route 73 west of Orwell and go right at the fork. The road will turn to gravel and once again will fork; take a sharp left-hand turn toward a small marina. The parking lot is on the left at the top of the hill.

Middlebury

★ ⑱ *17 mi north of Brandon, 34 mi south of Burlington.*

In the late 1800s Middlebury was the largest Vermont community west of the Green Mountains, an industrial center of river-powered wool and grain mills. This is Robert Frost country: Vermont's late poet laureate spent 23 summers at a farm east of Middlebury. Still a cultural and economic hub amid the Champlain Valley's serene pastoral patchwork, the town and countryside invite a day of exploration.

In the middle of town, **Middlebury College** (☎ 802/443–5000), founded in 1800, was conceived as a more godly alternative to the worldly University of Vermont. The college has no religious affiliation today, however. The early-19th-century stone buildings contrast provocatively with the postmodern architecture of the Center for the Arts and the sports center. Music, theater, and dance performances take place throughout the year at the **Wright Memorial Theatre** and **Center for the Arts.**

The **Middlebury College Museum of Art** has a permanent collection of paintings, photography, works on paper, and sculpture. ⊠ *Center for the Arts, Rte. 30* ☎ *802/443-5007* ☒ *Free* ☉ *Mid-Jan.–mid-Dec., Tues.–Fri. 10–5, weekends noon–5.*

In the Masonic Hall, the **Vermont Folklife Center** exhibits photography, antiques, folk paintings, manuscripts, and other artifacts and contemporary works that examine facets of Vermont life. ⊠ *3 Court St.* ☎ *802/388–4964* ☒ *Donations accepted* ☉ *Gallery May–Dec., Tues.–Sat. 11–4.*

The **Henry Sheldon Museum of Vermont History,** an 1829 marble-merchant's house, is the oldest community museum in the country. The period rooms contain Vermont-made textiles, furniture, toys, clothes, kitchen tools, and paintings. ⊠ *1 Park St.* ☎ *802/388–2117* ☒ *$4* ☉ *Mon.–Sat. 10–5.*

More than a crafts store, the **Vermont State Craft Center/Frog Hollow** mounts changing exhibitions and displays exquisite works in wood, glass, metal, clay, and fiber by more than 250 Vermont artisans. The center, which overlooks Otter Creek, sponsors classes taught by some of those artists. Burlington and Manchester also have centers. ⊠ *1 Mill St.* ☎ *802/388–3177* ⊕ *www.froghollow.org* ☉ *Call for hrs.*

The Morgan horse—Vermont's official state animal—has an even temper, stamina, and slightly truncated legs in proportion to its body. The University of Vermont's **UVM Morgan Horse Farm,** about 2½ mi west of Middlebury, is a breeding and training center where in summer you can tour the stables and paddocks. ⊠ *74 Battell Dr., off Morgan Horse Farm Rd. (follow signs off Rte. 23), Weybridge* ☎ *802/388–2011* ☒ *$4* ☉ *May–Oct., daily 9–4.*

About 10 mi east of town on Route 125 (1 mi west of Middlebury College's Bread Loaf campus), the easy ¾-mi **Robert Frost Interpretive Trail** winds through quiet woodland. Plaques along the way bear quotations from Frost's poems. A picnic area is across the road from the trailhead.

FORT TICONDEROGA FERRY – Established in 1759, the Fort Ti cable ferry crosses Lake Champlain between Shoreham and Fort Ticonderoga, New York, at one of the oldest ferry crossings in North America. The trip takes seven minutes. ⊠ *4675 Rte. 74 W, 18 mi southwest of Middlebury, 9 mi south of Brandon, Shoreham* ☏ *802/897–7999* ◿ *Cars, pickups, and vans with driver and passenger $8; bicycles $2; pedestrians $1* ◷ *May–last Sun. of Oct., 8–5:45.*

Where to Stay & Eat

$$–$$$ ✕ **Storm Café.** Locals rave about the eclectic ever-changing menu at this small restaurant in the old Frog Hollow Mill overlooking the Otter Creek Falls. Chef-owner John Goettelmann's creations include stormy Thai stew and Jamaican jerk-seasoned pork tenderloin, and melt-in-your-mouth desserts like an apricot soufflé. Outdoor seating by the river is available in nice weather. ⊠ *3 Mill St.* ☏ *802/388–1063* ▤ *MC, V* ◷ *Closed Sun. and Mon.*

★ **$–$$$** ✕ **Mary's at Baldwin Creek.** People drive from the far reaches of Vermont to eat at this restaurant in Bristol, 13 mi northeast of Middlebury. The innovative fare includes a superb garlic soup and entrées with whimsical names like Swimming with Noodles (shrimp, shiitake mushrooms, roasted tomato, and asparagus sautéed in garlic white wine and served over fettuccine), and What's Eating Gilbert Crepe (sesame-and-ginger-marinated tofu in a crepe). A café menu is also available. Four rooms above the restaurant have simple, comfortable furnishings. ⊠ *1869 Rte. 116, Bristol* ☏ *802/453–2432* ▤ *AE, DC, MC, V* ◷ *Closed Mon. and Tues. No lunch.*

¢–$$$ ✕ **Fire & Ice.** A 55-item salad bar (with all-you-can-eat peel-and-eat shrimp), prime rib, steak, fish, and a house specialty—homemade mashed potatoes—are all choices at this family-friendly spot. Although large, the space is divided into several rooms (each with a different theme) and has numerous intimate nooks and crannies for diners who seek privacy. Families may want to request a table next to the "children's corner," which is outfitted with cushions and a VCR. Sunday dinner begins at 1. ⊠ *26 Seymour St.* ☏ *802/388–7166 or 800/367–7166* ▤ *AE, DC, MC, V* ◷ *No lunch Mon.–Thurs.*

$$–$$$$ ⌂ **Swift House Inn.** The Georgian home of a 19th-century governor contains white-panel wainscoting, mahogany, and marble fireplaces. The rooms—most with Oriental rugs and nine with fireplaces—have period reproductions such as canopy beds, curtains with swags, and claw-foot tubs. Some bathrooms have double whirlpool tubs. Rooms in the gatehouse suffer from street noise but are charming; a carriage house holds six luxury accommodations. ⊠ *25 Stewart La., 05753* ☏ *802/388–9925* 🖷 *802/388–9927* ⊕ *www.swifthouseinn.com* ⇥ *21 rooms* ⟐ *Restaurant, sauna, steam room, pub, meeting room; no TV in some rooms* ▤ *AE, D, DC, MC, V* ⦿ *CP, MAP.*

Sports & the Outdoors

The **Bike Center** (⊠ 74 Main St. ☏ 802/388–6666) has bike sales, rentals, and repairs.

On Route 116, about 5½ mi north of East Middlebury, a U.S. Forest Service sign marks a dirt road that forks to the right and leads to the start of the two- to three-hour hike to **Abbey Pond,** which has a beaver lodge and dam as well as a view of Robert Frost Mountain.

Shopping

Historic Marble Works (✉ Maple St. ☎ 802/388–3701), a renovated marble manufacturing facility, is a collection of unique shops set amid quarrying equipment and factory buildings. **Danforth Pewter** (☎ 802/ 388–0098) sells handcrafted pewter vases, lamps, and tableware. **Holy Cow** (✉ 44 Main St. ☎ 802/388–6737) is where Woody Jackson sells his Holstein cattle–inspired T-shirts, memorabilia, and paintings.

Waitsfield & Warren

⑲ *32 mi northeast (Waitsfield) and 25 mi east (Warren) of Middlebury.*

Skiers discovered the high peaks overlooking the pastoral Mad River valley in the 1940s. Now the valley and its two towns, Waitsfield and Warren, attract the hip, the adventurous, and the low-key. The gently carved ridges cradling the valley and the swell of pastures and fields lining the river seem to keep further notions of ski-resort sprawl at bay. With a map from the Sugarbush Chamber of Commerce you can investigate back roads off Route 100 that have exhilarating valley views.

Where to Stay & Eat

\$\$\$–\$\$\$\$ ✕ **Spotted Cow.** Jay and Renate Young attract a steady clientele to their intimate dining room decorated with contemporary furnishings and warm woods. Lunch items include a fresh spinach salad with fried oysters and Bermuda codfish cakes. For dinner, try a ragout of seafood in puff pastry or the house specialty: sautéed medallions of New Zealand venison finished in lingonberry crème fraîche. ✉ *Bridge St., Waitsfield* ☎ *802/496–5151* ▭ *MC, V* ☉ *Closed Mon.*

\$\$–\$\$\$\$ ✕ **Common Man.** Eclectic New American cuisine using locally grown produce and meats is the emphasis here. The menu might include an appetizer of sautéed sweetbreads and apples, a salad of organic field greens, and entrées ranging from fish stew in tomato and saffron broth to grilled venison or sautéed and confited rabbit. The restaurant, a local institution since 1972, is housed in a mid-1800s barn with hand-hewn rafters and crystal chandeliers. Dinner is served by candlelight. ✉ *3209 German Flats Rd., Warren* ☎ *802/583–2800* ▭ *AE, DC, MC, V* ☉ *Closed Mon. mid-Apr.–mid-Dec. No lunch.*

\$–\$\$ ✕ **American Flatbread.** For ideologically and gastronomically sound pizza, you won't find a better place in the Green Mountains than this modest haven between Waitsfield and Warren. Organic flour and produce fuel mind and body, and Vermont hardwood fuels the earth-and-stone oven. The "punctuated equilibrium flat bread," made with olive-pepper goat cheese and rosemary, is a dream, as are more traditional pizzas. It's open Monday–Thursday 7:30 AM–8 PM for takeout, Friday and Saturday 5:30–9:30 for dinner. ✉ *Rte. 100* ☎ *802/496–8856* ⏺ *Reservations not accepted* ▭ *MC, V* ☉ *Closed Sun.*

\$\$\$\$ ✕▦ **Pitcher Inn.** Each guest room at Vermont's only Relais & Châteaux property has its own motif. A curved ceiling in the Mallard gives the illusion of a duck blind, and the windows are etched and frosted in the likeness of the banks of a marsh. All rooms have stereos; nine have fire-

FodorsChoice
★

places and six have steam showers. The formal dining room ($$$–$$$$) specializes in local produce and wild game; you can also dine in the private wine cellar. ✉ *275 Main St., Warren 05674* ☎ *802/496–6350 or 888/867–4824* 🖷 *802/496–6354* ⊕ *www.pitcherinn.com* ⤳ *9 rooms, 2 suites* ♿ *Restaurant, in-room VCRs, in-room data ports, hot tub, billiards; no kids under 16* ▭ *AE, MC, V* ❘⊙❘ *BP.*

$$ ✕▦ **1824 House.** A 10-gable farmhouse north of Waitsfield, this elegant inn has cozy rooms and featherbeds. A prix-fixe dinner ($$$$)—which might include lobster pancakes, filet mignon stuffed with blue cheese and wrapped in bacon, and a lemon sabayon pine-nut tart—and a less pricey à la carte menu are served in the intimate dining room (closed Monday and Tuesday). ✉ *2150 Main St., 05673* ☎ *802/496–7555 or 800/426–3986* 🖷 *802/496–7559* ⊕ *www.1824house.com* ⤳ *8 rooms* ♿ *Restaurant, hot tub; no room TVs* ▭ *AE, MC, V* ❘⊙❘ *BP, MAP.*

$$–$$$$ ▦ **Inn at the Round Barn Farm.** A Shaker-style round barn (one of only five in the state) dominates the farm's 215 acres. The inn's guest rooms, inside an 1806 farmhouse, are sumptuous, with eyelet-trimmed sheets, elaborate four-poster beds, rich-color wallpapers, and brass wall lamps for easy bedtime reading. Seven have fireplaces, four have whirlpool tubs, and five have steam showers. The inn also arranges snowshoe packages and tours. ✉ *1661 E. Warren Rd., 05673* ☎ *802/496–2276* 🖷 *802/496–2276* ⊕*www.theroundbarn.com* ⤳*12 rooms* ♿ *Wi-Fi, indoor pool, library, recreation room; no a/c in some rooms, no room TVs* ▭ *AE, D, MC, V* ❘⊙❘ *BP.*

Nightlife & the Arts

The Back Room at **Chez Henri** (✉ Sugarbush Village ☎ 802/583–2600) has a pool table and is popular with the après-ski crowds.

The **Eclipse Theater and Starlight Lounge** (✉ Rte. 100 ☎ 802/496–7787) presents soul, rock, country, blues, and jazz concerts. The **Green Mountain Cultural Center** (✉Inn at the Round Barn Farm, E. Warren Rd. ☎ 802/496–7722) hosts concerts and art exhibits, as well as educational workshops. The **Purple Moon Pub** (✉ Rte. 100 ☎ 802/496–3422) hosts live bands most weekends.

The **Valley Players** (✉ Rte. 100 ☎ 802/496–9612) present musicals, dramas, follies, and holiday shows.

Sports & the Outdoors

Clearwater Sports (✉ 4147 Main St. [Rte. 100] ☎ 802/496–2708) rents canoes, kayaks, and camping equipment and leads guided river trips and white-water instruction in the warm months; in winter, the store leads snowshoe and backcountry ski tours and rents telemark equipment, snowshoes, and one-person Mad River Rocket sleds.

GOLF Great views and challenging play are the trademarks of the Robert Trent Jones–designed 18-hole mountain course at **Sugarbush Resort** (✉ Golf Course Rd. ☎ 802/583–6725). The greens fees run from $48 to $58; a cart (sometimes mandatory) costs $18 per person.

SLEIGH RIDES **Mountain Valley Farm** (✉ 1719 Common Rd. ☎ 802/496–9255) specializes in horse-drawn carriage and sleigh rides. Advance reservations are required.

Shopping

ART & ANTIQUES **Cabin Fever Quilts** (✉ 4276 Main St. No. 1 [Rte. 100] ☏ 802/496–2287), inside a converted old church, sells fine handmade quilts. **Luminosity Stained Glass Studios** (✉ 4276 Main St. No. 1 [Rte. 100] ☏ 802/496–2231), which shares the premises with Cabin Fever Quilts, specializes in stained glass, custom lighting, and art glass.

CRAFTS **All Things Bright and Beautiful** (✉ Bridge St. ☏ 802/496–3997) is a 12-room Victorian house jammed to the rafters with stuffed animals of all shapes, sizes, and colors as well as folk art, prints, and collectibles. One of the rooms is a coffee and ice-cream shop.

Ski Areas

MAD RIVER GLEN The hundreds of shareholders who own Mad River Glen are dedicated, knowledgeable skiers devoted to keeping skiing what it used to be—a pristine alpine experience. Mad River's unkempt aura attracts rugged individualists looking for less-polished terrain: the area was developed in the late 1940s and has changed relatively little since then. It remains one of only three resorts in the country that ban snowboarding.

Downhill. Mad River is steep, with natural slopes that follow the mountain's fall lines. The terrain changes constantly on the 45 interconnected trails, of which 30% are beginner, 30% are intermediate, and 40% are expert. Intermediate and novice terrain is regularly groomed. Five lifts, including the last surviving single chairlift in the world, service the mountain's 2,037-foot vertical drop. Most of Mad River's trails (85%) are covered only by natural snow.

Telemark/snowshoe. The "Mecca of Free-Heel Skiing" sponsors telemark programs throughout the season. Every March, the North America Telemark Organization (NATO) Festival attracts up to 1,400 skiers to "MRG." There is a $5 fee to use the snowshoe trails, and rentals are available.

✉ *Rte. 17, 05673* ☏ *802/496–3551, 802/496–2001 snow conditions, 800/850–6742 cooperative office* ⊕ *www.madriverglen.com.*

SUGARBUSH Sugarbush has remade itself as a true skier's mountain, with steep, natural snow glades and fall-line drops. Not as rough around the edges as Mad River Glen, Sugarbush also has well-groomed intermediate and beginner terrain. A computer-controlled system for snowmaking has increased coverage to nearly 70%. At the base of the mountain are condominiums, restaurants, shops, bars, and a sports center.

Downhill. Sugarbush is two distinct, connected mountain complexes connected by the Slide Brook Express quad. Lincoln Peak, with a vertical of 2,400 feet, is known for formidable steeps, especially on Castlerock. Mount Ellen has more beginner runs near the bottom, with steep fall-line pitches on the upper half of the 2,650 vertical feet. There are 115 trails in all: 23% beginner, 48% intermediate, 29% expert. The resort has 18 lifts: 7 quads (including 4 high-speed versions), 3 triples, 4 doubles, and 4 surface lifts.

Summer and year-round activities. Open year-round, the **Sugarbush Health and Racquet Club** (☏ 802/583–6700), near the ski lifts, has cardio equipment and free weights; tennis, squash, and racquetball courts; a whirlpool, a sauna, and coed steam room; massage therapy; indoor and outdoor pools; a rock gym; and indoor golf lessons.

⊠ *Sugarbush Access Rd., accessible from Rte. 100 or Rte. 17* ✆ *Box 350, Warren 05674* ☎ *802/583–6300, 802/583–7669 snow conditions, 800/537–8427 lodging* ⊕ *www.sugarbush.com.*

CROSS-COUNTRY **Blueberry Lake Cross-Country Ski Area** (⊠ Plunkton Rd., Warren ☎ 802/
SKIING 496–6687) has 30 km (18 mi) of groomed trails through thickly wooded glades. **Ole's** (⊠ Airport Rd., Warren ☎ 802/496–3430) runs a popular cross-country center out of the tiny Warren airport. It has 45 km (30 mi) of groomed trails that span out into the surrounding woods from the landing strip.

Central Vermont A to Z

To research prices, get advice from other travelers, and book travel arrangements, visit www.fodors.com.

BUS TRAVEL

Vermont Transit links Rutland, White River Junction, Burlington, and many smaller towns.

🚍 Bus Information **Vermont Transit** ☎ 800/552-8737 ⊕ www.vermonttransit.com.

CAR TRAVEL

U.S. 4, the major east–west route, stretches from White River Junction in the east to Fair Haven in the west. Traffic can be slow through Woodstock. Route 100 is the scenic route. It splits the region in half along the eastern edge of the Green Mountains. Interstate 91 and the parallel U.S. 5 follow the state's eastern border; U.S. 7 and Route 30 are the north–south highways in the west. Interstate 89 links White River Junction with Montpelier to the north.

EMERGENCIES

🚑 Hospitals **Porter Hospital** ⊠ 115 Porter Dr., Middlebury ☎ 802/388-4701. **Rutland Regional Medical Center** ⊠ 160 Allen St., Rutland ☎ 802/775-7111.

LODGING

Sugarbush Reservations and the Woodstock Area Chamber of Commerce provide lodging referral services.

🛏 Reservation Services **Sugarbush Reservations** ☎ 800/828-4748. **Woodstock Area Chamber of Commerce** ☎ 802/457-3555 or 888/496-6378.

TOURS

Country Inns Along the Trail arranges self-guided hiking, skiing, and biking trips from inn to inn in Vermont. The Vermont Icelandic Horse Farm conducts year-round guided riding expeditions on easy-to-ride Icelandic horses. Ride for an hour, a day, or up to five days.

🚌 Tour Operators **Country Inns Along the Trail** ✆ Box 59, Montgomery 05470 ☎ 802/326-2072 or 800/838-3301 ⊕ www.inntoinn.com. **Vermont Icelandic Horse Farm** ⊠ N. Fayston Rd., Waitsfield 05673 ☎ 802/496-7141 ⊕ www.icelandichorses.com.

VISITOR INFORMATION
🔖 Tourist Information **Addison County Chamber of Commerce** ⊠ 2 Court St., Middlebury 05753 ☎ 802/388-7951 or 800/733-8376 ⊕ www.midvermont.com. **Quechee Chamber of Commerce** ⊠ 1789 Quechee St. ⬠ Box 106, Quechee 05059 ☎ 802/295-7900 or 800/295-5451 ⊕ www.quechee.com. **Rutland Region Chamber of Commerce** ⊠ 256 N. Main St., Rutland 05701 ☎ 802/773-2747 or 800/756-8880 ⊕ www.rutlandvermont.com. **Sugarbush Chamber of Commerce** ⊠ Rte. 100 ⬠ Box 173, Waitsfield 05673 ☎ 802/496-3409 or 800/828-4748 ⊕ www.madrivervalley.com. **Woodstock Area Chamber of Commerce** ⊠18 Central St. ⬠Box 486, Woodstock 05091 ☎802/457-3555 or 888/496-6378 ⊕ www.woodstockvt.com.

NORTHERN VERMONT

Vermont's northernmost region reveals the state's greatest contrasts. To the west, Burlington and its suburbs have grown so rapidly that rural wags now say that Burlington's greatest advantage is that it's "close to Vermont." The north country also harbors Vermont's tiny capital, Montpelier, and its highest mountain, Mt. Mansfield, site of the famous Stowe ski resort. To the northeast of Montpelier is a sparsely populated and heavily wooded territory that former Senator George Aiken dubbed the "Northeast Kingdom." It's the domain of loggers, farmers, and avid outdoors enthusiasts.

Our coverage of towns begins in the state capital, Montpelier; moves west toward Stowe and Burlington; then goes north through the Lake Champlain Islands, east along the boundary with Canada toward Jay Peak, and south into the heart of the Northeast Kingdom.

Montpelier

⑳ *38 mi southeast of Burlington, 115 mi north of Brattleboro.*

With only about 8,000 residents, Montpelier is the country's smallest capital city. The well-preserved downtown bustles with state and city workers walking to meetings or down the street for coffee or lunch. Unique shops, like the hip, made-in-Vermont children's clothing store **Zutano** (⊠ 79 Main St. ☎ 802/223-2229), attract locals and tourists alike.

The **Vermont State House**—with a gleaming gold dome and columns of Barre granite 6 feet in diameter—is home to the oldest legislative chambers in their original condition in the United States. The goddess of agriculture tops the gilded dome. Interior paintings and exhibits make much of Vermont's sterling Civil War record. ⊠ *115 State St.* ☎ *802/828-2228* 🖼 *By donation* ⊙ *Weekdays 8–4; tours July–mid-Oct., weekdays every ½ hr 10–3:30 (last tour at 3:30), Sat. 11–3 (last tour at 2:30).*

Next door to the capitol, in the Pavilion building, is the **Vermont Museum,** preserving all things Vermont, from a catamount to Ethan Allen's shoe buckles. ⊠ *109 State St.* ☎ *802/828-2291* ⊕ *www.state.vt.us/vhs* 🖼 *$5* ⊙ *May–Oct., Tues.–Sat. 10–4, Sun. noon–4.*

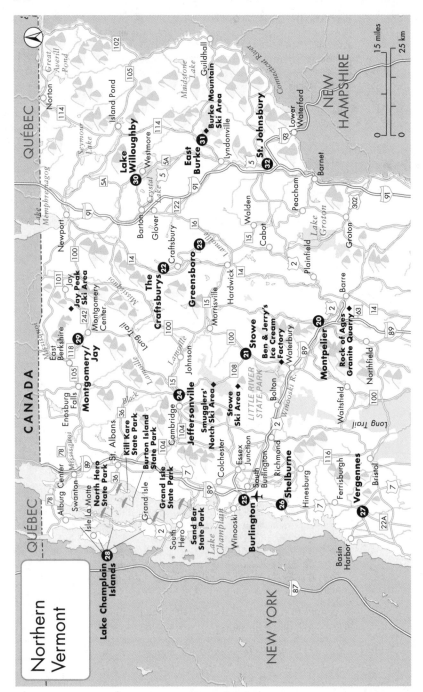

Northern Vermont

CANADA

QUÉBEC

QUÉBEC

NEW HAMPSHIRE

NEW YORK

Lake Champlain Islands 28

Norton
Great Averill Pond
102
Island Pond
105
114
Seymour Lake
Lake Memphremagog
Newport
91
Maidstone Lake
Guildhall
Burke Mountain Ski Area 31
East Burke
Lyndonville
St. Johnsbury 32
5
93
Lower Waterford
Barnet
Connecticut River
15 miles
25 km

Lake Willoughby 30
Westmore
114
Crystal Lake
5A
5A
5
5A
91
Barton
Glover
Craftsbury
122
16
The Craftsburys 22
Greensboro 23
Lamoille River
Walden
Cabot
15
Plainfield
Peacham
Lake Groton
302
Groton
91

100
101
Jay
Jay Peak Ski Area ◆
242
Montgomery Center
Montgomery/ Jay 29
East Berkshire
118
105
Enosburg Falls
78
Missisquoi
Long Trail
Lamoille
Johnson
100
15
Hardwick
Morrisville
14
15
Barre
2
Montpelier 20
Rock of Ages Granite Quarry ◆
63
14
89
Northfield
Waitsfield
100
Long Trail

Alburg Center
78
Swanton
Isle La Motte
89
36
Kill Kare State Park
St. Albans
Burton Island State Park
104
36
Grand Isle State Park
North Hero State Park
Grand Isle
Sand Bar State Park
2
South Hero
Lake Champlain
Black
Cambridge
104
Jeffersonville 24
Smugglers' Notch Ski Area ◆
15
Stowe Ski Area ◆
108
Stowe 21
Ben & Jerry's Ice Cream Factory ◆
Waterbury
LITTLE RIVER STATE PARK
Bolton
2
Winooski R.
89

Colchester
Essex Junction
South Burlington
Burlington 25 ✈
Winooski
Richmond
2
Hinesburg
Shelburne 26
7
116
Ferrisburgh
7
Vergennes 27
22A
Basin Harbor
Bristol
7

87

OFF THE BEATEN PATH

ROCK OF AGES GRANITE QUARRY – The attractions here range from the awe-inspiring (the quarry resembles the Grand Canyon in miniature) to the mildly ghoulish (you can consult a directory of tombstone dealers throughout the country). You might recognize the sheer walls of the quarry from *Batman and Robin*, the film starring George Clooney and Arnold Schwarzenegger. At the crafts center, skilled artisans sculpt monuments; at the quarries themselves, 25-ton blocks of stone are cut from sheer 475-foot walls by workers who clearly earn their pay. ⊠ *Exit 6 off I–89, follow Rte. 63, 7 mi southeast of Montpelier, Barre* ☎ *802/476–3119* 🖾 *Tour of active quarry $4, craftsman center and self-guided tour free* ☉ *Visitor center May–Oct., Mon.–Sat. 8:30–5, Sun. noon–5; narrated tour on Sat.*

CABOT CREAMERY – The major cheese producer in the state, midway between Barre and St. Johnsbury, has a visitor center with an audiovisual presentation about the dairy and cheese industry. You can taste samples, purchase cheese and other Vermont products, and tour the plant. ⊠ *2870 Main St. (Rte. 215), 3 mi north of U.S. 2, Cabot* ☎ *800/837–4261* 🖾 *$2* ☉ *June–Oct., daily 9–5; Nov., Dec., and Feb.–May, Mon.–Sat. 9–4; Jan., Mon.–Sat. 10–4; call ahead to check cheese-making days.*

Where to Stay & Eat

★ **$$–$$$** ✕ **Chef's Table.** Nearly everyone working here is a student at the New England Culinary Institute. Although this is a training ground, the quality and inventiveness are anything but beginner's luck. The menu changes daily. Dining is more formal than at the sister operation downstairs, the Main Street Bar and Grill (open daily for lunch and dinner). A 15% gratuity is added to the bill. ⊠ *118 Main St.* ☎ *802/229–9202, 802/223–3188 grill* ⊟ *AE, D, DC, MC, V* ☉ *Closed Sun. and Mon. No lunch.*

$–$$$ ✕ **Ariel's.** Well off the beaten path, this small restaurant overlooking a
Fodor'sChoice lake is worth the drive down a dirt road. Chef Lee Duberman prepares
★ eclectic treats such as scallop, lobster, and shrimp ravioli in a ginger shiitake broth. Husband-sommelier Ricard Fink recommends selections from the wine cellar. The full menu is offered Friday and Saturday; a pub menu ($–$$) is served Wednesday, Thursday, and Sunday. ⊠ *29 Stone Hill Rd., 8 mi south of Montpelier, Brookfield* ☎ *802/276–3939* ⊟ *DC, MC, V* ☉ *Closed Nov. and Apr.; Mon. and Tues. May–Oct., Mon.–Thurs. Dec.–Mar.*

$–$$ ✕ **Finkerman's.** The chef-owners of Ariel's opened this popular riverside barbecue in 2004. In addition to spareribs and pulled pork, the menu has marinated tempeh and garlic-lime chicken breast. A highlight of the restaurant is the children's playroom. ⊠ *188 River St.* ☎ *802/229–2295* ⊟ *AE, D, DC, MC, V.*

$–$$ ✕ **River Run Restaurant.** Mississippi-raised chef Jimmy Kennedy has brought outstanding Southern fare to northern Vermont. Fried catfish, hush puppies, collard greens, and whiskey cake are just a few of the surprises awaiting diners at this rustic, hip eatery. Try the buttermilk biscuits at breakfast. There is a full bar. ⊠ *Main St., 10 mi east of Montpelier, Plainfield* ☎ *802/454–1246* ⊟ *No credit cards* ☉ *Closed Mon.*

$–$$ ✕ **Sarducci's.** Legislative lunches have been a lot more leisurely since Sarducci came along to fill the trattoria void in Vermont's capital. These bright, cheerful rooms alongside the Winooski River are a great spot for pizza fresh from wood-fired ovens, wonderfully textured home-made Italian breads, and imaginative pasta dishes such as pasta *pugliese,* which marries penne with basil, black olives, roasted eggplant, porto-bello mushrooms, and sun-dried tomatoes. ⊠ *3 Main St.* ☎ *802/223–0229* ▱ *AE, MC, V* ⊘ *No lunch Sun.*

$$–$$$ 🍴 **Inn at Montpelier.** This inn built in the early 1800s was renovated with the business traveler in mind, but the architectural detailing, antique four-poster beds, Windsor chairs, and classical guitar on the stereo attract the leisure trade as well. The formal sitting room has a wide wraparound Colonial-revival porch, perfect for reading a book or watching the townsfolk stroll by. The rooms are small and can be chilly on cool summer days. ⊠ *147 Main St., 05602* ☎ *802/223–2727* 🖷 *802/223–0722* ⊕ *www.innatmontpelier.com* ↬ *19 rooms* ⚲ *Cable TV, meeting room* ▱ *AE, D, DC, MC, V* |⊙| *CP.*

**EN
ROUTE** On your way to Stowe from Interstate 89, be sure to stop at **Ben & Jerry's Ice Cream Factory,** the Valhalla for ice-cream lovers. Ben and Jerry began selling ice cream from a renovated gas station in Burlington in the 1970s. Famous for their social and environmental consciousness, the boys do good works while living off the butterfat of the land. The tour only skims the surface of the behind-the-scenes goings-on at the plant—a flaw forgiven when the free samples are dished out. ⊠ *Rte. 100, 1 mi north of I–89, Waterbury* ☎ *802/846–1500, 802/882–1260 recorded information* ⊕ *www.benjerry.com* 🎟 *Tour $3.*

Stowe

㉑
Fodor'sChoice
★

22 mi northwest of Montpelier, 36 mi east of Burlington.

Long before skiing came to Stowe in the 1930s, the rolling hills and val-leys beneath Vermont's highest peak, the 4,395-foot Mt. Mansfield, at-tracted summer tourists looking for a reprieve from city heat. Most stayed at one of two inns in the village of Stowe. When skiing made the town a winter destination, the arriving skiers outnumbered the hotel beds, so locals took them in. This spirit of hospitality continues, and many of these homes are now lovely country inns. The village itself is tiny, just a few blocks of shops and restaurants clustered around a picture-per-fect white church with a lofty steeple, but it serves as the anchor for Moun-tain Road, which leads north past restaurants, lodges, and shops on its way to Stowe's fabled slopes.

Mt. Mansfield, with its elongated summit ridge resembling the profile of a recumbent man's face, has long attracted the adventurous. The moun-tain is ribboned with hiking and ski trails. Mt. Mansfield's "Chin" area is accessible by the eight-seat **gondola.** At the gondola's summit station is the **Cliff House Restaurant** (☎ 802/253–3558 Ext. 237), where lunch is served daily 11–3. ⊠ *Mountain Rd., 8 mi off Rte. 100* ☎ *802/253–3000* 🎟 *Gondola $14* ⊘ *Mid-June–mid-Oct., daily 10–5; early Dec.–late Apr., daily 8–4.*

On a hillside overlooking the Stowe valley is the **Trapp Family Lodge** (⊠ Luce Hill Rd. ☎ 802/253–8511 or 800/826–7000). Built by the von

Trapp family, of *Sound of Music* fame, the Tyrolean lodge and its surrounding pastureland are the site of a popular outdoor music series in summer and an extensive cross-country ski-trail network in winter. The **Vermont Ski Museum** (☎ 802/253–9911) documents the state's skiing history with myriad exhibits.

Where to Stay & Eat

$$–$$$$ ✕ **Michael's on the Hill.** Swiss-born chef Michael Kloeti trained in Europe and New York before opening this dining establishment in a 19th-century farmhouse outside Stowe. His four-course prix-fixe menus ($$$$) highlight European cuisine such as roasted rabbit with mirepoix or ravioli with braised autumn vegetables. ⊠ *4182 Stowe-Waterbury Rd. (Rte. 100), 6 mi south of Stowe, Waterbury Center* ☎ *802/244–7476* ▭ *AE, DC, MC, V* ⊘ *Closed Tues. No lunch.*

★ $$–$$$ ✕ **Mes Amis.** At this small bistro, locals queue up for house specialties such as fresh oysters, lobster bisque, braised lamb shanks, roast duck (secret recipe), and bananas Foster. You can dine in the candlelit dining room or outside on the patio, especially on a warm summer's night. ⊠ *311 Mountain Rd.* ☎ *802/253–8669* ▭ *AE, D, MC, V* ⊘ *Closed Mon.*

$$–$$$ ✕ **Red Basil.** Stowe's new "in" dinner spot enhances its traditional Thai entrées with fresh cilantro, kaffir lime leaves, lemongrass, and ginger. The panang curry is smooth, just a bit hot, and delicious; you can also order from the sushi bar. The martini bar has 18 varieties of James Bond's favorite libation. ⊠ *294 Mountain Rd.* ☎ *802/253–4478* ▭ *AE, MC, V* ⊘ *No lunch weekends.*

$$$$ ✕🏨 **Topnotch at Stowe Resort and Spa.** One of the state's poshest resorts occupies 120 acres overlooking Mt. Mansfield. Floor-to-ceiling windows, a freestanding metal fireplace, and heavy stone walls distinguish the lobby. The spacious rooms are country-chic, with Anichini linens and other accents like painted barn-board walls. Maxwell's restaurant ($$–$$$$) serves contemporary continental cuisine. Service throughout the resort is impeccable. ⊠ *4000 Mountain Rd., 05672* ☎ *802/253–8585 or 800/451–8686* 🖶 *802/253–9263* ⊕ *www.topnotch-resort.com* ⚲ *71 rooms, 9 suites, 14 town houses* ♿ *2 restaurants, cable TV, 10 tennis courts (4 indoors), 2 pools (1 indoors), massage, sauna, spa, horseback riding, sleigh rides, bar, video game room, no-smoking rooms* ▭ *AE, D, DC, MC, V* ⦿ *BP, FAP, MAP.*

$$–$$$$ ✕🏨 **Green Mountain Inn.** Welcoming guests since 1850, this classic red-brick inn in downtown Stowe has all the amenities of a resort, such as an outdoor heated pool open year-round. But the rooms in the main building and annex still feel like a country inn, with Early American furnishings. Newer buildings have luxury rooms and suites. The Whip Bar & Grill ($$–$$$) puts an interesting twist on comfort food, as in cheddar-cheese-and-apple-stuffed chicken. ⊠ *18 Main St., 05672* ☎ *802/253–7301 or 800/253–7302* 🖶 *802/253–5096* ⊕ *www.greenmountaininn. com* ⚲ *105 rooms* ♿ *2 restaurants, Wi-Fi, pool, gym, hot tub, massage, sauna, recreation room* ▭ *AE, MC, V* ⦿ *BP.*

$$$$ 🏨 **Stone Hill Inn.** The amenities of a fine hotel and the intimacy of a B&B characterize this adult-oriented inn just off Mountain Road. Each elegantly decorated (and soundproof) guest room has a king-size bed, sitting area, and two-person whirlpool bath in front of a fireplace. Common

areas include a sitting room and a game room, and the 10 acres of grounds are beautifully landscaped with gardens and waterfalls. ☒ *89 Houston Farm Rd., 05672* ☎ *802/253–6282* 🖷 *802/253–7415* ⊕ *www. stonehillinn.com* ➳ *9 rooms* ♻ *Cable TV, in-room VCRs, Wi-Fi, outdoor hot tub, hiking, tobogganing, recreation room* ▱ *AE, D, DC, MC, V* ¦◎¦ *BP.*

$$$$ ⊞ **Stoweflake Mountain Resort and Spa.** Accommodations here range from standard hotel rooms to luxurious suites with fireplaces, refrigerators, double sinks, and whirlpool tubs. One- to three-bedroom town houses sit on the perimeter of the resort. The spa overlooks an herb and flower labyrinth and is connected to the fitness center via a faux covered bridge. The resort hosts Stowe's annual Hot Air Balloon Festival. ☒ *1746 Mountain Rd.* ⊕ *Box 369, 05672* ☎ *802/253–7355* 🖷 *802/ 253–6858* ⊕ *www.stoweflake.com* ➳ *94 rooms, 30 town houses* ♻ *2 restaurants, some kitchenettes, some microwaves, cable TV, driving range, putting green, 2 tennis courts, pool, gym, hair salon, sauna, spa, bicycles, sleigh rides, business services, meeting rooms* ▱ *AE, D, DC, MC, V* ¦◎¦ *BP, MAP.*

$$ ⊞ **Stowe Motel & Snowdrift.** This family-owned motel sits on 16 acres across the river from the Stowe recreation path. Accommodations range from one-room studios with small kitchenettes to modern two-bedroom fireplace suites. Late-model mountain bikes, kids' bikes, tricycles, bike trailers, and helmets are available to guests. The motel is owned by Peter Ruschp, whose father Sepp founded the Mt. Mansfield ski school in 1936. ☒ *2043 Mountain Rd. (Rte. 108), 05672* ☎ *802/253–7629 or 800/829–7629* 🖷 *802/253–9971* ⊕ *www.stowemotel.com* ➳ *52 rooms, 4 suites* ♻ *Some kitchenettes, refrigerators, cable TV, tennis court, 2 pools, outdoor hot tub, bicycles, mountain bikes, croquet, recreation room, some pets allowed (fee)* ▱ *AE, D, MC, V* ¦◎¦ *CP.*

Nightlife & the Arts

NIGHTLIFE The **Matterhorn Night Club** (☒ 4969 Mountain Rd. ☎ 802/253–8198) hosts live music and dancing Thursday–Saturday nights and has a separate martini bar. The **Rusty Nail** (☒ 1190 Mountain Rd. ☎ 802/253–6245) rocks to live music on weekends.

THE ARTS **Stowe Performing Arts** (☎ 802/253–7792) sponsors a series of classical and jazz concerts in July in the Trapp Family Lodge meadow. **Stowe Theater Guild** (☒ Town Hall Theater, Main St. ☎ 802/253–3961 summer only) performs musicals in July and August.

Sports & the Outdoors

A **recreation path** begins behind the Community Church in town and meanders for about 5½ mi along the river valley, with many entry points along the way. Whether you're on foot, skis, bike, or in-line skates, it's a tranquil spot to enjoy the outdoors.

BIKING The **Mountain Sports and Bike Shop** (☒ Mountain Rd. ☎ 802/253–7919) sells and rents bicycles.

CANOEING & **Umiak Outdoor Outfitters** (☒ 849 S. Main St. [Rte. 100], just south of
KAYAKING Stowe Village ☎ 802/253–2317) rents canoes and kayaks for day trips and leads overnight excursions. The store also operates a rental outpost

at Lake Elmore State Park in Elmore, on the Winooski River off Route 2 in Waterbury, at North Beach in Burlington, and on the Lamoille River in Jeffersonville.

FISHING The **Fly Rod Shop** (✉ Rte. 100, 1½ mi south of Stowe ☎ 802/253–7346 or 800/535–9763) provides a guiding service; gives fly-tying, casting, and rod-building classes in winter; rents fly tackle; and sells equipment, including classic and collectible firearms.

GOLF **Stowe Country Club** (✉ Mountain Rd. ☎ 802/253–4893) has a scenic 18-hole, par-72 course; a driving range; and a putting green. Greens fee is $45–$75; cart rental is $18.

HIKING An ascent of **Mt. Mansfield** makes for a scenic day hike. Trails lead from Route 108 (Mountain Road) to the summit ridge, where they meet the north-to-south Long Trail. Views from the summit take in New Hampshire's White Mountains, New York's Adirondacks across Lake Champlain, and southern Québec. The Green Mountain Club publishes a trail guide.

ICE-SKATING **Jackson Arena** (✉ Park St. ☎ 802/253–6148) is a public ice-skating rink, with skate rentals available.

TENNIS **Topnotch at Stowe Resort and Spa** has six outdoor and four indoor courts. Public courts are at Stowe's elementary school.

Shopping

In Stowe, **Mountain Road** is lined with shops from town up toward the ski area. North of Stowe, shops line Route 100 from Interstate 89. Watch apples pressed into cider at the **Cold Hollow Cider Mill** (✉ Rte. 100, 3 mi north of I–89 ☎ 802/244–8771 or 800/327–7537), a very popular tourist attraction. The on-site store sells cider, baked goods, Vermont produce, and specialty foods. On Route 100 south toward Waterbury, between the cider mill and Ben & Jerry's, you can visit the **Cabot Cheese Annex Store** (✉ Rte. 100, 2½ mi north of I–89 ☎ 802/244–6334). South of Waterbury, don't miss the freshly baked, maple-glazed sticky buns at the **Red Hen Baking Company** (✉ Rte. 100 ☎ 802/244–0966).

Ski Area

STOWE MOUNTAIN RESORT To be precise, the name of the village is Stowe and the name of the mountain is Mt. Mansfield, but to generations of skiers, the area, the complex, and the region are just plain Stowe. The resort is a classic that dates from the 1930s. Even today, the area's mystique attracts as many serious skiers as social skiers. Improved snowmaking, new lifts, and free shuttle buses that gather skiers from lodges, inns, and motels along Mountain Road have added convenience to the Stowe experience. Yet the traditions remain: the Winter Carnival in January, the Sugar Slalom in April, ski weeks all winter. Three base lodges provide the essentials, including two on-mountain restaurants. In 2004 the resort broke ground on its 10-year expansion plan at the Spruce Peak base area. Plans are to include new base lodges and lifts, a hotel, retail shops, and a golf course.

Downhill. Mt. Mansfield, with an elevation of 4,395 feet and a vertical drop of 2,360 feet, is one of the giants among eastern ski mountains. The mountain's symmetrical shape allows skiers of all abilities long, satisfying runs from the summit. The famous Front Four (National, Liftline, Starr, and Goat) are the intimidating centerpieces for tough, expert runs, yet there is plenty of mellow intermediate skiing, with 59% of the runs rated at that level. One long beginner trail, the Toll Road Trail, is 6 km 3½ mi). Mansfield's satellite sector is a network of intermediate trails and one expert trail off a basin served by a gondola. Spruce Peak, separate from the main mountain, is a teaching hill and a pleasant experience for intermediates and beginners. In addition to the high-speed, eight-passenger gondola, Stowe has 11 lifts, including 2 quads, 2 triples, and 5 double chairlifts, plus 1 handle tow, to service its 48 trails. Night-skiing trails are accessed by the gondola. The resort has 73% snow-making coverage. Snowboard facilities include a half pipe and two terrain parks—one for beginners, at Spruce Peak, and one for experts, on the Mt. Mansfield side.

Cross-country. The resort has 35 km (22 mi) of groomed cross-country trails and 40 km (24 mi) of backcountry trails. Four interconnecting cross-country ski areas have more than 150 km (90 mi) of groomed trails within the town of Stowe.

Summer activities. The resort provides hiking, in-line skating, an alpine slide, gondola rides, and an 18-hole golf course.

✉ *5781 Mountain Rd., 05672* ☎ *802/253–3000, 802/253–3600 snow conditions, 800/253–4754 lodging* ⊕ *www.stowe.com.*

The Craftsburys

㉒ *27 mi northeast of Stowe.*

The three villages of the Craftsburys—Craftsbury Common, Craftsbury, and East Craftsbury—are among Vermont's finest and oldest towns. Handsome white houses and barns, the requisite common, and terrific views make them well worth the drive. Craftsbury General Store in Craftsbury Village is a great place to stock up on picnic supplies and local information. The rolling farmland hints at the way Vermont used to be: the area's sheer distance from civilization and its rugged weather have kept most of the state's development farther south.

Where to Stay & Eat

$$–$$$$ ✕⬚ **Inn on the Common.** All guest rooms at these three renovated Federal-style homes are appointed with antiques and hand-stitched quilts and have sitting areas. Some rooms have fireplaces or woodstoves. The Trellis Restaurant ($$–$$$), which serves excellent "innovative country" cuisine, has indoor and outdoor seating overlooking the gardens. ✉ *1162 N. Craftsbury Rd., Craftsbury Common 05827* ☎ *802/586–9619 or 800/521–2233* 🖷 *802/586–2249* ⊕ *www.innonthecommon. com* ⇨ *14 rooms, 2 suites* ⚘ *Restaurant, cross-country skiing, library; no a/c, no room TVs* ⊟ *AE, D, DC, MC, V* ⦿| *BP, MAP.*

$$–$$$$ ⬚ **Craftsbury Outdoor Center.** This outdoors enthusiast's haven has standard accommodations and sporting packages. Cross-country skiing is terrific on 135 km (80 mi) of trails (85 km [50 mi] groomed); the rest of the year, sculling and running camps are held. You can ski, mountain bike, and canoe at day-use rates; equipment rental is available. Meals are served buffet-style. ✉ *535 Lost Nation Rd., Craftsbury Common 05827* ☎ *802/586–7767 or 800/729–7751* 📠 *802/586–7768* ⊕ *www. craftsbury.com* ⇨ *49 rooms, 10 with bath; 4 cabins; 2 efficiencies* ⚖ *Dining room, boating, mountain bikes, cross-country skiing, meeting room; no a/c, no room TVs* ☰ *MC, V* ⦿| *MAP.*

¢–$ 🏠 **Craftsbury Bed & Breakfast.** Craftsbury's longest-operating traditional B&B is a lovely place to unwind. Owner Margaret Ramsdell creates an air of peaceful informality at her farmhouse, right down to the absence of a TV. Common rooms include a spacious country kitchen with a woodstove and a living room. In summer, relax on lawn chairs in the big yard; in winter, ski on the property's cross-country ski trails, which are part of a 105-km (65-mi) network. ✉ *Wylie Hill, Craftsbury Common 05827* ☎ *802/586–2206* ⊕ *www.pbpub.com/craftsburybb* ⇨ *6 rooms without bath* ⚖ *No a/c, no room TVs* ☰ *MC, V* ⦿| *BP.*

Greensboro

❷❸ *10 mi southeast of Craftsbury Common.*

Tucked along the southern shore of Caspian Lake, Greensboro has been a summer resort for literati, academics, and old-money types for more than a century. Yet, it exudes an unpretentious, genteel character where most of the people running about on errands seem to know each other. A town beach is right off the main street.

Where to Stay & Eat

$$$ ✕🏠 **Lakeview Inn.** A quiet place to unwind, this 19th-century inn is close to the town center. Rooms are tastefully decorated with period antiques. Breakfast, lunch, and dinner ($–$$$; closed Monday and Tuesday) are served in the large airy dining room with views of Caspian Lake. Menus are seasonal, using products from 40 local farmers and growers. ✉ *295 Breezy Ave., 05841* ☎ *802/533–2291 or 888/251–0100* 📠 *802/533–9815* ⊕ *www.lakeviewinn.biz* ⇨ *9 rooms, 1 suite* ⚖ *Restaurant, some pets allowed* ☰ *AE, MC, V* ⦿| *MAP.*

$$$$ 🏠 **Highland Lodge.** Tranquillity reigns at this 1860 house overlooking a pristine lake. The lodge's 120 acres of rambling woods and pastures are laced with hiking and skiing trails (ski rentals available). Comfortable guest rooms have Early American–style furnishings; most have views of the lake. The one- to three-bedroom cottages are more private (four with gas stoves stay open in winter). The traditional dinner menu might include such entrées as roast leg of lamb. ✉ *1608 Craftsbury Rd., 05841* ☎ *802/533–2647* 📠 *802/533–7494* ⊕ *www.highlandlodge.com* ⇨ *11 rooms, 11 cottages* ⚖ *Restaurant, tennis court, lake, boating, hiking, cross-country skiing, recreation room; no a/c, no room TVs* ☰ *D, DC, MC, V* ⊘ *Closed mid-Mar.–late May and mid-Oct.–mid-Dec.* ⦿| *MAP.*

Shopping

The **Miller's Thumb** (✉ Main St. ☎ 802/533–2960 or 800/680–7886) sells Italian pottery, Vermont furniture, crafts and antiques, and April Cornell clothing and linens. **Willey's Store** (✉ Main St. ☎ 802/533–

2621) is a classic general store of the "If-we-don't-have-it-you-don't-need-it" kind.

Jeffersonville

㉔ *36 mi west of Greensboro, 18 mi north of Stowe, 28 mi northeast of Burlington.*

Jeffersonville is just over Smugglers' Notch from Stowe but miles away in feel and attitude. In summer, you can drive over the notch road as it curves precipitously around boulders that have fallen from the cliffs above, then pass open meadows and old farmhouses and sugar shacks on the way down to town. Below the notch, Smugglers' Notch Ski Resort is the hub of much activity year-round. Downtown Jeffersonville, once home to an artist colony, is quiet but has excellent dining and sophisticated art galleries.

West of town, **Boyden Valley Winery** (⊠ Junction of Rtes. 15 and 104, Cambridge ☎ 802/644–8151) conducts tours and tastings and showcases an excellent selection of Vermont specialty products and local handicrafts, including fine furniture. The winery is closed Monday, June–December, and Monday–Thursday, January–May.

Where to Stay & Eat

$–$$ ✕ **158 Main.** As soon as this restaurant opened in January 2004, locals were lining up at the door. Its menu selections range from sesame-seared yellowfin tuna with jasmine rice and wasabi to the locals' favorite breakfast: eggs, homemade toast, and home fries for $2.58. Portions are big, prices are not. Sunday brunch is served 8 AM–2 PM. ⊠ *158 Main St.* ☎ *802/644–8100* ⚅ *Reservations not accepted* ▤ *AE, DC, MC, V* ⊘ *Closed Mon. No dinner Sun.*

$$$$ 🏨 **Smugglers' Notch Resort.** From watercolor workshops to giant water
FodorśChoice parks to weeklong camps for kids, this family resort has a plethora of
★ activities. In winter, the main activity is skiing, but children's programs abound. Lodging is in clustered condominium complexes, with the condos set away from the resort center. Rates are packages for three, five, and seven nights and can include use of all resort amenities and lift tickets and ski lessons in season. ⊠ *4232 Rte. 108 S, 05464* ☎ *802/644–8851 or 800/451–8752* 🖨 *802/644–1230* ⊕ *www.smuggs.com* ⤦ *550 condominiums* ⚅ *4 restaurants, cable TV, 8 tennis courts, pools, hot tubs, downhill skiing, ice-skating, bar, babysitting, children's programs (ages 3–17), playgrounds; no a/c in some rooms* ▤ *AE, DC, MC, V.*

Sports & the Outdoors

Applecheek Farm (⊠ 567 McFarlane Rd., Hyde Park ☎ 802/888–4482) runs daytime and evening (by lantern) hay and sleigh rides, llama treks, and farm tours. **Green River Canoe & Kayak** (☎ 802/644–8336 or 802/644–8714), at the junction of routes 15 and 108 behind Jana's Restaurant, rents canoes and kayaks on the Lamoille River and leads guided canoe trips to Boyden Valley Winery. **Northern Vermont Llamas** (⊠ 766 Lapland Rd., Waterville ☎ 802/644–2257) conducts half- and full-day treks from May through October along the cross-country ski trails of

Smugglers' Notch. The llamas carry everything, including snacks and lunches. Advance reservations are essential.

Smugglers' Notch State Park (✉ 6 mi north of Stowe ☎ 802/253–4014) is good for picnicking and hiking on wild terrain among large boulders.

Shopping

ANTIQUES Route 15 between Jeffersonville and Johnson is dubbed the "antiques highway." The **Buggy Man** (✉ Rte. 15, 7 mi east of Jeffersonville ☎ 802/635–2110) sells American furniture and collectibles, including horse-drawn vehicles. The **Green Apple Antique Center** (✉ 60 Main St. ☎ 802/644–2989) has a good bakery in the back of the store. **Smugglers' Notch Antique Center** (✉ Rte. 108 ☎ 802/644–8321) sells antiques and collectibles of 60 dealers in a rambling barn.

CLOTHING The **Forget-Me-Not Shop** (✉ 942-B Rte. 15 W, 6½ mi east of Jeffersonville, Johnson ☎ 802/635–2335) sells men's and women's clothing, military surplus, and jewelry at incredibly low prices. **Johnson Woolen Mills** (✉ Main St., 9 mi east of Jeffersonville, Johnson ☎ 802/635–2271) is an authentic factory store with deals on woolen blankets, yard goods, and the famous Johnson outerwear.

CRAFTS **Vermont Rug Makers** (✉ Rte. 100C, 10 mi east of Jeffersonville, East Johnson ☎ 802/635–2434) weaves imaginative rugs and tapestries from fabrics, wools, and exotic materials. Its International Gallery displays rugs and tapestries from around the world.

Ski Area

SMUGGLERS' NOTCH RESORT This resort complex consistently wins accolades for its family programs. Its children's ski school is one of the best in the country—possibly *the* best. But skiers of all levels come here (Smugglers' was the first ski area in the East to designate a triple-black-diamond run—the Black Hole). All the essentials are available in the village at the base of the Morse Mountain lifts, including lodgings, restaurants, and several shops.

Downhill. Smugglers' has three mountains. The highest, Madonna, with a vertical drop of 2,610 feet, is in the center and connects with a trail network to Sterling (1,500 feet vertical). The third mountain, Morse (1,150 feet vertical), is adjacent to Smugglers' "village" of shops, restaurants, and condos; it's connected to the other peaks by trails and a shuttle bus. The wild, craggy landscape lends a pristine wilderness feel to the skiing experience on the two higher mountains. The tops of each of the mountains have expert terrain—a couple of double-black diamonds make Madonna memorable. Intermediate trails fill the lower sections. Morse has many beginner and advanced beginner trails. Smugglers' 70 trails are served by eight lifts, including six chairs and two surface lifts. Top-to-bottom snowmaking on all three mountains allows for 62% coverage. Several terrain parks are provided for snowboarders, including Prohibition Park, at 3,500 feet one of the longest in Vermont. Night skiing and snowboarding classes are given at the new Learning and Fun Park.

Cross-country/snowshoeing. The area has 27 km (18 mi) of groomed and tracked cross-country trails and 20 km (12 mi) of snowshoe trails.

Other activities. The self-contained village has outdoor ice-skating and sleigh rides. The numerous snowshoeing programs include family walks and backcountry trips. SmuggsCentral has an indoor pool, hot tub, Funzone playground with slides and miniature golf, and a teen center, open from 5 PM until midnight.

Summer and year-round activities. Smugglers' has a full roster of summertime programs, including pools, complete with waterfalls and waterslides; the Giant Rapid River Ride (the longest water ride in the state); lawn games; mountain biking and hiking programs; and craft workshops for adults. ⊠ *Rte. 108, 05464* ☎ *802/644–8851 or 800/451–8752* ⊕ *www.smuggs.com.*

Burlington

❷❺ *31 mi southwest of Jeffersonville, 76 mi south of Montréal, 349 mi north*
Fodor'sChoice *of New York City, 223 mi northwest of Boston.*
★

As you drive along Main Street toward downtown Burlington, it's easy to see why the city is so often called one of America's most livable small cities. Downtown is filled with hip restaurants and nightclubs, art galleries, and the Church Street Marketplace—a bustling pedestrian mall with trendy shops, craft vendors, street performers, and sidewalk cafés. Just beyond, Lake Champlain shimmers beneath the towering Adirondacks on the New York shore.

On the shores of the lake, Burlington's revitalized waterfront teems with outdoors enthusiasts who stroll along its recreation path and ply the waters in sailboats and motor craft in summer. A 500-passenger, three-level cruise vessel, **Shoreline Cruise's *Spirit of Ethan Allen III,*** takes people on narrated cruises and on dinner and sunset sailings with awesome views of the Adirondacks and Green Mountains. ⊠ *Burlington Boat House, College and Battery Sts.* ☎ *802/862–8300* ⊕ *www.soea.com* 🖂 *$12* ⊘ *Cruises late May–mid-Oct., daily 10–9.*

★ ♥ Part of the waterfront's revitalization, the **ECHO Leahy Center for Lake Champlain** is an aquarium and science center. Kids can check out the 100 hands-on, interactive wind and water exhibits and the sunken shipwreck. ⊠ *1 College St.* ☎ *802/864–1848* ⊕ *www.echovermont.org* 🖂 *$9* ⊘ *Daily 10–5, Thurs. until 8.*

Crowning the hilltop above Burlington is the campus of the **University of Vermont** (☎ 802/656–3131), known simply as UVM for the abbreviation of its Latin name, Universitas Viridis Montis—the University of the Green Mountains. With more than 10,000 students, UVM is the state's principal institution of higher learning. The most architecturally interesting buildings face the green, which contains a statue of UVM founder Ira Allen, Ethan's brother. The **Fleming Museum** (⊠ Colchester Ave. ☎ 802/656–0750) houses American portraits and landscapes, including works by Sargent, Homer, and Bierstadt; two Corots and a Fragonard; and an Egyptian mummy. Works by contemporary Vermont artists are also exhibited.

Burlington's **Intervale,** once a green floodplain along the Winooski River, the site of early farms, had been turned into a city dump by the 1970s.

Then the ecologically oriented founder of a gardening-equipment store jumpstarted a turnaround, and today the Invervale is again green, a zone of organic farms, community gardens, earthfriendly businesses, and nature trails. You can hike the trails or bike a 2-mi trail that connects with Burlington's 10-mi Cycle the City loop. **Gardener's Supply Company** (✉ 128 Intervale Rd. ☎ 802/660–3505 ⊕ www.gardeners.com), a major direct-mail gardening company, with greenhouses and outdoor display gardens, oversees the project. The company also provides maps, information, and a schedule of the many seasonal events held there.

One of the earliest residents of the Intervale was Ethan Allen, Vermont's Revolutionary-era guerrilla fighter, who remains a captivating figure. Exhibits at the **Ethan Allen Homestead** visitor center answer questions about his flamboyant life. The house contains such frontier hallmarks as rough saw-cut boards and an open hearth for cooking. A re-created Colonial kitchen garden resembles the one the Allens would have had. After the tour and multimedia presentation, you can stretch your legs on scenic trails along the Winooski River. ✉ *North Ave. off Rte. 127, north of Burlington* ☎ *802/865–4556* ⊕ *www.ethanallenhomestead.org* 🎟 *$5* ⊗ *May–Oct., daily.*

OFF THE BEATEN PATH

GREEN MOUNTAIN AUDUBON NATURE CENTER – This is a wonderful place to discover Vermont's outdoor wonders. The center's 300 acres of diverse habitats are a sanctuary for all things wild, and the 5 mi of trails provide an opportunity to explore the workings of differing natural communities. Events include dusk walks, wildflower and birding rambles, nature workshops, and educational activities for children and adults. The center is 18 mi southeast of Burlington. ✉ *255 Sherman Hollow Rd., Huntington* ☎ *802/434–3068* 🎟 *Donations accepted* ⊗ *Grounds daily dawn–dusk, center Mon.–Sat. 8–4.*

Where to Stay & Eat

$$–$$$ ✕ **Leunig's Bistro.** Church Street's café delivers alfresco dining, bistro cuisine, and live jazz Tuesday–Thursday evenings. Favorite entrées include rack of lamb and lavender-and-peppercorn-crusted tuna. A prix-fixe dinner for two for $30, served Sunday–Thursday 5–6, is one of the city's best bargains. ✉ *115 Church St.* ☎ *802/863–3759* ▭ *AE, D, DC, MC, V.*

★ **$$–$$$** ✕ **Trattoria Delia.** Didn't manage to rent that villa in Umbria this year? The next best thing, if your travels bring you to Burlington, is this superb Italian country eatery just around the corner from City Hall Park. Game and fresh produce are the stars, as in wild boar braised in red wine, tomatoes, rosemary, and sage served on soft polenta. Wood-grilled items are a specialty. ✉ *152 St. Paul St.* ☎ *802/864–5253* ▭ *AE, D, DC, MC, V* ⊗ *No lunch.*

$–$$$ ✕ **Cannon's.** Don't let the shopping center location deter you. This family-style Italian restaurant has more than just spaghetti on the menu. Pasta selections are diverse and include such items as fettuccine with sautéed chicken strips and snow peas, and noodle-less eggplant lasagna. Entrées range from traditional Italian (shrimp scampi) to American (sirloin steak). ✉ *1127 North Ave.* ☎ *802/652–5151* ▭ *DC, MC, V* ⊗ *No lunch Sat.*

$–$$$ ✕ **NECI Commons.** The initials stand for New England Culinary Institute, the respected Montpelier academy whose students and teachers run this busy restaurant and bar on Burlington's pedestrian mall. House specialties include rotisserie chicken with cheddar mashed potatoes and, on the lunch menu, a smoked salmon club sandwich. ⊠ *25 Church St.* ☏ *802/862–6324* ⊟ *AE, D, MC, V* ⊗ *Closed Mon.*

$–$$ ✕ **Ri Ra.** Brought to Burlington from Ireland in pieces and reassembled on-site, this Irish pub serves classic fare such as bangers-and-mash and fish-and-chips, along with burgers and fish. ⊠ *123 Church St.* ☏ *802/ 860–9401* ⊟ *AE, MC, V.*

$–$$ ✕ **A Single Pebble.** The creative, authentic Asian selections served here
Fodor'sChoice include traditional clay-pot dishes as well as wok specialties, such as sesame
★ catfish and kung po chicken. The dry-fried green beans (sautéed with flecks of pork, black beans, preserved vegetables, and garlic) are a house specialty. All dishes can be made without meat. ⊠ *133-135 Bank St.* ☏ *802/865–5200* ⌨ *Reservations essential* ⊟ *AE, D, MC, V* ⊗ *No lunch weekends.*

$$–$$$$ ✕▥ **Inn at Essex.** Billing itself as "Vermont's Culinary Resort," this inn and conference center is about 10 mi from downtown Burlington—next to Essex Outlet Fair—and has two restaurants ($$$$) run by the New England Culinary Institute. Butler's has a three-course prix-fixe menu, which might include pork tournedos with sweet pea puree or pan-seared halibut with lobster dumplings. At the Tavern, chicken puff pie and daily flat-bread pizza specials are among the highlights. Susan Sargent–designed rooms are adorned with her vibrant colors in everything from the wall paint to the pillow covers; 30 rooms have fireplaces. ⊠ *70 Essex Way, off Rte. 289, Essex Junction 05452* ☏ *802/878–1100 or 800/727–4295* ⎙ *802/878–0063* ⊕ *www.vtculinaryresort.com* ⇩ *119 rooms* ♨ *2 restaurants, cable TV, pool, bar, library, business services, meeting rooms* ⊟ *AE, D, MC, V.*

★ **$$–$$$$** ▥ **Willard Street Inn.** High in the historic hill section of Burlington, this ivy-covered grand house with an exterior marble staircase and English gardens incorporates elements of Queen Anne and Colonial–Georgian-revival styles. The stately foyer, paneled in cherry, leads to a more formal sitting room with velvet drapes. The solarium is bright and sunny with marble floors, many plants, and big velvet couches for contemplating views of Lake Champlain. All the rooms have down comforters and phones; some have lake views and canopied beds. Orange French toast is among the breakfast favorites. ⊠ *349 S. Willard St., 05401* ☏ *802/ 651–8710 or 800/577–8712* ⎙ *802/651–8714* ⊕ *www.willardstreetinn. com* ⇩ *14 rooms* ♨ *Cable TV, Internet room* ⊟ *AE, D, MC, V* ⏣ *BP.*

$$–$$$ ▥ **Lang House.** Within walking distance of downtown, this grand Victorian home is full of fine woodwork, plaster detailing, and stained-glass windows. Two rooms have tubs, one has a whirlpool tub, and two rooms have sitting areas in the home's three-story turret. ⊠ *360 Main St., 05401* ☏ *802/652–2500 or 877/919–9799* ⎙ *802/651–8717* ⊕ *www.langhouse. com* ⇩ *11 rooms* ♨ *Cable TV, Wi-Fi* ⊟ *AE, D, MC, V* ⏣ *BP.*

Nightlife & the Arts

NIGHTLIFE The music at the **Club Metronome** (⊠ 188 Main St. ☏ 802/865–4563) ranges from cutting-edge sounds to funk, blues, and reggae. National and local musicians come to **Higher Ground** (⊠ 1214 Williston Rd., S. Burlington ☎ 802/265–0777). The band Phish got its start at **Nectar's** (⊠ 188 Main St. ☎ 802/658–4771). This place is always jumping to the sounds of local bands and never charges a cover. **Ri Ra** (⊠ 123 Church St. ☎ 802/860–9401) hosts live entertainment with an Irish flair. **Vermont Pub and Brewery** (⊠ 144 College St. ☎ 802/865–0500) makes its own beer and fruit seltzers and is arguably the most popular spot in town. Folk musicians play here regularly.

THE ARTS The **Fire House Art Gallery** (⊠ 135 Church St. ☎ 802/865–7165) exhibits works by local artists. **Flynn Theatre for the Performing Arts** (⊠ 153 Main St. ☎ 802/652–4500 information, 802/863–5966 tickets ⊕ www. flynncenter.org), a grandiose old structure, is the cultural heart of Burlington; it schedules the Vermont Symphony Orchestra, theater, dance, big-name musicians, and lectures. **St. Michael's Playhouse** (⊠ St. Michael's College, Rte. 15, Colchester ☎ 802/654–2281 box office, 802/654–2617 administrative office) stages performances in the McCarthy Arts Center. The **UVM Lane Series** (☎ 802/656–4455 programs and times, 802/835–5966 Flynn box office) sponsors classical as well as folk music concerts in the Flynn Theatre, UVM Recital Hall, and St. Michael's College McCarthy Arts Center. The **Vermont Symphony Orchestra** (☎ 802/864–5741) performs throughout the state year-round and at the Flynn from October through May.

Sports & the Outdoors

BEACHES The **North Beaches** are on the northern edge of Burlington. Leddy Beach is popular for sailboarding. ⊠ *North Beach Park off North Ave.* ☎ *802/864–0123* ⊠ *Leddy Beach, Leddy Park Rd. off North Ave.*

BIKING Burlington's 10-mi Cycle the City loop runs along the waterfront, connecting several city parks and beaches. It also passes the Community Boathouse and runs within several blocks of downtown restaurants and shops. **North Star Cyclery** (⊠ 100 Main St. ☎ 802/863–3832) rents bicycles and provides maps of bicycle routes. **Ski Rack** (⊠ 85 Main St. ☎ 802/658–3313 or 800/882–4530) rents and services bikes and provides maps.

WATER SPORTS **Burlington Community Boathouse** (⊠ Foot of College St., Burlington Harbor ☎ 802/865–3377) rents 19-foot sailboats. **Waterfront Boat Rentals** (⊠ Foot of Maple St. on Perkins Pier, Burlington Harbor ☎ 802/864–4858) rents kayaks, canoes, rowboats, and skiffs, and Boston whalers.

Shopping

ANTIQUES **Architectural Salvage Warehouse** (⊠ 53 Main St. ☎ 802/658–5011) is a great place to hunt for claw-foot tubs, stained-glass windows, mantels, andirons, and other similar items. The large rhinoceros head bursting out of the **Conant Custom Brass** (⊠ 270 Pine St. ☎ 802/658–4482) storefront may tempt you in to see the custom work, including decorative lighting and bathroom fixtures.

CRAFTS In addition to its popular pottery, **Bennington Potters North** (⊠ 127 College St. ☎ 802/863–2221 or 800/205–8033) stocks interesting gifts, glassware, furniture, and other housewares. **Vermont State Craft Center/Frog**

Hollow (⊠ 85 Church St. ☎ 802/863–6458) displays contemporary and traditional crafts by more than 200 Vermont artisans.

MALLS &
MARKETPLACES
The remodeled **Burlington Square Mall** (⊠ Church St. ☎ 802/658–2545) has a Starbucks, a large Filene's department store, and a few dozen other shops. The **Champlain Mill** (⊠ U.S. 2/7, northeast of Burlington ☎ 802/655–9477), a former woolen mill on the banks of the Winooski River, holds three floors of stores, including several clothing shops and restaurants. **Church Street Marketplace** (⊠ Main St. to Pearl St. ☎ 802/863–1648), a pedestrian thoroughfare, is lined with boutiques, cafés, and street vendors. Look for bargains at the rapidly growing **Essex Outlet Fair** (⊠ Junction of Rtes. 15 and 289, Essex ☎ 802/878–2851), with such outlets as Brooks Brothers, Polo Ralph Lauren, and Levi's, among others. **University Mall** (⊠ Dorset St. ☎ 802/863–1066), housing Sears, Bon Ton, and JCPenney, continues to expand.

SPORTING GOODS
Burton (⊠ 80 Industrial Pkwy. ☎ 802/660–3200), the company that helped start snowboarding, sells equipment and clothing at its flagship store.

Shelburne

㉖ *5 mi south of Burlington.*

A few miles south of Burlington, the Champlain Valley gives way to fertile farmland, affording stunning views of the rugged Adirondacks across the lake. In the middle of this farmland is the village of Shelburne, chartered in the mid-18th century and now largely a bedroom community for Burlington. You can trace much of New England's history simply by wandering through the 45 acres and 37 buildings of the **Shelburne Museum.** The outstanding 80,000-object collection of Americana consists of 18th- and 19th-century period homes and furniture, fine and folk art, farm tools, more than 200 carriages and sleighs, Audubon prints, an old-fashioned jail, and even a private railroad car from the days of steam. The museum also has an assortment of duck decoys, an old stone cottage, a display of early toys, and the *Ticonderoga*, a side-wheel steamship, grounded amid lawn and trees. ⊠ *U.S. 7* ☎ *802/985–3346* ⊕ *www.shelburnemuseum.org* 🎫 *$18* ⊙ *May–Oct., daily 10–5.*

FodorsChoice
★

FodorsChoice
★
Founded in the 1880s as a private estate, the 1,400-acre **Shelburne Farms** is an educational and cultural resource center with, among other things, a working dairy farm, a Children's Farmyard, and a spot for watching the farm's famous cheddar cheese being made. Frederick Law Olmsted, cocreator of New York's Central Park, designed the magnificent grounds overlooking Lake Champlain. For an additional charge of $3, you can tour the 1891 breeding barn. ⊠ *West of U.S. 7 at Harbor and Bay Rds.* ☎ *802/985–8686* ⊕ *www.shelburnefarms.org* 🎫 *Day pass $6, tour an additional $5* ⊙ *Visitor center and shop daily 10–5; tours mid-May–mid-Oct. (last tour at 3:30); walking trails daily 10–4, weather permitting.*

On the 25-minute tour of the **Vermont Teddy Bear Company,** you'll hear more puns than you ever thought possible and learn how a few homemade bears, sold from a cart on Church Street, have turned into a multimillion-dollar business. A children's play tent is set up outdoors in summer, and you can wander the beautiful 57-acre property. ⊠ *6655*

Vermont on Two Wheels

VERMONT HAS MORE THAN 14,000 MI OF ROADS, and almost 80% of them are town roads that see little high-speed traffic, making them ideal for scenic bike rides. The state is also threaded with thousands of miles of dirt roads suitable for mountain biking. Although mountain-bike trails and old farm and logging roads wind through the Green Mountain State, most are on private property and are therefore not mapped. Several mountain-biking centers around the state have extensive trail networks (and maps) that will keep avid fat-tire fans happy for a few hours or a few days. To road bike in Vermont you'll want a bicycle with at least 10 gears and a map. The only roads that prohibit cycling are the four-lane highways and Rte. 7 and 4 in Rutland.

To make a relatively easy 16-mi loop, begin at the blinker on U.S. 7 in **Shelburne** and follow Mt. Philo Road south to Hinesburg Rd., then west to Charlotte. Lake Rd., Orchard Rd., and Mouth of River Rd. pass orchards and berry fields. Bostwick Rd. returns to U.S. 7. In the heart of the central Green Mountains is a moderate 18-mi loop on Rtes. 4, 100, and 100A that passes Calvin Coolidge's home in **Plymouth Notch.** West of **Rutland** is a beautiful 27-mi ride on Routes 140, 30, and 133 that passes swimming holes, then hugs the shore of Lake St. Catherine. Start in Middletown Springs. A scenic 43 mi ride in the **Northeast Kingdom** passes through picturesque Peacham and the birches and maples of Groton State Forest. Start in Danville and follow Peacham Rd., then Routes 302, 232, and U.S. 2. For a real test, try the 48-mi ride over **Middlebury and Brandon Gaps** on Rtes. 125 and 73. The routes connect via Routes 153 and 100.

Mountain Biking Centers:

Considered one of the best mountain-biking destinations in the U.S., the **Kingdom Trails** (⊠ Rte. 114, East Burke ☎ 802/626-0737 ⊕ www.kingdomtrails.org ☜ $7) are a continually growing 100+-mi network of singletrack trails and abandoned farm and logging roads maintained by the Kingdom Trail Association. The trails zigzag through fern grottos, climb into sugarbushes, and run through meadows and hayfields with views of working farms and forested mountains.

Closer to civilization, the **Catamount Outdoor Family Center** (⊠ 592 Governor Chittenden Rd., Williston ☎ 802/879-6001 ☜ $6) outside Burlington has mountain-biking trails throughout its 450 acres. With views of Mt. Mansfield and Lake Champlain, the trails wind through old pastures and into the woods. A Wednesday night race series from June to September is open to all abilities, and the center offers mountain-bike lessons and camps throughout the summer.

Two ski resorts have well-developed mountain-biking networks: **Mount Snow** (⊠ Rte. 100, West Dover ☎ 802/464-4040 ☜ $30 with lift, $10 for trails only) and **Killington** (⊠ Killington Access Rd., Killington ☎ 802/422-6232 ☜ $32 with lift, $8 for trails only) both have 45 mi of lift-served mountain-biking trails. Many of the singletrack trails are littered with slippery tree roots and rocks, making these networks best for advanced fat-tire riders. But Mount Snow's Mountain Bike School offers clinics in the summer.

3

Shelburne Rd. ☎ *802/985–3001* ⊒ *Tour $2* ⊙ *Tours Mon.–Sat. 9:30–5, Sun. 10:30–4; store daily 9–6.*

Where to Stay & Eat

★ **$$–$$$** ✕ **Café Shelburne.** This popular restaurant serves creative French bistro cuisine. Some specialties are sweetbreads in a port wine and mushroom sauce in puff pastry and homemade fettuccine with Vermont goat cheese. Desserts such as the sweet chocolate layered terrine and maple-syrup mousse with orange terrine are fabulous. ⊠ *U.S. 7* ☎ *802/985–3939* ⊟ *AE, MC, V* ⊙ *Closed Sun. and Mon. No lunch.*

$–$$ ✕ **La Villa Mediterranean.** Made-to-order pasta dishes, pizza (in three sizes), grilled items such as salmon and lamb chops, and an assortment of tasty appetizers make this family-friendly restaurant a popular choice for lunch and dinner. The large open dining room seats 60 at candlelit, linen-covered tables. Diners can watch chefs prepare their meals in the open kitchen. ⊠ *3762 Shelburne Rd. (Rte. 7), Tenneybrook Sq.* ☎ *802/985–2596* ⊟ *AE, D, MC, V* ⊙ *No lunch Sun.*

$$–$$$$ ✕⌂ **Inn at Shelburne Farms.** This turn-of-the-20th-century Tudor-style

FodorśChoice inn, once the home of William Seward and Lila Vanderbilt Webb, over-

★ looks Lake Champlain, the distant Adirondacks, and the sea of pastures that make up this 1,400-acre working farm. Each room is different, from the wallpaper to the period antiques. The dining room ($$–$$$$) defines elegance, and Sunday brunch (not served in May) is one of the area's best. Breakfast is served Monday–Saturday. ⊠ *Harbor Rd., 05482* ☎ *802/985–8498* ⊟ *802/985–1233* ⊕ *www.shelburnefarms.org* ⇨ *24 rooms, 17 with bath; 2 cottages* ⚭ *Restaurant, tennis court, lake, boating, fishing, billiards, hiking; no a/c, no room TVs* ⊟ *D, DC, MC, V* ⊙ *Closed mid-Oct.–mid-May.*

$$–$$$$ ⌂ **Heart of the Village Inn.** Each of the elegantly furnished rooms at this B&B in a handsomely restored 1886 Queen Anne Victorian across from Town Hall (and ½ mi from the Shelburne Museum) provides coziness and comfort. Five of the guest rooms are in the house itself, with four more and a suite in the carriage barn. In rooms with king-size beds, you can divide the beds into twins. ⊠ *5347 Shelburne Rd. (Rte. 7), 05482* ☎ *802/985–2800 or 877/808–1834* ⊟ *802/985–2870* ⊕ *www. heartofthevillage.com* ⇨ *8 rooms, 1 suite* ⚭ *Cable TV* ⊟ *AE, D, MC, V* ⍊ *BP.*

Shopping

When you enter the **Shelburne Country Store** (⊠ Village Green off U.S. 7 ☎ 802/985–3657) you'll step back in time. Walk past the potbellied stove and take in the aroma emanating from the fudge neatly piled behind huge antique glass cases. The store specializes in candles, weather vanes, glassware, and local foods.

Vergennes

㉗ *12 mi south of Shelburne.*

Vermont's oldest city, founded in 1788, is also the third oldest in New England. The downtown area is a compact district of Victorian homes and public buildings. Main Street slopes down to Otter Creek Falls, where cannonballs were made during the War of 1812. The statue of Thomas

MacDonough on the green immortalizes the victor of the Battle of Plattsburgh in 1814.

OFF THE
BEATEN
PATH
LAKE CHAMPLAIN MARITIME MUSEUM – This museum documents centuries of activity on the historically significant lake. Climb aboard a replica of Benedict Arnold's Revolutionary War gunboat moored in the lake, learn about shipwrecks, and watch craftsmen work at traditional boat-building and blacksmithing. Among the exhibits are a nautical archae-ology center, a conservation laboratory, and a restaurant. ⊠ *Basin Harbor Rd., 7 mi west of Vergennes, Basin Harbor* ☎ *802/475–2022* 🖃 *$9* ☉ *May–mid-Oct., daily 10–5.*

Where to Stay & Eat

$$$
FodorśChoice
★
× **Christophe's on the Green.** Amid simple elegance—high ceilings, crisp linens, fresh flowers—inside an old hotel in the center of town, this restau-rant serves classic, artfully prepared French cuisine. The seasonal menu might include a monkfish-and-crayfish flambé. Order à la carte or choose the three-course fixed-price dinner for $42 (there's also a pre-theater dinner for $35). ⊠ *5 Green St.* ☎ *802/877–3413* ▤ *MC, V* ☉ *Closed May–Oct., Sun. and Mon.; closed Nov. and Jan.; closed Dec., and Feb.–Apr., Sun.–Wed.*

$$–$$$
× **Starry Night Café.** Since it opened, this chic restaurant has become one of the hottest spots around, increasing in size to meet growing de-mand. Described as French-Asian cuisine, appetizers include house specials such as honey-chili glazed shrimp and gazpacho. Among the entrées are lobster-stuffed sole, pan-seared scallops, and grilled New York steak. ⊠ *5371 Rte. 7, 5 mi north of Vergennes, Ferrisburg* ☎ *802/877–6316* ⊕ *www.starrynightcafe.com* ▤ *MC, V* ☉ *Closed Mon. and Tues. No lunch.*

$$$$
FodorśChoice
★
×🖫 **Basin Harbor Club.** On 700 acres overlooking Lake Champlain, this family resort provides luxurious accommodations, a full roster of amenities, including an 18-hole golf course, boating (with a 40-foot tour boat), a 3,200-foot grass airstrip, and daylong children's programs. Some rooms in the guesthouses have fireplaces, decks, or porches. The cottages are charming and have one to three bedrooms. The restaurant menu ($–$$$$) is classic American, the wine list excellent. Jackets and ties are required in common areas after 6 PM from late-June through Labor Day. ⊠ *48 Basin Harbor Rd., 05491* ☎ *802/475–2311 or 800/622–4000* 🖷 *802/475–6545* ⊕ *www.basinharbor.com* 🛏 *36 rooms, 2 suites in 3 guesthouses, 77 cottages* ⚒ *3 restaurants, 18-hole golf course, 5 tennis courts, pool, health club, massage, boating, bicycles, children's programs (ages 3–15), some pets allowed; no a/c, no room TVs* ▤ *MC, V* ☉ *Closed mid-Oct.–mid-May* ⦿ *BP.*

$$–$$$$
🖫 **Whitford House.** Down a well-maintained dirt road, this remote late-18th-century country farmhouse sits on 37 acres of meadowlands. All three bedrooms in the main house have spectacular views of rolling dairy lands and the distant Adirondacks. The guest cottage, which sleeps four, has a microwave, refrigerator, and wet bar. ⊠ *912 Grandey Rd., 11 mi southwest of Vergennes, Addison 05491* ☎ *802/758–2704 or 800/746–2704* 🖷 *802/758–2089* ⊕ *www.whitfordhouseinn.com* 🛏 *3 rooms,*

1 cottage ♻ Bicycles, library, some pets allowed; no a/c, no room TVs ☰ MC, V ⏹ BP.

Shopping

Dakin Farm (✉ Rte. 7, 5 mi north of Vergennes ☎ 800/993–2546) sells cob-smoked ham, aged cheddar cheese, and other specialty foods. **Kennedy Brothers Marketplace** (✉ Rte. 22A ☎ 802/877–2975), in a large renovated creamery, displays the wares of local artisans.

Lake Champlain Islands

❷❽ *43 mi from Vergennes, 20 mi northwest of Shelburne, 15 mi northwest of Burlington.*

Lake Champlain, which stretches more than 100 mi southward from the Canadian border, forms the northern part of the boundary between New York and Vermont. Within it is an elongated archipelago composed of several islands—Isle La Motte, North Hero, Grand isle, South Hero—and the Alburg Peninsula. With a temperate climate, the islands hold several apple orchards and are a center of water recreation in summer and ice fishing in winter. A scenic drive through the islands on U.S. 2 begins at Interstate 89 and travels north to Alburg Center; Route 78 takes you back to the mainland.

Hyde Log Cabin, built in 1783 on South Hero, is often cited as the country's oldest surviving log cabin. ✉ *U.S. 2, Grand Isle* ☎ *802/828–3051* 💷 *$1* ☉ *July 4–Labor Day, Thurs.–Mon. 11–5.*

On the mainland east of the Alburg Peninsula, the **Missisquoi National Wildlife Refuge** (✉ Tabor Rd., 36 mi north of Burlington, Swanton ☎ 802/868–4781) consists of 6,642 acres of federally protected wetlands, meadows, and woods. It's a beautiful area for bird-watching, canoeing, or walking nature trails.

Herrmann's Royal Lipizzan Stallions, cousins of the noble white horses bred in Austria since the 16th century, perform intricate dressage maneuvers for delighted spectators for a brief period each summer on North Hero. These acrobatic horses, descendants of animals rescued from the turmoil of World War II by Gen. George Patton and members of the Herrmann family, their current owners, spend their winters in Florida. ✉ *U.S. 2, North Hero* ☎ *802/372–5683* 💷 *Barn visits free between performances, shows $17* ☉ *Early July–late Aug., Thurs. and Fri. at 6 PM, weekends at 2:30 PM.*

St. Anne's Shrine marks the site where French soldiers and Jesuits put ashore in 1665 and built a fort, creating Vermont's first European settlement. The state's first Roman Catholic Mass was celebrated here on July 26, 1666. ✉ *W. Shore Rd., Isle La Motte* ☎ *802/928–3362* 💷 *Free* ☉ *Mid-May–mid-Oct., daily 9–4.*

Snow Farm Vineyard and Winery has self-guided tours, a tasting room, and free concerts on the lawn Thursday evenings, mid-June through Labor Day. ✉ *190 W. Shore Rd., South Hero* ☎ *802/372–9463* 💷 *Free* ☉ *May–Dec., daily 10–5; tours at 11 and 2 through Oct.*

Where to Stay & Eat

$$ ✕🏨 **North Hero House Inn and Restaurant.** This inn overlooks Lake Champlain and has four buildings, including the 1891 Colonial-revival main house with nine guest rooms, the restaurant, a pub room, library, and sitting room. Many rooms have water views, and each is decorated with country furnishings and antiques. The Homestead, Southwind, and Cove House have adjoining rooms that are good for families. Dinner ($$–$$$) is served in the informal glass greenhouse or Colonial-style dining room. ⊠ *U.S. 2, North Hero 05474* ☎ *802/372–4732 or 888/525–3644* 🖷 *802/372–3218* ⊕ *www.northherohouse.com* 🛏 *26 rooms* ♿ *Restaurant, cable TV, hot tub, boating, pub, library, meeting rooms; no a/c in some rooms* ☰ *AE, MC, V* ⏞⊙⏞ *CP.*

$$ ✕🏨 **Ruthcliffe Lodge & Restaurant.** Good food and splendid scenery make this off-the-beaten-path motel and restaurant overlooking Lake Champlain worth the drive. Owner-chef Mark Infante specializes in Italian pasta, fish, and meat dishes; save room for the homemade desserts. Fixed-price dinners ($$–$$$$; reservations essential) include soup or salad, bread, an entrée, and coffee or tea. The motel rooms are small but overlook the lake. ⊠ *1002 Quarry Rd., Isle La Motte 05463* ☎ *802/928–3200* ⊕ *www.ruthcliffe.com* 🛏 *7 rooms* ☰ *MC, V* ⊙ *Closed Columbus Day–mid-May.*

$$ 🏨 **Shore Acres Inn and Restaurant.** This lakefront motel well off the main road has comfortable rooms overlooking the water and ½ mi of private lakeshore. Breakfast and dinner are served in the restaurant overlooking the lake. You have free access to a 9-hole, par-3 golf course. ⊠ *U.S. 2, North Hero 05474* ☎ *802/372–8722* ⊕ *www.shoreacres.com* 🛏 *23 rooms* ♿ *Restaurant, cable TV, 9-hole golf course, 2 tennis courts, croquet* ☰ *AE, MC, V* ⊙ *Closed mid-Oct.–Apr.* ⏞⊙⏞ *BP.*

Sports & the Outdoors

BIKING **Bike Shed Rentals** (⊠ W. Shore Rd., Isle La Motte ☎ 802/928–3440) rents bikes of all sizes and shapes. **Hero's Welcome** (⊠ U.S. 2, North Hero ☎ 802/372–4161 or 800/372–4376) rents bikes for adults and children.

BOATING **Apple Island Resort** (⊠ U.S. 2, South Hero ☎ 802/372–5398) rents sailboats, rowboats, canoes, kayaks, and motorboats. **Hero's Welcome** (⊠ U.S. 2, North Hero ☎ 802/372–4161 or 800/372–4376) has canoes, kayaks and paddleboats for rent.

STATE PARKS **Alburg Dunes State Park** has one of the longest sandy beaches on Lake Champlain and some fine examples of rare flora and fauna along the hiking trails. ⊠ *Off U.S. 2, Alburg* ☎ *802/796–4170* 🎟 *$2.50* ⊙ *Mid-May–Labor Day, daily dawn–dusk.*

Grand Isle State Park has a fitness trail, hiking trails, and boat rentals. ⊠ *U.S. 2, Grand Isle* ☎ *802/372–4300* 🎟 *$2.50* ⊙ *Mid-May–mid-Oct., daily dawn–dusk.*

North Hero State Park's 400 acres hold a swimming beach, nature trail, and campsites. You can rent rowboats and canoes. ⊠ *North Hero* ☎ *802/372–8727* 🎟 *$2.50* ⊙ *Mid-May–Labor Day, daily dawn–dusk.*

Sand Bar State Park, with one of Vermont's best swimming beaches, has a snack bar, changing room, and boat rental concession, but no campground. ⊠ *U.S. 2, South Hero* ☎ *802/893–2825* 🎫 *$3.50* 🕙 *Mid-May–Labor Day, daily dawn–dusk.*

Shopping

🕐 Open May–December, **Allenholm Farm** (⊠ 111 South St., South Hero ☎ 802/372–5566) has a farm store that sells local produce, a pick-your-own apple orchard (fall only), and farm animal petting paddock.

Montgomery/Jay

❷❾ *32 mi east of St. Albans, 51 mi northeast of Burlington.*

Montgomery is a small village near the Canadian border and Jay Peak ski resort. Amid the surrounding countryside are seven historic covered bridges. **Trout River Store** (⊠ Main St., Montgomery Center ☎ 802/ 326–3058), an old-time country store with an antique soda fountain, is a great place to stock up on picnic supplies, eat a hearty bowl of soup and an overstuffed sandwich, and check out local crafts.

OFF THE BEATEN PATH

LAKE MEMPHREMAGOG – Vermont's second-largest lake, Lake Memphremagog extends from Newport 33 mi north into Canada. Prouty Beach in Newport has camping facilities, tennis courts, and paddleboat and canoe rentals. Watch the sun set from the deck of the **East Side Restaurant** (⊠ Lake St., Newport ☎ 802/334–2340), which serves excellent burgers and prime rib. ⊠ *Veterans Ave.* ☎ *802/334–7951.*

Where to Stay & Eat

$$ ✕🏠 **Inn on Trout River.** Guest rooms at this 100-year-old riverside inn are decorated in a country-cottage style, and all have down quilts and flannel sheets in winter. Lemoine's Restaurant ($–$$$) specializes in American and continental fare. Try the raviolini stuffed with Vermont cheddar cheese and walnuts topped with pesto, and the medallions of pork tenderloin in a maple syrup demi-glace sauce. Hobo's Café, also at the inn, serves simpler fare. ⊠ *Main St., Montgomery Center 05471* ☎ *802/ 326–4391 or 800/338–7049* 🖨 *802/326–3194* ⊕ *www.troutinn.com* 📱*9 rooms, 1 suite* ⚬ *Restaurant, pub, library; no a/c, no room TVs* ⊟ *AE, DC, MC, V* ⏸ *BP, MAP.*

$$$$ 🏠 **Hotel Jay & Jay Peak Condominiums.** Centrally located in the ski resort's base area, the hotel and its simply furnished rooms are a favorite for families. Kids under age 14 stay and eat free, and during nonholiday times, they can ski free, too. Farther afield (but still mostly slopeside) are studio to five-bedroom condominiums and town houses, with fireplaces, modern kitchens, and washer/dryers. Complimentary child care is provided to hotel and condo guests 9 AM–4 PM for kids ages two–seven. ⊠ *Rte. 242, 05859* ☎ *802/988–2611, 800/451–4449 outside VT* 🖨 *802/988–4049* ⊕ *www.jaypeakresort.com* 📱 *48 rooms, 94 condominiums* ⚬ *Restaurant, cable TV, 2 tennis courts, pool, hot tub, sauna, hiking, downhill skiing, ice-skating, bar, recreation room; no a/c* ⊟ *AE, D, DC, MC, V* ⏸ *MAP.*

Ski Areas

JAY PEAK Sticking up out of the flat farmland, Jay averages 355 inches of snow a year—more than any other Vermont ski area. Its proximity to Québec attracts Montréalers and discourages eastern seaboarders; hence, the prices are moderate and the lift lines shorter than at other resorts. The area is renowned for its glade skiing and powder.

Downhill. Jay Peak has two interconnected mountains, the highest reaching nearly 4,000 feet with a vertical drop of 2,153 feet. The smaller mountain has straight-fall-line, expert terrain that eases mid-mountain into an intermediate pitch. The main peak is served by Vermont's only tramway and transports skiers to meandering but challenging intermediate trails. Beginners should stick near the bottom on trails off the Metro lift. Weekdays at 9:30 AM and 1:30 PM, mountain ambassadors conduct a free tour. The area's 76 trails, including 21 glades and two chutes, are served by eight lifts, including the tram and the longest detachable quad in the East. The area also has two quads, a triple, and a double chairlift; one T-bar; and a moving carpet. Jay has 80% snowmaking coverage. The area also has four terrain parks, each rated for different abilities.

Other activities. Snowshoes can be rented, and guided walks are led by a naturalist. Telemark rentals and instruction are available.

The child-care center for youngsters ages 2–7 is open from 9 AM to 9 PM. If you're staying at Hotel Jay and Jay Peak Condominiums, you receive this nursery care free, as well as evening care and supervised dining at the hotel. Infant care is available on a fee basis with advanced reservations. There are ski-school programs for children ages 3-18.

Summer activities. Jay Peak runs tram rides to the summit from mid-June through Labor Day, and mid-September through Columbus Day ($10).

✉ *Rte. 242, Jay 05859* ☎ *802/988–2611, 800/451–4449 outside VT* ⊕ *www.jaypeakresort.com.*

CROSS-COUNTRY **Hazen's Notch Cross Country Ski Center and B&B** (✉ Rte. 58 ☎ 802/326–
SKIING 4799), delightfully remote at any time of the year, has 64 km (40 mi) of marked and groomed trails and rents equipment and snowshoes.

▌ EN
ROUTE
Routes 14, 5, 58, and 100 make a scenic drive around the **Northeast Kingdom,** named for the remoteness and stalwart independence that have helped preserve its rural nature. You can extend the loop and head east on Route 105 to the city of Newport on Lake Memphremagog. You will encounter some of the most unspoiled areas in all Vermont on the drive south from Newport on either U.S. 5 or Interstate 91 (Interstate 91 is faster, but U.S. 5 is prettier).

Lake Willoughby

㉚ *30 mi southeast of Montgomery (summer route; 50 mi by winter route), 28 mi north of St. Johnsbury.*

The cliffs of Mt. Pisgah and Mt. Hor drop to the edge of Lake Willoughby on opposite shores, giving this beautiful, deep, glacially carved lake a striking resemblance to a Norwegian fjord. The trails to the top of Mt. Pisgah reward hikers with glorious views.

☾ The **Bread and Puppet Museum** is a ramshackle barn that houses a surrealistic collection of props used by the world-renowned Bread and Puppet Theater. The troupe has been performing social and political commentary with the towering (they're supported by people on stilts), eerily expressive puppets for about 30 years. They perform at the museum every Sunday June–August at 3 PM. ☒ *Rte. 122, 1 mi east of Rte. 16, Glover* ☎ *802/525–3031* ☜ *Donations accepted* ☉ *June–Oct., daily 10–6.*

Where to Stay

$$–$$$$ 🏠 **WilloughVale Inn.** On Lake Willoughby, this handsome inn, with wraparound veranda, has 11 spacious rooms overlooking the water. The dining room serves dinner Thursday through Monday in summer. The shorefront housekeeping cottages have fireplaces, screened porches, and private docks and sleep up to four people. Cottages rent by the week in July and August, and the renovated Pisgah cottage has a fireside whirlpool tub. ☒ *Rte. 5A, Westmore 05860* ☎ *802/525–4123 or 800/594–9102* 🖷 *802/525–4514* ⊕ *www.willoughvale.com* ↩ *11 rooms, 4 cottages* ⚭ *Dining room, some cable TV, boating; no a/c* ☲ *AE, MC, V* ⦿| *CP.*

East Burke

➌ *17 mi south of Lake Willoughby.*

Once a sleepy village, East Burke is now the Northeast Kingdom's outdoor-activity hub. The Kingdom Trails attract thousands of mountain bikers in summer and fall. In winter, many trails are groomed for cross-country skiing. Contact the **Kingdom Trails Association** (⌂ Box 204, East Burke 05832 ☎ 802/626–0737 ⊕ www.kingdomtrails.org) for information and maps.

Where to Stay & Eat

$–$$$$ ✕ **River Garden Café.** You can eat lunch, dinner, or brunch outdoors on the enclosed porch or the patio amid perennial gardens, or dine inside the bright and cheerful café. The excellent fare includes lamb tenderloin, warm artichoke dip, bruschetta, pastas, and fresh fish, and the popular salad dressing is bottled for sale. ☒ *Rte. 114, East Burke* ☎ *802/ 626–3514* ☲ *AE, D, MC, V* ☉ *Closed Mon. and Tues. Nov.–Apr.*

$$ ✕🏠 **Wildflower Inn.** The hilltop views are breathtaking at this rambling, family-oriented complex of old farm buildings on 500 acres. Guest rooms in the restored Federal-style main house and three other buildings are furnished with reproductions and contemporary furnishings. Junipers ($$–$$$; closed Sunday) serves comfort food such as meat loaf and lemon herb chicken, and includes a kids' menu. ☒ *2059 Darling Hill Rd., 5 mi west of East Burke, Lyndonville, 05851* ☎ *802/626–8310 or 800/627–8310* 🖷 *802/626–3039* ⊕ *www.wildflowerinn.com* ↩ *10 rooms, 13 suites, 1 cottage* ⚭ *Restaurant, some kitchenettes, tennis court, pool, hot tub, sauna, fishing, soccer, ice-skating, sleigh rides, snowmobiling, recreation rooms, playground, meeting room; no a/c in some rooms, no room TVs* ☲ *MC, V* ☉ *Closed Apr. and Nov.* ⦿| *BP.*

¢–$ ✕🏠 **Old Cutter Inn.** In 1977, Fritz and Marti Walther turned this small 19th-century farmhouse, ½ mi from the Burke Mountain base lodge, into a bit of their native Switzerland. The restaurant ($$–$$$) serves chateaubriand, rack of lamb, and rosti to hungry skiers and summer wayfarers. The rooms in the inn are quaint and simple, with small bathrooms. ☒ *143 Pinkham Rd., 05832* ☎ *802/626–5152 or 800/295–1943* ⊕ *www.oldcutterinn.com* ↩ *9 rooms, 5 with bath; 1 suite* ⚭ *Restau-*

rant, pool, bicycles, hiking, cross-country skiing, bar; no a/c, no room TVs ☐ *D, MC, V* ⊙ *Closed Apr. and Nov.*

$$ ⌂ **Inn at Mountain View Farm.** The renovated 1890 creamery on a hilltop has second-floor guest rooms furnished with antiques and handmade quilts. Cross-country skiing, snowshoe, hiking, and mountain-biking trails are right at the doorstep. There is a restaurant, but it is open only for special-event dining. ⊠ *Darling Hill Rd.* 🖃 *Box 355, 05832* ☎ *802/ 626–9924 or 800/572–4509* ⊕ *www.innmtnview.com* 🛏 *9 rooms, 5 suites* ♿ *Restaurant, hiking, cross-country skiing, sleigh rides, meeting room, some pets allowed; no room TVs* ☐ *AE, D, DC, MC, V* ⊙ *Closed Apr. and Nov.* ❄️ *BP.*

Sports & the Outdoors

East Burke Sports (⊠ Rte. 114, East Burke ☎ 802/626–3215) rents mountain bikes, kayaks, and skis, and provides guiding for cycling, hiking, paddling, skiing, and snowshoeing. **Village Sport Shop** (⊠ 511 Broad St., Lyndonville ☎ 802/626–8448) rents canoes, kayaks, bikes, Rollerblades, paddleboats, snowshoes, and cross-country and downhill skis.

Shopping

Bailey's & Burke, Inc. (⊠ Rte. 114 ☎ 802/626–9250) sells baked goods, pizza and sandwiches, wine, clothing, and sundries.

St. Johnsbury

㉜ *16 mi south of East Burke, 39 mi northeast of Montpelier.*

St. Johnsbury, the southern gateway to the Northeast Kingdom, was chartered in 1786. But its identity was established after 1830, when Thaddeus Fairbanks invented the platform scale, a device that revolutionized weighing methods. The Fairbanks family's philanthropic efforts gave the city a strong cultural and architectural imprint.

☯ Opened in 1891, the **Fairbanks Museum and Planetarium,** a redbrick building in the Romanesque-revival style of H. H. Richardson, houses the Fairbanks family's collections, as well as Vermont plants and animals, and worldwide ethnographic and natural-history collections. There's also a popular 45-seat planetarium. ⊠ *1302 Main St.* ☎ *802/748–2372* ⊕ *www. fairbanksmuseum.org* 🎫 *Museum $5, planetarium $3* ⊙ *Mon.–Sat. 9–5, Sun. 1–5; mid-Oct.–Apr., closed Mon. Planetarium shows July and Aug., daily at 11 and 1:30; Sept.–June, weekends at 1:30.*

FodorśChoice   The **St. Johnsbury Athenaeum,** with its dark rich paneling, polished Vic-
★   torian woodwork, and ornate circular staircases, is both the town library and one of the oldest art galleries in the country, housing over 100 original works mainly of the Hudson River School. Albert Bierstadt's enormous *Domes of Yosemite* dominates the gallery. ⊠ *1171 Main St.* ☎ *802/748–8291* ⊕ *www.stjathenaeum.org* 🎫 *Free* ⊙ *Mon. and Wed. 10–8; Tues., Thurs., and Fri. 10–5:30; Sat. 9:30–4.*

For folk art, visit **Dog Mountain,** artist–dog lover Stephen Huneck's art gallery (works are for sale) and sculpture garden. In the chapel, humans and their canine companions can meditate. ⊠ *Off Spaulding Rd.* ☎ *802/*

748–2700 or 800/449–2580 ⊕ *www.huneck.com* 🏷 *Free* ⊙ *Mon.–Sat.* *10–5, Sun. 11–4, and by appointment.*

East of downtown, the **Maple Grove Museum and Factory** is the world's oldest and largest maple candy factory. On a tour, watch how maple candy is made, then sample some in the gift shop. ⊠ *1052 Portland St., Rte. 2* ☎ *802/748–5141* ⊕ *www.maplegrove.com* 🏷 *Tour $1* ⊙ *May–Dec., weekdays 8–2.*

OFF THE
BEATEN
PATH

PEACHAM – Tiny Peacham, 10 mi southwest of St. Johnsbury, is on almost every tour group's list of "must-sees." With views extending to the White Mountains of New Hampshire and a white-steeple church, Peacham is perhaps the most photographed town in New England. *Ethan Frome,* starring Liam Neeson, was filmed here. One of the town's gathering spots, the **Peacham Store** (⊠ *Main St.* ☎ *802/592–3310*), sells gourmet soups and stews. Next door, the **Peacham Corner Guild** sells local handcrafts.

Where to Stay & Eat

$$–$$$ ✕ **Elements.** In a converted mill, this restaurant seeks to provide the "elements" of a fine dining experience. Local ingredients, such as farmstead cheeses and homemade breads, are used for the seasonal menus, which might include striped bass with pepper slaw and wasabi mashed potatoes or smoked trout and apple cakes. You can eat indoors or on the deck overlooking the Passumpsic River. Lunch is served Tuesday–Friday from Memorial Day through Columbus Day. ⊠ *98 Mill St.* ☎ *802/748–8400* 🖃 *MC, V* ⊙ *Closed Sun. and Mon.*

★ **$$$$** ✕🏨 **Rabbit Hill Inn.** Many of the spacious, elegant rooms have fireplaces, two-person whirlpool tubs, and views of the Connecticut River and New Hampshire's White Mountains. The intimate candlelit dining room serves a three- or five-course fixed-price dinner ($$$$) featuring contemporary new American and regional dishes such as grilled venison loin with cranberry-juniper orange glaze. Meat and fish are smoked on the premises. ⊠ *Rte. 18, 11 mi south of St. Johnsbury, Lower Waterford, 05848* ☎ *802/748–5168 or 800/762–8669* 🖷 *802/748–8342* ⊕*www.rabbithillinn.com* ⋙*19 rooms* ⌂ *Restaurant, hiking, cross-country skiing, pub; no a/c, no room TVs, no kids under 14* 🖃 *AE, D, MC, V* ⊙ *Closed 1st 3 wks in Apr., 1st 2 wks in Nov.* 🍴 *BP, MAP.*

Northern Vermont A to Z

To research prices, get advice from other travelers, and book travel arrangements, visit www.fodors.com.

BOAT & FERRY TRAVEL

Lake Champlain Ferries operates three ferry crossing routes between the lake's Vermont and New York shores: Grand Isle–Plattsburgh, NY; Burlington–Port Kent, NY; and Charlotte–Essex, NY. Two of the routes are in operation year-round, through thick lake ice in winter; the Burlington–Port Kent route functions from late-May to mid-October. This is a convenient means of getting to and from New York State, as well as a pleasant way to spend an afternoon.

🚢 Boat & Ferry Information **Lake Champlain Ferries** ☎ 802/864–9804 ⊕ www. lakechamplainferries.com.

BUS TRAVEL

Vermont Transit links Burlington, Waterbury, Montpelier, St. Johnsbury, and Newport.

🚌 Bus Information Vermont Transit ☎ 800/552-8737 ⊕ www.vermonttransit.com.

CAR TRAVEL

In north-central Vermont, Interstate 89 heads west from Montpelier to Burlington and continues north to Canada. Interstate 91 is the principal north–south route in the east, and Route 100 runs north–south through the center of the state. North of Interstate 89, Routes 104 and 15 provide a major east–west transverse. From Barton, near Lake Willoughby, U.S. 5 and Route 122 south are beautiful drives. Strip-mall drudge bogs down the section of U.S. 5 around Lyndonville.

EMERGENCIES

🚑 Hospitals & Emergency Services Copley Hospital ⊠ Washington Hwy., Morrisville ☎ 802/888-4231. **Fletcher Allen Health Care** ⊠ 111 Colchester Ave., Burlington ☎ 802/847-0000. **Northeastern Vermont Regional Hospital** ⊠ Hospital Dr., St. Johnsbury ☎ 802/748-8141.

TOURS

P.O.M.G. Bike Tours of Vermont leads weekend and five-day bike tours. True North Kayak Tours operates a guided tour of Lake Champlain and a natural-history tour; the company also customizes multiday trips and coordinates special trips for kids.

🚲 Tour Operators P.O.M.G. Bike Tours of Vermont ⊠ Richmond ☎ 802/434-2270 or 888-635-2453. **True North Kayak Tours** ⊠ 25 Nash Pl., Burlington ☎ 802/860-1910.

VISITOR INFORMATION

ℹ Tourist Information Lake Champlain Islands Chamber of Commerce ⊠ 3537 Rte. 2, Suite 100, North Hero 05474 ☎ 802/372-8400 or 800/262-5226 ⊕ www.champlainislands.com. **Lake Champlain Regional Chamber of Commerce** ⊠ 60 Main St., Suite 100, Burlington 05401 ☎ 802/863-3489 or 877/686-5253 ⊕ www.vermont.org. **Northeast Kingdom Chamber of Commerce** ⊠ 51 Depot Sq., Suite 3, St. Johnsbury 05819 ☎ 802/748-3678 or 800/639-6379 ⊕ www.nekchamber.com. **Northeast Kingdom Travel and Tourism Association** ⌂ Box 465, Barton 05822 ☎ 802/525-4386 or 800/884-8001 ⊕ www.travelthekingdom.com. The **Stowe Area Association** ⊠ Main St. ⌂ Box 1320, Stowe 05672 ☎ 802/253-7321 or 877/467-8693 ⊕ www.gostowe.com. **Vermont North Country Chamber of Commerce** ⊠ The Causeway, Newport 05855 ☎ 802/334-7782 or 800/635-4643 ⊕ www.vtnorthcountry.com.

VERMONT A TO Z

To research prices, get advice from other travelers, and book travel arrangements, visit www.fodors.com.

AIRPORTS & TRANSFERS

Continental, Delta, Jet Blue, United, and US Airways fly into Burlington International Airport (BTV). Rutland State Airport (RUT) has daily service to and from Boston on US Airways Express. West of Bennington and convenient to southern Vermont, Albany International Airport (ALB) in New York State is served by 10 major U.S. carriers.

🛪 Airport Information **Albany International Airport** ✉ 737 Albany Shaker Rd., Albany ☎ 518/242-2200 ⊕ www.albanyairport.com. **Burlington International Airport** ✉ 1200 Airport Dr., 4 mi east of Burlington off U.S. 2 ☎ 802/863-1889 ⊕ www.burlingtonintlairport.com. **Rutland State Airport** ✉ 1004 Airport Rd., North Clarendon ☎ 802/773-3348.

BIKE TRAVEL

Vermont is a popular destination for cyclists, who find villages and towns—with their inns, B&Bs, and restaurants—spaced closely enough for comfortable traveling. Vermont Bicycle Touring leads numerous tours in the state.

🛪 **Vermont Bicycle Touring** ✉ Monkton Rd., Bristol ☎ 802/453-4811 or 800/245-3868.

BUS TRAVEL

Vermont Transit connects Bennington, Brattleboro, Burlington, Rutland, and other Vermont cities and towns with Boston, Springfield, Albany, New York, Montréal, and cities in New Hampshire. Local service in Burlington and surrounding communities is provided by Chittenden County Transportation Authority.

🛪 Bus Information **Chittenden Country Transportation Authority** ☎ 802/864-0211. **Vermont Transit** ☎ 800/552-8737 ⊕ www.vermonttransit.com.

CAR TRAVEL

Interstate 91, which stretches from Connecticut and Massachusetts in the south to Québec in the north, serves most points along Vermont's eastern border. Interstate 89, from New Hampshire to the east and Québec to the north, crosses central Vermont from White River Junction to Burlington. Southwestern Vermont can be reached by U.S. 7 from Massachusetts and U.S. 4 from New York.

The official speed limit in Vermont is 50 mph, unless otherwise posted; on the interstates it's 65 mph. Right turns are permitted on a red light unless otherwise indicated. You can get a state map, which has mileage charts and enlarged maps of major downtown areas, free from the Vermont Department of Tourism and Marketing. The *Vermont Atlas and Gazetteer,* sold in many bookstores, shows nearly every road in the state and is great for driving on the back roads. For current road conditions, call 800/429-7623.

EMERGENCIES

🛪 Emergency Services **Ambulance, fire, police** ☎ 911. **Vermont Poison Control Center** ✉ Burlington ☎ 800/222-1222. **Vermont State Police** ☎ 802/244-7345.

LODGING

The Vermont Chamber of Commerce publishes the *Vermont Travelers' Guidebook,* which is an extensive list of lodgings, and additional guides to country inns and vacation rentals. The Vermont Department of Tourism and Marketing has a brochure that lists lodgings at working farms.

CAMPING Call Vermont's Department of Forests, Parks, and Recreation for a copy of the "Vermont Campground Guide," which lists state parks and other public and private camping facilities. Reservations can be made up to 11 months in advance.

Department of Forests, Parks, and Recreation ☎ 888/409-7579.

MEDIA

Vermont's largest newspaper is the *Burlington Free Press.* For upcoming events and performances, see its Thursday "Weekend" section. The *Rutland Herald,* winner of a 2001 Pulitzer prize for editorial writing, carries *New York Times* wire service stories and is available throughout much of the state. *Seven Days* is a Burlington-based, free alternative weekly with extensive arts and entertainment listings.

Vermont's two leading magazines are *Vermont Life,* published quarterly by the state, and the privately owned *Vermont,* a bimonthly that covers political as well as lifestyle issues and has a more upscale slant. *Yankee,* published 10 times yearly in Dublin, New Hampshire, covers all of New England and has events listings for each state.

SPORTS & THE OUTDOORS

A hotline has tips on peak foliage viewing locations and times, up-to-date snow conditions, and events in Vermont.

Foliage and Snow Hot Line ☎ 802/828-3239.

CANOEING Umiak Outdoor Outfitters has day excursions and customized overnight trips. Battenkill Canoe, Ltd. organizes canoe tours (some are inn-to-inn) and fishing trips.

Umiak Outdoor Outfitters ✉ 849 S. Main St., Stowe ☎ 802/253-2317 🌐 www.umiak.com. **Vermont Canoe Trippers/Battenkill Canoe, Ltd.** ✉ 6328 Rte. 7A, Arlington ☎ 802/362-2800 🌐 www.battenkill.com.

FISHING For information about fishing, including licenses, call the Vermont Fish and Wildlife Department. Strictly Trout will arrange a fly-fishing trip on any Vermont stream or river, including the Battenkill.

Strictly Trout ☎ 802/869-3116. **Vermont Fish and Wildlife Department** ☎ 802/241-3700 🌐 www.vtfishandwildlife.com.

HIKING The Green Mountain Club publishes hiking maps and guides. The club also manages the Long Trail, the north–south trail that traverses the entire state. New England Hiking Holidays leads guided walks with lodging in country inns.

Green Mountain Club ✉ 4711 Waterbury-Stowe Rd. (Rte. 100), Waterbury Center ☎ 802/244-7037 🌐 www.greenmountainclub.org. **New England Hiking Holidays** ✉ North Conway, NH ☎ 603/356-9696 or 800/869-0949.

HORSEBACK RIDING Kedron Valley Stables has one- to six-day riding tours with lodging in country inns. The Vermont Icelandic Horse Farm conducts year-round guided riding expeditions on easy-to-ride Icelandic horses.

Kedron Valley Stables ✉ South Woodstock ☎ 802/457-1480 or 800/225-6301. **Vermont Icelandic Horse Farm** ✉ N. Fayston Rd., Waitsfield 05673 ☎ 802/496-7141 🌐 www.icelandichorses.com.

SKIING For information, contact Ski Vermont/Vermont Ski Areas Association.

Vermont Ski Areas Association ✉ 26 State St. Box 368, Montpelier 05601 ☎ 802/223-2439 🌐 www.skivermont.com.

STATE PARKS

Vermont state parks open the last week in May and close after the Labor Day or Columbus Day weekend, depending on location. Day-use charges are $2.50 per person for ages 14 and up, $2 for ages 4–13; children under 4 are free. Call individual parks or the Department of Forests, Parks, and Recreation for information.

🚹 **Vermont State Parks** ☎ 802/241-3655 ⊕ www.vtstateparks.com.

TRAIN TRAVEL

Amtrak's *Vermonter* is a daytime service linking Washington, D.C., with Brattleboro, Bellows Falls, White River Junction, Montpelier, Waterbury, Essex Junction, and St. Albans. The *Adirondack,* which runs from New York City to Montréal, serves Albany, Ft. Edward (near Glens Falls), Ft. Ticonderoga, and Plattsburgh, allowing relatively convenient access to western Vermont. The *Ethan Allen Express* connects New York City with Fair Haven and Rutland.

🚹 Train Information **Amtrak** ☎ 800/872-7245 ⊕ www.amtrak.com.

VISITOR INFORMATION

🚹 Tourist Information **Forest Supervisor, Green Mountain National Forest** ⊠ 231 N. Main St., Rutland 05701 ☎ 802/747-6700. **Vermont Chamber of Commerce** 🗗 Box 37, Montpelier 05601 ☎ 802/223-3443. **Vermont Department of Tourism and Marketing** ⊠ 6 Baldwin St., Drawer 33, Montpelier 05633-1301 ☎ 802/828-3676 or 800/837-6668 ⊕ www.vermontvacation.com.

Massachusetts

WORD OF MOUTH

"In Boston alone, there is SO much: Harvard Square and campus, MIT, Museum of Science, Bunker Hill, the North End, and the downtown shopping district. If you want a great and scenic city to visit, with friendly people, fun things to see and do, and great food, it's the place to be!"

—bear900

"The Cape is a beachlover's paradise."

—zootsi

"I love the Berkshires, especially in the summer. Tanglewood, antiquing, Jacob's Pillow, Mass MoCA, all set in gorgeous greenery."

—HHoward

THE SEASIDE TOWNS OF MASSACHUSETTS—from Newburyport to Provincetown—were built before the Revolution, during the heyday of American shipping. Their grand old houses and bustling waterfronts evoke a bygone world of clipper ships, robust fishermen, and sturdy sailors bound for distant points. Lowell, on the Merrimack River, was the first American city to be planned around manufacturing. This textile town introduced the rest of the nation to the routines of the Industrial Revolution. In our own time, the high-tech firms of the greater Boston area helped launch the information age, and the Massachusetts Institute of Technology and Harvard supplied intellectual heft to deliver it to the wider world.

The Massachusetts town meeting set the tone for politics in the 13 original colonies. A century later, Boston was a hotbed of rebellion—Samuel Adams and James Otis, the "Sons of Liberty," started a war with words, inciting action against British Colonial policies with patriotic pamphlets and fiery speeches at Faneuil Hall. Twentieth-century heirs to Adams include Boston's flashy mid-century mayor James Michael Curley; Thomas "Tip" O'Neill, the late Speaker of the House; and, of course, the Kennedys. In 1961 the young senator from the Boston suburb of Brookline, John Fitzgerald Kennedy, became president of the United States. JFK's service to Massachusetts was family tradition: in the years before World War I, Kennedy's grandfather John "Honey Fitz" Fitzgerald served in Congress and as mayor of Boston. But political families are nothing new here—Massachusetts has sent both a father and a son (John Adams and John Quincy Adams) to the White House.

Massachusetts has an extensive system of parks, protected forests, beaches, and nature preserves. Like medieval pilgrims, readers of *Walden* come to Concord to visit the place where Henry David Thoreau wrote his prophetic essay. Thoreau's disciples can be found hiking to the top of the state's highest peak, Mt. Greylock; shopping for organic produce in an unpretentious college burg like Williamstown; or strolling the beaches of Cape Cod. For those who prefer the hills to the ocean, the rolling Berkshire terrain defines the landscape from North Adams to Great Barrington in the western part of the state. A favorite vacation spot since the 19th century, when eastern aristocrats built grand summer residences, the Berkshire Hills have been described as an inland Newport. This area attracts vacationers seeking superb scenery and food and an active cultural scene.

The list of Bay State writers, artists, and musicians who have shaped American culture is long indeed. The state has produced great poets in every generation: Anne Bradstreet, Phillis Wheatley, Emily Dickinson, Henry Wadsworth Longfellow, William Cullen Bryant, e. e. cummings, Robert Lowell, Elizabeth Bishop, Sylvia Plath, and Anne Sexton. Massachusetts writers include Louisa May Alcott, author of the enduring classic *Little Women*; Nathaniel Hawthorne, who re-created the Salem of his Puritan ancestors in *The Scarlet Letter*; Herman Melville, who wrote *Moby-Dick* in a house at the foot of Mt. Greylock; Eugene O'Neill, whose early plays were produced at a makeshift theater in Provincetown on Cape Cod; Lowell native Jack Kerouac, author of *On the Road*; and

GREAT ITINERARIES

Massachusetts is a small state but one packed with appealing sights; you could easily spend several weeks exploring it. In a few days you can get a feeling for Boston and some of the historic towns near the city. Those who have a week and would like to explore several areas should spend a few days in Boston and then head west for some historic and scenic highlights in the Pioneer Valley and the Berkshires. A leisurely one-week trip to Cape Cod and Martha's Vineyard is a classic summer vacation.

IF YOU HAVE 3 DAYS

Spend two days touring **Boston.** You can hit highlights such as the Public Garden, Beacon Hill, and the Freedom Trail on the first day; check out the Museum of Fine Arts or the Isabella Stewart Gardner Museum the morning of the next day; and either explore Harvard and Cambridge or do some shopping on Newbury Street in the afternoon. On the third day either swing west on Route 2 and tour **Lexington** and **Concord** or north on Route 1A and east on Route 129 to **Marblehead.** Explore Marblehead and have lunch there before heading west on Route 114 and north on Route 1A to **Salem.**

IF YOU HAVE 7 DAYS

Follow the three-day itinerary above, and spend your third night in **Salem.** On Day 4 take the Massachusetts Turnpike (Interstate 90) out of Boston and make a half-day stop at Old Sturbridge Village in **Sturbridge.** Afterward, continue west on Interstate 90 and north on Interstate 91, stopping briefly in **Northampton** before heading to **Deerfield,** where you'll spend the

night and Day 5. On Day 6 head to the Berkshires—from Deerfield head north on Interstate 91 to Greenfield, where you'll take Route 2 west to **Williamstown.** On the morning of Day 7 tour the Clark Art Institute in Williamstown. U.S. 7 south takes you through **Pittsfield**; detour west on U.S. 20 to Hancock Shaker Village before heading on to **Lenox.**

IF YOU HAVE 7 DAYS TO SPEND ON THE CAPE

Head south from Boston (take Interstate 93 to Route 3 to U.S. 6). Stop in **Plymouth** and visit Plimoth Plantation. Have lunch in **Sandwich** and tour the town before continuing on U.S. 6 to **Chatham,** where you'll stay the night (have dinner and stroll Main Street in the evening). The next day, drive to **Orleans** and spend the day at Nauset Beach. On Day 3 continue on U.S. 6 to **Provincetown,** stopping briefly in **Wellfleet** to tour the galleries and detouring east off U.S. 6 to Cahoon Hollow Beach. After dinner take a walk down Commercial Street. The morning of Day 4 head to Race Point Beach, go on a whale-watching cruise, or take a dune-buggy tour. On Day 5 take U.S. 6 to **Hyannis,** where you can catch the ferry to **Martha's Vineyard.**

4

John Cheever, chronicler of suburban angst. Painters Winslow Homer and James McNeill Whistler both hailed from the Commonwealth. Norman Rockwell, the quintessential American illustrator, lived and worked in Stockbridge. Celebrated composer and Boston native Leonard Bernstein was the first American to conduct the New York Philharmonic. Joan Baez got her start singing in Harvard Square, and contemporary Boston singer-songwriter Tracy Chapman picked up the beat with folk songs for the new age.

Exploring Massachusetts

Boston is full of historic sights, as are surrounding communities such as Concord and Lexington. That history class you thought was so boring may suddenly come rushing back to you as you pass places such as the Old North Church. Cape Ann and Cape Cod have beautiful beaches, seafood restaurants, and plenty of traffic. In the Berkshires and the Pioneer Valley you'll find centuries-old towns, antiques shops, and rolling green hills. There's beauty to be discovered after the tourists have gone, wandering through snowy fields or braving the elements on a winter beach, and sipping hot cider at the hearth of a local inn.

Numbers in the text and in the margin correspond to numbers on the maps: Cape Cod, Martha's Vineyard, Nantucket, The North Shore, The Pioneer Valley, and The Berkshires.

About the Restaurants

Massachusetts invented the fried clam, which appears on many North Shore and Cape Cod menus. Creamy clam chowder is another specialty. Eating seafood "in the rough"—from paper plates in shacklike buildings—is a revered local custom. On the Cape, specialties from the Portuguese community such as kale soup and linguiça sausage regularly appear on menus.

At country inns in the Berkshires and the Pioneer Valley you'll find creative contemporary fare that makes the most of local ingredients, as well as traditional New England "dinners" strongly reminiscent of old England: double-cut pork chops, rack of lamb, game, Boston baked beans, Indian pudding, and the dubiously glorified "New England boiled dinner."

WHAT IT COSTS				
$$$$	**$$$**	**$$**	**$**	**¢**
AT DINNER over $32	$25–$32	$15–$24	$8–$14	under $8

Prices are per person, for a main course at dinner.

About the Hotels

Boston has everything from luxury hotels to charming bed-and-breakfasts. The signature accommodation outside Boston is the country inn; in the Berkshires, where magnificent mansions have been converted into lodgings, the inns reach a very grand scale indeed. Less extravagant and less expensive are B&B establishments, many of them in pri-

PLEASURES & PASTIMES

BEACHES

Massachusetts has many excellent beaches, especially on Cape Cod, where the waves are gentle and the water cool. South-side beaches, on Nantucket Sound, have rolling surf and are warmer. Open-ocean beaches on the Cape Cod National Seashore are cold and have serious surf. Parking lots can fill up by 10 AM in summer. Beaches not restricted to residents charge parking fees; for weekly or seasonal passes, contact the local town hall.

Bostonians head for wide sweeps of sand along the North Shore (beware of biting blackflies in late May and early June), among them Singing Beach in Manchester, Plum Island in Newburyport, and Crane Beach in Ipswich. Boston city beaches are not particularly attractive and definitely not for swimming, though the ongoing rehabilitation of Boston Harbor has made them somewhat cleaner.

BOATING

Sea-kayaking is popular along the marshy coastline of the North Shore, where freshwater canoeing is also an option. Inland, the Connecticut River in the Pioneer Valley is navigable by all types of craft between the Turners Falls Dam, just north of Greenfield, and the Holyoke Dam. The large dams control the water level daily, so you will notice a tidal effect; if you have a large boat, beware of sandbanks. Canoes can travel north of Turners Falls beyond the Vermont border; canoeing is also popular in the lakes and small rivers of the Berkshires.

FISHING

Deep-sea fishing trips depart from Boston, Cape Cod, and the South and North shores; surf casting is popular on the North Shore. The rivers, lakes, and streams of the Pioneer Valley and Berkshire County abound with fish—bass, pike, and perch, to name but a few. Stocked trout waters include the Hoosic River (south branch) near Cheshire; the Green River around Great Barrington; Notch Brook and the Hoosic River (north branch) near North Adams; Goose Pond and Hop Brook around Lee; and the Williams River around West Stockbridge.

WHALE-WATCHING

In summer and fall, boats leave Boston, Cape Cod, and Cape Ann two or more times a day to observe the whales feeding a few miles offshore. It's rare not to have the extraordinary experience of seeing several whales, most of them extremely close up.

SHOPPING

Boston has many high-quality shops, especially in the Newbury Street and Beacon Hill neighborhoods, and most suburban communities have at least a couple of main-street stores selling old furniture and collectibles. Antiques can be found on the South Shore in Plymouth; on the North Shore in Essex, Newburyport, Marblehead, and elsewhere; in the northern towns of the Pioneer Valley (especially in Amherst or along the Mohawk Trail); and just about everywhere in the Berkshires, with particularly rich hunting grounds around Sheffield and Great Barrington. On Cape Cod, Provincetown and Wellfleet are centers for fine arts and crafts.

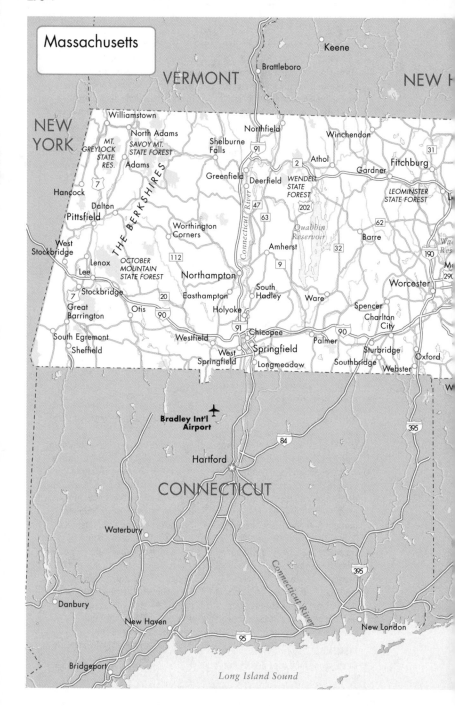

Massachusetts

VERMONT

NEW YORK

NEW H

Keene

Brattleboro

Williamstown

North Adams

Shelburne Falls

Northfield

Winchendon

Fitchburg

31

MT. GREYLOCK STATE RES.

SAVOY MT. STATE FOREST

Adams

91

2

Athol

Gardner

Hancock

Dalton

Greenfield

Deerfield

WENDELL STATE FOREST

LEOMINSTER STATE FOREST

7

THE BERKSHIRES

47

63

202

Pittsfield

Worthington Corners

Quabbin Reservoir

62

Barre

Wa Res

West Stockbridge

Lenox

OCTOBER MOUNTAIN STATE FOREST

112

Amherst

32

190

Lee

Northampton

9

Worcester

29(

Mc

Stockbridge

20

Easthampton

South Hadley

Ware

Spencer

7

Great Barrington

Otis

90

Holyoke

Charlton City

South Egremont

Westfield

91

Chicopee

Palmer

90

Sturbridge

Oxford

Sheffield

West Springfield

Springfield

Longmeadow

Southbridge

Webster

W

Bradley Int'l Airport

395

84

Hartford

CONNECTICUT

Waterbury

Connecticut River

395

Danbury

New Haven

95

New London

Bridgeport

Long Island Sound

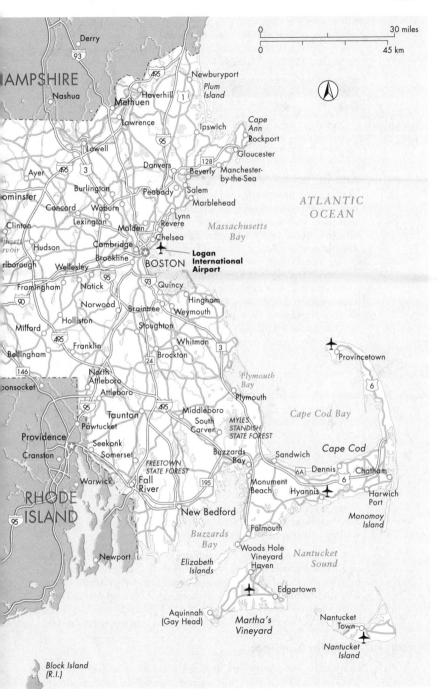

vate homes. On Cape Cod, inns are plentiful, and rental homes and condominiums are available for long-term stays. Be sure to make reservations for inns well in advance during peak periods: summer on the Cape and islands, summer through winter in the Berkshires.

	WHAT IT COSTS				
	$$$$	**$$$**	**$$**	**$**	**¢**
FOR 2 PEOPLE	over $325	$226–$325	$151–$225	$75–$150	under $75

Prices are for two people in a standard double room in high season, excluding 12.45% tax and service charges.

Timing

The dazzling foliage and cool temperatures make fall the best time to visit western Massachusetts, and it's the perfect season to see Boston as well. This is no secret, so make reservations well ahead. Summer, especially late in the season when the water is a bit warmer, is ideal for visits to the beaches. Bostonians often find their city to be too hot and humid in July and August, but if you're visiting from points south, the cool evening coastal breezes might strike you as downright refreshing. Many towns save their best for winter—inns open their doors to carolers, shops serve eggnog, and lobster boats parade around Gloucester harbor adorned with lights. The off-season is the perfect time to try cross-country skiing, take a walk on a stormy beach, or spend a night by the fire, tucked under a quilt, catching up on books by Hawthorne or Thoreau.

BOSTON

Updated by Diane Bair, Michael Blanding, Matthew Cordell, Alexandra Hall, Corey O'Hara, Andrew Rimas, Erica Silverstein, Emily J. Stebbins, and Pamela Wright

New England's largest and most important city—Boston—was the cradle of American independence. The city's most famous buildings are not merely civic landmarks but national icons, and its local heroes are known to the nation: John and Samuel Adams, Paul Revere, John Hancock, and many more who live at the crossroads of history and myth.

At the same time, Boston is a contemporary center of high finance and high technology, a place of granite and glass towers rising along what once were rutted village lanes. Its many students, artists, academics, and young professionals have made the town a haven for the arts, international cinema, late-night bookstores, ethnic food, alternative music, and unconventional politics.

Best of all, Boston is meant for walking. Most of its historical and architectural attractions are in neighborhoods that are easy to explore on foot. Its varied and distinctive enclaves reveal their character to visitors who take the time to stroll through them. Should you need to make short or long hops between neighborhoods, the "T"—the safe, easy-to-ride trains of the Massachusetts Bay Transportation Authority—covers the city.

Beacon Hill & Boston Common

Home of the old-money elite, Beacon Hill is Boston at its most Bostonian. The redbrick elegance of its narrow, cobbled streets transports you back to the 19th century. From the gold-topped splendor of the State House to the neoclassical panache of its mansions, Beacon Hill exudes power, prestige, and a calm yet palpable undercurrent of history. But its residents would never make the faux pas of being out of date. The neighborhood is home to hip boutiques and trendy restaurants, frequented by young, affluent professionals.

Beacon Hill is bounded by Cambridge Street to the north, Beacon Street to the south, the Charles River Esplanade to the west, and Bowdoin Street to the east. Just to the south of it is Boston Common, the country's oldest public park. In contrast to "the Hill," the Common has a more egalitarian feel, deriving, no doubt, from its original use as public land for cattle grazing.

Numbers in the text and in the margin correspond to numbers on the Boston map.

A Good Walk

Start at the **Park Street Church** ❶ ⌐, across the street from the T station. Next door to the church is the **Granary Burying Ground** ❷, final resting place of some of Boston's most illustrious figures, including John Hancock and Paul Revere. From here, head to **Boston Common** ❸. Get your maps and guides at the Boston Common Visitor Information Center, then meander past the Parkman Bandstand and toward the Central Burying Ground—where Tories and Patriots are interred side by side.

If you wish to view some of the grandest interiors in Boston, head up Beacon Street and take a tour of the august **Boston Athenaeum** ❹. From Charles Bulfinch's neoclassical masterpiece, the **State House** ❺, continue along Beacon Street. Turn right on Charles Street, then right on Chestnut and left on Willow to find Acorn Street—perhaps Boston's most photogenic byway—on your left. Continue on Willow across Mt. Vernon Street to reach the serene **Louisburg Square** ❻, then continue up Mt. Vernon Street to the **Nichols House** ❼, with its beveled bow window. A left on Joy Street takes you to the **Museum of Afro-American History** ❽. Here you can pick up a map for the Black Heritage Trail.

TIMING Allow yourself the better part of a day for this walk, particularly if you want to linger in the Common or browse through the antiques shops on Charles Street.

Sights to See

★ ❹ **Boston Athenaeum.** Founded in 1807 and occupying its present quarters since 1847, this library is a veritable cathedral of scholarship. Only 1,049 proprietary shares exist for membership in this institution, and most have been passed down for generations—though the Athenaeum is open for use by qualified scholars who may choose to become members on a yearly basis. Take the guided tour to spy one of the most marvelous sights in the world of Boston academe, the fifth-floor Reading Room, said by poet David McCord to combine "the best elements of the Bodleian, Monticello, the frigate *Constitution*, a greenhouse, and an old New England sitting room." ✉ *10½ Beacon St., Beacon Hill* ☎ *617/227–0270* ⊕ *www.bostonathenaeum.org* ✆ *Free* ⊙ *Mon. 9–8, Tues.–Fri. 9–5:30, Sat. 9–4. Tours Tues. and Thurs. at 3* Ⓜ *Park St.*

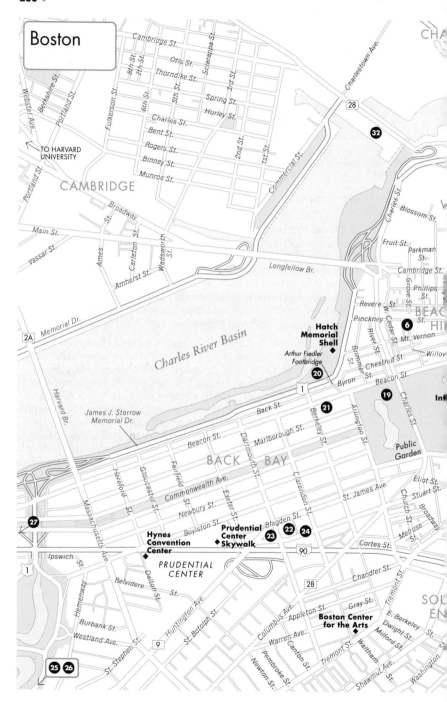

Boston

Cambridge St.
8th St.
7th St.
Otis St.
Thorndike St.
Sciarappa St.
3rd St.
Spring St.
Hurley St.
Patterson St.
6th St.
5th St.
Charles St.
Bent St.
2nd St.
Rogers St.
Binney St.
Munroe St.
1st St.
Commercial St.

Charlestown Ave.

28

32

Webster Ave.
Berkshire St.
Portland St.

TO HARVARD
UNIVERSITY

Portland St.

CAMBRIDGE

Broadway

Main St.
Vassar St.
Ames
Carleton
Wadsworth St.

Amherst St.

Memorial Dr.

2A

Charles St.
Blossom St.

Fruit St.
Parkman St.

Cambridge St.
Grove St.
Phillips St.

Revere St.
W. Cedar St.
Pinckney
River St.

BEAC
HI

6
Mt. Vernon

Willov

**Hatch
Memorial
Shell**

*Arthur Fiedler
Footbridge*

20

Brimmer St.
Byron
Chestnut St.
Beacon St.

19

Charles St.

Inf

Charles River Basin

1

Back St.

21

Berkeley St.

Arlington St.

Public
Garden

James J. Storrow
Memorial Dr.

Beacon St.

Marlborough St.

Dartmouth St.

BACK   BAY

Eliot St.

Harvard Br.

Fairfield

Gloucester St.

Commonwealth Ave.

Newbury St.

Exeter St.

Clarendon St.

St. James Ave.
St. James Ave.

Church St.
Stuart St.
Broadway

Hereford
Massachusetts Ave.

27

Ipswich St.

Boylston St.

**Hynes
Convention
Center**

◆

*Prudential
Center
Skywalk*

23 22 24

90

Melrose

Cortes St.

SOU
EN

Ipswich St.

1

9

Belvidere

Dalton St.

St.

*PRUDENTIAL
CENTER*

28

Chandler St.

Tremont St.

Hemenway

Burbank St.

Westland Ave.

Huntington Ave.

St. Botolph St.

St. Stephen St.

25 26

Columbus Ave.
Appleton St.
Gray St.

Warren Ave.

Canton St.

**Boston Center
for the Arts**
◆

E. Berkeley St.
Dwight St.
Milford St.

Pembroke St.
Newton St.

Tremont St.

Waltham

Shawmut Ave.

Washington

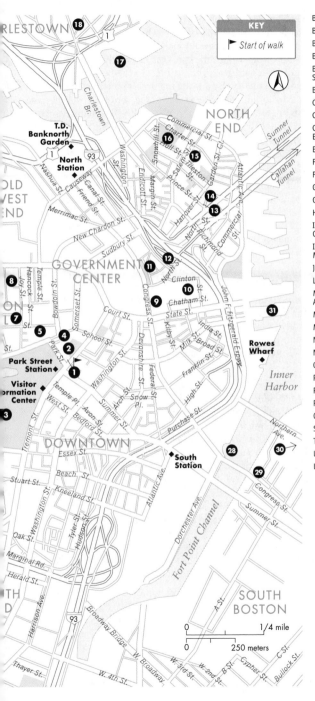

❸ Boston Common. The oldest public park in the United States is the largest and undoubtedly the most famous of the town commons around which New England settlements were traditionally arranged. As old as the city around it (it dates from 1634), the spot was originally set aside as the place where farmers could graze their cattle. On the Beacon Street side of the Common—actually, just outside the park's gates—is the **Robert Gould Shaw Memorial,** executed in deep-relief bronze by Augustus Saint-Gaudens in 1897. It honors the all-black 54th Massachusetts Regiment, portrayed in the 1989 movie *Glory.* The **Central Burying Ground,** along the Boylston Street side, is the final resting place of Tories and Patriots, as well as many British casualties of the Battle of Bunker Hill.

❷ Granary Burying Ground. "It is a fine thing to die in Boston," essayist A. C. Lyons once remarked—alluding to Boston's cemeteries, among the most picturesque and historic in America. If you found a resting place here at the Old Granary (as it's affectionately called), chances are your headstone was eloquently ornamented and your neighbors mighty eloquent, too: Samuel Adams, John Hancock, Benjamin Franklin's parents, and Paul Revere. ✉ *Entrance on Tremont St., Beacon Hill* ☉ *Daily 9–5* Ⓜ *Park St.*

★ **❻ Louisburg Square.** One of the most appealing corners in a neighborhood that epitomizes charm, Louisburg (pronounce the "s" as the locals do) Square is the very heart of Beacon Hill. Its houses—many built in the 1840s—have seen their share of famous tenants, including the Alcotts at No. 10 (Louisa May died here in 1888, on the day of her father's funeral). In 1852 the popular Swedish singer Jenny Lind was married in the parlor of No. 20. ✉ *Between Mt. Vernon and Pickney Sts., Beacon Hill* Ⓜ *Park St.*

★ **❽ Museum of Afro-American History.** Throughout the 19th century, abolition was Boston's intellectual elite's cause célèbre, and during that time a thriving black community lived on Beacon Hill. This museum, founded in 1964, occupies the first public school for black children in the United States, the **Abiel Smith School,** which was open from 1835 to 1855 and educated about 200 students. Rotating exhibits preserve local black history and help to underscore the importance of African Americans to Boston and New England history in general. Also part of the museum is the adjacent **African Meeting House,** built in 1806, the black community's center of social, educational, and political activity and a hotbed of abolitionist fervor. In 1832 the New England Anti-Slavery Society was formed here under the leadership of William Lloyd Garrison. ✉ *46 Joy St., Beacon Hill* ☏ *617/725–0022* ⊕ *www.afroammuseum.org* ✒ *Free* ☉ *Mon.–Sat. 10–4* Ⓜ *Charles/MGH.*

❼ Nichols House. The only Mt. Vernon Street home open to the public, the Nichols House—built in 1804 and attributed to Charles Bulfinch—belonged to Beacon Hill eccentric, philanthropist, and peace advocate Rose Standish Nichols, who was also one of the first female landscape designers. The house is a delightful mélange of styles. ✉ *55 Mt. Vernon St., Beacon Hill* ☏ *617/227–6993* ⊕ *www.nicholshousemuseum. org* ✒ *$7* ☉ *May–Oct., Tues.–Sat. noon–4; Nov.–Apr., Thurs.–Sat. noon–4. Tours on the ½ hr; last tour starts at 4* Ⓜ *Park St.*

▶ ❶ **Park Street Church.** If the Congregationalist Park Street Church could talk, what a joyful noise it would make. Samuel Smith's hymn "America" debuted here on July 4, 1831; two years earlier, William Lloyd Garrison began his long public campaign for the abolition of slavery. The 1810 church—designed by Peter Banner and called "the most impressive mass of brick and mortar in America" by Henry James—is easily recognized by its 217-foot steeple, considered by many to be the most beautiful in New England. ⊠ *1 Park St., Beacon Hill* ☎ *617/523–3383* ⊕ *www.parkstreet.org* ☉ *Tours mid-June–Aug., Tues.–Sat. 9:30–3:30; Sun. services at 8:30, 11, 4, and 6* Ⓜ *Park St.*

❺ **State House.** Charles Bulfinch's magnificent State House, one of the greatest works of classical architecture in America, is so striking that it hardly suffers for having been expanded in three directions by bureaucrats and lesser architects. The neoclassical design is poised between Georgian and Federal; its finest features are the delicate Corinthian columns of the portico, the graceful pediment and window arches, and the vast yet visually weightless dome, sheathed in copper from the foundry of Paul Revere. ⊠ *Beacon St. between Hancock and Bowdoin Sts., Beacon Hill* ☎ *617/727–3676* ⊕ *www.sec.state.ma.us/trs/trsidx.htm* 🖾 *Free* ☉ *Tours weekdays 10–3:30; call ahead to schedule* Ⓜ *Park St.*

Government Center & the North End

This is a section of town Bostonians love to hate. Not only does Government Center house what they can't fight—City Hall—but it also contains some of the bleakest architecture since the advent of poured concrete. This stark, treeless plain has been roundly jeered at for being user-unfriendly, but the expanse is enlivened by feisty political rallies, free summer concerts, and the occasional festival. Nearby are Faneuil Hall and the frenzied Quincy Market.

In the 17th century the North End *was* Boston—much of the rest of the peninsula was still underwater or had yet to be cleared. Today's North End is almost entirely a creation of the late 19th century, when brick tenements began to fill up with immigrants—first the Irish, then the Eastern European Jews, then the Portuguese, and finally the Italians. Despite a recent influx of yuppies of all ethnicities, you'll still find dozens of authentic eateries.

Interstate 93, which used to separate the North End from Government Center, has been buried as part of Boston's multibillion-dollar Central Artery/Tunnel project, aka the "Big Dig." For Bostonians, the project has meant a solid decade of construction disruption, but they are finally seeing the light at the end of the tunnel. Although the area is still unfinished and construction zones have not yet turned into public parkland as is planned, traffic is flowing better, the roads aren't quite so confusing, and the pedestrian ways in this area are also better marked. But don't feel shy about asking a local for help getting where you're going—you may still need it!

Numbers in the text and in the margin correspond to numbers on the Boston map.

A Good Walk

The stark expanse of Boston's City Hall Plaza introduces visitors to the urban renewal age, but across Congress Street is **Faneuil Hall** ❾ ➤, a site of political speech-making since Revolutionary times. Just beyond that is **Quincy Market** ❿. For more Bostonian fare, walk back toward Congress Street to the city's oldest restaurant, the **Union Oyster House** ⓫ for some oysters and ale. Around the corner to the north on Blackstone Street are the open-air produce stalls of **Haymarket** ⓬, always aflutter with activity on Friday and Saturday.

To sample Italian goodies, follow the Freedom Trail into the North End. From Salem Street, turn right on Cross Street and left on Hanover Street, the North End's main thoroughfare. From Hanover, turn right on Parmenter Street and left on North Street, following the Freedom Trail into North Square to reach the venerable brick **Pierce-Hichborn House** ⓭ and, beside it, the **Paul Revere House** ⓮. Take Prince Street to Hanover Street, and then continue on Hanover to St. Stephen's, the only remaining church designed by Charles Bulfinch. Directly across the street is the Prado, or Paul Revere Mall, dominated by a statue of the patriot and hero. At the end of the mall is the **Old North Church** ⓯, of "One if by land, two if by sea" fame. Continue following the Freedom Trail to Hull Street and **Copp's Hill Burying Ground** ⓰, the resting place of many Revolutionary War heroes.

TIMING   You can explore Faneuil Hall and Quincy Market in about an hour, more if you linger in the food stalls or shop. Give yourself another two to three hours to stroll through the North End. Finish the day with an Italian meal or at least a cappuccino.

Sights to See

⓰ **Copp's Hill Burying Ground.** An ancient and melancholy air hovers over this Colonial-era burial ground like a fine mist. Many headstones were chipped by practice shots fired by British soldiers during the occupation of Boston, and a number of musket-ball pockmarks can still be seen. ⊠ *Between Hull and Snowhill Sts., North End* ☉ *Daily 9–5* Ⓜ *North Station.*

★ ➤ ❾ **Faneuil Hall.** Faneuil Hall was erected in 1742 to serve as a place for town meetings and a public market. Inside are the great mural *Webster's Reply to Hayne,* Gilbert Stuart's portrait of Washington at Dorchester Heights, several worthwhile shops in the basement, and, on the top floors, the headquarters and museum of the Ancient and Honorable Artillery Company of Massachusetts, the oldest militia in the Western Hemisphere (1638). ⊠ *Faneuil Hall Sq., Government Center* ☎ *617/242–5690* ⊕ *www.cityofboston.gov/freedomtrail/faneuilhall.asp* ⊡ *Free* ☉ *Daily 9–5* Ⓜ *Government Center, Aquarium, State St.*

⓬ **Haymarket.** Here's an exuberant maze of a marketplace, packed with loudly self-promoting vendors who fill Marshall and Blackstone streets on Friday and Saturday from 7 AM until mid-afternoon. Pushcart vendors hawk fruits and vegetables against a backdrop of fish, meat, and cheese shops. ⊠ *Marshall and Blackstone Sts., Government Center* Ⓜ *Haymarket, Government Center.*

⑮ Old North Church. Also known as Christ Church, Old North is famous
Fodor'sChoice not only for its status as the oldest church in Boston (1723) but also for
★ the two lanterns that glimmered from its steeple on the night of April
18, 1775, signaling the departure by water of the British regulars to Lexington and Concord. Longfellow's poem aside, the lanterns—hung by
a young sexton named Robert Newman—were not a signal *to* Paul Revere but *from* him to the citizens of Charlestown across the harbor. ✉ *193*
Salem St., North End ☎ *617/523–6676* ⊕ *www.oldnorth.com* ☉ *Daily*
9–5; Sun. services at 9 and 11 AM Ⓜ *Haymarket, North Station.*

⊙ ⑭ Paul Revere House. It is an interesting coincidence that the oldest house
Fodor'sChoice standing in one of the oldest sections of Boston should also have been
★ the home of Paul Revere, patriot activist and silversmith. And it *is* a
coincidence, since many homes of famous Bostonians have burned or
been demolished over the years. It was saved from oblivion in 1902
and restored to an approximation of its original 17th-century appearance. The house was built nearly a hundred years before Revere's 1775
midnight ride through Middlesex County, on a site once occupied by
the parsonage of the Reverend Increase Mather's Second Church of
Boston. ✉ *19 North Sq., North End* ☎ *617/523–2338* ⊕ *www.*
paulreverehouse.org ✎ *$3, $4.50 with Pierce-Hichborn House*
☉ *Jan.–Mar., Tues.–Sun. 9:30–4:15; Nov., Dec., and 1st 2 wks Apr.,*
daily 9:30–4:15; mid-Apr.–Oct., daily 9:30–5:15 Ⓜ *Haymarket, Aquar-*
ium, Government Center.

⑬ Pierce-Hichborn House. One of the city's oldest brick buildings, this structure, just to the left of the Paul Revere House, was once owned by
Nathaniel Hichborn, a boatbuilder and Revere's cousin on his mother's
side. Built about 1711 for a window maker named Moses Pierce, the
Pierce-Hichborn House is an excellent example of early Georgian architecture. The home's symmetrical style was a radical change from the
wood-frame Tudor buildings, such as the Revere House, then common.
✉ *29 North Sq., North End* ☎ *617/523–2338* ✎ *$3, $4.50 with Paul*
Revere House ☉ *Daily guided tours 12:30 and 2:30; call ahead to con-*
firm Ⓜ *Haymarket, Aquarium, Government Center.*

⑩ Quincy Market. Also known as Faneuil Hall Marketplace, this pioneer
effort at urban recycling set the tone for many similar projects throughout America. The market consists of three block-long annexes: Quincy,
North, and South markets, each 535 feet long and built to the 1826 design of Alexander Parris. Abundance and variety have been the watch-
words of Quincy Market since its reopening in 1976. Some people
consider it hopelessly commercial, though in the peak summer season
50,000 or so visitors a day rather enjoy the extravaganza. ✉ *Bordered*
by Clinton, Commercial, and Chatham Sts., Government Center ☎ *617/*
523–1300 ⊕ *www.faneuilhallmarketplace.com* ☉ *Mon.–Sat. 10–9,*
Sun. noon–6. Restaurants and bars generally open daily 11 AM–2 AM;
food stalls open earlier Ⓜ *Government Center, State St., Aquarium.*

⑪ Union Oyster House. Billed as the oldest restaurant in continuous service in the United States, the Union Oyster House first opened its doors
as the Atwood & Bacon Oyster House in 1826. Charles Forster of
Maine was the first American to use the curious invention of the tooth-

pick on these premises. The menu hasn't changed much from the restaurant's early days (though the prices have). ⊠ *41 Union St., Government Center* ☎ *617/227–2750* ⊕ *www.unionoysterhouse.com* ☉ *Sun.–Thurs. 11–9:30, Fri. and Sat. 11–10; bar open until midnight* Ⓜ *Haymarket.*

Charlestown

Charlestown was a thriving settlement a year before Colonials headed across the Charles River to found Boston proper. The district holds two of the most visible—and vertical—monuments in Boston's history: the Bunker Hill Monument and the USS *Constitution.*

Numbers in the text and in the margin correspond to numbers on the Boston map.

A Good Walk

Charlestown can be reached by foot via the Charlestown Bridge; by Bus 93 from Haymarket Square, Boston; or on the Massachusetts Bay Transportation Authority (MBTA) water shuttle, which runs every 15 or 30 minutes year-round, from Long Wharf in downtown Boston. If you're walking, start at Copp's Hill Burial Ground; follow Hull Street to Commercial Street, and turn left to reach the bridge. The Charlestown Navy Yard will be on your right; ahead is the **USS *Constitution*** ⑰ museum and visitor center. From here, you can follow the Red Line of the Freedom Trail to the **Bunker Hill Monument** ⑱.

TIMING　Give yourself two or three hours for a Charlestown walk; the lengthy stroll across the bridge calls for endurance in cold weather. Many save Charlestown's stretch of the Freedom Trail for a second-day outing. You can avoid backtracking by taking the water shuttle back to Long Wharf.

Sights to See

⑱　**Bunker Hill Monument.** British troops sustained heavy losses on June 17,
Fodor'sChoice　1775, at the Battle of Bunker Hill—one of the earliest major confronta-
★　tions of the Revolutionary War. Most of the battle took place on Breed's Hill, which is where the monument, dedicated in 1843, actually stands. The famous war cry "Don't fire until you see the whites of their eyes" may not have been uttered by American colonel William Prescott or General Israel Putnam, but if either did shout it, he was quoting an old Prussian command that was necessary due to the inaccuracy of the musket. No matter. The Americans employed a deadly delayed-action strategy and proved themselves worthy fighters. Though they lost the battle, the engagement made clear that the British could be challenged. The monument's top is reached by a flight of 294 steps. There is no elevator, but the views from the observatory are worth the arduous climb—for those in good condition. In the lodge at the base, dioramas tell the story of the battle, and ranger programs are conducted regularly. ⊠ *Main St. to Monument St.* ☎ *617/242–5641* ▦ *Free* ☉ *Lodge daily 9–5, monument daily 9–4:30* Ⓜ *Community College.*

⊛ ⑰　**USS *Constitution*.** Better known as "Old Ironsides," the more than two-
Fodor'sChoice　centuries-old USS *Constitution* is docked at the Charlestown Navy
★　Yard. Launched in 1797, the oldest commissioned ship in the U.S. fleet is from the days of "wooden ships and iron men"—when she and her

Tours Worth Trying

CLOSE UP

FOR CENTURIES, the sea was Boston's lifeblood. In the early 18th century, this was the third-largest seaport in the British Empire. Reconnect with Boston's salty traditions on the **Boston Maritime Trail** (☎ 617/350-0358 ⊕ www. bostonbysea.org). This self-guided walk covers historic waterfront buildings, notable vessels, marine life, and the seaside parks.

The **Boston Women's Heritage Trail** (☎ 617/522-2872 ⊕ www.bwht.org) highlights remarkable women who played an integral role in shaping the history of Boston and the nation as patriots, intellectuals, abolitionists, suffragists, artists, and writers. More than a dozen self-guided walks make up the trail, although there are six main ones, all in the city center—Back Bay, Beacon Hill, Downtown, Jamaica Plain, North End, and South Cove/ Chinatown. A book ($12.95) detailing the major walks is sold at visitor centers and in most historic sites' bookstores; the remainder are sketched out in leaflet form. Check the Web site for further information.

Boston has always been on the cutting edge of science and technology. The **Innovation Odyssey** (☎ 617/350-0358 ⊕ www. innovationodyssey.com) bus tour connects sites where inventions— including the telephone, the Internet, modern surgery, and the mutual fund—came into being. The guide's running commentary, supplemented by video clips, makes sitting in Boston traffic with a bunch of strangers fun. The tour ($25) meets every second Saturday of each month at 2 PM in front of the **Old State House** (⊠ 206 Washington St., at State St., Downtown Ⓜ State St.).

Boston's long literary tradition has attracted and nurtured poets, novelists, and scholars. From May through October, the Literary Trail of Greater Boston conducts a two-hour **Athens of America: The Literary Trail in Boston** (☎ 617/621-4020 ⊕ www. literarytrailofgreaterboston.org) walking tour ($25.50) that begins at the Omni Parker House and visits the Boston Athenaeum and other sites, filling in the background of the extraordinary 19th-century cultural flowering that enabled the talents of Louisa May Alcott, Nathaniel Hawthorne, Harriet Beecher Stowe, Henry David Thoreau, Ralph Waldo Emerson, and others. The same organization also conducts a 90-minute Literary Trail in Cambridge walking tour ($25.50) tracing the footsteps of Henry Wadsworth Longfellow, W. E. B. Du Bois, E. E. Cummings, and others, and a four-hour Literary Trail in Concord tour (by van or limousine; $85 including lunch) that visits such sites as Louisa May Alcott's Orchard House and Thoreau's Walden Pond.

4

---

crew of 200 helped to assert the sovereignty of an improbable new nation. The ship's principal service was in the War of 1812. After her 42 engagements, her record was 42–0. ⊠ *55 Constitution Rd.* ☎ *617/ 242-5670* ⊕ *www.ussconstitution.navy.mil* ⊡ *Free* ⊙ *Apr.–Oct., Tues.–Sun. 10–5:50; Nov.–Mar., Thurs.–Sun. 10–3:50, last tour at 3:30* Ⓜ *North Station.*

The Back Bay

In the folklore of American neighborhoods, the Back Bay stands with New York's Park Avenue and San Francisco's Nob Hill as a symbol of propriety and high social standing. The main east–west streets—Beacon, Marlborough, Commonwealth, Newbury, and Boylston—are bisected by eight streets named in alphabetical order from Arlington to Hereford. Note that Huntington Avenue is also known as the Avenue of the Arts, but you'll hear locals use Huntington.

Numbers in the text and in the margin correspond to numbers on the Boston map.

A Good Walk

A walk through the Back Bay properly begins with the **Boston Public Garden** ⑲ ▶, the oldest botanical garden in the United States. Walk its meandering pathways to the corner of Commonwealth Avenue and Arlington Street, then venture out into the Back Bay through the gate at Arlington and Beacon streets. If you're in the mood for more greenery, take a right toward the Arthur Fiedler Footbridge to the **Esplanade** ⑳ for a river view, running paths, or perhaps a concert at the Hatch Memorial Shell. Backtrack to proceed on Beacon Street to the **Gibson House** ㉑. Follow Beacon to Berkeley and turn left to reach Commonwealth Avenue. Stroll the avenue to Clarendon, turn left, and head into **Copley Square** ㉒, where you will find the **Boston Public Library** ㉓ and **Trinity Church** ㉔. The John Hancock Tower looms above. From Copley Square, you can walk north on Dartmouth to Newbury Street and its posh boutiques.

TIMING   The Boston Public Garden is such a delight in spring and summer that you should give yourself at least an hour to explore it if this is when you're visiting. Distances between sights in the Back Bay are a bit greater than in other parts of the city, so allow one or two hours for a walk down Newbury Street.

Sights to See

🖰 ▶ ⑲   **Boston Public Garden.** The oldest botanical garden in the United States
Fodor'sChoice   is beloved by Bostonians and visitors alike. The park's pond has been
★   famous since 1877 for its foot-pedal-powered Swan Boats. Don't miss the *Make Way for Ducklings* bronzes sculpted by Nancy Schön, a tribute to the 1941 classic children's story by Robert McCloskey. ⊠ *Bounded by Arlington, Boylston, Charles, and Beacon Sts.* ☎ *617/522–1966* ⊕ *www.swanboats.com* 🎫 *Swan Boats $2.50* ☉ *Swan Boats mid-Apr.–June 20, daily 10–4; June 21–Labor Day, daily 10–5; Labor Day–mid-Sept., weekdays noon–4, weekends 10–4* Ⓜ *Arlington.*

★ ㉓   **Boston Public Library.** This venerable institution is a handsome temple to literature and a valuable research library. When the building was opened in 1895, it confirmed the status of architects McKim, Mead & White as apostles of the Renaissance-revival style, while reinforcing Boston's commitment to an enlightened citizenry that goes back 350 years, to the founding of the Public Latin School. Philip Johnson's 1972 addition emulates the mass and proportion of the original, though not its extraordinary detail; this skylighted annex houses the library's circulating collections. ✉ *700 Boylston St., at Copley Sq.* ☎ *617/536–5400* ⊕ *www.bpl.org* ☉ *Mon.–Thurs. 9–9, Fri. and Sat. 9–5; Oct.–May, also Sun. 1–5. Free guided art and architecture tours Mon. at 2:30, Tues. and Thurs. at 6, Fri. and Sat. at 11, Sun. at 2* Ⓜ *Copley.*

㉒ Copley Square. For thousands of folks in April, a glimpse of this square is a welcome sight; this is where Boston Marathon runners end their 26-mi race.

⑳ Esplanade. Near the corner of Beacon and Arlington Streets, the Arthur Fiedler Footbridge crosses Storrow Drive to the Esplanade and the **Hatch Memorial Shell.** The free concerts here in summer include the Boston Pops' immensely popular televised Fourth of July show. An impressive stone bust of the late maestro Arthur Fiedler watches over the walkers, joggers, picnickers, and sunbathers who fill the Esplanade's paths on pleasant days. The green is home port for the fleet of small sailboats that dot the Charles River Basin; they belong to Community Boating. Here, too, is the turn-of-the-20th-century **Union Boat Club Boathouse,** headquarters of the country's oldest private rowing club.

㉑ Gibson House. One of the first Back Bay residences (1859), the Gibson House is relatively modest in comparison with some of the grand mansions built during the decades that followed; yet its furnishings, from its circa-1790 Willard clock to the raised and gilded wallpaper to the multipiece faux-bamboo bedroom set, seem sumptuous to modern eyes. ✉ *137 Beacon St.* ☎ *617/267–6338* ⊕ *www.thegibsonhouse.org* 🎫 *$7* ☉ *Tours Wed.–Sun. at 1, 2, and 3 and by appointment* Ⓜ *Arlington.*

㉔ Trinity Church. In his 1877 masterpiece, architect Henry Hobson Richardson brought his Romanesque-revival style to maturity; all the aesthetic elements for which he was famous—bold masonry, careful arrangement of masses, sumptuously carved interior woodwork—come together magnificently. The church is undergoing renovation, but remains open during the project. ✉ *206 Clarendon St.* ☎ *617/536–0944* ⊕ *www. trinityboston.org* 🎫 *Church free, guided and self-guided tours $4* ☉ *Daily 8–6; Sun. services at 7:45, 9, and 11:15 AM, and 6 PM; Wed. services at 5:30 PM. Tours take place several times daily; call to confirm times* Ⓜ *Copley.*

The Fens

The marshland known as the Back Bay Fens gave this section of Boston its name, but two quirky institutions give it its character: Fenway Park and the Isabella Stewart Gardner Museum, the legacy of a 19th-century bon vivant Brahmin. Kenmore Square, a favorite haunt of college students, adds a bit of funky flavor to the mix.

Numbers in the text and in the margin correspond to numbers on the Boston map.

A Good Tour

The attractions in the Fens, best visited separately, are the **Museum of Fine Arts** ㉕, between Huntington Avenue and the Fenway, and the **Is-**

abella Stewart Gardner Museum ㉖. From the **Kenmore Square** T stop, **Fenway Park** ㉗ is a five-minute walk south along Brookline Avenue.

TIMING   The MBTA Green Line stops near the attractions on this tour. The Gardner is much smaller than the Museum of Fine Arts, but each can take up an afternoon if you take a break at their cafés.

Sights to See

㉗ **Fenway Park.** For 86 years the Boston Red Sox suffered a World Series dry spell, a streak of bad luck that fans attributed to the "Curse of the Bambino," which, stories have it, struck the team in 1920 when they sold Babe Ruth (the "Bambino") to the New York Yankees. All that changed in 2004, when the team broke the curse in a thrilling seven-game series. Fenway may be one of the smallest parks in the major leagues, but it's one of the most beloved, despite its oddball dimensions and the looming left-field wall, otherwise known as the Green Monster. ⊠ 4 *Yawkey Way, between Van Ness and Lansdowne Sts.* ☎ *617/267–1700 box office, 617/226–6666 tours* ⊕ *boston.redsox.mlb.com* 🎫 *Tours $10* ☉ *Tours daily 9–4; on game days, last tour is 3 hrs before game time and lasts only ½ hr* Ⓜ *Kenmore.*

㉖ **Isabella Stewart Gardner Museum.** This Venetian-style palazzo has a spectacular array of paintings, including masterpieces like Titian's *Rape of Europa,* Giorgione's *Christ Bearing the Cross,* Piero della Francesca's *Hercules,* and John Singer Sargent's *El Jaleo,* as well as rooms bought outright from great European houses, Spanish leather panels, Renaissance hooded fireplaces, and Gothic tapestries. An intimate restaurant overlooks the courtyard, and in spring and summer, tables and chairs spill outside. Note that a charming quirk of the museum's admission policy waives entrance fees to anyone named Isabella, forever. ⊠ *280 the Fenway* ☎ *617/566–1401, 617/566–1088 café* ⊕ *www.gardnermuseum.org* 🎫 *$10, $11 weekends* ☉ *Tues.–Sun. 11–5* Ⓜ *Museum.*

Fodor'sChoice
★

㉕ **Museum of Fine Arts.** The MFA's holdings of American art surpass those of all but two or three other U.S. museums. There are more than 50 works by John Singleton Copley, Colonial Boston's most celebrated portraitist, plus major paintings by Winslow Homer, John Singer Sargent, and Edward Hopper. Other artists represented include Mary Cassatt, Georgia O'Keeffe, and Berthe Morisot. The museum also has a sublime collection of French impressionists—including the largest collection of Monet's work outside France—and renowned collections of Asian, Egyptian, and Nubian art. Three excellent galleries showcase the art of Africa, Oceania, and the ancient Americas, expanding the MFA's emphasis on civilizations outside the Western tradition. In November 2005, the museum broke ground on an expansion that will ultimately double its size when complete in 2010. The museum will remain open during construction. ⊠ *465 Huntington Ave.* ☎ *617/267–9300* ⊕ *www. mfa.org* 🎫 *$15, free Wed. (donations accepted) 4–9:45* ☉ *Sat.–Tues. 10–4:45, Wed.–Fri. 10–9:45. West Wing open Thurs. and Fri. until 9:45* Ⓜ *Museum.*

Fodor'sChoice
★

Elsewhere in Boston

A bit off the beaten path, these sights are well worth seeing, several of them especially so if you have kids in tow.

Numbers in the margin correspond to numbers on the Boston map.

Sights to See

Boston Tea Party Ship & Museum. After a lengthy renovation, the museum is expected to reopen in the spring of 2007. The *Beaver II*, a replica of one of the ships forcibly boarded and unloaded the night Boston Harbor became a teapot, will return to the Fort Point Channel at the Congress Street Bridge, later to be joined by two tall ships, the *Dartmouth* and the *Eleanor.* Visitors will be able to explore the ships and museum exhibits, and ask questions of actors in period costumes. ⊠ *Fort Point Channel at Congress St. Bridge, Downtown* ☎ *617/269–7150* ⊕ *www. bostonteapartyship.com* ⊙ *Daily 9–5; call for updated information* Ⓜ *South Station.*

Children's Museum. Most children have so much fun here that they don't realize they're actually learning something. Creative hands-on exhibits demonstrate scientific laws, cultural diversity, and problem solving. Some of the most popular stops are also the simplest: bubble-making machinery, the two-story climbing maze, and Boats Afloat, where children can float wooden objects down a 28-foot-long replica of the Fort Point Channel. ⊠ *300 Congress St., Downtown* ☎ *617/426–6500, 617/426–8855 recorded information* ⊕ *www.bostonkids.org* ⊠ *$9, $1 Fri. 5–9* ⊙ *Sat.–Thurs. 10–5, Fri. 10–9* Ⓜ *South Station.*

Institute of Contemporary Art. Founded in 1936, the ICA is the oldest non-collecting contemporary-arts institution in the country, but that's about to change as it embarks on a project to collect 21st century art to be housed in its striking 65,000-square-foot new building on the Boston waterfront. The dramatic cantilevered edifice opened in September 2006, a fitting home for an institute that has backed many a groundbreaking artist. The ICA introduced Boston to Edvard Munch, Egon Schiele, and Oskar Kokoschka, among others, while Andy Warhol, Robert Rauschenberg, and Roy Lichtenstein each mounted pivotal exhibitions here early in their careers. The museum continues to present innovative work, including videos, installations, and multimedia shows, while pursuing its ambitions to establish a major international collection. ⊠ *Fan Pier, South Boston* ☎ *617/266–5152* ⊕ *www.icaboston. org* ⊠ *$7, free Thurs. 5–9* ⊙ *Tues., Wed., and Fri. noon–5, Thurs. noon–9, weekends 11–5. Tours on select Sun. at 2:30 and select Thurs. at 6:30* Ⓜ *South Station.*

Museum of Science. With 15-foot lightning bolts in the Theater of Electricity and a 20-foot-long *Tyrannosaurus rex* model, this is just the place to ignite any child's scientific curiosity. More than 550 exhibits cover astronomy, astrophysics, anthropology, progress in medicine, computers, the organic and inorganic earth sciences, and much more. The emphasis is on hands-on education. For instance, at the "Investigate!" exhibit children explore such scientific principles as gravity by balancing objects. The museum includes the **Mugar Omni Theater** (☎ 617/723–2500), a five-story dome screen. ⊠ *Science Park at the Charles River Dam, Old West End* ☎ *617/723–2500* ⊕ *www.mos.org* ⊠ *$15* ⊙ *July 5–Labor Day, Sat.–Thurs. 9–7, Fri. 9–9; Labor Day–July 4, Sat.–Thurs. 9–5, Fri. 9–9* Ⓜ *Science Park.*

↻ ㉛ **New England Aquarium.** More than just another pretty fish, this aquar-
FodorsChoice ium really shows you—or challenges you to imagine—life under (and
★ around) the sea. Seals bark outside the West Wing, its glass-and-steel exterior constructed to mimic fish scales; this section houses changing exhibits. Inside the main building are examples of more than 2,000 species of marine life from sharks to jellyfish, many of which make their homes in a four-story ocean-reef tank. Don't miss the five-times-a-day feeding time, a fascinating procedure that lasts nearly an hour. Educational programs, like the "Science at Sea" cruise, take place year-round. Sea-lion shows are held aboard *Discovery,* a floating marine-mammal pavil-ion; whale-watch cruises leave from the aquarium's dock from April to early November, and cost $31. ⊠ *Central Wharf between Central and Milk Sts., Downtown* ☎ *617/973–5200* ⊕ *www.neaq.org* ⊠ *$17.95, IMAX $9.50, entrance plus IMAX $22.95* ⊙ *July–early Sept., week-days 9–6, weekends 9–7; early Sept.–June, weekdays 9–5, weekends 9–6* Ⓜ *Aquarium, State St.*

Cambridge

Pronounced with either prideful satisfaction or a smirk, the nickname "People's Republic of Cambridge" sums up this independent city of nearly 100,000 west of Boston. Cambridge not only houses two of the coun-try's greatest educational institutions—Harvard University and the Massachusetts Institute of Technology—it also has a long history as a haven for freethinkers, writers, and activists of every stamp. Once a pub-lishing center, Cambridge is now known for its high-tech and biotech-nology firms.

Cambridge is easily reached on the Red Line train. The Harvard Square area is notorious for limited parking. If you insist on driving into Cam-bridge, you may want to avoid the local circling ritual by pulling into a garage.

Numbers in the text and in the margin correspond to numbers on the Cambridge map.

A Good Walk

Begin your tour in **Harvard Square** ❶ near the T station entrance. Enter Harvard Yard for a look at one of the country's premier educational in-stitutions: **Harvard University** ❷. Just past Memorial Hall (ask any student for directions) is Kirkland Street; turn right and then take a quick left onto Divinity Avenue. At 11 Divinity, you'll find an entrance to the complex of the **Peabody Museum of Archaeology & Ethnology** ❸ and the **Harvard Mu-seum of Natural History** ❹. From Harvard Square, it's about a 10-minute walk to Harvard's **Fogg Art Museum** ❺, on Quincy Street, and **Arthur M. Sackler Museum** ❻, on Broadway. The **Longfellow National Historic Site** ❼ is a 15-minute walk west of Harvard Square on Brattle Street.

In good weather, you can walk along Massachusetts Avenue through the bustle and ethnic diversity of urban Central Square and into the warehouselike openness of the Kendall Square area, where the campus of the **Massachusetts Institute of Technology** ❽ dominates the neighborhood. If the weather is poor, take the T Red Line heading inbound from Harvard Square two stops to Kendall Square.

TIMING Allow at least two hours to explore Harvard Square, plus at least three more if you plan to go to Harvard's museums. The walk down Massachusetts Avenue to MIT will take an additional 30 to 45 minutes, and you could easily spend an hour or two on the MIT campus admiring its architecture and visiting its museum or the List Visual Arts Center.

Sights to See

❻ **Arthur M. Sackler Museum.** The richness of the East and artistic treasures of the ancient Greeks, Egyptians, and Romans fill three of the four floors of this modern structure. The changing exhibits are first-rate, but if time is limited, make a beeline for the Ancient and Asian art galleries on the fourth floor, where you can gaze at bronze relics from a Chinese dynasty, Buddhist sculptures, Greek friezes, or Roman marbles. ⊠ *485 Broadway* ☎ *617/495–9400* ⊕ *www.artmuseums.harvard.edu* ⊠ *$7.50 includes admission to the Fogg Art Museum, free Sat. 10–noon* ☾ *Mon.–Sat. 10–5, Sun. 1–5* Ⓜ *Harvard.*

★ ❺ **Fogg Art Museum.** Seldom has so much been packed into so small a space. Harvard's most famous art museum is a virtual history of art, stunningly arranged in a way intended to stimulate, not overtax. Opened in 1895, and occupying its current space since 1927, the collection of more than 80,000 works focuses primarily on European, American, and East Asian art. It has notable collections of Italian Renaissance paintings and 19th-century French impressionists, including Renoir and Monet, plus works by van Gogh (*Self-Portrait Dedicated to Paul Gauguin*) and Degas (*The Rehearsal*). ⊠ *32 Quincy St.* ☎ *617/495–9400* ⊕ *www.artmuseums.harvard.edu* ⊠ *$6.50 includes admission to the Arthur M. Sackler Museum, free Sat. 10–noon* ☾ *Mon.–Sat. 10–5, Sun. 1–5* Ⓜ *Harvard.*

🐣 ❹ **Harvard Museum of Natural History.** Many museums promise something for every member of the family; the Harvard museum complex actually delivers. One fee admits you to all three museums. In the **Botanical Museum** is the Ware Collection of Glass Flowers—3,000 models of 847 plant species meticulously created between 1887 and 1936 by father and son glass artisans Leopold and Rudolph Blaschka in their studio near Dresden, Germany. The **Museum of Comparative Zoology** traces the evolution of animals (including dinosaurs) and humans. Oversize garnets and crystals are among the holdings of the **Mineralogical and Geological Museum,** which also has an extensive collection of meteorites. ⊠ *26 Oxford St.* ☎ *617/495–3045* ⊕ *www.hmnh.harvard.edu* ⊠ *$7.50 includes admission to Peabody Museum of Archaeology & Ethnology, free Sun. 9–noon throughout the year plus Wed. 3–5 Sept.–May* ☾ *Daily 9–5* Ⓜ *Harvard.*

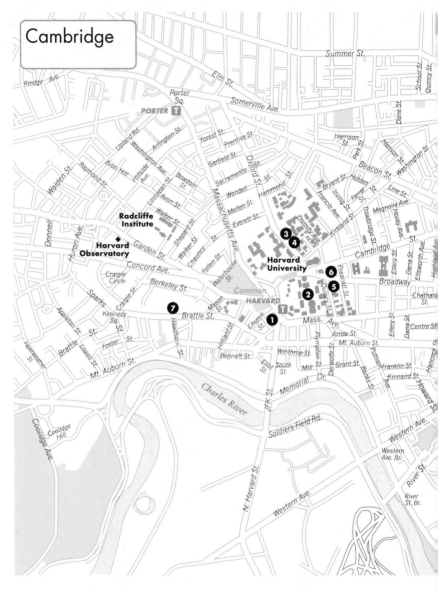

Cambridge

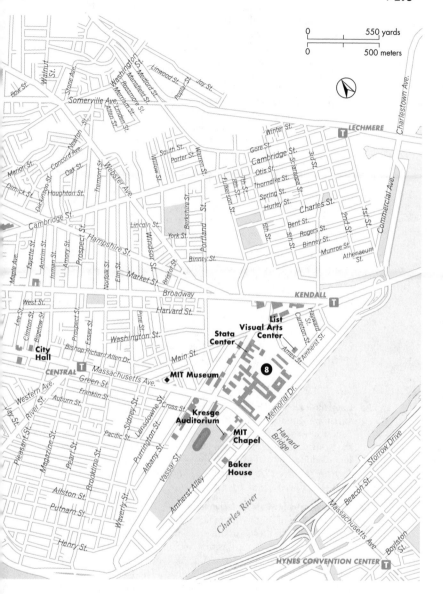

0   550 yards
0   500 meters

Walnut St.
Bow St.
Stone Ave.
Washington St.
Medford St.
Mansfield St.
Rossmore St.
Merriam St.
Linden St.
Allen St.
Somerville Ave.
Linwood St.
Poplar St.
Joy St.

LECHMERE T

Charlestown Ave.

Marion St.
Newton
Concord Ave.
Oak St.
Tremont St.
Webster Ave.
South St.
Porter St.
Warren St.
Winter St.
Gore St.
Cambridge St.
Sciarappa St.
3rd St.
Otis St.
Thorndike St.
Spring St.
Hurley St.
Charles St.
Commercial Ave.

Dickinson St.
Bishop St.
Houghton St.
Willow St.
Berkshire St.
Portland St.
Elkerson St.
7th St.
8th St.
6th St.
5th St.
Bent St.
Rogers St.
Binney St.
2nd St.
1st St.
Munroe St.
Athenaeum St.

Cambridge St.
Fayette St.
Antrim St.
Amory St.
Inman St.
Prospect St.
Hampshire St.
Windsor St.
Lincoln St.
York St.
Bristol St.
Binney St.

Maple Ave.

Norfolk St.
Elm St.
Market St.
Broadway
Harvard St.

KENDALL T

West St.
Lee St.
Clinton St.
Bigelow St.
Prospect St.
Essex St.
Bishop Richard Allen Dr.
2nd St.
Washington St.
Main St.
Stata Center
List Visual Arts Center
Carleton St.
Harvard St.
Ames St.
Amherst St.

City Hall
CENTRAL T
Massachusetts Ave.
Green St.
Franklin St.
MIT Museum ◆
❽
Memorial Dr.

Western Ave.
River St.
Jay St.
Auburn St.
Magazine St.
Pearl St.
Brookline St.
Sidney St.
Lansdowne St.
Cross St.
Kresge Auditorium
Purrington St.
Pacific St.
Albany St.
MIT Chapel
Baker House
Harvard Bridge

Pleasant St.
Allston St.
Putnam St.
Vassar St.
Waverly St.
Amherst Alley
Charles River
Storrow Drive
Beacon St.
Massachusetts Ave.

Henry St.

HYNES CONVENTION CENTER T
Boylston St.

1 **Harvard Square.** Gaggles of students, street musicians, people hawking
Fodor'sChoice the paper *Spare Change* (as well as asking for some), end-of-the-world
★ preachers, and political-cause proponents make for a nonstop pedestrian
flow at this most celebrated of Cambridge crossroads. Harvard Square
is where Massachusetts Avenue (locally, Mass Ave.), coming from
Boston, turns and widens into a triangle broad enough to accommodate a brick peninsula (beneath which the MBTA station is located). Sharing the peninsula is the Out-of-Town newsstand, a local institution that
occupies the restored 1928 kiosk that used to be the entrance to the MBTA
station. Harvard Square is flanked on two sides by banks, restaurants,
and shops and on the third by Harvard University. The **Cambridge Visitor Information Booth** (⊠ Harvard Sq. ☎ 617/497–1630 ⊕ www.
cambridge-usa.org), just outside the T station entrance, is a volunteer-
staffed kiosk with maps and brochures. The booth, which is open weekdays 9–5, Saturday 10–3, and Sunday 1–5, has maps for historic and
literary walking tours of the city and an excellent guide to the bookstores in the Square and beyond.

★ **2** **Harvard University.** The shade-dappled expanse of **Harvard Yard**—the
very center of Harvard University—has exuded quiet gentility for
more than 300 years. Named in 1639 for John Harvard, a young
Charlestown clergyman who left the college his entire library and half
his estate, Harvard remained the only college in the New World until
1693. The **Harvard University Events & Information Center** (⊠ Holyoke
Center, 1350 Massachusetts Ave. ☎ 617/495–1573) distributes maps
of the university area and offers free student-led tours of Harvard Yard.
⊠ *Bounded by Massachusetts Ave., Mt. Auburn St., Holyoke St., and
Dunster St.* ☎ *617/495–1000 for general information* ⊕ *www.harvard.
edu* Ⓜ *Harvard.*

7 **Longfellow National Historic Site.** Henry Wadsworth Longfellow—whose
stirring poem about Paul Revere's midnight ride thrilled 19th-century
America—once lived in this elegant mansion. He filled the house with
the exuberant spirit of his own work and that of his literary circle, which
included Ralph Waldo Emerson and Nathaniel Hawthorne. ⊠ *105
Brattle St.* ☎ *617/876–4491* ⊕ *www.nps.gov/long* 🖾 *$3* ☉ *Tours
May–Oct., Wed.–Sun. 10–4:30* Ⓜ *Harvard.*

8 **Massachusetts Institute of Technology.** MIT, at Kendall Square, occupies
135 acres 1½ mi southeast of Harvard, bordering the Charles River. The
campus, divided into east and west by Massachusetts Avenue, is studded with a public art collection including works by Henry Moore,
Jacques Lipchitz, Louise Nevelson, Alexander Calder, and Frank Stella,
and it has some extraordinary buildings. The Kresge Auditorium, designed by Eero Saarinen with a curving roof and unusual thrust, rests
on three, instead of four, points; it was dedicated in 1955 along with
the nondenominational MIT Chapel, a circular Saarinen design. Alvar
Aalto's Baker House dormitory, from 1947, is another post-war modernist landmark on the West Campus. On the East Campus, besides the
List Visual Arts Center in a building designed by MIT graduate I. M.
Pei, is the recently completed Stata Center for Computer, Information,
and Intelligence Sciences, a stunning design by Frank Gehry. An infor-

mation center (open weekdays 9–5), housed in one of MIT's original buildings of 1916, offers free campus tours at 10:45 and 2:45. ✉ 77 *Massachusetts Ave.* ☎ *617/253–1000, 617/253–4795 information center* ⊕ *web.mit.edu* Ⓜ *Kendall/MIT.*

🔄 **MIT Museum.** A place where art and science meet, the museum showcases photos, paintings, and scientific instruments and memorabilia. A popular ongoing exhibit is the "Hall of Hacks," a look at the pranks MIT students have played over the years. Most notable is a rare photo of Oliver Reed Smoot Jr., a 1958 MIT Lambda Chi Alpha pledge. Smoot's future fraternity brothers used the diminutive freshman to measure the length of the nearby Harvard Bridge, which spans the Charles. Every 5 feet or so became "One Smoot." To this day, the markings remain painted on the bridge. ✉ *265 Massachusetts Ave.* ☎ *617/253–4444* ⊕ *web.mit.edu/museum* 🎫 *$5* 🕐 *Tues.–Fri. 10–5, weekends noon–5* Ⓜ *Kendall/MIT.*

❸ Peabody Museum of Archaeology & Ethnology. With one of the world's outstanding anthropological collections, the Peabody (pronounced *pee-buh-dee*) focuses on Native American and Central and South American cultures; there are also interesting displays on Africa. The Hall of the North American Indian is outstanding, with its models of traditional dwellings and samples of traditional dress. ✉ *11 Divinity Ave.* ☎ *617/ 496–1027* ⊕ *www.peabody.harvard.edu* 🎫 *$7.50 includes admission to Harvard Museum of Natural History, free Sun. 9–noon, free Wed. 3–5 Sept.–May* 🕐 *Daily 9–5* Ⓜ *Harvard.*

Where to Eat

Back Bay/Beacon Hill

CONTEMPORARY

★ **$$$$**

✕ **Clio.** Years ago when Ken Oringer opened his snazzy leopard skin–lined hot spot in the tasteful boutique Eliot Hotel, the hordes fought over reservations. Things have quieted down since then, but the food hasn't. Luxury ingredients pack the menu, from foie gras and tiny eels called elvers to the sea urchins and Kobe beef Oringer serves at Uni, the small but adventurous sushi bar set up in a side room off the main dining room. ✉ *Eliot Hotel, 370 Commonwealth Ave., Back Bay* ☎ *617/536–7200* 🍴 *Reservations essential* 🟰 *AE, MC, V* Ⓜ *Hynes Convention Center/ ICA.*

$$$–$$$$

Fodor'sChoice

★

✕ **Excelsior.** Having proven his talents at Harvard Square's Harvest, Chef Eric Brennan brings his gift for creating exquisite handcrafted American cuisine to Excelsior, the cream of Boston's culinary crop. Brennan's appreciation for and innovative use of fresh local seafood serves him well here, especially with his selection of raw-bar items. Try to finagle a seat near the windows on the second floor for a terrific view of the Public Garden or snag a seat at the bar for one of the incomparable lobster pizzas and a hand-muddled bajito (made with rum, sugar and basil). ✉ *272 Boylston St., Back Bay* ☎ *617/426–7878* 🍴 *Reservations essential* 🟰 *AE, D, DC, MC, V* Ⓜ *Arlington.*

★ **$$$–$$$$**

✕ **The Federalist.** Inside the swanky Fifteen Beacon hotel, the Federalist's modern dining room clearly reflects the attitude around this part

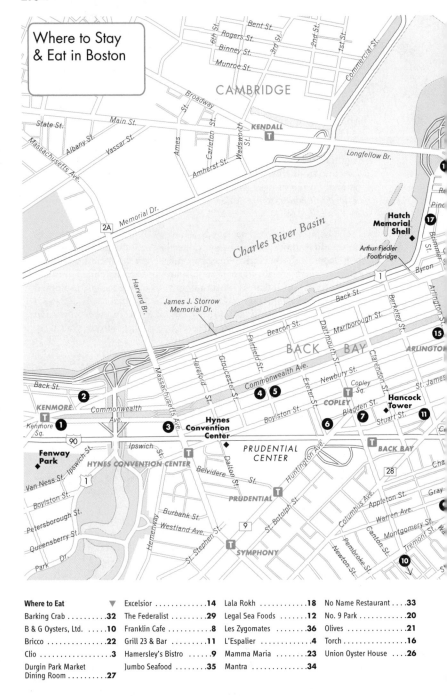

Where to Stay & Eat in Boston

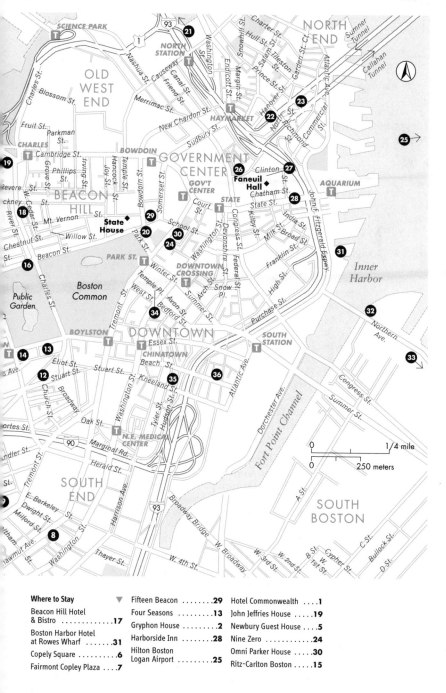

of town: refined, civilized, and all about luxury. The menu pushes traditional Boston dishes driven by local ingredients; look for a sherry-drizzled lobster bisque served beside a lobster and avocado salad. Be warned, though: the food is as rich as the pricetag. The wine list, with more than 1,000 entries including a few century-old bottles, is an impressive but expensive proposition. ⊠ *Fifteen Beacon Hotel, 15 Beacon St., Beacon Hill* ☎ *617/670–2515* ⚴ *Reservations essential* ⊟ *AE, D, DC, MC, V* Ⓜ *Park St.*

$$$–$$$$
Fodor's Choice
★
✕ **No. 9 Park.** In the shadow of the State House's golden dome, chef Barbara Lynch's stellar cuisine draws plenty of well-deserved attention of its own. Settle into the plush but unpretentious dining room and indulge in pumpkin risotto with rare lamb or the memorably rich prune-stuffed gnocchi drizzled with bits of foie gras. The wine list bobs and weaves into new territory but is always well chosen. ⊠ *9 Park St., Beacon Hill* ☎ *617/742–9991* ⊟ *AE, D, DC, MC, V* Ⓜ *Park St.*

FRENCH
$$$$
Fodor's Choice
★
✕ **L'Espalier.** From sole with black truffles to foie gras with quince, chef-owner Frank McClelland's masterpieces are every bit as impeccable and elegant as the Victorian town house in which they are served. You can skip the opulent menu by choosing a prix-fixe tasting, such as the innovative and flat-out fabulous vegetarian degustation. With two fireplaces and subtle decor in earthy colors, this is one of Boston's most romantic places. ⊠ *30 Gloucester St., Back Bay* ☎ *617/262–3023* ⚴ *Reservations essential* ⊟ *AE, D, DC, MC, V* ⊘ *Closed Sun. No lunch* Ⓜ *Hynes Convention Center/ICA.*

$$–$$$
✕ **Torch.** A little slice of the Marais hit Charles Street when Evan Deluty and wife Candice opened Torch. Deluty is a keen culinary editor, tweaking dishes with enough ingredients to enhance, but not obscure, the main flavors; witness the sweetly simple grilled chicken with lemon and tarragon. Follow it with the thoughtfully chosen cheese plate or a deep-chocolate mousse. ⊠ *26 Charles St., Beacon Hill* ☎ *617/723–5939* ⚴ *Reservations essential* ⊟ *AE, D, DC, MC, V* ⊘ *Closed Mon. No lunch* Ⓜ *Charles/MGH.*

PERSIAN
★ **$$**
✕ **Lala Rokh.** Persian miniatures and medieval maps cover the walls of this beautifully detailed and delicious fantasy of food and art. The focus is on the Azerbaijanian corner that is now northwest Iran, including exotically flavored specialties and dishes such as familiar (but superb here) eggplant puree, pilaf, kebabs, *fesanjoon* (the classic pomegranate-walnut sauce), and lamb stews. ⊠ *97 Mt. Vernon St., Beacon Hill* ☎ *617/720–5511* ⊟ *AE, DC, MC, V* Ⓜ *Charles/MGH.*

SEAFOOD
$–$$$$
✕ **Legal Sea Foods.** What began as a tiny restaurant over a Cambridge fish market has grown to important regional status, with more than 20 East Coast locations, plus a handful of national ones. The hallmark is the freshest possible seafood, whether you have it wood-grilled, in New England chowder, or doused with an Asia-inspired sauce. The smoked-bluefish pâté is delectable, and the clam chowder is so good it has become a menu staple at presidential inaugurations. A preferred-seating list allows calls ahead and this location boasts private dining inside its beautiful, bottle-lined wine cellar. ⊠ *26 Park Sq., Theater District* ☎ *617/426–4444* ⊟ *AE, D, DC, MC, V* Ⓜ *Arlington.*

STEAK ✕ **Grill 23 & Bar.** Pin-striped suits, dark paneling, comically oversize flat-
★ **$$–$$$$** ware, and waiters in white jackets give this steak house a posh de-
meanor. The food is anything but predictable, with dishes such as Kobe
beef carpaccio with smoked-onion compote and rotisserie tenderloin with
Roquefort mashed potatoes. Seafood specialties such as five-pepper
tuna au poivre give beef sales a run for their money. Desserts, like the
apple blackberry pot pie and the sticky toffee pudding, are far above
those of the average steak house. ⊠ *161 Berkeley St., Back Bay* ☎ *617/*
542–2255 ⌲ *Reservations essential* ▭ *AE, D, DC, MC, V* ⊗ *No lunch*
Ⓜ *Back Bay/South End.*

Cambridge

AMERICAN ✕ **Mr. Bartley's Burger Cottage.** It may be perfect cuisine for the student
¢–$ metabolism: a huge variety of variously garnished thick burgers, deli-
ciously crispy french fries (regular and sweet potato), and onion rings.
There's also a competent veggie burger. The nonalcoholic "raspberry
lime rickey," made with fresh limes, raspberry juice, sweetener, and soda
water, is the must-try classic drink. ⊠ *1246 Massachusetts Ave.* ☎ *617/*
354–6559 ⌲ *Reservations not accepted* ▭ *No credit cards* ⊗ *Closed*
Sun. Ⓜ *Harvard.*

CONTEMPORARY ✕ **Blue Room.** Totally hip, funky, and Cambridge, the Blue Room blends
$$–$$$ a host of cuisines from Southwestern to Mediterranean with fresh, local
ingredients. Brightly colored furnishings, counters where you can meet
others while you eat, and a friendly staff add up to a good-time place
that's serious about food. Try the seared scallops over green lentils, or
perhaps a cassoulet brimming with braised pork and wild-boar sausage.
An extraordinary buffet brunch with grilled meats and vegetables, as
well as regular breakfast fare and a gorgeous array of desserts, is served
on Sunday. ⊠ *1 Kendall Sq.* ☎ *617/494–9034* ▭ *AE, D, DC, MC, V*
⊗ *No lunch* Ⓜ *Kendall/MIT.*

$$–$$$ ✕ **Harvest.** The lavish menu of up-to-date dishes is hedged with tradi-
tional regional favorites made with locally-sourced ingredients. Starters
include raw seafood and a salad of braised rabbit and arugula; grilled
Block Island swordfish and honey-lacquered duck breast are among the
recommended main plates. The open kitchen makes some noise, but cus-
tomers at the ever-popular bar don't seem to mind. Warm weather lures
with the opening of a lush outdoor patio. ⊠ *44 Brattle St.* ☎ *617/868–*
2255 ⌲ *Reservations essential* ▭ *AE, D, DC, MC, V* Ⓜ *Harvard Sq.*

$–$$$ ✕ **East Coast Grill & Raw Bar.** Owner-chef-author Chris Schlesinger built
FodorśChoice his national reputation on grilled foods and red-hot condiments. The
★ Jamaican jerk, North Carolina pulled pork, and habañero-laced "pasta
from Hell" are still here, but this restaurant has made an extraordinary
play to establish itself in the front ranks of fish restaurants. Spices and
condiments are more restrained, and Schlesinger has compiled a wine
list bold and flavorful enough to match the highly spiced food. The dining space is completely informal. A killer brunch (complete with a do-
it-yourself Bloody Mary bar) is served on Sunday. ⊠ *1271 Cambridge*
St. ☎ *617/491–6568* ▭ *AE, D, MC, V* ⊗ *No lunch* Ⓜ *Central Sq.*

ECLECTIC ✕ **Chez Henri.** French with a Cuban twist—odd bedfellows, but it
$$–$$$ works for this sexy, confident restaurant. The dinner menu gets seri-

302 <

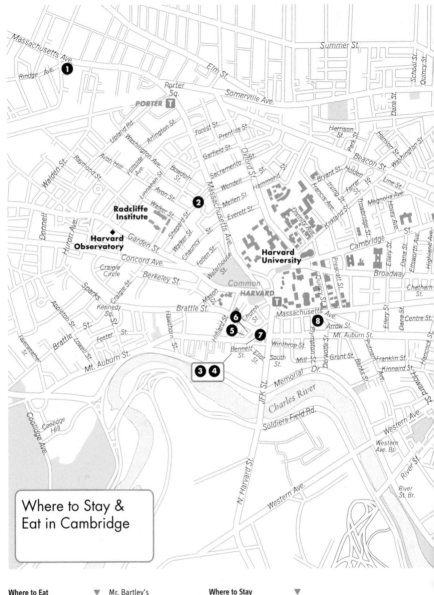

Where to Stay &
Eat in Cambridge

Where to Eat ▼

Blue Room **10**

Casablanca **6**

Chez Henri **2**

Harvest **5**

East Coast Grill
& Raw Bar **9**

Mr. Bartley's
Burger Cottage **8**

Rialto **4**

Where to Stay ▼

A Cambridge House
Bed & Breakfast **1**

Charles Hotel **3**

Harvard Square
Hotel **7**

Royal Sonesta
Hotel **11**

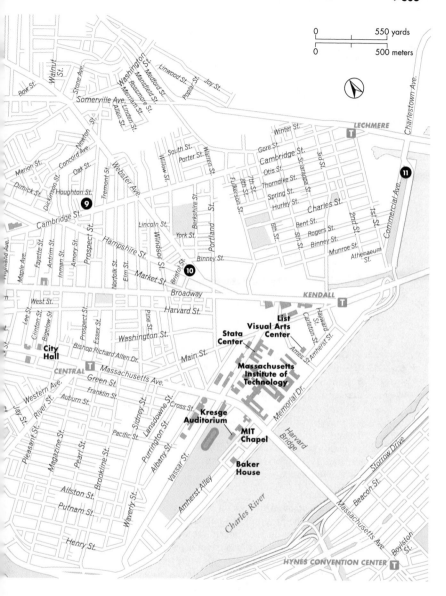

ous with rabbit paella and saffron rice, veal stew with buttered egg noodles, and sinfully sweet rum-laced pineapple cake. At the cozy bar you can sample spiced fries, clam fritters, and the best grilled three-pork Cuban sandwich in Boston. The place fills quickly with Cantabrigian locals—an interesting mix of students, professors, and sundry intelligentsia. ⊠ *1 Shepard St.* ☎ *617/354–8980* ⊟ *AE, DC, MC, V* ⊘ *No lunch* Ⓜ *Harvard.*

MEDITERRANEAN ✕ **Rialto.** The ultraposh dining room continues a pleasant drift from its
$$–$$$$ Mediterranean beginnings toward more French techniques and New England ingredients, such as Maine crab cakes and Macomber turnips (a local, sweet, white turnip). But the Tuscan-style sirloin steak with portobello and arugula salad is a lifetime commitment of chef Jody Adams, one of Boston's most admired kitchen wizards. ⊠ *Charles Hotel, 1 Bennett St., Harvard Sq.* ☎ *617/661–5050* ⊟ *AE, DC, MC, V* ⊘ *No lunch, except brunch Sun.* Ⓜ *Harvard Sq.*

★ $$ ✕ **Casablanca.** Long before the *Rocky Horror Picture Show,* Harvard and Radcliffe types would put on trench coats and head to the Brattle Theatre to see *Casablanca,* rising to recite the Bogart and Bergman lines in unison. Then it was on to this restaurant, where the walls are painted with scenes from the film, for more of the same. The path to this local institution is still well worn, thanks to its velvety, deep-flavored braised beef ribs and grilled quail with almond-honey butter. ⊠ *40 Brattle St.* ☎ *617/876–0999* ⊟ *AE, D, DC, MC, V* Ⓜ *Harvard Sq.*

Charlestown

MEDITERRANEAN ✕ **Olives.** No longer will you see chef Todd English tending the wood-
★ $$–$$$$ fire brick oven here—these days he's too busy watching over his many restaurants in New York and elsewhere. But don't worry, English's recipes are in good hands. Witness smart signature offerings such as the "Olives" house caesar with anchovy-caper dressing and jumbo lump crab. Crowded seating, noise, long lines, and abrupt service only add to the legend. Come early or late or be prepared for an extended wait: dinner reservations are taken only for groups of six or more at 5:30 or 8:30. ⊠ *10 City Sq.* ☎ *617/242–1999* ⊟ *AE, D, DC, MC, V* ⊘ *No lunch* Ⓜ *Community College.*

Chinatown

CHINESE ✕ **Jumbo Seafood.** Although this Cantonese/Hong Kong–style restaurant
$$–$$$ has much to be proud of, it's happily unpretentious. Have a whole sea bass with ginger and scallion to see what all the fuss is about. Nonoceanic offerings are equally outstanding—even such simple dishes as stir-fried sugar-snap-pea tendrils with white rice. The Hong Kong influence results in a lot of fried food; crispy fried calamari with salted pepper is a standout. The waiters are very patient with newcomers' questions, though some don't speak English fluently. ⊠ *7 Hudson St.* ☎ *617/ 542–2823* ⊟ *AE, MC, V* Ⓜ *Chinatown.*

Downtown

ECLECTIC ✕ **Mantra.** The refined fusion—a French-based Indian menu with as-
★ $$–$$$$ sorted other international flourishes—at this dark and sexy downtown spot is as elegant as it is inventive. Dishes such as rainbow trout with fenugreek tomato tartare and fava-bean compote are rich in flavor, and

if you're up for just a snack, catch the tuna tartare in the cushy lounge area. The expansive room, decked out in chain-mail curtains and marble walls, used to be a bank. ⊠ *52 Temple Pl.* ☎ *617/542–8111* ⌕ *Reservations essential* ⊟ *AE, D, DC, MC, V* ☽ *Closed Sun.* Ⓜ *Downtown Crossing.*

FRENCH
★ **$$-$$$**

✕ **Les Zygomates.** *Les zygomates is the French expression for the muscles on the human face that make you smile—and this combination wine bar–bistro inarguably lives up to its name, with quintessential French bistro fare that is both simple and simply delicious. The menu beautifully matches the ever-changing wine list, with all wines served by the 2-ounce taste, 6-ounce glass, or bottle. Prix-fixe menus are available at lunch and dinner, and could include oysters by the half dozen or pancetta-wrapped venison with roasted pears. There's live jazz several nights a week.* ⊠ *129 South St.* ☎ *617/542–5108* ⌕ *Reservations essential* ⊟ *AE, D, DC, MC, V* ☽ *Closed Sun. No lunch Sat.* Ⓜ *South Station.*

Faneuil Hall

AMERICAN
$$-$$$

✕ **Union Oyster House.** Established in 1826, this is Boston's oldest continuing restaurant. Consider having what Daniel Webster had—oysters on the half shell at the ground-floor raw bar, which is the oldest part of the restaurant and still the best. The rooms at the top of the narrow staircase are dark and have low ceilings—very Ye Olde New England—and plenty of nonrestaurant history. Uncomfortably small tables and chairs tend to undermine the simple, decent, but pricey food. There is valet parking after 5:30 PM. ⊠ *41 Union St., Government Center* ☎ *617/227–2750* ⊟ *AE, D, DC, MC, V* Ⓜ *Haymarket.*

$-$$$

✕ **Durgin Park Market Dining Room.** You should be hungry enough to cope with enormous portions, yet not so hungry you can't tolerate a long wait. Durgin Park was serving its same hearty New England fare (Indian pudding, baked beans, corned beef and cabbage, and a prime rib that hangs over the edge of the plate) back when Faneuil Hall was a working market instead of a tourist attraction. The service, once famously brusque, is these days much more good-natured. ⊠ *340 Faneuil Hall Market Pl., North Market Bldg., Government Center* ☎ *617/227–2038* ⊟ *AE, D, DC, MC, V* Ⓜ *Government Center.*

North End

ITALIAN
★ **$$-$$$$**

✕ **Bricco.** A sophisticated but unpretentious enclave of nouveau Italian, Bricco has carved out quite a following. And no wonder: the velvety butternut-squash soup alone is argument for a reservation. Simple but well-balanced main courses such as melt-in-your-mouth pistachio-crusted Kobe beef and rabbit loin wrapped in pancetta have a sweet smokiness that lingers. You're likely to want to linger in the warm room, too, gazing through the floor-to-ceiling windows while sipping a glass of Sangiovese. ⊠ *241 Hanover St.* ☎ *617/248–6800* ⌕ *Reservations essential* ⊟ *AE, DC, MC, V* Ⓜ *Haymarket.*

$$-$$$

✕ **Mamma Maria.** Don't let the clichéd name fool you: Mamma Maria is one of the most elegant restaurants in the North End, although some locals think it can feel stuffy. From the Maine lobster–filled tortellini to the innovative sauces and entrées to some of the best desserts in the North

End, you can't go wrong here. The view, meanwhile, is lovely: gaze out onto cobblestone-lined North Square as you finish your pappardelle layered with braised rabbit and savor a finale of limoncello. ✉ *3 North Sq.* ☎ *617/523–0077* ▤ *AE, D, DC, MC, V* Ⓜ *Haymarket.*

South End

CONTEMPORARY ✕ **Hamersley's Bistro.** Gordon Hamersley has earned a national repu-
$$$–$$$$ tation, thanks to such signature dishes as a grilled mushroom-and-gar-
Fodor'sChoice lic sandwich, roast chicken, and souffléed lemon custard. He's one of
★ Boston's great chefs and is famous for sporting a Red Sox cap instead of a toque. His place has a full bar, a café area with 10 tables for walk-ins, and a larger dining room that's a little more formal and decorative than the bar and café, though nowhere near as stuffy as it looks. ✉ *553 Tremont St.* ☎ *617/423–2700* ▤ *AE, D, DC, MC, V* Ⓜ *Back Bay/South End.*

$$ ✕ **Franklin Café.** This place has jumped to the head of the class by keeping things simple yet effective. (Its litmus: local chefs gather here to wind down after work.) Try anything with the great chive mashed potatoes and don't miss the double-thick brined pork chops. The vibe is generally more bar than restaurant, so be forewarned: it can get loud and smoky. Desserts are not served. ✉ *278 Shawmut Ave.* ☎ *617/350–0010* ✍ *Reservations not accepted* ▤ *AE, MC, V* Ⓜ *Back Bay/South End.*

SEAFOOD ✕ **B & G Oysters, Ltd.** Chef Barbara Lynch (of No. 9 Park fame) has made
$–$$ yet another fabulous mark on Boston with a style-conscious seafood
Fodor'sChoice restaurant that updates New England's traditional bounty with flair. De-
★ signed to imitate the inside of an oyster shell, the iridescent bar glows with silvery, candlelit tiles and a sophisticated crowd. They're in for the lobster roll, no doubt—an expensive proposition at $24, but worth every cent for its decadent chunks of meat in a perfectly textured dressing. ✉ *550 Tremont St.* ☎ *617/423–0550* ▤ *AE, D, MC, V* Ⓜ *Back Bay/ South End.*

Waterfront

SEAFOOD ✕ **Barking Crab.** It is, believe it or not, a seaside clam shack plunk in the
$–$$$ middle of Boston, with a stunning view of the downtown skyscrapers. An outdoor lobster tent in summer, in winter it retreats indoors to a warm-hearted version of a waterfront dive, with chestnuts roasting on a cozy woodstove. Look for the classic New England clambake—chowder, lobster, steamed clams, corn on the cob—or the spicier crab boil. ✉ *88 Sleeper St., Northern Ave. Bridge* ☎ *617/426–2722* ▤ *AE, DC, MC, V* Ⓜ *South Station.*

¢–$$ ✕ **No Name Restaurant.** Famous for not being famous, the No Name has
Fodor'sChoice been serving fresh seafood, simply broiled or fried, since 1917. Once
★ you find it, tucked off of New Northern Avenue (as opposed to Old Northern Avenue) between the World Trade Center and the Bank of America Pavilion, you can close your eyes and pretend you're in a little fishing village—it's not much of a stretch. Being right on the fish pier has its advantages. ✉ *15½ Fish Pier, off Northern Ave.* ☎ *617/338–7539 or 617/423–2705* ▤ *AE, D, DC, MC, V* Ⓜ *South Station.*

Where to Stay

If your biggest dilemma is deciding whether to spend $300 per night on old-fashioned elegance or extravagant modernity, you've come to the right city. The bulk of Boston's accommodations are not cheap, yet visitors with limited cash will find choices among the smaller, older establishments, the modern motels, or—perhaps the best option (if you can take early-morning small talk)—the B&B inn.

Back Bay

★ $$$$ ▦ **Four Seasons.** Overlooking the Public Garden, the Four Seasons is famed for luxurious personal service. You enter its antiques-filled public spaces through a large, sleek, black granite lobby. Oversize guest rooms have an understated elegance. Suites are enhanced with stereos, private bars, and 42-inch plasma TVs. The 51-foot lap pool, on the eighth floor, has views of the Public Garden. One of Boston's best restaurants, Aujourd'hui, is here. Relax in the Bristol Lounge over afternoon tea or an evening cocktail, when a pianist livens up the bar. ⊠ *200 Boylston St., 02116* ☎ *617/338–4400 or 800/819–5053* 🖷 *617/423–0154* ⊕ *www.fourseasons.com/boston* ↘ *197 rooms, 76 suites* ♿ *2 restaurants, room service, in-room safes, minibars, cable TV with movies and video games, in-room data ports, Wi-Fi, indoor pool, gym, massage, sauna, steam room, lounge, piano, babysitting, dry cleaning, laundry service, concierge, business services, meeting rooms, travel services, parking (fee), some pets allowed* ▤ *AE, D, DC, MC, V* Ⓜ *Arlington.*

$$$$ ▦ **Ritz-Carlton Boston.** A yearlong closure and impressive restoration has
Fodor'sChoice brought an updated vitality to this opulent gem that stands guard at the
★ corner of fashionable Newbury Street and the Public Garden. The Ritz's trademark devotion to its guests' comfort is apparent as soon as you walk into its bustling lobby. Fabric-covered corridors and soft hues of blue, gold, and apricot manage to make this grand dame—whose lavishness is manifested even in its small gym, with gilded sconces and luxurious window coverings—feel unexpectedly cozy. Fireplaces, technology, afternoon tea, and the gorgeous views and decadence of the club level are just some of the luxurious offerings that have long made the Ritz the choice for royalty. ⊠ *15 Arlington St., 02116* ☎ *617/536–5700 or 800/241–3333* 🖷 *617/536–1335* ⊕ *www.ritzcarlton.com/hotels/boston* ↘ *228 rooms, 45 suites* ♿ *Café, room service, in-room safes, minibars, refrigerators, cable TV with movies and video games, Wi-Fi, gym, massage, bar, lounge, shops, babysitting, dry cleaning, concierge, concierge floor, business services, meeting rooms, convention center, parking (fee), some pets allowed* ▤ *AE, D, DC, MC, V* Ⓜ *Arlington.*

★ $$$–$$$$ ▦ **Fairmont Copley Plaza.** Unabashedly romantic, this 1912 landmark underwent a $34 million renovation, updating rooms with new classically inspired decor, marble bathrooms, and high-speed Internet access. The grand public spaces have mosaic floors, marble pillars, and high gilded ceilings hung with glittering chandeliers. The mahogany-paneled Oak Room restaurant matches its former twin in New York's now-defunct Plaza Hotel; follow dinner with a trip to the equally stately—and tryst-worthy—Oak Bar, which has live music and one of the longest martini menus in town. Also new is Fairmont Gold, an ultradeluxe club level offering a dedicated staff, lounge, dining room, and library. ⊠ *138 St. James Ave., 02116* ☎ *617/267–5300 or 800/441–1414* ⊜ *617/375–9648* ⊕ *www.fairmont.com/copleyplaza* ⋟ *366 rooms, 17 suites* ⋞ *Restaurant, room service, in-room safes, minibars, cable TV with movies, in-room data ports, gym, bar, babysitting, dry cleaning, laundry service, concierge, concierge floor, business services, parking (fee), pets allowed (fee)* ⊟ *AE, D, DC, MC, V* Ⓜ *Copley, Back Bay.*

\$\$–\$\$\$ 🏨 **Copley Square.** This hotel has a quirky turn-of-the-20th-century charm—and its convenient Back Bay location is an all-around plus. The circa-1891 hotel, one of the city's oldest, is busy and comfortable, with winding corridors and repro-antique furniture. The idiosyncratic rooms have a few common denominators, such as coffeemakers, and some have couches. Complimentary afternoon tea is served daily in the lobby. The property is a favorite with international travelers. ⊠ *47 Huntington Ave., 02116* ☎ *617/536–9000 or 800/225–7062* ⊜ *617/267–3547* ⊕ *www. copleysquarehotel.com* ⋟ *148 rooms, 5 suites* ⋞ *2 restaurants, coffee shop, room service, in-room fax, in-room safes, cable TV with movies, Wi-Fi, bar, concierge, business services, parking (fee)* ⊟ *AE, D, DC, MC, V* Ⓜ *Copley.*

\$–\$\$ 🏨 **Newbury Guest House.** Book a few months in advance if you wish to stay at this elegant redbrick-and-brownstone 1882 row house. Its success is due to smart management, fine furnishings, and a location on Boston's most fashionable shopping street. Rooms with queen-size beds, natural pine floors, and elegant reproduction Victorian furnishings open off an oak staircase; prints from the Museum of Fine Arts enliven the walls. Some rooms have bay windows; others have decorative fireplaces. Limited parking is available at \$15 for 24 hours—a good deal for the area. ⊠ *261 Newbury St., 02116* ☎ *617/670–6100 or 800/437–7668* ⊜ *617/262–4243* ⊕ *www.newburyguesthouse.com* ⋟ *32 rooms* ⋞ *No-smoking rooms* ⊟ *AE, D, DC, MC, V* ⭘⬤⭘ *BP* Ⓜ *Hynes/Copley.*

Beacon Hill

\$\$\$\$ 🏨 **Fifteen Beacon.** At this stylish boutique hotel, inside a 1903 beaux arts
Fodor'sChoice building, old and new tastes are carefully juxtaposed—for instance, the
★ lobby has cage elevators and a newel post, while an abstract painting dominates the sitting area. Guests are made to feel like honored members of a plush private club. The rooms come with many small luxuries, from fresh flowers to 300-thread-count sheets. All are done in soothing taupe, cream, and espresso shades, and each has a four-poster queen-size bed, a gas fireplace, and surround-sound stereo. Studio rooms and suites have whirlpool tubs; all guest rooms have huge mirrors and heated towel bars. A nearby health club is available to hotel guests. ⊠ *15 Beacon St., 02108* ☎ *617/670–1500 or 877/982–3226* ⊜ *617/670–2525* ⊕ *www. xvbeacon.com* ⋟ *58 rooms, 2 suites* ⋞ *Restaurant, room service, in-room fax, in-room safes, minibars, cable TV with movies, in-room CD players, in-room broadband, gym, massage, bar, dry cleaning, laundry services, concierge, Internet, business services, parking (fee), some pets allowed (fee)* ⊟ *AE, D, DC, MC, V* Ⓜ *Government Center or Park St.*

★ \$\$\$ 🏨 **Beacon Hill Hotel & Bistro.** Two 19th-century town houses have been meticulously renovated to house this intimate boutique hotel on Beacon Hill. You can't beat the location on Charles Street, one of the city's premier addresses, within walking distance to the Public Garden, Back Bay, and the Government Center. Minimalist-style rooms are individually decorated with soft neutral colors and plush bed linens. Rooms have plenty of natural light filtering through the large windows overlooking city streets. There's a rooftop deck for lounging and a popular streetside bistro open for breakfast, lunch, and dinner. ⊠ *25 Charles St., 02114* ☎ *617/723–7575 or 888/959–2442* 📠 *617/723–7525* ⊕ *www. beaconhillhotel.com* 🛏 *12 rooms, 1 suite* ⚹ *Restaurant, cable TV with movies, in-room data ports, dry cleaning, laundry service* ▭ *AE, D, DC, MC, V* ¹⊚¹ *BP* Ⓜ *Arlington.*

$–$$
Fodor's Choice
★

▦ **John Jeffries House.** Once a housing facility for nurses, this turn-of-the-20th-century building across from Massachusetts General Hospital is now an elegant four-story inn. It's also one of the best values in town. The Federal-style double parlor has a cluster of floral-pattern chairs and sofas where you can relax with afternoon tea or coffee. Guest rooms are furnished with handsome upholstered pieces, and nearly all have kitchenettes. Triple-glazed windows block virtually all noise from busy Charles Circle; many rooms have views of the Charles River. Another plus: the inn is adjacent to Charles Street, home to lovely cafés, specialty boutiques, and antiques shops. ⊠ *14 David G. Mugar Way, 02114* ☎*617/ 367–1866* 📠 *617/742–0313* ⊕ *www.johnjeffrieshouse.com* 🛏 *23 rooms, 23 suites* ⚹ *Kitchenettes, in-room data ports, Wi-Fi, parking (fee)* ▭ *AE, D, DC, MC, V* ¹⊚¹ *CP* Ⓜ *Charles/MGH.*

Cambridge

$$$–$$$$
Fodor's Choice
★

▦ **Charles Hotel.** Gracious service and a great location on Harvard Square keep this first-class hotel in high demand. The New England Shaker interior is contemporary yet homey; antique quilts done by local artists hang throughout. Guest rooms come with terry robes, quilted down comforters, and Bose radios. If you're looking for a river or skyline view, ask for something above the seventh floor. Rooms facing the courtyard look down on an herb garden. Both of the hotel's restaurants—Rialto and Henrietta's Table—are excellent. ⊠ *1 Bennett St., 02138* ☎ *617/ 864–1200 or 800/882–1818* 📠*617/864–5715* ⊕*www.charleshotel.com* 🛏 *249 rooms, 45 suites* ⚹ *2 restaurants, room service, in-room safes, minibars, cable TV with movies, Wi-Fi, in-room data ports, indoor pool, health club, spa, 4 bars, library, nightclub, babysitting, dry cleaning, laundry service, concierge, business services, meeting rooms, parking (fee), some pets allowed, no-smoking floors* ▭ *AE, DC, MC, V* Ⓜ *Harvard.*

★ **$$$–$$$$**

▦ **Royal Sonesta Hotel.** An impressive collection of modern art, spread throughout the hotel, makes this otherwise cookie-cutter property a bit of a surprise. Its East Cambridge location, next to the Museum of Science and Galleria shopping center, and an attractive indoor/outdoor pool add to its appeal. Some rooms have superb views of Beacon Hill and the Boston skyline across the Charles River. Guest rooms are done in neutral earth tones, with modern amenities like Sony Playstation consoles, high-speed Internet, and CD clock radios. The hotel has great family excursion packages. ⊠ *5 Cambridge Pkwy., off Memorial Dr., 02142* ☎ *617/806–4200 or 888/782–9772* 📠 *617/806–4232* ⊕ *www.*

4

royalsonestaboston.com ⬧ *379 rooms, 21 suites* ⬧ *2 restaurants, room service, in-room safes, minibars, cable TV with movies and video games, Wi-Fi, pool, health club, spa, bicycles, 2 bars, dry cleaning, business services, parking (fee)* ▭ *AE, D, DC, MC, V* Ⓜ *Lechmere.*

$$–$$$ 🏨 **A Cambridge House Bed & Breakfast.** A gracious 1892 Greek-revival
Fodor'sChoice home listed on the National Register of Historic Places, A Cambridge
★ House has richly carved cherry paneling, a grand fireplace, elegant Victorian antiques, and polished wood floors overlaid with Oriental rugs. One of the antiques-filled guest rooms has fabric-covered walls, and many have four-poster canopy beds. Rooms in the adjacent carriage house are smaller, but all have fireplaces. Harvard Square is fairly distant, but public transportation is nearby. ⬧ *2218 Massachusetts Ave., 02140* ☎ *617/ 491–6300 or 800/232–9989* 📠 *617/868–2848* ⬧ *www.acambridgehouse. com* ⬧ *15 rooms* ⬧ *Free parking* ▭ *AE, MC, V* ⧣ *CP* Ⓜ *Davis.*

$$–$$$ 🏨 **Harvard Square Hotel.** Casual and family friendly, this hotel is an affordable option in the heart of Harvard Square, just steps from the neighborhood's many restaurants, shops, and lively street corners. Rooms are simple but clean and nicely decorated. The desk clerks are particularly helpful, assisting with everything from sending faxes to securing dinner reservations. There's a computer with Internet access in the lobby. ⬧ *110 Mt. Auburn St., 02138* ☎ *617/864–5200 or 800/458–5886* 📠 *617/864–2409* ⬧ *www.harvardsquarehotel.com* ⬧ *73 rooms* ⬧ *Refrigerators, cable TV, in-room data ports, Wi-Fi, laundry service, concierge, business services, car rental, parking (fee)* ▭ *AE, D, DC, MC, V* Ⓜ *Harvard.*

Downtown

$$$$ 🏨 **Boston Harbor Hotel at Rowes Wharf.** Red Sox owner John Henry
Fodor'sChoice parks his yacht here in summertime. The rest of us can arrive by boat
★ in a less grand fashion—the water shuttle runs from Logan Airport to the back door of this deluxe harborside hotel. Its dramatic entryway is an 80-foot archway topped by a rotunda, so eye-catching that it qualifies as a local landmark. The lobby, too, is stunningly elegant, with marble arches, antique maps, and a huge tumble of fresh flowers. Guest rooms have marble bathrooms, custom-made desks, 300-thread-count sheets, and down comforters. Many have views of the harbor. Meritage restaurant, under light fixtures that mimic a starry sky, has a unique, wine-inspired menu that pairs small plates with appropriate vintages. Want to work out in the hotel's health club, but forgot your exercise duds? Not to worry—they provide them for their guests. Now if only they would exercise for you. ⬧ *70 Rowes Wharf, 02110* ☎ *617/439–7000 or 800/ 752–7077* 📠 *617/330–9450* ⬧ *www.bhh.com* ⬧ *204 rooms, 26 suites* ⬧ *2 restaurants, café, room service, minibars, cable TV with movies, Wi-Fi, indoor pool, health club, hot tub, massage, sauna, spa, steam room, bar, shop, dry cleaning, laundry service, concierge, business services, meeting rooms, airport shuttle, parking (fee), some pets allowed (fee), no-smoking floors* ▭ *AE, D, DC, MC, V* Ⓜ *Aquarium or South Station.*

$$$–$$$$ 🏨 **Nine Zero.** When stepping into the sleek, chic stylings of Nine Zero
Fodor'sChoice you enter a startlingly cosmopolitan haven within the old-world charm
★ of downtown Boston. This hotel is the ultimate in style. Bold striped patterns and shimmering metallic curtains accent the common spaces,

and dramatic headboards bring a focal point to guest rooms. The Colonial wing chairs hearken to an older era, but their red hue and asymmetrical alignment bring you vividly to the present where luxuries abound. Enjoy a night on the town without leaving your hotel at the funky Spire restaurant and bar. ⊠ *90 Tremont St., 02108* ☎ *617/772–5800 or 866/646–3937* 🖷 *617/772–5810* ⊕ *www.ninezero.com* 🛏 *185 rooms, 5 suites* ⚘ *Restaurant, room service, in-room safes, minibars, cable TV with movies and video games, Wi-Fi, gym, massage, bar, dry cleaning, laundry service, concierge, business services, meeting rooms, parking (fee), some pets allowed* ⊟ *AE, D, DC, MC, V* Ⓜ *Park St., Government Center.*

★ **$$$–$$$$** 🏨 **Omni Parker House.** The oldest continuously operating hotel in the United States, the Parker House's original building opened in 1855 and counted Charles Dickens among its guests (his first reading of *A Christmas Carol* was in the Parker). A Colonial style adorns the lobby and guest rooms, which have custom-built furniture to accommodate the rooms' small sizes. Parker's Restaurant is known for two things: Parker House rolls and Boston cream pie, both of which were invented here and are still served. This historic hotel stands opposite old City Hall, on the Freedom Trail. ⊠ *60 School St., 02108* ☎ *617/227–8600 or 800/843–6664* 🖷 *617/742–5729* ⊕ *www.omniparkerhouse.com* 🛏 *551 rooms, 21 suites* ⚘ *2 restaurants, room service, cable TV with movies and video games, Wi-Fi, gym, 2 bars, shop, dry cleaning, laundry service, concierge, business services, meeting rooms, parking (fee), some pets allowed (fee)* ⊟ *AE, D, DC, MC, V* Ⓜ *Government Center, Park St.*

★ **$$** 🏨 **Harborside Inn.** One of the best values in town: the one-time 19th-century mercantile warehouse is now a plush, sedate inn with exposed brick and granite walls, hardwood floors, Turkish rugs, and Federal-style furnishings. Walk to popular Faneuil Hall, Quincy Market and the North End then return to the quiet and calm of this historic inn. Many of the snug, variously shaped rooms (no two are alike) have windows overlooking the small, open lobby, which extends eight stories up to the roof. If an outdoor view is important to you, request a room overlooking the city. ⊠ *185 State St., 02109* ☎ *617/723–7500 or 888/723–7565* 🖷 *617/670–6015* ⊕ *www.harborsideinnboston.com* 🛏 *52 rooms, 2 suites* ⚘ *Restaurant, café, in-room data ports, cable TV with movies, Wi-Fi, bar, dry cleaning, laundry service, concierge, Internet, parking (fee); no smoking* ⊟ *AE, D, DC, MC, V* Ⓜ *Aquarium.*

Kenmore Square

★ **$$$–$$$$** 🏨 **Hotel Commonwealth.** The Hotel Commonwealth is anything but common, blending old-world charm with modern conveniences for a sophisticated, boutiquey feel. Rich color schemes enhance the elegant rooms, and king- or queen-size beds are piled with down pillows and Italian linens. Choose rooms with views of bustling Commonwealth Avenue or Fenway Park. All rooms have marble baths and floor-to-ceiling windows. The award-winning seafood restaurant, Great Bay, makes you feel like you're sitting by the ocean, with diffused lighting and a sandy color scheme in a vast, shiplike room. ⊠ *500 Commonwealth Ave., 02215* ☎ *617/933–5000 or 866/784–4000* ⊕ *www.hotelcommonwealth.com*

⤴ *149 rooms, 1 suite* ⚄ *Restaurant, room service, in-room safes, mini-bars, cable TV with movies, in-room DVD players, Wi-Fi, gym, lounge, shops, dry cleaning, laundry service, concierge, Internet, business services, meeting rooms, parking (fee), no-smoking floors* ▭ *AE, D, DC, MC, V* Ⓜ *Kenmore.*

$–$$$ ⊡ **Gryphon House.** Many of the suites in this four-story, 19th-century

FodorsChoice brownstone are thematically decorated; one evokes rustic Italy, another

★ is inspired by neo-Gothic art. Among the many amenities—including gas fireplaces, wet bars, VCRs, CD players, and private voice mail—the enormous bathrooms with oversize tubs and separate showers are the most appealing. Even the staircase is extraordinary: a 19th-century wallpaper mural, *El Dorado*, wraps along the walls. (There is no elevator.) Trompe-l'oeil paintings and murals by local artist Michael Ernest Kirk decorate the common spaces and some rooms. Another nice touch: free passes to the Museum of Fine Arts and Isabella Stewart Gardner Museum. ✉ *9 Bay State Rd., 02215* ☏ *617/375–9003 or 877/375–9003* 🖷 *617/425–0716* ⊕ *www.gryphonhouseboston.com* ⤴ *8 suites* ⚄ *Refrigerators, minibars, in-room VCRs, Wi-Fi, Internet, free parking, no smoking* ▭ *AE, D, MC, V* ⋈ *CP* Ⓜ *Kenmore.*

Logan Airport

$–$$$ ⊡ **Hilton Boston Logan Airport.** They know they've got a captive audience, so maybe that's why they've got a bit of an attitude at this soaring Hilton hotel. The desk clerk was actually smug when she said, "You can stay for $119—unless a flight is cancelled, and we jack up the rates to $299!" OK, she didn't say "jack up," but you get the idea. If you can get past the indifferent-bordering-on-rude service, you'll do fine here. At least the location is good if you're looking for proximity to Logan Airport—there's a skywalk to terminals A and E. Rooms have granite countertops in the baths and desks with ergonomic chairs. There's an unremarkable restaurant and an Irish pub on the premises, along with a gym where a security guard presides. Give it a shot, just don't look too desperate when you check in! ✉ *One Hotel Dr., Logan Airport/East Boston, 02128* ☏ *617/568–6700* 🖷 *617/568–6800* ⊕ *www.hilton. com* ⤴ *595 rooms, 4 suites* ⚄ *Restaurant, coffee shop, room service, minibars, in-room data ports, cable TV with movies, Wi-Fi, indoor pool, health club, massage, sauna, spa, steam room, pub, concierge floor, business services, meeting room, parking (fee)* ▭ *AE, D, DC, MC, V* Ⓜ *Airport.*

Nightlife & the Arts

Nightlife

Good sources of nighttime happenings are the *Boston Globe* Thursday "Calendar" section, the *Boston Herald* Friday "Scene" section, and the listings in the *Boston Phoenix*, a free weekly that comes out on Thursday. The Friday "Music" and Sunday "Arts" sections in the *Boston Globe* and the Saturday and Sunday "Arts" sections in the *Boston Herald* also preview the week's top events. *Boston* magazine's "On the Town" gives a somewhat less detailed but still useful monthly overview. Call clubs to check cover charges, hours, and theme nights.

BARS & LOUNGES **Black Rose** (⊠ 160 State St., Faneuil Hall ☎ 617/742–2286 Ⓜ Government Center, Haymarket, State St.) is decorated with family crests, pictures of Ireland, and portraits of the likes of Samuel Beckett, Lady Gregory, and James Joyce—just like a Dublin pub. Music by contemporary and traditional Irish musicians makes it worth the crowds. **Boston Beer Works** (⊠ 61 Brookline Ave., Fens ☎ 617/536–2337 Ⓜ Kenmore, Fenway) is a "naked brewery," with all the works exposed—the tanks, pipes, and gleaming stainless-steel and copper kettles used in producing beer. ★ **Doyle's Café** (⊠ 3484 Washington St., Jamaica Plain ☎ 617/524–2345 Ⓜ Green St., Forest Hills) is a friendly, crowded neighborhood Irish pub that opened in 1882 and has been a Boston political landmark ever since. Despite its name, ★ **Saint** (⊠ 90 Exeter St., Back Bay ☎ 617/236–1134 Ⓜ Copley) draws patrons who are anything but. The spacious underground lounge consists of two rooms: an airy main space is decorated in blue and silver, with long couches to lounge on over appetizers while making eyes across the room. A more devilish "bordello room" is all plush red velvet and tasseled light fixtures. **Sonsie** (⊠ 327 Newbury St., Back Bay ☎ 617/351–2500 Ⓜ Hynes Convention Center/ICA), a European-style see-and-be-seen bistro, keeps the stereo volume at a manageable level. The bar crowd is full of trendy, cosmopolitan types and professionals; in warm weather, the crowd spills out to sidewalk tables. **Top of the Hub** (⊠ Prudential Center, 800 Boylston St., Back Bay ☎ 617/536–1775) has live jazz and fabulous views, making the steep drink prices worthwhile.

BLUES, FOLK, R& B CLUBS **Club Passim** (⊠ 47 Palmer St., Harvard Sq., Cambridge ☎ 617/492–5300 Ⓜ Harvard) ★ has seen Joan Baez, Bob Dylan, Suzanne Vega, and many other folkies on their way up. It's one of the country's first and most famous venues for live folk music. In the basement room, where the tables are close together, there's wait service and a counter where you can buy prepared food. **Johnny D's Uptown** (⊠ 17 Holland St., Davis Sq. Somerville ☎ 617/776–2004 Ⓜ Davis) books an eclectic mix of performers and musical styles: Cajun, country, Latin, blues, jazz, swing, acoustic, and more.

COMEDY **Comedy Connection,** which has been called the best comedy club in the country, has a mix of local and nationally known acts seven nights a week, with two shows Friday and Saturday (⊠ Faneuil Hall Marketplace, 245 Quincy Market, Faneuil Hall ☎ 617/248–9700 Ⓜ Government Center, Haymarket, State). ★ **ImprovBoston** (⊠ 1253 Cambridge St., Cambridge ☎ 617/576–1253 Ⓜ Central Sq., Kendall/MIT) turns audience suggestions into a situation comedy, complete with theme song and commercials. Be careful when you go to the restroom; you might be pulled onstage. **Nick's Comedy Stop** (⊠ 100 Warrenton St., Theater District ☎ 617/423–2900 Ⓜ Boylston) presents local comics Thursday–Saturday nights. Reservations are essential.

DANCE CLUBS **Avalon** (⊠ 15 Lansdowne St., Fens ☎ 617/262–2424 Ⓜ Kenmore) is Boston's premier nightclub—a 2,000-capacity pleasure palace renowned for its state-of-the-art sound-and-light systems. Top-name DJs spin on Friday and Saturday nights. On Sunday, Avalon sponsors a gay night. **Axis** (⊠ 13 Lansdowne St., Fens ☎ 617/262–2437 Ⓜ Kenmore) has high-energy dancing for more than 1,000 people. Theme nights include a Friday-night hip-hop session, and a Monday gay blockbuster. The **Roxy** (✉ 279 Tremont St., Theater District ☎ 617/338–7699 Ⓜ Boylston), one of Boston's biggest nightclubs, is renowned for theme events such as its reggae, salsa, swing, and Top 40 nights.

GAY & LESBIAN CLUBS For more on gay and lesbian nightlife, see the *Boston Phoenix* or *Bay Windows* newspaper.

Avalon (✉ 15 Lansdowne St., Fens ☎ 617/262–2424 Ⓜ Kenmore) sponsors a gay night on Sunday. The **Axis** (✉ 13 Lansdowne St., Fens ☎ 617/262–2437 Ⓜ Kenmore) hosts a Monday gay blockbuster. **Club Café & Lounge** (✉ 209 Columbus Ave., South End ☎ 617/536–0966 Ⓜ Back Bay/South End) is among the smartest spots in town for gay men and lesbians. It has a stylish restaurant, a piano bar, and a video bar.

JAZZ **Regattabar** (✉ Charles Hotel, 1 Bennett St., Harvard Sq., Cambridge ☎ 617/661–5000 or 617/876–7777 Ⓜ Harvard) attracts some of the top names in jazz. Reservations are essential. **Ryles Jazz Club** (✉ 212 Hampshire St., Inman Sq., Cambridge ☎ 617/876–9330) is one of the best places for both new and established performers, with a different group playing on each floor. Sunday jazz brunches are a local institution.

Fodor'sChoice ★ **Wally's Café** (✉ 427 Massachusetts Ave., South End ☎ 617/424–1408 Ⓜ Massachusetts Ave.) is a rare gem for blues and jazz fans. Founded in 1947, it continues to host big names like Branford Marsalis and Chick Corea, but is still best known for performances by local bands. It's open every night of the year and there is no cover.

ROCK CLUBS **Lizard Lounge** (✉ 1667 Massachusetts Ave., between Harvard and Porter squares, Cambridge ☎ 617/547–0759) is a low-key nightspot that often features more experimental and cult local bands. **Paradise Rock Club** (✉ 967-969 Commonwealth Ave., near Boston University, Allston ☎ 617/562–8800 or 617/562–8814) is a small place known for hosting big-name talent like Phish and the Indigo Girls. Two tiers of booths provide good sight lines anywhere in the club.

The Arts

DANCE **Boston Ballet** (✉ 19 Clarendon St., South End ☎ 617/695–6950 ⊕ www.bostonballet.org), the city's premier dance company, performs classical and modern works, primarily at the Wang Center for the Performing Arts, from October through May. Its annual *Nutcracker* is a Boston holiday tradition. **José Mateo's Ballet Theatre** (✉ 400 Harvard St., Cambridge ☎ 617/354–7467 ⊕ www.ballettheatre.org) is a young troupe building an exciting, contemporary repertory under Cuban-born José Mateo, the resident artistic director–choreographer. The troupe's performances include an original *Nutcracker,* and take place October through May at the Sanctuary Theatre, a beautifully converted former church at Massachusetts Avenue and Harvard Street in Harvard Square.

FILM The **Brattle Theatre** (✉ 40 Brattle St., Harvard Sq., Cambridge ☎ 617/876–6837 ⊕ www.brattlefilm.org Ⓜ Harvard) is a small downstairs cinema catering to classic-movie buffs and fans of new foreign and independent films. **Harvard Film Archive** (✉ Carpenter Center for the Visual Arts, 24 Quincy St., Cambridge ☎ 617/495–4700 ⊕ www.harvardfilmarchive.org

Ⓜ Harvard) screens the works of directors not usually shown at commercial cinemas.

MUSIC **Berklee Performance Center** (✉ 136 Massachusetts Ave., Back Bay ☎ 617/ 747–2261 ⊕ www.berkleebpc.com Ⓜ Hynes Convention Center/ICA) is best known for its jazz programs, but it also hosts folk performers such ★ as Arlo Guthrie and pop and rock stars such as Bryan Ferry. **Hatch Memorial Shell** (✉ Off Storrow Dr., Beacon Hill ☎ 617/626–1470 ⊕ www.mass. gov/dcr/events.htm Ⓜ Charles, Arlington), on the Charles River, is a wonderful acoustic shell where the Boston Pops perform their famous free summer concerts (including their traditional July 4 show, broadcast live ★ nationwide on TV). Jordan Hall at the **New England Conservatory** (✉ 30 Gainsborough St., Back Bay ☎ 617/585–1260 Ⓜ Symphony ⊕ www. newenglandconservatory.edu/concerts) is one of the world's acoustic treasures, ideal for chamber music, yet large enough to accommodate a full orchestra; the Boston Philharmonic often performs at the relatively intimate 1,000-seat hall. **Symphony Hall** (✉ 301 Massachusetts Ave., Back Bay ☎ 617/266–1492 ⊕ www.bostonsymphonyhall.org Ⓜ Symphony), one of the world's most perfect acoustical settings, is home to the Boston Symphony Orchestra, conducted by James Levine, and the Boston Pops, conducted by Keith Lockhart.

OPERA **Boston Lyric Opera Company** (✉ Shubert Theatre, 265 Tremont St., Theater District ☎ 617/542–6772) stages four full productions each season, which usually includes one 20th-century work.

THEATER **American Repertory Theatre** (✉ 64 Brattle St., Harvard Sq., Cambridge ★ ☎ 617/547–8300 ⊕ www.amrep.org Ⓜ Harvard) is a highly respected professional company that stages experimental, classic, and contemporary plays. Its home at the Loeb Drama Center has two theaters. The ★ **Boston Center for the Arts** (✉ 539 Tremont St., South End ☎ 617/426– 5000 ⊕ www.bcaonline.org Ⓜ Back Bay) houses more than a dozen quirky low-budget troupes in six performances spaces. **Harvard's Hasty Pudding Theatricals** at Harvard University calls itself the "oldest collegiate theatrical company in the United States." It produces one show annually, in February and March, and then goes on tour. The troupe also honors a famous actor and actress each year with an awards ceremony and a parade (in drag!) through Cambridge (✉ Hasty Pudding Theatre, 12 Holyoke St., Cambridge ☎ 617/495–5205 ⊕ www. hastypudding.org Ⓜ Harvard). The **Huntington Theatre Company** (✉ Boston University Theatre, 264 Huntington Ave., Back Bay ☎ 617/266–0800 ⊕ www.huntingtontheatre.org Ⓜ Symphony) performs a mix of established 20th-century plays and classics.

Sports & the Outdoors

FodorsChoice The islands making up **Boston Harbor Islands National Recreation Area** have ★ some of the most pleasant hiking and swimming near the city. Miles of hiking trails and uncrowded shoreline more than make up for unmanicured beaches and basic campsites (with neither electricity nor water). Lovell's, Peddock's, Grape, and Bumpkin islands allow camping with a permit from July through Labor Day. The park allows swimming at Lovell's, Grape, and Great Brewster islands, but posts lifeguards only at Lovell's. Pets and alcohol are not allowed on the Harbor Islands. To reach the islands, take the **Harbor Express** (☎ 617/222–6999 ⊕ www. harborexpress.com) ferry to George's Island from May through Labor Day. Shuttles run four times a day, at 10 AM, noon, 4 PM, and 6 PM, and cost $10 per adult, $6 per child. Beginning in late June, free shuttles travel from George's to the other islands.

Melting icicles in spring are signs for Bostonians to emerge from hibernation and get their bodies moving. Whenever a stray sunbeam escapes the cloud cover, runners, bikers, and in-line skaters throng to the **Charles River Reservation,** whether to the Esplanade along Storrow Drive, the Memorial Drive Embankment across the river in Cambridge, or any of the smaller and less-trafficked parks farther upriver. All through the city, both sides of the Charles are lined with bike paths and playgrounds, shady hollows and sunny slopes.

Fodor'sChoice

★ The six large public parks known as Boston's **Emerald Necklace** stretch 5 mi from the Back Bay Fens through Franklin Park, in Dorchester. Fredrick Law Olmsted's linear park design remains a well-groomed urban masterpiece. Locals take pride in and happily make use of its open spaces and its pathways and bridges connecting rivers and ponds.

Participant Sports

BIKING The **Dr. Paul Dudley White Bikeway,** about 14 mi long, follows both banks of the Charles River as it winds from Watertown Square to the
★ Museum of Science. The tranquil **Minuteman Bicycle Trail** courses 11 mi from the Alewife Red Line station in Cambridge through Arlington, Lexington, and Bedford. The trail, in the bed of an old rail line, cuts through a few busy intersections—be particularly careful in Arlington Center.

The **Pierre Lallement Bike Path** winds 5 mi through the South End and Roxbury, from Copley Place to Franklin Park.

Community Bicycle Supply (⊠ 496 Tremont St., at E. Berkeley St., South End ☎ 617/542–8623) rents cycles from April through September, at rates of $20 for 24 hours or $5 per hour, for a minimum of 2 hours.

BOATING **Community Boating** (⊠ 21 David Mugar Way, Beacon Hill ☎ 617/523–
★ 1038 ⊕ www.community-boating.org), near the Charles Street footbridge on the Esplanade, hosts America's oldest public sailing program. From April through October, an $80 registration fee nets you a 30-day introductory membership, including beginner-level classes and the use of sailboats and kayaks. Full memberships grant unlimited use of all facilities; splash around for 60 days for $135, or all season long for $190. Experienced sailors can rent a boat for $100 for two days, for use on the lower Charles.

IN-LINE SKATING Every Sunday from April through October, Memorial Drive on the Cambridge side of the Charles River is transformed into **Riverbend Park.** The area between the Western Avenue Bridge and Eliot Bridge is closed to auto traffic from 11 AM to 7 PM. Downstream, on the Boston side of the river, the **Esplanade** area swarms with skaters (and joggers) on weekends.

Beacon Hill Skate Shop (⊠ 135 S. Charles St., off Tremont St., near Wang Center for Performing Arts, South End ☎ 617/482–7400) rents blades (figure and hockey skates in winter) and safety equipment for $10 per hour or $25 for 24 hours. You'll need a credit card for a deposit.

Spectator Sports

The **Boston Bruins** (✉ 1 FleetCenter, Old West End ☎ 617/624–1000, 617/931–2222 Ticketmaster) of the National Hockey League hit the ice at the FleetCenter from October until April. The **Boston Celtics** (✉ Fleet-Center, Old West End ☎ 617/624–1000, 617/931–2222 Ticketmaster) of the National Basketball Association shoot their hoops at the Fleet-Center from October to May. The **Boston Red Sox** (✉ Fenway Park, Fens ☎ 617/267–1700 for tickets) play American League baseball at Fenway Park from April to early October. The **New England Patriots** (✉ Gillette Stadium, Rte. 1 off I–95 Exit 9, near Boston University, Foxboro, 30 mi southwest of Boston ☎ 800/543–1776 ⊕ www.patriots.com) of the National Football League play in Foxboro, 45 minutes south of the city, from August through the playoffs in January.

Fodor'sChoice
★

Every Patriots' Day (the third Monday in April), fans gather along the Hopkinton–to–Boston route of the **Boston Marathon** to cheer on more than 20,000 runners from all over the world. The race ends near Copley Square in the Back Bay.

Shopping

Boston's shops are generally open Monday through Saturday from 10 or 11 until 6 or 7 and Sunday noon to 5. Many stay open until 8 PM one night a week, usually Thursday. Malls are open Monday through Saturday from 9 or 10 until 8 or 9 and Sunday noon to 6. Most stores accept major credit cards and traveler's checks. There's no state sales tax on clothing. However, there's a 5% luxury tax on clothes priced higher than $175 per item; the tax is levied on the amount in excess of $175.

Shopping Districts

Boston's best shopping is around Quincy Market, the Back Bay, and Downtown. There are few outlet stores in the center city, but plenty of bargains nevertheless, particularly in the Downtown Crossing area. The South End's gentrification creates its own kind of consumerist milieus, from housewares shops to avant-garde art galleries. In Cambridge you can find lots of shopping around Harvard and Central squares, with independent boutiques migrating west along Massachusetts Avenue toward Porter Square and beyond.

BOSTON **Copley Place** (✉ 100 Huntington Ave., Back Bay ☎ 617/369–5000 Ⓜ Copley), an indoor shopping mall in the Back Bay, includes such high-end shops as Christian Dior, Louis Vuitton, and Gucci. A skywalk connects Copley Place to the **Prudential Center** (✉ 800 Boylston St., Back Bay ☎ 800/746–7778 Ⓜ Copley, Prudential Center). The Pru, as it's often called, contains moderately priced chain stores such as Ann Taylor and the Body Shop.

Downtown Crossing (✉ Washington St. from Amory St. to about Milk St., Downtown Ⓜ Downtown Crossing, Park St.) is a pedestrian mall with a Macy's, the famous Filene's Basement, and a handful of decent outlets. **Faneuil Hall Marketplace** (✉ Bounded by Congress St., Atlantic

Ave., the Waterfront, and Government Center, Downtown ☎ 617/523–1300 Ⓜ Government Center) is a huge complex that's also hugely popular, even though most of its independent shops have given way to Banana Republic, the Disney Store, and other chains. The place has plenty of history, and one of the area's great à la carte casual dining experiences, Quincy Market.

★ **Newbury Street** (Ⓜ Arlington, Copley, Hynes Convention Center/ICA) is Boston's version of New York's 5th Avenue. The entire street is a shoppers' paradise, from high-end names like Brooks Brothers to tiny specialty boutiques such as Dyptique. Parallel to Newbury Street is **Boylston Street,** where a few standouts, such as Shreve, Crump & Low, are tucked among the other chains and restaurants.

South End (Ⓜ Back Bay/South End) merchants are benefiting from the ongoing gentrification that has brought high-real-estate prices and trendy restaurants to the area. Revisit your childhood by picking up some Pixie Stix and jawbreakers at Olde Dutch Candy and Antiques before heading off to explore the chic home-furnishings and gift shops.

CAMBRIDGE **CambridgeSide Galleria** (✉ 100 CambridgeSide Pl. ☎ 617/621–8666 Ⓜ Lechmere, Kendall/MIT via shuttle) is a basic three-story mall with a food court. Traveling west along Massachusetts Avenue toward Harvard Square, you will pass through eclectic **Central Square,** which holds a mix of furniture stores, used-record shops, ethnic restaurants, and small, hip performance venues. **Harvard Square** comprises just a few blocks but contains more than 150 stores selling clothes, books and records, furnishings, and a range of specialty items. **Porter Square,** on Massachusetts Ave., has several distinctive clothing and home-furnishings stores, crafts shops, natural-food markets, and restaurants.

Department Stores
★ **Filene's Basement** (✉ 426 Washington St., Downtown ☎ 617/542–2011 Ⓜ Downtown Crossing) is a Boston institution. Though habitués bemoan a decline in quality over the past few years, the Basement is still the place for deals on designer labels—if you're willing to dig. Automatic markdowns are taken according to the number of days an item has been on the rack, so don't be surprised to find that perfect little black dress hidden for safekeeping among the men's sport jackets (✉ 426 Washington St., Downtown ☎ 617/542–2011 Ⓜ Downtown Crossing). **Lord & Taylor** (✉ 760 Boylston St., Back Bay ☎ 617/262–6000 Ⓜ Prudential Center) is a reliable stop for classic clothing. **Macy's** (✉ 450 Washington St., Downtown ☎ 617/357–3000 Ⓜ Downtown Crossing) carries men's and women's clothing, including top designers, as well as housewares, furniture, and cosmetics. It has direct access to the Downtown Crossing T station. **Neiman Marcus** (✉ 5 Copley Pl., Back Bay ☎ 617/536–3660 Ⓜ Back Bay/South End), the flashy Texas retailer, has three levels of high fashion, cosmetics, and housewares. **Saks Fifth Avenue** (✉ Prudential Center, 1 Ring Rd., Back Bay ☎ 617/262–8500 Ⓜ Prudential Center) stocks top-of-the-line clothing, from more traditional styles to avant-garde apparel, plus accessories and cosmetics.

Specialty Stores

ANTIQUES Though Newbury Street and the South End have several worthwhile shops, Charles Street has a clutch of stores where you can find everything from 18th-century paintings and early etchings of Boston landmarks to Chinese vases and complete sets of dinnerware. Don't miss the **Boston Antique Co-op** (⊠ 119 Charles St., Beacon Hill ☎ 617/227–9810 or 617/227–9811 Ⓜ Charles/MGH), a two-story, flea market–style collection of dealers that carries everything from vintage photos and paintings to porcelain, silver, bronzes, and furniture. **Cambridge Antique Market** (⊠ 201 Monsignor O'Brien Hwy., Cambridge ☎ 617/868–9655 Ⓜ Lechmere) is a bit off the beaten track but has a selection bordering on overwhelming, with four floors of dealers.

BOOKS If Boston and Cambridge have bragging rights to anything, it is their independent bookstores, many of which stay open late and sponsor author readings and literary programs. Don't come to **Barefoot Books** (⊠ 1771 Massachusetts Ave., Cambridge ☎ 617/349–1610 Ⓜ Porter) looking for the same old children's books. The store is full of beautifully illustrated, creatively told reading for all ages. These are the kind of books that kids remember and keep as adults. If the book you want is out of print, **Brattle Bookstore** (⊠ 9 West St., Downtown ☎ 617/542–0210 or 800/447–9595 Ⓜ Downtown Crossing) has it or can probably find it.

FodorsChoice ★

The literary and academic community is well served at the **Harvard Bookstore** (⊠ 1256 Massachusetts Ave., Cambridge ☎ 617/661–1515 Ⓜ Harvard). **Trident Bookseller and Café** (⊠ 338 Newbury St., Back Bay ☎ 617/267–8688 Ⓜ Hynes Convention Center/ICA) carries books, tapes, and magazines and stays open until midnight daily.

CLOTHING The terminally chic shop on Newbury Street, the hip hang in Harvard Square, and everyone goes downtown for the real bargains.

★ The Euro-dominated **Alan Bilzerian** (⊠ 34 Newbury St., Back Bay ☎ 617/536–1001 Ⓜ Arlington) sells avant-garde men's and women's fashions. **April Cornell** (⊠ Faneuil Hall Marketplace, North Market Bldg., Government Center ☎ 617/248–0280 Ⓜ Government Center ⊠ 43 Brattle St., Cambridge ☎ 617/661–8910 Ⓜ Harvard) carries frilly bohemian women's clothing, furniture, linens, and toiletries at 50% off original prices. **Betsy Jenney** (⊠ 114 Newbury St., Back Bay ☎ 617/536–2610 Ⓜ Copley) sells well-made, comfortable women's lines at moderate prices. Young trendsetters will be happiest at **Calypso** (⊠ 115 Newbury St., Back Bay ☎ 617/421–1887 Ⓜ Copley).

★ **Daniela Corte** (⊠ 91 Newbury St., Back Bay ☎ 617/262–2100 Ⓜ Copley) designs women's clothes that flatter at her sunny Back Bay studio. Look for gorgeous suiting, flirty halter dresses, and sophisticated formal frocks. **Wish** (⊠ 49 Charles St., Beacon Hill ☎ 617/227–4441 Ⓜ Charles/MGH) carries everything a hip young woman could wish for, from such designers as Katayone Adeli and Nanette Lepore.

You can travel back in time or to another country at many Boston gift shops. **Buckaroo's Mercantile** (✉ 1297 Cambridge St., Cambridge ☎ 617/ 492–4792 Ⓜ Central Sq.) rocks with retro kitsch, from pink poodle skirts to Barbie lamp shades—along with everything Elvis. **Flat of the Hill** (✉ 60 Charles St., Beacon Hill ☎ 617/619–9977 Ⓜ Charles/MGH) has something for everyone on your list—including Fido—with seasonal items, gourmet foods, hard-to-find toiletries, dolls, toys, pillows, and ★ pet products. At **Fresh** (✉ 121 Newbury St., Back Bay ☎ 617/482–9411 Ⓜ Copley), you won't know whether to wash with the soaps or nibble on them. The shea butter–rich bars come in such scents as clove-hazelnut and orange-cranberry. **Mayan Weavers** (✉ 268 Newbury St., Back Bay ☎ 617/262–4342 Ⓜ Copley) stocks reasonably priced boldly colored woven textiles, hand-carved furniture, and hand-painted tchotchkes.

Mohr & McPherson (✉ 281–290 Concord Ave., Cambridge ☎ 617/ 354–6662, 617/520–2000, or 617/520–2007 Ⓜ Porter ✉ 75 Moulton St., Cambridge ☎ 617/520–2000 Ⓜ Arlington) is a visual exotic feast of cabinets, tables, chairs, and lamps from Japan, India, China, ★ and Indonesia. **Nomad** (✉ 1741 Massachusetts Ave., Cambridge ☎ 617/ 497–6677 Ⓜ Porter) carries clothing as well as Indian good-luck *torans* (wall hangings), Mexican *milagros* (charms), silver jewelry, and curtains made from sari silk. **Tibet Emporium** (✉ 103 Charles St., Beacon Hill ☎ 617/723–8035 Ⓜ Charles/MGH) goes beyond the usual masks and quilted wall hangings with delicate beaded silk pillowcases, pashmina wraps in every color imaginable, and finely wrought but affordable silver jewelry.

Boston A to Z

To research prices, get advice from other travelers, and book travel arrangements, visit www.fodors.com.

AIRPORTS & TRANSFERS

Boston's major airport, Logan International (BOS), is across the harbor from downtown, about 2 mi outside the city center, and can be easily reached by taxi, water taxi, or subway (called the "T") via the Silver or Blue Line. Logan has five terminals, identified by letters A through E. A free airport shuttle runs between the terminals and airport hotels. Some airlines use different terminals for international and domestic flights. Most international flights arrive at Terminal E. Most charter flights arrive at Terminal D. A visitor center in Terminal C offers tourist information. Green Airport, in Providence, Rhode Island, and the Manchester Airport in Manchester, New Hampshire, are both about an hour from Boston.

Cabs can be hired outside each terminal. Fares to and from downtown average about $15–$18, assuming no major traffic jams. If you're driving from Logan to downtown Boston, the most direct route is by way of the Sumner Tunnel ($3 toll inbound; no toll outbound). On weekends and holidays and after 10 PM weekdays, you can get around Sumner Tunnel backups by using the Ted Williams Tunnel ($3 toll inbound; no toll outbound), which will steer you onto the Southeast Expressway south of downtown Boston. Follow the signs to Interstate 93 northbound to head back into the downtown area.

The subway's Blue and Silver lines run from the airport to downtown Boston in about 20 minutes. The Blue Line is best if you're heading to North Station, Fanueil Hall, North End/Waterfront, and Back Bay (Hynes Convention Center, Prudential Center area). Take the Silver Line to South Station, Boston Convention and Exhibition Center, Seaport World Trade Center, Chinatown Theater, and South End areas. From the North and South stations, you can reach the Red, Green, or Orange lines, or commuter rail. The T costs $1.25 for in-town travel. Visitor passes good for one day ($7.50), three days ($18), and seven days ($35) are also available for unlimited travel on all subway lines, local crosstown buses, and inner harbor ferries. You must pay a double fare if you're headed to some suburban stations such as Braintree; pay the second fare as you exit the station. Free 24-hour shuttle buses connect the subway station with all airline terminals. Shuttle Bus 22 runs between the subway and Terminal B, while Shuttle Bus 33 runs between the subway and Terminals C, D, and E.

Several companies offer shared van service to many Boston-area destinations. J. C. Transportation, Logan/Boston Hotel Shuttle, and Ace American provide door-to-door service to several major Back Bay and downtown hotels. Reservations are not required as vans swing by all terminals every 20 to 30 minutes. One-way fares run about $12 per person. Easy Transportation runs from the airport to the Back Bay Hilton, Radisson, and Lenox hotels from 7 AM to 10 PM. Star Shuttle operates vans from the airport to the Marriott Copley Place and Sheraton Copley every hour on the half-hour from 5:30 AM to 11:30 PM. Logan Express buses travel from the airport to the suburbs of Braintree, Framingham, Peabody, and Woburn. One-way fares are $11.

Several boat companies make runs between the airport and downtown destinations. City Water Taxi has an on-call boat service between the airport and 16 downtown locations from April through November. One-way fares to or from the airport are $10, and round-trip tickets are $17. Harbor Express water taxi service takes passengers between Logan Airport and Long Wharf in Downtown ($10) and Quincy on the South Shore ($12). Rowes Wharf Water Taxi ($10) offers a stunning glimpse of the city's skyline as it makes seven-minute trips across Boston Harbor between Logan Airport and Rowes Wharf.

🛈 Airport Information **Logan International** ☎ 617/561-1800, 800/235-6426 24-hr information ⊕ www.massport.com Ⓜ Airport.

🛈 Bus & Van Service **J.C. Transportation** ☎ 781/598-3433 or 800/517-2281 ⊕ www. jctransportationshuttle.com. **Ace American** ☎ 800/517-2281. **Logan/Boston Hotel Shuttle** ☎ 877/315-4700. **Easy Transportation** ☎ 617/445-1107. **Star Shuttle** ☎ 617/230-6005. **Logan Express** ☎ 800/235-6426 ⊕ www.massport.com.

🛈 Subway **MBTA** ☎ 617/222-3200, 800/392-6100, 617/222-5146 TTY ⊕ www.mbta.com.

🚹 Water Taxis **City Water Taxi** 🖀 617/422-0392 or 800/235-6426 ⊕ www.citywatertaxi. com. **Harbor Express** 🖀617/376-8417 or 617/222-6999 ⊕www.harborexpress.com. **Rowes Wharf Water Taxi** 🖀 617/406-8584 ⊕ www.roweswharfwatertaxi.com.

BUS TRAVEL TO & FROM BOSTON
South Station is the depot for most of the major bus companies that serve Boston.

🚹 Bus Information **South Station** ✉ 700 Atlantic Ave., at Summer St., Downtown Ⓜ South Station.

BUS TRAVEL WITHIN BOSTON
Buses of the Massachusetts Bay Transportation Authority (MBTA) criss-cross the metropolitan area and travel farther into suburbia than subway and trolley lines. Buses run roughly from 5:30 AM to 12:30 AM; the Night Owl service runs limited routes until 2:30 AM Friday and Saturday nights. Fares are 90¢ for trips within the city.

🚹 Bus Information **MBTA** 🖀 617/222-3200, 800/392-6100, 617/222-5146 TTY ⊕ www. mbta.com.

CAR TRAVEL
Boston is not an easy city to drive in because of the many one-way streets, the many streets with the same name, the many streets that abruptly *change* name in the middle, and the many illogical twists and turns. If you must bring a car, bring a good map, keep to the main thoroughfares, and park in lots rather than on the street to avoid tickets (signage is confusing at best, and meter patrol is preternaturally quick), accidents, or theft. Some neighborhoods have strictly enforced residents-only rules, with just a handful of two-hour visitor's spaces.

PARKING Major public lots are at Government Center and Quincy Market, beneath Boston Common (entrance on Charles Street), beneath Post Office Square, at the Prudential Center, at Copley Place, and off Clarendon Street near the John Hancock Tower. Smaller lots and garages are scattered throughout downtown, especially around the Theater District and off Atlantic Avenue in the North End. Most are expensive; expect to pay up to $8 an hour or $24 to park all day. The few city garages are a bargain at about $7–$11 per day. Theaters, restaurants, stores, and tourist attractions often provide customers with one or two hours of free parking. Some downtown restaurants offer valet parking.

DISCOUNTS & DEALS
BosTix booths in Copley Square and the Faneuil Hall Marketplace offer half-price, same-day dance, music, and theater tickets. Purchase tickets, with cash only, at BosTix beginning at 10 AM Monday–Saturday, 11 AM Sunday, or at www.artsboston.org. The BosTix Fanueil Hall location is closed on Monday.

The CityPass is a reduced-fee combination ticket, good for one year, to six major Boston sights: the John F. Kennedy Library & Museum, Prudential Center Skywalk, the Museum of Fine Arts, the Museum of Science, the New England Aquarium, and the Harvard University Museum of Natural History. The passes cost $39 and are available online, at participating attractions, and at the Greater Boston Convention & Visitors Bureau information booths.

The Go Boston Card, granting free admission to many of Boston's main tourist attractions and savings at shops and restaurants, is available in one-, two-, three-, five-, or seven-day increments. The price for the card, which is available at area hotels and online, starts at $45 for adults and $25 for children.

EMERGENCIES

⎘ Emergency Services 911 for police, fire, and ambulance. **Poison Control** ☎ 617/232–2120. **Travelers Aid Family Services** ☎ 617/542–7286 ⊕ www.taboston.org. **⎘ Hospitals Brigham and Women's Hospital** ✉ 75 Francis St., Brookline ☎ 617/732–5500 ⊕ www.brighamandwomens.org. **Children's Hospital** ✉ 300 Longwood Ave., Brookline ☎ 617/355–6000 ⊕ www.childrenshospital.org. **Massachusetts General Hospital** ✉ 55 Fruit St., Beacon Hill ☎ 617/726–2000 ⊕ www.mgh.harvard.edu. **⎘ 24-Hour Pharmacies CVS** ✉ 587 Boylston St. ☎ 617/437–8414. **Brooks** ✉ 14 McGrath Hwy., Somerville ☎ 617/776–3000. **Walgreens** ✉ 757 Gallivan Blvd., Dorchester ☎ 617/282–5246.

Sightseeing Tours

BOAT TOURS Boston has many waterways that offer stunning views back into the city skyline. Narrated sightseeing water tours generally run from spring through early fall, daily in summer, and on weekends in the shoulder seasons. (Labor Day weekend is often the cutoff point.) These trips normally last ¾–1½ hours and cost less than $20. Many companies also offer sunset or evening cruises with music and other entertainment.

The Boston Duck Tours, which gives narrated land-water tours on a World War II amphibious vehicle, are particularly popular. After driving past several historic sights, the vehicle dips into the Charles River to offer a view of the Boston skyline. These tours, costing $25 per person, run later than most, through late November.

Boston Harbor Cruises and Mass Bay Lines have tours around the harbor. Trips with Boston Duck Tours and the Charles Riverboat Company are along the Charles River Basin.

⎘ Fees & Schedules Boston Duck Tours ✉ Departures from Prudential Center, Huntington Ave. in front of Shaw's supermarket, and from the Museum of Science ☎ 617/267–3825 ⊕ www.bostonducktours.com. **Boston Harbor Cruises** ✉ 1 Long Wharf ☎ 617/227–4321 or 877/733–9425 ⊕ www.bostonharborcruises.com. **Charles Riverboat Company** ✉ 100 CambridgeSide Pl., Suite 320, Cambridge ☎ 617/621–3001 ⊕ www.charlesriverboat.com. **Mass Bay Lines** ✉ 60 Rowes Wharf ☎ 617/542–8000 ⊕ www.massbaylines.com.

BUS TOURS Boston Private Tours has customized tours in vans or limousines. Brush Hill has more traditional charter bus tours as well as smaller tours, with lots of prepackaged options and add-ons.

⎘ Fees & Schedules Boston Private Tours ☎ 800/620–1136 ⊕ www.bostonprivatetours.com. **Brush Hill Tours** ✉ Transportation Bldg., 16 Charles St. S ☎ 781/986–6100 or 800/343–1328 ⊕ www.brushhilltours.com.

TROLLEY TOURS Both Brush Hill and Old Town Trolley have 1½-hour narrated tours. Old Town Trolley tours focus on history.

■ Fees & Schedules Brush Hill Tours ☒ Transportation Bldg., 16 Charles St. S ☏ 781/
986-6100 or 800/343-1328 ⊕ www.brushhilltours.com. **Old Town Trolley** ☒ 380
Dorchester Ave., South Boston ☏ 617/269-7150 or 800/868-7482 ⊕ www.historictours.
com/boston.

Subways, Trains & Trolleys

The Massachusetts Bay Transportation Authority (MBTA)—or "T"
when referring to the subway line—operates subway trains, elevated trains,
trolleys, and, including the newly introduced Silver Line, rapid-transit
buses along five connecting lines. A 24-hour hotline and the MBTA Web
site offer information on routes, schedules, fares, wheelchair access, and
other matters. Free maps are available at the MBTA's Park Street Station information stand, open daily from 7 AM to 10 PM, and online at
www.mbta.com.

"Inbound" trains head into the city center and "outbound" trains head
away from downtown Boston. If you get on the Red Line at South Station, the train heading toward Cambridge is inbound. But once you pass
the Park Street station, the train becomes an outbound train. The best
way to figure out which way to go is to know the last stop on the train,
which is always listed. So, from downtown, the Red Line to Cambridge
would be the Alewife train and the Green Line to Fenway would be the
Boston College or Cleveland Circle train.

Trains operate from about 5:30 AM to about 12:30 AM. T fares are $1.25
for adults, 60¢ for children ages 5 through 11, and 35¢ for senior citizens. An extra fare is required heading inbound from distant Green Line
stops and both inbound and outbound on the most distant Red Line
stops (for example, the fare each way from Braintree is $2.50). Fares
on commuter rail—the Purple Line—vary widely; check with the MBTA.

MBTA visitor passes are available for unlimited travel on city buses and
subways for one-, three-, and seven-day periods (fares are $7.50, $18,
and $35, respectively). Buy passes at the following MBTA stations: Air-
port, South Station, North Station, Back Bay, Government Center, and
Harvard Square. Passes are also sold at the Boston Common Visitor Information Center and at some hotels.

ROUTES The Red Line originates at Braintree and Mattapan to the south; the
routes join near South Boston and continue to Cambridge. The Green
Line operates trolleys in the suburbs that dip underground in the city
center. The line originates at Cambridge's Lechmere, heads south,
and divides into four routes that end at Boston College (Commonwealth
Avenue), Cleveland Circle (Beacon Street), Riverside, and Heath Street
(Huntington Avenue). Buses connect Heath Street to the old Arbor-
way terminus.

The Blue Line runs weekdays from Bowdoin Square and weeknights and
weekends from Government Center to the Wonderland Racetrack in Revere, north of Boston. The Orange Line runs from Oak Grove in north
suburban Malden to Forest Hills near the Arnold Arboretum. The Silver Line consists of two rapid-transit bus lines. One, the Washington

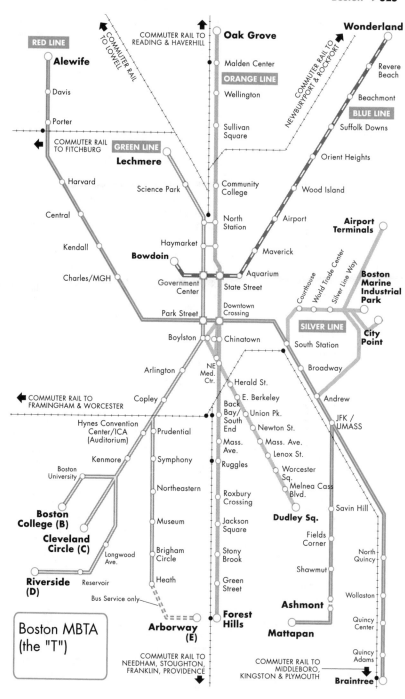

Boston MBTA (the "T")

Street route, connects Downtown Crossing and Boylston to Dudley Square. The other, the Silver Line Waterfront, is actually three bus routes that start out underground and surface before they reach their destination: SL1 goes from South Station to Logan Airport, SL2 from South Station to Boston Marine Industrial Park, and SL3 from South Station to City Point. Park Street Station (on the Common) and State Street are the transit system's major downtown transfer points.

🚇 **MBTA** ☎ 617/222-3200, 800/392-6100, 617/222-5146 TTY ⊕ www.mbta.com.

Taxis

Cabs may be hailed on the street; they're available around the clock. You can also call for a cab or find them outside most hotels. Taxis also generally line up in Harvard Square, around South Station, near Faneuil Hall Marketplace, at Long Wharf, near Massachusetts General Hospital, and in the Theater District. A taxi ride within the city of Boston starts at $1.75, and costs 30¢ for each ⅛ mi thereafter. Licensed cabs have meters and provide receipts. An illuminated rooftop sign indicates an available cab. If you're going to or from the airport or to the suburbs, ask about flat rates. Cab drivers sometimes charge extra for multiple stops. One-way streets often make circuitous routes necessary and increase your cost.

🚕 (Boston Cab Association) ☎ 617/536-3200. **Cambridge Checker Cab** ✉ Cambridge ☎ 617/497-1500. **Green Cab Association** ☎ 617/625-5000. **Independent Taxi Operators Association (ITOA)** ☎ 617/825-4000. **Town Taxi** ☎ 617/536-5000.

Train Travel

South Station and Back Bay Station are served by frequent Amtrak trains to and from New York, Philadelphia, Washington, D.C., and other points along the Northeast Corridor; the *Lake Shore Limited*, which travels daily between Boston and Chicago by way of Albany, Rochester, Buffalo, and Cleveland, also uses South and Back Bay stations. Only Amtrak's *Downeaster* service to New Hampshire and Portland, Maine, uses North Station. Amtrak's pricey high-speed Acela train has cut the travel time between Boston and New York from 4½ hours to 3½ hours. An additional Amtrak station with ample parking is just off Route 128 in suburban Westwood, southwest of Boston.

The MBTA runs commuter trains to points south, west, and north. Those bound for Worcester, Needham, Forge Park, Providence (RI), and Stoughton leave from South Station and Back Bay Station; those to Fitchburg, Lowell, Haverhill, Newburyport, and Rockport operate out of North Station. MBTA's Old Colony commuter line connects Boston's South Station with points south, running through Braintree to Plymouth/Kingston and Middleborough.

🚆 Train Information **Amtrak** ☎ 800/872-7245 ⊕ www.amtrak.com. **MBTA** ☎ 617/222-3200, 800/392-6100, 617/222-5146 TTY ⊕ www.mbta.com.

VISITOR INFORMATION

🚩 **Boston Common Visitor Information Center** ✉ Tremont St. where Freedom Trail begins ☎ 617/426-3115. **Greater Boston Convention & Visitors Bureau** ✉ 2 Copley Pl., Suite 105, 02116 ☎ 617/536-4100, 800/888-5515, or 888/733-2678 🖷 617/424-7664 ⊕ www.bostonusa.com.

AROUND BOSTON

Lexington

Updated by
Michael
Blanding

16 mi northwest of Boston.

Some of the first military encounters of the American Revolution took place in Lexington, and they are very much a part of present-day Lexington, a modern suburban town that sprawls out from the historic sites near its center. Although the downtown area is generally lively, with ice-cream and coffee shops, boutiques, and a great little movie theater, the town becomes especially animated each Patriots' Day, when costume-clad groups re-create the minutemen's battle maneuvers and Paul Revere's ride.

On April 18, 1775, Paul Revere went to the **Hancock-Clarke House** to warn patriots John Hancock and Sam Adams, who were staying there while attending the Provincial Congress in nearby Concord, of the advance of British troops. Hancock and Adams, on whose heads the British king had put a price, fled to avoid capture. The house, a parsonage built in 1698, is a 10-minute walk from Lexington Common. Inside are the pistols of the British major John Pitcairn as well as period furnishings and portraits. ⊠ *36 Hancock St.* ☎ *781/862–1703* ⊕ *www. lexingtonhistory.org* ☞ *$5; $12 combination ticket includes Buckman Tavern and Munroe Tavern* ⊙ *Mid-May–Oct, daily 11–2.*

It was on **Battle Green,** a 2-acre triangle of land, on April 19, 1775, that the first confrontation between British soldiers, who were marching from Boston toward Concord, and the colonial militia known as the minutemen took place. The minutemen—so called because they were able to prepare themselves at a moment's notice—were led by Captain John Parker, whose role in the American Revolution is commemorated in Henry Hudson Kitson's renowned 1900 *Minuteman* statue. Facing downtown Lexington at the tip of Battle Green, the statue's in a traffic island and therefore makes for a difficult photo op.

While waiting for the arrival of the British on the morning of April 19, 1775, the minutemen gathered at the **Buckman Tavern,** built in 1690. A half-hour tour takes in the tavern's seven rooms, which have been restored to the way they looked in the 1770s. Among the items on display is an old front door with a hole made by a British musket ball. ⊠ *1 Bedford St.* ☎ *781/862–1703* ⊕ *www.lexingtonhistory.org* ☞ *$5; $12 combination ticket includes Hancock-Clarke House and Munroe Tavern* ⊙ *Mid-Apr.–Oct., daily 10–4.*

The pleasant **Lexington Visitor Center,** across from the Battle Green, has a diorama of the 1775 clash, plus a gift shop. ⊠ *Lexington Chamber of Commerce, 1875 Massachusetts Ave.* ☎ *781/862–1450* ⊕ *www. lexingtonchamber.org* ⊙ *Apr.–Nov., daily 9–5; Dec.–Mar., daily 10–4.*

As April 19, 1775, dragged on, British forces met fierce resistance in Concord. Dazed and demoralized after the battle at Concord's Old North Bridge, the British backtracked and regrouped at the **Munroe Tav-**

ern (1695), 1 mi east of Lexington Common, while the Munroe family hid in nearby woods. The troops then retreated through what is now the town of Arlington. After a bloody battle there, they returned to Boston. Tours of the tavern last about 30 minutes. ⊠ *1332 Massachusetts Ave.* ☎ *781/862–1703* ⊕ *www.lexingtonhistory.org* ⬚ *$5; $12 combination ticket includes Hancock-Clarke House and Buckman Tavern* ⊘ *Mid-May–Oct., 1 tour daily at 3* PM.

The **National Heritage Museum** displays items and artifacts from all facets of American life, putting them in social and political context. An ongoing exhibit, "Lexington Alarm'd," outlines events leading up to April 1775 and illustrates Revolutionary-era life through everyday objects such as blacksmithing and farming tools, scalpels and bloodletting paraphernalia, and dental instruments, including a "tooth key" used to extract teeth. ⊠ *33 Marrett Rd., Rte. 2A at Massachusetts Ave.* ☎ *781/ 861–6559* ⊕ *www.monh.org* ⬚ *Donations accepted* ⊘ *Mon.–Sat. 10–5, Sun. noon–5.*

★ ⌖ West of Lexington's center stretches the 1,000-acre, three-parcel **Minute Man National Historical Park,** which also extends into nearby Lincoln and Concord. Begin your park visit at Lexington's **Minute Man Visitor Center** to see its free multimedia presentation, "The Road to Revolution," a captivating introduction to the events of April 1775. Then, continuing along Route 2A toward Concord, you pass the point where Revere's midnight ride ended with his capture by the British; it's marked with a boulder and plaque, as well as an enclosure where rangers sometimes give educational presentations. You can also visit the 1732 **Hartwell Tavern** (open May through October, daily 9:30–5:30), a restored drover's (driver's) tavern staffed by park employees in period costume; they frequently demonstrate musket firing or open-hearth cooking, and children are likely to enjoy the reproduction Colonial toys. ⊠ *Rte. 2A, ¼ mi west of Rte. 128* ☎ *978/369–6993* ⊕ *www.nps.gov/mima* ⊘ *May–Oct., daily 9–5; Nov.–Apr., call for times.*

Where to Eat

$–$$ ✕ **Bertucci's.** Part of a popular chain, this family-friendly Italian restaurant offers good food, reasonable prices, and a large menu. Specialties include ravioli, calzones, and brick-oven pizzas. ⊠ *1777 Massachusetts Ave.* ☎ *781/860–9000* ⊟ *AE, D, DC, MC, V.*

Concord

About 10 mi west of Lexington, 21 mi northwest of Boston.

The Concord of today is a modern suburb with a busy center filled with arty shops, places to eat, and (recalling the literary history made here) old bookstores. Autumn lovers, take note: Concord is a great place to start a fall foliage tour. From Boston, head west along Route 2 to Concord, and then continue on to find harvest stands and do-it-yourself apple-picking around Harvard and Stow.

To reach Concord from Lexington, take Routes 4/225 through Bedford and Route 62 west to Concord; or pick up Route 2A west from Massachusetts Avenue (known locally as Mass Ave.) at the National Heritage Museum or Waltham Street south from Lexington Center.

★ ☾ The **Minute Man National Historical Park,** along Route 2A, is a three-parcel park with 1,000 acres. The park contains many of the sites important to Concord's role in the Revolution, including Old North Bridge, as well as two visitor centers, one each in Concord and Lexington. Although the initial Revolutionary War sorties were in Lexington, word of the American losses spread rapidly to surrounding towns: when the British marched into Concord, more than 400 minutemen were waiting. A marker set in the stone wall along Liberty Street, behind the North Bridge Visitors Center, announces: "On this field the minutemen and militia formed before marching down to the fight at the bridge." The **North Bridge Visitor Center** (✉ 174 Liberty St. ☎ 978/369–6993) is open from May through October, daily 9–5. If you're visiting from November through April, call for hours. ✉ *Bounded by Monument St., Liberty St., and Lowell Rd.* ⊕ *www.nps.gov/mima* ☾ *Daily dawn–dusk.*

At the **Old North Bridge,** ½ mi from Concord center, the Concord minutemen turned the tables on the British on the morning of April 19, 1775. The Americans didn't fire first, but when two of their own fell dead from a redcoat volley, Major John Buttrick of Concord roared, "Fire, fellow soldiers, for God's sake, fire." The minutemen released volley after volley, and the redcoats fled. Daniel Chester French's famous statue *The Minuteman* (1875) honors the country's first freedom fighters. Inscribed at the foot of the statue are words Ralph Waldo Emerson wrote in 1837 describing the confrontation: BY THE RUDE BRIDGE THAT ARCHED THE FLOOD / THEIR FLAG TO APRIL'S BREEZE UNFURLED / HERE ONCE THE EMBATTLED FARMERS STOOD / AND FIRED THE SHOT HEARD ROUND THE WORLD. The lovely wooded surroundings give a sense of what the landscape was like in more rural times.

The Reverend William Emerson, grandfather of Ralph Waldo Emerson, watched rebels and redcoats battle from behind his home, the **Old Manse,** which was within sight of the Old North Bridge. The house, built in 1770, was occupied continuously by the Emerson family for almost two centuries, except for a 3½-year period during which Nathaniel Hawthorne rented it. Furnishings date from the late 18th century. Tours run throughout the day and last 45 minutes, with a new tour starting within 15 minutes of when the first person signs up. ✉ *269 Monument St.* ☎ *978/369–3909* 🎟 *$8* ☾ *Mid-Apr.–Oct., Mon.–Sat. 10–5, Sun. noon–5; last tour departs 4:30* ⊕ *www.oldmanse.org.*

The 19th-century essayist and poet Ralph Waldo Emerson lived briefly in the Old Manse in 1834–35, then moved to what is known as the **Ralph Waldo Emerson House,** where he lived until his death in 1882. Here he wrote the *Essays.* Except for items from Emerson's study, now at the nearby Concord Museum, the Emerson House furnishings have been preserved as the writer left them, down to his hat resting on the newel post. You must join one of the half-hour-long tours to see the interior. ✉ *28 Cambridge Tpke., at Lexington Rd.* ☎ *978/369–2236* 🎟 *$7* ☾ *Mid-Apr.–mid Oct., Thurs.–Sat. 10–4:30, Sun. 1–4:30; call for tour schedule.*

The original contents of Emerson's private study, as well as the world's largest collection of Thoreau artifacts, are in the **Concord Museum.** Set in a 1930 Colonial-revival building just east of the town center, the museum provides a good overview of the town's history, from its original Native American settlement to the present. Highlights include Native American artifacts, furnishings from Thoreau's Walden Pond cabin, and one of the two lanterns hung at Boston's Old North Church to signal that the British were coming by sea. If you've brought the children, ask for a free family activity pack. ⊠ *200 Lexington Rd., entrance on Cambridge Tpke.* ☎ *978/369–9763* ⊕ *www.concordmuseum.org* ⊠ *$8* ☼ *Apr. and May, Mon.–Sat. 9–5, Sun. noon–5; June–Dec. daily 9–5; Jan.–Mar., Mon.–Sat. 11–4, Sun. 1–4.*

The dark brown exterior of Louisa May Alcott's family home, **Orchard House,** sharply contrasts with the light, wit, and energy so much in evidence inside. Named for the apple orchard that once surrounded it, Orchard House was the Alcott family home from 1857 to 1877. Here, Louisa wrote *Little Women,* based on her life with her three sisters, and her father, Bronson, founded his school of philosophy; the building remains behind the house. Because Orchard House had just one owner after the Alcotts left and because it became a museum in 1911, many of the original furnishings remain, including the semicircular shelf-desk where Louisa wrote *Little Women.* The 30-minute tours start about every half hour daily from April through October; call for the off-season tour schedule. ⊠ *399 Lexington Rd.* ☎ *978/369–4118* ⊕ *www.louisamayalcott. org* ⊠ *$8, tours free* ☼ *Apr.–Oct., Mon.–Sat. 10–4:30, Sun. 1–4:30; Nov., Dec., and Jan. 16–Mar., weekdays 11–3, Sat. 10–4:30, Sun. 1–4:30. Half-hr tours begin every 30 mins Apr.–Oct.; call for off-season tour schedule.*

Nathaniel Hawthorne lived at the Old Manse in 1842–45, working on stories and sketches; he then moved to Salem (where he wrote *The Scarlet Letter*) and later to Lenox (*The House of the Seven Gables*). In 1852 he returned to Concord, bought a rambling structure called **The Wayside,** and lived here until his death in 1864. The subsequent owner, Margaret Sidney, wrote the children's book *Five Little Peppers and How They Grew* (1881). Before Hawthorne moved in, the Alcotts lived here, from 1845 to 1848. An exhibit center, in the former barn, provides information about the Wayside authors and links them to major events in American history. Hawthorne's tower-study is substantially as he left it, complete with his stand-up writing desk. ⊠ *455 Lexington Rd.* ☎ *978/ 369–6993* ⊕ *www.nps.gov/mima/* ⊠ *Free, tours $4* ☼ *May–Oct., call for tour schedule.*

Each Memorial Day, Louisa May Alcott's grave in the nearby **Sleepy Hollow Cemetery** is decorated in commemoration of her death. Along with Emerson, Thoreau, and Hawthorne, Alcott is buried in a section of the cemetery known as Author's Ridge. ⊠ *Bedford St. (Rte. 62)* ☎ *978/ 318–3233* ☼ *Daily dawn–dusk.*

★ A trip to Concord can include a pilgrimage to **Walden Pond,** Henry David Thoreau's most famous residence. Here, in 1845, at age 28, Thoreau moved into a one-room cabin—built for $28.12—on the shore of this

100-foot-deep kettle hole formed 12,000 years ago by the retreat of the New England glacier. Living alone for the next two years, Thoreau discovered the benefits of solitude and the beauties of nature. The essays in *Walden,* published in 1854, are a mixture of philosophy, nature writing, and proto-ecology. The site of the first cabin is staked out in stone. A full-size, authentically furnished replica of the cabin stands about ½ mi from the original site, near the Walden Pond State Reservation parking lot. Even when it's closed, you can peek through its windows. Now, as in Thoreau's time, the pond is a delightful summertime spot for swimming, fishing, and rowing, and there's hiking in the nearby woods. To get to Walden Pond State Reservation from the center of Concord—a trip of only 1½ mi—take Concord's Main Street a block west from Monument Square, turn left onto Walden Street, and head for the intersection of Routes 2 and 126. Cross over Route 2 onto Route 126, heading south for ½ mi. ⊠ *95 Walden St. (Rte. 126)* ☎ *978/369–3254* 🖾 *Free, parking $5* ☉ *Daily from 8* AM *until about ½ hr before sunset, weather permitting.*

Where to Eat

$$–$$$ ✕ **Walden Grille.** In this old brick firehouse-turned-dining-room, satisfy your appetite with tempting contemporary dishes. Lighter options include salads and sandwiches: try curried chicken on grilled Syrian bread. Heartier entrées may include seafood carbonara with shrimp and mussels or pan-seared duck breast with cherry and port wine sauce. ⊠ *24 Walden St.* ☎ *978/371–2233* ⊟ *AE, D, MC, V.*

$ ✕ **La Provence.** This little taste of France, a casual café and take-out shop opposite the Concord train station, makes a good stop for a light meal. In the morning you can start off with a croissant or a brioche, and at midday you can pick up sandwiches (perhaps pâté and cheese or French ham), quiches, or salads. Leave room for an éclair or a petite fruit tart. Just don't plan a late night here; the café closes at 7 PM during the week and at 5:30 on Saturday. ⊠ *105 Thoreau St.* ☎ *978/371–7428* ⊟ *D, MC, V* ☉ *Closed Sun.*

Lowell

30 mi northwest of Boston.

Everyone knows that the American Revolution began in Massachusetts. But the Commonwealth, and in particular the Merrimack Valley, also nurtured the Industrial Revolution. Lowell's first mill opened in 1823; by the 1850s, 40 factories employed thousands of workers and produced 2 million yards of cloth every week. The **Lowell National Historical Park** tracks the history of a gritty era when the power loom was the symbol of economic progress. It encompasses several blocks in the downtown area, including former mills–turned–museums, a network of canals, and a helpful visitor center.

The **American Textile History Museum,** a short walk southwest along Dutton Street from the National Park Visitor Center, is in a former Civil War–era mill. The museum's collection of working machines ranges from an 18th-century waterwheel to an 1860s power loom to a 1950s "weave room" where fabrics are still made. Special exhibitions are held periodically; these have an extra admission fee. ✉ *491 Dutton St.* ☎ *978/441–0400* ⊕ *www.athm.org* 🎫 *$6* ⊙ *Tues.–Fri. 9–4, weekends 10–5.*

The **Boott Cotton Mills Museum,** about a 10-minute walk northeast from the National Park Visitor Center, is the first major National Park Service museum devoted to industrialization. The textile worker's grueling life is shown with all its grit, noise, and dust. You know you're in for an unusual experience when you're handed earplugs—they're for the re-creation of a 1920s weave room, authentic down to the deafening roar of 88 working power looms. Other exhibits at the complex include weaving artifacts, cloth samples, video interviews with workers, and a large, meticulous scale model of 19th-century production. ✉ *Foot of John St.* ☎ *978/970–5000* 🎫 *$6* ⊙ *Apr.–Nov., daily 9:30–5; Dec., daily 9:30–4:30; Jan–Mar., Mon.–Sat. 9:30–4:30, Sun. 11–4:30.*

Plymouth

40 mi south of Boston.

On December 26, 1620, 102 weary men, women, and children disembarked from the *Mayflower* to found the first permanent European settlement north of Virginia. Today, Plymouth is characterized by narrow streets, clapboard mansions, shops, antiques stores, and a scenic waterfront. To mark Thanksgiving, the town holds a parade, historic-house tours, and other activities. Historic statues dot the town, including depictions of William Bradford, Pilgrim leader and govern of Plymouth Colony for more than 30 years, on Water Street; a Pilgrim maiden in Brewster Gardens; and Massasoit, the Wampanoag chief who helped the Pilgrims survive, on Carver Street. The largest freestanding granite statue in the United States, the allegorical **National Monument to the Forefathers** stands high on a grassy hill. Designed by Hammet Billings of Boston in 1854 and dedicated in 1889, it depicts Faith, surrounded by Liberty, Morality, Justice, Law, and Education and includes scenes from the Pilgrims' early days in Plymouth. ✉ *Allerton St.*

The **Mayflower II,** a seaworthy replica of the 1620 *Mayflower,* was built in England through research and a bit of guesswork, then sailed across the Atlantic in 1957. As you explore the interior and exterior of the ship, sailors in modern dress answer your questions about both the reproduction and the original ship, while costumed guides provide a 17th-century perspective. ✉ *State Pier* ☎ *508/746–1622* ⊕ *www.plimoth. org* 🎫 *$8, $24 with admission to Plimoth Plantation* ⊙ *Late Mar.–Nov., daily 9–5.*

A few dozen yards from the *Mayflower II* is **Plymouth Rock,** popularly believed to have been the Pilgrims' stepping-stone when they left the ship. Given the stone's unimpressive appearance—it's little more than a boulder—and dubious authenticity (as explained on a nearby plaque), the grand canopy overhead seems a trifle ostentatious.

Several historic houses are open for visits, including the 1640 **Sparrow House,** Plymouth's oldest structure. You can peek into a pair of rooms furnished in the spartan style of the Pilgrims' era. The contemporary crafts gallery also on the premises seems somewhat incongruous, but the works on view are high quality. ⊠ *42 Summer St.* ☎ *508/747–1240* ✉ *$2, gallery free* ⏱ *Apr.–late Nov., Thurs.–Tues. 10–5.*

From the waterfront sights it's a short walk to one of the country's oldest public museums. The **Pilgrim Hall Museum,** established in 1824, transports you back to the time of the Pilgrims' landing with objects carried by those weary travelers to the New World. Included are a carved chest, a remarkably well-preserved wicker cradle, Myles Standish's sword, John Alden's Bible, Native American artifacts, and the remains of the *Sparrow Hawk,* a sailing ship that was wrecked in 1626. ⊠ *75 Court St. (Rte. 3A)* ☎ *508/746–1620* ⊕ *www.pilgrimhall.org* ✉ *$6* ⏱ *Feb.–Dec., daily 9:30–4:30.*

⟳ Over the entrance of the **Plimoth Plantation,** 3 mi south of downtown
FodorśChoice Plymouth, is the caution: "You are now entering 1627." Believe it. Against
★ the backdrop of the Atlantic Ocean, a Pilgrim village has been carefully re-created, from the thatch roofs, cramped quarters, and open fireplaces to the long-horned livestock. Throw away your preconception of white collars and funny hats; through ongoing research, the Plimoth staff has developed a portrait of the Pilgrims that's more complex than the dour folk in school textbooks. Listen to the accents of the "residents," who never break out of character. You might see them plucking ducks, cooking rabbit stew, or tending garden. Feel free to engage them in conversation about their life, but expect only curious looks if you ask about anything that happened after 1627. "Thanksgiving: Memory, Myth & Meaning," an exhibit in the visitor center, offers a fresh perspective on the 1621 harvest celebration that is now known as "the first Thanksgiving." ⊠ *137 Warren Ave. (Rte. 3A)* ☎ *508/746–1622* ⊕ *www.plimoth.org* ✉ *$21, $24 with Mayflower II* ⏱ *Late Mar.–Nov., daily 9–5.*

Where to Stay & Eat

¢ ✕ **All-American Diner.** The look is nostalgia—red, white, and blue, with vintage movie posters. The specialty is beloved American food—omelets and pancakes for breakfast; burgers, salads, and soups for lunch. ⊠ *60 Court St.* ☎ *508/747–4763* ⊟ *AE, MC, V* ⏱ *No dinner.*

$$–$$$$ ✕⊡ **John Carver Inn.** This three-story, Colonial-style redbrick building is steps from Plymouth's main attractions. The public rooms are lavish, with period furnishings and stylish drapes. The guest rooms include six "environmentally sensitive" options with filtered air and water and four-poster beds. The suites have fireplaces and whirlpool baths. There's also an indoor pool with a *Mayflower* ship model and a waterslide. The hotel's Hearth 'n Kettle Restaurant ($–$$) serves a wide selection of American favorites, including seafood and hearty sandwiches, at reasonable prices. ⊠ *25 Summer St., 02360* ☎ *508/746–7100 or 800/274–1620* ⊠ *508/746–8299* ⊕ *www.johncarverinn.com* ↝ *79 rooms, 6 suites* ⟡ *Restaurant, cable TV with movies, indoor pool, bar, meeting rooms* ⊟ *AE, D, DC, MC, V.*

New Bedford

45 mi southwest of Plymouth, 50 mi south of Boston.

In 1652 colonists from Plymouth settled in the area that now includes the city of New Bedford. The city has a long maritime tradition, beginning as a shipbuilding center and small whaling port in the late 1700s. By the mid-1800s, it had developed into a center of North American whaling. Today, New Bedford has the largest fishing fleet on the East Coast. Although much of the town is industrial, the restored historic district near the water is a delight. It was here that Herman Melville set his masterpiece, *Moby-Dick*, a novel about whaling.

The city's whaling tradition is commemorated in the **New Bedford Whaling National Historical Park,** which takes up 13 blocks of the waterfront historic district. The park visitor center, housed in an 1853 Greek-revival building that was once a bank, provides maps and information about whaling-related sites. Free walking tours of the park leave from the visitor center at 10 AM and noon in July and August. ⊠ *33 William St.* ☎ *508/996–4095* ⊕ *www.nps.gov/nebe* ⊠ *Free* ☉ *Daily 9–5.*

☼ The **New Bedford Whaling Museum,** established in 1903, is the world's largest museum of its kind. A highlight is the skeleton of a 66-foot blue whale, one of only three on view anywhere. An interactive exhibit lets you listen to the underwater sounds of whales, dolphins, and other sea life—plus the sounds of a thunderstorm and a whale-watching boat—as a whale might hear them. You can also peruse the collection of scrimshaw, visit exhibits on regional history, and climb aboard an 89-foot, half-scale model of the 1826 whaling ship *Lagoda*—the world's largest ship model. ⊠ *18 Johnny Cake Hill* ☎ *508/997–0046* ⊕ *www. whalingmuseum.org* ⊠ *$10* ☉ *Fri.–Wed. 9–5, Thurs. 9–9.*

Seaman's Bethel, the small chapel described in *Moby-Dick*, is across the street from the New Bedford Whaling Museum. ⊠ *15 Johnny Cake Hill* ☎ *508/992–3295* ☉ *May–Columbus Day, weekdays 10–5.*

For a glimpse of upper-class life during New Bedford's whaling heyday, head ½ mi south of downtown to the **Rotch-Jones-Duff House & Garden Museum.** This 1834 Greek-revival mansion, amid a full city block of gardens, housed three prominent families in the 1800s and is filled with elegant furnishings from the era, including a mahogany piano, a massive marble-top sideboard, and portraits of the house's occupants. A free self-guided audio tour is available. ⊠ *396 County St.* ☎ *508/997–1401* ⊕ *www.rjdmuseum.org* ⊠ *$5* ☉ *Mon.–Sat. 10–4, Sun. noon–4.*

Where to Eat

$–$$$ ✕ **Davy's Locker.** A huge seafood menu is the main draw at this spot overlooking Buzzards Bay. Choose from more than a dozen shrimp preparations, or a choice of healthful entrées—dishes prepared with olive oil, vegetables, garlic, and herbs. For landlubbers, chicken, steak, ribs, and the like are also served. ⊠ *1480 E. Rodney French Blvd.* ☎ *508/992–7359* ⊟ *AE, D, DC, MC, V.*

$–$$ ✕ **Antonio's.** Sample the traditional fare of New Bedford's large Portuguese population at this friendly, unadorned restaurant. It serves up hearty portions of pork and shellfish stew, *bacalau* (salt cod), and grilled sardines, often on plates piled high with crispy fried potatoes and rice. ✉ 267 *Coggeshall St., near intersection of I–195 and Rte. 18* ☎ *508/990–3636* ▭ *No credit cards.*

Around Boston A to Z

To research prices, get advice from other travelers, and book travel arrange-ments, visit www.fodors.com.

BUS TRAVEL

The Massachusetts Bay Transportation Authority, or MBTA, operates buses to Lexington from Alewife station in Cambridge. Buses 62 and 76 make the trip in 25–30 minutes. Dattco offers service from Boston to New Bedford. Plymouth & Brockton Street Railway Co. buses link Plymouth and the South Shore to Boston's South Station with frequent service. From the Plymouth bus depot, you can take the Plymouth Area Link buses to the town center or to Plimoth Plantation.

🚍 Bus Information **Dattco** ☎ 800/453-5040. **MBTA** ☎ 617/222-3200, 800/392-6100, 617/222-5146 TTY ⊕ www.mbta.com. **Plymouth & Brockton** ☎ 508/746-0378 ⊕ www. p-b.com.

CAR TRAVEL

From Boston to Lexington, pick up Memorial Drive in Cambridge, and continue to the Fresh Pond Parkway, then to Route 2 west. Exit Route 2 at Routes 4/225 if your first stop is the National Heritage Museum; from Routes 4/225, turn left on Mass Ave. For Lexington Center, take the Waltham Street–Lexington exit from Route 2. Follow Waltham Street just under 2 mi to Mass Ave.; you'll be just east of the Battle Green. The drive takes about 30 minutes. To reach Concord by car, continue west on Route 2. Or take Interstate 90 (the Massachusetts Turnpike) to Interstate 95 north, and then exit at Route 2, heading west. Driving time is 40–45 minutes.

Lowell lies near the intersection of Interstate 495 and Route 3. From Boston, take Interstate 93 north to Interstate 495. Go south on Interstate 495 to Exit 35C, the Lowell Connector. Follow the Lowell Connector to Exit 5B, Thorndike Street. Travel time is 45 minutes to an hour. To get to Plymouth, take the Southeast Expressway Interstate 93 south to Route 3 (toward Cape Cod); Exits 6 and 4 lead to downtown Plymouth and Plimoth Plantation, respectively. To reach New Bedford from Boston, follow Interstate 93 to Route 24 south to Route 140 south, and continue to Interstate 195 east. Allow about one hour from Boston to Plymouth and about one hour from Plymouth to New Bedford.

EMERGENCIES

🚓 Police ☎ 911. **Emerson Hospital** ✉ 133 Old Rd., off Rte. 2, Concord ☎ 978/369-1400. **Jordan Hospital** ✉ 275 Sandwich St., Plymouth ☎ 508/746-2000. **Newton-Welles-ley Hospital** ✉ 2014 Washington St., Rte. 16, Newton ☎ 617/243-6000. **St. Luke's Hos-pital** ✉ 101 Page St., New Bedford ☎ 508/997-1515.

TRAIN TRAVEL

The MBTA's commuter rail (the Purple Line) offers service to many of the towns mentioned in this chapter. For destinations north and west of the city, trains depart from North Station, while trains to Plymouth depart from South Station. Concord is a 40-minute ride on the Fitchburg Line; the station is a short walk outside the town center. Lowell is a 45-minute ride on the Lowell Line—catch a Lowell Regional Transit Authority bus from the station.

🚆 Train Information **Lowell Regional Transit Authority** ✉ 145 Thorndike St., Lowell ☎ 978/452-6161 ⊕ www.lrta.com. **MBTA** ☎ 617/222-3200, 800/392-6100, 617/222-5146 TTY ⊕ www.mbta.com.

VISITOR INFORMATION

🚆 Tourist Information **Concord Chamber of Commerce** ✉ 100 Main St., Concord 01742 ☎ 978/369-3120 ⊕ www.concordchamberofcommerce.org. **Concord Visitor Center** ✉ 58 Main St., Concord 01742 ☎ 978/369-3120. **Lexington Visitor Center** ✉ 1875 Massachusetts Ave., Lexington ☎ 781/862-1450 ⊕ www.lexingtonchamber.org. **New Bedford Office of Tourism** ✉ Waterfront Visitors Center, Pier 3, New Bedford 02740 ☎ 508/979-1745 or 800/508-5353 ⊕ www.ci.new-bedford.ma.us. **Plymouth Visitor Information Center** ✉ 170 Water St., at Rte. 44, Plymouth 02360 ☎ 508/747-7533 or 800/872-1620 ⊕ www.visit-plymouth.com.

CAPE COD

Updated by Andrew Collins, Lori A. Nolin, and James W. Rohlf

A Patti Page song from the 1950s promises that "If you're fond of sand dunes and salty air, quaint little villages here and there, you're sure to fall in love with old Cape Cod." The tourism boom since the '50s has certainly proved her right. Continually shaped by ocean currents, this windswept land of sandy beaches and dunes has compelling natural beauty. Everyone comes for the seaside, yet the crimson cranberry bogs, forests of birch and beech, freshwater ponds, and marshlands that grace the interior are just as splendid. Local history is equally fascinating; whale-watching provides an exhilarating experience of the natural world; cycling trails lace the landscape; shops purvey everything from antiques to pure kitsch; and you can dine on simple fresh seafood, creative contemporary cuisine, or most anything in between.

Separated from the Massachusetts mainland by the 17½-mi Cape Cod Canal—at 480 feet the world's widest sea-level canal—and linked to it by two heavily trafficked bridges, the Cape is always likened in shape to an outstretched arm bent at the elbow, its Provincetown fist turned back toward the mainland. A bodybuilder "showing off his bulging bicep" is how one writer aptly described it.

Each of the Cape's 15 towns is broken up into villages, which is where things can get complicated. The town of Barnstable, for example, consists of Barnstable, West Barnstable, Cotuit, Marstons Mills, Osterville, Centerville, and Hyannis. The terms Upper Cape and Lower Cape can also be confusing. **Upper Cape**—think upper arm, as in the shape of the Cape—refers to the towns of Bourne, Falmouth, Mashpee, and Sandwich. **Mid Cape** includes Barnstable, Yarmouth, and Dennis. Brewster,

Harwich, Chatham, Orleans, Eastham, Wellfleet, Truro, and Province-town make up the **Lower Cape.**

Three major roads traverse the Cape. U.S. 6 is the fastest way to get from the mainland to Orleans. Route 6A winds along the North Shore through scenic towns; Route 28 dips south through some of the overdeveloped parts of the Cape. If you want to avoid malls, heavy traffic, and tacky motels, avoid Route 28 from Falmouth to Chatham. Past Orleans on the way out to Provincetown, the roadside clutter of much of U.S. 6 masks the beauty of what surrounds it.

Sandwich

★ ❶ *3 mi east of the Sagamore Bridge, 11 mi west of Barnstable.*

The oldest town on Cape Cod, Sandwich was established in 1637 by some of the Plymouth Pilgrims and incorporated in 1638. Today it is a well-preserved, quintessential New England village with a white-columned town hall and streets lined with 18th- and 19th-century houses.

From 1825 until 1888, the main industry in Sandwich was the production of vividly colored glass, made in the Boston and Sandwich Glass Company's factory. The **Sandwich Glass Museum** contains relics of the town's early history, a diorama of the factory in its heyday, and displays of shimmering blown and pressed glass. Glassmaking demonstrations are held in summer, and a gift shop sells attractive glass pieces. ⊠ *129 Main St.* ☎ *508/888–0251* ⊕ *www.sandwichglassmuseum.org* 🏷 *$4.50* ☾ *Apr.–Dec., daily 9:30–5; Feb. and Mar., Wed.–Sun. 9:30–4.*

Heritage Museums and Gardens is an impressive complex of museum buildings with specialty collections ranging from cars to toys. In 1967 pharmaceuticals magnate Josiah K. Lilly III purchased the estate and turned it into a nonprofit museum. A highlight is the Shaker Round Barn, which showcases classic and historic cars—including a 1930 yellow-and-green Duesenberg built for Gary Cooper, a 1919 Pierce-Arrow, and a 1911 Stanley Steamer—as well as art exhibitions. The American History museum has antique firearms, a collection of 2,000 hand-painted miniature soldiers, military uniforms, and Native American arts. The art museum has an extensive Currier & Ives collection, Americana (including a mechanical-bank collection), antique toys such as a 1920 Hubley Royal Circus, and a working 1912 Coney Island–style carousel that both adults and little ones can ride as often as they like. Paths crisscross the grounds, which include gardens planted with daylily, hosta, heather, herbs, and fruit trees. ⊠ *67 Grove St.* ☎ *508/888–3300* ⊕ *www. heritagemuseumsandgardens.org* 🏷 *$12* ☾ *May–Oct., Mon., Tues., and Thurs.–Sat. 9–6, Wed. 9–8, Sun. noon–6; Nov.–Apr., Wed.–Sat. 10–4, Sun. noon–4.*

FodorśChoice ★

The **Sandwich Boardwalk,** built over a salt marsh, a creek, and low dunes, leads to Town Neck Beach. Cape Cod Bay stretches out around the beach at the end of the walk, where a platform provides fine views, especially at sunset. From town cross Route 6A on Jarves Street, and at its end turn left, then right, and continue to the boardwalk parking lot.

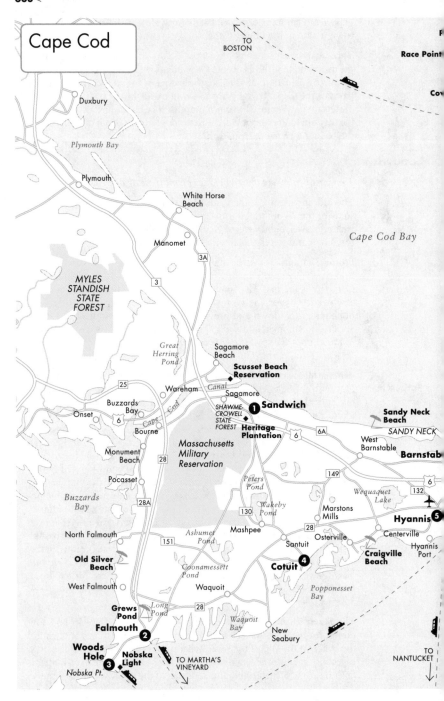

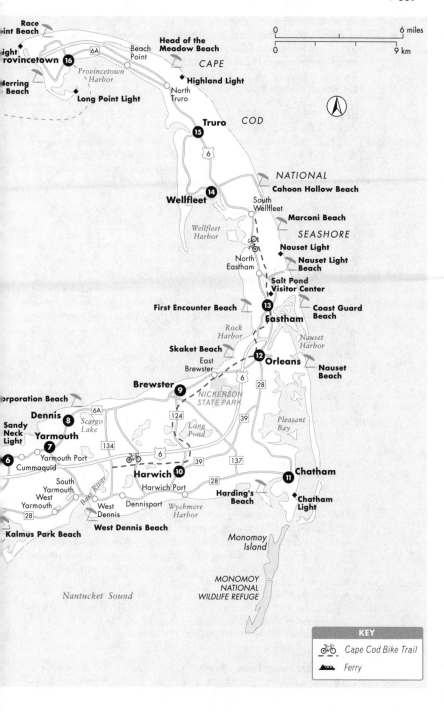

Race Point Beach

ight
Provincetown 16

6A

Beach Point

Head of the Meadow Beach

CAPE

Provincetown Harbor

North Truro

Highland Light

Herring Beach

Long Point Light

Truro 15

COD

6

NATIONAL

Cahoon Hollow Beach

Wellfleet 14

South Wellfleet

Marconi Beach

Wellfleet Harbor

SEASHORE

Nauset Light

North Eastham

Nauset Light Beach

Salt Pond Visitor Center

First Encounter Beach

Eastham 13

Coast Guard Beach

Rock Harbor

Nauset Harbor

Skaket Beach

East Brewster

Orleans 12

Nauset Beach

6

28

Brewster 9

NICKERSON STATE PARK

orporation Beach

6A

Dennis 8

Scargo Lake

124

Long Pond

39

Pleasant Bay

Sandy Neck Light

Yarmouth 7

134

6

Chatham 11

6

Yarmouth Port

39

137

Chatham Light

Cummaquid

Harwich 10

28

South Yarmouth

Harwich Port

Harding's Beach

West Yarmouth

Dennisport

West Dennis

Wychmere Harbor

28

Kalmus Park Beach

West Dennis Beach

Bass River

Monomoy Island

Nantucket Sound

MONOMOY NATIONAL WILDLIFE REFUGE

0   6 miles

0   9 km

KEY	
🚲	Cape Cod Bike Trail
⛴	Ferry

Where to Stay & Eat

★ **$–$$** ✕ **Aqua Grille.** At this smart-casual bistro by the marina, offerings range from Cape basics (clam chowder, fried seafood, boiled lobsters) to more creative contemporary fare. The excellent lobster salad, for example, is a hearty serving of greens, tomatoes, avocados, baby green beans, and big, meaty lobster chunks. Sandwiches (salmon burgers, turkey wraps), grilled seafood, pastas, and steaks are also available. ⊠ *14 Gallo Rd., 02563* ☎ *508/888–8889* ⊕ *www.aquagrille.com* ⊟ *AE, DC, MC, V* ☺ *Closed late Oct.–Mar.*

$$–$$$$ ✕▥ **Dan'l Webster Inn.** Built on the site of a 17th-century inn, the Dan'l Webster is a modern hotel with old New England friendliness. Guest rooms have fine reproduction mahogany and cherry furnishings. Contemporary dishes, such as Tuscan shrimp with white beans or horseradish-crusted salmon, take their places beside veal Oscar, broiled scrod, and other classics ($$). A casual tavern serves pizzas, burgers, and salads. ⊠ *149 Main St., 02563* ☎ *508/888–3622 or 800/444–3566* ▤ *508/888–5156* ⊕ *www.danlwebsterinn.com* ⇱ *45 rooms, 9 suites* ☼ *2 restaurants, room service, some in-room hot tubs, cable TV, pool, no-smoking rooms* ⊟ *AE, D, DC, MC, V.*

$–$$$ ✕▥ **Belfry Inne & Bistro.** This one-of-a-kind inn consists of a 1902 former church, the Abbey; a rectory of 1879, an authentic Victorian "painted lady"; and an 1830 Federal-style house, plus a fourth building—a 1638 former parish house, the oldest standing structure in Sandwich—just a short walk down the road. Room themes in each building nod to their respective histories. The luxurious rooms in the Abbey, named for the six days of creation, have whirlpool tubs and gas fireplaces, and are set along a corridor overlooking the restaurant below. The Bistro ($$–$$$), in the Abbey, serves creative interpretations of popular foods in a striking setting—look up at the church's original arches and stained glass as you dine. The Painted Lady Café ($–$$) serves light fare 11–9 PM, except Sunday and Monday. ⊠ *8 Jarves St., 02563* ☎ *508/888–8550 or 800/844–4542* ▤ *508/888–3922* ⊕ *www.belfryinn.com* ⇱ *28 rooms* ☼ *2 restaurants, some in-room hot tubs, bar; no kids under 10* ⊟ *AE, D, DC, MC, V* ☺ *No dinner Sun. and Mon., no lunch* ⍾ *CP.*

★ **$$–$$$** ▥ **Wingscorton Farm.** This is perhaps the Upper Cape's best-kept secret: an enchanting working farm with chickens, goats, horses, and other animals. Built in 1763, the main house, once a stop on the Underground Railroad, has a dining room with a fireplace with a 9-foot-long hearth, as well as two suites, each with a fireplace, wide-plank floors, and a smaller adjoining bedroom with twin beds. The property also includes a detached cottage with a kitchen, rented by the week in season. A stone carriage house has a fully equipped kitchen, a living room with a pullout sofa, and a wood-burning stove. ⊠ *11 Wing Blvd., off Rte. 6A, about 4½ mi east of Sandwich Center, East Sandwich 02537* ☎ *508/888–0534* ▤ *508/888–0545* ⇱ *2 suites, 1 carriage house, 1 2-bedroom cottage* ☼ *Dining room, some kitchens, refrigerators, beach, library, pets allowed (fee); no room phones* ⊟ *AE, MC, V* ⍾ *BP.*

Nightlife

Atmospheric **Bobby Byrne's Pub** (⊠ 65 Rte. 6A ☎ 508/888–6088) is a relaxing, convivial place to stop for a drink. The **British Beer Com-**

pany (✉ 46 Rte. 6A ☎ 508/833–9590) has a traditional "public house" atmosphere.

Shopping

Fodor'sChoice
★ The **Giving Tree** (✉ 550 Rte. 6A, East Sandwich ☎ 508/888–5446 or 888/246–3551 ⊕ www.givingtreegallery.com), an art gallery and sculpture garden, sells contemporary crafts, jewelry, ceramics, and prints. It has walking paths through a peaceful bamboo grove, along the marsh, and over a narrow wooden suspension bridge. **Titcomb's Bookshop** (✉ 432 Rte. 6A, East Sandwich ☎ 508/888–2331) stocks used, rare, and new books, including a large collection of Cape and nautical titles and Americana, as well as an extensive selection of children's books.

Falmouth

② *15 mi south of the Bourne Bridge, 4 mi north of Woods Hole.*

Falmouth, the Cape's second-largest town after Barnstable, was settled in 1660. Although much of Falmouth is suburban, with a large year-round population, the town center still includes sights from earlier times.

Between Falmouth and Cotuit, the **Waquoit Bay National Estuarine Research Reserve** encompasses 2,500 acres of estuary and barrier beach around the bay, making it a good birding site. Flat Pond Trail runs through several different habitats, including fresh- and saltwater marshes. ✉ *Rte. 28, 3 mi west of Mashpee rotary, Waquoit* ☎ *508/457–0495* ⊕ *www.waquoitbayreserve.org* ☉ *Exhibit center late June–early Sept., Mon.–Sat. 10–4; late May–late June, weekdays 10–4.*

Where to Stay & Eat

$–$$$
Fodor'sChoice
★ ✗ **La Cucina Sul Mare.** Northern Italian cooking is the specialty at this classy and popular place. The staff is friendly and the setting is both intimate and festive, if a bit crowded. Calamari, bruschetta, rigatoni à la vodka, and a variety of specials—including plenty of local fresh fish—adorn the menu. The *zuppa di pesce,* a medley of seafood sautéed in olive oil and garlic and finished in a white wine herb-and-tomato broth, is a specialty of the house. ✉ *237 Main St.* ☎ *508/548–5600* ▤ *AE, D, MC, V.*

$$–$$$ ✗▥ **Coonamessett Inn.** At this delightful old-Cape-style inn-restaurant, five buildings of one- or two-bedroom suites ring a landscaped lawn that leads to a scenic wooded pond. Rooms are casually decorated, with bleached wood or pine paneling and New England antiques or reproductions. A large collection of Cape artist Ralph Cahoon's work appears throughout the inn. In the main dining room ($$–$$$$), a few contemporary flourishes enhance the traditional menu; you can still find rack of lamb and baked-stuffed lobster, but you might also see cumin-scented scallops. ✉ *311 Gifford St., at Jones Rd., 02540* ☎ *508/548–2300* ⊕ *www.capecodrestaurants.org/coonamessett* ⇗ *28 suites, 1 cottage* ☖ *Restaurant, cable TV, bar* ▤ *AE, D, MC, V* ▢ *CP.*

★ $$$ ▥ **Mostly Hall B & B.** With its deep, landscaped yard and wrought-iron fence, this elegant inn with a wraparound porch resembles a private estate. (The house got its name when a young guest is said to have exclaimed, "Look! It's mostly hall!") The imposing 1849 Italianate house has an upscale European style with painted wall murals in several bedrooms; the Tuscan Room's walls suggest an intimate Tuscan garden. Three of the rooms are more traditionally decorated, with canopy beds and antiques. Breakfast is served in the formal parlor or outside on the veranda. ⊠ *27 Main St. (Rte. 28), 02540* ☎ *508/548–3786 or 800/682–0565* ⊠ *508/548–5778* ⊕ *www.mostlyhall.com* ⇨ *6 rooms* ♿ *Bicycles, library; no kids under 16* ⊟ *AE, D, MC, V* ☯ *Closed mid-Dec.–mid-Apr.* ⧆ *BP.*

Nightlife & the Arts

The **Nimrod Inn** (⊠ 100 Dillingham Ave. ☎ 508/540–4132) presents jazz and contemporary music at least six nights a week.

Sports & the Outdoors

BEACHES **Old Silver Beach,** a long crescent of white sand, is especially good for small children because a sandbar keeps it shallow at one end and creates tidal pools full of crabs and minnows. There are lifeguards, restrooms, showers, and a snack bar. ⊠ *Off Quaker Rd., North Falmouth* ⊞ *Parking $10 in summer.*

BIKING The **Shining Sea Trail** is an easy 3½-mi route between Locust Street in Falmouth and the Woods Hole ferry parking lot.

FISHING Freshwater ponds are good for perch, pickerel, trout, and more; you can obtain the required license (along with rental gear) at tackle shops, such as **Eastman's Sport & Tackle** (⊠ 150 Main St. [Rte. 28] ☎ 508/548–6900).

SHOPPING **Bean & Cod** (⊠ 140 Main St. [Rte. 28] ☎ 508/548–8840 or 800/558–8840 ⊕ www.beanandcod.com), a specialty food shop, sells cheeses, breads, and picnic fixings, along with pastas, coffees and teas, and unusual condiments.

Woods Hole

❸ *4 mi southwest of Falmouth, 19 mi south of the Bourne Bridge.*

Woods Hole is home to several major scientific institutions: the Woods Hole Oceanographic Institution, the Marine Biological Laboratory, the National Marine Fisheries Service, and the U.S. Geological Survey's Branch of Marine Geology. The town is also the departure point for ferries to Martha's Vineyard.

Scientific forces join together at the **Marine Biological Laboratory–Woods Hole Oceanographic Institution Library,** one of the best collections of biological, ecological, and oceanographic literature in the world. Unless you are a scientific researcher, the only way you can get to see the library is by taking a one-hour tour (mid-June–August, weekdays at 1, 2, and 3), led by retired scientists. You'll see the Marine Resources Center (where living sea creatures collected each day are kept), and one of the many working research labs. ⊠ *7 Marine Biological Laboratory St., off Water St.* ☎ *508/289–7623 for tour information* ⊕ *www.mbl.edu.*

The **National Marine Fisheries Service Aquarium** displays 16 tanks of regional fish and shellfish. Magnifying glasses and a dissecting scope help you examine marine life, and several hands-on pools hold banded lobsters, crabs, snails, starfish, and other creatures. The top attraction is two harbor seals, on view in the outdoor pool near the entrance in summer; you can watch their feedings daily at 11 and 4. ⊠ *Corner of Albatross and Water Sts.* ☎ *508/495–2267, 508/495–2001 recorded information* ⊕ *www.nefsc.nmfs.gov/nefsc/aquarium* ☒ *Free, donations accepted* ☉ *Call for hrs.*

Impressive **Nobska Light** (⊠ Church St.) has spectacular views from its base of the nearby Elizabeth Islands and of Martha's Vineyard, across Vineyard Sound.

Where to Eat

★ **$-$$** ✕ **Fishmonger's Café.** The seafood-centered menu at this top Woods Hole choice is ambitious, particularly the inventive daily specials. The hearty bruschetta with ricotta, basil, and olives is a treat, and many grilled seafood dishes come with tropical fruit glazes, such as a mango and cilantro sauce over grilled salmon. Vegetarians have lots of options here, too. The main dining room overlooks the water, and there's a handsome wood bar. ⊠ *56 Water St.* ☎ *508/540–5376* ⚱ *Reservations not accepted* ▤ *AE, MC, V* ☉ *Closed mid-Dec.–mid-Feb. and Tues. early Sept.–Mar.*

Cotuit

④ *16 mi northeast of Woods Hole.*

Once called Cotuit Port, this charming little town was formed around seven homesteads belonging to the family of 18th-century trader Winslow Crocker. Its center is not much more than a crossroads with a post office, old-time coffee shop, local pizza parlor, and general store.

The **Cahoon Museum of American Art** is in one of the old Crocker family buildings, a 1775 Georgian Colonial farmhouse that was once a tavern and an overnight way station for travelers on the Hyannis–Sandwich stagecoach line. Displays include selections from the permanent collection of American primitive paintings by Ralph and Martha Cahoon, along with works by other 19th- and early-20th-century artists. ⊠ *4676 Falmouth Rd. (Rte. 28)* ☎ *508/428–7581* ⊕ *www.cahoonmuseum.org* ☒ *$3* ☉ *Feb.–Dec., Tues.–Sat. 10–4.*

Where to Stay & Eat

$$$-$$$$ ✕ **Regatta of Cotuit.** This restaurant is in a restored Colonial stagecoach inn filled with wood, brass, and Oriental carpets. The classic yet original fare includes pâtés of rabbit, veal, and venison and a seared loin of lamb with cabernet sauce, surrounded by chèvre, spinach, and pine nuts. Chef Heather Allen's signature premium fillet of buffalo tenderloin is prepared differently each night, with seasonal starches and vegetables. ⊠ *4631 Falmouth Rd. (Rte. 28)* ☎ *508/428–5715* ⊕ *www.regattaofcotuit.com* ⚱ *Reservations essential* ▤ *AE, MC, V.*

$ ▦ **Josiah Sampson House.** Guest rooms in this 1793 Federal-style home have canopy beds, needlepoint rugs, antiques, and air-conditioning.

Hannah's Room, the most spacious, has a queen-size four-poster bed, built-in window seats, and a massive working fireplace. Upstairs, the Sampson Room has an extra-large bathroom and a view of the backyard. ⊠ *40 Old Kings Rd., off Main St.* ⬦ *Box 226, 02635* ☎ *508/428–8383 or 877/574–6873* 🖷 *508/428–0116* ⊕ *www.josiahsampson.com* ⇄ *6 rooms, 1 suite* ♨ *Outdoor hot tub, bicycles; no room phones, no room TVs, no kids under 10* ▭ *AE, MC, V* ¶◎ *BP.*

Shopping

The **Sow's Ear Antique Company** (⊠ 4698 Rte. 28 ☎ 508/428–4931), in a house that dates from the late 1600s next to the Cahoon Museum, specializes in folk art—dolls, ship's models, wood carvings, antique quilts, and paintings.

Hyannis

❺ *11 mi northeast of Cotuit, 23 mi east of the Bourne Bridge.*

Perhaps best known for its association with the Kennedy clan, the Hyannis area was also a vacation site for Ulysses S. Grant and Grover Cleveland. A bustling year-round hub of activity, Hyannis has the Cape's largest concentration of businesses, shops, malls, hotels and motels, restaurants, and entertainment venues.

The enlarged and annotated photographs at the **John F. Kennedy Hyannis Museum** document JFK's Cape years (1934–63). ⊠ *397 Main St., Downtown Hyannis* ☎ *508/790–3077* ⬱ *$5* ◔ *Mid-Apr.–Oct., Mon.–Sat. 9–5, Sun. and holidays noon–5; Nov.–early Dec. and mid-Feb.–mid-Apr., Thurs.–Sat. 10–4, Sun. and holidays noon–4.*

Where to Stay & Eat

$$–$$$$ ✕ **The Paddock.** The Paddock is synonymous with excellent formal din-
Fodor'sChoice ing on the Cape. Its authentic Victorian style includes sumptuous up-
★ holstery in the main dining room and old-style wicker on the breezy summer porch. The menu is traditional yet deceptively innovative, combining fresh ingredients in novel ways. Pistachio-crusted halibut with citrus beurre blanc is but one example. The steak au poivre, with several varieties of crushed peppercorns, is masterful. ⊠ *W. Main St. rotary, next to Melody Tent* ☎ *508/775–7677* ⊕ *www.paddockcapecod.com* ▭ *AE, DC, MC, V* ◔ *Closed mid-Nov.–Mar.*

$$–$$$$ ✕ **Roadhouse Café.** Candlelight flickers off the white-linen tablecloths and dark-wood wainscoting at this smart choice for a night out. Popular dishes include the pepper-and-goat-cheese appetizer and shrimp and basil pesto over linguine. In the more casual bistro and the mahogany bar, you can order from a separate menu, which includes thin-crust pizza as well as burgers and lighter fare. On Monday night year-round in the bistro is excellent straight-ahead jazz. ⊠ *488 South St., Downtown Hyannis* ☎ *508/775–2386* ⊕ *www.roadhousecafe.com* ⚏ *Reservations essential* ▭ *AE, D, MC, V* ◔ *No lunch.*

$–$$$ ✕ **Baxter's Fish N' Chips.** Since fried seafood is a Cape staple, you may want to pay homage to one of the best Fry-o-lators around. Right on Hyannis Harbor, it's been a favorite of boaters and bathers alike since 1955. Generous portions of fried clams are delicious and cooked hot to order. The picnic tables outside, some set up on an old floating ferry, allow you to lose no time in the sun while eating lobster, fish-and-chips, or something from the raw bar. If the weather's not on your side, there's indoor seating overlooking the harbor. ⊠ *Pleasant St., Hyannis Harbor* ☎ *508/775–4490* ⊕ *www.baxtersboathouse.com* ⌂ *Reservations not accepted* ▭ *AE, DC, MC, V* ✆ *Closed mid-Oct.–Apr. and weekdays early Sept.–mid-Oct.*

$–$$ ▣ **Breakwaters.** If these weathered-gray-shingle cottages were any closer to Nantucket Sound, they'd be in it. These privately owned condos rent by the week (or day if vacancies occur); divided into one-, two-, and three-bedroom units, the cottages offer all the comforts of home. Each unit has one or two full baths; kitchens with microwave, coffeemaker, refrigerator, toaster, and stove; TV and phone (local calls are free); and a deck or patio with grill and picnic table. ⊠ *432 Sea St.* ⌂ *Box 118, 02601* ☎☎ *508/775–6831* ⊕ *www.capecod.com/breakwaters* ⌁ *19 cottages* ⌂ *Kitchens, microwaves, refrigerators, cable TV, pool, beach, babysitting; no a/c* ▭ *No credit cards* ✆ *Closed mid-Oct.–Apr.*

★ $ ▣ **Sea Breeze Inn.** Each room in this comfortable cedar-shingle B&B two blocks from the beach has antique or canopied beds and is simply decorated with quilts or floral comforters and well-chosen antiques. There's also an efficiency unit with a stove and refrigerator. Breakfast is served in the dining room or in the outdoor gazebo, surrounded by winsome gardens. ⊠ *270 Ocean Ave., at Sea St., 02601* ☎ *508/771–7213* ▤ *508/862–0663* ⊕ *www.seabreezeinn.com* ⌁ *13 rooms, 1 efficiency* ⌂ *Kitchenette, refrigerator, cable TV* ▭ *AE, D, MC, V* ⦶◯⦶ *CP.*

Nightlife & the Arts

In 1950 the actress Gertrude Lawrence opened the **Cape Cod Melody Tent** (⊠ 21 W. Main St., at Old West End rotary, West End ☎ 508/775–5630, 800/347–0808 for tickets ⊕ www.melodytent.com) to showcase Broadway musicals. Today it's the Cape's top venue for performers such as Aretha Franklin, the Doobie Brothers, Tom Jones, Ziggy Marley, and Crosby, Stills & Nash.

The **Island Merchant** (⊠ 10 Ocean St., Downtown Hyannis ☎ 508/771–1337), a restaurant and lounge, serves comfort food with an island twist and showcases up-and-coming New England bands and musicians. The lineup includes acoustic, blues, bluegrass, jazz, rock, reggae, and Latin.

Sports & the Outdoors

Kalmus Park Beach is a wide beach with a section for windsurfers and a sheltered area for children. It has a snack bar, restrooms, showers, and lifeguards. ⊠ *South end of Ocean St.* ⛫ *Parking $10* ✆ *Memorial Day–Labor Day.*

Barnstable

❻ *4 mi north of Hyannis, 11 mi east of Sandwich.*

With nearly 50,000 year-round residents, Barnstable is the largest town on the Cape. It's also the second oldest—it was founded in 1639, two years after Sandwich. You can get a feeling for its age in Barnstable Village, on and near Main Street (Route 6A), a lovely area of large old homes.

The county courthouse, built in 1772, is the home of **Tales of Cape Cod** (⊠ 3018 Main St. [Rte. 6A] ☎ 508/362–8927), a historical society.

Where to Stay

$$–$$$ ⌂ **Honeysuckle Hill.** Innkeepers Mary and Bill Kilburn ran an inn in Vermont before relocating to the Cape, and their experience and graciousness shine through in lots of little touches: a guest fridge stocked with sodas and water bottles, beach chairs with umbrellas (perfect for nearby Sandy Neck Beach), and an always-full cookie jar. The airy, country-style guest rooms in this 1810 Queen Anne–style cottage have lots of white wicker, featherbeds, checked curtains, and pastel-painted floors. The spacious second-floor Wisteria Room overlooking the lush yard is a particularly comfortable retreat, and the screened-in porch is a peaceful place for early-morning coffee. ⊠ *591 Rte. 6A, West Barnstable 02668* ☎ *508/362–8418 or 866/444–5522* 🖷 *508/362–8386* ⊕ *www.honeysucklehill.com* ⊰ *4 rooms, 1 suite* ⚴ *No room phones, no TV in some rooms, no kids under 12* ☰ *AE, D, MC, V* ⎸⊙⎸ *BP.*

★ **$$** ⌂ **Beechwood Inn.** Debbie and Ken Traugot's yellow and pale green 1853 Queen Anne house has gingerbread trim and is wrapped by a wide porch with wicker furniture and a glider swing. Although the parlor is pure mahogany-and-red-velvet Victorian, guest rooms (all with queen- or king-size beds) have antiques in lighter Victorian styles; several have fireplaces, and one has a bay view. Bathrooms have pedestal sinks and antique lighting fixtures. ⊠ *2839 Main St. (Rte. 6A), 02630* ☎ *508/362–6618 or 800/609–6618* 🖷 *508/362–0298* ⊕ *www.beechwoodinn.com* ⊰ *6 rooms* ⚴ *Dining room, refrigerators, bicycles; no room phones, no TV in some rooms, no kids under 12* ☰ *AE, D, MC, V* ⎸⊙⎸ *BP.*

Sports & the Outdoors

Hovering above Barnstable Harbor and the 4,000-acre Great Salt Marsh, **Sandy Neck Beach** stretches 6 mi across a peninsula that ends at Sandy Neck Light. The beach is one of the Cape's most beautiful—dunes, sand, and sea spread east, west, and north. The lighthouse, a few feet from the eroding shoreline at the tip of the neck, has been out of commission since 1952. The main beach at Sandy Neck has lifeguards, a snack bar, restrooms, and showers. ⊠ *Sandy Neck Rd., West Barnstable* 🅿 *Parking $10 late May–early Sept.* ☉ *Daily 8 AM–9 PM, but staffed only until 5 PM.*

Yarmouth & Yarmouth Port

❼ *4 mi east of Barnstable, 21 mi east of the Sagamore Bridge.*

Yarmouth was settled in 1639 by farmers from the Plymouth Bay Colony. By 1829, when Yarmouth Port was incorporated as a separate village, the Cape had begun a thriving maritime industry. Many impressive sea captains' houses—some now B&Bs and museums—still line the streets, and Yarmouth Port has some real old-time stores.

🅲 Visit the **Edward Gorey House Museum** to explore the eccentric illustrations and offbeat humor of the late acclaimed artist in his home. The exhibitions, including displays of his drawings and rantings of oddball characters, reveal the mysterious psyche of the sometimes dark but always playful Gorey. ⊠ *8 Strawberry La.* ☎ *508/362–3909* ⊕ *www. edwardgoreyhouse.org* 🖻 *$5* ⊙ *May–Sept., Wed.–Sat. 10–5, Sun. noon–5; Oct.–Apr., Thurs.–Sat. 11–4, Sun. noon–4.*

★ ᕀ One of Yarmouth Port's most beautiful spots is Bass Hole, which stretches from Homer's Dock Road to the salt marsh. **Bass Hole Boardwalk** extends over a marshy creek. The 2½-mi **Callery-Darling nature trails** meander through salt marshes, vegetated wetlands, and upland woods. Gray's Beach is a little crescent of sand with calm waters. ⊠ *Trail entrance on Center St. near Gray's Beach parking lot.*

Where to Stay & Eat

$$–$$$ ✕ **Inaho.** Yuji Watanabe, the chef-owner of the Cape's best Japanese restaurant, makes early-morning journeys to Boston's fish markets to shop for the freshest local catch. His selection of sushi and sashimi is vast and artful, and vegetable and seafood tempura come out of the kitchen fluffy and light. If you're a teriyaki lover, you can't do any better than the chicken. One remarkable element of the restaurant is its artful lighting: small pinpoint lights on the food accentuate the presentation in a dramatic way. ⊠ *157 Main St. (Rte. 6A)* ☎ *508/362–5522* ⊟ *MC, V* ⊙ *Closed Sun. No lunch.*

FodorśChoice
★

$$–$$$ ✕ **Old Yarmouth Inn Restaurant & Tavern.** Established in 1696, this inn— the oldest on Cape Cod—now primarily functions as a restaurant (rooms are available in season). The restaurant comprises a main dining room, which is bright and airy, and two smaller and more intimate ones, plus the wood-paneled Tavern, which has a full bar and serves more casual fare. ⊠ *223 Rte. 6A* ☎ *508/362–9962* ⊕ *www.oldyarmouthinn.com* ⊟ *AE, D, MC, V* ⊙ *Closed Mon. Jan.–May.*

$–$$ 🏨 **Blueberry Manor.** The living room of this 19th-century Greek-revival pairs Victorian furnishings with modern amenities, including a TV-VCR, a stereo, and a stash of puzzles, games, and books. Guest-room furnishings are traditional, but there are no fussy lace treatments or curio shelves. The Lavender Room has a queen-size four-poster bed with a handmade quilt, an antique armoire, and a modern bath under the eaves. The Rose Room has an exquisitely painted queen-size bed and cheery pink walls. The Willow Garden Suite, with a loft and fireplace, accommodates up to four and is suitable for a family. ⊠ *438 Main St. (Rte. 6A), 02675* ☎ *508/362–7620* 🖨 *508/362–0053* ⊕ *www. blueberrymanor.com* 🛏 *3 rooms, 1 suite* ᕀ *No smoking* ⊟ *AE, MC, V* ⊙|⊙ *BP.*

Nightlife & the Arts
Oliver's (⊠ 6 Bray Farm Rd., off Rte. 6A ☎ 508/362–6062) has live music in a variety of genres in its tavern on weekends.

Shopping
Parnassus Book Service (⊠ 220 Main St. [Rte. 6A] ☎ 508/362–6420), in an 1840 building, formerly a general store, specializes in Cape Cod, maritime, and antiquarian books. **Peach Tree Designs** (⊠ 173 Main St. [Rte. 6A] ☎ 508/362–8317) carries home furnishings and accessories made by local craftspeople.

Dennis

8 *4 mi northeast of Yarmouth, 7 mi west of Brewster.*

The backstreets of Dennis still retain the Colonial charm of seafaring days. The town was named for the Reverend Josiah Dennis and incorporated in 1793. There were 379 sea captains living in Dennis when fishing, salt making, and shipbuilding were the main industries, and the elegant houses they constructed still line the streets.

The holdings of the **Cape Museum of Fine Arts** include more than 850 works by Cape-associated artists. Important pieces include a portrait of a fisherman's wife by Charles Hawthorne, the father of the Provincetown art colony. ⊠ *60 Hope La., on grounds of Cape Playhouse, off Rte. 6A* ☎ *508/385–4477* ⊕ *www.cmfa.org* ☜ *$7* ☉ *Late May–mid-Oct., Mon.–Sat. 10–5, Sun. noon–5; mid-Oct.–Jan. and early Apr.–late May, Tues.–Sat. 11–5, Sun. noon–5; Jan.–early Apr., Mon.–Sat. 10–4, Sun. noon–4.*

Where to Stay & Eat

$$–$$$ ✕ **Red Pheasant.** This is one of the Cape's best cozy country inns, with a consistently good kitchen, where hearty American food is prepared with elaborate sauces and herb combinations. For instance, rack of lamb is served with an intense port-and-rosemary reduction, and exquisitely grilled veal chops come with a dense red wine and portobello mushroom sauce. In fall look for the specialty game dishes, including venison and quail. ⊠ *905 Main St. (Rte. 6A)* ☎ *508/385–2133 or 800/480–2133* ⊕ *www.redpheasantinn.com* ☖ *Reservations essential* ▭ *D, MC, V* ☉ *No lunch.*

★ $–$$ ✕ **Captain Frosty's.** A great stop after the beach, this is where locals go to get their fried seafood. The modest joint has a counter where you order and take a number written on a french fries box. The staff is young and hardworking, pumping out fresh fried clams and fish-and-chips on paper plates. There's seating inside as well as outside on a shady brick patio. ⊠ *219 Main St. (Rte. 6A)* ☎ *508/385–8548* ☖ *Reservations not accepted* ▭ *No credit cards* ☉ *Closed Oct.–Mar.*

★ $–$$ ▦ **Isaiah Hall B&B Inn.** Lilacs and pink roses trail along the white picket fence outside this historic 1857 Greek-revival farmhouse on a quiet residential road near the bay. Innkeepers Jerry and Judy Neal set the scene for a romantic getaway with guest rooms that have country antiques, floral-print wallpapers, and such homey touches as quilts and Priscilla curtains. In the attached carriage house, rooms have three walls stenciled white and one paneled in knotty pine, and some have small balconies overlooking a wooded lawn with gardens, grape arbors, and berry bushes. ⊠ *152 Whig St.* ⌖ *Box 1007, 02638* ☎ *508/385–9928 or 800/736–0160* ⊟ *508/385–5879* ⊕ *www.isaiahhallinn.com* ⤻ *9 rooms, 1 suite* ♻ *Picnic area, in-room VCRs, Wi-Fi, badminton, croquet; no kids under 7* ▭ *AE, D, MC, V* ¹◎¹ *BP.*

Nightlife & the Arts

The oldest professional summer theater in the country is the **Cape Playhouse** (⊠ 820 Main St. [Rte. 6A] ☎ 508/385–3911 or 877/385–3911 ⊕ www.capeplayhouse.com), which produces Broadway-style plays as well as children's shows.

Sports & the Outdoors

BEACHES Parking at Dennis beaches is $10 per day for nonresidents from Memorial Day to Labor Day. Dennis's **Corporation Beach** (⊠ Corporation Rd.) on Cape Cod Bay is a beautiful crescent of white sand backed by low dunes; there are lifeguards, showers, restrooms, and a food stand. On the South Shore, one of the best beaches is the long, wide **West Dennis Beach** (⊠ Davis Beach Rd., West Dennis), which has bathhouses, lifeguards, a playground, and food concessions.

Brewster

❾ *7 mi northeast of Dennis, 5 mi west of Orleans.*

Brewster is the perfect place to learn about the natural history of the Cape: the area contains conservation lands, state parks, forests, freshwater ponds, and marshes. When the tide is low in Cape Cod Bay, you can stroll the beaches and explore tidal pools up to 2 mi from the shore on the Brewster flats.

★ ☉ For nature enthusiasts, a visit to the **Cape Cod Museum of Natural History** is a must. The museum and grounds include guided field walks, a shop, a natural-history library, lectures, classes, nature and marine exhibits such as a working beehive, and a pond- and sea-life room with live specimens. Walking trails wind through 80 acres of forest, marshland, and ponds, all rich in birds and other wildlife. ⊠ *869 Main St. (Rte. 6A)* ☎ *508/896–3867, 800/479–3867 in Massachusetts* ⊕ *www.ccmnh.org* ⊡ *$8* ☉ *June–Sept., daily 10–4; Apr. and May, Wed.–Sun. 10–4; Oct.–Dec., weekends 10–4.*

The **Brewster Store** (⊠ 1935 Main St. [Rte. 6A] ☎ 508/896–3744 ⊕ www.brewsterstore.com) is a local landmark. Built in 1852, this typical New England general store provides such essentials as the daily papers, penny candy, and benches out front for conversation.

The 1,961 acres of **Nickerson State Park** were once part of a vast estate belonging to Roland C. Nickerson. Roland and his wife, Addie, lavishly entertained such visitors as President Grover Cleveland at their private beach and hunting lodge in English country-house style, with coachmen dressed in tails and top hats and a bugler announcing carriages entering the front gates. The park consists of acres of oak, pitch pine, hemlock, and spruce forest dotted with seven freshwater ponds. ⊠ *3488 Rte. 6A, East Brewster* ☎ *508/896–3491* ⊕ *www.mass.gov/dcr/parks/southeast/nick.htm* ⊡ *Free* ☉ *Daily dawn–dusk.*

Where to Stay & Eat

$$$$ ✕ **Chillingsworth.** Generally regarded as the crown jewel of Cape restaurants, Chillingsworth combines formal presentation with an excellent Fodor'sChoice French menu and a diverse wine cellar to create a memorable dining experience. Super-rich risotto, roast lobster, and grilled venison are favorites. Dinner in the main dining rooms is prix fixe only and though it may seem pricey at first glance, it includes appetizer, soup, salad, sorbet, entrée, and dessert, plus coffee or tea. À la carte dinners ($$–$$$$) plus lunch and Sunday brunch are served in the more casual, patio-style Bistro. Inquire about on-site guest rooms if you decide to extend your stay.

✉ *2449 Main St. (Rte. 6A), East Brewster* ☎ *508/896–3640* ⊕ *www. chillingsworth.com* 🖃 *AE, DC, MC, V* ⊙ *Closed late Nov.–late May; Mon. mid-June–late Nov.; and some weekdays late May–mid-June and mid-Oct.–late Nov.*

\$–\$\$\$ ✗ **Spark Fish.** "Spark" refers to a wood-fire grill, which the kitchen uses often. Owner Steven Parrott's menu emphasizes simple ingredients—fresh herbs, garlic, and fruit salsas—and lets the flavors of local seafood, quality meats, and good vegetables shine through without complicated sauces. The inside is as unfussy as the menu and, like the food, is more about elegant understatement than elaborate decoration. A full wine list is available. The canopy-covered outdoor deck is the place to be in warm weather. In the off-season, there's comfortable fireside dining. ✉ *2671 Rte. 6A, East Brewster* ☎ *508/896–1067* 🖃 *AE, MC, V* ⊙ *Closed Mon. and Tues. off-season.*

\$–\$\$ 🏨 **Old Sea Pines Inn.** With its white-columned portico and wraparound
Fodor'sChoice veranda overlooking a broad lawn, Old Sea Pines resembles a vintage
★ summer estate. Climb the sweeping staircase to guest rooms decorated with reproduction wallpaper, antiques, and framed old photographs. Some are quite large; others have fireplaces. One of the more popular rooms has a sitting area in an enclosed sunporch. Rooms in a newer building are simple with bright white modern baths and cast-iron queen-size beds. Some rooms have shared bathrooms. ✉ *2553 Main St. (Rte. 6A)* 📪 *Box 1070, 02631* ☎ *508/896–6114* 🖶 *508/896–7387* ⊕ *www.oldseapinesinn.com* 🛏 *24 rooms, 19 with bath; 3 suites; 2 family-size rooms* ⚎ *Restaurant, cable TV, meeting rooms; no a/c, no room phones, no TV in some rooms, no kids under 8* 🖃 *AE, D, DC, MC, V* ⊙ *Closed Dec.–Mar.* ⦿¶ *BP.*

Nightlife & the Arts

The **Cape Cod Repertory Theatre Co.** (✉ 3379 Main St. [Rte. 6A], West Brewster ☎ 508/896–1888) performs several impressive productions, from original works to classics, in its indoor Arts and Crafts–style theater way back in the woods. The season runs from May to November.

Sports & the Outdoors

BIKING The **Cape Cod Rail Trail** has many access points in Brewster, among them Long Pond Road, Underpass Road, and Nickerson State Park.

BOATING **Jack's Boat Rentals** (✉ Flax Pond, Nickerson State Park, Rte. 6A, East Brewster ☎ 508/896–8556) rents canoes, kayaks, Seacycles, Sunfish, pedal boats, and sailboards; guide-led kayak tours are also offered.

Shopping

Kemp Pottery (✉ 258 Main St. [Rte. 6A], West Brewster ☎ 508/385–5782) has functional and decorative stoneware and porcelain. **Kingsland Manor** (✉ 440 Main St. [Rte. 6A], West Brewster ☎ 508/385–9741) sells everything "from tin to Tiffany." The **Spectrum** (✉ 369 Main St. [Rte. 6A], West Brewster ☎ 508/385–3322) purveys American arts and crafts, including art glass and pottery. **Sydenstricker Galleries** (✉ 490 Main St. [Rte. 6A], West Brewster ☎ 508/385–3272) is a working glass studio.

Harwich

❿ *3 mi south of Brewster.*

Originally known as Setucket, Harwich separated from Brewster in 1694 and was renamed after the famous seaport in England. Like other townships on the Cape, Harwich is actually a cluster of seven small villages, including bustling Harwich Port. Three naturally sheltered harbors on Nantucket Sound make the town, like its English namesake, a popular spot for boaters.

The Cape's famous cranberry industry took off in Harwich in 1844. Each September Harwich holds a **Cranberry Festival** to celebrate the importance of this indigenous berry.

The pillared 1844 Greek-revival building that houses the Harwich Historical Society and its **Brooks Academy Museum** was once the home of a private school offering early courses in navigation. In addition to a large photo-history collection and exhibits on artist Charles Cahoon (grandson of cranberry grower Alvin), the sociotechnological history of cranberry culture, and shoe making, the museum has antique clothing and textiles, china and glass, fans, and toys. ⊠ *80 Parallel St.* ☎ *508/432–8089* 🖅 *Donations accepted* 🕙 *June–mid-Oct., Wed.–Sat. 1–4 or by appointment.*

Where to Eat

$–$$ ✕ **Brax Landing.** In this local stalwart perched alongside busy Saquatucket Harbor, you can get a menu tip-off as you pass by tanks full of steamers and lobsters in the corridor leading to the dining room. The restaurant sprawls around a big bar that serves specialty drinks like the Banzai (frozen piña colada with a float of dark rum). The swordfish and the Chatham scrod are favorites, both served simply and well. And if you've been after the ultimate lobster roll—and never thought you could get full on one—sample this one, bursting with the meat of a 1¼-pound lobster. ⊠ *Rte. 28 at Saquatucket Harbor, Harwich Port* ☎ *508/432–5515* 🕭 *Reservations not accepted* ▤ *AE, DC, MC, V.*

Sports & the Outdoors

Whether you're in the mood to sail under the moonlight, hire a private charter, or learn to navigate yourself, **Cape Sail** (⊠ 337 Saquatucket Harbor, off Rte. 28, Harwich Port ☎ 508/896–2730) can accommodate any whim.

Chatham

⓫ *5 mi east of Harwich.*

At the bent elbow of the Cape, Chatham has all the charm of a quiet seaside resort, with relatively little commercialism. And it *is* charming: gray-shingle houses with tidy awnings and cheerful flower gardens, an attractive Main Street with crafts and antiques stores alongside homey coffee shops, and a five-and-ten. It's well-to-do without being ostentatious, casual and fun but refined, and never tacky.

Built by sea captain Joseph C. Atwood in 1752, the **Atwood House Museum** has a gambrel roof, variable-width floor planks, fireplaces, and an old kitchen with a wide hearth and a beehive oven. ⊠ *347 Stage Harbor Rd., West Chatham* ☎ *508/945–2493* ⊕ *www.chathamhistoricalsociety. org* ⊠ *$5* ⊙ *Mid-June–Sept., Tues.–Sat. 1–4.*

★ The famous view from **Chatham Light** (⊠ Main St. near Bridge St.)—of the harbor, the offshore sandbars, and the ocean beyond—justifies the crowds that gather to share it.

★ **Monomoy National Wildlife Refuge** is a 2,500-acre preserve including the Monomoy Islands, a fragile 9-mi-long barrier-beach area south of Chatham. A haven for bird-watchers, the island is an important stop along the North Atlantic Flyway for migratory waterfowl and shore birds. The only structure on the islands is the South Monomoy Lighthouse, built in 1849.

Where to Stay & Eat

$$–$$$
Fodor'sChoice
★

✕ **Vining's Bistro.** An exceptionally inventive menu and a determination not to rest on its laurels make this restaurant a standout. The wood grill infuses many dishes with a distinctive flavor heightened further by the chef's use of zesty rubs and spices from all over the globe. The "Golden Triangle" mixes shrimp and chicken simmered in Madras and Indonesian curry. Spit-roasted Jamaican chicken competes with a portobello mushroom sandwich as the restaurant's signature dish. ⊠ *595 Main St.* ☎ *508/945–5033* ⊕ *www.viningsbistro.com* ⚲ *Reservations not accepted* ▤ *AE, D, MC, V* ⊙ *Closed mid-Jan.–Apr.*

$–$$$
✕ **Christian's.** French and New England influences are found at this landmark town restaurant. The menu includes grilled prime meats and fresh Cape Cod seafood. The mahogany-panel bar and upstairs sunroom serve a lighter menu that remains strong on seafood but adds some Mexican influences, such as tacos and quesadillas, that are well suited to summer. ⊠ *443 Main St.* ☎ *508/945–3362* 📠 *508/945–8049* ⊕ *www. christiansrestaurant.com* ▤ *DC, MC, V* ⊙ *Closed weekdays Jan.–Mar.*

$$$$
Fodor'sChoice
★

✕🏨 **Wequassett Inn Resort & Golf Club.** Twenty Cape-style cottages and an attractive hotel make up this traditionally elegant resort by the sea. Set on 22 acres of shaded landscape partially surrounded by Pleasant Bay, the Wequassett is an informally upscale resort. Chef Bill Brodsky's creative globally inspired cuisine graces the menus of the three restaurants (the sophisticated Atlantic 28, the elegant loungelike Thoreau's, and the open-air Outer Bar & Grill), as well as that of the Pool Bar & Grill, which serves cocktails, beverages, snacks, and light lunch fare poolside. ⊠ *173 Orleans Rd. (Rte. 28), Pleasant Bay 02633* ☎ *508/432–5400 or 800/225–7125* 📠 *508/432–5032* ⊕ *www.wequassett.com* 🛏 *102 rooms, 2 suites* ♧ *3 restaurants, snack bar, room service, 4 tennis courts, pool, gym, windsurfing, boating, piano bar* ▤ *AE, D, DC, MC, V* ⊙ *Closed Nov.–Mar.* ⦿ *FAP.*

★ $$–$$$$
🏨 **Queen Anne Inn.** Built in 1840 as a wedding present for the daughter of a famous clipper-ship captain, the building first opened as an inn in 1874. Some of the large guest rooms have working fireplaces, balconies, and hot tubs. Lingering and lounging are encouraged—around the large heated outdoor pool, at the tables on the veranda, in front of the fire-

place in the cozy sitting room, or in the plush parlor. ⊠ *70 Queen Anne Rd., 02633* ☎ *508/945–0394 or 800/545–4667* 🖷 *508/945–4884* ⊕ *www.queenanneinn.com* ➪ *31 rooms* ⌂ *Restaurant, some in-room hot tubs, cable TV, pool, bar, meeting rooms* ⊟ *AE, D, MC, V.*

Nightlife & the Arts

Chatham Squire (⊠ 487 Main St. ☎ 508/945–0945), with four bars including a raw bar, is a rollicking year-round local hangout, drawing a young crowd to the bars and a mixed crowd of locals to the restaurant.

Sports & the Outdoors

Harding's Beach (⊠ Harding's Beach Rd. off Barn Hill Rd., West Chatham), west of Chatham center, is open to the public and charges daily parking fees to nonresidents in season.

Shopping

Cape Cod Cooperage (⊠ 1150 Queen Anne Rd., at Rte. 137, West Chatham ☎ 508/432–0788) sells traditional wooden ware made by an on-site cooper. At **Chatham Glass Co.** (⊠ 758 Main St. ☎ 508/945–5547) you can watch glass being blown and buy it, too. **Marion's Pie Shop** (⊠ 2022 Main St. [Rte. 28], West Chatham ☎ 508/432–9439) sells fruit breads, pastries, prepared foods, and, of course, pies, both savory and sweet. **Yellow Umbrella Books** (⊠ 501 Main St. ☎ 508/945–0144) has an excellent selection of new and used books.

Orleans

⑫ *8 mi north of Chatham, 35 mi east of the Sagamore Bridge.*

Orleans has a long heritage in fishing and seafaring, and many beautifully preserved homes remain from the Colonial era. Much of this beauty is found in the small village of East Orleans. In other areas of town, such as down by Rock Harbor, more modestly grand homes stand near the water's edge.

A walk along Rock Harbor Road, a winding street lined with gray-shingle houses, white picket fences, and neat gardens, leads to the bay-side **Rock Harbor,** a former packet landing and site of a War of 1812 skirmish in which the Orleans militia kept a British warship from docking.

Where to Stay & Eat

★ **$$-$$$** ✕ **Nauset Beach Club.** Locals stand by this long-established eatery. The kitchen produces seasonally inspired regional Italian food with an emphasis on locally harvested seafood and produce. Choose from a fixed-price option (offered daily at two early seatings) or the regular menu for such favorites as pistachio-crusted roast rack of lamb or tagliatelle with lobster. The off-season warms up with wood oven–fired dishes. ⊠ *222 Main St.* ☎ *508/255–8547* ⌂ *Reservations essential* ⊟ *AE, D, DC, MC, V* ⊙ *No lunch.*

$$ ✕ **Beacon Room.** Adorned with crisp linens, frilly curtains, and wood furnishings, this bistro serves a nice mix of seafood and meats enhanced with sophisticated and inventive flavors. Start with the Gorgonzola, sun-dried cranberry, and walnut salad, and then move on to such delights as salmon and pasta sauté or the house favorite, chicken saltimbocca. ✉ *23 West Rd.* ☎ *508/255–2211* ⚑ *Reservations not accepted* ▭ *D, MC, V.*

★ **$–$$** ⌨ **Nauset House Inn.** You could easily spend a day trying out all the places to relax here. There's a parlor with comfortable chairs and a large fireplace, an orchard set with picnic tables, and a lush conservatory with a weeping cherry tree in its center. Rooms in both the main building and the adjacent Carriage House have stenciled walls, quilts, and unusual antique pieces, as well as hand-painted furniture, stained glass, and prints done by one of the owners. A single room with a shared bath is a rare find. ✉ *143 Beach Rd.* ⌂ *Box 774, East Orleans 02643* ☎ *508/255–2195 or 800/771–5508* ⊕ *www.nausethouseinn.com* ⇆ *14 rooms* ▭ *D, MC, V* ⊙ *Closed Nov.–Mar.* ⦿ *BP.*

Nightlife & the Arts

The **Academy Playhouse** (✉ 120 Main St. ☎ 508/255–1963), one of the oldest community theaters on the Cape, stages 12 or 13 productions year-round, including some original works.

Sports & the Outdoors

BEACHES **Nauset Beach** (✉ Beach Rd.)—not to be confused with Nauset Light Beach farther north—is a 10-mi-long sweep of sandy ocean beach with low dunes and large waves good for bodysurfing or boardsurfing. There are lifeguards, restrooms, showers, and a food concession. Daily parking fees are $10. **Skaket Beach** (✉ Skaket Beach Rd. ☎ 508/240–3775) on Cape Cod Bay is a sandy stretch with calm, warm water good for children. There are restrooms, lifeguards, and a snack bar. Daily parking fees are $10.

BOATING & **Arey's Pond Boat Yard** (✉ 43 Arey's La., off Rte. 28, South Orleans ☎ 508/
FISHING 255–0994) has a sailing school with individual and group lessons.

Goose Hummock Shop (✉ 15 Rte. 6A ☎ 508/255–0455) sells licenses, which are required for fishing in Orleans's freshwater ponds.

Shopping

Bird Watcher's General Store (✉ 36 Rte. 6A ☎ 508/255–6974 or 800/562–1512) stocks nearly everything avian but the birds themselves: feeders, paintings, houses, books, binoculars, calls, bird-theme apparel, and more. **Fancy's Farm Stand** (✉ 199 Main St., East Orleans ☎ 508/255–1949) sells tasty sandwiches, homemade soup, ice cream, freshly baked breads, and other supplies for a great picnic.

Eastham

❸ *3 mi north of Orleans.*

Often overlooked on the speedy drive up toward Provincetown, Eastham is full of hidden treasures. Route 6 bisects the town, which is spread out on both Cape Cod Bay and the Atlantic. Amid the gas stations, convenience stores, restaurants, and large motel complexes, Eastham's wealth of natural beauty takes a little exploring to find.

★ ⟳ The approximately 28,000-acre **Cape Cod National Seashore,** stretching along 30 mi of shoreline from Chatham to Provincetown, encompasses superb ocean beaches, rolling dunes, wetlands, pitch pine and scrub oak forest, wildlife, and several historic structures. Self-guided nature, hiking, biking, and horse trails lace these landscapes. The seashore's main information center, the Salt Pond Visitor Center in Eastham, has a museum and offers guided tours, boat trips, and lectures, as well as evening beach walks and campfire talks in summer. ⊠ *Doane Rd. off U.S. 6* ☎ *508/255–3421* ◻ *Free* ⊙ *Mar.–June and Sept.–Dec., daily 9–4:30; July and Aug., daily 9–5; Jan. and Feb., weekends 9–4:30.*

Roads and bicycle trails lead to Coast Guard and Nauset Light beaches, which begin an unbroken 15-mi stretch of barrier beach, referred to as the "Great Beach," extending to Provincetown. This is the **"Cape Cod Beach"** of Thoreau's 1865 classic, *Cape Cod*. You can still walk its length, as Thoreau did. Tours of the much-photographed red-and-white **Nauset Light** (⊠ Ocean View Dr. and Cable Rd. ☎ 508/240–2612 ⊕ www. nausetlight.org) are given on weekends in season; call for schedule.

Where to Stay & Eat

$–$$ ✕ **Friendly Fisherman.** Not just another roadside lobster shack with buoys and nets for decoration, this place is serious about its fresh seafood. It's both a great place to pick up ingredients to cook at home—there's a fish and produce market on-site—and a good bet for dining out on such favorites as fish-and-chips, fried scallops, and lobster. ⊠ *Rte. 6, North Eastham* ☎ *508/255–6770 or 508/255–3009* ▭ *AE, MC, V.*

$$–$$$$ ▦ **Penny House Inn.** Tucked behind a wave of privet hedge, this rambling gray-shingle inn's spacious rooms are furnished with antiques, collectibles, and wicker. The luxurious accommodations are cozy rather than stuffy; many are romantic, with whirlpool tubs, fireplaces, or both. Some rooms are larger, with sitting areas; suites have separate bedrooms and sitting rooms and can sleep up to five. ⊠ *4885 Rte. 6, 02642* ☎ *508/ 255–6632 or 800/554–1751* ▤ *508/255–4893* ⊕ *www.pennyhouseinn. com* ⊅ *9 rooms, 4 suites* ⊘ *Some refrigerators, cable TV, in-room VCRs, Wi-Fi, saltwater pool, spa, library* ▭ *AE, D, MC, V* ⦿| *BP.*

★ $$–$$$$ ▦ **Whalewalk Inn.** This 1830 whaling master's home is on 3 landscaped acres. Wide-board pine floors, fireplaces, and 19th-century country antiques provide historical appeal. Rooms in the main inn have four-poster twin, double, or queen-size beds; floral fabrics; and antique or reproduction furniture. Suites with fully equipped kitchens are in the converted barn and guesthouse. A secluded saltbox cottage has a fireplace, kitchen, and private patio. ⊠ *220 Bridge Rd., 02642* ☎ *508/255– 0617 or 800/440–1281* ⊕ *www.whalewalkinn.com* ⊅ *11 rooms, 5 suites, 1 cottage* ⊘ *Some in-room hot tubs, kitchens, bicycles, spa* ▭ *MC, V* ⦿| *BP.*

Sports & the Outdoors

★ **Coast Guard Beach** (⊠ Off Ocean View Dr.), part of the National Seashore, is a long beach backed by low grass and heathland. A handsome former Coast Guard station is also here, though it's not open to the public. A great spot for watching sunsets over the bay, **First Encounter Beach** (⊠ Samoset Rd. off U.S. 6) is laden with history. A bronze marker commemorates the first encounter between local Indians and passengers from the *Mayflower,* who explored the area for five weeks in late 1620.

Wellfleet

⑭ *10 mi northwest of Eastham, 13 mi southeast of Provincetown.*

Famous for its succulent namesake oysters, Wellfleet is today a tranquil center for artists and writers. Less than 2 mi wide, it's one of the Cape's most attractive resort towns, with a number of fine restaurants, historic houses, and art galleries.

★ **Marconi Station,** on the Atlantic side of the Cape's forearm, is the site of the first transatlantic wireless station erected on the U.S. mainland. From here Italian radio and wireless-telegraphy pioneer Guglielmo Marconi sent the first transatlantic wireless message from the U.S. to Europe—"most cordial greetings and good wishes" from President Theodore Roosevelt to King Edward VII of England—on January 18, 1903. Off the parking lot, a 1½-mi trail and boardwalk lead through the Atlantic White Cedar Swamp, one of the most beautiful trails on the seashore. ⌂ *Marconi Site Rd., South Wellfleet* ☎ *508/349–3785* ⊕ *www.nps.gov/ caco* ☑ *Free* ☉ *Daily 8–4:30.*

↻ A trip to the Outer Cape isn't complete without a visit to the **Massachu-**
Fodor'sChoice **setts Audubon Wellfleet Bay Wildlife Sanctuary,** an 1,100-acre haven for
★ more than 250 species of birds attracted by the varied habitats found here. The jewel of the Massachusetts Audubon Society, the sanctuary is a superb place for walking, birding, and looking west over the salt marsh and bay at wondrous sunsets. The **Esther Underwood Johnson Nature Center** contains two 700-gallon aquariums that offer an up-close look at marine life common to the Cape's tidal flats and marshlands. Rotating exhibits illustrate different facets of the area's ecology and natural history. ⌂ *Off U.S. 6* ☎ *508/349–2615* ⊕ *www.wellfleetbay.org* ☑ *$5* ☉ *Trails daily 8 AM–dusk; nature center late May–mid-Oct., daily 8:30–5; mid-Oct.–late May, Tues.–Sun. 8:30–5.*

A good stroll around town would take in Commercial and Main streets, ending perhaps at **Uncle Tim's Bridge** (⌂ Off E. Commercial St.). The short walk across this arching landmark—with its beautiful, much-photographed view over marshland and a tidal creek—leads to a small wooded island.

Where to Stay & Eat

$–$$$ ✕ **Finely JP's.** This unassuming little roadside spot right on U.S. 6 gives
Fodor'sChoice no hint that chef John Pontius consistently turns out wonderful food
★ full of the best Mediterranean and local influences and ingredients. The dining room is small and noisy, but the fish and pasta dishes (which emphasize good olive oil and plenty of lemon) silence all. Appetizers are especially good, among them a warm spinach-and-scallop salad and a poached salmon with a tangy ginger-soy glaze. ⌂ *U.S. 6, South Wellfleet* ☎ *508/349–7500* ⌔ *Reservations not accepted* ▭ *D, MC, V* ☉ *Closed Mon.–Wed. late Nov.–late May; Mon. and Tues. late May–mid-June and Oct.–late Nov.*

$–$$$ ⌑ **Surf Side Colony Cottages.** Scattered on either side of Ocean View Drive, accommodations range from units in a piney grove to well-equipped oceanside cottages. The cottages are a one-minute walk from Maguire's Landing town beach (Le Count Hollow), a beautiful wide strand of sand, dunes, and surf. Though the exteriors are retro-cool Floridian, with pastel shingles and flat roofs, cottage interiors are Cape-style, including knotty-pine paneling. ⊠ *Ocean View Dr.* ⌂ *Box 937, South Wellfleet 02663* ☎ *508/349–3959* 🖷 *508/349–3959* ⊕ *www.surfsidevacation.com* ⇥ *18 cottages* ⚬ *BBQs* ⚬ *1-wk minimum in summer* ⊟ *No credit cards* ⊙ *Closed Nov.–Mar.*

$ 🏠 **Holden Inn.** If you're watching your budget, try this old-timey place on a tree-shaded street just outside the town center but within walking distance of several galleries and restaurants. Rooms are simply decorated with Grandma's house–type wallpapers, ruffled sheer or country-style curtains, and antiques such as brass-and-white-iron or spindle beds or a marble-top table. Single rooms are available. ⊠ *140 Commercial St.* ⌂ *Box 816, Wellfleet 02667* ☎ *508/349–3450* ⊕ *www.theholdeninn.com* ⇥ *26 rooms, 10 with bath* ⚬ *No smoking* ⊟ *No credit cards* ⊙ *Closed mid-Oct.–mid-Apr.*

Nightlife & the Arts
★ **Beachcomber** (⊠ Ocean View Dr. off U.S. 6, by Cahoon Hollow Beach ☎ 508/349–6055) is big with the college crowd. There's live music and dancing nightly in summer.

The drive-in movie is alive and well on Cape Cod at the **Wellfleet Drive-In Theater** (⊠ 51 U.S. 6, South Wellfleet ☎ 508/349–7176). The well-
★ regarded **Wellfleet Harbor Actors Theater** (⊠ Kendrick St. past E. Commercial St., near Wellfleet Harbor ☎ 508/349–6835 or 866/252–9428 ⊕ www.what.org) presents world premieres of American plays.

Sports & the Outdoors
BEACHES **Cahoon Hollow Beach** (⊠ Ocean View Dr.) attracts younger and slightly rowdier crowds; it's a big Sunday-afternoon party place. Parking is $10. **White Crest Beach** (⊠ Ocean View Dr.) is a prime surfer hangout where the dudes often spend more time waiting for waves than actually riding them. Lifeguards are on duty. Parking is $10.

BOATING **Jack's Boat Rental** (⊠ Gull Pond, south of U.S. 6 ☎ 508/349–7553) has canoes, kayaks, sailboards, Sunfish, pedal boats, surfboards, boogie boards, and sailboards. Guided tours are also available.

Shopping
★ The giant **Wellfleet Flea Market** (⊠ 51 U.S. 6, South Wellfleet ☎ 508/349–2520) sets up shop in the parking lot of the Wellfleet Drive-In Theater mid-April–June, September, and October, weekends and Monday holidays 8–4; July and August, Monday holidays, Wednesday, Thursday, and weekends 10–5.

Blue Heron Gallery (⊠ 20 Bank St. ☎ 508/349–6724 ⊕ www.blueheronfineart.com), one of the Cape's best galleries, carries contemporary works. **Kendall Art Gallery** (⊠ 40 Main St., Downtown Wellfleet ☎ 508/349–2482) carries eclectic modern works.

Truro

⑮ *2 mi north of Wellfleet, 7 mi southeast of Provincetown.*

Edward Hopper summered in Truro from 1930 to 1967, finding the Cape light ideal for his austere brand of realism. Many other artists follow in his footsteps. One of the Cape's largest towns in land area—almost 43 square mi—it's also the smallest in population, with about 1,400 year-round residents.

Truly a breathtaking sight, **Highland Light,** also called Cape Cod Light, is the Cape's oldest lighthouse. Tours of the lighthouse are given daily in summer. ⊠ *Off S. Highland Rd.* ☎ *508/487–1121* ✎ *$3* ☉ *Mid-June–Sept., daily 10–5:30.*

Where to Stay & Eat

$$–$$$ ✕ **Terra Luna.** An insider's favorite for a special breakfast, Terra Luna has also become a wonderful choice for dinner. The dining room seems cramped rather than intimate, but the food is stylish, with surprising sauces for both fish and meat dishes. The striped bass is grilled perfectly, and spicy stuffed lamb chops are an excellent alternative to the usual fish. ⊠ *104 Shore Rd. (Rte. 6A), North Truro* ☎ *508/487–1019* ▤ *AE, MC, V* ☉ *Closed late Oct.–May.*

$–$$ ▦ **Cape View Motel.** The real beauty of this roadside motel is its noble perch on the westward bluff, looking out to sunsets over Cape Cod Bay and the distant lights of Provincetown. Deluxe rooms have private balconies, as well as fully equipped kitchenettes and a king bed or two doubles. Inside, the style doesn't at all try to compete with the outside vistas, but rooms are clean, simple, reasonably priced, and a 10-minute drive to Provincetown. ⊠ *Junction of U.S. 6 and Rte. 6A, 02652* ☎ *508/ 487–0363 or 800/224–3232* ⊕ *www.capeviewmotel.com* ⇖ *32 rooms* ♧ *Some kitchenettes, refrigerators, cable TV, pool* ▤ *AE, MC, V* ☉ *Closed mid-Oct.–mid-May.*

Sports & the Outdoors

BEACH **Ballston Beach** (⊠ Pamet Rd.) lies at the end of the winding Pamet Road
★ and is backed by the golden hills that artist Edward Hopper made famous in his Truro paintings. Parking is reserved for residents and renters in season, although anyone can walk or bicycle in.

BIKING The **Head of the Meadow Trail** provides 2 mi of easy cycling between dunes and salt marshes from High Head Road, off Route 6A in North Truro, to the Head of the Meadow Beach parking lot.

Bayside Bikes (⊠ 102 Rte. 6A, North Truro ☎ 508/487–5735) rents bicycles by the hour, day, or week, with easy access to the Head of the Meadow Trail.

Provincetown

★ **⑯** *7 mi northwest of Truro, 27 mi north of Orleans, 62 mi from the Sagamore Bridge.*

Many people know that the Pilgrims stopped here at the curved tip of Cape Cod before proceeding to Plymouth. Historical records suggest that an earlier visitor was Thorvald, brother of Viking Leif Erikson, who came ashore here in AD 1004 to repair the keel of his boat and consequently named the area Kjalarness, or Cape of the Keel. Bartholomew Gosnold came to Provincetown in 1602 and named the area Cape Cod after the abundant fish he found in the local waters.

Incorporated in 1727, Provincetown was for decades a bustling seaport, with fishing and whaling as its major industries. Fishing is still an important source of income for many locals—you can watch the fishing fleet unloading the day's catch at MacMillan Wharf—although today the town is a major whale-watching, rather than hunting, mecca. The Portuguese families who have lived here for generations, the gay and lesbian summer residents who have made this one of the country's most popular gay-friendly destinations, and the stroller-pushing masses who come for the day on the ferry from Boston all peacefully coexist.

Artists began coming here in the late 1890s to take advantage of the unusual Cape Cod light—in fact, Provincetown is the nation's oldest continuous art colony. By 1916, with five art schools flourishing here, painters' easels were nearly as common as shells on the beach. This bohemian community, along with the availability of inexpensive summer lodgings, attracted young rebels and writers as well, including John Reed (*Ten Days That Shook the World*) and Mary Heaton Vorse (*Footnote to Folly*), who in 1915 founded the Cape's first significant theater group, the Provincetown Players. The young, then unknown, Eugene O'Neill joined them in 1916, when his *Bound East for Cardiff* premiered in a tiny wharf-side fish house.

Driving on 3-mi-long Commercial Street, the main drag, could take forever in season—walking is definitely the way to go. Many architectural styles—Victorian, Second Empire, Gothic, and Greek revival, to name a few—were used to build houses for sea captains and merchants. The Provincetown Historical Society publishes walking-tour pamphlets, available for about $1 at many shops in town. The quiet East End of town is mostly residential, although you'll also find some interesting galleries. The similarly quiet West End has a number of small inns with neat lawns and elaborate gardens.

The Pilgrims dropped anchor in Provincetown Harbor on November 21, 1620, after a difficult 63-day voyage; before they left the *Mayflower* they signed the Mayflower Compact, the first document to declare a democratic form of government in America. They stayed in the area for five weeks before moving on to Plymouth. The **Pilgrim Monument**, which stretches incongruously into the sky over the low-rise town, commemorates their landing. Climb the 252-foot-high tower (116 steps and 60 ramps) for a panoramic view—dunes on one side, harbor on the other, and the entire bay side of Cape Cod beyond. At the base is a museum of Lower Cape and Provincetown history. ⊠ *High Pole Hill Rd.* ☎ *508/487–1310* ⊕ *www.pilgrim-monument.org* ☜ *$7* ⊙ *Apr.–June and Sept.–Nov., daily 9–4:15; July and Aug., daily 9–6:15.*

The **Provincetown Portuguese Bakery** (⊠ 299 Commercial St. ☎ 508/487–1803) makes fresh Portuguese breads and pastries and serves breakfast and lunch all day from March to October. Although it may be difficult to choose among the sweet splendor, try the fried dough locals call *malassadas*.

Fodor'sChoice
★

Founded in 1914 to collect and show the works of artists with Provincetown connections, the **Provincetown Art Association and Museum** has a 1,650-piece permanent collection, displayed in changing exhibits that mix up-and-comers with established 20th-century figures. ⊠ *460 Commercial St., East End* ☎ *508/487–1750* ⊕ *www.paam.org* ☜ *$3 donation suggested* ☉ *Apr.–late May, weekends noon–5; late May–early July and Sept., daily noon–5, also Fri. and Sat. 8 PM–10 PM; early July–Aug., daily noon–5 and 8 PM–10 PM; Oct.–Mar., weekends noon–4.*

Where to Stay & Eat

★ $$$–$$$$ ✕ **Chester.** Named for a pet terrier, this single-room restaurant in a Greek-revival sea captain's house serves beautifully presented meals from a small, contemporary menu that changes regularly. In addition to locally procured meats and seafood, the chef collects tomatoes, herbs, and lettuces from a garden behind the restaurant. Try duck prosciutto and arugula salad with Vermont chèvre, toasted pine nuts, and balsamic vinaigrette, before moving on to grilled French pork chop with fig, walnut, and blue cheese stuffing, fig sauce, and roasted potatoes. ⊠ *404 Commercial St.* ☎ *508/487–8200* ⊕ *www.chesterrestaurant.com* ⌕ *Reservations essential* ▭ *AE, MC, V* ☉ *Closed Dec.–Mar.*

★ $$–$$$$ ✕ **Martin House.** It's a relief to find this sanctuary of calm and creative contemporary fare right on bustling Commercial Street. Original 18th-century woodwork lends a touch of history, and Provincetown paintings grace the walls. The menu leans toward regional fare with a sophisticated touch, including unusually flavorful chutneys, risotto, and wild game. ⊠ *157 Commercial St.* ☎ *508/487–1327* ▭ *AE, D, DC, MC, V* ☉ *Closed Jan. and Mon.–Wed. Feb.–Apr.*

★ $$–$$$ ✕ **Front Street.** Front Street is so good, so consistent, and so romantic that many locals rate it the best restaurant in P-town. Classic Italian cooking is linked to offerings from Greece, southern France, and even North Africa. There's a nightly char-grilled fish special: match salmon, swordfish, or tuna with a Latin, berber, or Cajun spice rub; lemon-caper butter; or a ginger-soy-wasabi glaze. Tuscan beef braciola with spinach, fresh mozzarella, and prosciutto is essentially a simple dish, but its vibrant flavors show off these traditional ingredients in a new light. ⊠ *230 Commercial St., Downtown Center* ☎ *508/487–9715* ⌕ *Reservations essential* ▭ *AE, D, MC, V* ☉ *Closed Jan.–mid-May.*

$–$$$ ✕ **Ciro & Sal's.** Tucked inside a cozy house down an alley behind Commercial Street, this longtime local favorite offers a low-key, romantic alternative to some of the town's busier locations. The most memorable tables are inside a cozy brick wine cellar; the rest fill a pair of art-filled dining rooms, one of them warmed by a huge fireplace. You can also relax with a cocktail on the garden patio. The restaurant is justly known for its fresh pastas and bountiful salads. Favorite entrées include calamari sautéed with anchovies, lemon, garlic, and cream; and chicken livers sautéed with prosciutto, marsala wine, and sage. ⊠ *4 Kiley Ct.,*

Downtown Center ☎ *508/487–6444* ▤ *AE, D, MC, V* ☯ *Closed Mon.–Thurs. Labor Day–late June. No lunch.*

$–$$$ ✕ **Lobster Pot.** Provincetown's Lobster Pot is fit to do battle with all the lobster shanties anywhere (and everywhere) on the Cape. This hardworking kitchen turns out classic New England cooking: lobsters, generous and filling seafood platters (try the linguine tossed with shrimp, scallops, lobster, and Newburg sauce), and some of the best chowder around. ⊠ *321 Commercial St., Downtown Center* ☎ *508/487–0842* ⌔ *Reservations not accepted* ▤ *AE, D, DC, MC, V* ☯ *Closed Dec.–Apr.*

¢–$$ ✕ **Clem & Ursie's.** It's worth the short drive or long walk from downtown
Fodor'sChoice to sample the tantalizing seafood prepared at this colorful café, market,
★ and bakery. The mammoth menu touches on just about every kind of food from the ocean: tuna steaks, crab claws, squid stew, Japanese baby octopus salad, hot lobster rolls, lobster scampi—even sushi. A nice range of nonfishy items are offered, too, from pulled pork barbecue to bacon cheeseburgers. Pay at the counter and grab a seat inside the decidedly casual dining room; they bring your chow out to you. ⊠ *85 Shank Painter Rd.* ☎ *508/487–2333* ▤ *D, MC, V* ☯ *Closed Jan.–early Apr.*

¢–$$ ✕ **Spiritus.** The local bars close at 1 AM, at which point this pizza joint becomes the town's epicenter. It's the ultimate place to see and be seen, pizza slice in hand and witty banter at the ready. ⊠ *190 Commercial St.* ☎ *508/487–2808* ▤ *No credit cards* ☯ *Closed Nov.–Apr.*

$$–$$$$ ✕▥ **Red Inn.** A rambling red 1915 house that once hosted Franklin and Eleanor Roosevelt, this small and luxurious inn has been completely refurbished. Most of the airy rooms afford bay views, and all are fitted with big plush beds with high-thread-count linens, goose-down comforters, and pillow-top mattresses. The low-key, intimate restaurant ($$–$$$$) serves superb contemporary fare. Start off with the sweet and chunky lobster-corn chowder, before moving on to pepper-crusted filet mignon with truffle-mashed potatoes and onion-garlic-butter sauce. The fresh salmon wrapped with rice paper and sesame seeds and served with ginger dressing, cucumber salad, and sticky rice is also excellent. ⊠ *15 Commercial St., 02657* ☎ *508/487–7334 or 866/473–3466* 🖷 *508/487–5115* ⊕ *www.theredinn.com* ➷ *4 rooms, 2 suites, 2 cottages* ⌔ *Restaurant, room service, in-room hot tubs, refrigerators, cable TV, in-room VCRs, in-room data ports, free parking; no kids under 18* ▤ *AE, MC, V* ◎| *CP.*

★ $$$–$$$$ ▥ **Crowne Pointe Historic Inn.** At this atmospheric inn, owners Tom Walter and David Sanford have not left a single detail unattended. Period furniture and antiques fill the common areas and rooms; a queen-size bed is the smallest you'll find, dressed in 250-thread-count linens, with treats on the pillow for nightly turndown service. Many rooms have fireplaces: in one room, view the flames from your bed or the whirlpool tub. Start the day with a full, hot breakfast and graze freshly baked treats and wine and cheese in the afternoon. ⊠ *82 Bradford St., 02657* ☎ *508/ 487–6767 or 877/276–9631* 🖷 *508/487–5554* ⊕ *www.crownepointe. com* ➷ *37 rooms, 3 suites* ⌔ *Some in-room hot tubs, some kitchens, some microwaves, refrigerators, cable TV, in-room DVD, in-room data ports, pool, 2 outdoor hot tubs, spa, laundry service, concierge, business services, airport shuttle, free parking* ▤ *AE, D, MC, V* ◎| *BP.*

★ **$$–$$$$** ⊞ **Brass Key.** One of Provincetown's most luxurious resorts, the Brass Key comprises a beautifully restored main house—originally an 1828 sea captain's home—and several other carefully groomed buildings and cottages. Rooms mix antiques with such modern amenities as Bose stereos. Deluxe rooms also come with gas fireplaces and whirlpool baths or French doors opening out to wrought-iron balconies. A widow's-walk sundeck has a panoramic view of Cape Cod Bay. Complimentary cocktails are served in the courtyard. As is true of many of Provincetown's smaller hotels, the Brass Key draws a largely gay clientele, especially in summer. ⊠ *67 Bradford St., 02657* ☎ *508/487–9005 or 800/ 842–9858* 🖷 *508/487–9020* ⊕ *www.brasskey.com* ↰ *42 rooms* ⌂ *In-room safes, some in-room hot tubs, cable TV, in-room DVD, pool, hot tubs; no kids under 16* ⊟ *AE, D, MC, V* ⊘ *Closed late Nov.–mid-Apr. except for New Year's wk* ⒪ *CP.*

$$–$$$ ⊞ **Snug Cottage.** Noted for its extensive floral gardens and its enviable perch atop one of the larger bluffs in town, this inn decked in smashing English country antiques and fabrics delights Anglophiles. The oversize accommodations have distinctly British names (Victoria Suite, Royal Scott); most are full suites with sitting areas, and many have wood-burning fireplaces and private outdoor entrances. The Churchill Suite has 10 big windows overlooking the flowers and bushes outside. ⊠ *178 Bradford St., east of Downtown Center, 02657* ☎ *508/487–1616 or 800/ 432–2334* 🖷 *508/487–5123* ⊕ *www.snugcottage.com* ↰ *3 rooms, 5 suites* ⌂ *Some kitchenettes, cable TV, in-room DVD, in-room data ports* ⊟ *AE, D, MC, V* ⒪ *BP.*

$–$$$ ⊞ **Fairbanks Inn.** This meticulously restored Colonial inn a block from Commercial Street includes the 1776 main house and auxiliary buildings. Guest rooms have four-poster or canopy beds, Oriental rugs on wide-board floors, and antique furnishings; some have fireplaces or kitchens. Many original touches remain here, from the 18th-century wallpaper to artifacts from the inn's first residents. The baths are on the small side, but they help preserve the Colonial integrity of the home. ⊠ *90 Bradford St., 02657* ☎ *508/487–0386 or 800/324–7265* ⊕ *www. fairbanksinn.com* ↰ *15 rooms, 1 efficiency* ⌂ *Some kitchens, cable TV, some in-room VCRs, free parking* ⊟ *AE, MC, V* ⒪ *CP.*

Nightlife & the Arts

NIGHTLIFE The **Atlantic House** (⊠ 4 Masonic Pl., Downtown Center ☎ 508/487–3821), the grandfather of the gay night scene, is the only gay bar open year-round. Better known as the A House, it has several lounge areas and an outdoor patio. The **Boatslip** (⊠ 161 Commercial St., Downtown Center ☎ 508/487–1669) holds a gay and lesbian tea dance on the outdoor pool deck from 4 to 7 daily in summer and on weekends in spring and fall. **Vixen** (⊠ 336 Commercial St., Downtown Center ☎ 508/487–6424), a lively women's club, gets packed on weekends. On most nights there's also live music and comedy.

THE ARTS Serving as home base for both the Provincetown Repertory Theatre and the Provincetown Theatre Company, the **Provincetown Theater** (⊠ 238 Bradford St., Downtown Center ☎ 508/487–7487 or 800/791–7487 ⊕ www.provincetowntheater.org) hosts a wide variety of performances throughout the year, but especially in summer high season.

Sports & the Outdoors

BEACHES **Herring Cove Beach,** a national seashore beach, is calmer (and a little warmer) than Race Point Beach, though it's not as pretty since the parking lot isn't hidden behind dunes. But the lot to the right of the bathhouse is a great place to watch the sunset, and there's a hot-dog stand. From mid-June through Labor Day, parking costs $10 per day. **Race Point Beach** (⊠ Race Point Rd.), at the end of U.S. 6, has a remote feeling, with a wide swath of sand stretching around the point. Because it faces north, the beach gets sun all day long. Parking is $10.

BIKING The **Province Lands Trail** is a 5¼-mi loop off the Beech Forest parking lot on Race Point Road, with spurs to Herring Cove and Race Point beaches and to Bennett Pond. The paths wind up and down hills amid dunes, marshes, woods, and ponds, affording spectacular views. More than 8 mi of bike trails lace through the dunes, cranberry bogs, and scrub pine of the National Seashore, with many access points, including Herring Cove and Race Point.

FISHING You can go for fluke, bluefish, and striped bass on a walk-in basis from spring through fall with **Cap'n Bill & Cee Jay** (⊠ MacMillan Wharf, Downtown Center ☎ 508/487–4330).

GUIDED TOUR **Art's Dune Tours** (⊠ Commercial and Standish Sts., Downtown Center FodorśChoice ☎ 508/487–1950 or 800/894–1951 ⊕ www.artsdunetours.com) has been ★ taking eager passengers into the dunes of Province Lands for more than 50 years. Bumpy but controlled rides transport you through sometimes surreal sandy vistas peppered with beach grass and along shoreline patrolled by seagulls and sandpipers.

WHALE-WATCHING One of the joys of Cape Cod is spotting whales while they're swimming in and around the feeding grounds at Stellwagen Bank, about 6 mi off the tip of Provincetown. Many people also come aboard for birding, especially during spring and fall migration. Several tour operators take whale-watchers out to sea for three- to four-hour morning, afternoon, or sunset trips.

Dolphin Fleet tours are accompanied by scientists from the Center for Coastal Studies in Provincetown who provide commentary while collecting data on the whale population they've been monitoring for years. They know many of the whales by name and will tell you about their habits and histories. ⊠ *Ticket office: chamber of commerce building at MacMillan Wharf, Downtown Center* ☎ *508/240–3636 or 800/826–9300* ⊕ *www.whalewatch.com* ☎ *$30* ⊙ *Tours Apr.–Oct.*

The **Portuguese Princess** sails with a naturalist on board to narrate. The snack bar sells Portuguese specialties. ⊠ *70 Shank Painter Rd., ticket office, east of Downtown Center* ⊠ *Whale Watchers General Store, 309 Commercial St., Downtown Center* ☎ *508/487–2651 or 800/442–3188* ⊕ *www.princesswhalewatch.com* ☎ *$30* ⊙ *Tours May–Oct.*

Shopping

Berta Walker Gallery (⊠ 208 Bradford St., east of Downtown Center, toward East End ☎ 508/487–6411) represents Provincetown-affiliated artists working in various media. **Giardelli Antonelli** (⊠ 417 Commercial St., toward East End, Downtown Center ☎ 508/487–3016) specializes in handmade clothing by local designers. **Remembrances of Things Past** (✉ 376 Commercial St., toward East End, Downtown Center ☎ 508/487–9443) deals in articles from the 1920s to the 1960s. **West End Antiques** (✉ 146 Commercial St., toward West End, Downtown Center ☎ 508/432–1604) specializes in variety: $4 postcards, a $3,000 model ship, handmade dolls, and glassware.

Cape Cod A to Z

To research prices, get advice from other travelers, and book travel arrangements, visit www.fodors.com.

AIRPORTS

Barnstable Municipal Airport, the Cape's main air gateway, is served by Cape Air/Nantucket Airlines, and US Airways Express. Provincetown Municipal Airport has Boston service through Cape Air.

🛪 Airport Information **Barnstable Municipal Airport** ✉ 480 Barnstable Rd., north of the Rte. 28 rotary, Hyannis ☎508/775-2020. **Provincetown Municipal Airport** ✉Race Point Rd. ☎ 508/487-0241.

BIKE TRAVEL

The Cape's premier bike path, the Cape Cod Rail Trail, follows the paved right-of-way of the old Penn Central Railroad. About 25 mi long, the easy-to-moderate trail passes salt marshes, cranberry bogs, ponds, and Nickerson State Park. The trail starts at the parking lot off Route 134 south of U.S. 6, near Theophilus Smith Road in South Dennis, and it ends at the post office in South Wellfleet. If you want to cover only a segment, there are parking lots in Harwich (across from Pleasant Lake Store on Pleasant Lake Avenue) and in Brewster (at Nickerson State Park). For bike and trailer rentals, try the Little Capistrano Bike Shop or the Rail Trail Bike Shop.

🛪 Bike Rentals **Little Capistrano Bike Shop** ✉ Salt Pond Rd. across from Salt Pond Visitor Center, Eastham ☎ 508/255-6515. **Rail Trail Bike Shop** ✉ 302 Underpass Rd., Brewster ☎ 508/896-8200.

BOAT & FERRY TRAVEL

Bay State Cruise Company offers both high-speed ferry and standard excursion service between Commonwealth Pier in Boston and MacMillan Wharf in Provincetown. High-speed service runs daily from late May through late September and costs $64 round-trip; the ride takes 90 minutes. Standard service runs Saturday and Sunday from mid-June through early September and costs $29 round-trip; the ride takes three hours. On either ferry, the round-trip charge for bikes is $10.

🛪 Boat & Ferry Information **Bay State Cruise Company** ☎ 617/748-1428 in Boston, 508/487-9284 in Provincetown ⊕ www.baystatecruisecompany.com.

BUS TRAVEL

Peter Pan Bonanza offers direct bus service to Bourne, Falmouth, and the Woods Hole steamship terminal from downtown Boston and Logan International Airport. Plymouth & Brockton Street Railway Co. provides bus service to Provincetown from downtown Boston and Logan, with stops en route. The company also has service between Boston and Provincetown, with stops at many towns in between, including Wellfleet and Truro.

The Cape Cod Regional Transit Authority operates several bus routes. The Lower Cape route, which operates year-round, begins in Hyannis and follows Route 28 all the way to Orleans, stopping in Harwich Port and Chatham. The Shuttle begins in Truro and continues to Provincetown along Route 6A, stopping wherever a passenger or roadside flagger dictates. The service is popular and reasonably priced ($1 for a single fare, $3 for a day pass). It runs from late May until mid-October, with more limited service in spring and fall.

🚍 Bus Information **Cape Cod Regional Transit Authority** ☎ 800/352-7155 ⊕ www. capecodtransit.org. **Peter Pan Bonanza** ✉ South Station Bus Terminal, 700 Atlantic Ave., Boston ☎ 617/720-4110 ✉ Depot Ave., Falmouth ☎ 508/548-7588 ✉ Steamship Authority Piers, Woods Hole ☎ 508/548-5011. **Plymouth & Brockton** ✉ South Station Bus Terminal, 700 Atlantic Ave., Boston ☎ 508/746-0378.

CAR RENTAL

Budget rents cars at the Barnstable and Provincetown airports.

🚍 Major Agency **Budget** ☎ 800/527-0700 ⊕ www.budgetrentacar.com.

CAR TRAVEL

From Boston (60 mi), take Interstate 93 south to Route 3 south, across the Sagamore Bridge, which becomes U.S. 6, the Cape's main artery. From western Massachusetts, northern Connecticut, and northeastern New York State, take Interstate 84 east to the Massachusetts Turnpike (Interstate 90 east) and take Interstate 495 south and east to the Bourne Bridge. From New York City, and all other points south and west, take Interstate 95 north toward Providence, where you'll pick up Interstate 195 east (toward Fall River/New Bedford) to Route 25 east to the Bourne Bridge.

From the Bourne Bridge, you can take Route 28 south to Falmouth and Woods Hole (about 15 mi), or go around the rotary, following the signs to U.S. 6; this will take you to the Lower Cape and central towns more quickly. On summer weekends, avoid arriving in the late afternoon. U.S. 6, Route 6A, and Route 28 are heavily congested eastbound on Friday evening, westbound on Sunday afternoon, and in both directions on summer Saturdays. When approaching one of the Cape's numerous rotaries (traffic circles), keep in mind that vehicles already in the rotary have the right of way.

EMERGENCIES

🚑 Hospitals **Cape Cod Hospital** ✉ 27 Park St., Hyannis ☎ 508/771-1800 ⊕ www. capecodhealth.org. **Falmouth Hospital** ✉ 100 Ter Heun Dr., Falmouth ☎ 508/548-5300. 🚑 Late-Night Pharmacies **CVS** ✉ 105 Davis Straits, Falmouth ☎ 508/540-4307 ✉ 176 North St., Hyannis ☎ 508/775-8346 ⊕ www.cvs.com.

LODGING

APARTMENT & VILLA RENTALS   Commonwealth Associates can assist in finding rentals in the Harwiches. Donahue Real Estate lists apartments and houses in the Falmouth area. Kinlin Grover GMAC Vacation Rentals has locations in eight towns and lists apartments and houses throughout the Cape; the Brewster office is one of the larger ones.

🏠 Local Agents **Commonwealth Associates** ✉ 551 Main St., Harwich Port 02646 ☎ 508/432-2618 🖷 508/432-1771 ⊕ www.commonwealthrealestate.com. **Donahue Real Estate** ✉ 850 Main St., Falmouth 02540 ☎ 508/548-5412 🖷 508/548-5418 ⊕ www.falmouthhomes.com. **Kinlin Grover GMAC Vacation Rentals** ✉ 1990 Main St., Brewster 02631 ☎ 508/896-7004 or 800/724-1307 🖷 508/896-7090 ⊕ www.vacationcapecod.com.

BED-AND- Bed & Breakfast Cape Cod represents dozens of B&Bs throughout the
BREAKFASTS Lower Cape and beyond.

🏠 Reservation Services **Bed & Breakfast Cape Cod** 📪 Box 1312, Orleans 02653 ☎ 508/255-3824 or 800/541-6226 🖷 508/245-0599 ⊕ www.bedandbreakfastcapecod.com.

CAMPING The Cape Cod Chamber of Commerce maintains a list of private campgrounds.

SPORTS & THE OUTDOORS

FISHING The Cape Cod Chamber of Commerce's *Sportsman's Guide* describes fishing regulations and surf-fishing access locations and contains a map of boat-launching facilities. Freshwater-fishing licenses are available for a nominal fee at bait and tackle shops. The Cape Cod Canal is a good place to fish; the Army Corps of Engineers operates a canal fishing hotline.

🏠 **Army Corps of Engineers canal fishing hotline** ☎ 508/759-5991.

TAXIS

🏠 **All Village Taxi** ✉ Falmouth ☎ 508/540-7200. **Cape Cab** ✉ Provincetown ☎ 508/487-2222. **Eldredge Taxi** ✉ Chatham ☎ 508/945-0068.

TOURS

The Cape Cod Central Railroad offers two-hour, 42-mi narrated rail tours from Hyannis to the Cape Cod Canal (admission $15) late May through October; trains generally run Tuesday to Sunday, but call for a schedule.

🏠 Tour-Operator **Cape Cod Central Railroad** ✉ Hyannis Train Depot, 252 Main St., Hyannis ☎ 508/771-3800 or 888/797-7245 ⊕ www.capetrain.com.

VISITOR INFORMATION

The Cape Cod Chamber of Commerce is open year-round, Monday–Saturday 9–5 and Sunday 10–4.

🏠 Local Information **Brewster** ✉ 2198 Main St. (Rte. 6A) 📪 Box 1241, 02631 ☎ 508/896-3500 ⊕ www.brewstercapecod.org. **Chatham** 📪 Box 793, 02633 ☎ 508/945-5199 or 800/715-5567 ⊕ www.chathamcapecod.org ✉ Visitor center ✉ 2377 Main St., South Chatham ✉ Information booth ✉ 533 Main St., Chatham. **Dennis** ✉ Junction of Rtes. 28 and 134, West Dennis 📪 Box 275, South Dennis 02660 ☎ 508/398-3568 or 800/243-9920 ⊕ www.dennischamber.com. **Falmouth** ✉ 20 Academy La. 📪 Box 582, 02541 ☎ 508/548-8500 or 800/526-8532 ⊕ www.falmouthchamber.com. **Harwich** 📪 1 Schoolhouse Rd., Harwich Port 02646 ☎ 508/432-1600 or 800/442-7942 ⊕ www.harwichcc.com. **Hyannis** ✉ 1481 Rte. 132, 02601 ☎ 508/362-5230 or 877/492-6647 ⊕ www.hyannis.com. **Orleans** 📪 Box 153, 02653 ☎ 508/255-1386 ✉ Information booth ✉ Eldredge Pkwy. off Rte. 6A ☎ 508/240-2484 ⊕ www.capecod-orleans.com. **Province-**

town ✉ 307 Commercial St. ☎ Box 1017, 02657 ☎ 508/487-3424 ⊕ www.ptownchamber. com. **Truro** ✉ U.S. 6 at Head of the Meadow Rd. ☎ Box 26, North Truro 02652 ☎ 508/ 487-1288 ⊕ www.trurochamberofcommerce.com. **Wellfleet** ☎ Box 571, 02667 ☎ 508/ 349-2510 ✉ Information center off U.S. 6 in South Wellfleet ⊕ www.wellfleetchamber. com. **Yarmouth** ✉ 424 Rte. 28, West Yarmouth 02673 ✉ Box 479, South Yarmouth 02664 ☎ 508/778-1008 or 800/732-1008 ⊕ www.yarmouthcapecod.com ✉ Information center ✉ U.S. 6 heading east between Exits 6 and 7 ☎ 508/362-9796.

⏎ Regional Information Cape Cod Chamber of Commerce ✉ Junction of U.S. 6 and 132 ☎ Box 790, Hyannis 02601 ☎ 508/862-0700 or 888/332-2732 ⊕ www. capecodchamber.org.

MARTHA'S VINEYARD

4

Updated by
Phyllis Meras

Far less developed than Cape Cod yet more cosmopolitan than Nantucket, Martha's Vineyard is an island with a double life. From Memorial Day through Labor Day the quieter, some might say real, Vineyard quickens into a vibrant, star-studded frenzy. The busy main port, Vineyard Haven, welcomes day-trippers fresh off a ferry or private yacht. Oak Bluffs, where pizza and ice cream emporiums reign supreme, has the air of a Victorian boardwalk. Edgartown is flooded with seekers of chic who wander tiny streets that hold boutiques, stately whaling captains' homes, and charming inns. Summer regulars include a host of celebrities, among them William Styron, Walter Cronkite, and Sharon Stone. If you're planning to stay overnight on a summer weekend, be sure to make reservations well in advance; spring is not too early. Things stay busy on September and October weekends, a favorite time for weddings, but begin to slow down soon after. In many ways the Vineyard's off-season persona is even more appealing than its summer self. There's more time to linger over pastoral and ocean vistas, free from the throngs of cars, bicycles, and mopeds.

The Vineyard, except for Oak Bluffs and Edgartown, is "dry." Restaurants don't serve liquor, but many allow you to bring your own beer or wine.

Vineyard Haven (Tisbury)

❶ *7 mi southeast of Woods Hole, 3½ mi west of Oak Bluffs, 8 mi northwest of Edgartown.*

Most people call this town Vineyard Haven for the name of the port where the ferry pulls in, but its official name is Tisbury. Not as high-toned as Edgartown or as honky-tonk as Oak Bluffs, Vineyard Haven blends the past and the present with a touch of the bohemian. Visitors arriving here step off the ferry right into the bustle of the harbor, a block from the shops and restaurants of Main Street.

One of two lighthouses that mark the opening to the harbor, the 52-foot white-and-black **West Chop Lighthouse** was built in 1838 of brick to replace an 1817 wood building. It has been moved back twice from the edge of the eroding bluff. ✉ *W. Chop Rd. (Main St.)* ⊕ *www. marthasvineyardhistory.org.*

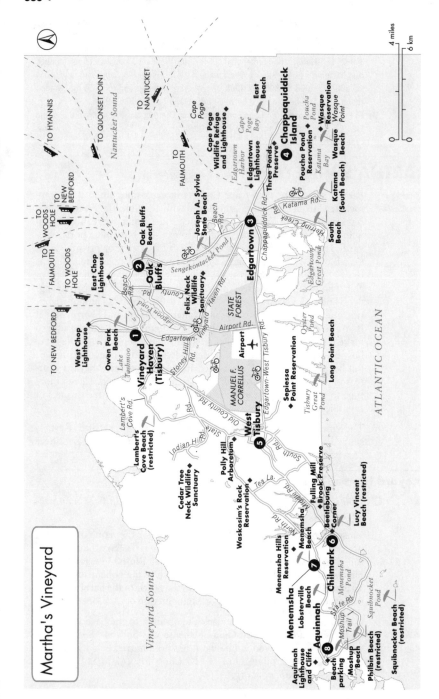

Martha's Vineyard

TO HYANNIS

TO QUONSET POINT

TO NANTUCKET

Nantucket Sound

TO FALMOUTH

TO NEW BEDFORD

TO WOODS HOLE

TO FALMOUTH

TO WOODS HOLE

TO NEW BEDFORD

Cape Pogue

East Beach

Cape Pogue Wildlife Refuge and Lighthouse

Cape Pogue Bay

Poucha Pond

Wasque Reservation

4 Chappaquiddick Island

Edgartown Harbor

Edgartown Lighthouse

Poucha Pond Reservation

Wasque Point

Three Ponds Preserve

Katama

Wasque Beach

Joseph A. Sylvia State Beach

Beach Rd.

Chappaquiddick Rd.

Katama Rd.

Katama (South Beach) Beach

3 Edgartown

Herring Creek

South Beach

2 Oak Bluffs

Oak Bluffs Beach

Sengekontacket Pond

County Rd.

Felix Neck Wildlife Sanctuary

East Chop Lighthouse

Beach Rd.

Vineyard Haven Rd.

STATE FOREST

Edgartown Great Pond

Oyster Pond

ATLANTIC OCEAN

West Chop Lighthouse

Owen Park Beach

1 Vineyard Haven (Tisbury)

Lake Tashmoo

Edgartown

Airport Rd.

Stoney Hill Rd.

Airport

MANUEL F. CORREILUS

Edgartown–West Tisbury Rd.

Long Point Beach

Lambert's Cove Rd.

Lambert's Cove Beach (restricted)

Sepiessa Point Reservation

Tisbury Great Pond

5 West Tisbury

State Rd.

Old County Rd.

Indian Hill Rd.

Cedar Tree Neck Wildlife Sanctuary

Polly Hill Arboretum

South Rd.

Tea La.

Waskosim's Rock Reservation

Fulling Mill Brook Preserve

Beetlebung Corner

Lucy Vincent Beach (restricted)

North Rd.

Middle Rd.

Menemsha Hills Reservation

Menemsha Beach

7

6 Chilmark

Menemsha Pond

Menemsha

Lobsterville Beach

State Rd.

Squibnocket Pond

8 Aquinnah

Moshup Trail

Squibnocket Beach (restricted)

Aquinnah Lighthouse and Cliffs

Beach parking

Moshup Beach

Philbin Beach (restricted)

Vineyard Sound

4 miles

6 km

Where to Stay & Eat

$$$–$$$$ ✕ **Le Grenier.** Up narrow stairs, above the M. V. Bagel Authority at the upper end of Vineyard Haven's downtown, owner-chef Jean Dupon has been serving classic French food since the late 1970s. Although some island restaurants have come and gone, and others shifted with the newest trends, Dupon has been consistently loyal to the French standards: frogs' legs, sweetbreads, and tournedos are among the entrées. The decor is hardly stuffy in the French tradition; rather, it's almost backyard casual, with a string of lightbulbs and souvenir wine-bottle corks lining the walls. ⊠ *Upper Main St.* ☎ *508/693–4906* ⊟ *AE, MC, V* 🍴 *BYOB* ☙ *No lunch.*

$$–$$$$ ✕ **Cafe Moxie.** Open year-round, this sophisticated restaurant has a handsome wooden bar (though it's a dry town) and island artists' work on the walls. A lunchtime favorite is Chef Austin Racine's mussels steamed in garlic and ginger served over noodles. Something fancier for dinner is duck breast wrapped in Swiss chard over a white-bean-and-duck ragout. You can eat lunch here for under $15. ⊠ *Main St. at Centre St.* ☎ *508/693–1484* ⊟ *MC, V* 🍴 *BYOB* ☙ *Closed Sun.–Wed. No lunch Oct.–Apr.*

$$–$$$ ✕ **Black Dog Tavern.** This island landmark, just steps from the ferry terminal in Vineyard Haven, remains a hangout for year-rounders in winter (when the lines aren't a mile long). In July and August, the wait can be as much as an hour as early as 8 AM or so. Why? Partly because the roaring fireplace, dark wood walls, maritime memorabilia, and a grand view of the water, make people feel so at home, as they have since its founding in 1971. The menu is heavy on local fish, chowders, and burgers. ⊠ *Beach St.* ☎ *508/693–9223* ⌦ *Reservations not accepted* ⊟ *AE, D, MC, V* 🍴 *BYOB.*

★ **$$$–$$$$** 🏠 **Thorncroft Inn.** On 3½ wooded acres about 1 mi from the ferry, this inn's main building, a 1918 Craftsman bungalow, combines fine Colonial and richly carved Renaissance-revival antiques with tasteful reproductions to create a somewhat formal environment. Ten of the rooms have working fireplaces. Most have canopy beds; three have two-person whirlpool baths, and two have private hot-tub spas. Rooms in the carriage house are more secluded and set apart from the main house via a breezeway. ⊠ *460 Main St.* 🗋 *Box 1022, 02568* ☎ *508/693–3333 or 800/332–1236* 🖷 *508/693–5419* ⊕ *www.thorncroft.com* 🛏 *14 rooms, 1 cottage* ⚒ *Dining room, some in-room hot tubs, some refrigerators, in-room VCRs, library; no kids under 13, no smoking* ⊟ *AE, D, DC, MC, V* ⧄ *BP.*

$$–$$$ 🏠 **Hanover House.** Set on a half-acre of landscaped lawn on a busy road but within walking distance of the ferry, this three-property inn consists of a classic, home-style bed-and-breakfast, a country inn, and a carriage house. Rooms are decorated with a combination of antiques and reproduction furniture. Each room has individual flair. In one, an antique sewing machine serves as the TV stand. The three carriage house suites have private decks or patios and two have kitchenettes. ⊠ *28 Edgartown Rd.* 🗋 *Box 2108, 02568* ☎ *508/693–1066 or 800/339–1066* ⊕ *www.hanoverhouseinn.com* 🛏 *12 rooms, 3 suites* ⚒ *Some kitchenettes, Wi-Fi* ⊟ *AE, D, MC, V* ⧄ *CP.*

Nightlife & the Arts

The **Vineyard Playhouse** (⊠ 24 Church St. ☎ 508/693–6450 or 508/696–6300) presents community theater, including summer programs at a natural amphitheater.

Sports & the Outdoors

Lake Tashmoo Town Beach (⊠ End of Herring Creek Rd.) invites swimming in the warm, relatively shallow, brackish lake or in the cooler, gentle Vineyard Sound. **Owen Park Beach** (⊠ Off Main St.), a small, sandy harbor beach, is just steps away from the ferry terminal in Vineyard Haven, making it a great spot for some last rays. **Tisbury Town Beach** (⊠ End of Owen Little Way off Main St.) is a public beach next to the Vineyard Haven Yacht Club.

Shopping

Bowl & Board (⊠ 35 Main St. ☎ 508/693–9441) is summer-home central. It carries everything you need to cozy up in a summer rental. **Bramhall & Dunn** (⊠ 19 Main St. ☎ 508/693–6437) carries crafts, linens, hand-knit sweaters, and fine antique country-pine furniture. **Bunch of Grapes Bookstore** (⊠ 44 Main St. ☎ 508/693–2291) sells new books and sponsors book signings. **Wind's Up!** (⊠ 199 Beach Rd. ☎ 508/693–4340) sells swimwear, windsurfing and sailing equipment, boogie boards, and other outdoor gear.

Oak Bluffs

❷ *3½ mi east of Vineyard Haven.*

Circuit Avenue is the bustling center of the Oak Bluffs action, with most of the town's shops, bars, and restaurants. Colorful gingerbread-trimmed guesthouses and food and souvenir joints enliven Oak Bluffs Harbor, once the setting for several grand hotels (the 1879 Wesley Hotel on Lake Avenue is the last remaining one). This small town is more high spirited than haute, more fun than refined.

The **East Chop Lighthouse** was built of cast iron in 1876 after its 1828 predecessor, which had been used as part of a semaphore system of visual signaling between the island and Boston, burned down. The 40-foot structure stands high atop a 79-foot bluff with spectacular views of Nantucket Sound. ⊠ *E. Chop Dr.* ☎ *508/627–4441* 🖼 *$3* ☉ *Late June–mid Sept., Sun. 1 hr before sunset–1 hr after sunset.*

☖ A National Historic Landmark, the **Flying Horses Carousel** is the nation's oldest continuously operating carousel. Handcrafted in 1876 (the horses have real horse hair and glass eyes), the ride gives children a taste of entertainment from a TV-free era. ⊠ *Oak Bluffs Ave.* ☎ *508/693–9481* 🖼 *Rides $1.50, book of 8 tickets $10* ☉ *Late May–early Sept., daily 10–10; Easter–late May, weekends 10–5; early Sept.–mid-Oct., weekdays 11–4:30, weekends 10–5.*

Where to Stay & Eat

$$$–$$$$ ✕ **Sweet Life Café.** Housed in a charming Victorian house, this island favorite, with its warm tones, low lighting, and handsome antique furniture, will make you feel like you've entered someone's home, but the

FodorsChoice
★

cooking is more sophisticated than home-style. Dishes on the menu are prepared in inventive ways. The duck breast is roasted with a lavender-honey-and-rosemary glaze. The desserts remain superb; try the warm chocolate fondant (a sort of soufflé) with toasted almond ice cream. There's outdoor dining by candlelight in a shrub-enclosed garden, with heaters for when it turns cold. ⊠ *Upper Circuit Ave. at far end of town* ☎ *508/696–0200* ⚠ *Reservations essential* ▭ *AE, D, MC, V* ☽ *Closed Jan.–Mar.*

★ $$–$$$$ ✕ **Tsunami.** In a quaint converted gingerbread house overlooking the harbor, this restaurant delivers an exclusively Asian-influenced menu, focusing on a Thai repertoire but also sampling flavors from Japan, China, Burma, and France. The small upstairs dining room is decorated with a minimalist's touch; downstairs is a handsome mahogany bar with several small tables. The dinner menu, which includes sushi and sake, is available on both levels. ⊠ *6 Circuit Ave.* ☎ *508/696–8900* ▭ *AE, MC, V* ☽ *Closed mid-Oct.–mid-May.*

$$–$$$ ▨ **Dockside Inn.** Just yards from the Oak Bluffs ferry and in the thick of the town's bustle, this gingerbread Victorian inn decked with broad porches sits right by the dock, steps from the ferry landing and downtown shops, restaurants, and bars. Kids are welcome, and they'll have plenty to do in town and at nearby beaches. Some rooms open onto building-length balconies. ⊠ *9 Circuit Ave. Exit* ✑ *Box 1206, 02557* ☎ *508/693–2966 or 800/245–5979* ▨ *508/696–7293* ⊕ *www.vineyardinns.com* ⇆ *19 rooms, 5 suites, 2 apartments* ⚷ *Some in-room hot tubs, some kitchens, some kitchenettes, cable TV* ▭ *AE, D, MC, V* ☽ *Closed late Oct.–mid-May* ⏀ *CP.*

★ $$–$$$ ▨ **Oak House.** The wraparound veranda of this courtly pastel-painted 1872 Victorian looks across a busy street to the beach and out across Nantucket Sound. Several rooms have private terraces or balconies; if you're bothered by noise, ask for a room at the back. Inside you will see richly painted oak in ceilings, wall paneling, wainscoting, and furnishings. All this well-preserved wood creates an appropriate setting for the choice antique furniture and nautical-theme accessories. An elegant afternoon tea with cakes and cookies is served in a glassed-in sunporch. ⊠ *75 Sea View Ave.* ✑ *Box 299, 02557* ☎ *508/693–4187 or 800/245–5979* ▨ *508/696–7385* ⊕ *www.vineyardinns.com/oakhouse.html* ⇆ *10 rooms, 2 suites* ⚷ *No kids under 10, no smoking* ▭ *AE, D, MC, V* ☽ *Closed mid-Oct.–mid-May* ⏀ *CP.*

Nightlife & the Arts

The island's only family brewpub, **Offshore Ale** (⊠ Kennebec Ave. ☎ 508/693–2626) hosts live Latin, folk, and blues year-round and serves its own beer and ales and a terrific pub menu. Cozy up to the fireplace with a pint on cool nights.

Sports & the Outdoors

BEACH **Joseph A. Sylvia State Beach** (⊠ Between Oak Bluffs and Edgartown, off Beach Rd.) is a 6-mi-long sandy beach with a view of Cape Cod across Nantucket Sound. The calm, warm water and food vendors make it popular with families.

FISHING **Dick's Bait & Tackle** (⊠ New York Ave. ☎ 508/693–7669) rents gear, sells accessories and bait, and keeps a current copy of the fishing regulations.

GOLF   **Farm Neck Golf Club** (✉ County Rd. ☎ 508/693–3057), a semiprivate club on marsh-rimmed Sengekontacket Pond, has 18 holes in a championship layout and a driving range. Reservations are required 48 hours in advance.

Shopping

Book Den East (✉ 71 New York Ave. ☎ 508/693–3946) stocks 20,000 out-of-print, antiquarian, and paperback books. **Laughing Bear** (✉ 33 Circuit Ave. ☎ 508/693–9342) carries women's wear made of Balinese or Indian batiks plus jewelry and accessories from around the world.

Edgartown

❸ *6 mi southeast of Oak Bluffs.*

Once a well-to-do whaling town, Edgartown remains the Vineyard's toniest town and has preserved some of its elegant past. Sea captains' houses from the 18th and 19th centuries, ensconced in well-manicured gardens and lawns, line the streets. The island's oldest dwelling is the 1672 **Vincent House.** A tour of this weathered-shingle farmhouse takes you along a time line that starts with the sparse furnishings of the 1600s and ends in a Federal-style parlor of the 1800s. ✉ *Main St.* ☎ *508/627–4440* ☜ *$3* ☺ *Late May–Oct., Mon.–Sat. 10–3.*

The **Edgartown Lighthouse,** surrounded by a public beach, provides a great view (but seaweedy bathing). The white cast-iron tower was floated by barge from Ipswich, Massachusetts, in 1938. ✉ *Off N. Water St.*

★ ☾ The 350-acre **Felix Neck Wildlife Sanctuary,** a Massachusetts Audubon Society preserve 3 mi out of Edgartown toward Oak Bluffs and Vineyard Haven, has 2 mi of hiking trails traversing marshland, fields, woods, seashore, and waterfowl and reptile ponds. Naturalist-led events include sunset hikes, stargazing, snake or bird walks, and canoeing. ✉ *Off Edgartown–Vineyard Haven Rd.* ☎ *508/627–4850* ☜ *$4* ☺ *Center June–Sept., daily 8–4; Oct.–May, Tues.–Sun. 9–4. Trails daily sunrise–7 PM.*

Where to Stay & Eat

$$$$ ✕ **L'étoile.** Perhaps the Vineyard's finest traditional French restaurant, L'étoile carries on a long history of excellent dining. Both the food and the setting in the stunningly appointed Charlotte Inn are unforgettable. The glass-enclosed dining room reminds you why hunter green, dark wood, and glass became so popular—and imitated. Preparations are at once classic and creative. Not to be missed are spice-crusted foie gras with sautéed nectarines and a "trilogy" of Chilmark lamb that includes a rack chop, a leg fillet, and homemade sausage with a warm chèvre-and-sunchoke napoleon. The outstanding wine list has selections from California and Europe that are solid, if a little pricey. ✉ *27 S. Summer St.* ☎ *508/627–5187* ⚐ *Reservations essential* ▤ *AE, MC, V* ☺ *Closed Jan.–mid-Feb., and Sun.–Wed. in Oct.–Dec. and late Feb.–Apr. No lunch.*

FodorsChoice
★

$$–$$$ ✕ **Grill on Main.** The space between the tables is what strikes you first in this low-key restaurant. Chef-owner Tony Saccoccia not only aims to provide some intimacy for his patrons but also creates inventive takes on seafood. For a starter, try the lobster turnover with a shrimp and lemon cream, then the baked codfish with a lump crab and smoked

scallop sauce for the entrée. If you want to see how it's all prepared, ask for a seat with a view of the kitchen. ⊠ *227 Upper Main St.* ☎ *508/ 627–8344* ▤ *AE, D, DC, MC, V.*

\$\$ ✕ **Lattanzi's Pizzeria.** Albert and Cathy Lattanzi's big brick oven gets fired up by 2:30 PM, and the pizza that slides out come evening is delicious—baby clams with plum tomatoes, oregano, spinach, roasted garlic, and Asiago cheese is just one example. Next dor is Lattanzi's Restaurant, which serves a broader Italian menu. ⊠ *Old Post Office Sq.* ☎ *508/ 627–9084* ▤ *D, DC, MC, V* ☻ *No lunch.*

★ **\$\$\$\$** ▦ **Harbor View.** The centerpiece of this historic hotel is a gray-shingle, 1891 Victorian building with wraparound veranda and a gazebo. Accommodations are also in a complex of nearby buildings in a residential neighborhood. Those in the contemporary town houses have cathedral ceilings, decks, kitchens, and large living areas with sofa beds. Rooms in other buildings, however, resemble upscale motel rooms, so ask for main-building or town-house rooms. A beach, good for walking, stretches ¾ mi from the hotel's dock. ⊠ *131 N. Water St.* ⌂ *Box 7, 02539* ☎ *508/ 627–7000 or 800/225–6005* 🖷 *508/742–1042* ⊕ *www.harbor-view. com* ⇨ *130 rooms, 22 suites* ♨ *2 restaurants, room service, some kitchenettes, refrigerators, 2 tennis courts, pool, dock, laundry service, concierge, business services* ▤ *AE, DC, MC, V.*

\$\$\$–\$\$\$\$ ▦ **Charlotte Inn.** From the moment you walk up to the dark-wood Scottish barrister's desk at check-in you'll be surrounded by the trappings and customs of a bygone era. Guests' names are handwritten into the register by the dignified and attentive staff. Beautiful antique furnishings, *objets,* and paintings fill the property—the book you pick up in your room might be an 18th-century edition of Voltaire, and your bed could be a hand-carved four-poster. All rooms have hair dryers and robes. This elegant atmosphere extends to the outstanding restaurant L'étoile. ⊠ *27 S. Summer St., 02539* ☎ *508/627–4751* 🖷 *508/627–4652* ⊕ *www. relaischateaux.com* ⇨ *21 rooms, 2 suites* ♨ *Restaurant, library; no kids under 14* ▤ *AE, MC, V* ▐◯▌ *CP.*

FodorśChoice
★

Nightlife & the Arts

NIGHTLIFE The **Atria Bar** (⊠ 137 Main St. ☎ 508/627–5850) is off the beaten path but is a quiet, comfortable place to escape the summer crowds. Enjoy one of the clever drinks, including the Green Bamboo (gin, mint, and fresh ginger), and the Espresso Martini (Ketel One vodka, Kahlúa, Tia Maria, and a shot of fresh espresso). **Hot Tin Roof** (⊠ Martha's Vineyard Airport, Edgartown–West Tisbury Rd. ☎ 508/693–1137), opened by Carly Simon in 1976, is a venue for big-name acts such as Medeski, Martin and Wood, Soulive, Kate Taylor, and the Derek Trucks Band.

Sports & the Outdoors

Bend-in-the-Road Beach (⊠ Beach Rd.), the town beach, is backed by low, grassy dunes and wild roses. **Little Beach** (⊠ End of Fuller St.) is a little-known beach that looks like a crooked pinkie that points into Eel Pond, a great place for bird-watching (be careful of the fenced-off piping plover breeding grounds in the dunes).

Big Eye Charters (☎ 508/627–3649) leads fishing charters that leave from Edgartown Harbor. **Coop's Bait and Tackle** (⊠ 147 W. Tisbury Rd.

☎ 508/627–3909) sells accessories and bait, rents fishing gear, and books fishing charters.

Shopping

David Le Breton, the owner of **Edgartown Books** (⊠ 44 Main St. ☎ 508/627–8463), is a true bibliophile and carries a large selection of current and island-related titles. He will be happy to make a recommendation for your summer reading. The **Edgartown Scrimshaw Gallery** (⊠ 43 Main St. ☎ 508/627–9439) showcases a large collection of scrimshaw, including some antique pieces. The **Old Sculpin Gallery** (⊠ 58 Dock St. ☎ 508/627–4881) is the Martha's Vineyard Art Association's headquarters. Don't miss the fabulous seaweed collages by Rose Treat.

Chappaquiddick Island

➍ *1 mi southeast of Edgartown.*

A sparsely populated area with many nature preserves, Chappaquiddick "Island" makes for a pleasant day trip or bike ride on a sunny day. The island is actually connected to the Vineyard by a long sand spit that begins in South Beach in Katama. It's a spectacular 2¾-mi walk, or you can take the ferry, which departs about every five minutes.

The **Cape Poge Wildlife Refuge** (⊠ East end of Dike Rd., 3 mi from Chappaquiddick ferry landing), on the easternmost shore of Chappaquiddick Island, is more than 6 square mi of wilderness—a conglomeration of habitats where you can swim, walk, fish, or just sit and enjoy the surroundings. Its dunes, woods, cedar thickets, moors, salt marshes, ponds, tidal flats, and barrier beach serve as an important migration stopover and nesting area for numerous sea and shore birds. The best way to get to the refuge is as part of a naturalist-led **jeep drive** (☎ 508/627–3599).

★ The 200-acre **Wasque Reservation** (pronounced *wayce*-kwee), mostly a vast beach, connects Chappaquiddick Island with the mainland of the Vineyard in Katama, closing off the south end of Katama Bay. You can fish, sunbathe, take the trail by Swan Pond, walk to the island's southeasternmost tip at Wasque Point, or dip into the surf—with caution, due to strong currents. Wasque Beach is accessed by a flat boardwalk with benches overlooking the west end of Swan Pond. It's a pretty walk skirting the pond, with ocean views on one side and poles for osprey nests on the other. Atop a bluff is a pine-shaded picnic grove with a spectacular, practically 180-degree panorama. *⊠ At east end of Wasque Rd., 5 mi from Chappaquiddick ferry landing ☎ 508/627–7260 ☄ Cars $3, plus $3 per adult late May–mid-Sept.; free rest of yr ☉ Property 24 hrs. Gatehouse late May–mid-Oct., daily 9–5.*

Sports & the Outdoors

BEACHES **East Beach,** one of the area's best beaches, is accessible by car from Dyke Road. There is a $3 fee to enter the beach. **Wasque Beach,** at the Wasque Reservation, is an uncrowded ½-mi sandy beach with sometimes strong surf and currents, a parking lot, and restrooms.

West Tisbury

5 *8 mi west of Edgartown, 6½ mi south of Vineyard Haven.*

West Tisbury retains its rural appeal and maintains its agricultural tradition at several active horse and produce farms. The town center looks very much the small New England village, complete with a white steepled church.

Long Point, a 633-acre Trustees of Reservations preserve with an open area of grassland and heath, provides a lovely walk with the promise of a refreshing swim at its end. The area is bounded on the east by freshwater Homer's Pond, on the west by saltwater Tisbury Great Pond, and on the south by fantastic, mile-long South Beach on the Atlantic Ocean. Long Cove Pond, a sandy freshwater swimming pond, is an ideal spot for bird-watchers. ⊠ *Mid-June–mid-Sept., turn left onto unmarked dirt road (Waldron's Bottom Rd., look for mailboxes) ³/₁₀ mi west of airport on Edgartown–West Tisbury Rd.; at end, follow signs to Long Point parking lot. Mid-Sept.–mid-June, follow unpaved Deep Bottom Rd. (1 mi west of airport) 2 mi to lot* ☎ *508/693–7392* ⊠ *Mid-June–mid-Sept., $7 per vehicle, $3 per adult; free rest of yr* ☉ *Daily 9–6.*

★ At the center of Martha's Vineyard, the **Manuel F. Correllus State Forest** is a 5,000-acre pine and scrub-oak forest crisscrossed with hiking trails and circled by a paved but rough bike trail (mopeds are prohibited). There's a 2-mi nature trail, a 2-mi par fitness course, and horse trails. The West Tisbury side of the state forest joins with an equally large Edgartown parcel to virtually surround the airport. ⊠ *Headquarters on Barnes Rd. by airport* ☎ *508/693–2540* ⊠ *Free* ☉ *Daily sunrise–sunset.*

A paradise for bird-watchers, **Sepiessa Point Reservation** consists of 164 acres on splendid Tisbury Great Pond, with expansive pond and ocean views, walking trails around coves and saltwater marshes, bird-watching, horse trails, swimming, and a boat launch. ⊠ *New La., which becomes Tiah's Cove Rd., off W. Tisbury Rd.* ☎ *508/627–7141* ⊠ *Free* ☉ *Daily sunrise–sunset.*

Where to Stay & Eat

$$$–$$$$ ✕ **Bittersweet.** A pronounced Mediterranean flavor enhances the progressive American cuisine that chef Job Yacubian creates here. Rosemary, olives, and celery hearts are part of the braised lamb shank, and the pan-roasted skate wing is flavored with kumquats and almonds, cauliflower, and capers. Despite its exciting menu, this place can be a bit noisy. ⊠ *State Rd.* ☎ *508/696–3966* ⚑ *Reservations essential* ▭ *MC, V* ⌂ *BYOB.*

$$–$$$$ ✕▣ **Lambert's Cove Inn.** A narrow road winds through pine woods and beside creeper-covered stone walls to this secluded inn surrounded by gardens and old stone walls. Rooms in the rambling 1790 farmhouse have light floral wallpapers and a sunny, country feel. Those in outbuildings have screened porches or decks. Except for a brief winter vacation, the inn is open year-round. You'll find soft candlelight and excellent contemporary cuisine in the restaurant ($$–$$$$; reservations essential). Especially good is the fresh cod with littleneck clams. ⊠ *Off Lambert's*

Cove Rd. 🕭 *R.R. 1, Box 422, Vineyard Haven 02568* 🕿 *508/693–2298*
🖷 *508/693–7890* ⊕ *www.lambertscoveinn.com* ➷ *15 rooms* ♻ *Restaurant, in-room DVDs, Wi-Fi, tennis court* ▭ *AE, MC, V* ⟡❘ *BP.*

Nightlife & the Arts

WIMP (✉ Grange Hall, State Rd. 🕿 508/939–9368), the island's premier comedy improvisation troupe, performs Wednesday at 8 PM from mid-June to mid-October.

Sports & the Outdoors

Lambert's Cove Beach (✉ Lambert's Cove Rd.), one of the island's prettiest, has fine sand and clear water. The Vineyard Sound Beach has calm waters good for children.

Shopping

The **Granary Gallery at the Red Barn** (✉ Old County Rd. 🕿 508/693–0455) exhibits artworks by island and international artists and displays Early American furniture.

Chilmark

❻ *5½ mi southwest of West Tisbury.*

Chilmark is a rural village whose ocean views, rustic woodlands, and lack of crowds have drawn chic summer visitors and resulted in stratospheric real estate prices. Laced with rough roads and winding stone fences that once separated fields and pastures, Chilmark reminds people of what the Vineyard was like in an earlier time, before developers took over.

Where to Stay & Eat

$$$–$$$$ ✕⬚ **Inn at Blueberry Hill.** Exclusive and secluded, this cedar-shingle retreat and its 56 acres of former farmland put you in the heart of the rural Vineyard. The restaurant, Theo's ($$–$$$$), is relaxed and elegant, and the fresh, health-conscious food is thoughtfully prepared. A cold breakfast is included in the room rate, and a box lunch is available for a picnic on the beach (the inn runs a guest shuttle to Lucy Vincent and Squibnocket beaches). Guest rooms are sparsely but tastefully decorated with simple island-made furniture. Most rooms have glass doors that open onto terraces or private decks. There is a large parlor-library with a fireplace. ✉ 74 North Rd., 02535 🕿 508/645–3322 or 800/356–3322 🖷 508/645–3799 ⊕ www.blueberryinn.com ➷ 25 rooms ♻ Restaurant, tennis court, pool, gym, hot tub, massage, meeting room, airport shuttle; no kids under 12, no smoking ▭ AE, MC, V ⊘ Closed Nov.–Apr. ⟡❘ CP.

Sports & the Outdoors

★ A dirt road leads off South Road to beautiful **Lucy Vincent Beach,** which in summer is open only to Chilmark residents and those staying in town.

Shopping

Chilmark Chocolates (✉ State Rd. 🕿 508/645–3013) sells superior chocolates and what may be the world's finest butter crunch, which you can sometimes watch being made in the back room.

Menemsha

★ **❼** *1½ mi northwest of Chilmark.*

Unspoiled by the "progress" of the past few decades, the working port of Menemsha is a jumble of weathered fishing shacks, fishing and pleasure boats, drying nets, and lobster pots. Several scenes of the movie *Jaws* were filmed here. The village is a must-see for cyclists, who can stop for an ice cream cone or a cup of chowder.

Where to Stay & Eat

$–$$ ✕ **Larsen's.** Basically a retail fish store, Larsen's also has a raw take-out
Fodor'sChoice counter and will boil lobsters for you as well. A plate of fresh littlenecks
★ or cherrystones goes for $9 a dozen. Oysters at $15 a dozen are not a bad alternative. There's also seafood chowder and a variety of smoked fish and dips. Bring your own bottle of wine or beer, buy your dinner here, and then set up on the rocks, on the docks, or at the beach: there's no finer alfresco rustic dining on the island. Larsen's closes at 6 PM weekdays, 7 PM weekends. ⊠ *Dutcher's Dock* ☎ *508/645–2680* ⊟ *MC, V* *BYOB* ☺ *Closed mid-Oct.–mid-May.*

★ **$$$–$$$$** ▦ **Beach Plum Inn.** This mansard-roof inn, surrounded by 7 acres of lavish formal gardens and lush woodland, sits on a bluff over Menemsha Harbor. The floral-theme rooms—five in the main house and four in cottages—have gorgeous furnishings; in the Daffodil room, bathed in shades of yellow and blue, you'll find a hand-painted queen bed and a romantic balcony. A vaulted, beamed ceiling rises over the bedroom of the secluded Morning Glory Cottage. ⊠ *North Rd., 02552* ☎ *508/645–9454 or 877/645–7398* ⊕ *www.beachpluminn.com* ⤳ *9 rooms* ☖ *Some in-room hot tubs, refrigerators, cable TV, tennis court, concierge; no smoking* ⊟ *AE, D, MC, V* ☺ *Closed Dec.–Apr.* ❖ *BP.*

Sports & the Outdoors

Menemsha Hills Reservation (⊠ North Rd. just north of Menemsha) has 4 mi of some of the most challenging, breathtaking, and steep hiking trails on the island, including a stroll up to the second-highest point of Martha's Vineyard and another ramble that descends down through the windswept valley to boulder-strewn Vineyard Sound Beach.

Aquinnah

❽ *6½ mi west of Menemsha, 10 mi southwest of West Tisbury, 17 mi southwest of Vineyard Haven.*

Aquinnah, called Gay Head until the town voted to change its name in 1997, is an official Native American township. The Wampanoag tribe is the guardian of the 420 acres that constitute the Aquinnah Native American Reservation. Aquinnah (pronounced a-*kwih*-nah), is Wampanoag for "land under the hill." The town is best known for the red-hued Aquinnah Cliffs.

Quitsa Pond Lookout (⊠ State Rd.) has a good view of the adjoining Menemsha and Nashaquitsa ponds, the woods, and the ocean beyond.

FodorsChoice   A National Historic Landmark, the spectacular **Aquinnah Cliffs** are part
★   of the Wampanoag reservation land. These dramatically striated walls
of red clay are the island's major sightseeing attraction, as evidenced by
the tour bus–filled parking lot. Native American crafts and food shops
line the short approach to the overlook, from which you can see the Elizabeth Islands to the northeast across Vineyard Sound and Noman's Land
Island—part wildlife preserve, part military bombing-practice site—3
mi off the Vineyard's southern coast. ⊠ *State Rd.*

The brick **Aquinnah Lighthouse** is stationed precariously atop the rapidly
eroding cliffs. The lighthouse is open to the public on summer weekends at sunset, weather permitting. ⊠ *Lighthouse Rd.* ☎ *508/645–
2211* ☞ *$2.*

Where to Stay & Eat

★ **$$$–$$$$**   ✕⛺ **Outermost Inn.** This B&B by the Aquinnah Cliffs stands alone on
acres of moorland. The house is wrapped in windows revealing views
of sea and sky in three directions. From the wide porch and patio are
great views of the Aquinnah Lighthouse. In the restaurant, open to the
public, dinner is served nightly in summer and is all prix fixe at $72 (reser-
vations are essential, and it's BYOB). The inn is clean and contempo-
rary, with white walls and polished light-wood floors. Each room has
a phone, and one has a whirlpool tub. The beach is a 10-minute walk
away. ⊠ *81 Lighthouse Rd.* ⌖ *R.R. 1, Box 171, 02535* ☎ *508/645–
3511* ⊟ *508/645–3514* ⊕ *www.outermostinn.com* ↷ *7 rooms* △ *Restau-
rant, some in-room hot tubs; no a/c, no kids under 12, no smoking* ⊟ *AE,
D, MC, V* ⊙ *Closed mid-Oct.–May* ⧖ *BP.*

Martha's Vineyard A to Z

*To research prices, get advice from other travelers, and book travel arrange-
ments, visit www.fodors.com.*

AIR TRAVEL

Cape Air connects the Vineyard year-round with Boston (including an
hourly summer shuttle), Hyannis, Nantucket, Providence, and New
Bedford. It offers joint fares and ticketing and baggage agreements with
several major carriers. Fares typically begin around $85 from Hyannis
to nearly $200 from Boston but vary depending on the time of year. Sev-
eral charter airlines also serve the island—these come and go, so it's best
to check with the chamber of commerce. Martha's Vineyard Airport is
in West Tisbury, near the center of the island.

🛂 Carrier **Cape Air** ☎ 800/352-0714 ⊕ www.flycapeair.com.

🛂 Airport Information **Martha's Vineyard Airport** ⊠ Edgartown–West Tisbury Rd.
☎ 508/693-7022.

BIKE TRAVEL

Martha's Vineyard is superb terrain for biking—you can pick up a map
that lists safety tips and shows the island's many dedicated bike paths
from the chamber of commerce. Several shops throughout the island rent
bicycles, many of them close to the ferry terminals. Martha's Vineyard
Strictly Bikes rents bike racks for your car.

🚲 Bike Rentals **DeBettencourt's** ✉ Circuit Ave. exit, Oak Bluffs ☎ 508/693-0011.
Martha's Vineyard Strictly Bikes ✉ 24 Union St., Vineyard Haven ☎ 508/693-0782.

BOAT & FERRY TRAVEL

Car-and-passenger ferries travel to Vineyard Haven from Woods Hole
on Cape Cod year-round and on to Oak Bluffs in season. Passenger-only
ferries from Falmouth and Hyannis on Cape Cod, and from New Bedford, serve Vineyard Haven and Oak Bluffs in season. All provide
overnight parking—fees are $6–$12 nightly. Service below is often limited fall through spring.

FROM FALMOUTH: The **Falmouth–Edgartown** passenger ferry makes the
approximately 45-minute trip to Edgartown late May through early October. During high season, the ferry runs daily, weekends in the slower
months. Reservations are recommended. (🚲 *Round-trip $30, bicycles
$8 additional; one-way $15, bicycles $4 additional.*) The *Island Queen,*
a 600-passenger ferry, sails from Falmouth Harbor to Oak Bluffs, a 35-
minute trip, daily from late May to mid-October. *Round-trip $12, bi-
cycles $6 additional.*

FROM HYANNIS: **Hy-Line** operates a high-speed passenger ferry that
makes the trip to Oak Bluffs in 55 minutes daily year-round. The traditional passenger ferry makes the 1¾-hour run to Oak Bluffs May to
late October. *High-speed: Round-trip June–late Oct. $54, rest of year
$27, bicycles $10 additional year-round; Traditional: Round-trip $31,
bicycles $10 additional.*

FROM NEW BEDFORD: **New England Fast Ferry Co.** makes daily passenger-only trips year-round to Vineyard Haven and also to Oak Bluffs
from mid-May to early October; the trip, leaving from the State Pier
in New Bedford, takes about an hour. *Round-trip $50, bicycles $10
additional.*

FROM WOODS HOLE: The **Steamship Authority** runs the only ferries carrying cars and trucks in addition to passengers; they make the 45-minute
trip to Vineyard Haven year-round and to Oak Bluffs from mid-May to
mid-October. If you plan to take a car, you'll definitely need a reservation in summer or on weekends in fall and spring (passenger reservations
are not necessary). *Passengers one-way year-round $6.50, bicycles $3 additional; cars one-way Apr.–mid-Oct. $62 or $72 depending on size, round-
trip excursion rates mid-May–mid-Sept. $73 and $93.*

🚲 Boat & Ferry Information **Falmouth-Edgartown Ferry** ✉ Falmouth Marine
☎ 508/548-9400 ⊕ www.falmouthferry.com. **Hy-Line** ✉ Ocean St. dock ☎ 508/
778-2600, 508/693-0112 in Oak Bluffs ⊕ www.hy-linecruises.com. ***Island Queen***
✉ Falmouth Heights Rd., Falmouth ☎ 508/548-4800 ⊕ www.islandqueen.com.
New England Fast Ferry ✉ Steamship Authority Dock, Oak Bluffs ☎ 617/748-
1428 or 866/453-6800 ⊕ www.mvfastferry.com. **Steamship Authority** ☎ 508/477-
8600 information and car reservations, 508/693-9130 on the Vineyard ⊕ www.
steamshipauthority.com.

🚲 Town Harbor Facilities **Edgartown** ☎ 508/627-4746. **Menemsha** ☎ 508/645-
2846. **Oak Bluffs** ☎ 508/693-9644. **Vineyard Haven** ☎ 508/696-4249.

BUS TRAVEL

The big buses of the Martha's Vineyard Transit Authority (VTA) provide regular service to all six towns on the island, with frequent stops in peak season and quite limited service in winter. The fare is $1 per town, including the town of departure. One day ($6), three-day ($15), and one-week ($25) passes are available at the Edgartown Visitors Center.

The VTA also has two free in-town shuttle-bus routes, one in Edgartown and one in Vineyard Haven.

🚌 Bus Information **Martha's Vineyard Transit Authority (VTA)** ☎ 508/693-9940 ⊕ www.vineyardtransit.com.

CAR RENTAL

You can book rentals through the Woods Hole ferry terminal free phone. The agencies listed below have rental desks at the airport. Cost is $80–$150 per day for a sedan. Renting a four-wheel-drive vehicle costs $150 per day (seasonal prices fluctuate widely).

🚗 Local Agencies **AAA Island** ☎ 508/627-6800. **Adventure Rentals** ✉ Beach Rd., Vineyard Haven ☎ 508/693-1959.

CAR TRAVEL

If you really want to see the whole island and tour freely among the different towns, it's worth having a car here. Bringing one over on the ferry in summer, however, requires reservations far in advance, costs almost double what it does off-season, and necessitates standing in long lines—it's sometimes easier and more economical to rent a car once on the island, and then only for the days you plan on exploring. Where you stay and what you plan on seeing can greatly influence your transportation plans; as soon as you've booked a room, discuss the different options for getting around the island with your innkeeper or hotel staff. Traffic can be a challenge, especially in season and in Vineyard Haven, Oak Bluffs, and Edgartown.

Note that permits, fees, and certain equipment are needed for driving on Katama Beach and Wasque Reservation. Contact the chamber of commerce or park rangers for details.

EMERGENCIES

Vineyard Medical Services provides walk-in care; call for days and hours. Leslie's Drug Store is open daily and has a pharmacist on 24-hour call for emergencies.

🏥 Hospital & Emergency Service **Martha's Vineyard Hospital** ✉ Linton La., Oak Bluffs ☎ 508/693-0410. **Vineyard Medical Services** ✉ State Rd., Vineyard Haven ☎ 508/693-6399.

💊 Late-Night Pharmacy **Leslie's Drug Store** ✉ 65 Main St., Vineyard Haven ☎ 508/693-1010.

TAXIS

Taxis meet all scheduled ferries and flights, and there are taxi stands by the Flying Horses Carousel in Oak Bluffs, at the foot of Main Street in Edgartown, and by the steamship office in Vineyard Haven. Fares range from $5 within a town to $35–$40 one-way from Vineyard Haven to

Aquinnah. Rates double between 1 AM and 7 AM. Note that limousine companies often provide service both on- and off-island.

Taxi Companies AdamCab ☎ 508/627-4462 ⊕ www.adamcab.com. **All Island Taxi** ☎ 508/693-2929. **Mario's** ☎ 508/693-8399. **Martha's Vineyard Taxi** ☎ 508/693-8660.

TOURS

Liz Villard's Vineyard History Tours leads walking tours of Edgartown's "history, architecture, ghosts, and gossip" that include visits to the Vincent House. Tours are run from April through December; call for times. Liz and her guides also lead similar tours of Oak Bluffs and Vineyard Haven. Walks last a little over an hour.

Tour Operator Vineyard History Tours ☎ 508/627-2529.

VISITOR INFORMATION

Martha's Vineyard Chamber of Commerce is two blocks from the Vineyard Haven ferry. The chamber information booth by the Vineyard Haven steamship terminal is open late May to the last weekend in June, Friday–Sunday 8–8; July–early September, daily 8–8; and early September–mid-October, Friday–Sunday 8:30–5:30. The chamber itself is open weekdays 9–5. There are also town information kiosks on Circuit Avenue in Oak Bluffs and on Church Street in Edgartown.

Tourist Information Martha's Vineyard Chamber of Commerce ⊠ Beach Rd. ⊡ Box 1698, Vineyard Haven 02568 ☎ 508/693-4486 ⊕ www.mvy.com.

NANTUCKET

Updated by
Sandy
MacDonald

At the height of its prosperity in the early 19th century, the little island of Nantucket was the foremost whaling port in the world. Its harbor bustled with whaling ships and merchant vessels; chandleries, cooperages, and other shops crowded the wharves. Burly ship hands loaded barrels of whale oil onto wagons, which they wheeled along cobblestone streets to refineries and candle factories. Sea breezes carried the smoke and smells of booming industry through town as its inhabitants eagerly took care of business. Shipowners and sea captains built elegant mansions, which today remain remarkably unchanged, thanks to a very strict building code initiated in the 1950s. The entire town of Nantucket is now an official National Historic District encompassing more than 800 pre-1850 structures within 1 square mi.

Day-trippers usually take in the architecture and historical sites, dine at one of the many delightful restaurants, and browse in the pricey boutiques, most of which stay open from mid-April through December. Signature items include Nantucket lightship baskets, originally crafted by sailors whiling away a long watch; artisans who continue the tradition now command prices of $700 and up, and the antiques are exponentially more expensive.

Nantucket Town

❶ *30 mi southeast of Hyannis, 107 mi southeast of Boston.*

Nantucket Town has one of the country's finest historical districts, with beautiful 18th- and 19th-century architecture and a museum of whal-

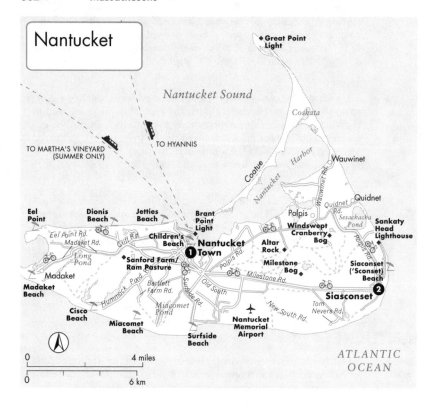

Nantucket

Great Point Light

Nantucket Sound

Coskata

TO MARTHA'S VINEYARD
(SUMMER ONLY)

TO HYANNIS

Wauwinet

Coatue

Nantucket Harbor

Wauwinet Rd.

Quidnet

Quidnet Rd.

Polpis

Sesachacha Pond

Eel
Point

Dionis
Beach

Jetties
Beach

Brant
Point
Light

Windswept
Cranberry
Bog

Sankaty
Head
Lighthouse

Eel Point Rd.
Madaket Rd.

Cliff Rd.

Children's
Beach

Nantucket
❶ Town

Altar
Rock ◆

Polpis Rd.

*Long
Pond*

Sanford Farm/
Ram Pasture

Milestone
Bog ◆

Siaconset
('Sconset)
Beach

Madaket

*Bartlett
Farm Rd.*

Hummock Pond

*Miacomet
Pond*

Old South Rd.

Surfside Rd.

Milestone Rd.

Siasconset ❷

Madaket
Beach

Cisco
Beach

Miacomet
Beach

Surfside
Beach

New South Rd.

Tom
Nevers Rd.

Nantucket
Memorial
Airport

ATLANTIC
OCEAN

0   4 miles
0   6 km

---

ing history. The **Nantucket Historical Association (NHA)** (☎ 508/228–1894 NHA ⊕ www.nha.org) maintains an assortment of these venerable properties, including the Whaling Museum. A $15 pass gets you into them all.

African Meeting House. When the island abolished slavery in 1773, Nantucket became a destination for free blacks and escaping slaves. The African Meeting House was built in the 1820s as a schoolhouse, and it functioned as such until 1846, when the island's schools were integrated. A complete restoration has returned the site to its authentic 1880s appearance. ⊠ *29 York St.* ☎ *508/228–9833* ⊕ *www.afroammuseum. org* ⊠ *Free* ☉ *July and Aug., Tues.–Sat. 11–3, Sun. 1–3.*

★ **Brant Point Light.** The 26-foot-tall, white-painted beauty has views of the harbor and town. Brant Point is the second oldest lighthouse station in the country (after Boston Light, 1716). The first lighthouse was built here in 1746, burned down, and was succeeded by many others—the present, much-photographed light was built in 1902. ⊠ *End of Easton St., across a footbridge.*

The tower of the **First Congregational Church** provides the best view of Nantucket—for those who climb the 92 steps. Rising 120 feet, the tower is capped by a weather vane depicting a whale catch. Peek in at the church's 1852 trompe l'oeil ceiling. ⊠ *62 Centre St.* ☎ *508/228–0950* ⊕ *www.nantucketfcc.org* ☜ *Tower tour $2.50 donation* ⊙ *Mid-June–mid-Oct., Mon.–Sat. 10–4; services Sun. 9 and 10 AM.*

★ ℭ Immersing you in Nantucket's whaling past with exhibits that include a fully rigged whaleboat and a skeleton of a 43-foot finback whale, the 1846 **Whaling Museum** is a must-see. Also exhibited are harpoons and other whale-hunting implements; portraits of sea captains; a large collection of exquisitely carved scrimshaw; a full-size tryworks once used to process whale oil aboard ship; replicas of cooper, blacksmith, and other ship-fitting shops; and the original 16-foot-high lens from Sankaty Head Lighthouse. ⊠ *13–15 Broad St.* ☎ *508/228–1894* ☜ *$10 or NHA pass* ⊙ *Late May–mid-Oct., daily 10–5; call for off-season hrs.*

4

Where to Stay & Eat

$$$$ ✕ **Company of the Cauldron.** The tiny dining room, a sconce-lighted haven of architectural salvage, is served by an even smaller kitchen, whence chef-owner All Kovalencik issues only one menu per evening. Adepts gladly forego multiple choice when the chef's choice is invariably so dead-on. (A rundown of the weekly roster of fixed-price dinners is available over the phone or online.) Given the close quarters, expect to come away not only sated but better acquainted with your near neighbors. ⊠ *5 India St.* ☎ *508/228–4016* ⌖ *Reservations essential* ▤ *MC, V* ⊙ *Closed Dec.–mid-Apr. No lunch.*

$$$$ ✕ **Straight Wharf.** This loftlike restaurant with harborside deck has enjoyed legendary status for two decades. At the helm since 1995, executive chef Steve Cavagnaro immediately inspires confidence with an intense lobster bisque with an undertone of caramel. The promise is upheld in subsequent dishes: everything from cuisine to service is just right. If you'd like a preview, try the less costly café menu at the adjoining bar—that is, if you can get in. ⊠ *6 Harbor Sq., Straight Wharf* ☎ *508/228–4499* ▤ *AE, MC, V* ⊙ *Closed late Sept.–mid-May. No lunch.*

$$–$$$ ✕ **Black-Eyed Susan's.** From a passing glance, you'd never peg this
Fodor'sChoice humble storefront as one of Nantucket's chic eateries—but as the
★ lines attest, it is. The luncheonette setup is offset by improbably fancy glass chandeliers, and foodies lay claim to the stools to observe chef Jeff Worster's often pyromaniacal "open kitchen." The dinner menu, which changes every three weeks, ventures boldly around the world and never lacks for novelty. The breakfasts (served until 1 PM) are just as stellar, including such eye-openers as sourdough French toast with orange, Jack Daniels butter, and pecans. ⊠ *10 India St.* ☎ *508/325–0308* ▤ *No credit cards* ⌖ *BYOB* ⊙ *Closed Nov.–Mar. No dinner Sun., no lunch.*

$$$$ ⌂ **White Elephant.** This 1920s behemoth right on Nantucket Harbor seems determined to keep raising the bar in terms of service and style. The complex, consisting of a main hotel plus several annexes treated to a breezy country-chic decor, hugs the harbor, leaving just enough room for an emerald lawn and the veranda of its in-house restaurant, the Brant Point Grill. Prices are up there but, for the echelon it attracts, not all that extreme. ⊠ *Easton St.* ⌂ *Box 1139, 02554* ☎ *508/228–2500 or 800/445–6574* 🖶 *508/325–1195* ⊕ *www.whiteelephanthotel.com* ⇲ *21*

rooms, 31 suites, 11 cottages ⚷ *Restaurant, room service, refrigerators, cable TV, in-room data ports, exercise equipment, dock, lounge, library, laundry service, concierge, business services, meeting rooms* 🖃 *AE, D, DC, MC, V* ✆ *Closed Nov.–Mar.* ⵔ *BP.*

★ **$$$–$$$$** ⊞ **Centerboard Guest House.** Victoriana, surprisingly, are in short supply on Nantucket: when the whaling boom fizzled, so did the island's disposable income. There's no dearth of the stuff here, however. Stained-glass lamps and antique quilts adorn rooms ornate with original woodwork. Standouts include a first-floor suite with 11-foot ceilings and its own living room–library with parquet floors, fireplace, and bar; its green-marble bath has a whirlpool tub. Also appealing is the "houseboat" room, which can sleep five; it even has a galley kitchen. ⊠ *8 Chester St.* ⬠ *Box 456, 02554* ☎ *508/228–9696* ⊕ *www.centerboardguesthouse. com* ⏎ *6 rooms, 1 suite* ⚷ *Refrigerators, cable TV; no smoking* 🖃 *MC, V* ⵔ *CP.*

★ **$$$–$$$$** ⊞ **Nantucket Whaler.** Let's not mince words: the suites carved out of this 1850 Greek-revival house are gorgeous. Neither Calliope Ligeles nor Randi Ott, the New Yorkers who rescued the place in 1999, had any design experience, but they approached the project as if preparing to welcome friends. Each suite has a private entrance and the wherewithal to whip up a meal. The spacious bedrooms are lavished with flowers, well-chosen antiques, and fine linens, including plush robes. Couples who have come to explore not so much the island as one another will scarcely have to come up for air. ⊠ *8 N. Water St.* ⬠ *Box 1337, 02554* ☎ *508/228–6597 or 800/462–6882* ⬔ *508/228–6291* ⊕ *www.nantucketwhaler. com* ⏎ *10 suites* ⚷ *Kitchenettes, cable TV, in-room DVD/VCR, in-room broadband, boccie, croquet; no kids under 12, no smoking* 🖃 *AE, MC, V* ✆ *Closed mid-Dec.–mid-Apr.*

★ **$$–$$$$** ⊞ **Jared Coffin House.** The largest house in town when it was built in 1845, this three-story brick manse is still plenty impressive. The antiques-filled parlors and formal dining room are a study in timeless good taste. The inn's umbrella extends to three other nearby buildings, the handsomest of which is the 1842 Greek-revival Harrison Gray House. Rooms vary greatly in terms of size and grandeur (the inn even has some very affordable singles), but one thing is assured: stay—or just breakfast or dine—here, and you'll have a better sense of what Nantucket's all about. ⊠ *29 Broad St.* ⬠ *Box 1580, 02554* ☎ *508/228–2405 or 800/248–2400* ⊕ *www.jaredcoffinhouse.com* ⏎ *60 rooms* ⚷ *Restaurant, café, cable TV, Wi-Fi, bar, concierge* 🖃 *AE, D, DC, MC, V* ⵔ *BP.*

★ **$$–$$$$** ⊞ **Pineapple Inn.** This 1838 Greek-revival captain's house, decorated with impeccable taste, makes an ideal retreat. Down quilts, marble-finished baths—no expense was spared in retrofitting this gem for its new role as pamperer. Breakfast is served in a formal dining room or beside the garden fountain. Whaling captains used to display a pineapple on their stoops upon completion of a successful journey, to signal the neighbors and invite them to come celebrate; here, that spirit prevails daily. ⊠ *10 Hussey St., 02554* ☎ *508/228–9992* ⬔ *508/325–6051* ⊕ *www. pineappleinn.com* ⏎ *12 rooms* ⚷ *Cable TV, in-room data ports* 🖃 *AE, MC, V* ✆ *Closed mid-Dec.–late Apr.* ⵔ *CP.*

Nightlife & the Arts

NIGHTLIFE The **Chicken Box** (✉ 14 Dave St., off Lower Orange St. ☎ 508/228–9717 ⊕ www.chickenbox.com) rocks! Live music—including some big-name bands—plays six nights a week in season, and weekends throughout the year. The **Club Car Lounge** (✉ 1 Main St. ☎ 508/228–1101) is an actual club car, salvaged from the narrow-gauge railroad that once ran out to Siasconset. Refined sorts find their way upstairs to the tiny bar at **Oran Mor** (✉ 2 S. Beach St. ☎ 508/228–8655) to sip fine wines and shots of single-malt Scotch: one such elixir inspired the restaurant's name.

Sports & the Outdoors

BEACHES A short ride from town, **Jetties Beach** (✉ Hulbert Avenue, 1½ mi north-west of Straight Wharf) is the most popular family beach because of its calm surf, lifeguards, restrooms, and snack bar.

BOATING On Jetties Beach, **Nantucket Community Sailing** (✉ 4 Winter St. ☎ 508/228–6600 ⊕ www.nantucketcommunitysailing.org), has sailboat and kayak rentals.

Shopping

ANTIQUES **Lynda Willauer Antiques** (✉ 2 India St. ☎ 508/228–3631) has amassed
★ a stellar cache of American and English furniture. **Rafael Osona Auctions** (✉ American Legion Hall, 21 Washington St. ☎ 508/228–3942) holds auctions of fine antiques most Saturday mornings from Memorial Day weekend to early December. **Sylvia Antiques** (✉ 6 Ray's Ct. ☎ 508/228–0960) has the richest stash of island-related antiquities.

CRAFTS **Four Winds Craft Guild** (✉ 6 Ray's Ct. ☎ 508/228–9623) sells antique and new scrimshaw and lightship baskets, as well as ship models, duck
★ decoys, and a kit for making your own lightship basket. **Nantucket Looms** (✉ 16 Federal St. ☎ 508/228–1908) stocks luscious woven-on-the-premises textiles and chunky Susan Lister Locke jewelry, among other adornments for self and home.

GALLERIES The **Artists' Association of Nantucket** (✉ 19 Washington St. ☎ 508/228–0772) is the best place to get an overview of the work being done on the island.

Siasconset

★ ❷ *7 mi east of Nantucket Town.*

First a fishing outpost and then an artist's colony (Broadway actors fa-vored it in the late 19th century), Siasconset—or 'Sconset, in the local vernacular—is a charming cluster of rose-covered cottages linked by drive-ways of crushed clamshells; at the edges of town, the former fishing shacks give way to magnificent sea-view mansions. The town per se consists of a market, post office, café, lunchroom, and liquor store–cum–lend-ing library.

★ **Altar Rock.** Altar Rock Road, a dirt track about 3 mi west on Polpis Road, leads to the island's highest point, Altar Rock, from which the view is spectacular. The hill overlooks open moor and bog land—technically called lowland heath—which is very rare in the United States. The entire area is laced with paths leading in every direction. Don't forget to keep track of the trails you travel in order to find your way back.

Where to Stay & Eat

$$–$$$$ ✕ **Sconset Café.** It looks like a modest lunchroom, with chockablock tables virtually within arm's reach of the open kitchen. But this tiny institution, treasured by summering locals since 1983, puts out wonderful breakfasts, great lunches, and outright astounding dinners. The nightly menus shift every two weeks to take advantage of seasonal bounty. If you have trouble getting in (it's not exactly undiscovered, and reservations are accepted for the 6 PM seating only), you can always order out and feast on the beach. (Call in the shoulder season before you head out to confirm that it's open.) ⊠ *Post Office Sq.* ☎ *508/257–4008* ▭ *No credit cards* 🍴 *BYOB* ☉ *Closed late Sept.–late May.*

$$$$ ✕▦ **Wauwinet.** This resplendently updated 1850 resort straddles a "haul
Fodor'sChoice over" poised between ocean and bay—which means beaches on both
★ sides. Head out by complimentary van or launch to partake of utmost pampering (the staff-to-guest ratio exceeds one-on-one). Optional activities include sailing, water-taxiing to a private beach, and touring the Great Point nature preserve by Land Rover. Of course, it's tempting just to stay put, what with the cushy country-chic rooms and a splendid restaurant, Topper's ($$$$). ⊠ *120 Wauwinet Rd., Wauwinet* 🖃 *Box 2580, Nantucket 02584* ☎ *508/228–0145 or 800/426–8718* 🖷 *508/228– 7135* ⊕ *www.wauwinet.com* 📨 *25 rooms, 5 cottages* 🝔 *Restaurant, room service, Wi-Fi, beach, boating, mountain bikes, croquet, bar, library, concierge, business services; no kids under 12, no smoking* ▭ *AE, DC, MC, V* ☉ *Closed Nov.–Apr.* ⵿ *BP.*

$$$–$$$$ ▦ **Summer House.** Perched on a bluff overlooking Siasconset Beach, this cluster of rose-covered cottages—cobbled from salvage in the 1840s— epitomizes Nantucket's enduring allure. The rooms, though small, are intensely romantic, with lace coverlets and pale pine armoires; most have marble baths with whirlpool tubs, and one has a fireplace. Contemplative sorts can claim an Adirondack chair on the lawn; others may want to race down to the beach, perhaps enjoying lunch beside the heated pool en route. ⊠ *17 Ocean Ave., 02564* ☎ *508/257–4577* 🖷 *508/ 257–4590* ⊕ *www.thesummerhouse.com* 📨 *10 rooms* 🝔 *2 restaurants, some in-room hot tubs, pool, bar, piano bar* ▭ *AE, MC, V* ☉ *Closed Nov.–late Apr.* ⵿ *CP.*

Sports & the Outdoors

BEACHES **Siasconset Beach** (⊠ End of Milestone Rd.) has a lifeguard (the surf runs moderate to heavy) but no facilities; restaurants are a short walk away.

BIKING The 6½-mi **'Sconset Bike Path** starts at the rotary east of Nantucket Town and parallels Milestone Road, ending in 'Sconset. It is mostly level, with some gentle hills.

Nantucket A to Z

To research prices, get advice from other travelers, and book travel arrangements, visit www.fodors.com.

AIRPORTS

Nantucket Memorial Airport is about 3½ mi southeast of town via Old South Road; rental cars are available at the airport. American Eagle/ American Airlines flies from Boston in season. Cape Air flies from Boston, Hyannis, New Bedford, and Providence year-round. US Airways Express has nonstops from New York (LaGuardia) year-round.

🛈 Airport Information **Nantucket Memorial Airport** ☎ 508/325-5300.

BIKE TRAVEL

In business since 1931, Young's Bicycle Shop rents all types of bicycles, including tandems. The staff will send you off with everything you need—an excellent touring map, a helmet, and a quaint little basket for your handlebars.

🛈 Bike Rentals **Young's Bicycle Shop** ✉ Steamboat Wharf ☎ 508/228-1151 ⊕ www. youngsbicycleshop.com.

BOAT & FERRY TRAVEL

FROM HYANNIS: **Hy-Line Cruises** makes one to three daily round-trips on its slower (1 hour 50 minutes each way) traditional passenger ferry between early May and late October, and five or six daily round-trips on its high-speed (one hour each way) ferry year-round. (⛴ Traditional one-way $15.50, high-speed one-way $36, bicycles one-way either vessel $5 additional.) The **Steamship Authority** runs car-and-passenger ferries to Nantucket year-round, from three to seven times daily (2 hours, 15 minutes each way). *One-way $14, bicycles $6 additional, cars one-way depending on size $175 or $200 high season and $115 or $135 off season.* Its fast, passenger-only ferry makes the trip in one hour, four or five times a day from late March through the end of December. *One-way $29.50, bicycles $6 additional.*

🛈 Boat & Ferry Information **Hy-Line Ferry** ✉ Ocean St. dock, Hyannis ☎ 508/778-2602 in Hyannis, 508/228-3949 on Nantucket ⊕ www.hy-linecruises.com. **Steamship Authority** ✉ South St. dock, Hyannis ☎ 508/477-8600 reservations, 508/228-0262 on Nantucket ⊕ www.steamshipauthority.com.

BUS TRAVEL

The Nantucket Regional Transit Authority (NRTA) runs shuttle buses in town and to Madaket, mid-island areas, the airport, Surfside Beach, Jetties Beach, and Siasconset. Service is available late May through September.

🛈 Bus Information **Nantucket Regional Transit Authority (NRTA)** ✉ 22 Federal St., Nantucket 02554 ☎ 508/228-7025 ⊕ www.shuttlenantucket.com.

CAR RENTAL

If you're determined to rent a car while on Nantucket, be sure to book early. Expect to spend about $85 a day during high season.

🛈 Local Agencies **Affordable Rentals** ✉ 6 S. Beach St. ☎ 508/228-3501 or 877/235-3500. **Nantucket Island Rent A Car** ✉ Nantucket Memorial Airport ☎ 508/228-9989 or 800/508-9972 ⊕ www.nantucketislandrentacar.com. **Nantucket Windmill** ✉ Nantucket Memorial Airport ☎ 508/228-1227 or 800/228-1227 ⊕ www.nantucketautorental.com.

EMERGENCIES

⚑ Hospital & Emergency Services **Police or fire** ☎ 911. **Nantucket Cottage Hospital** ✉ 57 Prospect St. ☎ 508/228-1200.

⚑ Late-Night Pharmacy **Nantucket Pharmacy** ✉ 45 Main St. ☎ 508/228-0180.

TAXIS

⚑ A-1 Taxi ☎ 508/228-3330. **All Point Taxi** ☎ 508/228-5779. **Breeze Taxi** ☎ 508/325-2170. **Lisa's Cab** ☎ 508/228-2223. **Roger's Taxi** ☎ 508/228-5779.

TOURS

Sixth-generation Nantucketer Gail Johnson of Gail's Tours narrates a lively 1½-hour van tour of island highlights.

⚑ Tour Operator **Gail's Tours** ☎ 508/257-6557 ⊕ www.nantucket.net/tours/gails.

VISITOR INFORMATION

You might want to stop by the Visitor Services and Information Bureau, open weekdays 9–5, to get your bearings. You'll find maps, brochures, and island information available year-round.

⚑ Tourist Information **Chamber of Commerce** ✉ 48 Main St., 2nd fl., 02554 ☎ 508/228-1700 ⊕ www.nantucketchamber.org. **Nantucket Visitor Services and Information Bureau** ✉ 25 Federal St., 02554 ☎ 508/228-0925 ⊕ www.nantucket.net/town/departments/visitor.html.

THE NORTH SHORE

Updated by
Michael
Blanding

The slice of Massachusetts's Atlantic Coast known as the North Shore extends past grimy docklands and through Boston's well-to-do northern suburbs to the picturesque Cape Ann region, and beyond Cape Ann to Newburyport, just south of the New Hampshire border. In addition to miles of fine beaches, the North Shore encompasses Marblehead, a classic New England sea town; Salem, which thrives on a history of witches, millionaires, and the maritime trades; Gloucester, the oldest seaport in America; colorful Rockport, crammed with crafts shops and artists' studios; and Newburyport, with its redbrick center and rows of clapboard Federal-style mansions. Bright and bustling during the short summer season, the North Shore is calmer between November and June, with many restaurants, inns, and attractions operating during reduced hours or closing entirely. It's worth calling ahead off-season.

Marblehead

 *17 mi north of Boston.*

Marblehead, with its narrow and winding streets, old clapboard houses, and sea captains' mansions, retains much of the character of the village founded in 1629 by fishermen from Cornwall and the Channel Islands. It's a sign of the times that today's fishing fleet is small compared to the armada of pleasure craft anchored in the harbor. This is one of New England's premier sailing capitals, and Race Week (usually the last week of July) attracts boats from all along the eastern seaboard. Parking in town can be difficult; try the lot at the end of Front Street, the lot on State Street by the Landing restaurant, or the metered areas on the street.

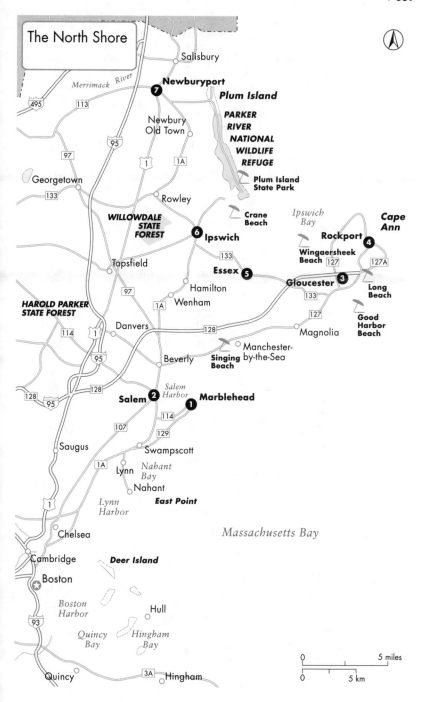

The North Shore

Marblehead's 18th-century high society is exemplified in the **Jeremiah Lee Mansion,** run by the town's historical society. Colonel Lee was one of the wealthiest people in the colonies in 1768, and although few furnishings original to the house remain, the rich mahogany paneling, unique hand-painted wallpaper, and other appointments, as well as a fine collection of traditional North Shore furniture, provide clues into the life of an American gentleman. ⊠ *161 Washington St.* ☎ *781/631–1768* ⊕ *www.marbleheadmuseum.org/LeeMansion.htm* ⊠ *Tours $5* ⊘ *June–Oct., Tues.–Sat. 10–4.*

The town's Victorian-era municipal building, **Abbott Hall,** built in 1876, displays Archibald Willard's painting *The Spirit of '76.* Many visitors, familiar since childhood with this image of the three Revolutionary veterans with fife, drum, and flag, are surprised to find the original in an otherwise unassuming town hall. Also on-site is a small naval museum exploring Marblehead's maritime past. ⊠ *188 Washington St.* ☎ *781/631–0000* ⊠ *Free* ⊘ *Mon., Tues., and Thurs. 8–5; Wed. 7:30–7:30; Fri. 8–1; weekends 10–5.*

Where to Stay & Eat

$–$$ ╳ **The Landing.** Crisply outfitted in nautical blues and whites, this pleasant restaurant sits right on Marblehead harbor, with walls of windows on two sides and a deck that's nearly in the water. The menu mixes classic New England fare (clam chowder, lobster, broiled scrod) with more contemporary dishes like boneless roast duck on a bed of wild rice. Brunch is served on Sunday. The pub area has a lighter menu. ⊠ *81 Front St.* ☎ *781/639–1266* ▭ *AE, D, DC, MC, V* ⊕ *www.thelandingrestaurant.com.*

$$–$$$ ⊡ **Harbor Light Inn.** Housed in a pair of adjoining 18th-century mansions, this elegant inn is handsomely appointed with Federalist antiques Fodor'sChoice sions, this elegant inn is handsomely appointed with Federalist antiques ★ and reproductions. Many rooms have brick fireplaces, skylights, and whirlpools; a soaring ceiling on the top floor reveals the original post-and-beam construction. Freshly baked cookies served with cider (winter) or lemonade (summer) help make a stay here special. ⊠ *58 Washington St., 01945* ☎ *781/631–2186* ⊟ *781/631–2216* ⊕ *www.harborlightinn.com* ⊅ *21 rooms* ⚬ *Cable TV, in-room VCRs, Wi-Fi, pool, hot tubs, meeting room; no kids under 8* ▭ *AE, MC, V* ⦿ *CP.*

Salem

➋ *16 mi northeast of Boston, 4 mi west of Marblehead.*

Salem unabashedly calls itself "Witch City." Witches astride broomsticks decorate the police cars; numerous witch-related attractions and shops, as well as resident witchcraft practitioners, recall the city's infamous connection with the witchcraft hysteria and trials of 1692. The incident began in January of that year, when several Salem-area girls fell ill and accused some of the townspeople of bewitching them. As the accusations continued and increased, more than 150 men and women were charged with practicing witchcraft, a crime punishable by death. After the resulting trials later that year, 19 innocent people were hanged and a 20th was "press'd to death" for refusing to be tried.

Witchcraft aside, Salem's charms include compelling museums, trendy waterfront stores and restaurants, and a wide common with a children's playground. Settled in 1626, the town has a rich maritime tradition: frigates out of Salem opened the Far East trade routes and generated the wealth that created America's first millionaires. Among its native sons are writer Nathaniel Hawthorne, navigator Nathaniel Bowditch, and architect Samuel McIntire.

★ The **House of the Seven Gables,** immortalized in Nathaniel Hawthorne's classic novel, should not be missed. Tours of the house, built in 1668 and also known as the Turner-Ingersoll Mansion, include a secret staircase, a garret containing an antique scale model of the house, and some of the finest Georgian interiors in the country. Also on the property is the small house where Hawthorne was born in 1804; built in 1750, it was moved from its original location a few blocks away. The Hooper–Hathaway House (1682) and the Retire Becket House (1655) are other 17th-century buildings in the complex originally located elsewhere in Salem. ⊠ *54 Turner St., off Derby St.* ☎ *978/744–0991* ⊕ *www.7gables.org* ⌕ *$11* ⊙ *Nov., Dec., and mid-Jan.–June, daily 10–5; July–Oct., daily 10–7.*

Near Derby Wharf is the 9¼-acre **Salem Maritime National Historic Site,** run by the National Park Service. The site focuses on Salem's heritage as a major seaport with a thriving overseas trade; it includes an orientation center with an 18-minute film; the 1762 home of Elias Derby, America's first millionaire; the 1819 Customs House, made famous in Nathaniel Hawthorne's *The Scarlet Letter*; and a replica of the *Friendship,* a 171-foot, three-masted 1797 merchant vessel. There's also an active lighthouse dating from 1871, as well as the nation's last surviving 18th-century wharves. ⊠ *193 Derby St.* ☎ *978/740–1660* ⊕ *www. nps.gov/sama* ⌕ *Free, tours $5* ⊙ *Daily 9–5.*

Fodor'sChoice Salem's vast maritime riches are celebrated at the **Peabody Essex Museum.**
★ The galleries are filled with maritime art and history and spoils of the Asian export trade, ranging from 16th-century Chinese blue porcelain to an entire Japanese carrying litter to Indian Colonial silver. ⊠ *East India Sq.* ☎ *978/745–9500 or 866/745–1876* ⊕ *www.pem.org* ⌕ *$13* ⊙ *Daily 10–5.*

For an informative, if somewhat hokey, introduction to the 1692 witchcraft hysteria, visit the **Salem Witch Museum.** A half-hour exhibit re-creates key scenes, using 13 sets, life-size models, and a taped narration. A 10-minute walk-through exhibit, "Witches: Evolving Perceptions," describes witch history and witch hunts through the years. The museum also sells an interesting pamphlet on the events that led to the witch trials. ⊠ *Washington Sq. N* ☎ *978/744–1692* ⊕ *www. salemwitchmuseum.com* ⌕ *$6.50* ⊙ *Sept.–June, daily 10–5; July and Aug., daily 10–7.*

The **Salem Witch Trials Memorial** honors those who died not because they were witches but because they refused to confess. This melancholy space, next to the central burial ground, provides an antidote to the re-

The First Witch Trial

It was in Danvers, not Salem, that the first witch trial was born, originating with the family of Samuel Parris, a minister who moved to the area in 1680 from Barbados, bringing with him two slaves, including one named Tituba. In 1691 Samuel's daughter, Betty, and niece, Abigail, began having "fits." Tituba, who had told Betty and Abigail stories of magic and witchcraft from her homeland, baked a "witch cake" in order to identify the witches who were harming the girls. The girls in turn accused Tituba of witchcraft. After three days of "questioning," which included beatings from Samuel and a promise from him to free her if she cooperated, Tituba confessed to meeting the devil (in the form of a black hog or dog). She also claimed there were other witches in the village, confirming the girls' accusations against Sarah Good and Sarah Osborne, but she refused to name any others. Tituba's trial prompted the frenzy that led to the deaths of 20 accused "witches."

lentless marketing of the merry-witches motif. A stone wall is studded with 20 stone benches, each inscribed with a victim's name. Look for the flagstones at one end of the plot that are engraved with protestations of innocence, sometimes cut off in midsentence. ⊠ *Off Liberty St. near Charter St.* ⊕ *www.salemweb.com/memorial.*

Where to Stay & Eat

$$–$$$ ✕ **Finz.** Walls of windows on three sides give this contemporary seafood restaurant on Pickering Wharf prime water views (there's a spacious deck, too). Fish-and-chips, seafood potpie, and lobster rolls highlight the lunch menu, while in the evening you might find sesame-crusted tuna or steamed lobster. ⊠ *76 Wharf St.* ☎ *978/744–8485* ⊕ *www.hipfinz. com* ▤ *AE, D, DC, MC, V.*

$$–$$$ ✕ **Strega.** Italian for "witch," the name of this restaurant hints at the
Fodor's Choice Italian alchemy in the kitchen. The bar has a broad selection of wines
★ by the glass and several small plates: calamari with garlic aioli, for example, or the very popular grilled pizza. The seasonal selection of large plates might include grilled salmon with lentils or apple-cured pork chops with sweet potato mash. ⊠ *94 Lafayette St.* ☎ *978/741–0004* ⊕ *www. stregasalem.com* ▤ *AE, D, MC, V* ☉ *Closed Mon. No lunch.*

$–$$ ▥ **Amelia Payson House.** Built in 1845, this Greek-revival house has been elegantly restored into an airy bed-and-breakfast; it's near all the historic attractions. With high ceilings, floral-print wallpaper, brass and canopy beds, and marble fireplaces, the four guest rooms are delicate and feminine. ⊠ *16 Winter St., 01970* ☎ *978/744–8304* ⊕ *www. ameliapaysonhouse.com* ☞ *4 rooms* ⌂ *Free parking* ▤ *AE, D, MC, V* ☉ *Closed Nov.–Mar.* ⊠◎ *CP.*

Shopping

Salem has dozens of offbeat shops related to the city's witchcraft history. The best-known store for "magickal" supplies is **Crow Haven Corner** (⊠ 125 Essex St. ☎ 978/745–8763 ⊕ www.crowhavencorner.net).

You can pick up blessed candles, incense, and herbs, as well as other witchy paraphernalia, at **The Cat, the Crow, & the Crown** (✉ 63R Wharf St. ☎ 978/744–6274 ⊕ www.lauriecabot.com), haunt of Laurie Cabot, the "Official Witch of Salem."

Gloucester

❸ *37 mi northeast from Boston, 8 mi northeast from Manchester.*

On Gloucester's fine seaside promenade is a famous statue of a man steering a ship's wheel, his eyes searching the horizon. The statue, which honors those "who go down to the sea in ships" was commissioned by the town citizens in celebration of Gloucester's 300th anniversary in 1923. The oldest seaport in the nation (and one with some of the North Shore's best beaches), this is still a major fishing port. Sebastian Junger's 1997 book, *A Perfect Storm,* was an account of the fate of the *Andrea Gail,* a Gloucester fishing boat caught in "the storm of the century" in October 1991. In 2000 the book was made into a movie, filmed on location in Gloucester.

The town's creative side thrives in the **Rocky Neck** neighborhood, the first-settled artists' colony in the United States. Its alumni include Winslow Homer, Maurice Prendergast, Jane Peter, and Cecilia Beaux. Rocky Neck is still a place that many artists call home; its galleries are usually open daily 10 to 10 in the busy summer months. From downtown, follow East Main Street.

The **Hammond Castle Museum** is a "medieval" stone castle built in 1926 by the inventor John Hays Hammond Jr., who is credited with more than 500 patents, including ones associated with the organ that bears his name. The museum contains medieval-style furnishings and paintings throughout, and the Great Hall houses an impressive 8,200-pipe organ. Walk into the serene Patio Room, with its pool and garden, and you may feel as if you've entered a 15th-century village. From the castle you can see "Norman's Woe Rock," made famous by Longfellow in his poem "The Wreck of the Hesperus." ✉ *80 Hesperus Ave., south side of Gloucester off Rte. 127* ☎ *978/283–2080 or 978/283–7673* ⊕ *www. hammondcastle.org* ☑*$8* ⊙ *Apr.–early Sept., daily 10–4; early Sept.–Mar, weekends 10–3.*

Where to Stay & Eat

$–$$$ ⤬ **Boulevard Ocean View Restaurant.** This clam shack has a Portuguese twist. Besides fried clams, burgers, and fish-and-chips, you can try Portuguese pork and clam stew, grilled shrimp, and salt cod. The water view from the front deck makes it a nice place to relax. ✉ *25 Western Ave.* ☎ *978/281–2949* ▭ *D, MC, V.*

$$ ⤬ **Franklin Cape Ann.** Under the same ownership as the Franklin Café in Boston's South End, this funky nightspot brings hip comfort food to the North Shore. Think bistro-style chicken, roast cod, and upscale meat loaf, perfect for the late-night crowd (it's open until midnight). Tuesday evening generally brings live jazz. Look for the signature martini glass over the door. ✉ *118 Main St.* ☎ *978/283–7888* ▭ *AE, D, MC, V* ⊙ *No lunch.*

$–$$ ⚏ **Cape Ann Motor Inn.** On the sands of Long Beach, this three-story, shingled motel has no-frills rooms with balconies and ocean views. Half have well-furnished kitchenettes. The Honeymoon Suite has a full kitchen, a fireplace, a whirlpool bath, a king-size bed, and a private balcony. ✉ *33 Rockport Rd., 01930* ☎ *978/281–2900 or 800/464–8439* 🖷 *978/281–1359* ⊕ *www.capeannmotorinn.com* ➫ *30 rooms, 1 suite* ☖ *Some kitchenettes, cable TV, some pets allowed; no a/c* ▭ *AE, D, MC, V* ⦿ *CP.*

$ ⚏ **Cape Ann's Marina Resort.** This year-round hostelry less than a mile from Gloucester really comes alive in summer, when two restaurants, a whale-watch boat, and deep-sea fishing excursions operate on and from the premises. The rooms all have balconies and water views; guests get a free river cruise during summer stays. The Gull restaurant is closed November–mid-April. ✉ *75 Essex Ave., 01930* ☎ *978/283–2116 or 800/ 626–7660* 🖷 *978-281-4905* ⊕ *www.capeannmarina.com* ➫ *31 rooms* ☖ *Restaurant, some kitchenettes, indoor pool, meeting rooms* ▭ *AE, D, DC, MC, V.*

Sports & the Outdoors

BEACHES Gloucester has some of the best beaches on the North Shore. From Memorial Day through mid-September, parking costs $15 on weekdays and $20 on weekends, when the lots often fill by 10 AM. **Good Harbor Beach** (✉ Signposted "S" from Rte. 127A) is a huge, sandy, dune-backed beach with a rocky islet just offshore. For excellent sunbathing, visit **Long Beach** (✉ Off Rte. 127A on Gloucester-Rockport town line). **Wingaersheek Beach** (✉ Exit 13 off Rte. 128) is a well-protected cove of white sand and dunes, with the white Annisquam lighthouse in the bay.

BOATING Consider a sail along the harbor and coast aboard the 65-foot schooner ***Thomas E. Lannon,*** (✉ 63 Rear Rogers St., Seven Seas Wharf ☎ 978/281–6634 ⊕ www.schooner.org) crafted in Essex in 1996 and modeled after the great boats built a century before. From mid-May through mid-October there are several two-hour sails, including those that let you enjoy the sunset or participate in a lobster bake.

Rockport

❹ *41 mi northeast of Boston, 4 mi northeast of Gloucester on Rte. 127.*

Rockport, at the very tip of Cape Ann, derives its name from the local granite formations, and many Boston-area structures are made of stone cut from its long-gone quarries. Today, the town is a tourist center, with hilly rows of colorful clapboard houses, historic inns, and artists' studios. Rockport has refrained from going overboard with T-shirt emporia and other typical tourist-trap landmarks: shops sell good crafts, clothing, and cameras, and the restaurants serve quiche, seafood, or home-baked cookies rather than fast food. Walk out to the end of Bearskin Neck for an impressive view of the Atlantic Ocean and the old, weather-beaten lobster shack known as "Motif No. 1" because of its popularity as a subject for amateur painters.

Where to Stay & Eat

$–$$ ✕ **Brackett's Ocean View.** A big bay window in this quiet, homey restaurant gives an excellent view across Sandy Bay. The menu includes baked scrod casserole, fish cakes, and other seafood dishes. ⊠ *25 Main St.* ☎ *978/546–2797* ▭ *AE, D, DC, MC, V* ☉ *Closed Nov.–Mar.*

¢–$$ ✕ **Portside Chowder House.** One of the few restaurants in Rockport open year-round, this casual seafood spot has big picture windows overlooking the harbor. Its popularity means that the wait for tables and food can be long. Chowder is the house specialty; it also serves lobster rolls, salads, burgers, and sandwiches. ⊠ *7 Tuna Wharf* ☎ *978/546–7045* ▭ *AE, MC, V* ☉ *No dinner Mon.–Thurs. in Dec.–Mar.*

$$–$$$$ 🖻 **Yankee Clipper Inn.** This imposing Georgian mansion sits on a rocky point jutting into the sea. Most guest rooms are spacious. Furnished with antiques, some have balconies or sitting areas, and all but one have an ocean view. Take in the seascape from the gazebo or one of the many Adirondack chairs on the grounds. ⊠ *127 Granite St., 01966* ☎ *978/ 546–3407 or 800/545–3699* 🖷 *978/546–9730* ⊕ *www.yankeeclipperinn. com* ⊅ *16 rooms* ♿ *Pool, meeting rooms, Internet* ▭ *AE, D, DC, MC, V* ☉ *Closed weekdays Dec.–Feb.* ⃒◯⃒ *BP.*

★ **$–$$** 🖻 **Addison Choate Inn.** Just a minute's walk from the center of Rockport, this 1851 inn sits inconspicuously among private homes. The sizable and beautifully decorated rooms have their share of antiques and local seascape paintings, as well as polished pine floors and large tile bathrooms; the captain's room contains a canopy bed, handmade quilts, and Oriental rugs. In the third-floor suite, huge windows look out over the rooftops to the sea. Two comfortably appointed duplex stable-house apartments have skylights, cathedral ceilings, and exposed wood beams. Rates include afternoon tea. ⊠ *49 Broadway, 01966* ☎ *978/ 546–7543 or 800/245–7543* 🖷 *978/546–7638* ⊕ *www.addisonchoateinn. com* ⊅ *5 rooms, 1 suite, 2 apartments* ♿ *Dining room; no room TVs* ▭ *MC, V* ☉ *Closed Jan.–Mar.* ⃒◯⃒ *CP.*

$–$$ 🖻 **Bearskin Neck Motor Lodge.** Near the end of Bearskin Neck, this small brick-and-shingle motel is in the thick of the shopping district and just a few minutes from the best local beaches. The simply appointed rooms, furnished with comfortable wooden furniture and white chenille spreads, provide the perfect backdrop for the breathtaking water views just outside your door. At night, you can go to sleep listening to the waves, and during the day, you can sun or read on the motel's large deck. ⊠ *64 Bearskin Neck, 01966* ☎ *978/546–6677 or 877/507–6272* 🖷 *978/ 546–8591* ⊕ *www.rockportusa.com/bearskin* ⊅ *8 rooms* ♿ *Cable TV; no a/c* ▭ *AE, D, MC, V* ☉ *Closed mid-Dec.–Mar.* ⃒◯⃒ *CP.*

$ 🖻 **Sally Webster Inn.** This inn was named for a member of Hannah Jumper's "hatchet gang," teetotalers who smashed up the town's liquor stores in 1856 and turned Rockport into the dry town it remains today. Sally lived in this house for much of her life, and the poshly decorated guest rooms are named for members of her family. Caleb's room is a romantic retreat with a canopy bed and floral quilts, and William's room has a crisply nautical theme. Other rooms have pine wide-board floors, nonworking brick fireplaces, rocking chairs, and four-poster, brass, or canopy beds. ⊠ *34 Mt. Pleasant St., 01966* ☎ *978/546–9251 or 877/*

FodorśChoice
★

546–9251 ⊕ www.sallywebster.com ⇆ 8 rooms ☁ Dining room, Wi-Fi, lounge; no room TVs ▭ MC, V ⊘ Closed Jan. ⫿◯⫿ CP.

Essex

⑤ *30 mi northeast of Boston, 12 mi west of Rockport. Head west out of Cape Ann on Rte. 128, turning north on Rte. 133.*

The small, seafaring town of Essex, once an important shipbuilding center, is surrounded by salt marshes and is filled with antiques stores and seafood restaurants. The **Essex Shipbuilding Museum,** still an active shipyard, traces the evolution of the American schooner, which was first created in Essex. The museum sometimes offers shipbuilding demonstrations. One-hour tours take in the museum's many buildings and boats, especially the *Evelina M. Goulart*—one of only seven remaining Essex-built schooners. ⊠ *66 Main St. (Rte. 133)* ☎ *978/768–7541* ⊕ *www. essexshipbuildingmuseum.org* ⊡ *$7* ⊘ *May–Columbus Day, Thurs.–Mon. 10–5; Columbus Day–Apr., Sat. and Sun. 10–5.*

Explore the area's salt marshes and rivers on a 1½-hour narrated cruise on the *Essex River Queen,* run by **Essex River Cruises** (⊠ Essex Marina, 35 Dodge St. ☎ 978/768–6981 or 800/748–3706 ⊕ www.essexcruises. com). Cruises are $22 and operate daily May–October.

Where to Eat

$–$$$ ✕ **Woodman's of Essex.** According to local legend, this is where Lawrence
Fodor'sChoice "Chubby" Woodman invented the first fried clam back in 1916. Today
★ this sprawling wooden shack with indoor booths and outdoor picnic tables is *the* place for seafood in the rough. Besides fried clams, you can tuck into clam chowder, lobster rolls, or shellfish from the raw bar. ⊠ *121 Main St. (Rte. 133)* ☎ *978/768–6451 or 800/649–1773* ⊕ *www. woodmans.com* ▭ *No credit cards.*

Shopping

Essex is a popular antiquing destination. **Chebacco Antiques** (⊠ 38 Main St. ☎ 978/768–7371) concentrates on lighting and country furniture, as well as Staffordshire plates and sterling silver. Open only on weekends, **Howard's Flying Dragon Antiques** (⊠ 136 Main St. ☎978/768–7282) is a general antiques shop that carries statuary and glass.

Ipswich

⑥ *36 mi north of Boston, 6 mi northwest of Essex.*

Quiet little Ipswich, settled in 1633 and famous for its clams, is said to have more 17th-century houses standing and occupied than any other place in America; more than 40 were built before 1725. Information and a booklet with a suggested walking tour are available at the **Visitor Information Center** (⊠ Hall Haskell House, 36 S. Main St. ☎ 978/ 356–8540 ⊘ Memorial Day–Columbus Day, Mon.–Sat. 9–5, Sun. noon–5).

The 59-room Stuart-style **Great House at Castle Hill,** built in 1927 for Richard Crane—of the Crane plumbing company—and his family, is part of the Crane Estate, a stretch of more than 2,000 acres along the Essex and Ipswich rivers, encompassing Castle Hill, Crane Beach, and the Crane Wildlife Refuge. Although the original furnishings of the mansion were sold at auction, it has been elaborately refurnished in period style; photographs in most of the rooms show their original appearance. One notable room is the library, with ornate wood carvings by 17th-century craftsman Grinling Gibbons. The Great House is open for one-hour tours and also hosts concerts and other events. ⊠ *Argilla Rd.* ☎ *978/356–4351* ⊕ *www.thetrustees.org* ⊠ *Tours $8* ☉ *June–Oct., Wed.–Thurs. 10–5, Fri. 9–noon.*

⏱ Kids can get in touch with their wild side at **Wolf Hollow**, a nonprofit wildlife sanctuary that's home to a pack of timber wolves. The one-hour tour lets visitors see and learn the truth about wolves. After the tour, everyone gets together to howl with the pack. ⊠ *114 Essex Rd.* ☎ *978/356–0216* ⊕ *www.wolfhollowipswich.org* ⊠ *$6* ☉ *Tours daily at 3:30.*

Where to Eat

$$–$$$ ✕ **Stone Soup Café.** It may look like nothing more than a simple storefront, but this cheery café in the center of town is booked days in advance for dinner. There are two seatings of eight tables a night for lobster bisque, porcini ravioli, or whatever contemporary fare the chef is inspired to cook from the day's farm-stand finds. If you can't book ahead, stop in for breakfast or lunch. ⊠ *0 Central St., off Rte. 1A* ☎ *978/356–4222* ⚑ *Reservations essential* ▭ *No credit cards* ☉ *No dinner Sun.–Wed., no lunch Sun.*

¢–$ ✕ **Clam Box.** Shaped like a giant fried clam box, this small roadside stand FodorsChoice is the best place to sample Ipswich's famous bivalves. Since 1938, locals and tourists have been lining up for clams, oysters, scallops, and onion rings. ⊠ *246 High St. (Rte. 1A)* ☎ *978/356–9707* ⊕ *www.ipswichma.com/clambox* ⚑ *Reservations not accepted* ▭ *No credit cards* ☉ *Closed mid-Dec.–Feb.*

Sports & the Outdoors

BEACHES **Crane Beach,** one of New England's most beautiful beaches, is a sandy, ★ 4-mi-long stretch backed by dunes and a nature trail. Public parking is available, but on a nice summer weekend, it's usually full before lunch. There are lifeguards and changing rooms. Check ahead before visiting mid-July to early-August, when greenhead flies terrorize sunbathers. ⊠ *Argilla Rd.* ☎ *978/356–4354* ⊕ *www.thetrustees.org* ⊠ *Free; parking $10 weekdays, $20 weekends mid-May–early Sept., $5 early Sept.–mid-May* ☉ *Daily 8–sunset.*

HIKING The Massachusetts Audubon Society's **Ipswich River Wildlife Sanctuary** has trails through marshland hills, where there are remains of early Colonial settlements as well as abundant wildlife. Get a trail map from the office. The Rockery Trail takes you to the perennial rock garden and the Japanese garden. ⊠ *87 Perkins Row, southwest of Ipswich, 1 mi off Rte. 97, Topsfield* ☎ *978/887–9264* ⊕ *www.massaudubon.org* ⊠ *$4* ☉ *Office: May–Oct., Tues.–Sun. 9–5; Nov.–Apr., Tues.–Fri. 9–4, weekends 10–4. Trails: Tues.–Sun. dawn–dusk.*

Newburyport

❼ *38 mi north of Boston, 12 mi north of Ipswich on Rte. 1A.*

Newburyport's High Street is lined with some of the finest examples of Federal-period (roughly, 1790–1810) mansions in New England. The city was once a leading port and shipbuilding center; the houses were built for prosperous sea captains. Although Newburyport's maritime significance ended with the decline of the clipper ships, the town's brick-front center is energetic once again. Inside the renovated buildings are restaurants, taverns, galleries, and shops that sell everything from nautical brasses to antique Oriental rugs. The civic improvements have been matched by private restorations of the town's housing stock, much of which dates from the 18th century, with a scattering of 17th-century homes in some neighborhoods.

Newburyport is a good walking city, and parking is free all day down by the water. A stroll through the **Waterfront Park & Promenade** gives a super view of the harbor and the fishing and pleasure boats that moor here. The **Custom House Maritime Museum,** built in 1835 in Greek-revival style, contains exhibits on maritime history, ship models, tools, and paintings. ⊠ *25 Water St.* ☎ *978/462–8681* ⊕ *www. themaritimesociety.org* ▨ *$5* ⊙ *Mar.–Dec., Tues.–Sat. 9–5, Sun. noon–4.*

A causeway leads from Newburyport to a narrow spit of land known as Plum Island, which harbors a summer colony (rapidly becoming year-round) at one end. The **Parker River National Wildlife Refuge** on Plum Island has 4,662 acres of salt marsh, freshwater marsh, beaches, and dunes; it's one of the few natural barrier beach–dune–salt marsh complexes left on the Northeast coast. Here you can bird-watch, fish, swim, and pick plums and cranberries. The refuge is such a popular place in summer, especially on weekends, that cars begin to line up at the gate before 7 AM. Only a limited number of cars are let in, although there's no restriction on the number of people using the beach. No pets are allowed in the refuge. ☎ *978/465–5753* ⊕ *www.parkerriver.org* ▨ *$5 per car, bicycles and walk-ins $2* ⊙ *Daily dawn–dusk. Beach usually closed during nesting season in spring and early summer.*

Where to Stay & Eat

$$–$$$$ ✕ **Glenn's.** The eclectic menu at this hip spot, a block from the waterfront parking lot, rambles from Asia to Latin America to the good ol' USA. The ever-changing menu might include sesame-crusted yellowfin tuna or house-smoked baby-back ribs. There's live jazz or blues on Sunday. ⊠ *44 Merrimac St.* ☎ *978/465–3811* ▭ *AE, D, DC, MC, V* ⊙ *Closed Mon. No lunch.*

★ **$–$$** ▦ **Clark Currier Inn.** This 1803 Federal mansion has been restored with care, taste, and imagination. It's one of the best inns on the North Shore. Guest rooms are spacious and furnished with antiques; one room has a glorious, late-19th-century sleigh bed. Rates include afternoon tea. ⊠ *45 Green St., 01950* ☎ *978/465–8363* ⊕ *www.clarkcurrierinn.com*

⊗ 8 rooms ⚫ Library; no room TVs, no kids under 11 ⊟ AE, D, MC, V ⟨O⟩ CP.

Nightlife & the Arts

The **Grog** (⊠ 13 Middle St. ☎ 978/465–8008 ⊕ www.thegrog.com) hosts blues and rock bands several nights weekly.

Sports & the Outdoors

Salisbury Beach State Reservation (⊠ Rte. 1A, 5 mi northeast of Newburyport, Salisbury ☎ 978/462–4481 ⊕ www.state.ma.us/dcr/parks/northeast/salb.htm ⊠ Free) has a long sandy beach, with an amusement area and arcades nearby. From Newburyport center, follow Bridge Road north, take a right on Beach Road, and follow it until you reach State Reservation Road. Parking is $7.

North Shore A to Z

To research prices, get advice from other travelers, and book travel arrangements, visit www.fodors.com.

BUS TRAVEL

The Cape Ann Transportation Authority, or CATA, provides local bus service in the Gloucester, Rockport, and Essex regions. The Coach Company bus line runs a commuter bus between Newburyport and Boston on weekdays; the ride takes 1–1¼ hours. Buses run by the Massachusetts Bay Transportation Authority, better known as the MBTA, leave for Marblehead and Salem daily from Central Square in Cambridge, and on weekdays in the early morning and evenings from Boston's Haymarket Station and Downtown Crossing. Travel time is about ½ hour from Cambridge and 1–1¼ hours from Boston. Look for Buses 441, 442, 448, or 449 for Marblehead and 455 or 459 for Salem.

🚌 Bus Information **Cape Ann Transportation Authority** ☎ 978/283-7278 ⊕ www.canntran.com. **Coach Company** ☎ 800/874-3377 ⊕ www.coachco.com. **MBTA** ☎ 617/222-3200, 800/392-6100, 617/222-5146 TTY ⊕ www.mbta.com.

CAR TRAVEL

The primary link between Boston and the North Shore is Route 128, which splits off from Interstate 95 and follows the coast northeast to Gloucester. To pick up Route 128 from Boston, take Interstate 93 north to Interstate 95 north to Route 128. If you stay on Interstate 95, you'll reach Newburyport. A less direct route is Route 1A, which leaves Boston via the Callahan Tunnel; once you're north of Lynn you'll pass through several pretty towns. Beyond Beverly, Route 1A travels inland toward Ipswich and Essex; at this point, Route 127 follows the coast to Gloucester and Rockport.

From Boston to Salem or Marblehead, follow Route 128 to Route 114 into Salem and on to Marblehead. A word of caution: this route is confusing and poorly marked, particularly returning to Route 128. An alternative route to Marblehead: follow Route 1A north, and then pick up Route 129 north along the shore through Swampscott and into Marblehead.

EMERGENCIES

🔲 **Police** ☎ 911.

🔲 **Late-Night Pharmacy Walgreens** ✉ 201 Main St., Gloucester ☎ 978/283-7361 ⊕ www. walgreens.com, open until 10 on weeknights, 6 on weekends.

TOURS

Essex River Cruises & Charters organizes narrated cruises of nearby salt marshes and rivers. Departure schedules often change, so call for reservations.

🔲 Tour Operator **Essex River Cruises & Charters** ✉ Essex Marina, 35 Dodge St., Essex ☎ 978/768-6981 or 800/748-3706 ⊕ www.essexcruises.com.

TRAIN TRAVEL

You can take MBTA's Newburyport/Rockport commuter rail line from Boston's North Station to Salem (25–30 minutes), Gloucester (55–60 minutes), Rockport (70–75 minutes), Ipswich (50–55 minutes), and Newburyport (60–65 minutes). The stations at Salem, Gloucester, Rockport, and Ipswich are within about ½ mi of the towns' historic sights. From the Newburyport station to downtown (about 1 mi), take the Merrimack Valley Regional Transit Authority Bus 51, but note that there's no Sunday service.

🔲 Train Information **MBTA** ☎ 617/222-3200, 800/392-6100, 617/222-5146 TTY ⊕ www. mbta.com. **Merrimack Valley Regional Transit Authority** ☎ 978/469-6878 ⊕ www. mvrta.com.

VISITOR INFORMATION

🔲 Tourist Information **Cape Ann Chamber of Commerce** ✉ 33 Commercial St., Gloucester 01930 ☎ 978/283-1601 ⊕ www.capeannvacations.com. **Destination Salem** ✉ 54 Turner St., Salem 01970 ☎ 978/741-3252 or 877/725-3662 ⊕ www.salem.org. **Ipswich Visitor Information** ✉ 36 S. Main St., Ipswich 01936 ☎ 978/356-8540 ⊕ www. ipswichma.com. **Marblehead Chamber of Commerce Information Booth** ✉ Corner of Pleasant and Spring Sts., Box 76, Marblehead 01945 ☎ 781/639-8469 ⊕ www. visitmarblehead.com. **Rockport Chamber of Commerce** ✉ 22 Broadway, Rockport 01966 ☎ 978/546-6575 ⊕ www.rockportusa.com.

THE PIONEER VALLEY

Updated by
Dave Simons

A string of historic settlements lines the majestic Connecticut River, the wide and winding waterway that runs through the heart of western Massachusetts. These communities are part of the Pioneer Valley, which formed the western frontier of New England from the early 1600s until the late 1900s. The river and its fertile banks first attracted farmers and traders, and later became a source of power and transport for the earliest industrial cities in America.

Educational pioneers came to this region as well and created a wealth of major colleges including Mt. Holyoke, America's first college for women; Amherst; Smith; Hampshire; and the University of Massachusetts. Northampton and Amherst, two hubs of higher learning, serve as the valley's cultural hubs; with the rise of the telecommunications era, both have become increasingly desirable places to live, drawing former city dwellers who relish the ample natural scenery, sophisticated cultural venues, and lively dining and shopping.

Northfield

❶ *88 mi northwest of Boston; 50 mi north of Springfield; 20 mi south of Brattleboro, Vermont.*

Just south of the Vermont and New Hampshire borders, this country town is known mainly as a center for hikers, campers, and other lovers of the outdoors.

The **Northfield Mountain Recreation & Environmental Center** has 26 mi of trails for biking, hiking, and horseback riding, and you can rent canoes, kayaks, and rowboats at the campground at Barton Cove. From here you can paddle to the Munn's Ferry campground, accessible only by canoe. The center also runs 1½-hour riverboat tours of the Pioneer Valley along a 12-mi stretch of the Connecticut River between Northfield and Gill, where you'll pass through a dramatically narrow gorge and get a close look at a nesting ground for bald eagles. The tours, offered between mid-June and mid-October, are Wednesday to Sunday at 11, 1:15, and 3. The cost is $9. In winter, the center rents cross-country skis and snowshoes and offers lessons. ⊠ *99 Miller's Falls Rd.* ☎ *413/863–9300 or 800/859–2960* ⊕ *www.nu.com/northfield* ☑ *Free* ☉ *Daily 9–5.*

Where to Stay & Eat

$–$$$ 🍽 **Centennial House.** Once home to presidents of the Mount Hermon School, this 1811 Colonial B&B has three spacious, antiques-filled guest rooms (two of them can be booked with additional adjoining bedrooms) and a third-floor suite with a kitchen that makes it perfect for families. The inn's large, glassed-in sunroom is a delightful place to curl up with a book; the pine-paneled living room has a huge fireplace. There are 2½ acres of grounds where guests gather to watch the sunset. ⊠ *Main St., 01360* ☎ *413/498–5921 or 877/977–5950* 🖷 *413/498–2525* ⊕ *www.thecentennialhouse.com* ⇨ *3 rooms, 1 suite* ⚐ *No room phones, no TV in some rooms* ☐ *AE, MC, V* ☒ *BP.*

Nightlife & the Arts

NIGHTLIFE Just south of Northfield, the honky-tonk **Route 63 Roadhouse** (⊠ Rte. 63, Miller's Falls ☎ 413/659–3384) is a spacious, pine-paneled music room hosting regional rock groups.

Shelburne Falls

❷ *24 mi southwest of Northfield.*

A tour of New England's fall foliage wouldn't be complete without a trek across the famed Mohawk Trail, a 63-mi section of Route 2 that runs past picturesque Shelburne Falls. The community, separated from neighboring Buckland by the Deerfield River, is filled with little art galleries. From May to October, an arched, 400-foot trolley bridge is transformed into the **Bridge of Flowers** (⊠ Water St. ☎ 413/625–2544), a promenade bursting with color.

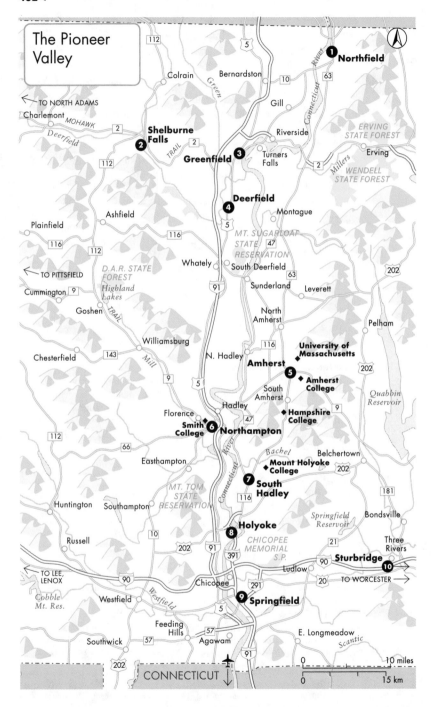

The Pioneer Valley

At the **Shelburne Falls Trolley Museum,** take a ride on this real working tribute to the old Colrain Street Railway Combine No. 10, the trolley car that served businesses in and around Shelburne during the early part of the 20th century. ⊠ *14 Depot St.* ☎ *413/625–9443* ⊕ *www.sftm. org* ⌑ *$2.50* ⊙ *May–Nov., weekends 11–5.*

Where to Stay

$ ⊞ **Penfrydd Farm.** In the middle of a 160-acre working farm, this serene B&B occupies a rejuvenated 1830s farmhouse with exposed beams, wide floorboards, skylights, and a big hot tub. The ideal place to get away from it all, it is across the valley from H. O. Cook State Forest, where there is fabulous fall foliage and trails for snowshoeing and cross-country skiing. The inn is 8 mi north of Shelburne Falls. ⊠ *105 Hillman Rd.* ⌑ *R.R. 1, Box 100A, Colrain 01340* ☎ *413/624–5516* ⊕ *www. penfrydd.com* ⌑ *4 rooms, 1 with bath* ⌑ *Some in-room hot tubs, hot tub; no kids under 10* ⊟ *AE, MC, V* ⦿ *BP.*

Sports & the Outdoors

White-water rafting in the Class II–III rapids of the Deerfield River is a popular summer activity. From April to October, **Zoar Outdoor** (⊠ 7 Main St., Rte. 2 ☎ 800/532–7483 ⊕ www.zoaroutdoor.com) conducts daylong rafting trips along 10 mi of challenging rapids, as well as family-friendly floats along gentler sections of the river.

Shopping

The **Salmon Falls Artisans Showroom** (⊠ 1 Ashfield St. ☎ 413/625–9833 ⊕ www.penguin-works.com/sfas) carries sculpture, pottery, glass (including handblown pieces by Josh Simpson), and furniture by more than 175 local artisans.

Greenfield

❸ *13 mi south of Northfield, 14 mi east of Shelburne Falls.*

In the 1990s, Greenfield made national news by stubbornly refusing to let Wal-Mart open a superstore downtown. Ironically, Greenfield, unlike other Pioneer Valley villages, is hardly a hotbed of political activism; its big-box opposition was merely an effort to preserve the sanctity of its downtown. Today, Main Street remains one of the few locales that time has left largely untouched, as evidenced by downtown mainstays such as Wilson's Department Store or the old-style Garden Cinemas.

 ⊙ Just west of downtown is **Old Greenfield Village,** a replica of an 1895 New England town. Among the 15 buildings are a general store, a church, a schoolhouse, and a print shop. ⊠ *Rte. 2* ☎ *413/774–7138* ⌑ *$5* ⊙ *Mid-May–mid-Oct., Sat. 10–4, Sun. noon–4.*

Where to Stay

$–$$$ ⊞ **Brandt House Country Inn.** This turn-of-the-20th-century Colonial-revival mansion is set on 3½ manicured acres. The sunlit, spacious common rooms are filled with plants, plump easy chairs, and handsome contemporary furnishings; the elegantly appointed guest rooms have featherbeds. The emphasis is on comfort and hominess. The stunning penthouse, with a full kitchen and sleeping loft, sleeps up to five. ⊠ *29 Highland Ave., 01301* ☎ *413/774–3329 or 800/235–3329* 🖷 *413/772–2908* ⊕ *www.brandthouse.com* ⇆ *9 rooms, 6 with bath; 1 suite* & *Some in-room hot tubs, refrigerators, some in-room VCRs, tennis court, meeting room, some pets allowed* ⊟ *AE, D, MC, V* ❍⫯ *BP.*

Nightlife

A microbrewery in the center of town, the **People's Pint** (⊠ 24 Federal St. ☎ 413/773–0333) serves robust handcrafted ales and porters, as well as freshly baked breads and healthy pub fare. It also books a wide range of folk and rock acts.

Sports & the Outdoors

High on a ridge between downtown Greenfield and the Connecticut River, **Poet's Seat Tower** (⊠ Rocky Mountain, follow signs from Maple St.) makes for one of the valley's most rewarding short jaunts. It's a 1-mi hike from the parking area, and from the summit are inspiring 360-degree views of the countryside.

Shopping

Occupying a dramatic bank building in downtown Greenfield, **Pushkin Gallery** (⊠ 332 Main St. ☎ 413/774–2891 or 413/549–4564) carries the works of prominent Russian painters, both contemporary and vintage.

Deerfield

❹ *18 mi southeast of Shelburne Falls.*

In Deerfield, a horse pulling a carriage clip-clops past perfectly maintained 18th-century homes, neighbors leave their doors unlocked and tip their hats to strangers, kids play ball in fields by the river, and the bell of the impossibly beautiful brick church peals from a white steeple. This is the perfect New England village, though not without a past darkened by tragedy. Its original Native American inhabitants, the Pocumtucks, were all but wiped out by deadly epidemics and a war with the Mohawks. English pioneers eagerly settled into this frontier outpost in the 1660s and 1670s, but two bloody massacres at the hands of the Native Americans and the French caused the village to be abandoned until 1707, when construction began on the buildings that remain today.

Fodor'sChoice ★ Although it has a turbulent past, **Historic Deerfield** now basks in a genteel aura. With 52 buildings on 93 acres, this village provides a vivid glimpse into 18th- and 19th-century America. Along the tree-lined main street are 13 museum houses, built between 1720 and 1850; two are open to the public on self-guided tours and the remainder are seen by guided tours that begin on the hour. A ticket that lets you visit all the houses can be purchased at the **Flynt Center of Early New England Life** (⊠ 37-D Old Main St.), which contains two galleries full of silver and pewter as well as needlework and clothing dating back to the 1600s. At the **Wells-Thorn House,** various rooms depict life as it changed from 1725 to 1850. The adjacent **Frary House** has arts and crafts from the 1700s on display; the attached Barnard Tavern was the main meeting place for Deerfield's villagers. Also of note is the **Hinsdale and Anna Williams House,** the stately home for this affluent early New England couple. Native American artifacts, quilts, and furnishings from early settlers, and other objects are on display at the **Memorial Hall Museum** (⊠ 8 Memorial St. ☎ 413/664–3768), one of the oldest museums in the country. Plan to spend at least one full day at Historic Deerfield. ⊠ *Old Main St.* ☎ *413/774–5581* ⊕ *www.historic-deerfield.org* 🕮 *$14* 🕒 *House museums and Flynt Center: Apr.–Dec. daily 9:30–4:30, Jan.–Mar. house museums open by appointment only, Flynt Center open Sat. and Sun. 9:30–4:30.*

🕲 Since it opened in fall 2001, **Magic Wings Butterfly Conservatory & Gardens** has rapidly become one of the region's most popular attractions.

Fodor'sChoice
★ The facility has an indoor conservatory garden where you can stroll among thousands of fluttering butterflies, as well as an extensive three-season outdoor garden filled with plants that attract local species. You can also observe the butterfly nursery, where throughout the day newborns experience the joy of flight. An extensive garden shop sells butterfly-friendly plants; there's also a snack bar and gift shop. ⊠ *281 Greenfield Rd., South Deerfield* ☎ *413/665–2805* ⊕ *www.magicwings.net* 🕮 *$8* 🕒 *Daily 9–5.*

The **Yankee Candle Company** not only displays a full review of its product line—including scented candles in such outlandish aromas as cantaloupe and banana-nut bread—but also has an array of other exhibits. In a small candle-making museum off the main showroom you can watch costumed docents practicing the art of candle dipping, using historically accurate implements. Highlights for younger kids include the Bavarian Christmas Village and Santa's Toy Factory, where electric trains chug by overhead and faux snow falls lightly. You can have lunch at either the pleasant café or the full-service restaurant. ⊠ *U.S. 5 and Rte. 10, near junction of Rte. 116, South Deerfield* ☎ *413/665–2929* ⊕ *www. yankeecandle.com* 🕮 *Free* 🕒 *Daily 9:30–6.*

Where to Stay & Eat

$$–$$$ ✕ **Sienna.** The atmosphere here is soothing and the service well mannered, but it's the food that really shines. Choices on the ever-changing menu might include a wild-mushroom crepe served with Roquefort cheese or pan-seared sea bass on a bed of Swiss chard accompanied by fingerling potatoes and a sweet corn flan. After an irresistible dessert such as a coconut panna cotta with persimmon compote, your evening ends with the personal touch of a handwritten bill on a sheet of stationery. ⊠ *6 Elm St., South Deerfield* ☎ *413/665–0215* ▭ *MC, V* 🕒 *Closed Mon. and Tues. No lunch.*

$$–$$$ ✕▥ **Deerfield Inn.** Period wallpaper decorates the rooms at this lovely
Fodor'sChoice lodging, which was built in 1884. Rooms are snug and handsomely ap-
★ pointed with both period antiques and reproductions; some rooms have four-poster or canopy beds. The restaurant ($$–$$$) showcases such creative American fare as pan-seared pheasant with crushed peppercorns and wild mushrooms in a cognac cream sauce with a truffle risotto cake.

✉ *81 Old Main St., 01342* ☎ *413/774–5587 or 800/926–3865* 🖶 *413/773–8712* ⊕ *www.deerfieldinn.com* 🖎 *23 rooms* ♨ *2 restaurants, coffee shop, bar* ▤ *AE, MC, V* ⦿ *BP.*

$ ✕🏚 **Whately Inn.** Antiques and four-poster beds slope gently on oldwood floors of the guest rooms at this informal Colonial-era inn. The dining room ($$–$$$; no lunch) has a fireplace and exposed beams; it's dimly lighted, with candles flickering on the tables. Prime Angus steaks, baked lobster with shrimp stuffing, rack of lamb, and other traditional entrées are served here or in the more casual lounge. There's no lunch during the week, but on Sunday dinner is served beginning at 1 PM. Enjoy the gorgeous east-facing view of the valley from the front veranda. ✉ *Chestnut Plain Rd., Whately Center 01093* ☎ *413/665–3044 or 800/942–8359* ⊕ *www.whatelyinn.com* 🖎 *4 rooms* ▤ *AE, D, MC, V.*

$ 🏚 **Sunnyside Farm Bed & Breakfast.** Maple antiques and family heirlooms decorate this circa-1800 Victorian farmhouse's country-style rooms, all of which are hung with fine-art reproductions and have views across the fields. A full country breakfast is served family-style in the dining room. The 50-acre farm is about 8 mi south of Deerfield, convenient to cross-country skiing, mountain biking, and hiking. ✉ *21 River Rd., Whately 01093* ☎ *413/665–3113* 🖎 *5 rooms without bath* ♨ *Dining room, pool* ▤ *No credit cards* ⦿ *BP.*

Nightlife & the Arts

Every weekend at the hotel-turned-roadhouse called **Hot-L-Warren** (✉ 13 Elm St., South Deerfield ☎ 413/665–2301) you can hear some of the best rock and country bands in the region.

Shopping

A short drive from Historic Deerfield, **Richardson's Candy Kitchen** (✉ 500 Greenfield Rd. ☎ 413/772–0443) makes and sells luscious cream-filled truffles as well as other handmade chocolates and confections.

Amherst

❺ *10 mi southeast of Deerfield.*

One of the most visited spots in all of New England, Amherst is known for its scores of world-renowned authors, poets, and artists. The aboveaverage intelligence quotient of its population is no accident, as Amherst is home to a trio of colleges—Amherst, Hampshire, and the University of Massachusetts. The high concentration of college-age humanity bolsters Amherst's downtown area, which includes a wide range of art galleries, music stores, and clothing boutiques.

Emily Dickinson Museum. The famed Amherst poet lived here her entire life (1830–86), and many of her belongings are contained within (though her manuscripts are housed elsewhere). The museum is outfitted with period accoutrements including original wall hangings and lace curtains. Next door is **The Evergreens** (✉ 214 Main St. ☎ 413/253–5272), an imposing Italianate Victorian mansion in which Emily's brother Austin and his family resided for more than 50 years. Tours of both buildings are conducted. ✉ *280 Main St.* ☎ *413/542–8161* ⊕ *www.*

emilydickinsonmuseum.org ⊠ *$8* ⊙ *June–Aug., Wed.–Sat. 10–5, Sun. 1–5; Sept.–Nov. and Mar.–May, Wed.–Sat. 1–5.*

Amherst History Museum at the Strong House. Housed in a mansion dating from the mid-1700s, this museum displays an extensive collection of household tools, furnishings, and clothing that reflects changing styles of interior decoration. Most items are Amherst originals, dating from the 18th to the mid-20th century. ⊠ *67 Amity St.* ☎ *413/256–0678* ⊕ *www.amhersthistory.org* ⊠ *$4* ⊙ *Feb.–Nov., Wed.–Sat. 12:30–3:30.*

<table>
<tr><td>

NEED A BREAK?

</td><td>

Newspapers and books are strewn about the tables at the **Black Sheep** (⊠ 79 Main St. ☎ 413/253–3442), a funky downtown café specializing in flavorful coffees and creative sandwiches such as the C'est la Brie (a baguette smothered with Brie, roasted peppers, spinach, and raspberry mustard) and the French Kiss (truffle pâté, Dijon mustard, and red onion on a baguette).

</td></tr>
</table>

⟲ **Eric Carle Museum of Picture Book Art.** This museum celebrates and preserves not only the works of renowned children's book author Eric Carle (who penned *The Very Hungry Caterpillar*) but also such luminaries as Maurice Sendak, Lucy Cousins, Petra Mathers, and Leo and Diane Dillon. Puppet shows, lectures, and storytelling are all part of the museum's ongoing calendar of events. ⊠ *125 W. Bay Rd.* ☎ *413/658–1100* ⊕ *www.picturebookart.org* ⊠ *$7* ⊙ *Tues.–Sat. 10–4, Sun. noon–4.*

★ **National Yiddish Book Center.** Founded in 1980 by a student on a mission to rescue Yiddish books from basements and dumpsters, this nonprofit organization has become a major force in the effort to preserve the Yiddish language and Jewish culture. On the campus of Hampshire College, the center is housed in a thatch-roof building that resembles a cluster of houses in a traditional Eastern European *shtetl*, or village. Inside, a contemporary space contains more than 1½ million books, a fireside reading area, a kosher dining room, and a visitor center with changing exhibits. The work here is performed out in the open: hundreds of books pour in daily, everything from family keepsakes to rare manuscripts among them. ⊠ *Rte. 116* ☎ *413/256–4900* ⊕ *www. yiddishbookcenter.org* ⊠ *Free* ⊙ *Weekdays 10–3:30, Sun. 11–4.*

Where to Stay & Eat

★ ¢–$$ ✕ **Bub's Bar-B-Q.** Back in 1979, Bub Tiley came up with the idea of opening an authentic Southern-style barbecue joint in Sunderland. A quarter century later, Bub's—which serves up ribs, chicken, and catfish with a slew of side dishes—is more popular than ever. Maybe it's the sauce, Tiley's's own tangy concoction. Pick up a jar before you leave. ⊠ *Rte. 116 north of Amherst town line, Sunderland* ☎ *413/548–9630* ▭ *MC, V* ⊙ *Closed Mon.*

¢–$$ ✕ **Judie's.** Since 1977, academic types have crowded around small tables on the glassed-in porch, ordering chicken ravioli with walnuts, shrimp
Fodor'sChoice tempura, gumbo popovers, Gorgonzola-and-mushroom burgers, and
★ probably the best bowl of French onion soup the town has to offer. The

atmosphere is hip and artsy; a painting covers each tabletop. ⊠ *51 N. Pleasant St.* ☎ *413/253–3491* ▭ *AE, D, MC, V* ☯ *Closed Mon.*

$–$$ ⬚ **Allen House Victorian & Amherst Inns.** A rare find, these late-19th-century inns a block apart from each other have been gloriously restored in accordance with the aesthetic of the Victorian era. Busy, colorful wall coverings reach to the high ceilings. Antiques include a burled-walnut headboard and dresser set, carved golden-oak beds, and wicker steamship chairs. Lace curtains and hand-stenciling grace the rooms, which have supremely comfortable beds with goose-down comforters. ⊠ *599 Main St. and 257 Main St., 01002* ☎ *413/253–5000* ⊕ *www.allenhouse. com* ⇝ *14 rooms* ⚬ *Wi-Fi, massage, business services; no room TVs, no kids under 10* ▭ *No credit cards* ⦿ *BP.*

Nightlife & the Arts

Live local bands perform Monday, Thursday, and Saturday nights at the place locals refer to as the "ABC," the **Amherst Brewing Company** (⊠ 24–36 N. Pleasant St. ☎ 413/253–4400). The pub has a decent-size dance floor and, as the name implies, a vast selection of beers brewed right on the premises. The earthy aroma from nearby Cowls Lumber fills the air as you stroll into the **Harp** (⊠ 163 Sunderland Rd., North Amherst ☎ 413/548–6900), a small but cozy tavern where regional rock and acoustic acts perform Thursday to Sunday nights.

Sports & the Outdoors

FISHING   The Connecticut River sustains shad, salmon, and several dozen other fish species. From May to October, at **Waterfield Farms** (⊠ 500 Sunderland Rd. ☎ 413/549–3558), you pay $3 per person to drop your line. Poles and bait are available.

Shopping

An institution in the Pioneer Valley, the **Atkins Farms Country Market** (⊠ Rte. 116, South Amherst ☎ 413/253–9528 or 800/594–9537) is surrounded by apple orchards and gorgeous views of the Holyoke Ridge. Hayrides are offered in fall, and children's events are hosted throughout the year. There's also a bakery and a deli.

Northampton

❻ *8 mi southwest of Amherst.*

The cultural center of western Massachusetts is without a doubt the city of Northampton, whose vibrant downtown scene reminds many people of lower Manhattan (hence its nickname "Noho"). No wonder John Villani ranked Northampton at the top in his book *The 100 Best Small Art Towns in America*. Packed with interesting eateries, lively clubs, and offbeat boutiques, the city attracts artsy types, academics, activists, lesbians and gays, and just about anyone else seeking the culture and sophistication of a big metropolis but the friendliness and easy pace of a small town.

Smith College, the nation's largest liberal arts college for women, opened its doors in 1875 (thanks to heiress Sophia Smith, who bequeathed her estate to the college's foundation). World renowned for its esteemed School of Social Work, Smith has a long list of distinguished alumnae, among them activist Gloria Steinem, chef Julia Child, and writer Margaret Mitchell. One of the most serene campuses in all of New England, the college is also a leading center of political and cultural activity. Worth visiting are the **Lyman Plant House** (☎ 413/585–2740) and the **Botanic Gardens of Smith College,** which cover the entirety of Smith's 150-acre campus.

The **Smith College Museum of Art** (✉ Brown Fine Arts Center, Elm St. ☎ 413/585–2760 ☞ $5, free 1st Sat. of month 10–noon ☉ Tues.–Sat. 10–4, Sun. noon–4) includes a new floor of skylighted galleries, an enclosed courtyard for performances and receptions, and a high-tech art history library. Highlights of the comprehensive permanent collection include European masterworks by Cézanne, Degas, Rodin, and Seurat. The fine representation of women's art ranges from Mary Cassatt to Alice Neel.

Historic Northampton maintains three houses that are open for tours: Parsons House (1730), Shepherd House (1798), and Damon House (1813). Together, they hold some 50,000 historical artifacts, including photographs, manuscripts dating back to the 17th century, fine furniture, ceramics, glass, and costumes. Exhibits in the main building chronicle the history of Northampton with some 50,000 documents, photos, and collectibles. ✉ *46 Bridge St.* ☎ *413/584–6011* ⊕ *www.historicnorthampton.org* ☞ *$3* ☉ *Main building Tues.–Fri. 10–4, houses weekends noon–4.*

Northampton was the Massachusetts home of the 30th president, Calvin Coolidge. He practiced law here and served as mayor from 1910 to 1911. At the **Forbes Library** (✉ 20 West St. ☎ 413/587–1011 ⊕ www.forbeslibrary.org/coolidge.html) the Coolidge Room contains a collection of his papers and memorabilia.

NEED A
BREAK?
☞ On the lower level of Thorne's Marketplace, **Herrell's Ice Cream** (✉ 8 Old South St. ☎ 413/586–9700) is famous for its chocolate pudding, vanilla malt, and cinnamon flavors of ice cream, as well as delicious homemade hot fudge.

William Cullen Bryant Homestead. About 20 mi northwest of Northampton, in the scenic hills west of the Pioneer Valley, is the country estate of the 19th-century poet and author, William Cullen Bryant. Inside the Dutch Colonial 1783 mansion are furnishings and collectibles from Bryant's life, work, and travels. Outside, the wild 465-acre grounds overlooking the Westfield River valley are a great venue for bird-watching, cross-country skiing, snowshoeing, fishing, hiking, and picnics. ✉ *207 Bryant Rd., Cummington* ☎ *413/634–2244* ⊕ *www.thetrustees.org* ☞ *$5* ☉ *House: late June–early Sept., Fri.–Sun. 1–5; early Sept.–mid-Oct., weekends 1–5. Grounds daily sunrise–sunset.*

Where to Stay & Eat

$–$$$ ✕ **Mulino's Trattoria.** In sleek quarters (which also contain the Brasserie 40-A downstairs and the Bishop's Lounge one flight up), this modern trattoria carefully prepares Sicilian-inspired home-style Italian food with authentic ingredients. You'll rarely taste a better carbonara sauce this side of the Atlantic, and don't overlook the smoked salmon in a lemon-caper-shallot sauce tossed with fettuccine. Portions are huge, and the wine list is extensive. ⊠ *41 Strong Ave.* ☎ *413/586–8900* ⊟ *AE, D, DC, MC, V* ⊗ *No lunch.*

$$

Fodor'sChoice

★

✕ **Spoleto.** A Noho mainstay since the 1980s, busy Spoleto, in the heart of Northampton's downtown, delivers top-flight Italian fare. Try the veal *forestiera,* sautéed veal with wild mushrooms in a peppercorn, cognac cream sauce—a can't-miss proposition. With an ever-changing menu and a cozy bar, this place is in a class by itself. Join the locals and stop by for the excellent Sunday brunch. ⊠ *50 Main St.* ☎ *413/586–6313* ⊟ *AE, DC, MC, V* ⊗ *No lunch, except brunch Sun. 11–2:30.*

$–$$ ✕ **Eastside Grill.** You might be 1,400 mi from Louisiana, but close your eyes while you're gobbling down this eatery's New Orleans–style barbecue shrimp and you'll swear you're in the heart of Crescent City. A Northampton mainstay, Eastside Grill presents a diverse bill of fare (which includes such old standbys as lobster corn chowder and pan-blackened rib eye); the service is consistent, and the martinis at the bar are always cold and dry. Be sure to try the superb Gorgonzola salad dressing. ⊠ *19 Strong Ave.* ☎ *413/586–3347* ⊟ *AE, D, DC, MC, V.*

$–$$ ✕ **Northampton Brewery.** In a rambling building behind Thorne's Marketplace, this often-packed pub and microbrewery has extensive outdoor seating on an airy deck. The kitchen serves tasty comfort food, including black-bean dip, chicken-and-shrimp jambalaya, and the black and blue burger (with blue cheese and caramelized onions). ⊠ *11 Brewster St.* ☎ *413/584–9903* ⊟ *AE, D, DC, MC, V.*

$$–$$$$ ▦ **Hotel Northampton.** Rooms at this 1927 downtown hotel include reproductions of period antiques, including graceful four-poster beds. Many rooms have whirlpool tubs, and balconies overlooking a busy street or the parking lot. Wiggins Tavern ($$–$$$) serves standard American fare and an elaborate Sunday brunch; the Coolidge Park Café serves lighter fare. ⊠ *36 King St., 01060* ☎ *413/584–3100 or 800/547–3529* 🖷 *413/584–9455* ⊕ *www.hotelnorthampton.com* ⇆ *106 rooms, 13 suites* ⚒ *2 restaurants, gym, bar, meeting rooms* ⊟ *AE, D, DC, MC, V* ⍒ *CP.*

Nightlife & the Arts

For decades, the stately **Calvin Theater** (⊠ 19 King St. ☎ 413/586–8686) was a classic old-time movie house, but it fell on hard times. Thanks to a grand restoration project, the Calvin is back and better than ever, hosting a variety of nationally recognized performing artists throughout the year.

The spacious **Diva's** (⊠ 492 Pleasant St. ☎ 413/586–8161) serves the region's sizable lesbian and gay community with great music that draws people to the cavernous dance floor. The reliable **Fitzwilly's** (⊠ 23 Main St. ☎ 413/584–8666) draws a friendly mix of locals and tourists for drinks and tasty pub fare. The dimly lighted **Hugo's** (⊠ 315 Pleasant St. ☎ 413/534–9800) has beer on tap, a rocking jukebox, and all the local color you'll ever want to see.

Sports & the Outdoors

☺ The **Norwottuck Rail Trail** (☎ 413/586–8706 ⊕ www.hadleyonline.com/railtrail), part of the Connecticut River Greenway State Park, is a paved 10-mi path that links Northampton with Belchertown by way of Amherst. Great for biking, rollerblading, jogging, and cross-country skiing, it runs along the old Boston & Maine Railroad route. Entry points include Route 9 in Northampton at the junction of Damon Road (near Coolidge Bridge) and Route 9 in Hadley at the junction of River Drive (Route 47 north).

Shopping
The **Williamsburg General Store** (⊠Rte. 9, Williamsburg ☎413/268–3036), a Pioneer Valley landmark, sells breads, penny candy, and gifts galore.

South Hadley

❼ *10 mi southeast of Northampton.*

Founded in 1837, **Mount Holyoke College** was the first women's college in the United States. Among its alumnae are poet Emily Dickinson and playwright Wendy Wasserstein. The handsome wooded campus, encompassing two lakes and lovely walking or riding trails, was landscaped by Frederick Law Olmsted. ⊠ *Rte. 116* ☎ *413/538–2000.*

The **Mount Holyoke College Art Museum** contains some 11,000 works including Asian, European, and American paintings and sculpture. ⊠*Lower Lake Rd.* ☎ *413/538–2245* ⊕ *www.mtholyoke.edu/offices/artmuseum* ⊠ *Free* ◷ *Tues.–Fri. 11–5, weekends 1–5.*

Where to Stay & Eat

$–$$ ✕ **Fedora's Tavern.** A favorite place with college students between classes and shoppers perusing the shops at the Village Commons, this dark and cozy English pub serves up a wide range of pub grub. Try the Maine crab cakes, portobello mushroom pasta, or a cup of what may be the best chili in the valley. ⊠ *25 College St.* ☎ *413/534–8222* ▤ *AE, D, MC, V.*

$ ▦ **Grandmary's Bed & Breakfast.** With three rooms from which to choose—the Primrose, the Princess Rose, and the Petit Rose—this soothing Victorian-era B&B fills up fast, especially during high season. The location, adjacent to the Mount Holyoke College campus and the shops of the Village Commons, couldn't be better. ⊠ *11 Hadley St., 01075* ☎ *413/533–7381* ⊕ *www.grandmarys.com* ➫ *3 rooms* ⚹ *No kids under 10* ▤ *No credit cards* ⊙∣ *BP.*

Shopping
In addition to stocking more than 50,000 new and used titles, the **Odyssey Bookshop** (⊠9 College St. ☎413/534–7307 ⊕www.odysseybks. com) has a packed schedule of readings and book signings by locally and nationally known authors. It's open Monday through Friday 10 to 8, Saturday 10 to 6.

Holyoke

❽ *5 mi south of South Hadley.*

Working hard to overcome its days as a textile-factory town, Holyoke has an imaginatively restored industrial city center with one of the most extensive and impressive collections of 19th-century commercial architecture in the country. Heritage Park sits in the middle of downtown and adjoins two museums. A walk along the streets near the park reveals some wonderfully innovative adaptations of vintage mill and factory buildings into office, condos, and retail space.

🕑 Check out the 134 separate **Dinosaur Footprints** that have been preserved in sandstone slabs along the banks of the Connecticut River. Some 190 million years ago Western Massachusetts was a favorite stomping ground (pardon the expression) for prehistoric creatures like the *Eubrontes giganteus* and *Anchisauripus sillimani.* ⊠ *U.S. 5, 2 mi north of Holyoke* ☎ *413/684–0148* ⊕ *www.thetrustees.org/dinosaurfootprints* 🔁 *Free* ⊙ *Apr.–Oct., daily sunrise–sunset.*

🕑 The visitor center in **Heritage State Park** tells the story of this papermaking community, the nation's first planned industrial town. Kids can ride a vintage merry-go-round with 48 hand-carved, hand-painted antique wooden horses. ⊠ *221 Appleton St.* ☎ *413/534–1723* 🔁 *Free* ⊙ *Tues.–Sun. noon–4.*

🕑 The **Holyoke Children's Museum,** which sits beside Heritage State Park in a converted mill, is packed with hands-on games and educational toys. Within the museum are a state-of-the-art TV station, a multitiered interactive exhibit on the human body, a giant bubble maker, and a sand pendulum. ⊠ *444 Dwight St.* ☎ *413/536–5437* 🔁 *$4* ⊙ *Tues.–Sat. 9:30–4:30, Sun. noon–5.*

Volleyball was invented at the Holyoke YMCA in 1895, and the **Volleyball Hall of Fame** pays homage to the sport with informative videos and displays of memorabilia. Interactive games let you test your skills. ⊠ *444 Dwight St.* ☎ *413/536–0926* ⊕ *www.volleyhall.org* 🔁 *$3.50* ⊙ *Tues.–Sun. noon–4:30.*

The **Wistariahurst Museum,** the mansion once owned by silk magnate William Skinner, peers into the lives of one of Pioneer Valley's most prosperous citizens. This 1874 Second Empire home, with a sweeping beaux arts staircase and elaborately landscaped grounds, overflows with priceless antiques and artworks. The house's leather wall coverings and meticulous woodwork remain perfectly intact. ⊠ *238 Cabot St.* ☎ *413/322–5660* ⊕ *www.wistariahurst.org* 🔁 *Donation suggested* ⊙ *Apr.–Oct., Wed. and weekends 1–5; Nov.–Mar., Wed. and weekends noon–4.*

Where to Stay & Eat

$$–$$$$ ✕ **Delaney House.** A meal at this popular eatery always feels like an event, partly because of the elegantly set tables and tasteful Victorian decor, and partly because of the music that flows from the comfortable lounge. The biggest plus is the food, beautifully presented in ample portions. Among the more ambitious creations are the shellfish lasagna and the veal sautéed with lobster, artichokes, mushrooms, and couscous. Well-known jazz musicians often play at the restaurant, which is about 5 mi north of downtown. ⊠ *U.S. 5, Smith's Ferry* ☎ *413/532–1800* ▭ *AE, D, DC, MC, V* ⊙ *No lunch.*

$ ✕⛶ **Yankee Pedlar Inn.** Antique furnishings and four-poster beds fill many of the charming guest rooms at this sprawling country inn at a busy cross-roads in Holyoke. The elaborate Victorian bridal suite is heavy on lace and curtains; the beamed carriage house has rustic appointments and simple canopy beds. Chicken potpie and hazelnut-crusted salmon with a raspberry vinaigrette are among the dishes served in the Grill Room ($–$$$), which has burgundy walls and is accented with stained glass. The more casual Oyster Bar hosts musicians many nights. ✉ *1866 Northampton St., 01040* ☎ *413/532–9494* 🖶 *413/536–8877* ⊕ *www. yankeepedlar.com* ↪ *21 rooms, 7 suites* ⚲ *Restaurant, bar, nightclub, meeting room* 🖃 *AE, D, DC, MC, V* ⍾❶ *CP.*

Nightlife & the Arts
A favored haunt for regional jazz performers, the **Red Cat Café** (✉ 274 High St. ☎ 413/532–5559) presents live music on Thursday and Friday evenings.

Sports & the Outdoors
A 3⅓-mi round-trip hike at the **Mt. Tom State Reservation** (✉ U.S. 5 ☎ 413/527–4805) leads to the summit, whose sheer basalt cliffs were formed by volcanic activity 200 million years ago. At the top are excellent views of the Berkshires. In winter, this is a favorite spot for cross-country skiers. The preserve is about 5 mi north of Holyoke.

Shopping
A restored 19th-century wood-and-brick factory building, **Open Square** (✉ 250 Open Square Way ☎ 413/532–5057) houses a number of charming boutiques and galleries.

Springfield

❾ *7 mi south of Holyoke; 90 mi west of Boston; 30 mi north of Hartford, Connecticut.*

Springfield is perhaps best known around the country as the birthplace of basketball, the game devised by local gym instructor James Naismith in 1891 as a last-minute attempt to keep a group of unruly teenagers occupied in winter. Today, the Basketball Hall of Fame stands as a permanent shrine to Naismith and the legions of basketball heroes who made the game a worldwide phenomenon.

You can glimpse Springfield's prosperous industrial past by exploring either of the city's most noted neighborhoods: the Maple Hill Historic District, which preserves several lavish mansions from the 1840s through the 1920s, and the McKnight Historic District, a Victorian neighborhood developed between 1870 and 1900, where you'll see a bounty of ornate Queen Anne, Tudor revival, and Italianate Victorian houses. Self-guided tour brochures of both neighborhoods are available at the Greater Springfield Convention & Visitors Bureau.

ⓒ Along the banks of the Connecticut River, the **Naismith Memorial Bas-**
Fodor'sChoice **ketball Hall of Fame** is dedicated to Springfield's own Dr. James Naismith,
★ who invented the game in 1891. This 80,000-square-foot facility includes

a soaring domed arena, dozens of high-tech interactive exhibits, and video footage and interviews with former players. The Honors Rings pay tribute to the hall's nearly 250 enshrinees. ⊠ *1150 W. Columbus Ave.* ☎ *413/781–6500 or 877/446–6752* ⊕ *www.hoophall.com* ⊡ *$16.99* ⊙ *Sun.–Fri. 10–5; Sat. 10–6.*

One of the most ambitious cultural venues in New England, the **Spring-field Museums** includes four impressive facilities. The most modest, the **Connecticut Valley Historical Museum** presents changing exhibits drawn from its collections of furniture, silver, industrial objects, autos, and firearms; its main draw is the in-depth genealogical library, where folks from all over the world come to research their family trees. The must-see **George Walter Vincent Smith Art Museum** houses a fascinating private art collection that includes 19th-century American paintings by Frederic Church and Albert Bierstadt. A Japanese antiquities room is filled with armor, textiles, and porcelain, as well as carved jade and rock-crystal snuff bottles. The **Museum of Fine Arts** has paintings by Gauguin, Monet, Renoir, Degas, Winslow Homer, and J. Alden Weir, as well as 18th-century American paintings and contemporary works by Georgia O'Keeffe, Frank Stella, and George Bellows. Rotating exhibits are open throughout the year. The **Springfield Science Museum** has an Exploration Center of touchable displays, the oldest operating planetarium in the United States, an extensive collection of stuffed and mounted animals, dinosaur exhibits, and the African Hall, through which you can take an interactive tour of that continent's flora and fauna. On the grounds is the **Dr. Seuss National Memorial Sculpture Garden,** an installation of five bronze statues depicting scenes from Theodore Geisel's famously whimsical children's books. Born in Springfield on 1904, Geisel was inspired by the animals at Forest Park Zoo, where his father served as director. The statues include a 4-foot Lorax and a 10-foot Yertle the Turtle. ⊠ *220 State St., at Chestnut St.* ☎ *413/ 263–6800* ⊕ *www.springfieldmuseums.org* ⊡ *$10* ⊙ *Tues.–Fri. noon–5, weekends 11–4.*

NEED A BREAK? Springfield's South End is the home of a lively Little Italy that supports some excellent restaurants, as well as **La Fiorentina Pastry Shop** (⊠ 883 Main St. ☎ 413/732–3151), which has been doling out heavenly pastries, butter cookies, and coffees since the 1940s.

Forest Park is a leafy 735-acre retreat, ideal for families. Hiking paths wind through the trees, paddleboats navigate Porter Lake, and hungry ducks float on a small pond. The zoo, where Theodore Geisel—better known as Dr. Seuss—found inspiration for his children's books, is home to nearly 200 animals, from black bears and bobcats to emus, lemurs, and wallabies. ⊠ *Off Sumner Ave.* ☎ *413/787–6461 or 413/733–2251* ⊕ *www.forestparkzoo.org* ⊡ *$4.50* ⊙ *Zoo: mid-Apr.–Labor Day, daily 10–5; Labor Day–mid-Nov., daily 10–4; mid-Nov.–mid-Apr., weekends 10–3.*

Four miles southwest of Springfield is **Six Flags New England,** the region's largest theme park and water park. It contains more than 160 rides and shows, including the Superman Ride of Steel, the tallest and fastest steel coaster on the East Coast; Batman–The Dark Knight floorless roller coaster; Mr. Six's Pandemonium, a spinning coaster; and the Typhoon water coaster. ⊠ *1623 Main St., Agawam* ☎ *413/786–9300* ⊕ *www. sixflags.com* 🖼 *$40* ⊙ *Late Apr.–late May and early Sept.–late Oct., Fri. and Sat. 10–10; late May–early Sept., daily 10–10.*

Where to Stay & Eat

$–$$ ✕ **Nadina's Café Lebanon.** This casual eatery, a short walk down the hill from the Springfield Museums, serves such authentic Lebanese dishes as lamb shank simmered in tomato sauce, charbroiled swordfish kabobs, and falafel with sesame sauce. There's live belly-dancing on some Saturday evenings. ⊠ *141 State St.* ☎ *413/737–7373* ▭ *AE, D, DC, MC, V* ⊙ *No lunch weekends.*

★ **$–$$** ✕ **Red Rose.** Outfitted with massive chandeliers and revolving dessert displays, the Red Rose is a big, brassy eatery where everyone from couples to huge parties can feel right at home. Go for the light and sumptuous eggplant Parmesan, one of the best items on the menu of Italian favorites. ⊠ *1060 Main St.* ☎ *413/739–8510* ▭ *AE, MC, V.*

¢–$$ ✕ **Theodore's.** "Booze, blues, and barbecue" are the specialties of this popular downtown restaurant, which stays open until 2 AM on weekends. You can dine saloon-style in the booths near the bar or in a small adjacent dining room. The decor is yard-sale chic, with framed old-time advertisements lending a whimsical air. The kitchen turns out standard pub fare—nothing special, but more people come here for the blues than the burgers. ⊠ *201 Worthington St.* ☎ *413/736–6000* ▭ *AE, D, MC, V* ⊙ *No lunch weekends.*

$$ ✕🖾 **Springfield Marriott.** One of the few business hotels in the Pioneer Valley, the Springfield Marriott makes a good base for vacationers, especially on weekends when the rates drop precipitously. Contemporary furnishings adorn the rooms, some of which face the Connecticut River. The restaurant, Currents ($$–$$$), is far better than you might expect of a chain hotel. Dine on such creative contemporary dishes as Block Island swordfish with sweet-potato fries, citrus pesto, and ginger, garlic, and lime marinade. ⊠ *Boland and Columbus Sts., 01115* ☎ *413/ 781–7111 or 800/229–9290* 🖨 *413/731–8932* ⊕ *www.marriott.com* ➥ *264 rooms* ⌂ *Restaurant, room service, indoor pool, health club, hot tub, sauna, 2 bars, business services, parking (fee)* ▭ *AE, D, DC, MC, V* ⦙◯⦙ *CP.*

Nightlife & the Arts

Worthington Street, the city's nightlife center, is lined with bars, clubs, and cafés. **Caffeine's** (⊠ 254 Worthington St. ☎ 413/731–5282), a contemporary bar and restaurant, hosts live music duos and combos on weekends. The **Pour House** (⊠ 280 Worthington St. ☎ 413/732–7934), a beautifully refurbished vintage pub, frequently stages such regional faves as NRBQ and the Ray Mason Band. If you're in the mood for a fresh Guinness draft, stop off at **Tilly's Irish Pub** (⊠ 1390 Main St. ☎ 413/732–3613), another weekend live-music haunt.

Sturbridge

❿ *34 mi east of Springfield, 60 mi southwest of Boston, 20 mi southwest of Worcester.*

Fodor'sChoice
★
Sturbridge is best known for **Old Sturbridge Village,** one of the country's finest re-creations of a Colonial-era village. Modeled on an early-19th-century New England town, the 200-acre site has more than 40 historic buildings that were moved here from other towns. Some of the village houses are filled with canopy beds and elaborate furnishings; in the simpler, single-story cottages, interpreters wearing period costumes demonstrate home-based crafts like spinning, weaving, and shoe making. The village store contains an amazing variety of goods necessary for everyday life in the 19th century. There are several industrial buildings, including a working sawmill. On the informative boat ride along the Quinebaug River, you can learn about river life in 19th-century New England and catch a glimpse of ducks, geese, turtles, and other local wildlife. ⊠ *1 Old Sturbridge Village Rd.* ☎ *508/347–3362 or 800/733–1830* ⊕ *www.osv.org* ⊠ *$20* ⊙ *Apr.–Oct., daily 9–5.*

At **Hyland Orchard & Brewery,** you can pick your own peaches, apples, and other fruit, depending on the season. Take a tour of the state-of-the-art brewery, check out the farm animals, or join a scenic hayride in fall. ⊠ *199 Arnold Rd.* ☎ *508/347–7500* ⊕ *www.hylandbrew.com* ⊠ *Free* ⊙ *Daily.*

Where to Stay & Eat

$$–$$$
Fodor'sChoice
★
✕ **Cedar Street.** This eatery, housed in a modest but charming Victorian house, sits just off Main Street. Inside, candlelit tables decked with fresh flowers fill the intimate dining room. The menu tends toward the simple but creative, with an emphasis on healthful cooking. Choices include handmade parsnip ravioli with walnut pesto as well as molasses-brined pork chop with a mango-rum glaze, fried plantains, and a ginger-coconut custard. ⊠ *12 Cedar St.* ☎ *508/347–5800* 🖃 *AE, MC, V* ⊙ *Closed Sun. No lunch.*

$$–$$$
✕ **Salem Cross Inn.** On a verdant 600-acre estate, the Salem Cross occupies a Colonial building built by the grandson of Peregrine White, the first child born on the *Mayflower.* It's a fitting legacy for a restaurant that prides itself on re-creating the Early American dining experience, both in terms of decor and dishes. A favorite event is the occasional Drover's Roasts, when prime rib is spiced and slow-roasted for hours in a fieldstone pit. A lavish and lengthy feast follows. Other times you'll find traditional American and Continental fare, such as broiled lamb chops and baked stuffed fillet of sole with lobster sauce. The inn is 12 mi northwest of Sturbridge. ⊠ *Rte. 9, West Brookfield* ☎ *508/867–8337* 🖃 *AE, D, MC, V* ⊙ *Closed Mon. No lunch Sat.*

$–$$
Fodor'sChoice
★
✕🖾 **Publick House Historic Inn.** Each of the three inns and the motel in this complex has its own character. The 17 rooms in the Publick House, which dates to 1771, are Colonial in design, with uneven plank floors and canopy beds. The neighboring Chamberlain House

consists of larger suites, and the Country Motor Lodge has more modern rooms. The Crafts Inn, about a mile away, has rooms with four-poster beds and painted wood paneling. The big, bustling Pub-lick House restaurant ($$–$$$) serves traditional Yankee fare with an inventive spin—pecan-dusted scrod or pan-seared barbecued scallops with bok choy and blue cheese–shallot mashed potatoes. Lighter fare is served in two taverns and a bakeshop. ☒ *Rte. 131, 01566* ☎ *508/347–3313 or 800/782–5425* 🖷 *508/347–5073* ⊕ *www.publickhouse. com* ➦ *116 rooms, 9 suites* ♿ *4 restaurants, tennis court, pool, shuf-fleboard, cross-country skiing, bar, playground, meeting rooms* ▭ *AE, D, DC, MC, V.*

$$ 🏨 **Sturbridge Host.** This hotel across the street from Old Sturbridge Village has luxuriously appointed bedrooms with Colonial decor and reproduction furnishings. Many rooms have fireplaces, and some have balconies or patios. Dinner is served nightly in Portobella's Ital-ian Restaurant; the Oxhead Tavern serves a lunch and dinner pub menu, which includes club sandwiches and burgers. ☒ *U.S. 20, 01566* ☎ *508/347–7393 or 800/582–3232* 🖷 *508/347–3944* ⊕ *www. sturbridgehosthotel.com* ➦ *233 rooms, 39 suites* ♿ *3 restaurants, miniature golf, pool, health club, sauna, boating, fishing, basketball, racquetball, bar, video game room, meeting rooms* ▭ *AE, D, DC, MC, V.*

$–$$ 🏨 **Sturbridge Country Inn.** The atmosphere at this 1840s Greek-revival farmhouse on Sturbridge's busy Main Street is between that of a coun-try inn and a plush business hotel. Guest rooms—all with working gas fireplaces and whirlpool tubs—have reproduction antiques; the best is the top-floor suite. ☒ *530 Main St., 01566* ☎ *508/347–5503* 🖷 *508/ 347–5319* ⊕ *www.sturbridgecountryinn.com* ➦ *6 rooms, 3 suites* ♿ *In-room hot tubs, hot tub, bar* ▭ *AE, D, MC, V* ⧖ *CP.*

Sports & the Outdoors

When state officials decided a reservoir was needed to provide drink-ing water for the metropolitan Boston area, they scoped out a remote area in western Massachusetts where the towns of Dana, Enfield, Greenwich, and Prescott stood. All four towns were subsequently taken by eminent domain, and when the waters of the Swift and Ware

★ rivers began to fill the **Quabbin Reservoir,** completed in the early 1940s, they flooded the towns and created the country's largest artificial lake. There are numerous hiking trails, bird observation posts, and pic-nic areas as well. ☒ *Rte. 9, Belchertown* ☎ *413/323–7221* ⧖ *Daily 9–4:30.*

Shopping

The **Seraph** (☒ 420 Main St. ☎ 508/347–2241) sells high-quality re-production furniture, all fashioned using period materials and designs. You'll also find Early American–style tin, pewter, and blown-glass ac-cessories. **Wild Bird Crossing** (☒ 4 Cedar St. ☎ 508/347–2473) carries every imaginable accoutrement for bird-watching, including birdbaths, binoculars, and books.

The Pioneer Valley A to Z

To research prices, get advice from other travelers, and book travel arrangements, visit www.fodors.com.

AIRPORTS

Bradley International Airport in Windsor Locks, Connecticut, is the most convenient airport for flying into the Pioneer Valley—it's 18 mi south of Springfield. American, America West, Continental, Delta, Northwest, Southwest, United, and US Airways serve Bradley.

🛪 Airport Information **Bradley International Airport** ✉ U.S. 20 (take Exit 40 off I-91) Windsor Locks, CT ☎ 860/292-2000 ⊕ www.bradleyairport.com.

BUS TRAVEL

Peter Pan Bus Lines links most major Northeast cities with Springfield, Holyoke, South Hadley, Northampton, Amherst, Deerfield, Greenfield, and Sturbridge and provides transportation to Bradley and Logan airports. Pioneer Valley Transit Authority provides service in 24 communities throughout the Pioneer Valley.

🚌 Bus Information **Peter Pan Bus Lines** ☎ 413/781-2900 or 800/237-8747 ⊕ www. peterpanbus.com. **Pioneer Valley Transit Authority** ☎ 413/781-7882 ⊕ www.pvta.com.

CAR TRAVEL

A car is your best way for exploring the region, as distances between attractions can be significant and public transportation impractical for most visitors. Interstate 91 runs north–south through the valley. Interstate 90 links Springfield to Boston. Route 2 connects Boston with Greenfield and, via U.S. 5, Deerfield.

EMERGENCIES

🏥 Hospitals & Emergency Services **Baystate Medical Center** ✉ 759 Chestnut St., Springfield ☎ 413/794-0000. **Cooley Dickenson Hospital** ✉ 30 Locust St., Northampton ☎ 413/582-2000. **Holyoke Hospital** ✉ 575 Beech St., Holyoke ☎ 413/534-2500.

TRAIN TRAVEL

Amtrak serves the Pioneer Valley with stops in Amherst and Springfield, with free parking at both stations. Express trains to New York City take three hours or less. Advance ticket purchases are often required, so book ahead.

🚆 Train Information **Amtrak** ☎ 800/872-7245 ⊕ www.amtrak.com.

VISITOR INFORMATION

The Greater Springfield Convention & Visitors Bureau serves the entire Pioneer Valley; it also operates the Riverfront Visitor Information Center, next to the Basketball Hall of Fame. Both the Northampton and Amherst chambers of commerce have useful visitor centers and Web sites. Additionally, the Franklin County Chamber of Commerce has more specific information about the northern end of the valley at its visitor center by the Route 2 exit of Interstate 91. The Sturbridge Area Tourist Association is your best resource for that area.

7 Tourist Information **Amherst Area Chamber of Commerce** ⊠ 409 Main St., Amherst 01002 ☎ 413/253-0700 ⊕ www.amherstarea.com. **Franklin County Chamber of Commerce** ⊠ 395 Main St. ⌂ Box 898, Greenfield 01302 ☎ 413/773-5463 ⊕ www.franklincc.org. **Greater Northampton Chamber of Commerce** ⊠ 99 Pleasant St., Northampton 01060 ☎ 413/584-1900 or 800/238-6869 ⊕ www.northamptonuncommon.com. **Greater Springfield Convention & Visitors Bureau** ⊠ 1441 Main St., Springfield 01103 ☎ 413/787-1548 or 800/723-1548 ⊕ www.valleyvisitor.com. **Sturbridge Area Tourist Association** ⊠ 380 Main St., Sturbridge 01566 ☎ 508/347-7594 or 800/628-8379 ⊕ www.sturbridge.org.

THE BERKSHIRES

Updated by
Gail M. Burns,
Carole
Owens, and
Eileen Pierce

More than a century ago, wealthy families from New York, Philadelphia, and Boston built "summer cottages" in the Berkshire Hills in western Massachusetts—great country estates that earned Berkshire County the nickname "inland Newport." Many of those grand houses have been razed, and still others are now occupied by schools or hotels. But the region's legacy as a desirable vacation getaway and cultural hub continues unabated.

Occupying the far western end of the state, the Berkshires lie about 2½ hours by car from Boston and New York City, yet the region lives up to the storybook image of rural New England, with wooded hills, narrow winding roads, and compact historic villages. Many cultural events take place in summer, among them the renowned Tanglewood classical music festival in Lenox. The foliage blazes brilliantly in fall, skiing is popular in winter, and spring is the time for maple sugaring. The scenic Mohawk Trail runs east to west across the northern section of the Berkshires.

North Adams

❶ *130 mi northwest of Boston; 73 mi northwest of Springfield; 20 mi south of Bennington, Vermont.*

Established as the military outpost Fort Massachusetts in the mid-18th century, North Adams started out as a part of East Hoosac, then became part of Adams, before incorporating as its own city in the late 19th century. By then its economy had become dependent upon its textile industry. After North Adams became a strong producer of electrical and radio parts, its fortunes waned just as did those of most other industrial New England cities following World War II.

In the past few years, however, the city has staged an impressive comeback as a center of contemporary art. In addition to the famous Mass MoCA arts space, North Adams has a bounty of mills and factory buildings that have been converted to artists' studios and residences. Additionally, Western Gateway Heritage State Park commemorates the city's industrial legacy. Downtown still is in somewhat of a transition, but preservation efforts continue to spruce things up, and new shops and eateries seem to open every few months.

Opened in 1999 to much fanfare, the **Massachusetts Museum of Contemporary Arts,** or Mass MoCA, is the nation's largest center for contemporary performing and visual arts. The vast, 13-acre 19th-century complex of 27 buildings once housed the now-defunct Sprague Electric Co. Six of the factory buildings have been transformed into more than 250,000 square feet of galleries, studios, performance venues, cafés, and shops. Its size enables the museum to display monumentally scaled works such as Robert Rauschenberg's ¼ *Mile or 2 Furlong Piece.* Exhibits and performances include everything from art exhibitions to dance and music concerts and film presentations. ⊠ *87 Marshall St.* ☎ *413/664–4111* ⊕ *www.massmoca.org* 🎟 *$10* ☉ *June–Sept., daily 10–6; Oct.–May, Wed.–Mon. 10–5.*

★ ☺ North Adams' best kept secret, the **North Adams Museum of History & Science** has more than 25 permanent exhibits on three floors of a building that was once part of a railroad yard. A store sells a number of North Adams Historical Society publications. ⊠ *Western Gateway Heritage State Park, Bldg. 5A, State St.* ☎ *413/664–4700* 🎟 *Free* ☉ *Jan.–Apr., Sat. 10–4, Sun. 1–4; May–Dec., Thurs.–Sat. 10–4, Sun. 1–4.*

★ ☺ **Western Gateway Heritage State Park** occupies the old Boston & Maine railroad yard. The visitor center houses exhibits that trace the impact that train travel had on the region. A 30-minute documentary provides a look at the intense labor that went into the construction of the nearby Hoosac Tunnel. ⊠ *115 State St.* ☎ *413/663–6312* ⊕ *www.mass.gov/dcr/parks/western/wghp.htm* 🎟 *Free* ☉ *Visitor center daily 10–5.*

Where to Stay & Eat

★ **$$** ✕ **Gramercy Bistro.** Occupying what was once a downtown diner, this casual, upbeat eatery has developed a loyal following. The intimate space, with a wood-beam ceiling and walls lined with black-and-white photos of the town, serves an eclectic mix of sandwiches and salads. Come by on weekends for the memorable brunch. ⊠ *24 Marshall St.* ☎ *413/663–5300* ▤ *AE, MC, V* ☉ *Closed Tues. No lunch.*

★ **$–$$** ✕ **Cafe Latino.** Formerly the stark, ultramodern Eleven, this restaurant in the Mass MoCA courtyard has taken on a Latin accent and gone warm and festive. At its signature back-lit bar, you can now order a Brazilian caipirinha or a wine from Argentina or Spain. Chef Omar Montoya, however, is from Peru, so while his menu ranges throughout Latin America, Peruvian influences predominate. Try his marinated and grilled skirt steak or his citrus-braised pork shoulder. The *tres leches* cake for dessert is formidable. ⊠ *1111 Mass MoCA Way* ☎ *413/662–2004* ▤ *AE, D, MC, V.*

¢ ✕ **Jack's Hot Dog Stand.** A North Adams institution since 1917, this hole-in-the-wall is where locals go for a frank. It also serves burgers and fries any way you like them. There is minimal seating, so be prepared to eat your wiener on the run. ⊠ *12 Eagle St.* ☎ *413/664–9006* ▤ *No credit cards.*

$$–$$$ 🏨 **Porches Inn.** These once-dilapidated mill workers' houses dating from the 1890s were refurbished to become one of New England's quirkiest hotels. They now strike a perfect balance between high-tech and historic—rooms have a mix of retro 1940s and '50s lamps and bungalow-style furnishings along with such contemporary touches as stunning bathrooms with slate floors, hot tubs, and mirrors fashioned out of old window frames. Some two-room suites have loft sleeping areas reached by spiral staircases. Suites have pull-out sofas and can sleep up to six. ⊠ *231 River St., 01247* ☎ *413/664–0400* ⊕ *www.porches.com* ⇌ *47 rooms, 12 suites* ♿ *Some in-room hot tubs, some kitchens, cable TV, in-room data ports, pool, exercise equipment, hot tub, sauna, bar, dry cleaning, laundry service, concierge, business services, meeting room* ▭ *AE, DC, MC, V* ⑩| *CP.*

★ **$–$$** 🏠 **Blackinton Manor B&B.** Dan and Betsy Epstein's meticulously restored 1849 Italianate mansion is furnished with antiques. The Epsteins are both professional musicians, and they often host concerts and chamber music workshops. Several of the elegantly appointed guest rooms have pianos. The mansion, one of many in the city built by textiles baron Sanford Blackinton, is notable for its intricate wrought-iron balconies, floor-to-ceiling windows, a spacious bay window, and decorative corbels. ⊠ *1391 Massachusetts Ave., 01247* ⊕ *www.blackinton-manor.com* ☎ *413/663–5795 or 800/795–8613* ⇌ *5 rooms* ♿ *Some in-room hot tubs, pool; no kids under 7* ▭ *MC, V* ⑩| *BP.*

Nightlife & the Arts

The historic Beaver Mill, which occupies 27 acres of woodland adjacent to Natural Bridge State Park, houses the **Contemporary Artists Center** (⊠ 189 Beaver St. ☎ 413/663–9555 ⊕ www.thecac.org), a 130,000-square-foot artists' residence and studio. The center has a small café that hosts exhibits.

Sports & the Outdoors

★ A hidden gem in the city is **Natural Bridge State Park** (⊠ Rte. 8 ☎ 413/663–6392 ⊕ www.mass.gov/dcr/parks/western/nbdg.htm), named for the 30-foot span that crosses Hudson Brook. The marble arch at the center of this 49-acre park sits in what was a marble quarry from the early 1880s to the mid-1900s. There are picnic sites, hiking trails, and well-maintained restrooms. In winter the park is popular for cross-country skiing.

Shopping

Delftree Mushroom Farm (⊠ 234 Union St. ☎ 413/664–4907 or 800/243–3742) raises Japanese shiitake mushrooms inside a 19th-century mill; you can see how the mushrooms are grown and buy them, too. Housed in the former J. J. Newberry storefront, **Moulton's General Store** (⊠ 75 Main St. ☎ 413/664–7770) sells Berkshire Ice Cream, Green Mountain Coffee, and all the penny candy you can eat.

Williamstown

❷ *5 mi west of North Adams.*

When Colonel Ephraim Williams left money to found a free school in what was then known as West Hoosac, he stipulated that the town's name be changed to Williamstown. Williams College opened in 1793 and even today, life in this placid town revolves around it. Williamstown looks nothing like North Adams, its gritty but colorful cousin to the east. Graceful campus buildings like the Gothic cathedral, built in 1904, line wide Main Street. Down Spring Street, you'll find a handful of upscale shops and lively eateries. The collection and exhibits at the **Williams College Museum of Art** focus on American and 20th-century art. More than 11,000 works span a broad range of eras and cultures, but the emphasis is on modern and contemporary American works. The original octagonal structure facing Main Street was built as a library in 1846. ⊠ *15 Lawrence Hall Dr.* ☎ *413/597–2429* ⊕ *www.williams.edu* 🎫 *Free* ۞ *Tues.–Sat. 10–5, Sun. 1–5.*

★ The **Chapin Library of Rare Books & Manuscripts** at Williams College contains original copies of the four founding documents of the United States—the Declaration of Independence, the Articles of Confederation, the Constitution, and the Bill of Rights. You'll also find 50,000 books, 40,000 manuscripts, and illustrations dating from as far back as the 9th century. Every Independence Day the Library holds an open house the highlight of which is readings of the founding documents by actors from the Williamstown Theatre Festival. ⊠ *26 Hopkins Hall Dr.* ☎ *413/597–2462* ⊕ *www.williams.edu* 🎫 *Free* ۞ *Weekdays 10–noon and 1–5.*

One of the nation's notable small art museums, the **Clark Art Institute** has more than 30 paintings by Renoir (among them *Mademoiselle Fleury in Algerian Costume*) as well as canvases by Monet and Pissarro. *The Little Dancer,* an important sculpture by Degas, is another exceptional work. Other items include priceless English silver, European and American photography from the 1840s through the 1910s, and Flemish and Dutch masterworks from the 17th and 18th centuries. ⊠ *225 South St.* ☎ *413/458–2303* ⊕ *www.clarkart.edu* 🎫 *July–Oct. $10, Nov.–May free* ۞ *Sept.–June, Tues.–Sun. 10–5; July and Aug., daily 10–5.*

Where to Stay & Eat

$–$$$ ✕ **Mezze Bistro & Bar.** This is, without a doubt, Williamstown's hot spot. On summer evenings it's not uncommon to find yourself rubbing elbows with stars from the Williamstown Theatre Festival. The interior mixes urban chic and rustic charm, with hardwood floors and exposed-brick walls. The spectacular menu is always in flux, but don't be surprised to encounter sashimi with watercress alongside filet mignon with roasted root vegetables. ⊠ *16 Water St.* ☎ *413/458–0123* ⊕ *www. mezzerestaurant.com* ⌕ *Reservations essential* ⊟ *AE, D, MC, V* ۞ *No lunch.*

★ **$$–$$$$** ✕🖵 **Orchards Hotel.** Although it's near Route 2 and surrounded by parking lots, this thoroughly proper, if rather stuffy, hostelry compensates with a beautiful courtyard filled with fruit trees and a pond stocked with koi. English antiques furnish most of the spacious accommodations. The inner rooms, which have windows looking onto the courtyard, are best for summer stays. The outer rooms have less-distinguished views, but their fireplaces add appeal for winter visits. The restaurant, Yasmin's

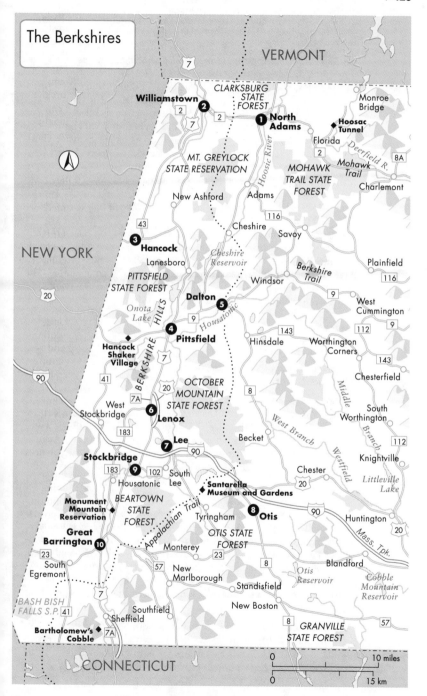

The Berkshires

VERMONT

CLARKSBURG STATE FOREST

Williamstown **2**

1 North Adams

◆ Hoosac Tunnel

Monroe Bridge

Florida

Deerfield R. 8A

MT. GREYLOCK STATE RESERVATION

MOHAWK TRAIL STATE FOREST

Mohawk Trail

Charlemont

New Ashford

Adams

Cheshire

Savoy

116

NEW YORK

20

3 Hancock

Lanesboro

Cheshire Reservoir

Berkshire Trail

Windsor

Plainfield

116

PITTSFIELD STATE FOREST

Onota Lake

Dalton **5**

West Cummington

9

Housatonic

9

143

112

4 Pittsfield

Hinsdale

Worthington Corners

143

◆ Hancock Shaker Village

41

20

OCTOBER MOUNTAIN STATE FOREST

8

South Worthington

Chesterfield

Middle Branch

90

West Stockbridge

7A

6 Lenox

183

Becket

West Branch

Westfield R.

112

Knightville

Littleville Lake

7 Lee

90

Stockbridge

183 **9** 102

South Lee

Chester

20

Huntington

20

Housatonic

◆ Santarella Museum and Gardens

BEARTOWN STATE FOREST

Tyringham

8 Otis

90

Mass. Tpk.

◆ Monument Mountain Reservation

Appalachian Trail

OTIS STATE FOREST

Blandford

Otis Reservoir

Cobble Mountain Reservoir

Great Barrington 10

23

Monterey

23

8

South Egremont

New Marlborough

Standisfield

New Boston

57

BASH BISH FALLS S.P. 41

7

57

Southfield

Sheffield

8

GRANVILLE STATE FOREST

◆ Bartholomew's Cobble 7A

CONNECTICUT

0   10 miles

0   15 km

($$–$$$$), serves such creative fare as sautéed scallops with a banana-shiitake salad. ✉ *222 Adams Rd., 01267* ☎ *413/458–9611 or 800/225–1517* 🖷 *413/458–3273* ⊕ *www.orchardshotel.com* 🛏 *49 rooms* ♿ *Restaurant, some refrigerators, pool, gym, hot tub, sauna, bar, meeting room, fireplace in some rooms* ▤ *AE, DC, MC, V.*

★ **$–$$$** ▦ **Guest House at Field Farm.** Built in 1948, this guesthouse contains a fine collection of art on loan from Williams College. The former owners, who gave part of their own art collection to the college, donated the 296-acre property to the Trustees of Reservations, which runs it as a B&B. The large windows in the guest rooms have expansive views of the grounds. Three rooms have private decks; two rooms have working tile fireplaces. You can prepare your own simple meals in the pantry. The grounds, open to the public, have miles of hiking trails. ✉ *554 Sloan Rd., 01267* ☎🖷 *413/458–3135* ⊕ *www.guesthouseatfieldfarm.org* 🛏 *5 rooms* ♿ *Pool; no kids under 12* ▤ *D, MC, V* ⦿ *BP.*

★ **$** ▦ **River Bend Farm.** On the National Register of Historic Places, this authentic 1770 Georgian Colonial was once the home and tavern of Colonel Benjamin Simonds. It has period details to make you feel cozy and just enough modern conveniences to make you comfortable. The guest rooms are sprinkled with antique pieces—chamber pots, washstands, wing chairs, and spinning wheels. Some bedrooms have wide-plank walls, curtains of unbleached muslin, and four-poster beds or rope beds. A gracious library awaits you downstairs. The kitchen contains an open-range stove and an oven hung with dried herbs. ✉ *643 Simonds Rd., 01267* ☎ *413/458–3121* ⊕ *www.riverbendfarmbb.com* 🛏 *4 rooms without bath* ♿ *No a/c, no room phones, no room TVs* ▤ *No credit cards* ⦿ *Closed Nov.–Mar.* ⦿ *CP.*

Nightlife & the Arts

Fodor'sChoice
★ At the Adams Memorial Theatre, the **Williamstown Theatre Festival** (✉ 1000 Main St. ☎ 413/597–3400 or 413/597–3399 ⊕ www.wtfestival.org) is summer's hottest ticket. From June through August, the long-running production presents well-known theatrical works with famous performers on the Main Stage and contemporary works on the Nikos Stage.

Sports & the Outdoors

The centerpiece of the 10,327-acre **Mt. Greylock State Reservation** (✉ Rockwell Rd., Lanesboro ☎ 413/499–4262 or 413/499–4263 ⊕ www.mass.gov/dcr/parks/western/mgry.htm) is 3,491-foot-high Mt. Greylock, the highest point in Massachusetts. The reservation, south of Williamstown, has facilities for cycling, fishing, horseback riding, camping, and snowmobiling. Many treks—including a portion of the Appalachian Trail—start from the parking lot at the summit, an 8-mi drive from the base of the mountain.

The **Green River** flows 11 mi from its headwaters on Sugarloaf Mountain in New Ashford to its confluence with the Hoosic River in Williamstown. There are several nice spots to picnic or fish along its banks, and locals enjoy taking a dip in some of its quieter pools or rafting along its gentle course in summer. The 489-acre Green River Wildlife Management Area is near the Five Corners intersection.

Shopping

Spring Street is downtown Williamstown's main drag, lined with up-scale shops, cafés, and businesses. At **Library Antiques** (⊠ 70 Spring St. ☎ 413/458–3436 ⊕ www.libraryantiques.com), you'll find an array of prints, folk art, jewelry, antiquarian books, and distinctive gifts. Some people consider tiny **Toonerville Trolley** (⊠ 131 Water St. ☎ 413/458–5229) the best music store in the world. One thing they appreciate is the vast musical knowledge of proprietor Hal March. Toon-erville carries hard-to-find jazz, rock, and classical recordings. Jam-packed with every imaginable toy and game, **Where'd You Get That?** (⊠ 100 Spring St. ☎ 413/458–2206 ⊕ www.wygt.com) also benefits from the warmth and enthusiasm generated by owners Ken and Michele Gietz.

Hancock

❸ *15 mi south of Williamstown.*

Tiny Hancock, the village closest to the Jiminy Peak ski resort, comes into its own in winter. It's also a great base for outdoors enthusiasts year-round, with biking, hiking, and other options in summer.

Established in the 1930s, the 600-acre **Ioka Valley Farm** (⊠ Rte. 43 ☎ 413/738–5915) is one of the best-known pick-your-own farms in the Berkshires. You can pick berries all summer, then apples and pumpkins in fall. In winter you can cut your own Christmas tree. Other activities include hayrides, pedal tractors for kids, and a petting zoo with pigs, sheep, goats, and calves.

Where to Stay

$$–$$$$ 🏨 **Country Inn at Jiminy Peak.** Massive stone fireplaces in its lobby and lounge lend this hotel a ski-lodge atmosphere. The modern condo-style suites accommodate up to four people and have kitchenettes separated from living areas by bars with high stools; the suites at the rear of the building overlook the slopes. Ski packages are available. ⊠ *Corey Rd., 01237* ☎ *413/738–5500 or 800/882–8859* 📠 *413/738–5513* ⊕ *www. jiminypeak.com* 🛏 *105 suites* ♨ *2 restaurants, kitchens, in-room VCRs, miniature golf, 5 tennis courts, pool, gym, 2 hot tubs, 2 saunas, fish-ing, hiking, cross-country skiing, downhill skiing, bar, video game room, meeting room* 🚭 *AE, D, DC, MC, V.*

Sports & the Outdoors

SKI AREA The only full-service ski and snowboard resort in the Berkshires, and the largest in southern New England, **Jiminy Peak** is also a splendid spot to stay during fall foliage season. A four-in-one Euro-bungee trampo-line, a two-story-high rock-climbing wall, summit rides on the Berkshire Express chairlift, and mountain biking make it a delightful alternative for families in summer.

Downhill. With a vertical of 1,150 feet, 40 trails, and 9 lifts, Jiminy has near-big-time status. It is mostly a cruising mountain—trails are groomed daily, and only on some are small moguls left to build up along the side of the slope. The steepest black-diamond runs are on the upper head walls; longer, outer runs make for good intermediate terrain. There's skiing nightly, and snowmaking covers 93% of the skiable terrain.

Other activities. Jiminy has a snowboard park and an old-fashioned ice rink.

Summer activities. The resort has a 3,000-foot alpine slide, a challenging 9-hole miniature golf course, rock climbing, mountain biking, tennis courts, swimming facilities, and trout fishing. You can ride up the mountain on a high-speed chairlift. ☒ *Corey Rd., 01237* ☎ *413/738–5500, 888/454–6469 outside Massachusetts, 413/738–7325 snow conditions* ⊕ *www.jiminypeak.com.*

Pittsfield

❹ *21 mi south of Williamstown, 11 mi southeast of Hancock.*

A mere agricultural backwater at the time of the American Revolution, the seat of Berkshire County grew steadily throughout the 19th century into an industrial powerhouse of textile, paper, and electrical machinery manufacturing. As recently as the 1930s, the WPA guidebook on Massachusetts described Pittsfield as possessing a "prosperous, tranquil look of general comfort and cultivation which makes it one of the most attractive industrial cities in the state." The city's economy took a nosedive following World War II, and much of that apparent prosperity diminished.

Modern Pittsfield has brushed off some of its bruises and blemishes of the past several decades and reclaimed a number of intriguing industrial buildings. Still, this is a workaday city without the monied urbanity of Great Barrington or the quaint, rural demeanor of the comparatively small Colonial towns that surround it. Along North Street, several new shops and eateries have opened, perhaps signaling a return to downtown prosperity.

☺ Opened in 1903, the **Berkshire Museum** houses three floors of exhibits, which display a varied and sometimes curious collection of objects relating to history, the natural world, and art. A highlight of the latter is a collection of Hudson River School paintings, including works by Frederic Church and Albert Bierstadt. An aquarium contains 26 tanks of sea creatures, including a touch tank; a 10-foot-high, 26-foot-long "Wally" the Stegosaurus highlights the Dinosaurs and Paleontology gallery. At the Dino Dig, kids and adults can dig together for touchable replicas of dinosaur bones. An ancient civilization gallery displays Roman and Greek jewelry and an ancient Egyptian mummy. ☒ *39 South St.* ☎ *413/443–7171* ⊕ *www.berkshiremuseum.org* ☒ *$7.50* ☺ *Mon.–Sat. 10–5, Sun. noon–5.*

FodorśChoice **Hancock Shaker Village** was founded in the 1790s, the third Shaker community in America. At its peak in the 1840s, the village had almost 300
★ inhabitants, who made their living farming, selling seeds and herbs, mak-

ing medicines, and producing crafts. The religious community officially closed in 1960, its 170-year life span a small miracle considering its population's vows of celibacy (they took in orphans to maintain their constituency). Many examples of Shaker ingenuity are visible at Hancock today: the **Round Stone Barn** and the **Laundry and Machine Shop** are two of the most interesting buildings. Also on-site are a farm, some period gardens, a museum shop with reproduction Shaker furniture, a picnic area, and a café. ⊠ *U.S. 20, 6 mi west of Pittsfield* ☎ *413/443–0188 or 800/817–1137* ⊕ *www.hancockshakervillage.org* ⊡ *$15, $10 in winter* ☉ *Late May–late Oct., daily 9:30–5 for self-guided tours; late Oct.–late May, daily 10–3 for guided tours.*

Where to Stay & Eat

$–$$$ ✕**Dakota.** Moose and elk heads watch over diners, and the motto is "Steak, seafood, and smiles" at this large and popular chain restaurant, decorated like a rustic hunting lodge. Meals cooked on the mesquite grill include steaks and salmon, shrimp, and trout; the 32-item salad bar has many organic foods. A hearty Sunday brunch buffet includes Belgian pancakes, omelets, ham, lox and bagels, fruit, salads, and rich desserts. ⊠ *1035 South St.* ☎ *413/499–7900* ▤ *AE, D, DC, MC, V* ☉ *No lunch Mon.–Sat.*

$–$$ ▦ **White Horse Inn.** Standing on Pittsfield's busy South Street, this early-20th-century Colonial-revival home provides comfortable rooms, appointed with handsome Colonial furnishings. The breakfast room has a wood-burning stove and overlooks a deck, where you can eat on warm summer mornings. ⊠ *378 South St., 01201* ☎ *413/442–2512* ⊟ *413/443–0490* ⊕ *www.whitehorsebb.com* ⊷ *8 rooms* ⌂ *Cable TV, in-room data ports* ▤ *AE, D, MC, V* ⦿❘ *BP.*

Nightlife & the Arts

For the serious music lover, **South Mountain Concerts** (⊠ U.S. 7 and 20, 2 mi south of Pittsfield center ☎ 413/442–2106) is one of the most distinguished centers for chamber music events in the country. Set on the wooded slope of South Mountain, the 500-seat auditorium presents concerts every September Sunday at 3.

Sports & the Outdoors

One of the highlights of the 65-acre **Pittsfield State Forest** (⊠ Cascade St. ☎ 413/442–8992 ⊕ www.mass.gov/dcr/parks/western/pitt.htm) is its paved ¾-mi Tranquility Trail. There are also 13 rustic campsites and 18 with flush toilets. Campground office hours are 8 AM–10 PM, and the regular camping season is from May to October.

The **Housatonic River** flows south from Pittsfield between the Berkshire Hills and the Taconic Range toward Connecticut, where it eventually empties into Long Island Sound. For guided canoe tours on the Housatonic River, contact **Berkshire Scenic Treks & Canoe Tours** (⊠ 151 Bullhill Rd. ☎ 413/442–2789).

SKI AREA Other areas have entered an era of glamour and high prices, but the **Bousquet Ski Area** remains an economical, no-nonsense place to ski. The inexpensive lift tickets are the same price every day, and there's night skiing except Sunday. You can go tubing for just $10 for the day when conditions allow.

Downhill. Bousquet, with a 750-foot vertical drop, has 21 trails, but only if you count every change in steepness and every merging slope. Though this is a generous figure, you will find some good beginner and intermediate runs, with a few steeper pitches. There are three double chairlifts, two surface lifts, and a small snowboard park.

Summer and year-round activities. Play Bousquet uses three drop funnels to pour kids out into a large activity pool and enough twists and turns and chute-to-chutes to scare the pants off many parents. A miniature-golf course, 24-foot climbing wall, go-karts, Thrill Sleds, and a scenic chairlift make Bousquet a suitable reward for children who have stoically accompanied their parents to the assortment of galleries, concerts, and plays that are the area's major tourism resource. The facilities at the **Berkshire West Athletic Club** (⊠ Dan Fox Dr. ☎ 413/499–4600), across the street from Bousquet, include four handball courts, indoor and outdoor tennis courts, cardiovascular and weight machines, and indoor and outdoor pools. ⊠ *101 Dan Fox Dr., off U.S. 7, near Pittsfield Airport, 01201* ☎ *413/442–8316, 413/442–2436 snow conditions* ⊕ *www.bousquets.com.*

Dalton

❺ *8 mi northeast of Pittsfield.*

The paper manufacturer Crane and Co., begun by Zenas Crane in 1801, is the major employer in working-class Dalton. Exhibits at the **Crane Museum of Paper Making,** in the handsomely restored Old Stone Mill (1844), trace the history of American papermaking from the 18th century to the present. A museum since 1930, the building sits on the banks of the Housatonic River. It's an impressive space with rough-hewn oak beams and Colonial-style chandeliers. ⊠ *E. Housatonic St. off Rte. 9* ☎ *413/684–6481* ⊠ *Free* ☉ *June–mid-Oct., weekdays 2–5.*

Where to Stay & Eat

¢ ✕ **Juice n' Java Coffee House.** This unassuming little café on Main Street serves fresh home-baked pastries, particularly muffins, that are downright memorable. Also available are specialty coffees, quiche, and designer sandwiches made on an Italian panini grill. ⊠ *661 Main St.* ☎ *413/684–5080* ☱ *AE, MC, V.*

$–$$ ⊞ **Dalton House.** Cheerful guest rooms decorated with an eclectic mix of Shaker and period furnishings, folk art, plants, and collectibles are spread among three interconnected buildings; the original structure was built in 1810 by a Hessian soldier. Common rooms include a living room with a stone fireplace and a sunny breakfast area. Two suites in the carriage house have sitting areas, exposed beams, and quilts. ⊠ *955 Main St., 01226* ☎ *413/684–3854, 800/694–3854* ☏ *413/684–0203* ⊕ *www. thedaltonhouse.com* ⬦ *9 rooms, 2 suites* ♿ *Cable TV, in-room data ports, pool; no kids under 8* ☱ *AE, MC, V* ⑩ *BP.*

Lenox

❻ *18 mi southwest of Dalton, 10 mi south of Pittsfield, 130 mi west of Boston.*

The famed Tanglewood music festival has been a fixture in upscale Lenox for decades, and it's a part of the reason the town remains fiercely popular in summer. Booking a room here or in any of the nearby communities can set you back dearly when music or theatrical events are in town. Many of the town's most impressive homes are downtown; others you can only see by taking to the curving, tortuous back roads that traverse the region. In the center of the village, a few blocks of shabby-chic Colonial buildings contain shops and eateries.

The **Berkshires Scenic Railway Museum,** in a restored 1903 railroad station in central Lenox, displays antique rail equipment, vintage exhibits, and a large working model railway. It's the starting point for the diesel-hauled **Berkshire Scenic Railway,** a 2½-hour narrated round-trip train ride between Lenox and Stockbridge. ✉ *Willow Creek Rd.* ☎ *413/637–2210* ⊕ *www.berkshirescenicrailroad.org* 🚆 *Train $13, museum free* ☉ *May–Oct., weekends 10–4.*

The sleek, modernist **Frelinghuysen Morris House & Studio** occupies a verdant 46-acre property and exhibits the works of American abstract artists Suzy Frelinghuysen and George L. K. Morris as well as those of contemporaries including Picasso, Braque, and Gris. ✉ *92 Hawthorne St.* ☎*413/637–0166* ⊕*www.frelinghuysen.org* 🚆*$10* ☉ *Mid-June–early Sept., Thurs.–Sun. 10–4; early Sept.–mid-Oct., Thurs.–Sat. 10–4.*

Fodor'sChoice ★ **The Mount,** a mansion built in 1902 with myriad classical influences, was the summer home of novelist Edith Wharton. The 42-room house and 3 acres of formal gardens were designed by Wharton, who is considered by many to have set the standard for 20th-century interior decoration. In designing the Mount, she followed the principles set forth in her book *The Decoration of Houses* (1897), creating a calm and well-ordered home. The Mount continues to undergo an extensive restoration, and only the downstairs rooms are finished. ✉ *2 Plunkett St.* ☎ *413/637–1899 or 888/637–1902* ⊕ *www.edithwharton.org* 🚆 *$16* ☉ *May–Oct. daily 9–5.*

Built in 1893, Ventfort Hall was the summer "cottage" of Sarah Morgan, the sister of financier J. P. Morgan. Inside is the **Museum of the Gilded Age,** which explores the role of Lenox and the Berkshires as the definitive mountain retreat during that fabled era. The building was in danger of being torn down when a group of preservationists formed to buy this 12-acre property in 1997. Since then a top restoration team has been hard at work repairing the elegant exterior brickwork and roofing, the ornate interior paneling and grand staircase, and the gabled carriage house. ✉ *104 Walker St.* ☎ *413/637–3206* ⊕ *www.gildedage.org* 🚆 *$9* ☉ *May–Oct., Mon.–Sat. tours on the hr 11:30–2:30; Nov.–Apr., Sat. tours at 10 and 11.*

Where to Stay & Eat

$–$$$$ ✕ **Café Lucia.** *Bistecca alla fiorentina* (porterhouse steak grilled with olive oil, garlic, and rosemary) and ravioli *basilico e pomodoro* (with fresh tomatoes, garlic, and basil) are among the dishes that change seasonally at this northern Italian restaurant. The sleek café has track lighting and photographs of the owners' Italian ancestors. Weekend reservations are essential up to a month ahead during the Tanglewood music festival. ⊠ *80 Church St.* ☎ *413/637–2640* ▭ *AE, DC, MC, V* ☾ *Closed July–Oct., Mon.; Nov.–June, Sun. and Mon. No lunch.*

$$–$$$ ✕ **Bistro Zinc.** Crisp lemon-yellow walls, warm tile floors, and tall windows are bright and inviting in this stellar French bistro, which feels like a country house in Provence. The kitchen turns out expertly prepared and refreshingly simple classics like steak frites, saddle of rabbit, and spinach lasagna. Zinc's long, wood bar, always full and determinedly sophisticated, is the best Lenox can offer for nightlife. If you can overlook the occasionally self-important attitudes of the staff, Zinc is top-notch. ⊠ *56 Church St.* ☎ *413/637–8800* ▭ *AE, MC, V.*

$$–$$$ ✕ **Church Street Café.** A little more laid-back than its nearby competitors, Church Street Café presents a no-less ambitious and intriguing menu of creative globally inspired dishes. From the baked onion–and–St. Andre Cheese tart to the miso-citrus–glazed salmon and the New Mexican home-style tortilla stuffed with barbecued brisket, the dishes served here are an international culinary treat. In warm weather you can dine on a shaded outdoor deck. ⊠ *65 Church St.* ☎ *413/637–2745* ▭ *MC, V* ☾ *Closed Sun. and Mon. mid-Oct.–May.*

$$–$$$ ✕ **Spigalina.** In an unprepossessing pale-green house in downtown
Fodor's Choice Lenox, Spigalina serves high-quality cuisine, reflecting the flavors of Spain,
★ southern France, Greece, and Morocco. The wild mushroom risotto is quite simply extraordinary, and the Greek-style spaghetti with sautéed shrimp and scallops as well as the rack of lamb are other standouts. ⊠ *80 Main St.* ☎ *413/637–4455* ▭ *AE, D, MC, V* ☾ *No lunch.*

$$–$$$$ ✕▥ **Gateways Inn.** The 1912 summer cottage of Harley Proctor (as in
Fodor's Choice Proctor and Gamble) has experienced some ups and downs during its
★ tenure as a country inn. But under the skillful direction of innkeepers Fabrizio and Rosemary Chiariello, it looks better than ever. Rooms come in a variety of configurations and styles, most with working fireplaces, detailed moldings, and plush carpeting. In the restaurant ($$–$$$; closed Mon.; no lunch weekdays) you might dine on sautéed medallions of venison or baked acorn squash with a wild rice–cranberry stuffing and roasted-chestnut ragout. The restaurant offers a light late-night menu during the Tanglewood season. ⊠ *51 Walker St., 01240* ☎ *413/637–2532* ▤ *413/637–1432* ⊕ *www.gatewaysinn.com* ↪ *11 rooms, 1 suite* ⚘ *Restaurant, some in-room VCRs, in-room data ports, bar, meeting room* ▭ *AE, MC, V* ❙◯❙ *BP.*

$$$$ ▥ **Blantyre.** Modeled after a castle in Scotland, this supremely elegant 1902 manor house sits amid nearly 100 acres of manicured lawns and woodlands. Lavishly decorated rooms in the main house have hand-carved four-poster beds, overstuffed chaise longues, and Victorian bathrooms. The rooms in the carriage house are well appointed but can't compete with the formal grandeur of the main house. The restaurant serves upscale country-house fare—no cream or heavy sauces, light on the butter. A typical entrée might be roasted Arctic char with fennel confit, crispy potatoes, mussels, crab, and saffron. ⊠ *16 Blantyre Rd., off U.S. 20, 01240* ☎ *413/637–3556* 🖷 *413/637–4282* ⊕ *www.blantyre.com* ⇗ *25 rooms, 5 suites, 1 cottage* ⚲ *Restaurant, some in-room hot tubs, 4 tennis courts, pool, hot tub, massage, sauna, croquet, hiking* ▭ *AE, DC, MC, V* ⊘ *Closed early Nov.–early May* ⦿ *CP.*

$$$–$$$$ 🏨 **Cranwell Resort, Spa, & Golf Club.** The best rooms in this 380-acre, five-building complex are in the century-old Tudor mansion; they're furnished with antiques and have marble bathrooms. Two smaller buildings have 20 rooms each, and there are several small cottages, each of which has a kitchen. Somewhat marring the property are an abundance of tightly spaced condos behind the hotel buildings. Most of the facilities are open to the public, as are the resort's restaurants, where you can dine formally or informally. There's also a full golf school. The 35,000-square-foot spa has a full complement of women's and men's treatments, plus several types of massage. ⊠ *55 Lee Rd., 02140* ☎ *413/637–1364 or 800/272–6935* 🖷 *413/637–4364* ⊕ *www. cranwell.com* ⇗ *116 rooms* ⚲ *4 restaurants, driving range, 18-hole golf course, 4 tennis courts, pool, health club, spa, bicycles, hiking, cross-country skiing, concierge, meeting rooms* ▭ *AE, D, DC, MC, V* ⦿ *CP.*

$$–$$$ 🏨 **Brook Farm Inn.** This 1870s Victorian and its gardens are tucked away in a beautiful wooded glen a short distance from Tanglewood. The innkeepers are music and literature aficionados and often have light opera, jazz, or Broadway tunes playing in the fireplace-lighted library, whose shelves contain copious volumes of verse. On Saturday poetry is read at afternoon tea. Rooms have antiques, light-pastel color schemes, and in many cases four-poster beds. Even the smallest units, with their eaved ceilings and cozy configurations, are highly romantic. ⊠ *15 Hawthorne St., 01240* ☎ *413/637–3013 or 800/285–7638* ⊕ *www.brookfarm. com* ⇗ *12 rooms, 1 suite* ⚲ *In-room data ports, pool, library; no room TVs, no kids under 15* ▭ *MC, V* ⦿ *BP.*

$$–$$$ 🏨 **Cliffwood Inn.** Six of the seven guest rooms in this 1889 Georgian-revival white-clapboard mansion have fireplaces, and four more fireplaces glow in the common areas, reflecting off the polished wooden floors. Many of the inn's ornate antiques come from Europe; most guest rooms have canopy beds. ⊠ *25 Cliffwood St., 01240* ☎ *413/637–3330 or 800/789–3331* 🖷 *413/637–0221* ⊕ *www.cliffwood.com* ⇗ *6 rooms, 1 suite* ⚲ *Some in-room hot tubs, some in-room VCRs, pool, hot tub; no room phones, no TV in some rooms, no kids under 11* ▭ *No credit cards* ⦿ *BP.*

$$–$$$ 🏨 **Harrison House.** An inviting white Victorian house with a sweeping wraparound porch across from Lenox's White Church on the Hill, this upscale inn is particularly notable for its attractive, mature landscaping. Rooms are lavish with decadent furnishings—every unit has a working fireplace, and a few have four-poster or canopy beds. Plush duvets, ceiling fans, and Victorian-style wallpaper add to the sense of romance. It's a bit smaller and less busy than most of the inns in Lenox, and the hosts are friendly and enthusiastic. The inn is close enough to walk into town but set nicely on a hillside away from the tourist bustle. Tea is served every afternoon. ⊠ *174 Main St., 01240* ☎ *413/637–1746* ⊕ *www.harrison-house.com* ↩ *6 rooms* ⚐ *No room phones* ☐ *AE, D, MC, V* ⚐ *BP.*

★ **$$–$$$** ⬚ **Whistler's Inn.** The antiques decorating the parlor of this eccentric 1820s English Tudor mansion are ornate, with a touch of the exotic. The library, formal parlor, music room (with a Steinway grand piano and Louis XVI original furniture), and gracious dining room all impress. Designer drapes and bedspreads adorn the rooms, three of which have working fireplaces. The carriage house is only open May through October; one room in it is done in African, and another in Southwestern style. The inn is nestled amid 7 acres of gardens and woods across from Kennedy Park. ⊠ *5 Greenwood St., 01240* ☎ *413/637–0975 or 866/637–0975* ⊟ *413/637–2190* ⊕ *www.whistlersinnlenox.com* ↩ *14 rooms* ⚐ *Badminton, croquet, library* ☐ *AE, D, MC, V* ⚐ *BP.*

$–$$$ ⬚ **Garden Gables.** This 1780s summer cottage on 5 acres of wooded grounds has been an inn since 1947. The three common parlors have fireplaces, and one long, narrow room has a rare five-legged Steinway piano. Rooms come in various shapes, sizes, and colors and have American country-style antiques; some have brass beds, and others have pencil four-posters. Some rooms have sloping ceilings, fireplaces, whirlpool baths, or woodland views. Three have private decks. Breakfast is served buffet-style in the airy dining room. ⊠ *135 Main St.* ⚐ *Box 52, 01240* ☎ *413/637–0193* ⊟ *413/637–4554* ⊕ *www.lenoxinn.com* ↩ *19 rooms* ⚐ *Some in-room hot tubs, cable TV, in-room data ports, pool; no TV in some rooms, no kids under 12* ☐ *AE, D, MC, V* ⚐ *BP.*

★ **$–$$** ⬚ **Yankee Inn.** Custom-crafted Amish canopy beds, gas fireplaces, and high-end fabrics decorate the top rooms at this immaculately kept property, one of several modern hotels and motels along U.S. 7. The more economical units contain attractive, if nondescript, country-style furnishings and such useful amenities as coffeemakers and irons with ironing boards. ⊠ *461 Pittsfield-Lenox Rd., U.S. 7 and 20, 01240* ☎ *413/499–3700 or 800/835–2364* ⊟ *413/499–3634* ⊕ *www.yankeeinn.com* ↩ *96 rooms* ⚐ *Refrigerators, in-room data ports, indoor pool, gym, hot tub, meeting rooms* ☐ *AE, D, MC, V* ⚐ *CP.*

Nightlife & the Arts

FodorsChoice **Tanglewood** (⊠ West St. off Rte. 183 ☎ 413/637–5165, 617/266–1492,
★ 617/266–1200 tickets from Symphony Charge ⊕ www.bso.org), the 200-acre summer home of the Boston Symphony Orchestra, attracts thousands every year to concerts by world-famous performers from mid-June to Labor Day. The 5,000-seat main shed hosts larger concerts; the Seiji Ozawa Hall (named for the former BSO conductor—James Levine took the helm in 2003) seats around 1,200 and is used for recitals, chamber music, and more intimate performances by summer program students and soloists. One of the most rewarding ways to experience Tanglewood is to purchase lawn tickets, arrive early with blankets or lawn chairs, and have a picnic. Except for the occasional celebrity concert, lawn tickets remain below $20, and concerts can be clearly heard from just about any spot on the lawn. Inside the shed, tickets vary in price, with most of the good seats costing between $38 and $100.

Shakespeare & Company (✉ 70 Kemble St. ☎ 413/637–1199, 413/637–3353 tickets) performs the works of Shakespeare and Edith Wharton from late May through October at the 466-seat Founders' Theatre and the 99-seat Spring Lawn Theatre. Also under way is the authentic reconstruction of an Elizabethan theater, the Rose Playhouse, the original of which stood on the south bank of London's Thames River in the sixteenth century.

Sports & the Outdoors

HIKING Part of the Massachusetts Audubon Society's system, the **Pleasant Valley Wildlife Sanctuary** (✉ 472 W. Mountain Rd. ☎ 413/637–0320 ⊕ www.massaudubon.org) abounds with beaver ponds, meadows, hardwood forests, and woodlands. Its 1,400 acres and 7 mi of trails offer excellent bird- and beaver-watching. The nature center is open daily July to Columbus Day.

HORSEBACK RIDING Travel along the beautiful shaded trails of Kennedy Park and Lenox Mountain and enjoy breathtaking views of Berkshire County when you book an hour, half-day, or overnight ride at **Berkshire Horseback Adventures** (✉ 293 Main St. ☎ 413/637–9090).

Shopping

One of the foremost crafts centers in New England, **Hoadley Gallery** (✉ 21 Church St. ☎ 413/637–2814) shows American arts and crafts with a strong focus on pottery, jewelry, and textiles. No one prepares picnics quite as elegant as **Perfect Picnics** (✉ 34A Main St. ☎ 413/637–3015), a small shop that has been packing picnics for those coming to Tanglewood since 1989. Depending on your budget, you can choose from either the Perfect or the Ultimate Perfect Picnic. **R. W. Wise** (✉ 81 Church St. ☎ 413/637–1589 ⊕ www.rwwise.com) produces high-quality creative jewelry and also sells estate and antique pieces.

Lee

❼ *5 mi south of Lenox.*

Founded after the Revolutionary War, Lee began as a farming community. Though the land was fertile, it was burdened with too many large stones, which turned out to be marble. Lee marble was one of the hardest marbles, making it perfect for public buildings, and soon quarries sprang up. Lee quarries produced the marble used for the 19th-century cottages of the Vanderbilts and Westinghouses. Today the bustling downtown contains a mix of touristy and workaday shops, and an outlet shopping center sits just off the Mass Pike highway exit.

You can see October Mountain, part of **October Mountain State Forest** from almost any point in Lee. To find the entrance drive down Main Street to Center Street, turn right and travel 2 mi to the electric plant and look for the entrance on your right. October Mountain is the largest state forest in Massachusetts, with 16,500 acres and 46 campsites, each with its own table and fireplace. ✉ *Woodland Rd.* ☎ *413/243–1778.*

Where to Stay & Eat

$–$$ ✕ **Bombay Bar & Grill.** As you enter this restaurant, you'll most likely encounter Indian music softly playing in the background. This is an authentic Indian restaurant, where such signature dishes as chicken *malai* kebab, chicken *tikka masala*, and lamb *kashmiri* fill out the menu. Set inside the Black Swan Inn, the restaurant overlooks Laurel Lake. ☒ *445 Laurel St.* ☎ *413/243–6731* ▭ *AE, D, MC, V* ☾ *Closed Mon.*

★ **$$–$$$$** ▥ **Applegate Inn.** This 1925 Georgian-revival mansion sits at the end of a regal circular drive, overlooking 6 acres of lush lawns and apple trees. The Greenock Golf Course is across the road. The inn has been exquisitely decorated: one room has a spacious steam shower and a fireplace, and another contains a French reproduction sleigh bed with fireplace and stunning views over the grounds to the mountains beyond. A carriage house contains two plush suites with stereos and wet bars; chocolates and crystal decanters filled with brandy and liqueurs add a touch of class. Owners Len and Gloria Friedman have attended to every detail in the house for a touch of elegance in the country. ☒ *279 W. Park St., 01238* ☎ *413/243–4451* ⊕ *www.applegateinn.com* ⇲ *6 rooms, 5 suites* ♿ *Some in-room hot tubs, some in-room VCRs, some in-room data ports, pool; no kids under 12* ▭ *MC, V* ⦿⦿ *BP.*

$$–$$$ ▥ **Devonfield Inn.** This grand, pale-yellow-and-cream Federal house sits atop a birch-shaded hillside dotted with a few quaint outbuildings and 29 acres of rolling meadows. The nine guest rooms have Colonial-style furnishings—many have Oriental rugs, lace-canopy four-poster beds, and working fireplaces. An immense penthouse suite is a favorite for special occasions, and a separate, contemporary cottage has its own kitchen with a pitched cathedral ceiling and private deck. A gracious pool and lanai sit behind the house. Expect such toothsome fare as vanilla-cinnamon French toast or baked pear pancakes at breakfast and details such as chocolates and spring water in each room; there is a video library and a butler's pantry with cookies, popcorn, and beverages. ☒ *85 Stockbridge Rd., 01238* ☎ *413/243–3298 or 800/664–0880* 🖷 *413/243–1360* ⊕ *www.devonfield.com* ⇲ *6 rooms, 3 suites, 1 cottage* ♿ *Some in-room hot tubs, in-room VCRs, tennis court, pool, bicycles, cross-country skiing; no kids under 12* ▭ *AE, MC, V* ⦿⦿ *BP.*

FodorsChoice
★

$$–$$$ ▥ **Historic Merrell Inn.** Built in the 1780s as a private residence (and converted to a stagecoach stop), this inn has good-size rooms, several with working fireplaces. Meticulously maintained, it has an unfussy authentic style, with polished wide-board floors, painted walls, and antiques. The sitting room has an open fireplace and the only intact "birdcage" bar—a semicircular bar surrounded by wooden slats—in the country. The purpose of a birdcage bar was to prevent thirsty Colonials from reaching across and helping themselves. Breakfast is cooked to order and served in the keeping room, where travelers have dined since 1786. ☒ *1565 Pleasant St., Rte. 102, 01260* ☎ *413/243–1794 or 800/243–1794* 🖷 *413/243–2669* ⊕ *www.merrell-inn.com* ⇲ *9 rooms, 1 suite* ▭ *AE, MC, V* ⦿⦿ *BP.*

$–$$$ ▥ **Chambery Inn.** A former 19th-century French country school houses this exceptional place is in downtown Lee. The rooms are quite large, some enough for two queen beds, with 13-foot-high embossed ceilings and state-of-the-art baths. Amish-style furniture fits nicely with the architecture and is attractive and comfortable. There are no common rooms; you choose breakfast from a breakfast card, and it's delivered to your room each morning in a basket. ⊠ *199 Main St., 01238* ☎ *413/243–2221 or 800/537–4321* 🖷 *413/243–1828* ⊕ *www.chamberyinn.com* ➷ *3 rooms, 6 suites* ⚠ *No kids under 12* ⊟ *AE, D, MC, V* ⎮⊙⎮ *BP.*

Shopping

At **Highlawn Farm** (⊠ 535 Summer St. ☎ 413/243–0672) you can visit the cows, watch the milking, and buy fresh milk, cream, butter, and blue cheese.

Otis

❽ *15 mi southeast of Lee.*

A more rustic alternative to the polish of Stockbridge and Lenox, Otis, with a ski area and 20 lakes and ponds, supplies plenty of what made the Berkshires desirable in the first place—the great outdoors. The dining options here are slim; your best bet is to pack a picnic of goodies from a Lenox gourmet shop. Nearby Becket hosts the outstanding Jacob's Pillow Dance Festival in summer.

Deer Run Maples (⊠ 135 Ed Jones Rd. ☎ 413/269–7588) is one of several sugarhouses where you can spend the morning tasting freshly tapped maple syrup that's been drizzled onto a dish of snow. Sugaring season varies with the weather; it can be anytime between late February and early April.

Where to Stay

$–$$ 🛏 **New Boston Inn.** The antique billiard table fits well in this historic treasure. Surrounded by woods and ponds, it has served travelers as an inn since 1737. You can still get a drink in the pub or dine on duck with a peach and brandy reduction, scampi, and other fine fare in the restaurant. ⊠ *101 N. Main St., Sandisfield 01255* ☎ *413/258–4477* ⊕ *www.newbostoninn.com* ➷ *7 rooms* ⚠ *Restaurant, pets allowed* ⊟ *AE, MC, V* ⎮⊙⎮ *BP.*

Nightlife & the Arts

For nine weeks each summer, the tiny town of Becket, 8 mi north of Otis, becomes a mecca of the dance world during **Jacob's Pillow Dance Festival** (⊠ 358 George Carter Rd., at U.S. 20 ☎ 413/327–1234 ⊕ www.jacobspillow.org), which showcases world-renowned performers of ballet, modern, and ethnic dance. Before the main events, works-in-progress and even some of the final productions are staged outdoors, often free of charge. You can picnic on the grounds or eat at the restaurant.

Sports & the Outdoors

SKI AREA The least-expensive ski area in New England, **Otis Ridge** has long been a haven for beginners and families, but experts will find slopes here, too. The remote location is quite stunning, the buildings historic. There are six downhill trails serviced by a pair of lifts. ⊠ *Rte. 23, 01253* ☎ *413/269–4444* ⊕ *www.otisridge.com.*

Stockbridge

9 *20 mi northwest of Otis, 7 mi south of Lenox.*

Stockbridge is the quintessence of small-town New England charm, untainted by industry or large-scale development. It is also the blueprint for small-town America as represented picture perfectly on the covers of the *Saturday Evening Post* by painter Norman Rockwell. From 1953 until his death in 1978, Rockwell lived in Stockbridge and painted its buildings and its residents, inspired by their simple charm. James Taylor sang about the town in his hit "Sweet Baby James," as did balladeer Arlo Guthrie in his famous Thanksgiving anthem "Alice's Restaurant," in which he tells what ensued when he tossed some garbage out the back of his Volkswagen bus down a Stockbridge hillside.

Indeed, Stockbridge is the stuff of story and legend. Travelers have been checking into the Red Lion Inn on Main Street since the 18th century, and Stockbridge remains only slightly altered in appearance since that time. In 18th- and 19th-century buildings surrounding the inn, you'll find a handful of engaging shops and eateries. The rest of Stockbridge is best appreciated via a country drive or bike ride over its hilly, narrow lanes.

The 15-acre **Berkshire Botanical Gardens** contain greenhouses, ponds, nature trails, and perennial, rose, day lily, and herb gardens of both exotic and native plantings—some 2,500 varieties in all. ✉ *Rtes. 102 and 183, 2 mi east of downtown* ☎ *413/298–3926* ⊕ *www.berkshirebotanical.org* ✐ *$7* ⊘ *May–Oct., daily 10–5.*

Fodor'sChoice **Chesterwood** was for 33 years the summer home of the sculptor Daniel
★ Chester French (1850–1931), who created *The Minuteman* in Concord and the Lincoln Memorial in Washington, D.C. Tours are given of the house, which is maintained in the style of the 1920s, and of the studio, where you can view the casts and models French used to create the Lincoln Memorial. The beautifully landscaped 122-acre grounds also make for an enchanting stroll. ✉ *Williamsville Rd. off Rte. 183* ☎ *413/298–3579* ⊕ *www.chesterwood.org* ✐ *$10* ⊘ *May–Oct., daily 10–5.*

★ **Naumkeag,** a Berkshire cottage once owned by Joseph Choate, a successful New York lawyer and an ambassador to Great Britain during the administration of President William McKinley, provides a glimpse into the gracious living of the gilded era of the Berkshires. The 26-room gabled mansion, designed by Stanford White in 1886, sits atop Prospect Hill. It is decorated with many original furnishings and art that spans three centuries; the collection of Chinese porcelain is also noteworthy. The meticulously kept 8 acres of formal gardens designed by Fletcher Steele are themselves worth a visit. ✉ *5 Prospect Hill Rd.* ☎ *413/298–3239* ⊕ *www.thetrustees.org* ✐ *$10* ⊘ *Memorial Day–Columbus Day, daily 10–5.*

The **Norman Rockwell Museum** traces the career of one of America's most beloved illustrators, beginning with his first *Saturday Evening*

Post cover in 1916. In addition to housing its collection of 570 Rockwell illustrations, the museum also mounts exhibits by other artists. Rockwell's studio was moved to the museum grounds and is complete in every detail. Stroll the 36-acre site, picnic on the grounds, or relax at the outdoor café. ✉ *Rte. 183, 2 mi from Stockbridge* ☎ *413/298–4100* 🌐 *www.nrm.org* 🎫 *$12.50* ⏲ *Weekdays 10–5, weekends 10–4.*

Where to Stay & Eat

$$–$$$ Fodor'sChoice ★ ✕ **Rouge.** In West Stockbridge, 5 mi northwest of Stockbridge, this little house with its gray-green shingles, illuminated small red sign, and simple and comfortable interior, reminds you of a restaurant in the French countryside. Owner-chef William Merelle is indeed from Provence, where he met his American wife (and co-owner) Maggie. They ensure that the food, wine, and surroundings give pleasure. Try the sesame-crusted salmon served with a honey-soy-sake glaze. ✉ *3 Center St. West Stockbridge* ☎ *413/232–4111* 💳 *AE, D, MC, V* ⏲ *Closed Mon. and Tues. No lunch.*

$–$$$ ✕ **Once Upon a Table.** The atmosphere is casual yet vaguely romantic at this little restaurant-in-the-mews off Stockbridge's Main Street. The Continental and contemporary American cuisine includes seasonal dishes, with appetizers such as potpie of escargots, and entrées that include seared crab cakes with horseradish-cream sauce as well as rack of lamb with garlic-mashed potatoes. At lunch try the Caesar salad or the wicked Reuben sandwich. ✉ *36 Main St.* ☎ *413/298–3870* ✍ *Reservations essential* 💳 *AE, MC, V.*

★ **$–$$** ✕ **Truc Orient Express.** Happy Pancake, Shaking Beef, and beef on rice noodles are just a few of the well-prepared Vietnamese specialties at this restaurant in West Stockbridge. Plenty of wood, windows, and artwork create a lovely setting. Portions tend to be on the small side but are beautifully presented. ✉ *3 Harris St. West Stockbridge* ☎ *413/232–4204* 💳 *AE, D, MC, V* ⏲ *Closed Tues. No lunch.*

$–$$$$ Fodor'sChoice ★ ✕🏨 **Red Lion Inn.** An inn since 1773, the Red Lion has hosted presidents, senators, and celebrities. It consists of a large main building and seven annexes, each of which is different (one is a converted fire station). If you like historic buildings filled with antiques, request a room in the main building: many of these units are small, and the furnishings are a tad worn in places, but this is the authentic inn. If you want more space and more modern furnishings, request a room in one of the annex buildings. In the restaurant, chef Brian Alberg, a James Beard Society member, emphasizes seasonal ingredients and locally grown produce. His menu includes roasted root vegetable hash with apple cider served with grilled pork tenderloin and a quiche made of spinach, caramelized onion, and goat-cheese. The main dining room ($$–$$$$) is somewhat formal; Widow Bingham's Tavern is cozier; for pub fare and live music, head to the Lion's Den. ✉ *30 Main St., 02162* ☎ *413/298–5545 or 413/298–1690* 📠 *413/298–5130* 🌐 *www.redlioninn.com* 🛏 *84 rooms, 71 with bath; 24 suites* 👍 *3 restaurants, cable TV, some in-room VCRs, pool, gym, massage, bar, meeting rooms* 💳 *AE, D, DC, MC, V* 🍽 *CP.*

$$–$$$ ⊞ **Inn at Stockbridge.** Antiques and feather comforters are among the
Fodor'sChoice   accents in the rooms of this 1906 Georgian-revival inn run by the at-
★   tentive Alice and Len Schiller. The two serve breakfast in their elegant
dining room, and every evening they provide wine and cheese. Each of
the rooms in the adjacent "cottage" building has a decorative theme such
as Kashmir, St. Andrews, or Provence; the junior suites in the new "carriage" building have Berkshire themes. The airy and posh rooms have
CD players, irons and ironing boards, hair dryers, and in some cases
gas fireplaces. ⊠ *U.S. 7* ⬧ *Box 618, 02162* ☎ *413/298–3337 or 888/
466–7865* 🖷 *413/298–3406* ⊕ *www.stockbridgeinn.com* ⬎ *8 rooms,
8 suites* ⚊ *Some in-room hot tubs, some in-room VCRs, pool; no TV
in some rooms* ⊟ *AE, D, MC, V* ⍻ *BP.*

Nightlife & the Arts

Since 1929, the **Berkshire Theatre Festival** (⊠ 6 Main St. ☎ 413/298–
5536, 413/298–5576 box office ⊕ www.berkshiretheatre.org) has presented plays nightly in summer. The four plays presented each summer
on the Main Stage tend to be better-known vehicles with established
actors. The Unicorn, a smaller theater, mounts experimental plays and
new works.

Shopping

The dynamic **Holsten Galleries** (⊠ 3 Elm St. ☎ 413/298–3044) shows
the wares of top contemporary glass sculptors, including Dale Chihuly
and Lino Tagliapietra. **Origins Gallery** (⊠ 36 Main St. ☎ 413/298–
0002) is filled with colorful carved animals, baskets, stone sculpture from
Zimbabwe, and other works from Africa.

Great Barrington

⑩   *7 mi southwest of Stockbridge; 13 mi north of Canaan, Connecticut.*

The largest town in South County became, in 1781, the first place in
the United States to free a slave under due process of law and was also
the birthplace, in 1868, of W. E. B. DuBois, the civil rights leader, author, and educator. The many ex–New Yorkers who live in Great Barrington expect great food and service, and the restaurants here deliver
complex, toothsome fare. The town is also a favorite of antiques hunters,
as are the nearby villages of South Egremont and Sheffield.

Bartholomew's Cobble is a natural rock garden beside the Housatonic River
(the Native American name means "river beyond the mountains"). The
277-acre site is filled with trees, ferns, wildflowers, and 5 mi of hiking
trails. The visitor center has a museum. ⊠ *Weatogue Rd., Rte. 7A*
☎ *413/229–8600* ⬧ *$5* ☉ *Daily dawn–dusk.*

Where to Stay & Eat

$$–$$$$ ✕ **Pearl's.** Run by the same owners as Lenox's trendy Bistro Zinc, Pearl's
adds a dash of big-city atmosphere to the Berkshires with its pressed-
tin ceilings, tall booths, exposed-brick walls, and well-coiffed crowd.
The menu updates the old bigger-is-better steak-house tradition by serv-
ing thick-and-tender chops, prime rib, wild game, raw oysters, and
fresh lobsters with innovative ingredients. Call ahead for a table on week-

ends, or simply hobnob and sip well-chosen wines and creative drinks at the elegant bar. ⊠ *47 Railroad St.* ☎ *413/528–7767* ☰ *AE, MC, V* ⊗ *No lunch.*

★ **$$–$$$** ✗ **Verdura.** This restaurant is a standout, even in Great Barrington's field of fancy culinary hot spots. The understated and classy interior, youthful and friendly staff, and superbly executed Tuscan cooking make for a satisfying experience. In a handsome storefront space with sponge-dappled ocher-and-pale-green walls, you can try saffron-lobster risotto with mascarpone or wood-grilled prosciutto-wrapped brook trout with lentils, roasted fennel, and sage-brown butter. The wild-mushroom pizza with leeks, chèvre, and white-truffle oil is another favorite. ⊠ *44 Railroad St.* ☎ *413/528–8969* ☰ *MC, V.*

$–$$$ ✗ **Helsinki Tea Company.** The emphasis is on Finnish, Russian, and Jewish cuisines, prepared with lots of spices and served in big portions, at this restaurant that suggests a lost world of old European elegance. A hodgepodge of colorful cushions, fringed draperies, and objets d'art creates the feeling of an intimate café. It doesn't get much cozier than sitting by a roaring fire, tucking into an order of Midnight Train to Moscow (chicken-apple bratwurst, hot cabbage slaw, and potato latkes), and then lingering over one of the numerous tea choices (or something stronger—the restaurant has a full liquor license). ⊠ *284 Main St.* ☎ *413/528–3394* ☰ *D, MC, V.*

$$ ✗ **Bizen.** Diners seeking authentic Japanese fare need look no farther than this sushi bar–cum–restaurant. A corridor edged with river rocks and carpeted with bamboo leads to individual dining areas, which typically bustle with patrons. In Japanese fashion, you remove your shoes and sit on cushions at low tables; you can also order from the sushi bar or sake lounge. Sushi, sashimi, hand rolls, soups, and a variety of grilled and cooked dishes fill out the menu. Prix-fixe meals are also offered; prices vary depending on the number of appetizers, entrées, and sakes. ⊠ *17 Railroad St.* ☎ *413/528–4343* ⌖ *Reservations essential* ☰ *AE, D, MC, V.*

$–$$$ ✗▣ **Egremont Inn.** The public rooms in this 1780 stagecoach inn are enormous, and each has a fireplace. Bedrooms are on the small side but have four-poster beds (some have claw-foot baths) and, like the rest of the inn, unpretentious furnishings. On weekends in July and August you can book only two-night packages, which include breakfast daily and one dinner during your stay. Windows sweep around two sides of the stylish restaurant ($$–$$$), where flames flicker in a huge fireplace. The menu changes frequently but might include pan-seared Chilean sea bass with shiitakes and leeks or filet mignon with mashed potato and a caramelized-onion sauce. There's live jazz twice weekly. ⊠ *10 Old Sheffield Rd., South Egremont 01258* ☎ *413/528–2111 or 800/859–1780* 🖷 *413/528–3284* ⊕ *www.egremontinn.com* ⇆ *22 rooms, 1 suite* ⌖ *Restaurant, tennis court, pool, bar, meeting rooms; no room phones, no room TVs* ☰ *AE, D, MC, V* ⌁ *CP, MAP.*

$–$$$ ▣ **Wainright Inn.** Built in 1766 as the Troy Tavern & Inn, this hostelry had one brief period as a private home, when it was inhabited by Franklin L. Pope. The portraits of the electrical innovator and his wife are displayed on the mantel in the front room. You enter the inn via the large wraparound porch into an antiques-filled parlor and dining room. The tables and sideboards are filled with fresh flowers and objets d'art. The rooms, many of which have fireplaces and four-poster beds, are appointed with a mix of modern and period furnishings. ⊠ *518 S. Main St., 01230* ☎ *413/528–2062* ⊕ *www.wainwrightinn.com* ⇨ *8 rooms* ⌂ *Wi-Fi; no room phones* ▤ *MC, V* ⦿*l BP.*

$–$$$ ⊡ **Weathervane Inn.** Set on 10 landscaped acres, this inn started out in 1785 as a farmhouse and received a Greek-revival addition in 1835. Guest rooms are period-appointed and there are comfortable sitting rooms. Home-baked cookies and cakes are served daily at afternoon tea. Spa services including yoga and massage are available, and golf courses and tennis courts are nearby. Three-night stays are required on weekends in late spring and summer; one-night stays are permitted midweek. ⊠ *Rte. 23* ⑤ *Box 388, South Egremont 01258* ☎ *413/528–9580 or 800/528–9580* 🖷 *413/528–1713* ⊕ *www.weathervaneinn. com* ⇨ *8 rooms, 2 suites* ⌂ *Pool, bar, meeting rooms; no TV in some rooms* ▤ *AE, MC, V* ⦿*l BP.*

Nightlife & the Arts

Club Helsinki (⊠ 284 Main St. ☎ 413/528–3394) draws some of the region's top jazz, blues, soul, and folk acts in the region; it's open mike on Sunday.

Sports & the Outdoors

HIKING On Route 23, about 4 mi east of where U.S. 7 and Route 23 intersect, is a sign for the **Appalachian Trail** and a parking lot. Enter the trail for a moderately strenuous 45-minute hike. A little way in, you will cross a stream. At the top of the trail is Ice Gulch, a gorge so deep and cold that there is often ice in it even in summer. Follow the Ice Gulch ridge to the shelter and a large flat rock from which you can see a wide panorama of valley.

SKI AREAS With a 1,000-foot vertical drop, 100% snowmaking capacity, and slow and even grades, **Catamount Ski Area** is ideal for family skiing. Nevertheless, the most varied terrain in the Berkshires is here, meaning that skiers of all abilities and tastes can find something to keep them happy.

Downhill. There are 28 trails, served by seven lifts, plus a snowboard area called Megaplex Terrain Park, which is separated from the downhill area and has its own lift and a 400-foot half pipe. The Sidewinder, an intermediate cruising trail, is more than 1 mi from top to bottom. There's also lighted nighttime boarding and skiing. ⊠ *Rte. 23, South Egremont 01258* ☎ *413/528–1262, 800/342–1840 snow conditions* ⊕ *www.catamountski.com.*

Ski Butternut has good base facilities, pleasant skiing, 100% snowmaking capabilities, and the longest quad lift in the Berkshires. Two top-to-bottom terrain parks are for snowboarders. Ski and snowboard lessons are available. Kids six and under ski free midweek on nonholidays if accompanied by a paying adult. In summer Butternut usually hosts a crafts show and children's activities. Call for details.

Cross-country. Butternut Basin has 8 km (6 mi) of groomed cross-country trails.

Downhill. Only a steep chute or two interrupt the mellow terrain on 22 trails, most of them intermediate. Eight lifts keep skier traffic spread out.

⊠ *Rte. 23* ☎ *413/528–2000 Ext. 112, 413/528–4433 ski school, 800/ 438–7669 snow conditions* ⊕ *www.skibutternut.com.*

Shopping

The Great Barrington area, including the small towns of Sheffield and South Egremont, has the greatest concentration of antiques stores in the Berkshires. Some shops are open sporadically, and many are closed on Tuesday. At the **Great Barrington Antiques Center** (⊠ 964 S. Main St., U.S. 7 ☎ 413/644–8848) 50 dealers crowd onto one floor, selling Oriental rugs, furniture, and smaller decorative pieces.

The country folk art merchandise at **Birdhouse Gallery** (⊠ 280 Main St., U.S. 7 ☎ 413/528–0984) is always fun and unusual. At the **Country Dining Room** (⊠ 178 Main St., U.S. 7 ☎ 413/528–5050) you can find elegant antique furniture, glass, and china. **Elise Abrams Antiques** (⊠ 11 Stockbridge Rd., U.S. 7 ☎ 413/528–3201) sells fine antique china, glassware, and furniture. **Emporium** (⊠ 319 Main St., U.S. 7 ☎ 413/528– 1660) specializes in art glass, sterling, and fine decorative arts.

Satisfy your sophisticated palate at **Bizalion** (⊠ 684 Main St. ☎ 413/ 644–9988), a French specialty food shop and café, where you can find imported cheeses, 10 different olive oils, cured meats, and brick-oven-baked baguettes and pastries. The **Chef Shop** (⊠ 31 Railroad St. ☎ 413/ 528–0135) is the place for cookware, bakeware, and much more. A mecca for the health-conscious, the **Co-op Market** (⊠ 42 Bridge St. ☎ 413/528– 9697) carries organic fruits and vegetables, multigrain breads, and homeopathic supplements.

The Berkshires A to Z

To research prices, get advice from other travelers, and book travel arrangements, visit www.fodors.com.

BUS TRAVEL

Bonanza Bus Lines connects Sheffield, Great Barrington, Stockbridge, Lenox, Lee, Pittsfield, Brodie Mountain, and Williamstown with Albany, New York City, and Providence. Peter Pan Bus Lines serves Lee, Lenox, and Pittsfield from Boston, Hartford, and Albany. Berkshire Regional Transit Authority provides transportation throughout the Berkshires.

🚌 Bus Information **Berkshire Regional Transit Authority** ☎ 800/292-2782. **Bonanza Bus Lines** ☎ 800/556-3815 ⊕ www.bonanzabus.com. **Peter Pan Bus Lines** ☎ 413/ 781-2900 or 800/237-8747 ⊕ www.peterpanbus.com.

CAR TRAVEL

The Massachusetts Turnpike (Interstate 90) connects Boston with Lee and Stockbridge and continues into New York, where it becomes the

New York State Thruway. To reach the Berkshires from New York City take either Interstate 87 or the Taconic State Parkway. The main north–south road within the Berkshires is U.S. 7. Route 2 runs from the northern Berkshires to Greenfield at the head of the Pioneer Valley and continues across Massachusetts into Boston. The scenic section of Route 2 known as the Mohawk Trail runs from Williamstown to Orange.

EMERGENCIES

🏥 Hospitals **Berkshire Medical Center** ⊠ 725 North St., Pittsfield ☎ 413/447–2000. **Fairview Hospital** ⊠ 29 Lewis Ave., Great Barrington ☎ 413/528–8600. **North Adams Regional Hospital** ⊠ 71 Hospital Ave., North Adams ☎ 413/663–3701.

SPORTS & THE OUTDOORS

BICYCLING The region's terrain is tremendously varied, and it tends to be hilly. However, the Berkshires are relatively uncongested and extremely popular for biking, affording cycling enthusiasts of all abilities miles of great riding. The Ashuwillticook (pronounced *Ash*-oo-will-ti-cook) Rail Trail runs from the Pittsfield–Cheshire town line north up through Adams. Partly paved, it traces the old rail line and passes through rugged woodland and Cheshire Lake. This is also a great venue for strolling, jogging, inline skating, and cross-country skiing. The Berkshires Visitors Bureau distributes a free Berkshire Bike Touring Route, which is a series of relatively short excursions along area roads.

BOATING With numerous lakes, rivers, and ponds throughout western Massachusetts, the region is rife with opportunities for sailing, canoeing, kayaking, rafting, and boating. Contact Mass Outdoors for more information. 🏖 **Mass Outdoors** ☎ 617/626–1600 ⊕ www.sport.state.ma.us.

HIKING A 90-mi swath of the Appalachian Trail cuts through the Berkshires. You'll also find hundreds of miles of trails elsewhere throughout the area's forests and parks.
🥾 **Appalachian National Scenic Trail** ⊠ NPS Park Office, Harpers Ferry Center, Harpers Ferry, WV 25425 ☎ 304/535–6331 or 304/535–6278 ⊕ www.nps.gov/appa.

TAXIS

Abbott's Limousine & Livery Service provides transportation to and from airports throughout the region, including New York, Boston, and Hartford. It requires 24-hour notice.
🚕 **Abbott's Limousine & Livery Service** ☎ 413/243–1645.

TRAIN TRAVEL

Amtrak runs the *Lake Shore Limited*, which stops at Pittsfield once daily in each direction on its route between Boston and Chicago.
🚆 Train Information **Amtrak** ☎ 800/872–7245 ⊕ www.amtrak.com.

VISITOR INFORMATION

ℹ️ Tourist Information **Berkshires Visitors Bureau** ⊠ 3 Hoosac St., Adams 01220 ☎ 413/743–4500 or 800/237–5747 ⊕ www.berkshires.org. **Mohawk Trail Association** 🏠 Box 1044, North Adams 01247 ☎ 413/743–8127 ⊕ www.mohawktrail.com. **Stockbridge Chamber of Commerce** ⊠ Elm St., Stockbridge ☎ 413/298–5200 or 866/626–5327 ⊕ www.stockbridgechamber.org. **South County Chamber of Commerce** ⊠ 362 Main

St., Great Barrington ☎ 413/528–1510 ⊕ www.southernberkshires.com. **Lee Chamber of Commerce** ✉ 3 Park St., Lee ☎ 413/243–0852.

MASSACHUSETTS A TO Z

To research prices, get advice from other travelers, and book travel arrangements, visit www.fodors.com.

AIRPORTS

Boston's Logan International Airport has scheduled flights by most major domestic and foreign carriers. Bradley International Airport in Windsor Locks, Connecticut, 18 mi south of Springfield on Interstate 91, has scheduled flights by major U.S. airlines.

🗗 Airport Information **Bradley International Airport** ☎ 860/292–2000 ⊕ www. bradleyairport.com. **Logan International** ☎ 617/561–1800, 800/235–6426 24-hr information ⊕ www.massport.com Ⓜ Airport.

BIKE TRAVEL

The Massachusetts Bicycle Coalition, an advocacy group that works to improve conditions for area cyclists, has information on organized rides and sells good bike maps of Boston and the state.

🗗 The **Massachusetts Bicycle Coalition** (MassBike) ✉ 44 Bromfield St., Boston 02178 ☎ 617/542–2453 ⊕ www.massbike.org.

BUS TRAVEL

Besides various regional bus companies, Massachusetts is served by national carriers Greyhound and Peter Pan.

🗗 Bus Information **Greyhound** ☎ 800/231–2222 ⊕ www.greyhound.com. **Peter Pan** ☎ 413/781–2900 or 800/237–8747 ⊕ www.peterpanbus.com.

CAR TRAVEL

Boston is the traffic hub of New England, with interstate highways approaching it from every direction. New England's chief coastal highway, Interstate 95, skirts Boston; Interstate 90 leads west through upstate New York. Interstate 91 brings visitors to the Pioneer Valley in western Massachusetts from Vermont and Canada to the north and Connecticut and New York to the south.

EMERGENCIES

🗗 Emergency Services **Ambulance, fire, police** ☎ 911.

SPORTS & THE OUTDOORS

FISHING For information about fishing and licenses, call the Massachusetts Division of Fisheries & Wildlife.

🗗 **Massachusetts Division of Fisheries & Wildlife** ☎ 617/626–1600 ⊕ www.mass. gov/dfwele/dfw/dfw_toc.htm.

TRAIN TRAVEL

The Northeast Corridor service of Amtrak links Boston with the principal cities between it and Washington, D.C. High-speed Acela service is available between the two cities. The *Lake Shore Limited,* which stops at Springfield and the Berkshires, carries passengers from Chicago to Boston.

🚆 Train Information **Amtrak** ☎ 800/872-7245 ⊕ www.amtrak.com.

VISITOR INFORMATION

🚆 Tourist Information **Massachusetts Office of Travel & Tourism** ✉ 10 Park Plaza, Suite 4510, Boston 02116 ☎ 617/973-8500, 800/447-6277 brochures ⊕ www. massvacation.com.

Rhode Island

WORD OF MOUTH

"We spent a day in Newport—not NEARLY enough time! Walked a good bit of the Cliffwalk, toured the Breakers, had dinner at the Black Pearl (steamed lobster—yum!)."

—neworleanslady

"We spent two days strolling around Newport, visiting mansions and other sites, one day over in Jamestown (Beavertail Lighthouse) and Wickford (charming colonial seaside village), and one day in Sakonnet (vineyard) and Little Compton. Perfect amount of time!"

—Tina6565

Updated by
Catherine
Bowen Brophy

Rhode Island, the smallest state in the nation—just 1,500 square mi (500 of that being water)—can be an enthralling destination. A Rhode Island getaway can encompass historic tours, visits to galleries, and fine dining in Providence; apple picking and canal boat rides in the Blackstone Valley; boating and beaching in South County or Block Island; biking in East Bay; and sunset sails and gilded-age mansions in Newport. Packed with American history, the state holds 20% of the country's National Historic Landmarks and has more restored Colonial and Victorian buildings than anywhere else in the United States.

In May 1776, before the Declaration of Independence was issued, Rhode Island and Providence Plantations—the state's official name to this day—passed an act removing the king's name from all state documents. This action was typical of the independent-thinking colony, which had been founded on principles of religious tolerance and attracted Baptists, Jews, Quakers, and others seeking refuge throughout the 17th and 18th centuries. The first public school was established in forward-thinking Newport in 1664. (Rhode Island continues to be a force in education, with 70,000 students at 10 colleges and universities.) In the 19th century the state flourished as its entrepreneurial leaders constructed some of the nation's earliest textile mills, silver foundries, and jewelry companies. Industry attracted workers from French Canada, Italy, Ireland, England, Portugal, and Eastern Europe, descendants of whom have retained much of their heritage in numerous ethnic enclaves all across the state.

Rhode Island does have some less-attractive elements: crowded state highways, especially around Providence, and, in certain areas, sprawling commercial development. But as tourism has become one of the state's biggest moneymakers, a more thoughtful approach to development seems to be the norm. Neighborhoods, remote villages, and even rough-hewn cities like Pawtucket and Woonsocket are now constructing bike paths, historic walkways, and visitor centers. The capital city of Providence is being aggressively reshaped by its leaders.

Rhode Island's 39 towns and cities—none more than 50 mi apart—all hold architectural gems and historic sights. Natural attractions, inspired culinary artistry, and fine accommodations complement the mix. With so much to see in such a compact space, it's easy to explore the Rhode Island that fits your interests.

Exploring Rhode Island

The Blackstone Valley region and the capital city of Providence compose the northern portion of Rhode Island. South County to the west and Newport County to the east make up the southern portion of the state. The museums and country roads of the Blackstone Valley make it a good family destination; Providence has history, intellectual and cultural vitality, and great food. Both southerly regions have beaches, boating, and historical sights, with Newport being more historically significant, more upscale, and more crowded.

GREAT ITINERARIES

By car it's less than an hour from any one place in Rhode Island to another. Though the distances are short, the state is densely populated, and getting around its cities and towns can be confusing; it's best to map out your route in advance. In five days, you can visit all four regions of the state, as well as Block Island. On a shorter visit of several days, you can still take in two regions, such as Providence and Newport. Most of the sights in Providence can be seen in one day. The Blackstone Valley will also occupy one day, but in fall foliage season, you will want to spend more time here. Newport has many facets and will require two busy days. South County, with its superb beaches, is generally a relaxing two-day destination.

IF YOU HAVE 3 DAYS

Spend a day and a half in the historic waterfront city of 🏨 **Newport**㊱ –㊹, and then make the 40-minute drive north to 🏨 **Providence**❶ –⓯. Though this city's attractions are less packaged than Newport's, they include sophisticated restaurants, historic districts, two large city parks, and an outdoor skating rink.

IF YOU HAVE 5 DAYS

Spend your first three days in 🏨 **Newport**㊱ –㊹ and 🏨 **Providence**❶ –⓯; then take two days to explore South County. With pristine beaches and no shortage of restaurants and inns, South County encourages a take-it-as-it-comes attitude that's just right for summer and fall touring. Shop and soak up the turn-of-the-20th-century elegance of 🏨 **Watch Hill**⑳, and then spend a day on the beach in

Charlestown㉒ or **South Kingstown**㉓ (try **Misquamicut**㉑ if you prefer beaches with a carnival atmosphere). 🏨 **Narragansett**㉔, which has great beaches and numerous B&Bs, is one option for a second South County night. A day trip to **Block Island**㉖ –㉞ allows enough time to see some of its treasures, but it's easy to linger longer.

5

Numbers in the text and in the margin correspond to numbers on the maps: Central Providence, the Blackstone Valley, South County and Newport County, Block Island, Downtown Newport, and Greater Newport.

About the Restaurants

Rhode Island has been winning national accolades for its restaurants, which serve cuisine from every part of the world. You can still find regional fare such as johnnycakes, a corn cake–like affair cooked on a griddle, and the native clam, the quahog (pronounced "*ko*-hog"), which is served stuffed, fried, and in chowder. "Shore dinners" consist of clam chowder, steamed soft-shell clams, clam cakes, sausage, corn-on-the-cob, lobster, watermelon, and Indian pudding (a steamed pudding made with cornmeal and molasses). The Federal Hill neighborhood in Providence holds superlative Italian restaurants, and several dozen other restaurants in the city rival many of Boston's finest eateries.

WHAT IT COSTS				
	$$$$	**$$$**	**$$**	**$**	**¢**
AT DINNER	over $28	$21–$28	$13–$20	$8–$12	under $8

Prices are per person, for a main course at dinner.

About the Hotels

The major chain hotels are represented in Rhode Island, but the state's many smaller bed-and-breakfasts and other inns provide a more down-home experience. Rates are very much seasonal; in Newport, for example, winter rates are often half those of summer. Many inns in coastal towns are closed in winter.

WHAT IT COSTS				
	$$$$	**$$$**	**$$**	**$**	**¢**
FOR 2 PEOPLE	over $220	$171–$220	$121–$170	$80–$120	under $80

Prices are for a standard double room during peak season and not including tax or gratuities. Some inns add a 15% service charge.

Timing

The best time to visit Rhode Island is between May and October. Newport hosts several high-profile music festivals in summer; Providence is at its prettiest; and Block Island and the beach towns of South County are in full swing (though not nearly as crowded as Newport). Because of the light traffic and the often gorgeous weather, October is a great time to come to Rhode Island. The colorful fall foliage of the Blackstone Valley is as bright and varied as any in New England.

PROVIDENCE

New England's second-largest city (with a population of 173,000, behind Boston) comes into the 21st century as a renaissance city. Once regarded, even by its own residents, as an awkward stepchild of greater Boston (50 mi to the north), Providence has metamorphosed from an

PLEASURES & PASTIMES

BEACHES

Rhode Island has 400 mi of shoreline with more than 100 salt- and fresh-water beaches. Almost all the ocean beaches around the resort communities of Narragansett, Watch Hill, Newport, and Block Island are open to the public. Deep sands blanket most Rhode Island beaches, and most waters are clear and clean—in some places, the water takes on the turquoise color of the Caribbean Sea. Newport's harbor glimmers from the beach at Fort Adams State Park; nearby Middletown has a long beach adjacent to a wildlife refuge; and Jamestown's Mackerel Cove Beach is sheltered from heavy surf, making it a good choice for families. With naturally occurring white sands and a rock reef to the north that's ideal for snorkeling, Mansion Beach on Block Island is one of the most splendid coastal stretches in New England.

BOATING

It should come as no surprise that a place nicknamed the Ocean State would attract boaters. Colonial Newport prospered from shipbuilding and trading, and even today boating is the city's second-largest industry after tourism. Point Judith Pond, close to deep Atlantic waters, harbors New England's second-largest commercial fishing fleet (behind that of New Bedford, Massachusetts) and nearly four dozen sportfishing charter boats. Block Island's Great Salt Pond is New England's busiest summertime harbor, hosting more than 1,700 boats on weekends. At the head of Narragansett Bay, Waterplace—Providence's riverfront park—is a destination for small boats, canoes, and kayaks. Many tidal rivers and salt ponds in South County are ideal for kayaking and canoeing.

SHOPPING

Newport is a shopper's—but not a bargain hunter's—city. You can find antiques, souvenirs, fine crafts, clothing, and marine supplies in abundance. Antiques are a specialty of South County; more than 30 stores are within an hour's drive of each other. Villages such as Wickford and Watch Hill have unique shops in postcard waterside settings. An upscale shopping mall in downtown Providence has 150 stores and several movie theaters, and the city's ethnic communities sell specialties such as Italian groceries and Hmong (Laotian) clothing. Providence's student population supports secondhand boutiques and funky shops on Wickenden and Thayer streets. The Blackstone Valley contains a handful of outlet stores; unlike suburban "factory outlets," these places, often modestly decorated, have great deals and are usually a short walk from the factory floor.

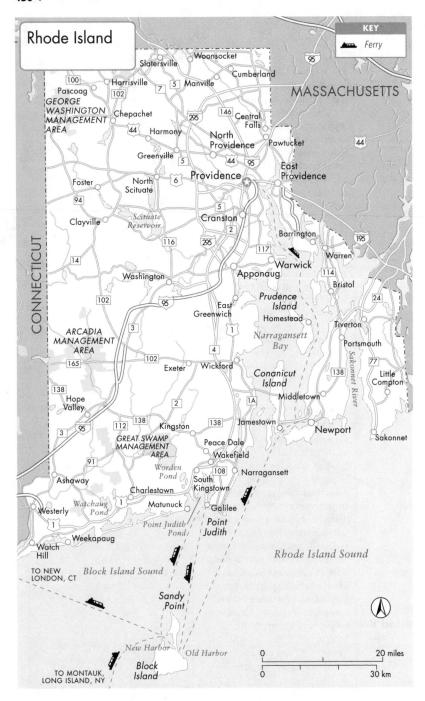

Rhode Island

MASSACHUSETTS

CONNECTICUT

Woonsocket

Slatersville

Cumberland

Pascoag
100
Harrisville
102
7
Manville
5

GEORGE WASHINGTON MANAGEMENT AREA

Chepachet
44
146
Central Falls

Harmony

North Providence

Pawtucket
44

Greenville
5

44
95

East Providence

Foster

North Scituate
6

Providence

94

Scituate Reservoir

5

Clayville

Cranston
2

Barrington

116
295

117
Warwick

Warren

14

Washington

Apponaug

Prudence Island

114
Bristol

102

East Greenwich

1

Homestead

Narragansett Bay

24

Tiverton

95

Portsmouth

ARCADIA MANAGEMENT AREA

3

4

Conanicut Island

77

165

102
Exeter

Wickford

138
Little Compton

138

Hope Valley

2

1A

Middletown

3
95

112
138
Kingston
138

Jamestown

Newport

Sakonnet

GREAT SWAMP MANAGEMENT AREA

Peace Dale

91

Worden Pond

Wakefield
108

Narragansett

Ashaway

Charlestown

South Kingstown

Westerly

Watchaug Pond
1

Matunuck

Galilee

Point Judith Pond

Point Judith

Rhode Island Sound

Watch Hill

Weekapaug

1

Block Island Sound

Sandy Point

New Harbor

Old Harbor

Block Island

0   20 miles

0   30 km

area that empties out at the end of a workday to a clean, modern, cultural and gastronomical hub. In the past decade, stretches of river downtown that had been paved over in the mid 20th century were uncovered and rerouted and parks were built along their banks. Railroad tracks were put underground, and money was spent on transportation improvements. Dilapidated neighborhoods began to be rejuvenated and luxury apartments and artists' lofts began to sprout downtown.

The focal point of this new Providence is Waterplace Park, a series of footbridges, walkways, and green spaces that run along both sides of the Providence River, which flows through the heart of downtown. Within walking distance of the park are a convention center and several hotels, an outdoor ice rink that's larger than New York's Rockefeller Center rink, and Providence Place, a glittering, upscale shopping center.

Providence's renaissance isn't all looks. Besides the glitzy new apartment buildings, the shopping center, and hotels and parks, the city has cultivated a more worldly, sophisticated spirit. As a result, it has, in recent years, hosted the National Governors Conference, the annual meeting of the International Association of Culinary Professionals, and the NCAA hockey finals. Time spent courting Hollywood deal makers has resulted in a string of movies filmed in the city, including *Federal Hill* and *Outside Providence,* as well as NBC's show *Providence.* With more restaurants per capita than any other major city in America, Providence—home to the Johnson and Wales University Culinary Institute—legitimately lays claim to being one of the nation's best places to eat.

Roger Williams founded Providence in 1636 as a refuge for freethinkers and religious dissenters escaping the dictates of the Puritans of Massachusetts Bay Colony. The city still embraces independent thinking in business, the arts, and academia. Brown University, the Rhode Island School of Design (RISD), and Tony award–winning Trinity Repertory Company are major forces in New England's intellectual and cultural life. Playing to that strength, Providence is striving to populate its once-abandoned downtown (now called Downcity, to erase the connotations of the old downtown) with artists and their studios.

The narrow Providence River cuts through the city north to south. West of the river lies the compact business district. An Italian neighborhood, Federal Hill, pushes west from here along Atwells Avenue. To the north you'll see the white-marble capitol. South Main and Benefit streets run parallel to the river, on the East Side. College Hill constitutes the western half of the East Side. At the top of College Hill, the area's primary thoroughfare, Thayer Street, runs north to south. Don't confuse East Providence, a city unto itself, with Providence's East Side.

A Good Walk & Tour

Begin at the **Rhode Island State House** ➤ ❶, where the south portico looks down over the city of Providence and the farthest reach of Narragansett Bay. After touring the capitol, proceed to Smith Street, at the north end of the State House grounds. Follow the road east to **Roger Williams Na-**

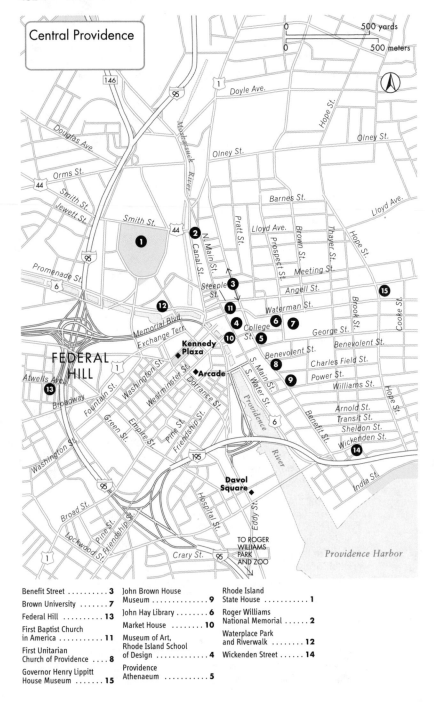

Central Providence

0   500 yards
0   500 meters

tional Memorial ➋. **Benefit Street** ➌ is one block east (up the hill). Walk south on this historic street to the **Museum of Art, Rhode Island School of Design** ➍ and the **Providence Athenaeum** ➎, with its changing exhibits from the library's collections.

Head east (away from the Providence River) on College Street and north (to the left) on Prospect Street to visit the **John Hay Library** ➏ and its specialized collections. The handsome **Brown University** ➐ campus is across the street. Walk east on Waterman Street; you can enter the grounds at Brown Street. After you've toured the campus, exit from the gate at George Street (to the south) and turn right, which will take you back to Benefit Street. Walk south for one block, where you'll see the Romanesque **First Unitarian Church of Providence** ➑. The magnificent **John Brown House Museum** ➒ is two blocks south of here. From the Brown house, walk one block downhill on Power Street and turn right on South Main Street. Proceed north until you reach the **Market House** ➓, a remnant of the Colonial economy, and, one block farther north, the Georgian **First Baptist Church in America** ⓫. Turn left at Steeple Street (also called Thomas Street), and you will shortly reach **Waterplace Park and Riverwalk** ⓬, centerpiece of the city's revitalization.

The Italian neighborhood of **Federal Hill** ⓭ and the fun shops of **Wickenden Street** ⓮ are best visited via car or taxi. The stately **Governor Henry Lippitt House Museum** ⓯ is at the eastern end of Providence; you'll need a car or taxi to visit.

TIMING If you stop for a half hour at most sights and an hour at the RISD Museum of Art, the walk from the State House to Waterplace Park will take about six hours. To see the rest of the sights, add several more hours.

What to See

➌ **Benefit Street.** The centerpiece of any visit to Providence is the "mile of
Fodor'sChoice History," where a cobblestone sidewalk passes a row of early-18th- and
★ 19th-century candy-color houses crammed shoulder-to-shoulder on a steep hill overlooking downtown. Romantic Benefit Street, with one of the nation's highest concentrations of historic architecture, is a reminder of the wealth brought to Colonial Rhode Island through the triangular trade of slaves, rum, and molasses. The **Providence Preservation Society** (✉ 21 Meeting St., at Benefit St., East Side ☎ 401/831–7440) distributes maps and pamphlets with self-guided tours. The **Rhode Island Historical Society** (☎ 401/438–0463 ⊕ www.rihs.org) conducts summer walks on Benefit Street. The 90-minute tours depart from the John Brown House Museum Tuesday–Sunday at 11 AM.

➐ **Brown University.** The nation's seventh-oldest college, founded in 1764, is an Ivy League institution with more than 40 academic departments, including a school of medicine. Gothic and beaux arts structures dominate the campus, which has been designated a National Historic Landmark. University tours leave weekdays at 10, 11, 1, 3, and 4 from the admissions office, in the Corliss-Brackett House. The university is on College Hill, a neighborhood with handsome 18th- and 19th-century architecture well worth a stroll. Thayer Street is the campus's principal commercial thoroughfare. The imposing gates are opened twice a year—in fall to welcome the students and in spring to bid adieu for the summer and goodbye to the graduating class. ⊠ *Corliss-Brackett House, 45 Prospect St., East Side* ☎ *401/863–2378, 401/863–2703 tour information.*

⑬ Federal Hill. You're as likely to hear Italian as English in this neighborhood, which is vital to Providence's culture and sense of self. The stripe down Atwells Avenue is repainted each year in red, white, and green, and a huge *pigna* (pinecone), an Italian symbol of abundance and quality, hangs on an arch soaring over the street. Hardware shops sell boccie sets and grocers sell pastas and Italian pastries. The neighborhood shines during the Federal Hill Stroll (usually held in the beginning of June) when festivalgoers enjoy music and sample signature cuisine at 20 eateries all within a ¾-mi stretch of Atwells Avenue.

⑪ First Baptist Church in America. This historic house of worship was built in 1775 for a congregation established in 1638 by Rhode Island founder Roger Williams and his fellow Puritan dissenters. The church, one of the finest examples of Georgian architecture in the United States, has a carved wood interior, a Waterford crystal chandelier, and graceful but austere Ionic columns. ⊠ *75 N. Main St., East Side* ☎ *401/751–2266* ☜ *Free, donations accepted* ⊙ *Guided tours June–Columbus Day, weekdays 10–noon and 1–4, Sun. at 11:15 after 10 AM service. Self-guided tours Columbus Day–Memorial Day, weekdays 10–noon and 1–3, Sun. at 12:15, after 11 AM service.*

❽ First Unitarian Church of Providence. This Romanesque house of worship made of Rhode Island granite was built in 1816. Its steeple houses a 2,500-pound bell, the largest ever cast in Paul Revere's foundry. ⊠ *1 Benevolent St., at Benefit St., East Side* ☎ *401/421–7970* ☜ *Free* ⊙ *Guided tours by appointment.*

⑮ Governor Henry Lippit House Museum. The two-term Rhode Island governor made his fortune selling textiles to both armies during the Civil War, and he spared no expense in building his home, an immaculate Renaissance Revival mansion, in 1863. The floor of the billiard room uses nine types of inlaid wood; the ceilings are intricately hand-painted (some look convincingly like tiger maple), and the neoclassical chandeliers are cast in bronze. The home was fitted with central heating and electricity, quite an extravagance at the time. ⊠ *199 Hope St., East Side* ☎ *401/ 453–0688* ☜ *$5* ⊙ *Daily. Tours by appointment only.*

★ ❾ John Brown House Museum. The four Brown brothers—John, Joseph, Moses, and Nicholas—were prominent Providence merchants who made a fortune trading with the West Indies, Europe, and, later, China. This three-story Georgian mansion, designed for John by his brother Joseph in 1786, has elaborate woodwork and is filled with furniture, decorative art, silver, and items from the China trade. John Brown was a patriot, famous for his role in the burning of the British customs ship *Gaspee* in 1772. He was also a slave trader: in fact, his abolitionist brother Moses brought charges against him for illegally engaging in the buying and selling of human lives. Despite his fame, it is not John who is remembered in Brown University, but his nephew, Nicholas Jr., whose gift to Rhode Island College in 1804 prompted it to change its name. Across the street and open Friday 1–4 is Nightingale House, built by a Brown business rival. ⊠ *52 Power St., East Side* ☎ *401/331–8575 or 401/273–7507* ⊕ *www.rihs.org* ☑ *$8* ☉ *Apr.–Dec., Tues.–Sat. 10–5; Jan.–Mar., Fri and Sat. 10–5.*

❻ John Hay Library. Built in 1910 and named for Abraham Lincoln's secretary, the "Hay" houses 11,000 items related to the 16th president. The noncirculating research library, part of **Brown University,** also stores American drama and poetry collections, 500,000 pieces of American sheet music, the Webster Knight Stamp Collection, the letters of horror and science-fiction writer H. P. Lovecraft, military prints, and a world-class collection of toy soldiers. ⊠ *20 Prospect St., East Side* ☎ *401/863–2146* ☑ *Free* ☉ *Weekdays 9–5.*

❿ Market House. Though this building is not open to the public, it is a historically significant site. Designed by Joseph Brown, this brick structure was central to Colonial Providence's trading economy. Tea was burned here in March 1775, and the upper floors were used as barracks for French soldiers during the Revolutionary War. From 1832 to 1878, Market House served as the seat of city government. A plaque shows the height reached by floodwaters during the Great Hurricane of 1938. ⊠ *Market Sq. and S. Main St., Downtown.*

🕲 **❹ Museum of Art, Rhode Island School of Design.** Deceiving from the exterior, this museum is a multilevel complex housing paintings, sculptures, prints, drawings, photographs, textiles, and decorative arts—80,000 works are in frequent rotation. The museum's permanent holdings include the Aldrich collection of Japanese prints, Gorham silver, American furniture, Latin American art, and French impressionist paintings including Monet, Manet, Degas, and Renoir. Also here are galleries filled with Greco-Roman, Egyptian, Asian, and Islamic art, as well as European and American art from the Middle Ages through the 20th century. Keep an eye out for purposeful juxtapositioning: a 19th-century bronze bust of an African woman is displayed in a gallery dominated by a formal family portrait of the Napoleonic era; a machine-age painting of flowers flanks a window to the museum's garden courtyard; an early Gauguin landscape hangs beside a Pissarro painted at the same site. Since this is a university museum, exhibits may include demonstration videos, or unfinished works by masters such as Cassatt and Cézanne. Popular with children are the 10-foot wooden statue of Buddha and the Egyptian mummy, which dates from 300 BC. Admission includes the adjoining **Pendleton House,** a replica of an early-19th-century Providence house. ⊠ *224 Benefit St., East Side* ☎ *401/454–6500* ⊕ *www.risdmuseum.org* ☑ *$8, free Sun. 10–1 and Fri. noon–1:30* ☉ *Tues.–Sun. 10–5.*

★ ❺ **Providence Athenaeum.** Established in 1753 and housed in a Greek-revival structure of 1838, this is among the oldest lending libraries in the world. The Athenaeum was the center of the intellectual life of old Providence. Here Edgar Allan Poe, visiting Providence to lecture at Brown, met and courted Sarah Helen Whitman, who was said to be the inspiration for his poem "Annabel Lee." The library holds Rhode Island art and artifacts, an original set of *Birds of America* prints by John J.

FodorsChoice ★

Audubon, and one of the world's best collections of travel literature. Changing exhibits showcase parts of the collection. ⊠ *251 Benefit St., East Side* ☎ *401/421–6970* ⊕ *www.providenceathenaeum.org* 🖃 *Free* ☉ *June–Labor Day, Mon.–Thurs. 9–7, Fri. 9–5, Sat. 9–1; Labor Day–May, Mon.–Thurs. 9–7, Fri. and Sat. 9–5, Sun. 1–5.*

❶ Rhode Island State House. Designed by the noted firm of McKim, Mead & White and erected in 1900, Rhode Island's capitol has an ornate white Georgia marble exterior and the fourth largest self-supporting dome in the world. The gilded statue that tops the dome, representing the Independent Man, is said to have been struck by lightning more than 25 times. Engraved on the south portico is a passage from the Royal Charter of 1663: "To hold forth a lively experiment that a most flourishing civil state may stand and best be maintained with full liberty in religious concernments." In the state room you'll see a full-length portrait of George Washington by Rhode Islander Gilbert Stuart. You'll also see the original parchment charter granted by King Charles to the colony of Rhode Island in 1663 and military accoutrements of Nathaniel Greene, Washington's second-in-command during the Revolutionary War. Although booklets are available for self-guided tours, guided tours are recommended. A gift shop is on the basement level. ⊠ *82 Smith St., Downtown* ☎ *401/ 222–2357* ☉ *Weekdays 8:30–4:30; tours weekdays 9–noon.*

❷ Roger Williams National Memorial. Roger Williams contributed so significantly to the development of the concepts that underpin the Declaration of Independence and the Constitution that the National Park Service dedicated a 4½-acre park to his memory. Displays provide a quick glimpse into the life and times of Rhode Island's founder, who wrote the first book on the languages of the North American native people. ⊠ *282 N. Main St., Downtown* ☎ *401/521–7266* 🖃 *Free* ☉ *Daily 9–4:30.*

OFF THE
BEATEN
PATH

🜚

ROGER WILLIAMS PARK AND ZOO – This beautiful 430-acre Victorian park is immensely popular. You can picnic, feed the ducks in the lakes, rent a paddleboat or miniature speedboat, or ride a pony. At Carousel Village, kids can ride the vintage carousel or a miniature train. The Museum of Natural History and Cormack Planetarium are also here; the Tennis Center has Rhode Island's only public clay courts. More than 900 animals of 156 different species live at the zoo. Among the attractions are the Tropical Rain Forest, the African Plains and Australasia exhibits, and polar bears. From downtown, take Interstate 95 south to U.S. 1 south (Elmwood Avenue); the park entrance is the first left turn. ⊠ *Elmwood Ave., South Providence* ☎ *401/785–9457 museum, 401/785–3510 zoo* 🖃 *Museum $2, planetarium $3 (includes museum), zoo $10* ☉ *Museum daily 10–5 (planetarium shows weekends 2), zoo daily 9–4.*

⓬ Waterplace Park and Riverwalk. Romantic Venetian-style footbridges, cobblestone walkways, and an amphitheater encircling a tidal pond set the tone at this 4-acre tract, which has won national and international design awards. The Riverwalk passes the junction of three rivers—the Woonasquatucket, Providence, and Moshassuck—a nexus of the shipping trade during the city's early years, but an area that had been covered over with highways and parking lots by the middle of the 20th century. The focus of an urban-renewal project that uncovered the buried rivers, rerouted them, and surrounded them with amenities for pedestrians rather than cars, Waterplace Park is now a gathering place for the city. It's also the site of the popular Waterfire, a multimedia installation featuring music and nearly 100 burning braziers that rise from the water and are tended from boats; the dusk-to-midnight Waterfire happens approximately a dozen and a half times a year and attracts 500,000 visitors annually. The Waterplace Amphitheater, renamed the Rosa Parks Amphitheater in December 2005, is the site of free concerts in summer. You can find out about the Waterfire schedule on the Web site or the hotline. ⊠ *1 Financial Way, Downtown* ☎ *401/272–3111* ⊕ *www.waterfire.org.*

🄯 **Wickenden Street.** The main artery in the Fox Point district, a working-class Portuguese neighborhood undergoing gentrification, Wickenden Street is chockablock with antiques stores, galleries, and trendy cafés. Professors, artists, and students are among the newer residents here. Many of the houses along Wickenden, Transit, Gano, and nearby streets are still painted the pastel colors of Portuguese homes.

Where to Eat

American/Casual

$–$$ ✕ **Union Station Brewery.** The historic brick building that houses this brewpub was once the freight house for the Providence Train Station. You can wash down tasty chicken enchiladas, an old-fashioned chicken potpie, classic meat loaf, or fish-and-chips with a pint of Providence cream ale or one of several other fine beers brewed here. If you can't decide on a beer, try a sampler tray. ⊠ *36 Exchange Terr., Downtown* ☎ *401/274–2739* ⊕ *www.johnharvards.com* ▤ AE, D, DC, MC, V.

Contemporary

$$$–$$$$ ✕ **Neath's.** The large open dining room of this converted warehouse and the views of the Providence River are wonderful, but it's the food that has made this a hot spot. The menu showcases a blend of French and Asian cuisine, such as crisp Cambodian spring rolls with bean sprouts and grilled shrimp, and yellowfin tuna steak with a soy and ginger glaze over a soba noodle gallette. Don't pass up the chocolate-stuffed fried wontons with homemade ginger ice cream for dessert. On Friday nights, the restaurant hosts live jazz in the lounge. ⊠ *262 S. Water St., Downtown* ☎ *401/751–3700* ⊕ *www.neaths.com* ▤ AE, D, MC, V ☉ *Closed Sun. and Mon. No lunch.*

$$–$$$$ ✕ **The Gatehouse.** Inside a redbrick building originally built to house the machinery and gatekeeper of the "swing" Red Bridge, which connected Providence with East Providence, this restaurant overlooks the serene Seekonk River. Soft candlelight and polished dark-wood furnishings make it feel elegant and romantic. Original works by the best area artists add to a sense of sophistication. On the menu are such appetizers as New England clam chowder and a caramelized Vidalia onion and chèvre tart, along with such entrées as South Shore cioppino and sage-roasted chicken. ⊠ *4 Richmond Sq., East Side* ☎ *401/521–9229* ⊕ *www. thegatehouse.com* ⊟ *AE, DC, MC, V* ☯ *Closed Mon. No lunch.*

$$–$$$$ ✕ **Mills Tavern.** Tile mosaics and paintings by the former head of the Rhode Island School of Design illustration department enhance this lively eatery. Specialties from the wood-burning stove include short ribs and a mustard-and-horseradish-crusted rack of lamb accompanied by goat-cheese mashed potatoes. ⊠ *101 N. Main St, Downtown* ☎ *401/272–3331* ⊟ *AE, D, DC, MC, V* ☯ *No lunch.*

$$–$$$$ ✕ **Rue de l'Espoir.** At this homey, longtime Providence favorite, dishes are designed to be fun. A few of the many eclectic choices include a lobster-and-mushroom Madeira crepe, and duck breast and sea scallops in a dried black fig and balsamic vinegar jus. Wide-plank pine floors, an ornate tin ceiling, and upholstered booths set the mood in the dining room. The spacious barroom, where many locals prefer to dine, has a large mural and a fine selection of jazz CDs. Weekday breakfast and weekend brunch are popular. ⊠ *99 Hope St., East Side* ☎ *401/751–8890* ⊕ *www.therue.com* ⊟ *AE, D, DC, MC, V* ☯ *Closed Mon.*

French

★ **$$–$$$** ✕ **Pot au Feu.** As night falls, business-driven downtown Providence clears out, and this bastion of French country cuisine lights up. Here the chefs work to perfect such dishes as pâté de foie gras, medallions of beef tenderloin, bouillabaisse Marseilles, and *pot de crème au chocolat*. The dining experience is more casual at the downstairs Bistro than at the upstairs Salon. ⊠ *44 Custom House St., Downtown* ☎ *401/273–8953* ⊕ *www.potaufeuri.com* ⊟ *AE, DC, MC, V* ☯ *Salon closed Sun. and Mon.; bistro closed Sun.*

Italian

$$$–$$$$ ✕ **Al Forno.** Al Forno means "from the oven" in Italian. And from the oven comes an exceedingly popular wood-grilled pizza. Try roasted clams and spicy sausage in a tomato broth or bistro steak. For dessert, choose from an array of fresh fruit tarts. Meals are served both upstairs, in the rustic dining room, and downstairs, in a room with white marble flooring. ⊠ *577 S. Main St., Fox Point* ☎ *401/273–9760* ⊕ *www. alforno.com* ⊜ *Reservations not accepted* ⊟ *AE, DC, MC, V* ☯ *Closed Sun. and Mon. No lunch.*

FodorsChoice ★

¢–$$ ✕ **Angelo's Civita Farnese.** In the heart of the "Hill," Angelo's is a lively (even boisterous) family-run place with old-world charm. Locals come here for its good-size portions of fresh, simply prepared pasta. ⊠ *141 Atwells Ave., Federal Hill* ☎ *401/621–8171* ⊕ *www.angelosonthehill. com* ⊟ *No credit cards.*

Japanese

$–$$ ✕ **Tokyo Restaurant.** Some say the Japanese cuisine served here is the best in the state. Choose regular or traditional Japanese seating—or take a stool at the sushi bar, where local fish such as tuna, mackerel, and eel are prepared alongside red snapper and fish from points beyond. The designer rolls include beef, squid, duck, and seaweed. ⊠ *388 Wickenden St., Fox Point* ☎ *401/331–5330* ⊟ *AE, D, MC, V* ⛾ *BYOB.*

Seafood

$$-$$$$ ✕ **Providence Oyster Bar.** In a neighborhood long known as the place for Italian food, this spirited seafood restaurant is a refreshing alternative. In a dining room handsomely turned out with polished wood floors, brick walls, and a tin ceiling, the raw bar serves more than a dozen varieties of fresh oysters. Favorite appetizers include ahi tuna tartare and coconut shrimp. For entrées, try grilled swordfish steak bouillabaisse or seared Georges Banks scallops. ✉ *283 Atwells Ave., Federal Hill* ☎ *401/272–8866* ⊕ *www.providenceoysterbar.com* ▭ *AE, DC, MC, V* ⊙ *Closed Sun. No lunch Sat.–Mon.*

Steak

$$-$$$$ ✕ **Capital Grille.** Dry-aged beef is the star, but lobster and fish also highlight the menu at this steak house. The mashed potatoes, cottage fries, and Caesar salads are served in portions that will sate even the heartiest appetite. Leather, brass, mahogany, oil portraits, mounted buffalo and moose heads, and Bloomberg News ticking away in the barroom lend this establishment the feel of an opulent men's club. ✉ *1 Union Station, Downtown* ☎ *401/521–5600* ⊕ *www.thecapitalgrille.com* ▭ *AE, D, DC, MC, V* ⊙ *No lunch weekends.*

Where to Stay

$$$$ ⌂ **Providence Biltmore.** Built in 1922, the Biltmore has a sleek art-deco exterior, an external glass elevator with delightful views of Providence, a grand ballroom, an Elizabeth Arden Red Door Spa, and an in-house Starbucks. The personal attentiveness of its staff, downtown location, and modern amenities make this hotel one of the city's best. Plus, with its skyscraping neon sign, this hotel couldn't be easier to find. ✉ *Kennedy Plaza, Dorrance and Washington Sts., Downtown, 02903* ☎ *401/421–0700 or 800/294–7709* 🖶 *401/455–3050* ⊕ *www.providencebiltmore. com* ⇆ *291 rooms, 139 suites* ⌂ *Restaurant, café, health club, meeting rooms, parking (fee)* ▭ *AE, D, DC, MC, V.*

★ **$$$$** ⌂ **Westin Providence.** The multi-turreted 25-story Westin towers over Providence's compact downtown, connected by skywalks to the city's gleaming convention center and the Providence Place mall. Its rooms have reproduction period furniture, and half have king-size beds; many have views of the city. The redbrick hotel's Agora restaurant has a superb wine cellar. ✉ *1 W. Exchange St., Downtown, 02903* ☎ *401/598–8000 or 800/937–8461* 🖶 *401/598–8200* ⊕ *www.westin.com* ⇆ *364 rooms, 22 suites* ⌂ *Restaurant, in-room broadband, pool, health club, hot tub, bar, meeting room, parking (fee)* ▭ *AE, D, DC, MC, V.*

$$$-$$$$ ⌂ **Courtyard by Marriott Providence.** One of the newest of Providence's hotels is housed in a seven-story redbrick building carefully designed to match the other buildings in its historic Union Station Plaza location. Nearly all of the large rooms, in tones of tans and greens with mauve accents, have views of either the State House, Waterplace Park, or the Financial District. The hotel is steps away from the Providence Place mall. ✉ *32 Exchange Terr., Downtown, 02903* ☎ *401/272–1191 or 800/321–2211* 🖶 *401/272–1416* ⊕ *www.marriott.com* ⇆ *210 rooms,*

6 *suites* ☼ *Restaurant, indoor pool, gym, hot tub, Internet room, meeting rooms* ☰ *AE, D, DC, MC, V.*

$$$–$$$$ 🏨 **Providence Marriott.** This modern, brick, six-story hotel near the capitol doesn't have the old-fashioned grandeur of the Providence Biltmore, but it has all the modern conveniences. Tones of mauve and green grace the good-size rooms. The Bluefin Grille restaurant specializes in creative American cuisine. ⊠ *1 Orms St., near Exit 23 off I–95, Downtown, 02904* ☎ *401/272–2400 or 800/937–7768* 🖷 *401/273–2686* ⊕ *www. marriottprovidence.com* ⇨ *346 rooms, 5 suites* ☼ *Restaurant, cable TV, in-room broadband, 2 pools (1 indoors), health club, sauna, bar, meeting rooms, free parking* ☰ *AE, D, DC, MC, V.*

$$–$$$ 🏨 **Old Court Bed & Breakfast.** This three-story Italianate inn on historic Benefit Street was built in 1863 as a rectory. Antique furniture, richly colored wallpaper, and memorabilia throughout the house reflect the best of 19th-century style. The comfortable, spacious rooms have high ceilings and chandeliers; most have nonworking marble fireplaces, and some have views of the State House and downtown. ⊠ *144 Benefit St., East Side, 02903* ☎ *401/751–2002* 🖷 *401/272–4830* ⊕ *www.oldcourt. com* ⇨ *10 rooms* ☰ *AE, D, MC, V* ⦿| *BP.*

★ $$ 🏨 **State House Inn.** The beautifully restored rooms of this inviting inn, in an 1880s Colonial-revival home near the State House, are furnished with Shaker- or Colonial-style pieces, and a few have working fireplaces. Some rooms are on the small side. ⊠ *43 Jewett St., Downtown, 02908* ☎ *401/351–6111* 🖷 *401/351–4261* ⊕ *www.providence-inn. com* ⇨ *10 rooms* ☼ *No smoking* ☰ *AE, D, MC, V* ⦿| *BP.*

$ 🏨 **C. C. Ledbetter's.** Innkeeper C. C. Ledbetter's mansard-roof 1770 home is in a great location on College Hill, the city's historic East Side. With its lively art, quilts, contemporary and antique furnishings, loads of books and magazines, plus a dog, you feel more like you're staying in someone's home instead of an inn. With reasonably priced rooms and a location across from the John Brown House Museum, this inn is a favorite of the parents of Brown University students. ⊠ *326 Benefit St., East Side, 02903* ☎🖷 *401/351–4699* ⇨ *5 rooms, 2 with bath* ☰ *D, MC, V* ⦿| *CP.*

Nightlife & the Arts

For events listings, consult the daily *Providence Journal* and the weekly *Providence Phoenix* (free in restaurants and bookstores). Brown University and the Rhode Island School of Design often present free lectures and performances.

Nightlife

BARS   The sub-street-level **Custom House Tavern** (⊠ 36 Weybosset St., Downtown ☎ 401/751–3630) is a convivial gathering place, with a copper-top bar stretching along most of one side of the narrow room. Fashionable with professionals, **Hot Club** (⊠ 575 S. Water St., Fox Point ☎ 401/861–9007) is where the waterside scenes in the movie *There's Something About Mary* were shot. **Snookers** (⊠ 145 Clifford St., Jewelry District ☎ 401/351–7665) is a stylish billiard hall in the Jewelry District that hosts live bands almost every night of the week. Through a double doorway at the rear of the billiard room is a '50s-style lounge where food is served.

MUSIC CLUBS **AS220** (✉ 115 Empire St., Downtown ☎ 401/831–9327 ⊕ www.as220.org) is a gallery and performance space where the musical styles run the gamut from techno-pop, hip-hop, and jazz to folk. Talent shows, poetry readings, and comedy nights are also scheduled. The **Call** (✉ 15 Elbow St., Jewelry District ☎ 401/751–2255) hosts touring modern rock bands. In the same building and under the same management as the Call is the **Century Lounge** (⊕ www.thecallnightclub.com), which hosts local progressive rock bands. Proclaiming itself "Rhode Island's number one reason to party," the **Complex** (✉ 180 Pine St., Jewelry District ☎ 401/751–4263) houses four different clubs, including house and hip-hop. The dance club can hold 1,400 people. The **Living Room** (✉ 23 Rathbone St., Downtown ☎ 401/521–5200) presents live entertainment nightly, often by prominent local blues musicians. **Lupo's at the Strand** (✉ 79 Washington St., Downtown ☎ 401/331–5876, 401/272–5876 concert line ⊕ www.lupos.com), housed in a historic, five-story theater downtown, hosts national alternative, rock, blues, and punk bands.

The Arts

FILM The **Cable Car Cinema & Café** (✉ 204 S. Main St., Downtown ☎ 401/272–3970 ⊕ www.cablecarcinema.com) showcases a fine slate of alternative and foreign flicks. You sit on couches and comfy chairs, and singers entertain prior to most evening shows. An espresso café substitutes for the traditional soda-and-popcorn concession.

GALLERY TOURS During **Gallery Night Providence** (☎ 401/751–2628 ⊕ www.gallerynight.info), held the third Thursday evening of every month, March–November, free art buses circulate along downtown, East Side, West Side, and Wickenden Street routes connecting some 25-plus participating art galleries and museums that hold open house and mount special exhibitions.

MUSIC Rock bands and country acts occasionally perform at the 14,500-seat **Dunkin' Donuts Center Providence** (✉ 1 LaSalle Sq., Downtown ☎ 401/331–6700 ⊕ www.dunkindonutscenter.com). The **Providence Performing Arts Center** (✉ 220 Weybosset St., Downtown ☎ 401/421–2787 ⊕ www.ppacri.org), a 3,200-seat theater and concert hall that opened in 1928, hosts touring Broadway shows, concerts, and other large-scale happenings. Its lavish interior is painted with frescoes and contains art-deco chandeliers. The **Rhode Island Philharmonic** (☎ 401/831–3123 ⊕ www.ri-philharmonic.org) presents concerts at Veterans Memorial Auditorium between October and May. The Philharmonic is also home to the Music School, a learning center for young musicians, which has its own children's orchestra. **Veterans Memorial Auditorium** (✉ 69 Brownell St., Downtown ☎ 401/272–4862) hosts concerts, plays, children's theater, and ballet.

THEATER **Brown University** (✉ Leeds Theatre, 77 Waterman St., East Side ☎ 401/863–2838 ⊕ www.brown.edu/tickets) mounts productions of contemporary, sometimes avant-garde, works as well as classics. The **Trinity Repertory Company** (✉ 201 Washington St., Downtown ☎ 401/351–4242 ⊕ www.trinityrep.com), one of New England's best theater companies, presents plays in the renovated Majestic movie house. The varied season generally includes classics, foreign plays, new works by groundbreaking young playwrights, and an annual version of *A Christmas Carol*.

Sports & the Outdoors

Basketball

The **Providence College Friars** play Big East basketball at the **Dunkin' Donuts Center Providence** (✉ 1 LaSalle Sq., Downtown ☎ 401/331–6700 events information ⊕ www.dunkindonutscenter.com).

Biking

The best biking in the Providence area is along the 14½-mi **East Bay Bicycle Path,** which hugs the Narragansett Bay shore from India Point Park through four towns before it ends in Independence Park in Bristol.

Boating

Prime boating areas include the Providence River, the Seekonk River, and Narragansett Bay. The **Narragansett Boat Club** (✉ River Rd., East Side ☎ 401/272–1838 ⊕ www.rownbc.org) has information about local boating.

Football

The **Brown Bears** (☎ 401/863–2773) football team (note that all of Brown University's athletic teams go by the same ursine name) play at **Brown Stadium** (✉ Elmgrove and Sessions Sts., East Side).

Hockey

The **Brown Bears** (☎ 401/863–2773) play high-energy hockey at **Meehan Auditorium** (✉ 235 Hope St., East Side). The **Providence Bruins** (☎ 401/331–6700), a farm team of the Boston Bruins, play at the **Dunkin' Donuts Center Providence** (✉ 1 LaSalle Sq., Downtown ☎ 401/331–6700 events information ⊕ www.dunkindonutscenter.com).

Ice-Skating

The popular **Fleet Skating Center** (✉ Kennedy Plaza, Downtown ☎ 401/331–5544 ⊕ www.fleetskating.com), an outdoor ice rink, is open mid-November–April, daily 10–8. Skates are available for rent.

Jogging

Three-mile-long **Blackstone Boulevard** draws joggers with its wide, level, and tree-lined trail.

Shopping

Antiques

Wickenden Street contains many antiques stores and several art galleries. **CAV** (✉ 14 Imperial Pl., Jewelry District ☎ 401/751–9164) is a large restaurant, bar, and coffeehouse (with music Friday and Saturday nights) in a revamped factory space. It sells fine rugs, tapestries, prints, portraits, and antiques. **Tilden-Thurber** (✉ 292 Westminster St., Downtown ☎ 401/272–3200 ⊕ www.stanleyweiss.com) carries high-end Colonial- and Victorian-era furniture, antiques, and estate jewelry. You can visit by appointment only.

Art Galleries

The **Bert Gallery** (✉ 540 S. Water St., Old Harbor/India Point ☎ 401/751–2628 ⊕ www.bertgallery.com) displays late-19th- and early-20th-century paintings by regional artists. **JRS Fine Art** (✉ 218 Wickenden St.,

Fox Point ☎ 401/331–4380) sells works by national, regional, and Rhode Island artists. The **Peaceable Kingdom** (⊠ 116 Ives St., East Side ☎401/351–3472) stocks folk art from around the world, including tribal weavings and rugs, ethnic clothing and jewelry, masks, musical instruments, and paintings.

Risdworks (⊠ 10 Westminster St. ☎ 401/277–4949 ⊕ www.risdworks. com) hosts changing exhibitions that showcase the work of Rhode Island School of Design alumni and faculty in a variety of media; works range from $1 greeting cards to $50 flatware patterns to $700 fine art.

Food

Constantino's Venda Ravioli (⊠ 275 Atwells Ave., Federal Hill ☎401/421–9105) sells imported and homemade Italian foods. **Roma Gourmet Foods** (⊠ 310 Atwells Ave., Federal Hill ☎ 401/331–8620) sells homemade pasta, bread, pizza, pastries, meats, cheeses, and custom food baskets. **Tony's Colonial** (⊠ 311 Atwells Ave., Federal Hill ☎ 401/621–8675), a superb Italian grocery and deli, stocks freshly prepared foods.

Malls

The **Arcade** (⊠ 65 Weybosset St., Downtown ☎401/598–1199), built in 1828, was America's first shopping mall. A National Historic Landmark, this graceful Greek-revival building has three tiers of shops and restaurants. Expect the unusual at **Copacetic Rudely Elegant Jewelry** (⊠ The Arcade, 65 Weybosset St., Downtown ☎401/273–0470), which sells the work of more than 100 artists. The **Game Keeper** (⊠ The Arcade, 65 Weybosset St., Downtown ☎401/351–0362) sells board games, puzzles, and gadgets. Downtown's upscale **Providence Place** (⊠ 1 Providence Pl., at Francis and Hayes Sts., Downtown ☎401/270–1000), with 150 shops, is anchored by Filene's, Lord & Taylor, and Nordstrom.

Maps

The **Map Center** (⊠ 671 N. Main St., East Side ☎ 401/421–2184) carries maps of all types and nautical charts.

Providence A to Z

To research prices, get advice from other travelers, and book travel arrangements, visit www.fodors.com.

BUS TRAVEL TO & FROM PROVIDENCE

Bonanza Bus Lines, Greyhound, and Peter Pan Bus Lines serve the Providence Bus Terminal. A shuttle service connects the terminal with Kennedy Plaza in downtown Providence, where you can board the local Rhode Island Public Transit Authority (RIPTA) buses, or the RIPTA Link trolley, whose two routes around downtown, the green and the gold lines, meet here. These two routes serve most points of interest. RIPTA fares range from $1.50 to $3. RIPTA buses also service T. F. Green Airport.

🖪 Bus Information **Bonanza Bus Lines** ☎ 800/556–3815. **Greyhound** ☎ 800/231–2222. **Peter Pan Bus Lines** ☎ 800/237–8747. **Providence Bus Terminal** ⊠ Bonanza Way off Exit 25 from I-95, Providence ☎ 401/751–8800 ⊠ Kennedy Plaza, Washington and Dorrance Sts., Providence. **Rhode Island Public Transit Authority** (RIPTA)

✉ Kennedy Plaza, Washington and Dorrance Sts., Downtown ☎ 401/781-9400, 800/244-0444 in Rhode Island ⊕ www.ripta.com.

CAR TRAVEL

Overnight parking is not allowed on Providence streets, and during the day it can be difficult to find curbside parking, especially downtown and on Federal and College hills. The Westin Providence downtown has a large parking garage; parking is also available at the Providence Place mall. To get from T. F. Green Airport to downtown Providence, take Interstate 95 north to Exit 22.

EMERGENCIES

🚑 Hospital **Rhode Island Hospital** ✉ 593 Eddy St., South Providence ☎ 401/444-4000.
🚑 24-Hour Pharmacy **Brooks Pharmacy** ✉ 1200 N. Main St. ☎ 401/272-3048.

TAXIS

Fares are $2 at the flag drop, then $2.50 per mile. The ride from the airport to downtown takes about 15 minutes and costs about $27. The Airport Taxi & Limousine Service shuttle costs $9 per person each way.
🚖 Taxi Companies **Airport Taxi & Limousine Service** ☎ 401/737-2868. **Checker Cab** ☎ 401/273-2222. **Economy Cab** ☎ 401/944-6700. **Yellow Cab** ☎ 401/941-1122.

TOURS

The Providence Preservation Society publishes the *PPS/AIAri Guide to Providence Architecture,* which describes a dozen walking tours of the city. From May through October, Conway Tours/Grayline Rhode Island runs a 90-minute Historic Providence bus tour that is a great way to learn the lay of the land; passengers are welcome to hop on and off the bus over the course of the day.
🚍 **Conway Tours/Grayline Rhode Island** ☎ 401/658-3400 ⊕ www.conwaytours. com. **Providence Preservation Society** ✉ 21 Meeting St., East Side ☎ 401/831-7440 ⊕ www.ppsri.org.

VISITOR INFORMATION

🛈 Tourist Information **Providence Warwick Convention and Visitors Bureau** ✉ 1 W. Exchange St., Downtown, 02903 ☎ 401/274-1636, 800/233-1636 in Rhode Island ⊕ www.pwcvb.com.

THE BLACKSTONE VALLEY

America's Industrial Revolution began in this region north of Providence in 1790, when the power of the Blackstone River, which runs south from Worcester, Massachusetts, was first harnessed at Pawtucket. The advent of water-powered factory mills along the 45-mi river catapulted a young agricultural United States into the Industrial Age. In the 1800s, Pawtucket and Woonsocket became large cities as a steady flow of French, Irish, and Eastern European immigrants came to work the mills, a system of canals, and later railroads came into being as distribution channels, and the local industry grew. Much of that industry is gone now, and the old mills are slowly but surely being renovated into condominiums, offices, and gallery space, but its heritage remains to be explored. The Blackstone River Valley National Heritage Corridor provides a backdrop to museums, historic villages, and country drives. Most of the Blackstone Valley experience is about taking in the history of the area, understanding its importance in the country's growths, and enjoying the slices of Americana it has to offer.

The Blackstone River and its valley are named after William Blackstone, who in 1628 became the first European to settle in Boston. In 1635, having grown weary of the ways of the Puritan settlers who had become his neighbors, this Anglican clergyman built a new home in what was wilderness and is now called Rhode Island.

Pawtucket

⑯ *5 mi north of Providence.*

In Algonquian, "petuket" (similar to standard Rhode Island pronunciation of the city's name today, accent on the second syllable) means "waterfalls." A small village was established at the falls in 1670 by Joseph Jenks Jr., who considered the area a prime spot for an iron forge. When Samuel Slater arrived 120 years later, he was delighted to find a corps of skilled mechanics ready to assist him in his dream of building a textile mill and bringing America's first factory system into being. Although many of Pawtucket's older buildings were torn down as part of urban renewal projects in the 1970s, significant portions of the city's history have been preserved and are worth a visit.

The **Blackstone Valley Visitor Center,** across the street from Slater Mill, has information kiosks, maps, hospitable tourism consultants, a café, and a gallery. Ask to see the 18-minute documentary on the region. ⊠ *175 Main St.* ☎ *401/724–2200 or 800/454–2882* ⊕ *www.tourblackstone. com* 🎫 *Free* ☉ *Daily 9–5.*

In 1793, Samuel Slater and two Providence merchants built the first factory in America to produce cotton yarn from water-powered machines. Today, the **Slater Mill Historic Site** consists of the old yellow clapboard mill, since restored and housing machinery illustrating the conversion of raw cotton to finished cloth, and the stone Wilkinson Mill, built in 1810, where a 9-ton reproduction of an 1826 waterwheel powers a 19th-century machine shop using a system of leather belts and pulleys to drive the machines. Interpreters demonstrate activities of daily family life in the 1758 Sylvanus Brown House and garden, and guides in period clothing conduct living history tours. ⊠ *67 Roosevelt Ave.* ☎ *401/ 725–8638* ⊕ *www.slatermill.org* 🎫 *$9* ☉ *Hrs vary.*

Slater Memorial Park stretches along Ten Mile River. Within the stately grounds are picnic tables, tennis courts, playgrounds, a river walk, and two historic sites. Eight generations of Daggetts lived in **Daggett House,** Pawtucket's oldest home, which was built in 1685. Among the antiques on display are Civil War memorabilia and bedspreads owned by Samuel Slater. The **Looff Carousel,** built by Charles I. D. Looff between 1880 and 1890, has 42 horses, three dogs, and a lion, camel, and giraffe that are the earliest examples of the Danish immigrant's work. The carousel animals don't go up and down, but they sure move fast. Bargains don't get much better than this: rides are 25¢. ⊠ *Newport Ave. (Rte. 1A)* ☎ *401/ 728–0500 Ext. 252 park information* 🎫 *Park free, Daggett House $2*

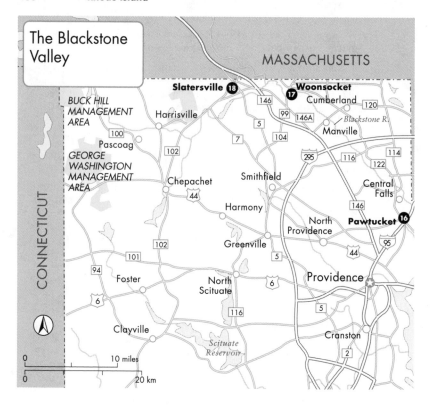

The Blackstone Valley

MASSACHUSETTS

Slatersville ⑱

Woonsocket ⑰

Cumberland 120

BUCK HILL MANAGEMENT AREA

Harrisville

146

99 146A

Blackstone R.

Manville

100

Pascoag

GEORGE WASHINGTON MANAGEMENT AREA

102

7

104

295

116

114

122

CONNECTICUT

Chepacet 44

Smithfield

Central Falls

Harmony

North Providence

146

Pawtucket ⑯

102

Greenville

5

44

95

101

94

Foster

North Scituate

6

Providence

116

5

Clayville

Scituate Reservoir

Cranston

2

0   10 miles

0   20 km

☉ Park daily dawn–dusk. Daggett House June–Sept., weekends 2–5. Carousel July–Labor Day, daily 10–4; late Apr.–June and Labor Day–Columbus Day, weekends 10–5.

Where to Eat

¢–$ ✕ **Modern Diner.** This 1941 Sterling Streamline eatery—a classic from the heyday of the stainless-steel diner—was the first diner to be listed on the National Register of Historic Places. The family-run Modern serves standard diner fare and some specialty items, including lobster Benedict and French toast with custard sauce and berries (usually served on weekends). ⊠ 364 East Ave. ☎ 401/726–8390 ▭ No credit cards ☉ No dinner.

Nightlife & the Arts

Known for its Shakespearian productions, the **Gamm Theatre** (⊠ 172 Exchange St. ☎ 401/723–4266 ⊕ www.gammtheatre.org) produces works of classic and contemporary theater in an intimate setting of 130 seats.

Woonsocket

⑰ 10 mi north of Pawtucket, 15 mi north of Providence.

A steep hill on the northern edge of Woonsocket looks down on the Blackstone River, which makes a dozen turns in its 5-mi course through town. Settled in the late 17th century, Woonsocket was inhabited by Quaker farmers for its first 100 years and was the site of a sawmill. Then the river's flow spawned textile mills that made the town a thriving community in the 19th and early 20th centuries; today a museum is dedicated to this industrial heritage. Woonsocket is Rhode Island's sixth-largest city (population 40,000), and manufacturing plants remain its leading employers.

☼ Set up in a former textile mill, the **Museum of Work and Culture** examines the lives of American factory workers and owners during the Industrial Revolution. Focusing on French Canadian immigrants to Woonsocket's mills, the museum's walk-through exhibits begin with a 19th-century Quebecois farmhouse, then continue with displays of life in a 20th-century tenement, in a parochial school, in church, and on the shop floor. The genesis of the textile workers' union is described, as are the events that led to the National Textile Strike of 1934. Youngsters may be interested in presentations about child labor. ⊠ *42 S. Main St.* ☏ *401/769–9675* ⊕ *www.rihs.org* ✉ *$6* ☉ *Weekdays 9:30–4, Sat. 10–5, Sun. 1–4.*

Where to Stay & Eat

¢–$ ✕ **Ye Olde English Fish & Chips.** Fresh fried fish and potatoes have been served at this Woonsocket institution for generations. The interior is unassuming—wood paneling and booths—so it must be the inexpensive and consistently excellent food that has kept folks coming back since 1922. ⊠ *Market Sq. and S. Main St.* ☏ *401/762–3637* ▭ *AE, D, MC, V* ☉ *Closed Sun. and Mon.*

$–$$ ▥ **Pillsbury House.** Stately Prospect Street stretches along the crest of the ridge north of the Blackstone River; its mansions, like the mansard-roof Pillsbury House, were built by mill owners in the late 1800s. The common room has a fireplace with a maple hearth. The three guest rooms on the second floor are furnished in Victorian style, with antiques, plants, high beds, and fringed lamp shades; the third-floor suite favors a more rustic-country aesthetic. Complimentary refreshments are available throughout the day. ⊠ *341 Prospect St., 02895* ☏ *800/205–4112* ☏▭ *401/766–7983* ⊕ *www.pillsburyhouse.com* ⤴ *3 rooms, 1 suite* ▭ *AE, D, DC, MC, V* ⦿ *BP.*

Nightlife & the Arts

The impressive entertainment lineup at **Chan's Fine Oriental Dining** (⊠ 267 Main St. ☏ 401/765–1900 ⊕ www.chanseggrollsandjazz.com) includes blues, jazz, and folk performers. Reservations are essential; ticket prices range from $10 to $24.

Slatersville

🔟 *3 mi west of Woonsocket.*

In 1803, Samuel Slater and his brother, John, purchased a small sawmill and blacksmith shop along the Branch River and began to turn the area (now part of the town of North Smithfield) into America's first company town, Slatersville. By 1807, the Slatersville Mill had been built, and because it was well removed from population centers, the Slaters and their partners went on to build homes, a general store, a town green, and a church for their workers. The village, west of the junction of Routes 102 and 146, has been well preserved, and though it doesn't have many amenities for visitors, it is a fine place for an afternoon stroll.

Where to Eat

$ ✕ **Wright's Farm Restaurant.** Chicken served family-style—all-you-can-eat bread, salad, roast chicken, pasta, and potatoes—a northern Rhode Island tradition, was born of a Woonsocket social club's need to feed many people efficiently. More than a dozen restaurants in the Blackstone Valley serve this food combo; Wright's Farm, the largest, dishes up 1 million pounds of chicken each year. ⊠ *84 Inman Rd., 2 mi west of Slatersville off Rte. 102, Burrillville* ☎ *401/769–2856* ▭ *No credit cards* ⊘ *Closed Mon. and Tues. No lunch Thurs. and Fri.*

Blackstone Valley A to Z

To research prices, get advice from other travelers, and book travel arrangements, visit www.fodors.com.

BUS TRAVEL

Rhode Island Public Transit Authority buses travel from Providence's Kennedy Plaza to towns in the Blackstone Valley.

🖪 Bus Information **Rhode Island Public Transit Authority** (RIPTA) ☎ 401/781-9400, 800/244-0444 in Rhode Island ⊕ www.ripta.com.

CAR TRAVEL

Pawtucket is north of Providence on Interstate 95. Woonsocket is northwest of Providence via Route 146, then north via Route 99; from Woonsocket, take Route 146A west to Route 102 to get to Slatersville.

The easiest way to explore the Blackstone Valley is by car, though a good map is needed because few signs exist. The detailed *Street Atlas Rhode Island,* published by Arrow Map, Inc., is available at many bookstores and gas stations.

EMERGENCIES

🖪 Hospital **Landmark Medical Center** ⊠ 115 Cass Ave., Woonsocket ☎ 401/769-4100.

TOURS

Blackstone Valley Explorer is a 49-passenger, canopied riverboat conducting various tours of the Blackstone River. Tours are given from June through October and depart from a number of landings along the river.

🖪 *Blackstone Valley Explorer* ⊠ 175 Main St., Pawtucket ☎ 800/454-2882 ⊕ www.tourblackstone.com.

VISITOR INFORMATION

The Blackstone Valley Tourism Council operates the Blackstone Valley Visitor Center, a good starting point for a visit to northern Rhode Island. A complete list of factory stores is also available.

🖪 Tourist Information **Blackstone Valley Tourism Council** ⊠ 175 Main St., Pawtucket 02860 ☎ 401/724-2200 or 800/454-2882 ⊕ www.tourblackstone.com.

SOUTH COUNTY

When the principal interstate traffic through Rhode Island shifted from U.S. 1 to Interstate 95 in the 1960s, the coastal part of the state—known locally as South County, although its true name is Washington County—was given a reprieve from the inevitabilities of development. In the past four decades, strong local zoning laws have been instituted and a park system established. In some communities, land trusts were set up to buy open space. Always a summertime destination, South County is now growing into a region of year-round residents. It is, indeed, the fastest-growing region in the state, but the changes are being well managed by the respective communities, and the area's appeal as a summer playground has not diminished. South County, where the living is easy, is a wonderfully slower-paced alternative to Newport and Providence, a place where you can savor more than 100 mi of beautiful beaches, 18 public golf courses, farm stands, outdoor sports, camping, historic sites, village boutiques, and family amusements.

5

Westerly

19 *50 mi southwest of Providence, 100 mi southwest of Boston, 140 mi northeast of New York City.*

Westerly is a busy little railroad town that grew up in the late 19th century around a major station on what is now the New York–Boston Amtrak corridor. Victorian and Greek-revival mansions line many streets off the town center, which borders Connecticut and the Pawcatuck River. During the Industrial Revolution and into the 1950s, Westerly was distinguished for its flawless red granite, from which monuments throughout the country were made. It has since sprawled out along U.S. 1 and grown to include seven villages—Westerly itself, or downtown Westerly, plus Watch Hill, Dunn's Corners, Misquamicut, Bradford, Shelter Harbor, and Weekapaug—encompassing a 33-square mi-area.

Watch Hill and Misquamicut are summer communities recognized without mention of the township to which they belong, Westerly. Casinos in Uncasville and Ledyard, Connecticut (less than an hour away), are slowly changing Westerly's economic climate. Many residents work in the Mohegan Sun and Foxwoods casinos, and Westerly's B&Bs are becoming popular alternatives to casino hotels.

Wilcox Park (⊠ 71½ High St. ☎ 401/596–8590 ⊕ www.westerlylibrary. org) is a 14½-acre Victorian strolling park in the heart of downtown Westerly. The park, designed and created in 1898 by Warren Manning (an associate of Fredrick Law Olmsted), has a pond, meadow, arboretum, perennial garden, sculptures, fountains, and monuments. Concerts, plays, and arts festivals are held periodically.

Where to Stay & Eat

$$$$ ✕🏠 **Weekapaug Inn.** Weekapaug is a picturesque coastal village 6 mi
Fodor'sChoice southeast of downtown Westerly. This inn, with a peaked roof and
★ huge wraparound porch, sits on a peninsula surrounded on three sides by salty Quonnochontaug Pond. The rooms are cheerful, and most are

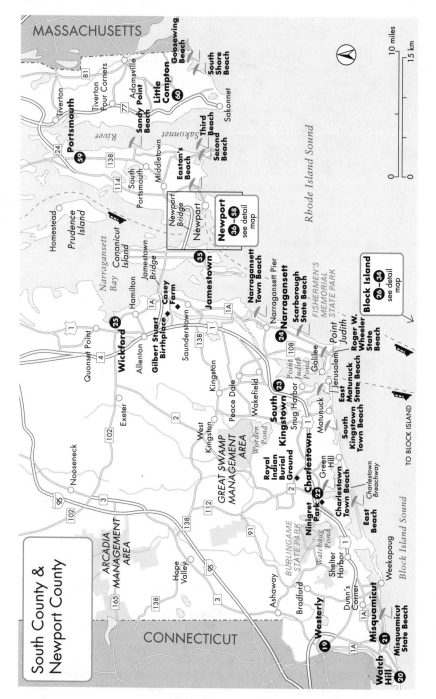

South County &
Newport County

MASSACHUSETTS

CONNECTICUT

Rhode Island Sound

Block Island Sound

Narragansett Bay

Sakonnet River

0   10 miles

0   15 km

Tiverton
Portsmouth **59**
Tiverton Four Corners
81
Adamsville
Sandy Point Beach
Little Compton **60**
Sakonnet
Goosewing Beach
South Shore Beach
77
Third Beach
Second Beach
Easton's Beach
Middletown
South Portsmouth
114
24
138
Newport **56–58**
see detail map
Newport Bridge
Newport

Homestead
Prudence Island
Conanicut Island
Jamestown Bridge
Hamilton
Jamestown **35**
Casey Farm
1A

Quonset Point
Wickford **25**
Gilbert Stuart Birthplace
Allenton
Saunderstown
4
1
138

Exeter
West Kingston
Kingston
2
Peace Dale
Wakefield
South Kingstown **23**
Snug Harbor
Point Judith Pond
108
Galilee
Jerusalem
Point Judith
Narragansett Town Beach
Narragansett **24**
Scarborough State Beach
FISHERMEN'S MEMORIAL STATE PARK
Roger W. Wheeler State Beach
Block Island **29–34**
see detail map

Nooseneck
102
GREAT SWAMP MANAGEMENT AREA
Worden Pond
Royal Indian Burial Ground
Matunuck
East Matunuck State Beach
South Kingstown Town Beach

95
3
102
112
91
138
ARCADIA MANAGEMENT AREA
165
Green Hill
Charlestown **22**
Ninigret Park
Charlestown Town Beach
East Beach
Charlestown Breachway
BURLINGAME STATE PARK
Watchaug Pond
Shelter Harbor

Hope Valley
Ashaway
Bradford
Dunn's Corner
Weekapaug
Westerly **19**
Misquamicut **21**
Misquamicut State Beach
Watch Hill **20**
TO BLOCK ISLAND

1A

big and bright, with wide windows and impressive views. Standards at the restaurant ($$$$), which has a full-time baker, are high: the menu emphasizes seafood and includes four to six entrées each day. ✉ *25 Spray Rock Rd., Weekapaug 02891* ☎ *401/322–0301* 🖷 *401/322–1016* ⊕ *www.weekapauginn.com* ⇔ *55 rooms* ☖ *Restaurant, tennis courts, hot tub, croquet, lawn bowling, shuffleboard, babysitting, children's programs (ages 3–10); no a/c, no room phones, no room TVs* ▭ *No credit cards* ۝ *Closed Oct.–May* ៧ *FAP.*

$–$$$$ ✕▦ **Shelter Harbor Inn.** This inn, about 6 mi east of downtown Westerly in a quiet, rural setting not far from the beach, started out as a summer musicians' colony in 1911. The rooms, many of which have fireplaces and decks, are furnished with a combination of Victorian antiques and reproduction pieces. The frequently changing menu at the excellent restaurant ($$–$$$$) might include pan-seared scallops, horseradish-crusted scrod, or hazelnut chicken. Breakfast is good every day, but Sunday brunch is extremely popular. ✉ *10 Wagner Rd., off U.S. 1, Shelter Harbor 02891* ☎ *401/322–8883 or 800/468–8883* 🖷 *401/322–7907* ⊕ *www.shelterharborinn.com* ⇔ *24 rooms* ☖ *Restaurant, hot tub, beach, croquet, paddle tennis* ▭ *AE, D, DC, MC, V* ៧ *BP.*

$–$$ ▦ **Grandview Bed and Breakfast.** Relaxed, homey, and affordable, this B&B on a rise above Route 1A has comfortable, if nondescript rooms. Those at the front have ocean views. The common room has a TV with VCR. Breakfast is served on the porch year-round. ✉ *212 Shore Rd., between Misquamicut and Weekapaug, Dunn's Corners 02891* ☎ *401/ 596–6384 or 800/447–6384* 🖷 *401/596–3036* ⊕ *www.grandviewbandb. com* ⇔ *8 rooms, 4 with bath* ▭ *AE, MC, V* ៧ *CP.*

Watch Hill

★ ⑳ *6 mi south of downtown Westerly.*

Watch Hill, a Victorian-era resort village, contains almost 2 mi of beautiful beaches. Many of its well-kept summerhouses are owned by wealthy families who have passed ownership down through generations. Sailing and socializing are the top activities for Watch Hill residents. Long before the first Europeans showed up, southern Rhode Island was inhabited by the Narragansetts, a powerful Native American tribe. The Niantics, ruled by Chief Ninigret in the 1630s, were one branch of the tribe. A statue of Ninigret stands watch over Bay Street, which is also a good place to shop for jewelry, summer clothing, and antiques.

The **Flying Horse Carousel,** at the beach end of Bay Street, is the oldest merry-go-round in America, built in 1867. It was part of a traveling carnival that stopped traveling in Watch Hill. The horses, suspended from above rather than fastened to the floor, swing out when in motion; the faster the ride, the more they seem to "fly." Each is hand-carved from a single piece of wood and has glass eyes and a real horsehair mane and tail. Adults are not permitted to ride the carousel. ✉ *Bay St.* ▱ *50¢* ۝ *Memorial Day–Columbus Day, weekdays 11–9, weekends 10–9.*

The **Watch Hill Lighthouse,** an active U.S. Coast Guard station, has great views of the ocean and of Fishers Island, New York. A tiny museum contains exhibits about the lighthouse. Parking is for the elderly only;

everyone else must walk from lots at the beach. The grounds here are worth a stroll, whether the museum is open or not. ⊠ *14 Lighthouse Rd.* ☏ *401/596–7761* ⌷ *Free* ☉ *Grounds daily 8–8; museum July and Aug., Tues.–Thurs.*

Where to Eat

★ $$–$$$ ✕ **Olympia Tea Room.** A step back in time, this small restaurant, which opened in 1916, has varnished wood booths and a soda fountain behind a long marble counter. It also has a view of the water, fun art, and a great reputation. The menu changes seasonally and is large and varied, centering around meats, seafood, and pasta. Favorites include lamb shanks, cod with capers, and lobster salad. Try to save room for the "world-famous Avondale swan" dessert—a fantasy of ice cream, whipped cream, chocolate sauce, and puff pastry. ⊠ *74 Bay St.* ☏ *401/348–8211* ⊕ *www.olympiatearoom.com* ⌷ *Reservations not accepted* ⊟ *AE, MC, V* ☉ *Closed Nov.–Mar.*

Shopping

Comina (⊠ 117 Bay St. ☏ 401/596–3218) displays international furnishings and accessories. **Puffins of Watch Hill** (⊠ 62 Bay St. ☏ 401/596–1140) carries fine American crafts, collectibles, pottery, jewelry, and gifts. **Sun-Up Gallery** (⊠ 95 Watch Hill Rd. ☏ 401/596–0800) has an extensive selection of unique clothing as well as fine crafts, jewelry, and gifts.

Misquamicut

㉑ *2½ mi northeast of Watch Hill.*

Motels with beach towels hanging over porch railings jostle for attention in Misquamicut, where a giant waterslide, a 1915-vintage carousel, miniature golf, a game arcade, children's rides, batting cages, and fast-food stands attract visitors by the thousands. The 7-mi-long beach, Rhode Island's longest state beach, is accessible year-round; the amusements are open between Memorial Day and Labor Day.

☽ **Atlantic Beach Park** (⊠ 337 Atlantic Ave. ☏ 401/322–0504) has more games and rides for kids than any other Misquamicut facility.

Where to Stay & Eat

$$–$$$$ ✕ **Paddy's Seafood Restaurant.** This tropical, turquoise hangout is directly on the sand in plain view of beach volleyball and the ocean. By day, the place is geared toward families; by night, live music and the bar are the focus. Seafood plates rule the menu, but you can also order pasta and salad. ⊠ *159 Atlantic Ave.* ☏ *401/596–2610* ⊕ *www.paddysbeach.com* ⊟ *MC, V.*

$$–$$$ ✕ **Maria's Seaside Cafe.** Although casual, this breezy and upbeat eatery serves such elegant dishes as sea scallops with Italian couscous and *ravioli fatti in casa* (homemade ravioli) with oven-roasted pepper cream sauce. If you have room, don't miss the chocolate lava cake. ⊠ *132 Atlantic Ave.* ☏ *401/596–6886* ⊕ *www.mariasseasidecafe. com* ⊟ *AE, MC, V.*

$$ ⌂ **Breezeway Resort.** The Bellone family takes great pride in its accommodations: summery rooms, suites, villas with fireplaces, and hot tubs. The grounds hold a pool, shuffleboard, and fountains. ⊠ *70 Winna-*

paug Rd. ✆ Box 1368, 02891 ☎ 401/348–8953 or 800/462–8872 🖷 401/596–3207 ⊕ www.breezewayresort.com ⇨ 52 rooms, 14 suites, 2 villas ⚿ Refrigerators, pool, recreation room, laundry service ⊟ AE, D, DC, MC, V ☉ Closed Nov. ⦿ CP.

Nightlife & the Arts

The **Windjammer** (⊠ 321 Atlantic Ave. ☎ 401/322–9283), open Memorial Day to Labor Day, hosts dancing to rock bands in a room that holds 1,000.

Sports & the Outdoors

Seven-mile-long **Misquamicut State Beach** (⊠ Atlantic Ave. ☎ 401/596–9097) has parking, shower facilities, and a snack bar at the state-run beach pavilion.

Charlestown

㉒ *12 mi northeast of Misquamicut.*

Charlestown stretches along the Old Post Road (Route 1A). The 37-square-mi town has parks, the largest saltwater marsh in the state, 7 mi of pristine beaches, and many oceanfront motels, summer chalets, and cabins.

Ninigret Park (⊠ Park La. off Rte. 1A ☎ 401/364–1227) is a 72-acre park with picnic grounds, ball fields, a bike path, tennis and basketball courts, nature trails, and a 3-acre spring-fed swimming pond. Also here is the **Frosty Drew Observatory and Nature Center** (☎ 401/364–9508 ⊕ www.frostydrew.org), which presents free nature and astronomy programs on Friday evenings.

Ninigret National Wildlife Refuge, a great spot for bird-watchers, consists of two stretches of beach lands and marshes, plus the abandoned naval air station on Ninigret Pond. Nine miles of trails cross 400 acres of diverse upland and wetland habitats—including grasslands, shrublands, wooded swamps, and freshwater ponds. ⊠ Rte. 1A ☎ 401/364–9124 ⬚ Free ☉ Daily dawn–dusk.

Many Narragansetts still live in the Charlestown area, but their historic sites are unmarked and easy to miss. The **Royal Indian Burial Ground,** on the left side of Narrow Lane north of U.S. 1, is the resting place of *sachems* (chiefs). You'll recognize it by the tall fences, but there's no sign. It's not open for visits except during the annual Narragansett meeting, usually the second Sunday in August, when tribal members from around the nation convene for costumed dancing and rituals.

Where to Stay & Eat

$–$$ ✕🏠 **General Stanton Inn.** For helping to pay the ransom of a native princess in 1655, Thomas Stanton was rewarded by the Narragansetts with the land on which this inn stands. Since the 18th century, it has provided dining and lodging in a Colonial setting. The rooms have low ceilings, uneven floorboards, small windows, and period antiques and wallpapers. The dining rooms in the restaurant ($–$$$; closed November–April) have brick fireplaces, beams, and wooden floors. Traditional New England fare—steaks, lobster, scrod, rack of lamb—is prepared; a tasty starter

is the Asian Lettuce Wrap. ✉ *4115-A Old Post Rd. (Rte. 1A), 02813*
☎ *401/364–8888* 🖶 *401/364–0800* ⊕ *www.generalstantoninn.com*
⌁ *16 rooms* ♨ *Restaurant, bar* ☰ *AE, D, DC, MC, V* ⑩ *BP.*

Sports & the Outdoors

The 2,100-acre **Burlingame State Park** (✉ 75 Burlingame Park Rd. ☎ 401/
322–7337 or 401/322–7994) has nature trails, picnic and swimming areas,
and campgrounds, as well as boating and fishing on Watchaug Pond.

BEACHES   The ½-mi **Charlestown Town Beach** (✉ Charlestown Beach Rd.) ends at
a breachway that is part of Ninigret National Wildlife Refuge. Glorious **East Beach** (✉ E. Beach Rd.), composed of 3½ mi of dunes backed
by the crystal-clear waters of Ninigret Pond, is a 2-mi hike from the breachway at Charlestown Town Beach. You'll find a snack bar and restrooms; parking is at the end of East Beach Road.

BOATING   **Ocean House Marina** (✉ 60 Town Dock Rd. ☎ 401/364–6040 ⊕ www.
oceanhousemarina.com), at the Cross Mills exit off U.S. 1, is a full-service marina with fuel, fishing supplies, and boat rentals.

Shopping

★ ☺ Follow the myriad pathways at the **Fantastic Umbrella Factory** (✉ 4820
Old Post Rd., off U.S. 1 ☎ 401/364–6616) to discover four rustic shops
and a barn built around a wild garden. For sale are hardy perennials
and unusual daylilies, jewelry, pottery, blown glass, penny candy, greeting cards, crafts, and incense. There is also an art gallery, greenhouse,
and café that serves organic foods. For 50¢ you can scoop a cone full
of seeds to feed the fenced-in ostrich, guinea hens, peacocks, and sheep.

South Kingstown

❷❸ *10 mi northeast of Charlestown.*

In summer, the 55-square-mi town of South Kingstown—encompassing Wakefield, Snug Harbor, Matunuck, Green Hill, Kingston, and 9
other villages—unfolds a wealth of history, outdoor recreation, beaches,
and entertainment. The town's seat of government is in Wakefield.

Where to Stay & Eat

$–$$ ✕ **Mews Tavern.** The food at this cheery tavern is consistently excellent.
Rhode Islanders consider it the best place in the state to get a hamburger
(buy one, get one free on Thursday night), but you can also order
seafood. Beer is also popular here; 69 varieties are on draft. ✉ *465 Main
St., Wakefield* ☎ *401/783–9370* ♨ *Reservations not accepted* ☰ *AE,
D, MC, V.*

$–$$ ✕▦ **Larchwood Inn.** This 1831 country inn with a Scottish flavor is set
in a grove of larch trees. Rooms range from suites with grand views to
smaller, back-of-the-house affairs. The dining room ($$) is open for three
meals daily; entrées include prime rib and lamb chops. Ask for a table
near the fireplace in winter or a patio spot under the trees in summer.
The inn is popular for its $1.49 breakfasts and is near a bike path. ✉ *521
Main St., Wakefield 02879* ☎ *401/783–5454 or 800/275–5450* 🖶 *401/
783–1800* ⊕ *www.xpos.com/larchwoodinn.html* ⌁ *18 rooms* ♨ *Restau-
rant* ☰ *AE, D, DC, MC, V.*

$–$$ 🛏 **Admiral Dewey Inn.** Victorian antiques furnish the rooms of this inn, which was built in 1898 as a seaside hotel—it's across the road from Matunuck Beach—and is now on the National Register of Historic Places. Some rooms have views of the ocean; others are tucked cozily under the eaves. Smoking is permitted only on the wraparound veranda, which is filled with old-fashioned rocking chairs. ✉ *668 Matunuck Beach Rd., Wakefield 02879* 📞 *401/783–2090* ⊕ *www.admiraldeweyinn. com* 🛏 *10 rooms, 8 with bath* ⊟ *MC, V* ❙❍❙ *CP.*

Nightlife & the Arts

Ocean Mist (✉ 895 Matunuck Beach Rd., Matunuck 📞 401/782–3740 ⊕ www.oceanmist.net) is a distinctive beachfront barroom with music nightly in summer and on weekends off-season. The hard-drinking crowd at this hangout of South County's younger generation can be as rough-hewn as the building.

Sports & the Outdoors

BEACHES **East Matunuck State Beach** (✉ Succotash Rd.) is popular with the college crowd for its white sand, picnic areas, pavilion with showers, and concessions. Crabs, mussels, and starfish populate the rock reef that extends to the right of **Matunuck Beach** (✉ Succotash Rd.). Southward, the reef gives way to a sandy bottom. When the ocean is calm, you can walk on the reef and explore its tidal pools. **Roy Carpenter's Beach** (✉ Matunuck Beach Rd.) is part of a cottage-colony of seasonal renters but is open to the public for a fee. **South Kingstown Town Beach** (✉ Matunuck Beach Rd.), with a playground, picnic tables, grills, and showers, draws many families.

FISHING At Snug Harbor it is not uncommon to see giant tuna and sharks weighing more than 300 pounds on the docks. **Snug Harbor Marina** (✉ 410 Gooseberry Rd., Wakefield 📞 401/783–7766) sells bait and arranges fishing charters.

Shopping

Dove and Distaff Antiques (✉ 365 Main St., Wakefield 📞 401/783–5714) carries home goods such as window treatments, slipcovers, and lamp shades. **Hera Gallery** (✉ 327 Main St., Wakefield 📞 401/789–1488 ⊕ www.heragallery.org), a women's art cooperative, exhibits the work of emerging local artists. It's open Wednesday–Friday 1–5, Saturday 10–4.

Narragansett

㉔ *5 mi east of South Kingstown.*

The popular beach town of Narragansett draws people for a scenic drive along the ocean (Route 1A) or for a stroll along its beach or its seawall. Set on the peninsula east of Point Judith Pond and the Pettaquamscutt River, the town has many grand old shingle houses that overlook the ocean and a handful of restaurants and shops directly across the street from the beach.

Narragansett Pier, the beach community often called simply the Pier, was named for an amusement wharf that no longer exists. The Pier—now populated by summertime "cottagers," college students, and commuting professionals—was a posh resort in the late 1800s linked by rail to

New York and Boston. Many summer visitors headed for the Narragansett Pier Casino, which had a bowling alley, billiard tables, tennis courts, a rifle gallery, a theater, and a ballroom. The grand edifice burned to the ground in 1900. Only the **Towers** (⊠ Rte. 1A ☎ 401/783–7121), the grand stone entrance to the former casino, remains. Most of the mansions built during Narragansett's golden age are along Ocean Road, from Point Judith to Narragansett Pier.

The village of **Galilee,** the third-largest fishing port in New England, is a busy, workaday fishing port from which whale-watching excursions, fishing trips, and the **Block Island Ferry** (⊠ Galilee State Pier ☎ 401/783–4613) depart. The occasionally pungent smell of seafood and bait will lead you to the area's fine restaurants and markets. From the port of Galilee it's a short drive to the **Point Judith Lighthouse** (⊠ 1460 Ocean Rd. ☎ 401/789–0444) and a beautiful ocean view. The lighthouse is open daily from dawn to dusk.

Set on the former estate of an early-19th-century Rhode Island governor, William Sprague, **South County Museum** houses 20,000 artifacts dating from 1800 to 1933. The campus consists of six exhibit buildings including a print shop, carpentry shop, transportation barn, and textile arts center. ⊠ *Strathmore St., off Rte 1A* ☎ *401/783–5400* ⊕ *www.southcountymuseum.org* ☑ *$3.50* ☉ *May, June, Sept., and Oct., Fri. and Sat. 10–4, Sun. noon–4; July and Aug., Wed.–Sat. 10–4, Sun. noon–4.*

Where to Stay & Eat

$$–$$$$ ✕ **Basil's.** French and continental cuisine are served in intimate surroundings within walking distance of Narragansett Town Beach. Dark floral wallpaper and fresh flowers enrich the small dining room. The specialty is veal topped with a light cream-and-mushroom sauce; among the other dishes are fish and duck à l'orange. ⊠ *22 Kingstown Rd.* ☎ *401/789–3743* ▭ *AE, DC, MC, V* ☉ *Closed Mon. and Tues., Oct.–June. No lunch.*

$$–$$$ ✕ **Coast Guard House.** This restaurant, housed in an 1888 building that served as a lifesaving station for 50 years, displays interesting photos of Narragansett Pier and the casino. Candles light the tables, and picture windows on three sides allow views of the ocean. The fare is American—seafood, pasta, veal, steak, and lamb. The upstairs lounge hosts entertainers and has a DJ on Friday and Saturday nights. ⊠ *40 Ocean Rd.* ☎ *401/789–0700* ⊕ *www.thecoastguardhouse.com* ▭ *AE, D, DC, MC, V.*

$–$$$ ✕ **George's of Galilee.** This restaurant at the mouth of the Point Judith Harbor has been a must for tourists since 1948. The "stuffies" (baked stuffed quahogs) are some of the best in the state. The menu lists fried and broiled seafood, chicken, steak, and pasta, all at reasonable prices. Its proximity to the beach and its large outside bar on the second floor make George's a busy place all summer. ⊠ *250 Sand Hill Cove Rd.* ☎ *401/783–2306* ♨ *Reservations not accepted* ▭ *D, MC, V* ☉ *Closed Dec. and weekdays Nov. and Jan.*

$–$$$ ✕ **Spain of Narragansett.** South County's only Spanish restaurant is
FodorsChoice   known for its generous portions and fine service by well-trained pro-
★   fessionals. Worthy appetizers include shrimp in garlic sauce, stuffed mush-

room caps, and Spanish sausage; veal chop, seafood and saffron rice, and paella are some of the main courses. Arched entryways and tall plants help create a Mediterranean mood. ⊠ *1144 Ocean Rd.* ☎ *401/783–9770* ▤ *AE, D, DC, MC, V* ☾ *Closed Mon. No lunch.*

$–$$$ ✕ **Turtle Soup.** Be prepared to wait for a table at this lively spot, with its sweeping views of the ocean. The dining room oozes simplicity and comfort, with its gleaming wood paneling and wood floors; a sitting room provides a fireplace and overstuffed chairs. The menu focuses on American dishes, many with an Italian flair. Favorites are lobster scampi, chicken piccata pasta, and capellini with shellfish. ⊠ *113 Ocean Rd.* ☎ *401/792–8683* ⊕ *www.turtlesoupri.com* ⌓ *Reservations not accepted* ▤ *AE, D, MC, V* ☾ *Closed Mon. Oct.–Mar. No lunch Tues.–Fri.*

$–$$ ✕ **Aunt Carrie's.** This popular family-owned restaurant has been serving up Rhode Island shore dinners, clam cakes and chowder, and fried seafood since 1920. At the height of the season the lines can be long; one alternative is to order from the take-out window and picnic on the grounds of the nearby lighthouse. ⊠ *Rte. 108 Sand Ocean Rd., Point Judith* ☎ *401/783–7930* ⌓ *Reservations not accepted* ▤ *MC, V* ☾ *Closed Oct.–Mar. and Mon.–Thurs. Apr., May, and Sept.*

$$–$$$ ▦ **The Richards.** Imposing and magnificent, this large, English-style stone mansion has a Gothic mystique that is quite different from the spirit of the typical summerhouse. French windows in the wood-paneled common rooms downstairs open up to views of a lush landscape, and a fishpond is the centerpiece of the gardens. A fire crackles in the library fireplace on chilly afternoons. Some rooms have 19th-century English antiques, floral-upholstered furniture, and fireplaces. ⊠ *144 Gibson Ave., 02882* ☎ *401/789–7746* ⊕ *www.virtualcities.com/ri/richards.htm* ⇘ *2 rooms, 2 suites* ▤ *No credit cards* ⦿ *BP.*

Sports & the Outdoors

BEACHES Popular mile-long **Narragansett Town Beach** (⊠ Rte. 1A) is regarded as a great surfing beach due to its smooth, curling waves. The beach is within walking distance of many hotels and guesthouses. Its pavilion has changing rooms, showers, and concessions. **Roger W. Wheeler State Beach** (⊠ Sand Hill Cove Rd., Galilee) has fine white sand, calm water, and a slight drop-off. There is a playground area, picnic tables, a bathhouse, and parking. **Scarborough State Beach** (⊠ Ocean Rd.), considered by many the jewel of the Ocean State's beaches, has a pavilion with showers and concessions, observation tower, and sitting areas along the boardwalk. On weekends, teenagers and college students blanket the sands.

FISHING The **Frances Fleet** (⊠ 33 State St., Point Judith ☎ 401/783–4988 or 800/662–2824 ⊕ www.francesfleet.com), with four vessels, operates day and overnight fishing trips. **Persuader** (☎ 401/783–5644) leads sportfishing charters. Excursions on the **Prowler** (☎ 401/783–8487) include tuna and striped bass fishing. The **Seven B's V** (☎ 401/789–9250 ⊕ www.sevenbs.com) is an 80-foot boat that holds up to 120 passengers.

WHALE-
WATCHING Whale-watching excursions aboard the **Lady Frances** depart at 1 PM and return at 5:30 PM. The fare is $35. The trips operate daily in July and August.

SURFING **Gansett Juice** (⊠74 Narragansett Ave. ☎401/789–7890) rents surfboards, body boards, and wet suits. Masters Surfing Champion Peter Pan gives lessons at nearby Narragansett Town Beach. Call 401/789–1954 for the daily surf report.

Wickford

★ ㉕ *12 mi north of Narragansett Pier, 15 mi south of Providence.*

The Colonial village of Wickford has a little harbor, dozens of 18th- and 19th-century homes, several antiques shops, and boutiques selling locally made jewelry and crafts, home accents and gifts, and clothing. This bayside spot is the kind of almost-too-perfect salty New England period piece that is usually conjured up only in books and movies. It is rumored that Wickford was John Updike's model for the New England of his novel *The Witches of Eastwick.*

Old Narragansett Church, now called St. Paul's, was built in 1707. It's one of the oldest Episcopal churches in America. ⊠ *55 Main St.* ☎ *401/ 294–4357* ◷ *July–Labor Day, Fri. and Sat. 11–4; Sun. services at 8, 9:30, and 10:30.*

Smith's Castle, built in 1678 by Richard Smith Jr., is a beautifully preserved saltbox plantation house on the quiet shore of an arm of Narragansett Bay. It was the site of many orations by Roger Williams, from whom Smith bought the surrounding property. The grounds have one of the first military burial grounds (open during daylight hours) in the country: a marked mass grave holding 40 colonists killed in the Great Swamp battle of 1675, during which the Narragansetts were nearly annihilated, ending King Philip's War in Rhode Island. ⊠ *55 Richard Smith Dr., 1 mi north of Wickford* ☎ *401/294–3521* ⊕ *www.smithscastle.org* 🏷 *$5* ◷ *Guided tours at noon, 1, 2, and 3 June–Aug, Thurs.–Mon.; May, Sept., and Oct., Fri.–Sun.*

Historic **Casey Farm,** whose mid-18th-century homestead overlooks Narragansett Bay off Route 1A south of Wickford, still functions much as it has since its earliest days. During the19th century the summer residence of the Casey family, who leased the land to tenant farmers, it is today a community-supported farm operated by resident managers who raise organically grown vegetables. Nearly 30 mi of stone walls surround the 300-acre farmstead. ⊠ *2325 Boston Neck Rd., Saunderstown* ☎ *401/295–1030* ⊕ *www.historicnewengland.org* 🏷 *$4* ◷ *June–mid-Oct., Sat. 11–5.*

⌐ EN
   ROUTE
Built in 1751, the **Gilbert Stuart Birthplace** was the home of America's foremost portraitist of George Washington. It lies on a pretty country road along little Mattatuxet River. The adjacent 18th-century snuff mill was the first in America. The site includes a gristmill and herring reserve, where river herring migrate up a fish ladder. You can hike the trail along the river. ⊠ *815 Gilbert Stuart Rd., Saunderstown* ☎ *401/294–3001* 🏷 *$5* ◷ *May–Oct., Thurs.–Mon. 11–4.*

Sports & the Outdoors

BOATING The **Kayak Centre** (⊠ 9 Phillip St. ☎ 401/295–4400), in bustling Wickford Harbor, rents kayaks and provides lessons.

Shopping

ANTIQUES The **Hour Glass** (⊠ 15 W. Main St. ☎ 401/295–8724) carries antique barometers, clocks, tide clocks, thermometers, and the like. **Mentor Antiques** (⊠ 7512 Post Rd. ☎ 401/294–9412) receives monthly shipments of antique English mahogany, pine, and oak furniture. **Wickford Antiques Centre** (⊠ 16 Main St. ☎ 401/295–2966) sells wooden kitchen utensils, country furniture, china, glass, linens, and jewelry.

CRAFTS Needlepoint pillows, leather journals, lamps, and woven throws are a few of the gifts and home furnishings at **Askham & Telham Inc.** (⊠ 12 Main St. ☎ 401/295–0891).

South County A to Z

To research prices, get advice from other travelers, and book travel arrangements, visit www.fodors.com.

AIRPORTS

The closest major airport is T. F. Green Airport in Warwick, south of Providence. Westerly Airport is served by New England Airlines, which operates scheduled flights from Westerly to Block Island and also provides charter service.

🚹 Airport Information **Westerly Airport** ⊠ Airport Rd., 2 mi south of Westerly off U.S. 1 ☎ 401/596-2357. **New England Airlines** ☎ 401/596-2460 or 800/243-2460.

BUS TRAVEL

Rhode Island Public Transit Authority provides service from Providence and Warwick to Kingston, Wakefield, and Narragansett.

🚹 Bus Information **Rhode Island Public Transit Authority** (RIPTA) ☎ 401/781-9400, 800/244-0444 in Rhode Island ⊕ www.ripta.com.

CAR TRAVEL

Interstate 95 passes 10 mi north of Westerly before heading inland toward Providence. U.S. 1 and Route 1A follow the coastline along Narragansett Bay and are the primary routes through the South County resort towns.

EMERGENCIES

🚹 Hospitals **South County Hospital** ⊠ 100 Kenyon Ave., Wakefield ☎ 401/782-8000. **Westerly Hospital** ⊠ 25 Wells St., Westerly ☎ 401/596-6000.
🚹 24-Hour Pharmacy **CVS Pharmacy** ⊠ 150 Granite St., Westerly ☎ 401/348-6088.

TRAIN TRAVEL

Amtrak trains running between Washington and Boston stop in Westerly and Kingston.

🚹 Train Information **Amtrak** ☎ 800/872-7245 ⊕ www.amtrak.com.

VISITOR INFORMATION

The state operates a visitor information center off Interstate 95 at the Connecticut border.

🚹 Tourist Information **Charlestown Chamber of Commerce** ⊠ 4945 Old Post Rd., Charlestown 02813 ☎ 401/364-3878. **Greater Westerly Chamber of Commerce** ⊠ 1

Chamber Way, Westerly 02891 ☎ 401/596-7761 or 800/732-7636. **Narragansett Chamber of Commerce** ✉ The Towers, 36 Ocean Rd., Narragansett 02882 ☎ 401/783-7121. **South County Tourism Council** ✉ 4808 Tower Hill Rd., Wakefield 02879 ☎ 401/789-4422 or 800/548-4662 ⊕ www.southcountyri.com.

BLOCK ISLAND

Block Island, 12 mi off Rhode Island's southern coast, is 7 mi long and 3 mi wide. With its 17 mi of beaches, Block Island has been a popular travel destination since the 19th century. Despite the number of visitors who come here each summer and thanks to the efforts of local conservationists, the island's beauty remains intact (40% of the land is preserved); its 365 freshwater ponds support more than 150 species of migrating birds.

The original inhabitants of the island were Native Americans who called it Manisses, or "isle of the little god." Following a visit in 1614 by the Dutch explorer Adrian Block, the island was given the name Adrian's Eyelant, and later Block Island. In 1661 the island was settled by farmers and fishermen from Massachusetts Bay Colony. They gave Block Island what remains its second official name, the Town of New Shoreham, when it became part of Rhode Island in 1672.

Block Island, with 800 year-round residents, is a laid-back community. People exchange phone numbers by the last four digits (466 is the prefix) alone, and you can dine at any of the island's establishments in shorts and a T-shirt. The busiest season is between May and Columbus Day—at other times, most restaurants, inns, stores, and visitor services close down. If you plan to stay overnight in summer, make reservations well in advance; for weekends in July and August, March is not too early.

Block Island has two harbors, Old Harbor and New Harbor. Approaching the island by sea from New London (Connecticut), Newport, or Point Judith, you'll see Old Harbor, the island's only village, and its group of Victorian hotels. Most of the smaller inns, shops, and restaurants are also here, and it's a short walk from the ferry landing to most of the interesting sights.

❷❻ Three docks, two hotels, and four restaurants huddled in the southeast corner of the Great Salt Pond make up the **New Harbor** commercial area. The harbor itself—also called Great Salt Pond—shelters as many as 1,700 boats on busy weekends, hosts sail races and fishing tournaments, and is the landing point for the Montauk, Long Island (New York), ferry and Hi-Speed Ferry from Galilee.

❷❼ The **Island Cemetery,** ½ mi west of New Harbor on West Side Road, has held the remains of island residents since the 1700s. At this well-maintained graveyard you can spot the names of long-standing Block Island families (Ball, Rose, Champlin) and take in fine views of the Great Salt Pond, the North Light, and the Rhode Island coast; on a clear day, the Jamestown–Newport Bridge will be visible to the northeast.

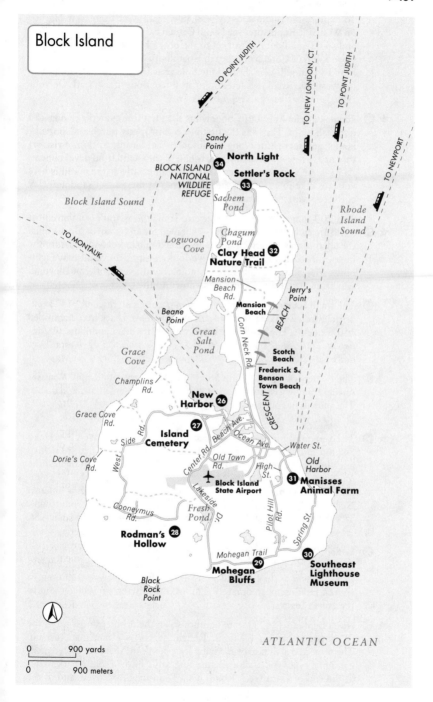

To explore the island's lovely **west side**, head west from New Harbor on West Side Road; after the Island Cemetery, you will pass a horse farm and some small ponds. You get to the beach by turning right on Dories Cove Road or Cooneymus Beach Road; both dirt roads dead-end at the island's tranquil west shore. One mile past Dories Cove Road, peaceful West Side Road jogs left and turns into Cooneymus Road. On your right ½ mi farther is a deep ravine.

★ ❷ **Rodman's Hollow** (⊠ Off Cooneymus Rd.) is a fine example of a glacial outwash basin. This was the first piece of property purchased in the island's quarter-century-long tradition of land conservation, an effort that has succeeded in saving nearly half of the island from development. At Rodman's you can descend along winding paths to the ocean, where you can hike the coastline, lie on beaches at the foot of sand and clay cliffs, or swim if the waters are calm.

★ ❷ The 200-foot cliffs along Mohegan Trail, the island's southernmost road, are called **Mohegan Bluffs**—so named for an Indian battle in which the local Manisses pinned down an attacking band of Mohegans at the base of the cliffs. From Payne Overlook, west of the Southeast Lighthouse Museum, you can see to Montauk Point, New York, and beyond. An intimidating set of stairs leads down to the beach.

❸ The small **Southeast Lighthouse Museum** occupies a "rescued" 1873 red-brick beacon with gingerbread detail that was moved back from the eroded 150-foot cliff. The lighthouse is a National Historic Landmark. ⊠ Mohegan Trail ☎ 401/466–5009 ▧ $5 ☉ Memorial Day–Labor Day, daily 10–4.

☾ ❸ The owners of the 1661 Inn and Hotel Manisses run a small **Manisses Animal Farm** with a collection of llamas, emus, sheep, goats, and ducks. The animals happily coexist in a meadow next to the hotel. ⊠ Off Spring St. or High St. ☎ 401/466–2063 ▧ Free ☉ Daily dawn–dusk.

★ ❸ The outstanding **Clay Head Nature Trail** meanders past Clay Head Swamp and along 150-foot-high ocean-side cliffs. Songbirds chirp and flowers bloom along the paths that lead to the beach or into the interior—an area called the Maze. The trailhead, recognizable by a simple white post marker, is at the end of a dirt road that begins at Corn Neck Road, just past Mansion Beach Road (about 2 mi from town). Trail maps are available at the **Nature Conservancy** (⊠ 352 High St. ☎ 401/466–2129).

❸ **Settler's Rock,** on the spit of land between Sachem Pond and Cow Beach, is a monument that lists the names of the original settlers and marks the spot where they landed in 1661 (with their cows swimming to shore). Hiking approximately 1 mi over sandy terrain will get you to the North Light.

★ ❸ **North Light,** an 1867 granite lighthouse on the northernmost tip of the Block Island National Wildlife Refuge, serves as a maritime museum. The protected area nearby is a temporary home to American oystercatchers, piping plovers, and other rare migrating birds. From a parking lot at the end of Corn Neck Road, it's a ¾-mi-long hike over sand to the lighthouse. ⊠ *Corn Neck Rd.* ☎ *401/466–3200* ⊑ *$2* ⊙ *July 5–Labor Day, daily 10–4.*

Where to Stay & Eat

$$$–$$$$ ✕ **Eli's.** A spaghetti eatery turned bistro, Eli's is Block Island's preferred
FodorśChoice restaurant. Pastas are the menu's mainstays, but the kitchen makes ex-
★ tensive excursions into local seafood, and steaks like the Carpetbagger,
a 12-ounce filet mignon filled with lobster, mozzarella, and sun-dried
tomatoes, topped with a béarnaise sauce. The food keeps people com-
ing back. ⊠ *457 Chapel St.* ☎ *401/466–5230* ⌖ *Reservations not ac-
cepted* ▭ *AE, D, MC, V* ⊙ *Closed Jan.–Apr.*

$–$$$$ ✕ **The BeacHead.** The food—especially the Rhode Island clam chowder—
is very good, the price is right, and you won't feel like a tourist at this
locals' hangout. Play pool, catch up on town gossip, or sit at the bar
and stare out at the sea. The menu and service are unpretentious; burg-
ers are served on paper plates with potato chips and pickles. ⊠ *Corn
Neck Rd.* ☎ *401/466–2249* ⌖ *Reservations not accepted* ▭ *MC*
⊙ *Closed Mon.–Wed. offseason.*

¢–$$$$ ✕ **Finn's.** A Block Island institution, Finn's serves reliable fried and
broiled seafood and prepares a wonderful smoked bluefish pâté. For lunch
try the Workman's Special platter—a burger, coleslaw, and french fries.
You can eat inside or out on the deck, or get food to go. Finn's raw bar
is on an upstairs deck that overlooks Old Harbor. ⊠ *Ferry Landing*
☎ *401/466–2473* ⌖ *Reservations not accepted* ▭ *MC, V* ⊙ *Closed
mid-Oct.–May.*

$$$–$$$$ ✕▦ **Atlantic Inn.** Perched on a hill of gardens and grounds, away from
FodorśChoice the hubbub of the Old Harbor area, this long, white, classic 1879 Vic-
★ torian resort has big windows, high ceilings, a sweeping staircase, and
lovely views. Most of the oak and maple furnishings in the rooms are
original to the building. Each morning the inn's pastry chef prepares a
buffet breakfast with fresh baked goods. The restaurant ($$$$; reser-
vations essential; closed late October–mid-April; no lunch) serves cre-
ative four-course prix-fixe meals that often include scallops and tuna.
⊠ *High St.* ⓓ *Box 1788, 02807* ☎ *401/466–5883 or 800/224–7422*
🖷*401/466–5678* ⊕*www.atlanticinn.com* ⇗*20 rooms, 1 suite* ⌂*Restau-
rant, 2 tennis courts, croquet, playground, meeting room* ▭ *D, MC, V*
⊙ *Closed late Oct.–mid Apr.* ▯⊙❘ *CP.*

$$$–$$$$ ✕▦ **Hotel Manisses.** The chef at the island's premier restaurant ($$$–$$$$;
closed November–April) for American cuisine uses herbs and vegeta-
bles from the hotel's garden and locally caught seafood to prepare su-
perb dishes such as littleneck clams Dijonnaise. Period furnishings,
floral wallpaper, white wicker, wrought iron, and heavily carved furni-
ture decorate the rooms in the 1872 mansion. The extras here include
picnic baskets, an animal farm, island tours, afternoon wine and hors
d'oeuvres in the parlor, and many rooms with whirlpool baths. ⊠*1 Spring
St., 02807* ☎ *401/466–2421 or 800/626–4773* 🖷 *401/466–3162*
⊕ *www.blockislandresorts.com* ⇗ *17 rooms* ⌂ *Restaurant, fans; no
a/c, no room TVs, no kids under 12* ▭ *MC, V* ▯⊙❘ *BP.*

★ $$$$ ▦ **1661 Inn and Guest House.** If your island vacation fantasy includes
lounging in bed while gazing at swans in marshes that <u>overlook the blue</u>

Atlantic, consider staying here. Loll on the inn's expansive deck or curl up in a chair on the lawn; you'll enjoy the panorama of the water below. The rooms reflect remarkable attention to detail: floral wallpaper in one room matches the colors of the hand-painted tiles atop its antique bureau. Rooms have a combination of ocean views, decks, canopy beds, whirlpool tubs, and gas fireplaces. The ample breakfast buffet might consist of fresh bluefish, corned-beef hash, sausage, Belgian waffles, scrambled eggs, and fresh muffins. ⊠ *Spring St., 02807* ☎ *401/466–2421 or 800/626–4773* 🖷 *401/466–2858* ⊕ *www.blockislandresorts.com* ⇆ *23 rooms, 19 with bath* ♨ *Some in-room hot tubs, some refrigerators, playground; no a/c, no room TVs* ⊟ *MC, V* ⊙| *BP.*

★ **$$–$$$$** 🏠 **Blue Dory Inn.** This Old Harbor district inn has been a guesthouse since its construction in 1898. Thanks to Ann Law, the dynamic owner-manager, its main building and three small shingle-and-clapboard outbuildings run efficiently. Though not large, the rooms are tastefully appointed with Victorian antiques, some have Jacuzzi tubs, and each has either an ocean or a harbor view. Couples looking for a romantic hideaway often enjoy the Tea House, which has a porch overlooking Crescent Beach. ⊠ *61 Dodge St.* 🖷 *Box 488, 02807* ☎ *401/466–2254 or 800/992–7290* ⊕ *www.thebluedoryinn.com* ⇆ *12 rooms, 4 cottages, 3 suites* ⊟ *AE, MC, V* ⊙| *BP.*

$$$ 🏠 **Barrington Inn.** This inn is quiet and bright with views of Trims Pond, Great Salt Pond, and Crescent Beach. Three rooms have private decks; there's also a large common deck. A hearty continental breakfast is served in the dining room and outside on the deck. Two apartments (rented by the week in season) in a separate building are good options for families. ⊠ *Beach Ave.* 🖷 *Box 397, 02807* ☎ *401/466–5510 or 888/279–9400* 🖷 *401/466–3103* ⊕ *www.thebarringtoninn.com* ⇆ *6 rooms, 2 apartments* ♨ *No kids under 12* ⊙ *Closed Nov.–Mar.* ⊟ *D, MC, V* ⊙| *CP.*

Nightlife

Nightlife is one of Block Island's highlights, and you have approximately two dozen places to grab a drink. Check the *Block Island Times* for band listings. **Ballard's** (⊠ On docks at Old Harbor ☎ 401/466–2231), a popular tourist destination, is a family restaurant with a beach and an outdoor bar by day. By night it becomes a dance club with live entertainment. **Captain Nick's Rock and Roll Bar** (⊠ 34 Ocean Ave. ☎ 401/466–5670), a fortress of summertime debauchery and host of June's Block Island Music Festival, has four bars and two decks on two floors. In season, bands play nightly. In one of the few year-round spots, **Club Soda** (⊠ 35 Connecticut Ave. ☎ 401/466–5397) has a 360-degree mural depicting Block Island in the 1940s. **McGovern's Yellow Kittens Tavern** (⊠ Corn Neck Rd. ☎ 401/466–5855) has darts, Ping-Pong, pool, and bands on summer weekend nights.

Sports & the Outdoors

Beaches

The east side of the island has a number of beaches. The 2½-mi **Crescent Beach** runs from Old Harbor to Jerry's Point. **Frederick J. Benson**

Town Beach, a family beach less than 1 mi down Corn Neck Road from Old Harbor, has a beach pavilion, parking, showers, and lifeguards. **Mansion Beach,** off Mansion Beach Road south of Jerry's Point, has deep white sand and is easily one of New England's most beautiful beaches; in the morning, you may spot deer on the dunes. Young summer workers congregate ½ mi north of Town Beach at **Scotch Beach** to play volleyball, surf, and sun themselves.

Boating

Block Island Boat Basin (⊠ West Side Rd., New Harbor ☎ 401/466–2631) is the island's best-stocked ship's store. **New Harbor Kayak** (⊠ Ocean Ave., New Harbor ☎ 401/466–2890) rents kayaks, paddleboats, and motorboats. **Oceans & Ponds** (⊠ Ocean and Connecticut Aves. ☎ 401/466–5131) rents kayaks, charters fishing boats and trimaran sail cruises, sells and rents fishing tackle, offers fishing guides, and sells outdoor clothing.

Fishing

Most of Rhode Island's record fish have been caught on Block Island. In fact, Block Island has held the striped bass fishing record since 1984. From almost any beach, skilled anglers can land tautog and bass. Bonito and fluke are often hooked in the New Harbor channel. Shellfishing licenses may be obtained at the town hall, on Old Town Road. **Oceans & Ponds** sells tackle and fishing gear, operates charter trips, and provides guide services. **Twin Maples** (⊠ Beach Ave. ☎ 401/466–5547) sells bait.

Hiking

The **Greenway,** a well-maintained trail system, meanders across the island, but some of the best hikes are along the beaches. You can hike around the entire island in about eight hours. Trail maps for the Greenway are available at the **Chamber of Commerce** (⊠ Water St. ☎ 401/466–2982) and at the **Nature Conservancy** (⊠ 352 High St. ☎ 401/466–2129). The Nature Conservancy conducts nature walks; call for times or check the *Block Island Times.*

Water Sports

Island Outfitters (⊠ Ocean Ave. ☎ 401/466–5502) rents wet suits, spearguns, and scuba gear. PADI-certification diving courses are available, and beach gear and bathing suits are for sale. **Parasailing on Block Island** (⊠ Old Harbor Basin ☎ 401/864–2474) will take you parasailing and also rents 5-person jet boats and 10-person banana boats.

Shopping

Scarlet Begonia (⊠ Dodge St. ☎ 401/466–5024) carries jewelry and crafts, including decoupage and handmade quilts. **Spring Street Gallery** (⊠ Spring St. ☎ 401/466–5374) shows and sells paintings, photographs, stained glass, serigraphs, and other work by island artists and artisans. **Watercolors** (⊠ Dodge St. ☎ 401/466–2538) showcases distinctive jewelry and clothing, much of it locally made.

Block Island A to Z

To research prices, get advice from other travelers, and book travel arrangements, visit www.fodors.com.

AIRPORTS

New England Airlines has regularly scheduled service from Westerly to Block Island Airport.

🛈 Airport Information **Block Island Airport** ✉ Center Rd. ☎ 401/466-5511. **New England Airlines** ☎ 401/466-5881 or 800/243-2460.

BIKE & MOPED TRAVEL

The best way to explore the island is by bicycle (about $15 a day to rent) or moped (about $40). Most rental places are open spring through fall and have child seats for bikes, and all rent bicycles in a variety of styles and sizes, including mountain bikes, hybrids, tandems, and children's bikes.

🛈 Bike Rentals **Island Bike & Moped** ✉ Weldon's Way ☎ 401/466-2700. **Moped Man** ✉ Weldon's Way and Water St. ☎ 401/466-5444. **Old Harbor Bike Shop** ✉ South of ferry dock ☎ 401/466-2029.

BOAT & FERRY TRAVEL

Two ferry lines run to Block Island from Galilee, Rhode Island. Block Island Ferry/Interstate Navigation Company operates ferry service year-round from Point Judith (Galilee) to Old Harbor; the 1-hour trip is $11.05 one-way, and the frequency varies from two to three times a day in winter to nine times a day in peak season. Make auto reservations well ahead. Foot passengers cannot make reservations; arrive 45 minutes ahead in high season—boats do fill up. From early June to mid-October Island Hi-Speed Ferry catamarans make a half dozen daily trips from Galilee to New Harbor; the 30-minute trip is $16 one-way. There is no auto service on the Hi-Speed; passenger reservations are accepted.

Block Island Ferry/Interstate Navigation also operates a seasonal service from Newport's Fort Adams State Park to Old Harbor. The passengers-only ferry leaves Newport for Block Island once a day from July through Labor Day at 9:15 AM and leaves Block Island at 4:45 PM. Same-day round-trip rates are $11.85. Approximate sailing time is 2 hours.

From late May to mid-October, a high-speed ferry operated by Block Island Express runs between New London, Connecticut, and Old Harbor. The ferry departs New London every 3 hours, four or five times a day, and takes a little more than an hour. Tickets are $17 one-way. Passenger reservations are recommended; there is no auto transportation.

Viking Fleet runs passenger service from Montauk, Long Island, from late May to mid-October. The boat departs Montauk at 10 AM and leaves Block Island at 4:30. Fare is $30 one-way. Travel time is 1 hour; the ferry docks at New Harbor.

All the above lines take bicycles; rates range from $3 to $10 one-way.

🛈 Boat & Ferry Information **Block Island Express** ✉ 2 Ferry St., New London ☎ 860/444-4624 ⊕ www.goblockisland.com. **Block Island Ferry/Interstate Navigation** ✉ Galilee State Pier, Narragansett ☎ 401/783-4613 ⊕ www.blockislandferry.com. **Is-**

land Hi-Speed Ferry ✉ No. 3 Galilee State Pier, Narragansett ☎ 877/733-9425 ⊕ www.islandhighspeedferry.com. **Viking Fleet** ☎ 631/668-5700 ⊕ www.vikingfleet.com.

CAR RENTAL

🎞 Local Agency **Block Island Car Rental** ✉ Ocean Ave. ☎ 401/466-2297.

LODGING

Inns and hotels on Block Island are booked well in advance for weekends in July and August. Many visitors rent homes for stays of a week or more. Many houses, however, are booked solid by April.

🎞 Local Agents **Ballard Hall Real Estate** ✉ Ocean Ave., 02807 ☎ 401/466-8883. **Sullivan Real Estate** ✉ Water St., 02807 ☎ 401/466-5521.

TAXIS

Taxis are plentiful at the Old Harbor and New Harbor ferry landings.

🎞 **Kirb's Cab** ☎ 401/466-2928. **Ladybird Taxi** ☎ 401/466-3133. **O. J.'s Taxi** ☎ 401/741-0500.

VISITOR INFORMATION

🎞 Tourist Information **Block Island Chamber of Commerce** ✉ Drawer D, Water St., 02807 ☎ 401/466-2982.

NEWPORT COUNTY

Perched gloriously on the southern tip of Aquidneck Island and bounded on three sides by water, Newport is one of the great sailing cities of the world and the host to world-class jazz, blues, folk, classical music, and film festivals. Colonial houses and gilded-age mansions grace the city. Besides Newport itself, Newport County also encompasses the two other communities of Aquidneck Island—Middletown and Portsmouth—plus Conanicut Island, also known as Jamestown, to the west, and Tiverton and Little Compton, abutting Massachusetts to the east. Little Compton is a remote, idyllic town that presents a strong contrast to Newport's quick pace.

Jamestown

㉟ *25 mi south of Providence, 3 mi west of Newport.*

The 9-mi-long, 1-mi-wide landmass that goes by the names Jamestown and Conanicut Island is encompassed by the east and west passages of Narragansett Bay. Valuable as a military outpost in days gone by, the island was once considered an impediment to commercial cross-bay shipping. In 1940 the Jamestown Bridge linked it to western Rhode Island, and in 1969 the Newport Bridge completed the cross-bay route, connecting Newport to the entire South County area. Summer residents have come to Jamestown since the 1880s, but never to the same extent as to Watch Hill, Narragansett, or Newport. The locals' "We're not a T-shirt town" attitude has resulted in a relatively low number of visitors, even in July and August, making this a peaceful alternative to the bustle of nearby Newport and South County.

The water conditions range from tranquil to harrowing at **Beavertail State Park,** which straddles the southern tip of Conanicut Island. The currents and surf here are famously deadly during rough seas and high winds; but on a clear, calm day, the park's craggy shoreline seems intended for sunning, hiking, and climbing. The **Beavertail Lighthouse Museum,** in what was the lighthouse keeper's quarters, has displays about Rhode Island's lighthouses. ⊠ *Beavertail Rd.* ☎ *401/423–3270* ⌨ *Free* ☉ *Museum June–Labor Day, daily 10–4; park daily.*

Thomas Carr Watson's family had worked the **Watson Farm** for 190 years before he bequeathed it to the Society for the Preservation of New England Antiquities when he died in 1979. The 285-acre spread, dedicated to educating the public about agrarian history, has 2 mi of trails along Jamestown's southwestern shore with amazing views of Narragansett Bay and North Kingstown. ⊠ *455 North Rd.* ☎ *401/423–0005* ⌨ *$3* ☉ *June–mid-Oct., Tues., Thurs., and Sun. 1–5.*

The English-designed **Jamestown Windmill,** built in 1789, ground corn for more than 100 years—and it still works. Mills like this one were once common in Rhode Island. ⊠ *North Rd. southeast of Watson Farm* ☎ *401/423–1798* ⌨ *Free* ☉ *Mid-June–Aug., weekends 1–4.*

A working 1859 hand tub and a horse-drawn steam pump are among
ⓒ the holdings of the **Jamestown Fire Department Memorial Museum,** an informal display of firefighting equipment in a garage that once housed the fire company. ⊠ *50 Narragansett Ave.* ☎ *401/423–1820* ⌨ *Free* ☉ *Daily 7–3; inquire next door at fire department if door is locked.*

Fort Wetherill State Park, an outcropping of stone cliffs at the tip of the southeastern peninsula, has been a picnic destination since the 1800s. There's great swimming at the small cove here, and it's a favorite spot for local snorkelers and scuba divers. ⊠ *Ocean St.* ☎ *401/423–1771* ⌨ *Free* ☉ *Daily dawn–dusk.*

The **Jamestown and Newport Ferry** stops in Newport at Bowen's Landing, Fort Adams, and Goat Island (and will stop at Rose Island upon request). The 35-foot passenger ferry departs on its half-hour voyage from Ferry Wharf about every 1½ hours, from 9:50 AM to 8 PM (until 9 PM on weekends). The last run leaves from Newport at 8:30 PM (9:45 on weekends). The ferry operates from Memorial Day to Labor Day. ⊠ *Ferry Wharf* ☎ *401/423–9900* ⌨ *$8 one-way, $14 round-trip.*

Where to Stay & Eat

$$–$$$ ✕ **Trattoria Simpatico.** A jazz trio plays on weekday evenings and sunny Sunday afternoons at Jamestown's signature restaurant, while patrons dine alfresco under a 275-year-old copper beech tree. An herb garden, fieldstone walls, and white linen complete the picture. You can munch on splendid salads, northern-Italian pasta dishes, or meats prepared with a continental flair. Memorable are the lobster spring rolls and scallop ravioli appetizers and the seared halibut fillet entrée. Reservations are essential on summer weekends. ⊠ *13 Narragansett Ave.* ☎ *401/423–3731* ▭ *AE, D, MC, V* ☉ *No lunch weekdays.*

$-$$$ ✕ **Jamestown Oyster Bar.** Whether you're ordering clam chowder and a
Fodor'sChoice $1.50 draft or grilled swordfish and a martini, you'll feel right at home
★ here. Freshly shucked oysters are kept on ice behind the bar, where ten-
ders pour fine microbrews and wines. The burgers are locally renowned,
but for something more delicate, try one of the seafood specials listed
on the chalkboard. ⊠ *22 Narragansett Ave.* ☎ *401/423–3380* ⚐ *Reser-
vations not accepted* ⊟ *AE, MC, V.*

$$$$ ⊡ **Bay Voyage.** In 1889 this Victorian inn was shipped from Newport
to its current location and named in honor of its trip. The one-bedroom
suites, furnished in floral prints and pastels, have been sold as time-shares,
which makes availability tight in summer. The facilities are plentiful, the
view memorable. The restaurant is known for its Sunday brunch, but
dinner, where you might find juniper-rubbed venison in an espresso demi-
glace, is first-rate, too. ⊠ *150 Conanicus Ave., 02835* ☎ *401/423–
2100* 🖷 *401/423–3209* ⊕ *www.bayvoyageinn.com* ⇱ *32 suites*
⚘ *Restaurant, kitchenettes, pool, gym, hot tub, sauna, bar* ⊟ *AE, D,
DC, MC, V.*

$-$$ ⊡ **East Bay B&B.** This 1896 Victorian is peaceful day and night, even
though it's only a block from Jamestown's two main streets and bustling
wharf. Rooms are generous in size; the common room has a fireplace.
The owner, a trained pastry chef, prepares a copious homemade breakfast. ⊠ *14 Union St., 02835* ☎ *401/423–0330 or 800/243–1107*
⊕ *www.eastbaybnb.com* ⇱ *4 rooms, 2 with bath* ⊟ *AE, MC* ⦿| *BP.*

Sports & the Outdoors

BEACHES Sandy **Mackerel Cove Beach** (⊠ Beavertail Rd.) is sheltered from the currents of Narragansett Bay, making it a great spot for families.

DIVING & **Ocean State Scuba** (⊠ 79 N. Main Rd. ☎ 401/423–1662 or 800/933–
KAYAKING 3483) rents kayaks and diving equipment.

GOLF **Jamestown Country Club** (⊠ 245 Conanicus Ave. ☎ 401/423–9930) has
a crisp 9-hole course for a mere $10.

Newport

30 mi south of Providence, 80 mi south of Boston.

The island city of Newport preserves Colonial industry and gilded-age
splendor like no other place in the country. Settled in 1639 by a small
band of religious dissenters from Massachusetts, Newport earned a
reputation for tolerance, and its prime location at the mouth of Narragansett Bay ensured its success. The golden age of Colonial Newport
ran from roughly 1720 to the 1770s, when products such as cheese, candles, clocks, furniture, and livestock, the best shipbuilders in North America, and the slave trade (although in 1774 progressive Rhode Island became
the first colony to outlaw trading in slaves) made Newport a leader in
New World maritime commerce.

In the 19th century, Newport became a summer playground for the
wealthy, those titans of the gilded age who built their fabulous "cottages"
overlooking the Atlantic. These mansions served as proving grounds for
the country's best young architects, who designed estates for the Van-

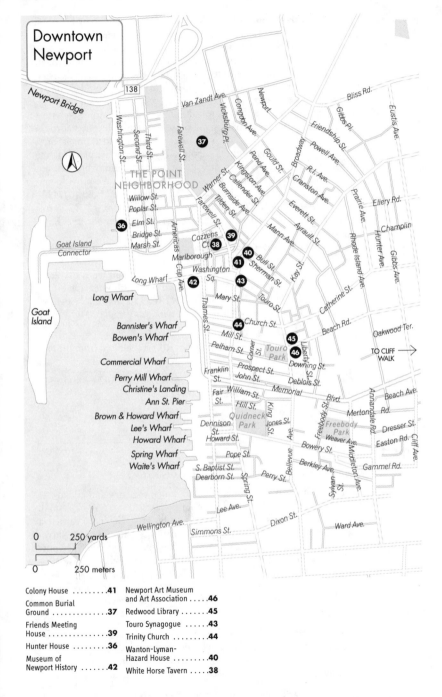

Downtown Newport

138

Newport Bridge

Washington St.

Second St.

Third St.

Farewell St.

THE POINT
NEIGHBORHOOD

Willow St.

Poplar St.

Elm St.

Bridge St.

Marsh St.

America's Cup Ave.

Goat Island
Connector

Goat
Island

Long Wharf

Long Wharf

Bannister's Wharf

Bowen's Wharf

Commercial Wharf

Perry Mill Wharf

Christine's Landing

Ann St. Pier

Brown & Howard Wharf

Lee's Wharf

Howard Wharf

Spring Wharf

Waite's Wharf

Van Zandt Ave.

Vicksburg Pl.

Congdon Ave.

Newport

Bliss Rd.

Gibbs Pl.

Friendship St.

Eustis Ave.

Warner St.

Kingston Ave.

Pond Ave.

Goulet St.

Powell Ave.

Broadway

R.I. Ave.

Cranston Ave.

Ellery Rd.

Callender St.

Burnside Ave.

Tilden St.

Farewell St.

Everett St.

Ayrault St.

Prairie Ave.

Rhode Island Ave.

Champlin

Hunter Ave.

Gibbs Ave.

Mann Ave.

Cozzens
Ct.

Marlborough

Washington
Sq.

Thames St.

Bull St.

Sherman St.

Kay St.

Catherine St.

Mary St.

Touro St.

Church St.

Mill St.

Beach Rd.

Oakwood Ter.

Corne St.

Touro
Park

Liberty St.

TO CLIFF
WALK

Pelham St.

Prospect St.

Downing St.

Franklin
St.

John St.

Deblois St.

Fair
St.

William St.

Hill St.

Memorial

Blvd.

Annandale Rd.

Beach Ave.

Mertondale Rd.

Quidneck
Park

Dennison
St.

King
St.

Jones St.

Freebody
Park

Freebody Ave.

Weaver Ave.

Dresser St.

Easton Rd.

Cliff Ave.

Howard St.

Pope St.

Bowery St.

Gammel Rd.

S. Baptist St.

Dearborn St.

Spring St.

Bellevue
Ave.

Berkley Ave.

Perry St.

Sylvan St.

Middleton Ave.

Lee Ave.

Wellington Ave.

Simmons St.

Dixon St.

Ward Ave.

0   250 yards

0   250 meters

derbilts, Berwinds, Astors, and Belmonts. Many of the mansions are now open to the public for tours.

Recreational sailing, a huge industry in Newport today, convincingly melds the attributes of two eras: the nautical expertise of the Colonial era and the conspicuous consumption of the late 19th century. Tanned young sailors often fill Newport's bars and restaurants. For those not arriving by water, a boat tour of the harbor is a great way to get your feet wet.

Newport has much to offer in a relatively small geographical area—mansions, beaches, seafood restaurants, art galleries, shopping, and, some say, more B&Bs per capita than anywhere else in the country. In summer, it can be crowded (3½ million people visit each year). Yet the quality of its sights and its arts festivals persuade many people to brave the crowds. In fall and spring, you can explore the city without having to stand in line.

Downtown Newport

More than 200 pre-Revolutionary buildings (mostly private residences) remain in Newport, more than in any other city in the country. Most of these treasures are in the neighborhood known as the Point.

With the exception of Ocean Drive, Newport is a walker's city. In summer, traffic is thick, and the narrow one-way streets can be mazelike. It's worth parking in a pay lot and leaving your car behind while you visit in-town sights; one lot is at the Newport Visitors' Information Center on America's Cup Avenue.

A GOOD WALK The ideal first sight in a walking tour is the Colonial-era **Hunter House** ㊱. From Hunter House walk north on Washington Street to Van Zandt Avenue, turn right, and proceed to the **Common Burial Ground** ㊲. Head southeast through the cemetery along aptly named Farewell Street. At the Marlborough Street intersection you'll pass the country's oldest bar and restaurant, the **White Horse Tavern** ㊳. Across Farewell Street stands **Great Friends Meeting House** ㊴. To the east, Marlborough intersects Spring Street and Broadway; ahead on your right you'll see the **Wanton-Lyman-Hazard House** ㊵, the oldest house in Newport. Follow Spring Street three short blocks south to Washington Street, which heads west into Washington Square. Over your left shoulder is the imposing **Colony House** ㊶, site of a number of historic events. At the bottom of Washington Square is the **Museum of Newport History** ㊷.

Walk two blocks east on Touro Street (on the south side of the square); **Touro Synagogue** ㊸, the country's oldest Jewish house of worship, will be on your left. Cross the road and follow High Street one block; then turn right on Church Street to see the immaculate **Trinity Church** ㊹. Proceed east on Church Street. Across Bellevue Avenue are the four pillars of the **Redwood Library** ㊺. The **Newport Art Museum and Art Association** ㊻ is one block south.

Timing. This walk covers 2½ mi. If you spend time inside each building, it might take about 4½ hours. It's best to do this walk one day and the mansions of Bellevue Avenue another. If you have only one day, you will have to limit the number of sights you visit.

WHAT TO SEE **Colony House.** This 1739 redbrick structure above downtown's Washington Square was the center of activity in Colonial Newport and Rhode Island. On July 20, 1776, the Declaration of Independence was read here to Newporters. In 1781, George Washington met here with French commander Count Rochambeau, cementing the alliance that led to the American victory at Yorktown. ⊠ *Washington Sq.* ☎ *401/846–0813* ⊙ *Tours by appointment.*

Common Burial Ground. Farewell Street is lined with historic cemeteries; the many tombstones at this 17th-century graveyard are fine examples of Colonial stone carving, much of it the work of John Stevens, who opened his stone-carving shop in 1705 (the business still thrives today).

Great Friends Meeting House. Built in 1699, this is the oldest house of worship in Rhode Island. With its wide-plank floors, simple benches, balcony, and beam ceiling (considered lofty by Colonial standards), the two-story shingle structure reflects the quiet reserve and steadfast faith of Colonial Quakers. ⊠ *29 Farewell St.* ☎ *401/846–0813* ⊠ *$4* ⊙ *Tours by appointment.*

★ **Hunter House.** The French admiral Charles Louis d'Arsac de Ternay used this lovely 1748 home as his Revolutionary War headquarters. The carved pineapple over the doorway was a symbol of welcome throughout Colonial America; a fresh pineapple placed out front signaled an invitation to neighbors to visit a returned seaman or to look over a shop's new stock. The elliptical arch in the central hall is a typical Newport detail. Pieces made by Newport artisans Townsend and Goddard furnish much of the house, which also contains the first commissioned painting by a young Gilbert Stuart, best known for his portraits of George Washington. ⊠ *54 Washington St.* ☎ *401/847–1000* ⊕ *www. newportmansions.org* ⊠ *$25* ⊙ *Late June–early Oct., daily 10–5.*

Museum of Newport History. This restored brick market building houses a museum that explores Newport's social and economic influences. Antiques such as the printing press of James Franklin (Ben's brother) inspire the imagination. Built in 1762 and designed by Peter Harrison, who was also responsible for the Touro Synagogue and the Redwood Library, the building also served as a theater and a town hall. The museum and the Newport Visitors' Information Center are departure points for walking tours of Newport; call for times. ⊠ *127 Thames St.* ☎ *401/841–8770* ⊕ *www.newporthistorical.org* ⊠ *$4 donation suggested* ⊙ *May–mid-June, Thurs.–Sat. 10–4, Sun. 1–4; mid-June–Labor Day, daily 10–4.*

Newport Art Museum and Art Association. Richard Morris Hunt designed the Stick-style Victorian building that houses this community-supported center for the arts. The galleries exhibit contemporary New England works. ⊠ *76 Bellevue Ave.* ☎ *401/848–8200* ⊕ *www.newportartmuseum.com* ⊠ *$6* ⊙ *Memorial Day–Labor Day, Mon.–Sat. 10–5, Sun. noon–5; Labor Day–Memorial Day, Mon.–Sat. 10–4, Sun. noon–4.*

Redwood Library. This Roman templelike building, complete with Doric columns, was built as a library in 1747 and has been in use for that purpose ever since, a record in America. Although it may look like a Roman temple, it is actually made of wood; the exterior paint is mixed with sand to make it resemble cut stone. The library's paintings include works by Gilbert Stuart and Rembrandt Peale. ⊠ *50 Bellevue Ave.* ☎ *401/847–0292* ⊕ *www.redwoodlibrary.org* ⊠ *Free* ☉ *Mon. and Fri. 9:30–5:30, Tues.–Thurs. 9:30–8, Sun. 1–5.*

43 **Touro Synagogue.** Jews, like Quakers and Baptists, were attracted by Rhode Island's religious tolerance; they arrived in Newport as early as 1658, possibly from Holland or the West Indies. At first they worshiped in homes, but by 1758 they were numerous enough to begin building a synagogue. Dedicated in 1763, the Touro Synagogue is the oldest surviving synagogue in the United States. Although simple on the outside, the Georgian building, designed by Peter Harrison, has an elaborate interior. Its classical style influenced Thomas Jefferson in the building of Monticello and the University of Virginia. ⊠ *85 Touro St.* ☎ *401/847–4794* ⊕ *www.tourosynagogue.org* ⊠ *Free* ☉ *Guided tours on the ½ hr: July 4–Labor Day, Sun.–Fri. 10–5; Memorial Day–July 4 and Labor Day–Columbus Day, weekdays 1–3, Sun. 1–3; Columbus Day–Memorial Day, Sun. 1–3, weekdays for 2 PM tour only. Services: 1 in morning and 1 in evening, call for times.*

44 **Trinity Church.** This Colonial beauty was built in 1724 and modeled after London churches designed by Sir Christopher Wren. A special feature of the interior is the three-tier wineglass pulpit, the only one of its kind in America. The lighting, woodwork, and palpable feeling of history make attending Episcopal services here an unforgettable experience. ⊠ *Queen Anne Sq.* ☎ *401/846–0660* ⊠ *Free* ☉ *May and June, weekdays 10–1; July and Aug., Mon.–Sat., 10–4; Sept.–mid-Oct., weekdays 10–1. Sun. services at 8 and 10.*

40 **Wanton-Lyman-Hazard House.** This late-17th-century residence presents a window on the fascinating Colonial and Revolutionary history of Newport. The dark-red building was the site of the city's Stamp Act riot of 1765. After the British Parliament levied a tax on most printed material, the Sons of Liberty stormed the house, which was occupied by a prominent and outspoken Loyalist. ⊠ *17 Broadway* ☎ *401/846–0813* ⊠ *$4* ☉ *Tours by appointment.*

38 **White Horse Tavern.** William Mayes, the father of a successful and notorious pirate, received a tavern license in 1687, which makes this building, built in 1673, the oldest tavern in America. Its gambrel roof, low dark-beam ceilings, cavernous fireplace, and uneven plank floors epitomize Newport's Colonial charm. ⊠ *26 Marlborough St.* ☎ *401/849–3600* ⊕ *www.whitehorsetavern.com.*

Greater Newport

The gilded-age mansions of Bellevue Avenue are what many people associate most with Newport. These late-19th-century homes are almost obscenely grand, laden with ornate rococo detail and designed with a determined one-upmanship.

The **Preservation Society of Newport County** (☎ 401/847–1000 ⊕ www. newportmansions.org) maintains 11 historic properties. Both guided tours and audio tours are available; you can purchase a combination ticket to see multiple properties for a substantial discount. (Astors' Beechwood, Belcourt Castle, and Rough Point, not operated by the preservation society, are not included in the combination ticket.) The hours and days the houses are open in fall and winter do change, so it's wise to call ahead. The Breakers, the Elms, and Marble House are decorated for Christmas and open for tours daily from mid-November to New Year's Day.

A GOOD TOUR At the corner of Memorial Boulevard and Bellevue Avenue is the **International Tennis Hall of Fame** ㊼, birthplace of the U.S. Open. Before you visit the mansions (or after you've finished), you can walk south on Bellevue Avenue, make a right on Bowery Street, and turn left at Thames Street to visit the **International Yacht Restoration School** ㊽. Back on Bellevue Avenue, catercorner from Newport Casino is **Kingscote** ㊾, a Victorian "cottage." The neoclassical **Elms** ㊿ is two blocks south. Three blocks farther is the Gothic-style **Chateau-sur-Mer** ㊾, and **Rosecliff** ㊾, modeled after the Grand Trianon, is four more blocks in the same direction. **Astors' Beechwood** ㊾ and the **Marble House** ㊾, a Vanderbilt mansion, are on the same side of this lengthy block of palaces. Farther down, at the corner of Lakeview and Bellevue, is **Belcourt Castle** ㊾. Beyond this mansion, Bellevue Avenue turns 90 degrees west and dead-ends at the south end of the Cliff Walk, a stunning promenade. From here you can take Cliff Walk down to **Rough Point** ㊾ to catch a backyard glimpse of the home of Doris Duke. Then you can stroll along the Rhode Island Sound to Newport's most renowned mansion, **The Breakers** ㊾, which can be reached from the Cliff Walk by heading west on Ruggles Avenue and north on Ochre Point Avenue.

You can walk the first part of this tour (although you may well prefer to save your energy for touring the houses), but you'll need a car to visit the **Museum of Yachting** ㊿ at Fort Adams State Park. From downtown Newport, drive south on Thames Street to Wellington Avenue. Turn right and follow Wellington along Newport Harbor to the bend where Wellington becomes Halidon Avenue. Turn right on Harrison Avenue. One mile to the right is the park entrance; the museum is at the end of Fort Adams Road. To get back to town, follow Ocean Drive to Bellevue Avenue. Be sure to take in the views of the ocean, rocky coast, and spectacular homes along the way. Consider stopping at Brenton State Park for a picnic or to take in the sunset.

Timing. If you have only one day, it's best to tour two or three mansions and see the others only from the outside. To avoid long lines in summer, go early or choose the less-popular but still splendid mansions— the Elms, Kingscote, and Belcourt Castle. (It is possible to call and make reservations for tours.) From Kingscote to Belcourt—the first and last mansions on Bellevue Avenue—the distance is less than 2 mi. The full Cliff Walk is 3½ mi long. Plan on spending one hour at each mansion you visit. Seeing the Tennis Hall of Fame, three mansions, walking the length of Bellevue Avenue, and returning via the Cliff Walk takes five or six hours. The driving portion of the tour is about 11 mi long.

SIGHTS TO SEE **Astors' Beechwood.** The original mistress of this oceanfront mansion, Caroline Schermerhorn Astor, was the queen of American society in the late 19th century; her list of the "Four Hundred" was the first social register. Her husband, William Backhouse Astor, was a member of one of the wealth-

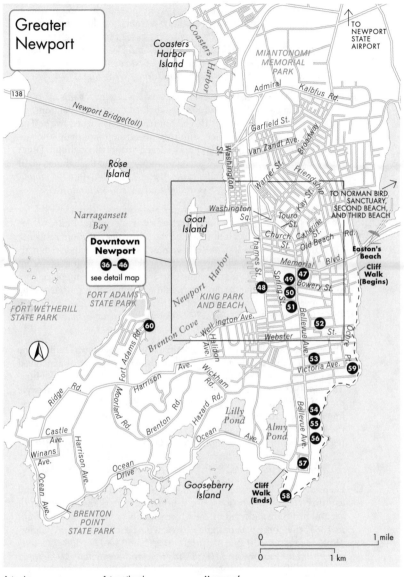

Greater Newport

iest families in the nation. As you're guided through the 1857 mansion, actors in period costume play the family, servants, and household guests. Murder mysteries and musical events are performed July through Oct; Victorian holiday events are held in November and December. ⊠ *580 Bellevue Ave.* ☎ *401/846–3772* ⊕ *www.astorsbeechwood.com* ⊠ *$15* ⊙ *Mid-May–Dec., daily 10–4; Feb.–mid-May, Wed.–Sun. 10–4.*

⑰ Belcourt Castle. Richard Morris Hunt based his design for this 60-room mansion, built in 1894 for wealthy bachelor Oliver H. P. Belmont, on the hunting lodge of Louis XIII. The home, privately owned by the Tinney family since 1956, is filled with treasures from more than 30 countries. Admire the stained glass and carved wood throughout. Don't miss the Golden Coronation Coach and inquire about the haunted chair and suit of armor. ⊠ *657 Bellevue Ave.* ☎ *401/846–0669* ⊕ *www. belcourtcastle.com* ⊠ *$10* ⊙ *Guided tours Wed.–Sun. noon–5.*

⑲ The Breakers. The largest of the Newport mansions was built in 1895 for Cornelius Vanderbilt II, president of the New York Central Railroad. Architect Richard Morris Hunt modeled the four-story, 70-room residence after the palaces of the Italian Renaissance. Its interiors include rich marbles and gilded rooms, with open-air terraces looking out at magnificent ocean views. A few of the marvels within are a blue marble fireplace, rose alabaster pillars in the dining room, and a porch with a mosaic ceiling that took Italian artisans six months, lying on their backs, to install. ⊠ *Ochre Point Ave.* ☎ *401/847–1000* ⊕ *www.newportmansions.org* ⊠ *$15* ⊙ *Jan.–Mar., daily 10–4; Apr.–Dec., daily 9–5.*

FodorśChoice ★

③ Chateau-sur-Mer. Bellevue Avenue's first stone mansion was built in the Victorian Gothic style in 1852 for William S. Wetmore, a tycoon involved in the China trade, and enlarged in the 1870s by Richard Morris Hunt. The Gold Room by Leon Marcotte and the Renaissance Revival–style dining room and library by the Florentine sculptor Luigi Frullini are sterling examples of the work of leading 19th-century designers. Upstairs, the bedrooms are decorated in the English Aesthetic style with wallpaper by Arts and Crafts designers William Morris and William Burges. ⊠ *Bellevue and Shepard Aves.* ☎ *401/847–1000* ⊕ *www. newportmansions.org* ⊠ *$10* ⊙ *Mid-Apr.–mid-Nov., daily 10–5.*

② Chepstow. This Italianate-style villa with a mansard roof is not as grand as other Newport mansions, but it houses a remarkable collection of art and furniture gathered by the Morris family of New York City. Built in 1861, the home was designed by Newport architect George Champlin Mason. ⊠ *120 Narragansett Ave.* ☎ *401/847–1000* ⊕ *www. newportmansions.org* ⊠ *$10* ⊙ *Mid-June–mid-Sept., daily 10–5; tours offered on the hr by reservation.*

FodorśChoice ★

Cliff Walk. This spectacular 3½-mi path runs south along Newport's cliffs from Easton's Beach (also called First Beach) to Bailey's Beach. The promenade has views of sumptuous mansions on one side and the rocky coastline on the other; walking any section of it is worth the effort. The Cliff Walk can be accessed from any road running east off Bellevue Avenue. The unpaved sections can be difficult for small children, strollers, or people with mobility problems.

51 The Elms. Architect Horace Trumbauer modeled this graceful 48-room French neoclassical mansion and its grounds after the Château d'Asnières near Paris. The Elms was built for Edward Julius Berwind, a bituminous-coal baron, in 1901 and was one of the first in Newport to be fully electrified. At the foot of the 10-acre estate is a spectacular sunken garden. ⊠ *Bellevue Ave.* ☎ *401/847–1000* ⊕ *www.newportmansions.org* 💺 *$10, guided tour $15* ⊙ *Mid-Apr.–Dec., daily 10–5; Jan.–Mar., weekends 10–4.*

47 International Tennis Hall of Fame. The photographs, memorabilia, and multimedia exhibits at the Hall of Fame chronicle the entire history of the game dating back to the 12th century and portray the sport's greatest champions and most memorable moments. The magnificent, shingle-style Newport Casino housing the collection was designed by Stanford White and built in 1880. Now a National Historic Landmark, it was commissioned by publisher James Gordon Bennett Jr., who had quit the nearby club, the Newport Reading Room, after a polo player—at Bennett's behest—rode a horse into the building and was subsequently banned. Built in retaliation, Bennett's casino quickly became the social and recreational hot spot of the gilded age. Today, the 6-acre venue has 13 grass courts, 1 clay court, a court-tennis facility, and 3 indoor courts—all available for public play. ⊠ *194 Bellevue Ave.* ☎ *401/849–3990* ⊕ *www.tennisfame.com* 💺 *$8* ⊙ *Daily 9:30–5.*

48 International Yacht Restoration School. This school, off Thames Street in a former power plant, lets you watch shipwrights and students as they overhaul historically significant sailboats and powerboats. Placards recount each boat's past. The 1885 racing schooner *Coronet* and the original "cigarette boat" are two standouts. ⊠ *449 Thames St.* ☎ *401/848–5777* ⊕ *www.iyrs.org* 💺 *Free* ⊙ *Apr.–Nov., daily 9–5; Dec.–Mar., Mon.–Sat. 10–5.*

50 Isaac Bell House. Considered one of the finest examples of American shingle-style architecture, this Bellevue Avenue home, currently being restored, is open to the public as a work in progress. Designed by McKim, Mead & White, the home was built in 1883 for wealthy cotton broker Isaac Bell. ⊠ *Bellevue Ave. and Perry St.* ☎ *401/847–1000* ⊕ *www.newportmansions.org* 💺 *$10* ⊙ *Mid-June–mid-Sept., daily 10–5.*

49 Kingscote. This Gothic Revival mansion, completed in 1841, was one of Newport's first summer cottages. Richard Upjohn designed Kingscote for George Noble Jones, a plantation owner from Savannah, Georgia. Decorated with antique furniture, glass, and Asian art, it contains one of the first installations of Tiffany glass windows in its dining room. ⊠ *Bowery St. off Bellevue Ave.* ☎ *401/847–1000* ⊕ *www.newportmansions.org* 💺 *$10* ⊙ *Mid-June–mid-Sept., daily 10–5.*

56 Marble House. One of the most opulent of the Newport mansions, Marble House is known for its extravagant gold ballroom. The house was built between 1888 and 1892 by William Vanderbilt, who gave it as a gift to his wife, Alva, in 1892. Alva divorced William in 1895 and married Oliver Perry Belmont, becoming the lady of Belcourt Castle. When Oliver died in 1908, she returned to Marble House and spent much of

Fodor'sChoice
★

her time campaigning for women's rights. She hosted many suffragette rallies in the intriguing Chinese teahouse that she had built behind the estate in 1914. It was designed by the sons of Richard Morris Hunt, who designed Marble House itself. ⊠ *Bellevue Ave. near Ruggles St.* ☎ *401/847–1000* ⊕ *www.newportmansions.org* 🎫 *$10* ☉ *Mid-Apr.–Dec., daily 10–5; Jan.–Mar., weekends 10–4.*

60 Museum of Yachting. The museum has four displays: the Single-Handed Sailors Hall of Fame, the World of Model Yachts, the Classic Wooden Boat Collection, and Seasonal Marine Art exhibits. You can also see the legendary two-time America's Cup winner and Rhode Island State Yacht *Courageous.* ⊠ *Ft. Adams State Park, Ocean Dr.* ☎ *401/847–1018* ⊕ *www.museumofyachting.org* 🎫 *$5* ☉ *Mid-May–Oct., daily 10–5.*

Norman Bird Sanctuary. Seven miles of trails, from ¼-mi to 1⅕-mi long, loop through this 300-acre sanctuary, which in summer provides refuge from downtown Newport's hustle and bustle. More than 300 species of birds, plus deer, fox, mink, dragonflies, turtles, and rabbits live in the fields and woodlands. From higher elevations you can see the ocean, some ponds, and the marshy lowlands. Exhibits at the visitor center explain the sanctuary's history and animal and plant life. ⊠ *583 3rd Beach Rd., Middletown* ☎ *401/846–2577* ⊕ *www.normanbirdsanctuary. org* 🎫 *$4* ☉ *Daily 9–5.*

54 Rosecliff. Newport's most romantic mansion was built in 1902, commissioned by Tessie Hermann Oelrichs, who inherited a Nevada silver fortune from her father. Stanford White modeled the palace after the Grand Trianon at Versailles. Rosecliff has a heart-shape staircase and Newport's largest private ballroom. ⊠ *Bellevue Ave.* ☎ *401/847–1000* ⊕ *www. newportmansions.org* 🎫 *$10* ☉ *Mid-Apr.–mid-Nov., daily 10–5.*

58 Rough Point. The late tobacco heiress and preservationist Doris Duke hosted such celebs as Elizabeth Taylor at her Newport mansion perched on Cliff Walk. The 105-room home (with 49 principal rooms) was built in the English-manor style in 1889. An avid collector of art and antiques, Miss Duke filled Rough Point with works by such masters as Renoir and Reynolds (of all the Newport mansions, Duke's has the best art collection). Furnishings range from the elaborate to the peculiar (count the mother-of-pearl bedroom suite among the latter). Tours include an annual changing exhibit. To tour the mansion, take the Rough Point shuttle from the Newport Visitors' Information Center. If you prefer to drive, you must make an online reservation. ⊠ *Bellevue Ave. and Ocean Dr.* ☎ *401/845–9130* ⊕ *www.newportrestoration.org* 🎫 *$25 (first-come, first-served basis)* ☉ *Tues.–Sat., tours leave from Newport Visitors' Information Center (23 America's Cup Ave.) and run every 30 mins.*

Where to Eat

$$$–$$$$ ✕ **Asterisk.** Fine dining is fun and colorful in this "New Yorkified," ren-
Fodor's Choice ovated auto-repair garage. Asian twists enliven the French-influenced
★ Mediterranean fare, accompanied by a carefully selected menu of wines, brandies, and aperitifs. The crispy salmon, butter-roasted lobster tails, and roasted duck with ginger lemon soy entrées melt in your mouth. High ceilings and an open floor lend to a lively metro vibe, and on Sun-

day, there's live jazz. ✉ *599 Thames St.* ☎ *401/841–8833* ▤ *AE, D, DC, MC, V* ☽ *No lunch.*

$$$–$$$$ ✗ **Restaurant Bouchard.** Regional takes on French cuisine fill the menu at this upscale yet homey restaurant. Sautéed sea scallops, for example, are finished with a red-wine-and-truffle-butter sauce. ✉ *505 Thames St.* ☎ *401/846–0123* ⊕ *www.restaurantbouchard.com* ▤ *AE, D, MC, V.*

$$$–$$$$ ✗ **22 Bowen's Wine Bar & Grille.** Newport's prime beef steak house also serves seafood, along with a 400-plus wine list. Distressed brick floors on the first floor, stained red oak wood on the second floor, white linens, leather chairs, and a mahogany bar lend a sumptuous air to the eatery. ✉ *Bowen's Wharf* ☎ *401/841–8884* ⊕ *www.22bowens.com* ▤ *AE, D, DC, MC, V.*

$$$–$$$$ ✗ **White Horse Tavern.** The first license to operate a tavern here was obtained in 1687 and almost uninterruptedly since then—the premises have served as a tavern, boardinghouse, or restaurant. Once a meetinghouse for Colonial Rhode Island's General Assembly, the tavern provides intimate dining with its low dark-beam ceilings, cavernous fireplace, and uneven plank floors. The service is black tie, the wine list top notch, and the American cuisine—including local seafood and beef Wellington, along with more exotic entrées such as orange-cognac duck breast—consistently excellent. ✉ *Marlborough and Farewell Sts.* ☎ *401/849–3600* ⊕ *www.whitehorsetavern.com* ⚑ *Reservations essential* ▤ *AE, D, DC, MC, V* ☽ *No lunch Mon.–Wed.*

$$–$$$$ ✗ **Clarke Cooke House.** Formal dining is on the upper level, on the Porch, a room with a timber-beam ceiling, green latticework, richly patterned cushions, and water views; there's open-air dining in warm weather. The refined, pricey Mediterranean menu incorporates local seafood; game dishes often appear as specials. On the middle levels are the Candy Store and the Grill Room; in summer, the large windows are opened so diners can view Bannister's Wharf. Late at night, the dark, downstairs Boom Boom Room comes alive with a DJ. A dance-floor cam provides a simulcast viewing of your dance moves at the TV across the bar. ✉ *Bannister's Wharf* ☎ *401/849–2900* ⚑ *Reservations essential* ▤ *AE, D, DC, MC, V.*

$$–$$$$ ✗ **Scales & Shells.** Busy, sometime noisy, but always excellent, this restaurant serves as many as 15 kinds of superbly fresh wood-grilled fish, including grilled lobster. Similar dishes are available in the more formal dining room upstairs at UpScales, open from Memorial Day through Labor Day. Reservations are not accepted downstairs. ✉ *527 Thames St.* ☎ *401/848–9378* ▤ *No credit cards.*

$$–$$$$ ✗ **Tucker's Bistro.** The red lacquered walls crowded with artwork, shelves lined with books, and gilded mirrors creates a vibe that is part library, part art gallery, and part bordello. Contemporary creations include sautéed scallops with morels, and halibut with chardonnay sauce; in winter, five-spiced duck is a popular choice. Regulars will never allow Tucker's to take favorite appetizers Thai shrimp nachos or pear salad off the menu. ✉ *150 Broadway* ☎ *401/846–3449* ⊕ *www.tuckersbistro.com* ▤ *D, MC, V* ☽ *No lunch.*

$–$$$$ ✗ **Black Pearl.** At this converted dock shanty, popular with yachters, clam chowder is sold by the quart. Dining is in the casual tavern or the formal Commodore's Room (jacket required, reservations essential). The latter serves an appetizer of black-and-blue tuna with red-pepper sauce. The French and American entrées include duck breast with green peppercorn sauce and swordfish with Dutch pepper butter. The outdoor patio is packed in summer. ⊠ *Bannister's Wharf* ☎ *401/846–5264* ▤ *AE, MC, V.*

$–$$ ✕ **Flo's Clam Shack.** With an old boat in front, peeling paint, and a bamboo-lined walkway leading to the order windows, this local favorite across from Easton's Beach is as casual as it gets. Fried seafood, steamed clams, cold beer, and a great raw bar keep the lines long here in summer. An upstairs bar serves baked, chilled lobster, and outside seating is available. ⊠ *4 Wave Ave.* ☎ *401/847–8141* ✍ *Reservations not accepted* ▤ *No credit cards* ☽ *Closed Jan.*

¢–$ ✕ **Ocean Coffee Roasters.** Known to locals as the Wave, this nonchalant diner draws fans aplenty for freshly roasted coffee and freshly baked muffins as well as bagels, salads, and homemade Italian soups. Breakfast is served until 2 PM. ⊠ *22 Washington Sq.* ☎ *401/846–6060* ✍ *Reservations not accepted* ▤ *MC, V* ☽ *No dinner.*

Where to Stay

$$$$ ✕▦ **Castle Hill Inn and Resort.** The 1874 main house and its lawn have
Fodor'sChoice views of Narragansett Bay, the Newport Bridge, and the Atlantic Ocean.
★ Amenities abound: Adirondack chairs to take in the view, patio dining, private beach, and trails to the Castle Hill Lighthouse. The tastefully appointed rooms, varied in style, are in the main house, harbor houses, and beach houses. The inn, 3 mi from the center of Newport, is also a perfect spot for a special meal ($$$–$$$$). The restaurant menus may include roasted king salmon, grilled Texas antelope, and vegetarian entrées; Sunday brunches with live jazz music; and prix-fixe tasting menus with wine pairings. ⊠ *590 Ocean Dr., 02840* ☎ *401/849–3800 or 888/466–1355* 🖷 *401/849–3838* ⊕ *www.castlehillinn.com* ⇨ *25 rooms* ⚲ *Restaurant, in-room hot tubs, 3 beaches* ▤ *AE, D, DC, MC, V* ⵔ *BP.*

$$$$ ▦ **Cliffside Inn.** Grandeur and comfort come in equal supply at this
Fodor'sChoice swank Victorian home on a tree-lined street near Cliff Walk. On the walls
★ are more than 100 paintings by artist Beatrice Turner, who lived in the house for many years and painted hundreds of self portraits. All rooms have one to three fireplaces and are furnished with Victorian antiques. The Governor's Suite (named for Governor Thomas Swann, of Maryland, who built the home in 1876) has a two-sided fireplace, a whirlpool bath, a four-poster king-size bed, and a brass birdcage shower. Afternoon tea is an experience here, complete with scones with Devonshire cream; finger sandwiches of salmon mousse, caviar, or cucumber; and a bevy of sweets. Breakfast may include poached eggs nestled on crab cakes or crepes lavish with berries. This inn is sister to the Adele Turner and Abigail Stoneman inns. ⊠ *2 Seaview Ave., 02840* ☎ *401/847–1811 or 800/845–1811* 🖷 *401/848–5850* ⊕ *www.legendaryinnsofnewport.com* ⇨ *8 rooms, 8 suites* ▤ *AE, D, DC, MC, V* ⵔ *BP.*

★ $$$$ ▦ **Francis Malbone House.** The design of this stately painted-brick house is attributed to the architect responsible for the Touro Synagogue and the Redwood Library. A lavish inn with period reproduction furnishings, the 1760 structure was tastefully doubled in size in the mid-1990s. The rooms in the main house overlook the courtyard, which has a fountain, or across the street to the harbor; all rooms have working fireplaces.

Breakfast is served in a domed ceiling dining room. ✉ *392 Thames St., 02840* ☎ *401/846–0392 or 800/846–0392* 🖷 *401/848–5956* ⊕ *www. malbone.com* ⇨ *17 rooms, 3 suites* ⚄ *In-room hot tubs, free parking* ▭ *AE, MC, V* ⦿❘ *BP.*

$$$$ ⛉ **Hotel Viking.** The elegant redbrick Hotel Viking, built in 1926, stands at the north end of Bellevue Avenue. The wood paneling and chandeliers evoke the hotel's sophisticated history. The stately rooms, adorned with reproduction Colonial furniture and appointments, resemble the homes of Colonial merchant seamen. One Bellevue Restaurant serves fresh seafood and afternoon tea service; Top of the Viking, a rooftop bar, is open in summer; Spa Terre provides Thai and Indonesian massage and body treatments. ✉ *1 Bellevue Ave., 02840* ☎ *401/ 847–3300 or 800/556–7126* 🖷 *401/848–4864* ⊕ *www.hotelviking. com* ⇨ *214 rooms, 8 suites* ⚄ *Restaurant, refrigerators, in-room VCRs, indoor pool, hot tub, sauna, spa, bar, meeting rooms* ▭ *AE, D, DC, MC, V.*

$$$$ ⛉ **Hyatt Regency Newport.** On Goat Island across from the Colonial Point district, the Hyatt has great views of the harbor and the Newport Bridge. Most rooms have water views. Although the hotel is a 10-minute walk to the center of Newport, bike and moped rentals are nearby. All rooms are decorated with light wood and dark granite-top furniture. The outdoor restaurant, Pineapples, is a little-known spot to watch the sunset in summer. ✉ *1 Goat Island, 02840* ☎ *401/851–1234* 🖷 *401/846–7210* ⊕ *www.hyatt.com* ⇨ *264 rooms* ⚄ *2 restaurants, tennis court, indoor pool, saltwater pool, health club, hair salon, sauna, spa, boating, racquetball, meeting rooms* ▭ *AE, D, DC, MC, V.*

$$$$ ⛉ **Vanderbilt Hall.** Built in 1909 as the Newport Men's Social Club, a Vanderbilt family gift to the Newport townspeople, this was turned into a YMCA during the Great Depression. It became a sophisticated inn with European flair in the 1990s and was closed during the first half of 2006 for further renovations meant, among other changes, to reduce the number of guestrooms by almost half. At the time of this writing, the ultimate disposition of the public rooms—until now furnished with antiques and oil paintings and looking as though the Vanderbilts might feel at home in them—was uncertain, as was whether the classy billiard room would turn into a spa, whether the martini bar would remain, and what the restaurant service would be. Most recently, an "anytime menu" of burgers, chicken, and a Caribbean jerk skewer, was served from noon to 10, with roast beef and lobster added on weekends. ✉ *41 Mary St., 02840* ☎ *401/846–6200* 🖷 *401/846–0701* ⊕ *www. vanderbilthall.com* ⇨ *30 rooms* ⚄ *Restaurant, microwaves, refrigerators, in-room data ports, indoor pool, sauna, billiards, bar; no smoking* ▭ *AE, D, MC, V.*

$$$–$$$$ ⛉ **Newport Marriott.** A light-filled atrium lobby with marble floors and a nautical theme unfolds as you enter this luxury hotel on the harbor at Long Wharf. Rooms overlook the atrium, city, or waterfront. Fifth-floor rooms facing the harbor have sliding French windows that open onto large decks. Rates vary greatly according to season and location; concierge and harbor-view rooms cost more. ✉ *25 America's Cup Ave., 02840* ☎ *401/ 849–1000 or 800/228–9290* 🖷 *401/849–3422* ⊕ *www.newportmarriott.*

com ⤳ *312 rooms, 7 suites* ⓑ *Restaurant, café, cable TV, indoor pool, health club, hot tub, sauna, racquetball, bar, laundry facilities, Internet room, meeting rooms, parking (fee)* ☰ *AE, D, DC, MC, V.*

$$–$$$$ ▦ **Admiral Fitzroy Inn.** This tidy 1854 Victorian provides a restful retreat in the heart of Newport's bustling waterfront district. Period antiques decorate the rooms, each of which has either an antique brass or hand-carved wood bed. All rooms have access to the rooftop deck with a view of the harbor. Two rooms have semiprivate decks and hot tubs. The inn's namesake, Admiral Fitzroy, commanded the *Beagle,* whose most famous passenger was Charles Darwin. ✉ *398 Thames St., 02840* ☎ *866/848–8780* 📠 *401/848–8006* ⊕ *www.admiralfitzroy.com* ⤳ *17 rooms* ⓑ *Refrigerators, cable TV, free parking* ☰ *AE, D, MC, V* ⦿ *CP.*

Nightlife & the Arts

Detailed events calendars can be found in *Newport This Week* and the *Newport Daily News.*

NIGHTLIFE   For a sampling of Newport's lively nightlife, you need only stroll down **Thames Street** after dark.

Aidan's Pub (✉ 1 Broadway ☎ 401/845–9311) occasionally hosts live Irish music. The **Candy Store** (✉ Bannister's Wharf ☎ 401/849–2900) in the Clarke Cooke House is a snazzy place for a drink. If you're up for dancing, head downstairs to the Boom Boom Room.

Newport Blues Café (✉ 286 Thames St. ☎ 401/841–5510), housed in a former bank, hosts great blues performers. **One Pelham East** (✉ 270 Thames St. ☎ 401/847–9460) draws a young crowd for live rock bands.

POP (✉ 162 Broadway ☎ 401/846–8456) is a martini/tapas bar, where a DJ spins on weekends.

Salvation Café (✉ 140 Broadway ☎ 401/847–2620), a funky, kitchy, eclectically decorated, happening spot, is popular with the local thirtysomethings. The tiki bar out back is open in summer.

The **JVC Newport Jazz Festival** (☎ 401/847–3700) takes place in mid-August at Fort Adams State Park. Performers have included Ray Charles, Dave Brubeck, Cassandra Wilson, Natalie Cole, Wynton Marsalis, Harry Connick Jr., and Ornette Coleman.

THE ARTS   Murder-mystery plays are performed on Thursday evenings at 8 PM from July to late October at **Astors' Beechwood** (✉ 580 Bellevue Ave. ☎ 401/846–3772); on Tuesday at 7, July through September, members of the Beechwood Theatre Company sing and dance in a mock 1920s-style speakeasy. The **Newport International Film Festival** (☎ 401/846–9100 ⊕ www.newportfilmfestival.com), an impressive six-day event, takes place at the beginning of June at the Jane Pickens Theater and other venues. **Newport Playhouse & Cabaret** (✉ 102 Connell Hwy. ☎ 401/848–7529) stages comedies and musicals; dinner packages are available.

Sports & the Outdoors

BEACHES   **Easton's Beach** (✉ Memorial Blvd.), also known as First Beach, is popular for its 50¢ carousel rides, aquarium, and playground. **Fort Adams State Park** (✉ Ocean Dr.), a small beach with a picnic area and lifeguards in summer, has views of Newport Harbor and is fully sheltered from ocean swells. **Sachuest Beach,** or Second Beach, east of First Beach in the Sachuest Point area of Middletown, is a beautiful, long, sandy beach adjacent to the Norman Bird Sanctuary. Dunes and a campground make it popular with young travelers and families. **Third Beach,** in the Sachuest Point area of Middletown, is on the Sakonnet River. It has a boat ramp and is a favorite of windsurfers.

BIKING   The 12-mi swing down Bellevue Avenue, along Ocean Drive and back, is a great route to ride your wheels. **Ten Speed Spokes** (⊠18 Elm St. ☎401/847–5609 ⊕ www.tenspeedspokes.com) rents specialized comfort bikes for $25 per day.

BOATING   **Adventure Sports** (⊠Behind Inn at Long Wharf ☎401/849–4820 ⊕www.newportwatersports.com) rents kayaks, outboard boats, and Wave Runners. **Oldport Marine Services** (⊠ Sayer's Wharf ☎ 401/847–9109) operates harbor tours and daily and weekly crewed yacht charters, rents moorings, and provides launch services. **Sail Newport** (⊠ 60 Ft. Adams Rd., Ft. Adams State Park ☎ 401/846–1983 ⊕ www.sailnewport.org) rents sailboats by the hour and provides lessons.

DIVING   **Newport Diving Center** (⊠ 550 Thames St. ☎ 401/847–9293 ⊕ www.newportdivingcenter.com) operates charter dive trips, refills Nitrox, conducts PADI training and certification, and has rentals, sales, and service.

FISHING   **Fishin' Off** (☎ 401/683–5557) runs charter-fishing trips on a 36-foot Trojan. The **Saltwater Edge** (⊠ 561 Thames St. ☎ 401/842–0062 ⊕ www.saltwateredge.com) sells fly-fishing and surf-casting tackle, gives lessons, and conducts guided trips. **Sam's Bait & Tackle** (⊠ 936 Aquidneck Ave. ☎ 401/849–5909) stocks gear and live bait.

Shopping

Many of Newport's shops and art and crafts galleries are on Thames Street, Spring Street, and at Bowen's and Bannister's wharves. The Brick Market area—between Thames Street and America's Cup Avenue—has more than 40 shops. Bellevue Avenue just south of Memorial Boulevard (near the International Tennis Hall of Fame) contains a strip of pricey shops with high-quality merchandise.

ANTIQUES   **Aardvark Antiques** (⊠ 9 Connell Hwy ☎ 401/849–7233) carries architectural pieces such as mantels, doors, and stained glass, plus fountains and garden statuary. The 125 dealers at the **Armory** (⊠ 365 Thames St. ☎ 401/848–2398), a vast 19th-century structure, carry antiques, china, and estate jewelry. **Harbor Antiques** (⊠ 134 Spring St. ☎ 401/848–9711) stocks unusual furniture, prints, and glassware.

ART & CRAFTS GALLERIES   **Arnold Art Store and Gallery** (⊠210 Thames St. ☎401/847–2273 ⊕www.arnoldart.com) collects marine-inspired paintings and prints. **DeBlois Gallery** (⊠138 Bellevue Ave. ☎401/847–9977 ⊕www.debloisgallery.com) exhibits the works of Newport's emerging artists. **MacDowell Pottery** (⊠138 Spring St. ☎401/846–6313) showcases the wares of New England potters. **Spring Bull Gallery** (⊠ 55 Bellevue Ave. ☎ 401/849–9166 ⊕ www.springbullgallery.com), an artists' cooperative, displays diverse local art. The delicate, dramatic blown-glass gifts at **Thames Glass** (⊠688 Thames St. ☎401/

846–0576 ⊕www.thamesglass.com) are designed by Matthew Buechner and created in the adjacent studio. **William Vareika Fine Arts** (⊠212 Bellevue Ave. ☎401/849–6149 ⊕www.vareikafinearts.com) exhibits and sells American paintings and prints from the 18th to the 20th century.

BEACH GEAR **Water Brothers** (⊠ 38 Broadway ☎401/849–4990) is the place to go for surf supplies, including bathing suits, wet suits, sunscreen, sunglasses, and surfboards.

BOOKS The **Armchair Sailor** (⊠ 543 Thames St. ☎401/847–4252) stocks marine and travel books, charts, and maps.

CLOTHING **Cathers & Coyne** (⊠ 18 Bowen's Wharf ☎401/849–5757) carries hot shoes for cool people. **JT's Chandlery** (⊠ 364 Thames St. ☎401/846–7256) stocks clothing, marine hardware, and equipment.

Karol Richardson (⊠ 24 Washington Sq. ☎401/849–6612 ⊕ www.karolrichardson.com) sells upscale, hip contemporary women's clothing and accessories. **Michael Hayes** (⊠202 and 204 Bellevue Ave. ☎401/846–3090) sells fine clothing for men, women, and children.

JEWELRY **Suydam & Diepenbrock** (⊠ 9 Bridge St. ☎401/848–9090) sells jewelry, functional art, and sculpture. Didi Suydam's jewelry work is contemporary yet classic. **Three Golden Apples** (⊠ 140 Bellevue Ave ☎401/846–9930) sells high-end jewelry.

Portsmouth

 11 mi north of Newport.

Portsmouth is now mainly a bedroom community for professionals who work in other parts of Rhode Island and Massachusetts. Its founder was Anne Hutchinson, a religious dissident and one of the country's first feminists, who led a group of settlers to the area in 1638 after being banished from the Massachusetts Bay Colony.

☘ **Green Animals Topiary Garden,** a large topiary garden on a Victorian estate, contains more than 80 shrubs sculpted in a variety of shapes including animals and geometric designs; among the oldest, begun before 1920, are an elephant, a camel, and a giraffe. Also here are flower gardens, winding pathways, a variety of trees, and the 1872 estate house, which displays original family furnishings and an antique toy collection. ⊠ *Cory's La. off Rte. 114* ☎ *401/847–1000* ⊕ *www.newportmansions. org* ⚄ *$10* ☉ *Mid-May–Oct., daily 10–5.*

Sports & the Outdoors

Sandy Point Beach (⊠ Sandy Point Ave.) is a choice spot for families and beginning windsurfers because of the calm surf along the Sakonnet River.

Little Compton

19 mi southeast of Portsmouth.

The rolling estates, lovely homes, farmlands, woods, and gentle western shoreline make Little Compton one of the Ocean State's prettiest areas. Little Compton and Tiverton were part of Massachusetts until

1747—to this day, residents here often have more roots in Massachusetts than in Rhode Island. "Keep Little Compton little" is a popular sentiment, but considering the town's remoteness and its steep land prices, there may not be all that much to worry about.

Little Compton Commons (⊠ Meetinghouse La.) is the epitome of a New England town square. As white as the clouds above, the spire of the Georgian-style United Congregational Church rises over the tops of adjacent oak trees. Within the triangular lawn is a cemetery with Colonial headstones, among them that of Elizabeth Padobie, said to be the first white girl born in New England. Surrounding the green is a rock wall and all the elements of a small community: town hall, community center, police station, and school.

A neatly kept relic of Rhode Island living, the 1680 **Wilbor House** was occupied by eight generations of Wilbors, the first of which included 11 children born between 1690 and 1712. Curiously, later generations used a half dozen variations on the spelling of the same last name. Rooms reflect life during the 17th, 18th, and 19th centuries. Other preserved buildings on the grounds include a carriage house with restored sleighs and coaches, a one-room schoolhouse, and two barns packed with an extraordinary array of historical objects. ⊠ 548 W. Main Rd. (Rte. 77) ☎ 401/635–4035 ➣ $5 ۞ Late June–Sept., Thurs.–Sun. 1–5; Oct., weekends 1–5.

Sakonnet Point, a surreal spit of land, reaches out toward three tiny islands. The point begins where Route 77 ends. The ½-mi hike to the tip of the spit passes tide pools, a beach composed of tiny stones, and outcroppings that recall the surface of the moon. Parking is sometimes available in the lot adjacent to Sakonnet Harbor.

Tours and tastings are free at **Sakonnet Vineyard,** New England's largest winery. Varietals include chardonnay, pinot noir, cabernet franc, and vidal blanc. ⊠ 162 W. Main Rd. ☎ 401/635–8486 ⊕ www.sakonnetwine. com ➣ Free ۞ Memorial Day–Oct., daily 10–6; Nov.–Memorial Day, daily 11–5.

HIKING **Wilbur Woods** (⊠ Swamp Rd.), a 30-acre hollow with picnic tables and a waterfall, is a good place for a casual hike. A trail winds along and over Dundery Brook.

Newport County A to Z

To research prices, get advice from other travelers, and book travel arrangements, visit www.fodors.com.

AIRPORTS & TRANSFERS
Newport State Airport is 3 mi northeast of Newport in Middletown. Charters fly from here to T. F. Green Airport in Warwick, south of Providence.

🚹 Airport Information **Newport State Airport** ☎ 401/846–9400.

Cozy Cab runs a shuttle service ($20) between T. F. Green Airport and the Newport Visitors' Information Center, as well as major hotels.

🚖 Taxi **Cozy Cab** ☎ 401/846-2500 or 800/846-1502.

BOAT & FERRY TRAVEL

The Jamestown and Newport Ferry Co. runs a passenger ferry about every 1½ hours from Newport's Bowen's Landing and Long Wharf (and, on request, Fort Adams and Goat Island) to Jamestown's Ferry Wharf. The ferry operates from Memorial Day to mid-October. Oldport Marine Company operates a water-taxi service for boaters in Newport Harbor.

🚢 Boat & Ferry Information **Jamestown and Newport Ferry Co.** ☎ 401/423-9900. **Oldport Marine Services** ☎ 401/847-9109.

BUS TRAVEL

Rhode Island Public Transit Authority buses connect Providence with Newport and also serve the city from other Rhode Island destinations.

🚌 Bus Information **Rhode Island Public Transit Authority** (RIPTA) ☎ 401/847-0209, 800/244-0444 in Rhode Island ⊕ www.ripta.com.

CAR TRAVEL

From Providence take Interstate 95 east into Massachusetts and head south on Route 24. From South County, take U.S. 1 north to Route 138 east. From Boston take Interstate 93 south to Route 24 south.

EMERGENCIES

🏥 Hospital **Newport Hospital** ✉ Friendship St., Newport ☎ 401/846-6400.

💊 Pharmacy **Walgreens Pharmacy** ✉ 12 E. Main Rd., Newport ☎ 401/847-8510.

LODGING

🏨 Local Agent **Newport Reservations** ✉ 174 Bellevue Ave. ☎ 800/842-0102 ⊕ www. newportreservations.com. Also visit www.gonewport.com, and click on "Where to Stay." This provides links to most Newport area hotels, inns, and B&Bs, as well as timeshares and camping/RV facilities.

TOURS

More than a dozen yacht companies operate tours of Narragansett Bay and Newport Harbor. Outings usually last 2 hours and cost about $25 per person. *Flyer Sailing,* a 57-foot catamaran, departs from Long Wharf. *Madeline,* a 72-foot schooner, departs from Bannister's Wharf. *RumRunner II,* a vintage 1929 motor yacht, once carried "hooch"; it leaves from Bannister's Wharf. *Sightsailing* departs from Bowen's Wharf and has three boats available for 1¼-hour tours of Newport Harbor and Narragansett Bay. The *Spirit of Newport,* a 200-passenger multideck ship, departs for tours of Narragansett Bay and Newport Harbor from the Newport Harbor Hotel, on America's Cup Avenue, from May to mid-October.

Viking Tours of Newport conducts trolley tours of Newport daily from May through October and on Saturdays the rest of the year; one-hour boat tours of Narragansett Bay operate from mid-May to Columbus Day weekend. The Newport Historical Society sponsors walking tours focusing on varying themes from April through December.

The Old Colony & Newport Railway follows an 8-mi route along Narragansett Bay. The vintage diesel train and coaches make 80-minute round-trips to Middletown on Sunday at 11:45 and 1:45.

🔲 Tour Operators **Flyer Sailing** ☎ 401/848-2100. **Madeleine** ☎ 401/847-0298. **Newport Historical Society** ✉ 82 Touro St., Newport ☎ 401/846-0813 ⊕ www.newporthistorical.org. **Old Colony & Newport Railway** ✉ 19 America's Cup Ave., Newport ☎ 401/849-0546 ⊕ www.ocnrr.com. **RumRunner II** ☎ 401/847-0299. **Sightsailing of Newport** ☎ 401/849-3333 or 800/709-7245 ⊕ www.sightsailing.com. **Spirit of Newport** ☎ 401/849-3575. **Viking Tours of Newport** ✉ Newport Visitors' Information Center, 23 America's Cup Ave., Newport ☎ 401/847-6921 ⊕ www.vikingtoursnewport.com.

VISITOR INFORMATION
Newport Visitors' Information Center has a welcome video and provides maps and advice.

🔲 Tourist Information **Newport County Convention and Visitors Bureau** ✉ Newport Visitors' Information Center, 23 America's Cup Ave., Newport ☎ 401/845-9123 or 800/326-6030 ⊕ www.gonewport.com.

RHODE ISLAND A TO Z

To research prices, get advice from other travelers, and book travel arrangements, visit www.fodors.com.

AIRPORTS
T. F. Green Airport, 10 mi south of Providence, has scheduled daily flights by several major airlines, including American, Delta, Northwest, Southwest, United, and US Air, with additional service by regional carriers. Westerly, Newport, and Block Island airports are the main regional airports in Rhode Island.

🔲 Airport Information **T. F. Green Airport** ✉ U.S. 1 (Exit 13 off I-95), Warwick ☎ 401/737-8222 or 888/268-7222.

BUS TRAVEL
Bonanza Bus Lines, Greyhound, and Peter Pan Bus Lines serve the Providence Bus Terminal. A shuttle service connects the Providence Bus Terminal with Kennedy Plaza in downtown Providence, where you can board the local public transit buses. Rhode Island Public Transit Authority buses crisscross the state.

🔲 Bus Information **Bonanza Bus Lines** ☎ 800/556-3815 ⊕ www.bonanzabus.com. **Greyhound** ☎ 800/231-2222. **Peter Pan Bus Lines** ☎ 800/237-8747 ⊕ www.peterpanbus.com. **Providence Bus Terminal** ✉ Bonanza Way off Exit 25 from I-95, Providence ☎ 401/751-8800 ✉ Kennedy Plaza, Washington and Dorrance Sts., Providence. **Rhode Island Public Transit Authority** (RIPTA) ☎ 401/781-9400, 800/244-0444 in Rhode Island ⊕ www.ripta.com.

CAR TRAVEL
Interstate 95, which cuts diagonally across the state, is the fastest route to Providence from Boston, coastal Connecticut, and New York City. Interstate 195 southeast from Providence leads to New Bedford, Massachusetts, and Cape Cod. Route 146 northwest from Providence leads

to Worcester and Interstate 90, passing through the northeastern portion of the Blackstone Valley. U.S. 1 follows much of the Rhode Island coast east from Connecticut before turning north to Providence. Route 138 heads east from Route 1 to Jamestown, Newport, and Portsmouth, in easternmost Rhode Island.

The speed limit on interstate highways varies from 55 mph to 65 mph; state routes vary, with 55 mph the top speed. Right turns are permitted on red lights after stopping, except in downtown Providence. Free state maps are available at all chambers of commerce and at visitor information centers in Providence and Newport and at T. F. Green Airport. The detailed *Street Atlas Rhode Island*, published by Arrow Map, Inc., is available at many bookstores and gas stations.

EMERGENCIES
🔳 Ambulance, fire, police ☎ 911.

SPORTS & THE OUTDOORS
For information on pricing and where to buy licenses for freshwater fishing, contact the Department of Environmental Management's Division of Licensing. No license is needed for saltwater fishing.

One of the best trail guides for the region is the *AMC Massachusetts and Rhode Island Trail Guide,* available at local outdoors shops or from the Appalachian Mountain Club. The Rhode Island Audubon Society leads interesting hikes and field expeditions around the state.
🔳 **Appalachian Mountain Club (AMC)** ⊠ 5 Joy St., Boston, MA 02114 ☎ 617/523-0636 ⊕ www.amcnarragansett.org. **Department of Environmental Management's Division of Licensing** ☎ 401/222-3576. **Rhode Island Audubon Society** ⊠ 12 Sanderson Rd., Smithfield 02917 ☎ 401/949-5454 ⊕ www.asri.org.

TRAIN TRAVEL
Amtrak service between New York City and Boston makes stops at Westerly, Kingston, and Providence. Providence Station is the city's main station. The Massachusetts Bay Transportation Authority (MBTA) commuter rail service connects Boston and Providence during weekday morning and evening rush hours for about half the cost of an Amtrak ride.
🔳 Train Information **Amtrak** ☎ 800/872-7245 ⊕ www.amtrak.com. **MBTA** ☎ 617/722-3200 ⊕ www.mbta.com. **Providence Station** ⊠ 100 Gaspee St., Providence ☎ 401/727-7379.

VISITOR INFORMATION
🔳 Tourist Information **Rhode Island Department of Economic Development, Tourism Division** ⊠ 1 W. Exchange St., Providence 02903 ☎ 401/222-2601 (ask to be transferred to Tourism Division), 800/556-2484 ⊕ www.visitrhodeisland.com.

Connecticut

WORD OF MOUTH

"Litchfield is a garden tour of itself, with lovely gardens, old homes, antiques, and quaint restaurants."
—LilMsfoodie

"Mystic Seaport is a great stop, especially with kids. It's a replication of an 1800s whaling village and has some really cool exhibits. It's also a working village and you can stop in at a blacksmith's to see how things were done back then."
—sjk

Updated by
Michelle
Bodak Acri

CONNECTICUT MAY BE the third-smallest state in the nation, but it is among the hardest to define. Indeed, you can travel from any point in the Nutmeg State, as it is known, to any other in less than two hours, yet the land you traverse—fewer than 60 mi top to bottom and 100 mi across—is as varied as a drive across the country. Connecticut's 253 mi of shoreline blows salty sea air over such beach communities as Old Lyme and Stonington. Patchwork hills and peaked mountains fill the state's northwestern corner, and once-upon-a-time mill towns line its rivers such as the Housatonic. Connecticut has seemingly endless farmland in the northeast, where cows just might outnumber people, as well as chic New York City bedroom communities such as Greenwich and New Canaan, where boutique shopping bags seem to be the dominant species. Unique as each section is, each defines Connecticut.

Just as diverse as the landscape are the state's residents, who numbered close to 3.5 million at last count. There really is no such thing as the definitive Connecticut Yankee, however. Yes, families can trace their roots back to the 1600s, when Connecticut was founded as one of the 13 original colonies, but the state motto is also "He who transplanted still sustains." And so the face of the Nutmegger is that of the family from Naples now making pizza in New Haven and the farmer in Norfolk whose land dates back five generations, the grandmother in New Britain who makes the state's best pierogi and the ladies who lunch in Westport, not to mention the celebrity nestled in the Litchfield Hills and the Bridgeport entrepreneur working to close the gap between Connecticut's struggling cities and its affluent suburbs.

A unifying characteristic of the Connecticut Yankee, however, is a propensity for inventiveness. You might say that Nutmeggers have been setting trends for centuries. They are historically known for both their intellectual abilities and their desire to have a little fun. As evidence of the former, consider that the nation's first public library was opened in New Haven in 1656 and its first statehouse built in Hartford in 1776; Tapping Reeve opened the first law school in Litchfield in 1784; and West Hartford's Noah Webster published the first dictionary in 1806. As proof of the latter, note that Lake Compounce in Bristol was the country's first amusement park; Bethel's P. T. Barnum staged the first three-ring circus; and the hamburger, the lollipop, the Frisbee, and the Erector set were all invented within the state's 5,009 square mi.

Not surprisingly, Nutmeggers have a healthy respect for their history. For decades, Mystic Seaport, which traces the state's rich maritime past, has been the premier tourist attraction. Today, however, slot machines in casinos in the southeastern woods are giving the sailing ships a run for their money. Foxwoods Casino near Ledyard, run by the Mashantucket Pequots, is the world's largest casino—it draws more than 40,000 visitors per day—and the Mohegan Sun Casino in nearby Uncasville is working hard to catch up. Thanks in large part to these lures, not to mention rich cultural attractions, cutting-edge restaurants, shopping outlets, first-rate lodgings, and abundant natural beauty (including 92 state parks and 30 state forests), tourism is now the state's

GREAT ITINERARIES

The Nutmeg State is a confluence of different worlds, where farm country meets country homes, and fans of the New York Yankees meet Down-Easter Yankees. To get the best sense of this variety, start in the scenic Litchfield Hills, where you can see historic town greens and trendy cafés juxtaposed in a way that's uniquely Connecticut. If you have a bit more time, head south to the wealthy southwestern corner of the state and then over to New Haven, with its cultural pleasures. If you have five days or a week, take in the capital city of Hartford and the surrounding towns of the Connecticut River valley and head down to the southeastern shoreline. If you have kids or an interest in the sea, Mystic alone could occupy a few days.

IF YOU HAVE 1 DAY

Begin a day in the Litchfield Hills in **New Preston**㉔ and then head for Lake Waramaug. In West Cornwall, near **Cornwall**㉖, have a look at the state's largest covered bridge. Turning south, spend a couple of hours in **Litchfield**㉙, where you can have lunch and tour historic houses before continuing south via **Bethlehem**㉛ to **Woodbury**㉝ to visit the town's churches and antiques shops.

IF YOU HAVE 2 DAYS

Old Saybrook㊸, once a lively shipbuilding and fishing town, is a picture-perfect example of the Connecticut shoreline. Start your day here with some shopping on Main Street or a stroll along the coastline. Next, head across the Connecticut River to **Old Lyme**㊹, home to the Florence Griswold Museum, where members of the Old Lyme ·

Impressionist Art Colony once lived and painted *en plein air*. Continue up the coast, stopping if you like in **Groton**㊽ to see the world's first nuclear-powered submarine and the Submarine Force Museum. On your way to **Mystic**㊾, stop in Noank for a late lunch or early dinner of lobster-in-the-rough seated at a picnic table at the edge of Noank Harbor. End your day in Mystic, where you'll find a wide assortment of hotels, inns, and restaurants to choose from. You won't have far to travel on Day 2: in Mystic, a visit to the highly esteemed Mystic Seaport and Mystic Aquarium and Institute for Exploration can easily fill your day. Afterward, if you have the stamina, head inland to **Ledyard**㊼ and try your luck at Foxwoods Resort Casino's 6,400-plus slot machines.

IF YOU HAVE 3 DAYS

Greenwich①, a wealthy community with grand homes and great restaurants, is a good starting point for a several-day tour that begins near New York. From here head to **Stamford**②, where you can visit the Stamford Museum and Nature Center or hit the mall. East along the coast is **Norwalk**③, whose SoNo commercial district and Maritime Aquarium are popular attractions. Have dinner in **Westport**⑤, and end your first day in ▦ **Ridgefield**④. After touring Ridgefield the next morning, head for the Litchfield Hills, driving north via **Cornwall**㉖ to **Norfolk**㉗. Then it's south to **Litchfield**㉙ and ▦ **New Preston**㉔, where you may want to conclude your day. If not, travel a little farther south to charming ▦ **Washington**㉜. Begin Day 3 in **Woodbury**㉝ and then head to **New Haven**㊱ –㊵.

second leading industry. Anyone who has explored even part of Connecticut will discover that a small state can be big in its appeal.

Exploring Connecticut

Southwestern Connecticut contains the wealthy coastal communities. Moving east of them along the coast (in most states you travel north or south along the coast, but in Connecticut you actually travel east or west), you come to New Haven and the southeastern coast, which is broken by many small bays and inlets. Northeast Connecticut's Quiet Corner, bordered by Rhode Island to the east and Massachusetts to the north, provides a tranquil countryside with rolling hills. West of it are the fertile farmlands of the Connecticut River valley and the state's capital, Hartford. In the northwestern part of the state is the Litchfield Hills area, covered with miles of forests, lakes, and rivers.

Numbers in the text and in the margin correspond to numbers on the maps: Southwestern Connecticut, Connecticut River Valley, Downtown Hartford, Litchfield Hills, Southeastern Connecticut, Downtown New Haven, and the Quiet Corner.

About the Restaurants

Call it the fennel factor or the arugula influx: southern New England has witnessed a gastronomic revolution. Preparation and ingredients reflect the culinary trends of nearby Manhattan and Boston; indeed, the quality and diversity of Connecticut restaurants now rival those of such sophisticated metropolitan areas. Although traditional favorites remain—such as New England clam chowder, buttery lobster rolls, Yankee pot roast, and fish-and-chips—Grand Marnier is now favored on ice cream over hot fudge sauce; sliced duck is wrapped in phyllo and served with a ginger-plum sauce (the orange glaze decidedly absent); and everything from lavender to fresh figs is used to season and complement dishes. Dining is increasingly international: you'll find Indian, Vietnamese, Thai, Malaysian, South American, and Japanese restaurants—even Spanish tapas bars—in cities and suburbs. Designer martinis are quite the rage, brewpubs have popped up around the state—even caviar is making a comeback. The one drawback of this turn toward sophistication is that finding an under-$10 dinner entrée is difficult.

	WHAT IT COSTS				
	$$$$	**$$$**	**$$**	**$**	**¢**
AT DINNER	over $28	$21–$28	$13–$20	$8–$12	under $8

Prices are per person, for a main course at dinner.

About the Hotels

Connecticut has plenty of business-oriented chain hotels and low-budget motels, along with many of the more unusual and atmospheric inns, resorts, bed-and-breakfasts, and country hotels that are typical of New England. You'll pay dearly for rooms in summer on the coast and in autumn in the hills, where thousands of visitors peek at the changing fo-

PLEASURES & PASTIMES

ANTIQUING

Although you'll find everything from chic boutiques to vast outlet malls in Connecticut, the state is an antiquer's paradise. The Litchfield Hills region, in the state's northwest corner, is the heart of antiques country. The Quiet Corner, east of the Connecticut River, runs a close second, with several hundred dealers and complexes. Mystic, Old Saybrook, Essex, and other towns along the coast are filled with markets, galleries, and shops, many specializing in antique prints, maps, books, and collectibles.

FISHING

Connecticut teems with possibilities for anglers, from deep-sea fishing in coastal waters to fly-fishing in the state's many streams. Try the Litchfield Hills region for freshwater fish: if you're just a beginner, don't fret—you'll be catching trout or bass in the Housatonic River in no time. Southeastern Connecticut is the charter- and party-boat capital of the state. Charter-fishing boats take passengers out on Long Island Sound for half-day, full-day, and overnight trips.

STATE PARKS

Sixty percent of Connecticut is forest land, some of it under the jurisdiction of the state parks division, which also manages several beaches on the southern shoreline. Many parks have campgrounds. Trails meander through most of the parks—the hiking is especially spectacular around the cool clear water at Lake Waramaug State Park and the 200-foot-high waterfall at Kent Falls State Park. Popular Gillette Castle State Park in East Haddam has

several trails, some on former railroad beds. Some state parks have no entrance fees year-round. At others the fee varies ($5–$14), depending on the time of year, day of the week, and whether or not your car bears a Connecticut license plate.

6

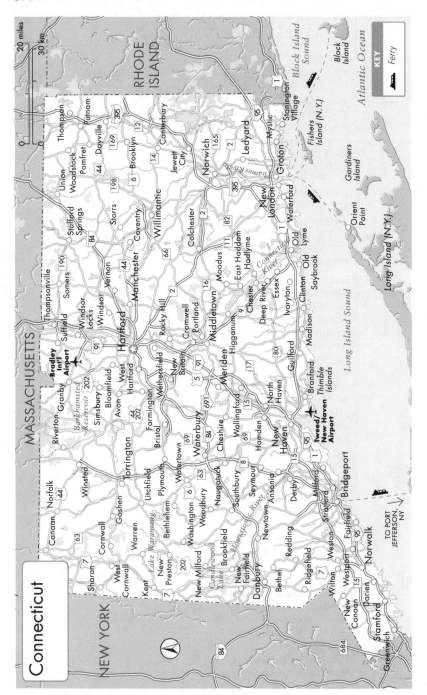

Connecticut

liage. Rates are lowest in winter, but so are the temperatures, making spring the best time for bargain seekers to visit.

WHAT IT COSTS				
$$$$	$$$	$$	$	¢
FOR 2 PEOPLE over $220	$171–$220	$121–$170	$80–$120	under $80

Prices are for a standard double room during peak season and not including tax or gratuities. Some inns add a 15% service charge.

Timing

Connecticut is lovely year-round, but fall and spring are particularly appealing times to visit. A fall drive along the state's back roads or the Merritt Parkway (a National Scenic Byway) is a memorable experience. Leaves of yellow, orange, and red color the fall landscape, but the state blooms in springtime, too—town greens are painted with daffodils and tulips, and blooming trees punctuate the rich green countryside. Many attractions that close in winter reopen in April or May. Summer, of course, is prime time for most attractions; travelers have the most options then but also plenty of company, especially along the shore.

SOUTHWESTERN CONNECTICUT

Southwestern Connecticut is a rich swirl of old New England and new New York. This region consistently reports the highest cost of living and most expensive homes of any area in the country. Its bedroom towns are home primarily to white-collar executives; some still make the hour-plus dash to and from New York, but most enjoy a more civilized morning drive to Stamford, which is reputed to have more corporate headquarters per square mile than any other U.S. city.

Venture away from the wealthy communities, and you'll discover cities struggling in different stages of urban renewal: Stamford, Norwalk, Bridgeport, and Danbury. These four have some of the region's best cultural and shopping opportunities, but the economic disparity between Connecticut's troubled cities and its upscale towns is perhaps nowhere more visible than in Fairfield County.

Greenwich

❶ *28 mi northeast of New York City, 64 mi southwest of Hartford.*

You'll have no trouble believing that Greenwich is one of the wealthiest towns in the United States when you drive along U.S. 1 (called Route 1 by the locals, as well as West Putnam Avenue, East Putnam Avenue, and the Post Road, among other monikers), where the streets are lined with ritzy car dealers, posh boutiques, oh-so-chic restaurants, and well-heeled, well-to-do residents clearly pleased to be able to call Greenwich "home." The median price of a house sold in Greenwich topped $1.5 million in 2004; the average was closer to $2 million. In other words, bring your charge cards.

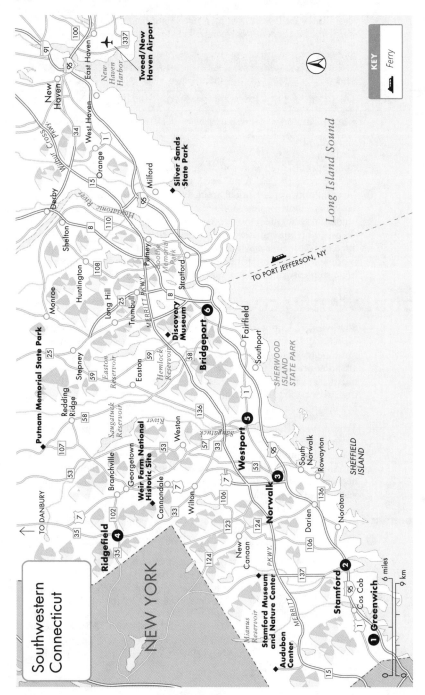

Southwestern Connecticut

NEW YORK

Long Island Sound

TO PORT JEFFERSON, NY

KEY

⛴ Ferry

Tweed/New Haven Airport

New Haven Harbor

New Haven

East Haven

West Haven

Orange

Milford

Silver Sands State Park

Derby

Shelton

Monroe

Huntington

Long Hill

Trumbull

Putney

Booth Memorial Park

Stratford

Discovery Museum

Bridgeport 6

Fairfield

Southport

SHERWOOD ISLAND STATE PARK

SHEFFIELD ISLAND

Stepney

Easton

Weston

Westport 5

South Norwalk

Rowayton

Putnam Memorial State Park

Redding Ridge

Branchville

Georgetown

Weir Farm National Historic Site

Cannondale

Wilton

Norwalk 3

Darien

Noroton

Ridgefield 4

New Canaan

Stamford 2

Stamford Museum and Nature Center

Audubon Center

Greenwich 1

Cos Cob

MERRITT PKWY.

WILBUR CROSS PKWY.

MERRITT PKWY.

Housatonic River

Saugatuck River

Saugatuck Reservoir

Easton Reservoir

Hemlock Reservoir

Mianus Reservoir

TO DANBURY

0   6 miles

0   9 km

The **Audubon Center** in northern Greenwich was established in 1942 as the National Audubon Society's first nature-education facility. A prime hawk-watching site—directly on the East Coast flyway—more than a dozen species have been spotted migrating during the Fall Hawkwatch Festival. Other annual events are the Spring into Audubon Festival and the summer and Christmas bird counts. Not only is the center filled with "real-life" interactive exhibits, galleries, and classrooms, but also observation decks that offer sweeping views of wildlife activity, a wildlife observation room with solar-powered video technology, and a 144-person capacity lecture hall. Outside, the sanctuary includes protected wildlife habitats and 10 mi of hiking trails on 285 acres of woodland, wetland, and meadow. ⊠ *613 Riversville Rd.* ☎ *203/869–5272* ⊕ *www.greenwich.center.audubon.org* ⊡ *$3* ☉ *Daily 9–5.*

The **Bruce Museum of Arts and Science** was built in 1853 as a private home. In 1908, its owner, wealthy textile merchant Robert Moffat Bruce, bequeathed it to the town of Greenwich with the stipulation that it be used "as a natural history, historical and art museum, for the use and benefit of the public." Today this diversity remains reflected in the museum's collection of some 15,000 objects in fine and decorative arts, natural history, and anthropology—including paintings by Childe Hassam, sculptures by Auguste Rodin and George Segal, and stained glass by Louis Comfort Tiffany and Dale Chihuly—from which the museum selects items for changing exhibitions. Permanently on display, however, is the spectacular mineral collection. Kids enjoy viewing the wiggly creatures in the Bruce's marine touch tank and listening to stories from long ago and far away in the full-size reconstruction of a Woodland Indian wigwam. ⊠ *1 Museum Dr. (I–95 Exit 3)* ☎ *203/869–0376* ⊕ *www.brucemuseum.org* ⊡ *$7, free Tues.* ☉ *Tues.–Sat. 10–5, Sun. 1–5.*

In the 1890s visitors from New York's Art Students League journeyed to the Cos Cob section of Greenwich to take classes taught by American impressionist John Henry Twachtman at a boardinghouse for artists and writers run by Josephine and Constant Holley. Thus the Cos Cob art colony, which flourished until 1920, was born. Today the 1730-vintage house is the **Bush-Holley Historic Site,** which displays a wonderful collection of 19th- and 20th-century artwork by sculptor John Rogers, potter Leon Volkmar, and painters Childe Hassam, Elmer Livingstone MacRae, and, of course, John Twachtman. The visitor center, set in the historic site's circa-1805 storehouse, holds changing exhibitions on art and history. ⊠ *39 Strickland Rd.* ☎ *203/869–6899* ⊕ *www.hstg.org* ⊡ *$6* ☉ *Mar.–Dec., Tues.–Sun. noon–4; Jan. and Feb., weekends noon–4.*

Where to Stay & Eat

$$$$
Fodor'sChoice
★

✕ **Restaurant Jean-Louis.** Chef Jean-Louis Gerin specializes in what he calls "la nouvelle classique" French cuisine, a style based on complex stocks and reductions—and his own dedication to excellence. A choice way to sample it is via the five-course menu degustation that explores the day's special offerings. Heady roses, signature fine china, custom glassware, and touches of lace create a romantic and sophisticated at-

mosphere. ⊠ *61 Lewis St.* ☎ *203/622–8450* ⊟ *AE, D, DC, MC, V*
⊘ *Closed Sun. No lunch Sat.*

$$$$ ✕⌂ **Delamar Greenwich Harbor Hotel.** This three-story luxury hotel with
yellow stucco exterior and terra-cotta tile roof resembles a private villa
on the Italian Riviera. Handcrafted furnishings from all over the world
enrich all rooms; many have working fireplaces and wrought-iron balconies overlooking Greenwich Harbor. Bathrooms have coral marble
vanities, hand-painted framed mirrors, and deep cast-iron tubs. The hotel
has its own 600-foot private dock on the harbor for boat owners to tie
up; it's just a few blocks from downtown Greenwich and one block from
the train station. The acclaimed L'Escale restaurant and bar ($$–$$$$),
which shares the hotel's superb water views, focuses on classic Provençal
dishes. ⊠ *500 Steamboat Rd., 06830* ☎ *203/661–9800 or 866/335–
2627* ⎙ *203/661–2513* ⊕ *www.thedelamar.com* ↩ *74 rooms, 8 suites*
△ *Restaurant, in-room DVDs, in-room data ports, gym* ⊟ *AE, D,
DC, MC, V.*

$$$$ ⌂ **Hyatt Regency Greenwich.** The Hyatt's vast but comfortable atrium
contains a flourishing lawn and abundant flora. The rooms are spacious,
with modern furnishings and many amenities. The pleasant Winfield's
restaurant serves innovative renditions of classic dishes. ⊠ *1800 E.
Putnam Ave., 06870* ☎ *203/637–1234* ⎙ *203/637–2940* ⊕ *www.
greenwich.hyatt.com* ↩ *373 rooms, 12 suites* △ *Restaurant, refriger-
ators, in-room data ports, indoor pool, health club, hair salon, sauna,
bar, shop, business services, meeting room* ⊟ *AE, D, DC, MC, V.*

Stamford

② *6 mi northeast of Greenwich, 38 mi southwest of New Haven, 33 mi
northeast of New York City.*

Glitzy office buildings, chain hotels, and major department stores are
among the landmarks in Stamford, the most dynamic city on the south-
western shore. Restaurants, nightclubs, and shops line Atlantic and
lower Summer streets, poised to harness the region's affluence and sat-
isfy the desire of suburbanites to spend an exciting night on the town
without having to travel to New York City.

The 91-acre **Bartlett Arboretum** is home to more than 2,000 varieties of
annuals, perennials, wildflowers, and woody plants; a visitor center with
an art gallery and research library; a greenhouse; marked ecology trails;
a 2-acre pond; and a boardwalk through a red maple swamp. Brilliant
purples, sunny yellows, and bold oranges make the wildflower garden
stunning in spring. Sunday afternoons are a prime time to visit for
guided walks that span the seasons. ⊠ *151 Brookdale Rd., off High Ridge
Rd. (Merritt Pkwy. Exit 35)* ☎ *203/322–6971* ⊕ *www.bartlettarboretum.
org* ☒ *$5 suggested donation* ⊘ *Grounds daily 8:30–dusk, visitor cen-
ter weekdays 8:30–4:30, greenhouse daily 10–noon.*

♺ Oxen, sheep, pigs, and other animals roam the **Stamford Museum and
Nature Center,** a 118-acre New England–style farmstead with many na-
ture trails to explore. Once the estate of Henri Bendel, the property in-
cludes a Tudor-revival stone mansion, which houses exhibits surveying
natural history, art, and Americana. Also here is a planetarium and ob-

servatory with a 22-inch research telescope—perfect for stargazing. ⊠ *39 Scofieldtown Rd. (Rte. 137)* ☎ *203/322–1646* ⊕ *www. stamfordmuseum.org* ⊠ *Grounds $6, planetarium an additional $2, observatory an additional $3* ☉ *Grounds daily 9–5; buildings and galleries daily 11–5, closed Mon. Jan.–Mar.; observatory Fri. evenings 8–10 Sept.–Apr., 8:30–10:30 May–Labor Day; planetarium shows 2nd Sun. each month.*

Where to Stay & Eat

$–$$$ ✕ **City Limits Diner.** This art deco deluxe diner, alive with bright colors and shiny chrome, likes to describe its food as running the gamut from "haute to homespun." Roughly translated, this is the place for everything from New York egg creams to French martinis to hot pastrami on New York rye to pan-roasted Atlantic salmon with Israeli couscous and shiitake mushrooms. ⊠ *135 Harvard Ave.* ☎ *203/348–7000* ⊟ *AE, D, DC, MC, V.*

$–$$$$ ⊞ **Stamford Marriott Hotel and Spa.** The Marriott stands out for its up-to-date facilities and convenience to trains and airport buses. Furnishings are modern and comfortable. ⊠ *2 Stamford Forum, 06901* ☎ *203/357–9555* ⊟ *203/358–0157* ⊕ *www.stamfordmarriott.com* ⟿ *500 rooms, 6 suites* ⊘ *3 restaurants, in-room data ports, pool, health club, hair salon, hot tub, sauna, racquetball, meeting rooms* ⊟ *AE, D, DC, MC, V.*

$–$$$$ ⊞ **Westin Stamford.** The ultramodern entrance of this downtown luxury hotel should prepare you for the dramatic atrium lobby. The attractive rooms are understated and elegant, with subdued colors and comfortable wing chairs; bathrooms are spacious. ⊠ *1 1st Stamford Pl., 06902* ☎ *203/967–2222* ⊟ *203/967–3475* ⊕ *www.starwood. com/westin* ⟿ *462 rooms, 28 suites* ⊘ *Restaurant, in-room data ports, 2 tennis courts, indoor pool, health club, meeting rooms* ⊟ *AE, D, DC, MC, V.*

Nightlife & the Arts

NIGHTLIFE At the **Terrace Club** (⊠ 1938 W. Main St. ☎ 203/961–9770) you can dance to everything from ballroom and country western to hip-hop and Latin.

The **Thirsty Turtle** (⊠ 84 W. Park Pl. ☎ 203/973–0300) is a combination of a pub, dance club, and shaken-not-stirred martini lounge. The Irish **Tigín Pub** (⊠ 175 Bedford St. ☎ 203/353–8444) hosts live music on Friday and Saturday nights.

THE ARTS The **Connecticut Grand Opera and Orchestra** (☎ 203/327–2867 ⊕ www. ctgrandopera.org) perform at the **Palace Theatre** (⊠61 Atlantic St.). Opera season runs from October to May. The **Stamford Center for the Arts** (☎ 203/325–4466) presents everything from one-act plays and comedy shows to musicals and film festivals. Performances are held at the **Rich Forum** (⊠ 307 Atlantic St.) and the **Palace Theatre** (⊠ 61 Atlantic St.). The **Stamford Symphony Orchestra** (☎ 203/325–1407) stages performances from October to April, including a family concert series.

Shopping

The **Stamford Town Center** (⊠ 100 Greyrock Pl. ☎ 203/356–9700) houses more than 130 chiefly upscale shops and restaurants, including Saks Fifth Avenue, Talbots, Pottery Barn, and Williams-Sonoma. Northern Stamford's **United House Wrecking** (⌧ 535 Hope St. ☎ 203/348–5371) sells acres of architectural artifacts, decorative accessories, antiques, nautical items, and lawn and garden furnishings.

Norwalk

❸ *14 mi northeast of Stamford, 47 mi northeast of New York City.*

In the 19th century, Norwalk became a major New England port and also manufactured pottery, clocks, watches, shingle nails, and paper. It later fell into a state of neglect, in which it remained for much of the 20th century. Since the 1990s, however, Norwalk's coastal business district has been the focus of a major redevelopment project. Art galleries, restaurants, bars, and trendy boutiques have blossomed on and around Washington Street. The stretch is now known as SoNo (short for South Norwalk), and in the evening especially it is without a doubt the place to be seen if you're young, single, and living the glamorous life in Fairfield County.

Norwalk is the home of Yankee Doodle Dandies: in 1756, Colonel Thomas Fitch threw together a motley crew of Norwalk soldiers and led them off to fight at Ft. Crailo, near Albany, New York. Supposedly, Norwalk's women gathered feathers for the men to wear as plumes in their caps in an effort to give them some appearance of military decorum. Upon the arrival of these foppish warriors, one of the British officers sarcastically dubbed them "macaronis"—slang for dandies. The name caught on, and so did the song.

The **Lockwood-Mathews Mansion Museum,** an ornate tribute to Victorian decorating, was built in 1864 as the summer home of LeGrand Lockwood. It remains one the oldest (and finest) surviving Second Empire–style country homes in the United States; it's hard not to be impressed by its octagonal skylighted rotunda and more than 50 rooms of gilt, frescoes, marble, intricate woodwork, and etched glass. ⌧ *295 West Ave.* ☎ *203/ 838–9799* ⊕ *www.lockwoodmathews.org* ▨ *$8* ⊙ *Mid-Mar.–Jan. 1, Wed.–Sun. noon–4, or by appointment.*

★ ☾ The cornerstone of the SoNo district is the **Maritime Aquarium at Norwalk,** a 5-acre waterfront center that explores the marine life and maritime culture of Long Island Sound. The aquarium's more than 20 habitats include some 1,000 creatures indigenous to the sound. You can see toothy bluefish and sand tiger sharks in the 110,000-gallon Open Ocean Tank, dozens of jellyfish performing their ghostly ballet in "Jellyfish Encounter," stately loggerhead sea turtles, winsome river otters, and happy harbor seals. The center also operates an Environmental Education Center and marine-mammal cruises aboard the *Oceanic,* and has a towering IMAX theater. ⌧ *10 N. Water St.* ☎ *203/852–0700* ⊕ *www.maritimeaquarium.org* ▨ *Aquarium $10.50, IMAX theater $8.50, combined $16.00* ⊙ *Labor Day–June, daily 10–5; July–Labor Day, daily 10–6.*

The 3-acre park at the **Sheffield Island Lighthouse** is a prime spot for a picnic. The 1868 lighthouse has four levels, 10 rooms to explore, and is adjacent to the Stewart B. McKinney U.S. Fish and Wildlife Refuge.

Clambakes with all the fixings are held Thursday evenings from June through September. ⊠ *Ferry service from Hope Dock (corner of Washington and North Water Sts.)* ☎ *203/838–9444 ferry and lighthouse* ⊕ *www.seaport.org* ⊠ *Round-trip ferry service and lighthouse tour $16* ☼ *Ferry early May–mid-June and late Sept.–mid-Oct., weekends at 11 and 3; mid-June–Labor Day, weekdays at 11 and 3, weekends at 11, 2, and 3:30.*

Except for the ColorCoaster, a 27-foot-high mechanical toy in constant motion, the exhibits at the **Stepping Stones Museum for Children** are not permanent, but they are always educational and encourage hands-on exploration. New exhibits are Rainforest Adventure, where kids under 10 can climb a kapok tree or explore a gorilla's nest, and Waterscape, where they can learn about weather and even role-play as weather reporters. For kids 3 and under, there's Toddler Terrain. ⊠ *Mathews Park, 303 West Ave.* ☎ *203/899–0606* ⊕ *www.steppingstonesmuseum. org* ⊠ *$8* ☼ *Labor Day–Memorial Day, Tues. 1–5, Wed.–Sun. 10–5; Memorial Day–Labor Day, daily 10–5.*

Where to Stay & Eat

$$–$$$ ✕ **Habana.** Ceiling fans, banana trees, and a high energy level characterize Habana, which serves contemporary Cuban cuisine with some Argentinian, Peruvian, Mexican, Puerto Rican, and Brazilian dishes thrown in for spice. Try the roasted sea bass with a crispy plantain crust or the baby back ribs with a spicy guava sauce, and top it off with a mojito. ⊠ *70 N. Main St.* ☎ *203/852–9790* ⊟ *AE, D, MC, V* ☼ *No lunch.*

$–$$$ ✕⊡ **Silvermine Tavern.** The simple rooms at this inn are furnished with hooked rugs and antiques along with some modern touches. The large, low-ceiling dining rooms ($$–$$$$; closed Jan.–Apr., Mon. and Tues., May–Dec., Tues.) are romantic, with eclectic Colonial appointments; many tables overlook a millpond. Traditional New England favorites receive modern accents—roast breast of duck with cranberries, for example. Sunday brunch is a local tradition. ⊠ *194 Perry Ave.* ☎ *203/847–4558 or 888/693–9967* ⊜ *203/847–9171* ⊕ *www.silverminetavern.com* ⊠ *10 rooms, 1 suite* ⊘ *Restaurant, shop; no room phones, no room TVs* ⊟ *AE, MC, V* ⏀ *CP.*

Ridgefield

❹ *11 mi north of New Canaan, 43 mi west of New Haven.*

In Ridgefield you'll find a rustic Connecticut atmosphere within an hour of Manhattan. The inviting town center is a largely residential sweep of lawns and majestic homes.

Cutting-edge art is not exactly what you'd expect to find in a stately 18th-century Main Street structure that was once a general store, Ridgefield's first post office, a private home, and, for 35 years, a church. But inside the **Aldrich Contemporary Art Museum** are 12 galleries, a screening room, a sound gallery, a 22-foot-high project space for large installations, a 100-seat performance space, and an education center. Outside is a 2-acre sculpture garden. ⊠ *258 Main St.* ☎ *203/438–4519* ⊕ *www. aldrichart.org* ⊠ *$7, free Tues.* ☼ *Tues.–Sun. noon–5.*

$–$$$ ✕⊞ **Stonehenge Inn & Restaurant.** The manicured lawns and bright white-clapboard buildings of Stonehenge are visible just off U.S. 7. Its tasteful rooms are a mix of Waverly and Schumacher fabrics; the gem of a restaurant ($$$–$$$$; closed Sunday; no lunch) provides an ever-changing menu that may include sautéed sea scallops topped with smoked salmon beurre blanc sauce or Piedmontese beef steak with a Roquefort crust. ⊠ *Stonehenge Rd. off U.S. 7* ☎ *203/438–6511* 📠 *203/ 438–2478* ⊕ *www.stonehengeinn-ct.com* ➴ *12 rooms, 4 suites* ♿ *Restaurant* 🖃 *AE, MC, V* ⁑◎⁑ *CP.*

Westwort

❺ *15 mi southeast of Ridgefield, 47 mi northeast of New York City.*

Westport, an artists' community since the turn of the 20th century, continues to attract creative types. Despite commuters and corporations, the town remains more artsy and cultured than its neighbors: if the rest of Fairfield County is stylistically five years behind Manhattan, Westport lags by just five months. Paul Newman and Joanne Woodward have their main residence here.

Summer visitors to Westport congregate at **Sherwood Island State Park,** which has a 1½-mi sweep of sandy beach, two water's-edge picnic groves, sports fields, interpretive programs, and several food concessions (open seasonally). ⊠ *I–95 Exit 18* ☎ *203/226–6983* 🚃 *$7–$14* ⊙ *Daily 8 AM–sunset.*

$$–$$$$ ✕ **Da Pietro's.** This romantic storefront café serves a savory mix of northern Italian and southern French specialties lovingly prepared by chef-owner Pietro Scotti. Black truffle risotto; sautéed veal tenderloins; and swordfish with raisins, lemon juice, white wine, olives, and tomato are possible choices. ⊠ *36 Riverside Ave.* ☎ *203/454–1213* 🖃 *AE, MC, V* ⊙ *Closed Sun. No lunch Mon. and Sat.*

★ **$$–$$$** ✕ **Tavern on Main.** This intimate restaurant takes the tavern concept to a new level—fresh flowers and soft music included. In winter the glow of fireplaces reaches every table, and in summer an outdoor terrace overlooking Main Street beckons. The sophisticated comfort food includes starters such as wild mushroom ravioli and lobster-and-shrimp spring rolls with tamarind dipping sauce. Among the notable entrées are potato-wrapped sea bass with cabernet sauce and roast duckling with a bing cherry and red zinfandel reduction. ⊠ *146 Main St.* ☎ *203/221– 7222* 🖃 *AE, D, DC, MC, V.*

★ **$$$$** ⊞ **Inn at National Hall.** Each whimsically exotic room at this towering Italianate redbrick inn in the heart of downtown Westport is a study in innovative restoration, wall stenciling, and decorative painting—including magnificent trompe l'oeil designs. The furniture collection is exceptional. Some rooms and suites have sleeping lofts and floor-to-ceiling windows overlooking the Saugatuck River. The Turkistan Suite—with its two-story-high bookcase, striped swag drapes, curving balcony, and king-size bed with Egyptian print canopy and painted valance—is one glorious example. ⊠ *2 Post Rd. W, 06880* ☎ *203/221–1351 or 800/*

628–4255 ⌂ *203/221–0276* ⊕*www.innatnationalhall.com* ⇗ *8 rooms, 8 suites* ⚲ *Refrigerators, in-room VCRs, meeting room* ⊟ *AE, DC, MC, V* ⎅ *CP.*

$$–$$$ ⎁ **Westport Inn.** Bedrooms in this upscale motor lodge have attractive contemporary furniture. Rooms surrounding the large indoor pool are set back nicely and are slightly larger than the rest. ⊠ *1595 Post Rd. E, 06880* ☎ *203/259–5236 or 800/446–8997* ⌂ *203/254–8439* ⊕*www. westportinn.com* ⇗ *115 rooms, 2 suites* ⚲ *In-room data ports, indoor pool, health club, sauna, some pets allowed* ⊟ *AE, D, DC, MC, V* ⎅ *CP.*

Nightlife & the Arts

The **Levitt Pavilion for the Performing Arts** (⊠ Jesup Rd. ☎ 203/221–4422) sponsors an excellent series of mostly free summer concerts that range from jazz to classical, folk rock to blues. The venerable **Westport Country Playhouse** (⊠ 25 Powers Ct. ☎ 203/227–4177 ⊕ www. westportplayhouse.org) celebrated its 75th anniversary in 2005, and in 2006 a new artistic director, Tazewell Thompson, succeeded Joanne Woodward, artistic director from 2001–2005. To mark the change, a season of winter plays was added to the traditional summer season.

Shopping

J. Crew, Ann Taylor, Crabtree Evelyn, Pottery Barn, and other fashionable shops have made Main Street in Westport the outdoor equivalent of upscale malls such as Stamford Town Center.

Bridgeport

❻ *10 mi east of Westport, 63 mi west of New London.*

Bridgeport, a city that has endured some economic hard times, is working hard to revitalize itself and overcome its negative image with improvements such as the Ballpark at Harbor Yard, opened in 1998, and the newer Arena at Harbor Yard sports and entertainment complex. A number of unique attractions make it a worthwhile stop.

☘ The Romanesque red sandstone-and-brick **Barnum Museum** stands out in downtown Bridgeport much like P. T. Barnum, the "Greatest Showman on Earth" and former mayor of Bridgeport, did in his day. The museum depicts the life and times of Barnum, who founded his circus in 1871 and presented performers such as General Tom Thumb and Jenny Lind, the Swedish Nightingale. Among the exhibits is a scaled-down model of Barnum's legendary five-ring circus containing more than 3,000 pieces. ⊠ *820 Main St.* ☎ *203/331–1104* ⊕ *www.barnum-museum.org* ⎙ *$5* ⊙ *Tues.–Sat. 10–4:30, Sun. noon–4:30.*

☘ The indoor walk-through South American rain forest at **Connecticut's Beardsley Zoo** alone justifies a visit. It's alive with dozens of species, some rare and endangered, such as keel-billed toucans, broad-snouted caimans, and black-and-gold howler monkeys living in a lush environment of waterfalls, ponds, greenery, and bamboo. The zoo itself has 36 acres of exhibits including bison, Amur (Siberian) tigers, timber wolves, and proud peacocks who freely roam the property right along with you. Also here is a working carousel and a New England farmyard. ⊠ *1875 Noble Ave.* ☏ *203/394–6565* ⊕ *www.beardsleyzoo.org* 🎟 *$8* ☉ *Park daily 9–4, rain forest daily 10:30–3:30.*

The **Discovery Museum and Planetarium** teaches visitors, young and old alike, about science and technology through hands-on exhibits that explore electricity, computers, sound, light, magnetism, and energy. Other draws include the *Challenger* learning center, which provides computer-simulated space missions, and the preschooler-friendly DiscoveryTown, with puppets and a life-size school bus. ⊠ *4450 Park Ave.* ☏ *203/372–3521* ⊕ *www.discoverymuseum.org* 🎟 *$8.50* ☉ *Sept.–June, Tues.–Sat. 10–5, Sun. noon–5; July and Aug., Mon.–Sat. 10–5, Sun. noon–5.*

HARTFORD & THE CONNECTICUT RIVER VALLEY

Westward expansion in the New World began along the meandering Connecticut River. Dutch explorer Adrian Block first explored the area in 1614, and in 1633 a trading post was set up in what is now Hartford. Within five years, throngs of restive Massachusetts Bay colonists had settled in this fertile valley. What followed was more than three centuries of shipbuilding, shad hauling, and river trading with ports as far away as the West Indies and the Mediterranean.

Less touristy than the coast and northwest hills, the Connecticut River valley is a swath of small villages and uncrowded state parks punctuated by a few small cities and a large one: the capital city of Hartford. South of Hartford, with the exception of industrial Middletown, genuinely quaint hamlets vie for attention with antiques shops, scenic drives, and trendy restaurants.

Essex

7 *29 mi east of New Haven.*

Essex, consistently named one of the best small towns in America, looks much as it did in the mid-19th century, at the height of its shipbuilding prosperity. So important to a young America was Essex's boat manufacturing that the British burned more than 40 ships here during the War of 1812. Gone are the days of steady trade with the West Indies, when the aroma of imported rum, molasses, and spices hung in the air. Whitewashed houses—many the former roosts of sea captains—line Main Street, which has shops that sell clothing, antiques, paintings and prints, and sweets.

The **Connecticut River Museum,** in an 1878 steamboat warehouse at the foot of Main Street, tells the story of the Connecticut River through paintings, maritime artifacts, interactive displays, and ship models. The riverfront museum even has a full-size working reproduction of the world's first submarine, the *American Turtle*; the original was built by David Bushnell in 1775 as a "secret weapon" to win the Revolutionary War. ⊠ *At dock, 67 Main St.* ☏ *860/767–8269* ⊕ *www.ctrivermuseum.org* 🎟 *$6* ☉ *Tues.–Sun. 10–5.*

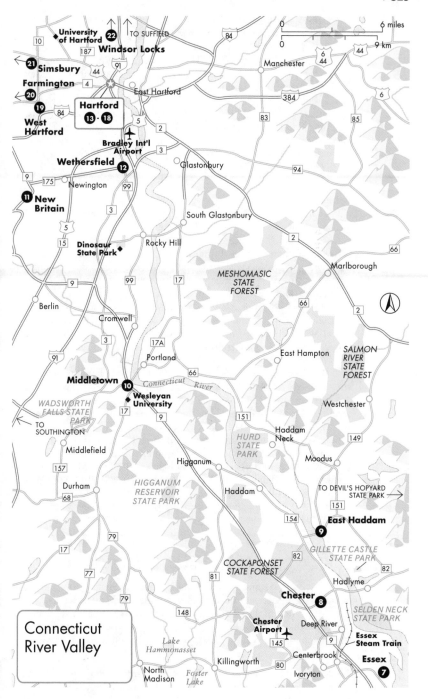

Connecticut
River Valley

The **Essex Steam Train and Riverboat** ride offers some of the best views of the Connecticut River valley from the vantage point of a restored train (1920s coaches pulled by a vintage steam locomotive) and an old-fashioned Mississippi-style riverboat. The train, traveling along the Connecticut River through the lower valley, makes a 12-mi roundtrip from Essex Station to Deep River Station; from there, if you wish to continue, you board the riverboat for a ride up the river to East Haddam (the open promenade deck on the third level has the best views). Special trains, including a dinner train and a wine train, as well as a Santa Special and hugely popular visits by Thomas the Tank Engine, occur periodically throughout the year. ⊠ *Valley Railroad Company, 1 Railroad Ave. (Rte. 9 Exit 3)* ☎ *860/767–0103* ⊕ *www.essexsteamtrain.com* 🎟 *Train fare $16, train-boat fare $24* ☉ *May–Dec.; call for schedule.*

Where to Stay & Eat

$$$–$$$$ ✕🏠 **Copper Beech Inn.** A magnificent copper beech tree shades this 1890 inn, set on 7 wooded Connecticut River valley acres. The venerable landmark has a luxe, sophisticated, even grand look. Rooms and suites, split between the main house and what was once a turn-of-the-20th-century carriage house, are all lavishly dressed with fine fabrics and furnishings, and all have fireplaces, radiant-heat flooring, and whirlpool baths. Crystal sparkles, silver shines, and candles glow in the dining room ($$$–$$$$; reservations essential; closed Monday; no lunch), lauded for its excellent French country cuisine. ⊠ *46 Main St., 4 mi west of Essex, Ivoryton 06442* ☎ *860/767–0330 or 888/809–2056* 🖷 *860/767–7840* ⊕ *www.copperbeechinn.com* 🛏 *11 rooms, 2 suites* ♿ *Restaurant, no-smoking rooms* ▭ *AE, D, DC, MC, V* ⏐◯⏐ *CP.*

$$–$$$$ ✕🏠 **Griswold Inn.** Two-plus centuries of catering to changing tastes at what's billed as America's oldest continuously operating inn has resulted in a kaleidoscope of decor—some Colonial, a bit of Federal, a little Victorian, and just as many modern touches as are necessary to meet present-day expectations. The chefs at the restaurant ($$–$$$) prepare country-style and more sophisticated dishes. The Tap Room, built in 1738 as a schoolhouse, is ideal for after-dinner drinks; a new wine bar (closed Monday and Tuesday) serves light meals. The "English Hunt Breakfast" is a Sunday event. ⊠ *36 Main St., 06426* ☎ *860/767–1776* 🖷 *860/767–0481* ⊕ *www.griswoldinn.com* 🛏 *17 rooms, 13 suites* ♿ *2 restaurants, bar, no-smoking rooms; no room TVs* ▭ *AE, MC, V* ⏐◯⏐ *CP.*

Chester

❽ *5 mi north of Ivoryton, 24 mi northwest of New London.*

Upscale boutiques and artisans' studios fill the chiefly 19th-century buildings along Chester's quaint and well-preserved Main Street. Chester sits on a portion of the Connecticut River that has been named "one of the last great places on earth" by the Nature Conservancy and is the starting point of the Chester–Hadlyme Ferry, which crosses the river in a grand total of five minutes.

Chester Airport arranges open-cockpit biplane rides over the lower Connecticut River valley. Bring your own bomber jacket and you're set. ⊠ *Off*

Rte. 9 ☎ *860/526–4321 or 800/752–6371* 🖂 *½ hr $125, 1 hr $225* ⊙ *By appointment.*

Sometimes the simple pleasures mean the most. The **Chester–Hadlyme Ferry** is the second-oldest continually operating ferry in the country. Although the trip across the Connecticut River to Hadlyme aboard the *Selden III*, the current vessel, is swift, you'll still catch nice views of the valley and Gillette Castle. 🖂 *148 Ferry Rd.* ☎ *860/526–2743* 🖂 *Vehicle and driver $3, walk-ons $1* ⊙ *Apr.–Nov., weekdays 7–6:45; weekends 10:30–5.*

Where to Eat

$$$–$$$$ ✕ **Restaurant du Village.** A black wrought-iron gate beckons you away from the boutiques of Chester's Main Street, and an off-white awning draws you through the door of this classic little Colonial storefront, painted in historic Newport blue and blooming with flower boxes. Here you can sample exquisite French country cuisine—escargots broiled in garlic and parsley sauce in the traditional Alsatian manner, pan-roasted filet mignon with a green peppercorn-and-cognac sauce—while recapping the day's shopping coups. 🖂 *59 Main St., 06412* ☎ *860/526–5301* 🖂 *Reservations essential* 🖃 *AE, MC, V* ⊙ *Closed Mon. and Tues. No lunch.*

$$–$$$ ✕ **River Tavern.** Sleek and sophisticated are words best used to describe this wildly popular tavern in the heart of Chester. The emphasis here is on freshness, so the menu changes frequently. Favorites have included a chanterelle-mushroom tart, Niman Ranch pork, and T-bone steak topped with roasted figs—an unexpectedly successful marriage. 🖂 *23 Main St.* ☎ *860/526–9417* 🖃 *AE, MC, V* ⊙ *Closed Tues.*

Shopping

Ceramica (🖂 36 Main St. ☎ 800/782–1238) carries hand-painted Italian tableware and decorative accessories. **Connecticut River Artisans** (🖂 5 W. Main St. ☎ 860/526–5575), a cooperative of local artists, sells traditional and contemporary handcrafts, from stained-glass kaleidoscopes to original watercolors. French country-style percales, upholstery fabrics, table linens, furnishings, and decorative accessories for the home are the focus at **Souleiado** (🖂 14 Main St. ☎ 860/526–1480).

East Haddam

❾ *7 mi north of Chester, 28 mi southeast of Hartford.*

Fishing, shipping, and musket making were the chief enterprises at East Haddam, the only town in the state that occupies both banks of the Connecticut River. This lovely community retains much of its old-fashioned charm, most of it centered around its historic downtown.

Sixty-foot cascades flow down Chapman Falls at the 860-acre **Devil's Hopyard State Park,** an idyllic spot for bird-watching, picnicking, fishing, camping, and hiking. 🖂 *366 Hopyard Rd., 3 mi north of junction of Rtes. 82 and 156* ☎ *860/873–8566* 🖂 *Free* ⊙ *Park daily 8 AM–dusk.*

★ **Gillette Castle State Park** holds the outrageous 24-room oak-and-fieldstone hilltop castle, modeled after medieval castles of the Rhineland, built between 1914 and 1919 by the eccentric actor and dramatist William Gillette. You can tour the castle and hike on trails near the remains of the 3-mi private railroad that chugged about the property until the owner's death in 1937. Gillette, who was born in Hartford, wrote two famous plays about the Civil War and was beloved for his play *Sherlock Holmes* (he performed the title role). In his will, he demanded that the castle not fall into the hands of "some blithering saphead who has no conception of where he is or with what surrounded." ⊠ *67 River Rd., off Rte. 82* ☎ *860/526-2336* ⌲ *Castle $5, grounds free* ☉ *Grounds daily 8–sunset; castle Memorial Day–Columbus Day, daily 10–4:30.*

★ The magnificent 1876 Victorian gingerbread **Goodspeed Opera House** is widely recognized for its role in the preservation and development of American musical theater. More than 16 Goodspeed productions have gone on to Broadway, including *Annie*. The "wedding cake" theater on the Connecticut River—so-called for all its turrets, mansard roof, and grand filigree—hosts performances from April to early December. ⊠ *6 Main St. (Rte. 82)* ☎ *860/873-8668* ⊕ *www.goodspeed.org* ⌲ *Tour $5* ☉ *Tours June–Oct; call for times.*

Middletown

⓾ *15 mi northwest of East Haddam, 24 mi northeast of New Haven.*

With its Connecticut River setting, easy access to major highways, and historic architecture, Middletown is a popular destination for recreational boaters and tourists alike. Originally named for its location halfway between Hartford and Long Island, the city is highlighted by the imposing campus of **Wesleyan University,** founded in 1831 and one of the oldest Methodist institutions of higher education in the United States. Its campus is traversed by High Street, which Charles Dickens once called "the loveliest Main Street in America"—even though Middletown's actual Main Street runs parallel to it a few blocks east. High Street is an architecturally eclectic thoroughfare. Note the massive, fluted Corinthian columns of the Greek-revival Russell House (circa 1828) at the corner of Washington Street, across from the pink Mediterranean-style Davison Art Center, built just 15 years later; farther on are gingerbreads, towering brownstones, Tudors, and Queen Annes. A few hundred yards up on Church Street, which intersects High Street, is the Olin Library. The 1928 structure, Wesleyan University's library, was designed by Henry Bacon, the architect of the Lincoln Memorial. The campus has roughly 2,700 undergrads, 150 graduate students, and a vibrant science-and-arts scene, which gives Middletown a contemporary college-town feel.

☾ Dinosaurs once roamed the area around **Dinosaur State Park,** north of Middletown. You can still see some 500 tracks, dating from the Jurassic period, 200 million years ago, preserved under a giant geodesic dome. You can even make plaster casts of tracks on a special area of the property; call ahead to learn what materials you need to bring. ⊠ *400 West St., east of I–91 Exit 23, Rocky Hill* ☎ *860/529–8423* ⊕ *www. dinosaurstatepark.org* ⌲ *$5* ☉ *Exhibits Tues.–Sun. 9–4:30, trails daily 9–4:30.*

If you are looking for a quintessential New England outing, **Lyman Orchards** (✉ Rtes. 147 and 157, Middlefield ☎ 860/349–1763 ⊕ www.lymanorchards.com) just south of Middletown is not to be missed. Here you can pick your own fruits and vegetables–berries, peaches, pears, apples, and even pumpkins from June to October.

Where to Stay & Eat

¢–$ ✕ **O'Rourke's Diner.** This steel, glass, and brick diner is the place to go for top-notch diner fare, an extensive weekend breakfast menu, delicious steamed cheeseburgers, and other innovative culinary creations. Get there early, however, as lines are often out the door and it closes at 2 PM. ✉ *728 Main St.* ☎ *860/346–6101* ▭ *AE, DC, MC, V* ⊙ *No dinner.*

$$–$$$ ⊞ **Inn at Middletown.** Opened in 2003, the Inn at Middletown is centrally located in a historic former National Guard Armory in the heart of Middletown. Rooms mix country-style furnishings with modern amenities, and all have views of the Connecticut River. ✉ *70 Main St., 06457* ☎ *860/854–6300 or 800/637–9851* ☎ *860/854–6301* ⊕ *www.innatmiddletown.com* ⊅ *88 rooms, 12 suites* ⌂ *Restaurant, cable TV, in-room broadband, indoor pool, gym, hot tub, dry cleaning, laundry service, meeting rooms,* ▭ *AE, D, DC, MC, V.*

Nightlife & the Arts

At Wesleyan University's **Center for the Arts** (✉ 283 Washington Terr. ☎ 860/685–3355) you can see modern dance or a provocative new play, hear top playwrights and actors discuss their craft, and take in an art exhibit or concert. At last count, **Eli Cannon's** (✉ 695 Main St. ☎ 860/347–3547) had more than 30 beers on draft and an extensive bottled selection, making it a hot late-night hangout.

Sports & the Outdoors

SKI AREA **Powder Ridge.** With a drop straight down from the 500-foot-high ridge; 18 trails designed for intermediate skiers, beginners and experts alike; a terrain park called Gnarly; and trails lighted for night skiing, this hill doesn't disappoint. Two triple chairlifts, one double to the top, and doubles and handle tows cover the mountain. Amenities include a full-service restaurant and ski instruction for children ages four and up. ✉ *99 Powder Hill Rd., Middlefield 06455* ☎ *860/349–3454 or 877/754–7434* ⊕ *www.powderridgect.com.*

Shopping

Wesleyan Potters (✉ 350 S. Main St. ☎ 860/347–5925) sells jewelry, clothing, baskets, pottery, weavings, and more. The shop also runs classes and workshops.

New Britain

❶ *13 mi northwest of Middletown, 10 mi southwest of Hartford.*

New Britain got its start as a manufacturing center producing sleigh bells. From these modest beginnings, it soon became known as "Hardware City," distributing builders' tools, ball bearings, locks, and other such items. No longer a factory town, this budding mecca for arts, business,

Garden Party

HAVE A GREEN THUMB—or wish you did? You're in luck. Nine extraordinary Connecticut gardens have banded together to form Connecticut's Historic Gardens, a statewide "trail" of natural beauties.

The re-created Colonial-revival garden at the **Webb-Deane-Stevens Museum** (✉ 211 Main St., Wethersfield ☎ 860/529-0612 ⊕ www.webb-deane-stevens.org) is a nostalgic presentation of old-fashioned flowers such as peonies, pinks, phlox, hollyhocks, larkspur, and antique roses.

A high-Victorian texture garden, a wildflower meadow, an antique rose garden, and a blue cottage garden are highlights of the **Harriet Beecher Stowe Center** (✉ 77 Forest St., Hartford ☎ 860/522-9258 ⊕ www.harrietbeecherstowecenter.org). The gardens also include Connecticut's largest magnolia tree and a 100-year-old pink dogwood. At the **Butler-McCook Homestead** (✉ 396 Main St., Hartford ☎ 860/247-8996 or 860/522-1806 ⊕ www.hartnet.org/als), landscape architect Jacob Weidenmann created a Victorian garden oasis smack in the center of downtown city life.

The centerpiece of the **Hill-Stead Museum** (✉ 35 Mountain Rd., Farmington ☎ 860/677-4787 ⊕ www.hillstead.org) is a circa-1920 sunken garden by Beatrix Farrand. The garden is enclosed in a yew hedge and surrounded by a wall of rough stone; at the center of the octagonal design is a summerhouse with 36 flowerbeds and brick walkways radiating outward. Farrand also designed the garden at **Promisek/Three Rivers Farm** (✉ 694 Skyline Ridge Rd., Bridgewater

☎ 860/354-1788), which overflows with beds of annuals and perennials such as hollyhocks, peonies, and always-dashing delphiniums.

Legendary British garden writer and designer Gertrude Jekyll designed only three gardens in the United States, and the one at the **Glebe House Museum** (✉ Hollow Rd., Woodbury ☎ 203/263-2855 ⊕ www.theglebehouse.org) is the only one still in existence. The garden is a classic example of Jekyll's ideas of color harmonies and plant combinations and is primarily composed of mixed perennials enclosed by an evergreen hedge of mixed shrubs.

A historic apple orchard and a spectacular circa-1915 formal parterre garden that blossoms with a collection of peonies, historic roses, and lilacs is the highlight of the **Bellamy-Ferriday House & Garden** (✉ 9 Main St. N., Bethlehem ☎ 860/247-8996 or 203/266-7596 ⊕ www.hartnet.org/als). The boxwood parterre garden at **Roseland Cottage** (✉ 556 Route 169, Woodstock ☎ 860/928-4074) includes 21 flowerbeds surrounded by 600 yards of boxwood hedge; each blooming bed of annuals and perennials is planted according to an 1850s plant-inventory list.

The gardens at the **Florence Griswold Museum** (✉ 96 Lyme St., Old Lyme ☎ 860/434-5542 ⊕ www.flogris.org), once the home of a prominent Old Lyme family and then a boardinghouse their daughter ran to shelter artists of the Old Lyme Colony early in the 20th century, have recently been restored to their appearance of 1910.

education, and sports is home to the Central Connecticut State College University and a first-rate museum of American art.

The **New Britain Museum of American Art,** an important stop for art lovers, more than doubled its exhibit space with the opening of a new building in 2006. The inauguration came not a moment too soon—the 100-year-old museum's collection of more than 5,000 works from 1740 to the present had seriously outgrown the turn-of-the-20th-century house that held it. Among the treasures are paintings by artists of the Hudson River and Ash Can schools; by John Singer Sargent, Winslow Homer, Georgia O'Keeffe, and others on up through Op Art works and sculpture by Isamu Noguchi. Deserving of special note is the selection of impressionist artists, including Mary Cassatt, William Merritt Chase, Childe Hassam, and John Henry Twachtman, as well as Thomas Hart Benton's five-panel mural *The Arts of Life in America.* The new space also allows for a café, an expanded shop, and a library of art books. ⊠ *56 Lexington St.* ☎ *860/229–0257* ⊕ *www.nbmaa.org* ⊠ *$9; free Sat. 10–noon* ⊙ *Tues., Wed., and Fri. 11–5; Thurs. 11–8; Sat. 10–5; Sun. noon–5.*

Wethersfield

⑫ *7 mi northeast of New Britain, 32 mi northeast of New Haven.*

Wethersfield, a vast Hartford suburb, dates from 1634 and has the state's largest—and, some say, most picturesque—historic district, with more than 100 pre-1849 buildings. Old Wethersfield has the oldest firehouse in the state, the oldest historic district in the state, and the oldest continuously operating seed company. Today, this "old" community is making improvements with new parks and new shops. But history is still Wethersfield's main draw.

Original tin signs still adorn the inviting post-and-beam buildings of **Comstock Ferre & Co.** (⊠ 263 Main St. ☎ 860/571–6590 ⊕ www.comstockferre.com), founded in 1820 and the country's oldest continuously operating seed company. The company sells more than 800 varieties of seeds and more than 2,000 varieties of perennials, as well as special seed collections so that you can create your own magical moonlight, Italian herb, or shade garden.

For a true sample of Wethersfield's historic past, stop by the **Webb-Deane-Stevens Museum.** The Joseph Webb House, the Silas Deane House, and the Isaac Stevens House—all next door to each other along Main Street and all built in the mid- to late 1700s—are well-preserved examples of Georgian architecture that reflect their owners' lifestyles as, respectively, a merchant, a diplomat, and a tradesman. The Webb House, a registered National Historic Landmark, was the site of the strategy conference between George Washington and the French general Jean-Baptiste Rochambeau that led to the British defeat at Yorktown. ⊠ *211 Main St. (I–91 Exit 26)* ☎ *860/529–0612* ⊕ *www.webb-deane-stevens. org* ⊠ *$8* ⊙ *May–Oct., Wed.–Mon. 10–4; Nov.–Apr., weekends 10–4 (last tour at 3).*

6

Hartford

4 mi north of Wethersfield, 45 mi northwest of New London, 81 mi northeast of Stamford.

Midway between New York City and Boston, Hartford is Connecticut's capital city. Founded in 1635 on the banks of the Connecticut River, Hartford was at one time home to authors Mark Twain and Harriet Beecher Stowe; inventors Samuel and Elizabeth Colt; landscape architect Frederick Law Olmsted; and Ella Grasso, the first woman to be elected a state governor. Today, Hartford, where America's insurance industry was born in the early 19th century, is poised for change, with a new convention center and new hotels (the Hilton Hartford and the Hartford Marriott Downtown) opened in 2005 and ground broken for the Connecticut Center for Science and Exploration (scheduled to open in 2008). Hartford, which already ranks in the top 6% of metropolitan areas in North America for its arts and culture, is a destination on the verge of discovery.

Bushnell Park, which fans out from the State Capitol building, was the first public space (1850) in the country with natural landscaping. The original designer, a Swiss-born landscape architect and botanist named Jacob Weidenmann, planted 157 varieties of trees and shrubs to create an urban arboretum. Added later were the Soldiers and Sailors Memorial Arch, dedicated to Civil War soldiers; the Corning Fountain; the Bushnell Park Carousel (open May through September), intricately hand-carved in 1914 by the Artistic Carousel Company of Brooklyn, New York; the Pumphouse Gallery; and a performance venue. An oasis of green, the park has about 750 trees, including 4 state champion trees, and a pond that is a popular summer lunch spot. ☎ *860/232–6710* ⊕ *www.bushnellpark.org.*

❶⑤ Hartford's oldest house, the **Butler-McCook Homestead,** was built in 1782 and continuously occupied by the same family until 1971. Inside are furnishings, family possessions, antiques, and Victorian-era toys that show the evolution of American taste over time. The beautifully restored Victorian garden, originally designed by Jacob Weidenmann, is a must-see. ⊠ *396 Main St.* ☎ *860/522–1806 or 860/247–8996* ⊕ *www.hartnet.org/als* ⊠ *$5* ⊗ *Wed.–Sat. 10–4 (1st Thurs. of most months until 8), Sun. 1–4, and by appointment.*

❶③ The Federal-style **Old State House,** with an elaborate cupola and roof balustrade, was designed in the early 1700s by Charles Bulfinch, architect of the U.S. Capitol. It served as Connecticut's state capitol until a new building opened in 1879, then became Hartford's city hall until 1915. In the 1820 Senate Chamber, where everyone from Abraham Lincoln to George Bush has spoken, you can view a portrait of George Washington by Gilbert Stuart, and in the Courtroom you can find out about the trial of the *Amistad* Africans in the very place where it was first held. In summer, enjoy the concerts and farmers' market. And don't forget to stop by the Museum of Natural and Other Curiosities. ⊠ *800 Main St.* ☎ *860/522–6766* ⊕ *www.ctosh.org* ⊠ *Free* ⊗ *Weekdays 10–4, Sat. 10–4.*

★ ⓱ Built in 1874, the **Mark Twain House & Museum** was the home of Samuel Langhorne Clemens, better known as Mark Twain, until 1891. While he and his family lived in this 19-room Victorian mansion, Twain published seven major novels, including *Tom Sawyer, Huckleberry Finn,* and *The Prince and the Pauper.* The home is one of only two Tiffany-designed domestic interiors open to the public. ⊠ *351 Farmington Ave., at Woodland St.* ☎ *860/247–0998* ⊕ *www.marktwainhouse.org* ⊠ *$12* ⊙ *May–Dec., daily 9:30–4:30; Jan.–Apr., Wed.–Sun. 9:30–4:30.*

⓲ The **Harriet Beecher Stowe Center** includes Stowe's Victorian Gothic cottage, erected in 1871 as a tribute to the author of the popular and influential antislavery novel, *Uncle Tom's Cabin.* Stowe (1811–96) spent her final years here. Inside the house, which is on the Connecticut Freedom Trail, are her personal writing table and effects. ⊠ *77 Forest St.* ☎ *860/522–9258 Ext. 317* ⊕ *www.harrietbeecherstowecenter.org* ⊠ *$8* ⊙ *Memorial Day–Columbus Day, Mon.–Sat. 9:30–4:30, Sun. noon–4:30; Columbus Day–Memorial Day, Tues.–Sat. 9:30–4:30, Sun. noon–4:30; Dec., Mon. 9:30–4:30.*

⓰ The gold-leaf dome of the **State Capitol** rises above Bushnell Park. Built in 1878, the building houses the state's executive offices and legislative chamber, as well as historical memorabilia. On a tour, you can walk through the Hall of Flags, gape at a statue of Connecticut state hero Nathan Hale, and observe the proceedings of the General Assembly from the public galleries, when in session. ⊠ *210 Capitol Ave.* ☎ *860/240–0222* ⊕ *www.cga.ct.gov/capitoltours* ⊠ *Free* ⊙ *Weekdays 9–3; tours weekdays 9:15–1:15; Apr.–Oct. also Sat. 10:15–2:15.*

With more than 50,000 artworks and artifacts spanning 5,000 years, ⓮ the **Wadsworth Atheneum Museum of Art** is the second-largest public art

Fodor\$Choice museum in New England and the oldest in the nation. The first American
★ ican museum to acquire works by Salvador Dalí and the Italian artist Caravaggio, the museum also houses 7,000 items documenting African-American history and culture in partnership with the Amistad Foundation. Particularly impressive are the museum's collections of baroque, impressionist, and Hudson River School artists. ⊠ *600 Main St.* ☎ *860/278–2670* ⊕ *www.wadsworthatheneum.org* ⊠ *$10* ⊙ *Wed.–Fri. 11–5 (1st Thurs. of most months until 8), weekends 10–5.*

Where to Stay & Eat

$$$–$$$$ ✕ **Max Downtown.** With its contemporary design, extensive array of mar-
Fodor\$Choice tinis and wines, and sophisticated cuisine, Max Downtown is a favorite
★ with the city's well-heeled and a popular after-work spot. Entrées include everything from pan-seared Canadian salmon to chophouse classics. Desserts such as the warm chocolate lava cake, pumpkin cheesecake, and banana cream pie are not to be missed. ⊠ *185 Asylum St.* ☎ *860/522–2530* ⊕ *www.maxrestaurantgroup.com/locations/down_index.php* ⌂ *Reservations essential* ⊟ *AE, DC, MC, V* ⊙ *No lunch weekends.*

$$–$$$ ✕ **Pastis.** Its warm Parisian style and French prints will make you feel that you've stepped into a brasserie in France. And the homey French cuisine with steak frites, coq au vin, and beef bourguignonne, among others, will make you feel like you've tasted France's finest. After dinner, stop in the Rhythm Room, a popular spot for live music and jazz

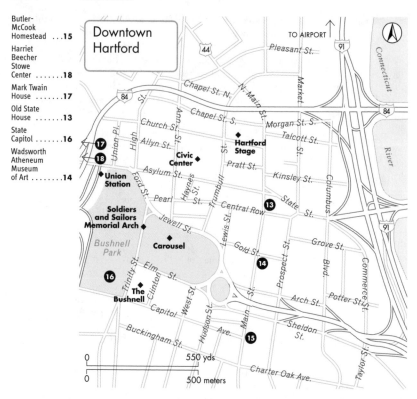

on weekends. ⊠ *201 Ann St., 06103* ☎ *860/278–8852* ⊕ *www. pastisbistro.com* ⊟ *AE, DC, MC, V* ⊘ *Closed Sun.*

$$–$$$ ✕ **Peppercorn's Grill.** This mainstay of Hartford's restaurant scene presents contemporary Italian cuisine in both a lively (colorful murals adorn the walls) and formal (tables are topped with white linen) setting. Look for house-made potato gnocchi, ravioli, and top-quality steaks, but save room for the warm chocolate bread pudding and the Valrohna chocolate cake. ⊠ *357 Main St., 06106* ☎ *860/547–1714* ⊟ *AE, DC, MC, V* ⊘ *Closed Sun.*

$$–$$$ ✕ **Trumbull Kitchen.** Upbeat, hip, and casual, Trumbull Kitchen is the place to see and be seen. The restaurant's menu is divided into categories including dim sum, tapas, and noshes; soups, noodles, and bowls; fondues; and stone pizzas and sandwiches. Expect to find everything from cutting-edge to home-style favorites, from Stilton cheese fritters with cranberry-orange chutney to steamed chicken dumplings and blackened yellowfin tuna. You decide in what order you'd like them served. ⊠ *150 Trumbull St., 06103* ☎ *860/493–7412* ⊕ *www.maxrestaurantgroup. com* ⊟ *AE, D, DC, MC, V* ⊘ *No lunch weekends.*

$–$$ ✕ **First and Last Tavern.** What looks to be a simple neighborhood joint south of downtown is actually one of the state's most hallowed pizza parlors. The long, old-fashioned wooden bar in one room is jammed most evenings with suburbia-bound daily-grinders shaking off their suits. The main dining room, which is just as noisy, has a brick outer wall covered with celebrity photos. ⊠ *939 Maple Ave., 06114* ☎ *860/ 956–6000* ⌕ *Reservations not accepted* ☰ *AE, D, DC, MC, V.*

★ **$–$$$$** ☑ **Goodwin Hotel.** Built in 1881, the Goodwin is an ornate, dark-red structure across the street from the civic center in the heart of the city. Rooms are tastefully appointed with rich wood furnishings, sleigh beds, and marble baths. The hotel's Pierpont's Restaurant is a popular breakfast spot with locals and hotel guests alike. ⊠ *1 Haynes St., 06103* ☎ *860/246– 7500 or 800/922–5006* 🖷 *860/247–4576* ⊕ *www.goodwinhotel.com* ⇥ *113 rooms, 11 suites* ⌕ *Restaurant, in-room data ports, gym, bar, meeting room* ☰ *AE, D, DC, MC, V.*

$$–$$$ ☑ **Residence Inn Hartford-Downtown Marriott.** Part of the rehabilitation project at the historic Richardson building, the all-suite Residence Inn is convenient to Pratt Street, Hartford Stage, and the Old State House. Rooms come with a kitchen, microwave, refrigerator, and coffeemaker, making it popular for longer stays. ⊠ *942 Main St., 06103* ☎ *860/524– 5550* 🖷 *860/524–0624* ⊕ *www.marriott.com* ⇥ *120 suites* ⌕ *Restaurant, cable TV with movies, in-room data ports, gym, meeting rooms* ☰ *AE, D, DC, MC, V* ☉︎ *BP.*

Nightlife & the Arts

NIGHTLIFE   The **Arch Street Tavern** (⊠ 85 Arch St. ☎ 860/246–7610) hosts local rock bands. For barbecue and blues head to **Black-Eyed Sally's** (⊠ 350 Asylum St. ☎ 860/278–7427). **Coach's** (⊠ 187 Allyn St. ☎ 860/522–6224) is one of the area's best sports bars. **Mozzicato–De Pasquale's Bakery, Pastry Shop & Caffe** (⊠ 329 Franklin Ave. ☎ 860/296–0426) serves late-night Italian pastries in the bakery, and espresso, cappuccino, and gelato in the café.

THE ARTS   The **Bushnell** (⊠ 166 Capitol Ave. ☎ 860/987–5900) hosts the **Hartford Symphony** (☎ 860/244–2999) and tours of major musicals. The **Hartford Conservatory** (⊠ 834 Asylum Ave. ☎ 860/246–2588) presents musical theater, concerts, and dance performances, with an emphasis on traditional works. The Tony Award–winning **Hartford Stage Company** (⊠ 50 Church St. ☎ 860/527–5151) puts on classic and new plays from around the world and premieres a fair number of productions that go on to become Broadway hits. The mammoth **New England Dodge Music Center** (⊠ 61 Savitt Way ☎ 860/548–7370), formerly the Meadows Music Center, hosts nationally known popular-music acts. **Real Art Ways** (⊠ 56 Arbor St. ☎ 860/232–1006) presents modern and experimental musical compositions in addition to avant-garde and foreign films. **TheatreWorks** (⊠ 233 Pearl St. ☎ 860/527–7838), the Hartford equivalent of off Broadway, presents experimental new dramas.

Sports & the Outdoors

SKI AREA   **Mt. Southington.** A 20-minute drive southwest of Hartford, Mt. Southington has a 425-foot vertical drop and 14 trails evenly split for beginners, intermediate, and advanced skiers. All trails are lighted for night skiing and are serviced by one triple chairlift, two doubles, two T-bars, and two handle tows. Snowboarders will find the Boarder Alpine Park, with its big air jump, as well as the Turkey Turn, noted for its boarder-friendly terrain. The ski school, for kids ages 4–12, uses learning terrain suited for younger skiers. And, when the whole family needs a break, the on-site restaurant is a perfect resting spot for all. ✉ *396 Mount Vernon Rd., Plantsville 06479* ☎ *860/628–0954.*

West Hartford

⑲ *5 mi west of Hartford.*

More metropolitan than many of its suburban neighbors, West Hartford is alive with a sense of community. Gourmet-food and ethnic grocery stores abound, as do unusual boutiques and oh-so-chic shops. A stroll around West Hartford Center (Interstate 84 Exit 42) reveals well-groomed streets busy with pedestrians and lined with coffee shops and restaurants with outdoor seating.

The **Noah Webster House/Museum of West Hartford History** is the birthplace of the famed author (1758–1843) of the *American Dictionary*. The 18th-century farmhouse contains Webster memorabilia and period furnishings; outside there is a garden planted with herbs, vegetables, and flowers that would have been available to the Websters when they lived here. ✉ *227 S. Main St.* ☎ *860/521–5362* ⊕ *www.noahwebsterhouse. org* ✉ *$6* ☉ *Thurs.–Mon. 1–4.*

Farmington

⑳ *5 mi southwest of West Hartford.*

Busy Farmington, incorporated in 1645, is a classic river town with lovely estates, a perfectly preserved main street, and the prestigious **Miss Porter's School** (✉ 60 Main St.), the late Jacqueline Kennedy Onassis's alma mater. Antiques shops can be found near the intersection of Routes 4 and 10, along with some excellent house museums.

★ The **Hill-Stead Museum** was converted from a private home into a museum by its talented owner, Theodate Pope, a turn-of-the-20th-century architect. The house has a superb collection of French impressionist art displayed in situ, including Monet's haystacks and Manet's *Guitar Player* hanging in the drawing room. Poetry readings by nationally known writers take place in the elaborate Beatrix Farrand–designed sunken garden every other week in summer. ✉ *35 Mountain Rd.* ☎ *860/ 677–4787* ⊕ *www.hillstead.org* ✉ *$9* ☉ *May–Oct., Tues.–Sun. 10–5 (last tour at 4); Nov.–Apr., Tues.–Sun. 11–4 (last tour at 3).*

Where to Stay & Eat

$$–$$$$ ✕ **Ann Howard's Apricots.** A white Colonial with dozens of windows overlooking gardens and the Farmington River is a long-term staple of the Hartford dining scene. American classics such as scrumptious meat loaf, duck breast, and rack of lamb are presented in a formal dining room; less-expensive fare is served in the downstairs pub. ✉ *1591 Farmington Ave., 06032* ☎ *860/673–5405* ▱ *AE, DC, MC, V.*

$$ ▥ **Farmington Inn.** Large guest rooms with four-poster canopied beds and European linens, antiques, and reproductions, highlight this stately inn.

Fresh flowers and paintings by local artists add homey touches. In the center of Farmington's historic district, the hotel is within walking distance of several excellent restaurants. ✉ *827 Farmington Ave., 06032* ☎ *860/677–2821 or 800/648–9804* 🖷 *860/677–8332* ⊕ *www. farmingtoninn.com* ↘ *59 rooms, 13 suites* ☖ *Cable TV, in-room VCRs, in-room data ports, business services, meeting room* ▤ *AE, D, DC, MC, V* ⑩ *CP.*

Simsbury

㉑ *12 mi north of Farmington via Rte. 10.*

Colonial-style shopping centers, a smattering of antiques shops, and a proliferation of insurance-industry executives define this chic bedroom community near Hartford. Once the home of many Revolutionary War soldiers, the community now offers great dining in addition to the shopping.

Headquarters of the Simsbury Historical Society, the **Phelps Tavern Museum** is set in a Colonial house built in 1771 for Captain Elijah Phelps and his family. Period-furnished rooms constitute the permanent exhibit, which highlights the home's use as a tavern from 1786 to 1849, when it was a stop on the Farmington Canal. You can learn about Simsbury's history, and on the 2-acre grounds you can visit research archives, a period garden, and the museum's shop. ✉ *800 Hopmeadow St.* ☎ *860/658–2500* ⊕ *www.simsburyhistory.org* 🖾 *$6* ☉ *Tues.–Sat. noon–4.*

Where to Stay

$$–$$$$ 🏨 **Simsbury 1820 House.** The rooms at this restored New England country manor on a hill overlooking Simsbury contain a judicious mix of antiques and modern furnishings. The main house was built in 1820 and has an 1890 addition on its west side. Rooms are decorated with period fabrics and antiques, and many have four-poster, mahogany canopy beds. ✉ *731 Hopmeadow St., 06070* ☎ *860/658–7658 or 800/879–1820* 🖷 *860/651–0724* ⊕ *www.simsbury1820house.com* ↘ *32 rooms, 3 suites* ☖ *Restaurant, in-room data ports, meeting rooms* ▤ *AE, D, DC, MC, V* ⑩ *CP.*

$–$$$ 🏨 **Avon Old Farms Hotel.** A country hotel at the base of Avon Mountain, this 20-acre compound of Colonial-style buildings with manicured grounds is midway between Farmington and Simsbury. The rooms, some with four-poster beds, are appointed with elegant furnishings and brass chandeliers. ✉ *279 Avon Mountain Rd., Avon 06001* ☎ *860/677–1651* 🖷 *860/677–0364* ⊕ *www.avonoldfarmshotel.com* ↘ *160 rooms* ☖ *Restaurant, Wi-Fi, pool, gym, sauna, pub, business services, meeting room* ▤ *AE, D, DC, MC, V* ⑩ *CP.*

Sports & the Outdoors

ICE-SKATING The **International Skating Center of Connecticut** is a world-class twin-rink facility used for practice by up-and-coming skating stars and national, international, and Olympic champions. Lessons and public skating sessions are offered, and ice shows are held periodically throughout the year. ✉ *1375 Hopmeadow St.* ☎ *860/651–5400* ✍ *Call for public hrs and rates.*

STATE PARK A roughly 1¼-mi climb from the parking lot at the southern section of **Talcott Mountain State Park** and up the 165-foot Heublein Tower, a former private home, rewards you with spectacular views of the Farmington Valley and, some say, four states. ✉ *Rte. 185* ☎ *860/242–1158* ✍ *Free* ☉ *Park daily 8* AM*–sunset. Tower late Apr.–Labor Day, Thurs.–Sun. 10–5; Labor Day–late Oct., daily 10–5.*

Shopping

Arts Exclusive Gallery (✉ 690 Hopmeadow St. ☎ 860/651–5824) represents more than 30 contemporary artists and has an inventory of more than 700 original works of art in the gallery at all times. The **Farmington Valley Arts Center** (✉ 25 Arts Center La., Avon ☎ 860/678–1867) provides studio space for more than 20 resident artists and shows and sells their works along with the works of other nationally known artists in its two galleries.

Windsor Locks

㉒ *13 mi northeast of Simsbury, 94 mi northeast of Greenwich, 48 mi northeast of New Haven, 56 mi northwest of New London.*

Incorporated in 1854, Windsor Locks is halfway between Hartford and Springfield, Massachusetts. Named for the locks of a canal built to bypass falls in the Connecticut River in 1833, this small suburban town is home to Bradley International Airport.

★ ☾ The more than 70 aircraft at the **New England Air Museum** include gliders and helicopters, a World War II–era P-47 Thunderbolt, and a B-29 Superfortress, along with other vintage fighters and bombers. There's even a jet fighter simulator. The museum also frequently holds open-cockpit days, allowing young and old to play pilot. Call to find out when the next day will be held. ✉ *Next to Bradley International Airport, off Rte. 75* ☎ *860/623–3305* ⊕ *www.neam.org* ✍ *$8.50* ☉ *Daily 10–5.*

THE LITCHFIELD HILLS

Here in the foothills of the Berkshires is some of the most spectacular and unspoiled scenery in Connecticut. Two scenic highways, Interstate 84 and Route 8, form the southern and eastern boundaries of the region. New York, to the west, and Massachusetts, to the north, complete the rectangle. Grand old inns are plentiful, as are sophisticated eateries. Rolling farmlands abut thick forests, and trails—including a section of the Appalachian Trail—traverse the state parks and forests. Two rivers, the Housatonic and the Farmington, attract anglers and canoeing enthusiasts, and the state's three largest natural lakes, Waramaug, Bantam, and Twin, are here. Sweeping town greens and stately homes anchor Litchfield and New Milford. Kent, New Preston, and Woodbury draw avid antiquers, and Washington and Norfolk provide a glimpse into New England village life as it might have existed two centuries ago.

Favorite roads for admiring fall foliage are U.S. 7, from New Milford through Kent and West Cornwall to Canaan; Route 41 to Route 4 from Salisbury through Lakeville, Sharon, Cornwall Bridge, and Goshen to Torrington; and Route 47 to U.S. 202 to Route 341 from Woodbury through Washington, New Preston, and Warren to Kent.

New Milford

㉓ *28 mi west of Waterbury, 46 mi northeast of Greenwich.*

If you're approaching the Litchfield Hills from the south, New Milford is a practical starting point to begin a visit. It was also a starting point for a young cobbler named Roger Sherman, who, in 1743, opened his shop where Main and Church streets meet. A Declaration of Independence signatory, Sherman also helped draft the Articles of Confederation and the Constitution. You'll find old shops, galleries, and eateries all within a short stroll of New Milford green—one of the longest in New England.

The **Silo at Hunt Hill Farm Trust,** formerly the property of the late Skitch Henderson, onetime music director of NBC and the New York Pops, consists of several attractions in the old buildings of two farms dating back to the 1700s. Inside a barn is the Silo Store, packed with *objets de cookery,* crafts, and assorted goodies and sauces; the Silo gallery presents art shows and literary readings; and the Silo cooking school draws culinary superstars to teach cooking classes between March and December. The latest addition, the Skitch Henderson Living Museum, focuses on Henderson's collections of musical memorabilia, including rare recordings and scores, as well as other items as diverse as the Steinway he used at NBC and an antique marble soda fountain. ⊠ *44 Upland Rd., 4 mi north of the New Milford town green on U.S. 202* ☎ *860/355–0300* ⊕ *www.thesilo.com* ✉ *Donation suggested* ☉ *Wed.–Mon. 10–5.*

Where to Stay & Eat

$$–$$$ ✕ **Adrienne.** Set in an 18th-century farmhouse with terraced gardens, Adrienne serves New American cuisine from a seasonal menu. You may be lucky enough to encounter Maine diver-scallop ravioli with pesto sauce or grilled American lamb chops with Peruvian Blue mashed potatoes. Sunday brunch (think eggs Florentine, seafood crepe, and vegetable scampi) on the outdoor terrace is also popular. ⊠ *218 Kent Rd., 06776* ☎ *860/354–6001* ⊕ *www.adriennerestaurant.com* ▭ *AE, D, DC, MC, V* ☉ *Closed Mon. No dinner Sun.*

$–$$ ▦ **Homestead Inn.** The Homestead, high on a hill overlooking New Milford's town green, was built in 1853 and opened as an inn in 1928. Breakfast is served in a cheery living room, where you can sit by the fire. Rooms are decorated in a mix of country antiques, reproductions, and an abundance of floral accents. The eight rooms in the main house have more personality than those in the motel-style structure next door. ⊠ *5 Elm St., 06776* ☎ *860/354–4080* 🖷 *860/354–7046* ⊕ *www.homesteadct.com* 🛏 *14 rooms* ▭ *AE, D, DC, MC, V* ⓧ *CP.*

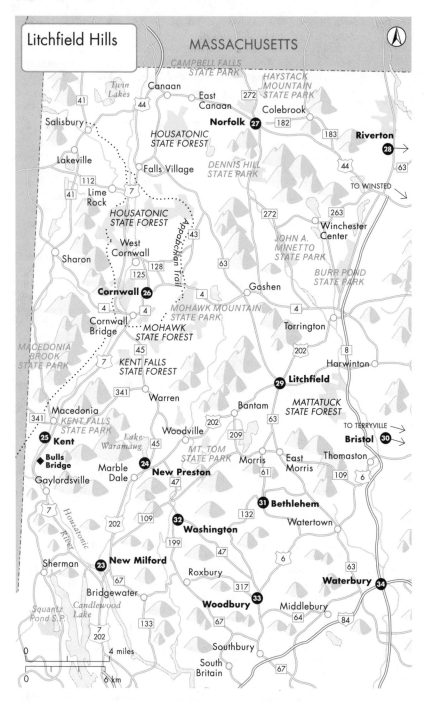

Litchfield Hills

New Preston

24 *4 mi north of New Milford.*

The crossroads village of New Preston, perched above a 40-foot water-fall on the Aspetuck River, has a little town center that's packed with antiques shops specializing in everything from 18th-century furnishings to out-of-print books.

Lake Waramaug, north of New Preston on Route 45, is an area that reminds many of Austria and Switzerland. The lake is named for Chief Waramaug, one of the most revered figures in Connecticut's Native American history. A drive around the 8-mi perimeter of the lake takes you past beautiful inns—many of which serve delicious food—and homes.

Lake Waramaug State Park (✉ 30 Lake Waramaug Rd. ☎ 860/868–0220 or 860/868–2592), at the northwest tip of the lake, is an idyllic 75-acre spread, great for picnicking and lakeside camping.

If you like your wine served with a water view try 35-acre **Hopkins Vineyard**, overlooking Lake Waramaug, which produces more than 11 varieties of wine, from sparkling to dessert. A weathered red barn houses a gift shop and a tasting room, and there's a picnic area. A wine bar in the hayloft serves a fine cheese-and-pâté board and has views of the lake. ✉ *25 Hopkins Rd.* ☎ *860/868–7954* ⊕ *www. hopkinsvineyard.com* ✉ *Free* ☉ *Jan. and Feb., Fri. and Sat. 10–5, Sun. 11–5; Mar. and Apr., Wed.–Sat. 10–5, Sun. 11–5; May–Dec., Mon.–Sat. 10–5, Sun. 11–5.*

6

Where to Stay & Eat

$$$$ ✕🏠 **Boulders Inn.** The most idyllic and prestigious of the inns along Lake

Fodor'sChoice Waramaug opened in 1940 but still looks like the private home it was

★ a century ago. Apart from the main house, a carriage house and several hillside cottages command panoramic views of the countryside and the lake. The rooms, four with double whirlpool baths, contain Victorian antiques and wood-burning fireplaces. The exquisite menu at the window-lined, stone-wall dining room ($$$–$$$$; closed Monday and Tuesday) changes seasonally but might include Thai crab cakes and wood-grilled fillet of beef with lobster. ✉ *E. Shore Rd. (Rte. 45), 06777* ☎ *860/868–0541 or 800/455–1565* 🖶 *860/868–1925* ⊕ *www. bouldersinn.com* ➟ *20 rooms* ⌂ *Restaurant, lake, exercise equipment, spa, beach, boating; no kids under 12, no smoking* ▭ *AE, MC, V* ¶◎¶ *BP.*

$$–$$$$ ✕🏠 **Birches Inn.** One of the area's poshest inns, the Birches is something of a Lake Waramaug institution. Antiques and reproductions enrich the rooms; three on the waterfront have private decks. The menu changes frequently in the lake-view dining room ($$–$$$; closed Monday–Wednesday; no lunch); you may be lucky enough to find pan-seared wild Atlantic salmon, oven-roasted Long Island duck, or grilled vegetable napoleon. ✉ *233 W. Shore Rd., 06777* ☎ *860/868–1735* 🖶 *860/868–1815* ➟ *12 rooms* ⌂ *Restaurant, beach; no kids, no smoking* ▭ *AE, MC, V* ¶◎¶ *CP.*

$–$$ ✕⬚ **Hopkins Inn.** A grand 1847 Victorian atop a hill overlooking Lake
Fodor'sChoice Waramaug, the Hopkins is one of the best bargains in the Hills. Most
★ rooms have plain white bedspreads, simple antiques, and floral wallpaper. In winter, the inn smells of burning firewood; year-round, it is redo-
lent with aromas from the rambling dining rooms ($$–$$$; closed
Monday and January–late March; reservations essential), which serve
outstanding Austrian dishes—sweetbreads Viennese is a favorite. When
the weather is kind, you can dine on the flagstone terrace underneath
the grand old horse chestnut tree and view the lake. ✉ *22 Hopkins Rd.
(1 mi off Rte. 45), 06777* ☎ *860/868–7295* 🖷 *860/868–7464* ⊕ *www.
thehopkinsinn.com* ⇨ *11 rooms, 2 suites* ⚲ *Restaurant, beach, no-smoking rooms* ▭ *AE, D, MC, V.*

Shopping

Dawn Hill Antiques (✉ 11 Main St. ☎ 860/868–0066) specializes in
18th- and 19th-century Swedish and French furniture. **J. Seitz & Co.** (✉ 9
E. Shore Rd. [Rte. 45] ☎ 860/868–0119) fills 5,000 square feet with
stylish home furnishings, fashions, and gifts.

Kent

㉕ *12 mi northwest of New Preston.*

Kent has the area's greatest concentration of art galleries, some nationally renowned. Home to a prep school of the same name, Kent once held
many ironworks. The Schaghticoke Indian Reservation is also here.
During the Revolutionary War, 100 Schaghticokes helped defend the
Colonies by transmitting messages of army intelligence from the Litchfield Hills to Long Island Sound, along the hilltops, by way of shouts
and drumbeats. **Bulls Bridge** (✉ U.S. 7 south of Kent), one of three covered bridges in Connecticut, is open to cars.

Hardware-store buffs and vintage-tool aficionados will feel right at
home at the **Sloane-Stanley Museum.** Artist and author Eric Sloane
(1905–85) was fascinated by Early American woodworking tools, and
his collection showcases examples of American craftsmanship from the
17th to the 19th century. The museum contains a re-creation of Sloane's
last studio and also encompasses the ruins of a 19th-century iron furnace. Sloane's books and prints, which celebrate vanishing aspects of
Americana such as barns and covered bridges, are on sale here. ✉ *U.S.
7* ☎ *860/927–3849* ⬚ *$4* ⊘ *Mid-May–Oct., Wed.–Sun. 10–4.*

Where to Stay & Eat

$$ ✕⬚ **Fife 'n Drum.** If you like to shop, eat, and rest your head in a cozy
place, you can do all three at this family-owned inn, restaurant, and gift
shop. The shop sells everything from cards and candles to jewelry and
accessories. The eight inn rooms (most above the shop) are decorated
with a pleasing assortment of antiques, reproductions, and flowery dec-
orative accessories. The restaurant ($$–$$$$) serves a mix of Continen-
tal and American choices such as filet mignon au poivre and roast rack
of lamb with a mustard crust. ✉ *53 N. Main St., 06757* ☎ *860/927–
3509* 🖷 *860/927–4595* ⊕ *www.fifendrum.com* ⇨ *8 rooms* ⚲ *Restaurant, shop* ▭ *AE, MC, V* ⊘ *Closed Tues.*

Sports & the Outdoors

The **Appalachian Trail**'s longest river walk, off Route 341, is the almost-8-mi hike from Kent to Cornwall Bridge along the Housatonic River. The early-season trout fishing is superb at 2,300-acre **Macedonia Brook State Park** (✉ Macedonia Brook Rd. off Rte. 341 ☎ 860/927–3238), where you can also hike and cross-country ski.

Shopping

The **Bachelier-Cardonsky Gallery** (✉ 10 N. Main St. ☎ 860/927–3129), one of the foremost galleries in New England, exhibits works by local artists and contemporary masters such as Alexander Calder, Carol Anthony, and Jackson Pollock. The **Paris–New York–Kent Gallery** (✉ Kent Station off U.S. 7 ☎ 860/927–4152) shows museum-quality contemporary works by local and world-famous artists. **Pauline's Place** (✉ 79 N. Main St. ☎ 860/927–4475) specializes in Victorian, Georgian, art deco, Edwardian, and contemporary jewelry.

EN ROUTE Heading north from Kent toward Cornwall, you'll pass the entrance to 295-acre **Kent Falls State Park** (✉ U.S. 7 ☎ 860/927–3238), where you can hike a short way to one of the most impressive waterfalls in the state and picnic in the green meadows at the base of the falls.

6

Cornwall

 12 mi northeast of Kent.

Connecticut's Cornwalls can get confusing. There's Cornwall, Cornwall Bridge, West Cornwall, Cornwall Hollow, East Cornwall, and North Cornwall. What this quiet corner of the Litchfield Hills is known for is its fantastic vistas of woods and mountains and its covered bridge, which spans the Housatonic and is easily one of the most photographed spots in the state.

A romantic reminder of the past, the wooden, barn-red, one-lane, covered **Cornwall Bridge** is not in the town of the same name but several miles up U.S. 7 on Route 128 in West Cornwall. The bridge was built in 1841 and incorporates strut techniques that were copied by bridge builders around the country.

With 11 mi of hiking trails, the **Sharon Audubon Center** provides myriad hiking opportunities. The 860-acre property is a mixture of forests, meadows, wetlands, ponds, and streams. It's also home to Princess, an American crow, who shares the visitor center with small hawks, an owl, and other animals in a live-animal display. Also here is a natural-history museum and children's adventure center. An aviary provides permanent housing for a bald eagle, a red-tailed hawk, and two turkey vultures. ✉ *325 Cornwall Bridge Rd., Sharon* ☎ *860/364–0520* ⊕ *www.audubon.org/local/sanctuary/sharon* ✍ *$3* ☉ *Tues.–Sat. 9–5, Sun. 1–5; trails daily dawn–dusk.*

Where to Stay & Eat

$$–$$$ ✕▦ **Cornwall Inn.** This 19th-century inn on scenic Route 7 combines country charm with contemporary elegance; eight rooms in the adjacent "lodge" are slightly more rustic in tone and have white cedar-post beds.

The restaurant ($–$$$; closed Monday–Wednesday; no lunch except Sunday brunch) serves a seasonally changing American menu. Entrées might include steak au poivre with cracked peppercorns and cognac sauce or fresh seafood. ⊠ *270 Kent Rd. (Rte. 7), 06754* ☎ *860/672–6884 or 800/786–6884* 🖨 *866/672–0352* ⊕ *www.cornwallinn.com* 🛏 *14 rooms* △ *Restaurant, in-room data ports, pool, hot tub, bar, no-smoking rooms, pets allowed* ⊟ *AE, D, MC, V* ⫿⊙⫿ *CP.*

Sports & the Outdoors

CANOEING & **Clarke Outdoors** (⊠ U.S. 7, West Cornwall ☎ 860/672–6365) rents ca-
KAYAKING noes, kayaks, and rafts and operates 10-mi trips from Falls Village to Housatonic Meadows State Park.

FISHING **Housatonic Anglers** (⊠ 26 Bolton Hill Rd. ☎ 860/672–4457) operates half- and full-day tours, as well as some evening outings, and provides fly-fishing instruction for trout and bass on the Housatonic and its tributaries. **Housatonic River Outfitters** (⊠ 24 Kent Rd., Cornwall Bridge ☎ 860/672–1010) operates a full-service fly shop; leads guided trips of the region; runs classes in fly-fishing, fly-tying, and casting; and stocks a good selection of vintage and antique gear.

SKI AREA **Mohawk Mountain.** Mohawk's 23 trails, ranging down 650 vertical feet, include plenty of intermediate terrain, with a few trails for beginners and a few steeper sections toward the top of the mountain. A small section is devoted to snowboarders. Trails are serviced by one triple lift and four doubles; 14 trails are lighted for night skiing. The base lodge has munchies and a retail shop, and the Pine Lodge Restaurant, halfway up the slope, has an outdoor patio. Mohawk's SKIwee program is for kids ages 5–12. There are facilities for ice-skating. ⊠ *46 Great Hollow Rd., off Rte. 4, 06753* ☎ *860/672–6100.*

STATE PARKS **Housatonic Meadows State Park** (⊠ U.S. 7, Cornwall Bridge ☎ 860/672–6772) is marked by its tall pine trees near the Housatonic River. Fly-fishers consider this 2-mi stretch of the river among the best places in New England to test their skills against trout and bass. The riverside campsites are excellent.

Shopping

Cornwall Bridge Pottery Store (⊠ Rte. 128, West Cornwall ☎ 860/672–6545) sells its own pottery, from dinnerware to garden pots, lamps, and vases. **Ian Ingersoll Cabinetmakers** (⊠ 422 Sharon Goshen Tpk., by the Cornwall Bridge, West Cornwall ☎ 860/672–6334) stocks handsome Shaker-style furniture.

Norfolk

❷ *7 mi southeast of Canaan, 59 mi north of New Haven.*

Norfolk, thanks to its severe climate and terrain, is one of the best-preserved villages in the Northeast. Notable industrialists have been summering here for two centuries, and many enormous homesteads still exist. The striking town green, at the junction of Route 272 and U.S. 44, has a fountain designed by Augustus Saint-Gaudens and executed by Stanford White at its southern corner. It stands as a memorial to Joseph Battell, who turned Norfolk into a major trading center.

Dr. Frederick Shepard Dennis, former owner of the 240 acres that are now **Dennis Hill State Park,** lavishly entertained guests, among them President Howard Taft and several Connecticut governors, in the stone pavilion at the summit of the estate. From its 1,627-foot height, you can see Haystack Mountain, New Hampshire, and, on a clear day, New Haven harbor, all the way across the state. Picnic on the park's grounds or hike one of its many trails. ⊠ *Rte. 272* ☏ *860/482–1817* 🎫 *Free* ☉ *Daily 8 AM–dusk.*

Where to Stay & Eat

★ ¢–$$ ✕ **The Pub.** Bottles of trendy beers line the shelves of this down-to-earth restaurant on the ground floor of a redbrick Victorian near the town green. Burgers and other pub fare are on the menu alongside more eclectic fare. This place is a real melting pot. ⊠ *U.S. 44, 06058* ☏ *860/ 542–5716* ▤ *AE, MC, V* ☉ *Closed Mon.*

$$–$$$$ 🏨 **Manor House.** Among this 1898 Bavarian Tudor's remarkable appoint-
Fodor's Choice   ments are its bibelots, mirrors, carpets, antique beds, and prints—not
★   to mention the 20 stained-glass windows designed by Louis Comfort Tiffany. The vast Spofford Room has windows on three sides, a king-size canopy bed with a cheery fireplace opposite, and a balcony. ⊠ *69 Maple Ave., 06058* ☏☏ *860/542–5690 or 866/542–5690* ⊕ *www. manorhouse-norfolk.com* ⇝ *8 rooms, 1 suite* ♨ *Some hot tubs; no room phones, no room TVs* ▤ *AE, MC, V* ⊙⧵ *BP.*

Nightlife & the Arts

The **Greenwoods Theatre at Norfolk** (⊠ U.S. 44 ☏ 860/542–0026) has its own professional resident company that performs June–September; a vintage-film series runs the rest of the year.

The **Norfolk Chamber Music Festival** (☏ 203/432–1966), at the Music Shed on the 70-acre Ellen Battell Stoeckel Estate at the northwest corner of the Norfolk green, presents world-renowned artists and ensembles on Friday and Saturday summer evenings. Students from the Yale School of Music perform on Thursday evening and Saturday morning. Early arrivals can stroll or picnic on the 70-acre grounds or visit the art gallery.

Sports & the Outdoors

One of the most spectacular views in the state can be seen from **Haystack Mountain State Park** (⊠ Rte. 272 ☏ 860/482–1817), via its challenging trail to the top or a road halfway up. **Loon Meadow Farm** (☏ 860/542–6085 ⊕ www.loonmeadowfarm.com) runs horse-drawn carriage, hay, and sleigh rides, by appointment only.

Shopping

Norfolk Artisans Guild (⊠ 24 Greenwoods Rd. E ☏ 860/542–5487) carries works by more than 60 local artisans—from hand-painted pillows to handcrafted baskets.

Riverton

28 *6 mi north of Winsted.*

Almost every New Englander has sat in a Hitchcock chair. Riverton, formerly Hitchcockville, is where Lambert Hitchcock made the first one, in 1826. The Farmington and Still rivers meet in this tiny hamlet. It's in one of the more unspoiled regions in the hills, and great for hiking and driving.

Where to Stay & Eat

$–$$$ ✕▨ **Old Riverton Inn.** This historic inn, built in 1796 and overlooking the west branch of the Farmington River, is a peaceful weekend retreat. Rooms are small—except for the fireplace suite—and the decorating, which includes Hitchcock furnishings, is for the most part ordinary, but the inn always delivers warm hospitality. The inviting dining room serves traditional New England fare ($$–$$$; closed Monday through Wednesday); the stuffed pork chops are local favorites. ⊠ *436 E. River Rd., 06065* ☎ *860/379–8678 or 800/378–1796* 🖷 *860/379–1006* ⊕ *www.rivertoninn.com/* 🛏 *11 rooms, 1 suite* ⚲ *Restaurant, bar* ☰ *AE, D, DC, MC, V* ��ⓄⱢ *BP.*

Sports & the Outdoors

American Legion and People's State Forests (⊠ Off Rte. 181 ☎ 860/379–2469, 860/379–0922 for camping information) border the west bank and the east bank, respectively, of the west branch of the Farmington River—a designated National Wild and Scenic River. You can picnic beneath 200-year-old pines along the riverbank, and the hiking, fishing, tubing, and canoeing are superb. **Farmington River Tubing** (⊠ Satan's Kingdom State Recreation Area, U.S. 44, New Hartford ☎ 860/693–6465) rents tubes and flotation devices for exhilarating rides down the scenic Farmington River.

SKI AREA **Ski Sundown.** This area has the state's most challenging trails as well as excellent facilities and equipment. The vertical drop is 625 feet. Of the 15 trails, 9 are for beginners, 3 for intermediates, and 3 for advanced skiers. All but one are lighted at night and serviced by three triple chairs and one double. Ski lessons are available for ages four and up. ⊠ *126 Ratlum Rd., New Hartford 06057* ☎ *860/379–7669 snow conditions.*

Litchfield

29 *19 mi southwest of Riverton, 48 mi north of Bridgeport, 34 mi west of Hartford.*

Everything in Litchfield, the wealthiest and most noteworthy town in the Litchfield Hills, seems to exist on a larger scale than in neighboring burgs, especially the impressive Litchfield Green and the white Colonial and Greek-revival homes that line the broad elm-shaded streets. Harriet Beecher Stowe, author of *Uncle Tom's Cabin,* and her brother, abolitionist preacher Henry Ward Beecher, were born and raised in Litchfield, and many famous Americans earned their law degrees at the Litchfield Law School. Today, lovely but exceptionally expensive boutiques and hot-spot restaurants line the downtown, attracting celebrities and the town's monied citizens.

Haight Vineyard is the state's oldest winery; it planted its first wine grapes in Connecticut in 1975. You can stop in for complimentary tastings and winery tours. Seasonal events include an annual barrel tasting in March and a harvest festival in September. ⊠ *29 Chestnut Hill Rd., Rte. 118 (1 mi east of Litchfield)* ☎ 860/567–4045 ⊕ *www. haightvineyards.com* ⊡ *Free* ⊙ *Mon.–Sat. 10:30–5, Sun. noon–5.*

At the **Litchfield History Museum,** furniture, clothing, household objects, and paintings provide glimpses into the evolution of this small New England town from its earliest days to the present, and seven well-organized galleries highlight family life and work during the 50 years after the American Revolution. The extensive reference library has information about the town's historic buildings, including the Sheldon Tavern (where George Washington slept on several occasions) and the Litchfield Female Academy, where in the late 1700s Sarah Pierce taught girls not just sewing and deportment but mathematics and history. ⊠ *7 South St., at Rtes. 63 and 118* ☎ 860/567–4501 ⊕ *www. litchfieldhistoricalsociety.org* ⊡ *$5 (includes Tapping Reeve House and Litchfield Law School)* ⊙ *Mid-Apr.–late Nov., Tues.–Sat. 11–5, Sun. 1–5.*

In 1773, Judge Tapping Reeve enrolled his first student, Aaron Burr, in what was to become the first law school in the country. (Before Judge Reeve, ★ students studied the law as apprentices, not in formal classes.) The **Tapping Reeve House and Litchfield Law School** is dedicated to Reeve's remarkable achievement and to the notable students who passed through its halls: Oliver Wolcott Jr., John C. Calhoun, Horace Mann, three U.S. Supreme Court justices, and 15 governors, not to mention senators, congressmen, and ambassadors. This museum is one of the state's most worthy attractions, with interactive multimedia exhibits, an excellent introductory film, and beautifully restored facilities. ⊠ *82 South St.* ☎ 860/567–4501 ⊕ *www.litchfieldhistoricalsociety.org* ⊡ *$5 (includes Litchfield History Museum)* ⊙ *Mid-Apr.–late Nov., Tues.–Sat. 11–5, Sun. 1–5.*

The chief attractions at 511-acre **Topsmead State Forest** are an English Tudor–style cottage built by architect Richard Henry Dana Jr. (and seemingly straight out of the English countryside) and a 40-acre wildflower preserve. The forest holds picnic grounds, hiking trails, and cross-country ski areas. ⊠ *Buell Rd. off E. Litchfield Rd.* ☎ 860/567– 5694 ⊡ *Free* ⊙ *Forest daily 8 AM–dusk; cottage tours June–Oct., 2nd and 4th weekends of month.*

A stroll through the landscaped grounds of **White Flower Farm** is always a pleasure, and will provide gardeners with myriad ideas. The farm is the home of a mail-order operation that sells annuals, perennials, shrubs, vines, bulbs, and houseplants to gardeners throughout the United States. ⊠ *Rte. 63, 3 mi south of Litchfield* ☎ 860/567–8789 ⊕ *www. whiteflowerfarm.com* ⊡ *Free* ⊙ *Apr.–Oct., daily 9–5:30.*

The **White Memorial Conservation Center,** at the heart of the White Memorial Foundation, a 4,000-acre nature preserve, houses top-notch natural-history exhibits and a gift shop. The foundation, one of the state's prime birding areas, contains some 30 bird-watching platforms; two self-guided nature trails; several boardwalks; campgrounds; boating facilities; fishing areas; and 35 mi of hiking, cross-country skiing, and horseback-riding trails. ✉ *U.S. 202 (2 mi west of village green)* ☎ *860/567–0857* ⊕ *www.whitememorialcc.org* ✍ *Conservation center $5, grounds free* ☉ *Conservation center Mon.–Sat. 9–5, Sun. noon–5; grounds daily.*

Where to Stay & Eat

★ $$–$$$$ ✕ **West Street Grill.** This sophisticated dining room on the town green is *the* place to see and be seen, both for patrons and for the state's up-and-coming chefs, many of whom got their start here. Imaginative grilled fish, steak, poultry, and lamb dishes are served with fresh vegetables and pasta or risotto. The ice cream and sorbets, made by the restaurant, are worth every calorie. ✉ *43 West St., 06759* ☎ *860/567–3885* ▭ *AE, MC, V.*

$$–$$$ ✕ **Village Restaurant.** The folks who run this storefront eatery in a red-brick town house serve food as tasty as any in town—inexpensive pub grub in one room, updated New American cuisine in the other. Whether you order a burger or herb-crusted pork chops, you're bound to be pleased. ✉ *25 West St., 06759* ☎ *860/567–8307* ▭ *AE, D, MC, V.*

$$–$$$$ ⌂ **The Litchfield Inn.** This reproduction Colonial-style inn lies little more than a mile west of the center of Litchfield. Period accents adorn its modern rooms, including themed "designer" rooms such as an "Irish" room (which has a four-poster bed draped in green floral chintz) and a "Southwestern" room (which employs a rustic picket fence as a headboard). ✉ *Rte. 202, 06759* ☎ *860/567–4503 or 800/499–3444* 📠 *860/567–5358* ⊕ *www.litchfieldinnct.com* ⌥ *32 rooms* �?⌂ *Restaurant, room service, cable TV, in-room data ports, bar, laundry service, business services, no-smoking rooms* ▭ *AE, DC, MC, V.*

Sports & the Outdoors

Lee's Riding Stables (✉ 57 E. Litchfield Rd. ☎ 860/567–0785) conducts trail and pony rides. At **Mt. Tom State Park** (✉ U.S. 202 ☎ 860/868–2592) you can boat, hike, swim, and fish in summer. The view from atop the mountain is outstanding.

Shopping

Jeffrey Tillou Antiques (✉ 39 West St. ☎ 860/567–9693) specializes in 18th- and 19th-century American furniture and paintings. The renowned **P. S. Gallery** (✉ 41 West St. ☎ 860/567–1059) showcases the works of area artists. At **Tina's Baskets** (✉ 3 West St., 2nd fl. ☎ 860/567–0385) artist Tina Puckett creates stunning handcrafted baskets and sculptures.

Bristol

③⓪ *17 mi southeast of Litchfield.*

There were some 275 clock makers in and around Bristol during the late 1800s—it is said that by the end of the 19th century just about every household in America told time by a Connecticut clock. Eli Terry (for whom nearby Terryville is named) first mass-produced clocks in the mid-19th century. Seth Thomas (for whom nearby Thomaston is named) learned under Terry and carried on the tradition.

You can set your watch by the **American Clock & Watch Museum,** one of the few museums in the country devoted entirely to clocks and watches. More than 1,400 timepieces make up the collection on display in this 1801 house, and though the majority of them are American timepieces from 1800 to 1940, the museum does have clocks dating from 1680 and watches dating from 1595. Many of the clocks are kept running and chiming, making the museum a prime place to be when the big hand strikes 12. ⊠ *100 Maple St.* ☎ *860/583–6070* ⊕ *www.clockmuseum. org* ⊠ *$5* ⊗ *Apr.–Nov., daily 10–5; Dec., Fri. and Sat. 10–5, Sun. 1–5; or by appointment.*

★ ☾ Known as the Lake, **Lake Compounce** opened in 1846 and is the oldest amusement park in the country. Today's attractions at the 325-acre facility include a lakefront beach; an ever-expanding water park with a wave pool, waterslides (high speed and otherwise), spray fountains, and a clipper ship with a 300-gallon bucket of water that gives unsuspecting guests a good dousing; and such hair-raising rides as the Sky Coaster, the Twister, and the Zoomerang. ⊠ *Rte. 229 N (I–84 Exit 31)* ☎ *860/ 583–3631* ⊕ *www.lakecompounce.com* ⊠ *$31.95* ⊗ *Memorial Day–Oct.; call for hrs.*

★ The **New England Carousel Museum** houses one of the largest collections of antique carousel pieces in the country. Full-size pieces in the Coney Island, Country Fair, and Philadelphia styles are on display, as are miniature carousels. The museum is also home to the **Bristol Center for Arts and Culture,** which hosts changing art exhibitions, and the **Museum of Fire History,** which displays firefighting photos, antique equipment, and memorabilia. The museum also oversees the Bushnell Park Carousel in Hartford (in operation May–October). ⊠ *95 Riverside Ave.* ☎ *860/ 585–5411* ⊕ *www.thecarouselmuseum.org* ⊠ *$5 (includes Bristol Center for Arts and Culture and Museum of Fire History)* ⊗ *Apr.–Nov., Mon.–Sat. 10–5, Sun. noon–5; Dec.–Mar., Thurs.–Sat. 10–5, Sun. noon–5.*

Where to Stay

$$–$$$ ▦ **Chimney Crest Manor.** All the rooms in this impressive 1930 Tudor mansion have spectacular views of the Farmington Valley. The 40-foot-long Garden Suite, in what was the mansion's ballroom, has gleaming hardwood floors, a fireplace, a queen-size canopy bed, its own kitchen, and tile walls with a dazzling sunflower motif. Breakfast, which might include yogurt pancakes, is served on fine china in the formal dining room or, more casually, on the grand fieldstone patio. Among the handsome public spaces are a sunroom and salon. ⊠ *5 Founders Dr., 06010* ☎ *860/582–4219* ☒ *860/584–8099* ↳ *5 rooms, 1 suite* ♿ *Library; no kids under 10, no smoking* ⊟ *AE, MC, V* ¶◎¶ *BP.*

Bethlehem

㉛ *16 mi west of Bristol.*

Come Christmas, Bethlehem is the most popular town in Connecticut. Cynics say that towns such as Canaan, Goshen, and Bethlehem were named primarily with the hope of attracting prospective residents and not truly out of religious deference. In any case, the local post office has its hands full postmarking the 220,000 pieces of holiday greetings mailed from Bethlehem every December.

The Benedictine nuns at the **Abbey of Regina Laudis,** who were made famous by their best-selling CD *Women in Chant,* sell their own pottery, candles, honey, cheese, herbs, beauty products, wool from abbey sheep, and more in an art shop near the main entrance to the abbey. The abbey's 18th-century Neapolitan crèche has more than 100 hand-carved baroque figures. Normally displayed in an 18th-century stable from Easter to Christmas, it closed in 2006 for restoration expected to take about a year. ⊠ *273 Flanders Rd.* ☎ *203/266–7637* ⊕ *www.abbeyofreginalaudis.com* ☯ *Mon., Tues., and Thurs.–Sun. 10–noon and 1:30–4.*

The **Bethlehem Christmas Town Festival** (☎ 203/266–5557), which takes place in early December, draws quite a crowd.

Washington

32 *11 mi west of Bethlehem.*

The beautiful buildings of The Gunnery prep school mingle with stately Colonials and churches in Washington, one of the best-preserved Colonial towns in Connecticut. The Mayflower Inn, south of The Gunnery on Route 47, attracts an exclusive clientele. Washington, which was settled in 1734, in 1779 became the first town in the United States to be named for the first president.

The **Institute for American Indian Studies** is a small but excellent and thoughtfully arranged collection of exhibits that detail the history and continuing presence of more than 10,000 years of Native American life in New England. Highlights include nature trails, a simulated archaeological site, and an authentically constructed Algonkian Village with wigwams, a longhouse, a rock shelter, and more. The Collections and Research Center has a research library, a large exhibit hall, and a gift shop that presents the work of some of the country's best Native American artists. The institute is at the end of a forested residential road (just follow the signs from Route 199 South). ⊠ *38 Curtis Rd., off Rte. 199* ☎ *860/868–0518* ⊕ *www.birdstone.org* ⊠ *$4* ☯ *Mon.–Sat. 10–5, Sun. noon–5.*

Where to Stay & Eat

$$$$ ╳▣ **Mayflower Inn.** Though the most-expensive suites at this inn cost
Fodor'sChoice an unbelievable $1,600 a night, the Mayflower is always booked
★ months in advance—and with good reason. Running streams, rambling stone walls, and rare specimen trees fill the country manor-style inn's 28 manicured acres. Fine antiques, 18th- and 19th-century art, and four-poster canopy beds define each of the rooms. The colossal baths have mahogany wainscoting, marble, and Limoges and brass fittings. At the posh restaurant ($$$–$$$$), the menu changes seasonally but may list entrées such as Parmesan-and-arugula-crusted halibut or oven-roasted free-range chicken breast. ⊠ *118 Woodbury Rd. (Rte. 47), 06793* ☎ *860/868–9466* ⊟ *860/868–1497* ⊕ *www.mayflowerinn.com* ⇖ *19 rooms, 11 suites* ☖ *Restaurant, in-room data ports, tennis court, pool,*

health club, spa, bar, meeting room, no-smoking rooms; no kids under 12 ⊟ AE, MC, V.

Woodbury

㉝ *10 mi southeast of Washington.*

There may very well be more antiques shops in the quickly growing town of Woodbury than in all the towns in the rest of the Litchfield Hills combined. Five magnificent churches and the Greek-revival King Solomon's Temple, formerly a Masonic lodge, line U.S. 6; they represent some of the best-preserved examples of Colonial religious architecture in New England.

The **Glebe House Museum and Gertrude Jekyll Garden** consists of the large, antiques-filled, gambrel-roof Colonial in which Dr. Samuel Seabury was elected America's first Episcopal bishop, in 1783, and its historic garden. The latter was designed in the 1920s by renowned British horticulturist Gertrude Jekyll. Small, it is a classic, old-fashioned English-style garden, the only one of the three gardens Jekyll designed in the United States still in existence. ⊠ *Hollow Rd.* ☎ *203/263–2855* ⊕ *www. theglebehouse.org* ⌗ *$5* ⊙ *Apr.–Oct., Wed.–Sun. 1–4; Nov., weekends 1–4; Dec.–Mar. by appointment.*

Where to Stay & Eat

$$$–$$$$
Fodor'sChoice
★

✕ **Good News Café.** Carole Peck is a well-known name in these parts, and her decision to open a restaurant in Woodbury was met with cheers. The emphasis is on healthful, innovative fare: wok-seared Gulf shrimp with new potatoes, grilled green beans, and a garlic aioli, or grilled East Coast swordfish with a watermelon salsa, curried basmati rice, and sesame green beans are good choices. ⊠ *694 Main St. S, 06798* ☎ *203/266–4663* ⊕ *www.good-news-cafe.com* ⊟ *AE, D, MC, V* ⊙ *Closed Tues.*

$–$$$

▥ **Dolce Heritage.** This sprawling resort has a modern Colonial look and extensive facilities. Guest rooms have dark traditional furniture and modern amenities; some have river or golf-course views. Drop by Schadrack's Tap Room for light fare or a drink after a day on the greens. ⊠ *522 Heritage Rd., Southbury 06488* ☎ *203/264–8200 or 800/932–3466* 🖷 *203/264–5035* ⊕ *www.heritage.dolce.com* ⇆ *163 rooms, 5 suites* ⚘ *Restaurant, in-room data ports, 18-hole golf course, 2 tennis courts, pool, health club, spa, racquetball, bar* ⊟ *AE, D, DC, MC, V.*

Sports & the Outdoors

SKI AREA **Woodbury Ski Area.** This small, laid-back ski area with a 300-foot vertical drop has 22 downhill trails of varying difficulty that are serviced by a double chairlift, one rope tow, two handle tows, two magic carpet lifts, and a T-bar. About half of the 9 mi of cross-country trails are groomed, and 1 mi is lighted and covered with snow from snowmaking machines when necessary. There's a snowboard and alpine park, a skateboard and in-line skating park, and a special area for sledding and tubing serviced by two lifts and three tows. Snowbiking and snowshoeing are other options. Lessons are given for both adults and children. ⊠ *Rte. 47, 06798* ☎ *203/263–2203.*

Shopping

Country Loft Antiques (⊠ 557 Main St. S ☎ 203/266–4500) specializes in 18th- and 19th-century country French antiques. **David Dunton** (⊠ Rte. 132 off Rte. 47 ☎ 203/263–5355) is a respected dealer of formal American Federal–style furniture. **Mill House Antiques** (⊠ 1068 Main St. N ☎ 203/263–3446) carries formal and country English and French furniture and has the state's largest collection of Welsh dressers. **Monique Shay Antiques & Design** (⊠ 920 Main St. S ☎ 203/263–3186) favors Canadian country antiques.

The **Woodbury Pewter Factory Outlet Store** (⊠ 860 Main St. S ☎ 203/263–2668) has discounts on fine reproductions of Early American tankards, Revere bowls, candlesticks, and more.

Waterbury

③④ *15 mi east of Woodbury, 28 mi southwest of Hartford, 28 mi north of Bridgeport.*

Waterbury, in the Naugatuck River valley, was once known as Brass City for its role as the country's top producer of brass products in the 19th and early-20th centuries. Evidence of the prosperity of the city's brass barons can still be seen in the hillside district northwest of downtown, where grand old Queen Anne, Greek and Georgian-revival, and English Tudor homes remain, a few of which have been turned into bed-and-breakfasts. Today Waterbury and its shops and restaurants serve as an urban center for people in the nearby Litchfield Hills. The dramatic 240-foot **Clock Tower** (⊠ 389 Meadow St.) in the historic downtown was modeled after the city-hall tower in Siena, Italy.

The **Mattatuck Museum** has a fine collection of 19th- and 20th-century paintings and sculptures by artists who have lived or worked in Connecticut. Pieces range from the 19th-century folk paintings of Erastus Salisbury Field and one of the celebrated "iceberg" paintings of Frederic Church to works by modern masters such as Josef Albers and Alexander Calder. The museum's Brass Roots exhibit looks back at the lives of the leaders and workers who transformed Waterbury into one of the nation's leading industrial centers. Within the Mattatuck, the Waterbury Button Museum exhibits approximately 10,000 of these miniature works of art from Waterbury and around the world. Also here is a 300-seat performing arts center and charming museum café. ⊠ *144 W. Main St.* ☎ *203/753–0381* ⊕ *www.mattatuckmuseum. org* 🎟 *$4* ☉ *Sept.–June, Tues.–Sat. 10–5, Sun. noon–5; July and Aug., Tues.–Sat. 10–5.*

The **Timexpo Museum,** housed in a renovated brass mill, curiously combines the history of Timex, which came into being as Waterbury Clock in the 1850s, with archaeological exhibits tracing the travels of Norwegian explorer Thor Heyerdahl. Additional components include a timepiece collection, interactive exhibits, and crafts activities. A museum store sells Timex watches, clocks, and related merchandise. ⊠ *175 Union St., Brass Mill Commons* ☎ *203/755–8463* ⊕ *www.timexpo.com* 🎟 *$6* ☉ *Tues.–Sat. 10–5, closed Sun. and Mon.*

Where to Stay & Eat

★ $$–$$$$ ✕ **Carmen Anthony Steakhouse.** A worthy re-creation of the steak houses of old, Carmen Anthony has rich wood paneling, handsome oil paintings on the walls, and white linen on the tables. You can order Delmonico, filet mignon, porterhouse, and other steaks served in all their charbroiled glory or go for something a bit fancier, like filet mignon Milanese. Seafood is also available; try the fresh Maine lobsters. ✉ *496 Chase Ave., 06704* ☎ *203/757–3040* ⊕ *www.carmenanthony.com* ▭ *AE, D, DC, MC, V* ◇ *No lunch weekends.*

★ $$–$$$ ✕ **Diorio Restaurant and Bar.** The dining room at Diorio, a Waterbury tradition for more than a half century, retains its original mahogany bankers' booth, marble brass bar, high tin ceilings, exposed brick, and white-tile floors. The dishes here are expertly prepared, from the fresh lobster ravioli with blue crab sauce to the dozens of pasta, chicken, veal, steak, and seafood plates. ✉ *231 Bank St.* ☎ *203/754–5111* ⊕ *www. diorios.com* ▭ *AE, D, DC, MC, V* ◇ *Closed Sun. No lunch Sat.*

$$–$$$ ⊞ **House on the Hill.** Owner-innkeeper Marianne Vandenburgh's fanciful B&B is surrounded by lush gardens in a historic hillside neighborhood. The three-story 1888 Victorian, former home of a brass baron, has a glorious exterior color scheme of teal, sage green, red, and ivory. The rich original woodwork and details remain, and guest rooms—four suites—are furnished in a welcoming blend of antiques and nostalgia. One suite has two bedrooms and another has a kitchenette. ✉ *92 Woodlawn Terr., 06710* ☎ *203/757–9901* ⊕ *www.houseonthehillbedandbreakfast.com* ⇨*4 suites* △ *In-room data ports, library, meeting room; no smoking* ▭*AE, D, DC, MC, V* ◇ *Closed mid-Dec.–mid-Jan* ⦿ *BP.*

Nightlife & the Arts

Seven Angels Theatre (✉ Hamilton Park Pavilion, Plank Rd. ☎ 203/757–4676) presents first-rate plays, musicals, children's theater, cabaret concerts, and youth programs.

Shopping

Howland-Hughes (✉ 120 Bank St. ☎ 203/753–4121) is stocked entirely with items made in Connecticut, from Wiffle balls to Pez candies, fine pottery to glassware.

NEW HAVEN & THE SOUTHEAST

As you drive northeast along Interstate 95, culturally rich New Haven is the final urban obstacle between southwestern Connecticut's overdeveloped coast and southeastern Connecticut's quieter shoreline. The remainder of the jagged coast, which stretches all the way to the Rhode Island border, consists of small coastal villages, quiet hamlets, and relatively undisturbed beaches. The only interruptions along this mostly undeveloped seashore are the industry and piers of New London and Groton. Mystic, Stonington, Old Saybrook, Clinton, and Guilford are havens for fans of antiques and boutiques. North of Groton, near the town of Ledyard, the Mashantucket Pequot Reservation owns and operates Foxwoods Casino and the Mashantucket Pequot Museum & Research Center. The Mohegan Indians run the Mohegan Sun casino in Uncasville.

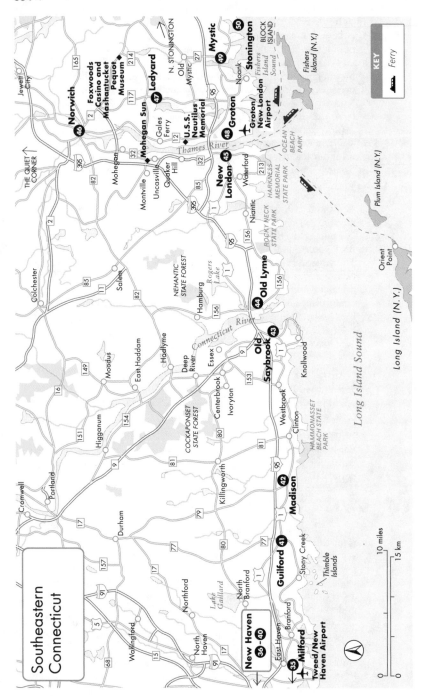

Southeastern Connecticut

KEY

⛴ Ferry

THE QUIET CORNER

165 Jewett City

2 **Norwich** 46

Foxwoods Casino and Mashantucket Pequot Museum ♦ 214

117 **Ledyard** 47

N. STONINGTON

27 Old Mystic

Mystic 50

Stonington 49

Noank

BLOCK ISLAND

Fishers Island Sound

Fishers Island (N.Y.)

395

82 Mohegan

Mohegan Sun ♦ 32

Gales Ferry 12

U.S.S. Nautilus Memorial ⚓

Groton 48

Thames River

95

Groton/New London Airport ✈

OCEAN BEACH PARK

Montville

Uncasville

Quaker Hill 85

New London 45

32

Plum Island (N.Y.)

Colchester

85 111

Salem 82

NEHANTIC STATE FOREST

Hamburg

Rogers Lake

156

395 1

Waterford 213

Niantic

156

ROCKY NECK STATE PARK

HARKNESS MEMORIAL STATE PARK

95

Long Island Sound

16

149

Moodus

East Haddam

Hadlyme

Connecticut River

156

Old Lyme 44

156

Orient Point

Long Island (N.Y.)

151

Higganum

154

9

Deep River

Essex

Ivoryton

Centerbrook

Old Saybrook 43

1

9

153

Knollwood

Cromwell

Portland

17

Durham 77

80

81

81

Killingworth

Clinton

Westbrook

HAMMONASSET BEACH STATE PARK

95

Madison 42

157

17

79

80

77

1

1

Guilford 41

Stony Creek

Thimble Islands

5 68

Wallingford

15

91

North Haven

Northford

North Branford

Lake Gaillard

Branford

New Haven 36–40

East Haven

Milford 35 ✈

Tweed/New Haven Airport

0 ⊢ 10 miles

0 ⊢ 15 km

Milford

35 *6 mi northeast of Stratford.*

Milford, established in 1639, is Connecticut's sixth-oldest municipality, and it retains the feel of a small coastal town despite its more than 48,000 residents and the commercial stretch of the Boston Post Road that runs through its center. The large town green is at the heart of this community, and it sparkles in winter with thousands of tiny white lights strung in its trees. The duck pond and waterfall behind city hall is a pleasant place to while away a spring afternoon, and Milford's many beaches, open to the public for the price of parking, are inviting in summer.

The **Connecticut Audubon Coastal Center,** on a barrier beach next door to an 840-acre reserve where the Housatonic River meets Long Island Sound, has educational exhibits, lectures, and classes indoors; outdoors are a 70-foot observation tower that provides a view of all the reserve has to offer, a boardwalk and observation platform at the water's edge, and an amazing assortment of birds year-round. ⊠ *1 Milford Point Rd.* ☎ *203/878–7440* ⊕ *www.ctaudubon.org/visit/milford.htm* ⊒ *Donation suggested at center, grounds free* ☉ *Center Tues.–Sat. 10–4, Sun. noon–4; grounds daily dawn–dusk.*

Where to Eat

\$\$–\$\$\$ ✕ **Jeffrey's.** This popular restaurant serves up-to-the-minute new American cuisine in a refined yet welcoming setting that includes an antique Dutch armoire and a grand piano. Some of the changing specials have included wasabi-encrusted ahi tuna over basmati rice and pan-seared filet mignon with a horseradish potato tart. ⊠ *501 New Haven Ave., 06460* ☎ *203/878–1910* ⊟ *AE, D, DC, MC, V.*

¢   ✕ **Paul's Famous Hamburgers.** "Not serving numbers, but generations" is the motto of this drive-in established in 1946. It's the place to go for extraordinarily fresh and juicy burgers, hot dogs on toasted buns, fries, Reubens, and milk shakes thick enough to stand a spoon in. ⊠ *829 Boston Post Rd.* ☎ *203/874–7586* ⊟ *No credit cards* ☉ *Closed Sun.*

Sports & the Outdoors

BEACHES   **Silver Sands State Park,** with its signature beach and old-fashioned wooden boardwalk, is an inviting spot to while away an afternoon— whatever the season. You can walk out to Charles Island (where Captain Kidd is rumored to have buried his treasure) at low tide. ⊠ *600 E. Broadway* ☎ *203/735–4311* ⊒ *Free* ☉ *Daily 8 AM–dusk.*

New Haven

9 mi east of Milford, 46 mi northeast of Greenwich.

New Haven's history goes back to the 17th century, when its squares, including a lovely central green for the public, were laid out. The city, a cultural center, is home to Yale University. The historic district surrounding Yale and the shops, museums, theaters, and restaurants on nearby Chapel Street are handsome and prosperous. Be careful, however, about exploring areas away from the campus and city common at night.

On a Roll

BEHOLD THE LOBSTER ROLL. Sweet, succulent, and sinfully rich, it's the ultimate buttery icon of a Connecticut summer. Other New England states may prefer to chill out with lobster rolls created from a cool mix of lobster meat, mayonnaise, and chopped celery, but Nutmeggers like their one-of-a-kind rolls served hot, hot, hot.

The traditional Connecticut lobster roll, said to have been invented in the early 1930s at Perry's, a now-defunct seafood shack on the Boston Post Road in Milford, consists of nothing more than plump chunks of hot lobster meat and melted butter served on a butter-toasted roll. In other words: heaven on a bun. From seafood shanties along the shore to more gourmet getaways farther inland, Connecticut is fairly swimming with eateries that offer these revered rolls. Three favorites: A roll at **Abbott's Lobster in the Rough** (✉ 117 Pearl St., Noank ☎ 860/536–7719 ⊕ www.abbotts-lobster.com) is best enjoyed seated at a picnic table at the edge of Noank Harbor watching the boats bob by. At **Lenny and Joe's Fish Tale Drive-in** (✉ 1301 Boston Post Rd., Madison ☎ 203/245–7289 ⊕ www.ljfishtale.com), kids of all ages love to eat outdoors by a hand-carved Dentzel carousel with flying horses (and a whale, frog, lion, seal, and more), which the restaurant runs from early May through early October. **Marnick's** (✉ 10 Washington Pkwy., Stratford ☎ 203/377–6288 ⊕ www. marnicks.nv.switchboard.com), on a small beach on the Long Island Sound, is a place where you can kick off your shoes for a picnic on the sand or leave them on and enjoy a leisurely after-dinner stroll along a sea wall.

㊱ Bordered on the west side by the Yale campus, the **New Haven Green** (✉ Between Church and College Sts.) is a fine example of early urban planning. As early as 1638, village elders set aside the 16-acre plot as a town common. Three early-19th-century churches—the Gothic-style **Trinity Episcopal Church,** the Georgian-style **Center Congregational Church,** and the predominantly Federal-style **United Church**—contribute to its present appeal.

★ New Haven as a manufacturing center dates from the 19th century, but the city owes its fame to merchant Elihu Yale. In 1718 Yale's contributions enabled the Collegiate School, founded in 1701 at Saybrook, to settle in New Haven, where it changed its name to **Yale University.** This is one of the nation's great universities, and its campus holds some handsome neo-Gothic buildings and a number of noteworthy museums. The university's knowledgeable guides conduct one-hour walking tours that include Connecticut Hall in the Old Campus, which counts Nathan Hale, William Howard Taft, and Noah Webster among its past residents. ✉ *Yale Visitor Center, 149 Elm St.* ☎ *203/432–2300* ⊕ *www.yale.edu/visitor* ☞ *Free* ◷ *Tours weekdays at 10:30 and 2, weekends at 1:30* ☞ *Tours start from 149 Elm St. on north side of New Haven Green.*

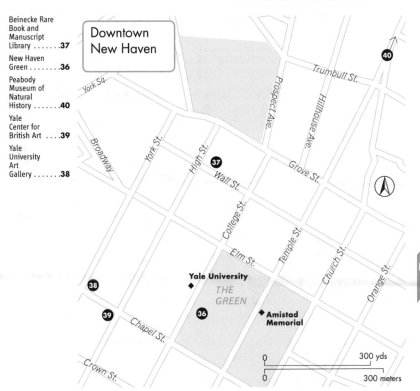

37 The collections at Yale's **Beinecke Rare Book and Manuscript Library** include a Gutenberg Bible, illuminated manuscripts, and original Audubon bird prints, but the building is almost as much of an attraction—the walls are made of marble cut so thin that the light shines through, making the interior a breathtaking sight on sunny days. ⊠ *121 Wall St.* ☎ *203/432–2977* ⊕ *www.library.yale.edu/beinecke* ⊠ *Free* ⊗ *Mon.–Thurs. 8:30–8, Fri. 8:30–5, Sat. 10–5.*

40 Yale's **Peabody Museum of Natural History** opened in 1876; with more than 11 million specimens, it's one of the largest natural history museums in the nation. In addition to exhibits on Andean, Mesoamerican, and Pacific cultures, the venerable museum has an excellent collection of birds, including a stuffed dodo and passenger pigeon. But the main attractions for children and amateur paleontologists alike are some of the world's earliest reconstructions of dinosaur skeletons. ⊠ *170 Whitney Ave.* ☎ *203/432–5050* ⊕ *www.peabody.yale.edu* ⊠ *$7* ⊗ *Mon.–Sat. 10–5, Sun. noon–5.*

39 The **Yale Center for British Art**, which surveys the development of English art, life, and thought from the Elizabethan period to the present, has the most comprehensive collection of British art outside Britain. The center's skylighted galleries, architect Louis I. Kahn's final work

Fodor'sChoice
★

(completed after his death), contain works by Constable, Hogarth, Gainsborough, Reynolds, and Turner, to name but a few. You'll also find rare books and paintings documenting English history. ⊠ *1080 Chapel St.* ☎ *203/432–2800* ⊕ *www.yale.edu/ycba* 🎟 *Free* ☉ *Tues.–Sat. 10–5, Sun. noon–5.*

❸❽ Since its founding in 1832, the **Yale University Art Gallery** has amassed more than 85,000 objects from around the world, dating from ancient Egypt to the present day. Highlights include works by van Gogh, Manet, Monet, Picasso, Winslow Homer, and Thomas Eakins, as well as Etruscan and Greek vases, Chinese ceramics and bronzes, early Italian paintings, and a collection of American decorative arts that is considered one of the world's finest. The gallery's landmark main building is also of note. Opened in 1953, it was Louis I. Kahn's first major commission and the first modernist building on the neo-Gothic Yale campus. Over the years, its extensive open spaces were subdivided into galleries, classrooms, and offices, but a major renovation, completed in 2006, restored it to Kahn's original conception. ⊠ *1111 Chapel St.* ☎ *203/432–0600* ⊕ *www.yale.edu/artgallery* 🎟 *Free* ☉ *Tues.–Sat. 10–5, Sun. 1–6.*

Where to Stay & Eat

$$–$$$ ✕ **Ibiza.** Owner Ignacio Blanco and chef Luis Bollo are *the* names in Span-
Fodor'sChoice ish cuisine in the state. Tall ceilings, multipaned windows, exposed
★ brick, and vibrant murals create a backdrop for such extraordinary dishes as Catalan noodle paella with codfish, salmon, shrimp, bay scallops, and cockles, and roasted eggplant cannelloni served over sautéed pepper, onions, tomatoes, and black olives. A tasting menu is available Monday–Thursday. ⊠ *39 High St., 06510* ☎ *203/865–1933* ⊕ *www. ibizanewhaven.com* ▭ *AE, MC, V* ☉ *Closed Sun. No lunch Fri.–Wed.*

★ **$–$$** ✕ **Frank Pepe's.** Does this place serve the best pizza in the world, as so many reviewers claim? If it doesn't, it comes close. Pizza is the only thing prepared here—try the justifiably famous white-clam pie. Expect to wait an hour or more for a table—or, on weekend evenings, come after 10. **The Spot,** right behind the restaurant, is owned by Pepe's and is sometimes open when Pepe's is not. ⊠ *157 Wooster St., 06510* ☎ *203/865– 5762* ⌕ *Reservations not accepted* ▭ *No credit cards* ☉ *No lunch Mon.–Thurs.*

¢ ✕ **Louis' Lunch.** This all-American luncheonette on the National Register of Historic Places claims to be the birthplace of the hamburger in America. Its first-rate burgers are cooked in an old-fashioned, upright broiler and served with either a slice of tomato or cheese on two slices of toast. And, as most customers who come from far and wide for these tasty morsels agree, it doesn't get much better than that. ⊠ *263 Crown St., 06510* ☎ *203/562–5507* ▭ *No credit cards* ☉ *Closed Sun. and Mon. No dinner Tues. and Wed.*

$$$–$$$$ ▥ **Omni New Haven Hotel at Yale.** This 19-floor Omni is the only large hotel in the city. With modern amenities, it's comfortable and convenient to the heart of New Haven. John Davenport's at the Top of the Park, the upscale rooftop restaurant, serves traditional American fare along with views of the Yale campus, New Haven Green, and Long Island Sound. ⊠ *155 Temple St., 06510* ☎ *203/772–6664* 🖶 *203/974–6777* ⊕ *www.*

omnihotels.com ☞ *299 rooms, 7 suites* ⟋ *Restaurant, in-room data ports, health club, lounge, business services, meeting room, some pets allowed* ▭ *AE, D, DC, MC, V.*

★ $$$ ⊡ **Three Chimneys Inn.** This 1870 Victorian mansion is one of the classiest small inns in the state. Rooms have posh Georgian furnishings: mahogany four-poster beds, oversize armoires, Chippendale desks, and Oriental rugs. The sitting room and library have working fireplaces—both good places in which to enjoy the inn's afternoon tea. ⊠ *1201 Chapel St., 06511* ☎ *203/789–1201* 📠 *203/776–7363* ⊕ *www.threechimneysinn. com* ☞ *11 rooms* ⟋ *Exercise equipment, library, business services, meeting room, no-smoking rooms* ▭ *AE, MC, V* ⦿ *BP.*

Nightlife & the Arts

NIGHTLIFE **Anna Liffey's** (⊠ 17 Whitney Ave. ☎ 203/773–1776) is one of the city's liveliest Irish pubs. **BAR** (⊠ 254 Crown St. ☎ 203/495–1111) is a cross between a nightclub, a brick-oven pizzeria, and a brewpub. **Richter's** (⊠ 990 Chapel St. ☎ 203/777–0400) is famous for its half-yard glasses of beer. Alternative and traditional rock bands play at **Toad's Place** (⊠ 300 York St. ☎ 203/624–8623).

THE ARTS The **New Haven Symphony Orchestra** (☎ 203/865–0831) plays at Yale University's **Woolsey Hall** (⊠ College and Grove Sts.).

The well-regarded **Long Wharf Theatre** (⊠ 222 Sargent Dr. ☎ 203/787–4282) presents works by contemporary writers and imaginative revivals of neglected classics. The **Shubert Performing Arts Center** (⊠ 247 College St. ☎ 203/562–5666) hosts Broadway musicals and dramas, usually following their run in the Big Apple, plus dance and classical-music performances.

The highly professional **Yale Repertory Theatre** (⊠ Chapel and York Sts. ☎ 203/432–1234) premieres new plays and mounts fresh interpretations of the classics.

Yale School of Music (☎ 203/432–4157) presents an impressive roster of performers, from classical to jazz; most events take place in the Morse Recital Hall in **Sprague Hall** (⊠ College and Wall Sts.).

Shopping

Chapel Street, near the town green, has a pleasing assortment of shops and eateries. **Atticus Bookstore & Café** (⊠ 1082 Chapel St. ☎ 203/776–4040), in the heart of Yale University, was one of the first stores to combine books and food; it's been a favorite among museum groupies and theatergoers for years.

EN
ROUTE The village of Stony Creek, roughly 9 mi east of New Haven, with a few tackle shops, antiques shops, a general store, and a marina, is the departure point for cruises around the **Thimble Islands.** This group of more than 90 tiny islands was named for its abundance of thimbleberries, which are similar to gooseberries. Legend has it that Captain Kidd buried pirate gold on one island. Three sightseeing vessels vie for your patronage: the *Islander* (☎ 203/397–3921), the *Sea Mist II* (☎ 203/488–8905 ⊕ www.seamistcruises.com), and the *Volsunga IV* (☎ 203/481–3345

⊕ www.thimbleislands.com). All three depart from Stony Creek Dock, at the end of Thimble Island Road, from May to Columbus Day.

Guilford

④ *5 mi northeast of Branford, 37 mi west of New London.*

The Guilford town green, crisscrossed by pathways, dotted with benches, and lined with historic homes and specialty shops, is considered by many to be the prettiest green in the state and is actually the third largest in the Northeast.

The **Henry Whitfield State Museum,** built in 1639, is the oldest house in the state and the oldest stone house in New England. The furnishings in the post-medieval-style building were made between the 17th and 19th centuries. The visitor center has two exhibition galleries, a research library, and a gift shop. ⊠ *248 Old Whitfield St.* ☎ *203/453–2457* ⊕ *www.whitfieldmuseum.org* 🎫 *$4* ☉ *Apr.–mid-Dec., Wed.–Sun. 10–4:30; mid-Dec.–Mar. by appointment.*

Where to Eat

$$–$$$ ✕ **Martin's.** A beautifully restored Victorian building with a wall of windows overlooking Guilford Green is the backdrop for this lively café's mix of traditional and contemporary American cuisine. You might find New York strip steak, filet mignon, or mango lobster coloring your plate. ⊠ *25 Whitfield St., 06437* ☎ *203/458–1300* ⊟ *AE, MC, V.*

Shopping

The **Guilford Arts Center** (⊠ 411 Church St. ☎ 203/453–5947) sponsors seven crafts exhibitions a year and has an excellent shop that represents more than 300 artists.

Madison

④ *5 mi east of Guilford, 62 mi northeast of Greenwich.*

Coastal Madison has an understated charm. Ice cream parlors, antiques stores, and quirky gift boutiques prosper along U.S. 1, the town's main street. Stately Colonial homes line the town green, site of many a summer antiques fair and arts-and-crafts festival. The Madison shoreline, particularly the white stretch of sand known as Hammonasset Beach and its parallel boardwalk, draws visitors year-round.

Hammonasset Beach State Park, the largest of the state's shoreline sanctuaries, has 2 mi of white-sand beaches, a top-notch nature center, excellent birding, and a hugely popular campground with about 550 sites. ⊠ *I–95 Exit 62* ☎ *203/245–2785 park, 203/245–1817 campground* 🎫 *Park $7–$14 mid-Apr.–mid.-Oct., free off-season* ☉ *Park daily 8 AM–dusk.*

Where to Stay & Eat

$$ ✕🏨 **Inn at Lafayette.** Skylights, painted murals, and handcrafted woodwork are among the design accents at this airy hostelry in a converted 1830s church. The rooms may be small, but they are decorated with beautiful fabrics and reproduction 17th- and 18th-century antique furniture. The modern marble baths come equipped with telephones. Fresh food and flawless service are highlights at Café Allegre ($$; closed Monday), the inn's popular restaurant. The menu is largely southern Italian, with French accents. ⊠ *725 Boston Post Rd., 06443* ☎ *203/245–7773 or 866/623–7498* 🖷 *203/245–6256* ⊕ *www.allegrecafe.com/innatlafayette.htm* 🛏 *5 rooms* ♿ *Restaurant, in-room data ports, bar, business services, meeting room* ⊟ *AE, D, DC, MC, V* ⅼ⊙⅃ *CP.*

Old Saybrook

🕸 *9 mi east of Madison, 29 mi east of New Haven.*

Old Saybrook, once a lively shipbuilding and fishing town, bustles with summer vacationers and antiques shoppers. Its downtown is an especially pleasing place for a window-shopping stroll. At the end of the afternoon, stop at the old-fashioned soda fountain, where you can share a sundae with your sweetie.

Where to Stay & Eat

★ **$$–$$$** ✕ **Café Routier.** "Campstyle" grilled trout with lyonnaise potatoes and a whole-grain mustard sauce, fried oysters with a chipotle rémoulade, and a duck-and-wild-mushroom ragout are among the favorites at this classy Yankee bistro. ⊠ *1353 Boston Post Rd., 5 mi west of Old Saybrook, Westbrook 06498* ☎ *860/399–8700* ⊕ *www.caferoutier.com* ⊟ *AE, D, DC, MC, V* ⊙ *No lunch.*

$–$$ ✕ **Pat's Kountry Kitchen.** Upbeat service and traditional New England fare have made this home-style restaurant a local institution and a family favorite. Best-sellers are the fresh clam hash, pork chops, and apple-cranberry-raisin pie. ⊠ *70 Mill Rock Rd. E, 06475* ☎ *860/388–4784* ⊟ *AE, D, DC, MC, V* ⊙ *Closed Wed.*

$$$$ ✕▦ **Saybrook Point Inn & Spa.** Rooms at the Saybrook are furnished mainly in 18th-century style, with reproductions of British furniture and impressionist art. The health club and pools overlook the inn's marina and the Connecticut River. The Terra Mar Grille ($$$–$$$$), which sits on the river, serves stylish Continental cuisine such as sautéed tilapia meunière with seared sea scallops, jasmine rice, and concasse of tomato. ⊠ *2 Bridge St., 06475* ☎ *860/395–2000 or 800/243–0212* 🖷 *860/388–1504* ⊕ *www.saybrook.com* 🛏 *68 rooms, 12 suites* ♿ *Restaurant, in-room data ports, 2 pools (1 indoor), health club, spa, marina, meeting room, some pets allowed* ⊟ *AE, D, DC, MC, V.*

★ **$$$$** ▦ **Water's Edge Inn & Resort.** With its spectacular setting on Long Island Sound, this traditional weathered gray-shingle compound in Westbrook is one of the Connecticut shore's premier resorts. The main building has warm, bright public rooms furnished with antiques and reproductions, and its upstairs bedrooms, with wall-to-wall carpeting and clean, modern bathrooms, afford priceless views of the sound. ⊠ *1525 Boston Post Rd., 5 mi west of Old Saybrook, Westbrook 06498* ☎ *860/399–5901 or 800/222–5901* 🖷 *860/399–6172* ⊕ *www.watersedgeresortandspa.com* 🛏 *162 rooms* ♿ *Restaurant, in-room data ports, 2 tennis courts, 2 pools (1 indoor), health club, spa, beach, volleyball, bar, business services, meeting room* ⊟ *AE, D, DC, MC, V.*

6

Shopping

More than 120 dealers operate out of the **Essex-Saybrook Antiques Village** (⊠ 345 Middlesex Tpke. ☎ 860/388–0689). **Beautiful Impressions** (⊠ 2 Pennywise La. ☎ 860/395–1229) sells both watercolors and ice cream sodas in a historic former general store–pharmacy. **North Cove Outfitters** (⊠ 75 Main St. ☎ 860/388–6585) is Connecticut's version of L. L. Bean. **Saybrook Country Barn** (⊠ 2 Main St. ☎ 860/388–0891) sells everything country, from tiger-maple dining-room tables to hand-painted pottery.

Old Lyme

44 *4 mi east of Old Saybrook, 40 mi south of Hartford.*

Old Lyme, on the other side of the Connecticut River from Old Saybrook, is renowned among art lovers for its past as the home of the Lyme Art Colony, the most famous gathering of impressionist painters in America. Artists continue to be attracted to the area for its lovely countryside and shoreline. The town also has handsome old houses, many built for sea captains.

Fodor'sChoice ★ Central to Old Lyme's artistic reputation is the **Florence Griswold Museum,** a grand late-Georgian-style mansion owned by Miss Florence Griswold that served as a boardinghouse for members of the Lyme Art Colony in the first decades of the 20th century. When artists such as Willard Metcalf, Clark Voorhees, Childe Hassam, and Henry Ward Ranger flocked to the area to paint its varied landscape, Miss Florence offered housing as well as artistic encouragement. The house was turned into a museum in 1947 and, recently closed for renovation, reopened in summer 2006 restored to its appearance in 1910, when the colony was in full flower (clues to the house's layout and decor in that era were provided by many of the members' paintings). The museum's 10,000-square-foot Krieble Gallery, opened in 2002 on the riverfront, hosts changing exhibitions of American art. ⊠ 96 *Lyme St.* ☎ 860/434–5542 ⊕ *www.florencegriswoldmuseum.org* ☜ *$7* ⊙ *Tues.–Sat. 10–5, Sun. 1–5.*

Where to Stay & Eat

$$–$$$$ ✕🏠 **Bee & Thistle Inn.** Behind a weathered stone wall in the Old Lyme
Fodor'sChoice ★ historic district is a three-story 1756 Colonial house with 5½ acres of broad lawns, formal gardens, and herbaceous borders. The scale of rooms throughout is small and inviting, with fireplaces in the parlors and dining rooms and light and airy curtains in the multipaned guest-room windows. Most rooms have canopy or four-poster beds. Fireplaces and candlelight exude romance in the restaurant ($$$–$$$$; closed Monday and Tuesday), where American cuisine—with entrées such as blackberry-braised duck breast—is served with style. ⊠ *100 Lyme St., 06371* ☎ *860/434–1667 or 800/622–4946* 🖷 *860/434–3402* ⊕ *www. beeandthistleinn.com* ⇥ *11 rooms* ₺ *Restaurant, no-smoking rooms; no kids under 12* ▭ *AE, DC, MC, V* ¶⚪❙ *BP.*

New London

45 *3 mi northeast of Waterford, 46 mi east of New Haven.*

New London, on the banks of the Thames River, has long had ties to the sea. In the mid-1800s it was the second-largest whaling port in the world. Today the U.S. Coast Guard Academy uses its campus on the Thames to educate and train its cadets. Ocean Beach Park, an old-fashioned beach resort with a wooden boardwalk, provides an up-close-and-personal view of New London's connection to the deep blue sea.

The **Lyman Allyn Art Museum,** housed in a neoclassical building that overlooks both the U. S. Coast Guard Academy and Long Island Sound, was founded in 1926 by Harriet Upson Allyn in memory of her whaling merchant father, Lyman Allyn. Inside is an impressive collection of more than 15,000 objects covering a span of 5,000 years. Works include contemporary, modern, and Early American fine arts; American impressionist paintings; and Connecticut decorative arts. European works from the 16th through the 19th centuries round out the permanent collection. ⊠ *625 Williams St.* ☎ *860/443–2545* ⊕ *www.lymanallyn.org* ⌑ *$5* ☉ *Tues.–Sat. 10–5, Sun. 1–5.*

The 100-acre cluster of redbrick buildings you see overlooking the Thames River is the **U.S. Coast Guard Academy,** one of the country's four military academies. A museum on the property explores the Coast Guard's 200 years of maritime service and includes some 200 ship models, as well as figureheads, paintings, uniforms, and cannon. The three-mast training bark, the USCGC *Eagle,* may be boarded Friday–Sunday 1–5 when in port. ⊠ *15 Mohegan Ave.* ☎ *860/444–8270* ⊕ *www.cga.edu* ⌑ *Free* ☉ *Weekdays 9–5, Sat. 10–5, Sun. noon–5.*

Where to Stay

$$–$$$$ ⬚ **Lighthouse Inn Resort and Conference Center.** This Mediterranean-style-mansion–turned–inn was built in 1902 as the summer home of a steel magnate. When it opened as an inn in 1927 it was a retreat for film stars such as Bette Davis and Joan Crawford. The hotel retains its original grandeur, including the grounds designed by renowned landscape architect Frederick Law Olmsted, designer of New York's Central Park. Rooms in the semicircular mansion are appointed with a mix of antiques and period pieces; some face Long Island Sound. ⊠ *6 Guthrie Pl., 06320* ☎ *860/443–8411 or 888/443–8411* ⊟ *860/437–7027* ⊕ *www.lighthouseinn-ct.com* ⟿ *52 rooms* ⌂ *Restaurant, in-room data ports, spa, beach, bar, lounge, meeting rooms* ⊟ *AE, MC, V* ⑩ *CP.*

Nightlife & the Arts

The **Garde Arts Center** (⊠ 325 State St. ☎ 860/444–7373) hosts touring Broadway shows, national and international opera and dance companies, and children's events. Connecticut College's **Palmer Auditorium** (⊠ 270 Mohegan Ave. ☎ 860/439–2787) plans a full schedule of dance and theater programs.

Sports & the Outdoors

At **Fort Trumbull State Park** (⊠ 90 Walbach St. ☎ 860/444–7591), on the Thames River and former location of the Naval Undersea Warfare Center, you'll find a 19th-century stonework and masonry fort, an extensive visitor center focusing on military history, a top-rate fishing pier, a boardwalk with fantastic views, and a picnic area for when you want to relax. **Ocean Beach Park** (⊠ 1225 Ocean Ave. ☎ 860/447–3031) has a ½-mi-long beach, an Olympic-size outdoor pool (with a waterslide), a miniature golf course, a video arcade, a boardwalk, and a picnic area.

Norwich

46 *15 mi north of New London, 37 mi southeast of Hartford.*

Outstanding Georgian and Victorian structures surround the triangular town green in Norwich, and more can be found downtown by the Thames River. The former mill town is hard at work at restoration and rehabilitation efforts. So eye-catching are these brightly colored structures that the Paint Quality Institute has designated the town one of the "Prettiest Painted Places in New England."

The **Slater Memorial Museum & Converse Art Gallery,** on the grounds of the Norwich Free Academy, houses one of the country's largest collections of Greek, Roman, and Renaissance plaster casts of some of the world's greatest sculptures, including the *Winged Victory, Venus de Milo,* and Michelangelo's *Pietà.* The Converse Art Gallery adjacent to the museum hosts six to eight shows a year, many of which focus on Connecticut artists and craftsmen as well as student work. ⊠ *108 Crescent St.* ☎ *860/887–2506* ⊕ *www.norwichfreeacademy.com/slater_museum* ⊠ *$3* ☉ *Tues.–Fri. 9–4, weekends 1–4.*

Where to Stay

$$$–$$$$ 🍽 **Spa at Norwich Inn.** This posh Georgian-style inn is on 42 rolling acres right by the Thames River. The spa, the state's finest, provides an entire spectrum of skin care, massages, body treatments, and fitness classes. You'll find four-poster beds, wood-burning fireplaces, and a complete galley kitchen in the luxe villas as well as comfy country furnishings in the guest rooms. The inn's elegant restaurant serves tasty, yet health-conscious, fare. The top-notch seafood scampi with fresh Maine lobster, sea scallops, and Gulf shrimp over linguine has just 425 calories—and you'd never know it. ⊠ *607 W. Thames St. (Rte. 32), 06360* ☎ *860/886–2401 or 800/ 275–4772* 🖨 *860/886–4492* ⊕ *www.thespaatnorwichinn.com* 🛏 *49 rooms, 54 villas* △ *2 restaurants, in-room data ports, 18-hole golf course, 2 tennis courts, indoor pool, hair salon, spa* ⊟ *AE, D, DC, MC, V.*

Ledyard

47 *10 mi south of Norwich, 37 mi southeast of Hartford.*

There's no doubt that Ledyard, in the woods of southeastern Connecticut between Norwich and the coastline, is known first and foremost for the vast Mashantucket Pequot Tribal Nation's Foxwoods Resort Casino. With the opening of the excellent Mashantucket Pequot Museum & Research Center, however, the tribe has moved beyond gaming to educating the public about its history, as well as that of other Northeast Woodland tribes.

Foxwoods Resort Casino, on the Mashantucket Pequot Indian Reservation near Ledyard, is the world's largest resort casino. The skylighted compound draws more than 40,000 visitors daily to its more than 6,400 slot machines, 350 gaming tables, 3,200-seat high-stakes bingo parlor, poker rooms, Keno station, theater, and Race Book room. This 4.7-million-square-foot complex includes the Grand Pequot Tower, the Great Cedar Hotel, and the Two Trees Inn, which have more than 1,400 rooms combined, as well as a full-service day spa, retail concourse, food court, and 24 restaurants. ⊠ *39 Norwich Westerly Rd., Ledyard* ☎ *860/312–3000 or 800/752–9244* ⊕ *www.foxwoods.com* ⊙ *Daily.*

⟳ The **Mashantucket Pequot Museum & Research Center,** a large complex a
Fodor'sChoice mile from the Foxwoods Resort Casino, brings the history and culture
★ of Northeastern Woodland tribes in general and the Pequots in particular to life in exquisite detail. Some highlights include re-creations of an 18,000-year-old glacial crevasse that you can travel right into, a caribou hunt from 11,000 years ago, and a 17th-century fort. Perhaps most remarkable is a sprawling "immersion environment"—a 16th-century village with more than 50 life-size figures and real smells and sounds—in which you use audio devices to obtain detailed information about the sights. The research center, open to scholars and schoolchildren free of charge, holds some 150,000 volumes. Also on-site is a full-service restaurant that serves both Native and traditional American cuisine. ⊠ *110 Pequot Trail, Mashantucket* ☎ *800/411–9671* ⊕ *www.pequotmuseum. org* ⊠ *$15* ⊙ *Daily 10–4.*

The Mohegan Indians, known as the Wolf People, operate the **Mohegan Sun** casino, which currently has more than 300,000 square feet of gaming space, including 6,000 slot machines and more than 250 gaming tables; the "Kids Quest" family entertainment complex; a 130,000-square-foot shopping mall; more than 30 restaurants and food-and-beverage suppliers; and a 1,200-room luxury hotel with a full-service spa. Free entertainment, including nationally known acts, is presented nightly in the Wolf Den; a 10,000-seat arena hosts major national acts and is home to the WNBA's Connecticut Sun; and a swanky 300-seat cabaret hosts intimate shows and comedy acts. The latest addition, Mohegan After Dark, is a 22,000-square-foot complex with three nightclubs: Lucky's Lounge, the East Coast version of a Las Vegas lounge; the Dubliner, an Irish pub; and the ultrachic, ultra-exclusive Ultra 88 Night Club. Uncasville is west of Ledyard, across the Thames River. ⊠ *Mohegan Sun Blvd. off I–395, Uncasville* ☎ *888/226–7711* ⊕ *www.mohegansun.com.*

Where to Stay & Eat

★ **$–$$$$** ✕☷ **Stonecroft.** A sunny 1807 Georgian Colonial on 6½ acres of green meadows, woodlands, and rambling stone walls is the center of Stonecroft. Although individually thematic, the rooms here and in the historic barn are united in their refined but welcoming country atmosphere; all have fireplaces and two-person whirlpool tubs. At the restaurant ($$$–$$$$; closed Monday; no lunch), try the garlic-grilled filet mignon served with parsley mashed potatoes. ⊠ *515 Pumpkin Hill Rd., 06339* ☏ *860/572–0771 or 800/772–0774* 🖷 *860/572–9161* ⊕ *www.stonecroft.com* ⇋ *10 rooms* ♨ *Restaurant, croquet, horseshoes; no smoking* ⊟ *AE, D, MC, V* ⑩ *BP.*

$$$$ 🏨 **Grand Pequot Tower.** Foxwoods' showcase hotel is an imposing 17 stories. Mere steps from the gaming floors, the expansive showpiece contains deluxe rooms and suites in pleasantly neutral tones. ⊠ *Rte. 2, Box 3777, Mashantucket 06339* ☏ *800/369–9663* 🖷 *860/312–5044* ⊕ *www.foxwoods.com* ⇋ *824 rooms* ♨ *4 restaurants, 2 18-hole golf courses, indoor pool, health club, hair salon, spa, 2 bars, meeting room* ⊟ *AE, D, DC, MC, V.*

$$$$ 🏨 **Mohegan Sun Hotel.** The emphasis of this 34-story hotel is on luxury. As you enter, towering red cedar trees (simulated, but real looking) form a canopy above you, gleaming glass and birch-lined walls surround you, and a stream and pool of water lead to the impressive Taughannick Falls across the lobby in the connecting Shops at Mohegan Sun. Guest rooms are large—a minimum of 450 square feet—and all have king or queen beds and marble baths. ⊠ *1 Mohegan Sun Blvd., Uncasville 06382* ☏ *888/777–7922* 🖷 *860/862–8328* ⊕ *www.mohegansun.com* ⇋ *1,020 rooms, 180 suites* ♨ *Some kitchenettes, in-room data ports, pool, health club, spa, business services, meeting rooms* ⊟ *AE, D, MC, V.*

Groton

48 *10 mi south of Ledyard.*

Home to the U. S. Navy's first submarine base, the Naval Submarine Base New London, and the Electric Boat Division of General Dynamics, designer and manufacturer of nuclear submarines, Groton is often referred to as the "submarine capital of the world." The submarine *Nautilus,* a National Historic Landmark, is a major draw, as is the Submarine Force Museum.

Ft. Griswold Battlefield State Park contains the remnants of a Revolutionary War fort whose American defenders were massacred in 1781 by British troops under the command of the American traitor Benedict Arnold. The 134-foot-tall Groton Battle Monument is a memorial to those who lost their lives; you can climb it for a sweeping view of the shoreline. The adjacent Monument House Museum has historic displays. ⊠ *Monument St. and Park Ave.* ☏ *860/445–1729* ⊕ *www.revwar.com/ftgriswold* 🎫 *Free* ☉ *Park daily 8 AM–dusk; museum and monument Memorial Day–Labor Day, daily 10–5.*

The world's first nuclear-powered submarine, the *Historic Ship Nautilus,* was launched and commissioned in Groton in 1954 and spent her 25-year active career as a show horse of U.S. technological know-how. ℭ She is permanently berthed at the **Submarine Force Museum,** where you're welcome to climb aboard and explore. The museum, outside the entrance to the submarine base, is a repository of artifacts, documents, and photographs detailing the history of the U.S. Submarine Force component of the U.S. Navy, and has educational and interactive exhibits. ⊠ *Crystal Lake Rd.* ☏ *860/694–3174* ⊕ *www.ussnautilus.org* 🎫 *Free* ☉ *Wed.–Mon. 9–5, Tues. 1–5.*

Where to Stay

$$$$ 🏨 **Mystic Marriott Hotel and Spa.** This six-story hotel, within Mystic Executive Park, has Georgian-style architecture and modern rooms accented with old-world touches such as rich fabrics, gleaming wood furnishings, and elegant detailing. An Elizabeth Arden Red Door Spa is attached. ⊠ *625 North Rd. (Rte. 117), 06340* ☎ *860/446–2600 or 866/449–7390* 🖷 *860/446–2696* ⊕ *www.marriott.com* ⋤*281 rooms, 4 suites* ⊘ *Restaurant, coffee shop, some in-room hot tubs, in-room data ports, pool, health club, sauna, spa, lounge, shop, business services, meeting rooms* ▭ *AE, D, DC, MC, V.*

Mystic

49 *8 mi east of Groton.*

Mystic has devoted itself to recapturing the seafaring spirit of the 18th and 19th centuries. Some of the nation's fastest clipper ships were built here in the mid-19th century; today's Mystic Seaport is the state's most popular museum. Downtown Mystic has an interesting collection of boutiques and galleries.

☾ The animals at **Mystic Aquarium and Institute for Exploration** go through 1,000 FodorsChoice pounds of herring, capelin, and squid each day. Inuk, a male beluga ★ whale, is responsible for consuming 85 pounds of that himself. He calls the aquarium's Alaskan Coast exhibit home. This exhibit, which holds 750,000 gallons of water, measures 165 feet at its longest point by 85 feet at its widest point, and ranges from just inches to 16½ feet deep, is, if you can believe it, just a small part of this revered establishment. You can also check out world-renowned ocean explorer Dr. Robert Ballard's Institute for Exploration and its "Challenge of the Deep" exhibition center (dedicated to revealing what lies on the world's deep ocean floors), as well as see African penguins, harbor seals, graceful sea horses, Pacific octopuses, and sand tiger sharks. ⊠ *55 Coogan Blvd.* ☎ *860/572–5955* ⊕ *www. mysticaquarium.org* ⊠ *$17.50* ☉ *Hrs vary seasonally; call for details.*

☾ **Mystic Seaport,** the world's largest maritime museum, encompasses 37 FodorsChoice acres of indoor and outdoor exhibits, with more than 1 million artifacts, ★ that provide a fascinating look at the area's rich shipbuilding and seafaring heritage. In the narrow streets and historic homes and buildings (some moved here from other sites), craftspeople give demonstrations of open-hearth cooking, weaving, and other skills of yesteryear. The museum's more than 480 vessels include the *Charles W. Morgan,* the last remaining wooden whaling ship afloat, and the 1882 training ship *Joseph Conrad.* You can climb aboard for a look or for sail-setting demonstrations and reenactments of whale hunts. ⊠ *75 Greenmanville Ave.* ☎ *860/572–0711* ⊕ *www.mysticseaport.org* ⊠ *$17* ☉ *Apr.–Oct., daily 9–5; Nov.–Mar., daily 10–4.*

Where to Stay & Eat

$–$$$ ✕ **Abbott's Lobster in the Rough.** If you want some of the state's best lob-FodorsChoice sters, mussels, crabs, or clams on the half shell, head down to this unas-★ suming seaside lobster shack in sleepy Noank, a few miles southwest of Mystic. Most seating is outdoors or on the dock, where the views of

6

Noank Harbor are magnificent. ✉ *117 Pearl St., Noank 06340* ☎ *860/ 536–7719* ⊕ *www.abbotts-lobster.com* ▭ *AE, MC, V* ☞ *BYOB* ☉ *Closed Columbus Day–1st Fri. in May and weekdays Labor Day–Columbus Day.*

$–$$$
Fodor'sChoice
★

✕ **Go Fish.** In this town by the sea, one hungers for seafood, and this sophisticated restaurant captures all the tastes—and colors—of the ocean. There's a raw bar, wine bar, coffee bar, and a black granite sushi bar, which, with its myriad tiny, briny morsels, is worth the trip in itself. The glossy blue tables in the two large dining rooms perfectly complement the signature saffron-scented shellfish bouillabaisse. The menu lists options for vegetarians and carnivores as well, but the lobster ravioli in a light cream sauce is a must-try. ✉ *Olde Mistick Village, Coogan Blvd. (I–95 Exit 90), 06355* ☎ *860/536–2662* ▭ *AE, D, MC, V.*

$$$–$$$$
Fodor'sChoice
★

✕⌂ **Inn at Mystic.** The highlight of this inn, which sprawls over 15 hilltop acres and overlooks picturesque Pequotsepos Cove, is the five-bedroom Georgian Colonial mansion. Almost as impressive are the rambling four-bedroom gatehouse (where Lauren Bacall and Humphrey Bogart honeymooned) and the unusually attractive motor lodge. The convivial, sun-filled Flood Tide restaurant ($$$–$$$$; open for lunch only in summer) specializes in contemporary Continental fare such as the mix of lobster, shrimp, and scallops in a sherry cream velouté. Brunch fans flock here on Sunday. ✉ *U.S. 1 and Rte. 27, 06355* ☎ *860/536– 9604 or 800/237–2415* 🖷 *860/572–1635* ⊕ *www.innatmystic.com* ➳ *67 rooms* ⌂ *Restaurant, tennis court, pool, dock, boating* ▭ *AE, DC, MC, V.*

$$–$$$$

✕⌂ **Whaler's Inn.** A perfect compromise between a chain motel and a country inn, this complex with public rooms furnished with lovely antiques is one block from the Mystic River and downtown. The motel-style guest rooms feel Victorian, with quilts and reproduction four-poster beds. The restaurant, Bravo Bravo ($$$), serves nouvelle Italian food: the lobster ravioli is bathed with a chive sauce. ✉ *20 E. Main St., 06355* ☎ *860/536–1506 or 800/243–2588* 🖷 *860/572–1250* ⊕ *www. whalersinnmystic.com* ➳ *49 rooms* ⌂ *Restaurant, outdoor café, in-room data ports, meeting room, no-smoking rooms* ▭ *AE, DC, MC, V.*

$$–$$$

⌂ **Old Mystic Inn.** This cozy inn, built in 1784, was once a bookshop specializing in antique books and maps. Today, all its rooms, in the main house and a carriage house, are named after New England authors. Some have working fireplaces and whirlpools, and each is a welcoming and comfortable mix of antiques and owner-innkeeper Michael Cardillo Jr.'s personal touches. You can enjoy a game of checkers by the oversize Colonial hearth in the keeping room; a full country breakfast is served by the fire in the dining room. ✉ *52 Main St., 06372* ☎ *860/572–9422* 🖷 *860/572–9954* ⊕ *www.oldmysticinn.com* ➳ *8 rooms* ⌂ *No room phones, no room TVs, in-room data ports in carriage house* ▭ *AE, MC, V* ⦿ *BP.*

Shopping

The **Finer Line Gallery** (✉ 48 W. Main St. ☎ 860/536–8339) exhibits nautical and other prints, including some local scenes. **Olde Mistick Village** (✉ Coogan Blvd. off I–95 Exit 90 ☎ 860/536–4941), a re-creation of what an American village might have looked like in the early 1700s, has more than 50 shops that sell everything from crafts and clothing to souvenirs and munchies. The duck pond and gazebo are favorite gathering spots for pint-size shoppers. **Whyevernot** (⌧ 17 W. Main St. ☎ 860/536–6209) is a colorful spot for clothing, jewelry, pottery, linens, handmade papers, and much more.

Stonington

50 *7 mi southeast of Mystic, 57 mi east of New Haven.*

The pretty village of Stonington pokes into Fishers Island Sound. A quiet fishing community clustered around white-spired churches, Stonington is far less commercial than Mystic. In the 19th century, though, this was a bustling whaling, sealing, and transportation center. Historic buildings line the town green and border both sides of Water Street up to the imposing Old Lighthouse Museum.

The **Old Lighthouse Museum** occupies a lighthouse that was built in 1823 and moved to higher ground 17 years later. Climb to the top of the tower for a spectacular view of Long Island Sound and three states. Six rooms of exhibits depict the varied history of the small coastal town. ⌧ *7 Water St.* ☎ *860/535–1440* ⊕ *www.stoningtonhistory.org/light.htm* ⌧ *$5* ☉ *May–Oct., daily 10–5; Nov.–Apr., by appointment.*

At **Stonington Vineyards,** a small coastal winery, you can browse through the works of local artists in the small gallery or enjoy a picnic lunch on the grounds. The vineyard's Seaport White, a vidal-chardonnay blend, is a nice accompaniment. ⌧ *523 Taugwonk Rd.* ☎ *860/535–1222* ⊕ *www.stoningtonvineyards.com* ⌧ *Free* ☉ *Daily 11–5, tours at 2.*

Where to Stay & Eat

$$–$$$$ ✕▥ **Randall's Ordinary.** The waiters dress in Colonial garb at this inn, which occupies the 17th-century John Randall farmhouse and is known for its open-hearth cooking. The prix fixe menu ($$$$; reservations essential for dinner) changes daily; choices might include tasty Nantucket scallops or smoked turkey. The inn's very simple accommodations are across the way in the early 19th-century barn; all have authentic early Colonial appointments, along with modern baths with whirlpool tubs and showers; some have fireplaces. There is also a cabin and a circular-shaped suite in the silo. ⌧ *Rte. 2, 7 mi north of Stonington* ♐ *North Stonington 06359* ☎ *860/599–4540 or 877/599–4540* ⊟ *860/599–3308* ⊕ *www.randallsordinary.com* ⇦ *11 rooms, 1 suite, 1 cabin* ♌ *Restaurant, meeting room* ⊟ *AE, MC, V.*

$$$–$$$$ ▥ **Inn at Stonington.** The views of Stonington Harbor and Fishers Island Sound are spectacular from this waterfront inn in the heart of Stonington Village. Each room is individually decorated; all have fireplaces, and most have whirlpool baths. Kayaks and bicycles are available for use. Those coming by boat can use the inn's 400-foot deepwater pier. ⌧ *60 Water St., 06378* ☎ *860/535–2000* ⊟ *860/535–8193* ⊕ *www. innatstonington.com* ⇦ *18 rooms* ♌ *Some in-room hot tubs, health club, bicycles; no kids under 14, no smoking* ⊟ *AE, MC, V* ⭥ *CP.*

THE QUIET CORNER

Few visitors to Connecticut experience the old-fashioned ways of the state's "Quiet Corner," a vast patch of sparsely populated towns that seem a world away from the rest of the state. The Quiet Corner has a reclusive allure: people used to leave New York City for the Litchfield Hills; now many are leaving for northeastern Connecticut, where the stretch of Route 169 from Brooklyn past Woodstock has been named a National Scenic Byway.

The cultural capital of the Quiet Corner is Putnam, a small mill city on the Quinebaug River whose formerly industrial town center has been transformed into a year-round antiques mart. Smaller jewels are Pomfret and Woodstock—two towns where authentic Colonial homesteads still seem to outnumber the contemporary, charmless clones that are springing up all too rapidly across the state.

Pomfret

🔟 *6 mi north of Brooklyn.*

Pomfret, one of the grandest towns in the region, was once known as the inland Newport because it attracted the wealthy, who summered here in large "cottages." Today it is a quiet stopping-off point along Route 169, designated one of the 10 most scenic byways in the country.

The **Connecticut Audubon Center at Pomfret** is adjacent to the Connecticut Audubon Bafflin Sanctuary's more than 700 acres of rolling meadows, grassland habitats, forests, and streams. The nature center presents environmental-education programs for all ages, seasonal lectures and workshops, and changing natural-history exhibits. Miles of self-guided trails provide excellent birding. ⊠ *189 Pomfret St. (Rte. 169)* ☎ *860/928–4948* ⊕ *www.ctaudubon.org/visit/pomfret.htm* 🎟 *Free* ☉ *Sanctuary daily dawn–dusk, center Wed.–Sun. noon–4.*

Sharpe Hill Vineyard is centered around an 18th-century-style barn in the hills of Pomfret. Tastings are given, and the vineyard serves lunch and dinner ($$$$) in a European-style wine garden and Fireside Tavern, Friday through Sunday, depending on the season. Its Ballet of Angels, a heavenly semidry white, just may be New England's top-selling wine. ⊠ *108 Wade Rd.* ☎ *860/974–3549* ⊕ *www.sharpehill.com* 🎟 *Free* ☉ *Fri.–Sun. 11–5.*

Where to Eat

$$$$

Fodor'sChoice

★

✕ **Golden Lamb Buttery.** Connecticut's most unusual dining experience has achieved almost legendary status. Eating here—in a converted barn on a 1,000-acre farm—is far more than a chance to enjoy good continental food: it's a social and gastronomical event. There is one seating each for lunch and dinner; choose from one of four entrées, which might include roast duck or chateaubriand. Owners Bob and Virginia "Jimmie" Booth have a hay wagon that you can ride before dinner (a musician accompanies you). ⊠ *499 Bush Hill Rd., off Rte. 169, Brooklyn* ☎ *860/774–4423* ⚐ *Reservations essential* 🖃 *AE, D, MC, V* ☉ *Closed Sun. and Mon. No dinner Tues.–Thurs.*

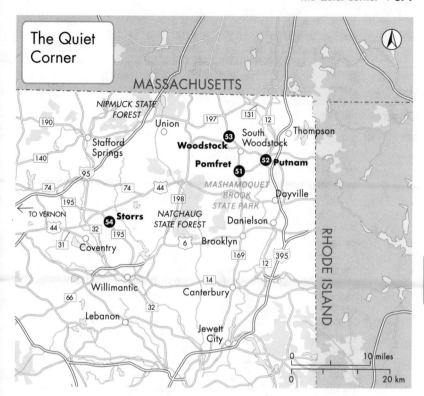

The Quiet Corner

$$–$$$ ✕ **The Harvest.** This romantic country restaurant is alive with fresh flowers, glimmering candles, antiques, and touches of chintz. It serves seafood, vegetable, and pasta dishes as well as a selection of steaks, fillets, and chops served with your choice of such accompaniments as béarnaise sauce, sautéed mushrooms, caramelized onions, or garlic-and-peppercorn butter. ⊠ *37 Putnam Rd., 06258* ☎ *860/928– 0008* ▭ *AE, MC, V* ⊘ *Closed Mon. No lunch Tues. and Sat.*

$–$$ ✕ **Vanilla Bean Café.** Homemade soups, sandwiches, and baked goods have long been a tradition at this comfortable café inside a restored 19th-century barn. Now, dinner entrées such as smoked mozzarella-and-basil ravioli and pan-seared sea scallops served over baby spinach are also becoming increasingly popular. Belgian waffles and blueberry pancakes are breakfast highlights. All this and an art gallery and folk entertainment, too. ⊠ *450 Deerfield Rd. (off U.S. 44, Rte. 97, and Rte. 169), 06258* ☎ *860/ 928–1562* ▭ *AE, MC, V* ⊘ *No dinner Mon. and Tues.*

Sports & the Outdoors

Mashamoquet Brook State Park (⊠ U.S. 44 ☎ 860/928–6121) is a 1,000-acre park with an attractive trail system, and swimming, fishing, and camping facilities.

Shopping

Majilly (⊠ 56 Babbitt Hill Rd. ☎ 860/974–3714) sells an upscale line of hand-painted ceramic pottery crafted in Italy. You can also pick up still-gorgeous seconds at 50%–70% off retail prices. **Martha's Herbary** (⊠ 589 Pomfret St. ☎ 860/928–0009), in a 1780 home, is an herb-theme gift shop and garden.

Putnam

➄ *5 mi northeast of Pomfret.*

Ambitious antiques dealers have reinvented Putnam, a mill town 30 mi west of Providence, Rhode Island, that became neglected after the Depression. Putnam's downtown, with more than 400 antiques dealers, is the heart of the Quiet Corner's antiques trade.

Where to Stay & Eat

$$–$$$ ✕ **85 Main.** This stylish trattoria-bistro is *the* place to go for a break from antiquing. If you go for lunch, your choice could be a curried chicken salad, a veal meatloaf sandwich, or a burger and fries; at dinner anything from a lobster risotto to the orange and coriander chicken with chipotle-mashed sweet potatoes, or a Guinness veal stew. There is also a raw bar dispensing clams, oysters, shrimp, and ceviche. ⊠ *85 Main St.* ☎ *860/928–1660* ⊕ *www.85main.com* ⊟ *AE, MC, V.*

¢–$ ⊡ **King's Inn.** Less than 2 mi from downtown Putnam, the King's Inn is a good base for antiquers. Half the rooms, which are decorated with cream-color walls or print wallpaper and straightforward wood furnishings, overlook a pond. ⊠ *5 Heritage Rd., 06260* ☎ *860/928–7961 or 800/541–7304* ☐ *860/963–2463* ⊕ *www.kingsinnputnam.com* ↷ *40 rooms, 1 suite* ☐ *Restaurant, some microwaves, some refrigerators, pool, bar, meeting rooms* ⊟ *AE, D, DC, MC, V* ⊙⌐ *CP.*

Shopping

The four-level **Antiques Marketplace** (⊠ 109 Main St. ☎ 860/928–0442) houses the wares of nearly 300 dealers, from fine furniture to tchotchkes and collectibles. **Arts & Framing** (⊠ 112 Main St. ☎ 860/963–0105) sells antique art and also provides art restoration and framing services. **Brighton Antiques** (⊠ 91 Main St. ☎ 860/928–1419) carries furniture and accessories from the 18th through 20th century.

Woodstock

➄ *5 mi northwest of Putnam.*

The landscape of this enchanting town is splendid in every season—the rolling hills seem to stretch for miles. Scenic roads take you past antiques shops, a country inn in the grand tradition, orchards, grassy fields and grazing livestock, and the fairgrounds of one of the state's oldest—and most popular—agricultural fairs held each Labor Day weekend.

Roseland Cottage is a pink board-and-batten Gothic-revival house built in 1846 as a summer home for New York silk merchant, publisher, and abolitionist Henry C. Bowen. The house and outbuildings (including a carriage house with its own private bowling alley) hold a prominent place in history, having hosted four U.S. presidents (Ulysses S. Grant, Rutherford B. Hayes, Benjamin Harrison, and William McKinley). The boxwood parterre garden includes 21 flower beds surrounded by 600 yards of boxwood hedge. ☒ *556 Rte. 169* ☏ *860/928–4074* ⊕ *www.spnea. org/visit/homes/roseland.htm* ⊠ *$8* ⊘ *June–mid-Oct., Fri.–Sun. 11–4.*

Where to Stay & Eat

$$–$$$ ✕☷ **Inn at Woodstock Hill.** This inn on a hill overlooking the countryside has sumptuous rooms with antiques, four-poster beds, fireplaces, pitched ceilings, and timber beams. The chintz-and-prints restaurant ($$$; reservations essential) serves excellent Continental and American variations on seafood, veal, beef, pork, and chicken dishes. ☒ *94 Plaine Hill Rd., South Woodstock 06267* ☏ *860/928–0528* ☒ *860/928–3236* ⊕ *www.woodstockhill.com* ⌁ *19 rooms, 3 suites* ⚴ *Restaurant, in-room data ports, meeting room* ⊟ *AE, D, MC, V* �Ⓞⅼ *CP.*

Shopping

Chocolate Saltbox Stenciler (☒ 1250 Rte. 171 ☏ 860/974–1437) has a library of more than 20,000 stencil designs from more than 50 stencil companies. Not a retail store, this is a catalog service; visitors' choices are filled via mail order by the pertinent company. The **Christmas Barn** (☒ 835 Rte. 169 ☏ 860/928–7652) has 12 rooms of country and Christmas goods. **Scranton's Shops** (☒ 300 Rte. 169 ☏ 860/928–3738) sells antiques and the wares of 90 local artisans. **Whispering Hill Farm** (☒ Rte. 169 ☏ 860/928–0162) sells supplies for rug hooking and braiding, quilting, and needlework mixed with an assortment of antiques.

Storrs

54 *25 mi southwest of Woodstock.*

The majority of Storrs's hillside and farmland is occupied by the 4,400 acres and some 18,000 students of the main campus of the University of Connecticut (UConn). Many cultural programs, sporting events, and other happenings take place here. University Parking Services and the Student Union supply campus maps.

Hand puppets, rod puppets, body puppets, shadow puppets, marionettes—the **Ballard Institute and Museum of Puppetry** has more than 2,000 puppets in its extraordinary collection. Half were created under the direction of Frank Ballard, a master of puppetry who established the country's first complete undergraduate and graduate degree program in puppetry at UConn more than three decades ago. Exhibits change seasonally. If you're lucky you might even catch Oscar the Grouch from *Sesame Street* on display. ☒ *Willimantic Cottage, University of Connecticut Depot Campus, Weaver Rd. off Route 44* ☏ *860/486–4605* ⊕ *www.bimp.uconn.edu* ⊠ *Donation suggested* ⊘ *Late Apr.–early Nov., Fri.–Sun. noon–5.*

The good news: the massive collection of the **Connecticut Archaeology Center and Connecticut State Museum of Natural History** documents more than 11,000 years of Connecticut's past via some 500,000 artifacts. The bad news (for now): while the building is undergoing renovations, which are not expected to be completed until late 2006, only one small changing exhibit area is open to the public (although a series of public programs, workshops, and lectures continues). ⊠ *University of Connecticut, 2019 Hillside Rd., Unit 1023* ☎ *860/486–4460* ⊕ *www.cac. uconn.edu* ⊡ *Free* ⊙ *Weekdays 9–4, Sun. 1–4.*

The permanent collection of the **William Benton Museum of Art** includes European and American paintings, drawings, prints, photographs, and sculptures from the 16th century to the present. Its galleries host changing exhibitions, lectures, recitals, and readings. The museum also has a café and museum shop. ⊠ *University of Connecticut, 245 Glenbrook Rd.* ☎ *860/486–4520* ⊕ *www.benton.uconn.edu* ⊡ *Free* ⊙ *Tues.–Fri. 10–4:30, weekends 1–4:30; café and shop weekdays 10–4:30, weekends 1–4:30.*

Where to Stay

$$ ⊡ **Nathan Hale Inn and Conference Center.** This five-floor inn and conference center on the University of Connecticut campus has comfortable contemporary rooms, appointed with a lot of mahogany. ⊠ *855 Bolton Rd., 06268* ☎ *860/427–7888* ⊟ *860/427–7850* ⊕ *www. nathanhaleinn.com* ⊲ *100 rooms* ⟁ *Restaurant, some microwaves, some refrigerators, in-room data ports, pool, health club, hot tub, lounge, business services, meeting rooms* ⊟ *AE, D, DC, MC, V.*

Nightlife & the Arts

The **Jorgensen Center for the Performing Arts** (⊠ University of Connecticut, 2132 Hillside Rd. ☎ 860/486–4226) presents a series of roughly 40 music, dance, and theater programs September through May. **Mansfield Drive-In** (⊠ Rtes. 31 and 32, Mansfield ☎ 860/423–4441), with three big screens, is one of the state's few remaining drive-in theaters.

CONNECTICUT A TO Z

To research prices, get advice from other travelers, and book travel arrangements, visit www.fodors.com.

AIRPORTS

Many people visiting Connecticut fly into New York City's John F. Kennedy International Airport or LaGuardia Airport, both of which are served by many major carriers. Another option is Bradley International Airport, north of Hartford.

🛈 Airport Information **Bradley International Airport** ☎ 860/292-2000 ⊕ www. bradleyairport.com. **John F. Kennedy International Airport** ☎ 718/244-4444 ⊕ www. panynj.gov/aviation/jfkframe.HTM. **LaGuardia Airport** ☎ 718/533-3400 ⊕ www.panynj. gov/aviation/lgaframe.HTM.

AIRPORT TRANSFERS Connecticut Limo operates bus and van service between Connecticut and the New York airports and to and from Bradley International Airport. Prime Time/Connecticut Airport Shuttle serves mainly New Haven and Fairfield counties with service to and from both New York airports.
🛈 Taxis & Shuttles **Connecticut Limo** ☎ 800/472-5466 ⊕ www.ctlimo.com. **Prime Time Shuttle** ☎ 800/733-8267 ⊕ www.primetimeshuttle.com.

BOAT & FERRY TRAVEL

From New London, Cross Sound Ferry operates year-round passenger and car service to and from Orient Point, Long Island, New York. Its high-speed passenger ferry can make the trip in 40 minutes. Fishers Island Ferry has passenger and car service to and from Fishers Island, New York, from New London. Interstate Navigation Co. operates passenger and car service from New London to and from Block Island, Rhode Island, from June to early September. From Bridgeport, the Bridgeport-Port Jefferson Steamboat Co. operates year-round.

🚢 Boat & Ferry Information **Bridgeport-Port Jefferson Steamboat Co.** ☎ 203/335-2040 ⊕ www.bpjferry.com. **Cross Sound Ferry** ☎ 860/443-5281 ⊕ www.longislandferry. com. **Fishers Island Ferry District** ☎ 631/788-7463 ⊕ www.fiferry.com. **Interstate Navigation Co.** ☎ 860/442-9553 ⊕ www.blockislandferry.com.

BUS TRAVEL

Bonanza Bus Lines connects Hartford, Farmington, Waterbury, Manchester, Torrington, Storrs, and Danbury with Boston and New York. Greyhound links Connecticut with most major cities in the United States. Peter Pan Bus Lines serves the eastern seaboard, including many New England cities.

🚌 Bus Information **Bonanza Bus Lines** ☎ 800/556-3815 ⊕ www.bonanzabus.com. **Greyhound Lines Inc.** ☎ 800/231-2222 ⊕ www.greyhound.com. **Peter Pan Bus Lines** ☎ 800/237-8747 ⊕ www.peterpanbus.com.

CAR TRAVEL

From New York City head north on Interstate 95, which hugs the Connecticut shoreline into Rhode Island, or, to reach the Litchfield Hills and Hartford, head north on Interstate 684, then east on Interstate 84. From Springfield, Massachusetts, go south on Interstate 91, which bisects Interstate 84 in Hartford and Interstate 95 in New Haven. From Boston take Interstate 95 south through Providence or take the Massachusetts Turnpike west to Interstate 84. Interstate 395 runs north–south from southeastern Connecticut to Massachusetts.

The interstates are the quickest routes between many points in Connecticut, but they are busy and ugly. The speed limits on Connecticut's interstates change, sometimes going from 65 mph to 45 mph and back quite quickly through the cities. Be certain to check for posted speed limits. Right turns on red are legal unless posted otherwise.

If time allows, skip the interstates in favor of the historic Merritt Parkway (Route 15), which winds between Greenwich and Middletown; U.S. 7 and Route 8, extending between Interstate 95 and the Litchfield Hills; Route 9, which heads south from Hartford through the Connecticut River valley to Old Saybrook; and scenic Route 169, which meanders through the Quiet Corner. Maps are available free from the Connecticut Office of Tourism.

EMERGENCIES

🏥 Hospitals **Hartford Hospital** ✉ 80 Seymour St. ☎ 860/545-5000 ⊕ www.harthosp. org. **Lawrence & Memorial Hospital** ✉ 365 Montauk Ave., New London ☎ 860/442-0711 ⊕ www.lmhospital.org. **Middlesex Hospital** ✉ 28 Crescent St., Middletown

☎ 860/344-6000 ⊕ www.midhosp.org. **New Milford Hospital** ⊠ 21 Elm St. ☎ 860/355-2611 ⊕ www.newmilfordhospital.org. **Norwalk Hospital** ⊠ 34 Maple St., Norwalk ☎203/852-2000 ⊕www.norwalkhosp.org. **St. Vincent's Medical Center** ⊠2800 Main St., Bridgeport ☎203/576-6000 ⊕ www.stvincents.org. **Windham Community Memorial Hospital** ⊠ 112 Mansfield Ave., Willimantic ☎ 860/456-9116 ⊕ www.windhamhospital.org. **Yale-New Haven Hospital** ⊠ 20 York St., New Haven ☎ 203/688-4242 ⊕ www.ynhh.org.

TOURS

The Connecticut Freedom Trail has more than 50 historic sights associated with the state's African-American heritage. The Connecticut Impressionist Art Trail is a self-guided tour of nine museums important to the 19th-century American impressionist movement. Write to the address below for a map. The Connecticut Wine Trail travels among 15 member vineyards.

🗐 **Connecticut Freedom Trail** ⊠ Historic Preservation and Museum Administration Division, 59 S. Prospect St., Hartford 06106 ☎ 860/566-3005 ⊕ www.ctfreedomtrail.com. **Connecticut Impressionist Art Trail** ⊕ Box 793, Old Lyme 06371 ⊕ www.arttrail.org. **Connecticut Wine Trail** ⊠ 131 Tower Rd., Brookfield 06804 ☎ 860/267-1399 ⊕ www.ctwine.com.

TRAIN TRAVEL

Amtrak runs from New York to Boston, stopping in Stamford, Bridgeport, and New Haven before heading either north to Hartford or east to Mystic. Metro-North Railroad trains from New York stop locally between Greenwich and New Haven, and a few trains head inland to New Canaan, Danbury, and Waterbury. Shoreline East commuter rail service provides weekday service between New Haven and New London.

🗐 Train Information **Amtrak** ☎ 800/872-7245 ⊕ www.amtrak.com. **Metro-North Railroad** ☎ 212/532-4900 in New York City, 800/638-7646 ⊕ www.mta.nyc.ny.us. **Shoreline East** ☎ 800/255-7433 toll free in CT, 203/777-7433 outside CT ⊕ www.shorelineeast.com.

VISITOR INFORMATION

State welcome centers, in Darien and Westbrook on Interstate 95 northbound, North Stonington on Interstate 95 southbound, Danbury on Interstate 84 eastbound, and Willington on Interstate 84 westbound, have visitor information.

🗐 Tourist Information **Central Regional Tourism District/River Valley/Connecticut** ⊠ 31 Pratt St., 4th fl., Hartford 06103 ☎ 860/244-8181 or 800/793-4480 ⊕ www.visitctriver.com. **Coastal Fairfield County Convention and Visitors Bureau** ⊠ Mathews Park, 297 West Ave., Norwalk 06850 ☎ 203/853-7770 or 800/866-7925 ⊕ www.coastalct.com. **Connecticut East-Home of Mystic Places and the Quiet Corner** ⊠ 32 Huntington St. ⊕ Box 89, New London 06320 ☎ 860/444-2206 or 800/863-6569 ⊕ www.mysticmore.com. **Greater New Haven Convention and Visitors Bureau** ⊠ 59 Elm St., New Haven 06510 ☎ 203/777-8550 or 800/332-7829 ⊕ www.newhavencvb.org. **Northwest Connecticut Convention and Visitors Bureau** ⊕ Box 968, Litchfield 06759 ☎ 860/567-4506 or 800/663-1273 ⊕ www.northwestct.com.

Antiquarian and Landmarks Society ⊠ 255 Main St., Hartford 06106 ☎860/247-8996 ⊕ www.hartnet.org/als. **Bureau of Parks and Forests** ⊠ 79 Elm St., Hartford 06106 ☎ 860/424-3200 ⊕ www.dep.state.ct.us/stateparks. **Connecticut Campground Own-**

ers Association ⊠ 14 Rumford St., West Hartford 06107 ☏ 860/521-4704 ⊕ www. campconn.com. **Connecticut State Golf Association** ⊠ 35 Cold Spring Rd., Suite 212, Rocky Hill 06067 ☏ 860/257-4171 ⊕ www.csgalinks.org. **Connecticut Commission on Culture & Tourism** ⊠ 505 Hudson St., Hartford 06106 ☏ 860/270-8080 or 888/ 288-4748 ⊕ www.ctvisit.com.

6

INDEX

NOTES

NOTES

NOTES

NOTES

NOTES

NOTES

ABOUT OUR WRITERS

Several writers worked on the Maine chapter. Stephen and Neva Allen have written extensively about travel for many newspapers and magazines. Lelah Cole, when not gardening or writing, enjoys hiking Acadia's mountains, biking, and cross-country skiing its carriage roads, and learning French. Mid-Coast Maine resident Sherry Hanson has written for many magazines, newspapers, and online publications. She has also worked on special projects for organizations such as Habitat for Humanity. As a Maine-based freelance writer, Mary Ruoff has enjoyed writing articles about Maine travel and other topics. Laura V. Scheel has written frequently for Fodor's, including the Maine chapter in *The Thirteen Colonies*, part of Fodor's Travel Historic America series.

Former Fodor's editor and New England native Andrew Collins, who revised the New Hampshire chapter as well as the Smart Travel Tips section, is the author of several books on travel in New England, including guides to Connecticut and Rhode Island. He's also a frequent contributor to *Travel + Leisure*, and numerous other newspapers and magazines.

Peggy Shinn is an award-winning freelance writer from central Vermont. She regularly travels to every corner of the Green Mountain State for her work covering travel, skiing, and cycling for a number of national ski magazines, New England newspapers, and MSNBC.com. She is also a contributing editor for the guidebook Ski America and Canada and its affiliated Web site skisnowboard.com.

For the Massachusetts chapter. Diane Bair and Pam Wright, Michael Blanding, Matthew Cordell, Alexandra Hall, Corey O'Hara, Andrew Rimas, Erica Silverstein, and Emily J. Stebbins all blended their first-hand insights of all-things-Boston with creative prose to create the Boston and Around Boston sections. Lori A. Nolin, James W. Rohlf, and Andrew Collins contributed to the Cape Cod section. Freelancer Phyllis Meras, Vineyard resident since the 1960s, is the author of 13 books, including a collection of essays about the island. New England travel guide writer and Nantucket resident Sandy MacDonald updated the Nantucket section. Author David Simons updated the Pioneer Valley. Berkshire residents and writers Gail M. Burns, Eileen Pierce, and Carole Owens updated the Berkshires section.

New England native Catherine Bowen Brophy resides in scenic Newport, Rhode Island (and absolutely loves it!). A freelancer and instructor at Salve Regina University in Newport, she writes about Rhode Island's rich history, picturesque sites, and tourist spots for national and local newspapers, magazines, and Web sites.

Michelle Bodak Acri, who updated the Connecticut chapter, has lived in the Nutmeg State for 36 years, the last 15 of them working as an editor and writer for, among other publications, *Connecticut* magazine. She enthusiastically shares her state's glories with the uninitiated.